economics

9th edition

economics

9th edition

David Begg
Stanley Fischer
Rudiger Dornbusch

**McGraw-Hill
Higher Education**

London Boston Burr Ridge, IL Dubuque, IA Madison, WI New York San Francisco
St. Louis Bangkok Bogotá Caracas Kuala Lumpur Lisbon Madrid Mexico City Milan
Montreal New Delhi Santiago Seoul Singapore Sydney Taipei Toronto

Economics 9th Edition
David Begg, Stanley Fischer and Rudiger Dornbusch
ISBN-13 9780077117870
ISBN-10 0077117875

McGraw-Hill
Higher Education

Published by McGraw-Hill Education
Shoppenhangers Road
Maidenhead
Berkshire
SL6 2QL
Telephone: 44 (0) 1628 502 500
Fax: 44 (0) 1628 770 224
Website: www.mcgraw-hill.co.uk

British Library Cataloguing in Publication Data
A catalogue record for this book is available from the British Library

Library of Congress Cataloging in Publication Data
The Library of Congress data for this book has been applied for from the Library of Congress

Acquisitions Editor: Catriona Watson
Development Editor: Hannah Cooper
Marketing Manager: Vanessa Boddington
Head of Production: Beverley Shields

Design by HL Studios
Text design by Wearset Ltd, Boldon, Tyne and Wear
Cover design by Ego Creative
Printed and bound in Italy by Rotolito Lombarda

ISBN-13 9780077117870
ISBN-10 0077117875

277876

The **McGraw-Hill** Companies

For Honora, Mary and Robin

Brief Table of Contents

Detailed Table of Contents

Detailed Table of Contents Continued

Detailed Table of Contents Continued

Detailed Table of Contents Continued

Detailed Table of Contents Continued

Detailed Table of Contents Continued

Preface

Economics is much too interesting to be left to professional economists. It affects almost everything we do, not merely at work or at the shops but also in the home and the voting booth. It influences how well we look after our planet, the future we leave for our children, the extent to which we can care for the poor and the disadvantaged, and the resources we have for enjoying ourselves.

These issues are discussed daily, in bars and on buses as well as in cabinet meetings and boardrooms. The formal study of economics is exciting because it introduces a toolkit that allows a better understanding of the problems we face. Everyone knows a smoky engine is a bad sign, but sometimes only a trained mechanic can give the right advice on how to fix it.

This book is designed to teach you the toolkit and give you practice in using it. Nobody carries an enormous toolbox very far. Useful toolkits are small enough to be portable but contain enough proven tools to deal with both routine problems and unforeseen circumstances. With practice, you will be surprised at how much light this analysis can shed on daily living. This book is designed to make economics seem as useful as it really is.

How much do economists disagree?

There is an old complaint that economists never agree about anything. This is simply wrong. The media, taxi-drivers and politicians love to talk about topics on which there is disagreement; it would be boring TV if all participants in a panel discussion held identical views. But economics is not a subject in which there is always an argument for everything. There are answers to many questions. We aim to show where economists agree – on what and for what reason – and why they sometimes disagree.

Economics in the twenty-first century

Our aim is to allow students to understand today's economic environment. This requires mastering the theory and practising its application. Just as the theory of genetics or of information technology is slowly progressing, so the theory of economics continues to make progress, sometimes in dramatic and exciting ways.

We believe in introducing students immediately to the latest ideas in economics. If these can be conveyed simply, why force students to use older approaches that work less well? Two recent developments in economics underlie much of what we do. One is the role of information, the other is globalization.

How information is transmitted and manipulated is central to many issues in incentives and competition, including the recent booming e-commerce. Ease of information, coupled with lower transport costs, also explains trends towards globalization, and associated reductions in national sovereignty, especially in smaller countries. Modern economics helps us make sense of our changing world, think about where it may go next, and evaluate choices that we currently face.

Learning by doing

Few people practise for a driving test just by reading a book. Even when you think you understand how to do a hill start, it takes a lot of practice to master the finer points. In the same way, we give you lots of examples and real-world applications not just to emphasize the relevance of economics but also to help you master it for yourself. We start at square one and take you slowly through the tools of theoretical reasoning and how to apply them. We do not use algebra and there are very few equations in the book. The best ideas are simple and robust, and can usually be explained quite easily.

How to study

Don't just read about economics, try to do it! It is easy, but mistaken, to read on cruise control, highlighting the odd sentence and gliding through paragraphs we have worked hard to simplify. Active learning needs to be interactive. When the text says 'clearly', ask yourself 'why' is it clear? See if you can construct the diagram before you look at it. As soon as you don't follow something, go back and read it again. Try to think of other examples to which the theory could be applied. The only way to check you really understand things is to try the review questions and see if you get the right answer. The ninth edition has comprehensive answers, which you will find on pages 712–38. You can also explore the online resources centre that accompanies this book for extra learning resources, and may also wish to consider using the student workbook that accompanies this text.

To assist you in working through this text, we have developed a number of distinctive study and design features. To familiarize yourself with these features, please turn to the Guided Tour on pages xvi–xvii.

Changes to the ninth edition

The ninth edition has been thoroughly revised, even though we have kept to the familiar and proven structure, to ensure that it keeps up with the latest thinking about our evolving world and the way in which economics can make sense of it.

Specific changes to the new edition include:

- Substantial new material on the economic effects of climate change.

- A thoroughly revised and updated Chapter 36 on poverty, development and globalization.

- New Activity Boxes added to each chapter, to encourage you to apply your learning of economics to the real world.

- New graded review questions, to create flexibility in the level and pace at which you learn and apply economic principles.

- Full updates throughout to include 2007/2008 data in graphs and tables, and many new contemporary boxes to illustrate key ideas with relevance to the real world.

- Revised design that aims to make the text easier to navigate and use.

- More resources provided for both students and lecturers.

Supplementary resources

Economics ninth edition offers a comprehensive package of resources for the teaching and learning of economics. The resources offered with the new edition have been developed in response to feedback from current users in order to provide lecturers with a variety of teaching resources for class teaching, lectures and assessment. Students are also offered a range of extra materials to assist in learning, revising and applying the principles of economics.

Online Learning Centre

An accompanying Online Learning Centre website has been developed to provide an unrivalled package of flexible, high quality resources for both lecturer and student. The ninth edition sees a new range of extra resources with this edition, including an interactive graphing tool, case studies with teaching notes, and enhanced assessment and revision tools, in a choice of delivery formats.

To access all of the free Online Learning Centre resources and to find out about enhanced options, simply visit the website at **www.mcgraw-hill.co.uk/textbooks/begg**.

To learn more about the resources available to lecturers and students online, go to our tour of the resources on pages xviii–xix (Technology to enhance learning and teaching).

Guided tour

Learning Outcomes

Each chapter opens with a set of learning outcomes, summarizing what knowledge, skills or understanding readers should acquire from each chapter. Part introductions explore these themes further.

Learning Outcomes

By the end of this chapter, you shoul

1 that economics is the study of ho

2 ways in which society decides w

3 the concept of opportunity c

4 positive and normative

Key Terms

Key terms are featured in margin definitions throughout each chapter. An ideal tool for last minute revision or to check definitions as your read.

are in the interests of society

v ideas
lf-interest,
You move
ces now
ss. Smith
, could

sts. In
works badly. Some

The **invisible hand** is the assertion that the individual pursuit of self-interest within free markets may allocate resources efficiently from society's viewpoint.

Figures and Tables

Each chapter provides a number of figures, illustrations and photos to help you to visualize economic examples.

industry, more work

Table 1.2 Production possibilities

Food workers	Output
4	25
3	22
2	17
1	10
0	0

The law of diminishing retur
d but other inputs

Boxed Examples

Each chapter includes short boxed examples. These aim to show how a particular economic principle can be applied in practice.

as and servic
ative mechanism of mar

Box 1.3 Poor Marx for central

During the Cold War, economists us
communism. But the Soviet bloc, fal
abandoned Marxist central planning
2003 fans of Chelsea Football Clu
had made his fortune in the marke
of Russia's leading oil companie

The Berlin Wall fell because th
difficulties that had emerg

mation

NEW! Activity boxes

These new boxes illustrate key economic concepts and then ask you to apply them – an excellent feature to develop the skill of applying economic ideas to the real world.

Activity box 1 Scarcely a h

Are we spending more on hea
government spending on heal
health services are being cut?
will rise from 23 per cent in 1
care. The same total spendi
have made available succ

Health spending is risin
ageing population,
care as in the

Chapter Summary

This briefly reviews and reinforces the main topics you have covered in each chapter to ensure you have acquired a solid understanding of the key topics. Use it as a quick reference to check you've understood the chapter.

Summary

- **Economics** analyses what, how a. reconcile the conflict between peo to produce goods and services to f

- The **production possibility fronti** produced given the output of the society in deciding what to prod unattainable. It is inefficient to

- The **opportunity cost of a** nit of the good. It is

Review Questions

These questions encourage you to review and apply the knowledge you have acquired from each chapter. They are a useful revision tool and can also be used by your lecturer as assignments or practice exam questions. Each chapter includes two harder questions and an essay question at the end of the standard review questions, allowing you to stretch yourself further once you have mastered the topic at a basic level.

Review questions

1 The police research department v unemployment rate. (a) How wou 'other things equal' problems wou

2 Use the data of Table 2.5 to plot a prices and the retail price index. data?

3 The table shows consumer s £ billion at 1995 prices. ome on the h

Also look out for the Interactive Graphing tool icon in the margins. This refers you to the OLC where you can practice drawing graphs relating to models in the book.

Technology to enhance learning and teaching

Online Learning Centre (OLC)

After completing each chapter, log on to the supporting Online Learning Centre website. Take advantage of the study tools offered to reinforce the material you have read in the text, and to develop your knowledge in a fun and effective way.

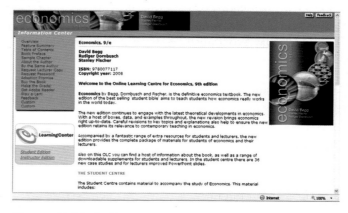

Resources for students include:

- Weblinks
- Solutions to the review questions in the book
- Interactive exercises
- Self-test questions
- Learning outcomes
- Chapter summaries
- Key terms
- NEW – interactive graphing tool
- NEW – searchable glossary of economics terms

Also available for lecturers:

- PowerPoint slides
- Chapter overviews
- Tutorial exercises
- Discussion questions with solutions
- Artwork from the book
- NEW – case study problems with teaching notes
- NEW – suggested course structures for teaching with Begg

EZTest

EZTest, a new computerized testbank format from McGraw-Hill, is available with this title. EZTest enables you to upload testbanks, select questions tagged by concept, difficulty and type, modify questions and add your own questions, thus creating a testbank that's totally unique to your course! Find out more at: http://mcgraw-hill.co.uk/he/eztest/

Visit www.mcgraw-hill.co.uk/textbooks/begg today

Custom Publishing Solutions: Let us help make our content your solution

At McGraw-Hill Education our aim is to help the lecturer find the most suitable content for their needs and the most appropriate way to deliver the content to their students. Our **Custom Publishing Solutions** offer the ideal combination of content delivered in the way which suits lecturer and students the best.

The idea behind our custom publishing programme is that, via a database of over two million pages called Primis, www.primisonline.com, the lecturer can select just the material they wish to deliver to their students:

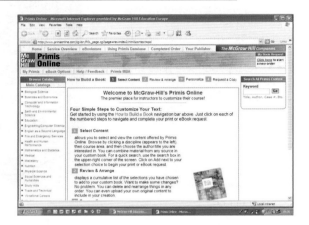

Lecturers can select chapters from:

- textbooks

- professional books

- case books – Harvard Articles, Insead, Ivey, Darden, Thunderbird and BusinessWeek

- Taking Sides – debate materials

Across the following imprints:

- McGraw-Hill Education

- Open University Press

- Harvard Business School Press

- US and European material

There is also the option to include material authored by lecturers in the custom product – this does not necessarily have to be in English.

We will take care of everything from start to finish in the process of developing and delivering a custom product to ensure that lecturers and students receive exactly the material needed in the most suitable way.

With a Custom Publishing Solution, students enjoy the best selection of material deemed to be the most suitable for learning everything they need for their courses – something of real value to support their learning. Teachers are able to use exactly the material they want, in the way they want, to support their teaching on the course.

Please contact your local McGraw-Hill representative with any questions or, alternatively, contact Warren Eels **e:** warren_eels@mcgraw-hill.com.

Make the grade!

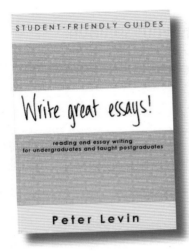
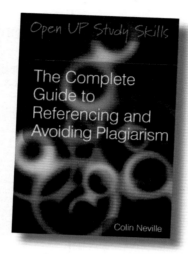

30% off any Study Skills book!

Our Study Skills books are packed with practical advice and tips that
are easy to put into practice and will really improve the way you study. Topics include:

- Techniques to help you pass exams
- Advice to improve your essay writing
- Help in putting together the perfect seminar presentation
- Tips on how to balance studying and your personal life

www.openup.co.uk/studyskills

Visit our website to read helpful hints about essays, exams, dissertations and much more.

Special offer! As a valued customer, buy online and receive 30% off any of our
Study Skills books by entering the promo code **getahead**

Acknowledgements for the 9th edition

We thank the team at McGraw-Hill for their support, advice and enthusiasm, and the many readers of previous editions who took the trouble to write with suggestions for improvements and ideas for the new edition.

We would like to thank the following reviewers who provided helpful suggestions and comments on the book as it progressed through its revision:

Alison Bailey, University of Reading
Mahmood Messkoub, University of Leeds
Giovanni Caggiano, Glasgow University
Roy Bailey, Essex University
Esa Mangeloja, Jyvaskyla University, Finland
Jerry Mushin, University of Wellington, New Zealand
Anthony Heyes, Royal Holloway, University of London
Kim Kaivanto, Lancaster University
Odile Poulsen, University of East Anglia

Every effort has been made to to trace and acknowledge ownership of copyright and to clear permission for material reproduced in this book. The publishers will be pleased to make suitable arrangements to clear permission with any copyright holders whom it has not been possible to contact.

About the lead author

Professor David Begg is Principal of the the business school at Imperial College London, currently ranked the world's fifth best university (*Times Higher Education Supplement*, November 2007).

Born in Glasgow, David went to Cambridge in the hope of playing cricket but became fascinated with economics. After also studying at Oxford, he won a Kennedy Scholarship to the Massachusetts Institute of Technology, where Stanley Fischer and Rudiger Dornbusch were his PhD supervisors.

David returned to jobs at Oxford then London universities. In 1983 he got together with Stan and Rudi to write what has become Europe's most successful economics textbook, featured by BBC Radio 4 in its series 'Student Bibles' along with other such classics as *Gray's Anatomy* (with over 100 years' start, now in its 39th edition!).

An expert on monetary and exchange rate policy, David has advised the IMF, the EU Commission, the Treasury, the Bank of England and several governments in emerging market economies.

He has always been committed to showing how useful economics is in making sense of the world around us. His other books include *Foundations of Economics* (now in its 3rd edition) and *Economics for Business* (co-authored with Damian Ward, now in its 2nd edition). The 9th edition of *Economics* remains the standard by which other economics textbooks are judged.

For those of you who keep asking about David's co-authors: after leaving MIT Stanley Fischer became Chief Economist of the World Bank, Deputy Head of the IMF, Vice Chairman of Citigroup and Governor of the Bank of Israel. Until his untimely death, Rudiger Dornbusch remained a professor at MIT; his analysis and recommendations were sought by countless governments and corporations. Stan and Rudi taught a generation of students – including Ben Bernanke, current Chairman of the US Federal Reserve.

Free with this book ...

Economics, 9th edition Interactive Workbook

Linked directly to the content in the book, and fully interactive, the *Economics, 9e* Workbook provides a range of tools and engaging activities, designed to consolidate your learning and give you the extra support you need to pass your principles course.

Features include:

- **Learning Outcomes checklists** to tick off and track progress as you complete the exercises
- **Important Concepts and Technical Terms matching exercises** to check your understanding of core economics concepts
- **Discussion questions** with feedback facility, to apply your knowledge to real economic scenarios
- **Interactive graphing questions**, where you can practise your graphing skills and view model answers
- **True/False questions** with feedback
- **Graded questions**, following the 'traffic light' signposting used in *Economics, 9e* to help you progress through different learning stages

Net Tutor

 NetTutor™ is an online tutoring service that meets the needs of instructors and students alike. Students experience fully customized tutoring powered by a specialized economics toolbar; gaining the benefits of immediate interactive sessions.

NetTutor™ is built on a rigorous tutor-training program and is available live seven days a week all year round. Our tutors know how to guide students in learning, rather than simply giving them an answer. Questions may also be submitted off-line any time, day or night, for review by tutors within the next business day. Threaded chat and tutorial archive centers offer further assistance. Matching students needing help with the quality of help educators expect, NetTutor™ represents the state-of the-art in online tutoring.

Log on to the Online Learning Centre: www.mcgraw-hill.co.uk/textbooks/begg for information on how to access these resources.

PART ONE

Introduction

Economics is all around you. It is about how society deals with the problem of scarcity. We cannot have everything we want, whether this refers to continuous holidays or perfectly clean air. We have to make choices. Economics is the study of how society makes these choices. Economics is not just about incomes, prices and money. Sometimes it makes sense to use markets, sometimes we need other solutions. Economic analysis helps us decide when to leave things to the market and when to override the market.

Chapter 1 introduces the central issues of scarcity and choice, and the extent of government involvement in these decisions. Chapter 2 outlines economic reasoning, discussing how our understanding is advanced by the interaction of theories and evidence. Chapter 3 illustrates markets in action.

Contents

Economics and the economy

Learning Outcomes

By the end of this chapter, you should understand:

1 that economics is the study of how society resolves the problem of scarcity

2 ways in which society decides what, how and for whom to produce

3 the concept of opportunity cost

4 positive and normative economics

5 microeconomics and macroeconomics

Every group of people must solve three basic problems of daily living: *what* goods and services to produce, *how* to produce them and *for whom* to produce them.

Goods are physical commodities, such as steel or strawberries. Services are activities such as massages or live concerts, consumed or enjoyed only at the instant they are produced. In rare cases some of the questions about what, how and for whom to produce have already been answered: until the arrival of Man Friday, Robinson Crusoe can ignore the 'for whom' question. Normally, society must answer all three questions.

> **Economics** is the study of how society decides what, how and for whom to produce.

By emphasizing the role of society, our definition places economics within the social sciences that study and explain human behaviour. Economics studies behaviour in the production, exchange and use of goods and services. The key economic problem for society is how to reconcile the conflict between people's virtually limitless desires for goods and services, and the scarcity of resources (labour, machinery and raw materials) with which these goods and services can be produced.

In answering what, how and for whom to produce, economics explains how scarce resources are allocated among competing claims on their use.

Although economics is about human behaviour, we describe it as a science. This reflects the method of analysis, not the subject matter, of economics. Economists develop theories of human behaviour and test them against the facts. Chapter 2 discusses the tools economists use and explains the sense in which this approach is scientific. This does not mean that economics ignores people as individuals. Moreover, good economics retains an element of art. Only by having a feel for how people actually behave can economists focus their analysis on the right issues.

> ### Box 1.1 Most output is service
>
> At the start of the twenty-first century, in advanced countries, agriculture comprises about 1 per cent of national output and industry less than 25 per cent. The rest is services, which include banking, transport, entertainment, communications, tourism, and public services (defence, police, education, health). In countries such as China and India, agriculture remains a higher share of GDP and services are not yet fully developed. Everywhere, services are the fastest growing part of output and of exports. Success in exporting banking, fashion and entertainment helps make the UK the second largest exporter of services in the world.
>
> In developed countries, services have for a long time been the largest component of national output. But until recently most international trade was trade in goods. The internet has changed all that. Accounting services can be outsourced to India and the advice of Indian accountants is as rapidly received by email in the UK as face to face in India.
>
> | % of national output | UK | USA | France | China | India |
> | --- | --- | --- | --- | --- | --- |
> | Agriculture | 1 | 1 | 2 | 13 | 19 |
> | Industry | 26 | 22 | 22 | 46 | 28 |
> | Services | 73 | 77 | 76 | 41 | 54 |
>
> *Source:* World Bank, *World Development Indicators* (http://devdata.worldbank.org).

1.1 Economic issues

Trying to understand what economics is about by studying definitions is like trying to learn to swim by reading an instruction manual. Formal analysis makes sense only once you have some practical experience. In this section we discuss two examples of how society allocates scarce resources between competing uses. In each case we see the importance of the questions what, how and for whom to produce.

Oil price shocks

Oil provides fuel for heating, transport and machinery and is an input for petrochemicals and household products ranging from plastic plates to polyester clothes. European economies can be brought to a halt by blockades of lorry drivers protesting about soaring fuel prices. What happens if continuing uncertainty in the Middle East or the ravages of climate change lead to very high oil prices? A little history lesson is useful in thinking about the likely results.

Up to 1973 the use of oil increased steadily. It was cheap and abundant. In 1973 OPEC – the Organization of Petroleum Exporting Countries (www.opec.org) – organized a production cutback by its members, making oil so scarce that its price tripled. Users could not quickly do without oil. Making oil scarce was very profitable for OPEC members.

Figure 1.1 shows the real (inflation-adjusted) price of oil, measured in US dollars, from 1970 to 2006. The price tripled in 1973–74, and doubled again in 1979–80, but then fell steadily until the mid-1990s. Markets found ways to overcome the oil shortage that OPEC had created. High oil prices

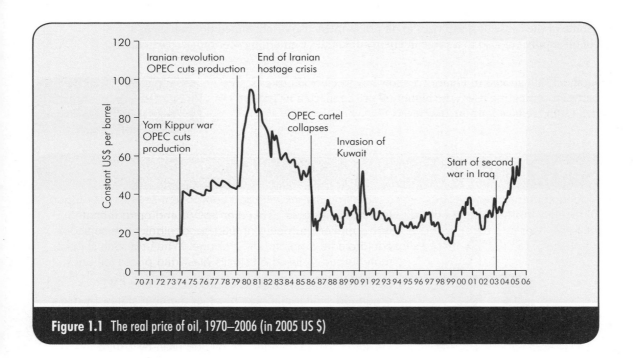

Figure 1.1 The real price of oil, 1970–2006 (in 2005 US $)

did not last indefinitely. Given time, the higher price induced consumers to use less oil and non-OPEC producers to sell more. These responses, guided by prices, are part of the way many societies determine what, how and for whom to produce. This suggests that the high oil prices since 1999 will lead eventually to a similar outcome.

Consider first *how* things are produced. When the price of oil jumps, firms cut their use of oil-based products. Chemical firms develop artificial substitutes for petroleum inputs, airlines order more fuel-efficient aircraft, and electricity is produced from more wind farms. Higher oil prices make the economy produce in a way that uses less oil.

How about *what* is being produced? Households install better insulation to economize on expensive central heating and they buy smaller cars. Commuters form car-pools or move to the city centre. High prices choke off the demand for oil-related commodities but also encourage consumers to purchase substitute commodities. Higher demand for these commodities bids up their price and encourages their production. Designers produce smaller cars, architects use solar energy, and research laboratories develop alternatives to petroleum in chemical production.

The *for whom* question in this example has a clear answer. The revenues of oil producers increased sharply. Much of their increased revenue was spent on goods produced in the industrialized Western nations. By contrast, oil-importing nations had to give up more of their own production in exchange for oil imports. In terms of goods as a whole, the rise in oil prices raised the buying power of OPEC and reduced the buying power of oil-importing countries such as Germany and Japan. The world economy was producing more for OPEC and less for Germany and Japan.

Figure 1.1 also shows that oil prices continue to fluctuate. After 1982 OPEC's power diminished as other oil supplies came on stream and users developed adequate substitutes. However, OPEC got its act together again in 1999, cut supply, forced up oil prices and prompted another fuel crisis in 2000, bringing lorry drivers on to the streets again. By 2004 the US and EU were pressing OPEC to increase oil supply in order to reverse the sharp rise in oil prices during uncertainties about Iraq and the Middle East.

Since 1999 some of the cause of sharp rises in oil prices must also be attributed not merely to a restriction of oil supply but also to a surge in energy demand by emerging economies, particularly China.

The oil price shocks illustrated in Figure 1.1 show how society allocates scarce resources between competing uses. The higher oil price reflected its greater scarcity when OPEC reduced production levels.

> A **resource** is **scarce** if the demand at a zero price would exceed the available supply.

Box 1.2 OPEC is back in charge of the oil price

In 2006, oil prices peaked at $80/barrel amid fears that, with suppliers pumping at full capacity, any adverse shock could create a painful oil shortage. When no such shocks materialized, unused oil stocks grew and prices fell back.

Saudi Arabia then reduced its production, and OPEC organized similar cutbacks by other member states. By mid-2007, OPEC production had fallen by 1 million barrels per day (mpd) compared with a year earlier. However, during the same period demand for oil had risen by 1 mpd. Leading forecasters started talking of $95 a barrel unless OPEC relented and increased oil supply again.

Writing in July 2007, *The Economist* noted that OPEC had every incentive not to kill the goose that keeps laying the golden egg. OPEC is likely to turn on the oil tap a bit if it perceives that oil prices have risen to such a height that they are seriously hurting the countries to which OPEC exports.

Adapted from *The Economist*, 21 July 2007.

Income distribution

You and your family have an annual income that lets you enjoy various goods and services and live in a particular place. Your standard of living includes the necessities of life – food, shelter, health, education – and something beyond, such as recreation. Your income is lower than some people's but higher than that of others.

> The **income distribution** (in a country or in the world) tells us how total income is divided between different groups or individuals.

Nations also have different levels of income. A nation's income, or national income, is the sum of the incomes of all its citizens. World income is the sum of all countries' incomes, hence also the sum of the incomes earned by all the people in the world.

Income distribution is closely linked to the what, how and for whom questions. Table 1.1 shows the percentage of world population that lives in different groups of countries. Twenty-one per cent of the world's population live in poor countries, such as Bangladesh and Indonesia. Seventy per cent live in middle-income countries, a group including Thailand, Brazil, Mexico and China. The rich countries, including the US, Western Europe, Canada and Japan, account for 9 per cent of world population.

Income per person indicates the average standard of living. Table 1.1 shows that in poor countries the average income per person is only £300 a year. In the rich industrial countries annual income is £17 700 per person, nearly sixty times larger. These are big differences.

Table 1.1 World population and income

	Country group		
	Poor	Middle	Rich
Income per head £	300	3900	17 700
% of world population	21	70	9
% of world income	3	19	78

Source: World Bank, *World Development Indicator.*

Table 1.1 also shows that poor countries account for one-fifth of the world's population but only 3 per cent of world income. Rich countries have 9 per cent of world population but 78 per cent of world income.

For whom does the world economy produce? Mainly, for the 9 per cent of its population living in the rich industrial countries. This answer also helps answer what is produced. World output is directed mainly to the goods and services consumed in the rich countries. These inequalities are part of what anti-capitalist protesters wish to highlight.

Why is inequality so great? This reflects how goods are produced. Poor countries have little machinery and few people with professional and technical training. One American worker uses power-driven earth-moving equipment to complete a task undertaken in Africa by many more workers equipped only with shovels. Workers in poor countries are less productive because they work under adverse conditions.

Income is unequally distributed within each country as well as between countries. In Brazil, the richest 10 per cent of families get 48 per cent of national income, but in the UK the richest 10 per cent get only 27 per cent of national income and in Denmark, only 20 per cent.

These differences partly reflect things we have already discussed. For example, state education increases access to education and training. However, in looking at income distribution within a country, we must include two extra things that are often less important when discussing differences in income per person between countries.

First, individual incomes come not just from working but also from owning assets (land, buildings, corporate equity) that earn rent, interest and dividends. In Brazil, ownership of land and factories is concentrated in the hands of a small group; in Denmark it is not.

Second, societies may decide whether to change their distribution of income. A pure socialist economy aims to achieve considerable equality of income and wealth. In contrast, in an economy of private ownership, wealth and power become concentrated in the hands of a few people. Between these extremes, the government may levy taxes to alter the income distribution that would otherwise emerge in a private ownership economy. One reason why Denmark has a more equal income distribution than Brazil is that Denmark levies high taxes on high incomes to reduce the buying power of the rich, and levies high taxes on inheritance to reduce the concentration of wealth in the hands of a few families.

The degree to which income is unequally distributed within a country affects not only for whom goods and services are produced, but also which goods are produced. In Brazil, where income is unequally distributed, the rich employ poor people as maids, cooks and chauffeurs. In Denmark, where equality is much greater, few people can afford to hire servants.

1.2 Scarcity and the competing use of resources

Consider an economy with 4 workers who can make food or films. Table 1.2 shows how much of each good can be made. The answer depends on how workers are allocated between the two industries. In each industry, more workers means more output of the good.

Table 1.2 Production possibilities

Food workers	Output	Film workers	Output
4	25	0	0
3	22	1	9
2	17	2	17
1	10	3	24
0	0	4	30

The law of diminishing returns applies when one input (such as labour) is varied but other inputs (such as equipment and land) remain fixed. Suppose workers in the film industry can use a fixed number of cameras and studios. The first worker has sole use of these facilities. With more workers, these facilities must be shared. Adding extra workers dilutes equipment per worker. Output per film worker falls as employment rises. A similar story applies in the food industry. Each industry faces diminishing returns to extra workers.

> The **law of diminishing returns** says each extra worker adds less to output than the previous extra worker added.

Table 1.2 shows combinations of food and films made if all 4 workers have jobs. By moving workers from one industry to the other, the economy can make more of one good but only by making less of the other good. There is a trade-off between food output and film output.

Figure 1.2 shows the maximum combinations of food and film output that the economy can produce. Point A plots the first row in Table 1.2, where food output is 25 and film output is 0. Points B, C, D and E correspond to the other rows of Table 1.2. The curve joining points *A* to *E* in Figure 1.2 is the 'production possibility frontier' or PPF.

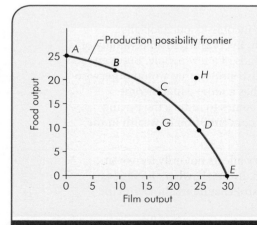

The frontier shows the maximum combinations of output that the economy can produce using all the available resources. The frontier displays a trade-off: more of one commodity implies less of the other. Points above the frontier need more inputs than the economy has available. Points inside the frontier are inefficient. By fully using available inputs the economy could expand output to the frontier.

Figure 1.2 The production possibility frontier

The frontier curves around the point given by zero output of both goods. This reflects the law of diminishing returns. Movements from A to B to C each transfer a worker from the food industry to the film industry. Each transfer reduces output per person in films but raises output per person in food. Each transfer yields less additional film output and gives up increasing amounts of food output.

> The **production possibility frontier** (PPF) shows, for each output of one good, the maximum amount of the other good that can be produced.

In Figure 1.2 suppose we begin at point A with 25 units of food but no films. Moving from A to B, we gain 9 films but lose 3 units of food. Thus, 3 units of food is the opportunity cost of producing the first 9 films. The slope of the PPF tells us the opportunity cost of a good: how much of one good we have to sacrifice to make more of another.

> The **opportunity cost of a good** is the quantity of other goods that must be sacrificed to get another unit of that good.

To see why the curve is a 'frontier', think about point G in Figure 1.2. Society makes 10 units of food and 17 films. This is feasible. From Table 1.2, it needs 1 worker in the food industry and 2 in the film industry. Society has spare resources. The fourth person is not employed. G is not a point on the PPF because we can make more of one good without sacrificing output of the other good. Employing the extra person in the food industry takes us to point C, with 7 extra units of food for the same film output. Employing the extra person to work in films takes us to point D, with 7 extra units of films but no less food output.

The PPF shows the points at which society is producing efficiently. Points such as G inside the frontier are inefficient because society is wasting resources. More output of one good would not require less output of the other. There would be no opportunity cost of expanding output of one good a bit.

Points outside the production possibility frontier, such as H in Figure 1.2, are unattainable. Given the inputs available, this output combination cannot be made. Scarce resources limit society to a choice of points inside or on the production possibility frontier. Society must choose how to allocate these scarce resources between competing uses.

> **Production efficiency** means more output of one good can be obtained only by sacrificing output of other goods.

Since people like food and films, society wants to produce efficiently. Points inside the PPF sacrifice output unnecessarily. Society chooses between the different points *on* the production possibility frontier. In so doing, it decides not only what to produce but how to produce. Table 1.2 shows how many workers must be allocated to each industry to make a particular output combination. As yet, our example is too simple to show for whom society produces.

How does society decide where to produce on the production possibility frontier? The government may decide. However, in most Western economies, the most important process that determines what, how and for whom goods are produced is the operation of markets.

1.3 The role of the market

Markets bring together buyers and sellers of goods and services. In some cases, such as a local fruit stall, buyers and sellers meet physically. In other cases, such as the stock market, business can be transacted by computer. We use a general definition of markets.

> A **market** is a process by which households' decisions about consumption of alternative goods, firms' decisions about what and how to produce, and workers' decisions about how much and for whom to work are all reconciled by adjustment of prices

Prices of goods and of resources (labour, machinery, land, energy) adjust to ensure that scarce resources are used to make the goods and services that society wants. You buy a hamburger for lunch because it is fast, convenient and cheap. You prefer steak but it is more expensive. The price of steak is high enough to ensure that society answers the 'for whom' question about lunchtime steaks in favour of someone else.

Activity box 1   Scarcely a hospital bed!

Are we spending more on health, or are hospitals in decline? Real (inflation-adjusted) government spending on health is 60 per cent higher than in 1990. So why do people think health services are being cut? First, we are living longer. Of the UK population, the over-65s will rise from 23 per cent in 1980 to 31 per cent by 2030. Older people need more health care. The same total spending means lower standards per person. Second, medical advances have made available successful but very expensive treatments. We all want them.

Health spending is rising a little faster than national output as a whole. However, with an ageing population, health spending must rise *faster* if people are to get the same standard of care as in the past. And to get any new treatment, however costly, health spending has to rise *much faster* still.

The real issue is *scarcity*: on what to spend our limited resources? Do we have fewer teachers and televisions in order to divert more resources to health? If not, we have to ration health care. Rationing can be done through markets (charging for health care so people choose to have less) or through rules (limiting access to treatment). Society's decision affects what is produced, how it is produced and, dramatically in this example, for whom it is produced.

Better health services do not come free. The *opportunity* cost of having more nurses and doctors is the quantity of education, entertainment and other outputs we have to sacrifice in order to divert more of our scarce resources into health care.

Questions

(a) A century ago, do you think health care was rationed? Explain why or why not?

(b) When the National Health Service made health care 'free at the point of delivery', did this mean **everyone** could have as much health care as they wished? If not, how did the NHS ration health care?

To check your answers to these questions, go to page 712.

McDonald's are in the business because, given the price of beefburger meat, the rent, and the wages for staff, they can still sell beefburgers at a profit. If rents were higher, they might sell beefburgers in a cheaper area or switch to luxury lunches for rich executives. The student behind the counter works there because a part-time job helps meet his tuition fees. If the wage were lower, he might not work at all. Conversely, the job is unskilled and there are plenty of students looking for such work, so McDonald's do not have to offer high wages.

Prices guide your decision to buy a beefburger, McDonald's decision to sell beefburgers, and the student's decision to take the job. Society allocates resources – meat, buildings and labour – into beefburger production through the price system. If people hated beefburgers, McDonald's sales revenue would not cover their cost. Society would devote no resources to beefburger production. People's desire to eat beefburgers guides resources into beefburger production.

However, when cattle contract BSE, consumers shun beefburgers in favour of bacon sandwiches, and the price of BLTs rises. As the fast food industry scrambles to get enough pork, the price of pigs rises but the price of beef falls. Adjustments in prices encourage society to reallocate land from beef to pig farming. At the height of the British beef crisis, caused by fears about 'mad cow' disease, pork prices rose 25 per cent but beef prices fell. Quite an incentive to reallocate!

The command economy

How would resources be allocated if markets did not exist? Such planning is very complicated. There is no complete command economy where all allocation decisions are undertaken in this way. However, in many countries, for example China, Cuba, and those formerly in the Soviet bloc, there was a large measure of central direction and planning. The state owned factories and land, and made the most important decisions about what people should consume, how goods should be produced, and how people should work.

This is a huge task. Imagine that you had to run by command the city or town in which you live. Think of the food, clothing, and housing allocation decisions you would have to make. How would you decide who should get what and the process by which goods and services are made? These decisions are being made every day, mainly by the allocative mechanism of markets and prices.

> In a **command economy** a government planning office decides what will be produced, how it will be produced, and for whom it will be produced. Detailed instructions are then issued to households, firms and workers.

Box 1.3 Poor Marx for central planners

During the Cold War, economists used to argue about the relative merits of capitalism and communism. But the Soviet bloc, falling increasingly behind the living standards of the West, abandoned Marxist central planning after 1990 and began transition to a market economy. By 2003 fans of Chelsea Football Club were celebrating their new owner Roman Abramovitch, who had made his fortune in the market economy, initially as an oil trader and then as chairman of one of Russia's leading oil companies.

The Berlin Wall fell because the Soviet bloc had fallen far behind market economies in the West. Key difficulties that had emerged were:

- **Information overload**   Planners could not keep track of the details of economic activity. Machinery rusted because nobody came to install it after delivery, crops rotted because storage and distribution were not co-ordinated.

- **Bad incentives**   Complete job security undermined work incentives. Factory managers ordered excess raw materials to ensure they got materials again the next year. Since planners could monitor quantity more easily than quality, firms met output targets by skimping on quality. Without environmental standards, firms polluted at will. Central planning led to low-quality goods and an environmental disaster.

- **Insufficient competition**   Planners believed big was beautiful. One tractor factory served the Soviets from Latvia to Vladivostok. But large scale deprived planners of information from competing firms, making it hard to assess efficiency. Managers got away with inefficiency. Similarly, without electoral competition, it was impossible to sack governments making economic mistakes.

The 'invisible hand'

Individuals in free markets pursue their own self-interest without government direction or interference. The idea that such a system could solve the what, how and for whom problems is one of the oldest themes in economics, dating back to the Scottish economist Adam Smith, whose book *The Wealth of Nations* (1776), remains a classic. Smith argued that individuals pursuing

> Markets in which governments do not intervene are called **free markets**.

their self-interest would be led 'as by an invisible hand' to do things that are in the interests of society as a whole.

Suppose you wish to become a millionaire. You play around with new ideas and invent something, perhaps the DVD. Although motivated by self-interest, you make society better off by creating new jobs and opportunities. You move society's production possibility frontier outwards – the same resources now make more or better goods – and become a millionaire in the process. Smith argued that the pursuit of self-interest, without any central direction, could produce a coherent society making sensible allocative decisions.

> The **invisible hand** is the assertion that the individual pursuit of self-interest within free markets may allocate resources efficiently from society's viewpoint.

This remarkable insight has been studied at length by modern economists. In later chapters, we explain when the invisible hand works well and when it works badly. Some government intervention may then be justified.

The mixed economy

The free market allows individuals to pursue their self-interest without government restrictions. The command economy allows little scope for individual economic freedom. Decisions are taken centrally by the government. Between these extremes lies the mixed economy.

> In a **mixed economy** the government and private sector jointly solve economic problems. The government influences decisions through taxation, subsidies, and provision of free services such as defence and the police. It also regulates the extent to which individuals may pursue their own self-interest.

Most countries are mixed economies, though some are close to command economies and others are much nearer the free market economy. Figure 1.3 illustrates this point. Even Cuba allows consumers some choice over the goods they buy. Conversely, even countries such as the United States, which espouse more enthusiastically the free market approach, still have substantial levels of government activity in the provision of public goods and services, the redistribution of income through taxes and transfer payments, and the regulation of markets.

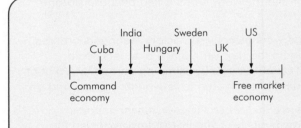

The role of the market in allocating resources differs vastly between countries. In the command economy resources are allocated by central government planning. In the free market economy there is virtually no government regulation of the consumption, production and exchange of goods. In between lies the mixed economy, where market forces play a large role but the government intervenes extensively.

Figure 1.3 Market orientation

1.4 Positive and normative

> **Positive economics** studies objective or scientific explanations of how the economy works.

In studying economics it is important to distinguish 'positive' and 'normative' economics.

The aim of positive economics is to analyse how society makes decisions about consumption, production, and exchange of goods. It aims both to explain why the economy works as it does, and to allow predictions about how the economy will respond to changes. In positive economics, we aim to act as detached scientists. Whatever our political sympathy or our ethical code, we examine how the world actually works. At this stage, there is no scope for personal value judgements. We are concerned with propositions of the form: if *this* is changed then *that* will happen. In this regard, positive economics is similar to the natural sciences such as physics, geology or astronomy.

> **Normative economics** offers recommendations based on personal value judgements.

Box 1.4 Green piece

Our planet is running out of rainforests and fish stocks, and climate change is threatening to destroy the planet completely. Why do we manage the environment so badly? An economist's response is 'because we do not price it like other commodities'. The market 'solved' the problem of scarcity when OPEC restricted oil supplies. High prices encouraged more supply and less demand. Why not price the environment, encouraging people to look after it?

Until now, the reason has been technology. Anyone can walk in a field, dump rubbish after dark, pump chemicals into a river, or drive down a public street. Gradually, however, electronic monitoring of usage is getting easier and cheaper. It is then possible to treat the environment as another commodity to be marketed. This prompts a vigorous debate about the 'what, how and for whom' questions.

We know how to charge cars for using a particular street at a particular time. A smart card in the car picks up signals as it passes each charge point. The driver gets a monthly bill like a credit card bill. Rush-hour traffic pays more when congestion is severe. The 'for whom' question can also be addressed. Residents can get a flat-rate annual payment, in exchange for supporting road pricing. Pricing the environment has a big advantage. It introduces a feedback mechanism. When society makes mistakes an alarm bell rings *automatically*. The price of scarce things rises.

This is one reason why so many economists think that establishing a comprehensive global market for carbon, the key component of emissions that lead to a build-up of greenhouse gases, is a necessary part of the solution to global warming.

Economists of widely differing political persuasions would agree that, when the government imposes a tax on a good, the price of that good will rise. The normative question of whether this price rise is desirable is entirely distinct.

As in any other science, there are unresolved questions where disagreement remains. These disagreements are at the frontiers of positive economics. Research in progress will resolve some of these issues but new issues will arise, providing scope for further research.

Competent and comprehensive research can in principle resolve many of the outstanding issues in positive economics; no such claim can be made about the resolution of issues in normative economics. Normative economics is based on subjective value judgements, not on the search for any objective truth. The following statement combines positive and normative economics: 'The elderly have very high medical expenses, and the government should subsidize their health bills.' The first part of the proposition is a statement in positive economics. It is a statement about how the world works. We can imagine a research programme that could determine whether or not it is correct. (Broadly speaking, it is.)

The second part of the proposition – the recommendation about what the government should do – could never be 'proved' true or false by any scientific research investigation. It is a subjective value judgement based on the feelings of the person making the statement. Many people might share this subjective judgement. Others might reasonably disagree. You might believe that it is more important to devote society's scarce resources to improving the environment not the health of the aged.

Economics cannot be used to show that one of these normative judgements is correct and the other is wrong. It all depends on the preferences or priorities of the individual or the society that has to make this choice. But we can use positive economics to clarify the menu of options from which society must eventually make its normative choice.

Most economists have normative views. Some economists are vociferous champions of particular normative recommendations. However, this advocacy role about what society should do must be distinguished from the role of the economist as an expert about the likely consequences of pursuing any course of action. In the latter case, the professional economist is offering expert advice on positive economics. Scrupulous economists distinguish their role as an expert adviser on positive economics from their status as involved private citizens arguing for particular normative choices.

1.5 Micro and macro

Many economists specialize in a particular branch of the subject. Labour economics deals with jobs and wages. Urban economics deals with land use, transport, congestion, and housing. However, we need not classify branches of economics by subject area. We can also classify branches of economics according to the approach used. The division of approaches into microeconomic and macroeconomic cuts across the subject groupings cited above.

> **Microeconomics** offers a detailed treatment of individual decisions about particular commodities.

For example, we can study why individuals prefer cars to bicycles and how producers decide whether to produce cars or bicycles. We can then aggregate the behaviour of all households and all firms to discuss total car purchases and total car production. We can examine the market for cars. Comparing this with the market for bicycles, we can explain the relative price of cars and bicycles and the relative output of these two goods. The sophisticated branch of microeconomics known as general equilibrium theory extends this approach to its logical conclusion. It studies simultaneously every market for every commodity. From this it is hoped to understand the complete pattern of consumption, production, and exchange in the whole economy at a point in time.

But this is very complicated. It is easy to lose track of the phenomena in which we were interested. The interesting task, that retains an element of art in economic science, is to devise judicious simplifications that keep the analysis manageable without distorting reality too much. Here, microeconomists and macroeconomists proceed down different avenues.

Microeconomists tend to offer a detailed treatment of one aspect of economic behaviour but ignore interactions with the rest of the economy in order to preserve the simplicity of the analysis. A microeconomic analysis of footballers' wages would emphasize the characteristics of footballers and the ability of football clubs to pay. It would largely neglect the chain of indirect effects to which a rise in footballers' wages might give rise (such as higher prices for luxury houses, leading to a boom in swimming pool manufacture). When microeconomic analysis ignores indirectly induced effects it is 'partial' rather than 'general' analysis.

> **Macroeconomics** emphasizes interactions in the economy as a whole. It deliberately simplifies the individual building blocks of the analysis in order to retain a manageable analysis of the complete interaction of the economy.

In some instances, indirect effects may not be important and it will make sense for economists to examine particular industries or activities in great detail. When indirect effects are too important to ignore, an alternative simplification must be found.

Macroeconomists rarely worry about the division of consumer goods into cars, bicycles, and videos. Instead, they treat them as a single bundle called 'consumer goods' because they want to study the interaction between household purchases of consumer goods and firms' decisions about purchases of machinery and buildings.

Because macroeconomic concepts refer to the whole economy, they get more media coverage than microeconomic concepts, which are chiefly of interest to those in a specific group. Here are three macroeconomic concepts you have probably encountered.

Gross domestic product (GDP)

After the terrorist attacks of 9/11, people worried that the global economy might face a recession. During a recession, GDP is falling or growing only very slowly.

> **Gross domestic product (GDP)** is the value of total output of an economy in a given period.

Aggregate price level

The prices of different goods may move differently. The aggregate price level tells us what is happening to prices on average. When this price level is rising, we say there is inflation.

> The **aggregate price level** measures the average price of goods and services.

Unemployment rate

The labour force is people of working age who have a job or want one. Some of the rich, the sick and the lazy are of working age but not looking for work. They are not in the labour force and not counted as unemployed.

> The **unemployment rate** is the fraction of the labour force without a job.

People dislike both inflation and unemployment. In the 1970s, oil price shocks and excessive money creation led to high inflation. Then, inflation fell but unemployment increased. By 2000 both inflation and unemployment had finally fallen back to low levels. Yet by 2007 inflation was beginning to increase again. Macroeconomists want to understand what generates these fluctuations.

Getting the most out of each chapter

There is a summary of the main points at the end of each chapter. Like learning to drive, the best way to check your progress is not to read more and more but to try to do it for yourself. Do the problems that follow the summary (answers follow Chapter 36). The accompanying *Workbook* has many more problems, also with answers: a self-contained driving instructor.

Summary

- **Economics** analyses what, how and for whom society produces. The key economic problem is to reconcile the conflict between people's virtually unlimited demands with society's limited ability to produce goods and services to fulfil these demands.

- The **production possibility frontier** (PPF) shows the maximum amount of one good that can be produced given the output of the other good. It depicts the trade-off or menu of choices for society in deciding what to produce. Resources are **scarce** and points outside the frontier are unattainable. It is inefficient to produce within the frontier.

- The **opportunity cost** of a good is the quantity of other goods sacrificed to make an additional unit of the good. It is the slope of the PPF.

- Industrial countries rely extensively on **markets** to allocate resources. The market resolves production and consumption decisions by adjustments in prices.

- In a **command economy**, decisions on what, how and for whom are made in a central planning office. No economy relies entirely on command.

- A **free market economy** has no government intervention. Resources are allocated entirely through markets in which individuals pursue their own self-interest. Adam Smith argued that an **'invisible hand'** would nevertheless allocate resources efficiently.

- Modern economies are **mixed**, relying mainly on the market but with a large dose of government intervention. The optimal level of intervention is hotly debated.

- **Positive economics** studies how the economy actually behaves. **Normative economics** recommends what should be done. The two should be kept separate. Given sufficient research, economists could agree on issues in positive economics. Normative economics involves subjective value judgements. There is no reason why people should agree about normative statements.

- **Microeconomics** offers a detailed analysis of particular activities in the economy. For simplicity, it may neglect some interactions with the rest of the economy. **Macroeconomics** emphasizes these interactions at the cost of simplifying the individual building blocks.

Review questions   To check your answers to these questions, go to page 712.

1   An economy has 5 workers. Each worker can make 4 cakes or 3 shirts however many others work in the same industry. (a) Draw the production possibility frontier. (b) How many cakes can society get if it does without shirts? (c) What points in your diagram are inefficient? (d) What is the opportunity cost of making a shirt? (e) Does the law of diminishing returns hold in this economy?

2   Communist Russia used prices to allocate production among different consumers. Central planners set production targets but then put output in shops, fixed prices and gave workers money to spend. Why not plan the allocation of particular goods to particular people as well?

3 Society abolishes higher education. Students have to find jobs immediately. If there are no jobs available, how do wages and prices adjust so those who want jobs can find them?

4 Which of the following statements are positive, and which are normative? (a) Annual inflation is below 2 per cent. (b) Because inflation is low the government should cut taxes. (c) Income is higher in the UK than in Poland. (d) Brits are happier than Poles.

5 Which statements refer to microeconomics, which to macroeconomics? (a) Inflation is lower than in the 1980s. (b) Food prices fell this month. (c) Good weather means a good harvest. (d) Unemployment in London is below the UK average.

6 **Common fallacies** Why are these statements wrong? (a) Since some economists are Tory but others Labour, economics can justify anything. (b) There is no such thing as a free lunch. To get more of one thing, you have to give up something else. (c) Economics is about people, and thus cannot be a science.

7 **Harder question** OPEC made a fortune for its members by organizing production cutbacks and forcing up prices. (a) Why have coffee producers not managed to do the same? (b) Could UK textile firms force up textile prices by cutting back UK textile production?

8 **Harder question** Suppose it becomes possible in 5 years' time to make as much energy as we want from biofuels provided the price is the equivalent of at least $50/barrel for oil. (a) What does this imply about the eventual price of oil in, say, 10 years' time? (b) Is it possible for oil prices to be substantially above $50/barrel for the next few years? (c) Do higher oil prices in the short run increase or reduce the incentive to look for alternative energy technologies?

9 **Essay question** Two similar countries take the decision to try to increase the health of their poorest people. One country raises taxes on the rich and gives more money to the poor. The other country raises taxes on the rich and provides more health care, free to patients, through its National Health Service. Which country do you think is more likely to meet its objective? Why?

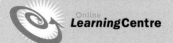

To help you grasp the key concepts of this chapter check out the extra resources posted on the Online Learning Centre. There are chapter summaries, self-test questions, an interactive graphing tool, weblinks and a searchable glossary, all for free!

To put your learning into practice and prepare for exams, an **Interactive Workbook** is also available online, containing a variety of question types and providing feedback on your answers.

If you'd like further help with economics, or have any questions, **NetTutor** is here to help! You will have a personalised tutorial service at your fingertips. Visit the online learning centre at: www.mcgraw-hill.co.uk/textbooks/begg for information on accessing all of these resources.

CHAPTER 2

Tools of economic analysis

Learning Outcomes

By the end of this chapter, you should understand:

1 why theories deliberately simplify reality

2 time-series and cross-section data

3 how to construct index numbers

4 nominal and real variables

5 how to build a simple theoretical model

6 how to plot data and interpret scatter diagrams

7 how to use 'other things equal' to ignore, but not forget, important influences

It is more fun to play tennis if you know how to serve, and cutting trees is much easier with a chainsaw. Every activity or academic discipline has a basic set of tools. Tools may be tangible, like the dentist's drill, or intangible, like the ability to serve in tennis. This chapter is about the tools of the trade. To analyse economic issues we use both *models* and *data*.

Models or theories – we use these terms interchangeably – are frameworks to organize how we think about a problem. They simplify by omitting some details of the real world to concentrate on the essentials. From this manageable picture of reality we develop an analysis of how the economy works.

> A **model** or **theory** makes assumptions from which it deduces how people will behave. It is a deliberate simplification of reality.

An economist uses a model as a tourist uses a map. A map of Glasgow misses out many features of the real world – traffic lights, roundabouts, speed bumps – but with careful study you get a good idea of how the traffic flows and the best route to take. The simplified picture is easy to follow, but helps you understand actual behaviour when you must drive through the city in the rush hour.

The data or facts interact with models in two ways. First, the data help us quantify the relationships to which our theoretical models draw attention. It is not enough to know that all bridges across the Clyde are likely to be congested. To choose the best route we need to know how long we have to queue at each bridge. We need some facts. The model is useful because it tells us which facts are likely to be the most important.

> **Data** are pieces of evidence about economic behaviour.

Second, the data help us to test our models. Like all careful scientists, economists must check that their theories square with the *relevant* facts. For example, for a while the number of Scottish dysentery deaths was closely related to UK inflation. Is this a factual coincidence or the key to a theory of inflation? The facts alert us to the need to ponder this question, but we can decide only by logical reasoning.

In this instance, we can find no theoretical connection. Hence, we view the close factual relationship between Scottish dysentery deaths and UK inflation as a coincidence that should be ignored. Without a logical underpinning, the empirical connection will break down sooner or later. Paying attention to a freak relationship in the data increases neither our understanding of the economy nor our confidence in predicting the future.

The blend of models and data is subtle. The data alert us to logical relationships we had overlooked. And whatever theory we wish to maintain should certainly be checked against the facts. But only theoretical reasoning can guide an intelligent assessment of what evidence has reasonable relevance.

When a theory that makes sense has for a long time survived exposure to the relevant economic data, we sometimes accord it the status of a law, such as the law of diminishing returns.

> A **behavioural law** is a sensible theoretical relationship not rejected by evidence over a long period.

Next we turn to the representation of economic data. Then we show how an economist might develop a theoretical model of an economic relationship. Finally, we discuss how actual data might be used to test the theory that has been developed.

2.1 Economic data

How might we present data to help us think about an economic problem?

Time-series data

The first two columns of Table 2.1 report a time series of monthly copper prices. It shows how the price changes over time. This information may be presented in tables or charts.

> A **time series** is a sequence of measurements of the same variable at different points in time.

Table 2.1 The price of copper, 2006 (US$/tonne)

Monthly	$/tonne	Quarterly	$/tonne
Sept	7599	III	7666
Oct	7498		
Nov	7027		
Dec	6671	IV	7065

Source: London Metal Exchange, www.lme.co.uk.

Figure 2.1 *plots*, or *graphs*, these data. Each point in the figure corresponds to an entry in the table. Point *A* shows that in September 2006 the price of copper was $7599 per tonne. The series of points or dots in Figure 2.1, in whichever colour, contains the same information as the first two columns of Table 2.1.

Charts or diagrams must be interpreted with care. The eye is easily misled by simple changes in presentation of the data. In Figure 2.1 the flat graph corresponds to the left-hand scale and the peaked graph corresponds to the enlarged scale on the right. Both graphs plot the same data but the peaked graph seems to move more. Diagrams can be manipulated in suggestive ways, a point well understood in advertising and politics.

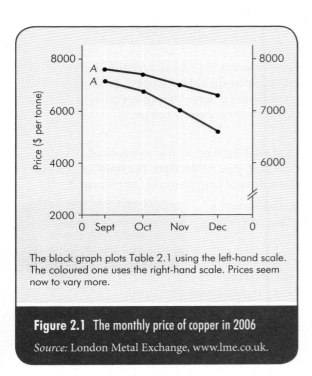

The black graph plots Table 2.1 using the left-hand scale. The coloured one uses the right-hand scale. Prices seem now to vary more.

Figure 2.1 The monthly price of copper in 2006

Source: London Metal Exchange, www.lme.co.uk.

Daily data usually contain too much detail. Imagine studying daily prices over 10 or 20 years! Averages over a month, a quarter (three months) or a year may be the best way to present data. The last two columns of Table 2.1 show quarterly averages for copper prices in 2006. The four quarters of the year are the periods January–March, April–June, July–September and October–December. For the fourth quarter of 2006, the data in the second and fourth columns of Table 2.1 overlap. The quarterly average of 7065 for the 2006 fourth quarter is a third of the sum of the monthly numbers for October, November and December.

Cross-section data

Time-series data record how a particular variable changes over time. Economists also use cross-section data. Table 2.2 shows a cross-section of unemployment rates in 2007.

Cross-section data record at a point in time the way an economic variable differs across different individuals or groups of individuals.

Table 2.2 Unemployment by country, 2007 (% of labour force)

USA	Japan	Germany	France	UK
4.9	3.7	7.5	8.4	5.8

Source: OECD, *Economic Outlook.*

2.2 Index numbers

To compare numbers without emphasizing units of measurement, we use index numbers.

Table 2.3 shows annual averages for aluminium and copper prices. We could choose 2001 as the base year and assign the value 100 to both the aluminium and the copper price index in this base year.

By 2004 the aluminium price of 1700 dollars per tonne was 1.13 times its price in 2001. If the aluminium prices had been 100 in 2001, this index must be 113 by 2004. To get the 2006 value, we divide the 2006 aluminium price of 2600 by the 2001 price of 1500 to get 1.73. Multiplying this by the starting value of 100 for the index in 2001 yields 173 for the aluminium index in 2006, as in Table 2.3. The price index for copper is calculated in the same way, dividing each price by the 2001 price, then multiplying by 100.

Now check that you understand this procedure. In 1992 average aluminium prices were 1000 dollars per tonne and average copper prices 2280. What were the values of the aluminium and copper price indices? (Answer: 67 and 134.)

Table 2.3 Prices of aluminium and copper (US$/tonne)

	2001	2004	2006
Aluminium price	1500	1700	2600
Copper price	1700	3000	6200
Aluminium Index (2001 = 100)	100	113	173
Copper Index (2001 = 100)	100	176	365
Metals Index (2001 = 100)	100	163	327

Source: London Metal Exchange, www.lme.co.uk.

Index numbers as averages

Now think about the price of metals as a whole. The prices of different metals change differently. To derive a single measure of metal prices we *average* different metal prices.

> An **index number** expresses data relative to a given base value.

Suppose aluminium and copper are the only metals. An index of metal prices in the fifth row makes a single time series by combining the time series in the third and fourth rows of Table 2.3. In the metal index, each metal has a weight or share that reflects the purpose for which the index is constructed. If it summarizes what firms pay for metal inputs, the weights should reflect the relative use of aluminium and copper as industrial inputs. Copper is much more widely used than aluminium. We might choose a weight of 0.8 for copper and 0.2 for aluminium. The weights always add up to 1.

The last row of Table 2.3 shows changes over time in the metal price index, the *weighted average* of the indices for aluminium and copper. In the base year 2001, the metals index is 100, being $(0.2 \times 100) + (0.8 \times 100)$. By 2004 the index is 163, which is $(0.8 \times 173) + (0.2 \times 113)$. In 2006 the index was 327.

The metals index, a weighted average of aluminium and copper prices, must lie between the indices for the two separate metals. The weights determine whether the metals index more closely resembles the behaviour of copper prices or aluminium prices.

The RPI and other indices

To keep track of the prices faced by consumers, countries construct a *consumer price index*. In the UK this is called the *retail price index* (RPI). The RPI is used to measure changes in the cost of living, the money that must be spent to purchase the typical bundle of goods consumed by a representative household.

> The **inflation rate** is the annual rate of change of the retail price index.

The RPI is constructed in two stages. First, index numbers are calculated for each category of commodity purchased by households. Then the RPI is constructed by taking a weighted average of the different commodity groupings. Table 2.4 shows the weights used and the main commodity groupings. A 10 per cent rise in food prices will change the RPI more than a 10 per cent rise in the price of leisure goods because food has a much larger weight than leisure goods.

Other examples of indices include the index of wages in manufacturing, a weighted average of wages in different manufacturing industries. The 'footsie', or FTSE, is the *Financial Times–Stock Exchange* index of share prices quoted on the London stock exchange. The *index of industrial production* is a weighted average of the *quantity* of goods produced by industry.

Table 2.4 RPI weights in the UK, 2006

Item	Weights
Food and non-alcoholic beverages	0.105
Alcoholic beverages and tobacco	0.096
Clothing and footwear	0.049
Housing, water, electricity, gas	0.255
Household goods	0.071
Household services	0.066
Transport	0.159
Personal goods and services	0.041
Leisure goods	0.041
Leisure services	0.067
Catering	0.050

Source: ONS, *Monthly Digest of Statistics*.

The procedure by which index numbers are calculated is always the same. We choose a base date at which to set the index equal to 100, then calculate other values relative to this baseline. Where the index refers to more than one commodity, we have to choose weights by which to average across the different commodities that the index describes.

2.3 Nominal and real variables

The first row of Table 2.5 shows the average price of a new house, which rose from £3100 in 1963 to £200 000 in 2007. Are houses really 65 times as expensive as in 1963? Not when we allow for inflation, which also raised incomes and the ability to buy houses.

Table 2.5 UK house prices (average price of a new house)

	1963	1983	2006
House price (£000s)	3.1	32.9	200
RPI (2007 = 100)	9.3	57.4	100
Real price of houses (2007 £000s)	33.3	57.3	200

Source: ONS, *Economic Trends*.

The second row of Table 2.5 shows the retail price index, using 2007 as the base year. Inflation led to substantial increases in the RPI during 1963–2007. The third row of Table 2.5 calculates an index of real house prices, expressed in 2007 prices. The value of house prices is the same in 2007 in the top and bottom rows.

To calculate the real price of houses in 1963, by expressing them at 2007 prices, we take the nominal price of £3100 and multiply by [(100)/(9.3)] to allow for subsequent inflation, yielding £33 300. Real prices have risen roughly sixfold since 1963 (from £33 300 to £200 000). Most of the 65-fold increase in nominal house prices in the top row of Table 2.5 was due to inflation.

> **Nominal values** are measured in the prices ruling at the time of measurement. **Real values** adjust nominal values for changes in the price level.

Real or relative prices

The distinction between nominal and real variables applies to all variables measured in money values. It does not apply to units of output, such as 4000 carpets per annum, which relate to physical quantities. Whatever the inflation rate, 4000 carpets is 4000 carpets. However, we do not know whether £100 is a large or a small amount until we know the general price level for goods.

The argument carries over to prices themselves. The nominal price of silver has risen a lot since 1970. To calculate an index of the *real price of silver*, divide an index of nominal silver prices by the retail price index and multiply by 100. Real prices indicate economic scarcity. They show whether the price of a commodity rose faster than prices in general. Hence, real prices are sometimes called *relative prices*.

Consider the price of televisions over the past 20 years. TV prices, measured in pounds, have hardly changed. The RPI has risen a lot. The real price of TVs has fallen. Advances in technology have reduced the cost of producing televisions. Because the real price has fallen, many households now have several TVs. It is misleading to base our analysis on nominal values of variables.

The purchasing power of money

When the price of goods rises, the purchasing power of money falls because £1 buys fewer goods. To distinguish real and nominal variables, we say that real variables measure nominal variables as if the purchasing power of money had been constant. Another way to express this idea is to distinguish nominal variables in *current* pounds and real variables in *constant* pounds.

> The **purchasing power of money** is an index of the quantity of goods that can be bought for £1.

Table 2.5 described real prices of houses measured in 2007 pounds. We could of course have used 1960 pounds instead. Although the level of the real price index for houses would have been different, it would have grown at exactly the same rate as the final row of Table 2.5.

Box 2.1 Millionaires galore

One in every 500 adults in Britain is now a millionaire. The Lottery created only a handful of Britain's 85 000 millionaires. It's mainly just the effect of inflation. The table below shows how much an old-fashioned millionaire would be worth at today's prices. Being a millionaire gets easier all the time.

£1 million in prices of year:	1988	1978	1968	1948	1938
= £ millions in 2000 prices	2	4	11	22	43

Sources: ONS, Economic Trends; UN, Economic Surveys of Europe.

> ## Box 2.2 Hyperinflation
>
> In 1918 the Allied victors demanded that Germany make reparations for the damage done and pay the pensions of Allied armed forces engaged in the war. By 1922, in economic ruin, Germany suspended reparations. In January 1923 French and Belgian troops occupied the Ruhr coalfields. German workers began a general strike and the government rolled the presses to print money to pay the 2 million workers involved.
>
> This was the last straw for the German economy. Prices spiralled out of control. Monthly inflation reached the equivalent of 1 million per cent a year. Paper money became almost worthless as its purchasing power evaporated.

2.4 Measuring changes in economic variables

During the BSE crisis in 1996, UK beef production fell from 90 000 tonnes in January to 50 000 tonnes in April. The *absolute change* was –40 000. The minus sign tells us it fell. The percentage change in UK beef output was $(100) \times (-40\,000)/(90\,000) = -44\%$. Absolute changes specify units (e.g. tonnes), but percentage changes are *unit-free*. Data are often shown this way.

> The **percentage change** is the absolute change divided by the original number, then multiplied by 100.

When we study time-series data over long periods such as a decade, we do not want to know just the percentage or absolute change between the initial date and the final date. Negative growth rates show percentage falls. Economists usually take *economic growth* to mean the percentage annual change in the national income.

> The **growth rate** is the percentage change per period (usually a year).

2.5 Economic models

Now for an example of economics in action. The London Underground, known locally as the tube, usually loses money and needs government subsidies. Might different policies help? You have to set the tube fare that will raise most revenue. How do you analyse the problem?

To organize our thinking, or build a model, we need to simplify reality, picking out the key elements of the problem. We begin with the simple equation

$$\textbf{Revenue} = [\textbf{fare}] \times [\textbf{number of passengers}] \tag{1}$$

London Underground can set the fare, but influences the number of passengers only through the fare that is set. (Cleaner stations and better service may help. We neglect these for the moment.)

The number of passengers may reflect habit, convenience and tradition, and be completely unresponsive to changes in fares. This is *not* the view an economist would adopt. It is possible to travel by car, bus, taxi or tube. Decisions about how to travel will depend on the relative costs of different modes of transport. Equation (1) requires a 'theory' or 'model' of what determines the number of passengers. We must model the *demand* for tube journeys.

First, the tube fare matters. Other things equal, higher tube fares reduce the number of tube journeys demanded. Second, if there are price rises for competing modes of taxis and buses, more people will use the tube at any given tube fare. Third, if passengers have higher income, they can afford more tube journeys at any given fare. We now have a bare-bones model of the number of tube passengers.

$$\text{Number of passengers} = f\left(\begin{array}{l}\textbf{tube fare, taxi fare, petrol price,}\\ \textbf{bus fare, passenger incomes} \dots\end{array}\right) \qquad (2)$$

The number of passengers 'depends on' or 'is a function of' the tube fare, the taxi fare, petrol prices, bus fares, incomes and some other things. The notation $f(\dots)$ is shorthand for 'depends on all the things listed inside the brackets'. The row of dots reminds us that we have omitted some possible determinants of demand to simplify our analysis. Tube demand probably depends on the weather. It is uncomfortable in the tube when it is hot. If the purpose of our model is to study *annual changes* in the number of tube passengers, we can neglect the weather provided weather conditions are broadly the same every year.

Writing down a model forces us to look for all the relevant effects, to worry about which effects must be taken into account and which can be ignored in answering the question we have set ourselves. Combining equations (1) and (2)

$$\begin{aligned}\textbf{Tube revenue} &= \textbf{tube fare} \times \textbf{number of passengers}\\ &= \textbf{tube fare} \times f\,(\textbf{tube fare, taxi fare, petrol price, bus fare, incomes} \dots) \qquad (3)\end{aligned}$$

Why all the fuss? You would have organized your approach along similar lines. That is the right reaction. Models are simply devices to ensure we think clearly about a problem. Clear thinking requires simplification. The real world is too complicated for us to think about everything at once. Learning to use models is more of an art than a science. Too much simplicity will omit a crucial factor from the analysis. Too much complexity and we lose any feel for why the answer turns out as it does.

Sometimes data guide us about which factors are crucial and which are not. At other times, as with tube fares, it is not enough to understand the forces at work. We need to quantify them. For both reasons, we turn now to the interaction of economic models and economic data.

2.6 Models and data

Equation (3) is our model of determinants of tube revenue. Higher fares give *more* revenue per passenger, but *reduce* the number of passengers. Theory cannot tell us which effect dominates. This is an *empirical* or factual issue: how many passengers are put off by higher fares?

Empirical evidence

We need some empirical research to establish the facts. *Experimental* sciences, including many branches of physics and chemistry, conduct controlled experiments in a laboratory, varying one factor at a time while holding constant all the other relevant factors. Like astronomy, economics is primarily a *non-experimental* science. Astronomers cannot suspend planetary motion to examine the relation between the earth and the sun in isolation; economists cannot suspend the laws of economic activity to conduct controlled experiments.

Most empirical research in economics must deal with data collected over periods in which many of the relevant factors were simultaneously changing. The problem is how to disentangle the separate influences on observed behaviour. We approach this in two stages. First, we proceed by examining the relationship of interest – the dependence of revenue on fares – neglecting the possibility that other relevant factors were changing. Then we indicate how economists deal with the harder problem in which variations in other factors are also included in the analysis.

Table 2.6 shows data on tube fares and passengers. When annual data are measured over overlapping calendar years – say from April 1992 to March 1993 – we show the year as 1992/93. Column (1) shows the real tube fare per passenger kilometre, column (2) shows tube demand, in billions of passenger kilometres a year, and column (3) shows real revenue.

Table 2.6 The tube, 1992/93–2004/05

	(1) Real fare (02/03 pence)	(2) No of trips (bn pass. km)	(3) Real revenue (02/03 £m)
1992/93	13.0	5758	751
1993/94	13.7	5814	799
1994/95	14.5	6051	877
1995/96	14.3	6337	906
1996/97	15.0	6153	922
1997/98	15.5	6479	1006
1998/99	15.8	6716	1059
1999/00	15.8	7171	1131
2000/01	15.7	7470	1172
2001/02	15.8	7451	1176
2002/03	14.2	8345	1185
2003/04	13.4	9388	1258
2004/05	14.2	9760	1386

Source: Transport for London.

It is useful to present evidence such as that in Table 2.6 in a *scatter diagram* such as Figure 2.2. The horizontal axis measures column (3), the real fare per passenger kilometre. The vertical axis measures column (1), real revenue in constant billion pounds. Real revenue is the real fare per passenger kilometre multiplied by the number of passenger kilometres travelled.

Other things equal, higher fares reduce the number of tube journeys, but if quantity demanded falls only a little, overall revenue may rise when fares are increased. Certainly, in some years, passenger use rose strongly despite higher fares. But we have not yet got to the bottom of things. We return to this issue in Section 2.8.

2.7 Diagrams, lines and equations

If we can draw a line or curve through all these points, this suggests, but does not prove, an underlying relationship between the two variables. If, when the points are plotted, they lie all over the place, this suggests, but does not prove, no underlying relationship between the two variables. Only if economics were an experimental science, in which we could conduct controlled experiments

A **scatter diagram** plots pairs of values simultaneously observed for two different variables.

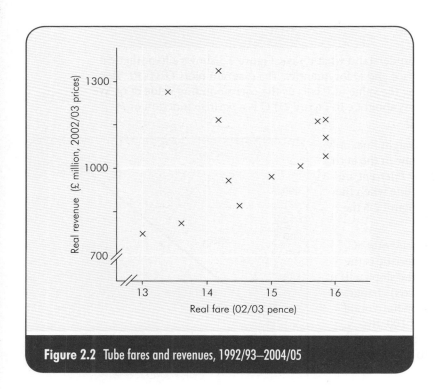

Figure 2.2 Tube fares and revenues, 1992/93–2004/05

guaranteeing that all other relevant factors had been held constant, could we interpret scatter diagrams unambiguously. Nevertheless, they often provide helpful clues.

Fitting lines through scatter diagrams

In Figure 2.2 we could draw a line through the scatter of points we plotted. The line would show the average relation between fares and revenue between 1992/93 and 2002/03. We could quantify the average relation between fares and usage.

Given a particular scatter of points, how do we decide where to draw the line, given that it cannot fit all the points exactly? The details need not concern us here, but the idea is simple. Having plotted the points describing the data, a computer works out where to draw the line to minimize the dispersion of points around the line.

After some practice, most people can work with two-dimensional diagrams such as Figure 2.2. A few gifted souls can even draw diagrams in three dimensions. Fortunately, computers can work in 10 or 20 dimensions at once, even though we cannot imagine what this looks like.

> **Econometrics** uses mathematical statistics to measure relationships in economic data.

This solves the problem of trying to hold other things constant. The computer measures the tube fare on one axis, the bus fare on another, petrol prices on a third, passenger incomes on a fourth, and tube revenue on a fifth, plots all these variables at the same time, and fits the average relation between tube revenue and each influence when they are simultaneously considered. Conceptually, it is simply an extension of fitting lines through scatter diagrams.

By disentangling separate influences from data where many different things move simultaneously, econometricians conduct empirical research even though economics is not an experimental science like physics. Although later chapters report the results of econometric research, in the text we never use anything more complicated than two-dimensional diagrams.

Reading diagrams

You need to be able to read a diagram and understand what it says. Figure 2.3 shows a hypothetical relationship between two variables: P for price and Q for quantity. The diagram plots $Q = f(P)$. The quantity Q is a function of price P. Knowing the value of P tells us the corresponding value of Q. We need to know values of P to make statements about Q. In Figure 2.3 Q is a *positive* function of P. Higher values of P imply higher values of Q.

When, as in Figure 2.3, the function is a straight line, only two pieces of information are needed to draw in the entire relationship between Q and P. We need the *intercept* and the *slope*. The intercept is the height of the line when the variable on the horizontal axis is zero. In Figure 2.3 the intercept is 100, the value of Q when $P = 0$.

Lots of different lines could pass through the point at which $Q = 100$ and $P = 0$. The other characteristic is the *slope* of the line, measuring its steepness. The slope tells us how much Q (the variable on the vertical axis) changes each time we increase P (the variable on the horizontal axis) by one unit. In Figure 2.3, the slope is 100. By definition, a straight line has a constant slope. Q rises by 100 whether we move from a price of 1 to 2, or from 2 to 3 or from 3 to 4.

Figure 2.3 shows a *positive* relation between Q and P. Since higher P values are associated with higher Q values, the line slopes *up* as we increase P and move to the right. The line has a positive slope. Figure 2.4 shows a case where Q is a *negative* function of P. Higher P values now imply smaller Q values. The line has a negative slope.

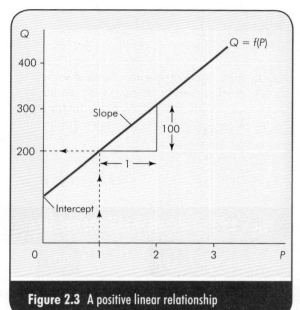

Figure 2.3 A positive linear relationship

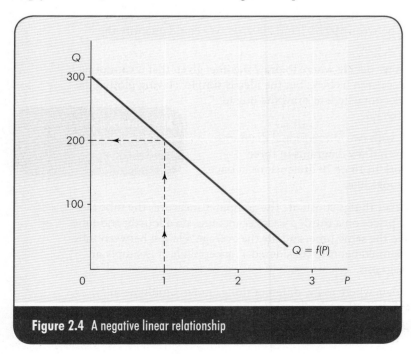

Figure 2.4 A negative linear relationship

Economic relationships need not be straight lines or linear relationships. Figure 2.5 shows a nonlinear relationship between two variables Y and X. The slope keeps changing. Each time we raise X by one unit we get a different rise (or fall) in Y. Consider the relationship between the income tax rate X and income tax revenue Y. When the tax rate is zero, no revenue is raised. When the tax rate is 100 per cent nobody bothers to work and revenue is again zero. Beginning from a zero tax rate, rises in tax rates initially raise total tax revenue. Beyond some tax rate, further rises in tax rates then reduce tax revenue, which becomes zero by the time the tax rate is 100 per cent. Diagrams display the essence of real-life problems.

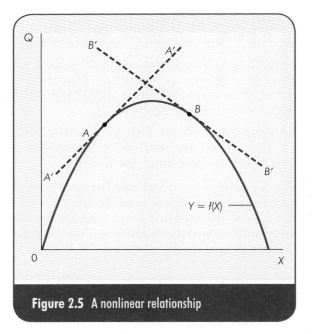

Figure 2.5 A nonlinear relationship

Activity box 2 Landing the big job

Two students, Gordon and Sarah, have to decide how hard to work for the final exam.

They need a mark of 70 to get the job with Greenpeace that they want. Their tutor has promised them that the exam will be just as hard (or easy) as previous exams. Gordon and Sarah have all the marks from their previous exams, and also know how hard they worked (minimum effort is 1, maximum effort is 5, and neither student worked all that hard in the exams leading up to their finals). From past experience, they know there is a linear relationship between effort and exam results.

Exam marks	Effort level		
	1	2	3
Gordon	20	40	60
Sarah	30	60	90

Questions

(a) What effort level must Gordon make in order to land his job with Greenpeace?

(b) What effort level does Sarah have to make?

(c) Which student is better at exams?

(d) Give 3 possible reasons for the different exam performance of Gordon and Sarah.

To check your answers to these questions, go to page 713.

2.8 Another look at 'other things equal'

A diagram might help London Underground think about tube fares. Apart from tube fares, the key determinants of passenger use are probably the incomes that passengers have available to spend, and the introduction of the congestion charge in 2003, which induced some Londoners to abandon their cars in favour of public transport.

In the period 1992/93 and 2004/05, Britain's national income, adjusted for inflation, grew strongly. Look again at Table 2.6. Even if tube fares had been constant, rising incomes should have led to (and did lead to) rising tube use and rising tube revenues.

Once we allow for movements in *both* tube fares *and* incomes of passengers our analysis makes more sense. Imagine two sub-periods, one in which incomes were low and one in which incomes were high. Figure 2.6 shows the relation between tube fare and tube revenue in each period separately. The red line corresponds to low incomes and hence low passenger demand for tube journeys. The black line shows greater demand for the tube at each and every potential level of tube fares.

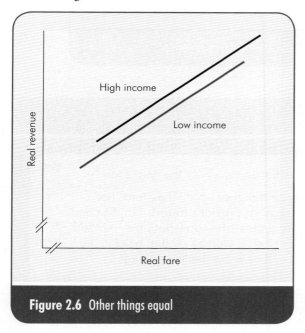

Figure 2.6 Other things equal

During 1992/93–2004/05 we moved from points near the bottom of the red line to points near the top of the black line. Tube revenue increased not merely because fares rose but because incomes rose. Similarly, the introduction of the congestion charge for car use in London will increase the demand for tube journeys at any particular level of fares and income.

The axes of Figure 2.6 encourage us to think about the relationship between fares and revenue. Other things equal, higher fares yield higher revenue and we move *along* the upsloping line. When one of these other things (like income or congestion charging) changes, we show this as a *shift* in the line. Now we can draw two-dimensional diagrams without neglecting other determinants. When things not drawn on the axes change, lines (or curves) shift.

> **Other things equal** is a device for looking at the relation between two variables, but remembering other variables also matter.

The same reasoning applies to the introduction of the congestion charge on vehicle use after 2003. Other things equal, fewer people drove cars and more people used the tube. As with the rise in income in Figure 2.6, the consequence of greater tube use is to generate more revenue at any particular level of tube fares. That is why, in Figure 2.4, the most recent data show much higher tube use than before at each level of tube fares.

2.9 Theories and evidence

Economists analyse a problem in three distinct stages. First, a phenomenon is observed or contemplated and the problem is formulated. By armchair reasoning or a cursory inspection of the data, we decide tube fares have something to do with tube revenues. We want to understand what this relationship is and why it exists.

Second, we develop a theory or model to capture the essence of the phenomenon. By thinking about incomes and the decision about which type of transport to use, we identify the things relevant to tube usage and hence tube revenue.

Third, we *test* the predictions of the theory by confronting it with economic data. An econometric examination of the data can quantify the things the model identifies. We can see if, on average, they work in the direction our model suggests. Indeed, by including in our econometric investigation some extra factors deliberately left out of our model in the quest for simplicity, we can check that the extra influences were sufficiently unimportant that it made sense to omit them from the analysis.

Suppose we confront our theory with the data and the two seem compatible. We *do not reject* our theory. If our model is rejected, we have to start again. If our model is not rejected by the data, this does not guarantee that we have found the correct model. There may be a better model that has escaped our attention but would also be compatible with our particular data. As time elapses, we acquire new data. We can also use data from other countries. The more we confront our model with different data and find that it is still not rejected, the more confident we become that we have found the true explanation of the behaviour in which we are interested. Relationships in which we have become very confident are sometimes called economic laws.

2.10 Some popular criticisms of economics and economists

This chapter has introduced the economist's toolkit. You may have some nagging doubts about it. We end this chapter by discussing some of the popular criticisms of economics and economists.

Box 2.3 Get a Becker view: use an economist's spectacles

Most people accept that the economic analysis of markets – thinking about how incentives affect resource allocation – helps us understand things like inflation or unemployment. Can the same tools be applied to other social behaviour? To crime? To marriage? To drug use?

Since much of economic analysis supposes that people are driven by self-interest, rather than an altruistic concern for others, some economists doubt whether economics can shed light on highly interactive 'social' situations. Other economists have no such fears. In 1992 Chicago economist Gary Becker was awarded the Nobel Prize for Economics for applying the logic of economic incentives to almost every facet of human behaviour. Some examples of Becker in action . . .

Marriage and divorce

'The courtroom is not a good place to make judgements about the unique circumstances of each marriage or relationship. We should replace judicial determination with marriage contracts that specify, among other things, the financial and child custodial terms of a divorce. Marriage contracts would become much more common if we set aside the legal tradition that they are not unenforceable.'

Drugs

Prohibition of alcohol gave the US Al Capone but failed to stop drinking. The end of Prohibition 'was a confession that the US experiment in banning drinking had failed dismally. It was not an

31

Box 2.3 Get a Becker view: use an economist's spectacles (Continued)

expression of support for heavy drinking or alcoholism.' Becker's solution for drugs is the same — legalize, boost government tax revenue, protect minors and cut out organized crime's monopoly on supply.

Becker's proposals have some merit. For example, in 2001 the police in Brixton were told not to arrest people smoking cannabis in public, part of a gradual policy switch to target hard drugs like cocaine and heroin. UK cannabis seizures in 2000 were only half those of 1997. As supply increased, the price on the street slumped.

Some people argue that implicit toleration of soft drugs should give way to decriminalization, allowing legal sales. With 1500 tonnes consumed annually in the UK, an excise duty of £3 a gram would raise up to £5 billion a year in tax revenue. Gains to the wider economy would be even greater. There would probably be cuts both in the £1.4 billion currently spent enforcing anti-drugs laws and in the £1.5 billion estimated as the cost of drug-related crime.

Sources: G. S. Becker and G. N. Becker, *The Economics of Life*, McGraw-Hill, 1997; *The Observer*, 8 July 2001.

No two economists ever agree

You need to distinguish positive economics and normative economics. Even if all economists agree on the positive economics of how the world works, there is huge scope to disagree on normative recommendations based on different value judgements. Many disagreements between economists fall under this heading.

There *are* disagreements in positive economics. Economics is only rarely an experimental science. It is prohibitively costly to make half of the population unemployed just to find out how the economy then works. Without controlled experiments, we have to disentangle different influences in past data to overcome the problem of other things equal. Using data over many years makes it easier to do this unravelling but introduces a new problem. Since attitudes and institutions are slowly changing, data from many years ago may no longer be relevant to current behaviour. The problems we confront are difficult ones and we have to do the best we can.

Finally, it is wrong to think that there are not serious disagreements between physicists or doctors or engineers. Most people do not pretend to know much about physics; everybody claims to know a bit about the problems that economists study.

Models in economics are so simple they have little to do with reality

A model is a deliberate simplification to help us think more clearly. A good model simplifies a lot but does not distort reality too much. It captures the main features of the problem. The test of a good model is not how simple it is, but how much of observed behaviour it can explain.

Sometimes we can get a long way with a simple model. You will see examples in later chapters. On other occasions, the behaviour we are studying is complex and a simple model may not suffice. Where a more realistic model would take us beyond the scope of this book, we still introduce a simple model to let you begin to see the elements of the problem.

People are not as mercenary as economists make out

Economists believe that most of the phenomena they study, such as whether to travel by bus or by tube, are mainly determined by economic incentives. This does not mean economic incentives are all that matter.

A successful advertising campaign by the tube would change tube usage. So would a change in social attitudes: it might become chic to take the tube. Knowledge of politics, sociology and psychology is needed for a more complete description of human behaviour. These are factors that economists subsume under the heading of 'other things equal'. Economics emphasizes the effect of economic incentives. Social attitudes change slowly and for many purposes may be treated as being held constant. However, if an economist discovered an important change in social attitudes, it would be easy to include this in the analysis.

Actions of human beings cannot be reduced to scientific laws

Physicists accept that individual molecules behave randomly but that we can construct and test theories based on their average or systematic behaviour. Economists take the same view about people. We shall never explain actions based on whim or because you got out of bed on the wrong side. However, random differences in behaviour tend to cancel out on average. We can describe average behaviour with a lot more certainty.

If behaviour shows no systematic tendencies – tendencies to do the same thing when confronted by the same situation – there is little to discuss. The past is no guide to the future. Every decision is a one-off decision. Not only is this view unhelpful, it is not supported by the data. The economic theories that survive are those consistently compatible with the data. The more random is human behaviour, the less is the systematic element about which we can form theories and use to make predictions. It is better to be able to say something about behaviour than nothing at all. Often, as you will shortly discover, we can say rather a lot.

Summary

- There is a continuing interplay between models and data in the study of economic relationships. A **model** is a simplified framework to organize how we think about a problem.

- **Data** or facts are essential for two reasons. They suggest relationships which we should aim to explain and they allow us to test our hypotheses and to quantify the effects that they imply.

- Tables present data in a form easily understood. **Time-series data** are values of a given variable at different points in time. **Cross-section data** refer to the same point in time but to different values of the same variable across different people.

- **Index numbers** express data relative to some given base value.

- Many index numbers refer to averages of many variables. The **retail price index** summarizes changes in the prices of all goods bought by households. It weights the price of each good by its importance in the budget of a typical household.

- The annual percentage change in the retail price index is the usual measure of **inflation**, the rate at which prices in general are changing.

- **Nominal or current price variables** refer to values at the prices ruling when the variable was measured. **Real or constant price variables** adjust nominal variables for changes in the general level of prices. They are inflation-adjusted measures.

- **Scatter diagrams** show the relationship between two variables plotted in the diagram. By fitting a line through these points we summarize the average relationship between the two variables. **Econometrics** uses computers to fit average relationships between many variables simultaneously. In principle this allows us to get round the '**other things equal**' problem, which always applies in two dimensions.

- Analytical diagrams are often useful in building a model. They show relationships between two variables holding other things equal. If we wish to change one of these other things, we have to shift the line or curve we have shown in our diagram.

- To understand how the economy works we need both theory and facts. We need theory to know what facts to look for: there are too many facts for the facts alone to tell us the correct answer. Facts without theory are useless, but theory without facts is unsupported assertion. We need both.

Review questions

To check your answers to these questions, go to page 712.

1   The police research department want to study whether the level of crime is affected by the unemployment rate. (a) How would you test this idea? What data would you want? (b) What 'other things equal' problems would you bear in mind?

2   Use the data of Table 2.5 to plot a scatter diagram of the relation between nominal house prices and the retail price index. Does this diagram plot time-series data or cross-section data?

3   The table shows consumer spending by households and income of households, both in £ billion at 1995 prices. (a) Plot a scatter diagram with consumption on the vertical axis, income on the horizontal axis. (b) Fit a line through these points. (c) Are consumption and income related?

UK	1995	1996	1997	1998	1999	2000	2001	2002	2003	2004	2005
Income	495	505	525	539	550	567	584	593	604	616	630
Consumption	454	471	489	509	530	548	564	575	587	601	607

4   The table shows unemployment rates in the capital and the rest of the country. One-third of the national population lives in the capital. Construct an index of national unemployment, treating 2000 as 100. What weights did you use for the two unemployment rates? Why?

Unemployment (%)	1997	1998	1999	2000	2001	2002	2003	2004	2005	2006
London	7	6	5	4	6	5	4	4	3	4
Rest of country	10	9	8	8	9	8	8	7	7	8

5   Plot a scatter diagram with variable Y on the vertical axis, variable X on the horizontal axis. Is the relation between X and Y positive or negative? Is it better to fit a straight line or a curve through these points?

Y	40	33	29	56	81	19	20
X	5	7	9	3	1	11	10

6   **Common fallacies** Why are these statements wrong? (a) The purpose of a theory is to let you ignore the facts. (b) Economics cannot be a science since it cannot conduct controlled laboratory experiments. (c) People have feelings and act haphazardly. It is misguided to reduce their actions to scientific laws.

7   **Harder question** The data in Question 3 confirm a very close relationship between household income and consumer spending. Why do other influences, particularly the changing level of interest rates, have only a small effect on household decisions about how much of their income to spend or save?

8   **Harder question** When we use economic data to test an economic theory, we must choose how high to set the bar in our test. If we say that whenever the data depart at all from the prediction of the theory, we will reject most of our theories, which were only approximations in the first place. Conversely, if we only reject theories when the data are a long way away from the prediction of the theory, we will hardly ever reject any theory. Which of these two possible mistakes is more dangerous?

9   **Essay question** Following the introduction of the congestion charge for driving into Central London, traffic levels initially fell by 20 per cent. Over the next few years, traffic increased back towards its original level. Does this show the congestion charge failed to reduce congestion? Even if it did, might it still be a good idea?

 Online **Learning Centre**

To help you grasp the key concepts of this chapter check out the extra resources posted on the Online Learning Centre. There are chapter summaries, self-test questions, an interactive graphing tool, weblinks and a searchable glossary, all for free!

To put your learning into practice and prepare for exams, an **Interactive Workbook** is also available online, containing a variety of question types and providing feedback on your answers.

If you'd like further help with economics, or have any questions, **NetTutor** is here to help! You will have a personalised tutorial service at your fingertips. Visit the online learning centre at: www.mcgraw-hill.co.uk/ textbooks/begg for information on accessing all of these resources.

Demand, supply and the market

By the end of this chapter, you should understand:

1 the concept of a market

2 demand and supply curves

3 equilibrium price and equilibrium quantity

4 how price adjustment reconciles demand and supply in a market

5 what shifts demand and supply curves

6 free markets and markets with price controls

7 how markets answer what, how and for whom to produce

Society has to find *some* way to decide what, how and for whom to produce. Modern economies rely heavily on markets and prices to allocate resources between competing uses. The interplay of *demand* (the behaviour of buyers) and *supply* (the behaviour of sellers) determines the quantity of the good produced and the price at which it is bought and sold.

3.1 The market

Shops and fruit stalls physically bring together the buyer and seller. The stock exchange uses intermediaries (stockbrokers) who transact business on behalf of clients. E-commerce is conducted on the internet. In supermarkets, sellers choose the price and let customers choose whether or not to buy. Antique auctions force buyers to bid against each other, with the seller taking a passive role.

> A **market** is a set of arrangements by which buyers and sellers exchange goods and services.

Although superficially different, these markets perform the same economic function. They determine prices that ensure that the quantity people wish to buy equals the quantity people wish to sell. Price and quantity cannot be considered separately. In fixing the price of a Bentley at 20 times the price of a Fiat, the market for motor cars ensures that production and sales of Fiats greatly exceed the production and sale of Bentleys. These prices guide society in choosing what, how and for whom to produce.

To understand this process more fully, we need to model a typical market. The ingredients are demand (the behaviour of buyers) and supply (the behaviour of sellers). We can then study how these interact to see how a market works.

3.2 Demand, supply and equilibrium

Demand is not a particular quantity, such as six bars of chocolate, but rather a full description of the quantity of chocolate buyers would purchase at each and every price that might be charged. The first column of Table 3.1 shows prices of chocolate bars. The second column shows the quantities demanded at these prices. Even if chocolate is free, only a finite amount is wanted. People get sick from eating too much chocolate. As the price of chocolate rises, the quantity demanded falls, other things equal. We assume nobody buys any chocolate if the price exceeds £0.40. Together, columns (1) and (2) describe the demand for chocolate as a function of its price.

> **Demand** is the quantity that buyers wish to purchase at each conceivable price.

Supply is not a particular quantity but a complete description of the quantity that sellers want to sell at each possible price. The third column of Table 3.1 shows how much sellers wish to sell at each price. Chocolate cannot be produced for nothing. Nobody would supply at a zero price. In our example, it takes a price of £0.20 before there is an incentive to supply chocolate. At higher prices it is more lucrative to supply chocolate bars and there is a rise in the quantity supplied. Together, columns (1) and (3) describe the supply of chocolate bars as a function of their price.

> **Supply** is the quantity of a good that sellers wish to sell at each possible price.

Note the distinction between *demand* and the *quantity demanded*. Demand describes the behaviour of buyers at every price. At a particular price there is a particular quantity demanded. The term 'quantity demanded' makes sense only in relation to a particular price. The same applies to *supply* and *quantity supplied*.

In everyday language, we say that when the demand for football tickets exceeds their supply some people do not get into the ground. Economists must be more precise. At the price charged for tickets, the quantity demanded exceeded the quantity supplied. A higher ticket price would have reduced the quantity demanded, leaving empty space in the ground. Yet there is no change in demand, the schedule describing how many people want admission at each possible ticket price. The quantity demanded only changed because the price changed.

The demand and supply schedules are each constructed on the assumption of 'other things equal'. In the demand for football tickets, one of the 'other things' is whether the game is televised. If it is, the quantity of tickets demanded at each and every price is lower than if the game is not televised.

Think again about the market for chocolate in Table 3.1. Other things equal, the lower the price of chocolate, the higher the quantity demanded. Other things equal, the higher the price of chocolate, the higher the quantity supplied. A campaign by dentists warning of the effect of chocolate on tooth decay, or a fall in household incomes, would change the 'other things' relevant to the demand for chocolate. Either of these changes would reduce the demand for chocolate, reducing the quantities demanded at each price. Cheaper cocoa beans, or technical advances in packaging chocolate bars, would change the 'other things' relevant to the supply of chocolate bars. They would tend to increase the supply of chocolate bars, increasing the quantity supplied at each possible price.

The equilibrium price

Assume, initially, that all these other things remain constant. We combine the behaviour of buyers and sellers to model the market for chocolate bars. At low prices, the quantity demanded exceeds the quantity supplied but the reverse is true at high prices. At some intermediate price, which we call the equilibrium price, the quantity demanded just equals the quantity supplied.

> The **equilibrium price** is the price at which the quantity supplied equals the quantity demanded.

In Table 3.1 the equilibrium price is £0.30, at which 80 bars is the *equilibrium quantity*, the quantity buyers wish to buy and sellers wish to sell. At prices below £0.30, the quantity demanded exceeds the

Table 3.1 Demand and supply of chocolate

(1) Price (£/bar)	(2) Demand (no. of bars)	(3) Supply (no. of bars)
0.00	200	0
0.10	160	0
0.20	120	40
0.30	80	80
0.40	40	120
0.50	0	160

quantity supplied and some buyers are frustrated. There is a shortage. When economists say there is *excess demand* they are using a shorthand for the more accurate expression: the quantity demanded exceeds the quantity supplied *at this price*.

Conversely, at any price above £0.30, the quantity supplied exceeds the quantity demanded. Sellers have unsold stock. Economists describe this surplus as *excess supply*, shorthand for an excess quantity supplied *at this price*. Only at £0.30, the equilibrium price, are quantity demanded and quantity supplied equal. The market clears. People's wishes are fulfilled at the equilibrium price.

> **Excess supply** exists when the quantity supplied exceeds the quantity demanded at the ruling price. **Excess demand** exists when the quantity demanded exceeds the quantity supplied at the ruling price.

Is a market automatically in equilibrium? What could bring this about? Suppose the price is initially £0.50, above the equilibrium price. Suppliers offer 160 bars but nobody buys at this price. Sellers cut the price to clear their stock. Cutting the price to £0.40 has two effects. It raises the quantity demanded to 40 bars and cuts the quantity producers wish to make and sell to 120 bars. Both effects reduce excess supply. Price cutting continues until the equilibrium price of £0.30 is reached and excess supply disappears. At this price the market clears.

If the price is below the equilibrium price the process works in reverse. At a price of £0.20, 120 bars are demanded but only 40 supplied. Sellers run out of stock and charge higher prices. This incentive to raise prices continues until the equilibrium price is reached, excess demand is eliminated and the market clears.

At a particular time, the price may not be the equilibrium price. If not, there is either excess supply or excess demand, depending on whether the price lies above or below the equilibrium price. But these imbalances provide the incentive to change prices towards the equilibrium price. Markets are self-correcting. Some of the key issues in economics turn on how quickly prices adjust to restore equilibrium in particular markets.

3.3 Demand and supply curves

> The **demand curve** shows the relation between price and quantity demanded, other things equal.

Table 3.1 shows demand and supply conditions in the chocolate market and allows us to find the equilibrium price and quantity. It is useful to analyse the same problem diagrammatically.

Figure 3.1 measures chocolate prices on the vertical axis and chocolate quantities on the horizontal axis. The demand curve *DD* plots the data in the first two columns of Table 3.1 and joins up the

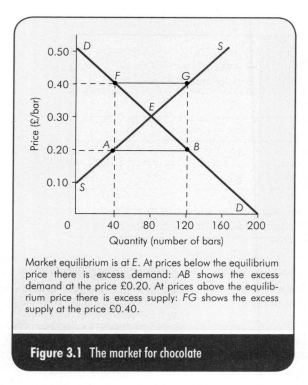

Market equilibrium is at *E*. At prices below the equilibrium price there is excess demand: *AB* shows the excess demand at the price £0.20. At prices above the equilibrium price there is excess supply: *FG* shows the excess supply at the price £0.40.

Figure 3.1 The market for chocolate

points. This demand curve happens to be a straight line, though it need not be. Our straight line has a negative slope. Larger quantities are demanded at lower prices.

Figure 3.1 plots columns (1) and (3) of Table 3.1. Joining up the different points yields the supply curve *SS*. Again, this happens to be a straight line but it need not be. It slopes up because suppliers only wish to increase the quantity supplied if they get a higher price.

> The **supply curve** shows the relation between price and quantity supplied, other things equal.

We can now re-examine excess supply, excess demand and equilibrium. A particular price is shown by a height on the vertical axis, a particular quantity by a length on the horizontal axis. Equilibrium is at point *E*. As in Table 3.1, this entails a price of £0.30 and a quantity of 80 bars. At any price below the equilibrium price, the horizontal distance between the supply curve and the demand curve is the excess demand at that price. At

£0.20, 40 bars are supplied but 120 bars are demanded. The distance *AB* is the excess demand of 80 bars. Conversely, above the equilibrium price there is excess supply. At £0.40, 40 bars are demanded, 120 bars are supplied and the horizontal distance *FG* is the excess supply of 80 bars at this price.

Suppose the price is £0.40. Only 40 bars are sold, even though sellers would like to sell 120 bars. Why are sellers – not buyers – frustrated when their wishes differ? Participation in a market is voluntary. Buyers are not *forced* to buy nor sellers *forced* to sell. When markets are not in equilibrium, the quantity transacted is the *smaller* of the quantity supplied and the quantity demanded. Any quantity above 40 bars at a price of £0.40 would force buyers into purchases they do not want. Similarly, at a price of £0.20, any quantity greater than 40 bars involves sellers in forced sales.

We can now reconsider *price determination* in the chocolate market. Figure 3.1 implies that there is excess supply at all prices above the equilibrium price of £0.30. Sellers react to unsold stocks by cutting prices. Once the price falls to the equilibrium price, excess supply is eliminated. Equilibrium is at point *E*. Conversely, at prices below £0.30 there is excess demand, which bids up the price of chocolate, eliminating excess demand until the equilibrium point *E* is reached. In equilibrium, buyers and sellers can trade as much as they wish at the equilibrium price. There is no incentive for any further price changes.

3.4 Behind the demand curve

The demand curve depicts the relation between price and quantity demanded *holding other things constant*. What are those 'other things'? The other things relevant to demand curves can usually be grouped under three headings: the price of related goods, the income of consumers (buyers) and consumer tastes or preferences. We look at each of these in turn.

The price of related goods

In Chapter 2 we discussed the demand for tube travel. A rise in bus fares or petrol prices would increase the quantity of tube travel demanded at each possible tube price. In everyday language, buses and cars are *substitutes* for the tube. Similarly, petrol and cars are *complements* because you cannot use a car without also using fuel. A rise in the price of petrol tends to reduce the demand for cars.

How do substitutes and complements relate to the demand for chocolate bars? Clearly, other sweets (jelly babies, say) are substitutes for chocolate. An increase in the price of other sweets increases the quantity of chocolate demanded at each possible chocolate price, as people substitute away from other sweets towards chocolate. If people buy chocolate to eat at the cinema, films would be a complement for bars of chocolate. A rise in the price of cinema tickets would reduce the demand for chocolate since fewer people would go to the cinema. Nevertheless, it is difficult to think of a lot of goods that are complements for chocolate. This suggests, correctly, that most of the time goods are substitutes for each other. Complementarity is usually a more specific feature (CD players and CDs, coffee and milk, shoes and shoelaces).

> A price increase for one good raises the demand for **substitutes** for this good but reduces the demand for **complements** to the good.

Consumer incomes

The second category of 'other things equal' when we draw a particular demand curve is consumer income. When incomes rise, the demand for most goods increases. Typically, consumers buy more of everything. However, there are exceptions.

> For a **normal good** demand increases when incomes rise. For an **inferior good** demand falls when incomes rise.

As their name suggests, most goods are normal goods. Inferior goods are typically cheap but low-quality goods that people prefer not to buy if they can afford to spend a little more.

Box 3.1 One little piggy went to market ..

The 1996 BSE crisis led to a collapse in the demand for British beef. With a lower demand curve, the equilibrium price of beef fell. Consumers switched to chicken and pork. The price of pig meat rose sharply. Many farmers switched from rearing cows to pigs. By 1998 the market was flooded with pork and pig prices collapsed again! By 2001 many fewer piggies were being reared for the market.

Source: ONS, Monthly Digest of Statistics.

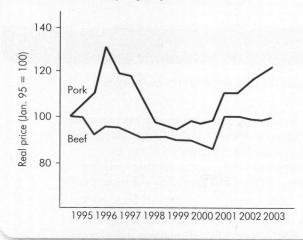

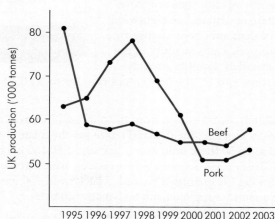

41

Tastes

The third category of things held constant along a particular demand curve is consumer tastes or preferences. In part, these are shaped by convenience, custom and social attitudes. The fashion for the mini-skirt reduced the demand for textile material. The emphasis on health and fitness has increased the demand for jogging equipment, health foods and sports facilities while reducing the demand for cream cakes, butter and cigarettes.

3.5 Shifts in the demand curve

We can now distinguish between movements along a given demand curve and shifts in the demand curve itself. In Figure 3.1 we drew the demand curve for chocolate bars for a given level of the three underlying factors: the price of related goods, incomes and tastes. Movements along the demand curve isolate the effects of chocolate prices on quantity demanded, holding other things equal. Changes in any of these three factors will change the demand for chocolate.

Figure 3.2 shows a rise in the price of a substitute for chocolate, say ice cream, which leads people to demand more chocolate and less ice cream. At each chocolate price there is a larger quantity of chocolate demanded when ice cream prices are high. People substitute chocolate for ice cream. This *shifts* the demand curve for chocolate from *DD* to *D'D'*. The entire demand curve shifts to the right. At each price on the vertical axis, a larger horizontal distance indicates a higher quantity demanded.

Changes in the price of ice cream have no effect on the incentives to supply chocolate bars: at each price of chocolate, suppliers wish to supply the same quantity of chocolate as before. The increase in demand, or rightward shift in the demand curve, changes the equilibrium price and quantity in the chocolate market. Equilibrium has changed from *E* to *E'*. The new equilibrium price is £0.40 and the new equilibrium quantity is 120 bars.

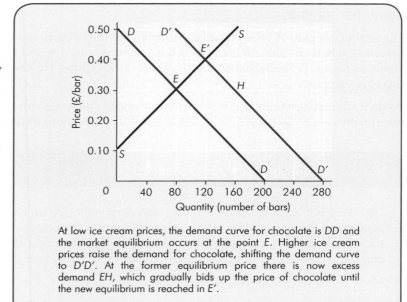

At low ice cream prices, the demand curve for chocolate is *DD* and the market equilibrium occurs at the point *E*. Higher ice cream prices raise the demand for chocolate, shifting the demand curve to *D'D'*. At the former equilibrium price there is now excess demand *EH*, which gradually bids up the price of chocolate until the new equilibrium is reached in *E'*.

Figure 3.2 An increase in chocolate demand

We can sketch the transition from the old equilibrium at *E* to the new equilibrium at *E'*. When the ice cream prices first rise, the demand curve for chocolate shifts from *DD* to *D'D'*. With the chocolate price still at £0.30 there is an excess demand *EH*: 160 bars are demanded but only 80 bars are supplied. This excess demand bids up prices, which gradually rise to the new equilibrium price of £0.40, choking the quantity demanded back from 160 bars to 120 bars and providing the incentive to raise the quantity supplied from 80 bars to 120 bars.

We draw two lessons from this example. First, the quantity demanded depends on four things: its own price, prices of related goods, incomes and tastes. We could draw a two-dimensional diagram showing the relation between quantity of chocolate demanded and any one of these four things. The other three things would then be the 'other things equal' for this diagram. In drawing demand curves, we single out the price of the commodity itself (here the price of chocolate bars) to put in the diagram with quantity demanded. The other three factors are the 'other things equal' for drawing a particular demand curve. Changes in any of these other three things shift the position of demand curves.

Why single out the price of the commodity itself to plot against quantity demanded? We want to study the market for chocolate. Prices of related goods, incomes and tastes are determined elsewhere in the economy. By focusing on the price of chocolate, we see the self-correcting mechanism by which the market reacts to excess demand or excess supply, inducing changes in chocolate prices within the chocolate market to restore equilibrium.

Second, our example illustrates analysis by *comparative statics*. The analysis is comparative because it compares the old and new equilibrium, and static because it compares only the equilibrium positions. In each equilibrium, prices and quantities are constant. Comparative static analysis is not interested in the dynamic path by which the economy moves from one equilibrium to the other, only in the point from which it began and the point at which it ends.

> **Comparative static analysis**
> changes one of the 'other things equal' and examines the effect on equilibrium price and quantity.

Using Figure 3.2 we can also analyse a change in one of the 'other things equal'. Suppose the demand curve is initially $D'D'$ and the market begins in equilibrium at E'. Then the demand for chocolate falls to DD. This might reflect a fall in the price of a chocolate substitute, a fall in consumer incomes or a change in tastes away from liking chocolate. When the demand curve shifts left to DD, showing less chocolate demanded at each price, the new equilibrium is at E. At the original price of £0.40 there is excess supply, which bids prices down to the new equilibrium price of £0.30. When the demand curve shifts to the left, there is a fall in both equilibrium price and equilibrium quantity.

3.6 Behind the supply curve

At low prices, only the most efficient chocolate producers make profits. As prices rise, producers previously unable to compete can now make a profit in the chocolate business and wish to supply. Moreover, previously existing firms may be able to expand output by working overtime, or buying fancy equipment unjustified when selling chocolate at lower prices. In general, higher prices are needed to induce firms to produce more chocolate. Other things equal, supply curves slope up as we move to the right.

Just as we studied the 'other things equal' along a demand curve, we now examine three categories of 'other things equal' along a supply curve: the technology available to producers, the cost of inputs (labour, machines, fuel, raw materials) and government regulation. Along a particular supply curve, all of these are held constant. A change in any of these categories shifts the supply curve, changing the amount producers wish to supply at each price.

Technology

A supply curve is drawn for a given technology. Better technology shifts the supply curve to the right. Producers supply more than previously at each price. Better cocoa refining reduces the cost of making chocolate. Faster shipping and better refrigeration lead to less wastage in spoiled cocoa beans. Technological advance enables firms to supply more at each price.

As a determinant of supply, technology must be interpreted broadly. It embraces all know-how about production methods, not merely the state of available machinery. In agriculture, the development of disease-resistant seeds is a technological advance. Improved weather forecasting might enable better timing of planting and harvesting. A technological advance is any idea that allows more output from the same inputs as before. In the terminology of Chapter 1, a technological advance shifts the production possibility frontier outwards.

Input costs

A particular supply curve is drawn for a given level of input prices. Lower input prices (lower wages, lower fuel costs) induce firms to supply more output at each price, shifting the supply curve to the right. Higher input prices make production less attractive and shift the supply curve to the left. If a late frost destroys much of the cocoa crop, scarcity will bid up the price of cocoa beans. Chocolate producers supply less chocolate at each price than previously.

Activity box 3   Movement along a curve versus shifts of the curve

From the initial point A, the figure shows two quite different 'increases in demand'. One is an increase in the quantity demanded, from Q_0 to Q_1, moving along the curve from A to B. This is the effect of a price cut but *not* an increase in demand since the demand curve DD is unaffected.

By an increase in demand we mean a shift in the demand curve, say from DD to $D'D'$, which also increases quantity demanded from Q_0 to Q_1 at the going price P_0. This shift in demand reflects an increase in the price of a substitute good (decrease in the price of a complement good), an increase in income or a change of taste.

Similarly, sellers adjust to higher prices by moving up a given supply curve. But an increase in supply means an upward shift in the whole supply curve, caused by lower input prices, new technology or less regulation.

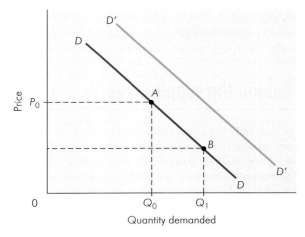

Other things equal, changes in price move us *along* demand and supply curves. When other determinants change, they shift these schedules.

Questions
Classify each of the following as an upward or downward shift in supply or demand curve:

(a)   New interactions between Europe and China make wages of unskilled European workers fall.

(b)   New interactions between Europe and China make the price of European coal increase.

(c)   The government ban on city parking by large cars reduces the price of Bentleys.

To check your answers to these questions, go to page 713

Government regulation

In discussing technology, we spoke only of technological advances. Once people have discovered a better production method they are unlikely subsequently to forget it.

Government regulations can sometimes be viewed as imposing a technological change that is *adverse* for producers. If so, the effect of regulations will be to shift the supply curve to the left, reducing quantity supplied at each price.

More stringent safety regulations prevent chocolate producers using the most productive process because it is quite dangerous to workers. Anti-pollution devices may raise the cost of making cars, and regulations to protect the environment may make it unprofitable for firms to extract surface mineral deposits which could have been cheaply quarried but whose extraction now requires expensive landscaping. Whenever regulations prevent producers from selecting the production methods they would otherwise have chosen, the effect of regulations is to shift the supply curve to the left.

3.7 Shifts in the supply curve

Along a given supply curve we hold constant technology, the prices of inputs and the extent of government regulation. We now undertake a comparative static analysis of what happens when a change in one of these 'other things equal' leads to a fall in supply. Suppose tougher safety legislation makes it more expensive to make chocolate bars in mechanized factories. Figure 3.3 shows a shift to the left in the supply curve, from SS to $S'S'$. Equilibrium shifts from E to E'.

The equilibrium price *rises* but equilibrium quantity *falls* when the supply curve shifts to the left. Conversely, a rise in supply shifts the supply curve from $S'S'$ to SS. Equilibrium shifts from E' to E. A rise in supply induces a *higher* equilibrium quantity and *lower* equilibrium price.

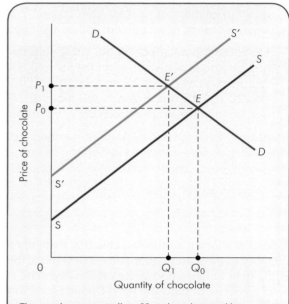

The supply curve initially is SS and market equilibrium is at E. A reduction in the supply of chocolate shifts the supply curve to the left to $S'S'$. The new equilibrium at E' has a higher equilibrium price and a lower equilibrium quantity than the old equilibrium at E.

Figure 3.3 A fall in supply

3.8 Free markets and price controls

Government actions may shift demand and supply curves, as when changes in safety legislation shift the supply curve, but the government makes no attempt to regulate prices directly. If prices are sufficiently flexible, the pressure of excess supply or excess demand will quickly bid prices in a free market to their equilibrium level. Markets will not be free when effective price controls exist. Price controls may be *floor* prices (minimum prices) or *ceiling* prices (maximum prices).

> **Free markets** allow prices to be determined purely by the forces of supply and demand.

Price ceilings make it illegal for sellers to charge more than a specific maximum price. Ceilings may be introduced when a shortage of a commodity threatens to raise its price a lot (such as food prices during war blockade). High prices are the way a free market rations goods in scarce supply. This

> **Price controls** are government rules or laws setting price floors or ceilings that forbid the adjustment of prices to clear markets.

45

Box 3.2 TUC concludes migrant workers boosted UK economy

Foreign workers made a positive net economic contribution to the UK economy, reported Britain's Trades Union Congress, with their share of tax paid exceeding the cost of supplying public services to migrants. However, it remains necessary to ensure that gangmasters and other unscrupulous employers provide proper employment conditions and adhere to the minimum wage. The UK saw an influx of migrant workers from Eastern Europe after 2004 when a host of new countries joined the European Union.

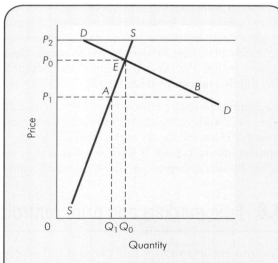

Increased labour supply in the UK should be expected to reduce wages relative to what they would have been in sectors such as construction, farming and domestic service.
The 2007 TUC report concluded that the strength of the UK economy had provided sufficient additional demand to absorb the extra labour supply without falls in the wages of the low paid.

Recent statistics suggest migrant numbers from Eastern Europe fell in 2007, partly because conditions had improved in Eastern Europe. Better employment opportunities in Poland and Hungary meant fewer casual workers for UK fruit picking.

Adapted from BBC online, 19 June 2007.

solves the allocation problem, ensuring that only a small quantity of the scarce commodity is demanded, but may be thought unfair, a normative value judgement. High food prices mean hardship for the poor. Faced with a national food shortage, a government may impose a price ceiling on food so that poor people can afford food.

Figure 3.4 shows the market for food. War has disrupted imports of food. The supply curve is far to the left and the free market equilibrium price P_0 is very high. Instead of allowing free market equilibrium at E, the government imposes a price ceiling P_1. The quantity sold is then Q_1 and excess demand is the distance AB. The price ceiling creates a shortage of supply relative to demand by holding food prices below their equilibrium level.[1]

The ceiling price P_1 allows the poor to afford food but it reduces total food supplied from Q_0 to Q_1. With excess demand AB at the ceiling price, rationing must be used to decide which potential buyers are actually supplied. This rationing system could be arbitrary. Food suppliers may sell supplies to their friends, not necessarily the poor, or may take bribes from the rich who jump the queue.

1 A price ceiling above the equilibrium price is irrelevant. The free market equilibrium at E is still to be attained.

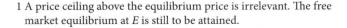

Free market equilibrium occurs at the point E. The high price P_0 chokes off quantity demanded to ration scarce supply. A price ceiling at P_1 succeeds in holding down the price but leads to excess demand AB. It also reduces quantity supplied from Q_0 to Q_1. A price ceiling at P_2 is irrelevant since the free market equilibrium at E can still be attained.

Figure 3.4 The effect of a price ceiling

Holding down the price of food may not help the poor after all. Ceiling prices are often accompanied by government-organized rationing by quota to ensure that available supply is shared out fairly, independently of ability to pay.

Whereas the aim of a price ceiling is to reduce the price for consumers, the aim of a floor price is to raise the price for suppliers. One example of a floor price is a national minimum wage. Figure 3.5 shows the demand curve and supply curve for labour. The free market equilibrium is at E, where the wage is W_0. A minimum wage below W_0 is irrelevant since the free market equilibrium can still be attained. Suppose, in an effort to help workers, the government imposes a minimum wage at W_1. Firms demand a quantity of labour Q_1 and there is excess supply AB. The lucky workers who manage to get work are better off than before but some workers are worse off since total hours worked fall from Q_0 to Q_1.

Many countries set floor prices for agricultural products. Figure 3.6 shows a floor price P_1 for butter. In previous examples we assumed that the quantity traded would be the smaller of quantity supplied and quantity demanded at the controlled price, since private individuals cannot be forced to participate in a market. There is another possibility: the government may intervene not only to set the control price but also to buy or sell quantities of the good to supplement private purchases and sales.

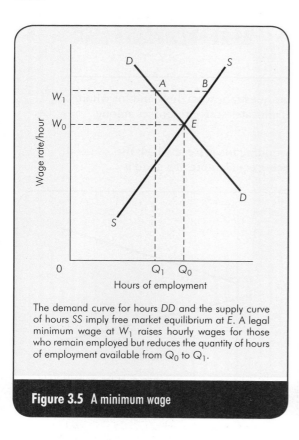

The demand curve for hours DD and the supply curve of hours SS imply free market equilibrium at E. A legal minimum wage at W_1 raises hourly wages for those who remain employed but reduces the quantity of hours of employment available from Q_0 to Q_1.

Figure 3.5 A minimum wage

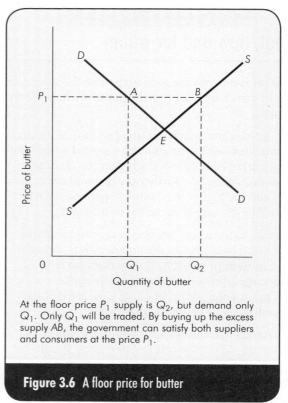

At the floor price P_1 supply is Q_2, but demand only Q_1. Only Q_1 will be traded. By buying up the excess supply AB, the government can satisfy both suppliers and consumers at the price P_1.

Figure 3.6 A floor price for butter

Box 3.3 Dunce's cap

California, home of Silicon Valley and Hollywood, is one of the richest places on earth. Yet in 2001 California suffered blackouts as electricity supplies ran out. Since poverty cannot be blamed, it must have been the result of poor policies. California privatized state electricity companies but then capped the price they could charge for electricity. However, the level of the price cap was far too low. Local electricity suppliers haemorrhaged money. Not only does an artificially low price lead sooner or later to a lower quantity supplied, it also raises the quantity demanded. A recipe for disaster.

Referring to Figure 3.6, at the floor price P_1 private individuals demand Q_1 but supply Q_2. In the absence of government sales or purchases the quantity traded will be Q_1, the smaller of Q_1 and Q_2.

However, the government may agree to purchase the excess supply AB so that neither private suppliers nor private demanders need be frustrated. Because European butter prices are set above the free market equilibrium price as part of the Common Agricultural Policy, European governments have been forced to purchase massive stocks of butter that would otherwise have been unsold at the controlled price. Hence the infamous 'butter mountain'.

3.9 What, how and for whom

The free market is one way for society to solve the basic economic questions what, how and for whom to produce. In this chapter we have begun to see how the market allocates scarce resources among competing uses.

The market decides how much of a good should be produced by finding the price at which the quantity demanded equals the quantity supplied. Other things being equal, more of a good is produced in market equilibrium the higher the quantity demanded at each price (the further the demand curve lies to the right) and the higher the quantity supplied at each price (the further the supply curve lies to the right).

The market tells us for whom the goods are produced: the good is purchased by all those consumers willing to pay at least the equilibrium price for it. The market also tells us who is producing: all those willing to supply at the equilibrium price. Later in this book we shall see that the market also tells us how goods are produced.

Finally, the market determines what goods are being produced. Nature supplies goods free of charge. People engage in costly production activities only if they are paid. The supply curve tells us how much has to be paid to bring supply. Figure 3.7 shows a good that will not be produced. The highest price P_1 that consumers are prepared to pay is still insufficient to persuade producers to produce.

Society may not like the answers the market provides. Free markets *do not* provide enough food to remove hunger or enough medical care to treat all the sick. They provide food and medical care for those willing and *able to pay* the

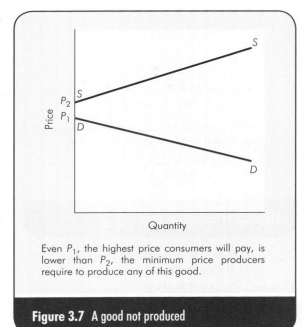

Even P_1, the highest price consumers will pay, is lower than P_2, the minimum price producers require to produce any of this good.

Figure 3.7 A good not produced

Box 3.4 Anatomy of price and quantity changes

How should we interpret the figure below showing data for the UK construction industry? What was happening? Was it a shift in demand, in supply or in both that caused this pattern during 1985–2005?

Suppose all the observations represent *equilibrium* prices and quantities in each year. Thus each point reflects the intersection of the demand and supply curve that year. What changes in the 'other things equal' determinants of supply and demand led to shifts in supply and demand curves and hence changed the location of the data points? Try drawing a diagram with a *given* demand curve and a *shifting* supply curve (do it now!). The equilibrium points you will trace out all lie on the *given* demand curve. If only supply shifts we expect a *negative* relation between price and quantity as we pick off different points on the same demand curve, which slopes downwards. Now, suppose the supply curve is *fixed* but the demand curve *shifts*. The equilibrium points then all lie on the *given* supply curve and exhibit a positive relation between price and quantity. The data in our example show a largely positive relationship between the price of construction and the quantity of construction, and hence principally correspond to a fixed supply curve for construction. It was demand for construction that must have been shifting around. Construction demand increased steadily during 1985–89, fell back in 1990–93, then grew again thereafter.

Having made a diagnosis, we now gather corroborating evidence. Economy-wide activity is an important determinant of the demand for construction. UK real income grew strongly during 1985–89, fell sharply during 1990–93 and grew fairly steadily thereafter. These changes in income nicely fit our theory that demand shifts mainly caused the data pattern in the figure.

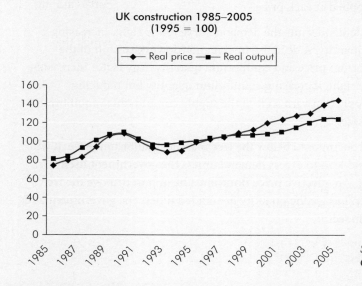

UK construction 1985–2005 (1995 = 100)

Sources: DEFRA; Association for Consultancy & Engineering.

equilibrium price. Society may adopt the normative judgement that the poor should get more food and medical care than they get in a free market. Society may also adopt the normative judgement that, although people are willing and able to pay for pornography, it is socially better to ban some of these activities. Few societies allow unrestricted free markets for all commodities. Governments intervene widely to alter market outcomes, through direct regulation, taxation and transfer payments such as unemployment benefit.

Summary

- **Demand** is the quantity that buyers wish to buy at each price. Other things equal, the lower the price, the higher the quantity demanded. Demand curves slope down.

- **Supply** is the quantity of a good sellers wish to sell at each price. Other things equal, the higher the price, the higher the quantity. Supply curves slope upwards.

- **The market clears, or is in equilibrium**, when the price equates the quantity supplied and the quantity demanded. At this point supply and demand curves intersect. At prices below the equilibrium price there is **excess demand** (shortage), which itself tends to raise the price. At prices above the equilibrium price there is **excess supply** (surplus), which itself tends to reduce the price. In a **free market**, deviations from the equilibrium price tend to be self-correcting.

- Along a given demand curve, the other things assumed equal are the prices of related goods, consumer incomes and tastes or habits.

- An increase in the price of a **substitute** good (or decrease in the price of a **complement** good) will raise the quantity demanded at each price. An increase in consumer income will increase demand for the good if the good is a **normal good** but decrease demand for the good if it is an **inferior good**.

- Along a given supply curve the other things assumed constant are technology, the price of inputs and the degree of government regulation. An improvement in technology, or a reduction in input prices, will increase the quantity supplied at each price.

- Any factor inducing an increase in demand shifts the demand curve to the right, increasing equilibrium price and equilibrium quantity. A decrease in demand (downward shift of the demand curve) reduces both equilibrium price and equilibrium quantity. Any factor increasing supply shifts the supply curve to the right, increasing equilibrium quantity but reducing equilibrium price. Reductions in supply (leftward shift of the supply curve) reduce equilibrium quantity but increase equilibrium price.

- To be effective, a **price ceiling** must be imposed below the free market equilibrium price. It will then reduce the quantity supplied and lead to excess demand unless the government itself provides the extra quantity required. An effective **price floor** must be imposed above the free market equilibrium price. It will then reduce the quantity demanded unless the government adds its own demand to that of the private sector.

Review questions

To check your answers to these questions, see page 713.

1 Supply and demand data for toasters are shown below. Plot the supply curve and demand curve and find the equilibrium price and quantity.

Quantity	Price					
	10	12	14	16	18	20
Demanded	10	9	8	7	6	5
Supplied	3	4	5	6	7	8

2 What is the excess supply or demand when the price is (a) 12, (b) 20? Describe the price movements induced by positions (a) and (b).

3 What happens to the demand curve for toasters if the price of bread rises? Show in a supply-demand diagram how the equilibrium price and quantity of toasters change.

4 How is the demand curve for toasters affected by the invention of the toaster oven if people prefer this new way of toasting? What happens to the equilibrium quantity and price of toasters?

5 You are a sheep farmer. Give three examples of a change that would reduce your supply of wool. Did you use a fall in the price of wool as one of your examples? Is it a valid example?

6 Goods with snob value are demanded because they are expensive. Does the demand curve for such goods slope upwards?

7 **Common fallacies** Why are these statements wrong? (a) Manchester United is a more famous football club than Wrexham. Man Utd will always find it easier to fill its stadium. (b) The European 'butter mountain' shows how productivity can be improved when farmers are inspired by the European ideal. (c) Holding down rents ensures plenty of cheap housing for the poor.

8 **Harder question** Consider the market for safe cities. Someone knocks on your door and asks if you wish to purchase a reduction in crime by subscribing to an enhanced city-wide police force. Your city has 1 million residents. (a) What happens if you do not subscribe but all your fellow city dwellers do? (b) What happens if you subscribe but nobody else subscribes? (c) What does this tell you about the possibility of a market for public goods such as safe cities? (d) How might society ensure that desirably safe cities are provided?

9 **Harder question** Profitable speculation should stabilize financial markets – successful speculators are those who buy when the price is below the equilibrium price and sell when it has risen, or sell when the price is above the equilibrium price and buy when it has fallen. Why, then, are financial market prices so volatile?

10 **Essay question** The UK government is discussing a change in the planning laws to allow the building of 3 million new homes by 2020. Discuss what this is likely to mean for (a) the price of houses for first-time buyers and (b) the demand for country houses in areas adjacent to new housing developments. (c) Does your answer to (b) depend upon whether new houses are accompanied by new infrastructure (better roads, shops, train services, flood protection)?

To help you grasp the key concepts of this chapter check out the extra resources posted on the Online Learning Centre. There are chapter summaries, self-test questions, an interactive graphing tool, weblinks and a searchable glossary, all for free!

To put your learning into practice and prepare for exams, an **Interactive Workbook** is also available online, containing a variety of question types and providing feedback on your answers.

If you'd like further help with economics, or have any questions, **NetTutor** is here to help! You will have a personalised tutorial service at your fingertips. Visit the online learning centre at: www.mcgraw-hill.co.uk/textbooks/begg for information on accessing all of these resources.

PART TWO
Positive microeconomics

Positive economics looks at how the economy functions. Microeconomics takes a detailed look at particular decisions without worrying about all the induced effects elsewhere. Part 2 studies in detail the demand behaviour of consumers and the supply behaviour of producers, showing how markets work and why different markets exhibit different forms of behaviour. By applying similar tools to the analysis of input markets, we can also understand why some people earn so much more than others.

Chapter 4 examines the responsiveness of demand and supply behaviour. Chapter 5 develops a theory of demand based on self-interested choice by consumers. Chapter 6 introduces different types of firm and considers motives behind production decisions. Chapter 7 analyses how costs of production influence the output that firms choose to supply. Chapters 8 and 9 explore how differences in market structure affect competition and the output decision of firms. Chapters 10 to 12 analyse input markets for labour, capital and land, which determine the distribution of income. Chapter 13 explains why people dislike risk, how institutions develop to shift risk on to those who can bear it more cheaply, and why informational problems can inhibit the development of markets for some commodities. Chapter 14 uses the microeconomic analysis of Part 2 to examine recent developments in the information economy.

Contents

By the end of this chapter, you should understand:

1 how elasticities measure responsiveness of demand or supply

2 the price elasticity of demand

3 how it affects the revenue effect of a price change

4 why bad harvests may help farmers

5 the fallacy of composition

6 how cross-price elasticity relates to complements and substitutes

7 income elasticity of demand

8 inferior, normal and luxury goods

9 elasticity of supply

10 how supply and demand elasticities affect tax incidence

In Chapter 3 we examined how the price of a good affects the quantity demanded. We saw also that changes in income, or in the price of related goods, shift demand curves, altering the quantity demanded at each price. We now study these effects in more detail.

4.1 The price responsiveness of demand

A down-sloping demand curve shows that lower prices increase quantity demanded. Often, we need to know by how much quantity will increase. Table 4.1 presents some hypothetical numbers relating ticket price and quantity demanded, other things equal. From columns (1) and (2), Figure 4.1 plots the demand curve, which happens to be a straight line.

How do we measure the responsiveness of the quantity of tickets demanded to the price of tickets? An obvious measure is the slope of the demand curve. Each price cut of £1 leads to 8000 extra ticket sales. Suppose we want to compare the price responsiveness of football ticket sales with that of cars. £1 is a trivial cut in the price of a car and has a negligible effect on the quantity of cars demanded.

In Chapter 2 we argued that when commodities are measured in different units it is often best to examine the percentage change, which is unit-free.

Table 4.1 The demand for football tickets

(1) Price (£/ticket)	(2) Tickets demanded (000s)	(3) Price elasticity of demand
12.50	0	—∞
10.00	20	−4
7.50	40	−1.5
5.00	60	−0.67
2.50	80	−0.25
0	100	0

Although we later introduce other demand elasticities – the cross-price elasticity and the income elasticity – the (own) price elasticity is the most often used of the three. If economists speak of the *demand elasticity* they mean the price elasticity of demand, as defined above.

Suppose a 1 per cent price rise reduces the quantity demanded by 2 per cent. The demand elasticity is the percentage change in quantity (−2) divided by the percentage change in price (+1) and is thus given by −2. The minus sign tells us quantity *falls* when price rises. If a price fall of 4 per cent increases the quantity demanded by 2 per cent, the demand elasticity is −1/2 since the quantity change (+2 per cent) is divided by the price change (−4 per cent). Since demand curves slope down, price and quantity changes always have opposite signs. The price elasticity of demand tells us about movements along a demand curve. The demand elasticity is a negative number.

> The **price elasticity of demand** (PED) is the percentage change in the quantity demanded divided by the corresponding percentage change in its price.
> PED = (% change in quantity)/ (% change in price).

For further brevity, economists often omit the minus sign. It is easier to say the demand elasticity is 2 than to say it is −2. When the price elasticity of demand is expressed as a positive number, it is implicit that a minus sign must be added (unless there is an explicit warning to the contrary). Otherwise, it implies that demand curves slope up, a rare but not unknown phenomenon.

The price elasticity of demand for football tickets is shown in column (3) of Table 4.1. Examining the effect of price cuts of £2.50, we calculate the price elasticity of demand at each price. Beginning at £10 and 20 000 tickets demanded, consider a price cut to £7.50. The price change is −25 per cent, from £10 to £7.50, the change in quantity demanded is +100 per cent, from 20 000 to 40 000 tickets.

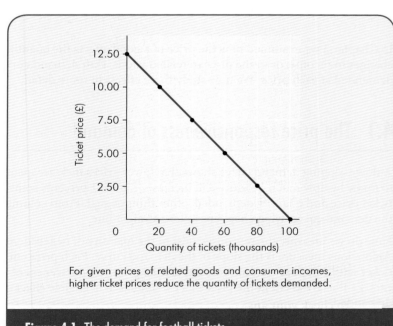

For given prices of related goods and consumer incomes, higher ticket prices reduce the quantity of tickets demanded.

Figure 4.1 The demand for football tickets

The demand elasticity at £10 is (100/−25) = −4. Other elasticities are calculated in the same way, dividing the percentage change in quantity by the corresponding percentage change in price. When we begin from the price of £12.50, the demand elasticity is minus infinity. The percentage change in quantity demanded is +20/0. Any positive number divided by zero is infinity. Dividing by the −20 per cent change in price, from £12.50 to £10, the demand elasticity is minus infinity at this price.

Price elasticity of demand = [% rise in quantity]/[% rise in price]

We say that the demand elasticity is *high* if it is a large negative number. The quantity demanded is sensitive to the price. The demand elasticity is *low* if it is a small negative number and the quantity demanded is insensitive to the price. 'High' or 'low' refer to the size of the elasticity, ignoring the minus sign. The demand elasticity falls when it becomes a smaller negative number and quantity demanded becomes less sensitive to the price.

Activity box 4 Practising calculation of price elasticity of demand (PED)

P = price (£)	1	2	3	4	5	6
Q = quantity demanded	10	8	6	4	2	1

The rows in the table above give price and quantity data for a particular demand curve. The table below shows five columns, labelled A–E, each corresponding to a situation in which the price changes by £1 and there is a corresponding change in the quantity demanded.

In column A, a 100 per cent price rise (from £1 to £2) induces a 20 per cent fall in quantity demanded (from 10 to 8), implying a price elasticity of demand of (−20/100) = −0.2. Similarly, in column C, a 50 per cent price reduction (from £2 to £1) induces a 25 per cent rise in quantity demanded (from 8 to 10), implying a price elasticity of (25)/(−50) = −0.5.

	A	B	C		D	E
(1) Initial P and Q	P = 1 Q = 10	P = 2 Q = 8	P = 2 Q = 8		P = 4 Q = 4	P = 5 Q = 2
(2) New P and Q	P = 2 Q = 8	P = 3 Q = 6	P = 1 Q = 10		P = 3 Q = 6	P = 6 Q = 1
(3) % change in P	100*(2−1)/1 = 100		100*(1−2)/2 = −50			
(4) % change in Q thus induced	100*(8−10)/10 = −20		100*(10−8)/8 = 25			
(5) PED = (4)/(3)	−0.2		−0.5			

Question
(a) Try to complete columns B, D and E for yourself.

To check your answers to this question, go to page 714.

The demand curve for football tickets is a straight line with constant slope: along its entire length a £1 cut in price always leads to 8000 extra ticket sales. Yet Table 4.1 shows the demand elasticity falls as we move down the demand curve from higher prices to lower prices. At high prices, £1 is a small percentage change in the price but 8000 tickets is a large percentage change in the quantity demanded. Conversely, at low prices £1 is a large percentage change in the price but 8000 is a small percentage change in the quantity. When the demand curve is a straight line, the price elasticity falls steadily as we move down the demand curve.[1]

It is possible to construct curved demand schedules (still, of course, sloping downwards) along which the price elasticity of demand remains constant. Generally, however, the price elasticity changes as we move along demand curves, and we expect the elasticity to be high at high prices and low at low prices.

If the demand curve is a straight line, we get the same size of quantity response (20 000 tickets) whether we raise or lower the price by £2.50. It does not matter whether we use price rises or price cuts to calculate the demand elasticity. When, as in Figure 4.2, the demand curve is not a straight line, we meet a minor difficulty. Beginning at point A where the price is P_0, moves to points B and C are percentage price changes of equal magnitude but opposite sign. Figure 4.2 shows that the quantity response (from Q_0 to either Q_1 or Q_2) differs for price rises and price falls when the demand curve is not a straight line.

For nonlinear demand curves, economists resolve this ambiguity about the definition of price elasticity of demand by defining it with respect to *very small* changes in price. If we move only a short distance either side of point A, the demand curve hardly has time to bend round. Over the very short distance corresponding to a small percentage price rise or fall, the demand curve is as near a straight line as makes no difference. With this amendment we can use the old definition.

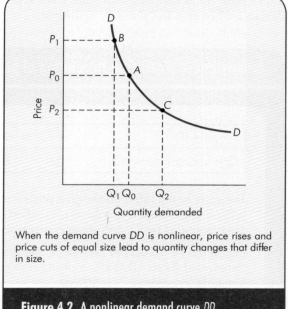

When the demand curve DD is nonlinear, price rises and price cuts of equal size lead to quantity changes that differ in size.

Figure 4.2 A nonlinear demand curve DD

Elastic and inelastic demand

Although elasticity typically falls as we move down the demand curve, an important dividing line occurs at the demand elasticity of –1. In Table 4.1 demand is elastic at all prices of £7.50 and above and inelastic at all prices of £5 and below.

> Demand is **elastic** if the price elasticity is more negative than –1. Demand is **inelastic** if the price elasticity lies between –1 and 0. If the demand elasticity is –1, demand is **unit-elastic**.

Although the price elasticity of demand typically changes as we move along demand curves, economists frequently talk of goods with high or low demand elasticities. For example, the demand for oil is price-inelastic (price changes have only a small effect on quantity demanded) but the demand for foreign holidays is price-elastic (price changes have a big effect on quantity demanded). Such statements implicitly refer to parts of the demand curve corresponding to prices usually charged for these goods or services.

Determinants of price elasticity

Why is the price elasticity of demand for a good high (–5) or low (–0.5)? The answer lies in consumer tastes. If it is a social necessity to own a television, higher TV prices have little effect on quantity

---

1 Except in two special cases of linear demand curves: a *horizontal* or infinitely elastic demand curve has an elasticity of minus infinity at all points since the *price* change is always zero; a *vertical* or completely inelastic demand curve has an elasticity of zero at all points since the *quantity* never changes.

demanded. If TVs are considered a frivolous luxury, the demand elasticity is much higher. Psychologists and sociologists can explain why tastes are as they are. As economists, we can identify some considerations likely to affect consumer responses to changes in the price of a good. *The most important consideration is the ease with which consumers can substitute another good that fulfils approximately the same function.*

Consider two extreme cases. Suppose the price of all cigarettes rises by 1 per cent. The quantity of cigarettes demanded will hardly respond. People who can easily quit smoking have already done so. In contrast, suppose the price of a particular brand of cigarettes rises by 1 per cent, all other brand prices remaining unchanged. We expect a much larger quantity response. Consumers switch from the dearer brand to other brands that also satisfy the nicotine habit. For a particular cigarette brand the demand elasticity is quite high.

Our example suggests a general rule. The more narrowly we define a commodity (a particular brand of cigarette rather than cigarettes in general), the higher will be the price elasticity of demand.

Measuring price elasticities

Table 4.2 confirms that the demand for broad categories of basic commodities, such as fuel, food or even household durable goods, is inelastic. As a category, only services such as haircuts, the theatre and sauna baths, have an elastic demand. Households simply do not have much scope to alter the broad pattern of their purchases.

Table 4.2 UK price elasticities of demand

Good (broad type)	Demand elasticity	Good (narrow type)	Demand elasticity
Fuel and light	−0.5	Dairy produce	−0.1
Food	−0.5	Bread and cereals	−0.2
Alcohol	−0.8	Entertainment	−1.4
Durables	−0.9	Expenditure abroad	−1.6
Services	−1.0	Catering	−2.6

Sources: J. Muellbauer, 'Testing the Barten Model of Household Composition Effects', *Economic Journal*, 1977; A. Deaton, 'The Measurement of Income and Price Elasticities', *European Economic Review*, 1975.

In contrast, there is a much wider variation in the demand elasticities for narrower definitions of commodities. Even then, the demand for some commodities, such as dairy produce, is very inelastic. However, particular kinds of services such as entertainment and catering have much more elastic demand.

Using price elasticities

Price elasticities of demand are useful in calculating the price rise required to eliminate a shortage (excess demand) or the price fall to eliminate a surplus (excess supply). One important source of surpluses and shortages is shifts in the supply curve. Harvest failures (and bumper crops) are a feature of agricultural markets. Because the demand elasticity for many agricultural products is very low, harvest failures produce large increases in the price of food. Conversely, bumper crops induce very large falls in food prices. When demand is very inelastic, shifts in the supply curve lead to large fluctuations in price but have little effect on equilibrium quantities.

Figure 4.3(a) illustrates this. *SS* is the supply curve in an agricultural market when there is a harvest failure and *S'S'* the supply curve when there is a bumper crop. The equilibrium price fluctuates between P_1 (harvest failure) and P_2 (bumper crop) but induces little fluctuation in the corresponding equilibrium quantities. Contrast this with Figure 4.3(b), which shows the effect of similar supply

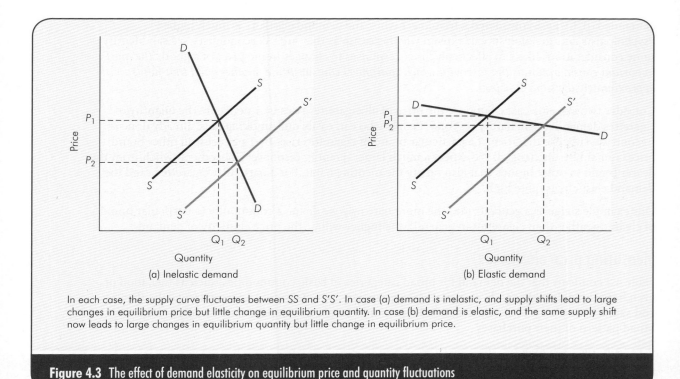

In each case, the supply curve fluctuates between *SS* and *S'S'*. In case (a) demand is inelastic, and supply shifts lead to large changes in equilibrium price but little change in equilibrium quantity. In case (b) demand is elastic, and the same supply shift now leads to large changes in equilibrium quantity but little change in equilibrium price.

Figure 4.3 The effect of demand elasticity on equilibrium price and quantity fluctuations

shifts in a market with very elastic demand. Price fluctuations are much smaller but quantity fluctuations are now much larger. Knowing the demand elasticity helps us understand why some markets exhibit volatile quantities but stable prices, while other markets exhibit volatile prices but stable quantities.

4.2 Price, quantity demanded and total expenditure

Other things equal, the demand curve shows how much consumers of a good wish to purchase at each price. At each price, total spending by consumers is the price multiplied by the quantity demanded. We now discuss the relation between total spending and price and show the relevance of the price elasticity of demand.

Figure 4.4 shows how total spending changes with price changes. In case A, we begin at *A* with price P_A and quantity demanded Q_A. Total spending is $P_A Q_A$, the area of the rectangle $OP_A A Q_A$. At the lower price P_B, consumers demand Q_B and total spending is $P_B Q_B$, the area of the rectangle $OP_B B Q_B$. How does total spending change when prices fall from P_A to P_B? Spending falls by the area marked (−) but rises by the area marked (+). In case A, the (+) area exceeds the (−) area and total spending rises. In the elastic range of the demand curve (towards the upper end) a lower price raises the quantity demanded by more than enough to offset the lower price. Total spending rises.

Case B examines the lower end of the demand curve, where demand is inelastic. Although the price cut raises the quantity demanded, the rise in quantity is insufficient to compensate for the lower price. The (+) area is smaller than the (−) area. Total spending falls. If price cuts increase total spend at high prices where the demand elasticity is high and reduce total spending at low prices where the demand elasticity is low, at some price in-between a fall in price will leave total spending unaltered. Case C shows this possibility. The higher quantity demanded exactly compensates for the lower price.

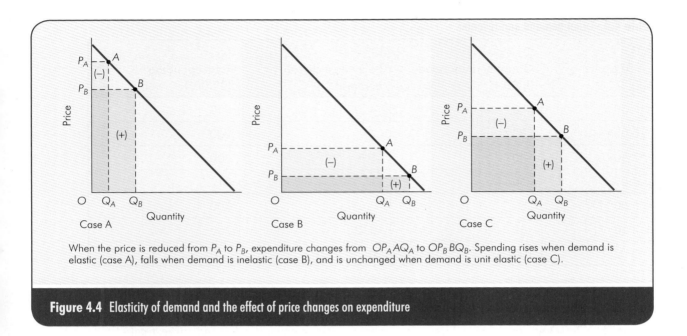

When the price is reduced from P_A to P_B, expenditure changes from $OP_A AQ_A$ to $OP_B BQ_B$. Spending rises when demand is elastic (case A), falls when demand is inelastic (case B), and is unchanged when demand is unit elastic (case C).

Figure 4.4 Elasticity of demand and the effect of price changes on expenditure

If quantity demanded rises 1 per cent when the price falls 1 per cent, total spending is unchanged. Case C shows the point on the demand curve at which the price elasticity of demand is –1 (quantity change –1 per cent, price change –1 per cent). If demand is elastic, a demand elasticity more negative than 1, as in case A, a 1 per cent price cut leads to an increase in quantity by *more* than 1 per cent. Hence total spending rises. Conversely, when demand is inelastic, a demand elasticity lying between 0 and 1, as in case B, a 1 per cent price cut leads to an increase in quantity by *less* than 1 per cent. Hence total spending falls. These results are summarized in Table 4.3.

Table 4.3 Demand elasticities and changes in spending

Change in total spending caused by	Price elasticity of demand		
	Elastic (e.g. –3)	Unit-elastic (–1)	Inelastic (e.g. –0.3)
Price rise	Fall	Unchanged	Rise
Price cut	Rise	Unchanged	Fall

Sources: J. Muellbauer, 'Testing the Barten Model of Household Composition Effects and the Cost of Children', *Economic Journal*, 1977; A. Deaton, 'The Measurement of Income and Price Elasticities', *European Economic Review*, 1975.

The price of football tickets

Think again about revenue from ticket sales. Table 4.4 shows the demand data of Table 4.1, but also shows the tickets demanded at a price of £6.25 per ticket. At this price the demand elasticity is –1. A 20 per cent price cut (–£1.25) induces a 20 per cent rise in the quantity demanded (10 000 tickets). Column (4) shows total spending on tickets at each price.

Beginning from the highest price of £12.50, successive price cuts first increase total spending on tickets, then reduce it. Table 4.4 explains why. When the price is high, demand is elastic: price reductions increase total spending. When demand is unit-elastic, at price £6.25, we reach a turning

Table 4.4 Ticket demand and revenue

(1) Ticket price (£)	(2) Quantity demanded ('000s)	(3) Price elasticity of demand	(4) Total spending (£'000s)
12.50	0	$-\infty$	0
10.00	20	-4	200
7.50	40	-1.5	300
6.25	50	-1	312.5
5.00	60	-0.67	300
2.50	80	-0.25	200
0	100	0	0

point. Above this price, price cuts have steadily increased total spending. Below this price, further price cuts reduce total spending because demand is then inelastic.

We can thus draw two conclusions. First, as we imagine moving down the demand curve, total spending is instantaneously unchanging as we move through the price £6.25 at which demand is unit-elastic. Second, *spending and revenue reach a maximum at the point of unit-elastic demand*. This idea, and the empirical knowledge that this occurs at the price of £6.25 per ticket, are the pieces of information the football club owner needs to know.

4.3 Further applications of the price elasticity of demand

The coffee frost

There's an awful lot of coffee in Brazil – the country supplies a large share of the world market. In 1994, people first realized that a frost in Brazil would cause havoc with the 1995 harvest. *The Economist* magazine (30 July 1994: www.economist.co.uk) reported estimates that the 1995 crop would not be the 26.5 million bags previously thought, but only 15.7 million bags. Obviously, coffee was going to be scarce in 1995. Anticipating this, speculators bought coffee in 1994, bidding up its price even before the supply fell.

Table 4.5 shows the effect on Brazilian exports during 1993–95. The first row shows that, even after adjusting for general inflation, coffee prices more than doubled in US dollars. The second row shows an index of the volume of Brazilian coffee exports. The final row shows Brazilian export revenue from coffee. Real revenue rose sharply in 1994: prices had risen *before* production had fallen too much. The interesting comparison is between 1993 and 1995. Brazilian export revenue from coffee *increased* despite the 'bad' harvest.

The demand for coffee is inelastic, despite an abundance of substitutes – tea, soft drinks and beer. This example emphasizes the importance of consumer tastes. If buyers refuse to abandon coffee drinking it is useless to point out that a blend of tea and Coca-Cola has as much caffeine as the average cup of coffee.

Table 4.5 Brazilian coffee exports

	1993	1994	1995
Price (US$/lb)	0.9	2.0	2.1
Export quantity (1990 = 100)	113	102	85
Price × quantity	102	204	179

Note: Prices are in 1995 US$.
Source: IMF, *International Financial Statistics.*

Farmers and bad harvests

This example illustrates a general result. When demand is inelastic farmers earn more revenue from a bad harvest than from a good one. When the supply curve shifts to the left it takes a big rise in price to eliminate excess demand when demand is inelastic. And price increases *raise* consumer spending and producer revenues when demand is inelastic. Demand elasticities are low for many commodities such as coffee, milk and wheat. They are part of our staple diet. Eating habits are slow to change, even when prices rise.

If bad harvests raise farmers' revenues and good harvests lead to a fall in agricultural prices and farmers' revenues, why don't farmers get together like OPEC to restrict their supply and increase revenues in the face of inelastic demand? If it were easy to organize such collusion between farmers, it would occur more frequently. Later we discuss the difficulties that arise in trying to maintain a co-operative policy to restrict supply.

When demand is inelastic, suppliers *taken together* are better off if supply can be reduced. However, if one farmer loses part of the crop but all other farmers' crops are unaffected, the unlucky farmer is worse off. The fall in a single farmer's output, unlike the reduction of all farmers' outputs simultaneously, has a negligible effect on supply. Market price is unaffected and the unlucky farmer simply sells less output at the price that would have prevailed in any case. This illustrates an important lesson in economics. The individual producer faces a demand that is very elastic – consumers can easily switch to the output of similar farmers – even if the demand for the crop as a whole is very inelastic.

> The **fallacy of composition** means that what is true for the individual may not be true for everyone together, and what is true for everyone together may not hold for the individual.

Box 4.1 Easy profits

Low cost airline pioneer Sir Stelios Haji-Ioannou, founder of easyJet and then the easyGroup, credits two things for his success. The first, which he says only half in jest, is coming from a rich family, which made it easier to get through the early years. The second, which he also proudly cites, is his economics degree, where the lecture on elasticity of demand helped underpin his conviction that low prices could generate large revenues by creating high sales volume. When he launched easyJet, conventional airlines were happy to fill 70 per cent of their seats on an average flight. easyJet now runs regularly at 85 per cent capacity on its 600 flights a day, which is a lot of extra revenue without any additional costs.

Source: www.easyJet.com

4.4 Short run and long run

> The **short run** is the period after prices change but before quantity adjustment can occur. The **long run** is the period needed for complete adjustment to a price change. Its length depends on the type of adjustments consumers wish to make.

The price elasticity of demand varies with the length of time in which consumers can adjust their spending patterns when prices change. The most dramatic price change of the past 50 years, the oil price rise of 1973–74, caught many households with a new but fuel-inefficient car. At first, they may not have expected the higher oil price to last. Then they may have *planned* to buy a smaller car with greater fuel economy. But in countries like the US few small cars were yet available. In the *short run*, households were stuck. Unless they could rearrange their lifestyles to reduce car use, they had to pay the higher petrol prices. Demand for petrol was inelastic.

Over a longer period, consumers had time to sell their big cars and buy cars with better fuel economy, or to move from the distant suburbs closer to their place of work. Over this longer period, they could reduce the quantity of petrol demanded much more than initially.

The price elasticity of demand is lower in the short run than in the long run when there is more scope to substitute other goods. This result is very general. Even if addicted smokers cannot adjust to a rise in the price of cigarettes, fewer young people start smoking and gradually the number of smokers falls.

How long is the long run?

Demand responses to a change in the price of chocolate should be completed within a few months, but full adjustment to changes in the price of oil or cigarettes may take years.

4.5 The cross-price elasticity of demand

> The **cross-price elasticity of demand** for good i with respect to changes in the price of good j is the percentage change in the quantity of good i demanded, divided by the corresponding percentage change in the price of good j.

The price elasticity of demand tells us about movements along a given demand curve holding constant all determinants of demand except the price of the good itself. We now hold constant the own-price of the good and examine changes in the prices of *related* goods. The cross-price elasticity tells us the effect on the quantity demanded of the good i when the price of good j is changed. As before, we use percentage changes.

The cross-price elasticity may be positive or negative. It is positive if a rise in the price of good j increases the quantity demanded of good i. Suppose good i is tea and good j is coffee. An increase in the price of coffee raises the demand for tea. The cross-price elasticity of tea with respect to coffee is positive. Cross-price elasticities tend to be positive when two goods are substitutes and negative when two goods are complements. We expect a rise in the price of petrol to reduce the demand for cars because petrol and cars are complements.

Table 4.6 shows estimates for the UK. Own-price elasticities for food, clothing and travel are given down the diagonal of the table, from top left (the own-price elasticity of demand for food) to bottom right (the own-price elasticity of demand for travel). Off-diagonal entries in the table show cross-price elasticities of demand. Thus, 0.1 is the cross-price elasticity of demand for food with respect to transport. A 1 per cent increase in the price of travel increases the quantity of food demanded by 0.1 per cent.

The own-price elasticities for the three goods lie between –0.4 and –0.5. For all three goods the quantity demanded is more sensitive to changes in its own price than to changes in the price of any other good.

Table 4.6 Cross-price and own-price elasticities of demand in the UK

% change in quantity	Caused by a 1% price change in demand for		
	Food	Clothing	Travel
Food	−0.4	0	0.1
Clothing	0.1	−0.5	−0.1
Travel	0.3	−0.1	−0.5

Source: R. Blundell *et al.*, 'What Do We Learn about Consumer Demand Patterns from Micro Data?', *American Economic Review*, 1993.

4.6 The effect of income on demand

Finally, holding constant the own price of a good and the prices of related goods, we examine the response of the quantity demanded to changes in consumer incomes. For the moment we neglect the possibility of saving. Thus a rise in the income of consumers will typically be matched by an equivalent increase in total consumer spending.

Chapter 3 pointed out that higher consumer incomes tend to increase the quantity demanded. However, demand quantities increase by different amounts as incomes rise. Thus the pattern of consumer spending on different goods depends on the level of consumer incomes. The budget share of a good is the fraction of total consumer spending for which it accounts.

> The **budget share** of a good is its price times the quantity demanded, divided by total consumer spending or income.

Table 4.7 reports the share of consumer spending in the UK devoted to food and drink and to recreation and cultural goods between 1997 and 2005. Real consumer spending (and incomes) rose during 1997–2005. Even though real spending on food and drink increased, its budget share fell. Spending on recreation and cultural goods rose so much that its budget share increased substantially. These changes in budget share mainly reflect changes in real consumer incomes and different income elasticities of demand.

> The **income elasticity of demand** for a good is the percentage change in quantity demanded divided by the corresponding percentage change in income.

Table 4.7 Budget shares, 1997–2005

	Real consumer spending (2003 £bn)	% budget share	
		Food and drink	Recreation and cultural goods
1997	558	10	3
2005	731	9	7

Source: ONS, *UK National Accounts.*

Normal, inferior and luxury goods

The income elasticity of demand measures how far the demand curve shifts horizontally when incomes change. Figure 4.5 shows two possible shifts caused by a given percentage increase in income. The income elasticity is larger if the given rise in income shifts the demand curve from DD to $D''D''$ than if the same income rise shifts the demand curve only from DD to $D'D'$. When an income rise shifts the demand curve to the left, the income elasticity of demand is a negative number, indicating that higher incomes are associated with smaller quantities demanded at any given prices.

In Chapter 3 we distinguished *normal* goods, for which demand increases as income rises, and *inferior* goods, for which demand falls as income rises. We also distinguish luxury goods and necessities.

All inferior goods are necessities, since their income elasticities of demand are negative. However, necessities also include normal goods whose income elasticity of demand lies between zero and one.

These definitions tell us what happens to budget shares when incomes are changed but prices remain unaltered. The budget share of inferior goods falls as incomes rise. Higher incomes and household budgets are associated with lower quantities demanded at constant prices. Conversely, the budget share of luxuries rises when income rises. Because the income elasticity of demand for luxuries exceeds one, a 1 per cent rise in income increases quantity demanded (and hence total spending on luxury goods) by more than 1 per cent. Rises in income *reduce* the budget share of normal goods that are necessities. A 1 per cent income rise leads to a rise in quantity demanded but of less than 1 per cent, so the budget share must fall.

Inferior goods tend to be low-quality goods for which there exist higher-quality, but more expensive, substitutes. Poor people satisfy their needs for meat and clothing by buying fatty meat and polyester shirts. As their incomes rise, they switch to better cuts of meat (steak) and more comfortable shirts (cotton). Rising incomes lead to an absolute decline in the demand for fatty meat and polyester shirts.

Luxury goods tend to be high-quality goods for which there exist lower-quality, barely adequate, substitutes: BMWs rather than small Fords, foreign rather than domestic holidays. Necessities that are normal goods lie between these two extremes. As incomes rise, the quantity of food demanded will rise but only a little. Most people still enjoy fairly simple home cooking even when their incomes rise. Looking back at Table 4.7, recreation and cultural goods are luxuries whose budget share increased from 3 to 7 per cent as UK incomes rose during 1997–2005. Food and drink cannot be a luxury, since its budget share fell as incomes rose, but it is not an inferior good either. At constant prices which adjust for the effects of inflation, during 1997–2007 real food spending *increased* from £56 billion (10 per cent of £558 billion) to £66 billion (9 per cent of £731 billion).

Table 4.8 summarizes the demand responses to changes in income holding constant the prices of all goods. The table shows the effect of income increases. Reductions in income have the opposite effect on quantity demanded and budget share.

Table 4.9 reports income elasticities of demand in the UK, for broad categories of goods in the first two columns and narrower categories in the last two columns. Again, the variation in elasticities is larger for narrower definitions of goods. Higher incomes have much more effect on the way in which households eat (more prawns, less bread) than on the amount they eat in total. Food is a normal good but not a luxury. Its income elasticity is 0.45.

The last column indicates that, within the food budget, higher income leads to a switch towards vegetables (whose income elasticity is higher than that for food as a whole) and away from bread,

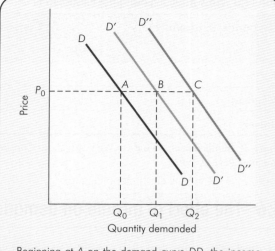

Beginning at A on the demand curve DD, the income elasticity measures the horizontal shift in the demand curve when income rises 1 per cent. At the given price P_0, a shift to B on the demand curve D'D' reflects a lower income elasticity than a shift to C on the demand curve D''D''. Leftward shifts in the demand curve when income rises indicate a negative income elasticity.

Figure 4.5 Income elasticity and shifts in the demand

A **normal good** has a positive income elasticity of demand. An **inferior good** has a negative income elasticity of demand.

A **luxury good** has an income elasticity above unity. A **necessity** has an income elasticity below unity.

Table 4.8 Demand responses to a 1% rise in income

Good	Income elasticity	Quantity demanded	Budget share	Example
Normal	Positive	Rises		
Luxury	Above 1	Rises more than 1%	Rises	BMW
Necessity	Between 0 and 1	Rises less than 1%	Falls	Food
Inferior	Negative	Falls	Falls	Bread

Table 4.9 UK income elasticities of demand

Broad categories	Income elasticity	Narrower categories	Income elasticity
Tobacco	0.5	Coal	2.0
Fuel	0.3	Bread and cereals	0.5
Food	0.5	Dairy produce	0.5
Alcohol	1.1	Vegetables	0.9
Clothing	1.2	Travel abroad	1.1
Durables	1.5	Leisure goods	2.0
Services	1.8	Wines and spirits	2.6

Sources: J. Muellbauer, 'Testing the Barten Model of Household Composition Effects', *Economic Journal*, 1977; A. Deaton, 'The Measurement of Income and Price Elasticities', *European Economic Review*, 1975.

Box 4.2 Car crazy

As countries develop and get richer, one of the first things people want is a car. The income elasticity of demand for cars has been estimated at around 2. China, one of the fastest-growing economies in the world, now has an insatiable appetite for cars. With rapidly rising incomes, the once common bicycle is fast giving way to the car. In 1949, the world's most populous economy had a mere 1800 cars. By 2005 that figure was 24 million, making China second only to the USA in the size of its car market. While in the 1970s a worker had to save for a year to buy a bicycle, incomes are now so high that they only have to save for a year to buy a car. With the financial sector also booming, it is anticipated that by 2015 almost half new car purchases will be financed by car loans.

Income elasticities of demand help us make confident predictions that rapidly rising living standards in countries such as China and India will lead to massive increases in the demand for cars, mobile phones, energy, air travel, and many other goods and services enjoyed in the affluent West. Since many of these are the source of emissions that lead to global warming, the very success of emerging economies adds new urgency to the need to find ways to reduce emissions, either by finding new, cleaner technologies or by co-ordinated government policies to discourage the activities with which harmful emissions are associated.

Source: http://news.bbc.co.uk/1/hi/business/6364195.stm.

for which the quantity demanded declines. Rich households can afford to eat expensive salads to avoid getting fat. Poor people need large quantities of bread to ward off the pangs of hunger. Notice that tobacco is an inferior good, with its largest budget share among poor people. Richer people get their kicks in other (more expensive) ways.

Using income elasticities of demand

Income elasticities help us forecast the pattern of consumer demand as the economy grows and people get richer. Suppose real incomes grow by 15 per cent over the next five years. The estimates of Table 4.9 imply that tobacco demand will fall by 7.5 per cent but the demand for wines and spirits will rise by 39 per cent. The growth prospects of these two industries are very different. These forecasts will affect decisions by firms about whether to build new factories and government projections of tax revenue from cigarettes and alcohol.

4.7 Inflation and demand

Elasticities measure the response of quantity demanded to separate variations in three factors – the own-price, the price of related goods and income. Chapter 2 distinguished *nominal* variables, measured in the prices of the day, and *real* variables, which adjust for inflation when comparing measurements at different dates. We end this chapter by examining the effect of inflation on demand behaviour.

Suppose all nominal variables double. Every good costs twice as much, wage rates are twice as high, rents charged by landlords and dividends paid by firms double in money terms. Whatever bundle of goods was previously affordable is still affordable. Goods cost twice as much but incomes are twice as high. If meat costs twice as much as bread it still costs twice as much. Nothing has really changed. Demand behaviour will be unaltered by a doubling of the nominal value of *all* prices and *all* forms of income.

How do we reconcile this with the idea that own-price elasticities measure changes in quantity demanded as prices change? Each of the elasticities (own-price, cross-price and income) measures the effect of changing that variable *holding constant all other determinants of demand*. When all prices and all incomes are simultaneously changing, the definitions of elasticities warn us that it is incorrect to examine the effect of one variable, such as the own price, on quantity demanded. We can decompose the change in quantity demanded into three components: the effect of changes in the own price alone, plus the effect of changes in price of other goods alone, plus the effect of changing incomes. When all nominal variables change by the same proportion, the sum of these three effects is exactly zero.

4.8 Elasticity of supply

Whereas the analysis of demand elasticities is quite tricky, the analysis of supply elasticities is refreshingly simple. We really need only keep track of the supply response to an increase in the own price of a good or service. The elasticity of supply measures the responsiveness of the quantity supplied to a change in the price of that commodity.

Supply elasticity = (% change in quantity supplied)/(% change in price)

Because supply curves slope upwards, the elasticity of supply is *always positive*. As we move along a supply curve, positive price changes are associated with positive output changes. The more elastic is supply, the larger the percentage increase in quantity supplied in response to a given percentage change in price. Thus, elastic supply curves are relatively flat and inelastic supply curves relatively steep.

Figure 4.6 shows a typical supply curve SS with a positive supply elasticity. If the supply curve is a straight line, the supply elasticity will change as we move along it. As we learned in relation to demand curves, a constant slope implies equal absolute changes in quantity as we successively increase price by one unit; however, these equal absolute changes imply different percentage changes, depending on the point from which we begin.

Figure 4.6 also shows two extreme cases. The vertical supply curve S'S' has a zero supply elasticity. A given percentage change in price is associated with a zero

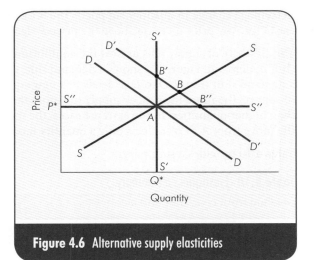

Figure 4.6 Alternative supply elasticities

Box 4.3 Coffee's bitter taste

In 2000 coffee prices slumped to a 20-year low. Higher incomes increased the demand for coffee, but supply increased more. New countries began coffee production, agricultural productivity increased and there was a collapse of the 1989 agreement to place quantity ceilings on coffee exports. For many third-world coffee producers – some of whom get 70 per cent of their export revenue from coffee – low prices have been a disaster. The power of the multinationals has not helped. In some cases, farmers get only 6 per cent of the retail price in the shops. Nestlé now controls about half the world market for instant coffee.

But the fair-trade movement is gathering steam. Starbucks recently agreed a wide-ranging accord with Ethiopia to support and promote the country's coffee, ending a long-running dispute over the issue. The US retailer will market, distribute and, in some cases, license Ethiopia's range of high-quality coffee brands. The new agreement acknowledges Ethiopian ownership of popular coffee designations such as Yirgacheffe, Harrar and Sidamo. It will also allow Starbucks to use coffee types in certain markets under agreed conditions.

Ethiopian farmers will not receive royalty payments from the deal, but it is hoped that more effective distribution and marketing will help boost demand and, in time, lift prices. 'This agreement marks an important milestone in our efforts to promote and protect Ethiopia's speciality coffee designations,' said Getachew Mengistie, director general of the Ethiopian Intellectual Property Office. 'Having the commitment and support of Starbucks will help enhance the quality of Ethiopian fine coffees and improve the income of farmers and traders.'

But fair-trade campaigners argue that this has done little so far to reward Ethiopian farmers, some of whom receive only $300 a year for their crop. Ethiopian officials said the ultimate aim of the agreement was to try to boost prices, which, for Starbucks purchases, averaged $1.42 per pound last year. Starbucks chairman Howard Schultz said, 'We are extremely pleased that this agreement supports both the Ethiopian speciality coffee industry and the farmers and their communities that produce these fine coffees, while allowing us to bring them to our customers. Ethiopia is Africa's largest coffee producer, ahead of Uganda and the Ivory Coast, and coffee is its largest source of foreign exchange.'

Source: BBC online, 21 June 2007.

percentage change in quantity supplied. The horizontal supply curve $S''S''$ has an infinite supply elasticity. Any price increase above the price P^* leads to an infinite increase in quantity supplied.

The elasticity of supply tells us how the equilibrium price and quantity will change when there is a shift in demand. Figure 4.6 shows a demand shift from DD to $D'D'$. Beginning from equilibrium at A, a demand shift from DD to $D'D'$ leads to a new equilibrium at B', B or B'' depending on the elasticity of supply. The more inelastic is supply the more the demand increase leads to higher prices rather than higher quantities. In the extreme cases, the move from A to B'' reflects only a price increase and the move from A to B'' reflects only a quantity increase.

Table 4.10 provides a summary.

Table 4.10 Elasticities: a summary

	% change in quantity demanded	% change in quantity supplied
	Induced by	
(Own-)Price elasticity of demand	1% rise in own price	
Cross-price elasticity of demand	1% rise in price of related good	
Income elasticity of demand	1% rise in income	
Elasticity of supply		1% rise in own price

4.9 Who really pays the tax?

By spending and taxing, the government affects resource allocation in the economy. By taxing cigarettes, the government can reduce the number of cigarettes smoked and thereby improve health. By taxing fuel it can discourage pollution, though it may incur the wrath of lorry drivers and motorists. By taxing income earned from work, the government affects the amount of time people want to work. Taxes loom large in the workings of a mixed economy and have a profound effect on the way society allocates its scarce resources.

Initially we discuss what are called *specific* taxes, those that specify a particular amount, such as £5 per bottle of vodka. We show how the effect of a specific tax is related to the slope of supply and demand curves. We then extend the argument to *ad valorem* taxes, which are measured as a percentage of the commodity's value. For example, VAT is usually levied at 17.5 per cent of the value of the good or service.

Just as specific taxes, in particular units, are related to slopes of supply and demand curves in particular units, so *ad valorem* or percentage taxes are related to *elasticities* of supply and demand, which are already expressed in percentages.

Either way, what we want to know is who ends up paying the tax. Suppose for simplicity we imagine a packet of cigarettes costs £1 and the government imposes a specific tax of 50p per packet. Do smokers end up paying the tax, or is it borne by cigarette producers? How much of the tax can producers pass on to the consumer? We now show that this depends on the slopes of the supply and demand curve.

The **incidence** of a tax describes who eventually bears the burden of it.

Figures 4.7(a) and 4.7(b) plot the (after-tax) price to the consumer on the vertical axis. DD' shows the demand curve, which depends on the price to smokers (consumers). Since the price received by the

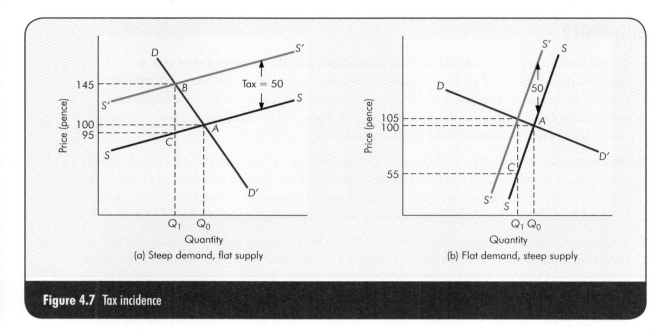

Figure 4.7 Tax incidence

producer is the consumer price minus the 50p tax per packet, the effect of the tax is to shift the supply curve from *SS* to *S'S'* in both diagrams. Each possible quantity supplied depends on the price received by the producer, which will be the same as before only if consumer prices are 50p higher: that is why we must shift the supply curve up by 50p.

In Figure 4.7(a), with a flat supply curve and steep demand curve, the tax is borne mainly by cigarette consumers. Point B is nearly 50p higher than point A. Since demand is insensitive to price, producers can pass on most of the tax in higher prices. Supply is price-sensitive, so the price received by producers cannot fall much. Consumers pay £1.45 and producers get £0.95 a packet.

In Figure 4.7(b), with a flat demand curve and a steep supply curve, most of the tax is borne by cigarette producers. Demand is price-sensitive, so attempts to pass on the tax in higher prices quickly lead to a drop in sales. Supply is price-insensitive and producers hardly cut back even though the price they receive has fallen nearly 50p. Consumers pay £1.05 and producers get £0.55 a packet.

The key implication is thus that the incidence of a tax has nothing to do with who initially hands over money to the government. The existence of the tax changes behaviour. This has induced effects on equilibrium price and quantity. These induced effects may be large or small, depending on the slopes of supply and demand curves.

Now that we understand the general principle, it is obvious that the same argument will carry over to the more commonly used *ad valorem* taxes. We simply need to remember to confront the change in the percentage tax rate with the relevant percentage measures of price responsiveness of supply and demand, namely the (own-price) supply and demand elasticities.

Hence, when demand is inelastic but supply elastic the case for percentages corresponding to the absolute change case in Figure 4.7(a), a rise in an *ad valorem* tax will largely be borne by buyers in the form of a higher price paid. Conversely, when demand is elastic, but supply inelastic the analogue of Figure 4.7(b), a higher *ad valorem* tax will fall mainly on suppliers, in the form of a lower price received. Thus, supply and demand elasticities help us think about the incidence of the commonest taxes, such as income tax, VAT and the corporation tax paid by companies, all of which are *ad valorem*.

Summary

- Unless otherwise specified, the **elasticity of demand** refers to the **own-price elasticity**. It measures the sensitivity of quantity demanded to changes in the own price of a good, holding constant the prices of other goods and income. Demand elasticities are negative since demand curves slope down. In general, the demand elasticity changes as we move along a given demand curve. Along a straight-line demand curve, elasticity falls as price falls.

- **Demand is elastic** if the price elasticity is more negative than –1 (for example –2). Price cuts then increase total spending on the good. **Demand is inelastic** if the demand elasticity lies between –1 and 0. Price cuts then reduce total spending on the good. **Demand is unit-elastic** if the demand elasticity is –1. Price changes then have no effect on total spending on the good.

- The demand elasticity depends on how long customers have to adjust to a price change. In the short run, substitution possibilities may be limited. Demand elasticities will typically rise (become more negative) with the length of time allowed for adjustment. The time required for complete adjustment varies from good to good.

- The **cross-price elasticity of demand** measures the sensitivity of quantity demanded of one good to changes in the price of a related good. Positive cross-elasticities tend to imply that goods are **substitutes**, negative cross-price elasticities that goods are **complements**.

- The **income elasticity of demand** measures the sensitivity of quantity demanded to changes in income, holding constant the prices of all goods.

- **Inferior goods** have negative income elasticities of demand. Higher incomes reduce the quantity demanded and the budget share of such goods. **Luxury goods** have income elasticities larger than 1. Higher incomes raise the quantity demanded and the budget share of such goods.

- Goods that are not inferior are called **normal goods** and have positive income elasticities of demand. Goods that are not luxuries are called **necessities** and have income elasticities less than 1. All inferior goods are necessities but normal goods are necessities only if they are not luxuries.

- Doubling all nominal variables should have no effect on demand since it alters neither the real value (purchasing power) of incomes nor the relative prices of goods. In examining data from economies experiencing inflation, it is often best to look at real prices and real incomes, adjusting prices and incomes for the effect of inflation.

- The **supply elasticity** measures the percentage response of quantity supplied to a 1 per cent increase in the price of the commodity. Since supply curves slope up, the supply elasticity is positive.

- **Tax incidence** measures who eventually pays the tax. Since taxes induce changes in equilibrium prices and quantities, this can be very different from the people from whom the government appears to collect the money.

- For **specific taxes**, slopes of supply and demand curves are relevant. For *ad valorem taxes*, elasticities of supply and demand are relevant. In either case, it is the more price-insensitive side of the market that bears more of the burden of a tax.

Review questions

To check your answers to these questions, go to page 713.

1 Your fruit stall has 100 ripe peaches that must be sold at once. Your supply curve of peaches is vertical. From past experience, 100 peaches are demanded if the price is £1. (a) Draw a supply and demand diagram, showing market equilibrium. (b) The demand elasticity is –0.5. You discover 10 of your peaches are rotten and cannot be sold. Draw the new supply curve. What is the new equilibrium price?

2 (a) Milk, dental services, beer; (b) chocolate, chickens, train journeys; (c) theatre trips, tennis clubs, films. For each of categories (a), (b) and (c), do you expect demand to be elastic or inelastic? Then rank the elasticities within each category. Explain your answer.

3 Where along a straight-line demand curve does consumer spending reach a maximum? Explain why. What use is this information to the owner of a football club?

4 The following table shows price and income elasticities for vegetables and catering services. For each good, explain whether it is a luxury or a necessity, and whether demand is elastic or inelastic.

	Price elasticity	Income elasticity
Vegetables	0.17	0.87
Catering services	2.61	1.64

5 In 1974 UK consumers spent £1.3 million on bread and cereals. In 2004 they spent over £5 million on bread and cereals, yet bread is an inferior good. Explain.

6 **Common fallacies** Why are these statements wrong? (a) Because cigarettes are a necessity, tax revenues from cigarettes will always increase when the tax rate is raised. (b) Farmers should take out insurance against bad weather that might destroy half of all their crops. (c) Higher consumer incomes always benefit producers.

7 **Harder question** (a) If the government wants to maximize revenue from cigarette tax, should it simply set a very high tax rate on cigarettes? (b) If the government achieves its objective, what is the elasticity of demand for cigarettes at the price corresponding to this tax rate? You may assume that cigarettes are essentially free to produce and the entire price reflects the tax. (c) A research company measures elasticity and concludes that the demand for cigarettes is price-elastic. Should you raise or lower the tax rate? (d) If you want not merely to get tax revenue but also to make people healthier, should you set a tax rate above or below that which maximizes revenue from cigarette taxation?

8 **Harder question** Air conditioners are a luxury good. (a) What does this imply, about which elasticity? (b) Which two countries would you guess have the highest per capita demand for air conditioners at present? (c) If people continue to get richer and global warming continues to increase, what is likely to happen to the quantity of air conditioners demanded? And what will this do to global warming? And hence to the demand for air conditioners? (d) Could this process spiral out of control?

9 **Essay question** Suppose climate change causes flooding that wipes out much of UK agriculture.

Discuss what happens to the price of food in the UK (a) in the short run and (b) in the long run. Did you assume that the UK made and consumed all food itself or did you allow for international trade? How does the outcome differ in these two cases?

To help you grasp the key concepts of this chapter check out the extra resources posted on the Online Learning Centre. There are chapter summaries, self-test questions, an interactive graphing tool, weblinks and a searchable glossary, all for free!

To put your learning into practice and prepare for exams, an **Interactive Workbook** is also available online, containing a variety of question types and providing feedback on your answers.

If you'd like further help with economics, or have any questions, **NetTutor** is here to help! You will have a personalised tutorial service at your fingertips. Visit the online learning centre at: www.mcgraw-hill.co.uk/textbooks/begg for information on accessing all of these resources.

Consumer choice and demand decisions

In previous chapters we introduced demand curves to represent consumer behaviour. To refine this theory of demand, we now build a formal model of consumer choice. It explains how buyers reconcile what they would like to do, as described by their tastes or preferences, with what the market will allow them to do, as described by their incomes and the prices of various goods. The model lets us predict how consumers will respond to changes in market conditions. It makes sense of the price and income elasticities examined in Chapter 4.

5.1 Demand by a single consumer

The model's four elements describe the consumer and the market environment. These elements are: (a) the consumer's income, (b) the prices at which goods can be bought, (c) the consumer's tastes, ranking different bundles of goods by the satisfaction they yield, and (d) the behavioural assumption that consumers pursue their own self-interest. Of the affordable consumption bundles, a consumer picks the bundle that maximizes her own satisfaction.

Each element in the model requires detailed discussion.

The budget constraint

A consumer's income and the market prices of goods define her budget constraint.

> The **budget constraint** describes the different bundles that the consumer can afford.

Consider a student with a weekly budget (income, allowance or grant) of £50 to be spent on meals or films. Each meal costs £5 and each film £10. What combination of meals and films can she afford? Going without films, she can spend £50 on 10 meals at £5 each. Going without meals, she can buy 5 cinema tickets at £10 each. Between these two extremes lie many combinations of meals and films that together cost exactly £50. These combinations are called the budget constraint.

The budget constraint shows the *maximum* affordable quantity of one good given the quantity of the other good being purchased.[1] Table 5.1 shows her budget constraint. Each row shows a bundle whose total value of £50 just exhausts her income.

Table 5.1 Affordable consumption baskets

Quantity of meals Q_M	Spending on meals £5 × Q_M	Quantity of films Q_F	Spending on films £10 × Q_F	Total spending £
0	0	5	50	50
2	10	4	40	50
4	20	3	30	50
6	30	2	20	50
8	40	1	10	50
10	50	0	0	50

Table 5.1 shows the *trade-off* between meals and films. Higher quantities of meals require lower quantities of films. For a given income, the budget constraint shows how much of one good must be sacrificed to obtain larger quantities of the other good. It is because there is a trade-off that she must *choose between* meals and films.

When the price of meals and films is fixed, independently of how many she buys, her budget constraint is a straight line, sometimes called the budget line. Figure 5.1 plots this budget line using the budget constraint data of Table 5.1.

The position of the budget line is determined by its end-points A and F, which have a simple interpretation. Point A is the most films the budget will buy if the student has no meals: £50 buys at most 5 film tickets at £10 each. Point F shows that £50 buys at most 10 meals at £5 each if she has no films. The budget line joins up points A and F. Intermediate points such as B and C show more balanced purchases of meals and films.

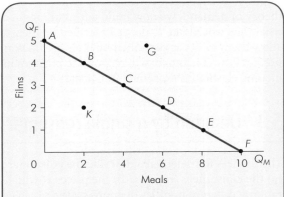

The budget line shows the maximum combinations of goods that the consumer can afford, given income and the prevailing prices. Points on the budget line use up the entire consumer budget. Points above the budget line are unaffordable. Points inside the budget line would allow additional spending.

Figure 5.1 The budget line

1 We assume that all income is spent. There is no saving. Later chapters discuss the important choice between spending and saving.

The slope of the budget line shows how many meals must be sacrificed to get another film. Moving from point *F* to point *E* reduces the quantity of meals from 10 to 8 but raises the quantity of films from 0 to 1. This trade-off between meals and films is constant along this budget line. Giving up 2 meals always yields the extra £10 to buy 1 extra film.

Since films cost twice as much as meals, 2 meals must be sacrificed to buy 1 more film ticket. *The slope of the budget line depends only on the ratio of the prices of the two goods.* The slope of a line is the change in the vertical distance divided by the corresponding change in the horizontal distance. In Figure 5.1 the slope of the budget line is –1/2. The (+1) change in films is divided by the (–2) change in meals. This example illustrates the general rule

$$\text{Slope of the budget line} = -P_H/P_V$$

where P_H is the price of the good on the horizontal axis and P_V is the price of the good on the vertical axis. In our example, the price of meals $P_H = £5$ and the price of films $P_V = £10$. The formula confirms that the slope of the budget line is –1/2. The minus sign reminds us that there is a trade-off. We have to *give up* one good to get more of the other good.

The two end-points of the budget line (here, *A* and *F*) show how much of each good the budget buys if the other good is not bought at all. The slope of the budget line joining these end-points depends only on the relative prices of the two goods.

Any point above the budget line (such as *G* in Figure 5.1) is unaffordable. The budget line shows the maximum quantity of one good that is affordable, given the quantity of the other good purchased and the budget available to spend. With an income of £50, *G* is out of reach: it would need £25 to buy 5 meals and £50 to buy 5 cinema tickets. Points such as *K*, which lie inside the budget line, leave some income unspent. Only on the budget line is there a trade-off where the student must choose *between* films and meals.

Tastes

The budget line shows the market environment (income and prices) faced by the consumer. We now consider the consumer's *tastes*, making three assumptions that seem plausible. First, the consumer can rank alternative bundles of goods according to the satisfaction or *utility* they provide. It is unnecessary to quantify this utility,[2] for example to say that one bundle yields twice as much utility as another bundle. We only require that the consumer can decide that one bundle is better than, worse than or exactly as good as another. We assume that this ranking of possible bundles is internally consistent: if bundle *A* is preferred to bundle *B* and bundle *B* is preferred to bundle *C*, then bundle *A* must be preferred to bundle *C*.

Second, we assume that the *consumer prefers more to less.* If bundle *B* offers more films but as many meals as bundle *K* we assume bundle *B* is preferred. What about things like pollution, which are not goods but 'bads'? Consumers do not prefer more pollution to less. We get round this problem by redefining commodities so that our assumption is satisfied. We analyse clean water rather than polluted water. More clean water is better than less.

Figure 5.2 examines the implications of these assumptions about tastes. Each point shows a consumption bundle of

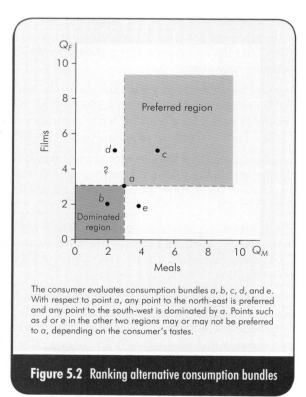

The consumer evaluates consumption bundles *a*, *b*, *c*, *d*, and *e*. With respect to point *a*, any point to the north-east is preferred and any point to the south-west is dominated by *a*. Points such as *d* or *e* in the other two regions may or may not be preferred to *a*, depending on the consumer's tastes.

Figure 5.2 Ranking alternative consumption bundles

2 In the Appendix, we analyse tastes based on measurable utility. This is a special case, but easier to master.

meals and films. We begin at bundle *a*. Since more is preferred to less, any point such as *c* to the north-east of *a* is preferred to *a*. Point *c* offers more of *both* goods than *a*. Conversely, points to the south-west of *a* offer less of both goods than *a*. Point *a* is preferred to points such as *b*.

Without knowing the consumer's exact tastes we cannot be sure how points in the other two regions (north-west, south-east) compare with *a*. At *d* or *e* the consumer has more of one good but less of the other good than at *a*. Someone who really likes food might prefer *e* to *a*, but an avid film buff would prefer *d* to *a*.

Box 5.1 To die for

David Beckham's advertising deals dwarf his income as a footballer and Thierry Henry is the public face of the Renault Clio. Why do the manufacturers pay superfees to superstars to promote their wares? They are trying to change your tastes. There are lots of small cars but only one has va-va-voom. It's the one to die for. No other will do.

You could buy a car magazine and find out whether the Clio's suspension geometry really is different. But that's not the point. This advertising is about *style*. Not what you think is nice, but what *other people* think is nice. Renault is assuring you that other people, stylish people, think it's cool to drive a Clio. Do so and you can be cool too. This *interdependence* of tastes is what opens the door for so much advertising and PR.

Consumers prefer more to less. An extra meal increases utility. To hold utility constant when a meal is added, the consumer must sacrifice some of the other good (films). The marginal rate of substitution tells us how many films the consumer could exchange for an additional meal without changing total utility.

> The **marginal rate of substitution** of meals for films is the quantity of films the consumer must sacrifice to increase the quantity of meals by one unit *without changing total utility*.

Suppose the student has 5 films and no meals. Having already seen 4 films, she does not enjoy the fifth film much. With no meals, she is *very* hungry. The utility of this bundle is low: being so hungry, she cannot enjoy films anyway. For the same low amount of utility she could give up a lot of films for a little food.

Suppose instead that she eats a lot of meals but sees few films. She is then reluctant to sacrifice much cinema attendance to gain yet another meal. It makes sense to sacrifice abundant films for scarce meals. Conversely, when the ratio of films to meals is already low, it does not make sense to sacrifice scarce films for yet more meals.

This common-sense reasoning about tastes or preferences is very robust. It can become a general principle, the third assumption we need to make about consumer tastes. It is the assumption of a diminishing marginal rate of substitution.

> Consumer tastes exhibit a **diminishing marginal rate of substitution** when, to hold utility constant, diminishing quantities of one good must be sacrificed to obtain successive equal increases in the quantity of the other good.

Our student might be equally happy with bundle *X* (6 films, 0 meals), bundle *Y* (3 films, 1 meal), and bundle *Z* (2 films, 2 meals). Beginning from bundle *X*, a move to *Y* sacrifices 3 films for 1 meal, but a further move from *Y* to *Z* sacrifices only 1 film for 1 extra meal. Such tastes satisfy the assumption of a diminishing marginal rate of substitution.

These three assumptions – that consumers prefer more to less, can rank alternative bundles according to the utility provided and have tastes satisfying a diminishing marginal rate of substitution – are all we require. It is now convenient to show how tastes can be represented as *indifference curves*.

Representing tastes as indifference curves

If we join up all the many points the student likes equally, we get an indifference curve. Figure 5.3 shows three indifference curves, U_1U_1, U_2U_2 and U_3U_3.

> An **indifference curve** shows all the consumption bundles yielding a particular level of utility.

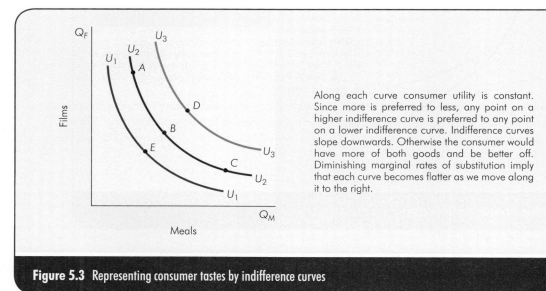

Along each curve consumer utility is constant. Since more is preferred to less, any point on a higher indifference curve is preferred to any point on a lower indifference curve. Indifference curves slope downwards. Otherwise the consumer would have more of both goods and be better off. Diminishing marginal rates of substitution imply that each curve becomes flatter as we move along it to the right.

Figure 5.3 Representing consumer tastes by indifference curves

Every point on U_2U_2 yields the same utility. Point C has many meals and few films, and point A offers many films but few meals. Because a consumer prefers more to less, *indifference curves must slope downwards*. Since more meals tend to increase utility, some films must simultaneously be sacrificed to hold utility constant.

The slope of each indifference curve gets steadily flatter as we move to the right. This reflects a diminishing marginal rate of substitution. At A, where films are relatively abundant compared with meals, the consumer will sacrifice a lot of films to gain a little more food. At B, where films are less abundant relative to meals, she will sacrifice fewer films to gain the same extra quantity of meals. And at C she has so many meals that hardly any films will be sacrificed for extra meals.

The marginal rate of substitution of meals for films is simply the slope of the indifference curve at the point from which we begin. These two properties of a single indifference curve – its downward slope and its steady flattening as we move to the right – follow directly from the assumptions that consumers prefer more to less and that their tastes satisfy the assumption of diminishing marginal rates of substitution.

Now consider point D on indifference curve U_3U_3. D offers more of both goods than B. Since consumers prefer more to less, utility at D is higher than utility at B. But all points on U_3U_3 yield the same utility as each other. Thus, every point on U_3U_3 yields more utility than every point on U_2U_2. Conversely, E must yield less utility than B since it offers less of both goods. Every point on U_1U_1 yields less utility than every point on U_2U_2.

Although Figure 5.3 shows only three indifference curves, we can draw in other indifference curves as well. Higher indifference curves are better because the consumer prefers more to less.

Indifference curves cannot cross. Figure 5.4 shows why. Suppose UU and $U'U'$ cross. Since X and Y lie on the indifference curve UU, the consumer is indifferent between these points. But Y and Z lie

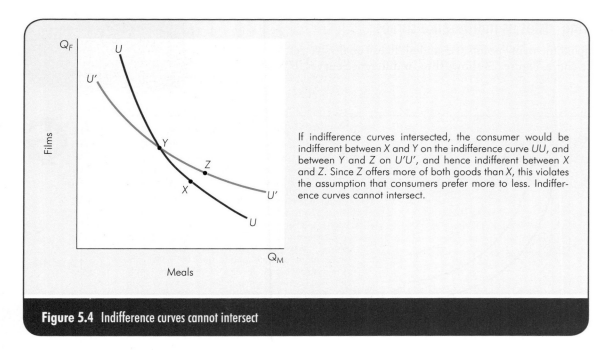

If indifference curves intersected, the consumer would be indifferent between X and Y on the indifference curve UU, and between Y and Z on U'U', and hence indifferent between X and Z. Since Z offers more of both goods than X, this violates the assumption that consumers prefer more to less. Indifference curves cannot intersect.

Figure 5.4 Indifference curves cannot intersect

on the indifference curve $U'U'$. Hence the consumer is indifferent between Y and Z. Hence, the consumer is indifferent between X and Z. This is impossible, since the consumer gets more of both goods at Z than at X. Intersecting indifference curves would violate our assumption that consumers prefer more to less. Our assumptions about consumer tastes rule out intersecting indifference curves.

Box 5.2 Other contour maps

When you look at a good map, you will see concentric rings or contours, each showing points of equal height. They are like indifference curves but do not have to obey the law of diminishing marginal rate of substitution and hence have stranger shapes. But they never intersect. Different contours are different heights.

As you rise through successive contours, you reach a dot marking the top of the mountain. In economics, we hardly ever reach the top. People are rarely satiated. But an indifference map for champagne and lobster might look like a mountain. Too much of either, and you are sick. The dot for the absolute best, or bliss point, equivalent to the top of the mountain, then shows the finite combination of champagne and lobster preferred above all others, however much is available. We are now violating our assumption that the consumer always prefers more to less. The part of the contours sloping up correspond to the range in which more is no longer better.

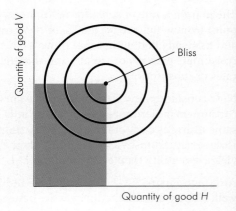

For broad categories of commodities, we are never satiated. It is as if we are confined to the shaded area of the diagram below.

We can represent the tastes of any consumer by drawing the complete *map* of his indifference curves. Figure 5.5 shows two consumers with different tastes. In each case, moves to a higher indifference curve imply an increase in utility. Figure 5.5(a) shows the indifference map for a glutton prepared to give up a lot of films to gain a little extra food. Figure 5.5(b) shows the indifference map for a weight-watching film buff, who will give up large quantities of food to see more films. Both indifference maps are valid: they satisfy our three basic assumptions about consumer tastes. Our theory can cope with extreme kinds of preferences as well as with more typical preferences in-between.

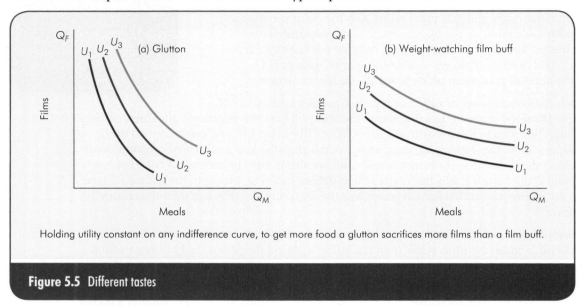

Holding utility constant on any indifference curve, to get more food a glutton sacrifices more films than a film buff.

Figure 5.5 Different tastes

Utility maximization and choice

The budget line shows affordable bundles given a consumer's market environment (his budget and the price of different goods). The indifference map shows his tastes. To complete the model, we assume *the consumer chooses the affordable bundle that maximizes his utility*. He cannot afford points above the budget line and will never choose points below the budget line (it is then possible to buy more of one good without sacrificing any of the other good). He will select a point on the budget line.

To find which point on the budget line maximizes utility we examine the consumer's tastes. Our glutton should pick a point with more meals and fewer films than the point our film buff selects. We first show how to use indifference curves to find the bundle the consumer chooses. Then we confirm that our model of consumer choice captures the different behaviour of the glutton and the film buff.

Figure 5.6 shows the budget line AF for the student who had £50 to spend on films (£10 each) and meals (£5 each). The indifference curves U_1U_1, U_2U_2 and U_3U_3 are part of the indifference map describing her tastes.

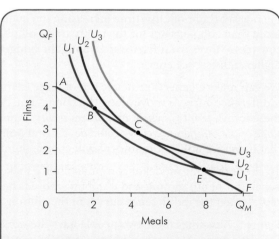

Points above the budget line AF are unaffordable. The consumer cannot reach the indifference curve U_3U_3. Points such as B and E are affordable but only allow the consumer to reach the indifference curve U_1U_1. The consumer will choose the point C to reach the highest possible indifference curve U_2U_2. At point C, the indifference curve and the budget line just touch and their slopes are equal.

Figure 5.6 Consumer choice in action

All points on U_3U_3 are unattainable since it lies entirely above the budget line AF. The student would like this high level of utility but cannot afford it. Next, suppose she considers the attainable point B on the indifference curve U_1U_1. She prefers this to point A, which must lie on a lower indifference curve (since indifferent curves cannot intersect, the indifference curve through A lies entirely below the indifference curve U_1U_1). Similarly, F must lie on a lower indifference curve than E and she prefers E to F.

However, she will choose neither B nor E. By moving to C she reaches a higher indifference curve and gets more utility. C is the point she chooses. Any other affordable point on the budget line is on a lower indifference curve. The budget line never crosses a higher indifference curve, such as U_3U_3, and crosses twice every lower indifference curve, such as U_1U_1. Point C is the point of maximum utility given the budget constraint.

> Hence, the **chosen bundle** will be the point at which an indifference curve just touches the budget line. The budget line is a tangent to the indifference curve at this point.

We can reach the same answer by different means. Consider again point B in Figure 5.6. The slope of the budget line shows the trade-off between affordable quantities of films and meals that the market environment will allow. When films cost £10 and meals £5, two meals can be traded for one film. The slope of the indifference curve at B (the marginal rate of substitution of meals for films) shows how the consumer would trade meals for films to maintain a constant level of utility. At point B the budget line is flatter than the indifference curve. Moves to the left would take the student on to a lower indifference curve because the market trade-off is less than the required utility trade-off.

Similarly, beginning at point E it makes no sense to move to the right along the budget line. The market trade-off of meals for films is less than the utility trade-off needed to hold utility constant. Moves from E to the right reduce utility and take the consumer to a lower indifference curve.

However, it makes sense to move from B to the right. The market trade-off of affordable meals for films exceeds the utility trade-off required to maintain constant utility. The student reaches a higher indifference curve and increases her utility. Similarly, it makes sense to move from E to the left. Again the market trade-off, this time increasing the quantity of affordable films in exchange for fewer meals, more than compensates for the utility trade-off, the slope of the indifference curve to keep utility constant. Moves from E leftwards along the budget line increase utility and allow her to reach a higher indifference curve.

We can make a general principle out of these examples. Wherever the budget line crosses an indifference curve, a move along the budget line in the smart direction will increase utility. Viewed in these terms, *point C, which maximizes utility, is the point at which the slope of the budget line and the slope of the indifference curve coincide.* Only at point C is there no feasible move along the budget line that increases utility. The student will choose point C since it maximizes utility.

To check that our model of consumer choice makes sense, consider what it implies for the observable behaviour of our glutton and film buff whose tastes between meals and films differ. Figure 5.5 represented the indifference curves of the glutton as steep and those of the film buff as flat.

Figure 5.7 assumes these two people have the *same* budget line. They have the same income and face the same prices for food and films. Only their tastes differ. Figure 5.7(a) shows the chosen point C for the glutton, with a lot of meals but few films. Figure 5.7(b) confirms that the film buff will choose a point C with many more films but much less food. Our theory of consumer choice successfully translates differences in tastes into observable differences in demands for the two goods.

Each person chooses a point at which their marginal rate of substitution equals the slope of the budget line, which depends only on the relative price of films and meals. The glutton has a strong preference for food (steep indifference curves): his chosen point is far to the right to give the indifference curve a long time to flatten out. The film buff has flat indifference curves: his chosen point is far to the left before indifference curves can become flatter than the budget line.

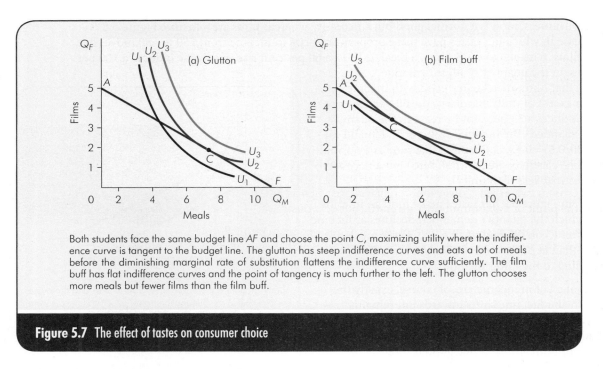

Both students face the same budget line *AF* and choose the point *C*, maximizing utility where the indifference curve is tangent to the budget line. The glutton has steep indifference curves and eats a lot of meals before the diminishing marginal rate of substitution flattens the indifference curve sufficiently. The film buff has flat indifference curves and the point of tangency is much further to the left. The glutton chooses more meals but fewer films than the film buff.

Figure 5.7 The effect of tastes on consumer choice

5.2 Adjustment to income changes

Chapter 4 introduced the income elasticity of demand to describe, other things equal, the response of quantity demanded to changes in consumer incomes. Now we can use our model of consumer choice to analyse this response in greater detail.

For given tastes and prices, Figure 5.8 shows the effect of a higher income. The student had an income of £50, faced the budget line *AF*, and chose point *C* to maximize utility. Suppose her income rises from £50 to £80. Prices of meals and films remain £5 and £10, respectively. With higher income, she can afford more of one or both of the goods. The budget line shifts outwards from *AF* to *A'F'*.

To find the exact position of this new line, again we calculate the end-points at which all income is spent on a single good. Point *A* shows that at most £80 buys 8 films at £10 each. Point *F* shows that £80 buys at most 16 meals at £5 each. Joining these points yields the new budget line *A'F'*. Since the slope of a budget line depends only on the relative price of the two goods, which is unchanged, the new budget line *A'F'* is parallel to the old budget line *AF*.

Which point on *A'F'* will the student choose? She chooses *C'*, at which the new budget line is tangent to the highest attainable indifference curve. However, the position of *C'* depends on the map of indifference curves that describe her tastes.

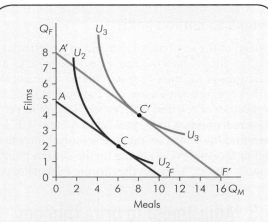

An increase in income from £50 to £80 induces a parallel shift in budget line from *AF* to *A'F'*. The new end-points *A'* and *F'* reflect the increase in purchasing power if only one good is purchased. The slope remains unaltered since prices have not changed. At the higher income the consumer chooses *C'*. Since both goods are normal, higher income raises the quantity of each good demanded but the percentage increase in film quantity is larger since its income elasticity is higher.

Figure 5.8 An increase in consumer income

For most consumers, food is a normal good but a necessity whereas films are a luxury. Figure 5.8 shows the case in which her tastes have these properties. A rise in income from £50 to £80 moves her from C (2 films, 6 meals) to C' (4 films, 8 meals). Thus, a 60 per cent rise in income induces a 100 per cent increase in the quantity of films demanded, confirming that films are a luxury good with income elasticity in excess of unity. Similarly, the 60 per cent rise in income induces a 33 per cent increase in the quantity of meals demanded. The income elasticity of demand for food is $(0.33/0.6) = 0.55$, confirming that food is a normal good (income elasticity greater than zero) but a necessity (income elasticity less than unity).

In contrast, in Figure 5.9 her tastes make food an inferior good, for which the quantity demanded declines as income rises. At point C' on the budget line $A'F'$ fewer meals are demanded than at point C on the budget line AF, corresponding to the lower income.

The effects of a fall in income are, of course, exactly the opposite. The budget line shifts inwards but remains parallel to the original budget line. When both goods are normal, lower consumer income reduces the quantity demanded for both goods. If one good is inferior, the quantity demanded will actually rise if income falls. Notice that both goods cannot be inferior: when income falls but prices remain unchanged it cannot be feasible for the consumer to consume more of both goods.

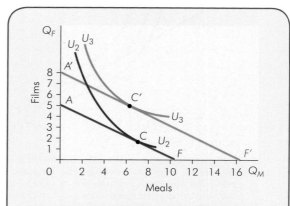

Again, income is increased from £50 to £80 and there is a parallel shift in the budget line from AF to $A'F'$. If meals were an inferior good, the quantity demanded would fall as income rose. The consumer then moves from C to C' when income rises.

Figure 5.9 An increase in income reduces demand for the inferior good

Income expansion paths

Instead of the response of demand to a particular change in income, we might want to know the response of demand to income over all possible variations in income. To study this we trace out the income expansion path. Look again at Figure 5.8. The budget lines AF and $A'F'$ correspond to incomes of £50 and £80, respectively. With yet higher incomes we could draw more budget lines, parallel to AF and $A'F'$ but higher up. We could then find the points on these new budget lines that the consumer would choose at these higher income levels. Joining up the chosen points (C and C' in Figure 5.8) and these new points (say, C'' and C'''), we get the income expansion path. Try drawing it for yourself.

> The **income expansion path** shows how the chosen bundle of goods varies with consumer income levels.

5.3 Adjustment to price changes

Having studied changes in tastes and in income, we now isolate the effect of a price change. Chapter 4 argued that a rise in price reduces the quantity demanded, other things equal. The own-price elasticity of demand measures this response, and is larger the easier it is to substitute towards goods whose prices have not risen.

We also introduced the cross-price elasticity of demand to measure the response of the quantity demanded of one good to a change in the price of another good. An increase in the price of good j tends to increase the quantity demanded of good i when the two goods are substitutes but tends to reduce the quantity demanded of good i when the two are complements. The empirical evidence was presented in Tables 4.2 and 4.6.

Are those propositions invariably true, or did the evidence we examined just happen to confirm our common-sense reasoning? We now offer a more formal analysis based on the model of consumer choice developed above.

Price changes and the budget line

Figure 5.10 raws the budget line *AF* for a consumer with an income of £50 facing prices of £10 and £5 for films and meals, respectively. Suppose meal prices increase to £10. Since the price of films remains unaltered, £50 still buys 10 films when all income is spent on films. Point *A* must lie on the new budget line as well as the old budget line. But when all income is spent on meals, £50 buys only 5 meals at £10 each instead of the 10 meals it used to buy at £5 each. Thus the other extreme point on the budget line shifts from *F* to *F'* when meal prices double. As usual, we join up these end-points to obtain the new budget line *AF'*. The effect of a rise in meal prices is to *rotate* the budget line inwards around the point *A* at which no meals are bought and higher meal prices are irrelevant.

Except at *A* itself, higher meal prices mean the consumer can now afford fewer meals for any given number of films, or fewer films for any given number of meals. The new budget line *AF'* lies inside the old budget line *AF*. The consumption bundles between *AF* and *AF'* are no longer affordable at the higher price of meals. In particular, the chosen point on the old budget line is no longer affordable unless it happens to be the end-point *A*. A price increase makes the consumer worse off by reducing consumption opportunities out of a fixed money income. The consumer's standard of living falls.

To check that you understand, try drawing diagrams to illustrate the effect on the budget line of: (1) a reduction in the price of meals (*hint*: Figure 5.10 can be used – how?); (2) an increase in the price of films (*hint*: around which point does the budget line rotate?).

Substitution and income effects

Our model of consumer choice is based on the interaction of affordable opportunities (the budget line) and tastes (indifference curves). To analyse the effect of price changes on the actual quantity of goods demanded, we must study how rotations of the budget line affect the highest indifference curve that the consumer can reach.

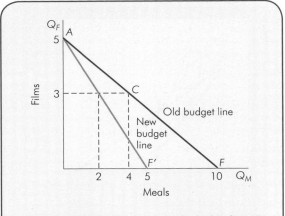

The consumer begins at point *C* on the budget line *AF*. Doubling meal prices halves the amount that can be spent on meals when no films are bought. The point *F* shifts to *F'*. The budget line rotates around the point *A* at which no meals are bought. Along the new budget line the consumer can no longer afford the original consumption bundle *C*. Consumption of one or both commodities must be reduced.

Figure 5.10 An increase in meal prices

> The **substitution effect** of a price change is the adjustment of demand to the relative price change alone. The **income effect** of a price change is the adjustment of demand to the change in real income alone.

A higher price of meals has two distinct effects on the budget line in Figure 5.10. First, the budget line becomes steeper, reflecting the rise in the relative price of meals. To get an extra meal more films must now be sacrificed. Second, the budget line *AF'* lies inside the original budget line *AF*. The purchasing power of a given money income is reduced by the price increase. Economists therefore break up the effect of a price increase into these two distinct effects: the change in the relative price of the two goods and the fall in the purchasing power of the given money income.

Figure 5.11 shows the response of demand quantities to a higher meal price. At the original prices, the consumer faced the budget line *AF* and chose *C* to reach the highest possible indifference curve U_2U_2. At a higher meal price, the budget line rotates to *AF'* and she chooses *E* to reach U_1U_1, the highest indifference curve now possible. In this example, higher meal prices reduce the quantity demanded of both meals and films.

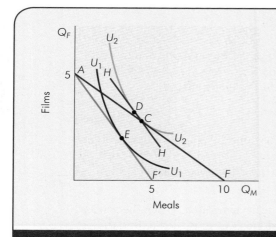

Higher meal prices rotate the budget line from *AF* to *AF'*. The consumer moves from *C* to *E*. This can be decomposed into a pure substitution effect, from *C* to *D*, the response to relative price changes at the old standard of living, plus a pure income effect, from *D* to *E*, the response to a fall in real income at constant relative prices. The substituion effect reduces the quantity of meals demanded. The income effect also reduces the quantity of meals demanded if meals are a normal good. Under these circumstance, price increases reduce the quantity demanded and demand curves slope downwards.

Figure 5.11 Income and substitution effects

The substitution effect

To isolate the effect of relative prices alone, imagine a *hypothetical* budget line *HH*, parallel to *AF'* but tangent to the original indifference curve U_2U_2. Because *HH* is a parallel to the new budget line *AF'* its slope reflects the new relative prices of films and meals after the price of meals has risen. Because *HH* is tangent to the old indifference curve U_2U_2, it restores the consumer to the original utility and standard of living shown by all points on U_2U_2.

If confronted with the hypothetical budget line *HH* the consumer would choose *D*. The move from *C* to *D* is the pure substitution effect, the adjustment of demand to relative prices when income is adjusted to maintain the old standard of living in the face of the new higher prices. *The substitution effect of an increase in the price of meals unambiguously reduces the quantity of meals demanded.* This result is perfectly general.[3] As meals become relatively more expensive, the consumer switches towards films, which have become relatively cheaper.

Box 5.3 Substitution: even rats do it

A white male albino rat was offered a choice between a Tom Collins cocktail and root beer. Facing equal prices for the two drinks, he chose a particular combination. Then the relative price of Tom Collins was increased fourfold but his income was adjusted, so that he could still afford the original combination. However, he responded to a lower relative price of root beer by choosing a new combination that substituted some root beer for some Tom Collins. That is the pure substitution effect in action. The rat's budget line was the number of times it had to push on levers to get the two kinds of drink. The quantity per push changed with the price of the drink.

Source: J. Kagel *et al.*, 'Experimental Studies of Consumer Demand Behaviour Using Laboratory Animals', *Economic Inquiry*, March 1975.

3 With only two goods, substitution away from meals must imply substitution towards films. However, when there are more than two goods, we cannot be sure that the substitution effects will tend to increase the quantity demanded for all other goods. We discuss this shortly under the heading 'Complements and substitutes'.

The income effect

To isolate the effect of the reduction in real income, holding relative prices constant, consider now the parallel shift in the budget line from the hypothetical position *HH* to the actual new position *AF'*. The consumer moves from *D* to *E*. When both goods are normal goods, a cut in real income will reduce the quantity demanded of both goods. Figure 5.11 shows *E* lying to the south-west of *D*.

The net effect of a price increase on the quantity demanded

The consumer moves directly from the original point *C* to the new point *E*. We can interpret this as a pure substitution effect from *C* to the hypothetical point *D* plus a pure income effect from *D* to *E*. If the good whose price has risen is a normal good, demand curves slope downwards as asserted in Chapter 4.

The substitution effect from *C* to *D* must reduce the quantity of meals demanded. When the price of meals rises, the budget line becomes steeper and we must move along U_2U_2 to the left to find the point at which it is tangent to *HH*. Similarly, the income effect must further reduce the quantity of meals demanded if meals are a normal good. *E* must lie to the left of *D*.

Inferior goods

Although the substitution effect must reduce the quantity of meals demanded when the price of meals increases, the income effect goes in the opposite direction if the good is inferior: reductions in real income increase the quantity demanded. We can even imagine a perverse case in which this effect is so strong that price rises actually increase the quantity of that good demanded. Demand curves then slope *upwards*!

This possibility is shown in Figure 5.12. A higher price of the inferior good rotates the budget line from *AF* to *AF'*. The substitution effect, from *C* to *D*, reduces the quantity of the inferior good demanded but is outweighed by the income effect, from *D* to *E*. Since *E* lies to the right of *C*, the net effect of a higher price of the inferior good is to raise the quantity demanded. Economists refer to such goods as 'Giffen goods', after a nineteenth-century economist who examined whether higher potato prices raised the quantity of potatoes demanded by the poor.

An inferior good need not be a Giffen good. It requires a very strong income effect – here an increase in demand in response to real income reductions – to offset the substitution effect that is always

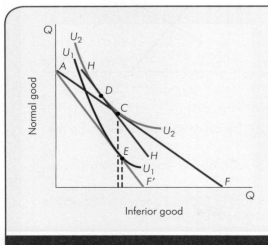

The price increase rotates the budget line from *AF* to *AF'*. The substitution effect, from *C* to *D*, reduces the quantity of the inferior good demanded. Since the good is inferior, the income effect, from *D* to *E*, increases the quantity of the inferior good demanded. For a Giffen good, the income effect dominates and *E* lies to the right of *C*. In practice, the income effect for inferior goods is less strong and the point *E*, although to the right of *D*, usually lies to the left of *C* so that the quantity demanded falls as the price of the inferior good rises.

Figure 5.12 A Giffen good

negative. When goods are inferior, theoretical reasoning cannot establish which effect dominates. We must look at the empirical evidence. After decades of empirical research, economists are convinced that Giffen goods are rare. In practice, goods are rarely so inferior that the income effect can reverse the substitution effect.

Activity box 5 Conspicuous consumption

When the next generation of Nike trainers comes out you simply have to have them, even though they cost a lot. In fact, the more they cost, the more exclusive they are and the more desirable they seem. Armani, Gucci, Porsche and all the other brand icons of fashion have understood this for years. Does this mean economists have got it wrong? Demand curves slope up: the higher the price, the greater the quantity demanded?

American economist Thorstein Veblen (1857–1929) first drew attention to 'conspicuous consumption' and consumers' desire for exclusivity. However, the existence of these Veblen goods are quite consistent with the model of consumer choice that we have been developing. The figure below shows demand curves for two brands of trainers, Exclusive and Bogstandard. For each, the demand curve slopes down as usual. But, since Exclusive are better than Bogstandard, people are willing to pay more for Exclusive – its demand curve EE lies above that BB for Bogstandard.

When people assert that demand curves slope upwards, they are usually comparing points such as Q_E and Q_B in the figure below, as if joining them up would reveal an upward-sloping demand curve. However, our old friend, the device of 'other things equal', allows us to make better sense of revealed behaviour.

Other things equal, if you could get the fabulous new trainers at a cheaper price you would want to buy more of them. What has to be kept equal in this experiment is their quality and perceived exclusiveness. However, if a low price is achievable *only* because the actual or perceived quality has been reduced, other things are no longer equal. We are talking about a different product, whose demand curve is at a different height. Conspicuous consumption in no way invalidates our theory of demand. But it does help explain why Thierry Henry and David Beckham are paid huge sums to convince consumers about the coolness of being associated with particular products, whose demand curve is then shifted upwards.

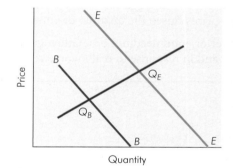

Questions
Which of these examples represent Veblen goods? Why, or why not?

(a) *What Car?* magazine declares the BMW 525 the best executive saloon. Sales go up the week after.

(b) Madonna announces she is buying another house in Marylebone. Local property prices surge.

(c) Celebrity chef Rick Stein praises a little-known restaurant in Scotland, and it is impossible to get a table for the next year because it quickly takes so many bookings.

To check your answers to these questions, go to page 715.

As an empirical judgement, economists have concluded that, even for inferior goods, the demand curve will usually slope downwards as price is increased. For the much more common case in which goods are normal, with a positive income elasticity of demand, the income and substitution effects both reduce the quantity demanded, as in Figure 5.11. The downward slope of the demand curves can then be proved by theoretical reasoning alone.

Cross-price elasticities of demand

How does a rise in the price of one good affect demand for other goods? Chapter 4 showed that cross-price elasticities may be negative or positive. We now illustrate these possibilities, highlighting the roles played by substitution and income effects.

Figure 5.13 shows a negative cross-price elasticity. A higher price of meals reduces the quantity of films demanded. Figure 5.13 has three properties. First, the two goods are poor substitutes. Indifference curves are very curved. Moving away from balanced combinations of the two goods requires large extra quantities of one good to compensate for small losses of the other good if a constant level of utility is to be preserved. When the price of meals is increased, the substitution effect towards films is small. Moving leftwards along $U_2 U_2$, we quickly attain the slope required to match the new relative prices of the two goods. The substitution effect from C to D adds little to the quantity of films demanded.

Second, films have a high income elasticity of demand. They are a luxury good. Hence the income effect, the move from D to E in response to the parallel downward shift in the budget line from HH to AF', leads to a lot fewer films demanded.

Finally, point C is well to the right on the original budget line AF. Meal expenditure is a large part of consumer budgets. Hence changes in meal prices lead to big changes in the purchasing power of consumer income. Not only is the number of films demanded very responsive to given changes in consumer real income, but also a given rise in meal prices has a large effect on consumer real income because meals are a large part of consumer budgets.

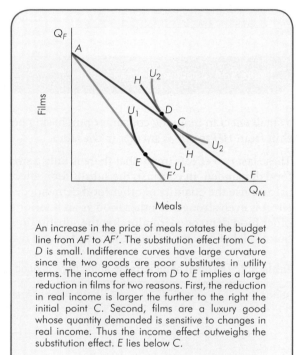

An increase in the price of meals rotates the budget line from AF to AF'. The substitution effect from C to D is small. Indifference curves have large curvature since the two goods are poor substitutes in utility terms. The income effect from D to E implies a large reduction in films for two reasons. First, the reduction in real income is larger the further to the right the initial point C. Second, films are a luxury good whose quantity demanded is sensitive to changes in real income. Thus the income effect outweighs the substitution effect. E lies below C.

Figure 5.13 A negative cross-price elasticity

These last two effects lead to a large income effect, which reduces the quantity of films demanded. Because the substitution effect in favour of films is small, the net effect is a reduction in the quantity of films demanded. An increase in meal prices reduces the quantity of films demanded. The cross-price elasticity of demand is negative.

Figure 5.14 shows the opposite case, a positive cross-price elasticity of demand. Suppose the consumer is choosing between bread and other food. If the price of bread rises, potatoes are a good substitute for bread. To maintain a given utility, consumers can substitute lots of cheap potatoes for expensive bread. Indifference curves are less curved than in Figure 5.13.

Suppose also that other food has a small income elasticity of demand. Although higher bread prices reduce real consumer income, this has a small income effect that reduces the quantity of other food demanded. Finally, if bread is a relatively small share in consumer budgets, higher bread prices have

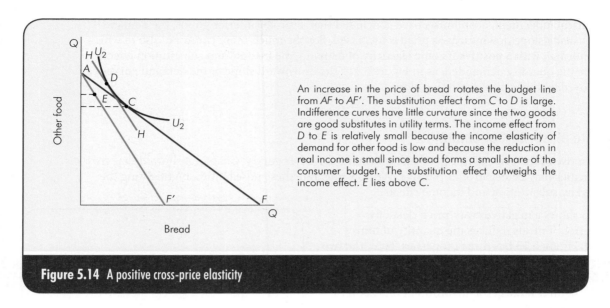

An increase in the price of bread rotates the budget line from *AF* to *AF′*. The substitution effect from *C* to *D* is large. Indifference curves have little curvature since the two goods are good substitutes in utility terms. The income effect from *D* to *E* is relatively small because the income elasticity of demand for other food is low and because the reduction in real income is small since bread forms a small share of the consumer budget. The substitution effect outweighs the income effect. *E* lies above *C*.

Figure 5.14 A positive cross-price elasticity

a small effect in reducing consumer purchasing power. Comparing Figures 5.13 and 5.14, the parallel shift from *HH* to *AF′* is smaller in the latter.

These last two effects imply that there is only a small income effect reducing the quantity of other food demanded. In contrast, the substitution effect towards other food is big. Hence higher bread prices raise the quantity of other food demanded. The cross-price elasticity is positive. This positive effect is even stronger if 'other food' is an inferior good. The income effect then raises the quantity of other food demanded, reinforcing the substitution effect. Table 5.2 summarizes the implications of our model of consumer choice for the demand response to a price change.

Table 5.2 The effect of an increase in the price of good *I* on the quantity demanded of goods *I* and *J*

Good	Type	Substitution effect	Income effect	Total effect
I	Normal	Negative	Negative	Negative
	Inferior	Negative	Positive	Ambiguous
J	Normal	Positive	Negative	Ambiguous
	Inferior	Positive	Positive	Positive

5.4 The market demand curve

The **market demand curve** is the sum of the demand curves of all individuals in that market.

We have now established that individual demand curves (almost always) slope downwards. For the rest of this book we assume that this is the case. Aggregating the demand curves of every individual consumer we get the market demand curve.

At each price, we find out how much each consumer demands. Adding the quantities demanded by all consumers at that price, we get the total quantity demanded at each price, the market demand curve. Since, as price is reduced, each person increases the quantity demanded, the total quantity demanded must also increase as price falls. The market demand curve also slopes downwards.

The market demand curve is the *horizontal addition of individual demand curves*. With prices on the vertical axis and quantities on the horizontal axis, we must add together individual quantities demanded at the same price. Figure 5.15 illustrates this idea for two consumers.

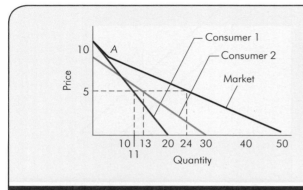

The market demand curve is the horizontal sum of individual demand curves. For example, if the price is £5, the quantity demanded by consumer 1 is 11 units, and the quantity demanded by consumer 2 is 13 units. The total quantity demanded in the market at £5 is thus 24 units, as shown in the market demand curve. The market demand curve is kinked at point A, the price at which consumer 2 first comes into the market.

Figure 5.15 Individual demand curves and the market demand curve

5.5 Complements and substitutes

Income and substitution effects are used to understand the effects of a price change. Whatever the direction of the income effect, with only two goods the substitution effect is always negative. The pure relative price effect leads the consumer to substitute away from the good whose relative price has risen towards the good whose relative price has fallen. Abstracting from income effects, goods are necessarily substitutes for one another in a two-good world.

With more than two goods, some goods may be consumed jointly – pipes and pipe tobacco, bread and cheese, electric cookers and electricity. These goods are *complements*.

Even with many goods, there is always a substitution effect *away* from goods whose relative price has risen. However, substitution may not be *towards* all other goods. Consumers substitute *away* from goods consumed jointly with the good whose price has risen.

Suppose the price of pipes rises. What will happen to the demand for pipe tobacco? (Ignore the income effect, since expenditure on pipes is a tiny fraction of household budgets, so real incomes are only slightly reduced.) Since pipes and pipe tobacco are used jointly, we expect the demand for pipe tobacco to fall along with the number of pipes demanded. The demand curve for pipe tobacco shifts to the left in response to the increase in pipe prices.

When goods are complements, a rise in the price of one good will reduce the demand for the complement both through the substitution effect (substituting away from the higher priced activity) and of course through the income effect (provided goods are normal).

5.6 Transfers in kind

Social security payments are a monetary transfer. Wages are not: the recipient provides labour services in exchange for wages. An example of a transfer in kind is food stamps, given to the poor to buy food. The stamps must be spent on food, not beer, films or petrol. We now use our model of

A **transfer** is a payment, usually by the government, for which no corresponding service is provided by the recipient. A **transfer in kind** is the gift of a good or service.

consumer choice to ask whether an in-kind transfer payment is preferred by the consumer to a cash transfer payment of the same monetary value.

The consumer has £100 to spend on food or films, each costing £10 per unit. Figure 5.16 shows the budget line *AF*. Suppose the government issues the consumer with stamps worth 4 food units. For any point on the old budget line *AF* the consumer can have 4 more units of food from the food stamps. Moving horizontally to the right by 4 food units, the new budget line is *BF′*. Since food stamps cannot buy films, the new budget line is *ABF′*. The consumer can still get at most 10 films.

Suppose the consumer originally chose *e* on the budget line *AF*. Since both goods are normal, the shift in the budget line to *ABF′* – effectively a rise in income – makes the consumer choose a point to the north-east of *e*, as he would have done had the transfer been in cash.

When food costs £10 per unit, the cash equivalent of 4 food units is £40, shifting the budget line to *A′F′*. Thus, if the consumer begins at *e* it makes no difference if the transfer is in cash or in kind.

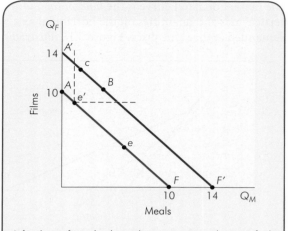

A food transfer in kind may leave consumers less satisfied than a cash transfer of the same value. A consumer at e′ might wish to spend less than the full allowance on food moving to c. The budget line is A′BF′ under a cash transfer. The in-kind transfer restricts the budget line to ABF′.

Figure 5.16 Transfers in cash and in kind

Suppose, however, that the consumer begins at *e′*. With a cash payment, the consumer might move to point *c* on the budget line *A′F′*. The transfer in kind, by restricting the consumer to the budget line *ABF′*, prevents the consumer reaching the preferred point *c*. Instead the consumer moves, say, to the feasible point *B*. *B* must yield the consumer less utility than *c*: when the consumer got a cash payment and could choose either point, *c* was preferred to *B*.

Cash transfers let consumers spend the extra income in any way that they wish. Transfers in kind may limit the consumer's option. Where they do, the increase in consumer utility is less than under a cash transfer of the same monetary value.

Yet transfers in kind are politically popular. The electorate wants to know that taxes are being wisely spent. Some people argue that the poor really do not know how to spend their money wisely and may spend cash transfers on 'undesirable' goods such as alcohol or gambling rather than on 'desirable' goods such as food or housing.

Do people act in their own best interests? This issue is not merely one of economics but also of philosophy, involving wider questions such as liberty and paternalism. In so far as people can judge their own self-interest, economic analysis is clear: people are better off, or at least no worse off, if they get transfers in cash rather than in kind.

Summary

- Given the **budget constraint**, the theory of demand assumes a consumer seeks to reach the **maximum possible level of utility**.

- The **budget line** shows the maximum affordable quantity of one good for each given quantity of the other good. The position of the budget line is determined by income and prices alone. Its slope reflects only relative prices.

- Because the **consumer prefers more to less**, he or she will always select a point on the budget line. The consumer has a problem of choice. Along the budget line, more of one good can be obtained only by sacrificing some of the other good.

- **Consumer tastes** can be represented by a map of non-intersecting **indifference curves**. Along each indifference curve, utility is constant. Higher indifference curves are preferred to lower indifference curves. Since the consumer prefers more to less, indifference curves must slope downwards. To preserve a given level of utility, increases in the quantity of one good must be offset by reductions in the quantity of the other good.

- Indifference curves exhibit a **diminishing marginal rate of substitution**. Their slope is flatter as we move along them to the right. To maintain given utility, consumers sacrifice ever smaller amounts of one good to get successive unit increases in the amount of the other good.

- **Utility-maximizing** consumers choose the consumption bundle at which the highest reachable **indifference curve is tangent to the budget line**. At this point the market trade-off between goods, the slope of the budget line, just matches the utility trade-off between goods, the slope of the indifference curve.

- At constant prices, an increase in income leads to a parallel outward shift in the budget line. If goods are normal, the quantity demanded will increase.

- A change in the price of one good rotates the budget line around the point at which none of that good is purchased. Such a price change has an income effect and a substitution effect. The **income effect of a price increase** is to reduce the quantity demanded for all normal goods. The **substitution effect**, induced by relative price movements alone, leads consumers to substitute away from the good whose relative price has increased.

- In a two-good world, goods must be substitutes. The substitution effect is unambiguous. With many goods, the pure substitution effect of a price increase also reduces demand for goods that are complementary to the good whose price has risen.

- A rise in the price of a normal good must lower its quantity demanded. For inferior goods, the income effect operates in the opposite direction but rarely seems to dominate the substitution effect. Demand curves slope downwards.

- The **market demand curve** is the horizontal sum of individual demand curves, at each price adding together the individual quantities demanded.

- **Consumers prefer to receive transfers in cash** rather than in kind, if the two transfers have the same monetary value. A transfer in kind may restrict the choices a consumer can make.

Review questions

To check your answers to these questions, go to page 714.

1 A consumer's income is £50. Food costs £5 per unit and films cost £2 per unit. (a) Draw the budget line. Pick a point e as the chosen initial consumption bundle. (b) The price of food falls to £2.50. Draw the new budget line. What can be said about the new consumption point e' if both goods are normal? (c) The price of films also falls to £1. Draw the new budget line and show the chosen point e''. (d) How does e'' differ from e? Why?

2 The own-price elasticity of demand for food is negative. The demand for food is inelastic. A higher food price raises spending on food. Higher food prices imply less is spent on all other goods. The quantity demanded of each of these other goods falls. Discuss each statement. Are they all correct?

3 Suppose films are normal goods but transport is an inferior good. How do the quantities demanded for the two goods change when income increases? Draw the old and new budget lines and illustrate the change in demand.

4 Suppose Glaswegians have a given income and like weekend trips to the Highlands, a three-hour drive. (a) If the price of petrol doubles, what is the effect on the demand for trips to the Highlands? Discuss both income and substitution effects. (b) Use a demand and supply diagram to show what happens to the price of Highland hotel rooms.

5 **Common fallacies** Why are these statements wrong? (a) Since consumers do not know about indifference curves or budget lines, they cannot choose the point on the budget line tangent to the highest possible indifference curve. (b) Inflation must reduce demand since prices are higher and goods are more expensive.

6 **Harder question** You begin with 5 coconuts and 5 fish. You can get extra fish by sacrificing 2 coconuts for each extra fish, or get extra coconuts by sacrificing 1 extra fish for each extra coconut. (a) Draw your budget line. (b) Draw an indifference map. (c) Where is it likely that you will choose to be? (d) Suppose there is a small change in the number of fish you can swap for an extra cocounut – is your behaviour likely to change?

7 **Harder question** You can invest in a safe asset or in a risky asset or in both. The safe asset has a guaranteed return of 3% a year. The risky asset has an expected return of 4% but it could be as much as 8% or as little as 0%. You decide to have some of your wealth in each asset. Now the expected return on the risky asset rises to 5%; it could be as high as 9% or as low as 1%. Given the increase in the expected return on the risky asset, do you invest more of your wealth in the risky asset?

8 **Essay question** We observe a person behaving differently in apparently similar situations. Either the situations were not similar or the person is 'irrational'. Which approach would an economist take? Why? Is it realistic to think that we account for behaviour in every situation?

Online Learning Centre

To help you grasp the key concepts of this chapter check out the extra resources posted on the Online Learning Centre. There are chapter summaries, self-test questions, an interactive graphing tool, weblinks and a searchable glossary, all for free!

To put your learning into practice and prepare for exams, an **Interactive Workbook** is also available online, containing a variety of question types and providing feedback on your answers.

If you'd like further help with economics, or have any questions, **NetTutor** is here to help! You will have a personalised tutorial service at your fingertips. Visit the online learning centre at: www.mcgraw-hill.co.uk/textbooks/begg for information on accessing all of these resources.

Appendix: Consumer choice with measurable utility

Our theory of consumer choice assumed that consumers can rank different bundles according to the utility or satisfaction they give. Saying bundle *A* gives more utility than bundle *B* just means the consumer prefers *A* to *B*. We do not need to know *by how much A* is preferred to *B*. Higher indifference curves are better. We do not need to know how much better.

> The **marginal utility** of a good is the increase in total utility obtained by consuming one more unit of that good, for given consumption of other goods.

Nineteenth-century economists believed utility levels could actually be measured, as if each consumer had a *utility meter* measuring his happiness. The further to the right the needle on his utility meter, the happier he was. The units on this meter were traditionally marked off in *utils*. Nowadays this seems a bit strange: are you 2.9 times as happy if you get an extra week's holiday?

Even so, analysis of consumer choice when utility *is* measurable is quite interesting, even though we derived all the main propositions in the text without this extra assumption. The (robot-like) individual whose utility is exactly calibrated in utils we shall call Fred.

> A consumer has **diminishing marginal utility** from a good if each extra unit consumed, holding constant consumption of other goods, adds successively less to total utility.

Fred goes to rock concerts and eats hamburgers. For a given consumption of one of these goods, he prefers more of the other to less. His utility goes up. If Fred gets 67 utils of utility from consuming 10 hamburgers and 1 rock concert, and 70 utils from 11 hamburgers but still 1 rock concert, his marginal utility from the eleventh hamburger is $(70 - 67 =)$ 3 utils.

Fred was not very hungry. He had 10 hamburgers at his only concert. He didn't get much from an eleventh hamburger, only an extra 3 utils. In contrast, if Fred had only 2 hamburgers at one concert (say, giving him 20 utils), he might rather have enjoyed a third hamburger (say, taking his utils to 27). The marginal utility of that extra hamburger is $(27 - 20 =)$ 7 utils. Fred's tastes obey the law of diminishing marginal utility.

Figure 5.A1 plots Fred's marginal utility of hamburgers. He gets fewer *extra* utils from extra consumption of hamburgers the more he is already consuming: his marginal utility schedule *MU* slopes down.

Fred has a given income to spend. Once we know the prices of rock concerts and hamburgers, we can work out his budget line. How does Fred choose the affordable point on this line at which to consume? He maximizes his utility.

The price of hamburgers in pounds is P_H and the price of concerts is P_C. If MU_H is Fred's marginal utility from another hamburger, he gets an extra util of MU_H/P_H for each extra pound spent on hamburgers and an extra MU_C/P_C util for each extra pound spent on concerts.

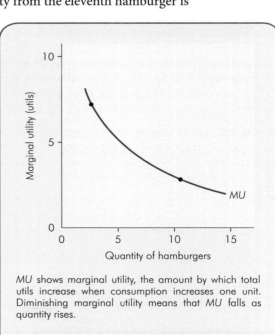

MU shows marginal utility, the amount by which total utils increase when consumption increases one unit. Diminishing marginal utility means that *MU* falls as quantity rises.

Figure 5.A1 Marginal utility

Suppose MU_H/P_H exceeds MU_C/P_C. An extra pound spent on hamburgers raises Fred's utility more than an extra pound spent on concerts. If Fred spends £1 more on hamburgers but £1 less on concerts his total utils rise: he gains more from hamburgers than he loses from concerts. He can increase utility *without spending more*. He will always want to transfer spending towards the good that yields more marginal utility per pound spent. To maximize utility, Fred spends all his income (he is on, not inside, his budget line) and adjusts his spending between hamburgers and concerts until

$$\textbf{MU}_H/\textbf{P}_H = \textbf{MU}_C/\textbf{P}_C \qquad\qquad \textbf{(A1)}$$

When this holds, Fred cannot rearrange the division of his total spending to increase his utility.[4] Fred maximizes utility by choosing the consumption bundle, on the budget line, at which the ratio of marginal utility to price is the same for every good.

Deriving demand curves

Suppose the price of hamburgers P_H falls. For given hamburger consumption, MU_H/P_H rises, and now exceeds MU_C/P_C for concerts, violating equation (A1). To maximize utility, Fred changes the quantities he demands.

If Fred buys *more* hamburgers when the price *falls*, the law of diminishing marginal utility means that MU_H falls as Fred buys more hamburgers. MU_H/P_H moves towards MU_H/P_C, as required by equation (A1). This is the *substitution effect* of the relative change in the price of hamburgers and concerts. On its own, the substitution effect suggests that *demand curves slope down*: when the price of hamburgers falls, the quantity demanded increases.

However, cheaper hamburger prices also raise the purchasing power of Fred's money income. This affects Fred's marginal utility. If hamburgers are a normal good, Fred buys more when the purchasing power of his income rises. Higher income shifts Fred's marginal utility schedule up in Figure 5.A2.

Box 5.4 Marginal utility and the water diamond paradox

Nineteenth-century economists wondered why the price of water, essential for survival, was so much lower than that for decorative diamonds. One answer is that diamonds are scarcer than water. Yet consumers clearly get more total utility from water (without it they die) than from diamonds. The concept of marginal utility solves the problem.

Equation (A1) tells us that consumers keep buying a good until the ratio of its *marginal* utility to price equals that for other goods. *At the margin*, the last litre of water we drink or use in the shower gives very little extra utility. At the margin, the last diamond still makes a big difference. People are willing to pay more for extra diamonds than for extra water.

In terms of a figure like Figure 5.A1, the marginal utility schedule *MU* is *very* high for the first few drops of water. Not dying is worth lots of utils. But most of us are a long way down this schedule, using lots of water to the point where its marginal value to us is low.

---

4 Equation (A1) implies $MU_H/MU_C = P_H/P_C$. Multiplying both sides by (-1), the right-hand side is the slope of the budget line, which depends only on relative prices. The left-hand side is the marginal rate of substitution: if the marginal utility of one hamburger is 2 and of one concert is 4, then $-MU_H/MU_C = -1/2$. One hamburger can be swapped for 1/2 a concert without altering total utility, precisely what the marginal rate of substitution measures. Equation (A1) implies that the slope of the indifference curve, the marginal rate of substitution, equals the slope of the budget line. This is the tangency condition of the test, derived without using measurable utility!

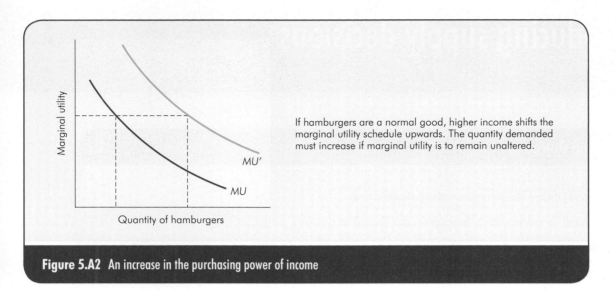

If hamburgers are a normal good, higher income shifts the marginal utility schedule upwards. The quantity demanded must increase if marginal utility is to remain unaltered.

MU'

MU

Marginal utility

Quantity of hamburgers

Figure 5.A2 An increase in the purchasing power of income

This *income effect* means that Fred finds that MU_H/P_H rises not only because P_H falls but also because MU_H rises at any particular level of hamburger consumption. Fred buys even more hamburgers, sliding down the higher marginal utility schedule, thereby reducing the marginal utility of hamburgers MU_H, until MU_H/P_H again equals MU_C/P_C. Thus for normal goods the income effect reinforces the substitution effect. Demand curves must slope down.

Suppose hamburgers are an inferior good. Figure 5.A2 then shows a downward shift in the MU_H schedule when the purchasing power of Fred's income increases. At his original consumption bundle, MU_H may fall by more than the fall in P_H, the price of hamburgers. If so, Fred has to *reduce* his hamburger consumption to increase its marginal utility and restore MU_H/P_H to equality with MU_C/P_C as utility maximization requires.

For inferior goods, the income effect goes in the opposite direction to the substitution effect. If the income effect is big enough, it could win out. Lower hamburger prices then reduce the quantity of hamburgers demanded. Demand curves slope upwards. As we discuss in the text, such Giffen goods are rare. It is safe to assume that demand curves slope down in practice.

Modern economists are pretty sniffy about measurable utility, preferring the more general indifference curve analysis used in the text. But indifference curves are tricky the first time you meet them. You need to practise using them to get comfortable with them. Measurable utility, and the simple idea of diminishing marginal utility, allows an easier introduction to the basic properties of demand curves and consumer choice developed in this chapter.

Introducing supply decisions

Learning Outcomes

By the end of this chapter, you should understand:

1 the legal forms in which businesses are owned and run

2 revenue, cost, profit and cash flow

3 accounts for flows and for stocks

4 economic and accounting definitions of cost

5 whether a firm chooses output to maximize profits

6 how this choice reflects marginal cost and marginal revenue

Having analysed demand, we turn now to supply. How do firms decide how much to produce and offer for sale? Can a single theory of supply describe the behaviour of different producers, from giant companies such as Shell to the self-employed ice cream vendor with a van?

For each possible output level a firm needs to calculate what it *costs* to make this output and how much *revenue* is earned by selling it. At each output, production costs depend on technology which determines the inputs needed and on the input prices that the firm faces. Sales revenue depends on the demand curve faced by the firm. The demand curve determines the price for which any output quantity can be sold and thus the revenue the firm earns.

Profits are the excess of revenues over costs. The key to the theory of supply is the assumption that all firms aim to make as much profit as possible. By examining how revenues and costs change with the level of output produced and sold, the firm chooses the output that maximizes its profits. To understand supply decisions, we need to analyse what determines revenues and costs.

The assumption of profit maximization is the cornerstone of the theory of supply. We conclude by discussing its plausibility and examine alternative views of what firms' aims might be.

6.1 Business organization

Businesses are self-employed sole traders, partnerships or companies. Sole traders, the commonest type of business organization, operate on a small scale. Partnerships are larger scale; companies are larger still.

> A **sole trader** is a business owned by a single individual.

A sole trader gets the revenue of the business and is responsible for any losses it makes. If he cannot meet these losses, he becomes personally bankrupt. His remaining assets, such as his house, are sold and the money shared out among the creditors.

If the business prospers, a sole trader may need money to expand. One way is to bring in new partners, who inject money in exchange for a share of the subsequent profits. Partnerships usually have *unlimited liability*. Like sole traders, partners are personally liable for the firm's losses, however large. Firms where trust is involved – solicitors or accountants – are often partnerships. Customers see that the people running the business are willing to put their own wealth behind the firm's obligations.

> A **partnership** is a business jointly owned by two or more people, sharing the profits and jointly responsible for any losses.

Any business needs money to start the business and finance its growth. Firms of lawyers, doctors or accountants, businesses relying on human expertise, need relatively little money for such purposes. The necessary funds can be raised from the partners and, possibly, by a bank loan. Businesses requiring large initial expenditure on machinery need much larger initial funds. It is too complicated to have a huge number of partners. Instead, it makes sense to form a company.

Unlike a partnership, a company has a legal existence distinct from that of its owners. Ownership is divided among shareholders. The original shareholders may now have sold shares of the profits to outsiders. By selling entitlements to share in the profits, the business can raise new funds.

> A **company** is an organization legally allowed to produce and trade.

Shareholders earn a return in two ways. First, the company makes regular *dividend* payments, paying out to shareholders that part of the profits that the firm does not wish to re-invest in the business. Second, the shareholders may make *capital gains* (or losses). If you buy Shell shares for £700 each but then people decide Shell profits and dividends will be unexpectedly high, you may be able to resell the shares for £750, making a capital gain of £50 per share. Unlike sole traders and partners, shareholders cannot be forced to sell their personal possessions if the business goes bust. At worst, the shares become worthless.

> Shareholders of a company have **limited liability**. The most they can lose is the money they spent buying shares.

Companies are run by boards of directors who submit an annual report to the shareholders, who can vote to sack the directors if it seems that other directors could do better. Companies are the main form of organization of big businesses.

6.2 A firm's accounts

Firms report two sets of accounts, one for stocks and one for flows.

The water *flowing* out of a tap is different per second and per minute. The measure needs a time interval to make sense of it. The *stock* of water in the basin at any instant is a number of litres, with no time dimension. A firm reports profit-and-loss accounts per year (flow accounts) and a balance sheet showing assets and liabilities at a point in time (stock accounts). The two are related, as they are for the basin of water. The inflow from the tap changes the stock of water over time, even though the stock is in litres at each point in time. We begin with flow accounts.

> **Stocks** are measured at a point in time; **flows** are corresponding measures during a period of time.

Flow accounts

These ideas are simple, but the calculation of revenue, cost and profit for a large firm is tricky. Otherwise we would not need so many accountants. Here is a simple example.

Rent-a-Person (R-a-P) is a firm that hires people whom it then rents out to other firms that need temporary workers. R-a-P charges £10 an hour

> **Revenue** is what the firm earns from selling goods or services in a given period, **cost** is the expense incurred in production in that period and **profit** is revenue minus cost.

per worker but pays its workers only £7 an hour. During 2007 it rented 100 000 hours of labour. Business expenses, including leasing an office, buying advertising space and paying phone bills, were £200 000. Table 6.1 shows the *income statement* or *profit-and-loss account* for 2007. Profits before tax were £100 000. Tax was £25 000. R-a-P's after-tax profits were £75 000. Now for the complications.

Table 6.1 R-a-P income statement, year to 31 December 2007

Revenue		
100 000 hours @ £10		£1 000 000
Cost		
Wages	£700 000	
Adverts	£50 000	
Office rent	£50 000	
Other expenses	£100 000	
		−£900 000
Pre-tax profit		£100 000
Tax		£25 000
Post-tax profit		£75 000

Unpaid bills

People do not always pay bills on time. At the end of 2007, R-a-P has unpaid bills for workers hired to other firms during the year. Nor has it yet paid its own telephone bill for December. From an economic viewpoint, the right definition of revenues and costs relates to the activities during the year whether or not payments have yet been made.

Actual receipts and payments thus may differ from economic revenue and cost. Profitable firms may still have a poor cash flow, for example when customers are slow to pay.

> A firm's **cash flow** is the net amount of money actually received during the period.

Capital and depreciation

R-a-P owns little physical capital. Instead, it leases office space, typewriters and desks. However, many firms do buy physical capital. Economists use 'capital' to denote goods not entirely used up in the production process during the period. Buildings and lorries are capital, to be used again in the next year. Electricity is not capital: purchases in 2007 do not survive into 2008. Economists also use 'durable goods' or 'physical assets' to describe capital goods.

> **Physical capital** is machinery, equipment and buildings used in production.

How is the cost of a capital good treated in calculating profit and cost? It is the cost of *using* rather than *buying* capital equipment that is part of the firm's costs within the year. If R-a-P leases all its capital equipment, its costs include merely the rentals paid in leasing capital goods.

> **Depreciation** is the loss in value of a capital good during the period.

Suppose R-a-P buys 8 computers in January for £1000 each. £8000 is not the cost of computers in calculating costs and profits for that year. Rather, the cost is the fall in value of the computers over the year. Suppose wear-and-tear and obsolescence reduce the value of a computer by £300 during the year. Part of the economic cost using 8 computers over the year is the £2400 by which they depreciate during the year.

Depreciation makes economic profit and cash flow differ. When a capital good is first bought there is a large cash outflow, much larger than the depreciation cost of using the good in the first year. Profits may be high but cash flow low. In later years, the firm makes no further cash outlay, having already paid for the capital goods, but must still calculate depreciation as an economic cost since the resale value of goods falls steadily. Cash flow is now higher than economic profit.

Treating depreciation, not the purchase price, as the true economic cost spreads the initial cost over the life of the capital goods but that is not why we calculate cost in this way. R-a-P could have sold its computers for £5600 after a year, restricting its costs to £2400. Since it chose to keep them for re-use in the next year, the latter strategy is even more profitable. Hence the true economic cost of using the computers in the first year is at most £2400.

Inventories

If production is instantaneous, firms can produce to meet orders as they arise. In fact, production takes time. Firms hold inventories to meet future demand.

> **Inventories** are goods held in stock by the firm for future sales.

Suppose at the start of 2007 Ford has a stock of 50 000 cars completed and available for sale. In 2007 it makes 1 million new cars and sells 950 000. By December its stock of finished cars is 100 000. What about profit? Revenue arises from selling 950 000 cars. Should cost reflect sales of 950 000 cars or the 1 million actually made?

Economic costs relate to the 950 000 cars actually sold. The 50 000 cars added to stocks are capital the firm made for itself, available for sale in the next period. There was a cash outflow to pay for the manufacture of 1 million cars but part of this cash outflow was used to buy inventories that will provide cash revenue the following year without any new cash outlay on production.

Borrowing

Firms usually borrow to finance their set-up and expansion costs, buying capital goods, solicitors' fees for the paperwork in registering the company, and so on. There is interest to be paid on the money borrowed. This interest is part of the cost of doing business and should be counted as part of the costs.

Stock accounts: the balance sheet

The income statement of Table 6.1 shows flows *in a given year*. We can also examine the firm at *a point in time*, the result of all its past trading operations. The *balance sheet* lists the assets the firm owns and the liabilities for which it is responsible at a point in time. Table 6.2 shows the balance sheet for Snark International on 31 December 2007.

Snark's assets are cash in the bank, money owed by its customers (accounts receivable), inventories in its warehouses and its factory (original cost £500 000, now worth only £330 000 because of depreciation). The total value of Snark assets is £540 000.

> A firm's **net worth** is the assets it owns minus the liabilities it owes.

Snark's liabilities are bills it has yet to pay, the mortgage on its factory and a bank loan for short-term cash needs. Its total liabilities (debts) are £300 000. The *net worth* of Snark International is £240 000, its assets minus its liabilities.

You make a takeover bid for Snark. Should you bid £240 000, its net worth? Probably more. Snark is a live company with good prospects and a proven record. You get not merely its physical and financial

Table 6.2 Snark's balance sheet at 31 December 2007

Assets	£000s	Liabilities	£000s
Cash	40	Accounts payable	90
Accounts receivable	70	Mortgage	150
Inventories	100	Bank loan	60
Factory (bought for 500)	330	**Total liabilities**	**300**
		Net worth	**240**
Total	540		540

assets minus liabilities but also its reputation, customer loyalty and a host of intangibles that economists call *goodwill*. If Snark is a sound company, bid more than £240 000. Alternatively, you may think Snark's accountants undervalued the resale value of its assets. If you can buy Snark for £240 000 you may make a profit by selling off the separate pieces of capital, a practice known as 'asset-stripping'.

Box 6.1 What a good name is worth

The consultancy Interbrand tries to calculate how much of a company's revenue is due simply to the marketing value of its brand image. US giants such as Coca-Cola and Microsoft top the worldwide list, but Nokia, Mercedes and Ikea are well up there. So are Nike and Adidas.

Rank	Company	Industry	Brand value ($bn) 2006
1	Coca-Cola	Drinks	67
2	Microsoft	Software	57
3	IBM	Computers	56
5	Intel	Computers	32
6	Nokia	Mobile phones	30
8	Disney	Entertainment	28
10	Mercedes	Cars	22
26	Sony	Electronics	12
31	Nike	Sports goods	11
41	Ikea	Furniture	9
57	Xerox	Copiers	6
71	Adidas	Sports goods	4

Source: www.interbrand.com.

Earnings

When a firm makes profits after tax, it can pay them out to shareholders as dividends, or keep them in the firm as retained earnings. Retained earnings affect the balance sheet. If kept as cash or used to purchase new equipment, they increase assets. Alternatively, they may reduce the firm's liabilities, by repaying the bank loan. Either way, the firm's net worth increases.

> **Retained earnings** are the part of after-tax profits ploughed back into the business.

Opportunity cost and accounting costs

The income statement and the balance sheet of a company provide two useful guides to how a firm is doing. But economists and accountants take different views of cost and profit. An accountant is interested in tracking the actual receipts and payments of a company. An economist is interested in how revenue and cost affect the firm's supply decision, the allocation of resources to particular activities. Accounting methods can mislead in two ways.

> **Opportunity cost** is the amount lost by not using a resource (labour, capital) in its best alternative use.

Economists identify the cost of using a resource not as the payment actually made but as its opportunity cost. To show that this is the right measure of costs, given the questions economists study, we provide two examples.

If you run your own firm you should take into account the cost of your labour time in the firm. You might draw up an income statement such as Table 6.1, find that profits are £20 000 a year and conclude that the firm is a good thing. This conclusion neglects the opportunity cost of your time. If you could have earned £25 000 a year working for someone else, being self-employed is losing you £5000 a year despite an accounting profit of £20 000. To understand the incentives that the market provides to guide people towards particular jobs, we must use the economic concept of opportunity cost, not the accounting concept of actual payments.

The second place where opportunity cost must be counted is with respect to capital. You put up the money to start the business. Accounting profits ignore the use of owned (as opposed to borrowed) financial capital. But this money could have been deposited in an interest-bearing bank account or used to buy shares in other firms. The opportunity cost of that money is part of the *economic* costs of the business but not its accounting costs. If it could earn 10 per cent elsewhere, the opportunity cost of your funds is 10 per cent times the money you put in. If, after deducting this cost and the true cost of your time, the business still makes a profit, economists call this 'supernormal profit'.

Supernormal profits are the true indicator of how well you are doing by tying up your time and funds in the business. Supernormal profits (or losses), not accounting profits (or losses), are the incentive to shift resources into (or out of) a business.

> **Supernormal profit** is pure economic profit and measures all economic costs properly.

6.3 Firms and profit maximization

Economists assume that firms choose output to *maximize profits*. Some economists and business executives question this assumption. A sole owner may prefer to work for herself even if she could earn more in total by working somewhere else. Her business decisions reflect maximization of her total job satisfaction not merely her monetary profit.

Ownership and control

A more significant reason to question profit maximization is that a large firm is run not by its owners but by a salaried board of directors. At the annual meeting, shareholders may dismiss the board but this is rare. The directors are the experts with the information. It is hard for the shareholders, even in bad times, to be sure that different directors would make more profits.

Economists call this a separation of ownership and control. Although shareholders want the maximum possible profit, the directors who actually make the decisions can pursue different objectives. Do directors have an incentive to act other than in the interests of the shareholders?

Directors' salaries are usually higher the larger is the firm. Directors may aim for size and growth rather than the maximum possible profit, spending big sums on costly adverts to boost sales.

Nevertheless, there are two reasons why the aim of profit maximization is a good place to begin. Even if the shareholders cannot recognize that profits are lower than they might be, other firms with experience in the industry may catch on faster. If profits are low, share prices will be low. By mounting a takeover, another company can buy the shares cheaply, sack the existing managers, restore profit-maximizing policies and make a handsome capital gain as the share price rises once the stock market sees the improvement in profits. Fear of takeover may induce directors to try to maximize profits.

Moreover, aware of the scope for directors' discretion, shareholders try to ensure that the interests of directors and shareholders coincide. By giving senior directors big bonuses tied to profitability or share performance – a small cost when spread over many shareholders but a major incentive for the existing management – shareholders try to make senior management care about profits as much as shareholders do.

The assumption that firms try to maximize profits is more robust than might first be imagined. Before using it to develop the theory of supply, we discuss the stock market in more detail.

6.4 Corporate finance and corporate control

Sources of finance include (a) borrowing from banks, (b) borrowing by selling pieces of paper (corporate bonds) whereby the firm promises to pay interest for a specified period and then repay the debt, and (c) using the stock market for selling new shares in the firm. Different countries have very different systems of corporate finance.

> **Corporate finance** refers to how firms finance their activities.

The US and the UK have market-based or outsider systems, relying on active stock markets trading existing shares and debt, and available to issue new shares and debt. Japan and much of continental Europe, notably Germany, have traditionally had an insider system, in which financial markets play only a small role. German companies got long-term loans from banks, who then sat on company boards with access to inside information about how the firm was doing.

Finance or control?

Large firms finance most of their new investment from their own retained profits. Roughly 90 per cent of UK corporate investment is financed in this way; less then 7 per cent comes from sales of new shares on the stock market. The key difference in the two systems of corporate finance lies not in the ease with which they provide firms with finance but in the way they award control rights to those providing that finance.

> **Corporate control** refers to who controls the firm in different situations.

In the bank-based insider system, representatives of the bank sit on the firm's board, using this inside position to press for changes when mistakes are made. The market-based system entails a smaller role for banks and a larger role for stock markets and debt markets. Failure to meet interest payments on debt usually gives debt-holders the right to make the firm bankrupt, a radical transfer of corporate control in which the existing management rarely survives. Similarly, the existence of publicly-quoted shares raises the possibility of a stock market takeover in which a new management team effectively buys control on the open market. Outsider market-based systems of corporate finance thus become markets for corporate control itself.

Hostile takeovers

In Germany, hostile takeovers have traditionally been rare. In contrast, many UK takeovers are hostile bids uninvited by existing managers. Some economists see hostile bids as a vital force for efficiency. However, the separation of ownership and control in public companies leads to a principal–agent problem. The agents (here, the managers) are tempted to act in their own interests rather than those of their principals (the shareholders).

The threat of hostile takeovers deters managers from departing too much from the profit-maximizing policies that shareholders want. Slack management leads to low profits, depressed share prices and opportunities for takeover raiders to buy the company cheaply. The threat of takeover provides a discipline that helps overcome the principal–agent problem.

> A principal or owner may delegate decisions to an agent. If it is costly for the principal to monitor the agent, the agent has inside information about its own performance, causing a **principal–agent problem**.

However, hostile takeovers also undermine the existing managers. Wanting workforce co-operation in moving to new production methods, you promise to reward employees well once productivity has risen. The workers know you keep your word, but cannot trust you. While the changes are being made, profits will temporarily fall and you could face a takeover raid. The new owner may fire workers to save money. So your workers reject your plan to bring sensible changes to the company.

Hostile takeovers, by undermining the ability of managers to make commitments to their workers, inhibit investment and encourage short-termism. However, the German and Japanese insider systems also have their problems, especially if radical action is required. The Japanese economy languished in the doldrums for ten years because its companies, particularly its banks, failed to make key changes after a property price collapse in the early 1990s. In the US and the UK, there would have been less patience, less concern about admitting failure and a swifter response.

As usual, the debates that rumble on – here, the relative merits of the two systems of corporate control – do so because there are good arguments on both sides. Box 6.2 has more details.

After this glimpse of what lies ahead of you if you opt for a career in high finance, we return to the supply decision by an individual firm.

6.5 The firm's supply decision

Suppose a firm makes spoons. Some ways to make spoons use lots of labour and few machines, other ways use many machines but little labour. The firm knows different techniques for making spoons and the cost of hiring inputs – the wage rate for workers and rental for leasing a machine. The firm also knows its demand curve and hence its revenue from selling different quantities of spoons at different prices.

To maximize profits the firm chooses the best level of output. Changing output affects both the costs of production and the revenues from sales. Costs and demand conditions jointly determine the output choice of a profit-maximizing firm.

Box 6.2 How private should private equity be?

If you start your own company, you probably have regular conversations with your bank manager but you do not need to make extensive disclosures to the general public. In contrast, a company with a public listing on the stock exchange can obtain more funding from shareholders but has to obey stock exchange rules, make its accounts transparent and inform current and potential shareholders about the state of the company. Because its shares are bought and sold on a daily basis, it worries about its short-term performance in case someone mounts a takeover raid.

Would it ever make sense for a large company to delist from the stock exchange and become private again, making takeover more difficult and allowing the management to take a longer-run perspective? Richard Branson thought so when, having launched Virgin as a public company, he then changed his mind and borrowed enough money to buy back all the shares and make Virgin private again.

In the past few years, an alternative vehicle for achieving a similar objective has been the rise of private equity funds. These funds obtain long-term loans (often 10 years) from pension funds and other investors, and then take over companies which the private equity (PE) fund then manages itself. On average they have been able to outperform the stock market. PE funds say it is because they have better management expertise and can adopt longer-run strategies. Critics say they sometimes engage in asset stripping, breaking up good companies and getting more for the sum of the parts than they paid for the whole entity. Or they find ways to impose tougher terms on company pension schemes.

Household names, such as Boots the chemist and Saga holidays, have recently been bought by private equity firms for huge amounts of money. By 2007 even companies such as Sainsbury's were rumoured to be targets. Amid mounting public concerns, the PE industry asked the Bank of England director, Sir David Walker, to recommend new measures for increased transparency and self-regulation by the industry.

The Walker Report concluded that PE funds controlled 8 per cent of UK private sector employment because they had been successful in stimulating productivity improvement and better management; that their longer-term approach to investment decisions could usefully be copied by other firms (crudely speaking, they should borrow more and issue fewer shares); and that greater public disclosure of their affairs would allow them to document their own success.

When partners of the top PE funds were required to testify in front of the Treasury Select Committee in 2007, much of the discussion addressed the huge payoffs that leading partners were earning, largely because they arrange for most of their remuneration to be received as capital gains from selling companies, rather than as conventional income incurring income tax. As Chancellor Gordon Brown had cut capital gains taxes for such activities, the masters of the PE universe noted that they were merely responding to the tax regime that the Chancellor himself had created. It made some people very rich, but it established London as a private equity centre, bringing huge wealth into the UK.

Adapted from BBC online, various dates.

Cost minimization

The firm certainly wants to make its chosen output level at the least possible cost. By producing the same output at lower cost it could increase profits. Thus a profit-maximizing firm must produce its chosen output as cheaply as possible.

The total cost curve

Knowing the available production methods and the costs of hiring workers and machines, the firm calculates the least cost at which each output can be made. It is not worth using many machines to make only a few spoons; to make more spoons, it makes sense to use more machines.

Table 6.3 shows various outputs in column (1). Column (2) shows the minimum cost at which each output can be made. The firm incurs a cost of £10 even when output is zero. This is the cost of being in business at all – running an office, renting a telephone line and so on. Thereafter, costs rise with output. Costs include the opportunity costs of all resources used in production. Total cost is higher the more is produced. At high levels of output, cost rises sharply as output increases: the firm has to pay the workers overtime to work weekends and nights.

Table 6.3 Cost, revenue, profit (weekly)

(1) Output	(2) Total cost (£)	(3) Price (£)	(4) Total revenue (1) × (3) (£)	(5) Profit (4) − (2) (£)
0	10	–	0	−10
1	25	21	21	−4
2	36	20	40	4
3	44	19	57	13
4	51	18	72	21
5	59	17	85	26
6	69	16	96	27
7	81	15	105	24
8	95	14	112	17
9	111	13	117	6
10	129	12	120	−9

Total revenue

The revenue from an output depends on price and hence demand. Column (3) of Table 6.3 shows the demand curve, the price at which each output can be sold. Column (4) calculates sales revenue, price times quantity. At a price of £21 the firm sells only one spoon. The lower the price, the greater the sales: its demand curve slopes down.

Profit

The last column shows profit, the difference between revenue and cost. At low output, profit is negative. At the highest output of 10, profit is again negative. At intermediate outputs, the firm makes positive profit.

The highest profit is £27 a week, at an output of 6 spoons. At £16 each, total revenue is £96. Production cost, properly calculated, is £69, leaving a profit of £27 a week. This chosen output, or supply decision, is the highlighted row in Table 6.3.

Maximizing profit is not the same as maximizing revenue. By selling 10 spoons a week the firm could earn £120, but it would cost £129 to make them. Making the last few spoons is expensive and brings in little extra revenue. It is more profitable to make fewer.

6.6 Marginal cost and marginal revenue

It is helpful to view the same problem from a different angle. At each output level, we now ask whether the firm should increase output still further. Suppose the firm makes 3 spoons and considers making 4 spoons. Table 6.3 shows this raises total cost from £44 to £51, a £7 increase in total cost. Revenue rises from £57 to £72, a rise of £15. Raising output from 3 to 4 spoons adds more to revenue than cost. Profit rises by £8 (£15 more revenue, minus £7 more cost). The firm then checks if it is also profitable to increase production from 4 to 5, and so on.

> **Marginal cost** is the rise in total cost when output rises 1 unit. **Marginal revenue** is the rise in total revenue when output rises 1 unit.

This approach – examining how 1 more unit of output affects profit – focuses on the marginal cost and marginal revenue of producing 1 more unit.

If marginal revenue exceeds marginal cost, the firm should raise output. Producing and selling an extra unit adds more to total revenue than to total cost, raising total profit. If marginal cost exceeds marginal revenue, the extra unit of output reduces total profit.

Thus we can use marginal cost and marginal revenue to calculate the output that maximizes profit. So long as marginal revenue exceeds marginal cost, keep increasing output. As soon as marginal revenue falls short of marginal cost, stop increasing output.

Marginal cost

Table 6.4 uses Table 6.3 to calculate the marginal cost of producing each extra unit of output. Increasing output from 0 to 1 raises total cost from £10 to £25. The marginal cost of the first unit is £15. Table 6.4 shows this marginal cost of each output level, the extra total cost of raising output by the last unit.

Marginal cost is large when output is low but also when output is high. Marginal cost is lowest when making the fourth unit, which adds only £7 to total costs.

As output increases, why do marginal costs start high, then fall, then rise again? The answer reflects different production techniques. At low output, the firm uses simple techniques. As output rises, more sophisticated machines are used, making extra output quite cheap. As output rises still further, the difficulties of managing a large firm emerge. Raising output gets hard and marginal costs rise.

Figure 6.1 plots this relation between output and marginal cost, which varies from firm to firm. In a coal mine that is nearly worked out, marginal cost rises steeply with extra output. In mass-production industries, as output increases marginal cost may decline and then become constant (see Figure 6.1 again).

Table 6.4 Total and marginal cost

Output	Total cost (£)	Marginal cost (£)
0	10	
1	25	15
2	36	11
3	44	8
4	51	7
5	59	8
6	69	10
7	81	12
8	95	14
9	111	16
10	129	18

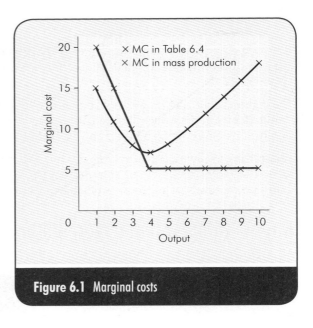

Figure 6.1 Marginal costs

Marginal revenue

Still based on Table 6.3, Table 6.5 shows marginal revenue, the extra total revenue when an extra unit of output is made and sold. Raising output from 0 to 1 raises revenue from £0 to £21. The marginal revenue of the first unit is £21. Raising output from 7 to 8 units raises revenue from £105 to £112, so marginal revenue is £7. Total revenue and marginal revenue depend on the demand curve for the firm's product.

Table 6.5 Price, total revenue and marginal revenue

Output	Price (£)	Total revenue (£)	Marginal revenue (£)
0	–	0	–
1	21	21	21
2	20	40	19
3	19	57	17
4	18	72	15
5	17	85	13
6	16	96	11
7	15	105	9
8	14	112	7
9	13	117	5
10	12	120	3

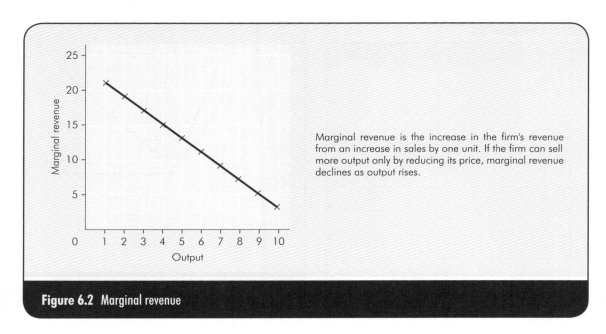

Marginal revenue is the increase in the firm's revenue from an increase in sales by one unit. If the firm can sell more output only by reducing its price, marginal revenue declines as output rises.

Figure 6.2 Marginal revenue

Marginal revenue, also shown in Figure 6.2, falls steadily as output rises and can be negative at high output levels. To sell 11 spoons, the price must be cut to £10 each. Total revenue is £110. Since 10 spoons earn £120 in Table 6.5, the marginal revenue from moving from 10 to 11 spoons is £110–£120, and thus –£10.

> **Marginal revenue = extra revenue from making and selling 1 more unit**
> **= [extra revenue from selling last unit alone] –**
> **[revenue lost selling existing units at a lower price]**

Demand curves slope down. To sell more output, the price must be cut. Selling an extra unit of output at this lower price is the first component of marginal revenue. However, to sell that extra unit the firm has to cut the price for which *all* previous units of output can be sold. This effect reduces the marginal revenue obtained from selling an extra unit of output.

Marginal revenue falls steadily for two reasons. First, because demand curves slope down, the extra unit must be sold at a lower price. Second, successive price reductions reduce the revenue earned from *existing* units of output, and at larger output there are more existing units on which revenue is lost when prices fall further. To sum up, (a) marginal revenue falls as output rises and (b) marginal revenue is less than the price for which the last unit is sold, because a lower price reduces revenue earned from existing output.

The shape of the marginal revenue curve reflects the shape of the firm's demand curve. A small firm in a huge market sells as much output as it wants without affecting the market price. That firm's demand curve is horizontal at the going price. In this special case, the price *is* the marginal revenue. No revenue is lost on existing output when more output is sold.

MR, MC and the output choice

Combining marginal cost (*MC*) and marginal revenue (*MR*), Table 6.6 examines the output that maximizes the firm's profits. If *MR* exceeds *MC*, a 1-unit increase in output will increase profits. The last column shows that this reasoning leads the firm to make at least 6 units of output.

The firm now considers increasing output from 6 to 7 units. Marginal revenue is £9 and marginal cost £12. Profits fall by £3. Output should *not* be expanded to 7 units, or to any level above this.

Box 6.3 So what is a firm?

Chapter 1 highlighted the spectrum from a pure command economy to a pure market economy. Oranges are traded in a market fruit stall, but the army relies on command. Firms do both. They trade with markets, but within the firm they rely on command. A boss wanting a coffee doesn't hold an auction, she tells a subordinate to get it. This prompts the interesting question of why some activities are more efficiently transacted through markets while others are more efficiently conducted in other ways. In turn, this provokes the question of what constitutes a firm? Economists have offered three types of answer.

Static synergies

One view is that firms capture 'static synergies', benefits from closely related activities. It makes sense to bundle together related production activities before selling the package, thereby reducing the overall cost of transacting in markets. It is cheaper, and therefore more efficient, to take advantage of these synergies within a firm than to assemble the same portfolio of activities within a market, for example because the search costs are reduced.

Transaction costs and institutional economics

A second view is that firms involve trust and teamwork, always long-run relationships. Firms are devices to cement together the long-run relationships that efficiency requires. Whereas anonymous markets may allow bad behaviour to go unpunished – because individual transactions are anonymous and unrepeated – familiarity, repeated contact, and information flows within the firm promote discipline and co-operation. There is nowhere to hide after bad behaviour, and sufficient management hierarchy to make punishment possible once bad behaviour has been detected. Hence firms promote co-operative good behaviour, with consequent efficiency gains. This view is associated with Professor Oliver Williamson.

Incomplete contracts

The third and most recent view is that firms reflect the impossibility of writing complete contracts. Suppose people could foresee everything that might happen in the future. They could then engage in a market transaction, signing a contract specifying what happens in every possible situation. But some future situations cannot be foreseen: no contract can take them into account. Our parents did not anticipate global warming would even be an issue. Authority – the hierarchy of decision making in the firm – specifies who adjudicates if a strange contingency arises that nobody has foreseen. It removes the ambiguity of what would happen if we had to leave everything to markets and contracts.

The firm should expand up to 6 units of output but no further. This output maximizes profits, as we know already from Table 6.5.

Total cost and revenue versus marginal cost and revenue

Table 6.3, based on total cost and total revenue, and Table 6.6, based on marginal cost and revenue, are different ways to study the same problem. Economists frequently use marginal analysis. Is there a small change that could make the firm better off? If so, the current position cannot be the best possible one and changes should be made.

Table 6.6 Using marginal revenue and marginal cost to choose output

Output	MR (£)	MC (£)	MR – MC (£)	Output decision
1	21	15	6	Raise
2	19	11	8	Raise
3	17	8	9	Raise
4	15	7	8	Raise
5	13	8	5	Raise
6	11	10	1	
7	9	12	–3	Lower
8	7	14	–7	Lower
9	5	16	–11	Lower
10	3	18	–15	Lower

Marginal analysis should be subjected to one very important check. It may miss an all-or-nothing choice. For example, suppose that *MR* exceeds *MC* up to an output level of 6 units but thereafter *MR* is less than *MC*. Six units is the best positive output level. However, if the firm incurs large costs whether or not it produces (for example, a vastly overpaid managing director), the profit earned from producing 6 units may not cover these fixed costs. Conditional on paying these fixed costs, an output level of 6 units is then the loss-minimizing output level. Shareholders might do better to shut the firm and fire the fat cat boss. We examine this issue in the next chapter.

To sum up, a profit-maximizing firm should expand output so long as marginal revenue exceeds marginal cost but stop expansion as soon as marginal cost exceeds marginal revenue. This rule guides the firm to the best positive level of output. If the firm is not making profits even in this position, it may do better to close down altogether.

6.7 Marginal cost and marginal revenue curves

Thus far we have assumed the firm produces an integer number of goods, such as 0, 1 or 2, rather than a quantity such as 1.5 or 6.7. Output is not usually confined to integer levels. For goods such as wheat or milk, the firm can sell in odd amounts. Even for goods such as cars, sold in whole units, the firm may be selling 75 cars every four weeks, or 18.75 cars a week. It is convenient to imagine that firms can vary output and sales levels continuously.

We can then draw smooth schedules for marginal cost *MC* and marginal revenue *MR* as in Figure 6.3. Profits are maximized where the schedules cross, at point *E*. The output Q_1 maximizes profits (or minimizes losses). At smaller outputs, *MR* exceeds *MC* and expansion increases profits (or reduces losses).

To the right of Q_1, *MC* exceeds *MR*. Expansion adds more to costs than revenue, and contraction saves more in costs than it loses in revenue. The profit incentive to increase output to the left of Q_1 and to reduce output to the right of Q_1 is shown by the arrows in Figure 6.3. This incentive guides the firm to choose Q_1, provided the firm should be in business at all. At Q_1 marginal revenue is exactly equal to marginal cost. Table 6.7 summarizes the conditions for determining the output that maximizes profits.

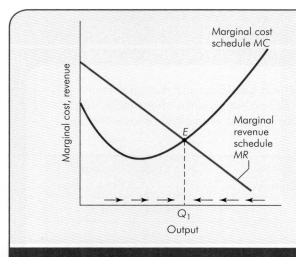

The marginal cost and marginal revenue schedules are shown changing smoothly. The firm's optimal output is Q_1, at which marginal revenue is equal to marginal cost. Anywhere to the left of Q_1, marginal revenue is larger than marginal cost and the firm should increase output, as shown by the arrows. Where output is greater than Q_1, marginal revenue is less than marginal cost and profits are increased by reducing output. If the firm is losing money at Q_1 it has to check whether it might be better not to produce at all than to produce Q_1.

Figure 6.3 Marginal cost and marginal revenue

Table 6.7 The firm's output choice

Marginal condition	Output decision	Check
$MR > MC$	Raise	
$MR < MC$	Cut	
$MR = MC$	Stay	If profits > 0, make this output. If not, quit.

Changes in cost

Suppose the firm faces a price rise for a raw material. At each output, marginal cost is higher than before. Figure 6.4 shows this upward shift from MC to MC'. The firm now produces at E'. Higher marginal costs reduce profit-maximizing output from Q_1 to Q_2.

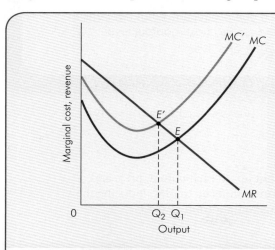

The marginal cost curve shifts up from MC to MC' as a result of an increase in the costs of using a factor of production; for instance, the wage may have risen. This upward shift moves the intersection of MC and MR curves from E to E'. Output falls from Q_1 to Q_2. Thus, when the firm's costs rise, it decides to produce less.

Figure 6.4 An increase in marginal cost reduces output

Activity box 6 The effect of taxation

The table below shows output; the marginal revenue, marginal cost and marginal profit on the last unit of output; and hence the output decision in the absence of any taxes. The firm chooses an output of 6, at which $MC = MR$. Does it matter which kind of taxes the firm faces?

Output	MR	MC	MR − MC (marginal profit)	Output decision
1	21	15	6	Raise
2	19	11	8	Raise
3	17	8	9	Raise
4	15	7	8	Raise
5	13	8	5	Raise
6	11	11	0	Remain
7	9	12	−3	Lower
8	7	14	−7	Lower
9	5	16	−11	Lower
10	3	18	−15	Lower

Questions

(a) Suppose first that the firm pays a 10 per cent tax on all profits. Do you think the firm reduces output? Why or why not?

(b) Now suppose that the firm faces a tax of 1 on each unit produced. What happens to marginal cost inclusive of taxation? Will the firm reduce its chosen output level?

To check your answers to these questions, go to page 715.

A demand shift

Suppose the firm's demand curve and marginal revenue curve shift up. At each output, price and marginal revenue are higher than before. In Figure 6.5 the MR curve shifts up to MR', inducing the firm to move from E to E''. Higher demand makes the firm expand output from Q_1 to Q_3.

Do firms know their marginal cost and revenue curves?

Do firms in the real world know their marginal cost and marginal revenue curves, let alone go through some sophisticated calculations to make sure output is chosen to equate the two?

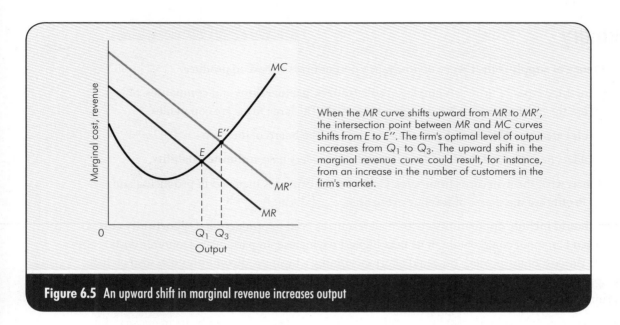

When the MR curve shifts upward from MR to MR', the intersection point between MR and MC curves shifts from E to E''. The firm's optimal level of output increases from Q_1 to Q_3. The upward shift in the marginal revenue curve could result, for instance, from an increase in the number of customers in the firm's market.

Figure 6.5 An upward shift in marginal revenue increases output

Such thought experiments by firms are not necessary for the relevance of our model of supply. If, by luck, hunch or judgement, a firm succeeds in maximizing profits, marginal cost and marginal revenue *must* be equal. Our formal analysis merely tracks the hunches of smart managers who get things right and survive in a tough business world.

In this chapter we introduced cost and revenue conditions. Later chapters fill in the details but we now have the basis for a theory of how much output firms choose to supply. Firms choose the output that maximizes profits. At this output, marginal cost equals marginal revenue.

Summary

- The **theory of supply** is the theory of how much output firms choose to produce.

- There are three types of firm: self-employed **sole traders**, **partnerships** and **companies**. Sole traders are the most numerous but are often very small. The large firms are companies.

- Companies are owned by their shareholders but run by the board of directors.

- Shareholders have **limited liability**. Partners and sole traders have **unlimited liability**.

- **Revenue** is what the firm earns from sales. **Costs** are the expenses incurred in producing and selling. **Profits** are the excess of revenue over costs.

- **Costs should include opportunity costs** of all resources used in production. **Opportunity cost** is the amount an input could obtain in its next highest paying use. In particular, economic costs include the cost of the owner's time and effort in running a business. **Economic costs** also include the opportunity cost of financial capital used in the firm. **Supernormal profit** is the pure profit accruing to the owners after allowing for all these costs.

- Firms are assumed to aim to **maximize profits**. Even though the firm is run by its managers, not its owners, profit maximization is a useful assumption in understanding the firm's behaviour. Firms that make losses cannot continue in business indefinitely.

- In aiming to maximize profits, firms necessarily produce each output level as cheaply as possible. Profit maximization requires minimization of costs for each output level.

- Firms choose the **optimal output level** to maximize total economic profits. This decision can be described equivalently by examining marginal cost and marginal revenue. **Marginal cost** is the increase in total cost when one more unit is produced. **Marginal revenue** is the corresponding change in total revenue and depends on the demand curve for the firm's product. **Profits are maximized at the output at which marginal cost equals marginal revenue**. If profits are negative at this output, the firm should close down if this reduces losses.

- An upward shift in the marginal cost curve reduces output. An upward shift in the marginal revenue curve increases output.

- It is unnecessary for firms to calculate their marginal cost and marginal revenue curves. Setting *MC* equal to *MR* is merely a device that economists use to mimic the hunches of smart firms who correctly judge, by whatever means, the profit-maximizing level of output.

Review questions

To check your answers to these questions, go to page 715.

1. How do the following affect the income statement for R-a-P in Table 6.1? (a) R-a-P owes £70 000 to its workers for work done in the year. (b) Instead of renting an office, R-a-P owns its office. (c) During the year R-a-P was paid by a creditor owing money from the year before.

2. R-a-P is run by an owner, who can earn £40 000 a year to manage another firm. She has also invested £20 0000 in R-a-P that could be earning 12 per cent elsewhere. What are the economic profits of R-a-P? (Use Table 6.1.)

3 (a) Snark International borrows another £50 000 from the bank and increases its inventories. How is its balance sheet affected (Table 6.2)? (b) How would interest on the loan appear in the income statement of Snark International?

4 (a) Do firms aim to maximize profits? (b) Should firms support charities, the arts and political campaigns? Is there any conflict with (a)?

5 In Table 6.3, assume total costs of making each output are higher by £40 than the costs in the second column of the table. What level of output should the firm produce? Explain.

6 A firm with the costs shown in Table 6.4 can now sell as much output as it wants at a price of £13. (a) Draw *MR* and *MC* curves. (b) What output will it produce?

7 **Common fallacies** Why are these statements wrong? (a) Firms with an accounting profit must be thriving. (b) Firms do not know their marginal costs. A theory of supply cannot assume that firms set marginal revenue equal to marginal cost. (c) To maximize profit, maximize sales.

8 **Harder question** Airbus makes 50 planes a year, which sell for $50 million each. If Airbus raises it price, Boeing will leave its prices unaltered, so Airbus loses market share. It faces an elastic demand curve. However, if Airbus cuts its price below $50 million, Boeing is forced to match the price cut so quantity demanded increases only to the extent that additional plane orders are placed when planes are cheaper. Each company faces inelastic demand when it cuts the price. (a) Draw the demand curve that Airbus thinks it faces. (b) Can you deduce what its marginal revenue schedule looks like?

9 **Harder question** (a) Unexpectedly, the government levies a once-off 'windfall' tax on the profits of a company making large profits. What is the company's optimal output response? (b) Suppose the company is worried that there will also be future 'unexpected windfall taxes'. If its cost and revenue schedules are given, should its behaviour be affected? (c) If the company had been intending to invest, spending money today to shift down cost curves in the future, could its present investment decision be affected by fears of future windfall taxes?

10 **Essay question** 'The industrial revolution was built on the ability of entrepreneurs to float companies and obtain funding. Today, it is often argued that stock exchanges force firms to be focused too much on the short term, making it hard to raise long-term funds. Private equity firms see themselves as addressing this shortcoming of stock markets. The amazing thing about private equity is not its recent appearance but that it took so long to appear.' Discuss.

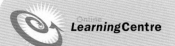
LearningCentre

To help you grasp the key concepts of this chapter check out the extra resources posted on the Online Learning Centre. There are chapter summaries, self-test questions, an interactive graphing tool, weblinks and a searchable glossary, all for free!

To put your learning into practice and prepare for exams, an **Interactive Workbook** is also available online, containing a variety of question types and providing feedback on your answers.

If you'd like further help with economics, or have any questions, **NetTutor** is here to help! You will have a personalised tutorial service at your fingertips. Visit the online learning centre at: www.mcgraw-hill.co.uk/textbooks/begg for information on accessing all of these resources.

Costs and supply

Chapter 6 introduced the theory of supply. Firms choose the output at which marginal cost equals marginal revenue. This maximizes profits (or minimizes losses). If profits are positive, the firm produces this output. If profits are negative, it checks whether losses are reduced by shutting down. This chapter develops the theory of supply in more detail.

We distinguish between the *short-run* and the *long-run* output decisions of firms. No firm stays in business if it expects to make losses for ever. We show how and why cost curves differ in the short run, when the firm cannot fully react to changes in conditions, and the long run in which the firm can fully adjust to changes in demand or cost conditions

Figure 7.1 summarizes the material of this chapter. The new material is all on the cost side. Because there are so many cost curves, you may find it useful to check back to Figure 7.1. We start by introducing the *production function*, which describes the firm's technology.

7.1 Input and output

> An **input** (or **factor of production**) is a good or service used to produce output.

Inputs include labour, machinery, buildings, raw materials and energy. Suppose our firm uses inputs to make snarks. This is an engineering and management problem. Making snarks is largely a matter of technology and on-the-job experience. The production function summarizes technically efficient ways to combine inputs to produce output. Since profit-maximizing firms are not interested in wasteful production methods, we restrict our attention to those that are technically efficient.

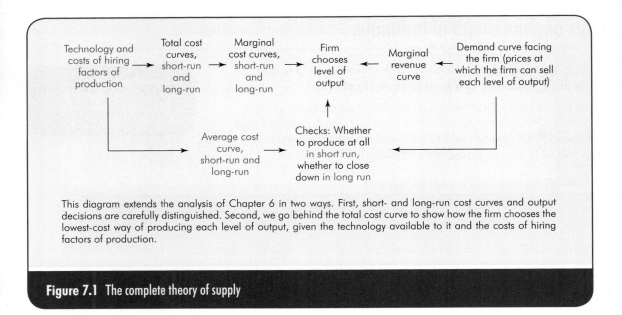

Figure 7.1 The complete theory of supply

To make 1 snark, Method A needs 2 workers and 1 machine, but Method B needs 2 workers and 2 machines. Method B is less efficient than method A. It uses more machines but the same labour to make the same output. Method B is not in the production function.

> A production technique is **technically efficient** if there is no other way to make a given output using less of one input and no more of the other inputs. The **production function** is the set of all technically efficient techniques.

Table 7.1 shows some technically efficient methods in the production function. The first two rows show two ways to make 100 snarks: 4 machines and 4 workers, or 2 machines and 6 workers. Beginning from the latter, the third row shows the effect of adding an extra worker. Output rises by 6 snarks. The last row shows that doubling both inputs in the second row also doubles the output, though this need not be so: overcrowding a small factory can slow people down.

Table 7.1 A production function

Output	Capital input	Labour input
100	4	4
100	2	6
106	2	7
200	4	12

Table 7.1 could be enlarged to include other combinations of labour and capital that are also technically efficient. A firm discovers its production function, the complete set of technically efficient production techniques, by asking its engineers, designers and time-and-motion experts – and by trial and error.

> A **technique** is a particular way to combine inputs to make output. **Technology** is the list of all known techniques.

A method previously technically efficient may become inefficient after a technical advance allows a better production technique. Technical progress alters the production function. For now, we assume a given technology and a given production function. Chapter 30 discusses growth and technical progress.

7.2 Costs and the choice of technique

The production function relates volumes of inputs to volume of output. To get costs, which are values, we also need to know input prices.

> **Technical progress** is a new technique allowing a given output to be made with fewer inputs than before.

Consider the lowest-cost way to make 100 snarks.[1] Assume there are two technically efficient techniques, the first two rows of Table 7.1, reproduced as the second and third columns of Table 7.2 and labelled techniques A and B. It costs £320 to rent a machine and £300 to hire a worker.

Table 7.2 Choosing the lowest-cost production technique

Technique	Capital input	Labour input	Rental per machine (£)	Wage per worker (£)	Capital cost (£)	Labour cost (£)	Total cost (£)
A	4	4	320	300	1280	1200	2480
B	2	6	320	300	640	1800	2440

To make 100 snarks, Table 7.2 shows that the total cost is £2480 with technique A and £2440 with technique B. The firm chooses B. 100 snarks at a total cost of £2440 is one point on the total cost curve for snarks. It is the *economically efficient* (lowest-cost) production method at the rental and wage rates in Table 7.2.

To get the whole total cost curve, we repeat the calculation for each output. The production function tells us the inputs needed by each technique. Using input prices, we calculate the cost using each technique and choose the lowest-cost production method. Joining up these points we get the total cost curve, which may switch from one production technique to another at different outputs. From the total cost curve we calculate the marginal cost curve – the rise in total cost at each output when output is increased by one more unit.

Factor intensity

A technique using a lot of capital and little labour is 'capital intensive'. One using a lot of labour but relatively little capital is 'labour intensive'. In Table 7.2, technique A is more capital intensive and less labour intensive than technique B. The ratio of capital input to labour input is 1 in technique A but only 1/3 in technique B.

Factor prices and the choice of technique

At the factor prices (prices per unit input) in Table 7.2, the more labour-intensive technique is cheaper. Suppose the wage rises from £300 to £340: labour is dearer but the rental on capital is unchanged. The *relative price* of labour has risen.

We ask two questions. First, what happens to the total cost of making 100 snarks? Second, is there any change in the preferred technique? Table 7.3 recalculates production costs at the new factor prices. Because both techniques use some labour, the total cost of making 100 snarks by each technique rises. Repeating this argument at all output, the total cost curve must shift *upwards* when the wage rate (or the price of any other input) rises.

In this example, the rise in the relative price of labour leads the firm to switch techniques: it switches to the more capital-intensive technique A.

1 Since output, revenue and cost are all flows, these should be measured per week or per year. We omit time units for brevity but do not forget they are flows not stocks!

Table 7.3 The effect of a higher wage rate

Technique	Capital input	Labour input	Rental per machine (£)	Wage per worker (£)	Capital cost (£)	Labour cost (£)	Total cost (£)
A	4	4	320	340	1280	1360	2640
B	2	6	320	340	640	2040	2680

7.3 Long-run total, marginal and average costs

Faced with an upward shift in its demand and marginal revenue curves, a firm will expand output, as we explained in Chapter 6. However, adjustment takes time. Initially, the firm can get its existing workforce to do overtime. In the long run, the firm can vary its factory size, switch techniques of production, hire new workers and negotiate new contracts with suppliers of raw materials.

The firm may be able to alter the shift length at once. Hiring or firing workers takes longer and it might be years before a new factory is designed, built and operational. In this section we deal with long-run cost curves, when the firm can make all the adjustments it desires.

Table 7.4 shows long-run total costs *LTC* and long-run marginal costs *LMC* of making each output. Since there is always an option to close down entirely, the *LTC* of producing zero output is zero. *LTC* describes the eventual costs after all adjustments have been made.

> The **long run** is the period long enough for the firm to adjust all its inputs to a change in conditions. In the **short run** the firm can make only *partial* adjustment of its inputs to a change in conditions.

> **Long-run total cost** is the minimum cost of producing each output level when the firm can adjust all inputs. **Long-run marginal cost** is the rise in long-run total cost if output rises permanently by one unit.

Table 7.4 Long-run costs

(1) Output	(2) Total cost (£)	(3) Marginal cost (£)	(4) Average cost (£)
0	0	–	–
1	30	30	30
2	54	24	27
3	74	20	24.67
4	91	17	22.75
5	107	16	21.40
6	126	19	21.00
7	149	23	21.29
8	176	27	22.00
9	207	31	23.00
10	243	36	24.30

Table 7.4 also shows long-run marginal cost *LMC*. *LTC* must rise with output: higher output always costs more to produce. *LMC* shows how much total cost is involved in making the last unit of output.

Can large firms produce goods at a lower unit cost than small firms? Might it be a disadvantage to be large? To answer these questions, we need to think about average cost per unit of output.

Table 7.4 shows long-run average cost *LAC* (column 2 divided by column 1). These *LAC* data are plotted in Figure 7.2. Average cost starts out high, then falls, then rises again. This common pattern of average costs is called the U-shaped average cost curve. To see why the U-shaped average cost curve is common in practice we examine 'returns to scale'.

> **Long-run average cost** is the total cost *LTC* divided by the level of output Q.

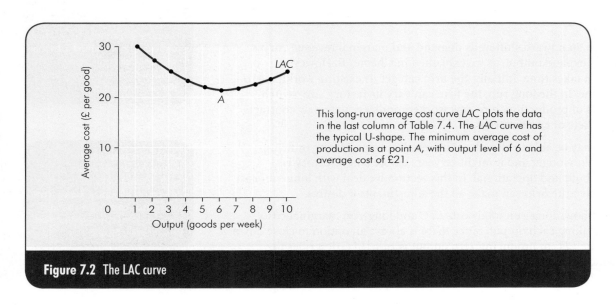

This long-run average cost curve *LAC* plots the data in the last column of Table 7.4. The *LAC* curve has the typical U-shape. The minimum average cost of production is at point A, with output level of 6 and average cost of £21.

Figure 7.2 The LAC curve

7.4 Returns to scale

Scale refers to the output of the firm. The three cases are shown in Figure 7.3.

In Figure 7.2 the U-shaped average cost curve had scale economies up to point *A*, where average cost was lowest. At higher outputs there were diseconomies of scale. Why are there scale economies at low output levels but diseconomies of scale at high output levels?

We draw a cost curve for given input prices. Changes in average costs as we move along the *LAC* curve cannot be explained by changes in factor prices. (Changes in factor prices *shift* cost curves.) The relationship between average costs and the output *LAC* curve depends on the technical relation between physical quantities of inputs and output, summarized in the production function.

> **Economies of scale** (or **increasing returns to scale**) mean long-run average cost falls as output rises. **Diseconomies of scale** (or **decreasing returns to scale**) mean long-run average cost rises as output rises. **Constant returns to scale** mean long-run average costs are constant as output rises.

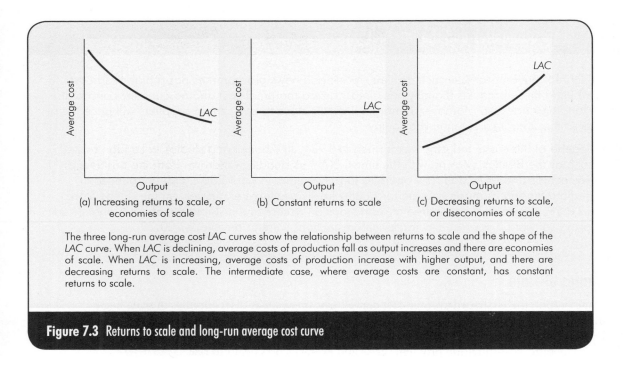

The three long-run average cost *LAC* curves show the relationship between returns to scale and the shape of the *LAC* curve. When *LAC* is declining, average costs of production fall as output increases and there are economies of scale. When *LAC* is increasing, average costs of production increase with higher output, and there are decreasing returns to scale. The intermediate case, where average costs are constant, has constant returns to scale.

Figure 7.3 Returns to scale and long-run average cost curve

Economies of scale

There are three reasons for economies of scale. The first is *indivisibilities* in the production process, a minimum quantity of inputs required by the firm to be in business at all whether or not output is produced. These are sometimes called *fixed costs*, because they do not vary with the output level. To be in business a firm requires a manager, a telephone, an accountant and a market research survey. The firm cannot have half a manager and half a telephone merely because it wishes to operate at low output levels.

Beginning from small output levels, these costs do not initially increase with output. The manager can organize three workers as easily as two. As yet there is no need for a second telephone. There are economies of scale because these fixed costs can be spread over more units of output as output is increased, reducing average cost per unit of output. However, as the firm expands further, it has to hire more managers and telephones and these economies of scale die away. The average cost curve stops falling.

The second reason for economies of scale is *specialization*. A sole trader must undertake all the different tasks of the business. As the firm expands and takes on more workers, each worker can concentrate on a single task and handle it more efficiently.

The third reason for economies of scale is closely related. Large scale is often needed to take advantage of better machinery. No matter how productive a robot assembly line is, it is pointless to install one to make five cars a week. Average costs would be enormous. However, at high output levels the machinery cost can be spread over a large number of units of output and this production technique may produce so many cars that average costs are low.

Box 7.1 Scale economies and the internet

Producing information products such as films, music and news programmes has a high fixed cost, but distributing these products digitally has almost a zero marginal cost and no capacity constraint. Scale economies are vast. Moreover, if marginal cost is close to zero, smart suppliers will price their products so that marginal revenue is also tiny.

EMI, a legend of the music industry, was formed in 1931. Its Abbey Road studios in London hosted giants such as the Beatles. Moving with the times, EMI has steadily withdrawn from the business of supplying records and CDs, and now operates largely online. In April 2007, EMI announced it would begin releasing its music as superior-quality tracks available exclusively on the iTunes Store. Costing £0.99, the tracks were be free of restrictions on access and distribution, and no longer had anti-copying software. Lower-quality tracks with restrictions were to be sold for £0.79.

Diseconomies of scale

Beyond some output, the U-shaped average cost curve turns up again as diseconomies of scale begin. Management is harder as the firm gets larger: there are *managerial diseconomies of scale*. Large companies need many layers of management, themselves needing to be managed. The company becomes bureaucratic, co-ordination problems arise and average costs begin to rise.

Geography may also explain diseconomies of scale. If the first factory is located in the best site, to minimize the cost of transporting goods to the market, the site of a second factory must be less advantageous. To take a different example, in extracting coal from a mine, a firm will extract the easiest coal first. To increase output, deeper coal seams have to be worked and these will be more expensive.

As output increases, the shape of the average cost curve thus depends on two things: how long economies of scale persist and how quickly the diseconomies of scale set in. The balance of these two forces varies from industry to industry and firm to firm.

Returns to scale in practice

To gather evidence on returns to scale we can talk to design engineers to see how production costs vary with output. It is much harder to quantify managerial diseconomies. Most empirical research focuses only on direct production costs. Because it ignores managerial diseconomies of scale, it overestimates scale economies.

Many such studies of manufacturing industry confirm that scale economies continue over a wide range of output.[2] The long-run average cost curve slopes down, albeit at an ever-decreasing rate. Economists have tried to measure the output at which all scale economies are first achieved: the point at which the average cost curve first becomes horizontal.

Table 7.5 contains some traditional estimates of the minimum efficient scale (*MES*) for firms in different industries in the UK and the US. The first column gives an idea of how steeply average costs fall before minimum efficient scale is reached. It shows how much average costs are higher if output is 1/3 the output of minimum efficient scale. The second and third columns show the *MES* output relative to the output of the industry as a whole. This provides a benchmark for the importance of economies of scale to firms in each industry. Since firms in the UK and the US essentially have access to the same technical

Minimum efficient scale (MES) is the lowest output at which the *LAC* curve reaches its minimum.

2 See F. M. Scherer and D. Ross, *Industrial Market Sstructure and Economic Performance* (3rd edn), Houghton Mifflin, 1990.

Table 7.5 Minimum efficient scale, selected industries, UK and USA

Industry	% increase in *LAC* at 1/3 *MES*	MES as % of market in	
		UK	USA
Cement	26	6	2
Steel	11	15	3
Glass bottles	11	9	2
Bearings	8	4	1
Fabrics	7	2	1
Refrigerators	6	83	14
Petroleum	5	12	2
Paints	4	10	1
Cigarettes	2	30	6
Shoes	2	1	1

Source: F. M. Scherer *et al.*, *The Economics of Multiplant Operation*, Harvard University Press, 1975, tables 3.11 and 3.15.

know-how, differences between the second and third columns primarily reflect differences in the size of the industry in the two countries rather than differences in the *MES* output level for an individual firm.

Scale economies in manufacturing industries are substantial. At low outputs, average costs are much higher than at minimum efficient scale. We would expect similar effects in aircraft and motor car manufacture, which have huge fixed costs for research and development of new models and which can utilize highly automated assembly lines once output is large. Yet in a large country such as the US, minimum efficient scale for an individual firm occurs at an output that is small relative to the industry as a whole. Most firms are producing on a relatively flat part of their average cost curve with few scale economies unexploited. In smaller countries such as the UK, the point of minimum efficient scale is larger relative to the industry as a whole.

However, Table 7.5 suggests that there are many industries, even in the manufacturing sector, where minimum efficient scale for a firm is small relative to the whole market and average costs are only a little higher if output is below minimum efficient scale. These firms will be producing in an output range where the *LAC* curve is almost horizontal.

Finally, there are many firms, especially outside the manufacturing sector, whose cost conditions are well represented by a U-shaped average cost curve. With only limited opportunities for economies of scale, these firms run into rising average costs even at quite moderate levels of output. Many service sector industries – hairdressers, doctors, decorators – have very modest scope for scale economies.

Globalization, technical change and scale economies

We described the estimates in Table 7.5 as 'traditional' rather than 'modern'. The data are more than a decade old. Some things have changed since then. Technical progress in transport has reduced the cost of shipping goods over vast distances. Technical progress in information technology has made it much easier to manage companies with global activities. Computers at courier companies such as Federal Express and DHL can track packages across the world. In 2001 the global activities of FedEx were temporarily halted not by a pilots' strike but by a computer virus.

Box 7.2 All drugged up

The appetite for mergers among the world's big pharmaceutical companies is as insatiable as ever. But it also raises the question of how much longer this consolidation can keep going.

Pfizer bid $60 billion for Pharmacia, only shortly after completing its mega merger with Warner Lambert. Previously, in 2003, GlaxoWellcome and Smith Kline Beecham became GlaxoSmithKline, GSK. Coming together can generate significant cost savings. GSK is estimated to have generated savings of $1.8bn during the 3 years post merger, or 15 per cent of expenses. Principally, such savings come from greater exploitation of scale economies within the salesforces. The merged salesforce can be used to target broader geographic regions, with a wider array of drugs from the two merged catalogues.

However, sales teams are growing faster than the number of doctors who prescribe drugs, with salespeople expecting no more than 60 seconds of time with a doctor. The challenge for pharmaceutical companies is how to generate value in the future. A growing trend is to downsize the company and focus on high value lines such as biotechnology. GSK has split its research into six key areas, all competing for research and development funds. Financially successful units are likely to be spun out – sold into the corporate marketplace, as small focused pharma companies where commercial strength will rest with the products under patent and not the economies of scale in selling.

Source: Investors' Chronicle, 12 March 2004.

Globalization is partly a matter of policy – countries are abandoning restrictions to keep out foreign businesses – but it is chiefly being driven by cost changes caused by technical progress. New technology and lower transport costs not merely enhance market size, they also reduce managerial diseconomies of scale. It gets easier to run big companies. The output of minimum efficient scale is rising. Global companies like Microsoft, Shell, Nike and Nokia keep popping up successfully in more and more countries: scale economies let them undercut the domestic competition.

> **Globalization** is the increasing integration of national markets that were previously much more segmented from one another.

The second sense in which the presentation of Table 7.5 is 'traditional' is that its final column presumes that the domestic market size is the relevant market size against which to assess minimum efficient scale. That would make sense if firms produced only for the home market. Globalization is making this obsolete too. Of course, the larger the potential market, the easier it is to justify large scale, and the more firms may seeks mergers in order to achieve that scale quickly.

For example, when Barclays Bank announced in 2007 its proposed £45bn takeover of Dutch counterpart ABN Amro, it hoped to cut 12 800 jobs from the combined workforce, with another 10 800 positions likely to be transferred to lower-cost locations. The two companies would then have a joint workforce of 217 000 worldwide, including 62 400 staff who work for Barclays in the UK.

Having discussed scale economies, we begin putting flesh on the bare-bones theory of supply we developed in Chapter 6. Despite the growing importance of scale economies, we begin by discussing the output decision of a firm with a U-shaped average cost curve. Then we show how this analysis must be amended when firms face significant economies of scale.

7.5 Average cost and marginal cost

Table 7.4 showed long-run marginal cost *LMC* and long-run average cost *LAC*. We now want to connect these two cost measures, whose behaviour is closely related.

The last two columns of Table 7.4 are plotted in Figure 7.4. At each output, *LAC* is total cost divided by output. To stress that marginal cost is incurred by moving from one output level to another, we plot *LMC* at points halfway between the corresponding outputs. The *LMC* of £30 for the first output unit is plotted at the output halfway between 0 and 1.

Two facts stand out from the table and diagram.

1 *LAC* is falling when *LMC* is less than *LAC*, rising when *LMC* is greater than *LAC*.
2 *LAC* is at a minimum at the output at which *LAC* and *LMC* cross.

Neither fact is an accident. The relation between average and marginal is a matter of arithmetic, as relevant for football as for production costs. A footballer with 3 goals in 3 games averages 1 goal a game. Two goals in the next game, implying 5 goals from 4 games, raise the average to 1.25 goals a game. In the fourth game the marginal goals were 2, raising total goals from 3 to 5. Because the marginal score exceeds the average score in previous games, the extra game must drag up the average.

The same holds for production costs. When the marginal cost of the next unit exceeds the average cost of the existing units, making the next unit must raise average cost. If the marginal cost of the next unit lies below the average cost of existing units, an extra unit of production drags down average costs. When marginal and average cost are equal, adding a unit leaves average cost unchanged. This explains fact 1.

Fact 2 follows from fact 1. In Figure 7.4 average and marginal cost curves cross at point *A*, which must be the point of minimum average cost. To the left of *A*, *LMC* is below *LAC* so average cost is still falling. To the right of *A*, *LMC* is above *LAC* so average cost is rising. Average cost is lowest at *A*. The marginal cost curve crosses the average cost curve from below at the point of minimum average cost. As in the football example, this rests purely on arithmetic.

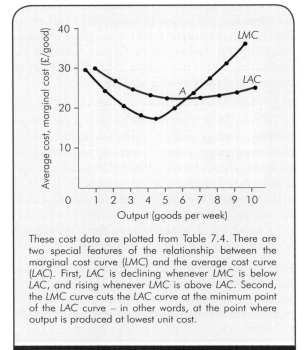

These cost data are plotted from Table 7.4. There are two special features of the relationship between the marginal cost curve (*LMC*) and the average cost curve (*LAC*). First, *LAC* is declining whenever *LMC* is below *LAC*, and rising whenever *LMC* is above *LAC*. Second, the *LMC* curve cuts the *LAC* curve at the minimum point of the *LAC* curve – in other words, at the point where output is produced at lowest unit cost.

Figure 7.4 Average and marginal cost curves

Table 7.6 summarizes this important relationship. It is true both for the relationship between *LMC* and *LAC* and for the relationship between short-run average cost (*SAC*) and short-run marginal cost (*SMC*).

Table 7.6 Marginal and average cost

	MC < AC	MC = AC	MC > AC
AC is:	Falling	Minimum	Rising

7.6 The firm's long-run output decision

Figure 7.5 shows smooth *LAC* and *LMC* curves for a firm not restricted to produce integer units of output. It also shows the marginal revenue *MR* curve. From Chapter 6 we know that the output of maximum profit, or minimum loss, is at *B*, the output at which marginal revenue equals marginal cost. The firm then checks whether it makes profits or losses at this output. It should not stay in business if it makes losses for ever.

Total profit is average profit per unit of output, multiplied by output. Total profit is positive only if average profit is positive. Average profit is average revenue minus average cost. But average revenue is simply the price for which each output unit is sold. Hence *if long-run average costs at B exceed the price for which the output Q1 is sold*, the firm makes losses in the long run and should close down. If, at this output, price equals *LAC*, the firm just breaks even. If price exceeds *LAC* at this output, the firm makes long-run profits and happily remains in business.

First we use the *marginal condition* (*LMC* = *MR*) to find the best output provided the firm stays in business. Then, we use the *average condition* (comparing *LAC* at this output with the price or average revenue received) to see if the best positive output yields a profit or a loss.

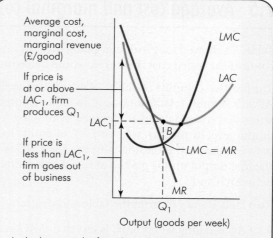

In the long run the firm chooses its output level at the point *B* where *MR* is equal to *LMC*. It has then to check whether it is making losses at that output level Q_1. If price is equal to or more than LAC_1, the long-run average cost corresponding to output Q_1, the firm is not making losses and stays in business. If the price is less than LAC_1, the firm's long-run output decision should be zero – it closes down permanently.

Figure 7.5 The firm's long-run output decision

7.7 Short-run costs and diminishing marginal returns

The short run is the period in which the firm cannot fully adjust to a change in conditions. In the short run the firm has some fixed factors of production. How long this short run lasts depends on the industry. It might take ten years to build a new power station but only a few months to open new restaurant premises if an existing building can be bought, converted and decorated.

> A **fixed factor of production** is an input that cannot be varied. A **variable factor** can be varied, even in the short run.

The existence of fixed factors in the short run has two implications. First, in the short run the firm has some fixed costs. These fixed costs must be borne even if output is zero. If the firm cannot quickly add to or dispose of its existing factory, it must still pay depreciation on the building and meet the interest cost of the money it originally borrowed to buy the factory.

> **Fixed costs** do not vary with output.

Second, because in the short run the firm cannot make all the adjustments it would like, its short-run costs must exceed its long-run costs. We now study these short-run costs in more detail.

Short-run fixed and variable costs

Table 7.7 presents data on short-run costs. The second column shows the fixed costs, which are independent of the output level. The third column shows the variable costs.

Table 7.7 Short-run costs of production

(1) Output	(2) SFC Short-run fixed cost	(3) SVC Short-run variable cost	(4) STC Short-run total cost	(5) SMC Short-run marginal cost
0	30	0	30	
1	30	22	52	22
2	30	38	68	16
3	30	48	78	10
4	30	61	91	13
5	30	79	109	18
6	30	102	132	23
7	30	131	161	29
8	30	166	196	35
9	30	207	237	41
10	30	255	285	48

Variable costs are the costs of hiring variable inputs, typically labour and raw materials. Firms may have long-term contracts with workers and material suppliers, which reduce the speed at which these inputs can be adjusted. Yet most firms retain some flexibility through overtime and short time, hiring or non-hiring of casual and part-time workers, and raw material purchases in the open market to supplement contracted supplies.

Variable costs change as output changes.

The fourth column of Table 7.7 shows short-run total costs:

Short-run total cost (*STC*) = short-run fixed cost (*SFC*) + short-run variable cost (*SVC*)   **(1)**

The final column shows short-run marginal costs *SMC*. Since fixed costs do not rise with output, *SMC* is the rise both in short-run total costs and in short-run variable costs as output is increased by 1 unit.

Whatever the output, fixed costs are £30 per week. Marginal costs are always positive. Short-run total costs rise steadily as output rises. Extra output adds to total cost, and adds more the higher the marginal cost. In the last column of Table 7.7, as output increases, marginal costs first fall then rise again. The short-run marginal cost curve has the same shape as the long-run marginal cost curve shown in Figure 7.5, but for a different reason.

In the long run the firm can vary all factors freely. As output expands, the firm enjoys some scale economies, then diseconomies of scale set in and marginal costs of further output increases start to rise again.

The short-run marginal cost curve assumes that there is at least one fixed factor, probably capital. Suppose there are two inputs in the short run: fixed capital and variable labour. To change output as we move along the short-run marginal cost curve, the firm adds ever-increasing amounts of labour to a given amount of plant and machinery. This explains the shape of the short-run marginal curve.

The marginal product of labour and diminishing marginal productivity

Table 7.8 shows how output rises as variable labour input is added to a fixed quantity of capital. With no workers, output is zero. The first worker raises output by 0.8 units. The first worker has a marginal product of 0.8 units. The third worker has a marginal product of 1.3 units, since 2 workers produce 1.8 units but 3 workers produce 3.1 units.

> The **marginal product** of a variable factor is the extra output from an extra unit of that input, holding constant all other inputs.

Table 7.8 Total and marginal products of labour

Labour input (workers)	Output (total product)	Marginal product of labour
1	0.8	0.8
2	1.8	1.0
3	3.1	1.3
4	4.3	1.2
5	5.4	1.1
6	6.3	0.9
7	7.0	0.7
8	7.5	0.5
9	7.8	0.3

At low levels of output and labour input, the first worker has a whole factory to work with; too many tasks to produce very much. A second worker helps and a third helps even more. Suppose the factory has three machines and the 3 workers are each specializing in fully running one of the factory's machines. The marginal product of the fourth worker is lower. With only three machines, the fourth worker gets to use one only when another worker is having a rest. There is even less useful machine work for the fifth worker to do. In fact, beyond 3 workers, the marginal product of each additional worker decreases steadily as the number of workers is increased. We say that there are diminishing returns to labour.

> Holding all factors constant except one, **the law of diminishing returns** says that, beyond some level of the variable input, further increases in the variable input lead to a steadily decreasing marginal product of that input.

This is a law about technology. Adding ever more workers to a fixed quantity of machinery gets less and less useful. The ninth worker's main role in production is to get coffee for the others. This contributes to output but not a great deal. Figure 7.6 summarizes our discussion of marginal productivity.

If capital was the variable factor and labour the fixed factor, adding more and more machines to a given labour force might initially lead to large increases in output but would quickly encounter diminishing returns as machines became under-utilized. Thus Figure 7.6, showing the marginal product of labour when labour is the variable factor, might also describe the behaviour of the marginal product of capital when capital is the variable factor.[3]

Marginal product is *not* the everyday meaning of 'productivity', which refers to the *average* product. The average product of labour, what is most commonly meant by 'productivity', is total output divided by total labour input. If the marginal product of labour lies above the average product, adding

3 Economists use *diminishing* returns to describe the addition of one variable factor to other fixed factors in the short run, but *decreasing* returns to describe diseconomies of scale when *all* factors are freely varied in the long run.

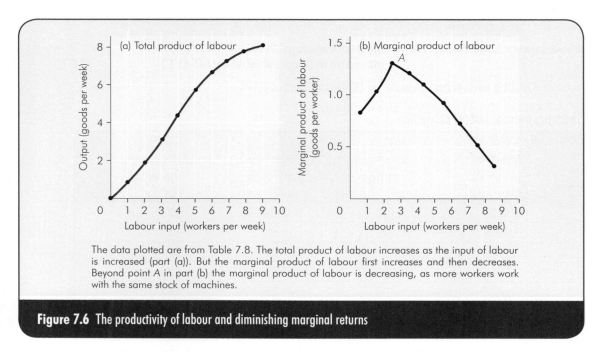

The data plotted are from Table 7.8. The total product of labour increases as the input of labour is increased (part (a)). But the marginal product of labour first increases and then decreases. Beyond point A in part (b) the marginal product of labour is decreasing, as more workers work with the same stock of machines.

Figure 7.6 The productivity of labour and diminishing marginal returns

another worker will raise the average product and 'productivity'. When diminishing returns set in, the marginal product will quickly fall below the average product and the latter will fall if further workers are added. If you do not see why this must be true, try calculating output per unit of labour input as an extra column in Table 7.8.

As usual, we must distinguish between movements along a curve and shifts in a curve. The marginal product curve is drawn for given levels of the other factors. For a higher given level of the fixed factors, the marginal product curve would be higher. With more machinery to work with, an extra worker will generally be able to produce more extra output than previously. The numbers in Table 7.8 and the height of the marginal product curve in Figure 7.6 depend on the number of fixed factors with which the firm began.

Short-run marginal costs

Table 7.7 shows that, as output is increased, short-run marginal costs first fall then rise. Every worker costs the firm the same wage. While the marginal product of labour is increasing, each worker adds more to output than the previous workers. Hence the extra cost of making extra output is falling. *SMC* is falling as long as the marginal product of labour is rising.

> **Short-run marginal cost** is the extra cost of making an extra unit of output in the short run while some inputs remain fixed.

Once diminishing returns to labour set in, the marginal product of labour falls and *SMC* starts to rise again. It takes successively more workers to make each extra unit of output. So the shape of the short-run marginal cost curve and hence the short-run total cost curve is determined by the shape of the marginal product curve in Figure 7.6, which in turn depends on the technology facing the firm.

Short-run average costs

Table 7.9 shows short-run *average* cost data corresponding to Table 7.7. Each number in Table 7.9 is obtained by dividing the corresponding number in Table 7.7 by the output level. The table also shows short-run marginal costs, taken from Table 7.7.

> **Short-run average fixed cost** (*SAFC*) equals short-run fixed cost (*SFC*) divided by output. **Short-run average variable cost** (*SAVC*) equals *SVC* divided by output and **short-run average total cost** (*SATC*) equals *STC* divided by output.

Figure 7.7 plots the three short-run average cost measures from Table 7.9.

Short-run average total cost (*SATC*) = short-run average fixed cost (*SAFC*) +
short-run average variable cost (*SAVC*)　　(2)

This follows from dividing each term in equation (1) by the output level.

Table 7.9　Short-run average costs of production

Output	SAFC Short-run average fixed cost	SAVC Short-run average variable cost	SATC Short-run average total cost	SMC Short-run marginal cost
1	30.00	22.00	52.00	22
2	15.00	19.00	34.00	16
3	10.00	16.00	26.00	10
4	7.50	15.25	22.75	13
5	6.00	15.80	21.80	18
6	5.00	17.00	22.00	23
7	4.29	18.71	23.00	29
8	3.75	20.75	24.50	35
9	3.33	23.00	26.33	41
10	3.00	25.50	28.50	48

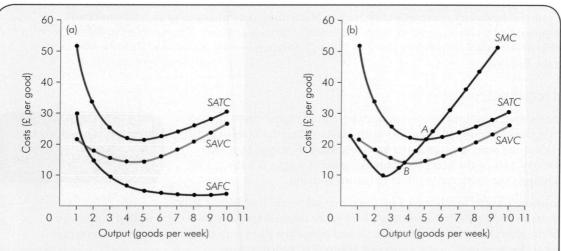

These diagrams plot the data of Table 7.9. Part (a) shows short-run average fixed, variable and total costs, *SATC* is equal to *SAFC* plus *SAVC*. The shape of the *SATC* curve is a result of the shapes of its two components. When both *SAVC* and *SAFC* are declining, so is *SATC*. When *SAVC* starts rising, the shape of *SATC* depends on whether *SAVC* is rising more rapidly than *SAFC* is falling. In part (b) the relationship between marginal and average cost curves established for the long run applies also to the short-run curves. The *SMC* curve goes through the minimum points of both the *SAVC* curve, at *B*, and the *SATC* curve, at *A*.

Figure 7.7　Short-run average cost and marginal cost curves

Look first at Figure 7.7(b). We already understand the shape of the *SMC* curve that follows from the behaviour of marginal labour productivity. The usual arithmetical relation between marginal and average explains why *SMC* passes through the lowest point *A* on the short-run average total cost curve. To the left of this point, *SMC* lies below *SATC* and is dragging it down as output expands. To the right of *A* the converse holds. That explains the shape of the *SATC* curve in Figure 7.7.

Variable cost is total cost minus fixed cost. Fixed cost does not change with output. Hence marginal cost also shows how much total *variable* cost is changing. The usual arithmetic between marginal cost and average *variable* cost must hold. Hence, *SMC* goes through the lowest point *B* on *SAVC*. To the left of *B*, *SMC* is below *SAVC* and *SAVC* is falling. To the right of *B*, *SAVC* is rising. Finally, since average total cost exceeds average variable cost by average fixed cost, *SAVC* lies below *SATC*. Point *B* must lie to the left of point *A*. That explains the shape of *SAVC* and its relation to *SATC* in Figure 7.7(b).

In Figure 7.7(a), *SAFC* falls steadily because total fixed cost ('overheads') is spread over ever larger output levels, thus reducing average fixed costs. The reasoning of Figure 7.7(b) is easily confirmed in Figure 7.7(a). Carrying over from Figure 7.7(b) the *SATC* and *SAVC* curves we can check that, at each output level, $SATC = SAVC + SAFC$, as in equation (2).

How can anyone remember all these curves and what use are they? Figure 7.1 helps. It shows the three basic costs: total, marginal and average. We have to distinguish between short run and long run, and between fixed and variable costs. These distinctions generate all the cost curves we have examined.

We make all these curves to understand a firm's output decision in the short run and in the long run. We have analysed the long-run output decision. Now we use short-run cost curves to analyse a firm's short-run output decision.

Box 7.3 The Rolls-Royce treatment

Rolls-Royce cars, once the badge of Britishness, are now made by BMW. But the Rolls-Royce aero engine business is booming and the company's market share has risen from 20 per cent to over 30 per cent within the past decade, making it the second largest aero engine manufacturer in the world. How was this success achieved? By recognizing the crucial role of scale economies.

Aircraft engines have huge costs in research and development, requiring large production runs to recover this initial investment. The company's change in strategy reflected two key insights.

First, it extended its initial investment so that its engines could service a wide range of aircraft, thereby increasing the chances of building up long-term relationships with particular aircraft manufacturers and the airlines that they supply. Second, by signing fixed-price agreements for the subsequent repair and maintenance of their engines, Rolls-Royce effectively insured the user against defective quality, thereby signalling their commitment to excellence and safety.

As a result, companies ordered Rolls-Royce engines in greater numbers and over longer time periods, creating the volume of business necessary to recoup the large costs of research and development.

Adapted from http://news.bbc.co.uk.

7.8 A firm's output decision in the short run

Figure 7.8 illustrates the firm's choice of output in the short run. Short-run marginal cost is set equal to marginal revenue to determine the output Q_1 that maximizes profits or minimizes losses.

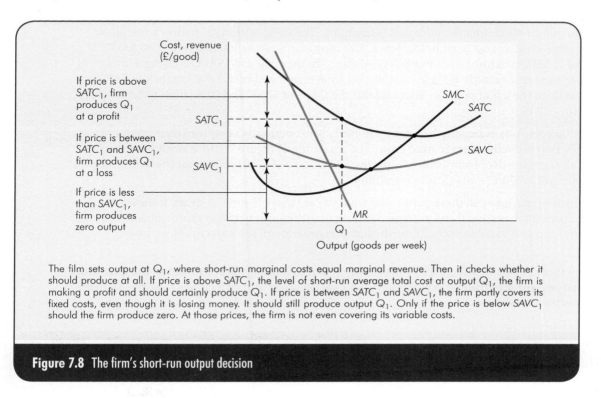

The film sets output at Q_1, where short-run marginal costs equal marginal revenue. Then it checks whether it should produce at all. If price is above $SATC_1$, the level of short-run average total cost at output Q_1, the firm is making a profit and should certainly produce Q_1. If price is between $SATC_1$ and $SAVC_1$, the firm partly covers its fixed costs, even though it is losing money. It should still produce output Q_1. Only if the price is below $SAVC_1$ should the firm produce zero. At those prices, the firm is not even covering its variable costs.

Figure 7.8 The firm's short-run output decision

Next, the firm decides whether or not to produce in the short run. Profit is positive at the output Q_1 if the price p at which this output is sold covers average total cost. It is the short-run measure $SATC_1$ at output Q_1 that is relevant. If p exceeds $SATC_1$, the firm makes profits in the short run and produces Q_1.

Suppose p is less than $SATC_1$. The firm is losing money because p does not cover costs. In the long run the firm closes down if it keeps losing money. In the short run, even at zero output the firm must pay its fixed costs. The firm needs to know whether losses are bigger if it produces at Q_1 or produces zero.

If revenue exceeds *variable cost* the firm is earning something towards its overheads. It produces Q_1 if revenue exceeds variable cost even though Q_1 may involve losses. The firm produces Q_1 if p exceeds $SAVC_1$. If not, it produces zero. Table 7.10 summarizes the short-run and long-run output decisions of a firm.

> The firm's **short-run output decision** is to supply Q_1, the output at which $MR = SMC$, if the price covers short-run average variable cost $SAVC_1$ at that output. If not, the firm supplies zero.

Table 7.10 The firm's output decisions

	Marginal condition	Check whether to produce
Short run	Choose the output at which $MR = SMC$	Produce this output if $p > SAVC$. Otherwise, produce zero.
Long run	Choose the output at which $MR = LMC$	Produce this output if $p > LAC$. Otherwise, produce zero.

Activity box 7 Marginal conditions and sunk costs

The theory of supply obeys two principles of good decision making in life. The first is the *marginal principle*. Once the best position is reached, no feasible change can improve things. To climb a hill, take small steps in an upwards direction. If you cannot move upwards, you are at the top.

There is also the big picture. Having equated marginal cost and marginal revenue, a firm checks it is not better to close down completely. Similarly, the marginal principle guides you to a local peak but looking around you may see a higher hill a mile away, but you have to go down a bit before you can scale it.

The second principle is that *sunk costs are sunk*. Costs already incurred should not affect new decisions. In choosing short-run output, the firm ignores fixed costs that are paid anyway. It is no use crying over spilt milk. Having read seven chapters of this book, should you read on? It depends on the costs and benefits you get from the rest of the book, not on the time already spent.

Questions

(a) A firm lasts for two periods and then dies. In the first period, it can choose to buy a very special piece of equipment that will be no use to any other firm and will have no resale value. It will however help the firm to make output in each of the two periods. When the second period arrives, should the cost of the machine be included in the marginal cost of the firm? In the first period, should it be included in the marginal cost of producing output? What is the smart way for the firm to think about this problem?

(b) Playing poker, you bet most of your chips on a single hand before getting a sinking feeling that you are going to lose the hand. Should you bet on? Why or why not?

To check your answers to these questions, go to page 716.

7.9 Short-run and long-run costs

Even if making losses in the short run, a firm stays in business if it covers its variable costs. In the long run it must cover all its costs to remain in business. We now discuss how a firm may reduce its costs in the long run, converting a short-run loss into a long-term profit.

Figure 7.9 shows a U-shaped *LAC* curve. At each point on the curve the firm is producing a given output at minimum cost. The *LAC* curve describes a time scale sufficiently long that the firm can vary *all* factors of production, even those that are fixed in the short run.

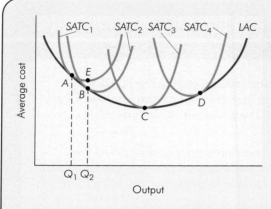

Suppose the plant size is fixed in the short run. For each plant size we obtain a particular SATC curve. But in the long run even plant size is variable. To construct the LAC curve we select at each output the plant size which gives the lowest SATC at this output. Thus points such as A, B, C and D lie on the LAC curve. Notice the LAC curve does not pass through the lowest point on each SATC curve. Thus the LAC curve shows the minimum average cost way to produce a given output when all factors can be varied, not the minimum average cost at which a given plant can produce.

Figure 7.9 The long-run average cost curve *LAC*

Suppose, for convenience, that 'plant' is the fixed factor in the short run. Each point on the *LAC* curve involves a particular quantity of plant. Holding constant this quantity of plant, we can draw the short-run average total cost curve for this plant size. $SATC_1$ corresponds to the plant size at point *A* on the *LAC* curve, and the $SATC_2$ and $SATC_3$ curves correspond to the plant size at points *B* and *C* on the *LAC* curve. In fact, we could draw an *SATC* curve corresponding to the plant size at each point on the *LAC* curve.

By definition, the *LAC* curve shows the least-cost way to make each output when all factors can be varied. *B* is the least-cost way to make an output Q_2. It *must* be more costly to make Q_2 using the wrong quantity of plant, the quantity corresponding to point *E*. For the plant size at *A*, $SATC_1$ shows the cost of producing each output including Q_2. Hence $SATC_1$ must lie above *LAC* at every point except *A*, the output level for which this plant size is best.

This argument can be repeated for other plant sizes. Hence $SATC_3$ and $SATC_4$, reflecting plant sizes at *C* and at *D*, must lie above *LAC* except at points *C* and *D* themselves. In the long run the firm can vary all its factors and can generally produce a particular output more cheaply than in the short run, when it is stuck with the quantities of fixed factors it was using previously. A firm currently suffering losses because demand has fallen may make future profits once it has had time to build a plant more suitable to its new output.

Summary

- This chapter discusses short-run and long-run decisions, based on the corresponding cost curves. In the **long run**, a firm can fully adjust all its inputs. In the **short run**, some inputs are fixed. The length of the short run varies from industry to industry.

- The **production function** shows the maximum output that can be produced using given quantities of inputs. The inputs are machines, raw materials, labour and any other factors of production. The production function summarizes the technical possibilities faced by a firm.

- The **total cost curve** is derived from the production function, for given wages and rental rates of factors of production. The **long-run total cost curve** is obtained by finding, for each output, the least-cost method of production when all inputs can be varied. If the relative price of using a factor of production rises, the firm substitutes away from that factor in its choice of production techniques.

- **Average cost** is total cost divided by output. The **long-run average cost curve (LAC)** is derived from the long-run total cost curve.

- *LAC* **is typically U-shaped**. As output rises, at first average costs fall because of indivisibilities in production, the benefit of specialization and engineering advantages of large scale. There are increasing returns to scale on the falling part of the U. The rising part of the U reflects diseconomies of scale.

- Much of manufacturing has **economies of scale**. For some industries, particularly personal services, economies of scale run out at quite low output levels.

- When **marginal cost** is below average cost, average cost is falling. When marginal cost is above average cost, average cost is rising. Average and marginal cost are equal only at the lowest point on the average cost curve.

- In the long run the firm supplies the output at which **long-run marginal cost (LMC)** equals *MR* provided price is not less than the level of long-run average cost at that level of output. If price is less than long-run average cost, the firm goes out of business.

- In the short run the firm cannot adjust some of its inputs. But it still has to pay for them. It has short-run fixed costs (*SFC*) of production. The cost of using the variable factors is short-run variable cost (*SVC*). Short-run total costs (*STC*) are equal to *SFC* plus *SVC*.

- The **short-run marginal cost curve (SMC)** reflects the marginal product of the variable factor holding other factors fixed. Usually we think of labour as variable but capital as fixed in the short run. When very little labour is used, the plant is too big for labour to produce much. Increasing labour input leads to large rises in output and *SMC* falls. Once machinery is fully manned, extra workers add progressively less to output. *SMC* begins to rise.

- Short-run average total costs (*SATC*) are equal to short-run total costs (*STC*) divided by output. *SATC* **is equal to short-run average fixed costs (SAFC) plus short-run average variable costs (SAVC)**. The *SATC* curve is U-shaped. The falling part of the U results both from declining *SAFC* as the fixed costs are spread over more units of output and from declining *SAVC* at low levels of output. The *SATC* continues to fall after *SAVC* begins to increase, but eventually increasing *SAVC* outweighs declining *SAFC* and the *SATC* curve slopes up.

- The *SMC* curve cuts both the *SATC* and *SAVC* curves at their minimum points.

- In the short run the firm supplies the output at which *SMC* is equal to *MR*, provided price is not less than short-run average variable cost. In the short run the firm is willing to produce at a loss provided it is recovering at least part of its fixed costs.

- The *LAC* curve is always below the *SATC* curve, except at the point where the two coincide. This implies that a firm is certain to have higher profits in the long run than in the short run if it is currently producing with a plant size that is not best from the viewpoint of the long run.

Review questions

To check your answers to these questions, go to page 716.

1 (a) What information does the production function provide? (b) Explain why the production function does not provide enough information for anyone actually to run a firm.

2 (a) What are economies of scale and why might they exist? (b) The table shows how output changes as inputs change. The wage rate is £5 and the rental rate of capital is £2. Calculate the lowest-cost method of making 4, 8 and 12 units of output. (c) Are there increasing, constant or decreasing returns to scale between those outputs? Which applies where?

Capital input	4	2	7	4	11	8
Labour input	5	6	10	12	15	16
Output	4	4	8	8	12	12

3 (a) For each output in the above table, say which technique is more capital intensive. (b) Does the firm switch towards or away from more capital-intensive techniques as output rises?

4 Suppose the rental rate of capital in Question 2 rose to £3. (a) Would the firm change its method of production for any levels of output? Say which, if any. (b) How do the firm's total and average costs change when the rental rate of capital rises?

5 (a) Calculate the marginal and average costs for each level of output from the following total cost data. (b) Show how marginal and average costs are related. (c) Are these short-run or long-run cost curves? Explain how you can tell.

Output	0	1	2	3	4	5	6	7	8	9
TC (£)	12	27	40	51	60	70	80	91	104	120

6 (a) Explain why it might make sense for a firm to produce goods that it can only sell at a loss. (b) Can it keep on doing this for ever? Explain.

7 **Common fallacies** Why are these statements wrong? (a) Firms making losses should quit at once. (b) Big firms can always produce more cheaply than smaller firms. (c) Small is always beautiful.

8 **Harder question** The 'big 3' car makers used to be Ford, General Motors (GM) and Chrysler. Now they are Toyota, Nissan and Honda. In 2007 Ford, GM and Chrysler announced record losses (again). Why do they remain in the industry? Who is financing their losses? What would you need to believe to be prepared to lend these companies more money at this point?

9 **Harder question** The marginal cost of supplying another unit of output of an electronic product on the internet is almost zero. If long run equilibrium has price equals marginal cost, internet firms will all go broke. Can you resolve the puzzle?

10 **Essay question** We choose between couriers such as DHL and Federal Express based on the quality, convenience and reliability of service that they offer, not just on the price that they quote. Once we recognize that service matters, the inevitability of scale economies is greatly reduced. Even Amazon have got to organize the distribution of the products that they sell. Do you agree?

Learning Centre

To help you grasp the key concepts of this chapter check out the extra resources posted on the Online Learning Centre. There are chapter summaries, self-test questions, an interactive graphing tool, weblinks and a searchable glossary, all for free!

To put your learning into practice and prepare for exams, an **Interactive Workbook** is also available online, containing a variety of question types and providing feedback on your answers.

If you'd like further help with economics, or have any questions, **NetTutor** is here to help! You will have a personalised tutorial service at your fingertips. Visit the online learning centre at: www.mcgraw-hill.co.uk/textbooks/begg for information on accessing all of these resources.

Perfect competition and pure monopoly

An industry is the set of all firms making the same product. The output of an industry is the sum of the outputs of its firms. Yet different industries have very different numbers of firms. Eurostar is the only supplier of train journeys from London to Paris. In contrast, the UK has 150 000 farms and 20 000 grocers.

Why do some industries have many firms but others only one? Chapter 9 develops a general theory of market structure, showing how demand and cost conditions together determine the number of firms and their behaviour.

First it is useful to establish two benchmark cases, extremes between which all other types of market structure must lie. These limiting cases are *perfect competition* and *monopoly*.

We focus on how the number of sellers affects the behaviour of sellers. Buyers are in the background. We simply assume there are many buyers whose individual downward-sloping demand curves can be aggregated into the market demand curve. Thus, we assume that the demand side of the market is competitive but contrast the different cases on the supply side.

> In a **perfectly competitive** market, both buyers and sellers believe that their own actions have no effect on the market price. In contrast, a **monopolist**, the only seller or potential seller in the industry, sets the price.

Perfect competition means that each firm or household, recognizing that its quantities supplied or demanded are trivial relative to the whole market, assumes its actions have no effect on the market price. This assumption was built into our model of consumer choice in Chapter 5. Each consumer's budget line took market prices as given, unaffected by the quantities then chosen. Changes in *market* conditions, applying to all firms and consumers, change the equilibrium price and hence individual quantities demanded, but each consumer neglects any feedback from his own actions to market price.

This concept of competition, which we now extend to firms and supply, differs from everyday usage. Ford and VW are fighting each other vigorously for the European car market but an economist would not call them perfectly competitive. Each has such a big share of the market that changes in its quantity supplied affect the market price. VW and Ford each take account of this in deciding how much to supply. They are not *price-takers*. Only under perfect competition can individuals make decisions that treat the price as independent of their own actions.

8.1 Perfect competition

If an individual's action doesn't affect the price, a perfectly competitive industry must have many buyers and many sellers. Each firm in a perfectly competitive industry faces a horizontal demand curve as in Figure 8.1. However much the firm sells, it gets the market price. If it charges a price above P_0 it won't sell any output: buyers will go to other firms whose product is just as good. Since the firm can sell as much as it wants at P_0, it won't charge less than P_0. The individual firm's demand curve is *DD*.

A *horizontal* demand curve, along which the price is fixed, is the key feature of a perfectly competitive firm. To be a plausible description of the demand curve facing the firm, the industry must have four attributes. First, there must be many firms, each trivial relative to the entire industry. Second, the product must be standardized. Even if the car industry had many firms it would not be a competitive industry. A Ford Mondeo is not a perfect substitute for a Vauxhall Vectra. The more imperfect they are as substitutes, the more it makes sense to view Ford as the sole supplier of Mondeos and Vauxhall as the sole supplier of Vectras. Each producer ceases to be trivial relative to the relevant market and cannot act as a price-taker. In a perfectly competitive industry, all firms must be making the same product, *for which they all charge the same price.*

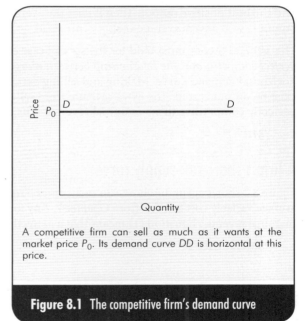

A competitive firm can sell as much as it wants at the market price P_0. Its demand curve *DD* is horizontal at this price.

Figure 8.1 The competitive firm's demand curve

Even if all firms in an industry made *homogeneous* or identical goods, each firm may have some discretion over the price it charges if buyers have imperfect information about the quality or characteristics of products. To rule this out in a competitive industry, we must assume that buyers have almost perfect information about the products being sold. They know the products of different firms in a competitive industry really are identical.

Why don't all the firms in the industry do what OPEC did in 1973–74, collectively restricting supply, to increase the price of their output by moving the industry up its market demand curve (see pages 4–5)?

The fourth crucial characteristic of a perfectly competitive industry is *free entry and exit*. Even if existing firms could organize themselves to restrict total supply and drive up the market price, the consequent rise in revenues and profits would simply attract new firms into the industry, thereby increasing total supply again and driving the price back down.

Conversely, as we shall shortly see, when firms in a competitive industry are losing money, some firms will close down and, by reducing the number of firms remaining in the industry, reduce the total supply and drive the price up, thereby allowing the remaining firms to survive.

To sum up, each firm in a competitive industry faces a horizontal demand curve at the going market price. To be a plausible description of the demand conditions facing a firm, the industry must have: (1) many firms, each trivial relative to the industry; (2) a homogeneous product, so that buyers would switch between firms if their prices differed; (3) perfect customer information about product quality, so that buyers know that the products of different firms really are the same; and (4) free entry and exit, to remove any incentive for existing firms to collude.

8.2 A perfectly competitive firm's supply decision

Chapter 7 developed a general theory of supply. The firm uses the marginal condition ($MC = MR$) to find the best positive output. Then it uses the average condition to check if the price for which this output is sold covers average cost.

This general theory must hold for the special case of perfectly competitive firms. *The special feature of perfect competition is the relationship between marginal revenue and price.* A competitive firm faces a horizontal demand curve. Making and selling extra output does *not* bid down the price for which existing output is sold. The extra revenue from selling an extra unit is simply the price received. A perfectly competitive firm's marginal revenue *is* its output price

$$MR = P \qquad \text{(1)}$$

A firm's short-run supply curve

Figure 8.2 shows again the short-run cost curves – marginal cost *SMC*, average total cost *SATC* and average variable cost *SAVC* – from Chapter 7. Any firm chooses the output at which marginal cost equals marginal revenue. Equation (1) means that a perfectly competitive firm chooses the output at which

$$SMC = MR = P \qquad \text{(2)}$$

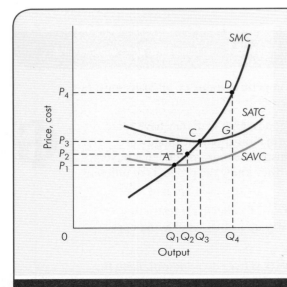

The perfectly competitive firm produces at that level of output at which price is equal to marginal cost, provided it makes more profit by producing some output than none at all. The firm's short-run supply curve is the *SMC* curve above the point *A*, the shutdown point below which the firm cannot cover average variable costs *SAVC* in the short run.

Figure 8.2 Short-run supply decisions of the perfectly competitive firm

Suppose the firm faces a horizontal demand curve at the price P_4 in Figure 8.2. From equation (2) the firm chooses the output Q_4 to reach point D, at which price equals marginal cost.

Next, the firm checks whether it would rather shut down in the short run. It shuts down if the price P_4 fails to cover short-run variable cost at this output. In Figure 8.2 P_4 exceeds $SAVC$ at the output Q_4. The firm supplies Q_4 and makes profits. Point D lies above point G, the short-run average total cost (including overheads) of producing Q_4. Hence profits are the rectangle obtained by multiplying the vertical distance DG (average profit per unit produced) by the horizontal distance OQ_4 (number of units produced).

> The **short-run supply curve** is the SMC curve above point A, at which the SMC curve crosses the lowest point on the $SAVC$ curve.

In the short run, the firm supplies positive output for any price above P_1. At a price P_2, the firm makes Q_2, the output at which price equals marginal cost. Any price below P_1 is below the minimum point on the $SAVC$ curve. The firm cannot find an output at which price covers $SAVC$. Between points A and C the firm is making short-run losses but recouping some of its overheads. At any price above P_3, at which the SMC curve crosses the lowest point on the $SATC$ curve, the firm is making short-run profits.

> The price P_1 is the **shutdown price**, below which the firm cuts its losses by making no output.

Remember that these are economic or supernormal profits after allowing for the economic costs, including the opportunity costs of the owners' financial capital and work effort, summarized in the $SAVC$ and $SATC$ curves.

A firm's long-run supply curve

Figure 8.3 shows the firm's average and marginal costs in the long run. The long-run marginal cost curve LMC is flatter than the SMC curve since the firm can adjust all inputs in the long run.

> A firm's **long-run supply curve**, relating output supplied to price in the long run, is that part of its LMC curve above its LAC curve.

Facing a price P_4, the firm chooses the long-run output Q_4 at point D, then checks if it is better to shut down than to produce this output. In the long run, shutting down means leaving the industry altogether. The firm exits

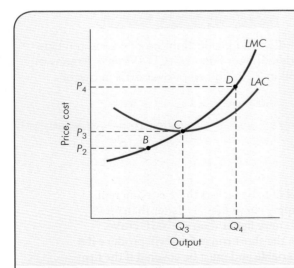

The perfectly competitive firm produces at that level of output at which P is equal to marginal cost, provided it makes more profit by producing some output than none at all. It therefore chooses points on the LMC curve. At any price above P_3 the firm makes profits because price is above long-run average cost (LAC). At any price below P_3, such as P_2, the firm makes losses because price is below long-run average cost. It therefore will not produce any output at prices below P_3. The long-run supply curve is the LMC curve above point C.

Figure 8.3 Long-run supply decisions of the perfectly competitive firm

the industry if price fails to cover long-run average cost *LAC* at the best positive output. At the price P_2, the best positive output is at point *B* in Figure 8.3 but the firm makes a loss and should exit the industry in the long run. At any price below P_3 the firm exits the industry. At the price P_3, the firm produces Q_3 and just breaks even after paying all its economic costs. It makes only normal profits.

> When economic profits are zero the firm makes **normal profits**. Its accounting profits just cover the opportunity cost of the owner's money and time.

Entry and exit

The price P_3 corresponding to the lowest point on the *LAC* curve in Figure 8.3 is the *entry or exit price*. Firms make only normal profits. There is no incentive to enter or leave the industry. The resources tied up in the firm are earning just as much as their opportunity costs, what they could earn elsewhere. Any price below P_3 induces the firm to exit the industry in the long run. P_3 is the minimum price required to keep the firm in the industry.

> **Entry** is when new firms join an industry. **Exit** is when existing firms leave.

We can also interpret Figure 8.3 as the decision facing a potential entrant to the industry. The cost curves now describe the post-entry costs. P_3 is the price at which entry becomes attractive. Any price above P_3 yields supernormal profits and encourages entry of new firms.

Box 8.1 Flat out

Prices of liquid crystal display (LCD) flat screen TVs have been tumbling, partly because the producers, the Dutch group Philips and South Korean manufacturer LG, have been scaling up. The new thin-film transistor (TFT) screens will boost them further. The Philips–LG joint venture LG Philips saw sales rise 45% in the year to June 2007. Industry leader Samsung shares the optimism.

Unlocking scale economies at a rapid speed is not an easy business. In 2004–05, a huge investment in new factories led to oversupply, causing top firms to take a breather in 2006, before investing again in 2007. Matching supply and demand during this bumpy ride is never easy. Investment bank Merrill Lynch forecast that supply in the flat screen industry will rise by 46% in 2007 and 33% in 2008, while demand will increase by a little more, taking up the temporary slack that appeared in 2006.

Scale economies, continuing technical improvements, and unsold production are of course a recipe for price cuts, which themselves help boost the quantity demanded. Sales of LCD TVs with screens of 32 inches or more will jump from 31 million to 55 million in 2007, a rise of over 80% in a year.

Adapted from *Newsweek*, 11 July 2007.

Supply decisions of a competitive firm

Figure 8.4 summarizes the preceding discussion. For each level of fixed factors there is a different *SMC* curve and short-run supply curve *SRSS*. The long-run supply curve *LRSS* is flatter than *SRSS* because extra factor flexibility in the long run makes the *LMC* curve flatter than the *SMC* curve. The *SRSS* curve starts from a lower shutdown price because, in the short run, a firm will produce if it can cover average variable costs. In the long run all costs are variable and must be covered if the firm is to stay in the industry. In either case, a competitive firm's supply curve is the part of its marginal cost curve above the point at which it is better to make no output at all. Table 8.1 sets out this principle.

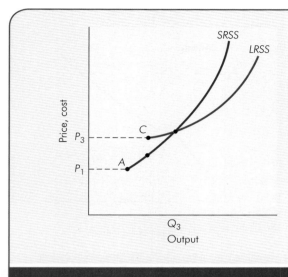

Taken from the two previous figures, the short-run supply curve SRSS is the firm's SMC curve above A and the long-run supply curve LRSS is the firm's LMC curve above C. P_1 is the shutdown price in the short run and P_3 the entry and exit price in the long run. If the firm happens to begin with the stock of fixed factors it would choose at the lowest point on its LAC curve, then C will actually lie on the SRSS curve.

Figure 8.4 Short- and long-run supply curves of the competitive firm

Table 8.1 Supply decisions of a perfectly competitive firm

Marginal condition	Average condition	
	Short-run	**Long-run**
Produce output where $P = MC$	If $P < SAVC$ shut down temporarily	If $P < LAC$ exit industry

8.3 Industry supply curves

A competitive industry comprises many firms. In the short run two things are fixed: the quantity of fixed factors used by each firm and the number of firms in the industry. In the long run, each firm can vary all its factors of production but the number of firms can also change through entry and exit from the industry.

The short-run industry supply curve

Figure 8.5 adds individual supply curves of firms to get the industry supply curve. At each price, we add the quantities supplied by each firm to get the total quantity supplied at that price.

In the short run, the number of firms in the industry is given. Suppose there are two firms, A and B. Each firm's short-run supply curve is the part of its SMC curve above its shutdown price. In Figure 8.5, firm A has a lower shutdown price than firm B. Firm A has a lower SAVC curve. It may have a better location or better technical know-how. Each firm's supply curve is horizontal at the shutdown price. At a lower price, no output is supplied.

At each price, the industry supply Q is the sum of Q^A, the supply of firm A, and Q^B, the supply of firm B. Thus if P_3 is the price, $Q_3 = Q_3^A + Q_3^B$. The industry supply curve is the horizontal sum of the separate supply curves. The industry supply curve is discontinuous at the price P_2. Between P_1 and P_2 only the lower-cost firm A is producing. At P_2 firm B starts to produce as well.

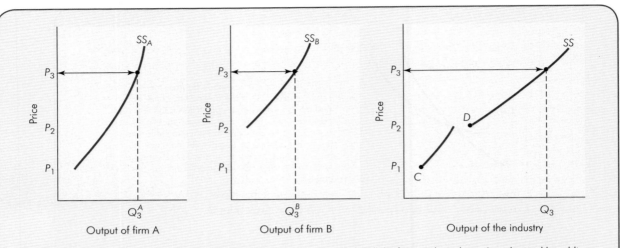

The industry supply curve SS shows the total quantity supplied at each price by all the firms in the industry. It is obtained by adding at each price the quantity supplied by each firm in the industry. With only two firms, A and B, the figure shows how, at a price such as P_3, we add Q_3^A and Q_3^B to obtain Q_3 on the industry supply curve. Since firms can have different shutdown prices or entry and exit prices, the industry supply curve can have step jumps at points such as C and D where an extra firm starts production. However, with many firms in the industry, each trivial relative to the industry as a whole, the step jumps in the industry supply curve when another starts production are so small that we can effectively think of the upward-sloping industry supply curve as smooth.

Figure 8.5 Deriving the industry supply curve

With many firms, each with a different shutdown price, there are many tiny discontinuities as we move up the industry supply curve. Since each firm in a competitive industry is trivial relative to the total, the industry supply curve is effectively smooth.

Comparing short-run and long-run industry supply curves

Figure 8.5 may also be used to derive the long-run industry supply curve. For each firm the individual supply curve is the part of its *LMC* curve above its entry and exit price. Unlike the short run, the number of firms in the industry is no longer fixed. Existing firms can leave the industry and new firms can enter. Instead of horizontally aggregating at each price the quantities supplied by the existing firms in the industry, we must horizontally aggregate the quantities supplied by existing firms *and firms that might potentially enter the industry.*

At a price below P_2 in Figure 8.5 firm B is not in the industry in the long run. At prices above P_2 firm B is in the industry. As the market price rises, total industry supply rises in the long run not just because each existing firm moves up its long-run supply curve but also because new firms join the industry.

Conversely, at low prices, high-cost firms lose money and leave the industry. Entry and exit in the long run are analogous to shutdown in the short run. In the long run, entry and exit affect the number of producing firms whose output is horizontally aggregated to get the industry supply. In the short run, the number of firms in the industry is given but some are producing while others are temporarily shut down. Again, the industry supply curve is the horizontal sum of those outputs produced at the given market price.

The long-run supply curve is flatter than its short-run counterpart. Each firm can vary its factors more appropriately in the long run and has a flatter supply curve. Moreover, higher prices attract extra firms into the industry. Industry output rises by more than the extra output supplied by the firms already in the industry.

Conversely, if the price falls, firms initially move down their (relatively steep) short-run supply curves. If short-run average variable costs are covered, firms may not reduce output very much. In the long run each firm reduces output further since all factors of production can now be varied. In addition some firms exit the industry since they are no longer covering long-run average costs. A price cut reduces industry output by more in the long run than in the short run.

The marginal firm

Suppose there are many firms, each making the same product for sale at the same price but having slightly different cost curves. Figure 8.6 shows cost curves for a low-cost firm A and a high-cost firm B. Some firms have costs lying between those of A and B, others have even higher costs than B.

> The **marginal firm** in an industry just breaks even.

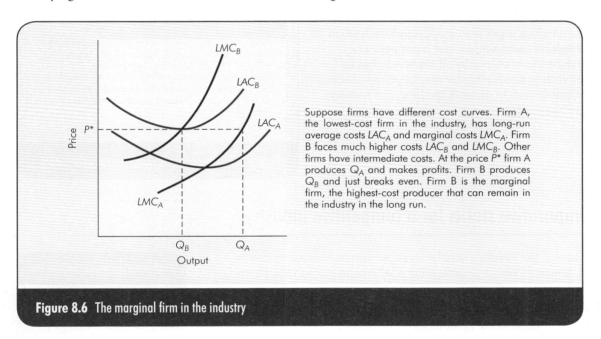

Suppose firms have different cost curves. Firm A, the lowest-cost firm in the industry, has long-run average costs LAC_A and marginal costs LMC_A. Firm B faces much higher costs LAC_B and LMC_B. Other firms have intermediate costs. At the price P^* firm A produces Q_A and makes profits. Firm B produces Q_B and just breaks even. Firm B is the marginal firm, the highest-cost producer that can remain in the industry in the long run.

Figure 8.6 The marginal firm in the industry

The long run is the period in which adjustment – both inputs and number of firms – is complete. There is no more entry and exit. Suppose the long-run price is P^* in Figure 8.6. The low-cost firm A makes Q_A and earns profits, since P^* exceeds LAC at the output Q_A. Slightly higher-cost firms are making slightly less profit. Firm B is the last firm that can survive in the industry.

All firms with higher costs than firm B cannot compete in the industry at a long-run price P^*. If a potential entrant has an LAC curve whose lowest point is only slightly above P^*, it is the marginal firm waiting to enter the industry. If anything makes P^* rise a little, this marginal firm can enter.

A horizontal long-run industry supply curve

Each firm has a rising LMC curve and thus a rising long-run supply curve. The industry supply curve is a bit flatter. Higher prices do not merely induce existing firms to produce more but also induce new firms to enter. In the extreme case, the industry long-run supply curve is horizontal if all existing firms and potential entrants have *identical cost* curves (Figure 8.7). Below P^* no firm wants to supply. It takes a price P^* to induce each individual firm to make Q_1.

At a price P_2 above P^*, each firm makes Q_2 and earns supernormal profits. Point D is above point E. Since potential entrants face the same cost curves, new firms flood into the industry. The industry supply curve is horizontal in the long run at P^*. It is not necessary to bribe existing firms to move up their individual supply curves. Industry output is expanded by the entry of new firms alone. Figure 8.7 shows the long-run industry supply curve $LRSS$, horizontal at the price P^*.

There are two reasons why a rising long-run industry supply curve is much more likely than a horizontal long-run supply curve for a competitive industry. First, it is unlikely that every firm and potential firm in the industry has identical cost curves. Second, even if all firms face the same cost curves, we draw a cost curve for given technology *and* given input prices. Although each small firm affects neither output prices nor input prices, collective expansion of output by all firms may bid up input prices. It then needs a higher output price to induce industry output to rise. In general, the long-run industry supply curve slopes up.

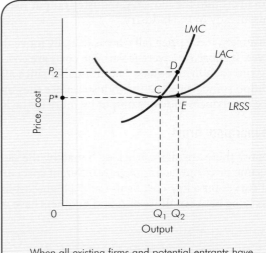

When all existing firms and potential entrants have identical costs, industry output can be expanded without offering a price higher than P^*. The long-run industry supply curve is the horizontal line $LRSS$ at P^*. Industry output can be indefinitely expanded at this price by increasing the number of firms that each produce Q_1.

Figure 8.7 The horizontal long-run industry supply

8.4 Comparative statics for a competitive industry

Having discussed the industry supply curve, we can now examine how supply and demand interact to determine equilibrium price in the short run and the long run.

We now examine equilibrium in a competitive industry and apply the method of comparative static analysis introduced in Chapter 3.

An increase in costs

Consider a rise in costs, such as a higher input price, that hits all firms in the industry. For simplicity, suppose all firms have the same cost curves and the long-run industry supply curve is horizontal.

In Figure 8.8 the competitive industry faces a downward-sloping demand curve DD. Initially, the long-run supply curve is $LRSS_1$. The market clears at the price P_1^* and the total output Q_1^*. The short-run industry supply curve is $SRSS_1$. The market is in short-run and long-run equilibrium.

The left-hand figure shows that each firm makes q_1^* at the lowest point on its average cost curve LAC_1. This is also the lowest point on its $SATC$ curve and hence also lies on its SMC curve, though the initial position of these two curves is not shown in Figure 8.8. N_1 firms in the industry each make output q_1^*. Total output is $Q_1^* = N_1 q_1^*$.

> In **short-run equilibrium** the price equates the quantity demanded to the total quantity supplied by the given number of firms in the industry when each firm is on its short-run supply curve.

> In **long-run equilibrium** the price equates the quantity demanded to the total quantity supplied by the number of firms in the industry when each firm is on its long-run supply curve and firms can freely enter or exit the industry.

> **Comparative statics** examines how equilibrium changes when demand or cost conditions shift.

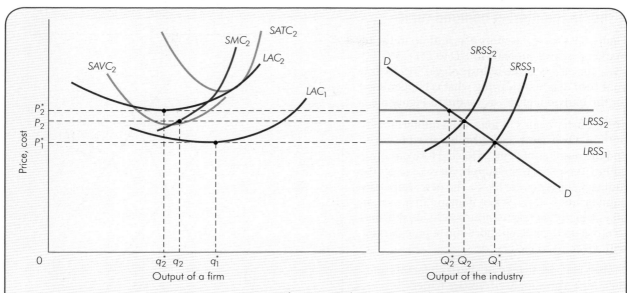

The industry begins in long-run equilibrium producing Q_1^* at a price P_1^*. Each identical firm produces q_1^* at the lowest point on LAC_1. The long run supply curve $LRSS_1$ is horizontal at P_1^*. When costs increase, firms have fixed factors and the number of firms is given in the short run. Each firm produces q_2 where the short-run equilibrium price P_2 equals SMC_2. Together these firms produce Q_2. Since firms are losing money, in the long run some firms leave the industry. The new long-run supply curve $LRSS_2$ for the industry is horizontal at P_2^*, the minimum point on each firms's new long-run average cost curve LAC_2. Each firm produces q_2^*. Industry output is Q_2^*.

Figure 8.8 A cost increase in a competitive industry

A rise in input prices raises costs for all firms. LAC_2 is the new long-run average cost curve for a firm. In the short run, a firm has some fixed factors. $SATC_2$ and $SAVC_2$ are average total and average variable costs given these fixed factors. Short-run marginal cost SMC_2 goes through the lowest point of both these curves. The part of SMC_2 above $SAVC_2$ is the firm's short-run supply curve. In the short run the number of firms remains fixed.

Horizontally adding these short-run supply curves for N_1 firms, we get the new industry short-run supply curve $SRSS_2$. The new short-run equilibrium is at P_2, where $SRSS_2$ crosses the demand curve. Each firm has $P_2 = SMC_2$ and supplies q_2. Together the N_1 firms supply Q_2. Firms cover variable costs, but not fixed costs, at the price P_2. They are losing money.

As time elapses, fixed factors are varied, and firms leave the industry. Long-run equilibrium is at the price P_2^* since the new long-run industry supply curve $LRSS_2$ is horizontal at P_2^*, which just covers minimum long-run average costs. Each firm supplies q_2^*. The number of firms N_2 is such that $Q_2^* = N_2 q_2^*$.

Figure 8.8 makes two points about the change in the long-run equilibrium. First, the rise in average costs is eventually passed on to the consumer in higher prices. In long-run equilibrium the marginal firm (here all firms, since they are identical) breaks even, so there is no incentive for further entry or exit. Hence, price rises to cover the increase in minimum average costs.

Second, since higher prices reduce the total quantity demanded, industry output must fall.

A shift in the market demand curve

Figure 8.9 shows the effect of a shift up in the market demand curve from *DD* to *D'D'*. We show the effects at the industry level. Try to draw your own diagram showing what is happening for the individual firm, as we did in Figure 8.8.

The industry begins in long-run equilibrium at point *A*. Overnight, each firm has fixed factors and the number of firms is fixed. Horizontally adding their short-run supply curves, we get the industry supply curve *SRSS*. The new short-run equilibrium is at *A'*. When demand first rises, it takes a big price rise to induce individual firms to move up their steep short-run supply curves with given fixed factors.

In the long run, firms can adjust all factors and their long-run supply curves are flatter. Moreover, supernormal profits attract extra firms into the industry. Figure 8.9 assumes that the long-run industry supply curve is rising. Either it takes higher prices to attract higher-cost firms into the industry, or the collective expansion bids up some input prices, or both. The new long-run equilibrium is at *A"*. Relative to short-run equilibrium at *A'* there is another rise in total output. However, a better choice of inputs and the entry of new firms raise supply and reduce the market-clearing price.

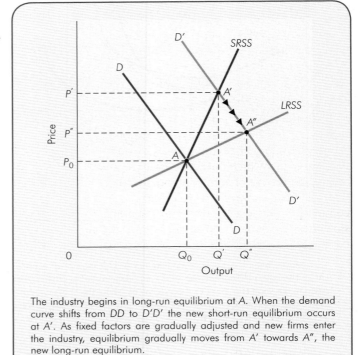

The industry begins in long-run equilibrium at A. When the demand curve shifts from DD to D'D' the new short-run equilibrium occurs at A'. As fixed factors are gradually adjusted and new firms enter the industry, equilibrium gradually moves from A' towards A", the new long-run equilibrium.

Figure 8.9 A shift in demand in a competitive

8.5 Global competition

Changes in conditions in domestic markets often reflect events abroad. Fish prices in Western Europe fell in the 1990s after suppliers from the ex-USSR joined the world economy. Wool prices in the EU rise when a drought in Australia hits sheep farmers there. Competitive markets in different countries are linked together by international trade.

When transport costs are low, a commodity's price in one country cannot vary much from its price in other countries. In the extreme case, the 'Law of One Price' holds. If there are no obstacles to trade and no transport costs, the price of a given commodity is the same all over the world. Suppliers sell in the market with the highest price but consumers buy in the market with the lowest price. Trade makes the two prices the same.

In practice, transport costs and trade restrictions such as tariffs (taxes levied on imports) allow some international differences in the price of a commodity. Nevertheless, unless transport costs and trade restrictions are prohibitive, international competition means that prices of the same good in different countries generally move in the same direction.

We now illustrate global competition in the extreme case without transport costs or trade restrictions. Producers and consumers throughout the world are then part of a unified world market for the commodity.

Equilibrium in the domestic market

Figure 8.10 shows the domestic supply curve *SS* and the domestic demand curve *DD* for such a commodity. Initially, there is no international trade, perhaps because the domestic country has big tariffs on imports. The domestic market equilibrium is at *A*, at a price P^* and quantity Q^*.

Now tariffs are abolished. There is a world supply curve, which horizontally aggregates the supply curve of each country, and a world demand curve, which horizontally aggregates the demand curve of each country. Together these determine a world price for the commodity. Suppose the domestic country is small relative to the world and cannot affect the world price. One of three things can happen. Figure 8.10 illustrates these cases. First, if the world price is P^*, the price that would have cleared the domestic market anyway, point *A* is still equilibrium in the domestic market. The Law of One Price holds. There is no incentive for international trade. Domestic supply exactly caters for domestic demand. Imports and exports are zero.

Second, at a world price P_1^*, below the initial domestic price, domestic consumers simply import the good and refuse to pay more than P_1^*. Domestic suppliers cannot get more than P_1^* wherever they sell. Hence they produce Q_1. Consumers buy Q_1', and imports are $(Q_1'-Q_1)$, the horizontal distance between *C* and *C'*.

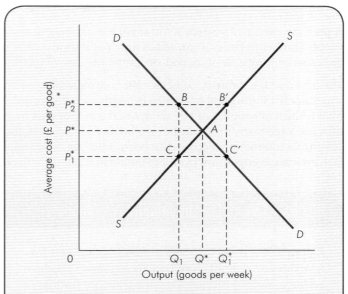

DD and SS show the domestic supply and demand curves for a commodity competitively traded in world markets. In the absence of trade, domestic equilibrium occurs at A. When trade is possible at the world price P^*, equilibrium occurs at A. When trade is possible at the given world price P_1^*, domestic producers supply Q_1 and domestic consumers demand Q_1'. The excess demand (the horizontal distance between C and C') is met from imports. Conversely, when world prices and P_2^*, domestic producers supply Q_1', domestic consumers demand Q_1, and the excess supply (the horizontal distance between B and B') is exported.

Figure 8.10 Domestic equilibrium and world prices

Third, at a world price P_2^*, domestic consumers buy Q_1 but domestic producers make Q'. The quantity $(Q_1'-Q_1)$, the horizontal distance between *B* and *B'*, is exported to consumers abroad.

World conditions and the home market

A rise in the world price affects the domestic market, as Figure 8.10 illustrates. The world oil price is P_1^*. UK oil companies supply Q_1 but oil-guzzling consumers import $(Q_1'-Q_1)$ since quantity demanded is Q_1'. Now OPEC restricts oil production and the world price of oil rises. This has two effects. First, it reduces the quantity of oil demanded in the UK. Second, UK producers can charge higher prices and move up their supply curve, expanding output.

Since the domestic quantity demanded falls but domestic output rises, the higher world oil price reduces imports. If the world price rises sufficiently, the country becomes a net exporter.

This first look at international trade also reminds us that the relevant definition of the market or the industry may be a good deal wider than that of the domestic economy. When transport costs are low and trade restrictions unimportant, it is in the world market that we must seek the forces that determine the equilibrium price of a good.

8.6 Pure monopoly: the opposite limiting case

A perfectly competitive firm is too small to worry about any effect of its output decision on industry supply and hence price. It can sell as much as it wants at the market price. We next discuss the opposite limiting case of market structure, the case of pure monopoly.

The firm and the industry coincide. The sole national supplier may not be a monopolist if the good or service is internationally traded. The Royal Mail is the sole supplier of UK stamps and a monopolist in them. Airbus is the only large plane maker in Europe but is not a monopolist since it faces cut-throat international competition from Boeing. Sole suppliers may also face invisible competition from potential entrants. If so, they are not monopolists.

> A **monopolist** is the sole supplier and potential supplier of the industry's product.

Box 8.2 The end of the telephone monopoly

Before 1997 many countries' domestic markets for telecommunications were heavily regulated. Early editions of this textbook used the national phone company as an example of a monopoly. Britain and the USA began deregulating telecoms in the 1980s. In 1997 68 countries signed an agreement to go even further, and the EU committed itself to complete liberalization of basic telecoms, including satellite networks and mobile phones, by 2003. The World Trade Organization (www.wto.org) forecast additional trade worth 4 per cent of the world's output.

In the 1995, an off-peak 3-minute long-distance call cost an average of 40 pence in France, Germany, Italy and Spain; even in the partially deregulated UK it cost 18 pence for 3 minutes, and more in peak hours. Nowadays, such rates are unthinkable, and the price of making calls has tumbled. We have mobile phone packages, texting and Skype, the free internet telephony network.

This example makes three points. First, many monopolies are the result of government policy to license only one supplier; such policies can change. Second, firm size must always be considered in relation to the relevant market. When technical breakthroughs in telecom technology made the relevant market much larger – satellites are no respecters of national boundaries – the national phone company was suddenly playing in a much larger game. Sooner or later policy makers had to recognize such realities. Third, technical progress can change not merely the geographical boundary of the market but the nature of the product as well. The inventors of texting did not expect it to catch on as a consumer activity. How wrong can you be?

First, we study the decisions of a private profit-maximizing monopolist who has no fear of entry or foreign competition. Some monopolies are state owned and not necessarily run for private profit. However, in the past two decades many countries have been 'privatizing' these state-run monopolies. The analysis in the rest of this chapter is relevant both to existing private monopolies and to how state-run monopolies might behave if restored to private ownership.

8.7 Profit-maximizing output for a monopolist

To maximize profits any firm chooses the output at which marginal revenue *MR* equals marginal cost (*SMC* in the short run and *LMC* in the long run). It then checks it is covering average costs (*SAVC* in the short run and *LAC* in the long run).

The special feature of a competitive firm is that *MR* equals price. Selling an extra unit of output does not bid down the price and reduce the revenue earned on previous units. The price at which the extra unit is sold is the change in total revenue.

In contrast, a monopolist's demand curve *is* the industry demand curve, which slopes down. Hence *MR* is less than the price at which the extra output is sold. The monopolist knows that extra output reduces revenue from *existing* units. To sell more, the price on all units must be cut.

For a down-sloping demand curve, Figure 8.11 reminds you how price, marginal revenue and total revenue are related. The more inelastic the demand curve, the more an extra unit of output bids down the price, reducing revenue from existing units. At any output, *MR* is further below the demand curve the more inelastic is demand. Also, the larger the existing output, the larger the revenue loss from existing units when the price is reduced to sell another unit. For a given demand curve, *MR* falls increasingly below price the higher the output from which we begin.

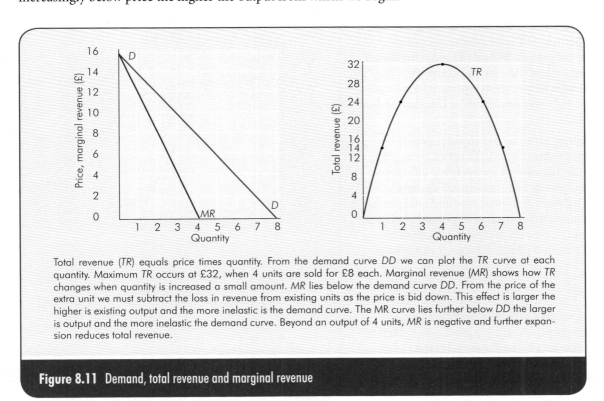

Total revenue (*TR*) equals price times quantity. From the demand curve *DD* we can plot the *TR* curve at each quantity. Maximum *TR* occurs at £32, when 4 units are sold for £8 each. Marginal revenue (*MR*) shows how *TR* changes when quantity is increased a small amount. *MR* lies below the demand curve *DD*. From the price of the extra unit we must subtract the loss in revenue from existing units as the price is bid down. This effect is larger the higher is existing output and the more inelastic is the demand curve. The MR curve lies further below *DD* the larger is output and the more inelastic the demand curve. Beyond an output of 4 units, *MR* is negative and further expansion reduces total revenue.

Figure 8.11 Demand, total revenue and marginal revenue

Beyond a certain output (4 in Figure 8.11), the revenue loss on existing output exceeds the revenue gain from the extra unit itself. Marginal revenue is negative. Further expansion reduces total revenue.

On the cost side, with only one producer, the cost curves for a single firm in Chapter 7 carry over directly. The monopolist has the usual cost curves, average and marginal, short-run and long-run. For simplicity we discuss only the long-run curves.

Profit-maximizing output

Setting MR equal to MC leads to the profit-maximizing level of positive output. Then the monopolist must check whether, at this output, the price (average revenue) covers average variable costs in the short run and average total costs in the long run. If not, the monopolist should shut down in the short run and leave the industry in the long run. Table 8.2 summarizes the criteria by which a monopolist decides how much to produce.

Table 8.2 Profit-maximizing monopoly

	Marginal condition			Average condition			
	$MR > MC$	$MR = MC$	$MR < MC$	Short-run		Long-run	
				$P > SAVC$	$P < SAVC$	$P > LAC$	$P < LAC$
Output decision	Raise	Optimal	Lower	Produce	Shut down	Stay	Exit

Figure 8.12 shows the average cost curve AC with its usual U-shape. The marginal cost curve MC goes through the lowest point on the AC curve. Marginal revenue MR lies below the down-sloping demand curve DD. Setting $MR = MC$, the monopolist chooses the output Q_1. To find the price for which Q_1 is sold we look at the demand curve DD. The monopolist sells output Q_1 at a price P_1. Profit per unit is $(P_1 - AC_1)$ and total profit is the shaded area $(P_1 - AC_1)\,Q_1$.

Even in the long run, the monopolist makes *supernormal* profits, sometimes called *monopoly* profits. Unlike the case in competitive industry, supernormal profits of a monopolist are not eliminated by entry of more firms and a fall in the price. A monopoly has no fear of possible entry. By ruling out entry, we remove the mechanism by which supernormal profits disappear in the long run.

Price-setting

Whereas a competitive firm is a *price-taker*, a monopolist sets prices and is a *price-setter*. Having decided to produce Q_1 in Figure 8.12, the monopolist quotes a price P_1 knowing that customers will then demand the output Q_1.

Elasticity and marginal revenue

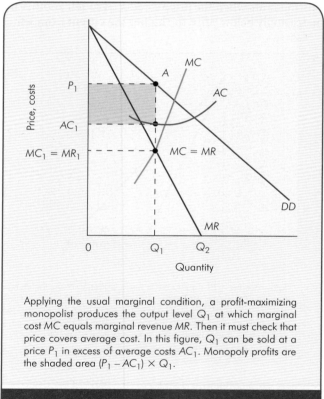

Applying the usual marginal condition, a profit-maximizing monopolist produces the output level Q_1 at which marginal cost MC equals marginal revenue MR. Then it must check that price covers average cost. In this figure, Q_1 can be sold at a price P_1 in excess of average costs AC_1. Monopoly profits are the shaded area $(P_1 - AC_1) \times Q_1$.

Figure 8.12 The monopoly equilibrium: $MC = MR$

When the elasticity of demand is between 0 and –1, demand is inelastic and a rise in output reduces total revenue. Marginal revenue is negative. In percentage terms, the fall in price exceeds the rise in quantity. All outputs to the right of Q_2 in Figure 8.12 have negative MR. The demand curve is inelastic at quantities above Q_2. At quantities below Q_2 the demand curve is elastic. Higher output leads to higher revenue. Marginal revenue is positive.

The monopolist sets $MC = MR$. Since MC must be positive, so must MR. The chosen output must lie to the left of Q_2. *A monopolist never produces on the inelastic part of the demand curve.*

Price, marginal cost and monopoly power

At any output, price exceeds the monopolist's marginal revenue since the demand curve slopes down. Hence, in setting $MR = MC$ the monopolist sets a price that exceeds marginal cost. In contrast, a competitive firm always equates price and marginal cost, since its price is also its marginal revenue. A competitive firm cannot raise price above marginal cost and has no monopoly power. The more inelastic the demand curve of a monopolist, the more marginal revenue is below price, the greater is the excess of price over marginal cost, and the more monopoly power it has.

> The excess of price over marginal cost is a measure of **monopoly power**.

Comparative statics for a monopolist

Figure 8.12 may also be used to analyse changes in costs or demand. Suppose a rise in costs shifts the MC and AC curves upwards. The higher MC curve must cross the MR curve at a lower output. If the monopolist can sell this output at a price that covers average costs, the effect of the cost increase must be to reduce output. Since the demand curve slopes down, lower output means a higher equilibrium price.

Similarly, for the original cost curves shown in Figure 8.12, suppose there is an outward shift in demand and marginal revenue curves. MR must now cross MC at a higher output. Thus a rise in demand leads the monopolist to increase output.

8.8 Output and price under monopoly and competition

We now compare a perfectly competitive industry with a monopoly. For this comparison to be of interest the two industries must face the same demand and cost conditions. How would the *same* industry change if it were organized first as a competitive industry then as a monopoly?

Chapter 9 explains why some industries are competitive but others are monopolies. If this theory is right, can the same industry be both competitive and a monopoly? Only in some special cases.

Comparing a competitive industry and a multi-plant monopolist

Consider a competitive industry in which all firms and potential entrants have the same cost curves. The horizontal $LRSS$ curve for this competitive industry is shown in Figure 8.13. Facing the demand curve DD, the industry is in long-run equilibrium at A at a price P_1 and total output Q_1. The industry $LRSS$ curve is horizontal at P_1, the lowest point on the LAC curve of each firm. Any other price leads eventually to infinite entry or exit from the industry. $LRSS$ is the industry's long-run marginal cost curve LMC_1 of expanding output by enticing new firms into the industry.

Each firm produces at the lowest point on its LAC curve, breaking even. Marginal cost curves pass through the point of minimum average costs. Hence, each firm is also on its SMC and LMC curves. Horizontally adding the SMC curves of each firm, we get $SRSS$, the short-run industry supply curve. This is the industry's short-run marginal cost curve SMC_1 of expanding output from existing firms with temporarily fixed factors. Since $SRSS$ crosses the demand curve at P_1, the industry is in both short-run and long-run equilibrium.

Beginning from this position, the competitive industry becomes a monopoly. The monopolist takes over each plant (firm) but makes central pricing and output decisions. Overnight, the monopolist still

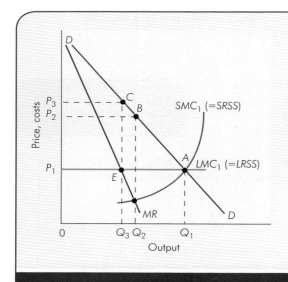

Long-run equilibrium in a competitive industry occurs at A. Total output is Q_1 and the price P_1. A monopolist sets MR equal to SMC_1, restricting output to Q_2 and increasing price to P_2. In the long run the monopolist sets MR equal to LMC_1, reducing output to Q_3 and increasing the price again to P_3. There are no entrants to compete away supernormal profits P_3CEP_1 by increasing the industry output.

Figure 8.13 A monopolist produces a lower output at a higher price

has the same number of factories (ex-firms) as in the competitive industry. Since the firm and the industry now coincide, SMC_1 remains the short-run marginal cost curve for the monopolist taking all plants together.[1] However, the monopolist knows that higher total output bids down the price.

In the short run the monopolist equates SMC_1 and MR, reaching equilibrium at B. Output is Q_2 and the price P_2. Relative to competitive equilibrium at A, *the monopolist raises price and reduces quantity*.

In the long run the monopolist can enter (set up new factories) or exit (close down existing factories). Whether making short-run profits or losses at B (we need to draw the $SATC$ curve to see which), a monopolist will now exit or retire some factories from the industry in the long run.

The monopolist cuts back output to force up the price. In the long run it makes sense to operate each factory at the lowest point on its LAC curve. To reduce total output some factories are closed. In the long run, the monopolist sets $LMC_1 = MR$ and reaches equilibrium at C. *Price has risen yet further to P_3 and output has fallen to Q_3.* Long-run profits are given by the area P_3CEP_1 since P_1 remains the long-run average cost when all plants are at the lowest point on their LAC curve.

Because MR is less than price, a monopolist produces less than a competitive industry and charges a higher price. However, in this example it is a legal prohibition on entry by competitors that allows the monopolist to succeed in the long run. Otherwise, with identical cost curves, other firms would set up in competition, expand industry output and compete away these supernormal profits. Absence of entry is intrinsic to the model of monopoly.

---

1 In a competitive industry each firm equates the price to its own marginal cost. Hence firms produce at the same marginal cost. We horizontally add individual SMC curves (at the same price) to get the industry SMC curve. A multi-plant monopolist need not equate MC across all plants but always finds it profitable to do so. If marginal costs in two plants differ, a monopolist can produce the same total output more cheaply by producing an extra unit in the low MC plant and one less unit in the high MC plant. Thus SMC for the monopolist across all plants remains the horizontal sum of the SMC curves for individual plants, as in a competitive industry.

Comparing a single-plant monopolist with a competitive industry

Instead of a multi-plant monopolist taking over many previously competitive firms, consider a monopolist meeting the entire industry demand from a single plant. This is most plausible when scale economies are big. There are huge costs in setting up a national telephone network. Yet the cost of connecting a marginal subscriber is low once the network has been set up.

Monopolies enjoying huge economies of scale – falling *LAC* curves over the entire range of output – are *natural monopolies*. Large-scale economies may explain why there is a sole supplier without fear of entry by others. Smaller new entrants would be at a prohibitive cost disadvantage.

Figure 8.14 illustrates a natural monopoly. In the long run it faces average and marginal cost curves *LAC* and *LMC*. Given the position of the demand curve, *LAC* is declining over the entire range of outputs that might be sold. The monopoly produces at *LMC* equal to *MR*, selling output Q_1 for a price P_1. At this output, price exceeds *LAC*. The monopoly makes supernormal profits and is happy to remain in business.

It makes no sense to compare this equilibrium with how the industry would behave if it were competitive. With such economies of scale, there is only one firm in the industry. *LAC* is the cost curve for each possible firm. If a lot of small firms each produced a small fraction of total output, their average costs would be huge. By expanding, a single firm could undercut them and wipe them out. This industry must have a sole supplier. This natural monopoly will maximize profits only by recognizing that its marginal revenue is not its price.

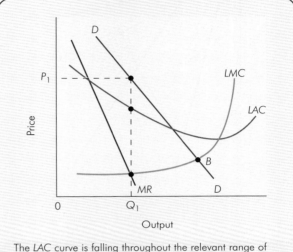

The *LAC* curve is falling throughout the relevant range of output levels. Economies of scale are large relative to the market size. The monopoly produces Q_1 at price P_1 and makes profits. If it tried to behave like a price-taking competitive firm it would produce at *B* where price equals *LMC* and make losses. By recognizing the effect of output on price the single firm monopoly can do much better. This industry cannot support a lot of small firms. Each would have very high average costs at low output. This cannot be a competitive industry.

Figure 8.14 A natural monopoly with economies of scale

8.9 A monopoly has no supply curve

A competitive firm sets price equal to marginal cost if it supplies at all. If we know its marginal cost curve we know how much it supplies at each price. Aggregating across firms, we also know how much the industry supplies at each price. We can draw the supply curve without knowing anything about the market demand curve. We then analyse how supply and demand interact to determine equilibrium price and quantity.

A monopolist's output affects marginal cost and marginal revenue simultaneously. Figure 8.15 shows a given *LMC* curve. How much will the monopolist produce at the price P_1? It all depends on demand and marginal revenue. When demand is *DD*, marginal revenue is *MR* and the monopolist produces Q_1 at a price P_1. If demand is *D'D'*, marginal revenue is *MR'*, and the monopolist produces Q_2 but still charges P_1.

A monopolist does not have a supply curve independent of demand conditions. Rather, a monopolist simultaneously examines demand (hence marginal revenue) and cost (hence marginal cost) to decide how much to produce and what to charge.

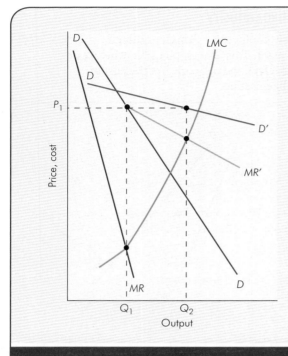

Given the demand curve DD and the corresponding marginal revenue curve MR, the monopolist produces Q_1 at a price P_1. However, lacking DD and MR, the monopolist produces Q_2 at a price P_1. Knowing the price, we cannot uniquely infer the quantity supplied unless we also know demand and marginal revenue. Because the monopolist knows that output affects both marginal cost and marginal revenue, the two must be considered simultaneously.

Figure 8.15 Absence of a supply curve under monopoly

Discriminating monopoly

Thus far we have assumed that all consumers are charged the same price. Unlike a competitive industry, where competition prevents any firm charging more than its competitors, a monopolist may be able to charge different prices to different customers.

> A **discriminating monopoly** charges different prices to different people.

Consider an airline monopolizing flights between London and Rome. It has business customers whose demand curve is very inelastic. They have to fly. Their demand and marginal revenue curves are very steep. The airline also carries tourists whose demand curve is much more elastic. If flights to Rome get too expensive, tourists visit Athens instead. Tourists have much flatter demand and marginal revenue curves.

The more inelastic is the demand curve, the more the marginal revenue curve lies below the demand curve. To sell another output unit requires a bigger price cut that hits existing revenue. Since demand elasticity determines the gap between marginal revenue and price, charging the same price to purchasers with different demand elasticities means that the marginal revenue from the last business traveller is less than the marginal revenue from the last tourist.

Whatever the total number of passengers (and total cost of carrying them), the airline then has the wrong *mix* between tourists and business travellers. Since the marginal revenue from the last tourist exceeds the marginal revenue from the last business traveller, the airline gains revenue with no extra cost by carrying one more tourist and one fewer business traveller. It pays to keep changing the mix until the marginal revenue from the types is equal.

To do this, the airline must charge the two groups *different* prices. Since tourist demand is elastic, the airline charges tourists a low fare to raise tourist revenue. Since business demand is inelastic, the airline charges business travellers a high fare to increase business revenue.

Profit-maximizing output satisfies two separate conditions. First, business travellers with inelastic demand pay sufficiently more than tourists with elastic demand that the marginal revenue from the two types is equal. Then there is no incentive to rearrange the mix by altering the price differential between the two groups. Second, the level of prices and the total number of passengers is determined to equate marginal cost to each of these marginal revenues. The airline operates at the most profitable scale as well as with the most profitable mix.

When a producer charges different customers different prices we say that the producer *price discriminates*. There are many examples of this in the real world. Rail companies charge rush-hour commuters a higher fare than midday shoppers whose demand for trips to the city is much more elastic.

Most examples of price discrimination refer to services consumed on the spot rather than to goods that can be resold. Price discrimination in a standardized commodity is unlikely to work. Those buying at the low price resell to those paying the high price, undercutting price discrimination. Effective price discrimination requires that the sub-markets can be quarantined to prevent resale.

Price discrimination illustrates again the absence of a supply curve under monopoly. Figure 8.16 shows *perfect price discrimination*. Each customer pays a different price for the same product.

If a monopolist charges every customer the same price, profit-maximizing output is Q_1 where MR equals MC and the price is P_1.

If the monopolist can perfectly price discriminate, the very first unit of output can be sold at a price E. Having sold the first unit to the highest bidder most desperate for the good, the next unit can be sold to the next highest bidder and so on. Moving down the demand curve DD we can read off the price for which each extra unit is sold. In reducing the price to sell extra output, the monopolist no longer reduces revenue from previously sold units. *Hence the demand curve is the marginal revenue curve under perfect price discrimination.* The marginal revenue of the last unit is simply the *price* for which it is sold.

Treating DD as the marginal revenue curve, a perfectly price-discriminating monopolist produces at point C where marginal revenue and marginal cost are equal. Two points follow immediately. First, if price discrimination is possible it is profitable to use it. Moving from the uniform pricing point A to the price discriminating point C, the monopolist adds the area ABC to profits. This is the excess of extra revenue over extra cost when output is increased.

The monopolist makes a second gain from price discrimination. Even the output Q_1 now earns more revenue than under uniform pricing. The monopolist also gains the area

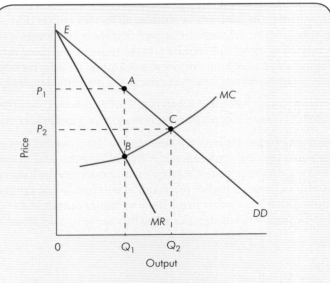

Charging all customers the same price the monopolist will produce at B where MC = MR. If each output unit can be sold for a different price the revenue from existing units is not reduced by cutting the price to sell another unit. The demand curve DD is the marginal revenue curve and the perfectly discriminating monopolist will produce at C. Output is higher and profits are higher. By price discrimination the monopolist gains an extra revenue EP_1A from selling Q_1 but also increases output beyond this level making a marginal profit of ABC in expanding from A to C.

Figure 8.16 Perfect price discrimination

EP_1A by charging different prices on the first Q_1 units of output rather than the single price P_1. In practice, one of the main ways management consultants raise the profits of firms that they advise is by devising new ways in which the firm can price discriminate.

Second, whether or not the firm can price discriminate affects its output choice. Uniform pricing leads to an output Q_1. Perfect price discrimination leads to an output Q_2. Uniform and discriminatory pricing lead to different outputs because they affect the marginal revenue obtained by a monopolist from a given demand curve.

8.10 Monopoly and technical change

Section 8.8 compared a monopoly and a perfectly competitive industry. When such a comparison was meaningful we discovered: (1) a monopoly will restrict output and drive up prices and (2) a monopoly may make economic profits permanently.

Joseph Schumpeter (1883–1950) argued that this comparison ignores technical advances that reduce costs, allowing price cuts and output expansion. A large monopolist with steady profits may find it easier to *fund* the research and development (R&D) necessary to make cost-saving breakthroughs. More importantly, a monopolist may have more *incentive* to undertake R&D.

In a competitive industry a firm with a technical advantage has only a temporary opportunity to earn high profits to recoup its research expenses. Imitation by existing firms and new entrants competes away profits. In contrast, by shifting all its cost curves downwards, a monopoly can enjoy higher profits for ever. Schumpeter argued that these two forces – more resources for R&D and a higher return on a successful venture – make monopolies more innovative than competitive industries. Taking a dynamic long-run view, not a static picture, monopolists enjoy lower cost curves. As a result, they charge lower prices, thus raising the quantity demanded.

This argument has some substance. Tiny firms often do little R&D. Many of the largest firms have excellent research departments. Even so, the Schumpeter argument may overstate the case.

Modern economies have a *patent* system. Inventors of new processes get a temporary legal monopoly for a fixed period. By temporarily excluding entry and imitation, patent laws raise the incentive to conduct R&D but do not establish a monopoly in the long run. Over the life of the patent, the inventor charges a higher price and makes handsome profits. Eventually, the patent expires and competition from other firms leads to higher output and lower prices. The real price of copiers and microcomputers fell significantly when the original patents of Xerox and IBM expired.

Activity box 8   How sorry should we feel for the drug giants?

Patents award firms a temporary legal monopoly, thereby creating the incentive to invest in expensive technologies. Because the patent eventually expires, in the long run everyone gets the benefits of the discovery at a more reasonable cost. Temporary monopoly profits on the drugs that work help finance losses on all the drug discovery projects that failed and never came to market. When we see a company making profits on a particular drug, we need to view this in context – only when we take account of all the invisible failures too can we get a complete picture.

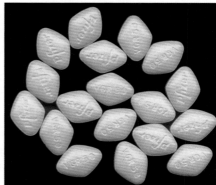

Pfizer is the world's largest drug company, responsible for successes such as Viagra. But it also has its bad days. In December 2006, its share price fell 11 per cent in a day when it abandoned its heart and cholesterol drug torcetrapib after tests linked it to increased deaths and heart disease among trial patients.

Abolishing patent rights would make existing drugs cheaper for consumers but also reduce the incentive to look for new drugs.

Questions

(a)   Suppose political pressure usually leads to patent rights being relaxed for poor importers, so that Africa is in practice allowed to import anti-HIV drugs cheaply or manufacture cheap 'generic' copies of the drugs. If you are a drug company, is there any difference to your profits between (i) signing up in advance for a scheme in which certain poorer countries are entitled to cut-price versions of your drug, and (ii) believing your patents can always be enforced throughout the world only to find either that poor countries gain political support for their being allowed cheaper versions, or (iii) believing they violate your patents and you find it unprofitable to take legal action against them.

(b)   Would your answer to (a) be different if the explicit acknowledgement of differential pricing then undermined your ability to charge high prices for successful drugs in rich countries?

(c)   What information would you require to decide whether or not drug companies charged prices that were on average 'too high'?

To check your answers to these questions, go to page 717.

Summary

- In a **competitive industry** each buyer and seller is a **price-taker**, believing individual actions have no effect on the market price. Competitive supply is most plausible when many firms make a standard product, with free entry and exit, and easy verification by buyers that the products of different firms really are the same.

- For a **competitive firm**, the price is its marginal revenue. Output equates price to marginal cost. The firm's supply curve is its *SMC* curve above *SAVC*. At a lower price, the firm temporarily shuts down. In the long run, the firm's supply curve is its *LMC* curve above its *LAC* curve. At a lower price, the firm eventually exits the industry.

- Adding at each price the quantities supplied by each firm, we obtain the **industry supply curve**. It is flatter in the long run both because each firm can fully adjust all factors and because the number of firms in the industry can vary. In the extreme case where all potential and existing firms have identical costs, the long-run industry supply curve is horizontal at the price corresponding to the lowest point on each firm's *LAC* curve.

- An increase in demand leads to a large price increase but only a small increase in quantity. The existing firms move up their steep *SMC* curves. Price exceeds average costs and the ensuing profits attract new entrants. In the long run output increases still further but the price falls back. In the long-run equilibrium the **marginal firm** makes only normal profits and there is no further change in the number of firms in the industry.

- An increase in costs for all firms reduces the industry's output and increases the price. In the long run the marginal firm must break even. A higher price is required to match the increase in its average costs.

- Markets for the same good in different countries will be closely linked if transport costs are small and there are no trade restrictions. In a competitive world market each country takes the world price of the commodity as given. Discrepancies between domestic supply and domestic demand are met through imports or exports. Foreign trade transmits foreign shocks to the domestic economy but acts as a shock absorber for domestic shocks.

- A **pure monopoly** is the only seller or potential seller of a good and need not worry about entry even in the long run. Though rare in practice, this case offers an important benchmark against which to compare less extreme forms of monopoly power.

- A **profit-maximizing monopolist has a supply rule** – choose output to set *MC* equal to *MR* – but not a supply curve uniquely relating price and output. The relation of price and MR depends on the demand curve.

- Where a monopoly and a competitive industry can meaningfully be compared, the monopolist produces a smaller output at a higher price. However, natural monopolies with large economies of scale could not exist as competitive industries.

- A **discriminating monopolist** charges different prices to different customers. To equate the marginal revenue from different groups, groups with an inelastic demand must pay a higher price. Successful price discrimination requires that customers cannot trade the product among themselves.

● Monopolies may have more internal resources available for research and may have a higher incentive for cost-saving research because the profits from technical advances will not be eroded by entry. Although small firms do not undertake much expensive research, it appears that the **patent laws** provide adequate incentives for medium- and larger-sized firms. There is no evidence that an industry has to be a monopoly to undertake cost-saving research.

Review questions

To check your answers to these questions, go to page 716.

1 Draw a diagram showing the positions of a competitive firm and of the industry in long-run equilibrium. Suppose this is the wool industry. The development of artificial fibres reduces the demand for wool. (a) Show what happens in the short run and the long run if all sheep farmers have identical costs. (b) What happens if there are high-cost and low-cost sheep farmers?

2 Suppose foot-and-mouth disease means many sheep are slaughtered. What happens to the price of wool in the short run and the long run?

3 (a) If the country can trade wool at given world prices, draw the domestic supply and demand curves. Show a price that would make the country a wool importer. (b) The government now taxes wool imports, raising their price in the domestic market. Show what happens to domestic output and the quantity of imports?

4 The table shows the demand curve facing a monopolist who produces at a constant marginal cost of £5. Calculate the monopolist's marginal revenue curve. What is the equilibrium output? Equilibrium price? What would be the equilibrium price and output for a competitive industry?

Price (£)	8	7	6	5	4	3	2	1	0
Quantity	1	2	3	4	5	6	7	8	9

5 Now suppose that, in addition to the constant marginal cost of £5, the monopolist has a fixed cost of £2. How does this affect the monopolist's output, price and profits? Why?

6 **Common fallacies** Why are these statements wrong? (a) Since competitive firms break even in the long run, there is no incentive to be a competitive firm. (b) By breaking up monopolies we always get more output at a lower price.

7 **Harder question** A competitive industry has free entry and exit. Why does free exit matter? How would the analysis change if it was costly to exit?

8 **Harder question** A firm's market power can be measured by its ability to raise price above marginal cost. Relative to the level of marginal cost, this measure is $(P - MC)/MC$. How do you expect this to be related to the elasticity of demand for the monopolist's output?

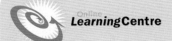

Market structure and imperfect competition

Perfect competition and pure monopoly are useful benchmarks of the extremes of market structure. Most markets are between the extremes. What determines the structure of a particular market? Why are there 10 000 florists but only a few chemical producers? How does the structure of an industry affect the behaviour of its constituent firms?

A perfectly competitive firm faces a horizontal demand curve at the market price. It is a price-taker. Any other type of firm faces a downward-sloping demand curve for its product and is *imperfectly competitive*.

For a pure monopoly, the demand curve for the firm and the industry coincide. We now distinguish two intermediate cases of an imperfectly competitive market structure.

The car industry is an oligopoly. The price of Rover cars depends not only on Rover's own output and sales but also the output of Ford and Toyota. The corner grocer's shop is a monopolistic competitor. Its output is a subtle package of physical goods, personal service and convenience for

> An **imperfectly competitive firm** faces a down-sloping demand curve. Its output price reflects the quantity of goods it makes and sells.

> An **oligopoly** is an industry with few producers, each recognizing their interdependence. An industry with **monopolistic competition** has many sellers of products that are close substitutes for one another. Each firm has only a limited ability to affect its output price.

local customers. It can charge a slightly higher price than an out-of-town supermarket. But, if its prices are too high, even local shoppers travel to the supermarket.

As with most definitions, the lines between different market structures can get blurred. One reason is ambiguity about the relevant definition of the market. Is Eurostar a monopoly in cross-channel trains or an oligopolist in cross-channel travel? Similarly, when a country trades in a competitive world market, even the sole domestic producer may have little influence on market price. We can never fully remove these ambiguities but Table 9.1 shows some things to bear in mind as we proceed through this chapter. The table includes the ease with which new firms can enter the industry, which affects the ability of existing firms to maintain high prices and supernormal profits in the long run.

Table 9.1 Market structure

Competition	Number of firms	Ability to affect price	Entry barriers	Example
Perfect	Lots	Nil	None	Fruit stall
Imperfect: Monopolistic	Many	Little	Small	Corner shop
Oligopoly	Few	Medium	Bigger	Cars
Monopoly	One	Large	Huge	Post Office

9.1 Why market structures differ

Some industries are legal monopolies, the sole licensed producers. Patent laws may confer temporary monopoly on producers of a new process. Ownership of a raw material may confer monopoly status on a single firm. We now develop a general theory of how demand and cost interact to determine the likely structure of each industry.

The car industry is not an oligopoly one day but perfectly competitive the next. Long-run influences determine market structures. Eventually, one firm can hire another's workers and learn its technical secrets.

Figure 9.1 shows the demand curve DD for the output of an industry in the long run. Suppose all firms and potential entrants face the average cost curve LAC_1. At the price P_1, free entry and exit means that each firm produces q_1. With the demand curve DD, industry output is Q_1. The number of firms in the industry is $N_1 (= Q_1/q_1)$. If q_1, the minimum average cost output on LAC_1, is small relative to DD, N_1 will be large. Each firm has a tiny effect on industry supply and market price. We have found a perfectly competitive industry.

Next, suppose that each firm has the cost curve LAC_3. Scale economies are vast relative to the market size. At the lowest point on LAC_3, output is big relative to the demand curve DD. Suppose initially two firms each make q_2. Industry output is Q_2. The market clears at P_2 and both firms break even. If one firm expands a bit, its average costs fall. Its higher output also bids the price down. With lower average costs, that firm survives but the other firm loses money. The firm that expands undercuts its competitor and drives it out of business.

This industry is a natural monopoly. Suppose Q_3 is the output at which its marginal cost and marginal revenue coincide. The price is P_3 and the natural monopoly makes supernormal profits. There is no room in the industry for other firms with access to the same LAC_3 curve.

> A **natural monopoly** enjoys such scale economies that it has no fear of entry by others.

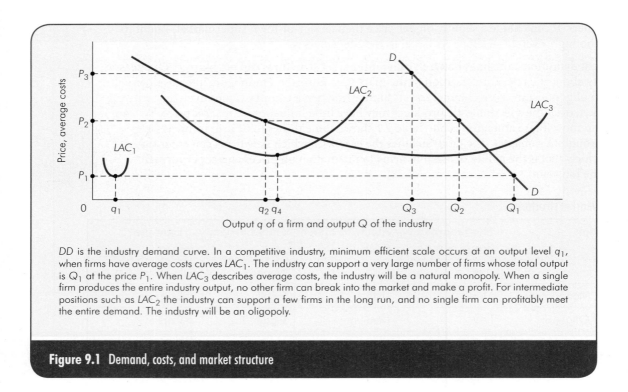

DD is the industry demand curve. In a competitive industry, minimum efficient scale occurs at an output level q_1, when firms have average costs curves LAC_1. The industry can support a very large number of firms whose total output is Q_1 at the price P_1. When LAC_3 describes average costs, the industry will be a natural monopoly. When a single firm produces the entire industry output, no other firm can break into the market and make a profit. For intermediate positions such as LAC_2 the industry can support a few firms in the long run, and no single firm can profitably meet the entire demand. The industry will be an oligopoly.

Figure 9.1 Demand, costs, and market structure

A new entrant needs a big output to get average costs down. Extra output on this scale so depresses the price that both firms make losses. The potential entrant cannot break in.

Finally, we show the LAC_2 curve with more economies of scale than a competitive industry but fewer than a natural monopoly. This industry supports at least two firms enjoying scale economies near the bottom of their LAC_2 curves. It is an oligopoly. Attempts to expand either firm's output beyond q_4 quickly meet decreasing returns to scale and prevent a firm driving competitors out of business.

The crucial determinant of market structure is minimum efficient scale relative to the size of the total market as shown by the demand curve. Table 9.2 summarizes our analysis of the interaction of market size and minimum efficient scale. When the demand curve shifts to the left, an industry previously with many firms may have room for only a few. Similarly, a rise in fixed costs, raising the minimum efficient scale, reduces the number of firms. In the 1950s there were many European aircraft makers. Today, the research and development costs of a major commercial airliner are huge. Apart from the co-operative European venture Airbus Industrie, only the American giant The Boeing Company survives.

> **Minimum efficient scale** is the lowest output at which a firm's *LAC* curve stops falling.

Monopolistic competition lies between oligopoly and perfect competition. Monopolistic competitors supply different versions of the same product, such as the particular location of a newsagent.

Table 9.2 Demand, cost and market structure

Minimum efficient scale relative to market size		
Tiny	Intermediate	Large
Perfect competition	Oligopoly	Natural monopoly

Evidence on market structure

The larger the minimum efficient scale relative to the market size, the fewer the number of plants – and probably the number of firms – in the industry. What number of plants (NP) operating at minimum efficient scale does a market size allow? Chapter 7 discussed estimates of minimum efficient scale in different industries. By looking at the total purchases of a product we can estimate market size. Hence we can estimate NP for each industry.

Even industries with only a few key players have some small firms on the fringe. The total number of firms can be a misleading indicator of the structure of the industry. Economists use the *N-firm concentration ratio* to measure the number of key firms in an industry. Thus, the 3-firm concentration ratio tells us the market share of the largest three firms. If there are three key firms, they will supply most of the market. If the industry is perfectly competitive, the largest three firms will only have a tiny share of industry output and sales.

> The **N-firm concentration ratio** is the market share of the largest N firms in the industry.

It would be nice to look at cross-country evidence to see if market structures always obey our theory. If this is to be an independent check, we really need national data before globalization and European integration became important. Table 9.3 examines evidence for the UK, France and Germany for the mid-1970s.

Table 9.3 Concentration and scale economies

Industry	UK		France		Germany	
	CR	NP	CR	NP	CR	NP
Refrigerators	65	1	100	2	72	3
Cigarettes	94	3	100	2	94	3
Refineries	79	8	60	7	47	9
Brewing	47	11	63	5	17	16
Fabrics	28	57	23	57	16	52
Shoes	17	165	13	128	20	197

Note: Concentration ratio CR is % market share of 3 largest firms; number of plants NP is market size divided by minimum efficient scale.
Sources: F. M. Scherer *et al.*, *The Economics of Multiplant Operation*, Harvard University Press, 1975; and F. M. Scherer, *Industrial Market Structure and Economic Performance*, Rand McNally, 1980.

CR is the 3-firm concentration ratio, the market share of the top three firms. NP is the number of plants at minimum efficient scale that the market size allows. If our theory of market structure is correct, industries with big scale economies relative to market size, and thus few plants NP, should have a large concentration ratio CR. Such industries should have few key firms. Conversely, where NP is very high, economies of scale are relatively unimportant and the largest three firms should have a much smaller market share. CR should be low.

Table 9.3 confirms that this theory of market structure fits these facts. Industries such as refrigerator and cigarette manufacture had room for few plants operating at minimum efficient scale: these industries had high degrees of concentration. The largest three firms controlled almost the whole market. Scale economies still mattered in industries such as brewing and petroleum refining: the top three firms had about half the market. Industries such as shoemaking quickly met rising average cost curves, had room for many factories operating at minimum efficient scale and thus were much closer to competitive industries. The top three firms in shoemaking had under one-fifth of the market.

Globalization and multinationals

Table 9.3 showed data before the rise of globalization and multinationals. Globalization reflects cheaper transport costs, better information technology and a deliberate policy of reducing cross-country barriers in order to get efficiency gains from large scale and specialization. Multinationals sell in many countries at the same time. They may, or may not, also produce in many countries.

> **Globalization** is the closer integration of markets across countries. **Multinationals** are firms operating in many countries simultaneously.

Box 9.1 Facing the music

Recorded music, from albums to digital, is now a global business owned by Sony–Bertelsmann 21.5 per cent, Universal Music 25.5 per cent, EMI 13.4 per cent, Warner Music 11.3 per cent, and by independents taking the final 28.4 per cent. While the global market is largely split among a few giants, the value of the global recorded music market is falling every year because of price competition and endemic internet piracy.

Source: http://en.wikipedia.org/wiki/Global_music_market.

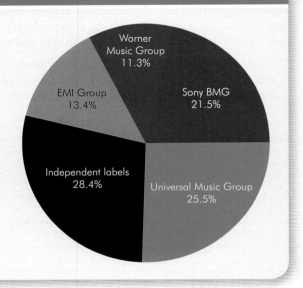

Multinationals affect the analysis implied by Figure 9.1 and Table 9.3. To what market size should we compare minimum efficient scale to estimate the number of plants that can survive in the long run? Multinationals can produce on a large scale somewhere in the world, where production is cheapest, enjoy all the benefits of scale economies, but still sell small quantities in many different markets.

This has three effects. First, it reduces entry barriers in a particular country. A foreign multinational entrant need not achieve a large market share, and therefore need not bid down the price a lot, to achieve scale economies. These now arise because of success in selling globally. Second, small domestic firms, previously sheltered by entry barriers, now face greater international competition and may not survive. Third, greater competition by low-cost producers leads *initially* to lower profit margins and lower prices.

However, if there are only a few multinationals, they may drive the higher-cost domestic firms out of business but then collude among themselves to raise prices again. Some of the debate about globalization hinges on which of these two outcomes dominates: the initial price fall or a possible subsequent price increase. We return shortly to the analysis of collusion. First, we study a simpler case.

9.2 Monopolistic competition

The theory of monopolistic competition envisages a large number of quite small firms so that each firm can neglect the possibility that its own decisions provoke any adjustment in other firms' behaviour. We also assume free entry and exit from the industry in the long run. In these respects, the industry resembles *perfect* competition. What distinguishes *monopolistic* competition is that each firm faces a *downward*-sloping demand curve.

Monopolistic competition describes an industry in which each firm can influence its market share to some extent by changing its price relative to its competitors. Its demand curve is not horizontal because different firms' products are only limited substitutes, as in the location of local shops. A lower price attracts some customers from another shop but each shop always has some local customers for whom convenience is more important than a few pence off the price of a jar of coffee.

Monopolistically competitive industries exhibit *product differentiation*. Corner grocers differentiate by location, hairdressers by customer loyalty. The special feature of a particular restaurant or hairdresser lets it charge a slightly different price from other firms in the industry without losing all its customers.

Monopolistic competition requires not merely product differentiation but also limited opportunities for economies of scale. Firms are small. With lots of producers, each can neglect its interdependence with any particular rival. Many examples of monopolistic competition are service industries where economies of scale are small.

The industry demand curve shows the total output demanded at each price if all firms in the industry charge that price. The market share of each firm depends on the price it charges and on the number of firms in the industry. For a given number of firms, a shift in the industry demand curve shifts the demand curve for the output of each firm. For a given industry demand curve, having more (fewer) firms in the industry shifts the demand curve of each firm to the left (right) as its market share falls (rises). But each firm faces a downward-sloping demand curve. For a given industry demand curve, number of firms and price charged by all other firms, a particular firm can raise its market share a bit by charging a lower price.

Box 9.2 Game wars

'Sony will continue its domination of the video console market through 2010, though its lead will likely shrink due to stronger competition from Microsoft and Nintendo,' according to market research specialists Research and Markets. 'Until 2010, the Sony PS3 will remain just over 50% of the installed base of next-generation consoles, while the Microsoft Xbox 360 will have 29%, and the Nintendo Revolution 21%.'

Microsoft will lead Nintendo in the next generation of consoles due to its head start in launching, its strength in the North American market, and its appeal to older gamers, an ever growing market. The research covers line-powered video game consoles but not portable platforms such as the Nintendo DS or Sony PSP.

Guessing how rivals will behave is critical in this market dominated by the Big 3. The tools of this chapter help us analyse how the strategic interactions play out.

Source: http://www.researchandmarkets.com/reports/c34649.

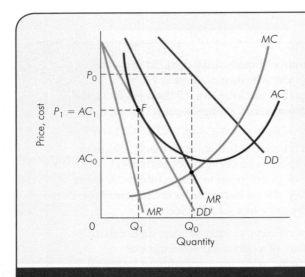

In the short run the monopolistic competitor faces the demand curve *DD* and sets *MC* equal to *MR* to produce Q_0 at a price P_0. Profits are $Q_0 \times (P_0 - AC_0)$. Profits attract new entrants and shift each firm's demand curve to the left. When the demand curve reaches *DD'* we reach the long-run tangency equilibrium at *F*. The firm sets *MC* equal to *MR'* to produce Q_1 at which P_1 equals AC_1. Firms are breaking even and there is no further entry.

Figure 9.2 Equilibrium for a monopolistic competitor

Figure 9.2 shows a firm's supply decision. Given its demand curve *DD* and marginal revenue curve *MR*, the firm makes Q_0 at a price P_0 making short-run profits $Q_0 (P_0 - AC_0)$. In the long run, these profits attract new entrants, diluting the market share of each firm in the industry, shifting their demand curves to the left. Entry stops when each firm's demand curve shifts so far left that price equals average cost and firms just break even. In Figure 9.2 this occurs when demand is *DD'*. The firm makes Q_1 at a price P_1 in the tangency equilibrium at *F*.

> In monopolistic competition, in the long-run **tangency equilibrium** each firm's demand curve just touches its *AC* curve at the output level at which *MC* equals *MR*. Each firm maximizes profits but just breaks even. There is no more entry or exit.

Note two things about the firm's long-run equilibrium at *F*. First, the firm is *not* producing at minimum average cost. It has excess capacity. It could reduce average costs by further expansion. However, its marginal revenue would be so low that this is unprofitable. Second, the firm has some monopoly power because of the special feature of its particular brand or location. Price exceeds marginal cost.

This explains why firms are usually eager for new customers prepared to buy additional output at the *existing* price. We are a race of eager sellers and coy buyers. It is purchasing agents who get Christmas presents from sales reps, not the other way round. In contrast, a perfectly competitive firm does not care if another buyer shows up at the existing price. With price equal to marginal cost, the firm is already selling as much as it wants to sell.

9.3 Oligopoly and interdependence

Under perfect competition or monopolistic competition, there are many firms in the industry. Each firm can ignore the effect of its own actions on rival firms. However, the key to an oligopolistic industry is the need for each firm to consider how its own actions affect the decisions of its relatively few competitors. Each firm has to guess how its rivals will react. Before discussing what constitutes a smart guess we introduce the basic tension between competition and collusion when firms know that they are interdependent. Initially, for simplicity, we neglect the possibility of entry and focus on existing firms.

The profits from collusion

As sole decision maker in the industry, a monopolist would choose industry output to maximize total profits. Hence, the few producers in an industry can maximize their total profit by setting their total output as if they were a monopolist.

> **Collusion** is an explicit or implicit agreement to avoid competition.

Figure 9.3 shows an industry where each firm, and the whole industry, has constant average and marginal costs at the level P_C. Chapter 8 showed that a competitive industry produces Q_C at a price P_C but a multi-plant monopolist maximizes profits by making Q_M at a price P_M. If the oligopolists collude to produce Q_M they act as a *collusive monopolist*. Having decided industry output, the firms agree how to share total output and profits among themselves.

However, it is hard to stop firms cheating on the collective agreement. In Figure 9.3 joint profit is maximized at a total output Q_M and price P_M. Yet each firm can expand output at a marginal cost P_C. Any firm can expand output, selling at a little below the agreed price P_M, and make extra profit since its marginal revenue exceeds its marginal cost. This firm gains at the expense of its collusive partners. Industry output is higher than the best output Q_M, so total profits fall and other firms suffer.

Oligopolists are torn between the desire to collude, in order to maximize joint profits, and the desire to compete, in order to raise market share and profits at the expense of rivals. Yet if all firms compete, joint profits are low and no firm does very well. Therein lies the dilemma.

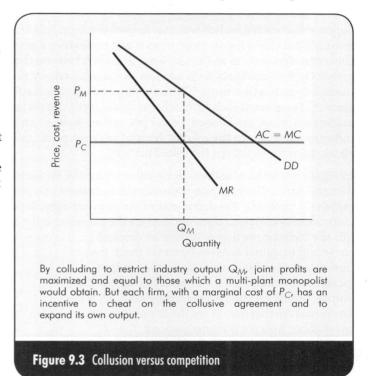

By colluding to restrict industry output Q_M, joint profits are maximized and equal to those which a multi-plant monopolist would obtain. But each firm, with a marginal cost of P_C, has an incentive to cheat on the collusive agreement and to expand its own output.

Figure 9.3 Collusion versus competition

Cartels

Collusion between firms is easiest if formal agreements are legal. Such arrangements, called *cartels*, were common in the late nineteenth century, agreeing market shares and prices in many industries. Cartels are now outlawed in Europe, the US and many other countries. There are big penalties for being caught, but informal agreements and secret deals are sometimes discovered even today.

Cartels across continents are harder to outlaw. The most famous cartel is OPEC, the Organization of Petroleum Exporting Countries. Its members meet regularly to set price and output. Initially, OPEC succeeded in organizing quantity reductions to force up the price of oil. Real OPEC revenues rose 500 per cent between 1973 and 1980. Yet many economists predicted that OPEC, like most cartels, would quickly collapse. Usually, the incentive to cheat is too strong to resist and once somebody breaks ranks others tend to follow. One reason that OPEC was successful for so long was the willingness of Saudi Arabia, the largest oil producer, to restrict its output further when smaller members insisted on expansion.

By 1986 Saudi Arabia was no longer prepared to play by these rules and refused to prop up the price any longer. The oil price collapsed from just under $30 to $9 a barrel. During 1987–98, apart from a brief period during the First Gulf War, oil prices fluctuated between $8 and $20 a barrel. Only after

1998 did OPEC recover the cohesion it displayed during 1973–85. The Second Gulf War and continuing uncertainty in the Middle East has continued to restrict supply in any case, also underpinning the high oil prices since 2003.

The kinked demand curve

Collusion is much harder if there are many firms in the industry, if the product is not standardized and if demand and cost conditions are changing rapidly. In the absence of collusion, each firm's demand curve depends on how competitors react. Firms must guess how their rivals will behave.

Suppose that each firm believes that its own price cut will be matched by all other firms in the industry, but that a rise in its own price will not induce a price response from competitors. Figure 9.4 shows the demand curve DD that each firm then believes that it faces. At the current price P_0 the firm makes Q_0. If competitors do not follow suit, a price rise by one firm alone leads to a large loss of market share to other firms. The firm's demand curve is elastic above A at prices above the current price P_0. However, if each firm believes that if it cuts prices this will be matched by other firms, market shares are unchanged. Lower prices then induce extra sales rises only because the whole industry moves down the market demand curve as prices fall. The demand curve DD is much less elastic for price cuts from the initial price P_0.

In Figure 9.4 we have to draw marginal revenue MR for each of the separate portions of the kinked demand curve. The firm jumps discontinuously from one part of MR to the other when it reaches the output Q_0. Below Q_0 the elastic part of the demand curve is relevant, and marginal revenue is high since additional output does not depress the price much for existing sales. At the output Q_0 the firm hits the inelastic portion of its kinked demand curve and marginal revenue becomes much lower: now that demand is less elastic, further output increases require much lower prices to sell the extra output, hitting revenue from existing sales. Q_0 is the profit-maximizing output for the firm, given its belief about how competitors respond.

Suppose the MC curve of a single firm shifts up or down by a small amount. Since the MR curve has a discontinuous vertical segment at Q_0, it remains optimal to make Q_0 and charge the price P_0. In contrast, a monopolist facing a continuously downward-sloping MR curve would adjust quantity and price when the MC curve shifted. The kinked demand curve model may explain the empirical finding that firms do not always adjust prices when costs change.

It does not explain what determines the initial price P_0. One interpretation is that it is the collusive monopoly price. Each firm believes that an attempt to undercut its rivals will provoke them to co-operate among themselves and retaliate in full. However, its rivals will be happy for it to charge a higher price and see it lose market share.

If we interpret P_0 as the collusive monopoly price, we can contrast the effect of a cost change for a single firm and a cost change for all firms. The latter

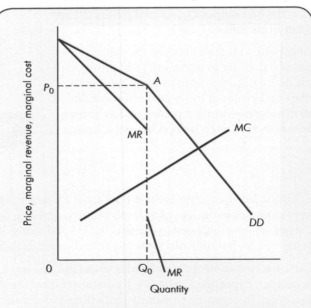

An oligopolist believes rivals will match price cuts but not price rises. The oligopolist's demand curve is kinked at A. Price rises lead to a large loss of market share, but price cuts increase quantity only by increasing industry sales. Marginal revenue is discontinuous at Q_0. The oligopolist produces Q_0, the output at which MC crosses the MR schedule.

Figure 9.4 The kinked demand curve

shifts the marginal cost curve up for the entire industry, raising the collusive monopoly price. Each firm's kinked demand curve shifts up since the monopoly price P_0 has risen. Hence, we can reconcile the stickiness of a firm's price with respect to changes in its own costs alone, and the speed with which the entire industry marks up prices when all firms' costs increase. Examples of the latter are higher taxes on the industry's product, or a union wage increase across the whole industry.

9.4 Game theory and interdependent decisions

A good poker player sometimes bluffs. You can win with a bad hand if your opponents misread it for a good hand. Similarly, by having bluffed in the past and been caught, you may persuade opponents to bet a lot when you have a terrific hand.

> A **game** is a situation in which intelligent decisions are necessarily interdependent.

Like poker players, oligopolists try to anticipate their rivals' moves to determine their own best action. To study interdependent decision making, we use *game theory*. The *players* in the game try to maximize their own *payoffs*. In an oligopoly, the firms are the players and their payoffs are their profits in the long run. Each player must choose a strategy. Being a pickpocket is a strategy. Lifting a particular wallet is a move.

> A **strategy** is a game plan describing how a player acts, or moves, in each possible situation.

As usual, we are interested in equilibrium. In most games, each player's best strategy depends on the strategies chosen by other players. It is silly to be a pickpocket when the police have CCTV cameras or to play four centre backs when the opponents have no proven goalscorers.

Nobody then wants to change strategy, since other people's strategies were already figured into assessing each player's best strategy. This definition of equilibrium, and its application to game theory, was invented by a Princeton University mathematician, John Nash.[1]

> In **Nash equilibrium**, each player chooses the best strategy, *given* the strategies being followed by other players.

Dominant strategies

Sometimes (but not usually) a player's best strategy is independent of those chosen by others. We begin with an example in which each player has a dominant strategy.

> A **dominant strategy** is a player's best strategy *whatever* the strategies adopted by rivals.

Figure 9.5 shows a game[2] between the only two members of a cartel. Each firm can select a high-output or low-output strategy. In each box of Figure 9.5 the coloured number shows firm A's profits and the black number firm B's profits for that output combination.

When both have high output, industry output is high, the price is low and each firm makes a small profit of 1. When each has low output, the outcome is like collusive monopoly. Prices are high and each firm does better, making a profit of 2. Each firm does best (a profit of 3)

		Firm B output	
		High	Low
Firm A output	High	1 1	3 0
	Low	0 3	2 2

The coloured and black numbers in each box indicate profits to firms A and B, respectively. Whether B pursues high or low output, A makes more profit going high; so does B, whichever A adopts. In equilibrium both go high. Yet both would make greater profits if both went low!

Figure 9.5 The Prisoner's Dilemma game

1. Nash, who battled schizophrenia, won the Nobel Prize in Economics for his work on game theory. A film about his life, *A Beautiful Mind*, starred Russell Crowe.
2. The game, called the Prisoner's Dilemma, was first used to analyse the choice facing two people arrested and in different cells, each of whom could plead guilty or not guilty to the only crime that had been committed. Each prisoner would plead innocent if only he or she knew the other would plead guilty.

when it alone has high output: the other firm's low output helps hold down industry output and keep up the price. In this situation we assume the low-output firm makes a profit of 0.

Now we can see how the game will unfold. Consider firm A's decision. It first thinks what to do if firm B has a high-output strategy. Firm A will thus be in one of the two left-hand boxes of Figure 9.5. Firm A gets a profit of 1 by choosing high but a profit of 0 by choosing low. If firm A thinks firm B will choose high output, firm A prefers high output itself.

But firm A must also think what to do if firm B chooses a low-output strategy. This puts firm A in one of the two right-hand boxes. Firm A *still* prefers high output for itself, which yields a profit of 3 whereas low yields a profit of only 2. Firm A has a dominant strategy. Whichever strategy B adopts, A does better to choose a high-output strategy.

Firm B also has a dominant strategy to choose high output. If firm B anticipates that firm A will go high, facing a choice of the two boxes in the top row, firm B prefers to go high. If B thinks A will go low, B faces a choice from the two boxes in the bottom row of Figure 9.5, but B still wants to go high. Firm B does better to go high whichever strategy A selects. Both firm A and firm B have a dominant strategy to go high. Equilibrium is the top left-hand box. Each firm gets a profit of 1.

Yet both firms would do better, getting a profit of 2, if they colluded to form a cartel and both produced low – the bottom right-hand box. But neither can risk going low. Suppose firm A goes low. Firm B, comparing the two boxes in the bottom row, will then go high, preferring a profit of 3 to a profit of 2. And firm A will be screwed, earning a profit of 0 in that event. Firm A can figure all this out in advance, which is why its dominant strategy is to go high.

This shows vividly the tension between collusion and competition. In this example, it appears that the output-restricting cartel will never be formed, since each player can already foresee the overwhelming incentive for the other to cheat on such an arrangement. How, then, can cartels ever be sustained? One possibility is that there exist binding commitments.

> A **commitment** is an arrangement, entered into voluntarily, that restricts future actions.

If both players in Figure 9.5 could simultaneously sign an enforceable contract to produce low output they could achieve the co-operative outcome in the bottom right-hand box, each earning profits of 2. This beats the top left-hand box, which shows the Nash equilibrium of the game when collusion cannot be enforced. Without a binding commitment, neither player can go low because then the other player goes high. Binding commitments, by removing this temptation, let both players go low. Both players gain.

This idea of commitment is important and we shall encounter it many times. Just think of all the human activities that are the subject of legal contracts, a simple commitment simultaneously undertaken by two parties or players.

Although this insight is powerful, its application to oligopoly requires care. Cartels within a country are usually illegal and OPEC is not held together by a contract enforceable in international law. Is there a less formal way in which oligopolists can avoid cheating on the collusive low-output solution to the game? If the game is played only once, this is difficult.

Repeated games

In the real world, the game is repeated many times: firms choose output levels day after day. Suppose two players try to collude on low output: each announces a *punishment strategy*. If firm A ever cheats on the low-output agreement, firm B says that it will subsequently react by raising its output. Firm A makes a similar promise.

Suppose the agreement has been in force for some time and both firms have stuck to their low-output deal. Firm A assumes that firm B will go low as usual. Figure 9.5 shows that firm A makes a *temporary* gain today if it cheats and goes high. Instead of staying in the bottom right-hand box with a profit of

Activity box 9 Sustaining a competitive advantage

Harvard Business School guru Michael Porter pioneered the analysis of the strategy that a firm uses to build and sustain a competitive advantage over its actual and potential rivals. A competitive advantage exists when a firm can earn supernormal profits (also called economic rents). To sustain a competitive advantage, a firm must erect entry barriers that prevent other firms joining the party, increasing industry output, and bidding down the price. The key element of strategy, according to Porter, is to create something distinctive and choose a bundle of activities that reinforce one another, making the sum of the parts even harder for rivals to copy.

For example, BMW launched the 1-series to complete its product range and lock in successful professionals. Previously, a successful company director with a BMW 525 might have bought a VW Golf for her ageing mother. When the BMW 1-series became available, it might be more convenient for both the family BMWs to be serviced at the same local garage. Someone wanting this convenience might have previously chosen an Audi A6 as their company car because mum already had a Golf.

Professor Porter recognized that, while it sometimes takes only a little piece to complete the jigsaw, the brand is much less powerful without it. Good strategy creates interlocking advantages, and thereby makes it much more expensive for rivals to compete. One implication of this view is that a particular firm's best strategy is very sensitive to its history. You need to know which pieces of the jigsaw already exist in order to advise on the best way in which to enhance the value of the interlocking pieces.

Nor does it follow that all attempts at strategy succeed. Some motoring journalists responded to the launch of the BMW 1-series by claiming it would *diminish* the BMW brand. The deliberately conservative image of the 1-series might not appeal to boy racers or trendy young professionals. If instead they bought a Golf GTI, they might subsequently remain in the VW-Audi family and graduate to an Audi A4 rather than a 3-series BMW.

Questions
Which of these meet the Porter test for building competitive advantage?

(a) An oil company diversifies its business by buying a mobile phone company.

(b) A mobile phone company does a deal with an internet provider to make internet access available on mobile phones.

(c) A grocery supermarket provides in-store banking facilities to become a one-stop-shop for customers.

To check your answers to these questions, go to page 718.

2, it can move to the top right-hand box and make 3. However, from tomorrow onwards, firm B will also go high and firm A can then do no better than continue to go high too, making a profit of 1 for evermore. But if A refuses to cheat today it can continue to stay in the bottom right-hand box and make 2 for ever. In cheating, A swaps a temporary gain for a permanent reduction in future profits. Thus, punishment strategies can sustain an explicit cartel or implicit collusion even if no formal commitment exists.

It is all very well to promise punishment if the other player cheats. But this will affect the other player's behaviour only if your threat is credible.

> A **credible threat** is one that, after the fact, is still optimal to carry out.

In the preceding example, once firm A has cheated and gone high, it is then in firm B's interest to go high anyway. Hence a threat to go high if A ever cheats is a credible threat.

These insights shed light on the actual behaviour of OPEC in 1986, when Saudi Arabia dramatically raised its output, leading to a collapse of oil prices. In the 1980s, other members of OPEC had gradually cheated on the low-output agreement, trusting that Saudi Arabia would still produce low to sustain a high price and the cartel's prestige. They hoped Saudi threats to adopt a punishment strategy were empty threats. They were wrong. Figure 9.5 shows that, once the others went high, Saudi Arabia had to go high too.

9.5 Reaction functions

In the previous example, in a one-off game each player had a dominant strategy, to produce high output whatever its rival did. This led to a poor outcome for both players because they were not co-operating despite being interdependent. When the game is repeated, commitments and punishment strategies help players co-operate to find an outcome that is better for both of them.

> In the **Cournot model**, each firm treats the *output* of the other firm as given.

In punishing a rival, a player's actions change in response to bad behaviour by the rival. Dominant strategies are rare. More usually, each player's best action depends on the actual or expected actions of other players. How a player reacts depends on what it assumes about its rivals' behaviour. For simplicity we analyse *duopoly* in which there are only two players.

Cournot behaviour

In 1838 French economist Augustin Cournot analysed a simple model of duopoly.

Imagine a duopoly in which both firms have the same constant marginal costs MC. Figure 9.6 draws the decision problem for firm A. If firm A assumes that firm B produces 0, firm A gets the whole industry demand curve D_0. This shows what output firm A can sell given the prices that it charges. From this, firm A calculates the marginal revenue MR_0, and produces Q_0 to equate its marginal cost and marginal revenue.

If instead firm A assumes that firm B makes 3 units, firm A faces a demand curve D_3 obtained by shifting the market demand D_0 to the left by 3 units. Firm B gets 3 units and the residual demand is available for firm A. For this demand curve D_3, firm A computes the marginal revenue curve MR_3 and chooses output Q_3 to equate marginal cost and marginal revenue.

Similarly, if firm A expects firm B to make 5 units, firm A shifts D_0 to the left by 5 units to get D_5, and produces Q_5 in order to equate marginal cost and its marginal revenue MR_5. The larger the output that firm 2 is expected to make and sell, the smaller the optimal output of firm A. Q_5 is smaller than Q_3, which is smaller than Q_0.

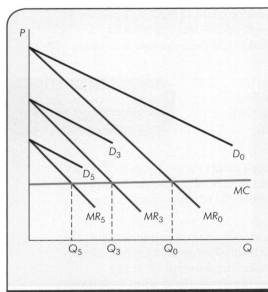

Assuming firm B makes 0, firm A faces the market demand curve D_0 and maximizes profits by producing Q_0 to equate marginal cost and marginal revenue. If firm B is assumed to make 3 units, firm A faces the residual demand curve D_3 lying 3 units left of D_0. Firm A then makes Q_3. If firm B is assumed to make 5 units, firm A faces D_5 and makes Q_5. Optimal output for firm A is lower the higher the output that it assumes firm B will make.

Figure 9.6 Cournot behaviour

Repeating this exercise for every possible belief that firm A has about the output of firm B, yields the reaction function of firm A.

> A firm's **reaction function** shows how its optimal output varies with each possible action by its rival.

In the Cournot model, a rival's action is its output choice. Figure 9.7 shows the two outputs Q^A and Q^B. From Figure 9.6, firm A makes less the more it thinks that firm B will make. In Figure 9.7, firm A's optimal output choice is the reaction function R^A. If firm B is expected to produce 1 unit less, firm A chooses to raise output by less than 1 unit. This ensures total output falls, raising the price. Because this lets firm A earn more on its previous output units, it is not worth raising its output by as much as it expects the output of B to fall. Equivalently, in Figure 9.6 firm A's demand curve shifts more than its marginal revenue curve, hence its output rise is smaller than the conjectured fall in the output of firm B.

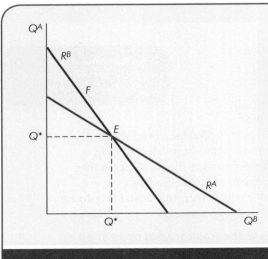

R^A is the reaction function of firm A, showing how its optimal output varies with the output it assumes firm B will make and sell. Since firms are similar, R^B is the similar reaction function for firm B, showing its best output given the assumed output by firm A. With these Cournot assumptions about its rival's behaviour, point E is the Nash equilibrium. Each firm's guess about its rival's behaviour is then correct, and neither firm wishes to change its behaviour. If the firms are identical, their reaction functions are asymmetric, and both make the same output Q^*.

Figure 9.7 Nash–Cournot equilibrium

In the duopoly, both firms are the same. Hence firm B faces a similar problem. It makes guesses about the output of firm A, calculates the residual demand curve for firm B, and chooses its best output. Figure 9.7 shows the reaction function R^B for firm B, which also makes less the more that it assumes its rival will produce.

Along each reaction function, each firm makes its best response to the assumed output of the other firm. Only in equilibrium is it optimal for the other firm actually to behave in the way that has been assumed. In Nash equilibrium, neither firm wishes to alter its behaviour even after its conjecture about the other firm's output is then confirmed.

> **Nash equilibrium** is where the two reaction functions intersect.

Since both firms face the same industry demand curve, their reaction functions are symmetric if they also face the same marginal cost curves in Figure 9.6. The two firms then produce the same output Q^* as shown in Figure 9.7. If costs differed, we could still construct (different) reaction functions and their intersection would no longer imply equal market shares.

Suppose the marginal cost curve of firm A now shifts down in Figure 9.6. At each output assumed for firm B, firm A now makes more. It moves further down any MR schedule before meeting MC. Hence in Figure 9.7 the reaction function R^A shifts up, showing firm A makes more output Q^A at any assumed output Q^B of its rival. The new intersection of the reaction functions, say at point F, shows what happens to Nash equilibrium in the Cournot model.

It is no surprise that the output of firm A rises. Why does the output of firm B fall? With lower marginal costs, firm A is optimally making more. Unless firm B cuts its output, the price will fall a lot. Firm B prefers to cut output a little, in order to prop up the price a bit, preventing a big revenue loss on its existing units.

As in our discussion of the Prisoner's Dilemma game in Section 9.4, the Nash–Cournot equilibrium does not maximize the joint payoffs of the two players. They fail to achieve the total output that maximizes joint profits. By treating the output of the rival as given, each firm expands too much. Higher output bids down prices for everybody. In neglecting the fact that its own expansion hurts its rival, each firm's output is too high.

Each firm's behaviour is correct given its assumption that its rival's output is fixed. But expansion by one firm induces the rival to alter its behaviour. A joint monopolist would take that into account and make more total profit.

Bertrand behaviour

To show how the assumption about rivals' behaviour affects reaction functions and hence Nash equilibrium, consider a different model suggested by another French economist, Joseph Bertrand.

> In the **Bertrand model** of oligopoly, each firm treats the *prices* of rivals as given.

Each firm decides a price (and hence an output), reflecting the price it expects its rival to set. We could go through a similar analysis to the Cournot model, find reaction curves showing how the *price* set by each firm depends on the *price* set by its rival, and hence find the Nash equilibrium in prices for the Bertrand model. Knowing the equilibrium price, we could work out equilibrium quantity. If the firms are identical, again they divide the market equally. However, in the Bertrand model, it is easy to see what the Nash equilibrium must be. It is the perfectly competitive outcome – price equals marginal cost. How do we know?

Suppose firm B sets a price above its marginal cost. Firm A can grab the whole market by setting a price a little below that of firm B. Since firm B can anticipate this, it must set a lower price. This argument keeps working until, in Nash equilibrium, both firms price at marginal cost and split the market between them. There is then no incentive to alter behaviour.

Comparing Bertrand and Cournot

Under Bertrand behaviour, Nash equilibrium entails price equal to marginal cost, so industry output is high. Under Cournot behaviour, Nash equilibrium entails lower industry output and a higher price. Because marginal and average costs are constant, each firm makes profits since the price is higher. But the firms do not co-operate. A joint monopolist would make more profit by co-ordinating output decisions. Industry output would be even lower and the price even higher.

Thus, Nash equilibrium depends on the *particular* assumption each firm makes about its rival's behaviour. Generally, economists prefer the Cournot model. In practice, few oligopolies behave like a perfectly competitive industry, as the Bertrand model predicts.

Moreover, since prices can be changed rapidly, treating a rival's *price* as fixed does not seem plausible. In contrast, we can interpret the Cournot model as saying that firms first choose *output capacity* and then set price. Since capacity takes time to alter, this makes more sense.

First-mover advantage

So far we have assumed that the two duopolists make decisions simultaneously. Suppose one firm can choose output before the other. Does it help to move first?

To anticipate how firm B behaves once the output of firm A is fixed, firm A examines the reaction function of firm B as derived in Figures 9.6 and 9.7. In setting output, firm A then takes account of how its own output decisions *affect* output by firm B.

Firm A thus has a different reaction function. Figure 9.7 showed the Cournot reaction function R^A treating Q^B as chosen independently of Q^A. Now firm A uses the reaction function R^B to deduce that a higher output Q^A induces a *lower* output Q^B. Hence, firm A expects its own output expansion to bid the price down *less* than under Cournot behaviour. Its marginal revenue schedule is higher up. Firm A knows that firm B will help prop up the price by cutting Q^B in response to a rise in Q^A.

Facing a higher *MR* schedule as a *Stackelberg leader* than under Cournot behaviour, firm A produces more than under Cournot behaviour. Firm B makes less because it must react to the fact that a high output Q^A is already a done deal. Firm A ends up with higher output and profits than under Cournot behaviour but firm B has lower output and lower profit. Firm A has a first-mover advantage.

> In the **Stackelberg model,** firm B can observe the output already fixed by firm A. In choosing output, firm A must thus anticipate the subsequent reaction of firm B.

Moving first acts like a commitment that prevents your subsequent manipulation by the other player. Once firm A has built a large output capacity, firm B has to live with the reality that firm A will make large output. The best response of firm B is then low output. By propping up the output price, this helps firm A. Being smart, firm A had already figured all that out.

> A **first-mover advantage** means that the player moving first achieves higher payoffs than when decisions are simultaneous.

In some industries, firms are fairly symmetric and Cournot behaviour is a good description of how these oligopolists behave. Other industries have a dominant firm, perhaps because of a technical edge or privileged location. That firm may be able to act as a Stackelberg leader and anticipate how its smaller rivals will then react.

9.6 Entry and potential competition

So far we have discussed imperfect competition between existing firms. To complete our understanding of such markets, we must also think about the effect of potential competition from new entrants to the industry on the behaviour of existing or incumbent firms. Three cases must be distinguished: where entry is trivially easy, where it is difficult by accident and where it is difficult by design.

Contestable markets

Free entry to, and exit from, the industry is a key feature of perfect competition, a market structure in which each firm is tiny relative to the industry. Suppose, however, that we observe an industry with few incumbent firms. Before assuming that our previous analysis of oligopoly is needed, we must think hard about entry and exit. The industry may be a contestable market.

> A **contestable market** has free entry and free exit.

By free entry, we mean that all firms, including both incumbents and potential entrants, have access to the same technology and hence have the same cost curves. By free exit, we mean that there are no *sunk* or irrecoverable costs: on leaving the industry, a firm can fully recoup its previous investment expenditure, including money spent on building up knowledge and goodwill.

A contestable market allows *hit-and-run* entry. If the incumbent firms, however few, do not behave as if they were a perfectly competitive industry ($p = MC = $ minimum LAC), an entrant can step in, undercut them and make a temporary profit before quitting again.

As globalization proceeds, we should remember that foreign suppliers are important potential entrants. This can take two forms. First, if monopoly profits are too high in the domestic market, competition from imports may augment supply, bidding down prices and profits in the domestic market. In the extreme case, in which imports surge in whenever domestic prices rise above the world price, we are back in the competitive world analysed in Chapter 8.

Globalization also raises the likelihood that foreign firms will set up production facilities in the home market, a tangible form of entry. By raising the supply of potential entrants, globalization increases the relevance of contestable markets as a description of market structure. Moreover, we normally think of an entrant as having to start from scratch. When an existing foreign firm enters the domestic market, its production and marketing expertise may already be highly developed.

Globalization may be a two-edged sword. On the one hand, it raises the size of the relevant market and makes entry easier. On the other hand, by allowing multinationals to become vast by operating in many countries simultaneously, globalization may encourage the formation of large firms that then have substantial market power wherever they operate. Coke and Pepsi are slugging it out for global dominance and Virgin Cola provides only limited competition, even in the UK.

The theory of contestable markets remains controversial. There are many industries in which sunk costs are hard to recover or where the initial expertise may take an entrant some time to acquire, placing it at a temporary disadvantage against incumbent firms. Nor, as we shall shortly see, is it safe to assume that incumbents will not change their behaviour when threatened by entry. But the theory does vividly illustrate that market structure and incumbent behaviour cannot be deduced simply by counting the number of firms in the industry.

In the previous chapter, we were careful to stress that a monopolist is a sole producer *who can completely discount fear of entry*. We now refine the classification of Table 9.1 by discussing entry in more detail.

> **Box 9.3 Barriers at the checkout**
>
> In 2004 the Morrisons supermarket chain finally completed its takeover of rival Safeway. At a stroke, Morrisons was catapulted from the supermarket minnow, with a 6 per cent market share, to a big league player with 17 per cent of the UK market, only marginally less than Sainsbury's, one-time leader of the supermarket industry.
>
> The takeover of Safeway was contested, with Tesco, Asda and Sainsbury's all mounting rival bids to Morrisons'. At one stage, Philip Green, the owner of high street retailer British Home Stores (Bhs), also registered an interest in Safeway. Safeway was such an attractive target because it provided the last chance to enter the supermarket industry. Without access to land, and facing difficulty getting planning permission for new supermarkets, the only entry mode was a takeover. With Safeway now in the hands of Morrisons, and the industry consolidated into large players, the next takeover will be even more difficult.

Innocent entry barriers

Our discussion of entry barriers distinguishes those that occur anyway and those that are deliberately erected by incumbent firms.

> An **innocent entry barrier** is one not deliberately erected by incumbent firms.

The American economist Joe Bain distinguished three types of entry barrier: product differentiation, absolute cost advantages and scale economies. The first of these is not an innocent barrier, as we shall shortly explain. Absolute cost advantages, where incumbent firms have lower cost curves than those that entrants will face, may be innocent. If it takes time to learn the business, incumbents will face lower costs, at least in the short run. If they are smart, they may already have located in the most advantageous site. In contrast, if incumbents have undertaken investment or R&D specifically with a view to deterring entrants, this is not an innocent barrier. We take up this issue shortly.

Figure 9.1 showed the role of scale economies as an innocent entry barrier. If minimum efficient scale is large relative to the industry demand curve, an entrant cannot get into the industry without considerably depressing the market price, and it may prove simply impossible to break in at a profit.

The greater such innocent entry barriers, the more appropriate it is to neglect potential competition from entrants. The oligopoly game then reduces to competition between incumbent firms along the lines we discussed in the previous section. Where innocent entry barriers are low, one of two things may happen. Either incumbent firms accept this situation, in which case competition from potential entrants will prevent incumbent firms from exercising much market power – the outcome will be closer to that of perfect competition – or else incumbent firms will try to design some entry barriers of their own.

9.7 Strategic entry deterrence

A strategy is a game plan when decision making is interdependent. The word 'strategic' is used in everyday language but it has a precise meaning in economics.

> A **strategic move** is one that influences the other person's choice, in a manner favourable to oneself, by affecting the other person's expectations of how one will behave.

In Figure 9.8 a single incumbent firm plays a game against a potential entrant. The entrant can come in or stay out. If the entrant comes in, the incumbent can opt for the easy life, accept the new rival and agree to share the market – or it can fight. Fighting entry means producing at least as much as before, and perhaps considerably more than before, so that the industry price collapses. In this *price war*, sometimes called *predatory pricing* by the incumbent, both firms do badly and make losses. The top row of boxes in Figure 9.8 show the profits to the incumbent (in black) and the entrant (in colour) in each of the three possible outcomes.

If the incumbent is unchallenged it does very well, making profits of 5. The entrant of course makes nothing. If they share the market, both make small profits of 1. In a price war, both make losses. How should the game go?

Suppose the entrant comes in. Comparing the left two boxes of the top row, the incumbent does better to cave in than to fight. The entrant can figure this out. Any threat by the incumbent to resist entry is not a credible threat – when it comes to the crunch, it will be better to cave in. Much as the incumbent would like the entrant to stay out, in which case the incumbent would make profits of 5, the equilibrium of the game is that the entrant will come in and the incumbent will not resist. Both make profits of 1, the top left-hand box.

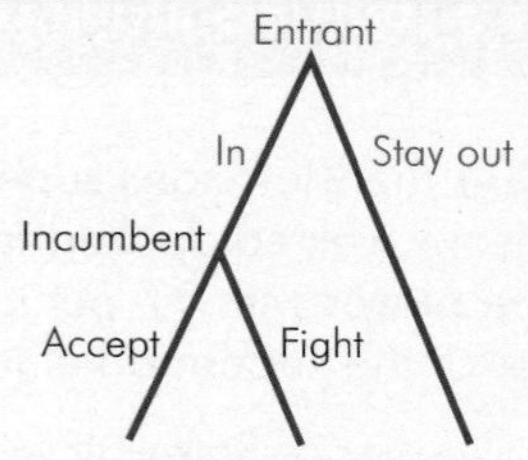

	Entrant		
	In		Stay out
Incumbent			
Accept		Fight	

Profits without	1,	1	−1, −2	5,	0
Profits with	−2,	1	−1, −1	2,	0

In the absence of deterrence, if the entrant enters, the incumbent does better to accept entry than to fight. The entrant knows this and enters. Equilibrium is the top left-hand box, and both firms make a profit of 1. But if the incumbent pre-commits an expenditure of 3 which is recouped *only* if there is a fight, the incumbent resists entry, the entrant stays out and equilibrium is the bottom right-hand box. The incumbent does better, making a profit of 2.

Figure 9.8 Strategic entry deterrence

The incumbent, however, may have got its act together before the potential entrant appears on the scene. It may be able to invent a binding pre-commitment, forcing itself to resist entry and thereby scare off a future challenge. The incumbent would be ecstatic if a Martian appeared and guaranteed to shoot the incumbent's directors if they ever allowed an entry to be unchallenged. Entrants would expect a fight, would anticipate a loss of 1, and would stay out, leaving the incumbent with a permanent profit of 5.

In the absence of Martians, the incumbent can achieve the same effect by economic means. Suppose the incumbent invests in expensive spare capacity that is unused at low output. The incumbent has low output in the absence of entry or if an entrant is accommodated without a fight. Suppose in these situations the incumbent loses 3 by carrying this excess capacity. The second row of boxes in Figure 9.8 reduces the incumbent's profits by 3 in these two outcomes. In a price war, however, the incumbent's output is high and the spare capacity is no longer wasted; hence we do not need to reduce the incumbent's profit in the middle column of boxes in Figure 9.8. Now consider the game again.

If the entrant comes in, the incumbent loses 2 by caving in but only 1 by fighting. Hence entry is resisted. Foreseeing this, the entrant does not enter, since the entrant loses money in a price war. Hence the equilibrium of the game is the bottom right-hand box and no entry takes place. Strategic entry deterrence has been successful. It has also been profitable. Even allowing for the cost of 3 of carrying the spare capacity, the incumbent still makes a profit of 2, which is better than the profit of 1 in the top left-hand box when no deterrence was attempted and the entrant came in.

> **Strategic entry deterrence** is behaviour by incumbent firms to make entry less likely.

Does deterrence always work? No. Suppose in Figure 9.8 we change the right-hand column. In the top row the incumbent gets a profit of 3 if no entry occurs. Without the pre-commitment, the equilibrium is the top left-hand box as before. But if the incumbent has to spend 3 on a spare capacity pre-commitment, it now makes a profit of 0 in the bottom right-hand box when entry is deterred. The entrant is still deterred but the incumbent would have done better not to invest in spare capacity and to let the entrant in.

Box 9.4 Why advertise so much?

Advertising is not always meant to erect entry barriers to potential entrants. Sometimes it really does aim to inform consumers by revealing inside information that firms have about the quality of their own goods.

When consumers can tell at a glance the quality of a product, even before buying it, there is little gain from advertising. Black rotten bananas cannot be advertised as fresh. Information is freely available and attempts to deceive consumers are detected. However, for most goods, consumers cannot detect quality before purchase and discover it only by using the good for a while.

The firm then has inside information over first-time buyers. A conspicuous (expensive) advertising campaign *signals* to potential consumers that the firm believes in its product and expects to make enough repeat sales to recoup the fixed cost of initial advertising. Firms whose lies are quickly discovered do not invest much in advertising.

What about goods like refrigerators, essentially a once-off purchase, usually not replaced for a decade or more? Consumers would really benefit from truthful advertising but producers of high-quality goods have no incentive to advertise. It would pay lying advertisers to advertise too (since it is ages before they are found out). A willingness to advertise no longer signals the quality of the product. So little advertising occurs.

The table below shows advertising spending as a fraction of sales revenue for the four types of good identified above. The theory fits the facts rather well.

Advertising spending as a percentage of sales revenue

Quality detected	Time until buy again	Example	Advertising as % of sales revenue
Before buy	Irrelevant	Bananas	0.4
Soon after buy	Soon	Biscuits	3.6
Long after buy	Irrelevant	CD player	1.8

Source: E. Davis, J. Kay and J. Star, 'Is Advertising Rational?', *Business Strategy Review*, Autumn 1991, Oxford University Press.

This model suggests that price wars should never happen. If the incumbent is really going to fight, then the entrant should not have entered. This of course requires the entrant to know accurately the profits of the incumbent in the different boxes and therefore correctly predict its behaviour. In the real world, entrants sometimes get it wrong. Moreover, if the entrant has much better financial backing than the incumbent, a price war may be a good investment for the entrant. The incumbent will exit first and thereafter the entrant will be able to cash up and get its losses back with interest.

Is spare capacity the only pre-commitment available to incumbents? Pre-commitments must be irreversible, otherwise they are an empty threat, and they must increase the chances that the incumbent will fight. Anything with the character of fixed and sunk costs may work: fixed costs artificially increase scale economies and make the incumbent more keen on high output, and sunk costs cannot be reversed. Advertising to invest in goodwill and brand loyalty is a good example. So is product proliferation. If the incumbent has only one brand, an entrant may hope to break in with a different brand. But if the incumbent has a complete range of brands or models, an entrant will have to compete across the whole product range.

9.8 Summing up

Few industries in the real world are like the textbook extremes of perfect competition and pure monopoly. Most are imperfectly competitive. This chapter introduced you to types of imperfect competition. Game theory in general, and concepts such as commitment, credibility and deterrence, allow economists to analyse many of the practical concerns of big business.

What have we learned? First, market structure and the behaviour of incumbent firms are determined *simultaneously*. Economists used to start with a market structure, determined by the extent of scale economies relative to the industry demand curve, then deduce how the incumbent firms would behave (monopoly, oligopoly, perfect competition), then check out these predictions against performance indicators, such as the extent to which prices exceeded marginal cost. Now we realize that strategic behaviour by incumbent firms can affect entry, and hence market structure, except where entry is almost trivially easy.

Second, and related, we have learned the importance of *potential* competition, which may come from domestic firms considering entry, or from imports from abroad. The number of firms observed in the industry today conveys little information about the extent of the market power they truly exercise. If entry is easy, even a single incumbent or apparent monopolist may find it unprofitable to depart significantly from perfectly competitive behaviour.

Finally, we have seen how many business practices of the real world – price wars, advertising, brand proliferation, excess capacity or excessive research and development – can be understood as strategic competition in which, to be effective, threats must be made credible by prior commitments.

Summary

- **Imperfect competition** exists when individual firms believe they face downward-sloping demand curves. The most important forms are monopolistic competition, oligopoly and pure monopoly.

- **Pure monopoly** status can be conferred by legislation, as when an industry is nationalized or a temporary patent is awarded. When **minimum efficient scale** is very large relative to the industry demand curve, this innocent entry barrier may be sufficiently high to produce a natural monopoly in which all threat of entry can be ignored.

- At the opposite extreme, entry and exit may be costless. The market is **contestable**, and incumbent firms must mimic perfectly competitive behaviour to avoid being flooded by entrants. With an intermediate size of entry barrier, the industry may be an oligopoly.

- **Monopolistic competitors** face free entry to and exit from the industry but are individually small and make similar though not identical products. Each has limited monopoly power in its special brand. In long-run equilibrium, price equals average cost but exceeds marginal revenue and marginal cost at the tangency equilibrium.

- **Oligopolists** face tension between collusion to maximize joint profits and competition for a larger share of smaller joint profits. **Collusion** may be formal, as in a cartel, or informal. Without **credible threats** of punishment by its partners, each firm faces a temptation to cheat.

- **Game theory** analyses interdependent decisions in which each player chooses a strategy. In the Prisoner's Dilemma game, each firm has a dominant strategy. With binding commitments, both players could do better by guaranteeing not to cheat on the collusive solution.

- A **reaction function** shows one player's best response to the actions of other players. In **Nash equilibrium** reaction functions intersect. No player then wishes to change his decision.

- In **Cournot behaviour** each firm treats the output of its rival as given. In **Bertrand behaviour** each firm treats the price of its rival as given. Nash–Bertrand equilibrium entails pricing at marginal cost. Nash–Cournot equilibrium entails lower output, higher prices and profits. However, firms still fail to maximize joint profits because each neglects the fact that its output expansion hurts its rivals.

- A firm with a **first-mover advantage** acts as a **Stackelberg leader**. By deducing the subsequent reaction of its rival, it produces higher output, knowing the rival will then have to produce lower output. Moving first is a useful commitment.

- **Innocent entry barriers** are made by nature, and arise from scale economies or absolute cost advantages of incumbent firms. **Strategic entry barriers** are made in boardrooms and arise from credible commitments to resist entry if challenged. Only in certain circumstances is strategic entry deterrence profitable for incumbents.

Review questions

To check your answers to these questions, go to page 717.

1 An industry faces the demand curve:

Q	1	2	3	4	5	6	7	8	9	10
P	10	9	8	7	6	5	4	3	2	1

(a) Suppose it is a monopolist whose constant $MC = 3$: what price and output are chosen?
(b) Now suppose there are two firms, each with $MC = AC = 3$: what price and output maximize joint profits if they collude? (c) Why might each firm be tempted to cheat if it can avoid retaliation by the other?

2 With the above industry demand curve, two firms, A and Z, begin with half the market each when charging the monopoly price. Z decides to cheat and believes A will stick to its old output level. (a) Show the demand curve Z believes it faces. (b) What price and output would Z then choose?

3 Vehicle repairers sometimes suggest that mechanics should be licensed so that repairs are done only by qualified people. Some economists argue that customers can always ask whether a mechanic was trained at a reputable institution without needing to see any licence. (a) Evaluate the arguments for and against licensing car mechanics. (b) Are the arguments the same for licensing doctors?

4 Think of five adverts on television. Is their function primarily informative, or the erection of entry barriers to the industry?

5 A good-natured parent knows that children sometimes need to be punished but also knows that, when it comes to the crunch, the child will be let off with a warning. Can the parent undertake any pre-commitment to make the threat of punishment credible?

6 **Common fallacies** Why are these statements wrong? (a) Competitive firms should get together to restrict output and drive up the price. (b) Firms would not advertise unless they expected advertising to increase sales.

7 **Harder question** 'Since a firm's optimal behaviour depends on how it believes that its rival(s) will react, there are as many output decisions, and hence equilibria, as there are guesses about what rivals will do.' How do economists try to narrow down the assumptions that firms make about their rivals?

8 **Harder question** Many of the interesting games are games against the government. Think of a European airline, until recently state-owned, now private but losing money under the pressure of high oil prices and the growth of low-cost airlines. Believing that the government will bail it out if the worst comes to the worst, the airline has no incentive to take the tough measures today needed to make its business profitable. How can the government signal that it will not bail out the airline, forcing the airline to improve or go bust?

9 **Essay question** 'Globalization, by increasing the size of the market, reduces market power of individual firms and the need to address strategic interactions.' 'Globalization increases the payoff to scooping the pool, making mergers more attractive and enhancing worries about market power.' Are either of these views correct? Both of them?

To help you grasp the key concepts of this chapter check out the extra resources posted on the Online Learning Centre. There are chapter summaries, self-test questions, an interactive graphing tool, weblinks and a searchable glossary, all for free!

To put your learning into practice and prepare for exams, an **Interactive Workbook** is also available online, containing a variety of question types and providing feedback on your answers.

If you'd like further help with economics, or have any questions, **NetTutor** is here to help! You will have a personalised tutorial service at your fingertips. Visit the online learning centre at: www.mcgraw-hill.co.uk/textbooks/begg for information on accessing all of these resources.

The labour market

By the end of this chapter, you should understand:

1 a firm's demand for inputs in the long run and short run

2 marginal value product, marginal revenue product and marginal cost of a factor

3 the industry demand for labour

4 labour supply decisions

5 transfer earnings and economic rent

6 labour market equilibrium and disequilibrium

7 how minimum wages affect employment

8 isoquants and the choice of production technique

In winning a golf tournament, a top professional earns more in a weekend than a professor earns in a year. Students studying economics can expect higher career earnings than those of equally smart students studying philosophy. An unskilled worker in the EU earns more than an unskilled worker in India. Few market economies provide jobs for all their citizens wanting to work. How can we explain these aspects of the real world?

In each case the answer depends on the supply and demand for that type of labour, the subject of the next two chapters. We begin our analysis of the markets for the factors of production – labour, capital and land. We discuss what determines the equilibrium prices and quantities of these inputs in different industries and in the whole economy. We begin with the factor called 'labour'. Chapter 12 applies the same principles to the markets for other production inputs.

We have already studied the market for goods. There is nothing intrinsically different about our approach to factor markets. You should be able to guess the structure of this chapter: demand, supply, equilibrium, problems of disequilibrium and adjustment.

Table 10.1 gives data on UK earnings (full-time males) in 2005 and compares these with inflation-adjusted data for 1993. By 2005 male workers in financial services earned £155 a week more than the national average. Workers in energy and water were also doing well in their high-tech industry at a time of high oil prices. Conversely, construction workers' wages were subject to downward pressure from immigrant workers.

Although the economics of factor markets still focuses on supply and demand, there is something special about demand in factor markets. It is not a direct or final demand, but a derived demand. Firms demand inputs

> The demand for inputs is a **derived demand**, reflecting demand for the firm's output.

Table 10.1 Weekly real earnings, UK (full-time males, 2005 £)

	1993	2005
Whole economy	378	519
Financial services	452	664
Construction	367	470
Energy and water	495	646

Source: ONS, *Labour Market Trends.*

only because they want to produce output. Each firm simultaneously decides how many outputs to supply and how many inputs to demand. The two are inextricably linked.

On the supply side we distinguish between the supply of factors to the economy and to an individual firm or industry. A firm can gain factors by attracting them away from other firms. However, the economy as a whole may be able to expand particular inputs only slowly. It takes time to build factories or train skilled workers.

In the short run, the supply of pilots to the economy may be fixed. Any rise in the total demand for pilots raises their equilibrium wage. In the longer run, high wages for pilots then act as a signal for school leavers to abandon plans to become train drivers and go to flying school instead. Thus, we need to distinguish labour supply in the short run and long run.

Combining demand and supply leads to equilibrium prices and quantities in the labour market. How quickly does the labour market return to equilibrium? Whereas some output markets may return to equilibrium relatively quickly, labour market adjustment is often more sluggish. We examine reasons why the labour market may be slow to adjust.

10.1 The firm's demand for factors in the long run

In the long run all inputs can be adjusted. Chapter 7 studied a firm's long-run costs. Chapters 8 and 9 considered various descriptions of the demand curve facing a firm and showed how a firm would choose output supplied to maximize profits. Although part of the same decision, we now focus not on the firm's supply of output but on its corresponding demand for inputs.

The firm thinks about the least-cost way of making each possible output and then selects the output that maximizes profit. In producing any particular output by the cheapest available technique, a rise in the price of labour relative to capital makes the firm switch to a more capital-intensive technique. Conversely, if capital becomes relatively more expensive, the least-cost technique for a given output is now more labour-intensive. The firm substitutes away from the factor of production that has become relatively more expensive.

This principle helps explain cross-country differences in capital–labour ratios in the same industry. European farmers face high wages relative to the rental of a combine harvester. Mechanized farming economizes on expensive workers. Indian farmers, facing cheap and abundant labour but scarce and expensive capital, use labour-intensive techniques. Workers with scythes and shovels do the jobs done by combine harvesters and bulldozers in the UK.

A higher wage makes the firm substitute capital for labour in making a given output. But it also raises the total cost of producing any output. Firms still use *some* labour, for which they now pay more than before. With higher marginal costs, but unchanged demand and marginal revenue curves, the firm chooses to make less output.

Thus a rise in the price of one factor not merely changes factor intensity at a given output, but also changes the profit-maximizing level of output. Studying consumer decisions in Chapter 5, we saw that a change in the price of a good has both a substitution effect and an income effect. The substitution effect reflects the change in relative prices of different goods and the income effect reflects changes in real income as a result of the price change. The demand for production inputs works exactly the same way.

There is a pure substitution effect at a given level of output. A higher relative price of labour compared with capital leads firms to substitute capital for labour. But there is also an output effect, the analogue of the income effect in consumer demand theory. By raising the marginal cost of producing output, a rise in the price of labour leads to a lower output.

In the long run a rise in the wage *will* reduce the quantity of labour demanded. The substitution effect leads to less demand for labour and each output and the output effect reduces the demand for all inputs.

A rise in the wage also affects the long-run demand for capital and other inputs. At any particular output, the firm substitutes capital for labour. However, with lower output it needs less capital input. The overall effect could go either way. The easier it is to substitute capital for labour, the more likely is the substitution effect to dominate. Firms will substitute a lot of capital for labour. The quantity of capital demanded will rise.

The demand for factors of production is a derived demand. It depends on demand for the firm's output. The output demand curve affects the output effect on the demand for inputs when an input price changes.

In Figure 10.1 at the original wage, the long-run marginal cost curve LMC of output is LMC_0. A rise in the wage shifts this up to LMC_1. The original profit-maximizing point is A. If the firm faces a horizontal demand curve DD, output falls from Q_0 to Q_1. With the less elastic demand curve $D'D'$, the firm still begins at A where LMC_0 equals MR, the marginal revenue curve corresponding to $D'D'$. Now the shift to LMC_1 leads to a much smaller fall in output. The new output is Q_2 and the firm is at C.

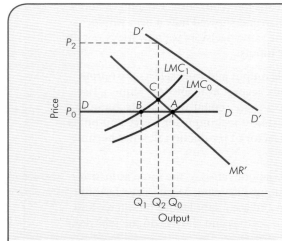

A wage increase will have a substitution effect leading firms to substitute relatively more capital-intensive techniques. Nevertheless, total costs and marginal costs of producing output will be greater than before. Facing the horizontal demand curve DD, a shift from LMC_0 to LMC_1 will lead the firm to move from A to B and output will fall from Q_0 to Q_1. This tends to reduce the demand for all factors of production. Facing the demand curve $D'D'$ and corresponding marginal revenue curve MR', the upward shift from LMC_0 to LMC_1 leads the firm to move from A to C at which marginal cost and marginal revenue are again equal. The output effect reduces output only from Q_0 to Q_2.

Figure 10.1 The output effect of a wage increase

The more elastic the demand curve for the firm's output, the more a given rise in the price of an input, and a given shift in the *LMC* curve for output, leads to a big fall in output. The larger the output effect, the greater the fall in the quantity of all factors demanded.

The Appendix (page 211) shows that we can also analyse factor demands using techniques like the indifference curves and budget lines used to study household demands for goods in Chapter 5.

10.2 The firm's demand for labour in the short run

In the short run the firm has some fixed factors of production. We now consider the firm's short-run demand for labour when its capital input is fixed.

> The **marginal product of labour** is the extra total output when an extra worker is added, with other input quantities unaltered.

Table 10.2 shows a firm's variable labour input and corresponding output, holding capital input fixed. Column (3) shows the marginal product of labour (*MPL*). This marginal product rises as the first workers are added. It is hard for the first and second worker to carry all the tools. After the third worker has been added, the *diminishing marginal productivity* of labour sets in. With existing machines fully utilized, there is less and less for each new worker to do.

Table 10.2 Short-run output supply and labour demand

(1) Workers	(2) Output	(3) MPL	(4) MVPL (£)	(5) Extra profit (£)
1	0.8	0.8	400	100
2	1.8	1.0	500	200
3	3.1	1.3	650	350
4	4.3	1.2	600	300
5	5.4	1.1	550	250
6	6.3	0.9	450	150
7	7.0	0.7	350	50
8	7.5	0.5	250	−50

As in our discussion of output, we use the *marginal principle*. Does the cost of a new worker exceed the benefit of a new worker? Table 10.2 shows a competitive firm hiring workers at a wage of £300 and selling output at a price of £500. Column (4) shows the extra revenue from taking on another worker.

> The **marginal value product of labour** is the extra revenue from selling the output made by an extra worker.

Since the firm is perfectly competitive, the marginal value product of another worker is the marginal product in physical goods multiplied by the (constant) price for which the extra goods are sold. From this extra revenue from the extra worker, the firm subtracts the extra wage cost. The last column of Table 10.2 shows the extra profit from an extra worker.

The firm hires more workers if the marginal value product of another worker exceeds the wage cost. It is profitable to hire 7 workers. The seventh worker has a marginal value product of £350, just above the cost of £300 for this extra worker. An eighth worker's marginal value product is only £250, below the £300 another worker costs. The firm hires 7 workers.

In so doing, the firm chooses both labour input and goods output: the shaded row shows that 7 workers make 7 units of output. The firm gets the same answer, namely maximum profit, whether it compares the marginal revenue from another output unit with the marginal cost of making that output unit, or compares the marginal revenue from hiring another unit of the variable factor with the marginal cost of hiring that variable factor.

The firm's employment rule is thus: expand (contract) employment if the marginal value product of labour is greater than (less than) the wage of an extra worker. If labour can be smoothly adjusted, for example if labour input is measured in [hours] × [workers], the firm's demand for labour must satisfy the condition

Wage = marginal value product of labour ($MVPL$) (1)

Figure 10.2 illustrates this principle. If we assume diminishing marginal productivity at all employment levels, the marginal value product of labour ($MVPL$) slopes down. A competitive firm can hire labour at the constant wage rate W_0. It is a price-taker in the labour market.

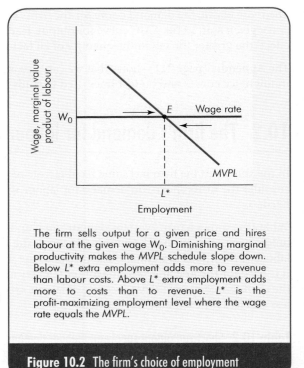

The firm sells output for a given price and hires labour at the given wage W_0. Diminishing marginal productivity makes the $MVPL$ schedule slope down. Below L^* extra employment adds more to revenue than labour costs. Above L^* extra employment adds more to costs than to revenue. L^* is the profit-maximizing employment level where the wage rate equals the $MVPL$.

Figure 10.2 The firm's choice of employment

Below L^* profits are increased by raising employment, since $MVPL$ exceeds the wage rate or marginal cost of hiring extra labour. Above L^* it is profitable to shrink employment, since the wage exceeds the $MVPL$. Thus L^* is the profit-maximizing level of employment.

Monopoly and monopsony power

This theory is easily amended when the firm has *monopoly power* in its output market (a downward-sloping demand curve for its product) or *monopsony power* in its input markets (an upward-sloping supply curve for its inputs: the firm must then offer a higher factor price to attract a larger quantity of that input).

For a perfectly competitive firm, the $MVPL$ schedule is its marginal revenue from an extra worker. We use the term *marginal value product of labour ($MVPL$)* for competitive firms who are price-takers in their output markets. $MVPL$ is simply the marginal product of labour in physical goods MPL multiplied by the output price. We reserve the term *marginal revenue product of labour ($MRPL$)* for firms with a downward-sloping demand curve for their output.

To find $MRPL$, we use the marginal physical product of labour MPL to work out the extra quantity of output when an extra worker is hired, then calculate the change in the firm's total revenue when it sells these extra goods.

> A firm with **monopsony power** faces an upward-sloping factor supply curve and must offer a higher factor price to attract more factors. The marginal cost of the input exceeds the factor price. In expanding inputs, the firm bids up the price paid on all inputs already employed.

> The **marginal revenue product of labour** is the change in total output revenue when a firm sells the extra goods that an extra unit of labour input allows it to produce.

Figure 10.3 shows the $MVPL$ and $MRPL$ schedules for two firms with the same technology. Both schedules slope down because of diminishing marginal productivity – a technical property of production – but the $MRPL$ schedule slopes down more steeply because the firm faces a downward-sloping demand curve for its output and recognizes that additional output reduces the price and hence the revenue earned on previous units of output.

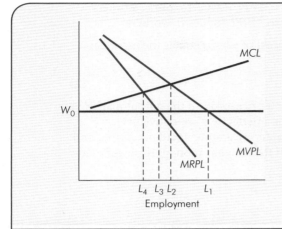

A perfectly competitive firm sets MVPL equal to W_0 and employs L_1 workers. Facing a downward-sloping demand curve in its output market, an imperfectly competitive firm recognizes that its marginal revenue from extra output will be less than MVPL. It sets MRPL equal to W_0 and employs L_3 workers. A monopsonist recognizes that additional employment bids up wages for existing workers so that MCL depicts the marginal cost of an extra worker. Facing a given goods price, the monopsonist sets MCL equal to MVPL to employ L_2 workers, but facing a downward-sloping demand curve in the output market, the monopsonist would set MCL equal to MRPL to employ L_4 workers. Thus, monopoly and monopsony power tend to reduce the firm's demand for labour.

Figure 10.3 Monopoly and monopsony power

Similarly, although W_0 is the marginal cost of labour for a competitive firm that is a price-taker in its input market, a monopsonist recognizes that expanding employment bids up the wage. If all workers are paid the same wage, the marginal cost of an extra worker is not just the wage paid to that worker but also the rise in the wage bill for previously employed workers. The monopsonist's marginal cost of labour exceeds the wage, and rises with the level of employment. It is shown in Figure 10.3 as the MCL schedule.

Any firm maximizes profits by equating the marginal revenue and marginal cost of an extra worker. Otherwise, the firm has the wrong employment level. A firm that is a price-taker in both output and input markets sets $W_0 = MVPL$ to hire L_1 workers in Figure 10.3. A firm that is a price-taker in the labour market but not in the output market sets $MRPL = W_0$ and hires L_3 workers. A firm that is a

Box 10.1 How common is monopsony?

Economists have often assumed that small firms probably face a pretty horizontal labour supply curve – they can attract extra workers without bidding the wage up much. If so, monopsony is more of a special case for textbook writers than something to worry about much in the real world.

However, in the past decade this view has been increasingly challenged. Even small firms not requiring very many extra workers may have difficulty in attracting the workers they need without bidding up the wage they have to offer.

For example, Professors Alan Manning and Steve Machin studied residential care homes in southern England. Towns like Bournemouth and Eastbourne are famous as places in which the elderly cluster in their retirement. Manning and Machin collected data on the wages paid to individual care workers in individual retirement homes and discovered a surprising fact. There is a very large wage dispersion across care homes, even after controlling for identifiable differences in their workers. This is difficult to reconcile with a labour market in which each firm is a price-taker for labour. Monopsony may be more relevant than you first thought.

Adapted from S. Machin and A. Manning, 'The structure of wages in what should be a competitive labour market', Centre for Economic Performance, LSE, 2002.

price-taker in its output market but not in the labour market sets $MVPL = MCL$ to hire L_2 workers. A firm that is both a monopolist and a monopsonist sets $MCL =$ to $MRPL$ to hire L_4 workers.

In all cases, the firm hires up to the point at which the marginal cost of labour equals the marginal revenue product of labour:

$$MCL = MRPL \tag{2}$$

For a price-taker in the labour market, MCL is just the wage. For a price-taker in the output market, $MRPL$ is simply the marginal value product of labour $MVPL$. For a perfectly competitive firm, equation (2) thus reduces to equation (1). For the rest of this chapter we assume that both output and labour markets are competitive. The analysis is easily amended if the firm has monopoly power in its output market or monopsony power in the labour market.

Changes in the firm's demand for labour

Consider a rise in the wage W_0 faced by a competitive firm. Using Figure 10.2 or 10.3, the firm hires fewer workers than before. The marginal cost of labour has risen. Diminishing labour productivity makes the $MVPL$ schedule slope down. Hence lower employment is needed to raise the marginal value product of labour in line with its higher marginal cost.

Suppose that a competitive firm faces a higher output price. The MPL remains unaltered in physical goods, but this output now earns more money. The $MVPL$ schedule shifts up at each level of employment. Hence in Figure 10.2 or 10.3 the horizontal line through the wage W_0 crosses the new $MVPL$ schedule at a higher employment level. With the marginal cost of labour unaltered and the marginal revenue from labour increased, output and employment expand until diminishing marginal productivity drives $MVPL$ back down to the wage W_0.

Finally, suppose the firm had begun with a higher capital stock. Each worker has more machinery with which to work and makes more output. Although wages and prices are unchanged, there is a rise in MPL in physical goods at each employment level. The $MVPL$ schedule shifts up, since $MVPL$ equals MPL times output price. As with a higher output price, this upward shift in the $MVPL$ schedule leads the firm to expand employment and output.

For a competitive firm there is a neat way to combine our first two results. Noting that $MVPL$ equals the output price P times MPL, the extra physical product of another worker, the firm's profit-maximizing condition is wage $W = P \times MPL$. Dividing both sides of this equation by P gives

$$W/P = MPL \tag{3}$$

A profit-maximizing competitive firm demands labour up to the point at which the marginal physical product of labour equals its *real* wage, the nominal divided by the output price.

The position of the MPL schedule depends on technology and the existing capital stock. Since these are fixed in the short run we can alter MPL only by moving along the schedule. Diminishing returns imply that, with more workers, the marginal physical product of the last worker is lower. From the particular level of the marginal physical product of labour we can deduce how many workers are being employed.

Equation (3) tells us that if nominal wages and output prices both double, real wages and employment are unaffected. But changes in either the nominal wage or the output price, if not matched by a change in the other, alter employment by affecting the real wage. Lower real wages move the firm down its MPL schedule, taking on more workers until the marginal physical product of labour equals the real wage.

Having studied the firm's demand for labour in the short run, we now turn to the demand by the industry as a whole. Although each competitive firm regards itself as a price-taker in both its output

A few years ago, the Bank of England admitted that it was having difficulty recruiting staff with good postgraduate degrees in economics. British students account for less than 10 per cent of PhD students in economics in leading UK universities. Why is this figure so low? One reason is because a good undergraduate economics degree is worth so much in the City. Economics undergraduates can easily earn £40 000 a year in their mid-twenties, rising to over £125 000 a year by retirement. Until recently, government institutions such as the Bank of England and the Treasury could not match these salaries. Increasingly, they have now been forced to pay market rates to get the best people.

A second reason why there are so few British PhD students in economics in British universities is that the market for postgraduate students is increasingly global. Many students good enough to be admitted to a PhD programme are capable of getting scholarships from top US universities. Why add to student debt by doing a British PhD when you can be paid to do one in the USA?

Questions

(a)   In an increasingly global world, does it make sense for all UK students to study at UK universities?

(b)   Why do US universities have more scholarships than UK universities?

(c)   Does it make sense for the Bank of England only to hire students from UK universities?

To check your answers to these questions, go to page 718.

To check your answers to these questions, go to page 718.

and input markets, an expansion by the whole industry will change output prices and wages. In moving from the firm's demand curve to the industry demand curve for labour, we take account of these effects.

10.3   The industry demand curve for labour

For a given price P_0 and wage W_0, each firm in a competitive industry chooses employment to equate the wage and the $MVPL$. Figure 10.4 horizontally adds the marginal value product of labour curves for each firm to obtain the $MVPL_0$ schedule for the industry. At the wage W_0 and the price P_0, the industry is at E_0. This is a point on the industry demand curve for labour.

However, $MVPL_0$ is *not* the industry demand curve for labour. It is drawn for a particular output price P_0. Suppose the wage is cut from W_0 to W_1. At the output price P_0 each firm wants to move down its $MVPL$ schedule and the industry expand output and employ labour to point E_1 in Figure 10.4. In terms of the supply and demand for output, the cut in wages has shifted the industry supply curve to the right.

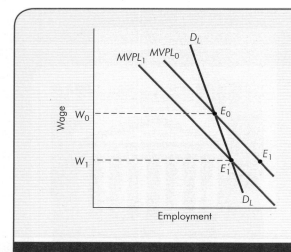

$MVPL_0$ is the horizontal sum of each firm's $MVPL$ schedule at the price P_0. Each firm and the industry as a whole sets $MVPL$ equal to W_0. Hence E_0 is a point on the industry demand curve for labour. A lower wage W_1 leads each firm and the industry as a whole to move down their $MVPL$ schedules to a point E_1. Extra employment and output by the whole industry (a shift to the right in the industry supply curve of goods) leads to excess goods supply at the original price P_0. To clear the output market the price must fall, and this shifts to the left each firm's $MVPL$ schedule. The new industry schedule is $MVPL_1$ and the chosen point is E_1'. Joining all the points such as E_0 and E_1', we obtain the industry demand curve $D_L D_L$.

Figure 10.4 The industry demand for labour

At the given price P_0 there is now an excess supply of goods. This bids down the price for the industry's product to a lower price P_1. The lower price shifts each firm's $MVPL$ schedule to the left. $MVPL_1$ is thus the new $MVPL$ schedule for the industry at the new price P_1. The industry chooses the point E_1' at the new wage W_1.

Connecting points such as E_0 and E_1' we get the *industry demand for labour schedule $D_L D_L$* in Figure 10.4. Each firm constructs its $MVPL$ schedule as if it were a price-taker but the industry demand curve has a steeper slope, since a lower wage shifts the industry output supply curve to the right and reduces the equilibrium price.

The slope of the $MVPL$ schedule reflects the production technology. The more MPL diminishes as labour input rises, the steeper is the $MVPL$ schedule of the firm and of the industry. The slope of the industry demand curve for labour also depends on the elasticity of the market demand curve for the industry's product. The more inelastic output demand is, the more a wage cut – by raising the supply of output – bids down the output price and shifts $MVPL$ schedules to the left, and the steeper is the industry demand curve $D_L D_L$ for labour.

The demand for factors of production is a *derived* demand. Firms want factors only because they see a demand for their output that it is profitable to supply. The elasticity of input demand reflects the elasticity of output demand.

10.4 The supply of labour

We now discuss the supply of labour, for the individual, the industry and the whole of the economy. We can then combine labour demand and labour supply to determine the equilibrium level of wages and employment.

Individual labour supply: hours of work

We analyse labour supply in two stages: how many hours people work once in the labour force and whether people join the labour force at all.

Once in the labour force, how many hours will a person wish to work? This depends on the *real* wage, W/P, the nominal wage divided by the

> The **labour force** is all individuals in work or looking for work.

price of goods, which shows the quantity of goods that labour effort will purchase. It is the real wage that affects labour supply decisions.

Figure 10.5 shows two possible labour supply curves, relating hours of work supplied to the real wage. The curve SS_1 slopes up. Higher real wages make people want to work more. The labour supply curve SS_2 is *backward-bending*. Beyond A, further real wage rises make people want to work fewer hours.

The alternative to working another hour is staying at home and having fun. Each of us has 24 hours a day to divide between work and leisure. More leisure is nice but by working longer we can get more real income with which to buy consumer goods. How should an individual trade off leisure against consumer goods in deciding how much to work?

This is an application of the model of consumer choice in Chapter 5. The choice is now between goods as a whole and leisure. An individual will want to work until the marginal utility derived from the goods that an extra hour of work will provide is just equal to the marginal utility from the last hour of leisure.

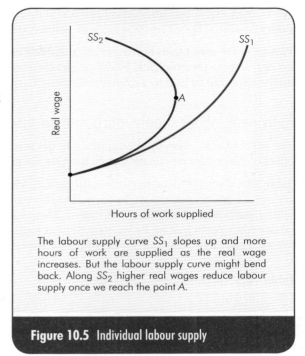

The labour supply curve SS_1 slopes up and more hours of work are supplied as the real wage increases. But the labour supply curve might bend back. Along SS_2 higher real wages reduce labour supply once we reach the point A.

Figure 10.5 Individual labour supply

A higher real wage increases the quantity of goods an extra hour of work will purchase. This makes working more attractive than before and tends to increase the supply of hours worked. But there is a second effect. Suppose you work to get a target bundle of goods. You work to get enough to be able to eat, pay the rent, run a car and have a holiday. With a higher real wage you need to work fewer hours to earn the same target bundle of goods.

These two effects are precisely the *substitution and income effects* introduced in the consumer choice model of Chapter 5. An increase in the real wage increases the relative return on working. It leads to a substitution effect or pure relative price effect that makes people want to work more. But a higher real wage also tends to raise people's real income. This has a pure income effect. Since leisure is probably a luxury good, the quantity of leisure demanded increases sharply when real incomes increase. This income effect tends to make people work less. The overall effect of a real wage rise, and the shape of the supply curve for hours worked, depends on which effect is larger.

To decide whether or not the substitution effect will dominate the income effect, we must look at actual data on what people do. Economists have tried three techniques in an attempt to discover how people actually behave. Interview studies ask people how they behave. Econometric studies, of the kind discussed in Chapter 2, try to disentangle the separate effects from data on actual behaviour. And experiments have been conducted by giving different people different amounts of take-home pay and recording their behaviour.

The empirical evidence for the UK, the US and most other Western economies is as follows. For adult men, the substitution effect and the income effect almost exactly cancel out. A change in the real wage has almost no effect on the quantity of hours supplied. The supply curve of hours worked is almost vertical.[1]

---

1 This conclusion applies to small changes in real wage rates. In most Western countries, the large rise in real wages over the past 100 years has been matched by reductions of ten hours or more in the working week.

For women, the substitution effect just about dominates the income effect. The supply curve for hours slopes upward. Higher real wages make women work longer hours.

Workers care about take-home pay after deductions of income tax. Lower income tax rates raise after-tax real wages. The empirical evidence on labour supply implies that lower income tax rates should not be expected to lead to a dramatic increase in the supply of hours worked.

Individual labour supply: participation rates

The effect of real wages on the supply of hours is smaller than often supposed. The more important effect of real wages on labour supply is on the incentive to join the labour force.

Table 10.3 gives UK data on participation rates. Most men of working age are in jobs or are seeking employment, but this percentage is gradually falling, particularly with early retirement. There has been a big rise in labour force participation by women. Similar patterns are seen in other Western countries. Can our model of choice explain these trends?

> The **participation rate** is the fraction of the population of working age who join the labour force.

Table 10.3 UK participation rates (%)

	1971	2006
Men	95	84
Women	59	74

Source: http://www.statistics.gov.uk.

We now develop a model in which labour force participation is higher (a) the more their tastes favour the benefits of working (goods or job status) relative to the benefits of leisure, (b) the lower their income from non-work sources, (c) the lower the fixed costs of working and (d) the higher the real wage rate.

Figure 10.6 plots leisure on the horizontal axis. The maximum leisure a day is 24 hours. The vertical axis plots total real income from work and other sources. This shows the ability to buy consumer goods and services. We begin with budget constraint. Suppose the individual has a non-labour income given by the vertical distance *BC*. This may be income earned by a spouse, income from rent or dividends, or welfare payments received from the government.

Someone not working at all can have 24 hours of leisure a day plus a daily income *BC*. She can consume at point *C*. Now suppose she works. There may be fixed costs in working. Unemployment benefit from the government may be lost immediately, the right clothes or uniform must be purchased, travel expenses must be incurred to get to the place of work, childcare must be found for the children. These costs are independent of the number of hours worked provided any work is done. They are a fixed cost of working.

Figure 10.6 shows these costs as the vertical distance *AC*. Instead of being able to consume at *C*, the net non-labour income *BC* is reduced to *BA* after these fixed costs of working are incurred. Having decided to work, she can then move along the budget line *AD*, sacrificing leisure to gain wage income. The higher the real wage, the steeper the budget line *AD*.

Fixed costs of working lead to a kinked budget line *CAD*. Working a few hours reduces total real income. The small wage income does not cover the fixed costs of working. The lower the real wage rate, the flatter is the line *AD* and the more hours she has to work merely to recoup the fixed costs. This is sometimes called the *poverty trap*. Unskilled workers face such a low wage that they actually lose out by working.

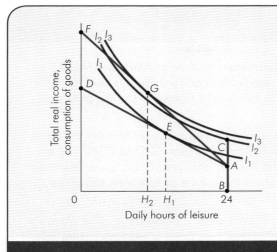

With a non-labour income BC the individual can do no work and consume at C on the indifference curve I_2I_2. Any work incurs the fixed cost AC. At a low hourly wage rate the total budget line is CAD and the best point attainable by working is E. Thus this lies on the indifference curve I_1I_1 and the individual is better off at C where no work is done. At a higher hourly wage rate the new budget line is CAF. By working $(24 - H_2)$ hours the individual can reach G on the indifference curve I_3I_3 which is better than being at C. The higher the real hourly wage rate the more likely is the individual to participate in the labour force.

Figure 10.6 Labour force participation

To complete the model of consumer choice we superimpose an indifference map on the kinked budget line CAD. Individuals like both leisure and goods. Each indifference curve has the usual slope and curvature. A higher indifference curve means the individual is better off. We can now analyse the participation decision and establish the four effects we cited above.

The indifference curve I_2I_2 shows how well off she is by not participating. She can start to consume at C. Given the budget line CAD, the best she can do by working is to work $(24 - H_1)$ hours, consume H_1 hours of leisure and choose point E, reaching the indifference curve I_1I_1. But she can reach the higher indifference curve I_2I_2 by not working. She chooses not to work.

Now suppose the real wage rises. Each hour of leisure could now earn a higher real wage. AD rotates to AF and the complete budget line is now CAF. By choosing point G, she can reach the indifference curve I_3I_3 and is better off than at C. Hence higher real wages raise the number of people wishing to join the labour force.

A reduction in AC, the fixed cost of working, also raises participation. Point C is fixed but point A shifts up. There is a parallel upward shift in the sloping part of the budget line such as AD or AF. It is more likely that the highest indifference curve attainable by working will lie above the zero-work indifference curve I_2I_2.

Although not shown in Figure 10.6, lower non-labour income BC also raises labour force participation. Changes in non-labour income have no effect on the relative return of an hour's work and an hour's leisure. There is no substitution effect but there is an income effect. Lower non-labour income reduces the quantity demanded of all normal goods including leisure. People are more likely to work.

Finally, consider a change in tastes. People decide leisure is less important and work more important. Each indifference curve in Figure 10.6 is flatter: people are prepared to sacrifice more leisure for the direct and indirect benefits of extra work. Consider again the budget line CAD. The flatter the indifference curves are, the more likely it is that the indifference curve through C will cross the portion of the budget line AD on which work is done. But if it crosses AD there must be another point on AD yielding even higher utility. In Figure 10.6 it is possible to attain a higher indifference curve by choosing the point G on AF. Exactly the same argument applies if the flatter indifference curve through C crosses the line AD.

Box 10.2 Boosting UK labour supply

New Labour's labour market policies fell under two main headings, *Welfare to Work* and *Making Work Pay*. Both were based on the belief that work allows people to acquire skills and new opportunities: work is a ladder allowing people gradually to climb out of poverty. Did the policy boost UK labour supply?

Welfare to Work had two elements: more help in finding a job and possible loss of benefits for those making little effort to find work. The budget line in diagram (a) changes from *CAD* to *FGH*. The fall from *C* to *F* reflects lower benefits for those out of work, and the rise from *A* to *G* the lower fixed cost of working once the government helps. In diagram (a) we show the choice of someone drawn into the labour force by the change in policy.

Making Work Pay dealt with the part of the budget line once some work is being done. The Working Families Tax Credit gave money to *workers* with children, provided the parent is working a minimum number of hours a week. Diagram (b) shows the discontinuity *JK* when the benefit kicks in. The indifference map shows a person who would not work facing *CAD* but for whom *K* is better than *F* once the budget line becomes *FGJKM*. Or so the government hoped! (See www.newdeal.gov.uk.)

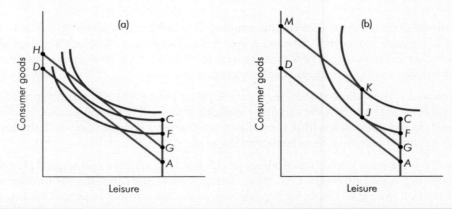

Thus labour force participation rises with (a) a higher real hourly wage rate, (b) lower fixed costs of working, (c) lower income from non-labour sources and (d) changes in tastes in favour of more work and less leisure. Is this why participation by married women increased?

First, there was a change in social attitudes to work, especially to work by married women. Indifference curves became flatter. Second, pressure for equal opportunities for women raised women's real wages. The budget line for women working rotated from *AD* to *AF* in Figure 10.6. Finally, the fixed costs of working fell. Automatic ovens, labour-saving devices for housework, a second family car and many other changes, not least in the attitude of husbands, reduce the cost of work, especially for married women.

We have reached two conclusions. First, a higher real wage rate raises total labour supply but perhaps by less than is commonly thought. Second, this operates more by sucking people into the labour force than by greatly raising the supply hours of those already in the labour force.

This analysis relates best to the supply of unskilled workers. Acquiring skills takes time. We examine decisions about whether or not to acquire training and skills in the next chapter.

The supply of labour to an industry

Now we discuss an individual industry. Suppose it is small relative to the economy and wishes to employ workers with common skills. It has to pay the going rate for the job. Jobs in different industries have different non-monetary characteristics, such as risk, comfort or anti-social hours like night shifts. The going rate must be adjusted industry by industry to allow for the *equilibrium wage differential* that offsets these non-monetary characteristics and makes workers indifferent to where they work. Dangerous, nasty industries have to pay more than pleasant, safe industries if they are to attract workers.

Adjusted in this way, this determines the wage at which a small industry can hire as many workers as it wants from the economy-wide labour pool. At this wage, the industry faces a horizontal labour supply curve.

Many industries are not this small relative to all the skills they wish to employ. The steel industry is a big user of welders, the freight industry a big user of lorry drivers. When an industry is a significant user of a particular skill, higher employment in the industry bids up the wages of that particular skill in the whole economy. In the short run, the industry's labour supply curve slopes upwards.

In the long run, the industry's labour supply curve may be flatter. When short-run expansion bids up the wages of computer programmers, more school-leavers train in this skill. In the long run, the economy-wide supply rises and the wages of these workers fall back a bit. An individual industry does not have to offer such a high wage in the long run to increase the supply of that type of labour to the industry.

In the short run, the supply of a given skill may be nearly fixed. To get a larger share of the total pool an individual industry has to offer higher relative wages than other industries to bid workers away from them.

10.5 Industry labour market equilibrium

Figure 10.7 shows equilibrium in the labour market for an industry. Its labour demand curve $D_L D_L$ slopes down and crosses the upward-sloping labour supply curve $S_L S_L$ at the equilibrium point E. Employment is L_0 and the wage W_0. We do not distinguish long-run and short-run supply curves, though this is easily done.

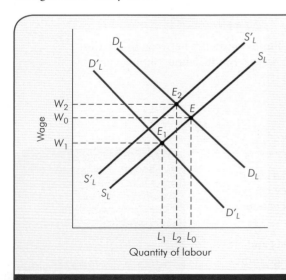

The industry labour market supply curve $S_L S_L$ slopes up. Higher wages are needed to attract workers into the industry. For a given output demand curve, the industry's labour demand curve $D_L D_L$ slopes down because of diminishing marginal labour productivity and because higher industry output bids down its output price. A leftward shift in the output demand curve thus shifts the derived demand for labour from $D_L D_L$ to $D'_L D'_L$ and moves labour market equilibrium from E to E_1. An increase in wages elsewhere in the economy shifts the industry's labour supply curve from $S_L S_L$ to $S'_L S'_L$ and shifts equilibrium from E to E_2.

Figure 10.7 Equilibrium in an industry labour market

We draw the industry labour demand curve $D_1 D_1$ for a given output demand curve. A recession in the building industry would shift the demand curve for cement to the left. The equilibrium price of cement falls. This shifts to the left the marginal value product of labour curve $MVPL$ for each cement manufacturer. Hence $D_1 D_1$ shifts to $D'_1 D'_1$ for the cement industry. At the new equilibrium E_1, wages and employment are lower in the industry.

Conversely, suppose there is a spurt of investment in new machinery in every industry except cement. With more capital to work with, labour is more productive in other industries. Setting wages equal to the $MVPL$, these industries pay higher wages. This shifts up the supply curve of labour to the cement industry to $S'_L S'_L$. At each wage in the cement industry, the industry attracts fewer workers from the general pool.

The new equilibrium for cement workers is at E_2. Employment falls from L_0 to L_2. Since the remaining workers have more capital to work with, they have a higher marginal product. In addition, the contraction in cement output shifts the output supply curve to the left and bids up the cement price. Together these effects move the industry up its demand curve $D_L D_L$ and allow it to pay a higher wage rate to its remaining workers.

Thus wage increases in one industry spill over into other industries. The crucial link between industries is labour mobility. It is because cement workers are lured away from the industry by wage rises elsewhere that the cement industry's labour supply curve shifts to the left in Figure 10.7. The degree of labour mobility between industries affects not only how much an industry's labour supply curve shifts when conditions change elsewhere, but also the slope of the industry's labour supply curve. Consider two extreme cases.

Suppose first that workers can move effortlessly between similar jobs in different industries. If each industry is small relative to the economy, it will face a completely elastic (horizontal) labour supply curve at the going wage rate (adjusted for non-monetary advantages). When all other industries pay higher wages, the horizontal supply curve of labour to the cement industry shifts up by the full amount of the wage increase elsewhere. Unless the cement industry matches the going rate, it loses all its workers.

At the opposite extreme, consider the market for concert pianists. Suppose they can do no other job. The supply curve of concert pianists is vertical. If all other industries pay higher wages, this has no effect on the market for concert pianists. There is no possible entry or exit from the occupation of concert pianists.

The general case of Figure 10.7 is between these extremes. With limited mobility between industries, the cement industry can attract more workers by offering higher wages. But its labour supply curve shifts when wages change elsewhere.

10.6 Transfer earnings and economic rents

Top pianists and top footballers are delighted with their high salaries but might have chosen the same career even if paid less. Why do they get paid so much? We need to distinguish between transfer earnings and economic rent.

In Figure 10.8 DD is the labour demand curve for concert pianists and SS the supply of pianists to the music industry. Even at a zero wage some dedicated musicians would be concert pianists. Higher wages attract into the industry concert pianists who could have done other things. The supply curve slopes upwards.

> The **transfer earnings** of a factor in a particular use are the minimum payments needed to induce the input to work in that job. **Economic rent** (not to be confused with income from renting out property) is the payment a factor receives in excess of the transfer earnings needed to induce it to supply its services in that use.

Because all workers are paid the same wage, equilibrium is at E with a wage W_0 and a number of pianists L_0. W_0 may be a large wage. Each firm in the music industry pays W_0 because their workers are very talented, with a high marginal product. In the output market (concerts) firms earn a large revenue. The derived demand curve DD for concert pianists is very high.

The supply curve SS shows the transfer earnings that the industry pays to attract pianists into the industry. The first A pianists would work for nothing. A wage W_1 is needed to expand the supply of pianists to B, and W_0 must be paid to increase supply to L_0. If the industry can pay each individual pianist a different amount, paying only the minimum required to attract each to the industry, triangle AL_0E is the total transfer earnings paid to attract L_0 pianists.

At the equilibrium E the last pianist enticed into the industry has transfer earnings W_0 since E is on the supply curve SS. This last pianist's marginal value product is also W_0 since E is on the demand curve DD. However, when an industry has to pay all workers the same wage, all previous workers are paid W_0 even though the labour supply curve SS implies they would have worked for less than W_0. These workers, with transfer earnings below W_0, earn *economic rent*, a pure surplus arising because W_0 is needed to attract the last pianist. Rent reflects differences in pianists' *supply* decisions, not their *productivity* as musicians.

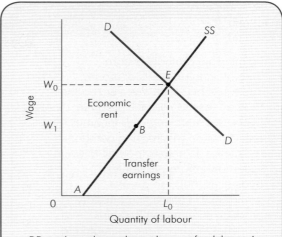

D ... SS

W_0 ... E

Wage

Economic rent

W_1 ... B

D

Transfer earnings

A

0 ... L_0

Quantity of labour

DD is the industry demand curve for labour. A quantity A of labour would work in the industry even at a zero wage. Higher wages attract additional workers to the industry. SS is the industry labour supply curve. If each worker was paid only the transfer earnings required to attract them to the industry (to keep them on their supply curve), the industry need only pay AL_0E in wages. If all workers must be paid the highest wage rate necessary to attract the last workers to the industry, equilibrium at E implies workers as a whole derive economic rent $OAEW_0$. For workers who would work for a zero wage rate, W_0 is economic rent, a pure bonus.

Figure 10.8 Transfer earnings and economic rent

In Figure 10.8 the industry makes total wage payments equal to the rectangle OW_0EL_0. It pays L_0 workers W_0 each. These payments comprise the total transfer earnings AL_0E and the economic rent $OAEW_0$.

Economic rent arises if the factor supply curve is not horizontal. With a horizontal supply curve, no worker earns more than the going rate required to keep pianists in the industry. All earnings are transfer earnings.

Note the distinction between the firm and the industry. Economic rent is an unnecessary payment as far as the industry is concerned. By colluding in order to wage-discriminate, paying each worker his transfer earnings alone, the industry could retain all its workers without paying them economic rent. But the entire wage W_0 is a transfer earning as far as a single competitive firm is concerned. If it fails to pay the going rate, its workers will go to another firm.

In the UK football industry[2] and the US baseball industry, it is often said that high player salaries are bankrupting the industry. But wages are high because the derived demand is high – crowds at the ground and television rights make it profitable to supply this output – and because the supply of talented players is scarce. The supply curve of good players is steep: even very high wages cannot increase the number of good players by much. There is no simple link between high salaries and the ruin of the game. If supplying the output was not profitable, the derived demand for players would be lower and their wages reduced.

2 Football clubs pay transfer fees to another club from whom they wish to take over a player. These transfer fees between clubs should not be confused with the economist's concept of transfer earnings of players, the amount needed to keep them in the industry.

Box 10.3 Premiership wages

Premiership footballers earn breathtaking amounts of money. The wage bill in UK Premier League football rose to over £1 billion in 2004/05. Spiralling club incomes reflect not only increasing demand as satellite TV retails football to ever wider (and more profitable) audiences, but also greater proficiency in marketing ancillary products such as replica shirts. Manchester United are estimated to earn around 40 per cent of their income from games, 33 per cent from TV rights and 27 per cent from commercial activities. Such breadth and depth to football teams' revenues has led to players trying to get their hands on all of the club's additional revenue.

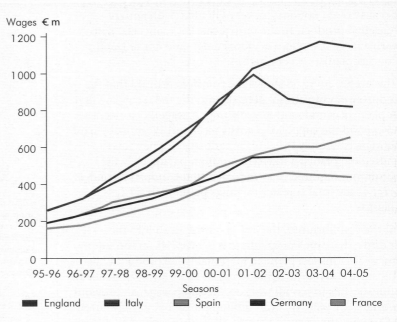

As clubs lose revenue from TV or commercial deals, downward pressure on wages begins. When teams are relegated to lower divisions, expensive players are offloaded. Any change in the generosity of sponsorship is likely to feed into wages as a whole. The financial success of the premier league was caused by its ability to sell TV rights and market its products. Its ability to attract top foreign players was the consequence not the cause of this success, though it then reinforced further successes.

Source: www.bbc.co.uk.

10.7 Do labour markets clear?

So far we have assumed that wages are flexible. The equilibrium wage equates labour supply and labour demand. In Part 4 you will see that many questions in macroeconomics turn on whether wage flexibility is sufficient to keep labour markets near their equilibrium positions. It may not be possible to take labour market equilibrium for granted.

Minimum wage agreements

The UK minimum wage is £5.35 an hour. Figure 10.9 shows the demand curve $D_L D_L$ and the supply curve $S_L S_L$ for a particular skill in a particular industry. Free market equilibrium is at E. For skilled workers, the equilibrium wage W_0 exceeds a minimum wage at W_1 which is thus irrelevant.

Suppose the minimum wage is W_2, above the free market equilibrium wage W_0. At W_2 there is excess labour supply $L_2 - L_1$. Since firms cannot be forced to hire workers they do not want, employment is L_1 and the quantity of workers $L_2 - L_1$ are involuntarily unemployed.

> Workers are **involuntarily unemployed** if they would work at the going wage but cannot find jobs.

A national minimum wage may exceed the free market equilibrium wage for low-skill occupations. If so, those workers lucky enough to find jobs get higher wages than before but the total amount of employment is lower than in free market equilibrium. Minimum wages may explain involuntary unemployment among low-skilled workers.

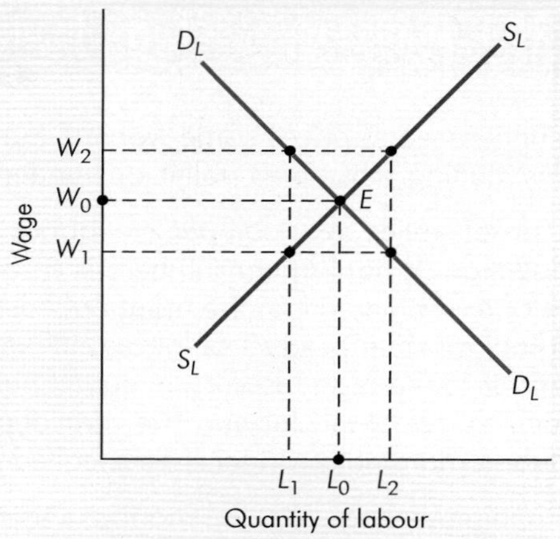

Trade unions

A strong trade union may act in a similar way. Figure 10.9 implies that, if unions in an industry force firms to pay a wage W_2, above the wage W_0 under free competition, the result is fewer jobs in the industry. By raising the wage from W_0 to W_2, the union reduces employment from L_0 to L_1. How unions trade off higher wages for lower employment is discussed in the next chapter. The effect is already clear. If the union chooses a wage W_2, the resulting unemployment is collectively voluntary – members of the union chose this action – but may be involuntary for the unlucky union members who lose their jobs. To say more, we need to discuss how decisions are made within unions.

Scale economies

Involuntary unemployment may reflect scale economies and imperfect competition. These create entry barriers and prevent new firms from joining an industry. Entry barriers prevent the unemployed from starting new firms even if unemployed workers would work for a lower wage than that paid in existing firms.

Free market equilibrium occurs at the wage W_0 and a quantity of employment L_0. A minimum wage W_1 below W_0 is irrelevant. However, a minimum wage W_2 above W_0 will restrict the actual quantity of employment to L_1, leaving a quantity $L_2 - L_1$ of workers involuntarily unemployed. They would like to work at this wage rate but cannot find jobs.

Figure 10.9 A minimum wage

Insiders and outsiders

> **Insiders** have jobs and are represented in wage bargaining. **Outsiders** do not have jobs and are unrepresented in wage bargaining

The previous explanation emphasizes entry barriers in forming new firms. Insider–outsider theories emphasize barriers to entering employment in existing firms.

Entry barriers have many forms. It is costly to advertise for workers, interview them, evaluate what sort of job they should be offered, train them in activities specific to the firm, build up teamwork and allow new employees to master their new jobs. In the terminology of Chapter 9, these are innocent entry barriers.

But existing workers (insiders) may also erect strategic barriers to entry by outsiders, even without the presence of formal trade unions. For example, insiders may threaten industrial disruption if too many outsiders are admitted too quickly or if outsiders offer to work at a lower wage than that being paid to insiders.

When such entry barriers confront outsiders, the insiders can raise their own wage above that for which outsiders would be prepared to work *without* inducing a spate of hiring of outsiders.

Efficiency wages

> **Efficiency wages** are high wages that raise productivity through their incentive effect.

Thus far, we have assumed that information is cheap to come by. In practice, firms face two problems: it is hard to tell whether a job applicant will be a productive worker (a matter of innate ability) and hard to monitor whether workers shirk after being employed.[3]

3 Economists refer to these problems as adverse selection and moral hazard. We discuss them in detail in Chapter 13 when we examine the economics of information.

Box 10.4 Minimum wages hurt jobs, don't they?

A minimum wage prices some workers out of a job: by raising wages, it slides firms up their demand curves, cutting jobs. Even politicians understand. Right?

The 'proof' relies on a competitive labour market. People's intuition is often based on perfect competition. What happens if there is a sole employer? A monopsonist's new hiring bids up the price of existing workers: the marginal cost of labour exceeds the wage. The diagram shows the marginal revenue product of labour, the labour supply curve facing the firm, and the marginal cost of labour to the monopsonist. In equilibrium, $MRPL = MCL$. Employment is N_1 and a wage W_1 is needed to attract this labour. The vertical gap between LS and $MRPL$ shows workers are paid less than their marginal product. This is called *exploitation*.

At a minimum wage W_2, the monopsonist faces a *horizontal* labour supply at W_2, at least until N_2 people are hired. W_2 is now the marginal cost of labour. The firm hires N_2 workers to equate the marginal cost and marginal benefit of hiring. By offsetting exploitation, the minimum wage boosts jobs from N_1 to N_2.

Beginning at free market equilibrium at a wage W_1, successive rises in the minimum wage *boost* jobs (sliding the firm along the labour supply curve LS) until the minimum wage reaches W_2 at which employment is maximized. Still higher minimum wages now move the firm up its demand curve, *reducing* jobs thereafter. When firms have some monopsony power, a minimum wage slightly above the free market equilibrium is good for jobs – it offsets the distortion caused by the market power of employers – but a minimum wage substantially above the free market equilibrium is bad for jobs.

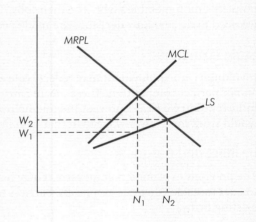

Whether the minimum wage is too high to boost jobs is thus an *empirical* question. A study of EU countries found no evidence that minimum wages cut adult employment, but some evidence they cut youth employment. The productivity of the young and unskilled is low. Minimum wages, even at lower rates for youths, are often above the intersection of LS and $MRPL$.

Source: J. Dolado *et al.*, 'The Economic Impact of Wages in Europe', *Economic Policy*, 1996.

Given the cost of evaluating new workers, and the subsequent cost of monitoring their performance on the job, what is the best policy for a firm? The efficiency wage theory argues that it is profitable for firms to pay existing workers a wage above their transfer earnings.

First, suppose workers quit their job if they get a better offer elsewhere. If firms pay a wage that is the average of that faced by productive and unproductive workers, it is the productive workers who are more likely to find better offers elsewhere and quit. Eventually, the firm will be left only with the low-quality workers. Paying a wage premium helps retain high-quality workers, even if the firm has some trouble telling which these are.

Second, when workers shirk on the job they may get caught. If caught, they get sacked. How big is the penalty for being caught? It is the difference between the current wage and what the worker gets in unemployment benefit or in a subsequent job. The higher the wage paid by the existing employer, the larger the penalty of being caught shirking. To increase the penalty and reduce the incentive to shirk, firms pay existing workers a higher wage than on average is necessary to get them to supply their labour.

Again, the implication is that some workers may be involuntarily unemployed. They may be happy to work for wages at or below those paid to existing workers but have little practical chance of securing a job at such wages.

Minimum wage agreements, trade union power, scale economies, insider–outsider distinctions and efficiency wages are *possible* explanations for insufficient wage flexibility in the short run to maintain the labour market in continuous equilibrium. Whether the labour market is always in equilibrium, and the length of time for which disequilibrium persists, are questions to which we return repeatedly in Part 4.

10.8 UK wages and employment

We began the chapter by looking at real earnings in energy, financial services and construction. By re-examining these industries, we draw together some of the themes of the chapter.

Table 10.4 shows real earnings and employment during 1993–2006. In the economy, real earnings rose 37 per cent. Technical advances, better machinery and better skills raised labour's marginal value product, shifting the labour demand curve to the right. But this process differed in different industries.

Table 10.4 UK jobs and real earnings, males (% cumulative change)

	Real earnings 1993–2005	Jobs 1993–2006
Whole economy	+37	+15
Financial services	+47	+55
Construction	+28	+13
Energy and water	+41	−50

Source: ONS, *Labour Market Trends.*

In construction, immigration has tended to increase labour supply to this sector, in itself putting downward pressure on wages, which rose less than the national average. So why then does Table 10.4 record higher real incomes as well as more jobs? Demand must have risen strongly, because of a housing boom partly caused by lower interest rates, and because higher incomes raised demand as well.

In financial services (such as banking and insurance), wages and employment both increased sharply. Demand increases were more than sufficient to offset any tendency for information technology or global outsourcing to reduce the need for workers.

Technical progress and capital investment in the basic utilities – energy and water supply – meant that jobs continued to contract sharply in the sector. With so much capital per worker, workers are very productive and are highly paid. High energy prices – in part caused by global rises in the price of oil – meant that energy companies declared record profits. The competition for workers meant that incomes in the industry rose sharply.

Summary

- In the long run, a firm chooses a **production technique** to minimize the cost of a particular output. By considering each output, it constructs a **total cost curve**.

- In the long run, a **rise in the price of labour** (capital) has a **substitution effect** and an **output effect**. The substitution effect reduces the quantity of labour (capital) demanded as the capital–labour ratio rises (falls) at each output. But total costs and marginal costs of output increase. The more elastic the firm's demand curve and marginal revenue curve, the more the higher marginal cost curve reduces output, reducing demand for both factors. For a higher price of a factor, the substitution and output effects both reduce the quantity demanded.

- In the short run, the firm has **fixed factors**, and probably a **fixed production technique**. The firm can vary short-run output by varying its variable input, labour, which is subject to diminishing returns when other factors are fixed. The **marginal physical product of labour** falls as more labour is hired.

- A profit-maximizing firm produces the output at which marginal output cost equals marginal output revenue. Equivalently, it hires labour until the **marginal cost of labour** equals its **marginal revenue product**. One implies the other. If the firm is a price-taker in its output market, the *MRPL* is its **marginal value product**, the output price times its marginal physical product. If the firm is a price-taker in the labour market, the marginal cost of labour is the wage rate. A perfectly competitive firm equates the real wage to the marginal physical product of labour.

- The downward-sloping marginal physical product of labour schedule is the **short-run demand curve for labour** (in terms of the real wage) for a competitive firm. Equivalently, the marginal value product of labour schedule is the demand curve in terms of the nominal wage. The *MVPL* schedule for a firm shifts up if the output price increases, the capital stock increases or if technical progress makes labour more productive.

- The **industry's labour demand curve** is not merely the horizontal sum of firms' *MVPL* curves. Higher industry output in response to a wage reduction also reduces the output price. The industry labour demand curve is steeper (less elastic) than that of each firm, and more inelastic the more inelastic is the demand curve for the industry's output.

- Labour demand curves are **derived demands**. A shift in the output demand curve for the industry will shift the derived factor demand curve in the same direction.

- For someone already in the labour force, a **rise in the hourly real wage** has both a **substitution effect** tending to increase the supply of hours worked, and an **income effect** tending to reduce the supply of hours worked. For men, the two effects cancel out almost exactly in practice but the empirical evidence suggests that the substitution effect dominates for women. Thus women have a rising labour supply curve; for men it is almost vertical.

- Individuals with non-labour income may prefer not to work. Four things raise the **participation rate in the labour force**: higher real wage rates, lower fixed costs of working, lower non-labour income and changes in tastes in favour of working. These explain the trend for increasing labour force participation by married women over the past few decades.

- The **industry supply curve of labour** depends on the wage paid relative to wages in other industries using similar skills. **Equilibrium wage differentials** are the monetary compensation for differences in non-monetary characteristics of jobs in different industries undertaken by workers with the same skill. Taking monetary and non-monetary rewards together, there is then no incentive to move between industries.

- When the labour supply curve to an industry is less than perfectly elastic, the industry pays higher wages to expand employment. For the marginal worker, the wage is a pure **transfer earning**, required to induce that worker into the industry. For workers prepared to work in the industry at a lower wage, there is an element of **economic rent** (the difference between income received and transfer earnings for that individual).

- In free market equilibrium, some workers choose not to work at the equilibrium wage rate. They are **voluntarily unemployed**. **Involuntary unemployment** is the difference between desired supply and desired demand at a disequilibrium wage rate. Workers would like to work but cannot find a job.

- There is considerable disagreement about how quickly labour markets can get back to equilibrium if initially in disequilibrium. Possible causes of involuntary unemployment are **minimum wage** agreements, **trade unions**, **scale economies**, **insider–outsider** distinctions and **efficiency wages**.

Review questions
To check your answers to these questions, go to page 718.

1 (a) Explain why the marginal product of labour eventually declines. (b) Show in a diagram the effect of an increase in the firm's capital stock on its demand curve for labour.

2 (a) Over the past 100 years the real wage has risen but the length of the working week has fallen. Explain this result using income and substitution effects. (b) Explain how an increase in the real wage could cause everyone in employment to work fewer hours but still increase the total amount of work done in the economy.

3 Why should the labour supply curve to an industry slope upwards even if the aggregate labour supply to the economy is fixed?

4 Answer the questions with which we began the chapter. (a) Why can a top golfer earn more in a weekend than a university professor earns in a year? (b) Why can students studying economics expect to earn more than equally smart students studying philosophy?

5 **Common fallacies** Why are the following statements wrong? (a) There is no economic reason why a sketch that took Picasso one minute to draw should fetch £100 000. (b) Higher wages must raise incentives to work.

6 **Harder question** 'A minimum wage set sufficiently high will always reduce jobs, but whether a modest level of minimum wage reduces or increases employment depends entirely on the degree of competition in the labour market.' Explain.

7   **Harder question** Could a university degree increase your subsequent job prospects even if the subject that you studied at university had no relevance whatsoever for your subsequent career?

8   **Essay question** In the past 50 years, there has been a dramatic increase in female participation in the labour force. Three possible explanations are (a) a change in social attitudes to women working, (b) technological advances that make it easier to accomplish household chores (shopping, cleaning, etc.) without women themselves having to remain at home full time, and (c) the possibility that material goods are a luxury and that people wish to buy disproportionately more of them as living standards rise. What evidence would you gather in order to test these different hypotheses?

To help you grasp the key concepts of this chapter check out the extra resources posted on the Online Learning Centre. There are chapter summaries, self-test questions, an interactive graphing tool, weblinks and a searchable glossary, all for free!

To put your learning into practice and prepare for exams, an **Interactive Workbook** is also available online, containing a variety of question types and providing feedback on your answers.

If you'd like further help with economics, or have any questions, **NetTutor** is here to help! You will have a personalised tutorial service at your fingertips. Visit the online learning centre at: www.mcgraw-hill.co.uk/textbooks/begg for information on accessing all of these resources.

Appendix: Isoquants and the choice of production technique

The choice of technique can be examined with techniques similar to the indifference curve–budget line approach used to study consumer choice in Chapter 5. Figure 10.A1 plots input quantities of capital K and labour L. Points A, B, C and D show the *minimum* input quantities needed to make 1 unit of output using each of four different techniques. Technique A is the most labour intensive, requiring L_A units of labour and K_A units of capital to make 1 unit of output. Technique D is the most capital intensive. Connecting A, B, C and D yields an *isoquant* (iso = the same, quant = quantity).

Figure 10.A1 shows 4 techniques but we can imagine that there are other techniques. Figure 10.A2 shows smooth isoquants. Isoquant I corresponds to a particular output. Each point on isoquant I reflects a different technique, from very capital intensive to very labour intensive.

Higher isoquants, such as I, show higher output levels since more inputs are required. Each isoquant shows different input combinations to make a given output. The isoquants constitute an isoquant map.

Three properties of isoquants are important. First, they cannot cross. Each isoquant refers to a different output. Second, each isoquant slopes down. To make a given output, a technique can use more capital only if it uses less labour and vice versa. Hence isoquants must slope down. Third, each isoquant becomes flatter as we move along it to the right, as Figure 10.A2 shows. Moving down a given isoquant, it takes more and more extra capital input to make equal successive reductions in the labour input required to produce a given output.

Points A, B, C and D show different input combinations required to produce 1 unit of output. By connecting them we obtain an isoquant that shows the different input combinations which can produce a particular level of output.

Figure 10.A1 An isoquant

> An **isoquant** shows minimum combinations of inputs to make a given output. Different points on an isoquant reflect different production techniques.

In Figure 10.A2 the line L_0K_0 is an *isocost* line. It shows different input combinations with the *same* total cost. For a given cost, the firm can use more units of capital only if it uses fewer units of labour. Facing given prices at which different inputs may be hired, we can say two things about isocost lines.

First, the slope of the isocost line reflects the relative price of the two factors of production. Beginning at K_0, where all the firm's money is spent on capital, the firm can trade off 1 unit of capital for more units of labour the cheaper the wage rate relative to the rental cost of capital. Second, facing given factor prices, by raising spending a firm can have more capital and more labour. A higher isocost line parallel to L_0K_0 shows a higher spending on inputs. Along the isocost line L_1K_1 the firm spends more on inputs than along the isocost line L_0K_0.

To minimize the cost of making a given output, a firm chooses the point of tangency of that isoquant to the lowest possible isocost line. At this point, the (negative) slope of the isocost line equals the (negative) slope of the isoquant. If w is the wage rate and r the rental cost of a unit of capital, the slope of the isocost line is r/w. What about the slope of the isoquant?

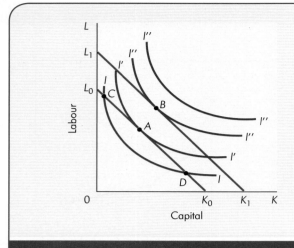

Each isoquant such as I shows a particular output level. Higher isoquants such as I'' show higher output levels. Straight lines such as L_0K_0 are isocost lines showing different input combinations having the same total cost. The slope of an isocost line depends only on relative factor prices. A higher isocost line such as L_1K_1 implies a larger total cost. To produce a given output, such as that corresponding to the isoquant I', the firm chooses the point of tangency of that isoquant to the lowest possible isocost line. Thus point A is the cost-minimizing way to produce the output level on I' and point B the cost-minimizing way to produce the output level on I''.

Figure 10.A2 Cost minimization

With an extra unit of capital, the firm gains MPK units of output, where MPK is the marginal physical product of capital. But along an isoquant output is constant. By shedding a unit of labour the firm gives up MPL units of output. Lowering labour input by $[-MPK/MPL]$ keeps output constant when capital input is 1 unit higher. The isoquant's slope $[-MPK/MPL]$ tells us by how much labour is changed to keep output constant when capital is 1 unit higher. Hence the tangency condition in Figure 10.A2 implies

Slope of isocost line $= r/w = -MPK/MPL$
$$= \text{slope of isoquant} \tag{A1}$$

Point A in Figure 10.A2 is the least-cost way to make the output shown by isoquant I'. We can repeat this analysis for every other isoquant showing different outputs. That is how we derive the total cost curve discussed in the text.

How does the firm find the profit-maximizing output? Suppose at point A the marginal product of labour exceeds the wage rate w. Equation (A1) tells us that in the long run the marginal product of capital must also exceed the rental rate r. Only then can the factor price ratio r/w equal the ratio of the marginal products MPK/MPL. But if the marginal product of each factor exceeds the price at which the firm can hire that factor, it is profitable to expand output. In the long run, the firm expands output and factor use until the marginal product of each factor equals the price for which that factor can be hired. In Figure 10.A2, long-run profit-maximizing output is at a point such as B at which

$$MPL = w \quad \text{and} \quad MPK = r \tag{A2}$$

If equation (A2) holds, equation (A1) is automatically satisfied. Profits are maximized only if the chosen output is produced in the cost-minimizing way.

Finally, we show the effect of a rise in the price of one factor. Figure 10.A3 shows the initial position B where the isocost line L_1K_1 is tangent to the isoquant I''. Suppose the wage rate rises. Each isocost line then becomes less steep. Sacrificing a unit of labour allows more extra capital at any given total cost. At the original output on isoquant I'' this leads to a pure substitution effect from B to B', the point on the old isoquant tangent to an isocost line with the new flatter slope. But a higher wage rate also shifts up the total cost curve and the marginal cost curve for output. Profit-maximizing output falls.

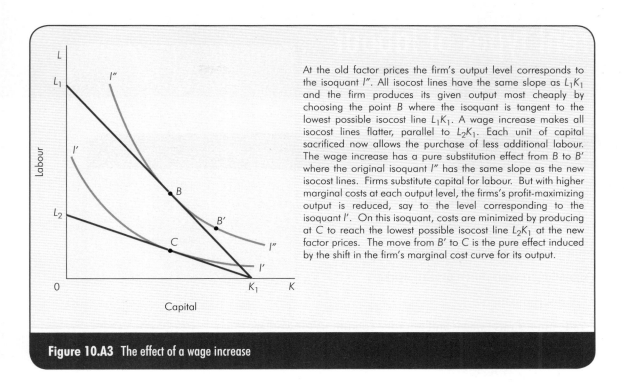

At the old factor prices the firm's output level corresponds to the isoquant I''. All isocost lines have the same slope as L_1K_1 and the firm produces its given output most cheaply by choosing the point B where the isoquant is tangent to the lowest possible isocost line L_1K_1. A wage increase makes all isocost lines flatter, parallel to L_2K_1. Each unit of capital sacrificed now allows the purchase of less additional labour. The wage increase has a pure substitution effect from B to B' where the original isoquant I'' has the same slope as the new isocost lines. Firms substitute capital for labour. But with higher marginal costs at each output level, the firms's profit-maximizing output is reduced, say to the level corresponding to the isoquant I'. On this isoquant, costs are minimized by producing at C to reach the lowest possible isocost line L_2K_1 at the new factor prices. The move from B' to C is the pure effect induced by the shift in the firm's marginal cost curve for its output.

Figure 10.A3 The effect of a wage increase

The lower isoquant I shows the new profit-maximizing output. L_2K_1 is the lowest attainable isocost line embodying the flatter slope corresponding to the new relative input prices. The firm now chooses point C. The move from B' to C is the pure output effect of a higher wage rate. The actual move from B to C can be decomposed into a substitution effect from B to B' and an output effect from B' to C. Both effects reduce the quantity of labour demanded.

Different types of labour

In most EU countries men earn more than women and whites earn more than non-whites. Does this reflect discrimination in the labour market or simply differences in the productivity of different workers?

This chapter is about differences in workers by sex, race, age, experience, education, training, innate ability and whether or not they belong to a trade union. How do these differences affect pay? Figure 11.1 shows that women earn only 80 per cent as much as men, although the gender gap is gradually closing.

The gender gap partly reflects continuity of employment. Single women earn almost 90 per cent as much as men. Whether we view this as discrimination against women who take time off to raise a family is central to our view about how society should be organized.

Table 11.1 examines pay differentials for men, the group for whom most data are available. It shows separate estimates for workers in trade unions and not in unions. The effect of unions is considered later in the chapter.

Table 11.1 highlights four sources of pay differentials. People with more education and training earn more. These returns to education do not depend much on whether the worker is in a union or not. It is not just vocational degrees, such as engineering, that enhance earning power. Philosophy and history graduates also earn more than those without degrees.

Personal characteristics also matter. Table 11.1 shows that ethnic minorities are paid less *even after allowing for differences in education and work experience*. This is *prima facie* evidence of discrimination. It may understate the

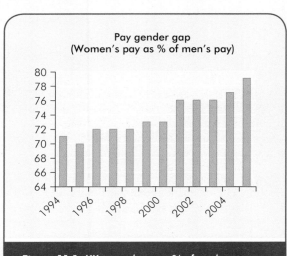

Figure 11.1 UK women's pay as % of men's pay,

Table 11.1 Pay differentials for UK men

% extra pay for	Union	Non-union
Education and training		
GCSEs	+5	+13
A-levels	+16	+21
University degree	+32	+47
Postgraduate degree	+50	+50
Other higher education	+18	+21
Apprenticeship	+11	+9
Personal		
Ethnic minority	−1	−5
Years' experience		
5	+13	+10
10	+23	+20
15	+30	+28
30	+35	+32
Job character		
South-east	+15	+16
London	+23	+15
Manual	+17	−21
Shift work	+12	+8
% overtime	+52	+47

Source: A. Booth, 'Seniority, Earnings and Unions', *Economica*, 1996.

true disadvantage of such minorities if they also have lower educational achievement because of discrimination elsewhere, for example in schools.

Work experience adds to earnings, though at a diminishing rate, especially in manual work, where older workers cannot match their strong, young colleagues. But experience still matters, even in manual work. Table 11.1 shows that job characteristics also affect pay. Shift work and overtime typically involve additional payments (equalizing wage differentials). Manual workers, perhaps with fewer skills, earn less than non-manual workers. And firms in the busy (and expensive) south-east region, including London, have to pay workers more.

Section 11.1 examines reasons why different workers have different productivity. If workers are paid their marginal product of labour, different workers earn different incomes. Section 11.2 discusses discrimination and equality of opportunity in the labour market. Section 11.3 studies the role of trade unions.

11.1 Productivity differences

This section contrasts two views of why workers have different productivity levels: either they acquired them or they were born with them.

Human capital

Human capital is the result of past investment in order to raise future incomes. The cost of investing in another year of school education or a further qualification is the direct cost, such as tuition fees, plus the opportunity cost of the time involved, namely delaying paid employment. The benefit of the investment is a higher future monetary income or a future job yielding more job satisfaction.

> **Human capital** is the stock of expertise accumulated by a worker to enhance future productivity.

The human capital approach assumes that wage differentials reflect differences in the productivity of different workers. Skilled workers have a higher marginal value product and earn more. The problem for workers is to decide how much to invest in improving their own productivity.

Age–earnings profiles and education

Table 11.1 shows that education and work experience contribute to higher earnings. Figure 11.2 shows how earnings typically change with age. It shows profiles for workers with three different levels of educational qualification: university or other higher degrees, A-levels or equivalent and no formal qualifications at all.

The figure makes two points. People with more educational qualifications typically earn more but the disparity grows steadily with age and experience. Healthy young people without qualifications can work hard and make good money but they cannot look forward to steadily rising real wages. By the age of 45 their earnings have peaked. In contrast, the highly educated start at wage rates only a little above those of the unqualified but they then face steadily rising incomes over most of their working lifetime. The most highly educated go into the most difficult jobs that take a long time to master. With increasing experience, productivity and earnings rise steadily.

The market for educated workers

Suppose higher education contributes to productivity. Figure 11.3 shows the market for workers with higher education. The vertical axis plots the difference between wages for workers with higher education and for workers without higher education. It is the *wage premium* for higher education. The horizontal axis shows the fraction of the workforce with higher education.

DD is the demand curve for workers with higher education. At point *B* the wage differential is high and firms want only a small proportion of their workers to

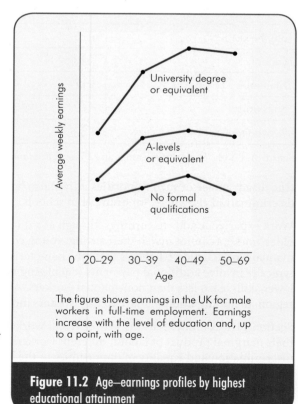

The figure shows earnings in the UK for male workers in full-time employment. Earnings increase with the level of education and, up to a point, with age.

Figure 11.2 Age–earnings profiles by highest educational attainment

have this extra education. At the lower differential at point *C* the demand for educated workers is much higher. The demand curve *DD* thus assumes that workers with higher education are more productive but that firms face diminishing returns in employing educated workers. At any instant, the supply of such workers is fixed by past education decisions. The short-run supply curve *SS* is vertical.

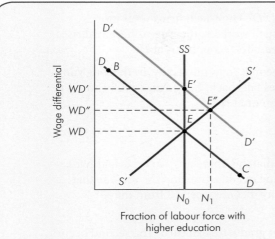

In the short run the supply of educated workers is fixed at N_0, but in the long run an increase in the wage differential for educated workers will induce more people to go to university. The long-run supply curve is *S'S'*. *DD* is the downward-sloping demand curve for educated workers. From the initial equilibrium at *E*, with a wage differential *WD*, an upward shift in the demand for educated workers leads initially to a sharp increase in the differential to *WD'*. Gradually more people get higher education and the new long-run equilibrium is at *E''*.

Figure 11.3 The market for highly educated workers

Box 11.1 Higher education pays off

Nowadays most students have to contribute to the cost of their higher education. What can we tell them about the financial benefits likely to accrue in the future? The table below shows the results of a major empirical study on determinants of people's wages by the time they are 33 years old.

The research suggests that degrees add a lot to future earning power but that the subject studied also matters. Economics students can expect to earn much more than history or languages students.

	% extra wage in Britain at age 33 for	
	Men	Women
First degree	+15	+32
Postgraduate degree	+15	+35
Extra effect by subject		
Arts	−10	+5
Economics	+10	+24
Chemistry/biology	−17	−11
Maths/physics	+9	+16

Source: R. Blundell *et al.*, 'Returns to Higher Education in Britain', *Economic Journal*, 2000.

In the long run, the supply curve $S'S'$ of workers with higher education slopes up. The greater the payoff to higher education, measured by the wage differential, the more school leavers delay work and acquire more education. The market begins in short-run and long-run equilibrium at E. The wage differential WD just compensates workers for the cost of acquiring further qualifications and for the wages they forgo while in higher education.

Suppose the demand curve for educated workers shifts up to $D'D'$. High-tech firms want more educated workers. In the short run, with a fixed supply SS of such workers, the wage differential rises to WD'. Competing for scarce workers, firms bid up their wages. The economy is at E'.

The premium on higher education is now so high that more people go to university. In the long run, the supply of graduates rises. The premium on scarce graduates falls back. Long-run equilibrium is at E'' with a higher number of educated workers and a wage differential WD''.

Investing in human capital: cost–benefit analysis

Will a school leaver continue in education or take a job immediately? There are two costs and two benefits. The immediate costs are for books and fees to continue in education and the income that could have been earned by taking a job immediately (*minus* any income received from the government as an educational grant).

The first benefit, in the future, is the stream of *extra* wages that graduates can earn. The second occurs immediately but in a non-monetary form. It is the fun or consumption value of going to college or university. Most students have a good time.

To decide whether to go to college, a school leaver compares current cost with the future stream of benefits. Figure 11.4 compares the income profile of a school leaver entering the labour force at 18 with the income profile of a graduate starting work at 21. The cost of higher education, the grey area, is the income forgone by not having a job between 18 and 21, *plus* the direct cost of fees and books, *minus* the money school leavers would have paid to enjoy the pleasures of being a student. The benefit, the coloured area, is the stream of extra income earned after the age of 21.

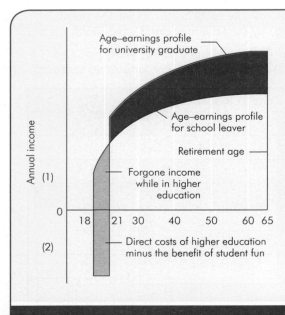

The diagram shows the age–earnings profiles for a worker leaving school at 18 to enter the labour force and for a student who delays working until 21. The coloured area shows how much extra the student will eventually earn. The grey area above 0 shows the income forgone while at university. The grey area below 0 shows the money value of the other costs and benefits of being at university: the diagram assumes that these costs outweigh the benefits. The decision whether or not to go to university depends on comparing the coloured area with the total grey area.

Figure 11.4 Investment in higher education

Box 11.2 University a distant dream for poorest

University is as distant as Pluto for many youngsters on Merseyside's poorest estates, Alan Johnson, the minister for further and higher education, said yesterday. He said top-up fees would encourage poorer children to go to university because it would put less financial pressure on their families.

Tricia Jenkins, head of widening participation at Liverpool University, said: 'It is not that young people in 55 per cent of the wards of Liverpool, Halton and Knowsley are not as capable but what they have not got is the choice of getting into higher education. A lot of it is because there is no family expectation and no community expectation that it is normal to go to university.'

Using top-up fees to fund bursaries for poorer university students should lower the cost of a university education and, within our framework, increase the value of a university education to students from poorer backgrounds. However, the problem appears to be one of recognizing the value of a university education. If education is not valued within poorer communities, and individuals are not expected to undertake university-based studies, then no increase in the net present value of a degree will alter access rates.

Adapted from *The Guardian*, 21 May 2004.

More education makes sense if the benefits outweigh the costs. But the benefits accrue in the future. Most people would prefer £100 today to a promise of £100 in five years' time. To compare like with like, we need to *discount*, or reduce the value of, future benefits (or future costs) to place them on a par with benefits or costs incurred today. Chapter 12 shows in detail how this should be done.

For the moment we skip the technical details. The general idea will suffice. If the present value, however calculated, of the benefits outweighs the present value of the costs incurred, the educational investment in improving human capital by further education makes sense. If the present value of the benefits is less than the present value of the costs, higher education is a bad investment. It is better to start work immediately.

In terms of Figure 11.4, higher education is a good deal for the student if the present value of the coloured area (the extra future earnings better education generates) more than offsets the present value of the grey area (the net cost of being in higher education).

On-the-job training and age–earnings profiles

Figure 11.1 showed that education raises future earning power. But earnings also rise with experience on the job, especially in the difficult jobs usually done by workers of higher ability and education. Learning on the job is central to the age–earnings profiles of the better educated but less important for the unqualified who do relatively routine jobs that can be mastered quickly.

If on-the-job training increases worker productivity, why don't workers pay firms for the valuable learning opportunities that firms provide? In part they do. To understand how and why we must distinguish between two kinds of skills.

Firm-specific skills

Firm-specific human capital could be as simple as knowing how the filing system works or as complicated as mastering the most efficient way to combine the various production processes of a particular factory. In either case, the skill is virtually worthless to any other firm.

> **Firm-specific skills** raise a worker's productivity only if he or she works for that particular firm.

General skills

Examples are learning how to use Microsoft Word or understanding how the stock market works.

> **General skills** enhance productivity in many jobs, not just the current one.

The firm can afford to pay for training in firm-specific skills. Workers' productivity is then higher with that firm than with any other firm. The firm is unlikely to lose the worker. The more general or transferable the skill, the more the firm wants the worker to pay the cost of training. No firm will invest heavily in training its workers only to see them move to other firms.

Firms offering general or transferable training try to make the workers pay for it. Firms offer an age–earnings profile that starts off below the worker's marginal product but is guaranteed to rise steeply over time. Apprenticeships, both in industry and in the professions, are examples. The worker pays for training by working for less than his immediate marginal product. Workers pay this cost of investing in human capital because the firm commits to an age–earnings profile that lets the worker recoup the initial investment with interest at a later date. In Figure 11.2 age–earnings profiles rise much more steeply for educated people, doing jobs that involve more training, than they do for unqualified workers whose training is likely to be limited.

Signalling

Human capital theory says that education and training raise worker productivity. An alternative theory of education is the theory of *signalling*. This theory says it could be rational to invest in costly education *even if education adds nothing directly to a worker's marginal product*. This theory may be more helpful in explaining why history graduates earn big money in banking.

> **Signalling** is the decision to undertake an action in order to reveal inside information.

The theory assumes that people are born with different innate ability. Some people are good at most things, other people are less smart and less productive. Not all smart people have blue eyes. The problem for firms is to tell which applicants are the smart ones with high productivity. Looking at their eyes is not enough.

Suppose higher education contributes nothing to productivity. Signalling theory says that, in going on in education, people who know that they are smart send a signal to firms that they are the high-productivity workers of the future. Higher education *screens out* the smart high-productivity workers. Firms can pay university graduates more because they know that they are the high-ability workers.

> **Screening** is the process of learning inside information by observing differences in behaviour.

To be effective, the screening process must separate the high-ability workers from the others. Why don't lower-ability workers go to university and fool firms into offering them high wages? Lower-ability workers could not be confident of passing. If studying adds to productivity, firms should offer higher wages to people who *attend* university, whether or not they pass the final exam. If university screens out the good people, firms will care not about attendance but *academic performance*.

Some firms hire university students before they sit their final exams. Is this evidence against the signalling theory? Not necessarily. Screening works in a second way. Since most people know their own ability, firms may take it on trust that people who have stuck it out till their final year at university believe themselves to be at the high end of the ability range.

It seems probable that education (even at the highest level) contributes something to productivity. But there may also be an element of screening. Engineering, law and business degrees presumably contribute more to productivity than philosophy, history or medieval French.

Activity box 11 Asymmetric information

The 2001 Nobel Prize for economic science was shared by three economists who pioneered the analysis of inside information, where people know more about themselves than others can easily discover. This means that those with the information have the power to exploit those without it, and those who fear they that they do not have access to inside information are driven to take defensive measures in case they get exploited.

Why does a new car depreciate by 15 per cent when you drive it out of the car showroom? George Akerlof of the University of California at Berkeley first analysed behaviour in the used car market, where sceptical buyers fear that sellers may try to offload useless cars about which the seller has much more information than the buyer. Akerlof showed that in market equilibrium buyers assume all cars are bad. Sellers of good cars cannot get a fair price. If you try to sell your recently purchased car, it might or might not be because you have discovered a fault. Potential buyers, unable to tell why you are selling, have to assume the worst in order not to be exploited. Hence your car depreciates a lot when you first buy it. The same analysis helps us understand loan sharks, junk bonds and some forms of discrimination against minorities. Chapter 12 discusses this **adverse selection** in greater detail.

Michael Spence of Stanford University showed that this problem is partly solved if those knowing they have good characteristics take costly actions to reveal credibly that they must be the good guys. His own research emphasized how education can **signal** innate talent. Smart students, knowing their own characteristics, sign up for tough courses that less smart students would fail. By passing the course, they reveal to prospective employers that they are smart and can work hard. There would be no point less talented or less dedicated students mimicking this behaviour – if they tackled the tough course they would fail and be found out. Tough courses allow people with good job prospects to signal their innate ability, which might otherwise be difficult for firms to discover before making costly hiring decisions. Signalling also explains how firms use dividends to signal their optimism about future profits to the stock market.

Joseph Stiglitz of Columbia University, recently Chief Economist of the World Bank, developed an alternative solution to Akerlof's adverse selection problem, relying on **screening** by the uninformed rather than signalling by the informed. By offering a lower premium in exchange for a higher deductible (the part of an insurance claim that will not be reimbursed), insurance companies can induce those who know they are low risk to reveal themselves. People who intend to drive slowly are happy to sign up for a large deductible in exchange for a lower insurance premium. Boy racers expect to have lots of accidents and would not find such an offer attractive since they would keep getting hit with the deductible. Similarly, a steep age–earnings profile for wages, beginning very low but ending very high, is attractive only to workers knowing that they do not intend to quit the labour force early. Those planning to hop in and out of the labour force want more of their pay up front.

221

Activity box 11 Asymmetric information (Continued)

Questions

Classify each of these activities as signalling, screening or adverse selection:

(a) A good risk borrower cannot get a loan at a decent interest rate because the lender fears that the borrower may not be able to repay, and cannot discover easily that this is a good risk borrower.

(b) An applicant for health insurance undertakes a health check at her own expense to confirm that she is not a smoker.

(c) A health insurance company pays for applicants to have prior health checks.

(d) The army makes all recruits go to a very tough boot camp despite the expense to the army.

(e) People enlisting for the army are prepared to go to the horrible camp.

(f) Students in their final year at school undertake a range of extracurricular activities in the hope of impressing the university to which they have applied.

To check your answers to these questions, go to page 719.

For other Nobel Prize winners, see www.nobelprize.org.

If education raises productivity directly, it is good for society. It raises the amount of output that the labour force can eventually produce. What if the only function of higher education is to signal the high-ability workers? It still makes sense for individuals to go to university. It raises their future incomes. Does it make sense for society as a whole? The social gain to learning who are the smart workers is that, by matching smart workers to difficult jobs, society gets higher output.

If the only function of higher education is to screen out the high-ability workers, there is a cheaper way for society to achieve the same result. A national IQ test, with results adjusted for disadvantages of background and previous opportunity to learn, might screen just as well (possibly even better!) at much less cost to society as a whole.

11.2 Discrimination

Figure 11.1 showed that women earn less than men. Table 11.4 showed that ethnic minorities earn less than whites. Is this evidence of sex and race discrimination in the UK labour market?

Some jobs pay more than others. Differences in average earnings of different groups can arise for two distinct reasons. Different groups may get different shares of the high-paying jobs, or may get paid different amounts for doing the same job.

> **Discrimination** is the different treatment of people whose relevant characteristics are identical.

Differences between men and women

Few women do manufacturing jobs, most have jobs in services. Yet the pattern of employment is not the major cause of the fact that women on average earn 80 per cent as much as men. Sector by sector, women systematically get paid substantially less than men. The main reason that women earn less is that they earn less than men whatever job they do.

The percentage of women in professional or managerial occupations is comparable with that for men but few women are on the boards of major companies.

Why do firms promote or train women more slowly? Suppose firms bear some of the cost of training. The firm makes a hard-nosed investment decision. Assuming men and women are of inherently equal ability and educational attainment, it costs the firm the same to train either sex.

Suppose firms believe women are more likely than men to interrupt, or even end, their careers at a young age. As a matter of biology, women have babies. Firms may conclude that the present value of the extra productivity benefits in the future is lower for women than men simply because many women work fewer years in the future. It is more profitable to train and promote men.

Some women plan to have a full-time career, either remaining childless or returning to work almost immediately after any children are born. It would make sense for firms to invest in such people. How is a firm to tell which young women are planning to stay? Asking is pointless. There is no incentive for young women to tell the truth.

Suppose firms offer young workers the choice between a relatively flat age–earnings profile and a steep profile that begins at a lower wage but pays a much higher wage later in a worker's career. In this way, firms can make the two profiles of equal value to someone planning a lifetime career. The early sacrifice (low wages) is recouped with interest later (high wages). Someone planning to quit the labour force, say at the age of 30, will never opt for the steeper profile.

Age–earnings profiles may induce recruits to reveal their true career plans. If women, or any other group with a high risk of quitting at a young age, accept the steeper profile, the firm can embark on training with some confidence that its investment will not be wasted.

Some firms may still try to pay female workers less than male workers who are identical in every respect, including the risk of quitting. This is overt discrimination.

Box 11.3 Snakes and ladders for career women

Top staff in the big consulting firms are nearly all men. Even though half the graduate intake is women, the share of women falls off rapidly as one moves up the career ladder. By 2010 KPMG wants a quarter of its partners to be women; Deloitte is aiming for 31 per cent by 2009.

According to recent research, 37 per cent of all professional women drop out of work at some point, and only 40 per cent of those make it back into full-time employment. If they do, they suffer a huge salary gap: with a three-year career break, they are likely then to earn 38 per cent less than those women who had remained in full-time work.

Smart employers are now starting to offer a variety of more flexible working: unpaid leave for career breaks, project-based work for those who wish to be part-time, compressed working that better fits school holidays and other forms of flexitime. As people live longer, people have to reconcile not merely work and childcare but looking after elderly relatives as well.

Adapted from *The Economist*, 21 July 2007

Society may discriminate against women in more subtle ways. Our analysis suggests that paternity leave for fathers, the provision of crèches for working parents, or a greater acceptance of part-time working by both sexes, would reduce the incentive for hard-nosed firms to decide to favour the training of men. Whether or not society wishes to organize its work and home life on such principles is not just a matter of economics.

Access to education

Some firms may treat innately similar workers equally but still pay men more than women because men have more educational qualifications than women. The cause of pay differences by sex then lies not in the labour market but in education.

Table 11.2 shows full-time and part-time UK students in three types of education: FE colleges, university undergraduates and postgraduates. In 1971 male students greatly outnumbered female students in all forms of further and higher education. This gender gap has now disappeared.

Table 11.2 UK students 1971–2002 (thousands)

	Male		Female	
	1971	2002	1971	2002
Further education				
Full time	116	569	95	559
Part time	891	1665	630	2562
Undergraduate				
Full time	241	519	173	620
Part time	127	263	19	412
Postgraduate				
Full time	33	94	10	93
Part time	15	133	3	153

Source: ONS, Social Trends.

Nevertheless, current data on earnings patterns reflect education over many previous decades. Today's top executive in his fifties finished university in around 1975. Past inequalities in education cast a long shadow over today's job market.

Racial discrimination

The same general principles apply to racial discrimination and earnings differences between whites and non-whites. Many studies have confirmed the data in Table 11.3. On average, non-whites earn less than whites.

Age–earnings profiles for non-white men are much flatter than those for white men. White men are much more likely to achieve steady promotion and rising earnings. In turn, this provides an incentive for whites to do more difficult jobs where training and experience are important. Part of the problem for non-white men is the type of education they receive. The payoff to education is often low for non-whites who attend a typical inner-city school.

Table 11.3 Ethnic groups, UK, 2002

	Participation rate (%)		Unemployment rate (%)	
	Men	Women	Men	Women
Whites	85	75	5	4
Blacks	77	64	17	13
Indian	80	69	6	8
Pakistani	74	36	14	19
Bangladeshi	75	22	21	16

Source: ONS, *Labour Market Trends.*

Whether this reflects lack of resources or the disadvantaged background of many pupils, firms may believe that these potential workers will have lower productivity and be harder to train. Hence, these workers get less training. A higher proportion of non-whites are restricted to unskilled and low-paying jobs.

Table 11.3 completes our examination of racial discrimination. Muslim women from Pakistan and Bangladesh have low rates of labour force participation. This reflects a different willingness to supply their labour as well as any evidence of discrimination in the demand for their labour. However, most minority groups have unemployment rates well above those for whites.

Again, it is hard to draw a line between discrimination in the labour market and elsewhere in society. Firms have to act in the interest of their shareholders. So long as firms perceive that different groups of workers already have acquired different characteristics, or will behave differently during their working lifetimes, firms will wish to treat different groups differently. Unless society removes these differences in characteristics, opportunities and behaviour of different groups of workers, the eradication of blatant racism or sexism will go only part of the way to eliminating pay differentials between groups of workers.

11.3 Trade unions

Trade unions are worker organizations set up by workers to affect pay and working conditions. Do unions protect workers from exploitation by powerful employers or do they use their power to secure unjustified pay increases and oppose technical change and productivity improvements that might threaten the jobs of their members?

In 1980 half the civilian labour force in the UK belonged to a trade union. Figure 11.5 shows changes since 1910. After a steady increase in union membership until 1920 there was a massive decline during the Depression of the 1930s. After a sharp recovery until 1950, the degree of unionization of the labour force remained fairly constant until the late 1960s. The 1970s saw a sharp rise in union membership, which peaked in 1979, since when it has been falling sharply.

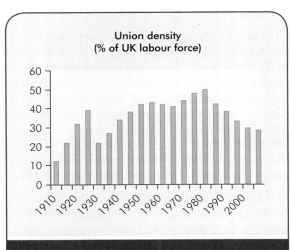

Figure 11.5 Union membership (% of civilian labour force)

Sources: Bain and Elsheik, *Union Growth and the Business Cycle*, Basil Blackwell, 1976; ONS, *Labour Market Trends.*

Declining unionization reflects several trends. First, as the share of the service sector in national output rises, the share in traditional industry, manual and male, has shrunk. Second, the public sector, in which unions were traditionally well organized, has been shrunk with privatization and cuts in the size of the public sector. Third, computers and other technical advances have made production much more flexible and small scale, circumstances in which it is harder to organize a trade union. Fourth, increased female participation in the labour force has often been in part-time jobs in which union organization is harder. Finally, globalization has had a powerful impact, as we explain shortly. First we need to analyse further what unions actually do.

What unions do

The traditional view of unions is that they offset the power that a firm enjoys in negotiating wages and working conditions. A single firm has many workers. If each worker must make a separate deal with the firm, the firm can make a take-it-or-leave-it offer. A worker with firm-specific human capital, which will be pretty useless in any other firm, may face a large drop in productivity and wages if she rejects the firm's offer. The firm is in a strong bargaining position if it can make separate agreements with each of its workers. In contrast, by presenting a united front, the workers may be able to impose large costs on the firm if they *all* quit. The firm can replace one worker but not its whole labour force. The existence of unions evens up the bargaining process.

Once a union is established, it aims not merely to protect its members but to improve their pay and conditions. To be successful the union must be able to restrict the firm's labour supply. If the firm can hire non-union labour, unions will find it hard to maintain the wage above the level at which the firm can hire non-union workers. This is one reason why unions are keen on closed-shop agreements with individual firms.[1]

> A **closed shop** is an agreement that all a firm's workers will be members of a trade union.

How do unions raise wages by restricting supply? Figure 11.6 shows an industry's downward-sloping labour demand curve *DD*. The wage in the rest of the economy is W_0, and we assume the industry faces a perfectly elastic labour supply curve at the wage rate W_0. In the absence of unions, equilibrium is at E_0 with employment N_0.

Now suppose everyone in the industry must belong to a trade union and the union restricts labour in this industry to N_1. The industry faces a vertical labour supply curve at N_1. Equilibrium is at E_1. By sacrificing employment in the industry, the union raises the wage for each employed member from W_0 to W_1. At a higher wage and marginal cost of production, each firm is forced to raise its price. The full effect of the trade union is not merely to raise wages and lower employment in the industry but also to raise the output price and lower equilibrium output of the industry.

This analysis raises two questions. What determines how far the union will trade off lower employment for higher wages in the industry? And what determines how much power unions have to control the supply of labour to particular industries?

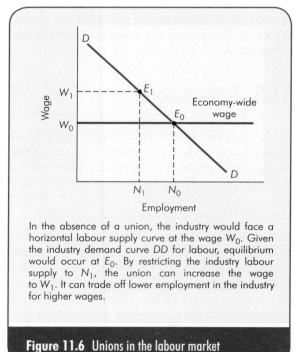

In the absence of a union, the industry would face a horizontal labour supply curve at the wage W_0. Given the industry demand curve *DD* for labour, equilibrium would occur at E_0. By restricting the industry labour supply to N_1, the union can increase the wage to W_1. It can trade off lower employment in the industry for higher wages.

Figure 11.6 Unions in the labour market

1 Unions frequently argue that, in the absence of a closed shop, non-union workers will benefit from improvements in pay and conditions achieved through the efforts of the union. Non-union members are getting a 'free ride' without paying their union subscriptions.

Assume that the union has full control over the supply of labour to a firm or an industry. It can trade off employment for wage rises. How far it will go depends on the preferences or tastes of the union and its members. It might try to maximize total income (wage times employment) of its members, or it might try to maximize per capita income (wages) of those in employment. A lot depends on the power and decision structure within the union.

The more the union cares about its senior members, the more it is likely to maximize the wage independently of what happens to employment. Senior workers have the most firm-specific human capital and are the least likely to be sacked if total employment in the industry must fall. Conversely, the more the union is democratic, and the more it cares about its potential members as well as those actually in employment, the less likely it is to restrict employment to ensure higher wages for those who remain employed in the industry.

A given reduction in labour supply raises wages most when labour demand is most inelastic. Figure 11.7 illustrates. Without unions, industry equilibrium is at E_0, where the horizontal labour supply curve intersects the labour demand curve. DD shows an inelastic labour demand curve and $D'D'$ a more elastic labour demand curve. The more inelastic labour demand is, the larger the wage increase a union will secure by restricting labour supply from N_0 to N_1.

When the car industry was unionized, initially the derived demand curve for car workers was quite inelastic. By restricting employment to N_1 the unions increased car workers' wages from W_0 to W_1. Then Japanese car producers began competing in the UK market. Each UK firm's output demand curve became more price-elastic.

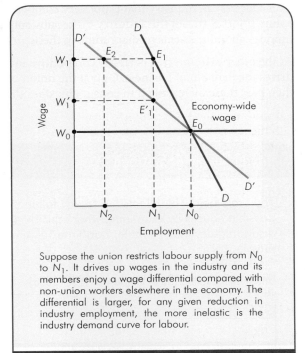

Suppose the union restricts labour supply from N_0 to N_1. It drives up wages in the industry and its members enjoy a wage differential compared with non-union workers elsewhere in the economy. The differential is larger, for any given reduction in industry employment, the more inelastic is the industry demand curve for labour.

Figure 11.7 Wage differentials and the demand for labour

Hence, its derived demand curve for labour also became more elastic, rotating DD to $D'D'$ in Figure 11.7. At the wage rate W_1 domestic firms lost market share and union employment fell from N_1 to N_2.

Unionization and wage differentials

Table 11.4 shows estimates of the union wage differential, how much more a union member earns than a non-union worker. Union members earn 7.5 per cent more than people not belonging to a union in unskilled jobs, but only 1.5 per cent extra in skilled jobs. Union power has been falling over time. So has the union wage differential.

Table 11.4 Union wage differentials

% extra for union in	1984	1990
Unskilled	10.5	7.5
Semi-skilled	10.5	6.5
Skilled	3.5	1.5

Source: M. Stewart, 'Union Wage Differentials in an Era of Declining Unionisation', *Oxford Bulletin of Economics and Statistics*, 1995.

Trade union power also varies across industries. Figure 11.7 identified the slope of the labour demand curve as the key determinant of trade union power to raise wages without a large loss of jobs. Chapter 10 noted that the demand for labour is a derived demand, reflecting the demand for a firm's output.

Consider first an industry that is not very competitive, with few domestic firms and little foreign competition. Firms in this industry make substantial supernormal profits. By threatening to strike, unions can induce firms to share some of these profits, in the form of higher wages.

At the other extreme, in a perfectly competitive industry, if a union in a single firm raises wages it drives the firm out of business. Only if the union can organize across *the whole industry*, which can then pass these increases on to consumers, does the union stand a chance of raising wages.

Box 11.4 The unions flag

The table below highlights the steady fall in union membership. We can learn more about its possible causes by examining where this decline has occurred. The table examines various ways to disaggregate: male/female, part-time/full-time, manual/non-manual, industry/services and public/private.

Union membership (% of employees 1990–2003)

	1990	2003	Change
Male	43	29	−14
Female	32	29	−3
Full-time	43	32	−11
Part-time	22	21	−1
Manual	42	26	−16
Non-manual	35	29	−6
Industry	44	27	−17
Services	37	30	−7
Public	65	58	−7
Private	24	12	−12

Source: ONS, *Labour Market Trends.*

Not only have full-time manual male jobs been shrinking as manufacturing industry has become less important to the UK economy, *union membership has fallen sharply even as a percentage of those who have remained in such jobs*. This has been a real double whammy for union membership.

Finally, the outlook for union membership looks bleak, with enormous variations in membership by age. Only 14 per cent of workers aged between 16 and 24 are union members, compared with 40 per cent of workers over the age of 50.

Studying a large number of industries, Mark Stewart of Warwick University showed that this is exactly what happens in practice.[2] In competitive industries facing significant foreign competition, unions get no wage differential. In industries sheltered from foreign competition but with many domestic firms, union differentials exist only if the whole industry is unionized. But unions get big mark-ups in industries with few domestic firms and little foreign competition.

Globalization is affecting unions. Greater international competition in more and more industries is eliminating pockets of domestic monopoly whose profits were tempting targets for unions. As greater competition makes the derived demand for labour more elastic, unions face an ever-worsening trade-off between wages and employment. Restricting labour supply only raises wages by sacrificing many jobs. As the trade-off gets less attractive, it is less worth belonging to a union.

Union wages as compensating differentials

Union wage differentials arise not only from the successful restriction of labour supply. Union work has certain characteristics – a structured work setting, inflexibility of hours, employer-set overtime and a faster work pace – a whole set of conditions that might be regarded as unpleasant. To some degree, higher wages in such industries are merely *compensating wage differentials* for these non-monetary aspects of the job.

There are two competing views. The first is that, after unions take over and raise wages, firms respond by taking advantage of unions to raise productivity. Work patterns are standardized and the union assists in implementing these new practices. Firms finance higher wages by making workers operate in less pleasant but more productive ways.

The alternative view is that changed work practices are not an employer *response* to union restriction of labour supply to raise wages, but rather the reason why unions exist. Unions emerge in industries where large productivity gains are possible but cause unpleasant working conditions. The union exists not to restrict labour supply but to ensure workers receive proper compensating differentials for the unpleasant work practices that firms find it profitable to introduce. On this view, the unions do not make separate deals for pay and working conditions. They secure pay rises in exchange for changes in working conditions.

To sum up, unions secure higher wages for their members for two distinct reasons. First, they restrict labour supply, trading off lower employment in the industry for higher wages. Second, they negotiate changes in working practices that raise productivity and channel part of this gain to the workforce.

Bargaining and strikes

How serious are strikes? Table 11.5 shows days of work lost per employee because of industrial disputes. Strikes now cost the economy less than one day per employee per year. Days lost through industrial disputes have been falling since the 1970s.

Why do strikes occur? Although employers and workers are fighting for a share of the firm's total revenue, they have a common interest too. If the firm does better, it can pay more. Typical bargaining between a firm and a union is completed without a strike. If strikes are avoided, there is more money to divide between the shareholders and the workers.

Given a common interest, why do strikes occur at all? If both parties knew the settlement reached after a strike, it would be better to settle immediately on the same share-out and avoid the loss of output and revenue that the strike induces. One reason for strikes is that one party misjudges the other's position. As the strike proceeds, each side learns the needs of the other side.

2 M. Stewart, 'Union Wage Differentials, Product Market Influences and the Division of Rents', *Economic Journal*, 1990.

Table 11.5 Industrial disputes: annual days lost per 1000 workers, 1975–2005

	1975–79	1985–89	1990–94	1995–99	2000–05
Italy	1510	300	240	77	110
Canada	940	424	231	218	189
UK	510	180	37	21	25
USA	260	86	43	38	38
France	210	57	30	105	46

Source: ONS, *Labour Market Trends*.

Not all strikes are mistakes that would have been avoided with better initial perceptions of the other side's needs. Strikes also occur to establish long-term credibility. If a firm believes that the workers will strike unless they get a fair deal, the firm may offer a fair deal at once. After a few years of co-operation the firm begins to feel that the union is a pushover. The union may then strike not merely because of the current dispute but to remind the firm that it will strike unless the firm is fair. Investing in one strike may earn the union a fair deal for many years to come.

Why have strikes fallen since the 1970s? Part of the answer is a falling rate of unionization of the labour force. But even unionized industries are striking less. In the private sector, this is another aspect of globalization and the presence of outside competitors. In the public sector, it reflects government commitments to clear and well-publicized spending targets that leave less room for unions to fight about wages and conditions.

Summary

- Different workers get different pay. This reflects personal characteristics such as education, job experience, sex, race and union status.

- **Skills** are the most important source of wage differentials. **Human capital** formation includes both formal schooling and on-the-job training. Earnings profiles confirm that workers with more education and training earn higher lifetime incomes.

- How much more employers pay for skilled workers depends on the production technology. The demand for skilled workers depends on the extent to which skilled and unskilled workers can be substituted and on the output demand for industries that use skilled workers relatively intensively.

- Skilled labour is relatively scarce because it is costly to acquire human capital. Education beyond minimum age has not only direct costs but also the opportunity cost of earnings forgone by not working immediately. The investment decision for human capital involves comparing the present costs with the **present value** of extra income or other benefits in the future.

- These considerations are reinforced by the role of education as a **screening** or **signalling** device, which indicates to employers the workers of innate ability. Thus education has a return to high-ability workers even if it does not directly increase their productivity.

- Women and non-whites on average receive lower incomes than white men. Women and non-whites are concentrated in relatively unskilled jobs with fewer opportunities for promotion. This need not reflect blatant sexism or racism by employers. It may reflect educational or other disadvantages before young workers reach the labour market. It may also reflect a low perceived rate of return by firms on the money spent in training such workers or by such workers on the time spent in education and skill acquisition.

- Under one-third of the UK labour force now belongs to a **trade union**. Unions restrict the labour supply to firms or industries, thereby raising wages but lowering employment. Unions move firms up their demand curve for labour.

- Unions achieve a higher **wage differential** for their members the more inelastic the demand for labour and the more they are willing or able to restrict the supply of labour. However, some union wage differentials are compensating wage differentials, which unions have secured in return for changes in work practices that raise productivity but reduce job satisfaction.

Review questions

To check your answers to these questions, go to page 719.

1 A worker can earn £20 000 a year for the next 33 years. Alternatively, the worker can take three years off to go on a training course whose fees are £10 000 per year. If the interest rate is zero, what future income must the worker then earn to make the investment in training profitable?

2 Suppose economists form a union and establish a certificate that is essential for practising economics. How would this help to raise the relative wage of economists? How would the union restrict entry to the economics profession?

3 Does your answer to Question 2 explain why young hospital doctors are forced to work ridiculous hours?

4 If EU membership raises competition between European firms, what is likely to happen to the wages of European workers? Why? Would it be appropriate for European trade unions then to amalgamate across EU countries?

5 **Common fallacies** Why are these statements wrong? (a) If women earn less than men, employers must be sexists. (b) Free schooling from 16 to 18 ensures that children from poor families can stay on in education. (c) Since many low-paid workers belong to a trade union, unions have little effect on improving pay and conditions.

6 **Harder question** Suppose you have to give up your summer holiday to acquire some skills, which may be general or specific to a particular employer. If the skills are equally easy to acquire, which do you prefer? Why? How might a firm requiring firm-specific skills induce you to learn them? Suppose the firm has the choice of paying for your training or paying a wage premium for each year you work for the firm. Which will the firm prefer? Why?

7 **Harder question** Despite the assumptions of consumer choice theory, there is little evidence that people get happier as general living standards rise, and Vanuatu, in the Pacific, was recently judged the happiest country despite its material poverty. (a) Can this latter finding be reconciled with the economics you have learned so far in this book? (b) Could the former finding be partly explained by the importance of one's income and living standards relative to one's peer group?

8 **Essay question** 'The only coherent response to a global market is a global trade union.' Is this logic correct? What problems do you foresee in trying to implement it?

To help you grasp the key concepts of this chapter check out the extra resources posted on the Online Learning Centre. There are chapter summaries, self-test questions, an interactive graphing tool, weblinks and a searchable glossary, all for free!

To put your learning into practice and prepare for exams, an **Interactive Workbook** is also available online, containing a variety of question types and providing feedback on your answers.

If you'd like further help with economics, or have any questions, **NetTutor** is here to help! You will have a personalised tutorial service at your fingertips. Visit the online learning centre at: www.mcgraw-hill.co.uk/ textbooks/begg for information on accessing all of these resources.

Factor markets and income distribution

The previous two chapters focused on labour. We now examine the other inputs with which labour co-operates in production. Some issues can be dealt with briefly. You already know how a firm chooses a production technique in the long run, when all factors can be freely varied, and you are familiar with the concept of a factor's marginal product.

Apart from investment in human capital, many aspects of labour market behaviour are easily analysed within a short-run time horizon. Labour is a variable input even in the short run. Since it takes much longer to adjust other factor inputs, decisions about their use must take a longer view.

One theme of this chapter is how the future affects the present. We examine how decisions today should value future benefits and costs, and show how to discount future payments or receipts to calculate their *present value*.

Our interest in the markets for capital and land goes beyond the equilibrium quantity of capital or the equilibrium price of land. There are two reasons to study factor markets as a whole. First, firms rarely use a single input. Decisions about inputs of capital and land affect the demand curve for labour and the equilibrium wage, just as decisions about labour inputs affect the demand for other factors of production.

Second, having completed our analysis of factor markets, we can discuss what determines the *income distribution*. The price of a factor, multiplied by the quantity used, tells us its income. We need to know the prices and quantities of all productive factors to understand how the economy's total income is distributed. We end this chapter by examining income distribution in the UK.

Apart from labour, the other principal inputs to production are capital and land.

> **Physical capital** is the stock of produced goods that are inputs to production of other goods and services.

The stock of physical capital includes assembly-line machinery used to make cars, railway lines making transport services, school buildings producing education services, dwellings that produce housing services, and consumer durables, such as televisions, that produce entertainment services.

Physical capital is distinguished from land by the fact that the former is produced.

> **Land** is the factor of production that nature supplies.

Although nature can change the quantity of land – through earthquakes, fires, and the deposit of silt – economists treat land as fixed in supply. Its quantity is largely unaffected by economic decisions, whereas capital can be produced. The distinction between land and capital can become blurred. Fertilizer and irrigation can 'produce' better land. Because land and capital may be hard to disentangle, we discuss them in the same chapter. However, the distinction is often useful.

Chapter 6 introduced *depreciation*, the extent to which an asset or durable good is used up within the period of analysis. Capital and land are both assets. Capital depreciates a little every year, though new capital can be produced. In treating land as fixed, we assume it does not depreciate.

> Together, capital and land are the **tangible wealth** of the economy.

Capital and land are wealth or assets because they are durable. They are tangible because they are physical and we could touch them. Financial wealth is not tangible, and not a physical input to production, though it can hire such inputs. We distinguish between *physical* capital – plant, machinery and buildings, which henceforth we call 'capital' – and *financial* capital, or money and paper assets.

12.1 Physical capital

Table 12.1 shows the level and composition of physical capital in the UK in 2005. (Data on capital takes ages to collect!) Dwellings are houses and flats. Productive fixed capital is plant, machinery and buildings. Productive capital that is not fixed is called working capital: inventories or stocks of manufactured goods awaiting sale, partially finished goods (work in progress), and raw materials held for future production. Inventories are capital because they are produced goods that contribute to future production.

Table 12.2 shows productive fixed capital (PFK) used in production in the UK in 1997 and 2005. The capital input to production is about twice the value of annual national output. The final row shows that, at 2003 prices, the quantity of capital per employed worker rose from £77 000 to £90 000 during 1997–2005.

Table 12.1 UK capital stock, 2005

	£bn	%
Dwellings	1558	45
Productive fixed capital	1874	55
Total capital stock	3432	100

Source: ONS, *UK National Accounts.*

Table 12.2 Capital input to UK production

	1997	2005
PFK	1558	1778
PFK/GDP	2	2
PFK/employed worker	77	90

Note: PFK in £bn. PFK per worker in £000, both at 2003 prices.
Source: ONS, *UK National Accounts.*

Investment in physical capital is increasing capital as a production input, not only in absolute terms but relative to the number of workers employed. Even in a decade, production techniques have become more *capital intensive*. Each worker has more capital with which to work.

Because capital depreciates, it takes some investment in new capital goods merely to stand still.

If net investment is positive, gross investment more than offsets depreciation. The capital stock rises. Conversely, if low gross investment may fail to offset depreciation, the capital stock falls.

> **Gross investment** is the production of new capital goods and the improvement of existing capital goods. **Net investment** is gross investment minus depreciation of the existing capital stock.

12.2 Rentals, interest rates and asset prices

Table 12.3 distinguishes *stocks* and *flows*, and distinguishes *rental payments* and *asset prices*. The price for hiring labour services is the wage. Rather loosely, we call it the 'price of labour' but the wage is the *rental payment* to hire labour. There is no asset price for buying the physical asset called a 'worker'. We no longer have slavery, ownership of workers by firms.

Table 12.3 Stock and flow concepts

	Capital	Labour
Flow input to hourly production	Capital services	Labour services
Payment for flow	Rental rate (£/machine hour)	Wage rate (£/labour hour)
Asset price	£/machine	£/slave, if purchase allowed

Capital assets and capital services can be bought and sold. We have to be more careful.

Rental payments and asset prices correspond to flows and stocks.

Tourists rent a car for the weekend. Building contractors pay a rental rate to lease earth-moving equipment. Sometimes there is no rental market. It is impossible to rent a power station. When firms make a once-and-for-all purchase of a capital asset or stock they must calculate how much it is implicitly costing them to use their capital. We return to this question in Section 12.4.

> A **stock** is the quantity of an asset at a point in time. A **flow** is the stream of services an asset provides in a period of time.

> The cost of using capital services is the **rental rate** for capital.

Unlike labour, capital goods can be bought and have an asset price.

Buying a car for £9000 entitles you to a stream of future transport services. You might even obtain a stream of future rental payments by letting your friend drive it.

What will a buyer pay for a capital asset? This reflects the value of the future income from capital services that the asset stock provides. However, we cannot simply add the future rental payments over the life of the capital asset to calculate its current asset price or value? We have to pay attention to the role of *time* and *interest payments*.

> The **price of an asset** is the sum for which the asset can be purchased outright. The owner of a capital asset gets the future stream of capital services from this asset.

Interest and present values

A lender makes a loan to a borrower, who agrees to repay the initial sum (the principal) *with interest* at some future date. A loan of £100 for a year at 10 per cent interest must be repaid at £110 by the end of the year. The extra £10 (10 per cent of £100) is the interest cost of borrowing £100 for a year. *Interest rates* are quoted as a percentage per annum.

Suppose we lend £1 and re-lend the interest as it accrues. The first row of Table 12.4 shows what happens if the annual interest rate is 10 per cent. After a year we have £1 plus an interest payment of £0.10. Re-lending the whole £1.10, we have £1.21 by the end of the second year. Because of *compound interest*, the absolute amount by which our money grows increases every year. The first year we increase our money by £0.10, which is 10 per cent of £1. Since we re-lend the interest, our money grows by £0.11 in the next year since we earn 10 per cent on £1.10. If we lend for yet another year, our money will grow by £0.121 to £1.331 at the end of the third year.

Table 12.4 Interest and present value (PV)

	Year		
	0	1	2
At 10% interest rate:			
Value of £1 lent today in:	£1	£1.10	£1.21
PV of £1 earned in:	£1	£0.91	£0.83
At 5% interest rate:			
Value of £1 lent today in:	£1	£1.05	£1.10
PV of £ earned in:	£1	£0.95	£0.91

At 10 per cent interest per annum, £1 in year 0 is worth £1.10 in year 1 and £1.21 in year 2. Now ask the question the other way round. If we offered you £1.21 in two years' time, what sum today would be just as valuable? The answer is £1. If you had £1 today you could always lend it out to get exactly £1.21 in two years' time. The second row of Table 12.4 extends this idea. If £1.21 in year 2 is worth £1 today, then £1 in year 2 must be worth £[1/1.21] = £0.83 today. £0.83 today could be lent out at 10 per cent interest to accumulate to £1 in year 2. Similarly, £1 in year 1 is worth only £[1/1.10] = £0.91 today.

> The **present value** of a future £1 is the sum that, if lent today, would cumulate to £1 by that date.

Compound interest implies that lending £1 today cumulates to ever-larger sums the further into the future we keep the loan and re-lend the interest. Conversely, the present value of £1 earned at some future date becomes smaller the further into the future the date at which the £1 is earned.

The present value of a future payment also depends on the interest rate. Table 12.4 shows that a loan of £1 accumulates less rapidly over time if the interest rate is lower. At 5 per cent interest a loan of £1 cumulates to only £1.10 after two years, compared with £1.21 after two years when the interest rate was 10 per cent in row 1. Hence the bottom row of Table 12.4 shows that the present value of £1 in year 1 or year 2 is larger when the interest rate is only 5 per cent than in the corresponding entry when the interest rate is 10 per cent.

Figure 12.1 illustrates the same points, showing how lending £1 today cumulates at compound interest rates of 5 and 10 per cent. After 10 years, the loan fund is worth £2.59 at 10 per cent interest but only £1.62 at 5 per cent interest. Higher interest rates imply more rapid accumulation through lending. The same diagram can be used for present values. A payment of £2.59 in 10 years' time has a present value of £1 if the annual interest rate is 10 per cent. The present value of £1 in 10 years' time is thus £1/[2.59] = £0.386. If interest rates are 5 per cent, the value of £1 in 10 years' time is £1/[1.62] = £0.617.

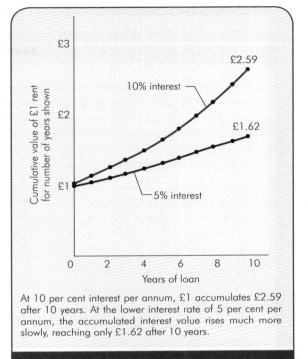

At 10 per cent interest per annum, £1 accumulates £2.59 after 10 years. At the lower interest rate of 5 per cent per annum, the accumulated interest value rises much more slowly, reaching only £1.62 after 10 years.

Figure 12.1 Accumulation through interest

Activity box 12 A Stern view of discount rates

Private investors have several benchmarks against which to assess what rate at which to discount the future. Every day, by the decisions they make in pricing assets that are entitled to future income streams, the financial markets reveal what discount rates are being used by market participants.

But what rate should society use in discounting future costs and benefits when making policy decisions? Nowhere is this more clearly illustrated than in the controversy surrounding Sir Nicholas Stern's review of the economics of climate change, commissioned by the UK government and published in 2006.

The figure below shows a 1000-year history of temperatures on the planet. Suppose we could all agree on the science of global warming. This would allow statements of the form, 'if we continue producing emissions at the current rate, global temperatures will rise according to the following profile, with the following consequences in terms of flooding, volatile weather, drought, and so on'.

Suppose too that there was only one country in the world, so we did not have to worry about whether the USA or India participated in trying to slow down climate change. The central issue then would be 'how much pain should we inflict on today's generation in order to mitigate the problem for future generations?'

Activity box 12 A Stern view of discount rates (Continued)

The lower the discount rate we use in this calculation, the greater the present value of the benefits of helping future generations; the lower the discount rate we use, the less today we care about helping future generations. The Stern Review's recommendation that we should take urgent action to reduce emissions substantially follows inexorably from its analysis provided we agree with its assumption that we should *not* discount the welfare of future generations in making this policy decision today.

Others, such as Professor William Nordhaus of Yale University, have argued that today's decision makers should discount the welfare of future generations – not least because they are still likely to be richer than us and have better options than we face – in which case the optimal policy response to climate change is a slower mitigation of emissions today, albeit then requiring that future generations will have to take much more drastic action.

The discount rate is not an academic abstraction. It affects key valuations and decisions, whether in the stock market or in the politics of controlling global warming.

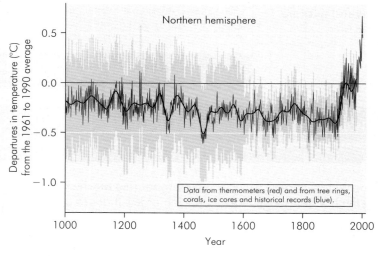

Source: Intergovernmental Panel on Climate Change, Fourth Assessment, 2007

Questions

(a) If we wish to weight equally the utility of current and future generations, what discount rate should we apply to future utility?

(b) Still weighting utility equally, suppose future generations are richer than us and we believe in the principle of diminishing marginal utility of consumption. Will a unit of consumption be worth more today when we are poor or tomorrow when we are rich?

(c) Suppose, by sacrificing consumption today, we invest in physical capital that would make future generations richer. Say on average this investment has a rate of return of 5 per cent a year in real terms. What return would an environmental investment (e.g. preventing climate change) have to yield in order for future generations to be pleased with the decisions we made today?

To check your answers to these questions, go to page 720.

Using interest rates to calculate present values of future payments tells us the right way to add together payments at different points in time. For each payment at each date we calculate its present value. Then we add together the present values of the different payments.

To relate the price of a capital asset to the stream of future payments earned from the capital services it provides, we calculate the present value of the rental payment earned by the asset in each year of its working life, and add these present values together. This is what the asset is worth today. In equilibrium it should be the asset price.

Asset valuation

How much would you bid for a machine that earns £4000 in rental for two years and is then sold for scrap for £10 000? If you bid anything without finding out the interest rate you misunderstood the previous section! Suppose the annual interest rate is 10 per cent. The first two rows of Table 12.5 show the money received each year. The final column shows the present value of these receipts. From Table 12.4, £1 next year is worth only £0.91 today, and £1 in year 2 only £0.83 today. The present value PV of £4000 in year 1 is £3640 (£4000×0.91), and the PV of the £14 000 received from rental earnings and sale for scrap in year 2 is £11 620 (£14 000×0.83). Adding these present values for years 1 and 2, the asset price should be £15 260.

Table 12.5 Present values and asset prices (at annual interest rate of 10%)

Year	Rental (£)	Scrap value (£)	Present value (£)
1	4000		3 640
2	4000 +	10 000	11 620
Asset price in year 0			15 260

Note: From Table 12.4, the present value of each £1 in year 1 is £0.91 and in year 2 is £0.83.

£15 260 is much smaller than the £18 000 actually earned from two years of rental income and the scrap value. Present values *discount* the future.

These principles can be used to calculate the present value of any future income stream once the interest rate is known. The appendix shows more detail. The calculation is very simple in one special case: when the asset lasts for ever and the income stream per time period is constant. Governments sometimes borrow by selling a *perpetuity*, a bond (simply a piece of paper) promising to pay the owner a constant interest payment (called the 'coupon') for ever. In the UK, these are called 'consols' (after a famous bond issue called Consolidated Stock). The PV of a consol, the price the stock market will offer for this piece of paper, obeys the formula

$$PV = \frac{\text{constant annual coupon payment}}{\text{interest rate per annum}} \tag{1}$$

In the financial pages of a newspaper you will find 2.5 per cent consols. This perpetuity promises to pay £2.50 per annum for ever. £2.50 was 2.5 per cent of the original sale price of £100. If the current rate of interest is 5 per cent, 2.5 per cent consols should be worth around £50 (the annual coupon £2.5, divided by 0.05, the annual interest rate as a decimal fraction). If interest rates rise to 10 per cent per annum, the consol is then worth only £25 [= (£2.5)/(0.10)].

Real and nominal interest rates: inflation and present values

Thus far we have discussed future payments valued in nominal terms. The first column of Table 12.5 shows rental receipts in actual pounds. The interest rate of 10 per cent tells us how many actual pounds we earn by lending £1 for a year.

At a nominal interest rate of 10 per cent, £100 lent today accumulates to £110 by next year. But we want to know how many goods that £110 will then buy.

> The **nominal interest rate** tells us how many actual pounds are earned by lending £1 for a year.

Suppose the nominal interest rate is 10 per cent but inflation is 6 per cent. Lending £1 for a year gives £1.10, but after a year it costs £1.06 to buy goods we could have bought for £1 today. With £1.10 to spend next year, our purchasing power rises by only 4 per cent. The real interest rate is 4 per cent. Thus

> The **real interest rate** on a loan is the extra quantity of goods that can be purchased.

$$\text{Real interest rate} = \frac{\text{nominal interest rate}}{\text{inflation rate}}$$

To use this formula, try a second example. Nominal interest rates are 17 per cent and inflation is 20 per cent. Lending £100 for a year, you get £117. But it will cost you £120 to buy goods you could have bought today for £100. You are worse off by 3 per cent by delaying purchases for a year and lending your money at the apparently high rate of 17 per cent. Real interest rates are *negative*. The real interest rate is −3 per cent. In real terms it *costs* you to be a lender. The nominal interest rate does not compensate for higher prices of goods you ultimately wish to buy.

What determines the real interest rate?

Two forces lead to positive real interest rates. First, people are impatient. Given the choice of an equal number of goods tomorrow or today, we'd rather have them today. To delay spending on goods and services, savers have to be bribed with a positive real interest rate that lets them consume *more* goods in the future if they postpone consumption and lend today.

Second, there must be a way of earning positive real returns, or borrowers would never borrow. Borrowers pay positive real interest rates because they can buy capital goods that provide a stream of returns more than sufficient to meet the interest cost.

Impatience to consume and the productivity of physical capital are the two forces that lead us to expect a positive real interest rate. Real interest rates are usually small and positive. Since real interest rates change little, big changes in nominal interest rates usually occur to offset big changes in inflation rates, keeping real interest rates in their normal range, determined by the forces of impatience and capital productivity. A good rule of thumb is that each percentage point rise in inflation is matched by a percentage point rise in nominal interest rates, leaving real interest rates the same as before

To calculate present values, we must be consistent. If we wish to calculate the present value of a future payment expressed in nominal terms, we must discount by the nominal interest rate. If the future payment is expressed in real terms, we must discount using the real interest rate.

The following is a common mistake. You want to buy a farm whose rental this year is £10 000. Today's interest rate is 10 per cent. You reckon that the farm's output should not change much over time. You use the formula of equation (1) for a perpetuity, divide £10 000 by 0.1, and get £100 000. The farmer wants £150 000 for the farm so you decide not to buy.

You missed a financial killing. Nominal interest rates are 10 per cent only because the market thinks inflation will be about 7 per cent, leaving a real interest rate of 3 per cent. Doing the calculation in real terms at constant prices, we divide £10 000 for ever by 0.03 to obtain £333 000 as the right price for the farm. Equivalently, to calculate in nominal terms, we can use discount factors based on the

10 per cent nominal interest rate, but remember that the likely inflation rate of around 7 per cent will steadily increase the nominal farm rental over time. If we do this calculation, we shall again conclude that £100 000 for the farm is a bargain.

12.3 Saving, investment and the real interest rate

Figure 12.2 shows the production possibility frontier *AA′*, feasible combinations of current and future consumption goods that the economy can produce. At *A* the economy only produces for current consumption, at *A′* only for future consumption.

The frontier *AA′* shows different amounts of *investment* in the capital stock. At *A* not only is no investment undertaken, the existing capital is sold off (to foreigners). Future consumption is zero.

At *A′* all current resources are going in investment to raise the capacity to make consumption goods in the future. Current consumption is zero. Moving down *AA′*, more and more resources are transferred from future to current consumption. As usual, the curvature of the production possibility frontier reflects diminishing returns in this trade-off.

The slope of the frontier is the extra future consumption from sacrificing a unit of current consumption. The slope has magnitude $-(1+i)$ where i is the rate of return on investment. The minus sign reminds us we sacrifice current consumption to add to future consumption.

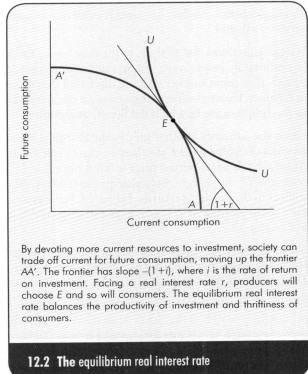

By devoting more current resources to investment, society can trade off current for future consumption, moving up the frontier *AA′*. The frontier has slope $-(1+i)$, where i is the rate of return on investment. Facing a real interest rate r, producers will choose E and so will consumers. The equilibrium real interest rate balances the productivity of investment and thriftiness of consumers.

12.2 The equilibrium real interest rate

What about consumer tastes? Both current and future consumption are desirable, so we can imagine a standard indifference map. The more impatient are consumers for current consumption, the steeper their indifference curves. Impatient people will give up lots of future consumption to get a bit more today. Thrifty people have flatter indifference curves.

In Figure 12.2 *UU* is the highest indifference curve that can be reached and *E* is the best allocation of current resources between consumption and investment.

The real interest rate may adjust to accomplish this outcome, even though decisions to add to the capital stock are taken by firms, and decisions about saving are taken by households.

Firms will invest until the real rate of return i equals the real interest rate r at which they can borrow money. Households face a budget line of slope $-(1+r)$, since by saving and lending they can exchange £1 of consumption today for £$(1+r)$ of consumption in the future. Households save up to the point at which their indifference curve is tangent to their budget line with slope $-(1+r)$.

> **Saving** is the difference between current income and current consumption.

Equilibrium occurs where saving equals investment. Households and firms are happy with the same transfer of resources from the present to the future. Figure 12.2 shows the equilibrium real interest rate r. Firms wish to be at E, where the rate of return i equals the cost of borrowing r [the slope of the frontier $-(1+i)$ is tangent to the line $-(1+r)$]. Households want to be at the *same* point E, where their indifference curve *UU* is tangent to the line $-(1+r)$.

12.4 The demand for capital services

The analysis of the demand for capital services by an industry closely parallels the analysis of labour demand in Chapter 10. The rental rate for capital replaces the wage rate. Each is the cost of hiring factor services. We emphasize the *use* of *services* of capital. The example to bear in mind is a firm renting a vehicle or leasing office space. In demanding capital services, a firm considers how much extra output another unit of capital services will add.

We can generalize our analysis to the case where the firm has monopoly power in its output market or monopsony power in its input market. Having discussed that extension in Chapter 10, we confine our discussion of capital services to the simpler case in which the firm is competitive.

> The **marginal value product of capital** is the extra value of the firm's output when another unit of capital services is used, all other inputs being held fixed.

Given the amounts of other inputs, the marginal value product of capital *MVPK* declines as more capital is used. Although the firm's output price is fixed since it is competitive, the marginal physical product of capital is subject to diminishing returns. Figure 12.3 shows a downward-sloping *MVPK* curve, just like the *MVPL* curve in Chapter 10.

A firm rents capital up to the point at which its marginal cost – the rental rate – equals its marginal value product. The firm demands K_0 capital services at the rental rate R_0.

For given rental rates and quantities of other factors of production, *MVPK* is the firm's demand curve for capital services at each rental rate for capital services. The firm's *MVPK* curve showing its capital demand curve can be shifted outwards by one of three things: (1) an increase in its output price, which makes the marginal *physical* product of capital more valuable, (2) an increase in the level of other factors (chiefly labour) with which capital works to produce output, making capital more productive, or (3) a technical advance that makes capital more productive.

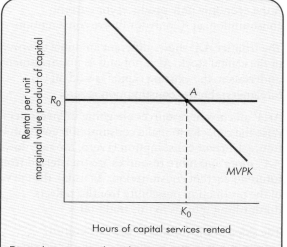

Diminishing marginal productivity implies a falling *MVPK* schedule as captial input is increased holding constant the quantity of other inputs. At any given rental, the firm hires capital services up to the point at which the rental per unit equals the *MVPK*. Thus the *MVPK* curve is also the firm's demand curve for capital services. For example, at a rental rate R_0 the firm will hire K_0 capital services.

Figure 12.3 The demand for capital services

The industry demand curve for capital services

As with labour, we can move from the firm's demand for capital services to the industry demand curve for capital services by horizontally adding the marginal value product of each firm. Again we must recognize that, in expanding output, the industry bid down the price of its output.

Thus the industry demand curve for capital services is steeper than the horizontal sum of each firm's *MVPK* curves. The industry demand curve recognizes that output prices fall as output rises. The more inelastic the demand curve for the industry's output, the more inelastic is the industry's derived demand curve for capital services.

12.5 The supply of capital services

Capital services are produced by capital assets. We analyse the market for capital services, then consider what this implies for the market for capital assets. In so doing, we assume that the flow of capital services is directly determined by the stock of capital assets, such as machines.

This is a simplification. By working overtime shifts, a firm can alter the effective flow of machine services it gets from a given machine bolted to the factory floor. It can also leave machines idle.

Even so, in normal times firms have limited ability to vary the flow of capital services from a given capital stock. We shall grasp the key features of the market for capital if we assume that the flow of capital services is determined by the stock of capital available. Our analysis must distinguish the long run and the short run, and examine both the supply of capital services to the economy and to a particular industry.

The short-run supply of capital services

In the short run, the total supply of capital assets (machines, buildings, and vehicles), and thus the services they provide, is fixed to the economy. New factories cannot be built overnight. The supply curve for capital services is vertical at a quantity determined by the existing stock of capital assets. Some types of capital are fixed even for an individual industry. The steel industry cannot change overnight its number of blast furnaces. However, by offering a higher rental rate for delivery vans, the supermarket industry can attract a larger share of the delivery vans that the economy currently has. For such capital services, an industry faces an upward-sloping supply curve. It can bid services away from other industries.

The supply of capital services in the long run

In the long run the quantity of capital in the economy can be varied. New machines and factories can be built. Conversely, without new investment in capital goods the existing capital stock will depreciate and gradually fall. Similarly, individual industries can adjust their stocks of capital.

At what rental rates will owners of capital *assets* be willing to buy or build?

> The **required rental on capital** just covers the opportunity cost of owning the asset.

You buy a machine to rent out as a business. The machine costs £10 000, which you borrow. How much must the machine earn if you are to break even? First you have to cover the interest cost. Suppose the *real*, or inflation-adjusted, interest rate is 5 per cent. You have to pay the bank £500 (= £10 000 × 0.05) a year in real terms.

Then you have spending on maintenance. Also, the resale value of the machine depreciates each year. In real terms, maintenance and depreciation cost you £1000 per annum, 10 per cent of the purchase price. The depreciation rate is 10 per cent a year. The annual cost of renting out a machine is £500 for the opportunity cost of the funds and £1000 for depreciation.

To break even, the *required rental* is £1500 a year at constant prices. The asset cost £10 000. Hence the *required real rate of return* is 15 per cent a year.[1] It is worth borrowing if the real interest rate on the loan is less than 15 per cent a year.[2]

1 To simplify the calculation, assume the machine and the bank loan last for ever. We can then use our formula for the present value of a perpetuity. The price p of a perpetuity is the annual payment c divided by the required rate of return r that lenders could get by lending to a bank. If $p = c/r$, then $r = c/p$. When c is the annual cost and p is the initial price of a machine, you need a rate of return $r = c/p$ to make it worth renting out machines.
2 If the firm using the capital services also owns the capital good, the required rental is the cost the firm should charge itself to use the capital when calculating economic costs (see our discussion of accounting versus economic costs in Chapter 6).

What determines the required rental?

The required rental rate, or cost of using capital, depends on three things: the price of the capital good, the real interest rate and the depreciation rate. Depreciation depends largely on technology; on how fast the machine wears out with use and age. The real interest rate is determined by economy-wide forces and changes only slowly. Treating the depreciation rate and the real interest rate as given, we examine how the purchase price of capital goods affects the required rental on capital.

The long-run supply curve for the economy

In the long run, the quantity of capital services must earn the required rental. If it earns more, people will build extra capital goods. If it earns less, owners of capital will let assets depreciate without building new ones.

Figure 12.4 shows the long-run supply curve of capital services to the economy. Capital services come from capital goods. The construction industry produces buildings and the motor industry produces container lorries. Each industry has an upward-sloping supply curve. The higher the price of the capital good, the more the capital goods producing industry will choose to supply.

In the long run, a larger flow of capital services needs a higher capital stock. But capital depreciates. The higher the capital stock, the larger is total depreciation. Thus, a higher long-run flow of capital services needs a higher capital stock, which needs a higher flow of new capital goods to offset depreciation and maintain the capital stock intact.

Producers need a higher price for capital goods to make more new capital goods. To maintain the required rate of return on assets, we need a higher rental rate for capital services. In the long run a higher flow of capital services is supplied only if the rental rate on capital rises to match the higher price of capital goods needed to induce producers of new capital goods to keep pace with higher absolute levels of depreciation.

Figure 12.4 shows the long-run supply curve for capital services. *SS* slopes upwards in the long run when plotted against the rental rate on capital. We draw *SS* for a given real interest rate. If the real interest rate rises, the opportunity cost of holding capital assets rises. For a given purchase price of capital goods, the required rental must rise. Suppliers of capital services need a higher return to offset the higher opportunity cost of the money they tie up in purchasing capital goods.

In Figure 12.4, higher real interest rates shift leftwards the long-run supply curve for capital services, from *SS* to *S'S'*. Higher rentals at each level of capital services (and hence capital assets) provide the higher real return to match the increase in the real interest rate.

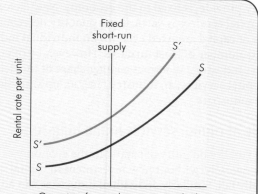

In the short run, the stock of capital goods, and the services they supply, is fixed by past investment decisions, new capital goods cannot be produced overnight. In the long run, the higher rental rate is requied to call forth a higher supply of capital services and a permanently higher capital stock. The higher rental rate just offsets the higher price for capital goods required to induce higher output of new capital goods to match the higher total depreciation of a larger capital stock. Thus the required rate of return is met at all points on *SS*. If real interest rates increase, the required rate of return will also increase to match the opportunity cost of funds tied up in capital goods. Hence the long-run supply curve of capital services shifts up to *S'S'* providing a higher rental level at each level of the capital stock and its corresponding purchase price. Each point on *S'S'* matches the new required rate of return.

Figure 12.4 The supply of capital services to the economy

The long-run supply curve for the industry

The preceding analysis determines the supply of capital services to the economy. In the long run, a small industry can get as much of this capital as it wishes, provided it pays the going rental rate. A larger industry may bid up the rental rate as it attracts a large fraction of the economy-wide supply of capital. Such an industry faces an upward-sloping supply curve for capital services.

We analyse the case of a small industry facing a horizontal long-run supply curve for capital services at the going rental rate. The analysis is easily extended to an industry facing an upward-sloping long-run supply curve for capital services.

12.6 Equilibrium and adjustment in the market for capital services

Figure 12.5 shows the market for capital services for a particular industry. Long-run equilibrium is at E, where the horizontal long-run supply curve $S'S'$ crosses the industry demand curve DD derived from firms' $MVPK$ curves. The industry hires K_0 capital services at the going rental R_0.

Adjustments in the market for capital services

Suppose workers in the industry get a wage increase. In the long run this has a *substitution effect* and an *output effect*. The substitution effect makes firms switch to more capital-intensive techniques, raising the demand for capital services. However, by raising costs, a wage increase reduces the quantity of output supplied. This output effect reduces demand for all inputs. The second effect is more likely to dominate the more elastic is the demand for the industry's output.

Short-run and long-run adjustment

Suppose in Figure 12.5 the wage rise reduces demand for capital services from DD to $D'D'$. The industry begins in equilibrium at E. Initially, the short-run supply of capital services SS is vertical at K_0. When demand shifts from DD to $D'D'$, the industry cannot immediately cut its input of capital services. With a vertical short-run supply curve, the new short-run equilibrium is at E'. The rental on capital falls from R_0 to R_1.

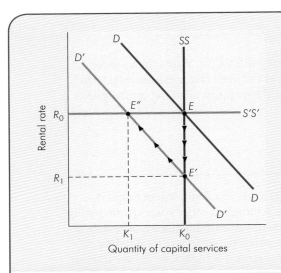

The industry begins in equilibrium at E. Overnight its short-run supply of capital is fixed at K_0, but in the long run it faces the horizontal supply curve $S'S'$ at the going rental, R_0. Suppose a wage increase shifts the demand curve for capital from DD to $D'D'$. The new short-run equilibrium is at E'. Since the rental R_1 fails to provide the required rate of return, owners of capital goods allow these goods slowly to depreciate without buying any new capital goods. The industry's capital stock and the services it provides gradually fall back. Eventually the industry reaches long-run equilibrium at E''. Since capital is again earning the required rate of return, owners of capital goods now replace goods as they depreciate.

Figure 12.5 Short- and long-run adjustment of capital to a wage rise

The industry faces a long-run supply curve $S'S'$ for capital services. Eventually it must pay the going rate. At E' owners of capital do not get the required rental for the capital services they supply. They let their capital stock depreciate. Over time, the industry's capital stock and supply of capital services fall until equilibrium is reached at E''. The capital services used by the industry have fallen to K_1. Less capital means a higher marginal product of capital and higher rentals. At E'' users of capital again pay the required rental R_0.

Box 12.1 Factor markets: a summary

Chapters 10–12 examined markets for production inputs. In the long run, when all inputs can be freely varied, the firm's choice of technique at each output level is determined by technology and relative factor rentals. At a given output, a higher relative price of one factor makes the firm substitute towards techniques using that factor less intensively. The long-run total cost curve shows the cheapest way to produce each output level when production techniques are optimally chosen. From long-run total cost, we calculate long-run marginal cost and hence the output at which marginal cost and marginal revenue are equal.

For each factor, the firm's demand is a derived demand that reflects the factor's marginal physical product in making extra output and the marginal revenue from selling that extra output. A competitive firm's demand curve for a factor is the marginal value product schedule, which assumes a given output price, given quantities of all other inputs, and given technology. Changes in any of these shift the marginal value product schedule. In the short run, a competitive firm demands that quantity of its variable factor that equates its marginal value product and its factor rental. In the long run, every factor can be varied. Each factor is demanded to the point at which its factor rental equals its marginal value product given the quantity of all other factors, *each having been adjusted in the same way*.

What distinguishes labour, capital and land is mainly the speed with which their supply can adjust. The input of casual labour on construction sites or during crop picking is easily variable, even in the short run. The supply of skilled workers with extensive training can be changed less quickly and the supply of capital goods takes even longer to adjust. Land is the factor whose total supply can never be adjusted. The slower the speed of adjustment, and the more irreversible the process, the more current decisions reflect beliefs about the future. The latter, neglected in our discussion of unskilled labour in Chapter 10, were central to our analysis of investment in human capital (Chapter 11) and physical capital (Chapter 12).

The arrows in Figure 12.5 show the dynamic path that the industry will follow. When demand for capital falls, there is a sharp fall in the rental on capital. Owners of the fixed factor cannot adjust the quantity of capital services supplied. As time elapses, they adjust the quantity, allowing capital goods to depreciate, and the rental gradually recovers.

12.7 The price of capital assets

We now turn from capital services to capital assets, demanded by firms wishing to supply capital services. Think of Hertz renting out cars, or property companies renting out office space. Anticipating a stream of rentals, suppliers of capital services work out the present value of this stream of rentals at the going interest rate. This tells us how much they should be prepared to pay to buy a capital asset. The price of capital assets is higher when (a) the anticipated rental stream is higher, or (b) the interest rate is lower. Both raise the present value of the future rental stream.

People anticipating a higher stream of rental earnings pay a high purchase price for capital assets. At a lower price, people with lower anticipated streams then find it profitable to demand capital goods. There is a downward-sloping demand curve for capital goods. The lower the price, the higher the quantity demanded. The upward-sloping supply curve and downward-sloping demand curve together determine the equilibrium price and quantity of capital goods for the economy. This determines the flow supply of capital services that this stock will provide.

What happens when an individual industry faces a fall in its derived demand for capital services, as in Figure 12.5? In the short run, the rental on capital services falls to R_1. Moreover, everyone can work out that it will take some time before the rental rate climbs back to R_0. At the going interest rate, the present value of rental earnings on new capital goods in this industry falls.

Now the industry is no longer willing to pay the economy-wide equilibrium price for capital assets. It does no new investment, and its capital stock depreciates. Its capital stock falls until capital services get so scarce that the rental rate returns to its original level. The present value of future rentals then matches the price of capital goods in the whole economy. The industry now buys capital goods to replace goods as they depreciate. The capital stock is constant, and the industry is in its new long-run equilibrium.

The long-run equilibrium price of a capital asset is both the price that induces suppliers to make enough new assets to offset depreciation and keep the capital stock constant, and the price that buyers of capital goods are prepared to pay for that quantity. That price is the present value of the anticipated rental stream for capital services discounted at the going rate of interest.

12.8 Land and rents

Land is essentially a capital good in fixed supply to the economy, even in the long run. This is not literally true. The Dutch reclaimed from the sea some areas of low-lying land, and fertilizers enhance the effective input of land for farming. Nevertheless, it makes sense to think about a factor whose total long-run supply is fixed.

Box 12.2 The best address

Since land is in fixed supply, land prices are dearest where demand is greatest. The table below shows the ten most expensive places to buy a two-bedroom apartment in 2006.

Top 10 most expensive cities	
1. Moscow	6. Osaka
2. Seoul	7. Geneva
3. Tokyo	8. Copenhagen
4. Hong Kong	9. Zurich
5. London	10. Oslo, New York (tied)

Source: www.money.cnn.com.

Figure 12.6 shows the derived demand curve *DD* for land services. With a fixed supply *SS*, the equilibrium rental per acre is R_0. A rise in the derived demand, for example because wheat prices rise, raises the rental to R_1. The quantity of land services is fixed by assumption.

Consider a tenant farmer who rents land. Wheat prices have risen but so have rents. Not only may the farmer be no better off, the connection between the two rises may be unrecognized. The farmer complains that high rents make it hard to earn a decent living. As in our discussion of footballers' wages in Chapter 10, it is the high derived demand combined with the inelastic factor supply that cause the high payments for factor services.[3]

Because land is *the* asset in fixed supply, economists have taken over the word 'rent', the payment for land services, to the concept of *economic rent*, the excess of actual payments over transfer earnings, introduced in Chapter 10. Economic rent is large when supply is inelastic.

12.9 Income distribution in the UK

The income of a factor is its rental rate multiplied by the quantity of the factor employed. We pull together our discussion of factor markets to examine the distribution of income in the UK.

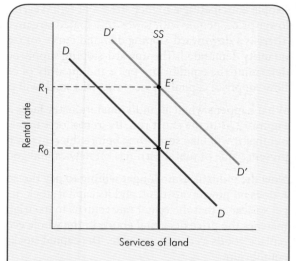

The total supply of land is fixed to the economy. The supply curve is vertical. The derived demand curve for land services reflects the marginal value product of land. Its derivation is exactly the same as the demand curves for labour and capital from the *MVPL* and *MVPK* schedules. The demand curve *DD* for land services determines the equilibrium land rental rate R_0. If the derived demand curve for land services shifts up to $D'D'$, the equilibrium land rental will increase to R_1.

Figure 12.6 The market for land services

The functional distribution of income

Table 12.6 shows the total earnings of the different factors of production in the UK in 2006 and compares their shares of national income with the shares they received during 1981–89. There have been only small changes in the shares of different factors of production. As the real incomes increased, the real incomes of the different production inputs broadly kept pace.

> The **functional income distribution** is the division of national income among different factors of production.

Aggregate labour supply to the economy is relatively inelastic. Hence, the total number of employed workers was little higher in 2002 than in 1981. Table 12.6 shows that the UK capital per worker increased. Technical progress also boosted productivity. For both reasons, labour's marginal product

Table 12.6 UK functional income distribution, 1981–2006 (% of national income)

Source (factor of production)	1981–89 average	2006
Employment	64	64
Self-employment	7	10
Profits and property rents	29	26

Source: ONS, UK National Accounts.

3 If most farmers rent their land, agricultural subsidies, such as the EU Common Agricultural Policy, increase land rentals as well as the price farmers get from crops. It is the landowners who really benefit!

schedule shifted outwards. Confronted with an almost vertical labour supply curve, this steady rise in the demand for labour raised the equilibrium real wage. Labour income from employment rose as national income rose.

Table 12.6 shows that the share of income from profits and rents fell slightly during 1989–2006, with a slight rise in income from self-employment. The quantity of capital employed rose steadily, at about the same rate as national output. Since the ratio of capital to output has been fairly constant, a declining real return on capital has accounted for the evolution of the share of capital earnings in national output.

If the quantity of capital rose substantially without a substantial fall in its rate of return, the economy cannot simply have moved down a given marginal product of capital schedule; otherwise, the rental on capital and its rate of return would have been reduced. Rather, the marginal product schedule must have shifted outwards. This outward shift mainly reflected by technical progress.

The supply of land is very inelastic. As national income increased, the derived demand curve for land shifted upwards. Property rentals have risen at least in line with national income.

Box 12.3 Widest rich–poor gap in 40 years

Britain is becoming an ever more segregated society, with the gap between rich and poor reaching its highest level for 40 years, a report from the Rowntree Foundation concluded in 2007. In the past 15 years, there has been a rise in the number of households living below the poverty line, while the wealthy have become even more wealthy. In this move to the extremes, fewer UK households are now classed as neither rich nor poor.

Although inequality has therefore increased, the number of people living in extreme poverty has fallen. Why the discrepancy? Because in most developed countries the poverty line is a relative concept, a certain percentage of average earnings. As living standards rise, the poverty line rises too. In Britain, when we say more people live in poverty, this is really the same thing as saying that inequality has increased.

In contrast, in looking at the poorest areas of the world, international agencies such as the World Bank often use measures of absolute poverty, such as the number of people living on less than $1 a day. If this number rises, the poorest are getting absolutely poorer. Given that the world as a whole is getting richer, an increase in absolute poverty means an increase in relative poverty. The UK shows that the converse need not always be true – relative poverty has increased in the UK but absolute poverty has declined.

We should also be interested in the social consequences. Different groups were also becoming geographically more segregated. If the rich retreat into affluent areas where they meet only other rich people, and travel only in their luxury cars rather than on public transport, their awareness of the problems of the poor may diminish. The Rowntree report concluded that urban clustering of poverty had increased, while wealthy households were becoming concentrated in the outskirts and surrounds of major cities.

The personal income distribution

The personal income distribution is relevant to issues such as equality and poverty. Table 12.7 excludes the very poor, whose income is so low that the Inland Revenue does not record what they earn. Even confining attention to people who pay income tax, pre-tax income is unequal in the

> The **personal income distribution** is the division of national income across individuals, regardless of the factor services from which these individuals earn their income.

UK. Based on 29.7 million taxpayers, the top row of Table 12.7 shows that the poorest 2.7 million households had an average taxable income of less than £7500 in 2006/07, whereas the bottom 3 rows show that the richest 1.9 million households all had taxable incomes in excess of £50 000.

Table 12.7 UK personal income distribution, 2006/07

Taxable income band £000 per annum	Million taxpayers
<7.5	2.7
7.5–10	3.4
10–15	6.0
15–20	4.9
20–30	6.4
30–50	4.4
50–100	1.4
100–200	0.4
200+	0.1

Source: ONS, Social Trends.

Why do some people earn so much while others earn so little? Chapters 10 and 11 discussed some reasons why people earn different wages and salaries. Unskilled workers have little training and low productivity. Workers with high levels of training and education earn much more. Some jobs, such as coal mining, pay high compensating differentials to offset unpleasant working conditions. Pleasant, but unskilled, jobs pay much less since many people are prepared to do them. Talented superstars in scarce supply but strong demand earn very high economic rents.

Table 12.7 refers not just to income from the supply of labour services. One reason why the distribution of personal income is so unequal is that the ownership of wealth, which provides income from profits and rents, is even more unequal. Table 12.8 gives details for 1991–2003.

The most wealthy 1 per cent of the population owns 21 per cent of UK marketable wealth and the most wealthy 25 per cent of the population own 72 per cent of UK marketable wealth. The stream of profit and rent income to which such wealth gives rise plays a large part in determining the personal distribution of pre-tax *income*.

Table 12.8 UK distribution of marketable wealth, 1991–2003

	1991	2003
Percentage of wealth owned by:		
Most wealthy 1%	17	21
Most wealthy 25%	71	72
Most wealthy 50%	92	93
Total marketable wealth (£ billion)	1711	3783

Note: Table applies to adults aged 18 and over.
Source: ONS, Social Trends.

Summary

- **Physical capital** comprises real assets yielding services to producing firms or consuming households. The main categories of physical capital are plant and machinery, residential structures, other buildings, consumer durables, and inventories. **Tangible wealth** is physical capital plus land.

- **Present values** convert future receipts or payments into current values. Because lenders can earn – and borrowers must pay – interest over time, a pound tomorrow is worth less than a pound today. How much less depends on the interest rate. The higher the interest rate, the lower the present value of any future payment.

- Since lending or borrowing cumulates at compound interest, for any given annual interest rate the present value of a given sum is smaller the further into the future that sum is earned or paid.

- The present value of a **perpetuity** is the constant annual payment divided by the rate of interest (expressed as a decimal fraction).

- **Nominal interest rates** measure the monetary interest payments on a loan. The inflation-adjusted **real interest rate** measures the extra goods a lender can buy by lending for a year and delaying purchases of goods. The real rate of interest is the nominal interest rate minus the inflation rate over the same period.

- In the long run, the real interest adjusts to make investment equal to saving, and is determined by the return on firms' investment and the degree of impatience of households.

- The demand for capital services is a derived demand. The **firm's demand for capital services** is its marginal value product of capital curve. Higher levels of the other factors of production and higher output prices shift the derived demand curve up. **The industry demand for capital services** is less elastic than the horizontal sum of each firm's curve because it also allows for the effect of an industry expansion in bidding down the output price.

- In the short run the supply of capital services is fixed. In the long run it can be adjusted by producing new capital goods or allowing the existing capital stock to depreciate.

- The **required rental** is the rental that allows a supplier of capital services to break even on the decision to purchase the capital asset. The required rental is higher, the higher is the interest rate, the depreciation rate or the purchase price of the capital good.

- A rise in the industry wage has two effects on the derived demand curve for capital services. By reducing labour input it reduces the marginal physical product of capital. By reducing the industry output it increases the output price. When output demand is very inelastic the latter effect will dominate. When output demand is very elastic the former effect dominates.

- The **asset price** is the price at which a capital good is bought and sold outright. In long-run equilibrium it is both the price at which suppliers of capital goods are willing to produce and the price at which buyers are willing to purchase. The latter is merely the present value of anticipated future rentals earned from the capital services that the good provides in the future.

- **Land** is the special capital good whose supply is fixed even in the long run. However, land and capital can move between industries in the long run until rentals on land or on capital are equalized in different industries.

- Technology and the ease of factor substitution dictate the very different capital intensity of different industries. Most industries are becoming more capital intensive over time, but at different rates. This reflects the ease with which industries can substitute capital for labour, the rise in wage rates relative to capital rentals, and technical advances in different industries.

- The **functional distribution of income** shows how national income is divided between the factors of production. The share of each factor has remained fairly constant over time. This conceals a rise in the quantity of capital relative to labour, and a corresponding fall in the ratio of capital rentals to labour wages.

- The **personal distribution of income** shows how national income is divided between different individuals regardless of the factor services from which income is earned. A major cause of income inequality in the UK is a very unequal distribution of income-earning wealth.

Review questions   To check your answers to these questions, go to page 719.

1 (a) Consumer durables such as washing machines are part of the capital stock but do not generate any financial income for their owners. Why do we include consumer durables in the capital stock? (b) To wash your clothes you can take them to a laundrette and spend £2 per week indefinitely or buy a washing machine for £400. It costs £1 per week (including depreciation) to run a washing machine, and the interest rate is 10 per cent per annum. Does it make sense to buy the washing machine? Does this help you answer part (a)?

2 A bank offers you £1.10 next year for every £0.90 you give it today. What is the implicit interest rate?

3 A firm buys a machine for £10 000, earns rentals of £3600 for each of the next two years, and then sells it for scrap for £9000. Use the data of Table 12.4 to determine if the machine is worth buying when the interest rate is 10 per cent per annum.

4 The interest rate falls from 10 to 5 per cent. Discuss in detail how this affects the rental on capital services and the level of the capital stock in an industry in the short and long run.

5 Suppose a plot of land is suitable only for agriculture. Can the farming industry experience financial distress if there is an increase in the price of land? Is your answer affected if the land can also be used for housing?

6 **Common fallacies** Why are these statements wrong? (a) Inflation leads to high nominal interest rates. This reduces the present value of future income. (b) If the economy continues to become more capital intensive, eventually there will be no jobs left for workers to do. (c) Since the economy's supply of land is fixed, it would be supplied even at a zero rental, which should therefore be the equilibrium rental in the long run.

7 **Harder question** What should be the impact of globalization on assets in fixed supply, particularly land. Can you think of an example in which globalization might induce a fall in land prices?

8 **Harder question** Some pension funds work as follows. Young workers pay a fraction of their salary into the scheme and retired workers withdraw money from the scheme. The scheme does not invest contributions into any fund. Year by year, it simply calculates what to charge young workers in order to meet obligations that year to old workers. (a) In a country that had a baby boom a couple of decades ago, is it easy or difficult to run such a scheme? (b) Suppose babies dry up and life expectancy increases. What happens to such pension schemes? (c) You are the government. What are your options now?

To help you grasp the key concepts of this chapter check out the extra resources posted on the Online Learning Centre. There are chapter summaries, self-test questions, an interactive graphing tool, weblinks and a searchable glossary, all for free!

To put your learning into practice and prepare for exams, an **Interactive Workbook** is also available online, containing a variety of question types and providing feedback on your answers.

If you'd like further help with economics, or have any questions, **NetTutor** is here to help! You will have a personalised tutorial service at your fingertips. Visit the online learning centre at: www.mcgraw-hill.co.uk/textbooks/begg for information on accessing all of these resources.

Appendix: The simple algebra of present values and discounting

Suppose we lend £K today at an annual interest rate i. After one year our money has grown to £$K(1+i)$. With $K=100$ and $i=0.1$, we get £110 back after a year. If we re-lend the money for another year at the same interest rate, we get back £$\{K(1+i)\}(1+i)$ at the end of the second year. For example, our £100 has grown to £121 after two years. If we lend this sum for yet another year we get back £$K(1+i)^3$ at the end of the third year. Hence, after N years we get back £$K(1+i)^N$.

Conversely, the present value of £X to be received N years later is £$X/[(1+i)^N]$, and we call $\{1/[(1+i)^N]\}$ the discount factor. Since the interest rate i is a positive number, the discount factor must be a positive fraction. Higher interest rates imply lower discount factors. The table shows the present value of £1 N years from now when the interest rate is 10 per cent a year ($i=0.1$).

Present value (PV) of £1 N years from now, annual interest rate of 10 per cent						
N	1	5	10	20	30	40
PV	£0.91	£0.62	£0.39	£0.15	£0.06	£0.02

To calculate the present value of a whole stream of future payments, we multiply the face value of each payment by the relevant discount factor. Thus the present value of £100 after 10 years and £200 after 40 years is $(£100 \times 0.39) + (£200 \times 0.02) = £43$. Payments not received or made for many years have a very small present value.

When the asset is a perpetuity, earning £K a year for ever, our formula implies that the present value of this stream is £K/i, as we pointed out in Section 12.2.

CHAPTER 13

Risk and information

Learning Outcomes

By the end of this chapter, you should understand:

1 risk aversion and diminishing marginal utility

2 risk pooling and risk spreading

3 how inside information leads to moral hazard and adverse selection

4 how an asset return reflects its cash income and its capital gain (loss)

5 how correlation of asset returns affects risk pooling

6 asset market efficiency

7 spot and forward markets

8 how hedging shifts the burden of risk

Every action today has a future outcome that is not certain. It is risky. When you start studying economics, you have only a rough idea of what is involved, and even less idea about how it will be used once the skill is acquired. This chapter examines how risk affects our actions, and how economic institutions have evolved to help us deal with the risky environment in which we live.

Some activities reduce risk, but others increase it. We spend billions of pounds on insurance, but also on the lottery and gambling on horse races. People generally dislike risk and are prepared to pay to have their risks reduced. This explains the existence of many economic institutions that, at a price, allow people who dislike risk most to pass on their risks to others more willing or more able to bear these risks. By the end of the chapter, we need to explain the allure of the lottery!

13.1 Individual attitudes to risk

A risky activity has two characteristics: the likely outcome, and the degree of variation in the possible outcomes. Suppose you are offered a 50 per cent chance of making £100 and a 50 per cent chance of losing £100. On average you make no money by taking such gambles.

In contrast, a 30 per cent chance of making £100 and a 70 per cent chance of losing £100 is an *unfair* gamble. On average you lose money. With the probabilities of winning and losing reversed, the gamble would on average be profitable. The odds are then *favourable*.

> A **fair gamble** on average yields zero monetary profit.

Compare a gamble with a 50 per cent chance of making or losing £100 and a gamble with the same chances of winning or losing £500. Both are fair gambles, but the second is *riskier*. The range of possible outcomes is greater.

We turn now to individual tastes. Economists classify people as risk-averse, risk-neutral or risk-loving. The key issue is whether or not a person would accept a fair gamble. A *risk-neutral* person ignores the dispersion of possible outcomes, betting if and only if the odds on a monetary profit are favourable.

A risk-averse person may bet if the odds are very favourable. The probable monetary profit overcomes the inherent dislike of risk. The more risk-averse the individual, the more favourable must be the odds before she takes the bet.

> A **risk-neutral** person is interested only in whether the odds yield a profit *on average*. A **risk-averse** person will refuse a fair gamble.

The more risk-loving the individual, the more unfavourable must be the odds before the individual will not bet.

Insurance is the opposite of gambling. Suppose you own a £100 000 house. There is a 10 per cent chance it burns down by accident. You have a 90 per cent chance of continuing to have £100 000 but a 10 per cent chance of having nothing. Our risky world forces you to take this bet. On average, you end up with £90 000, which is 90 per cent of £100 000 plus 10 per cent of nothing.

> A **risk-lover** bets even when the odds are unfavourable.

An insurance company offers to insure the full value of your house for a premium of £15 000. Whether or not your house burns down, you pay the insurance company the £15 000 premium. They pay you £100 000 if it burns down. Whatever happens, you will end up with £85 000.

Would you insure? The insurance company is offering unfavourable odds, which is how they make their money. Uninsured, on average you are worth £90 000, insured only £85 000. A risk-neutral person would not insure on these terms. The mathematical calculation in monetary terms says it is on average better to stand the risk of a fire. The risk-lover will also decline insurance. Not only are the odds poor, there is also the added enjoyment of standing the risk. But a person who is sufficiently risk-averse will accept the offer, happy to give up £5000 on average to avoid the possibility of catastrophe. Table 13.1 summarizes this discussion of attitudes to risk.

Table 13.1 Behaviour towards risk

Tastes	Betting	Insurance at unfair premium
Risk-averse	Needs favourable odds	May buy
Risk-neutral	Except at unfavourable odds	Won't buy
Risk-lover	Even if odds against	Won't buy

Diminishing marginal utility

Decisions about gambling or insurance depend on two considerations. First, there is the thrill of the activity. The thrill of a flutter on the Grand National is a pleasure, like seeing a good film. Having a lottery ticket provides excitement. In part it is pure entertainment. Gambling for fun is a legitimate form of consumption. We are prepared to pay for this modest form of entertainment. Unfair odds are the implicit price of our fun.

Such leisure activities form only a trivial part of the risk that we face in our everyday lives. This approach is unhelpful in thinking about the risk of our house burning down, or the risk a firm takes in building a new factory. These are not leisure pursuits. Serious money is at stake.

Suppose you are starving and broke. Getting £1000 would yield you a lot of utility or happiness, by allowing you some basic food. If you got another £1000, there are still things to spend it on that you really need. Clothes and shelter, for example. Having dealt with your immediate needs, the next £1000 is still helpful, but of less extra value than when you were desperate.

Thus, the marginal utility of the first £1000 is very high. You really needed it. The marginal utility of the next £1000 is not quite so high. As you get more, the marginal utility of the extra consumption tends to diminish.

Of course, there are exceptions to this general rule. Some people *really* want a yacht, and their utility takes a huge jump when they can finally afford one. But most of us first spend our money on the things we most need, and get less and less extra satisfaction out of successive equal increases in our spending power.

> People's tastes exhibit a **diminishing marginal utility**. Successive equal rises in consumption quantities add less and less to total utility.

You have £11 000 and are offered an equal chance of winning or losing £10 000. This is a fair bet in money terms since the average profit is £0. But it is not a fair bet in utility terms. Diminishing marginal utility implies that the extra utility you enjoy if the bet wins, taking your total wealth from £11 000 to £21 000, is much smaller than the utility you sacrifice if the bet loses, taking your wealth from £11 000 to £1000. You get a few extra luxuries with the £10 000 you might win, but you have to give up almost everything if you lose and have to survive on only £1000.

A risk-averse person declines a fair bet in money terms. The hypothesis of diminishing marginal utility implies that, except for the occasional gamble for pure entertainment, people should generally be risk-averse. They should refuse fair money gambles because they are not fair utility gambles. As we shall see, this story fits many of the facts.

Two implications of this analysis recur throughout the chapter. First, *risk-averse people devote resources to finding ways to reduce risk*. As the booming insurance industry confirms, people will pay to get out of some of the risks that the environment otherwise forces them to bear. Second, *individuals who take over the risk have to be rewarded for doing so*. Many economic activities consist of the more risk-averse bribing the less risk-averse to take over the risk.

Box 13.1 What a lottery

The UK's original National Lottery game, first introduced in 1994, is based on drawing 6 balls without replacement from a stock of 49 balls. The odds on matching all 6 balls are about 1 in 14 million. Only 45 per cent of sales revenue is returned as prizes, worse odds than received by a blind punter at a horse race. You get better odds still in a casino playing roulette: with a 0 and a 00 on a roulette wheel plus 36 other numbers, the casino only makes regular money on 2 of the 38 possible outcomes. Why are lotteries so popular?

People like giving to good causes. Since some lottery profits go to charity, people buy lottery tickets instead of giving to OXFAM or Comic Relief. These charities' other revenues did fall when the National Lottery was introduced. So did revenue in betting shops such as Ladbrokes. The thrill of the lottery was a substitute for the thrill of the 3.30 at Newmarket.

But this is not the whole story. Purchasers of lottery tickets are not a random sample of the population. The poorest 20 per cent of the population account for over a third of all spending on the National Lottery. Lotteries are an inferior good. This raises issues for government policy. If people have diminishing marginal utility, extensive gambling (even at fair odds) is as bad an investment for poor people as for rich people. One concern is that those with less access to education may be less able to calculate the true chances of winning.

13.2 Insurance and risk

A farmer and an actress have risky incomes. Each gets 10 in a good month, 0 in a bad month. But the risks are *independent*. Whether the farmer has a good month is unconnected with whether the actress has a good month. Individually, their incomes are very risky. Collectively they are less so.

In Table 13.2 they *pool* their incomes and their risk, each getting half of their joint income. If they both have a good month (top left entry) or both have a bad month (bottom right entry), the pooling arrangement makes no difference. They each get what they would have got on their own. In the other two cases, the success of one partner offsets the failure of the other. Together, their income is more *stable* than as individuals. If the farmer and the actress are risk-averse, they gain by pooling their risky incomes. If it were not so hard to set up such deals (lawyers' fees, the problem of cheating, tax problems) we would see more of them.

Table 13.2 Risk-pooling of incomes: sharing joint incomes

Actress		Farmer	
		Good month, 10	Bad month, 0
Good month, 10		10	5
Bad month, 0		5	0

Pooling independent risks is the key to insurance. Suppose mortality tables show that on average 1 per cent of people aged 55 will die during the next year. Deaths result from heart disease, cancer, road accidents, and other causes, in predictable proportions.

Now randomly choose any 100 people aged 55 knowing nothing about their health. Throughout the nation, 1 per cent of such people will die in the next year. In our sample of 100 people, it could be 0, 1 or 2 per cent, or even more. The larger the sample, the more likely it is that around 1 per cent will die in the next year. With 1 million 55-year-olds we could be pretty confident that around 10 000 would die, though we could not of course say which ones. By putting together more and more people we reduce the risk or dispersion of the aggregate outcome.[1]

Life assurance companies take in premium payments in exchange for a promise to pay a big amount to the family if the insured person dies. The company can make this promise with great certainty because it pools risks over many clients. Since the company cannot guarantee that exactly 1 per cent of its many 55-year-olds will die in any one year, there is a small element of residual risk for the company to bear, and it makes a small charge for this in calculating its premiums. However, the company's ability to pool the risk means that it will make only a small charge. If life assurance companies try to charge more, new entrants join the industry knowing that the profits more than compensate for the small residual risk to be borne.

Risk-pooling does not work when all individuals face the same risk. Suppose there is a 10 per cent risk of a nuclear war in Europe in the next 10 years. If it happens, everyone in Europe dies, leaving money to their nearest surviving relative in the rest of the world. Ten million people in Western Europe offer to buy insurance from an American company.

Despite the number of people, the risk cannot be pooled. If everybody in Europe dies if anybody dies, the insurance company either pays out to everybody's relatives or it pays nothing. In the aggregate there is still a 10 per cent chance of having to pay out, just as individual Europeans face a 10 per cent chance of disaster. When the same thing happens to everybody, if it happens at all, the aggregate behaves like the individual. There is no risk reduction from pooling.

1 This is 'Law of Large Numbers'. A proof can be found in most statistics textbooks.

Many insurance companies do not insure against what they call 'acts of God' – floods, earthquakes, epidemics. Such disasters are no more natural or unnatural than a heart attack. But they affect large numbers of the insurance company's clients if they happen at all. The risk cannot be reduced by pooling. Companies cannot quote the low premium rates that apply for heart attacks, where risks are independent and the aggregate outcome is fairly certain.

There is another way to reduce the cost of risk bearing. This is known as *risk sharing*, and the most famous example is the Lloyd's insurance market in London. Risk sharing is necessary when it has proved impossible to reduce the risk by pooling. Lloyd's offer insurance on earthquakes in California, and insurance of a film star's legs.

> **Risk pooling** aggregates independent risks to make the aggregate more certain.

To understand risk sharing we return to diminishing marginal utility. We argued that the utility benefit from an extra £10 000 is less than the utility sacrificed when £10 000 is given up. However, this difference in marginal utility for equivalent monetary gains and losses is tiny if the size of the stake is tiny. The marginal utility from an extra £1 is only fractionally less than the utility lost by sacrificing £1. For small stakes, people are almost risk neutral. You would probably toss a coin with us to win or lose £0.10, but not to win or lose £10 000. The larger the stake, the more diminishing marginal utility bites.

You go to Lloyd's to insure the US space shuttle launch for £20 billion, a big risk. Only part of this risk can be pooled as part of a larger portfolio of risks. It is too big for anyone to take on at a reasonable premium.

> **Risk-sharing** works by reducing the stake.

The Lloyd's market in London has hundreds of 'syndicates', each a group of 20 or so individuals who have each put up £100 000. Each syndicate takes perhaps 1 per cent of the £20 billion deal and then resells the risk to yet other people in the insurance industry. By the time the deal has been subdivided and subdivided again, each syndicate or insurance company holds a tiny share of the total. And each syndicate risk is further subdivided among its 20 members. The risk is shared out until each individual's stake is so small that there is a tiny difference between the marginal utility from a gain and the marginal loss of utility in the event of a disaster. It now takes only a small premium to cover this risk. The package can be sold to the client at a premium low enough to attract the business.

By pooling and sharing risks, insurance allows individuals to deal with many risks at affordable premiums. But two things inhibit the operation of insurance markets, reducing the extent to which individuals can use insurance to buy their way out of risky situations.

Moral hazard

Insurance companies calculate the statistical chances of particular events. They work out how many cars are stolen each year. Since different thefts are largely independent risks, we expect insurance firms to pool the risk over many clients and charge low premiums for car theft.

Sitting in a restaurant, you remember that your car is unlocked. Do you abandon your nice meal and rush outside to lock it? Not if you know the car is *fully* insured against theft. If the act of insuring changes the odds, we call this the problem of *moral hazard*.

Statistical averages for the whole population, some of whom are uninsured and take greater care, are no longer a reliable guide to the risks the insurance company faces and the premiums it should charge. Moral hazard makes it harder to get insurance and more expensive when you do get it.

> **Moral hazard** is the use of inside information to exploit the other party to a contract.

Insurance companies insure your car or house only up to a certain percentage of its replacement cost. They take over a big part of the risk, but you are worse off if the nasty thing happens. The company gives you an incentive to hold down the chance of the nasty thing happening. By limiting moral hazard, they pay out less frequently and can charge a lower premium.

Adverse selection

Some people smoke cigarettes but others do not. People who smoke reduce their life expectancy. Individuals know whether they themselves smoke, but suppose the insurance company cannot tell the difference and must charge all clients the same premium rate for life assurance.

Suppose the premium is based on mortality rates for the nation as a whole. People who do not smoke know they have an above-average life expectancy and find the premium too expensive. Smokers know their life expectancy is low and realize that the premium is a bargain. Even though the insurance company cannot tell the difference between the two groups, it knows a premium based on the national average will attract only the high-risk people.

One solution is to assume that all clients smoke and charge the correspondingly high premium to all clients. Non-smokers cannot get insurance at what they believe is a reasonable price. They might pay for a medical examination to try to prove they are low-risk clients who should be charged a lower price. Medical examinations are now compulsory for many insurance contracts.

> **Adverse selection** occurs when individuals use their inside information to accept or reject a contract. Those who accept are not an average sample of the population.

To check that you understand the difference between moral hazard and adverse selection, say which is which in the following examples. (1) A person with a fatal disease signs up for life insurance. (2) Reassured by the fact that he took out life assurance to protect his dependants, a person who has unexpectedly become depressed decides to commit suicide. (The first was adverse selection, the second moral hazard.)

13.3 Uncertainty and asset returns

There are many ways to carry wealth from the present to the future. People can hold money, government bills or bonds, company shares, housing, gold, and so on. We now compare the rates of return on shares and Treasury bills, two particular ways of holding wealth.

Treasury bills are issued usually for a period of three months. The Treasury sells a bill for, say, £99 and simultaneously promises to buy back the bill for £100 in three months' time. People who buy the bill, and later resell it to the government, earn around 1 per cent on their money in three months. By re-investing the proceeds to buy three more bills in the course of the year, they will earn around 4 per cent a year. Each time an individual buys a bill, the implicit nominal interest rate over the three-month period is known for certain since the government has guaranteed the price at which the bill will be re-purchased.

The *real return* is the nominal return minus the inflation rate over the period the bill is held. People have a pretty good idea about what inflation is *likely* to be in the next three months. The real return on Treasury bills is not very risky.

Company shares offer a return in two different ways. If a share is bought at a low price and later sold at a high price, this contributes to the return earned while holding the share. The *rate of return* is the return as a percentage of the money initially invested. Hence

> **Dividends** are the regular payments of profit to shareholders. The **capital gain (loss)** is the rise (fall) in the share price while it is held.

$$\text{Rate of return} = \frac{[\text{dividend} + \text{capital gain}]}{\text{initial purchase price}}$$

To compute the real rate of return, we subtract the inflation rate from the nominal rate of return. For 1900–2005, Table 13.3 compares the average annual real rate of return on company shares (equities) with that on government bonds (gilts) and on short-term assets, such as Treasury bills or interest-bearing liquid loans, and on company shares in the UK during 1900–2005. It shows that, on average, equities yield substantially higher returns.

Table 13.3 Average annual real rates of return 1990–2005 (% per annum)

	2005	1985–2005	1900–2005
Equities	18.9	5.0	5.2
Gilts	6.0	5.6	1.2
Short-term liquid assets	2.7	2.9	1.0

Source: Barclays Capital, *Equity Gilt Study.*

However, the real rate of return on company shares is much more variable than that on Treasury bills. The latter varied little, but the annual real return on shares was as high as 130 per cent during 1975 and as low as –70 per cent in 1974. There are many years when the real return on shares exceeded 20 per cent or fell below –10 per cent. Shares are much riskier than Treasury bills.[2] This larger risk is

Box 13.2 Stock market volatility

The chart below shows an index of corporate share prices, the Financial Times Stock Exchange index of 100 top companies since 1985. Notice that the vertical scale is logarithmic, which implies that equal vertical distances correspond to equal *percentage* changes. The graph shows that, even for a broad average over 100 individual companies, the index fell by half during 2000–03, then doubled during 2003–07. Inclusive of these capital gains or losses, annual returns have therefore varied from –20% to +20% at a time of low and stable inflation, implying that real returns are very volatile.

Why such wild swings? Largely because the market is having to extrapolate current information to make guesses about the entire stream of future earnings of these companies. In volatile sectors, small changes in current information can lead to rapid reassessments about future earnings. Since the share price embodies the future earnings that a company will earn, share prices can change dramatically when uncertainty about a sector is great.

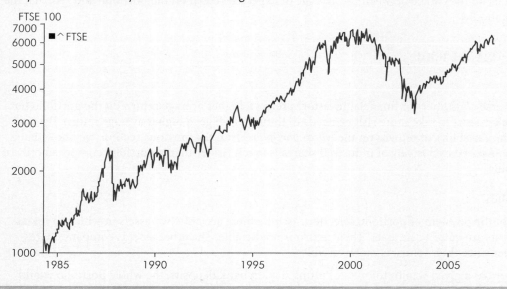

2 Large positive or negative returns on shares were probably not forecast by the market. If people had foreseen a real return of 30 per cent they would have bought shares earlier, bidding up share prices earlier. If large capital losses had been foreseen, share prices would already have been lower, as people tried to dump these shares before they fell.

compensated *on average* by a higher return. Since the risk is big – people recently lost fortunes as shares in dotcom companies plummeted – it needs a large real return on average to induce people to take this risk.

Shares are riskier for two reasons. First, nobody is sure what dividend the firm will pay. It depends what profit the firm makes and how confident it is about the future. When firms anticipate tough times, they cut dividends in order to keep a contingency reserve within the firm.

Second, views about the likely capital gains change radically. Stock market investors paid high prices for dotcom companies in the late 1990s, even though profits were still years away. People thought the present value of distant dividends was big. Discounting reduces the value of future dividends, but people were projecting spectacular growth and eventually huge dividends. Growth projections were slashed as reality crept in, and estimated present values changed a lot. Share prices in Amazon and Yahoo! fell by 80 per cent or more during 2000–01. Box 13.2 gives details over a longer period. It is revisions in beliefs about capital gains that cause volatile share prices and share returns.

13.4 Portfolio selection

The *portfolio* of a financial investor is the bundle of financial and real assets – bank deposits, Treasury bills, government bonds, shares in industrial companies, gold, works of art – in which wealth is held. How does a risk-averse investor select his portfolio or wealth composition?

Chapter 5 set out the basic model of consumer choice. The budget line summarized the market opportunities, the goods that a given income would buy. Indifference curves showed individual tastes, and the consumer chose the bundle on the highest possible indifference curve given the budget constraint describing which bundles were affordable.

We use the same approach for the choice of a portfolio. Instead of a choice between different goods, we now focus on the choice between the average or expected return on the portfolio and risk that the portfolio embodies.

The risk–return choice

Tastes

The risk-averse consumer (or financial investor) prefers a higher average return on the portfolio but dislikes higher risk. To take more risk he needs to think he will get a higher average return. By 'risk' we mean the variability of returns on the *whole portfolio*. From the previous section, we know that a portfolio composed exclusively of industrial shares is much riskier than a portfolio composed only of Treasury bills.

Opportunities

To highlight the problem of portfolio selection, assume there are only two assets in which to invest. Bank deposits are quite a safe asset. Their return is predictable. The other asset is company shares, much riskier since their return is more variable.

The investor has a given wealth to invest. Putting it all in bank deposits, the whole portfolio would earn a small but riskless return. The higher the fraction of the portfolio held in shares, the larger the average return on the whole portfolio but the greater its risk.

Portfolio choice

A very risk-averse investor will put the whole portfolio into the safe asset. To consider buying the risky asset, he must believe the average return on the risky asset is much higher than on the safe asset. Suppose this is the case. How much of the portfolio will he put into the risky asset? Generally, the fraction of the portfolio held in the risky asset will be higher (1) the higher the average return on the risky asset compared with the safe asset, (2) the less risky is the risky asset, and (3) the less risk-averse is the investor.

Diversification

When there are several risky assets the investor may be able to reduce the risk on the whole portfolio *without* having to accept a lower average return on the portfolio. We illustrate using Table 13.4, whose structure resembles the problem of the actress and the farmer in Table 13.2. There are two risky assets: oil shares and bank shares. Each has two possible returns: £4 if things go well and £2 if things go badly. Each industry has a 50 per cent chance of good times and a 50 per cent chance of bad times. Finally, we assume that returns in the two industries are independent. Good times in the oil industry tell us nothing about whether the banking industry is having good or bad times.

You have £2 to invest, and oil and bank shares each cost £1. Which portfolio gives the best risk–return combination? A bank share and an oil share have the same risk and expected return. You are indifferent between buying only oil shares and only bank shares. But a superior strategy is to buy one of each and *diversify* the portfolio.

Diversification means not putting all your eggs in one basket. If you put your eggs in one basket, buying say 2 oil shares for your £2, you have a 50 per cent chance of earning £8 and a 50 per cent chance of earning £4. It depends whether the oil industry has good or bad times. The average return is £6, but the actual return will either be £4 or £8.

> **Diversification** pools risk across several assets whose individual returns behave differently from one another.

Table 13.4 A diversified portfolio

Oil	Banking	
	Good	**Bad**
Good	£8	£6
Bad	£6	£4

Table 13.4 shows a diversified portfolio with one bank share and one oil share. If both industries do well you will make £8, but this is only a 25 per cent chance. There is a 50 per cent chance oil does well; since returns in the two industries are independent, on only half of those occasions will banking also be doing well. Similarly, there is a 25 per cent chance of both industries doing badly at the same time. There is also a 25 per cent chance that one industry does well while the other one does badly. Each of the four portfolio returns shown in Table 13.4 is a 25 per cent chance.

The average return on the portfolio is still £6, as if you put your £2 in one basket, but the variability of returns is smaller. Instead of a 50/50 chance of £4 or £8, you now have only a 25 per cent chance of each extreme, and a 50 per cent chance of earning the average return of £6.

Diversification reduces the risk by pooling it without altering the average rate of return. It offers you a better deal. As in our earlier discussion of risk-pooling by insurance companies, the greater the number of risky assets with independent returns across which the portfolio pools the risk, the lower will be the total risk of the portfolio.

Figure 13.1 shows the typical relationship between the total portfolio risk and the number of independent assets in the portfolio. Portfolio risk declines as the number of independent risky assets is increased. However, most of the risk reduction through diversification comes very quickly. Even a few assets cut the total risk a lot. Your car has one spare tyre, not five.

Because it is more expensive to buy in small quantities, small investors typically hold a dozen different shares rather than a hundred. They get most of the benefit of diversifying without needing lots of small packages of shares. People who are more risk-averse and want a large number of shares can buy shares in a mutual fund or unit trust, a professional fund that buys large quantities of shares in many firms, and then retails stakes in the fund to small investors.

Diversification when asset returns are correlated

Risk-pooling works because asset returns are independent of each other. When asset returns move together, we say that they are *correlated*. When returns on two assets tend to move in the same direction we say they are *positively correlated*. For example, a boom in the whole economy will tend to be good for bank shares and shares in TV companies. If returns tend to move in opposite directions, we say they are *negatively correlated*. For example, if people buy gold shares during financial crises, gold shares will tend to rise when other shares are falling, and vice versa.

Positive and negative correlations affect the way in which diversification changes risk. Suppose bank shares and oil shares always rise or fall together. Buying one of each is like putting all your money in either share. Diversification achieves nothing. When returns are perfectly positively correlated risk-pooling does not work, just as it fails for 'acts of God' in the insurance industry.

Conversely, diversification is a spectacular success when returns are negatively correlated. Suppose bank shares do well only when gold shares do badly, and vice versa. Buying one of each, you earn either £4 from oil and £2 from gold or £2 from oil and £4 from gold. On the diversified portfolio, you earn £6 for certain. You have diversified away all the risk, even though each share is individually risky.

In practice, returns on different shares are never perfectly correlated. Some *tend* to vary together and some *tend* to vary in opposite directions, but over any particular period actual returns on two shares may not exhibit their usual correlation. Thus it is impossible to completely diversify away all portfolio risk. But smart fund managers are always on the lookout for an asset that tends to have a negative correlation with the assets in the existing portfolio. On average, extending the portfolio to include that asset will improve the risk–return characteristics of the portfolio.

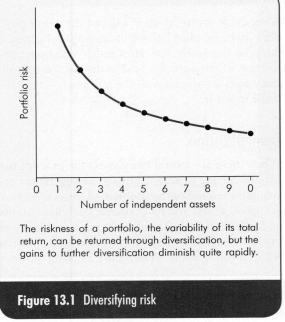

The riskness of a portfolio, the variability of its total return, can be returned through diversification, but the gains to further diversification diminish quite rapidly.

Figure 13.1 Diversifying risk

Beta

Table 13.5 gives some examples. The first row shows returns on the market as a whole in booms, normal times and slumps. A share with beta = 1 moves the same way as the whole market. A high beta share does even better when the market is up, even worse when the market is down. A low beta share moves in the same general direction as the market but more sluggishly than the market. Negative beta shares move against the market.

> **Beta** measures how much an asset's return moves with the return on the whole stock market.

Table 13.5 Share returns and beta

Asset	Return (%)		
	Boom	Normal	Slump
Whole market	14	6	22
High beta	20	10	28
Beta = 1	14	6	22
Low beta	5	4	3
Negative beta	2	3	5

Most shares move pretty much with the market and have a beta close to one. There are not too many negative beta shares, but some gold shares have betas close to zero. Most people should have some gold shares in their portfolios.

Bankers and stockbrokers calculate betas from the past behaviour of individual shares and the whole stock market. Ideally, they are looking for negative beta shares that greatly reduce the risk of a portfolio whose other components vary with the market as a whole. Even low beta shares are partly independent of the rest of the market and allow some risk to be pooled. High beta shares are undesirable. Including them in the portfolio adds to its total risk.

Box 13.3 Too smart?

A financial asset is really a bundle of different characteristics which people gradually realized could be unbundled and traded separately. Derivative markets boomed for financial products such as options (the right to buy or sell in the future at a particular price). Like a giant game of fantasy football, participants bought and sold hypothetical teams of players and made side bets whose outcome depended on what happened in the real match.

When the price of a characteristic differed in different markets, you could buy in one market and sell in others to make sure profits. Traders boasted that, in making fortunes, they helped make financial markets more efficient.

Long-Term Capital Management (LTCM) was a dream team of Wall Street bond dealers and hot-shot academics (in 1997 Bob Merton and Myron Scholes won the Nobel Prize in economics). Using fancy mathematics and huge computers, they exploited small arbitrage opportunities other people missed. Betting billions at a time, they turned small profit margins into big bucks. During February 1994 to April 1998, LTCM made $95 million a month!

In August 1998 LTCM had huge quantities of Russian bonds, offset by fancy contracts to insure against changes in the rouble exchange rate. It looked safe to LTCM. They forgot that the Russians might default. LTCM lost $1.8 billion in August 1998.

Markets began to panic. Who had lent to LTCM? Who else had lost money in Russia? Asset prices collapsed, and people were reluctant to trade. LTCM could not trade in sufficient volume to insure its other supposedly riskless bets. By late September LTCM had lost $4.6 billion and was out of business.

How was confidence restored? The Fed (the US equivalent of the Bank of England) 'persuaded' leading private banks to stump up for LTCM losses, and Fed Chairman Alan Greenspan said he would cut interest rates as much as needed to restore market confidence. The Fed cut interest rates three times in seven weeks. Markets got the message and the crisis subsided.

A share with a low (or even negative) beta will be in high demand. Risk-averse purchasers are anxious to buy low beta shares whose inclusion in their portfolios reduce the total portfolio risk. High demand bids up the share price and reduces the average return: since it costs more to buy the shares, people get less per pound invested. However, investors are happy to trade off a lower return for the fact that low beta shares reduce the total risk of their portfolios.

In stock market equilibrium, low beta shares have high prices and low rates of return on average. Conversely, high beta shares add to investors' portfolio risk and are purchased only because they have low prices and on average offer high rates of return that compensate for their undesirable risk characteristics. Figure 13.2 shows the results of a pioneering study by Professors Black, Jensen, and Scholes using stock market data from 1931 to 1965. Average returns on individual shares rise steadily with the shares' beta as the theory predicts. Table 13.6 shows recent estimates of beta for selected sectors of the Financial Times Stock Exchange index.

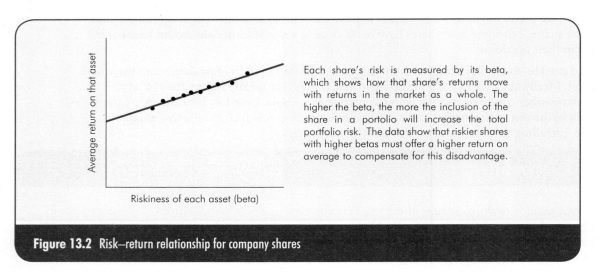

Each share's risk is measured by its beta, which shows how that share's returns move with returns in the market as a whole. The higher the beta, the more the inclusion of the share in a portolio will increase the total portfolio risk. The data show that riskier shares with higher betas must offer a higher return on average to compensate for this disadvantage.

Figure 13.2 Risk–return relationship for company shares

Table 13.6 Beta for selected sectors

Retailing	0.96	Media	1.2
Cosmetics	0.66	Defence	1.14
Banks	1.27	Paper	0.99
Chemicals	0.81	Mining	1.19
Energy	0.82	Textiles	0.27
Brewing	0.66	Personal Products	0.63
Tobacco	0.59	Clothing	0.71

Source: Risk Management Services, 2003.

To sum up, individual share prices depend both on expected or average returns and on risk characteristics. The risk characteristics of a firm's shares determine the expected return its shares must offer to compete with other shares. For a given required return, higher anticipated income (dividends or capital gains) means a higher current share price.

The riskiness of a firm's shares refers not to variability of the share's return in isolation from the rest of the market. This is why beta matters. Adding a risky asset to the portfolio reduces the risk of the portfolio provided the share's beta is less than 1. Low beta shares can be individually risky; nevertheless, taken with other shares they reduce portfolio risk and are therefore desirable. Low beta shares have an above-average price and a below-average rate of return to offset this advantage; high beta shares must offer an above-average expected return to be competitive.

Activity box 13 Beta in action

The table below shows three possible outcomes – boom, slump and normal times – and three possible assets – the FTSE index, an asset with negative beta that moves against the general stock market trend, and a high beta asset that moves in the same direction as the stock market but even more so.

Question

1   Complete the table by showing for each outcome (boom, normal, slump) the level of portfolios A, B and C, respectively (for example in portfolio A, half your money is invested in the FTSE index and half in the low beta asset).

Outcome	Asset price			Portfolio value		
	(a) FTSE index	(b) Low beta asset	(c) High beta asset	A ½ of (a) + ½ of (b)	B ⅓ of (a) + ⅔ of (b)	C ½% of (a) + ½ of (c)
Boom	120	90	150			
Normal	100	100	100			
Slump	80	110	50			

To check your answers to these questions, go to page 721.

Diversification in other situations

Risk is all around us, and diversification happens all the time. Countries diversify their sources of raw materials. Otherwise, if anything disrupts the sole supplier's ability or willingness to sell, the country may face a disaster. Similarly, a farmer is reluctant to rely on a single crop. It may be better for a navy to have two small aircraft carriers than a large one. If the only aircraft carrier sinks, there is no air cover.

13.5 Efficient asset markets

There are two basic images of the stock market. One is that of a casino, without any rational basis for speculation; it is all a matter of luck. The other view – the theory of *efficient markets* – is that the stock market is a sensitive processor of information, quickly responding to new information to adjust share prices correctly.

The second view recognizes that share prices fluctuate a lot but argues that these fluctuations are the appropriate response to new information as it becomes available.

> An **efficient asset market** already incorporates existing information properly in asset prices.

Companies with high average returns and low betas should be valued both by society and by the stock market. The higher the share price, the more money a company raises from a new share issue, and the more likely is the company to invest in plant and machinery financed by this new share issue. High share prices are guiding the right firms to invest. Companies with low average returns and high betas are valued neither by financial investors nor by society. Low share prices make it harder for them to finance new plant and equipment, and they will tend to contract.

It matters which of the two views of the stock market is correct. If share prices correctly reflect prospective dividends and risk characteristics – the efficient market view – a free market in industrial shares is guiding society's scarce resources towards the right firms. But if share prices are purely pot luck, as in a casino, the wrong firms may expand just because their share prices are high.

Testing for efficiency

Suppose everybody has all the information available today about the likely risks and returns on different shares. Equilibrium share prices should equate the likely return on all shares with the same risk characteristics. Otherwise there would be an obvious opportunity to switch from the low return shares to higher return shares with equivalent risk characteristics. If the market has got it right, it does not matter which share you buy in any risk class. They are all expected to yield the same return. The efficient market view says there is no way of beating the market to earn an above-average return on a share of a given risk class.

If the market neglects some available information, you could use this information to beat the market. If the market failed to spot that hot weather increases ice cream sales it would never mark up share prices in ice cream companies when good weather occurred. By buying ice cream shares when the sun shone you would make money and beat the market. The market would be surprised by high dividends from ice cream companies. But you bought them, having figured all this out by using extra information. You knew ice cream shares would pay a higher rate of return than the market thought. You spotted an inefficiency in the market.

In contrast, the efficient market view says all the relevant available information is immediately incorporated in the share price. Given the long-range weather forecast, the market makes the best guess about profits and dividends in the ice cream industry and sets the current price to give the required rate of return for shares with the same risk characteristics as ice cream shares. If the weather forecast is correct, the return will be as predicted. If unexpectedly there is a hot spell, the market will immediately mark up ice cream shares to reflect the new information that ice cream profits will be higher than previously expected. How high are ice cream shares marked up? To the price that reduces the expected rate of return back to the average for that risk class.

The crucial implication of the efficient market theory is that asset prices correctly reflect all existing information. It is unforeseen new information that changes share prices as the market quickly incorporates this unanticipated development to restore expected returns to the required level. Existing information cannot systematically be used to get above-average returns for that risk class of asset.

The theory of efficient markets has been tested extensively to see whether there is any *currently available* information that would allow an investor systematically to earn an above-average return for that risk class. The vast majority of all empirical studies conclude that there is no readily available information that the market neglects. Rules of the form 'buy shares when the price has risen two days in a row' do not work. Nor do rules that use existing information about how the economy or the industry is doing. Smart investors have taken this information on board as it became available. It is already in the price.

The empirical literature usually concludes you may as well stick a pin in the financial pages of a newspaper as employ an expensive financial adviser. Paradoxically, it is because the market has *already* used all the relevant economic information correctly that there are no bargains around. The theory of efficient markets does not say share prices and returns are unaffected by economics; it says that, because the economics has been correctly used to set the price, there are no easy pickings left.

Financial newspapers and stock market institutions run competitions for the investor of the year. If the theory of efficient markets is right, why do some portfolios do better than others? Why, indeed, are financial portfolio advisers in business at all? The world is uncertain, and there will always be surprises that could not have been forecast. As this new information is incorporated in share prices some lucky investors will find they happen to have already invested in shares whose price has unexpectedly risen. Others are unlucky, holding shares whose price unexpectedly falls.

Box 13.4 Behavioural finance

'PEOPLE make barmy decisions about the future. The evidence is all around, from their investments in the stockmarkets to the way their run their businesses. In fact, people are consistently bad at dealing with uncertainty, underestimating some kinds of risk and overestimating others.

'Daniel Kahneman, now a professor at Princeton, noticed as a young research psychologist in the 1960s that the logic of decision science was hard for people to accept. …In the past decade the fields of behavioural finance and behavioural economics have blossomed, and in 2002 Mr Kahneman shared a Nobel prize in economics for his work.' (*The Economist*, 22 January 2004)

So far, the economics that we have examined assumes that people are completely rational and that the cost of acquiring information is either free or can be modelled in simple ways. This leads to an incredibly powerful set of economic tools that help us understand many complicated situations. But it is not the whole story. Here is a glimpse of how we could complicate our analysis.

Suppose there is a fixed cost of either acquiring information or of taking the time to make a decision. This leads to 'bounded rationality'. It is no longer optimal to examine every possible decision in great detail – you would incur too many fixed costs – so instead you incur costs once, have a good think, and then come up with a simple decision rule that you implement automatically until it no longer fits the facts, at which point you incur some more thinking costs and try to improve your rule. Simple rules may explain why people extrapolate the recent past rather than conduct extensive research all the time.

Such behavioural rules are a large part of the concern of psychologists, who have conducted a lot of empirical research on how accurate these rules are. Often, people err in systematic ways, over time because they have not updated their old rules, and across people because they are using similar short cuts that are making the same mistake. For example, most people's optimism rises the longer the time horizon. Forty per cent of Americans think they will some day be in the top 1 per cent of income earners! Recently, economists have applied these ideas to financial markets, in the search for systematic mistakes in asset pricing.

One reason that economists have been sceptical about applications that make use of departures from full rationality is that there is only one way to be rational but a million ways in which to be irrational. Anyone can explain a particular event by invoking a particular kind of irrationality – it then takes a lot of data to establish whether there is anything systematic in this irrationality or whether it was just a coincidence invoked by someone trying to be wise after the event.

Thus one interpretation of why some investors do better than others is pure chance. This story could even explain why some investors have above-average returns for several years in a row. Even with a fair coin there is roughly one chance in a thousand of tossing ten consecutive heads. Even if there is no systematic way to beat the market, there are thousands of investors, and someone is going to have a lucky streak for ten years.

But there is also a more subtle interpretation. When a piece of new information first becomes available someone has to decide *how* share prices should be adjusted. The price does not change by magic. And there is an incentive to be quick off the mark. The first person to get the information, or correctly to calculate where the market will soon be setting the price, may be able to buy a share just before everyone else catches on and the share's price rises.

The non-specialist investor cannot use *past* information to make above-average profits. But specialist investors, by reacting very quickly, can make capital gains or avoid capital losses within the first few hours of new information becoming available. It is their actions that help to change the price, and the profits that they make from fast dealing are what pay for City salaries. It is the economic return to their time and effort in gathering and processing information.

Speculative bubbles

Consider the market for gold. Unlike shares or bonds, gold pays no dividend or interest payment. Its return accrues entirely through the capital gain. Today's prices depend on the anticipated capital gain, which in turn depends on expectations of tomorrow's price. But tomorrow's price will depend on the capital gain then expected, which will depend on expectations of the price the day after; and so on.

In such markets there is no way for the *fundamentals*, the economic calculations about future dividends or interest payments, to influence the price. It all depends on what people today think people tomorrow will expect people the next day to expect. Such a market is vulnerable to *speculative bubbles*. If everyone believes the price will rise tomorrow, it makes sense to purchase the asset today. So long as people expect the price to keep rising, it makes sense to keep buying even though the price may already have risen a lot.

A famous example of a speculative bubble is the South Sea Bubble of 1720. A company was set up to sell British goods to people in the South Seas and to bring home the wonderful and exotic goods produced there. The shares were issued long before any attempt was made actually to trade these goods. It sounded a great idea and people bought the shares. The price rose quickly, and soon people were buying not in anticipation of eventual dividends but purely to resell the shares at a profit once the price had gone even higher. The price rose even faster, till one day it became apparent that the company's proposal was a fiasco with no chance of success and the bubble burst. Sir Isaac Newton lost £2000 (over half a million pounds at today's prices).

The great English economist John Maynard Keynes argued that the stock market is like a casino, dominated by short-term speculators who buy not in anticipation of future dividends but purely to resell at a quick profit. Since next period's share price depends on what people then think the following period's share price will be, Keynes compared the stock market to a beauty competition in a newspaper, where the winner is the reader who guesses the beauty getting most votes from all readers. Share prices reflect what average opinion expects average opinion to be.

Undoubtedly, financial markets sometimes exhibit temporary bubbles. The overpricing of shares in dotcom companies was a recent example. Nevertheless, bubbles *are* usually temporary. Eventually it is obvious that the share price cannot be justified by fundamentals. Bubbles are less likely for assets whose income is mainly from dividends or interest rather than capital gains.

13.6 More on risk

Risk is central to economic life. Every topic in this book could be extended to include risk. Individual applications differ, but two features recur: individuals try to find ways to reduce risk, and those who take over the bearing of risk have to be compensated for so doing.

Hedging and forward markets

There are forward markets for many commodities and assets, including corn, coffee, sugar, copper, gold and foreign currencies.

> A **spot market** deals in contracts for immediate delivery and payment. A **forward market** deals in contracts made today for delivery of goods at a specified future date at a price agreed today.

Suppose the current price of copper is £800 a tonne and people expect the price to rise to £880 a tonne after 12 months. Some people will hold copper in their portfolios. The expected capital gain is 10 per cent of the purchase price, and it may be interesting to diversify a portfolio by including copper. However, that is not our concern at present.

You own a copper mine and will have 1 tonne of copper to sell in 12 months' time. The *spot* price of copper is the price for immediate delivery. Today's spot price is £800 and people expect the spot price to be £880 at this time next year. One option is for you simply to sell your copper at the spot price at this time next year. You expect that to be £880 but you cannot be sure today what the price next year will actually be. It is risky.

Alternatively, you can *hedge* against this risk in the forward market for copper.

> **Hedging** is the use of forward markets to shift risk on to somebody else.

Suppose today you can sell 1 tonne of copper for delivery in 12 months' time at a price of £860 agreed today. You have hedged against the risky future spot price. You know for certain what you will receive when your copper is available for delivery. But you have sold your copper for only £860, even though you expect copper then to sell for £880 on the spot market. You regard this as an insurance premium to get out of the risk associated with the future spot price.

To whom do you sell your copper in the forward market? You sell it to a trader whom we can call a speculator.

> A **speculator** temporarily holds an asset in the hope of making a capital gain.

The speculator has no interest in 1 tonne of copper *per se*. But the speculator, having promised you £860 for copper to be delivered in one year's time, currently expects to resell that copper immediately it is delivered. The speculator expects to get £880 for that copper in the spot market next year. He expects to make £20 as compensation for bearing your risk. If spot copper prices turn out to be less than £860 next year the speculator will lose money. £20 is the risk premium necessary to attract enough speculators into the forward market to take up the risky positions that hedgers wish to avoid.

Someone buying spot copper today at £800 for possible resale next year at £880 must compare the expected capital gain of 10 per cent with returns and interest rates on offer in other assets. Copper must cover the opportunity cost of the returns that could have been earned by using this money elsewhere. The speculator in the forward market need not make this comparison. No money is currently tied up in the forward contract. Although the price has been agreed today at £860, the money is handed over only next year when the copper is delivered. Provided the speculator then resells in next year's spot market, no money is actually tied up. All the speculator has to think about is the likely spot price in 12 months' time and how much it could vary either side of this estimate. The riskier the future spot price, the larger premium the speculator will need and the more the current forward price will lie below the expected future spot price.

Box 13.5 Spot markets and forward markets

At first most people find it hard to keep track of all the different terms – spot price, future spot price, expected future spot price, and forward price. Have you got them straight? Suppose there is a spot market for copper and a forward market for copper. Suppose the only type of forward contract that exists is for delivery of copper one year after the deal is struck but at a price agreed immediately. The money only changes hands when the copper is delivered in one year's time.

Term	Definition	Example
Today's spot price	Price of copper today for delivery and payment today	£800
Future spot price	Spot market price of copper in a year's time	£900
Expected future spot price	The best guess today about spot price in a year's time	£880
Forward price	Price today in forward market at which copper is being traded for delivery and payment in a year's time	£860
Risk premium	Expected future spot price minus the current forward price. The sum a hedger expects on average to lose by making a forward contract rather than by taking a chance on the future spot price. Hence, what the hedger expects to pay, and the speculator expects to make, by transferring the risk from hedger to speculator.	£880–£860 = £20

This speculator had an open position, having taken forward delivery of copper without yet having a purchaser to whom to resell. However, other firms use copper as an input to production, and may wish to *buy* copper for delivery in 12 months' time at a price agreed today. They too wish to hedge against the risky future spot price. A speculator who can make two forward contracts, one to take delivery of copper from the copper miner, the other to sell copper to a copper user, does not have an open position. The speculator's book is balanced, without any residual risk. The risky future spot price is irrelevant.

In forward markets with roughly equal numbers of people wishing to hedge by buying and by selling, speculators' books roughly balance and residual risk is small. Speculators need only a little compensation to cover this residual risk and the administration costs. The current price of forward copper is close to the expected future spot price.

However, speculation is a risky business if buyers and sellers cannot be matched up in the forward market. In practice, the spot prices that subsequently transpire can vary by a large amount on either side of the estimate implicitly contained in the current forward price.

Why do forward markets exist for copper and silver but not for BMWs? The answer again is moral hazard and adverse selection. Suppose today you contract for delivery of a new car model in 12 months' time. You thought you were buying a luxury car, but the company brings out a low-quality car and says 'this is our new model'. By making all these forward contracts, the car maker affects its own quality incentives.

Forward markets do not exist for most goods because it is impossible to write legally binding and cheaply enforceable contracts that adequately specify the characteristics of the commodity being traded. Where forward markets exist they are for very standardized commodities – 18-carat gold, Japanese yen – that are easily defined. Forward markets are an important way by which individuals can reduce the risks they face, but there are only a limited number of risks that can be hedged in this way.

Compensating differentials in the return to labour

Since people are risk-averse, we expect people with risky jobs to earn more on average than people whose jobs are safe. Broadly speaking this is confirmed by the facts. Divers who inspect North Sea oil pipelines earn high hourly rates because the death rate in this activity is high. University academics earn relatively low wages in the UK because many of them have secure jobs, unlike industrial managers who face the sack if their company has a bad spell.

Profits are often seen as a reward to entrepreneurs, individuals who set up and run firms, for taking big risks. The average person who starts a business works long hours for small rewards initially. In the early stages there is the continual threat of failure, and most small firms never get off the ground. The possibility of becoming a millionaire, like Richard Branson of Virgin or Bill Gates of Microsoft, is the carrot needed to persuade people to embark on this risky activity.

Summary

- **Risk** pervades economic life. Some people gamble for fun, some addicts gamble in spite of themselves. Most people are **risk-averse**. They volunteer to take risks only if offered favourable odds that on average yield a profit. Conversely, most people **insure**, despite less than fair odds, to reduce the risks they otherwise face.

- **Risk-aversion** reflects the **diminishing marginal utility of wealth**. A fair gamble in monetary terms yields less extra utility when it succeeds than it sacrifices when it fails. Hence people refuse fair gambles, except for very small stakes. The prevalence of risk aversion means that people look for ways to reduce risk, and must pay others to take over their risk-bearing.

- Insurance **pools** risks that are substantially independent to reduce the aggregate risk, and **spreads** any residual risk across many people so that each has a small stake in the risk that cannot be pooled away.

- Insurance markets are inhibited by **adverse selection** and **moral hazard**. The former means that high-risk clients are more likely to take out insurance; the latter means that the act of insuring increases the likelihood that the undesired outcome will occur.

- Company shares have a higher average return but a much more variable return than that on Treasury bills or bank deposits.

- Portfolio choices depend on the investor's tastes – the trade-offs between risk and average return that yield equal utility – and on the opportunities that the market provides – the risk and return combinations on existing assets.

- When risks on different asset returns are independent, the risk of the whole portfolio can be reduced by diversification across assets.

- The risk that an asset contributes to a portfolio is not measured by the variability of that asset's own return but on the correlation of its return with the return on other assets. An asset that is negatively correlated with other assets will actually reduce the risk on the whole portfolio even though its own return is risky. Conversely, assets with a strong positive correlation with the rest of the portfolio increase the overall risk. The value of **beta** for an asset measures its correlation with other assets.

- In equilibrium risky assets earn higher rates of return on average to compensate portfolio holders for bearing this extra risk. High beta assets have high returns. If an asset is offering too high an expected return for its risk class, people will buy the asset, bidding up its price until the expected return is forced back to its equilibrium level.

- In an **efficient market** assets are priced to reflect the latest available information about their risk and return. There are no easy systematic investment opportunities to beat the market unless you systematically get or use new information faster than other people. Evidence from share prices is compatible with stock market efficiency, but speculative bubbles sometimes occur.

- **Forward markets** set a price today for future delivery of and payment for goods. They allow people to **hedge** against risky spot prices in the future by making a contract today. **Speculators** take over this risk and require a premium unless they can match buyers and sellers.

Review questions

To check your answers to these questions, go to page 720.

1 A fair coin is to be tossed. If it comes down heads the player wins £1. If it comes down tails the player loses £1. Person A doesn't mind whether or not she takes the bet. Person B will pay £0.02 to play the game. Person C demands £0.05 before being willing to play. Characterize the three people's attitude to risk. Which is most likely to take out insurance for car theft?

2 You see an advert for life insurance for anyone over 45 years old. No medical examination is required. Do you expect the premium rates to be high, low or average? Why?

3 In which of the following are the risks being pooled: (a) life insurance, (b) insurance against the Thames flooding, (c) insurance for a pop star's voice?

4 You set up a firm to advise the unemployed on the best way to use their time to earn money. Your firm issues shares on the stock market. In equilibrium, will your shares be expected to earn a higher or lower return than the stock market average? Why?

5 Why are stock markets regulated to prevent 'inside trading', where a firm's managers use inside information about the firm to buy and sell its shares?

6 **Common fallacies** Why are the following statements wrong? (a) Economists cannot predict changes in the stock market. This proves that economics is useless in thinking about share prices. (b) It is silly to take out insurance. If the insurance company is making money, its clients are losing money. (c) Prudent investors should not buy shares whose returns are volatile.

7 **Harder question** We know from many situations that people will pay to avoid risk. Name three risky products that you choose to buy. In each case, explain the motive.

8 **Harder question** Suppose the stock exchange is expected to yield a return of 5 per cent next year, but this is risky and could be several percentage points either side of the central forecast. You are also aware that it is possible to hold gold as an asset and that gold is known to have a small negative beta. People buy gold in a panic so the gold price rises when the stock market is doing badly. Today's price of gold is £500. (a) If people are risk-neutral, what is the best estimate of next year's gold price? (b) If people are risk-averse, what do you think is the best estimate of next year's gold price?

9 **Essay question** You run a pension fund and know that in 20 years' time you need to make a lot of payments to people who will then have retired. Should you (a) invest in bonds that mature in 20 years' time so you know exactly how much you will then have, (b) invest in equities because historically their average return has been greater than bonds in the long run, or (c) begin mainly in equities but switch gradually into bonds as the 20-year period elapses?

To help you grasp the key concepts of this chapter check out the extra resources posted on the Online Learning Centre. There are chapter summaries, self-test questions, an interactive graphing tool, weblinks and a searchable glossary, all for free!

To put your learning into practice and prepare for exams, an **Interactive Workbook** is also available online, containing a variety of question types and providing feedback on your answers.

If you'd like further help with economics, or have any questions, **NetTutor** is here to help! You will have a personalised tutorial service at your fingertips. Visit the online learning centre at: www.mcgraw-hill.co.uk/textbooks/begg for information on accessing all of these resources.

The information economy

A century ago, fortunes were made in railways, steel and oil. John D. Rockefeller (1839–1937), founder of Standard Oil, amassed a fortune worth $200 billion if valued at 2004 prices. Today, the richest people on the planet are in the information business. Bill Gates of Microsoft (www.microsoft.com) is currently worth about $55 billion. The information revolution is here. It is big business and it is changing people's lives. Yet the laws of economics continue to provide a reliable framework in which to understand what is going on. This chapter is about microeconomics in action.

First, we discuss the key attributes of information products. Then we examine how consumers and producers of these products behave, and hence how the market will develop. How does competition occur? What forms of pricing and other strategic behaviour emerge?

14.1 E-products

> An **e-product** can be digitally encoded then transmitted rapidly, accurately and cheaply.

Figure 14.1 shows the rapid rise in digital technology in UK households, for entertainment, communication and information. The same applies in the corporate world, where 93 per cent of UK businesses had information and communications technology by 2006 and 70 per cent had a website. UK sales over the internet – from last-minute plane tickets to used car sales – topped £100 billion for the first time in 2005. The use of email has led to a collapse in the use of letters and the sale of stamps.

Examples of e-products include music, films, magazines, news, books and sport. Information is expensive to assemble and produce but very cheap to distribute. The fixed cost of creating a usable product is large; the marginal cost of distributing it is tiny. This cost structure implies vast scale economies in production. We discuss the implications for market structure and competition in Section 14.3. First, we examine key attributes of information products as viewed by users. These users or consumers of information are not merely households but businesses themselves.

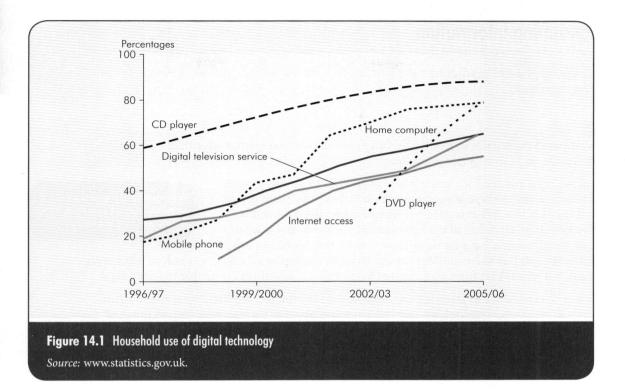

Figure 14.1 Household use of digital technology

Source: www.statistics.gov.uk.

Box 14.1 Web sights

The table shows the UK's leading websites in October 2006. There is an interesting mix of information/news/search sites, shopping and education. Internet transactions do not use cash. The Bank of England is studying the implications for monetary policy. The Treasury is examining effects on VAT revenue. The information economy seems like nothing that has gone before, but in fact is a nice illustration that the laws of economics are very robust.

	Million		Million
Total UK internet audience	29.5	Ask	11.8
Google	24.8	Fox Interactive Media	9.3
Microsoft	24.7	Wikipedia	8.6
eBay	19.9	DMGT	8.0
Yahoo!	19.4	British Sky Broadcasting (BSkyB)	7.6
BBC	16.4	Apple Computer	7.5
Time Warner	13.0	YouTube.com	7.3
Amazon	12.4		

Source: comScore World Metrix.

14.2 Consuming information

From the viewpoint of users, e-products have four key features: experience, overload, switching costs and network externalities.

Experience

We first encountered experience in Box 9.4, which examines how experience affects advertising strategies. Information is an experience product.

The first time we try something we find out how useful it is to us. Most goods and services that we buy are repeat purchases. We no longer buy them just to find out what they are like. What is different about information is that it is nearly always new. If we already had the information, we would not need to buy it. We say 'nearly always' because we all have a video that we like to watch more than once. People buy videos of Manchester United's Champions' League triumph to watch over and over again, but rent DVDs from Blockbuster, from whom a new thrill is rentable the next night.

> An **experience good or service** must be sampled before the user knows its value.

The importance of experience in assessing the demand for information products gives rise to many familiar tactics of suppliers, who look for ways to whet your appetite without revealing so much of their information that there is then no need for you to buy it. Free samples, previews, headlines, opportunities to browse are marketing tactics for experience goods and services. Suppose you supply such a product. Without free samples, people may never discover how great your product really is. How do you decide how many free samples to give away?

For simplicity, suppose the marginal cost of reproducing the information product is zero, so your only aim is to maximize revenue. Giving away more samples reduces sales you might have made today but, by raising awareness of your product, enhances the demand for your product in the future. You give away free copies up to the point at which the marginal loss of sales revenue today equals the (present value of) the marginal revenue from induced extra sales in the future.

A second way in which suppliers of experience products increase the demand for their output, and make a market in information itself, is through branding and reputation. Think first of a one-off deal. Do you want to buy a particular piece of information that costs £100? Without seeing the information, you do not know its worth; but, having seen it, you no longer need to buy it.

If every deal is a one-off, sellers face big temptations to rip off customers and customers are so wary that few trades occur. Firms invest in reputation (by previous good behaviour) in order to earn trust that yields returns in the present and the future. The demand curve for their products is higher the better the reputation they have previously established.

Box 14.2 Been here, got the e-shirt

The production and distribution of information dates back to the first conversation between our most primitive ancestors. Distribution costs have been falling ever since. The printing press slashed costs – think of those monks previously transcribing by hand – and so did the postal service and the telephone. Mail order catalogues are a century old. Browsing did not begin on the internet, it has merely been taken to another dimension. The information economy is different not merely because the distribution costs are dramatically lower but because the distribution of information is now interactive. Customers can manipulate the information they receive, and follow-up questions can be processed instantly and cheaply.

Information overload

Families with two Sunday newspapers rarely read the six sections in each paper. On the internet, the problem is compounded many times. There is so much information, it is hard to know where to start. Box 1.3 in Chapter 1 highlighted information overload as a fault line through central planning in the Soviet bloc. Search is much easier after someone else narrows down your options. Rich people looking for a house do not spend weeks driving round Belgravia. They hire an agent to narrow things down, and look only at the agent's shortlist. Similarly, a firm seeking a new director often employs a specialist 'headhunter' to produce a shortlist of suitable candidates.

Just as the agent charges a fee for the screening service, suppliers of internet screening have a valuable product that they can sell. Search engines such as Yahoo! are among the most visited websites on the internet, and hence offer valuable opportunities to advertisers.

Pre-screening explains why makers of yachts advertise in yachting magazines not football club fanzines. The internet allows the yacht producer to target customers even more accurately. One reason why internet firms may supply services without charge is that their register of customers, with customers' permission, can be retailed not just to advertisers but to others doing internet business. Similarly, the next time you buy a TV and complete your personal details on the 'free' guarantee

> **Information overload** arises when the volume of available information is large but the cost of processing it is high. Screening devices are then very valuable.

form, remember that the guarantor is 'buying' information about TV customers – where they live, and what they spend. This information helps other businesses target their sales more accurately. It is a valuable commodity.

Switching costs

Whereas compiling an ever-better customer database may provide a permanent reason to subsidize an information product, a second motive is strictly temporary. Suppliers may provide free services during an initial period to lock users into a particular supplier. Such users then face switching costs.

If Britain had to start from scratch, it might decide to drive not on the left but on the right. British cars would no longer be different from those in continental Europe. Car makers would find it much harder to charge British people premium prices for cars if similar cars were easily imported across the Channel. However, the UK has made many investments in driving on the left. Any switch would entail changing street signs and

> **Switching costs** arise when existing costs are sunk. Changing supplier then incurs extra costs.

motorway slip roads, scrapping most of the existing stock of left-hand-drive cars, and teaching drivers to do things the other way round. During the transition there would be accidents and expense. Even though Britons would benefit from cheaper right-hand-drive cars, switching costs may be so high that it is better to leave things unaltered.

Similarly, the cost of switching out of nicotine dependence is large. Someone who has never smoked and someone smoking 20 cigarettes a day make different decisions. The past matters. So does the future. Switching costs force users and suppliers to take a long-run view in the first place. Do not start smoking on the assumption it is easy to quit. You get locked in.

Table 14.1 illustrates this. A service can be bought from supplier A or supplier B. The latter is now a better supplier. Its service yields a benefit (net of any charges to consumers) of £700. The former yields a benefit of only £500. Without any switching costs, everyone would use supplier B.

However, if switching costs are £300, people who began using supplier A will not switch. The gain is £200 but the cost is £300. So they stay with supplier A and get benefits of £400. People who began with supplier B are delighted to stay with that supplier and get benefits of £700.

Table 14.1 Switching costs

	Supplier A	Supplier B
User benefit	£500	£700
Switching cost = £300		
Net benefit If began with A If began with B	£500 £200	£400 £700

Why did anyone start out with supplier A. Perhaps, previously, this supplier had offered a great deal that tempted some customers who believed that the good deal would last, or were too short-sighted to realize that a long-run decision was needed. In Table 14.1 it is best to interpret the benefits as present values of the benefits over all the future time that the user needs the service. It is the difference in these present values that must be compared with the once-off switching cost.

In Chapter 9 we distinguished innocent and strategic entry barriers, one made by nature, the other planned in boardrooms. Switching costs have both aspects. Smart suppliers devise strategies to lock in users. Air miles and reward points are obvious examples made possible by the information economy. Previously, it was too costly to keep separate track of individual retail customers.

Modern computing changed all that. Once individuals can be distinguished, they can be 'incentivized'. Reward points offer customers a small reward for staying with a particular supplier. The customer may care little whether she flies BA or Virgin, or shops at Tesco or Sainsbury's, but to the airline or supermarket it makes a big difference. Yahoo! and Freeserve were initially free. Once you are familiar with their systems they can charge you for the same services in the future, just as leading football clubs used satellite TV to reach wide audiences but then set up their own pay-TV stations.

The information economy did not invent these practices but is pushing to the limit things done more crudely for years. For decades, high street banks have known that today's students are tomorrow's profitable customers. Banks compete for space on campus and offer students subsidized banking, relying on the later cost of switching banks to lock in the customer, offering a future opportunity to get back their original investment with interest. Banks could always distinguish students and non-students. The information economy takes this principle to the limit, distinguishing individual customers and working out when early subsidies earn later returns.

Network externalities

From the user viewpoint, the final attribute of information products is that they have network externalities.

There is no point having a phone if nobody else has one, nor any reason to master Esperanto if this new language doesn't catch on. The fax was invented in 1843 and the first email was sent in 1969. It was not until other people adopted the technologies that they became popular.[1]

> A **network externality** arises when an additional network member conveys benefits to those already on the network.

Figure 14.2 shows how usage affects demand for a product exhibiting network externalities. It parallels our discussion of costs in Chapter 7. There, we saw that firms have different cost curves in the short run and long run. Even when short-run cost curves are U-shaped, long-run average costs may fall for a long time, exhibiting scale economies in production. Producing more can lower average costs.

1 These, and many other, fascinating examples are quoted in Carl Shapiro and Hal Varian, *Information Rules*, Harvard University Press, 1999.

Network externalities give rise to a similar phenomenon on the demand side: cutting prices can boost demand a lot, especially in the long run. Figure 14.2 shows the initial short-run demand curve D_1D_1, the demand for the product for a *given* number of users already on the network. Suppose A is the point at which the number of people using the network is the same as in the previous period. There is no reason for the demand curve to shift.

Now, however, suppose the supplier cut the price and induced extra customers today, moving down the demand curve D_1D_1 from A to B. With more people on the network, the product is now more valuable to everyone and the demand curve shifts up next period to D_2D_2. At the price p_2 the quantity demanded then rises to q_2. Further reductions in the price will shift the short-run demand curve even further to the right. The long-run demand curve DD, formed by joining up points such as A and C, is more elastic than the short-run demand curve.

Even without switching costs, network externalities may justify a price subsidy – even free provision – early in the life of a product. The supplier is investing in enhancing the network. Once customers build up, the price can be raised.

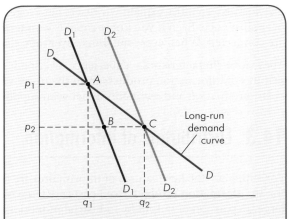

Each short-run demand curve reflects the number of people already using the network. Reducing the price from p_1 to p_2 not only causes a move from A to B it also induces a shift in demand curve since the network is more valuable. The long-run demand curve, joining points such as A and C, is more elastic.

Figure 14.2 A demand curve with network externalities

Box 14.3 *Britannica* shelved

Serious parents used to purchase their children a bookshelf filled with *Encyclopaedia Britannica* (www.britannica.co.uk). This prestige reference work was the market leader for two centuries after its launch in 1768, despite commanding a premium price, which peaked at £1000. Annual sales reached £450 million in 1990. Since 1990 sales revenue has collapsed. The CD-ROM destroyed the printed encyclopaedia. The marginal cost of making a CD-ROM is about £1. The marginal cost of *Encyclopaedia Britannica* had been about £150 for the books, plus several hundred pounds in commission for the doorstep salesforce.

The first challenge came when Microsoft decided to produce software for an encyclopaedia, called *Encarta*, at a thirtieth of the price of *Britannica*. *Encarta* was not only cheaper but also easier to carry around. Being shorter, it fitted on a single CD-ROM. *Britannica* was not brought down by a new entrant to the 24-volume book business but by a new technology that changed the nature of the niche.

During the 1990s, *Britannica* gradually figured out how best to respond to *Encarta*'s entry. It produced its own CD-ROM. The door-to-door salesforce got fired. Those using computers pay more attention to website advertising than doorstep sales patter. *Britannica* has tried to emphasize that, now with similar technology to *Encarta*, it remains longer and therefore more informative. *Encarta* is trying to get bigger to undermine the new niche that *Britannica* is hoping to create. Nowadays, a hardback set of *Britannica* costs almost £1000 but you can buy a DVD for £60, and *Encarta* for around £40.

Alternatively, you can visit the free online encyclopaedia Wikipedia at www.wikipedia.org, which has 75 000 active volunteers working on over 5 million articles in 100 languages.

Sources: P. Evans and T. Wurster, *Blown to Bits*, Harvard Business School Press, 1999; R. Melcher, 'Dusting off the Britannica', *Business Week*, 20 October 1997.

Network externalities explain why users herd together, slow to take up the new product then crossing over all at once. Even if you know email is wonderful, it is no use until your friends (and customers) are connected. When everyone thinks everyone else is ready, people all switch within a very short time.

These four characteristics – experience, overload, switching costs and network externalities – are key features of information products from the users' viewpoint. We turn now to the special features of costs, production and competition between suppliers.

14.3 Distributors of information

For suppliers, the key features of information are that it is expensive to create but cheap to distribute: for an information product, fixed costs are large but marginal costs tiny. Hence, scale economies are large. Expansion of output by industrial monopolists is eventually limited by their existing capacity, but reproduction of information products faces no such capacity constraint. The industrial economy was made up largely of oligopolists – Ford, Vauxhall, Fiat, etc. – but we should expect the information economy to be made up largely of monopolies. Moreover, as demonstrated by the precocious childhood of companies like Amazon, Yahoo! and Freeserve, even existing monopolists are always under threat from unexpected newcomers.

From our discussion in Chapters 8 and 9, you would expect – correctly – that these monopolies would take one of two forms. The first is a dominant firm with a fringe of smaller competitors. Microsoft, inventor of DOS and then Windows, fits the bill. Microsoft's income stream is now so large that, like Boeing in the airliner business, it can devote vast sums to R&D. Both enjoy huge scale economies and have become the low-cost producer of the industry's standard product.

Other forms of monopoly operate in smaller, niche markets, carefully targeted on particular groups of consumers whose diversity of preferences allows these niches to co-exist. Internet firms distribute many products, from airline tickets to dealings in stocks and shares. Monopolistic competition describes these market structures well. However, since the incumbent's advantage depends on the segmentation of the market into small niches, its temporary monopoly is vulnerable to competitors who can jump across niches. Amazon soon realized it had no reason to confine its activities to internet sales of books alone.

Monopolistic competition is consistent with entry and exit. The past few years have seen lots of both. Entry was easier than the incumbents had hoped, so many of their niches were harder to defend than they initially anticipated. When the market was flooded with entrants, few firms could make a profit. When the bubble burst, many firms went bankrupt and exited the industry. We discuss the boom and bust at the end of the chapter.

Pricing information products

Armed only with the preceding chapters, you set up as a consultant (on the internet, of course) to advise firms on how to price information products. Since marginal cost is very low, you expect to drive marginal revenue down almost to zero. But you also want to make profits. Like a phone company, you should use a two-part tariff.

Does anyone implement this on the internet? AOL, BT and Wanadoo charge an annual membership fee and then provide free services. Economic theory suggests that in the long run some form of annual fee may be part of the solution. Internet suppliers need to earn revenue just like every other business. Unless they can make this revenue from advertising or from selling customer information to other suppliers, membership fees may become part of how pricing develops.

> A **two-part tariff** levies an annual charge to cover fixed costs, and a small price per unit related to marginal cost.

Another lesson you will remember from Chapter 8 is that a monopolist earns more by price discriminating than by charging a uniform price. In revenue terms, the latter allows it to earn the best available rectangle (price × quantity) under the demand curve, whereas perfect price discrimination – a different price for each customer – allows the monopolist the entire (much larger) area under the demand curve.

Where suppliers simply quote a price without knowing the characteristics of the buyer that will show up, it is hard to price discriminate. Sometimes, differences in buyers are obvious, as with package holidaymakers and business travellers. However, in many instances, suppliers of goods and services have simply not been able to engage in much price discrimination.

The information revolution means that suppliers often have detailed data on individual buyers. This lets them price discriminate, quoting different prices to different customers based on the actual or likely characteristics of the customer. Since this yields so much more revenue, suppliers are willing to buy lists of customer information from other suppliers. So far, Chapters 8 and 9 are standing you in good stead. Let's look at price discrimination in more detail.

What we have described to date is customer-specific price discrimination. Nice work if you can get it. However, distributors of information products have two other tricks even when they cannot buy or establish information about particular customers.

Versioning

Why do publishers supply both hardback and paperback versions of a book, and at very different prices? It is a form of price discrimination to raise total sales revenue. Note that the 'benefit' of the hardback, that justifies the higher price, is not just its superior physical quality. It is also the fact that it comes out several months earlier. In the information business, old news is no news.

We'll take a bet that you are reading a paperback version of this textbook. It is a safe bet, since there is no hardback version! Delaying publication makes little sense when a student's course starts at a particular time; nor do students need the book to last for 20 years (even though the principles continue to be relevant!). So little *additional* benefit can be created for a hardback version; given the additional production costs, it is not worth doing it.

> **Versioning** is the deliberate creation of different qualities to facilitate price discrimination.

On the internet, the cost calculation is different. Once the product exists, packaging it in various forms incurs little extra cost. Marginal cost of all versions is close to zero. Even small revenue gains from differentiating the product to achieve price discrimination are worthwhile.

Sometimes this involves making one version of the product deliberately worse in order to enhance the value of the premium version. Think again about airlines, whose scheduled flights have economy class and business class. Do businessmen really need a continuous diet of smoked salmon? Is it really optimal to squeeze economy passengers in quite so tight?

Even within Europe, business fares can cost double an economy fare; on transatlantic flights the difference can be between £3000 for a business fare and £500 for a standard economy fare. Anything that makes people choose business class rather than economy is very profitable. It may enhance revenue to make economy class worse than it need have been.[2] Once again, suppliers of information products, who have made a fine art out of versioning, are merely taking previous ideas to their logical conclusion.

---

2 This trick is over 100 years old. Dupuit, a nineteenth-century French economist who was an early advocate of marginal cost pricing in state-run activities, noted that railway companies deliberately provided no roof for third-class carriages in order to boost the demand for second class, where much more revenue could be earned (quoted in Hal Varian, 'Versioning Information Goods', mimeo, University of California at Berkeley, 1997).

Bundling

Versioning creates different qualities of the same product in order to allow price discrimination. It occurs when suppliers do not know the characteristics of any individual, but can guess differences across groups of potential purchasers. A different tactic of suppliers is bundling.

> **Bundling** is the joint supply of more than one product to reduce the need for price discrimination.

Price discrimination is needed only when different customers behave differently. Suppose one really wants a news channel and another really wants a sports channel. Table 14.2 shows the valuations Edward and Camilla put on each channel. Their tastes for a particular channel differ a lot. Their tastes for a bundle of channels are more similar.

Table 14.2 Bundling TV channels (user value in £000s)

	News	Sports
Edward	6	10
Camilla	10	6

If Sky TV knows the exact characteristics of each viewer, it gets £32 000 in revenue by perfect price discrimination. It charges Edward £6000 to receive the news channel, and £10 000 for the sports channel; and charges Camilla £10 000 for the news channel and £6000 for the sports channel. If the prices were higher, Edward and Camilla would not sign up to Sky TV.

Now assume Sky executives do not have enough detailed information about users to charge different prices to different people. They have to set a single price per channel. For the news channel, if they charge £10 000 only Camilla will sign up. If they charge £6000 they can get both to sign up. Sky does best by charging £6000 for each channel, making £24 000 total revenue (2 × 2 × £6000). This is way below the £32 000 that price discrimination would yield. However, to sell a channel to the second subscriber, Sky has to cut the price a lot for the person who would have happily paid more.

Bundling reduces this diversity of tastes. Suppose Sky only offers the two channels as a package. Edward would pay up to £16 000 to get both, so would Camilla. Sky gets £32 000. Bundling is just as good as perfect price discrimination in this example because Edward and Camilla place the same total value on the total package. By bundling news, sports and film channels, Sky TV gets more revenue than by selling channels separately at a uniform price to each user.

Although bundling beats uniform pricing across users, it is usually less effective than perfect price discrimination. Suppose in Table 14.2 that the sports channel is worth £4000 rather than £6000 to Camilla. The most she will pay for a total package is £14 000. Selling a package for £14 000 to each of Edward and Camilla earns Sky £28 000. Note that since Edward still values the total at £16 000, price discrimination across users would earn Sky (£16 000 + £14 000), an extra £2000 in revenue for Sky. However, Sky's informational requirement about individual customers would then be huge. Bundling is often the best suppliers can do in the circumstances. You get bundled all the time. That's why the Sunday papers have all these sections, and why tour operators offer holidays with a week in Florence plus a week on an Adriatic beach. Perhaps Camilla likes frescoes more than Edward, who prefers swimming.

Competition versus collaboration

Bundling suggests that most products have more than one attribute or component. From this it is a short step to the idea that different components are made by *different* firms. More generally, the production and sales of products that are complements not substitutes is increasingly prevalent.

Activity box 14 The fine art of price discrimination

If two individual customers have different demand curves from one another, they will have different marginal revenue schedules MR_1 and MR_2. A profit-maximizing producer with the same marginal cost of supplying each of these customers will always want $MC = MR_1 = MR_2$. Generally, this requires charging different prices to the different customers. If it is possible, price discrimination is profitable. *Bundling* reduces the need for price discrimination by supplying joint products – news and sports, museums and beaches – for which demand curves are more similar across people. *Versioning* is the creation of different qualities in order to charge different prices to different customers. Quality differences make it harder for customers to switch between products in response to price differences.

Note that these types of price discrimination are based on demand differences across customers. Different prices may also reflect different marginal costs of supply and have nothing to do with demand. For example, if life expectancy of women is several years longer than that of men, an insurance company will wish to charge different prices to men and women. Saga has a minimum age limit, thereby excluding costly young people for which the statistics show that the risk of accidents is greater.

Sheilas' Wheels is not an Australian insurance company but rather a division of esure – one of the UK's leading direct insurers. esure understood that women drivers were statistically lower risk than men and opposed an EU directive for equal premiums that in practice would have seen women forced to subsidize men through their car insurance premiums. By supplying insurance to women alone, Sheilas' Wheels can charge the appropriate price to women without having to offer the same price to men.

Questions

In the examples below, state the source of the motive for price discrimination:

(a) Seats in the Grand Circle of the theatre are more expensive.

(b) Off-peak gym membership is cheaper.

(c) Buy one get one free.

(d) Discounts on health insurance for non-smokers.

(e) The Sky TV/internet/telephone package.

To check your answers to these questions, go to page 721.

Software and hardware is an obvious example. Most Microsoft products operated in computers driven by Intel chips. Nowadays, Apple is unusual in producing both hardware and software. Apple's early success was gradually overhauled by the strategic alliance of Microsoft and Intel.

Strategic alliances are occurring in other industries. For example, BA is currently in the One World partnership with Canadian Airlines, Qantas, Finnair, Iberia and American Airlines. These alliances allow the different partners to specialize in segments that largely complement one another – travel within the Americas, travel across the Atlantic and within Europe, and travel within Asia and Australasia.

> A **strategic alliance** is a blend of co-operation and competition in which a group of suppliers provide a range of products that partly complement one another.

Alliances seek many of the benefits that occur when vertical integration of different production stages occurs within any firm – cost reduction from closer co-ordination and greater specialization. However, an alliance is not a complete merger. It preserves a degree of competition, even between the partners. This keeps partners on their toes and helps assure customers that future profit margins will not become excessive. Whenever switching costs play a prominent role, current users will pay considerable attention to such signals about possible future behaviour of suppliers.

14.4 Setting standards

One process in which strategic alliances are especially useful is in the competition to set standards, norms around which economic behaviour is organized.

The UK decision to drive on the left is one standard, the width of railway tracks another, the type of electric plug socket a third. Each is a strong example of a network externality. There is little point having an AC power supply if the rest of the country has DC power supply.

Standards are originally determined by the outcome of competition, which may be economic, political or both. Strategic alliances help tip the balance in favour of the standard those partners want by demonstrating that a number of key players are already on this particular network. Underpopulated networks are not worth joining. Sometimes differences in standards are the easiest way to distinguish one network from another.

> A **standard** is the technical specification that is common throughout a particular network.

Typically, as a result of this initial competition to set the standard, one standard is increasingly adopted by everyone. For some of the early networks, this is a valuable triumph as their own standard becomes adopted more widely. Other networks wither as theirs is rejected. Sony ploughed a lot of R&D into the Betamax technology for video cassette recorders, but the world adopted its rival, the VHS system.

Alliances, explicit or implicit, help resolve the standards war in favour of the well organized. Why did UK mobile phone company Vodafone launch a takeover bid for its US counterpart Air Touch, rather than the other way round? The answer lies in standard setting. Early in the 1990s the Europeans agreed a standard for mobile telephony, creating sufficient of a single market to let European firms grow rapidly and enjoy scale economies. American firms were not late into the game. Rather, they had three competing standards and never managed to agree which to adopt. While US firms competed with one another inside fragmented regional markets, the Europeans forged ahead to such an extent that their standard was quickly adopted in other continents.

Once standards have been set, competition switches from rivalry over standards to rivalry within the standard. As we explained earlier, this often leads either to a dominant firm (e.g. Microsoft, Intel) using its scale to achieve cost advantages over rivals in current production and greater R&D to sustain this position in the future; or else to a series of temporary monopolies in niche markets, well described by the monopolistic competition model in Chapter 9.

14.5 Recap

So far, two lessons stand out. First, while the information revolution is changing our lives, few of its activities or market tactics are unprecedented. The cost of distributing information has been falling since the printing press was invented. The history of industries such as newspapers, book publishing and telephones already contains examples of most of the phenomena we described in the chapter. Standards, bundling, versioning, alliances, price discrimination, selling customer lists, switching costs – we've seen them all before. What is new about the information economy is the extent to which these tactics are routinely practised.

Second, the revolution in technology has not required any corresponding revolution in economic theory. The existing laws of economics work just fine. Indeed, they are much the best way to make sense of what is happening.

14.6 Boom and bust of the dotcom companies

The stock market boom in dotcom companies peaked in December 1999. Figure 14.3 shows how the value of Microsoft, Amazon and Yahoo! had soared in only a few years, valuing them at or above the value of industrial giant General Motors. On both sides of the Atlantic, investors blindly piled into TMT shares, those in Technology, Media and Telecommunications that seemed the main beneficiaries of the new information economy.

Some students have conservative views and like reading *The Times*. Others hate its politics but like its crossword. Both get to read acerbic columns by its Economics Editor, Anatole Kaletsky. Every January, Kaletsky makes predictions for the coming year. In January 2000, at the height of the stock market boom in internet companies, he bravely forecast that their share prices would halve within a year. It turned out to be an underestimate of the fall.

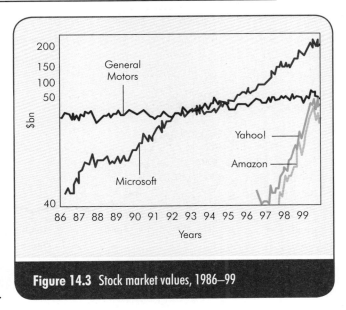

Figure 14.3 Stock market values, 1986–99

Within ten months he was reporting on the carnage:

> I was driving around San Francisco and found my way blocked by a delivery truck from Webvan.com. I recalled that this online delivery company was expected last year to become the biggest food business in America, but was soon forced to cut back its operations to just a few towns. … Another sure-fire winner was stamps.com, a company briefly worth almost $1 billion, after acquiring a supposedly priceless asset, the first licence from the American Government to sell postage stamps online. … It is becoming apparent that all internet companies, including even the giants, are as grotesquely overvalued as were the industrial giants of Japan in the bubble economy of 1989. If this is true, then the massacre of internet and technology firms has hardly even begun. This may be hard to believe for investors in companies such as Yahoo! who have already suffered losses of 70 per cent from this year's peak, Amazon.com (down 75 per cent), or even Microsoft (down 55 per cent).
>
> (*The Times*, 20 October 2000)

He was right again. In October 2000, 'new economy' companies took a further battering. Figure 14.4 shows the rise and fall of share prices in online giants Amazon and Yahoo!, and of the Nasdaq index of high-tech stocks.

Yahoo! had fallen from a peak share price of around $220 to a low of $11, a fall of 95 per cent. In the courtroom-addicted United States, people sued investment banks whose so-called experts advised people to invest in these stocks just before they collapsed. Why couldn't people see it coming?

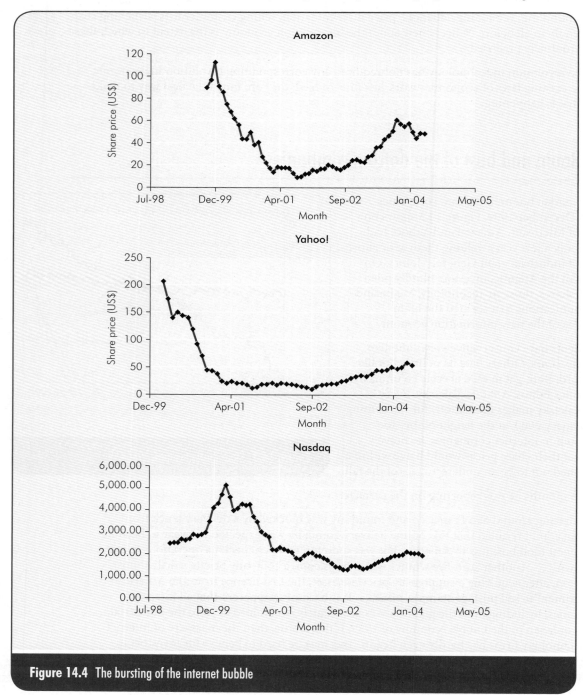

Figure 14.4 The bursting of the internet bubble

Asset price bubbles

Suppose the 'right' price of a share is £10. This price is justified by the 'fundamentals' of the company, sensible projections of its future performance. Suppose everybody agrees what these are. Everybody agrees what the right price is. One equilibrium is that the price is £10. Disturbingly, there are other equilibria.

Could £11 be an equilibrium for the share price today? Anything other than £10 is called a bubble, a departure from the fundamentals.

Suppose the market thinks there is a 50 per cent chance the bubble will continue tomorrow, and a 50 per cent chance it will burst. If it bursts, the share reverts to its fundamentals price.

> An **asset price bubble** is a departure of the price from that justified by fundamental characteristics of the asset. Bubbles are self-fulfilling prophecies.

You wonder whether to hold the share that is currently trading at £11. If the bubble bursts, you lose £1 because tomorrow the price will be £10. Suppose you think the price will go up to £12 if the bubble doesn't burst. Hence you have a 50 per cent chance of making £1 and a 50 per cent chance of losing £1. The market is offering you a fair bet. You are happy to hold the share at £11.

Tomorrow arrives and, as it happens, the bubble has not burst. The price is now £12. Should you keep holding the share? Now a bust means you lose £2 if the price reverts to £10. But you will still happily hold the share if you think that, provided the bubble continues, the price will be £14 tomorrow. You then have a 50–50 chance of winning or losing £2.

Maybe the bubble then bursts. If not, the next day the price stands at £14, and it takes the belief that it will rise to £18 – a possible gain of £4 to offset the danger of a loss of £4 – to keep you on the speculative bandwagon.

The key feature of asset price bubbles is therefore that the price must *accelerate* while the bubble lasts. Every extra day, the price is dangerously further from the sane price implied by the fundamentals, and it takes the lure of an ever-larger gain to offset this risk.

Eventually the bubble bursts. Precisely when is impossible to predict. But the bubble could last a while. During this period, everyone knows a bubble is going on, but a clear financial calculation makes it rational to participate.

In the preceding example, a bubble could arise even though everyone agreed on the price implied by the fundamentals. An additional difficulty in the case of dotcom companies was that estimates of the prices implied by fundamentals differed greatly. Would new business opportunities expand at 8 per cent a year, 12 per cent a year or 20 per cent a year? Extrapolations over the next 20 years yielded radically different answers depending on which growth rate was assumed. And past evidence was only vaguely relevant to making future guestimates for this new technology.

The past few years have provided the first data with which to make better assessments. We now know that take-up of the next generation of mobile phones, with full internet capability, has been slower than originally forecast. It is not merely the quantities of activity that have now been reassessed: the greatest change of mind has concerned the ability to earn revenue and hence make profits.

> Things look a little gloomy for the telecommunications companies that paid a total of £22.5 billion for UK third generation mobile telephone licences in April last year.
>
> (*Financial Times*, 28 March 2001)

The *Financial Times* then went on to note:

> 'classical economics' dictates that licences are a 'sunk cost' which cannot be reclaimed. ... If companies holding licences would not have colluded to push up prices before the auctions for licences had been dreamt up, so this argument goes, they will not do so afterwards.

The *Financial Times* noted that fears of bankruptcy might make phone companies so desperate that they will find a way to behave like OPEC, getting together to collude to raise prices and inhibit competition. Whether or not they would get away with it depends partly on how watchful the telephone regulator turns out to be.

Mobile phones are an example of where the new technology *was* profitable, but the government, by auctioning off the right to use the airwaves, managed to grab these profits for the taxpayer. Since the auction occurred at the peak of the optimism, with hindsight the phone companies bid too much. That is why their finances suddenly took a dive.

In other cases, the bad news came not from the government appropriating the profits but from the (distant prospect of profits) being competed away by ever more entry of new firms into the same market. Everyone wanted to start their own Lastminute.com. As the market flooded, and estimates rose of the time the initial loss-making phase would continue, the ability to survive often depended more on a firm's relations with its bankers than the soundness of its underlying idea.

Markets that can be exuberantly high can also overreact to the subsequent fall. Figure 14.4 shows that the staggering losses during 1999–2002 were followed by spectacular gains during 2003–04. Gains have not continued at this pace subsequently.

Summary

- **Information** is expensive to produce but very cheap to copy and distribute.

- From the users' viewpoint, e-products have four key attributes: experience, overload, switching costs and network externalities. Buyers' need to **experience** explains why sellers allow sampling and browsing. Sellers also invest in a good reputation to reduce the need for buyers to sample. Potential **information overload** explains why specialist agents develop to pre-screen material.

- **Switching costs** make future opportunities depend on current choices. Users should therefore take a long-run view from the outset. It is optimal for sellers to subsidize initial use and to manufacture artificial switching costs using reward schemes for loyalty.

- **Network externalities** arise when the value of a network depends on how densely it is populated. Producers will respond by subsidizing early entry to the network.

- Information products, with high fixed costs but low marginal cost, are potential monopolies. R&D, learning by doing, switching costs and network externalities may lead to natural monopolies. Where niche markets are smaller, monopolistic competition may prevail. Many existing markets are contestable by new entrants, so many monopolies are temporary.

- Monopolists want to **price discriminate** when users differ. Information technology may allow **personalized pricing**. Otherwise, sellers produce different **versions** of the product, to make discrimination easier, or **bundle** different products to reduce the need for discrimination.

- **Standards** are a key feature of a **network**. Initially, there is competition between networks to set the standard. Once one standard is dominant, there is competition within the network to supply according to that standard.

- Share prices of dotcom companies rose incredibly rapidly in the late 1990s. Since January 2000 many share prices have fallen by 80 or 90 per cent, and some firms have gone bankrupt. This does not mean that the new technologies were unwanted. More often it reflected anticipated profits being delayed or competed away by new entrants.

- An **asset price bubble** is a self-fulfilling prophecy about a departure of the asset price from the fundamentals. Staying on a bubble requires an acceleration of price growth. Hence eventually all bubbles burst.

- People know bubbles will burst, but if they knew when a bubble would burst they would get out in advance, bringing forward the burst. The bursting of a bubble is a random event.

Review questions

To check your answers to these questions, go to page 721.

1 You get invited to a free day 'trial membership' of a David Lloyd Sports Club. Is this because the product (a) has aspects of an experience good, (b) has network externalities, or (c) has switching costs?

2 Why do most undergraduate courses require students to take particular courses in their first year but give them a wide range of options in their final year? Of which supplier tactic in the chapter is this an example?

3 Give three of your own examples of versioning.

4 'If price discrimination is good for producers, it must be bad for consumers.' Do you agree? Does it matter which consumer you are?

5 What is the difference between a strategic alliance and a cartel?

6 **Common fallacies** Why are these statements wrong? (a) The internet is free, so fortunately it has little to do with economics. (b) Price discrimination requires monopoly and must therefore be bad. (c) Firms currently losing money cannot justify high share prices.

7 **Harder question** You are Chief Justice of the newly appointed Global Supreme Court, and you have just argued in favour of allowing Microsoft's dominant position to continue. What arguments did you use?

8 **Harder question** You are setting up a new network. There are three women and three men in the world, all at present belonging to a different network from which they each get a benefit of 1 whatever their gender. If all six people switch to your network, each man gets a benefit of 2 and each woman a benefit of 3. If fewer than six switch, there is no benefit to anyone from joining your network. (a) In the absence of switching costs, will individuals decide to join your network? (b) How could you co-ordinate them so that they all join? (c) If the switching cost is 1, who will join your network? (d) Is there any way to get them all to join?

9 **Essay question** 'The advent of the internet has led to many new forms of behaviour. It is a natural experiment with which to test the robustness of the laws of economics, which pass the test with flying colours.' Do you agree? Are there examples that economics has difficulty explaining?

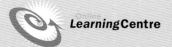 *Online* **LearningCentre**

To help you grasp the key concepts of this chapter check out the extra resources posted on the Online Learning Centre. There are chapter summaries, self-test questions, an interactive graphing tool, weblinks and a searchable glossary, all for free!

To put your learning into practice and prepare for exams, an **Interactive Workbook** is also available online, containing a variety of question types and providing feedback on your answers.

If you'd like further help with economics, or have any questions, **NetTutor** is here to help! You will have a personalised tutorial service at your fingertips. Visit the online learning centre at: www.mcgraw-hill.co.uk/textbooks/begg for information on accessing all of these resources.

PART THREE

Welfare economics

Normative or welfare economics is concerned with making value judgements and using these to recommend which policies are desirable. Much of economics is about reconciling the goals of efficiency and fairness. Part 3 discusses reasons for market failures that give rise to inefficiencies, then investigates how government might intervene to improve the market. Such intervention may itself be subject to failures: well-meaning intervention can sometimes make things worse. As globalization begins to undermine the economic sovereignty of nation states, it is also necessary to think about when national policies will suffice and when cross-border co-operation is beneficial.

Chapter 15 introduces welfare economics, defines efficiency and equity (fairness), and examines reasons for market failure. Chapter 16 focuses on direct government intervention through taxes and public spending. Chapter 17 deals with government attempts to influence the market through industrial policy and competition policy. Chapter 18 discusses whether natural monopolies should be taken over by the state or regulated in the private sector.

Contents

Welfare economics

Learning Outcomes

By the end of this chapter, you should understand:

1 what we mean by welfare economics

2 horizontal and vertical equity

3 the concept of Pareto efficiency

4 how the 'invisible hand' may achieve efficiency

5 the concept of market failure

6 why partial removal of distortions may be harmful

7 the problem of externalities and possible solutions

8 how monopoly power causes market failure

9 distortions from pollution and congestion

10 why missing markets create distortions

11 the economics of climate change

Chapter 1 noted that markets are not the only way society can resolve what, how and for whom to produce. Communist economies relied heavily on central direction or command. Are markets a good way to allocate scarce resources? What is a 'good' way? Is it fair that some people earn much more than others in a market economy? These are not positive issues about how the economy works but normative issues about how well it works. They are normative because the assessment depends on the value judgements adopted by the assessor.

Left- and right-wing parties disagree about how well a market economy works. The right believes the market fosters choice, incentives and efficiency. The left emphasizes the market's failings and the need for government intervention. What lies behind the disagreement? Two themes recur in our discussion of welfare economics in Part 3. The first is *allocative efficiency*. Is the economy getting the most out of its scarce resources or are they being squandered? The second is *equity*. How fair is the *distribution* of goods and services among different members of society?

> **Welfare economics** deals with normative issues. It does not describe how the economy works but assesses how well it works.

15.1 Equity and efficiency

Equity

Whether or not either concept of equity – horizontal or vertical – is desirable is a pure value judgement. Horizontal equity rules out discrimination between people whose economic characteristics and performance are identical. Vertical equity is the Robin Hood principle of taking from the rich to give to the poor.

Many people agree that horizontal equity is a good thing. In contrast, although few people believe that the poor should starve, the extent to which resources should be redistributed from the 'haves' to the 'have-nots' to increase vertical equity is an issue on which people disagree.

> **Horizontal equity** is the identical treatment of identical people. **Vertical equity** is the different treatment of different people in order to reduce the consequences of these innate differences.

Efficient resource allocation

Suppose that allocations are made by a central dictator. Feasible allocations depend on the technology and resources available to the economy. The ultimate worth of any allocation depends on consumer tastes – how people value what they are given.

> A **resource allocation** is a complete description of who does what and who gets what.

Figure 15.1 shows an economy with only two people, David and Susie. The initial allocation at A gives David a quantity of goods Q_D and Susie a quantity Q_S. Are society's resources being wasted? By reorganizing things, suppose society can produce at B, to the north-east of A. If David and Susie assess utility by the quantity of goods they get themselves, and if they would each rather have more goods than less, B is a better allocation than A. Both David and Susie get more. It is inefficient to produce at A if production at B is possible. Similarly, a move from A to C makes both David and Susie worse off. If it is possible to be at A, it is inefficient to be at C.

What about a move from A to E or F? One person gains, the other person loses. Whether this change is desirable depends on how we value David's utility relative to Susie's. If we think David's utility is very important we might prefer A to F, even though Susie's utility is reduced.

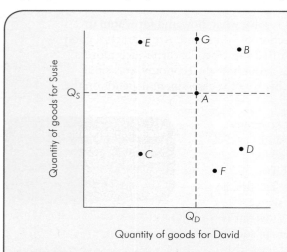

Provided people assess their own utility by the quantity of goods that they themselves receive, B is a better allocation than A which in turn is a better allocation than C. But a comparison of A with points such as D, E or F, requires us to adopt a value judgement about the relative importance to us of David's and Susie's utility.

Figure 15.1 Allocating goods to two people

Value judgements about equity or fairness get mixed up with our attempt to make statements about waste or inefficiency. Since different people will make different value judgements, there is no unambiguous answer to the question of whether a move from A to D, E or F is desirable. It depends who makes the assessment.

To try to separate the discussion of equity from the discussion of efficiency, modern welfare economics uses the idea of *Pareto efficiency*, named after the economist Vilfredo Pareto.

For a given set of consumer tastes, resources and technology, an allocation is **Pareto-efficient** if there is no other feasible allocation that makes some people better off and nobody worse off.

In Figure 15.1 a move from A to B or A to G is a *Pareto gain*. Susie is better off, David no worse off. If B or G is feasible, A is *Pareto-inefficient*. A free lunch is available.

A move from A to D makes David better off but Susie worse off. The Pareto criterion has nothing to say about this change. To evaluate it, we need a judgement about the relative value of David's and Susie's utility. The Pareto principle is of limited use in comparing allocations on efficiency grounds. It only allows us to evaluate moves to the north-east or the south-west in Figure 15.1. Yet it is the most we can say about efficiency without making value judgements about equity.

Figure 15.2 takes the argument a stage further. By reorganizing production, we can make the economy produce anywhere inside or on the frontier AB. From inside the frontier, a Pareto gain can be achieved by moving to the north-east on to the frontier. Any point inside the frontier is Pareto-inefficient. Someone can be made better off without making the other worse off. But *all* points on the frontier are Pareto-efficient. One person can get more only by giving the other person less. Since no Pareto gain is possible, every point on the frontier is Pareto-efficient.

Thus society should never choose an inefficient allocation inside the frontier. Which of the efficient points on the frontier is most desirable will depend on the value judgement about the relative value of David's and Susie's utility, a judgement about equity.

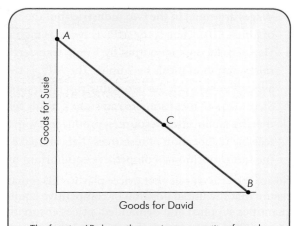

The frontier AB shows the maximum quantity of goods which the economy can produce for one person given the quantity of goods being produced for the other person. All points on the frontier are Pareto-efficient. David can only be made better off by making Susie worse off, and vice versa. The distribution of goods between David and Susie is much more equal at point C than at points A or B.

Figure 15.2 The efficient frontier

15.2 Perfect competition and Pareto efficiency

Will a free market economy find a Pareto-efficient allocation, or must it be guided there by government intervention?

Competitive equilibrium in free markets

Suppose there are many producers and many consumers, but only two goods, meals and films. Each market is a free, unregulated market and is perfectly competitive. In equilibrium, suppose the price of meals is £5 and the price of films is £10. Labour is the variable factor of production and workers can move freely between industries. We now argue through seven steps:

1   The last film yields consumers £10 worth of extra utility. If it yielded less (more) extra utility than its £10 purchase price, the last consumer would buy fewer (more) films. Similarly, the last meal must yield consumers £5 worth of extra utility. Hence consumers could swap 2 meals (£10 worth of utility) for 1 film (£10 worth of utility) without changing their utility.

2   Since each firm sets price equal to marginal cost MC, the MC of the last meal is £5 and the MC of the last film is £10.

3   Labour earns the same wage rate in both industries in competitive equilibrium. Otherwise, workers would move to the industry offering higher wages.

4   The MC of output in either industry is the wage divided by the marginal physical product of labour MPL. Higher wages raise marginal cost, but a higher MPL means fewer extra workers are needed to make an extra unit of output.

5   Wages are equal in the two industries but the marginal cost of meals (£5) is half the marginal cost of films (£10). Hence, the MPL is twice as high in the meal as in the film industry.

6   Hence reducing film output by 1 unit, transferring the labour thus freed to the meals industry, raises output of meals by 2 units. The MPL is twice as high in meals as in films. Feasible resource allocation between the two industries allows society to swap 2 meals for 1 film.

7   Step 1 says that consumers can swap 2 meals for 1 film without changing their utility. Step 6 says that, by reallocating resources, producers swap an output of 2 meals for 1 film. Hence there is no feasible reallocation of resources that can make society better off. Since no Pareto gain is possible, the initial position – competitive equilibrium in both markets – is Pareto-efficient.

Notice the crucial role that prices play in this remarkable result. Prices do two things. First, they ensure that the initial position of competitive equilibrium is indeed an *equilibrium*. By balancing the quantities supplied and demanded, prices ensure that the final quantity of goods being consumed can be produced. They ensure that it is a feasible allocation.

But in *competitive* equilibrium prices perform a second role. Each consumer and each producer is a price-taker and cannot affect market prices. In our example, each consumer knows that the equilibrium price of meals is £5 and the equilibrium price of films is £10. Knowing nothing about the actions of other consumers and producers, each consumer automatically ensures that the last film purchased yields twice as much utility as the last meal purchased. Otherwise that consumer could rearrange purchases out of a given income to increase her utility.

Thus by her individual actions facing given prices, each consumer arranges that 1 film could be swapped for 2 meals with no change in utility. Similarly, every producer, merely by setting its own marginal cost equal to the price of its output, ensures that the marginal cost of films is twice the marginal cost of meals. Thus it takes society twice as many resources to make an extra film as it does to make an extra meal. By rearranging production, transferring labour between industries, society can swap 2 meals for 1 film, exactly the trade-off that leaves consumer utility unaffected.

Thus, as if by an 'invisible hand', prices are guiding individual consumers and producers, each pursuing only self-interest, to an allocation of the economy's resources that is Pareto-efficient. Nobody can be made better off without someone else becoming worse off.

Figure 15.3 makes the same point. DD is the market demand curve for one of the goods, say films. At a price P_1, a quantity of films Q_1 is demanded. The last film demanded yields consumers P_1 pounds worth of utility; otherwise they would buy a different quantity. Hence DD shows also the marginal utility of the last unit of films which consumers purchase. When Q_1 films are purchased, the last film yields exactly P_1 pounds worth of extra utility to consumers.

In a competitive industry, the supply curve for films SS is also the marginal cost of films. The variable factor, labour, is paid its marginal value product in each industry. Labour mobility ensures wage rates are equal in the two industries. Hence the marginal cost of making the last film is the value of the meals sacrificed by using the last worker to make films not meals.

Prices ensure that both industries are in equilibrium. Figure 15.3 shows that in equilibrium at E the marginal utility of the last film equals its marginal cost. But the marginal cost of the last film is the value of meals sacrificed, the price of meals multiplied by the meals forgone by using labour to make that last film. However, the meals industry is also in equilibrium. An equivalent diagram for the meals industry shows that the equilibrium price of meals is also the marginal utility of the last meal purchased. Hence the value of meals sacrificed to make the last film is also the marginal utility of the last meal times the number of meals sacrificed.

Thus, provided the *meals* industry is in competitive equilibrium, the marginal cost curve for the *film* industry is the extra pounds worth of utility sacrificed by using scarce resources to make another film instead of extra meals. It is the opportunity cost in utility terms of the resources being used in the film industry. And equilibrium in the film industry, by equating the marginal utility of films to the marginal utility of the meals sacrificed to make the last film, guarantees that society's resources are allocated efficiently.

At any output of films below the equilibrium quantity Q^*, the marginal consumer benefit of another film exceeds the marginal consumer valuation of the meals that would have to be sacrificed to produce that extra film. At any output of films above Q^*, society is devoting too many resources to the film industry. The marginal value of the last film is less than the marginal value of the meals that could have been produced by transferring resources to the meals industry. Competitive equilibrium ensures that there is no resource transfer between industries that would make all consumers better off.

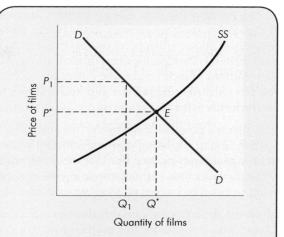

At any output such as Q_1 the last film must yield consumers P_1 pounds worth of extra utility; otherwise they would not demand Q_1. The supply curve SS for the competitive film industry is also the marginal cost of films. If the meals industry is in competitive equilibrium, the price of a meal is also the value of its marginal utility to consumers. Thus the marginal cost of a film is not only its opportunity cost in meals but also the value of the marginal utility consumers would have derived from those meals. Hence at any film output below Q^* the marginal utility of films exceeds the marginal utility of meals sacrificed to produce an extra film. Above Q^* the marginal utility of films is less than the marginal utility of meals sacrificed. The equilibrium point E for films and the corresponding equilibrium point in the market for meals thus ensure that resources are efficiently allocated between the two industries. No reallocation could make all consumers better off.

Figure 15.3 Competitive equilibrium and Pareto efficiency

Equity and efficiency

The previous section showed that there are many Pareto-efficient allocations, each with a different distribution of utility between different members of society. A competitive equilibrium in all markets generates a particular Pareto-efficient allocation. What determines which one?

People have different innate abilities, different human capital and different wealth. These differences mean people earn different incomes in a market economy. They also affect the pattern of consumer demand. Brazil, with a very unequal distribution of income and wealth, has a high demand for luxuries such as servants. In more egalitarian Denmark, nobody can afford servants.

Different inheritances of ability, capital and wealth thus imply different demand curves and determine different equilibrium prices and quantities. In principle, by varying the distribution of initial income-earning potential, we could make the economy pick out each possible Pareto-efficient allocation as its competitive equilibrium.

Here is an attractive idea. The government is elected to express the value judgements of the majority. If the market gets the economy to the Pareto-efficient frontier, the government can make the value judgement about which point on this frontier the economy should attain. Every competitive equilibrium is Pareto-efficient. Different efficient allocations correspond to different initial distributions of income-earning potential in a competitive economy. Can the government confine itself to redistributing income and wealth through taxation and welfare benefits *without having to intervene to ensure that resources are allocated efficiently*?

This seems a powerful case for the free enterprise ideal. The government should let markets get on with the job of allocating resources efficiently. We do not need regulations, investigatory bodies or state-run enterprises. Nor need the free enterprise ideal be uncompassionate. The government can redistribute income without impairing the efficient functioning of a free market economy. The right-wing case can be backed up by rigorous economic arguments.

However, the left-wing case can also be made. Remember the qualifications in the above argument. *Under certain conditions* free markets lead to a Pareto-efficient allocation. These conditions explain the difference between the two views of how a market economy works. The right believes that they are *minor* qualifications that do not seriously challenge the case for a free market economy. The left believes that the qualifications are so serious that substantial government intervention is necessary to *improve* the way the economy works.

15.3 Distortions and the second best

Competitive equilibrium is efficient because the independent actions of producers setting marginal cost equal to price, and consumers setting marginal benefits equal to price, ensure that the marginal cost of producing a good just equals its marginal benefit to consumers.

> A **distortion** exists if society's marginal cost of producing a good does not equal society's marginal benefit from consuming that good.

Taxation as a distortion

To finance subsidies to the poor, a government must tax the incomes of rich people or the goods rich people buy. Suppose everyone buys meals, but only the rich can afford to go to the cinema. A subsidy for the poor can be financed by a tax on films.

In Figure 15.4 the pre-tax price of films to consumers exceeds the post-tax price received by makers of films. The difference between the two prices is the tax on each film. Consumers equate the tax-inclusive price to the value of the marginal benefit they receive from the last film, but suppliers equate the marginal cost of films to the lower net-of-tax price of films.

In competitive equilibrium, the price system no longer equates the social marginal cost of making films with the social marginal benefit of consuming films. The marginal benefit of another film exceeds its marginal cost. The tax on films induces too few films. Making another film adds more to social benefit than to social cost.

Earlier, we showed that the marginal cost of a film equals the value of the extra meals that society could have had instead. When films are taxed, the marginal social benefit of another film exceeds its marginal cost, and hence exceeds the marginal social benefit of the extra meals that society could have had by using resources differently. By transferring labour from meals into films, society could make some people better off without making anyone else worse off.

A similar argument holds for any other commodity we tax. A tax causes a discrepancy between the price the purchaser pays and the price the seller receives. The 'invisible hand' no longer equates marginal social benefits of resources in different uses.

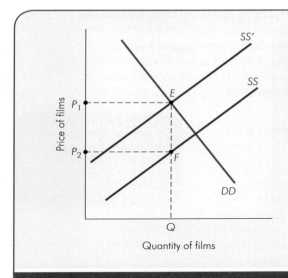

DD shows the demand for films and the marginal benefit of the last film to consumers. SS shows the quantity of films supplied at each price received by producers and is also the marginal social cost of producing films. Suppose each unit of films bears a tax equal to the vertical distance EF. To show the tax-inclusive price required to induce producers to produce each output, we must draw the new supply curve SS' that is a constant vertical distance EF above SS. The equilibrium quantity of films is Q. Consumers pay a price P_1, producers receive a price P_2 and the tax per film is the distance EF. At the equilibrium quantity Q the marginal benefit is P_1 but the marginal social cost is P_2. Society would make a net gain by producing more films. Hence the equilibrium quantity

Figure 15.4 A tax on films

The choice between efficiency and equity is now clear. If the economy is perfectly competitive, and if the government is happy with the current income distribution, competitive free-market equilibrium is efficient and the income distribution desirable.

However, if as a pure value judgement, the government dislikes this income distribution, it has to tax some people to provide subsidies for others. Yet the very act of raising taxes *introduces a distortion.* The resulting equilibrium has a more desirable distribution but is less efficient. Governments may have to make trade-offs between efficiency and equity.

One explanation for differing political attitudes to the market economy is a difference in value judgements about equity. Later, we will see that there may also be disagreements in positive economics. We consider other distortions in the next section. Before leaving our tax example, there is one final point to make.

The second best

When there is no distortion in the market for *meals*, a tax on *films* leads to an inefficient allocation. If we could abolish the tax on films neither industry would be distorted and we get the *first-best* allocation.

Suppose, however, that we cannot get rid of the tax on films. The government needs tax revenue to pay for national defence or its EU budget contribution. Given an unavoidable tax on films, at least it should not tax meals as well.

> The **first-best allocation** has no distortions and is fully efficient.

This plausible view is in fact *quite wrong.* Suppose both industries are in equilibrium but there is a tax on films. Above, we saw that too few films are produced and consumed. By implication, too many meals are therefore produced and consumed. Given an inevitable tax on films, a tax on meals would help not hinder.

A suitable tax on meals could restore the original relative price of meals and films. With only two goods this would restore the first best. However, there is always a third good, leisure. Households reduce consumption of leisure in order to supply labour for work. Taxing meals and films gets the right balance between meals and films, but makes the price of both wrong relative to the price of leisure. With higher taxes, the net wage falls, changing the implicit price of leisure.

In contrast to the *first-best* allocation, when we achieve full efficiency by removing all distortions, we have now developed the principle of the *second best*. Suppose we care only about efficiency but there is an inevitable distortion somewhere else in the economy that we cannot remove. It is inefficient to treat other markets as if that distortion did not exist. In the meals industry it is inefficient to equate private marginal cost and private marginal benefit, the efficient outcome in the absence of a film tax. Rather, it is efficient to deliberately introduce a new distortion in meals to help counterbalance the unavoidable distortion in the meals industry.

The theory of the second best says that, if there must be a distortion, it is a mistake to concentrate the distortion in one market. It is more efficient to spread its effect more thinly over a wide range of markets.

> The **first-best** removes all distortions. The **second-best** is the most efficient outcome that can be achieved conditional on being unable to remove some distortions.

Several applications of this general principle are found in the ensuing chapters. The real world in which we live provides several inevitable distortions. Given their existence, the argument of this section implies that the government may *increase* the overall efficiency of the whole economy by introducing *new* distortions to offset those that already exist. By now you will want to know the source of these inevitable distortions that the government could take action to offset.

15.4 Market failure

In the absence of any distortions, competitive equilibrium is efficient. We use the term *market failure* to cover all the circumstances in which market equilibrium is inefficient. Distortions then prevent the 'invisible hand' from allocating resources efficiently. We now list the possible sources of distortions that lead to market failure.

Imperfect competition

Only perfect competition makes firms equate marginal cost to price and thus to marginal consumer benefit. Under imperfect competition, producers set marginal cost equal to marginal revenue, which is below the price for which the last unit is sold. Since consumers equate price to marginal benefit, marginal benefit exceeds marginal cost in imperfectly competitive industries. Such industries produce too little. Higher output would add more to consumer benefit than to production costs or the opportunity cost of the resources used.

Equity

Redistributive taxation induces allocative distortions by driving a wedge between the price the consumer pays and the price the producer receives.

Externalities

Externalities are things like pollution, noise and congestion. One person's actions have direct costs or benefits for other people, but the individual does not take these into account. Much of the rest of this chapter examines this distortion. The problem arises because there is no market for things like noise. Hence markets and prices cannot ensure that the marginal benefit you get from making a noise equals the marginal cost of that noise to other people.

Other missing markets: future goods, risk and information

These are also commodities for which markets are absent or limited. In Chapter 13 we saw how moral hazard and adverse selection inhibit the setting up of insurance markets to deal with risk. As with externalities, we cannot expect markets to allocate resources efficiently if the markets do not exist.

Box 15.1 Rent seeking

In America, lobbyists get the early plane to Washington, DC. In Europe, they go to Brussels. Over expense-account lunches, the business of persuasion is conducted. What has this to do with efficiency or inefficiency? If the aim is to provide information to policy makers, it is possible that, like informative advertising, efficiency is increased. But lobbying goes much further.

Suppose a lecturer walks into a class and deposits on the table an open suitcase containing £10000 in used banknotes. She gives a brilliant class for an hour, but nobody is listening. The students are working out if there is a way to make off with the loot. Ian Ironfist is worried how to stop his rival Sam Slugger doing likewise. Ironfist and Slugger can be seen in the lecture parting with their own cash to assemble rival armies of students to fight the lunchtime battle for the suitcase. Microeconomic theory absorbed during the hour's lecture? Zero.

Sources of inefficiency? Everybody's time was wasted. At the start of the class, society has one suitcase with £10000, plus loose change in people's pockets. After the lunchtime fight, society will still have one suitcase, £10000 and some loose change. There was no net increase in goods and services during the morning. It was a zero-sum game that had no value added for society. The prospect of economic rent or pure surplus – a suitcase worth £10000 – led the students to spend their valuable resources (cash in their pocket, time available for learning economics) trying to compete for and capture the jackpot. Distributional fights are a source of inefficiency. Successful societies keep these to a minimum.

Government intervention in the economy to offset market failures can, in principle, improve efficiency. It can also create opportunities for rent seeking. Suppose the government regulates the award of franchises to operate railway lines, TV stations or lotteries. Rival bidders use up huge amounts of real resources trying to outdo one another. Privately, winning is so important that it is worth spending a lot to raise the chances of success. But socially it is close to a zero-sum game. One supplier of railway, TV or lottery services may be little better than another. Encouraging competition between prospective suppliers is good only if the social gain from finding the best supplier rather than an inferior one outweighs the social value of the resources the bidders use up in their war to win the award. Where society decides to intervene to combat market failure, it should still think which form of intervention minimizes government failure. Rent seeking is one channel through which such government failure may occur.

15.5 Externalities

A chemical firm discharges waste into a lake, polluting the water. It affects the production of anglers (fewer fish, harder to catch) or the consumption of swimmers (dirty water). Without a 'market' for pollution, the firm can pollute the lake without cost. Its self-interest leads it to pollute until the marginal benefit of polluting (cheaper production of chemicals) equals its own marginal cost of polluting, which is zero. It ignores the marginal cost that pollution imposed on anglers and swimmers.

> An **externality** arises if one person's production or consumption physically affects the production or consumption of others.

Conversely, by painting your house you make the whole street look nicer and give consumption benefits to your neighbour. But you paint only up to the point on which your own marginal benefit equals the marginal cost of the paint you buy and the time you spend. Your marginal costs are also society's marginal costs, but society's marginal benefits exceed your own. Hence, there is too little house painting.

In both cases there is a divergence between the individual's comparison of marginal costs and benefits and society's comparison of marginal costs and benefits. Free markets cannot induce people to take account of indirect effects if there is no market in these indirect effects.

Divergences between private and social costs and benefits

Suppose a chemical firm pollutes a river, the quantity of pollution rising with output. Downstream, companies use river water as an input in making sauce for baked beans. At low chemical output, pollution is negligible. The river dilutes the small amounts of pollutant discharged by the chemical producer. As the discharge rises, the costs of pollution rise sharply. Food processors must worry about water purity, and build expensive purification plants. Still higher levels of pollution start to corrode their pipes.

Figure 15.5 shows the marginal private cost *MPC* of producing chemicals. For simplicity, we treat *MPC* as constant. It also shows the marginal *social cost MSC* of chemical production. At any output, the divergence between marginal private cost and marginal social cost is the marginal *production externality*. The demand curve *DD* shows how much consumers will pay for the output of the chemical producer. If that firm is a price-taker, equilibrium is at *E* and the chemical producer's output is *Q*, at which the marginal private cost equals the price of the firm's output.

At this output *Q*, the marginal social cost *MSC* exceeds the marginal social benefit of chemicals, given by the height of the demand curve *DD*. The market for chemicals ignores the production externality inflicted on other firms. At *Q* the marginal social benefit of the last output unit is less than the marginal social cost inclusive of the production externality. Output *Q* is inefficient. By reducing the output of chemicals, society saves more in social cost than it loses in social benefit. Society could make some people better off without making anyone worse off.

The efficient output is *Q'*, at which the marginal social benefit equals the marginal social cost. *E'* is the efficient point. How much does society lose by producing at the free market equilibrium *E* not the efficient point *E'*? The vertical distance between the marginal social cost *MSC* and the marginal social benefit shows the marginal social loss of producing the last output unit. By overexpanding from *Q'* to *Q*, society loses the triangle *E'FE* in Figure 15.5. This is the social cost of the market failure caused by the production externality of pollution.[1]

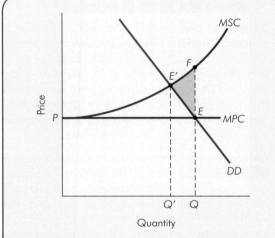

Competitive equilibrium occurs at *E*. The market clears at a price *P* which producers equate to marginal private cost *MPC*. But pollution causes a production externality which makes the marginal social cost *MSC* exceed the marginal private cost. The socially efficient output is at *E'* where marginal social cost and marginal social benefit are equal. The demand curve *DD* measures the marginal social benefit because consumers equate the value of the marginal utility of the last unit to the price. By inducing an output *Q* in excess of the efficient output *Q'* free market equilibrium leads to a social cost equal to the area of the triangle *E'FE*. This shows the excess of social cost over social benefit in moving from *Q'* to *Q*.

Figure 15.5 The social cost of a production externality

Production externalities make social and private marginal costs diverge. A consumption externality makes private and social marginal benefits diverge. Figure 15.6 shows a beneficial consumption externality. Planting roses in your front garden also makes your neighbours happy.

1 Conversely, a farmer who spends money on pest control reduces pests on nearby farms. If production externalities are beneficial, the marginal social cost is below the marginal private cost. Suppose we swap the labels *MSC* and *MPC* in Figure 15.5. Free market equilibrium is at *E'* but *E* is now the efficient allocation.

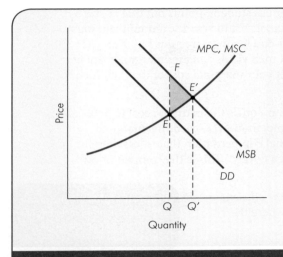

With no production externality, marginal private cost and marginal social cost coincide. *DD* measures the marginal private benefit, and the market equilibrium occurs at *E*. The beneficial consumption externality makes marginal social benefit *MSB* exceed marginal private benefit. *E'* is the socially efficient point. By producing *Q* instead of the efficient output *Q'*, free market equilibrium wastes the triangle *EFE'*.

Figure 15.6 A beneficial consumption externality

With no production externality, *MPC* is both the private and social marginal cost of planting roses. It is the cost of the plants and the opportunity cost of your time. *DD* is the marginal private benefit. Comparing your own costs and benefits, you plant a quantity *Q* of roses.

But you ignore the consumption benefit to your neighbours. The marginal social benefit *MSB* exceeds your marginal private benefit. The free market equilibrium is at *E*, but the efficient output is *Q'* since marginal social benefit and marginal social cost are equated at *E'*.

Society could gain the triangle *EFE'*, the excess of social benefits over social costs, by increasing the quantity of roses from *Q* to *Q'*. This triangle measures the social cost of the market failure that makes equilibrium output too low.

Property rights and externalities

Your neighbour's tree obscures your light, a harmful consumption externality. If the law says that you must be compensated for any damage suffered, your neighbour has to pay up or cut back the tree.

He likes the tree and wants to know how much it would take to compensate you to leave the tree at its current size. Figure 15.7 shows the marginal benefit *MB* that he gets from the last inch of tree and the marginal cost *MC* to you of that last inch. At the tree's current size S_1 the total cost to you is the area $OABS_1$. This is the marginal cost *OA* of the first inch, plus the marginal cost of the second inch, and so on to the existing size S_1. The area $OABS_1$ is what you need in compensation if the tree size is S_1.

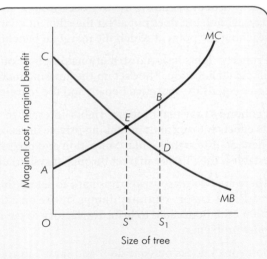

MB and MC measure the marginal benefit to your neighbour and marginal cost to you of a tree of size S. The efficient size is S* where the marginal cost and benefit are equal. Beginning from a size S_1, you might bribe your neighbour the value $S*EDS_1$, to cut back to S*. Below S* you would have to pay more than it is worth to you to have the tree cut back further. Alternatively, your neighbour might pay you the value OAES* to have a tree of size S*. Property rights, in this case whether you are legally entitled to compensation for loss of light to your garden, determine who compensates whom but not the outcome S* of the bargain.

Figure 15.7 The efficient quantity of an externality

Your neighbour is about to pay up when his daughter, an economics student, points out that at size S_1 the marginal benefit of the last inch to him is less than the marginal cost to you, the amount you must be compensated for that last inch on the tree. It is not worth her dad having a tree this big. Nor, she points out, is it worth cutting the tree down altogether. The first inch yields a higher marginal benefit to him than the amount that you need in compensation to offset your marginal cost of that first inch. A tiny tree has little effect on your light.

At the efficient tree size S^* the marginal benefit to your neighbour equals the marginal cost to you. Above S^* he cuts back the tree, since the marginal cost (and compensation) exceeds his marginal benefit. Below S^* he increases the tree size, and pays you marginal compensation that is less than his marginal benefit. At the efficient size S^* your total cost is the area $OAES^*$. This is the compensation you are paid.

Since a larger tree benefits one party but hurts the other party, *the efficient tree size and efficient quantity of the externality is not zero*. It is where the marginal benefit equals the marginal cost.

> **Property rights** are the power of residual control, including the right to be compensated for externalities.

Property rights affect who compensates whom, a distributional implication. Suppose there is no law requiring compensation. Instead of letting his tree grow to S_1, inflicting a huge cost on you, you bribe your neighbour to cut it back. You compensate him for the loss of his marginal benefit. You would pay to have the tree cut back as far as S^* but no further. Beyond that size, you pay more in compensation for loss of marginal benefit than you save yourself in lower cost of the externality. So you pay a *total* of S^*EDS_1 to compensate for the loss of benefit in cutting the tree back from S_1 to S^*. Who has the property rights determines who pays whom, but does not affect the efficient quantity that the bargain determines. It is always worth reaching the point at which the marginal benefit to one of you equals the marginal cost to the other.

Property rights have a distributional implication – who compensates whom – but also achieve the efficient allocation. They set up the 'missing market' for the externality. The market ensures that the price equals the marginal benefit and the marginal cost, and hence equates the two.

Economists say that property rights 'internalize' the externality. If people must pay for it they will take its effects into account in making private decisions and there will no longer be market failure. Why, then, do externalities, like congestion and pollution, remain a problem? Why don't private individuals establish the missing market through a system of bribes or compensation?

There are two reasons why it is hard to set up this market. The first is the cost of organizing the market. A factory chimney dumps smoke on a thousand gardens nearby, but it is costly to collect £1 from each household to bribe the factory to cut back to the efficient amount. Second, there is a *free-rider* problem.

Someone knocks on your door and says: 'I'm collecting bribes from people who mind the factory smoke falling on their gardens. The money will be used to bribe the factory to cut back. Do you wish to contribute? I am going round 1000 houses nearby.' Whether you mind or not, you say: 'I don't mind, and won't contribute.' If everybody else pays, the factory will

> A **free rider**, unable to be excluded from consuming a good, has no incentive to buy it.

cut back and you cannot be prevented from getting the benefits. The smoke will not fall exclusively on your garden just because you alone did not pay. Regardless of what other people contribute, your dominant strategy is to be a *free-rider*. Everyone else reasons similarly; hence no one pays, even though you are all better off paying and getting the smoke cut back.

Activity box 15 Climate change

The postscript to this chapter examines the economics of climate change, but let us see if you can discover some of the answers for yourself, based on what you have learned so far.

Questions

(a) Is it easier to address the problem of climate change if there are 150 nation states or a single world government? Why? Do you see any problems with your answer?

(b) What market failures (if any) are responsible for the 'problem' of climate change?

(c) To what extent should the current generation bear more pain in order to make life easier for the next generation?

(d) If we had a government capable of enforcing a 50 per cent reduction in carbon emissions, would it be more efficient to accomplish this by quotas, by taxes or by setting up a market?

To check your answers to these questions, go to page 722.

15.6 Environmental issues

When there is no implicit market for pollution, pollutants are overproduced. Private producers ignore the costs they impose on others. In equilibrium, social marginal cost exceeds social marginal benefit.

If the private sector cannot organize charges for the marginal externalities pollution creates, perhaps government can? By charging (through taxes) for the divergence between marginal private and social cost, the government can induce private producers to take account of the costs inflicted on others. This argument for pollution taxes or congestion charges is examined in the next chapter.

Pollution taxes, especially for water pollution, are used in many countries. But most policy takes a different approach, imposing pollution standards to regulate the quantities of pollution allowed.

Air pollution

Since the Clean Air Act of 1956, UK governments have designated clean air zones in which certain pollutants, notably smoke caused by burning coal, are illegal. The number of designated clean air zones has risen steadily. Table 15.1 shows a big fall in smoke pollution in the UK.

Table 15.1 Smoke emission, UK (million tonnes per annum)

1958	1974	2003
2.0	0.8	0.1

Sources: Digest of Environmental Protection and Water Statistics; ONS, Social Trends.

Adding lead to petrol improves the fuel economy of cars. However, lead emissions from car exhausts are an atmospheric pollutant harmful to people's health. Since 1972 the UK government has steadily reduced the quantity of lead permitted in petrol. Lead emission into the UK atmosphere has fallen from over 8000 tonnes a year in 1975 to only 1000 tonnes a year, even though consumption of petrol has risen dramatically.

Water pollution

Since 1951 governments in the UK have also imposed controls on discharges into inland waters. Although we think of *industrial* effluent, sewage is a more important source of pollution. Since 1970 regional water authorities in England and Wales have spent (at 2000 prices) over £3 billion a year on water purification and sewage treatment. Another key source of water pollution is nitrates used to fertilize agricultural land. The EU has laid down tough standards for water purity that will take many years to achieve.

Evaluating UK pollution policy

Direct regulation of pollution has been a mixed success. Cutting smoke pollution, which used to mix with winter fog to create dense 'smog', has been a big success. Many rivers are also cleaner, and fish have reappeared. In other cases, regulation was less successful. It is hard to enforce regulations such as those that prevent ships discharging oil at sea. UK beaches still feature on the EU blacklist. Coal-fired power stations still emit large quantities of sulphur dioxide.

Was the government tough enough on polluters? Recall that the efficient quantity of pollution is not zero. The fact that pollution still exists does itself not prove that policy has been too feeble.

Pollution control has often been crude and simple. Calculations of social marginal costs and benefits of cutting back pollution are rare. Measuring costs and benefits is difficult. In deciding how much to cut lead emissions from cars, we can estimate the marginal social cost of producing cars with anti-pollution exhaust systems and the marginal social cost of cars that use more fuel per mile. But even if doctors were unanimous about the effects of lead emission on health, how should society value a marginal increase in the health of current and future generations?

This is not merely a question of efficiency but also of equity, both within the current generation – poor inner-city children are more vulnerable to arrested development caused by inhaling lead-polluted air – and across generations. Today's consumers bear the cost of the clean-up, but its benefits accrue largely to future consumers.

Prices versus quantities

If free markets tend to overpollute, society can cut pollution either by regulating the quantity of pollution or by using the price system to discourage such activities by taxing them. Is it more sensible to intervene through the tax system than to regulate quantities directly?

Many economists prefer taxes to quantity restrictions. If each firm is charged the same price or tax for a marginal unit of pollution, each firm equates the marginal cost of reducing pollution to the price of pollution. Any allocation in which different firms have different marginal costs of reducing pollution is inefficient. If firms with low marginal reduction costs contract further and firms with high marginal reduction costs contract less, lower pollution is achieved at less cost.

The main problem with using taxes not quantity restrictions is uncertainty about the outcome. Suppose pollution beyond a critical level has disastrous consequences, for example irreversibly damaging the ozone layer. By regulating the quantity directly, society can ensure a disaster is avoided. Indirect control, through taxes or charges, runs the risk that the government does its sums wrong and sets the tax too low. Pollution is then higher than intended, and may be disastrous.

Regulating the total quantity of pollution, with spot checks on compliance by individual producers, is a simple policy that avoids the worst outcomes. However, by ignoring differences in the marginal cost of reducing pollution across different polluters, it does not reduce pollution in a way that is cost minimizing to society.

Lessons from the United States

The US has gone furthest in trying to use property rights and the price mechanism to cut back pollution efficiently. The US Clean Air Acts established an environmental policy that includes an *emissions trading programme* and *bubble policy*.

The Acts lay down a minimum standard for air quality, and impose pollution emission controls on particular polluters. Any polluter emitting less than their specified amount gets an *emission reduction credit* (ERC), which can be sold to another polluter wanting to exceed its allocated pollution limit. Thus, the total quantity of pollution is regulated, but firms that can cheaply reduce pollution have an incentive to do so, and sell off the ERC to firms for which pollution reduction is more expensive. We get closer to the efficient solution in which the marginal cost of pollution reduction is equalized across firms.

When a firm has many factories, the bubble policy applies pollution controls to the firm as a whole. The firm can cut back most in the plants in which pollution reduction is cheapest.

Thus, the US policy combines 'control over quantities' for aggregate pollution, where the risks and uncertainties are greatest, with 'control through the price system' for allocating efficiently the way these overall targets are achieved.

15.7 Other missing markets: time and risk

The previous two sections were devoted to a single idea. When externalities exist, free market equilibrium is inefficient because the externality itself does not have a market or a price. People take no account of the costs and benefits their actions inflict on others. Without a market for externalities the price system cannot bring marginal costs and marginal benefits of these externalities into line. We now discuss other 'missing markets', those for time and for risk.

The present and the future are linked. People save, or refrain from consumption, today in order to consume more tomorrow. Firms invest, reducing current output by devoting resources to training or building, in order to produce more tomorrow. How should society make plans today for the quantities of goods produced and consumed in the future? Ideally everyone makes plans such that the social marginal cost of goods in the future just equals their social marginal benefit.

Chapter 13 discussed a *forward market*, in which buyers and sellers make contracts today for goods delivered in the future at a price agreed today. Suppose there is a forward market for copper in 2008. Consumers equate the marginal benefit of copper in 2008 to the forward price, which producers equate to the marginal cost of producing copper for 2008. With a complete set of forward markets for all commodities for all future dates, producers and consumers today make consistent plans for future production and consumption of all goods, and the social marginal benefit of every future good equals its social marginal cost.

Chapter 13 explained why few forward markets exist. You can trade gold but not cars or washing machines. Since nobody knows the characteristics of next year's model of car or washing machine, we cannot write legally binding contracts to be easily enforced when the goods are delivered. Without these forward markets, the price system cannot equate the marginal cost and marginal benefits of planned future goods.

There are also few *contingent* or insurance markets for dealing with risk. People usually dislike risk. It reduces their utility. Does society undertake the efficient amount of risky activities?

A complete set of insurance markets lets risk be transferred from those who dislike risk to those who will bear risk at a price. The equilibrium price equates social marginal costs and benefits of risky activities. However, adverse selection and moral hazard inhibit the organization of private insurance markets. If some risky activities are uninsurable at any price, the price system cannot guide society to equate social marginal costs and benefits.

Future goods and risky goods are examples of commodities with missing markets. Like externalities, these are market failures. Free market equilibrium is generally efficient. And the theory of the second best tells us that when some markets are distorted, we probably do not want other markets to be completely distortion free.

15.8 Quality, health and safety

Information is incomplete because gathering information is costly. This leads to inefficiency. A worker unaware that exposure to benzene may cause cancer may work for a lower wage than if this information is widely available. The firm's production cost understates the true social cost and the good is overproduced. Governments regulate health, safety and quality standards because they recognize the danger of market failure.

UK examples include the Health and Safety at Work Acts, legislation to control food and drugs production, the Fair Trading Act governing consumer protection, and various traffic and motoring regulations. Such legislation aims to encourage the provision of information that lets individuals more accurately judge costs and benefits, and aims to set and enforce standards designed to reduce the risks of injury or death.

Providing information

Figure 15.8 shows the supply curve *SS* for a drug that is potentially harmful. *DD* is the demand curve if consumers do not know the danger. In equilibrium at *E*, the quantity *Q* is produced and consumed. With full information about the dangers, people would buy less of the drug. The demand curve *DD′* shows the marginal consumer benefit with full information. The new equilibrium at *E′* avoids the deadweight burden *E′EF* from overproduction of the drug.

If information were free to collect, everyone would know the true risks. From the social gain *E′EF* we should subtract the resources needed to discover this information. Free market equilibrium is at *E* because it is not worth each individual checking up privately on each drug on the market. It makes sense for society to have a single regulatory body to check drugs, and a law whose enforcement entitles individuals to assume that drugs have been checked out as safe.

Certification of safety or quality need not be carried out by the government. Sotheby's certify Rembrandts, the AA will check out a used car for you, and drunk drivers may send half their blood sample to a private certification agency to corroborate the results of the police analysis.

Two factors inhibit the use of private certification in many areas of health and safety. First, the public perceives a conflict between the profit motive and the incentive to tell the truth. Public officials may be less easily swayed.

Second, a private certification agency might have to decide standards. What margin of error should be built into safety regulations? How safe must a drug be to get a certificate? These are issues of public policy. They involve externalities and have distributional implications. Even if society uses private agencies to *monitor* regulations, it usually sets the standards itself.

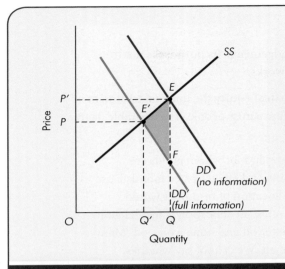

Consumers cannot individually discover the safety risks associated with a particular good. Free market equilibrium occurs at *E*. A government agency now provides information about the product. As a result, the demand curve shifts down and the new equilibrium is at *E'* where the *true* or full information value of an extra unit of the good equals its marginal social cost. Providing information prevents a welfare cost *E'EF* that arises when uninformed consumers use the wrong marginal valuation of the benefits of the good.

Figure 15.8 Information and unsafe goods

Imposing standards

The public interest is important when little is known about a product and where the consequences of any error may be catastrophic. Few believe that safety standards for nuclear power stations can be adequately determined by the private sector.

In imposing standards, governments raise the private cost of production by preventing firms from adopting the cost-minimizing techniques they otherwise would use. Sometimes the government has better information than the private sector. Sometimes standards compensate for externalities neglected by the private firm. Sometimes standards reflect a pure value judgement based on distributional considerations. One contentious area is the value of human life itself.

Politicians often claim, ridiculously, that human life is beyond economic calculation and must be given absolute priority at any cost. The UK government repeated this assurance after the Paddington rail disaster in October 1999. An economist will make two points in reply. First, it is *impossible* to implement such an objective. It is too costly in resources to try to eliminate *all* risks of premature death. Sensibly, we do not go this far. Second, in occupational and recreational choices, for example driving racing cars or going climbing, people take risks. Society must ask how much more risk-averse it should be than the people it is trying to protect.

Beyond some point, the marginal social cost of further risk reduction exceeds the marginal social benefit. It takes a huge effort to make the world just a little safer, and the resources might have been used elsewhere to greater effect. Zero risk does not make economic sense. We need to know the costs of making the world a little safer, and we need to encourage society to decide how much it values the benefits. By shying away from the 'unpleasant' task of spelling out the costs and benefits, society induces an inefficient allocation in which marginal costs and marginal benefits of saving life are very different in different activities.

Summary

- **Welfare economics** deals with normative issues or value judgements. Its purpose is not to describe how the economy works but to assess how well it works.

- **Horizontal equity** is the equal treatment of equals, and **vertical equity** the unequal treatment of unequals. Equity is concerned with the distribution of welfare across people. The desirable degree of equity is a pure value judgement.

- A **resource allocation** is a complete description of what, how and for whom goods are produced. To separate as far as possible the concepts of equity and efficiency, economists use Pareto efficiency. An allocation is **Pareto-efficient** if no reallocation of resources would make some people better off without making others worse off. If an allocation is inefficient it is possible to achieve a Pareto gain, making some people better off and none worse off. Many reallocations make some people better off and others worse off. We cannot say whether such changes are good or bad without making value judgements to compare different people's welfare.

- For a given level of resources and a given technology, the economy has an infinite number of Pareto-efficient allocations that differ in the distribution of welfare across people. For example, every allocation that gives all output to one individual is Pareto-efficient. But there are many more allocations that are inefficient.

- Under strict conditions, competitive equilibrium is Pareto-efficient. Different initial distributions of human and physical capital across people generate different competitive equilibria corresponding to each possible Pareto-efficient allocation. When price-taking producers and consumers face the same prices, marginal costs and marginal benefits are equated to prices (by the individual actions of producers and consumers) and hence to each other.

- In practice, governments face a conflict between equity and efficiency. Redistributive taxation drives a wedge between prices paid by consumers (to which marginal benefits are equated) and prices received by producers (to which marginal costs are equated). Free market equilibrium will not equate marginal cost and marginal benefit and there will be inefficiency.

- **Distortions** occur whenever free market equilibrium does not equate **marginal social cost** and **marginal social benefit**. Distortions lead to inefficiency or **market failure**. Apart from taxes, there are three other important sources of distortions: imperfect competition (failure to set price equal to marginal cost), externalities (divergence between private and social costs or benefits), and other missing markets in connection with future goods, risky goods or other informational problems.

- When only one market is distorted the **first-best** solution is to remove the distortion, thus achieving full efficiency. The first-best criterion relates only to efficiency. Governments caring sufficiently about redistribution might still prefer inefficient allocations with more vertical equity. However, when a distortion cannot be removed from one market it is not generally efficient to ensure that all other markets are distortion-free. The theory of the **second best** says that it is more efficient to spread inevitable distortions thinly over many markets than to concentrate their effects in a few markets.

- **Production externalities** occur when actions by one producer directly affect the production costs of another producer, as when one firm pollutes another's water supply. **Consumption externalities** mean one person's decisions affect another consumer's utility directly, as when my garden gives pleasure to neighbours. Externalities shift indifference curves or production functions.

- Externalities lead to divergence between private and social costs or benefits because there is no implicit market for the externality itself. When only a few people are involved, a system of **property rights** may establish the missing market. The direction of compensation will depend on who has the property rights. Either way, it achieves the efficient quantity of the externality at which marginal cost and marginal benefit are equated. The efficient solution is rarely a zero quantity of the externality. **Transactions costs** and the **free-rider problem** may prevent implicit markets being established. Equilibrium will then be inefficient.

- When externalities lead to market failure the government could set up the missing market by pricing the externality through taxes or subsidies. If it was straightforward to assess the efficient quantity of the externality and hence the correct tax or subsidy, and straightforward to monitor the quantities produced and consumed, such taxes or subsidies would allow the market to achieve an efficient resource allocation.

- In practice, governments often regulate externalities such as **pollution** or **congestion** by imposing standards that affect quantities directly rather than by using the tax system to affect production and consumption indirectly. Overall quantity standards may fail to equate the marginal cost of pollution reduction across different polluters, in which case the allocation will not be efficient. However, simple standards may use up fewer resources in monitoring and enforcement and may prevent disastrous outcomes when there is uncertainty.

- **Moral hazard**, **adverse selection** and **other informational problems** prevent the development of a complete set of **forward markets** and **contingent markets**. Without these markets the price system cannot equate social marginal cost and benefit for future goods or risky activities.

- **Incomplete information** may lead to inefficient private choices. Health, quality and safety regulations are designed both to provide information and to express society's value judgements about intangibles, such as life itself. By avoiding explicit consideration of social costs and benefits, government policy may be inconsistent in its implicit valuation of health or safety in different activities under regulation.

Review questions

To check your answers to these questions, go to page 721.

1. An economy has 10 units of goods to share out between two people. [x, y] means that the first person gets a quantity x, the second person a quantity y. For each of the allocations (a) to (e), say whether they are (i) efficient and (ii) equitable: (a) [10, 0], (b) [7, 2], (c) [5, 5], (d) [3, 6], (e) [0, 10]. What does 'equitable' mean? Would you prefer allocation (d) to allocation (e)?

2. The price of meals is £1 and of films £5. There is perfect competition and no externality. What can we say about (a) the relative benefit to consumers of a marginal film and a marginal meal, (b) the relative marginal production cost of films and meals, or (c) the relative marginal product of variable factors in the film and meal industries? Why is this equilibrium efficient?

3   In deciding to drive a car in the rush hour, you think about the cost of petrol and the time of the journey. Do you slow other people down by driving? Is this an externality? Will too many or too few people drive cars in the rush hour? Should commuter parking in cities be restricted?

4   In 1885, 200 people died when the steam boiler exploded on a Mississippi river boat. Jeremiah Allen and three friends formed a private company offering to insure any boiler that they had inspected for safety. Boiler inspections caught on, and explosion rates plummeted. Would Jeremiah Allen's company have been successful if it had certified boilers but not insured them as well? Explain.

5   (a) Why might society ban drugs that neither help nor harm the diseases they are claimed to cure? (b) If regulatory bodies are blamed for bad things that happen despite regulations (a train crash) but not blamed for preventing good things through too much regulation (rapid availability of a safe and useful drug), will regulatory bodies overregulate activities under their scrutiny?

6   **Common fallacies** Why are these statements wrong? (a) Society should ban all toxic discharges. (b) Anything governments can do the market can do better. (c) Anything the market can do the government can do better.

7   **Harder question** Much of the economics of efficiency is about ensuring that we equate the marginal cost of producing the last unit with the marginal benefit of that unit to the last consumer. Suppose the marginal cost of preventing the planet overheating is £10 000 billion. How would you attempt to assess the marginal benefit?

8   **Harder question** A government needs to raise £10 billion from taxes. It knows that taxes create deadweight burden triangles, and it taxes a number of activities and products. In the most efficient outcome possible, say whether the tax rate on each of the following should be low, average or high: (a) mobile international capital, (b) unskilled domestic labour, (c) food, (d) tobacco.

9   **Essay question** Why do politicians pretend that trains can be made perfectly safe and hospitals can supply all the health care that we know how to supply, when it is perfectly obvious that we do not have the resources to do these things and that it would be highly wasteful to try.

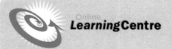

Online LearningCentre

To help you grasp the key concepts of this chapter check out the extra resources posted on the Online Learning Centre. There are chapter summaries, self-test questions, an interactive graphing tool, weblinks and a searchable glossary, all for free!

To put your learning into practice and prepare for exams, an **Interactive Workbook** is also available online, containing a variety of question types and providing feedback on your answers.

If you'd like further help with economics, or have any questions, **NetTutor** is here to help! You will have a personalised tutorial service at your fingertips. Visit the online learning centre at: www.mcgraw-hill.co.uk/textbooks/begg for information on accessing all of these resources.

There is increasing evidence that global temperatures are rising. The science of climate change means that we are also likely to see greater fluctuations in climate as well. Hence, extreme events will become much more frequent. Large parts of Bangladesh may disappear under water for ever; and English villages, from Yorkshire to Cornwall, have already experienced flash flooding. Conversely, regions of the world that are currently temperate may become arid and uninhabitable. Figure 15.P1 shows the dramatic change in global temperatures in recent years.

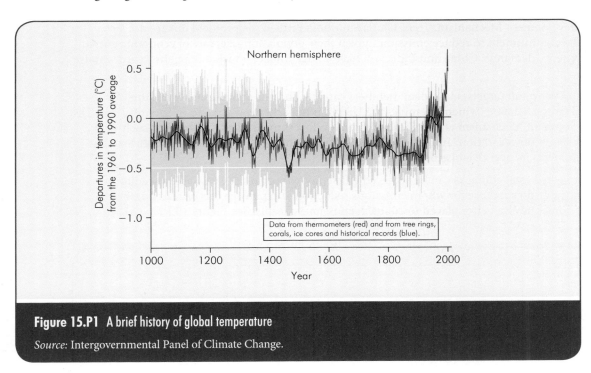

Figure 15.P1 A brief history of global temperature

Source: Intergovernmental Panel of Climate Change.

The science of climate change

The earth's climate is affected by many things, from solar radiation to the consequences of human behaviour. The ebb and flow of previous ice ages reminds us that human behaviour is not the only cause of climate change. Even so, there is increasing evidence that we must look to ourselves as a major cause of recent global warming.

Greenhouse gases – including carbon dioxide and methane – shield the earth from solar radiation, but also trap the heat underneath. Without them, all heat would escape and we would freeze to death. But we need just the right amount. Too much greenhouse gas, and the earth overheats, causing global warming.

The recent build-up of greenhouse gases reflects large emissions of carbon dioxide from households, from power stations and from transport. This may cause ice to melt and water to expand, causing sea levels to rise. A catastrophic eventual consequence would be melting of permafrost in Siberia, releasing such volumes of methane that a large rise in temperature would then be inevitable, perhaps threatening human survival.

Carbon, a key constituent of all greenhouse cases, is a useful common denominator. Slowing, let alone reversing, global warming requires the emission of much less carbon.

The Kyoto Protocol

In 1997 a group of countries signed an amendment to the UN International Treaty on Climate Change, committing themselves to cut greenhouse gas emissions. By 2006, 169 countries (though not the USA) had signed.

Developed countries accept the obligation to reduce emissions by 2012 to 5 per cent below the level of their emissions in 1990. Developing countries have not yet any commitment but can take part in the Clean Development Mechanism. Thus, China and India ratified the protocol but are not yet bound by the commitment to reduce emissions: given their population size, rate of economic growth and future energy demands, China and India will have a huge impact on what happens to greenhouse gases.

Within the EU's overall targets, individual members can buy and sell obligations within the EU Emissions Trading Scheme (which resembles the US pollution scheme discussed in Section 15.6). The Clean Development Mechanism allows India or China to invest in emissions reduction, such as by building a cleaner power station, and sell the emissions credit to a UK or German company so that Europe then meets its overall emissions obligations.

Thus the projected total cutbacks can be achieved efficiently – those most easily able to reduce emissions cheaply do so; those for whom emissions reduction is expensive can instead purchase a credit from someone else better placed to cut back emissions cheaply. See Figure 15.P2.

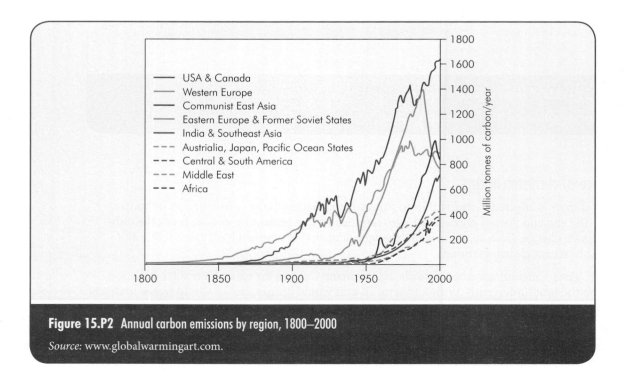

Figure 15.P2 Annual carbon emissions by region, 1800–2000

Source: www.globalwarmingart.com.

Cost–benefit analysis

Even if we accept the science, what should we do, and how quickly? This gets to the core of the what, how and for whom question of Chapter 1. The for whom question is particularly acute. How much pain should the current generation take in order to make life nicer for future generations? Can we expect China and India to slow their economic development to make life nicer for citizens in Europe and the US who begin with many more economic advantages?

The Kyoto targets are modest, and as yet fail to include the key economies of the US, China and India, on whom much will actually depend. Kyoto supporters see these targets as the thin end of the wedge, creating a political dynamic that will allow tougher targets soon; which is precisely why they are opposed by those who would potentially lose out (for example, the air-conditioned affluent citizens of the United States and Australia whose current energy consumption is enormous).

In 2006, the UK government published a report on the economics of climate change written by Sir Nicholas Stern, a London School of Economics professor, and ex-Chief Economist of both the World Bank and the European Bank for Reconstruction and Development. The Stern Review (details available on www.hm-treasury.gov.uk) concluded that 1 per cent of global GDP must be invested from now on if we are to head off the worst effects of climate change; and that failure to act now risks a future cost of up to 20 per cent of global GDP.

Sir Nicholas Stern

Many of the world's leading economists – including economics Nobel Prize winners Sir James Mirrlees, Amartya Sen, Joe Stiglitz and Bob Solow, and Professor Jeffrey Sachs, Director of the Earth Institute at Columbia University in New York – have come out strongly in support of the Stern Review. The principal point of subsequent debate has been the appropriate interest rate at which to discount future costs and benefits, a topic we discussed in Box 12.1 of Chapter 12. The decision about how much to discount the welfare of future generations affects the present value of the benefits of tackling climate change today, and hence both the optimal pace of action and estimates of the cost of inaction. Although the quantitative conclusions change, the qualitative conclusions do not.

Government spending and revenue

Learning Outcomes

By the end of this chapter, you should understand:

1 different kinds of government spending

2 why public goods cannot be provided by a market

3 average and marginal tax rates

4 how taxes can compensate for externalities

5 supply-side economics

6 why tax revenue cannot be raised without limit

7 how cross-border flows limit national economic sovereignty

8 the political economy of how governments set policy

The scale of government rose steadily until the 1970s. Then many people felt it had become too big, using resources better employed in the private sector. High taxes were thought to be stifling private enterprise. Electorates in many countries turned to the political leaders who promised to reduce the scale of government.

Now the pendulum is swinging back. In the US, even a Republican president, George W. Bush, promised massive government resources to rebuild New York after the terrorist attacks. In the UK the tax burden rose in the 1990s, after falling under Mrs Thatcher. Labour won the 2001 election on a promise of higher government spending on health, education and transport.

For historical perspective, Table 16.1 shows how government grew everywhere in the last century. Table 16.2 confirms that UK government spending fell after the 1970s, and decomposes total government spending into government purchases of goods and services – schools, defence, the police – and transfer payments, such as social security, state pensions and debt interest.

> A **transfer payment** requires no good or service in return during that time period.

Most government spending is financed by tax revenue. However, just as you may overspend your student income by borrowing now and repaying later, the government need not balance its spending and revenue in any particular period. Table 16.3 shows that by 2005 the US, UK, France and Germany were expected to have small budget deficits.

> The **budget surplus** (deficit) is the excess (shortfall) of its spending over its revenue.

After this broad background, we now examine microeconomic issues. First, we distinguish marginal and average tax rates.

> The **marginal tax rate** is the fraction of the last pound of income paid in tax. The **average tax rate** is the fraction of total income paid in tax.

Table 16.1 Government spending (% of GDP)

	1880	1960	2007
Japan	11	18	36
USA	8	28	37
Germany	10	32	45
UK	10	32	45
France	15	35	54
Sweden	6	31	55

Sources: World Bank, *World Development Report*; OECD, *Economic Outlook*.

Table 16.2 UK government spending (% of GDP)

	1956	1976	2007
Total spending	34	47	45
Goods and services	21	26	30
Transfer payments	13	21	15

Sources: ONS, *UK National Accounts;* HM Treasury, *Budget 2007.*

Table 16.3 Government activity in 2005 (% of GDP)

	UK	USA	France	Germany
Spending	45	37	54	45
Tax revenue	43	34	51	44
Budget surplus	−2	−3	−3	−1

Source: OECD, *Economic Outlook.*

In a *progressive* tax structure, the average tax rate rises with an individual's income. The government takes proportionately more from the rich than from the poor. In a *regressive* tax structure, the average tax rate falls as income level rises, taking proportionately less from the rich.

Table 16.4 shows that the UK, like most countries, has a progressive income tax structure. Figure 16.1 explains why. We plot pre-tax income on the horizontal axis and post-tax income on the vertical axis. The line *OG*, with a slope of 45 degrees, implies no taxes. A pre-tax income *OA* on the horizontal axis matches the same post-tax income *OA* on the vertical axis. Now suppose there is an income tax, but the first *OA* of income is untaxed. If the marginal tax rate on taxable income is constant, individuals face a schedule *OBCD*, keeping a constant fraction of each pound of pre-tax income above *OA*. The higher the marginal tax rate, the flatter is *BC*.

To calculate the average tax rate at a point such as *D*, we join up *OD*. The flatter the slope of this line, the higher is the average tax rate. Even with a constant marginal tax rate, and a constant slope along *BC*, the initial tax allowance makes the tax structure progressive. The higher an individual's gross income, the smaller is the tax allowance as a percentage of gross income, so the larger is the fraction of total income on which tax is paid.

Table 16.4 UK income tax rates, 1978–2008

Taxable income (000s of 2004 £)	Marginal tax rate (%)	
	1978/79	2008/09
2020	34	20
5000	34	20
10000	34	20
20000	45	20
31400	50	20
40000	70	40
70000	83	40

Note: Taxable income after deducting allowances. In 2008/09 a single person's allowance is almost £5500.

Sources: HMSO, *Financial Statement and Budget Report*; ONS, *Budget 2007*.

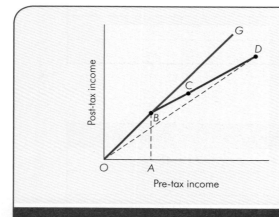

The 45 degree line OG shows zero taxes or transfers so that pre-tax and post-tax income coincide. With an allowance OA then a constant marginal tax rate *t*, the post-tax income schedule is OBCD. The slope depends only on the marginal tax rate [on BCD it is (1–*t*)]. The average tax rate at any point D is the slope of OD. A tax is progressive if the average tax rate rises with pre-tax income.

Figure 16.1 A progressive income tax

But Table 16.4 shows that *marginal* tax rates may also rise with income. As individuals move into higher tax bands they pay higher marginal tax rates, moving on to even flatter portions of the tax schedule. The average tax rate now rises sharply with income.

Table 16.4 shows that UK marginal tax rates have fallen a lot in the past two decades, especially for the very rich. A millionaire paying an 83 per cent tax rate on all taxable income except the first £70000 in 1978 paid only 40 per cent in 2008/09.

The UK was not alone in cutting tax rates. There was a worldwide move to cut tax rates, especially for the very rich. In part this reflected the belief that tax rates were previously so high that distortions had been large. However, it also reflected increasing competition between governments to attract mobile resources (physical and human capital) to their country. At the end of the chapter we discuss how cross-border mobility undermines national sovereignty.

16.1 Taxation and government spending

Government spending, and the taxes that finance it, are now about 45 per cent of national output. Figure 16.2 shows the composition of government spending and revenue in 2007/08.

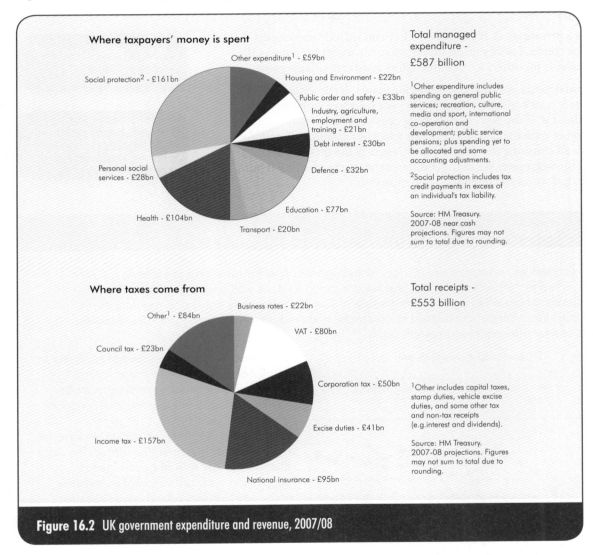

Where taxpayers' money is spent

Other expenditure[1] - £59bn
Social protection[2] - £161bn
Housing and Environment - £22bn
Public order and safety - £33bn
Industry, agriculture, employment and training - £21bn
Debt interest - £30bn
Personal social services - £28bn
Defence - £32bn
Health - £104bn
Education - £77bn
Transport - £20bn

Total managed expenditure - £587 billion

[1]Other expenditure includes spending on general public services; recreation, culture, media and sport, international co-operation and development; public service pensions; plus spending yet to be allocated and some accounting adjustments.

[2]Social protection includes tax credit payments in excess of an individual's tax liability.

Source: HM Treasury. 2007-08 near cash projections. Figures may not sum to total due to rounding.

Where taxes come from

Other[1] - £84bn
Business rates - £22bn
Council tax - £23bn
VAT - £80bn
Corporation tax - £50bn
Excise duties - £41bn
Income tax - £157bn
National insurance - £95bn

Total receipts - £553 billion

[1]Other includes capital taxes, stamp duties, vehicle excise duties, and some other tax and non-tax receipts (e.g.interest and dividends).

Source: HM Treasury. 2007-08 projections. Figures may not sum to total due to rounding.

Figure 16.2 UK government expenditure and revenue, 2007/08

Nearly a third of total government spending went on transfer payments such as social protection on pensions, jobseeker's allowance (formerly unemployment benefit) and debt interest. Of the remaining spending directly on goods and services, the most important spending categories are health, defence and education. Figure 16.2 also shows how this government spending is financed

The most important direct taxes are income tax, and corporation tax on company profits. The most important indirect taxes are value added tax (VAT) and customs duties. Note that since state provision of retirement pensions is included on the expenditure side as a transfer payment, pension contributions under the national insurance scheme are included on the revenue side.

> **Direct taxes** are taxes on income and wealth. **Indirect taxes** are taxes on spending and output.

16.2 The government in the market economy

How do we justify government spending in a market economy?

Public goods

Ice cream is a private good. If you eat an ice cream nobody else can eat that particular ice cream. For any given supply, your consumption reduces the quantity available for others to consume. Most goods are private goods.

Clean air and defence are examples of public goods. If the air is pollution-free, your consumption of it does not interfere with our consumption of it. If the Navy is patrolling coastal waters, your consumption of national defence does not affect our quantity of national defence. We all consume the same quantity, namely the quantity is supplied in the aggregate. We may get different amounts of utility if our tastes differ, but we all consume the same quantity.

> A **private good**, if consumed by one person, cannot be consumed by others.

> A **public good**, if consumed by one person, must be consumed by others in exactly the same quantity.

Box 16.1 Market infrastructure

In poor economies, resources are scarce, including resources for government itself. As a Czech minister noted in 1990, 'Initially, the best we are going to do is wild-west capitalism.' Even the United States took a while to establish the rule of law, clear property rights and regulate many private activities. Without confidence in contracts, and credible procedures to resolve disputes, markets cannot allocate resources efficiently.

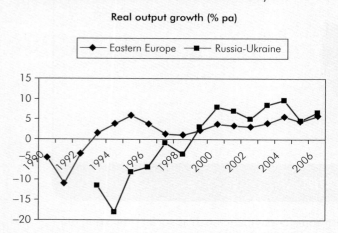

Real output growth (% pa)

— Eastern Europe — Russia-Ukraine

The Soviet bloc gave up central planning in 1990 because the system was failing. Lacking the initial infrastructure to make markets operate reliably, the early years of transition were difficult. Output fell substantially. But these transition economies have now firmly turned the corner. The data confirm the key role of government in supporting successful market economies.

Source: IMF, World Economic Outlook.

The key aspects of public goods are (1) that it is technically possible for one person to consume without reducing the amount available for others, and (2) the impossibility of excluding anyone from consumption except at a prohibitive cost. A football match can be watched by many people, especially if it is on TV, without reducing the quantity consumed by other viewers; but *exclusion* is possible. The ground holds only so many, and some Premier League clubs now charge to watch their games live on their own TV stations. The interesting issues arise when, as with national defence, exclusion of certain individuals from consumption is impossible.

Free riders

Chapter 15 introduced the *free-rider problem* when discussing why bribes and compensation for externalities might not occur. Public goods are wide open to the free-rider problem if they are supplied by the private sector. Since you get the same quantity of national defence as everyone else, *whether or not you pay for it*, you never buy national defence in a private market. Nor does anyone else. No defence is demanded even though we all want it.

Public goods are like a strong externality. If you buy defence everyone else also gets the benefits. Since marginal private and social benefits diverge, private markets will not produce the socially efficient quantity. Government intervention is needed.

The marginal social benefit

Suppose the public good is a pure public water supply. The more infected the water, the more people are likely to get cholera. Figure 16.3 supposes there are two people. The first person's demand curve for water purity is $D_1 D_1$. Each point on the demand curve shows what he would pay for the last unit of purer water, his marginal benefit. $D_2 D_2$ shows the marginal benefit of purer water to the second person.

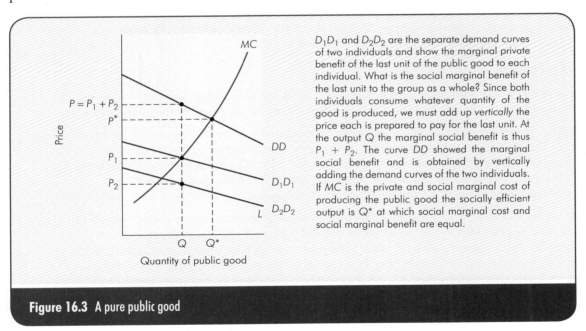

$D_1 D_1$ and $D_2 D_2$ are the separate demand curves of two individuals and show the marginal private benefit of the last unit of the public good to each individual. What is the social marginal benefit of the last unit to the group as a whole? Since both individuals consume whatever quantity of the good is produced, we must add up *vertically* the price each is prepared to pay for the last unit. At the output Q the marginal social benefit is thus $P_1 + P_2$. The curve DD showed the marginal social benefit and is obtained by vertically adding the demand curves of the two individuals. If MC is the private and social marginal cost of producing the public good the socially efficient output is Q^* at which social marginal cost and social marginal benefit are equal.

Figure 16.3 A pure public good

Curve DD is the marginal social benefit of purer water. At each level of the public good, we *vertically* sum the marginal benefit of each individual to get the marginal social benefit. At the output Q the marginal social benefit is $P = P_1 + P_2$. We sum vertically at *a given quantity* because everyone consumes the same quantity of a public good.

Figure 16.3 also shows the marginal cost of the public good. If there are no production externalities the marginal private cost and marginal social cost coincide. The socially efficient output of the public good is Q^*, where the marginal social benefit equals the marginal social cost.

What happens if the good is privately produced and marketed? Person 1 might pay P_1 to have a quantity Q produced by a competitive supplier pricing at marginal cost. At the output Q, the price P_1 just equals the marginal private benefit that person 1 gets from the last unit of the public good. Person 2 will not pay to have the output of the public good increased beyond Q. Person 2 cannot be excluded from consuming the output Q that person 1 has commissioned. At the output Q, person 2's marginal private benefit is only P_2, less than the current price P_1. Person 2 will not pay the higher price needed to induce a competitive supplier to expand output beyond Q. Person 2 free rides on person 1's purchase of Q. This quantity privately produced and consumed in a competitive market is below the efficient quantity Q^*.

Revelation of preferences

If it knows the marginal social benefit curve DD, the government can decide the efficient output of the public good. How does the government discover the individual demand curves that must be vertically added to get DD? If people's payments for the good are related to their individual demand curves, everyone will lie. People will understate how much they value the good in order to reduce their own payments, just as in a private market. Conversely, we are all for safer streets if we do not have to contribute to the cost.

In practice, democracies try to resolve this problem through elections of governments. Politics lets society get closer to the efficient answer than the market can. Different parties offer different quantities of public goods, together with a statement of how it will be financed by taxes. By asking 'How much would you like, given that everyone is charged for the cost of providing public goods?' society comes closer to providing the efficient quantities of public goods. However, with only a few parties competing in an election and many policies on which they offer a position, this remains a crude way to decide the quantities of public goods provided.

Government production

The output of public goods must be *decided* by the government not the market. This need not mean government must produce the goods itself. Public goods need not be produced by the public sector.

National defence is a public good largely produced in the public or government sector. We have few private armies. Street-sweeping, though a public good, can be subcontracted to private producers, even if local government determines its quantity and pays for it out of local tax revenue. Conversely, state hospitals involve public sector production of private goods. One person's hip replacement operation prevents the busy surgeon from operating on someone else.

In the next chapter we examine why the public sector may wish to produce private goods. Whether public goods need be produced by the public sector depends not on their consumption characteristics, on which our definition of public good relies, but on their production characteristics. There is nothing special about street-sweeping. In contrast, armies rely on discipline and secrecy. Generals and admirals may believe, and society may agree, that offences against these regulations should receive unusual penalties not generally sanctioned in private firms. Few people believe that insubordination is an important offence for street-sweepers.

Transfer payments and income redistribution

Government spending on transfer payments is primarily concerned with *equity* and *income redistribution*. By spending money on the unemployed, the old and the poor, the government alters the distribution of income and welfare that a free market economy would otherwise have produced: there is a minimum standard of living below which no citizen should fall. The specification of this standard is a pure value judgement.

To finance this spending, the government taxes those who can afford to pay. Taken as a whole, the tax and transfer system takes money from the rich and gives it to the poor. The poor get cash transfers but also enjoy the consumption of public goods paid for by income taxes raised from the rich. Figure 16.4 shows estimates of the cumulative effect of government intervention during 1997–2005. The richest 10 per cent of the population lost 4 per cent of their disposable incomes as a result of measures undertaken by the Labour government while Gordon Brown was Chancellor. In contrast, the poorest 10 per cent of the population benefited from changes to the tax and benefit system by an amount equal to 11 per cent of their initial disposable income. Labour redistributed spending power significantly.

The desirable amount of redistribution is a value judgement on which people and parties will disagree. There is also the trade-off between efficiency and equity. To redistribute more the government has to raise tax rates, driving a larger wedge between the price paid by the purchaser and the price received by the seller. Since the price system achieves efficiency by inducing each individual to equate marginal cost or marginal benefit to the price received or paid, and hence to one another, taxes are generally distortionary and reduce efficiency.

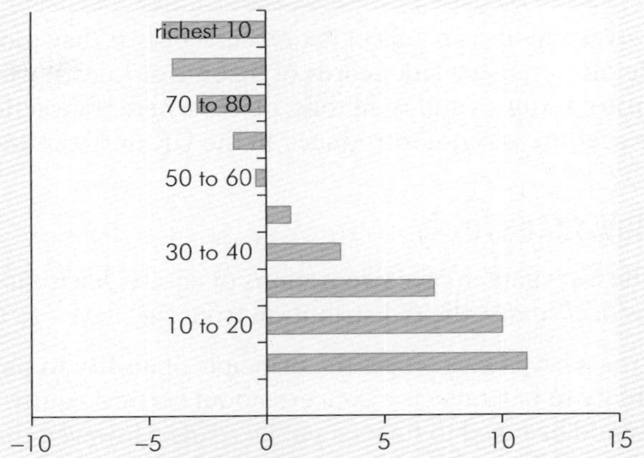

Figure 16.4 Net effect of changes to tax and benefits 1997–2005 (% of initial disposable income)

Source: Institute for Fiscal Studies.

Merit and demerit goods

Merit goods include education and health. Demerit goods include cigarettes and heroin. Since society places a different value on these goods from the value placed on them by the individual, individual choice in a free market leads to a different allocation from the one that society wishes.

Merit (demerit) goods are goods that society thinks everyone should have (not have) regardless of whether an individual wants them.

There are two reasons for merit goods. The first is externalities. If more education raises the productivity not merely of an individual worker but of the workers with whom she co-operates, she ignores this production externality when choosing how much education to acquire. If people demand too little education, society should encourage the provision of education.

Conversely, if people ignore the burden on state hospitals when deciding to smoke and damage their health, society may regard smoking as a demerit to be discouraged. Taxing cigarettes may offset externalities that individuals fail to take into account.

The second aspect of merit goods is if society believes that individuals no longer act in their own best interests. Addiction to drugs, tobacco or gambling are examples. Economists rarely subscribe to paternalism. The function of government intervention is less to tell people what they ought to like than to allow them better to achieve what they already like. However, the government sometimes has more information or is in a better position to take a decision. Many people hate going to school, but later are glad they did.

The government may spend money on compulsory education or compulsory vaccination because it recognizes that otherwise individuals act in a way they will subsequently regret.

16.3 The principles of taxation

This section is in three parts. First we consider different taxes through which the government can raise revenue. Then we consider equity implications of taxation. Finally, we examine efficiency implications of taxation.

Types of taxes

Governments can collect tax revenue only if they monitor and enforce the activities being taxed. Before sophisticated records of income or sales, governments raised most of their revenue from customs duties and road tolls, places where transactions were easily monitored. Income tax in peacetime was not introduced in the UK until the 1840s, and VAT not until the 1970s.

How to tax fairly

The last chapter gave two notions of equity: *horizontal equity*, or the equal treatment of equals, and *vertical equity*, the redistribution from the 'haves' to the 'have-nots'.

Progressive taxes reflect the principle of **ability to pay**. The principle of ability to pay reflects a concern about vertical equity. Thus, car users should be taxed to finance public roads. However, the benefits principle often conflicts with the principle of ability to pay. If those most vulnerable to unemployment pay the highest contributions to a government unemployment insurance scheme, it is hard to redistribute income or welfare. If the main objective is vertical equity, ability to pay must take precedence.

> The **benefits principle** is that people getting most benefit from public spending should pay most for it.

Two factors make the entire tax and benefit structure more progressive than an examination of income tax alone would suggest. First, transfer payments actually give money to the poor. The old receive pensions, the unemployed receive unemployment benefit, and, as a final safety net, anyone whose income falls below a certain minimum is entitled to supplementary benefit. Second, the state provides public goods that can be consumed by the poor, even if they have not paid any taxes to finance these goods.

However, the system of tax, transfer and spending has some *regressive* elements that take proportionately more from the poor. Beer and tobacco taxes are huge earners for the government. Yet the poor spend a much higher proportion of their income on these goods than do the rich. Regressive taxes inhibit redistribution from the rich to the poor.

Tax incidence

The ultimate effect of a tax can be very different from its initial effect. Figure 16.5 shows the market for labour. *DD* is the demand curve and *SS* the supply curve. Without an income tax (a tax on wages), labour market equilibrium is at *E*.

> **Tax incidence** is the final tax burden once we allow for all induced effects of a tax.

Now the government imposes an income tax. If we measure the gross wage on the vertical axis, the demand curve *DD* is unaltered. Firms' demand for labour depends on the gross wage that they pay. Workers' preferences are unchanged, but it is the wage net-of-tax that workers compare with the marginal value of their leisure in deciding how much labour to supply. *SS* continues to show labour supply in terms of the net-of-tax wage, but we must draw in the higher schedule *SS'* to show the supply of labour in terms of the gross or tax-inclusive wage. The vertical distance between *SS'* and *SS* is the tax on earnings from the last hour's work.

DD and *SS'* show the behaviour of firms and workers at any gross wage. At the new equilibrium *E'*, the gross wage is *W'* and firms demand *L'* workers. The vertical distance between *A'* and *E'* is the tax paid on the last hour of work. The net-of-tax wage is *W''* at which workers supply *L'* hours.

The tax on wages has raised the pre-tax wage to *W'*, but lowered the after-tax wage to *W''*. It has raised the wage that firms pay but lowered the take-home wage for workers. The incidence of the tax falls on *both* firms and workers.

> The **tax wedge** is the gap between the price paid by the buyer and the price received by the seller.

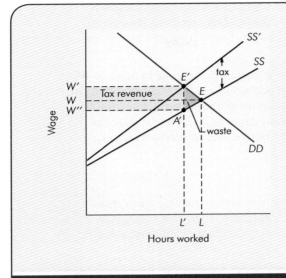

With no tax, equilibrium is at E and the wage is W. A wage tax raises the gross wage paid by firms above the net wage received by workers. Measuring gross wages on the vertical axis, the demand curve DD is unaltered by the imposition of the tax. Firms demand labour to equate the gross wage to the marginal value product of labour. SS continues to show labour supply, but as a function of the net wage. To get labour supply in terms of the gross wage we draw the new supply curve SS'. SS' lies vertically above SS by a distance reflecting the tax on earnings from the last hour worked. The new equilibrium is at E'. The hourly wage paid by firms is W' but the net wage received by workers is W''. The vertical distance A'E' shows the tax rate. Whether the government collects the tax from firms or from workers, the incidence of the tax is the same. It falls partly on firms, who pay a higher gross wage W' and partly on workers, who receive the lower net wage W''. The area of pure waste A'E'E is discussed in the text.

Figure 16.5 A tax on wages

The incidence or burden of a tax cannot be established by looking at who hands over the money to the government. Taxes alter equilibrium prices and quantities and these induced effects must be taken into account. However, we can draw one very general conclusion. The more inelastic the supply curve and the more elastic the demand curve, the more the final incidence will fall on the seller rather than the purchaser.

Figure 16.6 shows the extreme case in which supply is completely inelastic. With no tax, equilibrium is at E and the wage is W. Since the vertical supply curve SS means that a fixed quantity of hours L is supplied whatever the after-tax wage, a tax on wages leads to a new equilibrium at A'. Only if the gross wage is unchanged will firms demand the quantity L that is supplied. Hence the entire incidence falls on the workers.

To check you have grasped the idea of incidence, draw for yourself a market with an elastic supply curve and an inelastic demand curve. Show that the incidence of a tax will now fall mainly on the purchaser.[1]

Taxation, efficiency and waste

Taxes have efficiency effects as well as equity effects. We can use Figure 16.5 again. Before the tax is imposed, labour market equilibrium is at E. The wage W measures both the marginal social benefit of the last hour of work

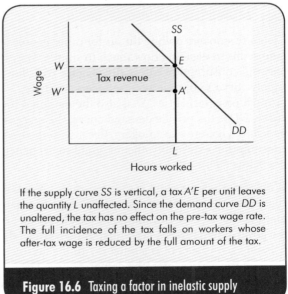

If the supply curve SS is vertical, a tax A'E per unit leaves the quantity L unaffected. Since the demand curve DD is unaltered, the tax has no effect on the pre-tax wage rate. The full incidence of the tax falls on workers whose after-tax wage is reduced by the full amount of the tax.

Figure 16.6 Taxing a factor in inelastic supply

1 Does a tax always shifts the supply curve? Yes, if we measure the gross price on the vertical axis. If we measure the net-of-tax price on the vertical axis, the tax shifts not the supply curve but the demand curve. In Figures 16.5 and 16.6, in terms of the net wage the demand curve shifts down until it passes through A'. The distance between A' and E still measures the tax and we get exactly the same conclusions as before.

and its marginal social cost. The demand curve *DD* tells us the marginal benefit of the extra goods produced. The supply curve *SS* tells us the marginal value of the leisure being sacrificed in order to work another hour, the marginal social cost of extra work. At *E* marginal social cost and benefit are equal, which is socially efficient.

When the tax is imposed, the new equilibrium is at *E'*. The tax *A'E'* increases the wage to firms to *W'* but reduces the after-tax wage for workers to *W''*. But there is an additional tax burden or deadweight loss that is pure waste. It is the triangle *A'E'E*. By reducing the quantity of hours from *L* to *L'*, the tax drives a wedge between marginal benefit, the height of the demand curve *DD*, and marginal social cost, the height of the supply curve *SS*. This distortion makes free market equilibrium inefficient.

Must taxes distort?

Government needs tax revenue to pay for public goods and make transfer payments. Figure 16.6 shows what happens when a tax is levied but supply is completely inelastic. There is no change in equilibrium quantity. Hence there is no distortionary triangle. The equilibrium quantity remains the efficient quantity.

We can make this into a general principle. When either the supply or the demand curve for a good or service is very inelastic, a tax leads to a small change in equilibrium quantity. Hence the deadweight burden triangle is small. Given that the government must raise some tax revenue, waste is smallest when the goods that are most inelastic in supply or demand are taxed most heavily.

In the UK tax system, the most heavily taxed commodities are alcohol and tobacco. Alcohol and tobacco have inelastic demand.

So far, we have discussed the taxes that do least harm to efficiency. Sometimes taxes improve efficiency and reduce waste. The most important example is when externalities exist.

Cigarette smokers pollute the air for other people but ignore this in deciding how much to smoke. They cause a harmful consumption externality. Figure 16.7 shows the supply curve *SS* of cigarette producers. With no production externalities, *SS* is also the marginal social cost curve. *DD* is the private demand curve, the marginal benefit of cigarettes to smokers. Because of the harmful consumption externality, the marginal social benefit *DD'* lies below *DD*.

With no tax, equilibrium is at *E*, but there are too many cigarettes. The efficient quantity is *Q**, which equates marginal social cost and marginal social benefit. Suppose the government levies a tax, equal to the vertical distance *E*F*, on each packet of cigarettes. With the tax-inclusive price on the vertical axis, the demand curve *DD* is unaffected, but the supply curve shifts up to *SS'*. Each point on *SS'* then allows producers to receive the corresponding net-of-tax price on *SS*.

The tax shifts equilibrium to *F*. The efficient quantity *Q** is produced and consumed. Consumers pay *P'* and producers get *P''* after tax is paid at the rate *E*F* per packet.

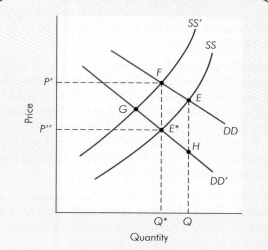

Given private demand *DD* and supply *SS* free market equilibrium is at *E* with a quantity *Q*. With a negative consumption externality, the social marginal benefit is *DD'* lying below *DD*. *E** is the socially efficient point at which output is *Q**. At this output the marginal externality is *E*F*. By levying a tax of exactly *E*F* per unit, the government can shift the private supply curve from *SS* to *SS'* leading to a new equilibrium at *F* at which the socially efficient quantity *Q** is produced and the deadweight burden of the externality *E*HE* is eliminated.

Figure 16.7 Taxes to offset externalities

The tax rate E^*F guides the free market to the efficient allocation. A lower tax rate (including zero) leads to too much consumption and production of cigarettes. A higher tax rate than E^*F moves consumers too far up their demand curve, causing too little consumption and production.

A tax rate E^*F leads to the efficient quantity because this is the size of the marginal externality when the efficient quantity Q^* is produced. A tax at this rate makes consumers behave as if they took account of the externality, though they think only about the tax-inclusive price.

When externalities induce distortions, the government can improve efficiency by levying taxes. The fact that alcohol and tobacco have harmful externalities is another reason to tax them heavily.

16.4 Taxation and supply-side economics

Suppose the government cuts spending and tax rates. What are the effects? First, by spending less on goods and services, the government frees some resources for use by the private sector. If the private sector is more productive than the public sector, the transfer of resources may directly raise output. Whether the private sector actually uses resources more productively than the government is unclear. It seems to do many things better but some things worse.

> **Supply-side economics** analyses how taxes and other incentives affect national output when the economy is at full capacity.

What about the effects of lower tax rates? Figure 16.7 suggests that tax distortions cause inefficiency. Lower taxes mean a lower deadweight burden. The size of this gain depends on supply and demand elasticity. If either elasticity is small, the social gain is low.

For example, Chapter 10 argued that labour supply is fairly inelastic for those in employment, but a bit more elastic for those thinking of joining the labour force. Cutting income tax rates *will* increase labour supply, but perhaps by less than many advocates of tax cuts believe.

The Laffer curve

We now discuss the relation between tax rates and tax revenues. Professor Laffer was an adviser to US President Ronald Reagan.

> The **Laffer curve** shows how much tax revenue is raised at each possible tax rate.

Figure 16.8 shows that with a zero tax rate the government gets zero revenue. At the opposite extreme, with a 100 per cent income tax rate,

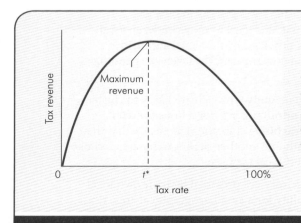

The Laffer curve shows the relationship between tax rates and tax revenue. Moderate tax rates raise some revenue. Beyond t^*, higher tax rates reduce revenue because disincentive effects greatly reduce the supply of the quantity being taxed. At 100 per cent tax rate, supply and revenue will be zero again.

Figure 16.8 The Laffer curve

there is no point working and again tax revenue is zero. Beginning from a zero rate, a small increase in the tax rate yields some tax revenue. Initially tax revenue rises with the tax rate, but beyond the tax rate t^* higher taxes have major disincentive effects on work effort and revenue falls.

Professor Laffer's idea was that 'big government–big tax' countries were at tax rates above t^*. If so, tax cuts were the miracle cure. The government would get *more* revenue by cutting taxes. By reducing the tax distortion and increasing the amount of work *a lot*, lower tax rates would be more than offset by higher incomes to tax.

The shape of the Laffer curve is not in dispute. However, many economists disputed the view that *in fact* tax rates were above t^*. Most economists' reading of the empirical evidence is that our economies were always to the left of t^*. Cutting income tax rates may eliminate some of the deadweight burden of distortionary taxation, but governments should probably expect their tax revenue to fall if tax rates are cut. Governments wishing to avoid borrowing need to cut their spending if they wish to cut the tax rate.

16.5 Local government

So much for central government. What about local government? Local government spends on things from sweeping the streets to providing local schooling. This is financed both by local taxes and by money from central government financed by national taxes. Local government is also responsible for some types of regulation, for example land use or *zoning* laws.

Economic principles

Why don't we make central government responsible for everything? First, diversity matters. People are different and do not want to be treated the same. Civic pride is necessarily local. Second, people feel that central government is remote from their particular needs. Even if central government paid attention to local considerations, it would find it hard to do so efficiently.

We examine two important models of local government. The *Tiebout model*[2] emphasizes diversity. Some people want high spending, good public services and high local taxes; others want low local taxes even if this means poor public services. If all local governments are the same, everyone hates the compromise. The Tiebout model is sometimes called the *invisible foot*: people cluster in the area providing the package of spending and taxes they want. The invisible foot allocates resources efficiently via competition *between* local governments.

In practice, the invisible foot is a crude incentive structure. First, it is hard to move between local authorities. You may lose your place in the queue for housing provided by that local authority. Second, if much of local authority revenue comes from central government, the levels of spending and taxes may be insensitive to the wishes of local residents.

Even if the invisible foot led to efficiency, it might also lead to inequity. The rich are likely to cluster together in suburbs. Then they pass zoning laws specifying a minimum size for a house and its garden. The poor cannot move into that area. By forming an exclusive club, the rich ensure that their taxes do not go to supporting the poor. The poor get stuck with one another in inner-city areas whose governments face the biggest social needs but have the smallest local tax base.

The Tiebout model assumes that residents consume the public services provided by their own local authority. When each unit of local government has responsibility for a small geographical area, this may be a bad assumption. If a city supplies free art galleries, financed by taxes on city residents, the

2 Charles Tiebout, 'A Pure Theory of Local Expenditures', *Journal of Political Economy*, 1956

rich still come in from the suburbs to use these facilities. Conversely, urban trendies spend their Sundays enjoying countryside facilities supported by rural taxes. In both cases, provision of public services in one area confers a beneficial externality on nearby areas.

Economic theory suggests an answer to this problem. Widen the geographical area of each local government until it includes most of the people who use the public services it provides. It may make sense to have an integrated commuter rail service and inner-city subway, and to subsidize it to prevent people driving through congested streets. However, only a local government embracing both the suburbs and the inner city is likely to get close to the efficient policy.

The Tiebout model favours a lot of small local government jurisdictions to maximize choice and competition between areas. However, the presence of externalities across areas suggests larger jurisdictions to 'internalize' externalities that would otherwise occur. The right answer may involve a bit of both.

16.6 Economic sovereignty

Nowadays, no country is an economic island, cut off from the rest of the world. We examine the world economy in Part 5, but some issues cannot be postponed till then. In a democratic country insulated from the rest of the world, the government is sovereign: while it retains democratic support and observes existing laws, it has the final say in policy design. Sometimes central government chooses to delegate powers to local government. Section 16.5 discussed when it is efficient to do so. What this account ignores is the existence of other countries. How do interactions with the rest of the world affect the sovereignty of national governments?

Even in a quarantined economy, governments cannot do anything they like. Within market economies they have to work within the forces of supply and demand. For example, in Section 16.3 we argued that it is generally more efficient to have high tax rates on things for which the demand or supply is inelastic: high tax rates on things with elastic supply and demand induces large distortions since equilibrium quantity is very sensitive to the price. We now apply this insight to economies open to interactions with the rest of the world.

> **Economic sovereignty** is the power of national governments to make decisions independently of those made by other governments.

Box 16.2 Betting tax scrapped early

The tax on punters will be abolished three months ahead of schedule on the first weekend in October, the Financial Secretary Paul Boateng announced today [13 July 2001]. Gordon Brown announced in his March budget that by 1 January 2002, the current tax on betting stakes would be replaced with a tax on bookmakers' gross profits, a radical reform which means Britain's bookmakers will end the deductions they currently charge punters, and look to grow their domestic and international business from a UK base.

(www.hm-treasury.gov.uk)

This example illustrates the limits to government sovereignty. Betting tax had been a big earner for the Treasury. Competition from offshore bookies offering online betting put an end to this. The government was forced to change betting tax to stop onshore bookies being wiped out. How the internet and globalization are changing the nation state is a recurring theme of our analysis. Economics helps you understand better what is going on.

International capital is now highly mobile across countries. Suppose the UK government tries to levy a large tax on capital in Britain. Lots of capital will quickly move elsewhere to escape the high taxes. The *tax base*, in this example the quantity of capital available for taxing in Britain, quickly shrinks. So the high tax *rates* may raise little tax *revenue*. In contrast, since people are much less mobile than capital across national boundaries, the tax base for taxing workers' incomes in Britain is much less sensitive to tax rates than the tax base for capital taxes.

Even people are more mobile across national boundaries than they were a few decades ago. Communication is easier, transport costs are lower and satellites pay no attention to national frontiers on a map. Migration affects not just taxation but government spending as well. Suppose a country wishes to implement a generous welfare state. As a closed economy, all it has to worry about is how much of its tax base disappears from work into leisure. If welfare is too generous, people may not work enough. As an open economy, it also has to worry whether more generous welfare provision will lead to more migration into the country as foreigners take advantage, legally or illegally, of the generous welfare provision.

Closer economic integration with other countries – through trade in goods and movement of factors of production – effectively undermines the sovereignty of nation states. If the tax rate was 80 per cent in Liverpool but 20 per cent in Manchester, one would expect big movements of capital and people from Liverpool to Manchester. The tax base in Liverpool would evaporate (even die-hard Everton supporters could commute from Manchester). The local government of Liverpool has limited local sovereignty because it is effectively in competition with Manchester.

As modern technology undermines even barriers between countries, the same process is at work. The economic sovereignty of nation states, their freedom to do what they want, is steadily being constrained by competition from foreign countries. More than one in ten cans of beer now consumed in England was bought by British households in France, hopping across the Channel to take advantage of lower alcohol taxes in France. UK Chancellors, caught between the pressure to raise revenue and support jobs in the UK drinks industry, have been cutting the real value of UK alcohol taxes. They have already lost the sovereignty to set tax rates at the high levels that they would have liked.

National sovereignty is undermined not just by competition between countries for tax bases but by two other forces. The first is other cross-country spillovers such as acid rain, greenhouse gases or the threat of pollution from a nuclear accident. Banning nuclear power generation in southern England has limited value if northern France is studded with nuclear power stations.

The second is the scope for redistribution. Economics is about equity as well as efficiency. In an important sense, the right jurisdiction for government is the area within which citizens feel sufficient identity with one another that the rich are prepared to pay for the poor, and the fortunate are prepared to assist the unlucky. European nation states have long histories and strong national identities. But these are not always set in stone. Countries such as Belgium, Italy, Spain and the UK have faced strong internal pressures to allow part of their country to secede. In the opposite direction, some Europeans now feel as much a citizen of Europe as of their own particular nation.

Nation states are not yet obsolete. But they are coming under pressure. Further developments in technology will increase the transnational scope of economic interactions and cultural identity. The proliferation of e-commerce and the internet will only accelerate this process.

16.7 Political economy: how governments decide

Firms are in business to make profits for their owners. Individuals buy affordable combinations of goods that yield them most satisfaction. These simple assumptions let economists explain most consumer and business decision making. What about government decision making?

Government is the most important single player in the economy. It is important to develop theories of how governments behave. There is no point analysing the consequences of a policy that a sane government will never implement.

> **Political economy** is the study of how governments make decisions.

Voters elect governments to set spending and taxing, pass new laws and establish new regulations. The electorate chooses among alternative policy *packages* offered by competing parties, but is rarely allowed a referendum on each issue.

The government does not simply do the bidding of society. Government has its own agenda, which may be to promote what it thinks is good for the public or may simply be to get re-elected.

The median voter

If everyone was identical and of one mind, public decision making would be trivial. Through the political process, society tries to reconcile different views and different interests.

Figure 16.9 shows 17 different voters and how much each wants the government to spend on the police. A dot shows each voter's preferred amount. Assume that a voter whose ideal amount is £250 will think that £300 is better than £400 if these are the only choices on offer, and will prefer £200 to £100. Each person has *single-peaked* preferences, being happier with an outcome the closer it is to his peak or preferred level.

There is a vote on how much to spend on the public good called police. A proposal to spend £0 is defeated by 16 votes to 1. Only the voter, who is the left-hand dot in Figure 16.9, votes for £0 rather than £100. From either extreme, as we move to the centre more people vote for a particular proposal. With 17 voters, the median voter is the person who wants to spend the ninth-highest amount on the police. Eight voters want to spend more, eight want to spend less.

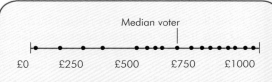

Each dot represents the preferred expenditure of each of 17 voters. The outcome under majority voting will be the level preferred by the median voter. Everybody to the left will prefer the median voter's position to any higher spending level. Everybody to the right will prefer it to any lower spending level. The median voter's position is the only position that cannot be outvoted against some alternative. Hence it will be chosen.

Figure 16.9 The median voter

Any proposal for higher spending than the median voter's preferred amount can be defeated. The median voter, plus the eight voters below him, all vote against. But any proposal for lower spending is also defeated. The median voter, and the eight voters above him, all vote against. Hence, the median voter gets his way by majority voting.

> The **median voter** on an issue is the person whose preferences are such that half the population's preferences on the issue lie on one side and half the population's preferences on the other side.

Logrolling

So far we have assumed each issue is voted on independently. Making decisions through legislative compromises is much more complicated when votes can be traded between different issues. Groups of politicians form parties or coalitions within which some vote trading can take place.

> **Logrolling** is a vote for another person's preferred outcome on one issue in order to exchange for their vote your preferred outcome on another issue.

For two issues, A and B, and three politicians, Tom, Dick and Harry, Table 16.5 shows the value of each outcome to each politician. Suppose each person votes for a proposal only if the outcome is positive. Tom votes against A and B, Dick votes against A but for B, and Harry votes for A but against B. Both issues are defeated on a majority vote.

Activity box 16 Hunting the median voter

After Labour lost the 1979 general election it moved to the left. This pleased party activists but took the party too far away from the preferences of the median voter. The Conservatives were in power for the next 17 years. After heavy defeat in 1983, successive Labour leaders slowly moved the party back to the middle ground that the median voter inhabits. Labour focus groups interviewed people directly to clarify the median voter's view on different issues. The result? Labour victories in 1997, 2001 and 2005.

Did Labour abandon its principles to win and keep office? It gave up old traditions of high welfare spending and high, visible taxes. But, Chancellor of the Exchequer Gordon Brown helped the poor substantially without frightening the middle classes. As a result of his budgets, the post-tax income of the poorest 20 per cent of people rose by over 10 per cent (see Figure 16.4 again).

How did he do it? Not by raising income tax or VAT. Some of it was financed by stealth taxes, such as the tax treatment of pension funds, which the median voter did not initially notice or understand. Some was financed by making transfer payments more selective. Instead of a universal benefit, scarce resources were concentrated only on those who really needed them. Some of it was financed by economic growth: as incomes grew, given tax rates yielded more tax revenue, which was given mainly to the poor.

Unusually, Labour has *not* taken credit for the extent it has helped the poor. This has kept the median voter sweet (the middle classes are not told repeatedly how they are paying too much to support the poor) but has upset some traditional Labour supporters (who will probably vote Labour anyway).

Questions

(a) In a country with two parties, suppose both end up with almost identical policies in the centre ground. What does this tell you about (i) the ideology of the party leaders and (ii) the extent to which party activists trade off the desire for power and their political beliefs?

(b) Suppose we could order voters from left to right with equal numbers of voters holding each possible opinion. If everyone votes for the party nearest their own beliefs, where should the two parties locate to maximize their vote?

(c) Now, however, suppose that people abstain if the party is not close to the voters' ideal positions. Does this change the optimal positioning of party manifestos?

To check your answers to these questions, go to page 723.

Now suppose Dick and Harry vote together. They vote for A, which Harry really wants, and for B, which Dick really wants. Dick gains 4 since B passes, and loses only 3 when A passes. Harry gains 6 when A passes and loses only 1 when B passes. By forming a coalition that allows them to express the intensity of their preferences they do better than under independent majority voting, when neither A nor B would have passed.

Many decisions in the European Union reflect logrolling. Individual countries get favourable decisions on issues they really mind about, but are expected to repay the favour on other issues.

Table 16.5 Logrolling

Politician	Issue A	Issue B
1	−4	−1
2	−3	4
3	6	−1

Commitment and credibility

Chapter 9 introduced credibility and commitment in the context of games between firms. Similar ideas apply to the political economy of policy design. Because expectations about the future affect current decisions, politicians are tempted to make optimistic promises about the future in the hope of influencing people today.

Our discussion of strategic entry deterrence in Chapter 9 gives you all the clues you need to think about political credibility. Project your imagination into the future and think how politicians will then want to behave. Use this insight to form smart guesses today about which promises are credible and which are not.

> A **credible** promise about future action is one that is optimal to carry out when the future arrives. A **commitment** is a current device to restrict future room for manoeuvre to make promises more credible today.

For example, most postwar Labour governments were big spenders, which required high taxation. When out of office, Labour promises of low spending and low taxes when next in government were not very credible. Gordon Brown's Code for Fiscal Stability was an attempt to enhance Labour's credibility by openly and repeatedly committing to a tough policy that would then be politically costly to abandon. With so much political capital invested in prudence and the Code for Fiscal Stability, the government would look very stupid if it subsequently abandoned it.

Recently, many countries have adopted a commitment that has been very successful. They have made the central bank operationally independent of government control, as Labour did with the Bank of England in 1997. The government chooses the aim of monetary policy – to keep inflation low – but the Bank alone now decides what interest rates are needed to achieve this. By keeping the government's hands off interest rates, central bank independence removes the temptation for the government to overheat the economy in pursuit of a pre-election boom.

Policy co-ordination

Chapter 9 contained another useful insight for modern political economy. In discussing games between oligopolists, we showed that collectively they make more profit acting as a joint monopolist than by acting without co-ordination. In the language you later learned in Chapter 15, when actions are interdependent and externalities matter, the efficient solution needs to take these spillovers fully into account. Internalizing externalities means stopping free-riding.

The more interdependent different nation states become, the more it may be necessary to co-ordinate national policies rather than formulate them in isolation. Global warming is one example, but many forms of regulation and taxation fall under this heading.

French tax rates on alcohol are so much lower than UK rates that UK Chancellors can no longer set UK alcohol taxes as high as they would like. The UK would like continental tax rates on alcohol to be higher. Conversely, continental Europeans complain about low levels of worker protection in the UK and the competitive edge this may give UK firms. Pressures for closer policy co-ordination are likely to increase as globalization continues.

> **Policy co-ordination** is the decision to set policies jointly when two interdependent areas have big cross-border spillovers.

Summary

- Government revenues come mainly from **direct taxes** on personal incomes and company profits, **indirect taxes** on purchases of goods and services and **contributions** to state-run social security schemes. Government spending comprises **government purchases** of goods and services and **transfer payments**.

- Governments intervene in a market economy in pursuit of distributional equity and allocative efficiency. A **progressive tax-and-transfer system** takes most from the rich and gives most to the poor. The UK system is mildly progressive. The less well off receive transfer payments and the rich pay the highest tax rates. Although some necessities, notably food, are exempt from VAT, other goods intensively consumed by the poor, notably cigarettes and alcohol, are heavily taxed.

- **Externalities** are cases of market failure where intervention may improve efficiency. By taxing or subsidizing goods that involve externalities, the government can induce the private sector to behave as if it takes account of the externality, eliminating the **deadweight burden** arising from the misallocation induced by the externality distortion.

- A **public good** is a good for which one person's consumption does not reduce the quantity available for consumption by others. Together with the impossibility of effectively excluding people from consuming it, this implies all individuals consume the same quantity, but they may get different utility if their tastes differ.

- A free market will undersupply a public good because of the **free-rider problem**. Individuals need not offer to pay for a good that they can consume if others pay for it. The socially **efficient** quantity of a public good equates the marginal social cost of production to the sum of the marginal private benefits over all people at this output level. Individual demand curves are vertically added to get the social demand or marginal benefit curve.

- Except for taxes to offset externalities, taxes are **distortionary**. A **wedge** between the sale price and purchase price prevents the price system equating marginal costs and marginal benefits. The size of the **deadweight burden** is higher the higher is the marginal tax rate and the size of the wedge, but also depends on supply and demand elasticities for the taxed commodity or activity. The more inelastic are supply and demand, the less the tax changes equilibrium quantity and the smaller is the deadweight burden.

- **Tax incidence** describes who ultimately pays the tax. The more inelastic is demand relative to supply, the more incidence falls on buyers not sellers.

- Rising tax rates initially increase tax revenue but eventually lead to such large falls in the equilibrium quantity of the taxed commodity or activity that revenue falls. Cutting tax rates will usually reduce the deadweight tax burden but might increase revenue if taxes were initially very high. Few economies are in this position. Lower tax rates usually reduce tax revenue.

- The **economic sovereignty** of nation states is reduced by cross-border mobility of goods, capital, workers and shoppers. Policy co-ordination may increase efficiency by making decisions reflect previously neglected policy spillovers.

- **Political economy** examines political equilibrium and incentives to adopt particular policies.

- When all those voting have single-peaked preferences, majority voting achieves what the **median voter** wants.

Review questions

To check your answers to these questions, go to page 722.

1 Which of the following are public goods? (a) The fire brigade, (b) clean streets, (c) refuse collection, (d) cable television, (e) social toleration, (f) the postal service.

2 Why does society try to ensure that every child receives an education? Discuss the different ways this could be done and give reasons for preferring one method of providing such an education.

3 How would you apply the principles of horizontal and vertical equity in deciding how much to tax two people, each capable of doing the same work, but one of whom chooses to devote more time to sunbathing and therefore has a lower income?

4 Classify the following taxes as progressive or regressive. (a) 10 per cent tax on all luxury goods, (b) taxes in proportion to the value of owner-occupied houses, (c) taxes on beer, (d) taxes on champagne.

5 There is a flat-rate 30 per cent income tax on all income over £2000. Calculate the average tax rate (tax paid divided by income) at income levels of £5000, £10 000 and £50 000. Is the tax progressive? Is it more or less progressive if the exemption is raised from £2000 to £5000?

6 **Common fallacies** Why are these statements wrong? (a) If government spends all its revenue, taxes are not a burden on society as a whole. (b) Taxes always distort. (c) Political economy is just an excuse to waffle, and cannot be made rigorous.

7 **Harder question** (a) Suppose labour supply is completely inelastic. Show why there is no deadweight burden if wages are taxed. Who bears the incidence of the tax? (b) Now suppose labour supply is quite elastic. Show the area that is the deadweight burden of the tax. How much of the tax is ultimately borne by firms and how much by workers? (c) For any given supply elasticity show that firms bear more of the tax the more inelastic is the demand for labour.

8 **Harder question** Hypothecation is the promise to use tax revenue from a product to achieve benefits for the group who bear the tax, for example using the London congestion charge to improve London's public transport or using tobacco taxes to build health centres for smokers. (a) Why are politicians attracted by hypothecation and (b) why are economists not attracted by hypothecation?

9 **Essay question** Imagine a new UK government, to the surprise of everyone, announces that income tax rates will rise by 15 percentage points in order to provide decent schools and hospitals. Describe the good and bad consequences. How did you decide what you meant by good and bad?

LearningCentre

To help you grasp the key concepts of this chapter check out the extra resources posted on the Online Learning Centre. There are chapter summaries, self-test questions, an interactive graphing tool, weblinks and a searchable glossary, all for free!

To put your learning into practice and prepare for exams, an **Interactive Workbook** is also available online, containing a variety of question types and providing feedback on your answers.

If you'd like further help with economics, or have any questions, **NetTutor** is here to help! You will have a personalised tutorial service at your fingertips. Visit the online learning centre at: www.mcgraw-hill.co.uk/textbooks/begg for information on accessing all of these resources.

CHAPTER 17

Industrial policy and competition policy

Learning Outcomes

By the end of this chapter, you should understand:

1 competition policy and industrial policy to offset market failures

2 how patents boost investment in R&D

3 market failures in sunrise and sunset industries

4 locational externalities

5 consumer surplus and producer surplus

6 the social cost of monopoly

7 the design of competition policy

8 types of merger and why merger booms occur

9 regulation of potential mergers

What do Durex and cornflakes have in common with Heathrow Airport and mobile phones? The London Rubber Company, Kelloggs, British Airports Authority and Vodafone were all investigated by the Competition Commission, which monitors how large firms behave and examines possible abuse of monopoly power.[1]

In Chapter 15 we explained how welfare depends on efficiency and equity.

Competition policy entails rules about conduct of firms or the structure of industries. The former aims to prevent abuse of a monopoly position. The latter seeks to prevent monopolies arising.

> **Competition policy** tries to enhance efficiency by promoting or safeguarding competition.

Some industries are natural monopolies. Scale economies are so large that breaking them up makes no sense, and competition from other firms provides no discipline. In many countries, especially in Europe, these became nationalized industries, run by the state in the social interest. After 1980 the UK pioneered the privatization of many of these firms. Other countries have followed suit. Since scale economies do not vanish with privatization, continuing regulation has been necessary in many instances. We describe this regulatory revolution in the next chapter. First, we deal with cases in which scale economies are less acute. Competition policy is then a more promising avenue for intervention.

---

1 Before 1999, the Competition Commission was called the Monopolies and Mergers Commission.

Before so doing, we discuss other motives for intervention to increase production efficiency. If inefficiency arises not from scale economies and market power, nor from the environmental externalities we discussed in Chapter 15, what other market failures do we have in mind? Essentially, all the other externalities associated with production.

We discuss four such market failures: piracy of intellectual property; spillovers across national borders that make national policies inefficient; capital market failures that explain why new businesses are so hard to start; and locational externalities that explain why top car producers – Ferrari, Maserati, Lamborghini – cluster in the Italian town of Modena and Chinese restaurants cluster in London's Soho district.

> **Industrial policy** aims to offset externalities affecting production decisions by firms.

17.1 Industrial policy

Intellectual property: inventions, patents and copyright

Information is a very special economic commodity that frequently causes indigestion in freely competitive markets. It is hard to trade information: the buyer needs to see it but, having seen it, then has no incentive to pay for it.

One example is invention, the discovery of new information about production. A company develops a product in secret, and then markets it. If other firms quickly imitate the new invention, competition bids away the profits on this new product. Everyone can foresee that this will occur, so few resources are devoted to searching for inventions, even though they are socially valuable.

The problem arises because the inventor cannot privately appropriate the benefits since imitators cannot be excluded. The solution to this market failure is a system of property rights that temporarily award the inventor the right to treat this knowledge as an asset called intellectual property. During this period, the creator of the knowledge can therefore profit from the use of their intellectual property. Knowing in advance that successful knowledge creation will be so rewarded is what provides the incentive to invest in the knowledge creation industry in the first place.

The legal monopoly is temporary to prevent successful inventors having a permanent entry barrier that prevents competition for ever. A successful patent system provides a big enough incentive for invention, but does not suppress competition indefinitely.

> **Intellectual property** is the recognition that the creator of new knowledge may, for a period, own it as an asset from which income may be derived. This temporary legal monopoly is called a **patent** in the case of inventions and is called a **copyright** in the case of works of literature or music.

There is no perfect solution to this tension – the need to protect intellectual property in order to create the right incentives for knowledge creation, and the wish to disseminate new knowledge as quickly as possible in order to maximize the benefits of competition. Industrial policy has to strike a balance, and the optimal duration of the initial property rights may vary from product to product. In practice, the legal system tends to standardize the life of patents and copyrights before they expire.

These issues are even more complicated when strategic behaviour takes place. Incumbent firms may discover and patent a new process, but *not* introduce it. Knowing they will be met with the launch of this new product, potential entrants are deterred from entry. Pre-emptive patenting is an effective strategic entry barrier. Intelligent industrial policy and competition policy must work hand in hand. Evidence of pre-emptive patenting is the type of information the Competition Commission seeks in evaluating whether incumbents are abusing their market power.

Research and development (R&D)

Most countries subsidize R&D, which accounts for around 2 per cent of national output in advanced countries. What are the market failures in R&D that the patent system can offset?

> **Research** is the process of invention, the creation of new knowledge. **Development** is the process of innovating to make research commercially viable.

First, large projects are risky for an individual company. Boeing, the large plane manufacturer, describes a project as 'betting the company': failure of one new project could threaten its existence as a company. Chapter 13 described why private individuals are risk-averse. So are executives of large firms. Private firms may undertake less R&D than is socially desirable.

The social return exceeds the private return to those making the decisions. Society needs a lower rate of return, or uses a lower discount rate to evaluate the project's future benefits, for two reasons. First, the government can *pool* the risks across many projects in its portfolio. Second, even if a project goes wrong, the government can spread the burden thinly across the population: 1 per cent on everybody's income tax rate for a year should cover even the biggest disaster. Thus, society needs a smaller risk premium than that required by executives who may lose their well-paid jobs if a project turns sour. This is one reason to subsidize R&D. Here is a second.

Sir Isaac Newton said he stood on the shoulders of giants. Each invention or discovery makes it easier for the next inventor. But no inventor can take out a patent for the future inventions that others invent as a result of a particular discovery. Hence, the private benefit to the inventor is less than the social benefit. This is a second reason to subsidize R&D.

Strategic international competition

Consider again the commercial airliner industry. Effectively, there are two large firms left in the world market, the US giant Boeing-McDonnell-Douglas and the European consortium Airbus, a division of EADS.[2]

Suppose Airbus asks the governments of its member producers for *launch aid*, a grant or loan on favourable terms to help with R&D on new aircraft. In addition to the standard arguments for R&D support, what extra issues does international competition raise?

First, Airbus may succeed even without government support. If so, public subsidies are simply a transfer payment to Airbus shareholders – a poor idea.

Second, launch aid may affect *whether* Airbus succeeds. If Airbus pulls out, Boeing-McDonnell-Douglas will be the sole producer without fear of competition. Boeing would surely raise the price of aircraft. European airlines and ultimately European consumers would pay high prices, and Boeing would earn monopoly profits. It may be worth preventing this.

Financial support is a commitment by European governments not to let Airbus be bullied out of the industry. Boeing may conclude that there is no point attempting a price war to force Airbus to exit. A European commitment may *prevent* a price war that would otherwise occur. Strategic international competition can provide a rationale for strategic industrial policy. Of course, once Airbus is as large as Boeing, it is no longer likely to be forced out of the industry. The case for government support then diminishes.

---

2 Airbus was originally a consortium of aerospace firms from France, Germany, Spain and the UK. In 2000, the French, German and Spanish companies merged to create EADS, which owned 80 per cent of Airbus, with British Aerospace continuing to own 20 per cent. In 2006, BAe pulled out, selling its stake to EADS.

Box 17.1 UK plc

Harvard Business School guru Michael Porter is famous for his work on what gives companies and countries a competitive edge. He gives the UK low marks when deriving commercial benefit from science and technology. Rather, Nordic countries, Singapore, South Korea and Taiwan have been significantly better at improving innovation rates. Both UK patent application rates and the quality of the patents are at best only average in a global perspective, reflecting how UK manufacturing spend less of their turnover on R&D than their European peers. For example, where the UK generates 75 patents per million of population, the Germans manage 150 per million of population.

Every year, Porter and his team publish an index of national competitiveness. In 2006 the United States and Germany continued to top an annual review of the business competitiveness of 121 countries. Porter's index of national competitiveness measures the underpinnings of a country's prosperity, emphasizing microeconomic underpinnings of productivity such as the level of company sophistication and quality of the business environment.

The annual report identifies national competitive strengths and weaknesses, highlights global economic trends and signals the ingredients of successful economic development. The US, ranked top in four of the last six years, scored high on business environment, financial markets and innovative capacity. Germany benefited from its orientation on exports, the unique competitive positions of its companies and the quality of its legal and regulatory framework.

Rounding out the Top 10 were Finland, Switzerland, Denmark, the Netherlands, Sweden, the United Kingdom, Japan and Hong Kong. Other high-income nations increasing their ranking included Qatar, Norway and Malta. Advanced economies on the decline included Cyprus, the Czech Republic, Taiwan and France.

China fell nine places to 64, because of higher levels of corruption, weaker assessment of buyer sophistication and concerns about labour relations, the study found. Also contributing were weak property rights, poor board governance and low quality of management education. India moved up four rankings to 27, aided by improvements in its business environment and increasing levels of company sophistication.

Among the dozens of variables analysed are production process sophistication, per capita internet and mobile phone use, intensity of local competition, financial market sophistication and intellectual property protection.

The report also attempts to gauge the ingredients necessary for long-term, sustainable growth. Although institutional stability, sound macroeconomic policies, market opening and privatization are often seen as keystones to success, they are not by themselves sufficient for economic development. Microeconomic activity such as the sophistication of company operations account for 80 per cent of the variation in GDP per capita across countries, according to the report. Macroeconomic factors create a favourable business environment while microeconomic activity contributes to the productivity and competitiveness of individual firms.

Source: http://hbswk.hbs.edu/item/5454.html.

Sunrise and sunset industries

More generally, this alerts us to the importance of dynamic change, the rise and fall of industries and the firms within them.

Currently, sunrise industries include computing and genetics. Sunset industries in Western economies include the old heavy industries, such as steel and shipbuilding, now suffering from massive excess capacity, undercut by more efficient producers in the Pacific basin.

> **Sunrise** industries are the emerging new industries of the future. **Sunset** industries are those of the past, now in long-term decline.

Why not leave such changes to market forces? What market failures might justify government intervention through industrial policy? We begin with the sunrise industries.

Two types of market failure are put forward to justify the case for intervention. First, there may be imperfections in the market for lending to new companies and new industries. Banks and other lenders may be too risk-averse, or too unfamiliar with the new business, to lend the money needed through the early loss-making years. Second, the market may be slow to provide the relevant training and skills: Catch 22 (until the industry exists, people will not perceive the need for developing such skills; but without the skills, the industry cannot exist).

These arguments may justify industrial policy to subsidize sunrise industries. But two questions must first be answered. First, why are markets short-sighted and uninformed? Second, even if markets get it wrong, can the government do better? The strategy of trying to outguess the market by 'picking winners' is now highly discredited. Civil servants or politicians are unlikely to beat analysts in industry and finance. If industrial policy is to be pursued, it is better to diagnose the cause of the market failure and provide a generalized incentive that market decision makers then take into account when undertaking their professional analysis.

Sunset industries present different problems. A government may care about local unemployment when industries with a heavy geographical concentration are allowed to go under. It *may* be desirable to spend what could otherwise be dole money on temporarily subsidizing lame ducks to ease the transition. Sometimes, a sharp shock is needed to signal the extent of the adjustment eventually required and the government's commitment to seeing the adjustment take place.

Strategic considerations are important here, too. Suppose there are two remaining firms in an industry that can now support only one. Each firm wants the other one to exit. One of two things may happen, neither of which is socially desirable. First, the industry survives with two firms for much longer than is socially efficient. Second, the firm with the smaller financial backing is the first to crack, even if it could produce at lower cost than its richer rival. An industrial policy that seeks faster and more efficient rationalization of the sunset industry may be advantageous.

17.2 Economic geography

Consumer electronics – TVs, sound systems, home computers – can be found in many ring-road superstores, but people in south-east England still go to Tottenham Court Road, London, for cheap deals, just as in the 1960s their parents bought flower-power clothes in Carnaby Street. Ferrari apart, most Formula 1 racing teams are based in the Thames Valley.

'Economic geography' – the idea that locational externalities are significant and require special analysis – was popularized by Professor Paul Krugman in the early 1990s, but the idea dates back to Alfred Marshall, a Cambridge professor at the turn of the last century. Why

> **Economic geography** means that a firm's location affects its production costs. A beneficial **locational externality** occurs if a firm's costs are reduced by locating near similar firms.

might a firm's costs of production depend on its proximity to other firms? Explanations fall under three headings: the interaction of scale economies and risk, transport and transactions costs, and technological spillovers.

Suppose a worker invests in very specific skills, such as designing racing cars or persuading customers that floral shirts are essential. With only one firm in the local labour market, the worker is very dependent on a particular employer. Having skills this specific is risky. With a cluster of similar employers, workers' risks fall. They no longer require such a large 'risk premium' or 'compensating differential' in their wage. Labour is cheaper for firms. Where did scale economies come into the argument? Without them, each locality could have a tiny smattering of every firm. It is the presence of (some) scale economies that forces firms into all or nothing choices between different locations.

A second reason for clustering of producers is transport costs. Shops may cluster because of transport costs for consumers – one trip gets you to a street with lots of shops stocking what you want – but larger producers cluster because of features of production. Closeness to raw materials is an obvious example. Discovering a coal seam or iron ore leads to a profusion of heavy industrial businesses in the locality.

Box 17.2 State Aids in the EU

Every time a government gives yet another 'final subsidy' to its ailing national airline, there is a howl of protest from other airlines trying to compete. The EU is cracking down on State Aids, preferential government treatment of its national firms, distorting competition. Examples are ad hoc subsidies and special tax breaks, but not aid open to firms of all nationalities. Getting rid of State Aids is not easy. But they are falling, and have gone in the UK.

EU policy views State Aids as bad for efficiency, the traditional view of economists. However, in economics you get out what you put in. In models with few market failures, State Aids add a wasteful market failure and diminish efficiency. However, State Aids may offset other market failures. Section 17.1 discusses strategic international competition, as between Boeing and Airbus. Knowing that Airbus has State Aids may affect Boeing's behaviour in ways favourable to Europe.

Second, locational externalities may provide incentives for governments to bid for inward investment (e.g. Japanese car producers), which then augments the industrial base of its host nation. For the EU as a whole, it is desirable that inflows go where contribution is largest. An implicit auction, with member states bidding to attract investment (offering tax advantages, investment grants, etc.) may be an efficient way to reveal where locational externalities are greatest.

Most significant of all is the spillover in technology itself. Famous examples include Silicon Valley in California, and Route 128 around Boston, clusters of computer-based producers who find it advantageous to be in proximity. Although in competition with one another, they also feed off each other's ideas just as the most competitive of university professors attend each other's seminars. Although articles get published two years later in journals, at which point ideas become accessible worldwide, discussions with the professor next door about a new idea may yield a competitive edge over professors elsewhere. The same holds good in businesses from software design to satellite technology.

In these examples, one firm's cost curve depends on how many other similar firms are nearby. This concept of a locational externality clarifies a concept that politicians have discussed for years but which previously economists have had trouble providing with a coherent interpretation.

The emphasis on 'industrial' carries the presumption that the externalities are more significant for producers than for consumers, because of the specificity of investments required and minimum size that scale economies impose. Although ring-road superstores cluster together to offer adjacent carpet stores, DIY shops and garden centres, competition between *different* local clusters is intense. The degree of market failure is small.

> The **industrial base** of a country or region is a measure of the stock of existing producers available to provide such locational externalities.

In contrast, if the minimum efficient scale of specific investments is large, countries or regions may find there are two possible outcomes: one in which nobody enters and one in which many firms enter, each enjoying benefits from the presence of the other. Yet achieving the second outcome efficiently requires co-ordination of the entry decision of different producers to internalize the externality facing each firm: it neglects the benefits that its own entry creates for other firms.

Before taking this as a blank cheque for industrial subsidies, remember that in the 1970s and 1980s industrial policy had some spectacular failures in many countries. Any time a large private firm faced difficulties, intervention was demanded to 'preserve skills' or 'maintain an international presence' in the industry. The new economic geography is not an alibi for backing losers or for freezing the industrial structure in a changing world.

17.3 The social cost of monopoly power

In the absence of market failure, competitive equilibrium is efficient. Each industry expands output to the point at which price equals marginal cost. The former equals social marginal benefit, the latter equals social marginal cost. Resource reallocation cannot make everyone better off.

When an industry is imperfectly competitive, each firm has some *monopoly power*. Since demand curves slope down, price exceeds marginal revenue. Each firm produces an output at which price exceeds marginal cost. The excess of price over marginal cost is a firm's monopoly power.

The price and social marginal benefit of the last output unit then exceed the private and social marginal cost of producing that last output unit. From society's viewpoint, industry output is too small. Expanding output adds more to social benefit than to social cost. How should we measure the social cost of monopoly power and inefficient resource allocation?

Chapter 18 takes up the case of pure monopoly. We begin with a more general discussion of imperfect competition. Intermediate forms of imperfect competition need some scale economies to limit the number of firms an industry can support. Nevertheless, to introduce the idea of the social cost of monopoly power it is convenient to ignore economies of scale altogether.

What happens if a competitive industry is taken over by a single firm that then operates as a multi-plant monopolist? In Figure 17.1, under perfect competition LMC is both the industry's long-run marginal cost curve and its supply curve. With constant returns to scale, LMC is also the long-run average cost curve of the industry. Given the demand curve DD, competitive equilibrium is at B. The competitive industry produces an output Q_C at a price P_C.

Now the industry becomes a monopolist, producing output Q_M at a price P_M, thus equating marginal cost and marginal revenue. The area $P_M P_C AC$ is the monopolist's profits from selling Q_M at a price above marginal and average cost. The triangle ACB is the social cost of monopoly power. At Q_M the social marginal benefit of another unit of output is P_M but the social marginal cost is only P_C. Society would like to raise output up to the competitive point B, at which social marginal benefit and social marginal cost are equal. The triangle ACB is the social gain from this output expansion. By reducing output to Q_M the monopolist imposes a social cost ACB.

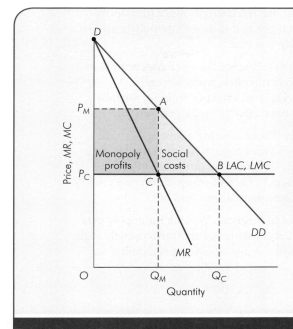

The industry has horizontal long-run average and marginal costs. A perfectly competitive industry produces at B, but a monopolist sets $MR = MC$ to produce only Q_M at a price P_M. The monopolist earns excess profits $P_M P_C CA$, but there is a social cost or deadweight burden equal to the triangle ACB. Between Q_M and Q_C social marginal benefit exceeds social marginal cost and society would gain by expanding output by Q_C. The triangle ACB shows how much society would gain by this expansion.

Figure 17.1 The social cost of monopoly

The demand curve measures the marginal benefit to consumers of each unit of output and the marginal cost curve measures the extra resources used to make each unit of output. Hence, the area between DD and LMC up to that output measures the total surplus to be divided between producers and consumers.

In Figure 17.1, at the output Q_M producer surplus is the rectangle labelled profits and consumer surplus is the triangle DAP_M above this. This output is inefficient because it does not maximize the sum of consumer and producer surplus. That is maximized at output Q_C, at which the area between the demand curve and the LMC curve is maximized.

For the economy, the social cost of monopoly is found by adding together the deadweight burden triangles such as ACB for all industries in which marginal cost and marginal revenue are less than price and social marginal benefit.

Is the social cost of monopoly power large? Economists who believe in market forces tend to think it is small. Professor George Stigler, a Nobel Prize winner, once quipped, 'Economists might serve a more useful purpose if they fought fires or termites instead of monopoly.' Other economists believe the social cost of monopoly is much larger.

Why such a disagreement? First, the area of the deadweight burden triangle in Figure 17.1 depends on the elasticity of the demand curve. In calculating the size of deadweight burden triangles under monopoly, different economists used different estimates of the demand elasticity.

> **Producer surplus (profit)** is the excess of revenue over total costs. Total costs are the area under the *LMC* curve up to this output.[3] **Consumer surplus** is the triangle showing the excess of consumer benefits over spending. It is the area under the demand curve at this output, minus the spending rectangle.

> The **social cost of monopoly** is the failure to maximize social surplus.

> At an output below the efficient level, the **deadweight burden** triangle shows the loss of social surplus.

3 The area under the *LMC* curve actually measures total variable costs. Thus producer surplus equals profit only if fixed costs are zero. In the long run, all costs are variable costs and producer surplus exactly equals profit. In the short run, profit is producer surplus minus fixed costs.

Second, the welfare cost of monopoly is not just the deadweight burden triangle. Since monopoly may yield high profits to the firm, firms spend a lot trying to acquire and secure monopoly positions. Box 15.1 gave more details on why such 'rent-seeking' is socially wasteful.

Similarly, firms may devote large quantities of resources trying to influence the government in ways that enhance or preserve their monopoly power. They may also deliberately maintain extra production capacity to create a credible threat to flood the market if an entrant comes in. Socially, resources devoted to lobbying the government or maintaining overcapacity are largely wasted.

Modern economic analysis also stresses the role of information. Those running a monopoly have inside information about the firm's true cost opportunities. They know more than shareholders or a regulator. Perhaps the monopolist could have lower costs if only its managers put in the effort. Economists sometimes call this 'managerial slack' or 'X-inefficiency'. Lack of competition gives the firm an 'information monopoly' on its own cost possibilities. Outsiders cannot find out.

If a competitive firm gets lazy it loses market share and goes out of business. When a monopoly gets lazy it simply makes a bit less profit. From the social viewpoint, its cost curves are unnecessarily high. Society spends more resources to make this output than it would if X-inefficiency was eliminated.

In Figure 17.2, LMC is the marginal cost of a cost-efficient firm. A monopolist takes advantage of its information monopoly to enjoy an easy life and has higher costs LMC'. Suppose the monopolist is broken up into identical firms (possible, if there are constant returns to scale). Competition between firms not merely makes each firm set price equal to marginal cost, it also reveals managerial slack and forces firms to attain the lower cost curve LMC. The monopolist produced output Q_M at a price P_M. The competitive industry produces Q_C at a price P_C. Thus the economy moves from E' to E. The social gain is much larger than the triangle $E'FG$.

At the monopoly output Q_M, consumer surplus, the excess of their benefits over what they paid, was $P_M JE'$. $HFE'P_M$ was the declared profit of the monopolist, $KFHP_C$ the hidden profit that the monopolist took as the easy life, and $OQ_M KP_C$ the costs that even an efficient firm would incur.

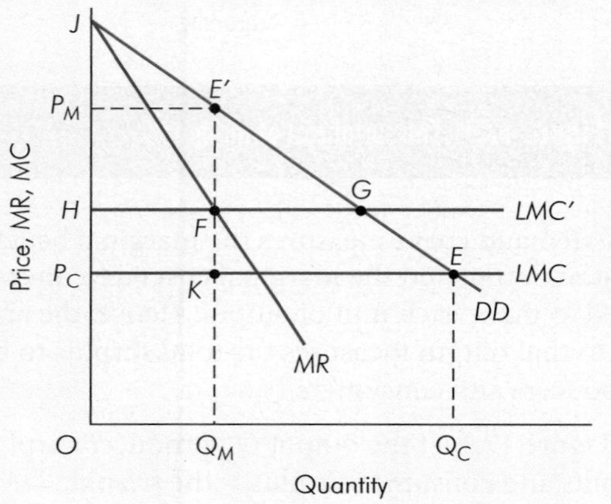

A monopolist with inside information about costs may allow LMC to rise to LMC', and produce at E'. A competitive industry would produce at E and reveal that true costs were LMC.

Figure 17.2 An information monopoly

When equilibrium moves from E' to E, the *additional* social profits are the whole triangle $E'KE$. With the industry now competitive, and the cost curve LMC, total consumer surplus is JEP_C, the gap between the demand curve and the rectangle $OQ_C EP_C$ that consumers actually pay. Notice that the rectangle $HFKP_C$ has effectively been redistributed from the slack monopolist to consumers once society finds out that costs are LMC and prices accordingly.

So far we have assumed monopolists are lazy 'fat cats'. If it takes resources (effort, investment, etc.) to lower costs, the gain from abolishing monopoly is smaller than in Figure 17.2 but still larger than the triangle $E'FG$.

For these reasons, the precise extent of the social cost of monopoly remains controversial. Nevertheless, few governments believe that the social cost of monopoly can be ignored.

Activity box 17 Just Yell

In 1996 *Yellow Pages*, then owned by BT, was investigated by the Competition Commission and forced to undertake not to abuse its dominant market position. In 2001 *Yellow Pages* was sold to a company called Yell. Nowadays, 98% of the UK market for printed telephone directories comprises *Yellow Pages* (which has about 75% of the total market), Thompson, and BT, which still produces the *Phone Book*. Because of its dominant position, Yell undertook to reduce the real price of advertising in its directory by 6% a year.

Since these directories are given away free, the market is measured not by copies distributed but by revenues from advertising in the directories. And of course people get more and more information from the internet, which raises the question of whether the relevant market is that for printed directories or should also include internet usage, which would dilute the estimated market shares of the printed directory companies.

A new investigation by the Competition Commission, completed in 2006, considered whether the benefits of large market share outweighed their cost, and in particular (a) whether Yell had honoured its previous commitments to cut prices; (b) whether it still enjoyed significant market power, or whether the internet and other print directory companies provided sufficient competition; and (c) whether new regulation of Yell's behaviour was therefore required.

The Commission concluded that the internet was largely a complement to, not a substitute for, print directories; and that the presence of Thompson and BT was not sufficient to prevent the potential of Yell to exert market power in this market. Accordingly, it imposed new price controls on Yell, for a minimum period of a further three years. Whatever scale economies and lower cost base Yell was achieving, it was not sufficient to offset the monopoly power that it enjoyed. On balance, it needed to be regulated (via price ceilings) to get the best outcome for society as a whole. Perhaps by the next time the Commission investigates, the internet will be providing more effective competition and the need for intervention through regulation may have diminished.

Source: www.competition-commission.org.uk.

Questions

(a) If Yell has such a dominant position, why did the Competition Commission not recommend that Yell be broken up into two or more companies so that there are more players in the industry and the prospect of more equal competition?

(b) Suppose you were trying to decide whether the internet and print directories were complements or substitutes. What evidence would you wish to gather? Why?

To check your answers to these questions, go to page 724.

Price discriminating monopoly

The social cost of monopoly arises because the monopolist cannot price discriminate. Perfect price discrimination makes the demand curve and marginal revenue curve coincide – selling new units no longer bids down the price on existing sales. Then, price is marginal revenue and hence equals marginal cost. The monopolist produces the socially efficient output.

This would then remove the first case for intervention – failure to price at marginal cost – but might still leave a case for intervention if, by deterring entry of competitors, the incumbent has become lazy and is incurring unnecessarily high costs that competitive pressure would reduce.

Of course, all this requires price discrimination to be possible in the first place. Consumers must not be able to set up a second-hand market. Price discrimination is possible only if the producer can establish separate sub-markets. Price discrimination in services is easier since resale is impossible: a service is consumed at the point at which it is produced. Price discrimination by large monopolists is sometimes precluded by a 'universal service requirement' legally forcing the monopolist to supply (e.g. letter delivery) to all parts of the country at a uniform price, even though costs of rural delivery are much higher.

The distribution of monopoly profits

Society does not care just about the inefficiency of imperfect competition. It may also care about two other aspects of monopoly power: the *political* power that large companies exert, and the *distributional* issue of fairness of the large profits a monopolist can earn.

Monopoly profits are a private tax. Should society tolerate them? The ultimate recipients of monopoly profits are the monopolist's shareholders. Much of the stock market is held by pension funds and insurance companies that eventually make payments to workers. Some monopoly profits go to the less well off. But most do not.

Suppose the government imposes a profits tax: how does this affect the monopolist's output decision? It doesn't! At any tax rate below 100 per cent, the way to maximize after-tax profits is to maximize pre-tax profits. For a given tax rate, higher pre-tax profits must raise post-tax profits. Hence the monopolist produces exactly the same output as in the absence of a profits tax and, facing the same demand curve, will charge the same price as before.[4]

A monopolist cannot shift the tax on to anybody else. Society can tax as much of the monopolist's profits as it wants without affecting the monopolist's behaviour, at least in the short run.

A monopolist may have sunk costs in the past, through R&D or by building factory capacity. Viewed from today, these costs are incurred and bygone. The position of today's cost curves is independent of whether or not the government taxes monopoly profits. However, had the firm known that profits would be subject to a windfall tax, the monopolist would never have incurred large R&D costs in the first place.

An occasional surprise windfall tax may remove monopoly profits without adverse incentive effects on efficiency. However, the expectation of regular resort to such taxes will undermine incentives to invest. Costs would then become higher than they need have been.

Must liberalization help?

By now you may be assuming that more competition is always better. But in Chapter 15 we introduced the theory of the second best. Beginning from a distorted position, elimination of all market failures would always increase efficiency. But partial elimination or reduction can occasionally make things worse: sometimes two distortions somewhat offset each other. Removing just one makes the other one worse.

Here is the first example. Unlike Figures 17.1 and 17.2, suppose there are large economies of scale and a falling average cost curve. A monopolist is bad for the reasons outlined already, but it does at least

---

4 Since profit maximization implies $MC = MR$, output is adjusted till the marginal profit of the last unit is zero. Hence profits taxation has no effect on the marginal condition used by the firm to find the best output.

produce on a large scale and lets society benefit from scale economies. Suppose the government insists on more competition, say entry of a second producer. Dividing the market, both firms fail to reap scale economies. More competition may reduce profit margins and drive price closer to marginal cost; it may also reduce information monopolies (we can see what the other firm is charging), forcing more expenditure on cost reduction to shift cost curves down. But if scale economies are big enough, both producers still have larger costs than the original monopolist. Society may be worse off because it has to spend more resources on production.

The second example is called cream-skimming.

Suppose a postal monopoly has a uniform service provision: it must deliver anywhere in the UK at the same price. A private entrant would want to take on profitable parcel delivery in cities but not unprofitable parcel delivery to remote rural areas. If it is allowed to cream-skim the profitable bits, it reduces the scale economies of the large producer in other areas and may even jeopardize the entire operation.

> **Cream-skimming** confines entry to profitable parts of the business, thereby undermining scale economies elsewhere.

With this brief discussion of market power, we can now understand more clearly the role of competition policy.

17.4 Competition policy

Figure 17.3 is a useful guide to the rest of this chapter and the chapter that follows. It divides possible outcomes into four regions. In the top left box, competition is possible and desirable, the normal case. In the top right box, some kind of competition is possible but undesirable. In this box, scale economies are important and entry by other firms leads to cream-skimming or to small-scale, high-cost activities by all firms. In the bottom right, the situation is natural monopoly. Huge scale economies preclude competition. In the bottom left box, the incumbent has sufficient power to deter entry if things are left to the market. But scale economies are not that significant. Society would gain more from greater competition, if only it could be secured, than it would lose from giving up economies of large scale by allowing entry.

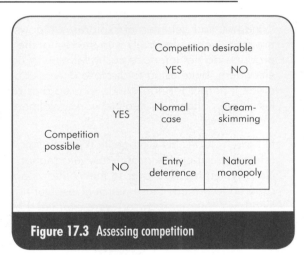

Figure 17.3 Assessing competition

Figure 17.3 divides up our analysis into competition policy, the topic in the remainder of this chapter, and regulation, the topic of the next chapter. Competition policy is about the two boxes in the left-hand column. It concerns situations in which promotion of competition is likely to be beneficial. This can be achieved by setting rules for conduct or by taking steps to ensure a market structure in which competition can then take place.

UK competition policy

Broadly speaking, competition policy can be divided into policies to deal with monopoly power that already exists, and policies to deal with mergers that may increase monopoly power. We begin with policies to address existing monopoly power. Since the UK belongs to the European Union, EU competition law takes precedence where it is relevant, essentially in the case of larger businesses with significant European or global activities.

EU competition law

The original Common Market was created by the 1956 Treaty of Rome. The modern and enlarged EU is largely underpinned by the 1999 Treaty of Amsterdam.

Article 81 of this Treaty prohibits anti-competitive agreements that have an appreciable effect on trade between EU member states and which prevent or distort competition within the EU. Article 82 prohibits the abuse of any existing dominant position.

Responsibility for enforcement of these Articles lies with the European Commission. During 1999–2004, the Commissioner specifically responsible for competition policy was Mario Monti, a former economics professor who is now Rector of Bocconi University in Milan. Box 17.4 discusses Monti in action, over the Microsoft case.

Box 17.3 The full Monti: the taming of Microsoft

After more than five years of investigation, the European Commission has fined Microsoft almost €500m for monopolistic abuses and given it four months to make life easier for competitors in the server and media-player markets.

(*The Economist*, 2 March 2004)

The success of Microsoft is partly built on the way it bundles products together, making it hard for competitors to compete on individual components without offering the entire package. If you buy Windows, you get Internet Explorer, Windows Media Player and perhaps even Microsoft Office. Each program works effectively with the rest of the Windows family. Rival producers complain that their products do not interface easily with the Windows family, thereby deterring customers from buying elsewhere. By refusing to disclose access codes for interoperability in workgroup servers, Microsoft made it harder for non-Windows programs run on office networks to access Windows systems. And RealPlayer, offered by RealNetworks, claimed to be disadvantaged in comparison with Windows Media Player.

In March 2004, EU Competition Commissioner Mario Monti ruled (a) that Microsoft had illegally refused to supply the proprietary information needed for interoperability and (b) that Microsoft had illegally tied Media Player to the Windows operating system. Microsoft was fined €497 million and ordered to remedy these deficiencies. During 1998–2002, similar issues (the monopoly position of Windows' internet browser) were examined by the US Department of Justice, though the case was finally settled out of court.

The Microsoft case not merely illustrates competition policy in action, it also demonstrates why firms operating in global markets need to face competition authorities that operate on a similar scale. Imagine if Microsoft had been investigated separately by national authorities in the UK, France, Germany, Sweden and Ireland, each with its own national rules and possibly leading to different judgments.

UK competition law

Although global businesses are increasingly subject to transnational competition law, many businesses still operate primarily within a country; national decisions are then appropriate. Within the UK, these are governed by the Competition Act 1998 and the Enterprise Act 2002. The latter made it a criminal offence, punishable by a jail sentence, to engage in a dishonest cartel.

Two key institutions of UK competition policy are the Office of Fair Trading (OFT) and the Competition Commission.

In particular, the OFT has the power to refer cases to the Competition Commission for a detailed investigation in cases in which existing monopoly power may be leading to a 'substantial lessening of competition'.

Prior to the Enterprise Act 2002, the Competition Commission was asked instead to evaluate whether or not a monopoly was acting 'in the public interest', without any presumption that monopoly was bad, and many previous judgments of the Commission concluded that companies were acting in the public interest, for example because they had an excellent record of innovation, *despite* having a monopoly position.

The change in 2002 therefore emphasized competition more strongly and made the Competition Commission more accountable by defining its objectives more clearly. This also brought UK law more clearly into line with EU competition law, by placing measures of competition at the centre of the evaluation of competition policy.

> The **Office of Fair Trading** is responsible for making markets work well for consumers, by protecting and promoting consumer interests while ensuring that businesses are fair and competitive.

> The **Competition Commission** investigates whether a monopoly, or potential monopoly, acts as 'a substantial lessening of competition'.

UK competition policy in practice

Prior to 2002, the Competition Commission investigated a wide range of cases, from beer to breakfast cereals, from contraceptives to cross-Channel ferries. Because the Commission looked at each case with an open mind, its judgments stressed different aspects of behaviour in different cases. Uncompetitive behaviour did not always attract an unfavourable judgment.

Since 2002, the Commission's reports have focused more narrowly on the implications for competition itself. During 2004, the Commission was investigating whether 'store cards' issued by particular retailers were substantially reducing competition. In 2003, the Commission reported on a similar investigation into the extended warranties that retailers often offer when you buy a new camera or TV.

Annual sales of domestic electrical goods are between £15 billion and £20 billion in the UK, and consumers spend nearly £1 billion a year buying extended warranties (multi-year insurance and service agreements), usually purchased from the retailer of the goods at the time the goods are bought. If you are buying a new camera in one shop, it is difficult for a different supplier simultaneously to be offering you a warranty.

The Commission concluded that this monopoly power led to prices on warranties being up to 50 per cent higher than they would have been in a competitive market. To remedy this, the Commission demanded that retailers be required to provide consumers with much more transparent written information about the cost of warranties, and that consumers should be allowed to cancel warranties (with a full refund) for up to 45 days after their initial purchase.

This judgment illustrates what has long been a distinction between the US and UK approaches to competition policy. US competition law often seeks a structural change in the industry to *prevent* the potential for monopoly power. UK competition law has more frequently sought to *control* behaviour of those with monopoly power rather than to restructure the industry altogether.

In Chapter 9, Figure 9.1 emphasized that market structure often reflects the tension between output required for minimum efficient scale and the size of the market as given by demand for the product. Large countries, facing large demand, may have room for many firms operating at minimum efficient scale. Small countries, with smaller markets, will typically have room for fewer firms at minimum efficient scale.

Putting it differently, large countries can break up monopolies more easily, since subdivided firms may still enjoy substantial scale economies. In smaller countries, with smaller markets, breaking up monopolies may imply such small scale that average costs become prohibitively large. Developing policies to contain monopoly behaviour may then be preferable to policies that outlaw monopoly itself.

Not only may this help make sense of the historical differences between UK and US competition policy, it also has implications for the evolution of competition policy with the EU as European integration proceeds and the EU market is increasingly unified. With a larger market, the preceding logic then implies that it will be sensible for the EU increasingly to adopt the US approach of outlawing monopoly itself rather than to worry about how to contain monopoly behaviour.

17.5 Mergers

Two firms can unite in two different ways: via a takeover bid or via merger. When a firm makes a takeover bid, managers of the 'victim' firm usually resist since they are likely to lose their jobs, but the shareholders will accept if the offer is sufficiently attractive.

From now on we use mergers as shorthand for both forms of union. Are mergers in the public interest, or do they just create private monopolies?

The production process typically has several stages. The first stage might be iron ore extraction, the second stage steel manufacture from iron ore, and the third stage production of cars from steel.

A horizontal merger may allow more economies of scale. One large car factory may be better than two small ones if each firm was previously producing below minimum efficient scale. In vertical mergers there may be gains to co-ordination and planning. It may be easier to make long-term decisions about the best size and type of steel mill if a simultaneous decision is taken on the level of car production to which steel output forms an important input. Since conglomerate mergers involve companies with completely independent products, these mergers have little opportunity for a direct reduction in production costs.

> A firm makes a **takeover bid** for another firm by offering to buy out the shareholders of the second firm.

> A **merger** is the voluntary union of two firms that think they will do better together.

> A **horizontal merger** is the union of two firms at the same production stage in the same industry. A **vertical merger** is the union of two firms at different production stages in the same industry. In a **conglomerate merger**, the production activities of the two firms are unrelated.

Two other factors are frequently mentioned as potential benefits of mergers. First, if one company has an inspired management team, it may be more productive to allow this team to run both businesses. Managers love this explanation for mergers. Economists are more sceptical. Second, by pooling their financial resources, the merged firms may enjoy access to cheaper borrowing, letting them take more risks and finance larger research projects. There may also be economies of scale in marketing. Managerial and financial gains could explain why mergers make sense even for firms producing completely distinct products.

If companies achieve any of these benefits, they will increase productivity and lower costs. These private gains are also social gains. If these were the only considerations, social and private calculations would coincide.

However, private and social assessments may diverge. First, the merger of two large firms gives them monopoly power from a large market share. The merged company is likely to restrict output and increase prices, a deadweight burden for society as a whole.

Second, the merged company can use its *financial* power. This danger is especially apparent in conglomerate mergers. A car producer and a food manufacturer can use their joint financial resources to start a price war in one of these industries. With large financial resources, they are not the first firm to go bust. By forcing out existing competitors, or merely holding this threat over potential entrants, they raise their market share, deter entry and charge high prices for ever.

Merger policy must thus compare the social gains (potential cost reduction) with the social costs (larger monopoly power).

Mergers in practice

Table 17.1 shows annual averages of takeovers and mergers involving UK firms. It shows dramatic merger booms in the late 1980s and late 1990s, which coincided with high values of the stock market, which raised the value of both firms involved in the merger.

Table 17.1 UK takeovers and mergers, 1972–2006 (annual averages)

	Number	Value (1998 £bn)
1972–85	560	3
1986–89	1300	43
1990–98	585	20
1999–00	540	61
2001–06	600	30

Sources: British Business Trends 1989; Business Trends 1997; ONS, First Release.

Mergers are often associated with opportunities to rationalize industrial structure. Two major developments in European markets were the periods preceding the creation of the Single European Market in 1992 and the launch of the euro in 1999. A larger market raises scope for scale economies (a greater private incentive to create large firms) and enhances competition (reducing the need for society to worry about mergers creating monopoly power).

The combination of new technology and deregulation has been changing market structure both in the UK and in its main trading partners. Segmentation of national markets has been breaking down in telecoms, financial services and many other industries. Cross-border mergers have allowed leading players to respond to larger markets. Figure 17.4 confirms that substantial cross-border activity, such as the spectacular acquisition of US mobile phone company AirTouch by Vodafone for £39 billion.

The increase in effective market size in the past 15 years has also influenced the type of mergers taking place. Conglomerate mergers had grown steadily in the 1960s and 1970s, becoming a third of all mergers by the early 1980s. However, financial deregulation has made it easier to raise finance and reduced the importance of the financial muscle that provided one of the motives for conglomerate mergers. Disappointing performance of these hybrid companies has increasingly led to demerger and a renewed focus on the original core business. In contrast, the erosion of segmented national markets has led to a boom in horizontal mergers.

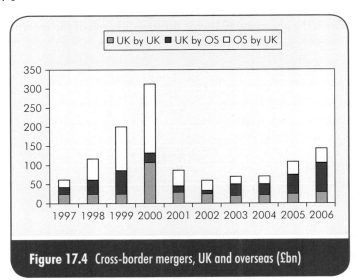

Figure 17.4 Cross-border mergers, UK and overseas (£bn)

Merger policy

The proliferation of large companies through merger would not have been possible if there had been a tough anti-merger policy.

353

There are currently two grounds for referring a prospective merger to an investigation by the Competition Commission: (1) that the merger will promote a new monopoly as defined by the 25 per cent market share used in deciding references for existing monopoly positions, or (2) that the company taken over has an annual UK turnover of at least £70 million.[5]

Since the merger legislation was introduced in 1965, only 4 per cent of all merger proposals have been referred to the Competition Commission. For much of the period, government policy has been to consent to, or actively encourage, mergers.

In believing that the benefits would outweigh the costs, UK merger policy reflected two assumptions. The first was that the cost savings from economies of scale and more intensive use of scarce management talent could be quite large. The second was that the UK was part of an increasingly competitive world market so that the monopoly power of the merged firms, and the corresponding social cost of the deadweight burden, would be small. Large as they were, the merged firms were small in relation to European or world markets, and would face relatively elastic demand curves, giving little scope to raise price above marginal cost.

Nevertheless, nearly half of the mergers actually referred to the Competition Commission were subsequently prohibited. However, investigation was a lengthy process taking many months, a delay during which company share prices could change, upsetting the original negotiations about the terms on which the relative shares of the companies should be valued. In practice, even the threat that a merger might be referred was often sufficient for the companies to abandon the merger.

Finally, as with competition policy, EU legislation takes precedence where this is appropriate. It is not appropriate in assessing whether a merger of two UK supermarkets should be allowed, since this predominantly affects only UK consumers. However, the European Commission will investigate mergers involving enterprises with an aggregate worldwide annual turnover of over €5 billion and where the aggregate EU-wide turnover of each of the enterprises exceeds €250 million.

---

5 In addition simply to competition considerations, wider considerations of the public interest are still applied to mergers in two particular industries: national security, and cross-media mergers in which the monopolization of information itself might be an issue.

Summary

- The **social cost of monopoly power** arises because marginal cost is set equal to marginal revenue, which is less than price and marginal consumer benefit. The social cost is the cumulative difference between the value that consumers place on the lost output and its marginal production cost. The social cost is higher if market power allows firms to have cost curves that are unnecessarily higher than they might have been.

- **X-inefficiency** arises from the **information monopoly** that a monopolist has about its cost possibilities. The easy life may lead monopolists to make inadequate efforts to reduce costs, adding to the social cost of monopoly.

- **Industrial policy** seeks to offset production market failures except those arising from scale economies and imperfect competition; offsetting these is the aim of **competition policy**.

- **Intellectual property** is conferred through the award of **patents and copyrights**, a temporary legal monopoly for successful knowledge creators. Patents provide an incentive to look for inventions. Otherwise, inventors, foreseeing that profits on successful inventions will quickly be competed away by imitators, will devote few resources to invention.

- **R&D** has a beneficial externality: spending by one firm benefits other firms.

- The industrial policies of national governments towards their own 'national champions' is a **commitment** that affects the bargaining power of their firms in the international market.

- **Sunrise and sunset industries** involve other market failures. This is not a general licence for active industrial policy to manage change. Governments must identify the market failure and show that intervention is preferable. Picking winners has not been a success, but decentralized incentives may be effective if their rationale has been clearly identified.

- **Economic geography** reflects **locational externalities** arising in training, transport and knowledge creation. The **industrial base** is the existing stock of locational capital.

- In the UK, the **Office of Fair Trading** is responsible for consumer protection and the efficient operation of markets. It can refer a market to a detailed investigation by the **Competition Commission** to assess whether competition is being substantially reduced by the current market structure and the conduct of firms within it.

- UK firms are subject to EU competition law if their activities extend substantially beyond UK borders.

- **Mergers** may be **horizontal**, **vertical** or **conglomerate**. Conglomerate mergers have the smallest scope for economies of scale. The recent merger boom has largely been in horizontal mergers to take advantage of larger markets caused by globalization, European integration and deregulation.

- In principle, mergers can be referred to the Competition Commission if they will create a firm with a 25 per cent market share or if they involve taking over a firm with an annual turnover of over £70 million. In practice, few mergers satisfying these criteria are actually referred. In part this may be justified because the UK competes in large world markets where the firms will have little monopoly power.

Review questions

To check your answers to these questions, go to page 723.

1. With constant $AC = MC = £5$, a competitive industry produces 1 million units. Taken over by a monopolist, output falls to 800 000 units and the price rises to £8. AC and MC are unchanged. What is the social cost of monopoly?

2. Suppose, when the monopolist takes over in Question 1, AC and MC increase to £6 and output falls to 600 000 units at a price of £11. What is the social cost of monopoly now?

3. Explain the difference between UK and US policy towards monopolies and mergers.

4. UK policy provides substantial tax breaks for those investing in small firms. Do the issues discussed in this chapter justify such a policy?

5. Most footballs in the world are made in a small village in Pakistan. Why do makers of footballs cluster together? Why not in Switzerland?

6. **Common fallacies** Why are these statements wrong? (a) Monopolies make profits and must be well-run companies. (b) Monopolies create social waste. We should ban firms from having over 20 per cent of the market. (c) Mergers are beneficial; otherwise companies would not merge.

7. **Harder question** During 2005–07 many companies, of increasingly large size, were taken over by private equity firms. (a) Why did anyone believe that private equity firms could run companies better than the incumbent management? (b) By 2007, the US mortgage market was starting to experience a number of bankruptcies which started to spook financial markets in general. How could this impact the takeover activity of private equity firms?

8. **Harder question** Suppose locational externalities imply that R&D by one Formula 1 constructor to locate in the Thames Valley enhances the productivity of other F1 constructors located in the Thames Valley. (a) Is there any case for the UK government providing a subsidy to Ferrari to move from Italy to the Thames Valley? (b) Why haven't existing UK-based teams already clubbed together to try to induce Ferrari to move? (c) Would the Italian government be likely to acquiesce in the move of Ferrari?

9. **Essay question** There is quite a lot of evidence that when two firms merge, their post-merger performance does not improve in the first few years. Adjudicate among the following possible explanations. (a) Firms only merge because trouble was on the way – if they do even reasonably well post-merger, the merger itself has been a success. (b) Top management time is eaten up both during the merger talks and in the subsequent forging of a single company out of two companies; it is therefore unsurprising that management gets diverted from the business itself. (c) Mergers alert the competition authorities to potential monopoly power, so the merged company has to go easy for a while in order to avoid an intrusive competition investigation.

Online LearningCentre

To help you grasp the key concepts of this chapter check out the extra resources posted on the Online Learning Centre. There are chapter summaries, self-test questions, an interactive graphing tool, weblinks and a searchable glossary, all for free!

To put your learning into practice and prepare for exams, an **Interactive Workbook** is also available online, containing a variety of question types and providing feedback on your answers.

If you'd like further help with economics, or have any questions, **NetTutor** is here to help! You will have a personalised tutorial service at your fingertips. Visit the online learning centre at: www.mcgraw-hill.co.uk/textbooks/begg for information on accessing all of these resources.

Natural monopoly: public or private?

By the end of this chapter, you should understand:

1 the problem of natural monopoly

2 nationalization as one solution to that problem

3 social marginal cost pricing

4 social cost–benefit analysis of investment decisions

5 two-part tariffs and peak-load pricing

6 privatization and the Private Finance Initiative

7 regulation of a private natural monopoly

8 how globalization reduces natural monopoly

> In every great monarchy in Europe the sale of the Crown lands would deliver a much greater revenue than any which these lands ever afforded to the Crown. When the Crown lands had become private property, they would, in the course of a few years, become well improved and well cultivated.
>
> Adam Smith, *The Wealth of Nations* (1776)

Chapter 17 discussed the role of policy in cases where promoting competition was feasible and likely to enhance efficiency. Now, we discuss cases in which scale economies are large. Competition may not be feasible or may sacrifice scale economies to an extent that competition is undesirable.

These cases may be entire industries, but natural monopoly can also occur in merely a segment of an industry. For example, there may be many creators of TV programming, but in some parts of the country the only access to digital television channels is through a particular cable or satellite company. Although natural monopoly therefore exists in several forms, it is most dramatic when it applies at the level of the industry itself.

Before 1980 such industries were thought to require so much regulation that they might as well be state owned. After 1980 the UK pioneered a programme of privatization, subsequently emulated in many countries.

After privatization, it was initially hoped that the privatized companies would need to be only lightly regulated. Hence, the changes were sometimes called deregulation. In industries without major scale economies, or facing extensive international competition, this is what happened. In the industries on which we focus in this chapter – utilities such as electricity, gas and water – more extensive regulation was needed whenever international competition was not vigorous.

> **Nationalization** is the acquisition of private companies by the public sector.
> **Privatization** is the return of state enterprises to private ownership and control.

18.1 Natural monopoly

Figure 18.1 shows an industry with steadily falling long-run average costs as output rises. Only one private firm can survive in such an industry. Any firm that expands output can cut costs and undercut its rivals. Facing a demand curve DD and marginal revenue curve MR, the resulting monopolist produces Q_M and earns profits P_MCBE.

At this output the social marginal benefit P_M exceeds the social marginal cost at A. The monopolist makes too little. Social marginal cost and marginal benefit are equal at the output Q' and the efficient point for society is E'. The private monopoly creates a deadweight burden AEE'.

> A **natural monopoly**'s average costs keep falling as its output rises. It undercuts all smaller competitors.

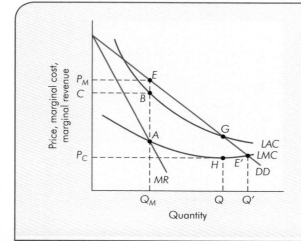

The efficient point E' equates long-run marginal cost LMC and marginal benefit DD. A private monopolist sets $MR = MC$, produces Q_M and earns profits P_MCBE. The deadweight loss under private monopoly is AEE'. If by law the monopolist was forced to charge a fixed price P_C, the monopolist would face a horizontal demand curve P_CE' up to the output Q'. Since P_C would then also be marginal revenue, the monopolist would produce at E' where the marginal revenue and marginal cost coincide. Although efficient, society cannot force the monopolist to produce here in the long run. Since E' lies below LAC the monopolist is making losses and would rather go out of business.

Figure 18.1 Natural monopoly

You sit on the Competition Commission investigating this monopolist. If you split up the firm, a lot of small firms each produce at higher average cost, a waste of society's resources. You could order the firm to produce at the efficient point E'. You will get the desired output Q', but the price P_C is below the firm's average costs at Q'. It makes losses. Since marginal cost always lies below average cost when average cost is falling, forcing a natural monopolist to price at marginal cost is always loss making. You cannot force a private firm to make losses. It will shut down.

One solution is a regulatory body, such as OFGEM that regulates gas and electricity markets in the UK. It aims to get close to the efficient allocation E' while letting the monopolist break even after allowing a proper deduction for all economic costs. By making the monopolist produce Q at the price corresponding to average cost at this output, the deadweight burden is cut from AEE' to GHE'.

An even better solution is to allow the monopolist to charge a two-part tariff.

A two-part tariff uses fixed charges to pay for fixed costs, and marginal charges to cover marginal costs. In Figure 18.1 the monopolist is told to charge P_C for each unit of the good. Consumers demand the socially efficient quantity Q'. Since the monopolist is now a price-taker at the controlled price P_C, it is loss-minimizing for the monopolist to produce Q', at which both price and marginal revenue equal marginal cost. The

> A **two-part tariff** charges a fixed sum for access to the service and then a price per unit that reflects the marginal cost of production.

regulator then allows the monopolist to levy the minimum fixed charge necessary to ensure that it breaks even after allowing for all relevant economic costs.

A third solution to the natural monopoly problem is to order the monopolist to produce at the efficient point E' at the price P_C and for the government to provide a subsidy to cover the losses entailed. It is socially desirable to make the efficient output Q' in the cost-minimizing way. If the subsidy solution is adopted, there is pressure for the government to get involved in the entire running of the industry so that operations can be carefully monitored.

Three problems recur with all these solutions to the problem of natural monopoly. First, information is costly for monitors to acquire. It is hard to ensure that the industry strives to keep its cost curves at their lowest possible positions. Unnecessarily high costs can be passed on under average cost pricing (solution 1), can result in a higher fixed charge to ensure break-even under a two-part tariff (solution 2), or can require a larger subsidy (solution 3). In each case the regulatory body has the difficult task of trying to make the natural monopoly as efficient as possible.

The second problem is regulatory capture. Regulated companies devote considerable time, effort and money to lobbying the regulator. Of necessity, regulators build up contacts with the regulated. Eventually, the regulator can come to sympathize with the problems of the regulated.

> **Regulatory capture** implies that the regulator gradually comes to identify with the interests of the firm it regulates, becoming its champion not its watchdog.

Third, regulators find it hard to make credible commitments regarding their future behaviour. For example, the regulator may encourage the monopolist to invest by promising 'light' regulation in the future. Once the investment is made and the cost sunk, the regulator then faces temptations to change the ground rules, toughening requirements. Foreseeing all this, the monopolist never invests in the first place. There is underinvestment if the regulator faces commitment problems.

During 1945–80, many European governments concluded that the least bad solution to these problems was nationalization.

18.2 Nationalized industries

Nationalized industries are state-owned firms making private goods and services for sale in a market. Even by 2005 some UK firms remained in state ownership (e.g. British Nuclear Fuels and the UK Atomic Energy Authority). How should society want state-owned firms to behave?

Investment decisions

A private investment project is profitable if the present value of the stream of future operating profits exceeds the initial cost of the new capital. Private firms do the most profitable projects first. Investment proceeds until the marginal project is reached. At this point the present value of future profits just equals the cost of the capital. The same statement can be made using flows instead of stocks. Investment proceeds as long as the rate of return exceeds the interest rate that is the opportunity cost of the funds tied up.

The same principles carry over into social investment decisions provided we use social not private measures of costs, benefits and the discount rate.

The initial cost of capital good

Without other distortions, this is simply the private cost of the capital project. However, local unemployment may reduce the social cost of construction workers below the market wage. Without the project, the workers may make no other goods. Production externalities may also lead to a divergence of private and social values. Where *building* capital goods fosters production externalities (e.g. skill development), the 'social price' of the capital good is reduced.

Valuing the stream of future costs and benefits

Society uses social not private values of costs and benefits. Externalities cause a divergence between private and social. An underground system that reduces road congestion has social benefits beyond the revenue raised from underground fares. Discovering a new drug may have social benefits that extend well beyond the benefits to the consumer of the drug herself.

Investment decisions also require the discounting of future costs and benefits to assess their present value. Society may also wish to use a different discount rate from that used by the private sector. For example, the private sector may worry more about risk. A disastrous project can bankrupt a private firm, but in the public sector may lead to only a tiny change in tax rates. Knowing this, public sector projects might use a lower discount rate than private sector projects.

> The **discount rate** is the interest rate used to calculate present values of future streams of benefits or costs.

To sum up, investment decisions in state-owned firms should use social valuations not private (market) valuations.

Pricing decisions

Public sector firms should set prices at social marginal cost. Private marginal cost should be adjusted for any production or consumption externalities that arise, ensuring that society equally values the marginal cost and marginal benefit from the last unit of output.

Short-run or long-run marginal cost pricing?

The once-off cost of building a plant is a *stock* concept. The cost is incurred at the point the plant is built. But *LMC* is a *flow* concept, relating to the cost *per period* of producing output. Chapter 12 explained how stocks and flows are related. At the discount rate r, the present value PV (a stock concept) of a permanent flow of c_k per period is given by the perpetuity formula $PV = c_k/r$. Conversely, the per period cost c_k of an initial outlay PV can be expressed as $c_k = r \times PV$. The flow cost of the resources tied up in the plant is the initial capital cost multiplied by the discount rate r.

Figure 18.2 shows the short-run marginal cost SMC_0. For simplicity, we assume existing plant has a maximum capacity of Q_0 and SMC_0 is constant at c up to full capacity, but then becomes vertical. No matter how much is spent, output cannot be increased beyond Q_0 given the existing level of capacity.

Since SMC_0 measures the marginal social opportunity cost in the short run of the resources used to produce this good, price should be set at SMC_0 to equate marginal social cost and marginal social benefit. If demand is low, the industry should produce Q_1 and operate at less than

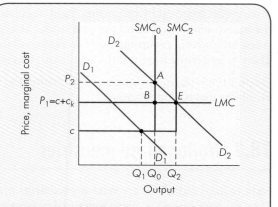

Assume that short-run marginal cost is constant at c up to full capacity and then vertical. SMC_0 corresponds to capacity Q_0 and SMC_2 to capacity Q_2. Suppose SMC_0 is relevant and demand is D_1D_1. In the short run the efficient output is Q_1 and the price should be set at c. If demand is D_2D_2, pricing at short-run marginal cost leads to a price P_2 on the vertical part of SMC_0. *LMC* also includes the capital charge c_k. Beginning from the plant size Q_0, in the long run society can gain the triangle ABE by expanding capacity until *LMC* equals social marginal benefit at E. At plant size Q_2 the price P_1 still lies on the short-run marginal cost curve which is now SMC_2. Short-run marginal cost pricing equates immediate marginal costs and marginal benefits. In the long run it is by efficient investment decisions that capacity is adjusted to ensure that this price also reflects long-run marginal cost.

Figure 18.2 Marginal cost pricing

full capacity. Given the higher demand curve D_2D_2, short-run marginal cost pricing will lead to a price P_2 and the industry will produce at full capacity. Since output cannot be increased above Q_0, a price P_2 above c is needed to keep the quantity demanded equal to the maximum quantity that can be supplied.

In the long run the industry can build more factories. With a higher capital stock, the industry will face the short-run marginal cost curve SMC_2 with constant marginal cost c up to the new level of full capacity Q_2, after which marginal cost is vertical.

But LMC also includes the per-period opportunity cost of the resources tied up in the capital stock, the capital charge c_k, whose calculation we described above. Thus in Figure 18.2 we draw the LMC curve as a horizontal line at the height $P_1 = c + c_k$. The long-run marginal cost of another output unit is the marginal operating cost plus the capital charge per unit of output.

Suppose the demand curve, reflecting social marginal benefit, is D_2D_2 and that the industry begins with a capital stock for which Q_0 is the maximum output and SMC_0 the short-run marginal cost curve. Pricing at short-run marginal cost, the industry charges a price P_2. Although socially efficient in the short run, it is not efficient in the long run. Once capacity can be varied society wants to produce at E, where marginal social benefit equals long-run social marginal cost LMC. By increasing the capital stock until its maximum output is Q_2, society gains the triangle ABE, the excess of marginal benefit over marginal cost when output is increased from Q_0 to Q_2.

Pricing and investment decisions are thus interconnected. In the short run output should be priced at SMC, the social opportunity cost of the resources employed. However, in the long run society should invest if the present value of future benefits exceeds the cost of adding to the capital stock. Instead of this stock evaluation of investment decisions we can use the equivalent flow evaluation. The capital stock should be increased if the marginal social benefit exceeds the long-run marginal cost inclusive of the capital charge. Thus, although prices are set according to SMC, in the long run investment will change capacity and shift the SMC curve.

Hence, although prices are set according to SMC, in the long run investment will adjust the capital stock and full capacity output until price also equals LMC. In the long run the efficient allocation is at point E in Figure 18.2, where marginal benefit, SMC, and LMC coincide.

Finally, note that many of these ideas carry over to a private monopolist. We simply replace social by private assessments of benefit and cost, and use the relevant private discount rate. However, smart (profit-maximizing) behaviour still recognizes the interdependence of pricing and investment decisions.

Peak load pricing

Chapter 8 argued that a monopolist makes higher profits if it can price-discriminate, charging different prices to customers whose demand curves are distinct. Price discrimination in *goods* induces low-price customers to resell to high-price customers, undermining price discrimination. Resale is not a problem if the commodity is a service (train journeys, electricity supply) that must be consumed as it is purchased.

A producer of electricity faces a high demand for electricity at breakfast and dinner, moderate demand in the rest of the day, and little demand at night. To cater for peak demand, it has to build extra power stations that are idle most of the day. In the long run, the capacity cost of building the extra power stations implies a high marginal cost of supplying peak users.

Users at different times impose very different marginal costs on society. It makes sense to charge peak users higher prices to reflect the higher marginal costs they impose.

Peak load pricing has two attractive effects. Not only do peak users pay for the high marginal costs they impose, users who do not mind consuming at a different time (e.g. households with night storage heaters, who can use electricity when marginal cost is low) are induced by cheaper prices to switch to consuming at off-peak times. By spreading total daily consumption more evenly, society reduces peak demand and need devote fewer resources to building power stations to cope with peak usage.

> **Peak load pricing** is price discrimination to charge peak-time users extra because of the higher marginal cost of supplying them.

In Figure 18.2, the efficient pricing policy makes prices vary with short-run marginal cost. Off-peak users, with the demand curve D_1D_1, pay the marginal operating cost c exclusive of capacity charges for the marginal plant. Peak users, with the demand curve D_2D_2, pay a higher price P_2 on the vertical part of the SMC curve through which their demand curve passes.

Given this efficient pricing structure, what is the efficient quantity of investment? Investment should increase capacity up to the point at which the once-and-for-all cost of a new plant equals the present value of operating profits when the efficient pricing structure is in operation. Equivalently, on a flow basis, the average daily price (in Figure 18.2, the average of the prices P_2 and c, weighted by the fraction of the day for which the demand curves D_1D_1 and D_2D_2 are relevant) should cover long-run marginal cost inclusive of capacity costs. Thus in Figure 18.2 the efficient level of capacity might be Q_0 if the weighted average of P_2 and c is equal to $P_1 = c + c_k$.

To sum up, prices should be set at short-run marginal cost, the actual opportunity cost of the resources to society. Given a daily or seasonal pattern in demand, peak load pricing reflects the different short-run marginal costs of supplying different customers at different times. The amount of total demand met on the vertical part of short-run marginal cost curves depends on the level of total capacity. At low capacity, prices will frequently be high since they are set on the vertical part of the short-run marginal cost curves. In the long run, investment and the efficient level of capacity should be determined to ensure that, when pricing at short-run marginal cost, average daily or yearly prices equal long-run marginal cost.

Implications for private firms

A private monopoly should also want to use two-part tariffs and peak load prices. Connecting to a network and subsequent use of the network are different products for which different prices are appropriate. Similarly, rush-hour travel and breakfast-time electricity are different products from mid-morning travel or mid-afternoon electricity, and profit-maximizing behaviour will set different prices for these different times of day that effectively constitute different markets.

So how then will private behaviour differ from efficient public sector behaviour? Recall that a monopolist, who must worry about additional output bidding down the price for which existing units of output can be sold, will generally charge higher prices than an equivalent firm that is behaving competitively. Hence, although a private monopolist's prices will vary by the time of day (if consumers view usage at different times of day as poor substitutes for one another), in general the private monopolist's prices will be higher throughout the day than the corresponding pattern of competitive pricing.

Phone pricing in the UK

Next time you see a quarterly telephone bill, look at it in closer detail. You are charged a quarterly rental independent of the number of calls made, plus a charge per minute that you make a call: a two-part tariff. The rental is related to the capacity charge in Figure 18.2, while the price per unit is related to short-run marginal cost SMC. The latter itself obeys the principle of peak load pricing.

People arrive at work in the morning impatient to start making phone calls. By evening, there are fewer people left to call, and by midnight most of us are asleep. Figure 18.2 implies that those who wish to make daytime calls should pay the high price needed to choke off demand at full capacity. Conversely, when the weekend network is deserted because business is asleep, *SMC* and price should be much lower.

Table 18.1 shows that actual prices of British Telecom closely follow both principles: two-part tariff and peak load pricing. In the past three decades, BT has evolved from nationalized industry to heavily regulated private monopoly to a less regulated firm facing extensive competition. But in all these market structures it has retained both a two-part tariff and peak load pricing, even though the details of pricing strategy have depended on the details of the market competition that BT was facing.

Table 18.1 BT price of a local call, 2007

	Day	Evening and weekend
Pence/minute	3	0.09

Note: Monthly fixed rental £10.50.
Source: BT.

Nationalized industries' performance

By 1970 the large UK public sector was following the sophisticated principles of pricing and investment set out above. Civil servants who helped run these industries were masters of the intricacies of the social discount rate, peak load pricing, two-part tariffs and consumer surplus. But three things went wrong.

First, the analysis assumed perfect (costless) information. In practice, firms always had inside information and the government became worried that it was hard to prevent unnecessary cost escalation. Cost curves were higher than they should have been.

Second, there were commitment problems. The government found it hard to resist pressure for wage increases in the public sector. Managers of nationalized industries could not argue that the Treasury could not afford it, and hence found it hard to resist wage claims. They also found it hard to fire people. Strikes against dismissals made politicians nervous. Sometimes the minister would pick up the phone and work out a deal.

Commitment problems also applied to investment. Investment by nationalized industries is part of government spending and contributes to the budget deficit. It also contributes to future government earnings, but short-sighted politicians had a habit of cancelling long-term investment. So nationalized industries had too little investment. However much the privatized utilities are now blamed for poor infrastructure in railways or water supply, half a century of underinvestment while state owned obviously contributed to the problem.

There were other types of 'government failure'. Politicians wanted plants located in their constituencies, and wanted individual state-owned industries adjusted to the temporary needs of the national economy, distorting decision making within nationalized industries. Nationalized to solve a market failure, they were undermined by government failure.

Third, people began to realize that a goldfish looks big in a jar but small in a lake. Increasing integration of different national economies began to introduce competition through imports or entry by foreign companies. As the size of the relevant market increased, the potential market power of firms of a given size diminished. If industries previously viewed as natural monopolies became subject to more international competition, the case for state control diminished.

18.3 Public versus private

Efficiency does not fall like rain from the sky. It needs sustained effort and leadership by management. How do incentives differ in the public and private sectors?

Incentives for private managers

In theory, private managers' performance is monitored by actual and potential shareholders. If directors do badly, they may be voted out of office at the annual general meeting of shareholders. Moreover, if bad management is perceived by the stock market, share prices will be lower than they might have been and a takeover raider may see an opportunity to buy up the company, install a better management, improve profits and hence make capital gains when share prices subsequently rise. These threats are supposed to discipline managers and keep them on their toes.

In practice, the threats are weak and not very credible. First, individual shareholders face a free-rider problem: if other shareholders monitor the management, everything will be fine. So everyone tends not to bother. Second, takeover raids typically bid up the share price significantly; the incumbent management has considerable leeway before it is likely to get into trouble and be out of a job. Finally, incumbent managers have a lot of insider information about the true state of the firm, information not available to existing shareholders or potential raiders.

Because shareholders know all this, they try to give managers a direct incentive to care about profits and cost reduction. Senior executives get big profit-related bonuses. However, recent years have seen chief executives earn spectacular bonuses even when their companies did poorly.

Private management is more likely to be efficient when subject to effective scrutiny, either from other competitors in the marketplace or from a tough and watchful regulatory body. When the private firm is very large, and therefore subject to little domestic competition, and also produces in a sector sheltered from imports and foreign competition, it is likely to be a relatively sleepy monopolist unless it has regulators with real teeth to whom it must account. And these regulators must be capable of resisting regulatory capture.

Incentives for public managers

Private managers sometimes face a weak market mechanism for discipline and control. Public sector managers used to face no market mechanism at all. Everything depended on the effectiveness of the government as a watchdog.

In principle, the government could be as effective as private markets. It could offer performance-related bonuses. On the other hand, its civil servants may have less training in business evaluation than do private sector analysts. Finally, there is the political temptation for the government to hijack the nationalized industries and make them an instrument of the urgent problem of the day.

Box 18.1 The Shareholder Executive

The Shareholder Executive was created in September 2003 to improve the government's performance as a shareholder in businesses that it owns. By 2007, the Shareholder Executive dealt with 27 government-owned businesses, including the Royal Mail, the Royal Mint, British Energy and the Met Office, creating boards of directors and management teams to help these organizations perform better, and advising ministers and officials on a wide range of shareholder issues, including objectives, governance, strategy, performance monitoring, board appointments and remuneration.

Box 18.2 Airline deregulation

Lessons from the United States

Internal US flights were deregulated in 1978. Entry barriers fell. By 1984 the number of airlines had risen from 36 to 120, fares were down 30 per cent and passenger use up 50 per cent. Fuller planes meant lower costs. More frequent services made flying more popular. Safety records did not deteriorate. Free marketeers rejoiced as their predictions came true.

However, after 1984 cutthroat competition led to bankruptcies and mergers. By 1989 the top 12 airlines had 97 per cent of the market. Fares rose, as did profits. Powerful incumbent airlines erected strategic entry barriers to consolidate their market share. They moved to a single airport (the hub) out of which long-haul flights operated. A system of feeder services (the spokes) first flew passengers to the hub. The hub-and-spoke system made it hard for small airlines to challenge the major airlines. The majors also owned the reservation system used by travel agents to locate empty seats. By programming the computer to show their own flights first, they put new entrants at a disadvantage. They also offered air miles that could be cashed in only with the same airline.

Regulation in Europe

European scheduled air travel was extensively regulated until 1997. Flights between European capitals were often restricted to one airline from each country, such as Iberia and Alitalia on the Madrid–Rome route. Competition was often nominal; the two airlines shared their joint revenue. Fares were strictly controlled. Scheduled air travel was exempt from EC competition law.

Hence fares were high. When firms have extensive product market power, trade unions will grab a big slice of these excess profits: lack of competition will show up as much in inflated costs as in high profits. The table shows how beautifully this theory fits the facts. European airlines pay much higher wages than their US counterparts, *despite* having lower living standards.

European airlines are gradually becoming subject to EU competition law. But incumbents still have big advantages. Because of congestion at major airports, new entrants operate out of secondary airports. While incumbents retain access to prime 'landing and takeoff slots' at favoured airports, life is hard for entrants.

The cost of flying in Europe will fall when the airline market becomes more competitive and when more countries finally privatize their state-owned airlines. An empirical study by Ng and Seabright estimates that ending state ownership typically reduces costs by 15–20 per cent, as workers are forced to accept more realistic wages.

The impact of 9/11

Following the terrorist attacks on New York, the airline industry imploded as demand collapsed. This led to renewed state involvement as governments bailed out ailing airlines. However, it also created a competitive opportunity for low-cost airlines like easyJet and Ryanair, which were quick to cut prices and take advantage of the withdrawal of incumbents. For the next few years, low cost airlines expanded rapidly.

Sources: F. McGowan and P. Seabright, 'Deregulating European Airlines', *Economic Policy*, 1990; C. Ng and P. Seabright, 'Competition, Privatisation and Productive Efficiency: Evidence from the Airline Industry', *Economic Journal*, July 2001.

The importance of ownership

In light of the above, the transfer of *ownership* from the public to the private sector may not in itself be the most important issue. Neither public nor private owners are good at monitoring management. If ownership transfer to the private sector has a direct benefit, it is probably by making it harder for governments to use industries to meet the requirements of other political dictates.

Thus, most economists agree that the key issue is not ownership itself but rather the severity of the market competition, or its substitute regulatory policy, which the industry faces. Sheltered monopolies are tempted to be slack no matter who owns them.

Selling the family silver?

Does selling off state assets mortgage a country's future. You already know enough to work out the answer for yourself. The market price of an asset is the present value of the net income stream to which it entitles the owner. Suppose a fair price is £100. If we sell you the asset, we get £100 in cash but you get an asset worth £100. Neither of us is better or worse off than before, though one of us has more cash to spend today.

How could the government be better off by privatization? Essentially for the reason first advanced by Adam Smith in the quotation at the start of this chapter. If nationalized industries previously had bad performances, they would have been worth little had they been sold at that stage. If management policy is changed to prepare for privatization, the present value of future profits rises at this point.

Finally, the question of mortgaging the future hinges crucially on what is done with the privatization revenue. It is not imprudent to invest this money in physical capital for the public sector, spend it on education that adds to human capital and hence to future earning power and the future tax base, or use it to pay off government debt. The government has then exchanged one asset for another. Only if privatization revenues are 'blown', for example on a tax-cut-financed consumer boom, is the government piling up financial trouble for future governments.

18.4 Privatization in practice

At 2007 prices, over £100 billion in revenue has been raised since 1980 from privatization of state industries such as British Telecom, British Gas, British Airways, British Steel, the water companies and most electric power. People found that buying shares at the offer price was a good deal; hence the queues of eager buyers featured on the TV news. However, the attempt to encourage wider share ownership was largely frustrated. Having made their capital gains, individuals soon sold their shares to the big pension funds and insurance companies eager to have a portfolio close to the market average.

Some companies that had previously been large fish in a small domestic pond now faced sufficient international competition that no additional regulation was necessary. Examples include British Airways, British Aerospace and Jaguar.

A second group of companies were closer to being true natural monopolies, facing substantial scale economies and, initially at least, facing little international competition. In particular, this group included the public utilities, energy and transport. In each of the water, electricity and railway industries, the state-owned monopoly was broken up into different private companies in the hope of partial competition. In contrast, British Telecom and British Gas were privatized intact.

Whatever the mode of privatization of these giant firms, regulation was needed, at least until globalization introduced sufficient international competition. This has happened in telecoms, but has some way to go in the other utilities.

When natural monopoly exists, letting private firms exploit market power is inefficient. Yet nationalization was not a success either. Moreover, we are gradually learning in Europe that the alternative policy response – leave natural monopolists in the private sector but regulate their activities – is also full of difficulties. In the US, where regulation was always preferred to public ownership, the same conclusion was reached long ago: regulatory capture and informational problems still pose serious difficulties for public policy.

Instead of imperfectly intervening to control a monopolist in a small market, why not expand the market? A large market may support competition between many firms, each large enough to exploit scale economies. This was a key aspect of the programme to 'complete the internal market' within the European Union after 1992.

18.5 Regulating private monopolies

What were the lessons from the earlier experience of nationalizing natural monopolies? First, regulators need to be independent of government to make credible the promise not to interfere all the time. This was accomplished by establishing the independent regulators whose acronyms punctuate the financial media: OFTEL, OFWAT, OFGEM and so on.[1] Each regulator has objectives clearly laid down by Parliament but is responsible for their implementation.

Even so, credibility is not always easily established. For example, when regulated companies make unforeseen profits, it may be hard for the regulator to allow the private monopoly to keep these. Failures of regulatory commitment are more important the more an industry depends on sustained investment for ongoing success. For example, if regulatory failure is severe enough, it might be better to privatize telecoms altogether in order to safeguard the incentive to keep investing.

Second, attention must be paid to information asymmetries and possible cost escalation by natural monopolists. In essence, two systems of regulation of *conduct* are possible: a price ceiling or a ceiling on the rate of return (sometimes called 'cost-plus'). Regulatory design faces a trade-off when the firm has an information monopoly on its true costs. A price ceiling gives the monopolist all the benefit of cost reduction that is unobservable by the regulator; a cap on the rate of return means that cost cuts lead to lower prices.

If that was the only problem, a price cap offers better incentives. But if the monopolist faces other risks, rate of return regulation enables unforeseen developments to be passed on to consumers, whereas a price cap makes the monopolist bear all of the risk. Efficient risk-sharing may use some elements of rate-of-return regulation.

Despite the case for some compromise between these two methods, UK regulation has, until recently, plumped largely for the price-cap method, putting the full force of regulation behind the pressure for cost reduction. This was pioneered with the privatization of BT in 1984, subject to an '$RPI - X$' price ceiling. *Nominal* prices could rise by the same percentage as the retail price index, minus X per cent.

---

1 Initially, telecoms, gas, electricity and other private monopolies each had their own regulator, such as OFTEL and OFGAS, but these have gradually been replaced by regulators for entire sectors. Thus OFGEM now regulates gas *and* electricity markets and OFCOM regulates not merely telecoms but other communications industries such as radio and broadband as well.

X is the annual cut in *real* prices. Since telecommunications enjoy rapid technical progress, BT could reduce costs year after year in real terms. Initially, the regulator OFTEL set X at 3 per cent a year, but later raised it to 4.5 per cent and then 6.25 per cent. During its first ten years as a private company, BT cut its real price by 43 per cent.

Box 18.3 Better deals for mobile phone users

Chapter 17 introduced the role of the Competition Commission in regulating the conduct of firms with monopoly power. Now that we have also studied the role of $(RPI - X)$ regulation, we can examine some Competition Commission judgments in relation to mobile phones.

In 1999, after an investigation by the Competition Commission critical of charges for mobile phones, Vodafone and BT Cellnet (later renamed O_2) were set a price ceiling of $RPI - 9$ in each of 1999 and 2000.

By 2003, the Competition Commission was involved again, this time investigating the claim that termination charges from mobile phones to fixed land lines were too high. The Commission concluded that the cost of terminating calls made by fixed line users was at least 40 per cent higher than the fair rate. Mobile network operators suggested that the high termination price was used to subsidize new mobile handsets. The Commission argued that not all fixed line users were mobile users and so did not benefit from this subsidy. Furthermore it was also questioned whether the 'churn' of new handsets was economically efficient.

As a result, during 2002–06 the Commission required Vodafone and O_2 to cut their real termination charges by 15 per cent a year, and required Orange and T-Mobile to reduce their real termination charges by 14 per cent a year.

Increasingly, because of growing competition from mobile phones, foreign suppliers and cable companies, regulation of telecoms is moving from the regulation of *final* prices to regulation of *intermediate* prices and access to networks. Just as the European Commission forced Microsoft to allow competitors to interface with its servers, OFCOM now thinks about the price that BT charges its competitors to use its national distribution network. With more potential suppliers, competition in the final output market rises.

As one would expect, competition between water companies has proved harder to stimulate – each company is effectively a local monopoly – so the original framework for regulation after privatization is essentially still in place. In regulating the water companies, OFWAT adopted $RPI + K$. The real price of water rises by K per cent a year to allow water companies to improve quality (and indeed quantity!) by substantial investment so long neglected when water was a nationalized industry. K initially averaged around 5 per cent but has subsequently been reduced. Even so, the consequence of regulation by OFWAT is that the real price of water to households rose by a cumulative 49 per cent during 1989–2007.

Regulating *conduct* is not the only option available to regulators. It is also possible to break up a company to change the *structure* of the industry. In the 1980s, the US phone company AT&T was broken up into 'baby Bells', each serving a region of the US but sharing the same network for interregional calls.

Problems of regulating giant companies has led regulators to think harder and harder about whether some parts of the business could survive competition. The British Gas monopoly has subsequently been broken down by allowing regional gas and electricity companies to compete in supplying both gas and electricity. These and other industries are vertically integrated, combining an upstream facility, the basic transmission network, with downstream activities such as local distribution. The basic network is a natural monopoly – we only want one national grid for electricity – but downstream activities offer more opportunities for competition. Obviously, access to the network has to be available at reasonable prices, and the regulator needs to monitor this. A key issue is whether the firm that runs the network should also be allowed to compete with other downstream distributors. The answer depends on whether either vertical externalities or opportunities for strategic behaviour give the network monopolist undue power in the downstream market.

Similarly, in 1994 privatization of British Rail led to the creation of Railtrack to supply the infrastructure network, and the award of regional operating franchises to companies such as Virgin Trains, Great Western Trains and Scotrail. Spillovers across activities show that breaking up companies does not always offer an easy solution. Railtrack was persistently criticized for underinvestment.

Since the direct beneficiaries of better railway lines were the rail operating companies, Railtrack's incentives depended on how directly the regulator tied Railtrack's income to its delivery of better railway infrastructure. The answer turned out to be 'not enough'. In 2002 as Railtrack went bankrupt, the government stepped in to reorganize the railways yet again, leading eventually to the creation of Network Rail.

The unhappy experience of rail privatization also shows that commitment problems do not vanish merely because an industry is privatized.

18.6 The Private Finance Initiative

In 1992 the UK government introduced the Private Finance Initiative (PFI). The government claimed it used private sector expertise to finance and manage public projects. Critics viewed it largely as a scam to cut the apparent size of the budget deficit. The argument has been raging ever since.

The PFI transforms government departments and agencies from owners and operators of assets to ongoing purchasers of services from the private sector. Private firms become long-term service providers not just upfront asset builders. Rather than paying for the capital cost of road building, the government becomes a continuing renter of miles of maintained highway.

During 1992–2002 £30 billion such deals were signed, including the building of the Channel Tunnel Rail Link, other transport schemes such as roads, bridges and rail and tram developments, and hospitals and other health sector projects. The remainder went on IT, defence, education, and prison and other accommodation. In 1996 the scheme was extended to local authorities as the Public Private Partnership (PPP) Programme. Table 18.2 shows that during 2006–08 annual new investment via PFI was running around £4.5 billion a year.

Table 18.2 UK PFI investment and subsequent payments (£bn)

	New investment	Repayments to PFI investor-operators
2006/07	4.8	–
2007/08	4.5	–
2006/07	–	6.9
2016/17	–	8.9
2026/27	–	5.0

Source: HM Treasury, Budget Report 2007.

By financing this initial cost, the private sector was removing a current burden from the taxpayer but only in exchange for a future burden. Table 18.2 shows that by 2007, based on all the PFI projects undertaken during 1992–2007, the Treasury was predicting future annual payments to private operators peaking at £8.9 billion in 2016/17. Since new PFI contracts continue to be signed, by the time we get to this date, the figure will be larger still.

The Treasury insists the principal aim is to draw on private sector management expertise and risk control. Projects are built and operated by consortia of firms with synergies between construction, financing, risk management and operational expertise.

The government was fed up with cost overruns on public projects. Under the PFI, the private sector is responsible for risks within its control. The government is only responsible for overruns arising from wider risks outside the contractors' control. Of course, the dividing line is ambiguous. London and Continental Railway, responsible for the largest PFI project, the Channel Tunnel Rail Link, kept asking for more money than the level specified in its original bid.

What about the budgetary implications? First, any benefit of private sector efficiency has to be set against the fact that the government can borrow more cheaply than the private sector. The private sector bears the initial construction costs, which it finances by borrowing. Yet the lower credit rating of privately financed projects (compared with a government rating of AAA, Greenwich Hospital's bonds are rated BBB and Docklands Light Railway bonds rated A) can mean anything up to an extra one percentage point on the interest rate that must be paid. When average interest rates are only 5 or 6 per cent, this adds a lot to the cost of a project. Private sector efficiency has to offset more than this if the government is to benefit.

Second, the PFI lets the government escape the initial capital cost of building a road or a prison in exchange for incurring two future costs. The first is ongoing 'renting' of the road or prison service from the asset provider, the second is possible liability for cost increases outside the control of the private supplier. Making proper allowance for the latter in today's budget estimates is no easy matter.

What about exchanging the capital cost for a future liability to rent the service instead? Suppose a road costs £100 million to build, and interest rates are 10 per cent. The private provider will have to charge £10 million a year just to cover the opportunity cost of the money tied up in the project. In the early years, the government has its road and is spending a lot less than the £100 million it would have to spend to build the road. Initially, it needs less tax revenue. It is like hidden borrowing. The present value of the future road rental charges it will have to pay does not show up in government debt.

Many future flows are not properly accounted for in the government accounts. When the UK first discovered North Sea Oil, the present value of all the future tax levied on oil extraction was not immediately included as a government asset. This is not how the stock market behaves. Think of all the internet companies valued at billions of pounds merely because the market thought they would earn revenues at some future date.

Conversely, many governments already know that they face huge future pension obligations, because of ageing populations and generous state pensions (not a feature of the UK!), yet this liability does not show up anywhere in their accounts today. It should be recorded not in the flow account of current income and spending, but ideally in the current assessment of assets and liabilities. Since it is not, as PFI projects gradually build up the flow of fees to be paid to private service providers of what were previously public projects, this will automatically tend to raise the flow of government spending in the future.

Activity box 18 Down the tube

In 2007, Metronet, a private sector consortium responsible for maintenance and upgrading of most of the London Underground network – including the Bakerloo, Victoria and Central lines – declared it was bankrupt. Metronet ran out of money after a long dispute with Transport for London, the company responsible for the tube, about who should pay for the spiralling cost of upgrading the network's infrastructure.

Metronet had planned to invest £17 billion over the next 30 years under the terms of a public–private partnership scheme (PPP schemes involve local government, PFI schemes involve central government), a method of funding and financing large projects opposed by Mr Livingstone (the mayor of London) but supported by the government. Since the tube is old, there was bound to be considerable uncertainty about the cost of maintenance and infrastructure upgrading. When it went bust, Metronet reckoned it would have been overspent by £2 billion by 2010.

Did the collapse of Metronet mean the end of PFI schemes in general? Many private finance projects for schools and hospitals have in fact gone well. The tube deal was larger, more complex and operated over a very long period.

As Chancellor, Gordon Brown had insisted on the tube PPP because he was fed up with cost overruns on public projects. For example, the Jubilee line extension cost £4 billion, nearly three times its original estimate. The PPP was supposed to transfer risk from the government to the contractors. Yet the costs of Metronet's failure fell on the state. Station renewals will almost certainly be scaled back.

We live in a world with risks. Some exist anyway and we have to deal with them (i.e. decide who bears them), the extent of others is affected by the contractual and incentive structure we put in place. Generations of defence procurement specialists have wrestled with this issue – if the government bears the risk, defence contractors have insufficient incentive to hold down costs; if the contractor bears the risk, as in a fixed-price contract, the contractor skimps on quality whenever unexpected costs appear. Second-best considerations suggest a mixture of the two incentive systems may be the least bad outcome.

PFI and PPP do not eliminate this dilemma. Sometimes, with better management they may indeed curtail the risk somewhat, but they will not eliminate it, especially on mega-projects. Where joint ventures have a legal entity distinct from the constituent companies, it is always an option to declare the venture bankrupt without dragging down the companies that had invested in the project. In these circumstances, the government is always residually liable for the risk. PFI may be helpful if well operated, but it cannot work magic.

Adapted from BBC online, 18 July 2007 and *The Guardian*, 19 July 2007.

Questions

(a) Explain the difference to the public finances (budget deficit, government debt) of paying for the capital cost of a project out of government money versus using PFI or PPP.

(b) Suppose it was possible to distinguish between risks that existed anyway and risks that arose because of contractor behaviour. Would you wish to treat these differently in a procurement contract?

To check your answers to these questions, go to page 725.

Summary

- **Nationalization** is the acquisition of private companies by the public sector. **Privatization** is the sale of public sector firms to the private sector.

- A **natural monopoly** faces a falling average cost curve. Marginal cost lies below average cost. Pricing at marginal cost implies losses.

- A **two-part tariff** lets the monopolist set the appropriate marginal charge and recover losses via the fixed charge. With an information monopoly, however, an inefficient firm will try to recover unnecessary losses via the fixed charge.

- Ideally, state-run firms should price at marginal social cost and invest until price just covers long-run marginal social cost, including the annual interest cost of the initial capital expenditure.

- **Regulatory capture** occurs when the regulator becomes the champion of the industry that it is supposed to regulate.

- Privatization was a response to the view that some state companies were not natural monopolies, and that even natural monopolies were better handled by arms' length regulation that committed the government not to intervene perpetually.

- Transfer of ownership makes credible the fact that the firm does not have limitless government backing (though governments do bail out even private companies from time to time!).

- Selling assets at a fair price leaves government wealth unaltered. If prospects of tougher treatment in the future lead to productivity improvements in state firms, the government becomes better off when productivity improvement first becomes likely, not when the firm is sold.

- Many privatized firms now face intense competition, often from abroad. However, natural monopolies have required a new framework of regulation. This has favoured price capping, administered by independent regulatory agencies, and subject to periodic review.

- Increasingly, the UK has been driven to regulate not merely conduct but market structure. This presupposes that some parts of a natural monopoly can become suitable for competition. In practice, this has usually been downstream activities in a vertically related industry.

- The **Private Finance Initiative** uses private finance to build projects and private management to run them. The government then pays a service charge to use the asset.

Review questions

To check your answers to these questions, go to page 724.

1 Why do sports clubs have both an initial membership fee and an annual subscription for people who are already members?

2 An MP has suggested that since British Telecom is regulated by OFCOM it would make sense to establish OFAIR to regulate British Airways. Would it?

3 'Cheap season tickets keep commuters off congested rush-hour roads.' 'Commuters should pay extra since most trains lie idle the rest of the day.' Adjudicate between these views. Does the answer depend on how cars and parking are being priced?

4 'The Channel Tunnel, built with private money, was then unable to keep up the interest payments on its debts. It should never have been built.' Discuss.

5 Did you remember the distinction between private and social valuation of costs and benefits in answering Question 4? Identify five sources of difference between private and social costs and benefits.

6 **Common fallacies** Why are these statements wrong? (a) Nationalized industries that lose money must be inefficient. (b) A private monopoly is always inferior to a public monopoly. (c) Since conduct can be regulated, there is no need ever to break up monopolies.

7 **Harder question** When the Ministry of Defence orders the design and manufacture of a new fighter aircraft, it could issue a fixed-price contract or a cost-plus contract. Explain how incentives differ in the two contracts. When would cost-plus be socially desirable? Why is the Private Finance Initiative a compromise between fixed-price and cost-plus contracts?

8 **Harder question** You are in charge of designing the UK's first comprehensive road pricing system that will reflect both congestion and pollution. You have satellite technology that can identify every vehicle's location around the clock. What principles would determine your answer? Would pollution and congestion be treated differently from one another?

9 **Essay question** Could nuclear energy ever be privatized? Why or why not?

Online
Learning Centre

To help you grasp the key concepts of this chapter check out the extra resources posted on the Online Learning Centre. There are chapter summaries, self-test questions, an interactive graphing tool, weblinks and a searchable glossary, all for free!

To put your learning into practice and prepare for exams, an **Interactive Workbook** is also available online, containing a variety of question types and providing feedback on your answers.

If you'd like further help with economics, or have any questions, **NetTutor** is here to help! You will have a personalised tutorial service at your fingertips. Visit the online learning centre at: www.mcgraw-hill.co.uk/textbooks/begg for information on accessing all of these resources.

PART FOUR

Macroeconomics

Part 4 studies the economy as an interrelated system. Output is demanded by firms, by households, by the government and by foreigners. Since interest rates affect the demand for output, the financial sector interacts with the real economy. Price and wage adjustments help restore output to full capacity, but monetary policy and fiscal policy also play a role. Together, all this affects inflation and unemployment. Economies are increasingly open to foreign trade and foreign capital. The balance of payments records transactions with foreigners. The dynamics of the national economy also depend on the exchange rate policy pursued. By the end of Part 4, we can explain business cycles around full capacity and long-run growth in full capacity output.

Chapter 19 introduces the macroeconomy. Chapters 20–21 develop a basic model of output determination in the short run. Chapters 22–23 describe money, banking, and how interest rates are set. Chapter 24 examines monetary and fiscal policy. Chapter 25 introduces aggregate supply and price adjustment. Chapters 26–27 look at inflation and unemployment, and Chapters 28–29 at exchange rates and the balance of payments. Chapter 30 discusses long-run growth and Chapter 31 analyses short-run business cycles. After thirteen chapters of macroeconomics, Chapter 32 takes stock.

Contents

CHAPTER 19

Introduction to macroeconomics

Learning Outcomes

By the end of this chapter, you should understand:

1 macroeconomics as the study of the whole economy

2 internally consistent national accounts

3 the circular flow between households and firms

4 why leakages always equal injections

5 more comprehensive measures of national income and output

We now turn to the big issues, such as unemployment, inflation and economic growth. Macroeconomics sacrifices details to study the big picture.

The distinction between microeconomics and macroeconomics is more than the difference between economics in the small and economics in the large, which the Greek prefixes *micro* and *macro* suggest. The purpose of their analysis is also different.

> **Macroeconomics** is the study of the economy as a system.

A model simplifies to focus on the key elements of a problem and think about them clearly. We could study the whole economy by piecing together a microeconomic analysis of every market, but it would be hard to keep track of all the economic forces at work. Our brains do not have a big enough Pentium chip to make sense of it.

Microeconomics and macroeconomics take different approaches to keep the analysis manageable. Microeconomics stresses a detailed understanding of particular markets. To achieve this detail, many interactions with other markets are suppressed. In saying a tax on cars reduces the equilibrium quantity of cars, we ignore what the government does with the tax revenue. If government debt is reduced, interest rates and the exchange rate may fall, boosting competitiveness and car output.

Microeconomics is like looking at a horse race through a pair of binoculars. It is great for details, but sometimes we get a clearer picture of the whole race by using the naked eye. Because macroeconomics studies the interaction of different parts of the economy, it uses a different simplification to keep the analysis manageable. Macroeconomics simplifies the building blocks in order to focus on how they fit together and influence one another.

Macroeconomics stresses broad aggregates such as the total demand for goods by households or the total spending on machinery and building by firms. As in watching the horse race through the naked eye, our notion of individual details is more blurred but our full attention is on the big picture. We are more likely to notice the horse sneaking up on the rails.

19.1 The big issues

Here are some key questions that form the theme of the analysis in Part 4.

Why did unemployment rise after the 1960s but fall in the 1990s? Did workers price themselves out of jobs by greedy wage claims? Does technical progress destroy jobs? Can the government create more jobs? These are questions we need to answer in Part 4.

What determines real GNP? Why was there a boom in the late 1990s, a slowdown after 2000 and a rise in activity after 2003? Why do some countries grow faster than others?

The price level is a weighted average of the prices households pay for goods and services.

What causes inflation? Money growth, oil price rises or a budget deficit? Have we now learned how to defeat inflation?

Almost every day the media discuss inflation, unemployment and economic growth. These issues help determine elections, and make people interested in macroeconomics.

> The **labour force** is people at work or looking for work. It excludes people neither working nor looking for work. The **unemployment rate** is the fraction of the labour force without a job.

> Real **gross national product** (GNP) measures the income of an economy, the quantity of goods and services the economy can afford to purchase. **Economic growth** is a rise in real GNP.

> The **inflation rate** is the percentage increase in the average price of goods and services.

19.2 The facts

We begin with some facts about unemployment, economic growth and inflation. Table 19.1 opposite puts recent performance in perspective, showing data for past 50 years.

The two decades before 1970 were a golden age of low unemployment, rapid growth and low inflation. In the early 1970s, with the world economy booming, OPEC quadrupled the price of oil. The rest of the 1970s saw high inflation, low growth and rising unemployment. After another oil price hike in 1979–80, the 1980s were another tough period. Table 19.1 shows that it was not until the 1990s that inflation and unemployment fell. Table 19.2 gives more details on the rise and fall of unemployment, trends that few countries escaped.

Figure 19.1 takes a longer look at UK inflation, which soared in 1970s. The Thatcher government reduced inflation after 1980, but lost control in the late 1980s when it let the economy grow too rapidly, leading to more inflation. Subsequent Chancellors – John Major, Norman Lamont, Kenneth Clarke and Gordon Brown – gradually got the UK back on an even keel, not least by giving the Bank of England much more independence in decisions about monetary policy.

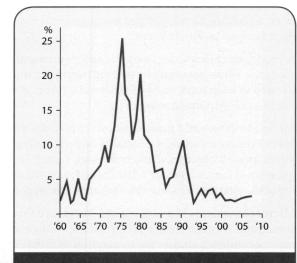

Figure 19.1 The inflation rate in the UK

Source: ONS, Economic Trends.

Table 19.1 Inflation, unemployment and output growth, 1960–2008 (annual, %)

	UK	USA	Germany
Unemployment			
1960–73	3	5	1
1973–81	6	7	3
1981–90	10	7	7
1991–2008	6	5	8
Real growth			
1960–73	3	4	5
1973–81	1	2	2
1981–90	3	3	2
1991–2008	2	3	2
Inflation			
1960–73	5	3	3
1973–81	15	9	5
1981–90	6	5	3
1991–2008	2	2	2

Source: OECD, Economic Outlook.

Table 19.2 Unemployment (%)

	1980	1989	2008
France	5.8	9.4	8.2
Italy	5.6	9.8	6.4
UK	6.2	7.3	5.9
Belgium	9.3	7.5	7.8
Holland	6.0	6.9	2.5

Source: OECD, Economic Outlook.

19.3 An overview

The economy comprises millions of individual economic units: households, firms, and the departments of central and local government. Together, their individual decisions determine the economy's total spending, income and output.

The circular flow

Initially, we ignore the government and other countries. Table 19.3 shows transactions between households and firms. Households own the factors of production (inputs to production). Households rent labour to firms in exchange for wages. Households are also the ultimate owners of firms and get their profits. Capital and land, even if held by firms, are ultimately owned by households.

The first row of Table 19.3 shows that households supply factor services to firms that use these inputs to make output. The second row shows the corresponding payments. Households earn factor incomes (wages, rents, profits), payments by firms for these factor services. The third row shows that households spend their incomes buying the output of firms, giving firms the money to pay for production inputs. Figure 19.2 shows this *circular flow* between firms and households.

Table 19.3 Transactions by households and firms

Households	Firms
Supply factor services to firms	Use factors to make output
Receive factor incomes from firms	Rent factor services from households
Buy output of firms	Sell output to households

The inner loop shows flows of real resources between the two sectors. The outer loop shows the corresponding flows of money in a market economy. A centrally planned economy could arrange the resource transfers on the inner loop without using the outer loop.

> The **circular flow** shows how real resources and financial payments flow between firms and households.

Figure 19.2 suggests three ways to measure economic activity in an economy: (a) the value of goods and services produced, (b) the level of factor earnings, which represent the value of factor services supplied, or (c) the value of spending on goods and services. All payments are the counterparts of real resources. For the moment, we assume all payments are spent buying real resources. Hence, we get the same estimate of total economic activity whether we use the value of production, the level of factor incomes or spending on goods and services.

Factor incomes equal household spending if all income is spent. The value of output equals total spending on goods and services if all goods are sold. The value of output also equals the value of household incomes. Since profits are residually defined as the value of sales minus the rental of factor inputs, and since profits accrue to the households that own firms, household incomes – from supplying land, labour and capital, or from profits – equals the value of output.

Our model is still very simple. What happens if firms do not sell all their output? What happens if firms sell output not to households but to other firms? What happens if households do not spend all their incomes? The next section answers these questions. Having done so, our conclusion will be unchanged: the level of economic activity can be measured by valuing total spending, total output or total earnings. All three methods give the same answer.

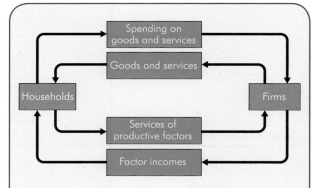

The inner loop shows the flow of real resources. Households supply the services of factors of production to firms who use these factors to produce goods and services for households. The outer loop shows the corresponding flow of payments. Firms pay factor incomes to households but receive revenue from households' spending on goods and services that the firms produce.

Figure 19.2 The circular flow between firms and households

The circular flow diagram in Figure 19.2 lets us keep track of some key interactions in the economy as a whole. But the diagram is too simple. It leaves out important features of the real world: saving and investment, government spending and taxes, transactions between firms and with the rest of the world. We need a comprehensive system of national accounts.

Box 19.1 Emerging markets act as locomotive for world economy

In April 2007, the International Monetary Fund on Wednesday raised its 2007 and 2008 forecasts for world economic growth to 5.2 percent, and said China was poised to become its most powerful driver. 'The global economy continued to expand at a brisk pace in the first half of 2007,' the IMF said in a statement. 'The major upward revisions have been for emerging markets and developing countries, with growth projections substantially marked up for China, India and Russia.' China is expected to see growth of 11 percent in 2007, India 9 percent, and Russia 7 percent.

In 2007, with strong Chinese growth and a United States slowdown to only 2 percent growth, for the very first time, China contributed the largest part to the increase in the global growth – one quarter of the annual growth rate of the world economy; adding in Russia and India as well, over half of global growth came from emerging market countries.

In contrast, the IMF expected Japan to grow by 2.6 percent in 2007, the same rate as Europe's 27-nation eurozone.

Source: IMF World Economic Outlook, April 2007.

19.4 National income accounting

Measuring GDP

GDP measures the value of output in the economy. Initially we discuss a *closed economy*, not linked to the rest of the world, in which output and income are the same.

First, we extend our simple circular flow diagram. Transactions do not take place exclusively between a single firm and a single household. Firms hire labour services from households but buy raw materials and machinery from *other* firms. To avoid double counting, we use value added.

To get value added, we take the firm's output then deduct the cost of the input goods used up to make that output. Closely related is the distinction between final goods and intermediate goods.

Thus, ice cream is a final good. Steel is an intermediate good, made by one firm but used as an input by another firm. Capital goods are final goods because they are *not* used up in subsequent production. They do not fully depreciate.

An example will clarify these concepts. Study it until you have mastered them. We assume that there are four firms in the economy: a steel maker, a producer of capital goods (machines) for the car industry, a tyre maker and a car producer who sells to the final user, households. Table 19.4 calculates GDP for this simple economy.

> **Gross domestic product** (GDP) measures the output made in the domestic economy, regardless of who owns the production inputs.

> **Value added** is the increase in the value of goods as a result of the production process.

> **Final goods** are purchased by the ultimate user, either households buying consumer goods or firms buying capital goods such as machinery. **Intermediate goods** are partly-finished goods that form inputs to a subsequent production process that then uses them up.

The steel firm makes £4000 worth of steel, one-quarter sold to the machine maker and three-quarters sold to the car maker. If the steel producer also mines the iron ore from which the steel is produced, all £4000 is value added or net output of the steel firm. This revenue is paid out in wages and rents, or is residual profits that also accrue to households as income. Hence the first two rows of the last column also add up to £4000. Firms have spent £4000 buying this steel output, but it is not expenditure on final goods. Steel is an intermediate good, used up in later stages of the production process.

Table 19.4 Calculating GDP

(1) Good	(2) Seller	(3) Buyer	(4) Transaction value	(5) Value added	(6) Spending on final goods	(7) Factor earnings
Steel	Steel maker	Machine maker	£1000	£1000	–	£1000
Steel	Steel maker	Car maker	£3000	£3000	–	£3000
Machine	Machine maker	Car maker	£2000	£1000	£2000	£1000
Tyres	Tyre maker	Car maker	£500	£500	–	£500
Cars	Car maker	Households	£5000	£1500	£5000	£1500
Total transactions			£11 500			
GDP			£7000	£7000	£7000	

The machine maker spends £1000 buying steel input, then converts it into a machine sold to the car maker for £2000. The value added by the machine maker is £2000 less the £1000 spent on steel input. This net revenue of £1000 accrues directly or indirectly to households as income or profit. Since the car firm intends to keep the machine, the full value of £2000 is then shown under 'final expenditure'.

Like the steel producer, the tyre manufacturer makes an intermediate output that is not final expenditure. If the tyre manufacturer also owns the rubber trees from which the tyres were made, the entire output of £500 is value added and contributes to household incomes. If the tyre company bought rubber from a domestic rubber producer, we subtract the input value of rubber from the tyre manufacturer's output to get value added or net output, but add another row in the table showing activity of the rubber producer.

The car producer spends £3000 on steel and £500 on tyres. Since both are used up during the period in which cars are made, we subtract £3500 from the car output of £5000 to get the value added of the car maker. This net revenue pays households for factor services supplied, or is paid to them as profits.

Finally, the car producer sells the car for £5000 to the final consumer–households. Only then does the car become a final good. Its full price of £5000 is final expenditure.

Table 19.4 shows that the gross value of all the transactions is £11 500. This overstates the value of the goods the economy has actually produced. For example, the £3000 that the steel producer earned by selling steel to the car producer is already included in the final value of car output. It is double-counting to count this £3000 again as output of the steel producer.

Column (5) shows the value added at each stage in the production process. £7000 is the true net output of the economy. Since each firm pays the corresponding net revenue to households either as direct factor payments or indirectly as profits, household earnings are £7000 in the last column of the table. If we add up payments made to households as income and profits, we get the same measure of GDP.

Table 19.4 confirms that we also get the same answer if we measure spending on *final* goods and services. In this case final users are households buying cars and the car producer buying the (everlasting) machinery used to make cars.

Investment and saving

This example explains value added, and the distinction between intermediate and final goods. It also deals with a second complication. Total output and household incomes are each £7000, but households spend only £5000 on cars. What do they do with the rest of their incomes? And who does the rest of the spending? To resolve these issues, we need investment and saving.

> **Investment** is the purchase of new capital goods by firms. **Saving** is the part of income not spent buying goods and services.

Households spend £5000 on cars. Since their income is £7000, they save £2000. The car maker spends £2000 on investment, buying new machinery. Figure 19.3 shows how to amend the circular flow diagram of Figure 19.2. The bottom half of the figure shows that incomes and factor services are each £7000. But £2000 leaks out from the circular flow when households save. Only £5000 finds its way back to firms as household spending on cars.

The top half of the figure shows that £5000 is the value of output of consumer goods and of household spending on these goods. Since GDP is £7000, where does the other £2000 come from? If not from

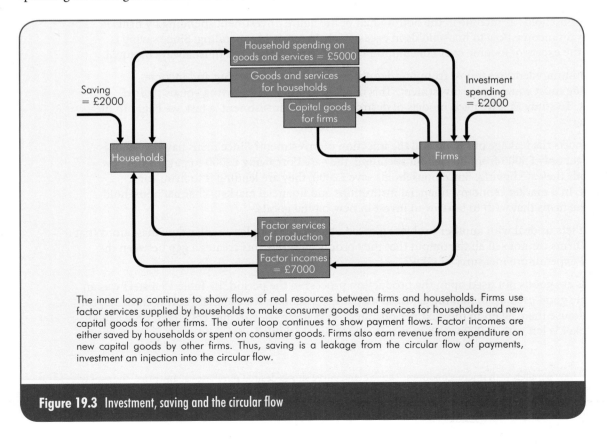

The inner loop continues to show flows of real resources between firms and households. Firms use factor services supplied by households to make consumer goods and services for households and new capital goods for other firms. The outer loop continues to show payment flows. Factor incomes are either saved by households or spent on consumer goods. Firms also earn revenue from expenditure on new capital goods by other firms. Thus, saving is a leakage from the circular flow of payments, investment an injection into the circular flow.

Figure 19.3 Investment, saving and the circular flow

household spending, it must come from spending by firms themselves. It is the £2000 of investment expenditure made by the car producer buying machinery for car production.

The numbers in Table 19.4 relate to flows of output, expenditure and income in a particular period, such as a year. During this period the economy goes once round the inner and outer loops of Figure 19.3. On the inner loop, firms make an output of £5000 for consumption by households and an output of £2000 of capital goods for investment by firms. On the outer loop, which relates to money payments, saving is a *leakage* of £2000 from the circular flow and investment spending by firms on new machinery is an *injection* of £2000 to the circular flow.

Two questions immediately arise. First, is it coincidental that household savings of £2000 exactly equal investment expenditure of £2000 by firms? Second, if not, how is the money saved by households transferred to firms to allow them to pay for investment spending?

> A **leakage** from the circular flow is money no longer recycled from households to firms. An **injection** is money that flows to firms without being cycled through households.

Suppose Y denotes GDP, which also equals the value of household incomes, C denotes household spending on consumption, and S saving. By definition saving is unspent income, so $Y \equiv C + S$, where the symbol $\equiv$ means 'is identically equal to, as a matter of definition'. Since one definition of GDP is the sum of final expenditure, $Y = C + I$. Putting these two definitions together

$$S \equiv I \tag{1}$$

since both are identical to $(Y - C)$.

It is thus no accident that saving and investment are each £2000 in our example. Equation (1) tells us that saving and investment are always equal, in the absence of government and foreign sectors.

Look again at the outer loop of Figure 19.3. All household spending in the top half of the figure returns to households as income in the bottom half of the figure. Investment spending by firms is matched by an income flow to households in excess of their consumer spending. Since saving is defined as the excess of income over consumption, investment and savings must always be equal.

These accounting identities follow from our definitions of investment, saving and income. *Actual* saving must equal *actual* investment. This need not mean *desired* saving equals *desired* investment. To study that we need models of desired saving and investment, a task we begin in the next chapter.[1]

What connects the leakage of saving and the injection of investment? Since firms pay households £7000 but get only £5000 from household spending, they are borrowing £2000 to pay for the new capital goods they are buying. Since households save £2000, they are lending it to firms for investment. In a market economy, financial institutions and financial markets channel household saving to the firms that wish to borrow to invest in new capital goods.

Investment lets us deal with another problem glossed over in our simpler circular flow diagram. What happens if firms cannot sell all the output that they produce? Surely this creates a gap between the output and expenditure measures of GDP?

Final goods are goods not used up in the production process in the period. In Table 19.4 steel was an intermediate good used up in making cars and machines; machines were a final good because the car maker could use them again in the next period. Suppose that car sales are not £5000 but only £4000. The car maker is left with £1000 worth of cars that must be stockpiled.

---

1 It helps to draw parallels with microeconomics. The demand curve shows desired purchases at any price, the supply curve desired sales at any price. In equilibrium desired purchases equal desired sales. When the price is too high there is excess supply and some desired sales are frustrated. But since every transaction has a buyer and a seller, actual purchases equal actual sales whether or not the market is in equilibrium.

The car producer may hold stocks of steel, an input to production of cars in the next period, or stocks of finished cars awaiting sale to consumers in the next period.

> **Inventories** or **stocks** are goods currently held by a firm for future production or sale.

In Chapter 6 we described stocks as *working capital.* Not used up in production and sale during the current period, stocks are classified as capital goods. Adding to stocks is investment in working capital. When stocks are depleted, we treat this as negative investment or disinvestment.

Now we can keep the national accounts straight. When the car firm sells only £4000 of the £5000 worth of cars made this period, we treat the inventory investment of £1000 by the car producer as final expenditure. As in Table 19.4, the output and expenditure measures of GDP are each £7000, including the output and expenditure on the machinery for making cars. But spending on final goods is now: car firm (£2000 on machines, £1000 on stocks), household-consumer (£4000 on cars).

This can be confusing. The trick is to distinguish between classification by commodity and classification by economic use. Steel is an intermediate commodity but that is not important. When a steel producer makes *and sells* steel we show this as production of an intermediate good. Since it has been passed on to someone else, our expenditure measure picks it up further up the chain of production and sales. But when a firm adds to its stocks we must count that as final expenditure because it will not show up anywhere else in the national accounts. The firm is temporarily adding to its capital. When it later uses up these stocks, we treat this as negative investment to keep the record straight.

We now introduce the government sector.

The government

Governments raise revenue both through direct taxes T_d on incomes (wages, rents, interest and profits) and through indirect taxes or expenditures taxes T_e (VAT, petrol duties and cigarette taxes). Taxes finance two kinds of expenditure. Government spending on goods and services G is purchases by the government of physical goods and services. It includes the wages of civil servants and soldiers, the purchase of computers, tanks, and military aircraft, and investment in roads and hospitals.

Governments also spend money on *transfer payments* or benefits, B. These include pensions, unemployment benefit and subsidies to firms. Transfer payments are payments that do not require the provision of any goods or services in return.

Transfer payments do not affect national income or national output. They are not included in GDP. There is no corresponding net output. Taxes and transfer payments merely redistribute existing income and spending power away from people being taxed and towards people being subsidized. In contrast, spending G on goods and services produces net output, gives rise to factor earnings in the firms supplying this output and also to additional spending power of the households receiving this income. Hence government spending G on goods and services is part of GDP. It is final expenditure since government is now an additional end user of the output.

National income accounts aim to provide a logically coherent set of definitions and measures of national output. However, taxes drive a wedge between the price the purchaser pays and the price the seller receives. We can choose to value national output either at market prices inclusive of indirect taxes on goods and services, or at the prices received by producers after indirect taxes have been paid.

> **GDP at market prices** measures domestic output inclusive of indirect taxes on goods and services. **GDP at basic prices** measures domestic output exclusive of indirect taxes on goods and services. The former exceeds the latter by the amount of revenue raised in indirect taxes.

Measuring consumption C, investment I and government spending G on goods and services at market prices inclusive of indirect taxes, the value added or net output of the economy is now

$$\text{GDP at market prices} \equiv \text{final spending} \equiv C + I + G \qquad (2)$$

Higher indirect taxes increase the price of goods and services. Although the value of output increases at market prices, the physical quantity of output is unchanged. It makes more sense to measure GDP at basic prices. Thus, subtracting indirect taxes T_e,

$$Y \equiv \textbf{GDP at basic prices} \equiv (C + I + G) - T_e \qquad (3)$$

This measure is independent of indirect taxes. Higher tax rates increase the value of $(C + I + G)$ but also raise T_e, leaving GDP at basic prices unchanged. From now on, we use Y to denote GDP at basic prices.

Figure 19.4 shows how direct taxes and transfer benefits affect the circular flow of payments once we add the government sector. Household incomes at basic prices Y are supplemented by benefits B less direct taxes T_d. This gives us personal disposable income $(Y + B - T_d)$.

> **Personal disposable income** is household income after direct taxes and transfer payments. It shows how much households have available for spending and saving.

Hence, saving is now the part of disposable income not spent on consumption:

$$S \equiv (Y + B - T_d) - C \quad \text{and} \quad Y \equiv S + C + T_d - B \qquad (4)$$

Round the top loop of Figure 19.4, consumption C at market prices is now supplemented by injections of investment spending I and government spending G. From $(C + I + G)$ or GDP at market prices, we subtract indirect taxes T_e to get Y or GDP at basic prices:

$$Y \equiv C + I + G - T_e \qquad (5)$$

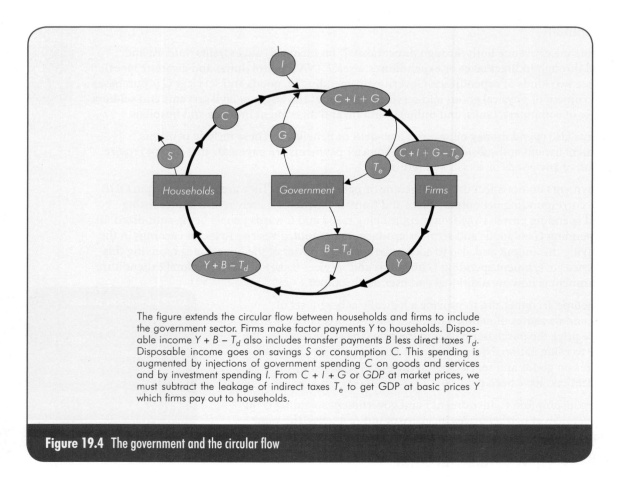

The figure extends the circular flow between households and firms to include the government sector. Firms make factor payments Y to households. Disposable income $Y + B - T_d$ also includes transfer payments B less direct taxes T_d. Disposable income goes on savings S or consumption C. This spending is augmented by injections of government spending C on goods and services and by investment spending I. From $C + I + G$ or GDP at market prices, we must subtract the leakage of indirect taxes T_e to get GDP at basic prices Y which firms pay out to households.

Figure 19.4 The government and the circular flow

Comparing this with the second part of equation (4):

$$S + T_d + T_e - B \equiv I + G \qquad (6)$$

Our national income accounts make sense. The left-hand side of equation (6) is leakages from the circular flow of payments between firms and households. Money leaks out through household savings and taxes (net of benefit subsidies) to the government. The right-hand side of equation (6) tells us the injections to the circular flow: investment spending by firms and government spending on goods and services. Total leakages must equal total injections; otherwise we have made a bookkeeping error and the sums will not add up. In the special case where $T_d \equiv T_e \equiv G \equiv B \equiv 0$, there is no government sector and equation (6) implies $S = I$, as in equation (1).

Notice too that equation (6) can be rewritten as

$$T_d + T_e - B - G \equiv I - S \qquad (7)$$

The left-hand side is the financial surplus of the government, total revenue minus its total spending. The right-hand side is the private sector deficit, the excess of investment spending over household saving. As a matter of definition, the private sector can run a deficit only if the government runs a surplus, and vice versa.

The foreign sector

So far we have studied a closed economy not transacting with the rest of the world. We now examine an *open economy* that deals with other countries.

Households, firms and the government may buy imports Z that are not part of domestic output and do not give rise to domestic factor incomes. These goods are not in the output measure of GDP, the *value added* by domestic producers. However, imports show up in final expenditure. There are two solutions to this problem. We could subtract the import component separately from C, I, G and X and measure only final expenditure on the domestically made bit of consumption, investment, government spending and exports. But it is easier to continue to measure total final expenditure on C, I, G and X and then to subtract from this total expenditure on imports Z. It comes to exactly the same thing.

Exports (X) are domestically produced but sold abroad. **Imports (Z)** are produced abroad but purchased for use in the domestic economy.

Hence in an open economy we recognize foreign trade by redefining GDP at basic prices as

$$Y \equiv C + I + G + X - Z - T_e \equiv C + I + G + NX - T_e \qquad (8)$$

where NX denotes net exports $(X - Z)$.

What about leakages and injections? Imports are a leakage, money not recycled to domestic firms, but exports are an injection, a revenue source not arising from domestic households. Hence, using equations (8) and (6):

$$S + (T_d + T_e - B) + Z \equiv I + G + X \qquad (9a)$$

$$(S - I) \equiv (G + B - T_e - T_d) + NX \qquad (9b)$$

Equation (9a) makes the usual point that total leakages must equal total injections. Imports are an extra leakage from, exports an extra injection to, the circular flow.

Equation (9b) extends equation (7) to an open economy. A private sector surplus $S - I$ is a leakage from the circular flow. It must be matched by an injection of the same amount. This injection can come either from a government deficit $(G + B - T_e - T_d)$ or from net exports NX, the excess of export earnings over import spending. Since our trade surplus is foreigners' trade deficit, equation (9b) says that the surplus of the private sector must be matched by the budget deficit of the government plus the trade deficit of foreigners.

From GDP to GNP or GNI

To complete the national accounts we must face two final problems. So far we have assumed all factors of production are domestically owned: all net domestic output accrues to domestic households as factor incomes. But this need not be so. When Nissan owns a car factory in the UK, some of the profits are sent back to Japan to be spent or saved by Japanese households.

Conversely, UK households earn income from owning foreign assets. This income from interest, dividends, profits and rents is shown in the national accounts as the flow of *property income* between countries. The net flow of property income into the UK is the excess of inflows of property income from factor services supplied abroad over the outflows of property income from factor services by foreigners in the UK.

When there is a net flow of property income between the UK and the rest of the world, the output and expenditure measure of GDP will no longer equal the total factor incomes earned by UK citizens. We use the terms *gross national product* (GNP) or *gross national income* (GNI) to measure GDP adjusted for net property income from abroad.

If the UK has an inflow of £2 billion of property income from abroad but an outflow of £1 billion of property income accruing to foreigners, UK GNP, measuring income earned by UK citizens, will exceed UK GDP, measuring the value of goods produced in the UK, by £1 billion.

> **GNP (or GNI)** measures total income earned by domestic citizens regardless of the country in which their factor services were supplied. GNP (or GNI) equals GDP plus net property income from abroad.

Table 19.5 shows actual data for UK GDP and GNP in 2005. Official statistics often decompose *G*, government spending on goods and services, into government consumption and government investment. Table 19.5 therefore shows data on consumption by households, consumption by government (and non-profit organizations) and on combined investment by government and private firms.

Table 19.5 UK national accounts, 2005 (£bn, current prices)

Expenditure measure		Income measure	
At market prices:		Income source: employment	685
C by households	759	Profits and rents	274
C by government and non-profit organizations	301	Other	113
I by private firms and government	210	GDP at basic prices	1072
NX	−45	Indirect taxes	153
GDP at market prices	1225	GDP at market prices	1225
Net property income from abroad	63		
GNP (GNI) at market prices	1288		

Sources: ONS, *UK National Accounts*; OECD, *Economic Outlook*.

From GNP to national income

The final complication is depreciation.

Depreciation is a flow concept telling us how much our effective capital stock is being used up in each time period. Depreciation is an economic cost because it measures resources being used up in the production process.

> **Depreciation** or capital consumption is the rate at which the value of the existing capital stock declines per period as a result of usage or obsolescence.

Our simple example in Table 19.4 ignored depreciation completely. The machine bought by the car maker lasted for ever. We now recognize that machinery wears out. In consequence, the *net* output of the economy is lower. The part of the economy's gross output used merely to replace existing capital is not available for consumption, investment in net additions to the capital stock, government spending or exports.

Similarly, we need to reduce our measure of the incomes available for spending on these goods. Thus, we subtract depreciation from GNP to get net national product (NNP) or national income.

> **National income** is the economy's net national product. It is calculated by subtracting depreciation from GNP at basic prices.

National income measures how much the economy can spend or save, after setting aside enough resources to maintain the capital stock intact by offsetting depreciation.

We have now developed a complete set of national accounts. Figure 19.5 may keep you straight.

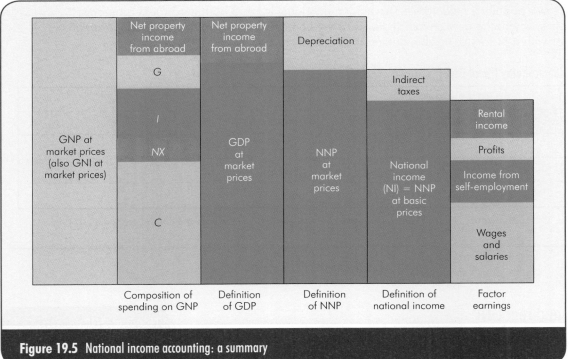

Figure 19.5 National income accounting: a summary

19.5 What GNP measures

A firm's accounts show how the company is doing. Our national income accounts let us assess how the economy is doing. Just as a firm's accounts may conceal as much as they reveal, we must interpret the national income accounts with care.

We focus on GNP as a measure of economic performance. Since depreciation is rather difficult to measure, and consequently may be treated differently in different countries or during different time periods, using gross national product avoids the need to argue about depreciation.

In this section we make three points. First, we recall the distinction between nominal and real variables. Second, we show how per capita GNP can provide a more accurate picture of the standard of living of an average person in an economy. Finally, we discuss the incompleteness of GNP as a measure of the activities that provide economic welfare to members of society.

Box 19.2 Hidden GNP

Gangster Al Capone, never charged with murder, was eventually convicted of tax evasion. Taxes are evaded by smugglers and drug dealers but also by gardeners, plumbers and everyone else doing things 'for cash'. Since GNP data are based on tax statistics, the 'hidden' economy is unreported.

Economists have various ways to estimate its size. One way is to count large-denomination banknotes in circulation. People with fistfuls of £50 notes are often engaged in tax evasion. Another way is to guess people's income by studying what they spend. Maria Lacko has used the stable relationship between household use of electricity and its main determinants – income and weather temperature – to estimate incomes from data on electricity consumption and temperature. She confirms two popularly held views. The hidden economy is large both in former communist economies, where the new private sector is as yet unrecorded, and in several Mediterranean countries with a history of trouble getting their citizens to pay tax.

The hidden economy (% of GNP)

Poland	34	Finland	11
Hungary	31	USA	10
Spain	21	UK	10
Greece	20	France	6
Italy	16	Japan	3

Source: M. Lacko, *Hungarian Hidden Economy in International Comparisons*, Institute of Economics, Budapest, 1996.

Nominal and real GNP

Since it is physical quantities of output that yield people utility or happiness, it can be misleading to judge the economy's performance by looking at nominal GNP.

Table 19.6 presents a simple hypothetical example of a whole economy. Nominal GNP rises from £600 to £1440 between 1980 and 2007. If we take 1980 as the base year, we can measure real GNP in 2007 by valuing output quantities in 2007 using 1980 prices. Real GNP rises only from £600 to £860. This rise of 43 per cent in real GNP gives a truer picture of the extra quantity of goods made by the economy as a whole.

> **Nominal GNP** measures GNP at the prices prevailing when income was earned.

> **Real GNP**, or GNP at constant prices, adjusts for inflation by measuring GNP in different years at the prices prevailing at some particular date known as the *base year*.

Table 19.6 Nominal and real GNP

		1980	2007
Quantity:	apples	100	150
	chickens	100	140
Price £	apples	2	4
	chickens	4	6
Value in current £	apples	200	600
	chickens	400	840
	Nominal GNP	600	1440
Value in 1980 £	apples	200	300
	chickens	400	560
	Real GNP	600	860

The GNP deflator

Chapter 2 introduced the consumer price index (CPI), an index of the average price of goods purchased by consumers. The most common measure of the inflation rate in the UK is the percentage rise in the CPI over its value a year earlier.

However, consumption expenditure is only one part of GNP, which also includes investment, government spending and net exports. To convert nominal GNP to real GNP we need to use an index showing what is happening to the price of all goods. This index is called the GNP deflator.

To express the deflator as an index, we take the ratio of nominal to real GNP and multiply by 100. In Table 19.7, if we measure real values at 1995 prices, we set the GNP deflator at 100 for 1995. Nominal and real GNP are both £750 billion in that year because we are using that year's prices to index the GNP deflator. For 2005 the ratio of nominal to real GNP is 1.30 and the GNP deflator index is therefore 130.

> The **GNP deflator** is the ratio of nominal GNP to real GNP expressed as an index.

Table 19.7 gives UK data over four decades. Nominal GNP in the UK rose from £25 billion in 1960 to £1288 billion in 2007. Without knowing what happened to the price of goods in general we cannot judge what happened to the quantity of output over the period. The second row of Table 19.8 answers this question. On average, prices in 2007 were 30 per cent higher than in 1995. Hence, the change in real GNP was much smaller than the change in nominal GNP in the same period. It is important to distinguish between nominal and real GNP.

Table 19.7 UK GNP, 1960–2005

	1960	1995	2005
Nominal GNP (current £bn)	25	750	1288
GNP deflator (1995 = 100)	8	100	130
Real GNP (£bn, 1995 prices)	316	750	991

Source: ONS, *Economic Trends.*

The contrast is even more marked if we go back to 1960 since there was a lot of inflation in the 1970s. Whereas nominal GNP rose 50-fold between 1960 and 2005, real GNP only tripled. The rest of the growth in nominal GNP simply reflected inflation.

Per capita real GNP

Real GNP is a simple measure of the real income of an economy. The annual percentage rise in real GNP tells us how fast an economy is growing. Table 19.8 shows the average annual growth rate of real GNP in three countries over two decades. The first column shows that the annual growth rate of real GNP during 1980–2005 was highest in Jordan and lowest in Denmark. Although this tells us about the growth of the whole economy, we may be interested in a different question: what was happening to the standard of living of a representative person in each of these countries? To answer this question we need to examine per capita real GNP.

Table 19.8 Growth, 1980–2005 (% per annum)

	Real GNP	Per capita real GNP
Denmark	2.3	2.2
UK	2.7	2.3
Jordan	4.1	0.1

Source: World Bank, *World Development Report.*

For a given real GNP, the larger the population, the smaller the quantity of goods and services per person. Table 19.8 shows growth of per capita real GNP. The ranking is reversed. To get a simple measure of the standard of living enjoyed by a person in a particular country, it is better to look at per capita real GNP, which adjusts for population, than to look at total real GNP.

> **Per capita real GNP** is real GNP divided by the total population. It is real GNP per head.

Even per capita real GNP is only a crude indicator. Table 19.8 does *not* say that every person in Denmark got 2.3 per cent more goods and services each year. It shows what was happening on average. Some people's real incomes increased by a lot more, some people became absolutely poorer. The more the income distribution changes over time, the less reliable is the change in per capita real GNP as an indicator of what is happening to any particular person.

A comprehensive measure of GNP

Because we use GNP to measure the income of the economy, the coverage of GNP should be as comprehensive as possible. In practice, we encounter two problems in including all production in GDP and GNP. First, some outputs, such as noise, pollution and congestion, are 'bads'. We should subtract them from GDP and GNP. This is a sensible suggestion but hard to implement. These nuisance goods are not traded through markets, so it is hard to quantify their output or decide how to value their cost to society.

Similarly, many valuable goods and services are excluded from GNP because they are not marketed and therefore hard to measure accurately. These activities include household chores, DIY activities and unreported jobs.

Deducting the value of nuisance outputs and adding the value of unreported and non-marketed incomes would make GNP a more accurate measure of the economy's production of goods and services. But there is another important adjustment to make before using GNP as the basis for national economic welfare. People enjoy not merely goods and services but also leisure time.

Activity box 19 'Asia's greenhouse gas to treble'

Well-run firms spend serious money on information systems that let their managers make intelligent decisions. In contrast, governments often have to make do with economic data gathered on the cheap. Many data are simply the by-product of tax records. Published GDP data ignore valuable commodities like leisure, and omit important harmful outputs like environmental pollution.

Citing a study by the Asian Development Bank, the BBC noted that Asian emissions of greenhouse gases would treble in the next 25 years. If so, Asia will overtake the OECD as the world's biggest source of greenhouse gas pollutants. Environmental degradation means that almost 40 per cent of the region's population now live in areas prone to drought and erosion. With the Asian population set to triple in the next 20 years, and half these people living in cities, air pollution will reach new records. Nor is access to clean water much better.

Asian countries from Thailand to the Philippines have had three decades of very rapid GDP growth. Because of this success, they are often called the Asian tigers. But if national accounts had to keep proper account of environmental depreciation, many of these countries would have much less impressive growth records. We might start calling them the Asian snails.

Source: BBC online, 14 December 2006.

Questions

(a) How does depreciation of ordinary machinery and buildings enter calculations of GDP?

(b) What measure properly reflects depreciation of physical capital?

(c) How are conventional estimates of depreciation made?

(d) What would be entailed in following the same procedures for environmental capital?

(e) How would environmental capital for the whole planet affect national accounts?

To check your answers to these questions, go to page 725.

Suppose Leisurians value leisure more highly than Industrians. Industrians work more and produce more goods. Industria has a higher measured GNP. It is silly to say this proves that Leisurians have lower welfare. By choosing to work less hard they reveal that the extra leisure is worth at least as much as the extra goods they could have made by working more.

Because it is difficult and expensive to collect regular measurements on non-marketed and unreported goods and bads, and to make regular assessments of the implicit value of leisure, real GNP inevitably remains the commonest measure of economic activity. Far from ideal, it is the best measure available on a regular basis.

Summary

- **Macroeconomics** examines the economy as a whole.

- Macroeconomics sacrifices individual detail to focus on the interaction of broad sectors of the economy. Households supply production inputs to firms that use them to make output. Firms pay factor incomes to households, who buy the output from firms. This is the **circular flow**.

- **Gross domestic product (GDP)** is the value of net output of the factors of production located in the domestic economy. It can be measured in three equivalent ways: value added in production, factor incomes including profits, or final expenditure.

- **Leakages** from the circular flow are those parts of payment by firms to households that do not automatically return to firms as spending by households on the output of firms. Leakages are saving, taxes net of subsidies and imports. **Injections** are sources of revenue to firms that do not arise from household spending. Investment expenditure by firms, spending on goods and services by the government, and exports are injections. By definition, total leakages equal total injections.

- **GDP at market prices** values domestic output at prices inclusive of indirect taxes. **GDP at basic prices** measures domestic output at prices exclusive of indirect taxes. **Gross national product (GNP)**, also called gross national income (GNI), adjusts GDP for net property income from abroad.

- **National income** is net national product (NNP) at basic prices. NNP is GNP minus the **depreciation** of the capital stock during the period. In practice, many assessments of economic performance are based on GNP since it is not hard to measure depreciation accurately.

- **Nominal GNP** measures income at current prices. **Real GNP** measures income at constant prices. It adjusts nominal GNP for changes in the GNP deflator as a result of inflation.

- **Per capita real GNP** divides real GNP by the population. It is a more reliable indicator of income per person in an economy, but only an average measure of what people get.

- Real GNP and per capita real GNP are crude measures of national and individual welfare. They ignore non-market activities, bads such as pollution, valuable activities such as work in the home, and production unreported by tax evaders. Nor do they measure the value of leisure.

- Because it is expensive, and sometimes impossible, to make regular and accurate measurements of all these activities, in practice GNP is the most widely used measure of national performance.

Review questions

To check your answers to these questions, go to page 725.

1 Car firms buy in raw materials (steel), intermediate goods (windscreens, tyres) and labour to make cars. Windscreen and tyre companies hire workers and also buy raw materials from other industries. What is the value added of the car industry (the three firms shown below)?

Producer of	Output	Intermediate goods used	Raw materials used	Labour input
Cars	1000	250	100	100
Windscreens	150		10	50
Tyres	100		10	30

2 GNP at market prices is £300 billion. Depreciation is £30 billion, indirect taxes £20 billion. (a) What is national income? (b) Why does depreciation cause a discrepancy between GNP and national income? (c) Why do indirect taxes enter the calculation?

3 GNP = 2000, C = 1700, G = 50 and NX = 40. (a) What is investment I? (b) If exports are 350, what are imports? (c) If depreciation = 130, what is national income? (d) In this example net exports are positive. Could they be negative?

4 Given the data below: (a) What is 2005 GNP in 2004 prices? (b) What is the growth rate of real GNP from 2004 to 2005? (c) What is the inflation rate?

Year	Nominal GDP	GNP deflator
2004	2000	100
2005	2400	110

5 Should these be in a comprehensive measure of GNP: (a) time spent by students in lectures; (b) the income of muggers; (c) the wage paid to traffic wardens; (d) dropping litter?

6 **Common fallacies** Why are these statements wrong? (a) Unemployment benefit props up national income in years when employment is low. (b) A high per capita real GNP is always a good thing. (c) In 2007 *Crummy Movie* earned £1 billion more at the box office than *Gone With the Wind* earned 50 years ago. *Crummy Movie* is already a bigger box office success.

7 **Harder question** You are head of the Leisure Commission that has to recommend to the government how to include the value of leisure in GDP. How do you come up with an estimate?

8 **Harder question** The price of a new television has remained roughly constant for the last 30 years. What does this show?

9 **Essay question** 'Economists are preoccupied with what they can measure. GDP is so misleading an indicator of welfare that it is almost pointless to gather statistics about it, either for international comparison across countries or to assess how well particular governments are doing.' How useful is GDP? Could we easily have a better indicator?

To help you grasp the key concepts of this chapter check out the extra resources posted on the Online Learning Centre. There are chapter summaries, self-test questions, an interactive graphing tool, weblinks and a searchable glossary, all for free!

To put your learning into practice and prepare for exams, an **Interactive Workbook** is also available online, containing a variety of question types and providing feedback on your answers.

If you'd like further help with economics, or have any questions, **NetTutor** is here to help! You will have a personalised tutorial service at your fingertips. Visit the online learning centre at: www.mcgraw-hill.co.uk/textbooks/begg for information on accessing all of these resources.

CHAPTER 20

Output and aggregate demand

Learning Outcomes

By the end of this chapter, you should understand:

1 actual output and potential output

2 why output is demand determined in the short run

3 short-run equilibrium output

4 consumption and investment demand

5 how aggregate demand determines short-run equilibrium output

6 the marginal propensity to consume *MPC*

7 how the size of the multiplier affects the *MPC*

8 the paradox of thrift

During 1960–2005 UK real output grew on average by 2.3 per cent a year, but fluctuated around this trend. Real output actually fell during 1973–75, 1979–81 and 1989–92, grew strongly during 1975–79, 1981–89 and 1992–1995, and has grown steadily since 1995. Words used by economists to describe these fluctuations – recession, recovery, boom and slump – are part of everyday language.

Why does real GDP fluctuate? To construct a simple model, we ignore discrepancies between national income, real GNP and real GDP. We use income and output interchangeably. First, we distinguish *actual* output and *potential* output.

Potential output tends to grow over time as the supply of inputs grows. Population growth adds to the labour force. Investment in education, training and new machinery adds to human and physical capital. Technical advances let given inputs produce more output. Together, these explain UK average growth at 2.3 per cent a year since 1960.

> **Potential output** is the economy's output when inputs are fully employed.

We study the theory of long-run economic growth in potential output in Chapter 30. First, we focus on deviations of actual output from potential output in the short run. Since potential output changes slowly, we begin with a short-run analysis of an economy with a fixed potential output.

Potential output is not the maximum an economy can conceivably make. With a gun to our heads, we could all make more. Rather, it is the output when every market in the economy is in long-run equilibrium. Every worker wanting to work at the equilibrium wage can find a job, and every machine that can profitably be used at the equilibrium rental for capital is in use. Thus, potential output includes an allowance for 'equilibrium unemployment'. Some people do not want to work at the equilibrium wage rate. Moreover, in a constantly changing economy, some people are temporarily between jobs. Today, UK potential output probably entails an unemployment rate of about 4–5 per cent.

Suppose actual output falls below potential output. Workers are unemployed and firms have idle machines or spare capacity. A key issue in macroeconomics is how quickly output returns to potential output. In microeconomics, studying one market in isolation, we assumed excess supply would quickly bid the price down, eliminating excess supply to restore equilibrium. In macroeconomics, this cannot be taken for granted. Disturbances in one part of the economy induce changes elsewhere that may feed back again, exacerbating the original disturbance.

We cannot examine this issue by *assuming* that the economy is always at potential output, for then a problem could never arise. We must build a model in which departures from potential output are possible, examine the market forces then set in motion and decide how successfully market forces restore output to potential output.

Thus our initial model has two crucial properties. First, all prices and wages are fixed at a given level. Second, at these prices and wage levels, there are workers without a job who would like to work, and firms with spare capacity they could profitably use. The economy has spare resources. It is then unnecessary to analyse the supply side of the economy in detail. Any rise in demand is happily met by firms and workers until potential output is reached.

Below potential output, firms happily supply whatever output is demanded. Total output is demand-determined.

Later, we shall relax the assumption that prices and wages are fixed. Not only do we want to study inflation, we also want to examine how quickly market forces, acting through changes in prices and wages, can eliminate unemployment and spare capacity. But first we must learn to walk. We postpone the analysis of price and wage adjustment until Chapter 25.

> Since markets trade the smaller of supply and demand, **output is demand-determined** when there is excess supply, and wages and prices have yet to adjust to restore long-run equilibrium. Output then depends only on aggregate demand.

Until then, we study the demand-determined model of output and employment developed by John Maynard Keynes in *The General Theory of Employment, Interest and Money*, published in 1936. Keynes used the model to explain high unemployment and low output in the Great Depression of the 1930s.

Most young economists soon became *Keynesians*, advocating government intervention to keep output close to potential output. By the 1950s, this approach was challenged by *monetarists*, led by Milton Friedman. They argued that Keynesian analysis, although helpful in studying recession, was a poor tool for studying inflation, which monetarists attribute to money creation. We develop an approach that uses the best insights of both Keynesians and monetarists.

In the 1970s unemployment rose again, despite Keynesian policies. Some economists discarded Keynesian economics completely. Not only did they deny the effectiveness of government policy to stabilize output, they argued that stabilizing output may not even be desirable.

This has now prompted a fightback by *New Keynesians*, who believe that the central messages of Keynes, right all along, can be understood better by using modern microeconomics to explain the market failures that justify Keynesian intervention. To scale these peaks of economic research, we need to begin at the foothills.

Chapter 19 introduced the circular flow of income and payments between households and firms. Households buy the output of firms. Firms' revenue is ultimately returned to households. We now build a simple model of this interaction of households and firms. The next chapter adds the government and the foreign sector.

20.1 Components of aggregate demand

Without a government or a foreign sector, there are two sources of demand: consumption demand by households and investment demand by firms. Using AD to denote aggregate demand, C for consumption demand and I for investment demand,

$$AD = C + I \qquad\qquad (1)$$

Consumption demand and investment demand are chosen by different economic groups and depend on different things.

Consumption demand

Households buy goods and services from cars to cinema tickets. These consumption purchases account for about 90 per cent of personal disposable income.

With no government, disposable income is simply the income received from firms. Given its disposable income, each household plans how much to spend and to save. Deciding one decides the other. One family may save to buy a bigger house; another may spend more than its income, or 'dissave', taking the round-the-world trip it always wanted.

> **Personal disposable income** is the income households receive from firms, plus transfer payments received from the government, minus direct taxes paid to the government. It is the net income households can spend or save.

Many things affect consumption and saving decisions. We examine these in detail in Chapter 24. To get started, one simplification takes us a long way. We assume that, in the aggregate, households' consumption demand rises with aggregate personal disposable income.

Figure 20.1 shows real consumption and real personal disposable income in the UK. Because the scatter of points lies close to the line summarizing this relationship, our simplification is helpful. Nevertheless, the points do not lie *exactly* along the line. Our simplification omits some other influences on consumption demand that we take up in Chapter 24.

The consumption function

This positive relation between disposable income and consumption demand is shown in Figure 20.2 and is called the *consumption function.*

The consumption function tells us how to go from personal disposable income Y to consumption demand C. If A is a positive constant, and c is a positive fraction between zero and one,

$$C = A + cY \qquad\qquad (2)$$

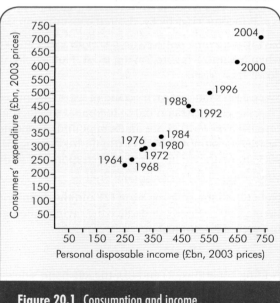

Figure 20.1 Consumption and income

Source: ONS.

Our bare-bones model has no government, no transfer payments and no taxes. Personal disposable income equals national income. Figure 20.2, and equation (2), then relate consumption demand to *national* income Y. The consumption function is a straight line. A straight line is completely described by its intercept – the height at which it crosses the vertical axis – and its slope – the amount it rises for each unit we move horizontally to the right.

> The **consumption function** shows aggregate consumption demand at each level of personal disposable income.

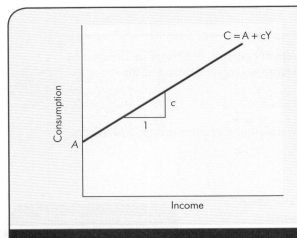

The consumption function shows aggregate consumption demand at each aggregate income. With zero income, autonomous consumption is A. The marginal propensity to consume c is the slope of the line, the fraction of each extra pound that households wish to spend. The remaining $(1 - c)$ they wish to save.

Figure 20.2 The consumption function

The intercept is A. We call this *autonomous* consumption demand. Autonomous means unrelated to income. Households wish to consume A even if income Y is zero.[1] The slope of the consumption function is the marginal propensity to consume.

In Figure 20.2 and equation (2), the marginal propensity to consume *MPC* is c. If income rises by £1, desired consumption rises by £c.

Saving is income not consumed. Figure 20.2 and equation (2) imply that when income Y is zero, saving is $-A$. Households are dissaving, or running down their assets.

Since a fraction c of each pound of extra income is consumed, a fraction $(1 - c)$ of each extra pound of income is saved. The *marginal property to save MPS* is $(1 - c)$. Since an extra pound of income leads either to extra desired consumption or to extra desired saving, $MPC + MPS = 1$. Figure 20.3 shows the *saving function* corresponding to the consumption function in Figure 20.2.

Note too that, using equation (2) and the definition of saving $Y \equiv C + S$, we can deduce the saving function shown in Figure 20.3. It must be

$$S = -A + (1 - c)Y \qquad (3)$$

Adding equations (2) and (3), the left-hand side gives desired consumption plus desired saving, the right-hand side gives income Y, as it should. Planned saving is the part of income not planned to be spent on consumption.

The **marginal propensity to consume** is the fraction of each extra pound of disposable income that households wish to consume.

The **saving function** shows desired saving at each income level.

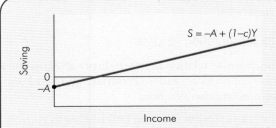

The saving function shows desired saving at each income level. Since all income is saved or is spent on consumption, the saving function can be derived from the consumption function or vice versa.

Figure 20.3 The saving function

1 A is the minimum consumption needed for survival. How do households finance it when their incomes are zero? In the short run they dissave and run down their assets. But they cannot do so for ever. The consumption function may differ in the short run and the long run, an idea we discuss in Chapter 24.

Investment spending

Income is the key determinant of household consumption or spending plans as described by the consumption function. What about the factors determining the investment decision by firms?

Firms' investment demand depends chiefly on firms' current guesses about how fast the demand for their output will increase. Sometimes output is high and rising, sometimes it is high and falling. Since there is no close connection between the current *level* of income and firms' guesses about how the demand for their output is going to *change*, we make the simple assumption that investment demand is autonomous. Desired investment I is constant, independent of current output and income. In Chapter 24 we discuss investment demand in more detail.

> **Investment demand** is firms' desired or planned additions to physical capital (factories and machines) and to inventories.

Activity box 20 The *AD* schedule: moving along it or shifting it?

The aggregate demand *AD* schedule is a straight line whose position depends on its intercept and its slope. The intercept, the height of the schedule when income is zero, reflects autonomous demand: part of consumption demand and all of investment demand. The slope of the schedule is the *MPC*. Changes in income induce movements along a given *AD* schedule.

Autonomous demand is influenced by many things that we study in Chapter 24. It is not fixed for ever. But it *is* independent of income. The *AD* schedule separates out the change in demand directly induced by changes in income. All other sources of changes in aggregate demand are shown as shifts in the *AD* schedule. If firms get more optimistic about future demand and invest more, autonomous demand rises. The new *AD* schedule is parallel to, but higher than, the old *AD* schedule.

Questions
In each case, decide whether the *AD* schedule is shifting or whether the economy is moving along a given *AD* schedule:

(a) The crisis that occurs if the American subprime mortgage market leads to a wave of pessimism among UK consumers who decide to play safe and save more.

(b) UK consumer spending rises because households are having a good year and enjoying high incomes.

(c) The 2012 Olympic Games in London are causing an investment boom in the construction industry.

To check your answers to these questions, go to page 726.

20.2 Aggregate demand

In our simple model, aggregate demand is simply households' consumption demand *C* plus firms' investment demand *I*.

Figure 20.4 shows the *aggregate demand schedule*. To the previous consumption function it adds a constant amount *I* for desired investment. Each extra unit of income adds *c* to consumption demand but nothing to investment demand: aggregate demand rises by *c*. The *AD* schedule is parallel to the consumption function. The slope of both is the marginal propensity to consume.

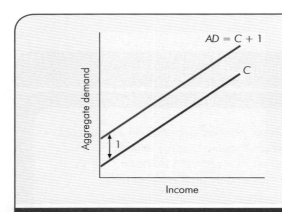

Aggregate demand is what households plan to spend on consumption and firms plan to spend on investment. Since we assume investment demand is constant, consumption is the only part of aggregate demand that increases with income. Vertically adding the constant investment demand to the consumption function *C* gives the aggregate demand schedule *AD*.

Figure 20.4 Aggregate demand

20.3 Equilibrium output

Wages and prices are *fixed*, and output is demand determined. If aggregate demand falls below potential output, firms cannot sell as much as they would like. There is *involuntary* excess capacity. Workers cannot work as much as they would like. There is *involuntary* unemployment.

To define short-run equilibrium we cannot use the definition used in microeconomics, the output at which both suppliers and demanders are happy with the quantity bought and sold. We wish to study a situation in which firms and workers would like to supply more goods and more labour. Suppliers are frustrated. At least we can require that demanders are happy.

Thus, spending plans are not frustrated by a shortage of goods. Nor do firms make more output than they can sell. In short-run equilibrium, actual output equals the output demanded by households as consumption and by firms as investment.

Figure 20.5 shows income on the horizontal axis and planned spending on the vertical axis. It also includes the 45° line, along which quantities on the horizontal and vertical axes are equal.

We draw in the *AD* schedule from Figure 20.4. This crosses the 45° line at *E*. On the 45° line, the value of output (and income) on the horizontal axis equals the value of spending on the vertical axis. Since *E* is the *only* point on the *AD* schedule also on the 45° line, it is the only point at which output and desired spending are equal.

Hence Figure 20.5 shows equilibrium output at E. Firms produce Y^*. That output is equal to income. At an income Y^* the AD schedule tells us the demand for goods is also Y^*. At E planned spending is exactly equal to the output produced.

At any other output, output is not equal to aggregate demand. Suppose output and income are only Y_1. Aggregate demand exceeds actual output. There is excess demand. Spending plans cannot be realized at this output level.

Figure 20.5 shows that, for all outputs below the equilibrium output Y^*, aggregate demand AD exceeds income and output. The AD schedule lies *above* the 45° line along which spending and output are equal. Conversely, at all outputs above the equilibrium output Y^*, aggregate demand is less than income and output.

Adjustment towards equilibrium

Suppose in Figure 20.5 the economy begins with an output of Y_1, below equilibrium output Y^*. Aggregate demand AD_1 exceeds output Y_1. If firms have inventories from the past, they can sell more than they have produced by running down stocks for a while. Note that this destocking is *unplanned*; planned changes of stocks are already included in the total investment demand I.

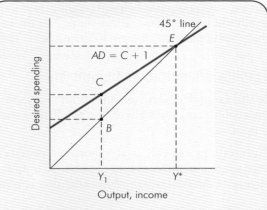

The 45° line reflects any value on the horizontal axis onto the same value on the vertical axis. The point E, at which the AD schedule crosses the 45° line, is the only point at which aggregate demand AD is equal to income. Hence E is the equilibrium point at which planned spending equals actual output and actual income.

Figure 20.5 The 45° diagram and equilibrium output

If firms cannot meet aggregate demand by unplanned destocking, they must turn away customers. Either response – unplanned destocking or turning away customers – is a signal to firms to raise output above Y_1. Hence, at *any* output below Y^*, aggregate demand exceeds output and firms get signals to raise output.

Conversely, if output is initially above its equilibrium level, Figure 20.5 shows that output will then exceed aggregate demand. Firms cannot sell all their output, make *unplanned* additions to inventories and respond by cutting output.

Box 20.1 The output response to a confidence crisis

What do you think caused the sharpest attack of the jitters in the last decade? The immediate aftermath of the terrorist attacks on 11 September 2001, which shattered business and consumer confidence, according to a survey reported by the news agency Reuters. How did firms respond to the sudden collapse in demand for their products?

The survey of 2500 companies showed that output, new orders, employment and inventories of inputs all hit new lows. Firms stopped buying raw materials and ran down their own stocks of raw materials. New orders, the most easily adjusted item in the survey, fell especially sharply after 9/11.

Firms also added to stocks of unsold finished goods. Production fell less quickly than demand. Companies used these devices to avoid expensive and rapid changes in production. However, if lower demand persists, firms have to reduce output in line with lower demand.

Hence, when output is below its equilibrium level, firms raise output. When output is above its equilibrium level, firms reduce output. At the equilibrium output Y^* firms sell all their output and make no unplanned changes to their stocks. There is no incentive to change output.

Equilibrium output and employment

In this example, short-run equilibrium output is Y^*. Firms sell all the goods they produce, and households and firms buy all the goods they want. But nothing guarantees Y^* is the level of potential output.

The economy can end up at a short-run equilibrium output below potential output, with no forces then present to move output to potential output. At the given level of prices and wages, a lack of aggregate demand will prevent expansion of output above its short-run equilibrium level.

20.4 Another approach: planned saving equals planned investment

Equilibrium income equals the demand from investment and consumption. Hence, planned investment equals equilibrium income minus planned consumption. Thus $I = Y - C$. This is not a definition, but holds only when output and income are at the right level to achieve equilibrium output. However, planned saving S is always the part of income Y not devoted to planned consumption C. Thus $S \equiv Y - C$.

Thus $Y - C$ is equal to planned investment but also to planned saving. Since the latter depends on income and output, and since household plans are met only in equilibrium, equilibrium output occurs where planned investment equals planned savings:

$$I = S \qquad\qquad (4)$$

In modern economies, firms make investment decisions, and the managers of these firms are not the same decision-units as the households making savings and consumption plans. But household plans depend on their income. Since planned saving depends on income but planned investment does not, equation (4) implies that equilibrium income adjusts to make households plan to save as much as firms are planning to invest. Figure 20.6 illustrates.

Planned investment I is autonomous, and so a horizontal line. Planned saving is $-A + (1-c)Y$. It slopes up since the marginal propensity to save is positive. Equilibrium output makes planned saving equal planned investment. Thus $I = -A + (1-c)Y^*$. Hence equilibrium output Y^* is

$$Y^* = [A + I]/[1 - c] \qquad\qquad (5)$$

This had better be the same equilibrium output we got by equating actual output to aggregate demand! Of course it is. For then we get $Y^* = C + I = [A + I] + cY^*$, which leads to the same equilibrium output as in equation (5). An example may dispel any doubts.

Suppose investment demand is 10 and the saving function is $S = -10 + 0.1Y$. Hence, equilibrium output Y is 200. At this Y, planned saving is $[-10 + 20] = 10$. Hence 10 is both planned saving and planned investment.

If the saving function is $S = -10 + 0.1Y$, the consumption function must be $C = 10 + 0.9Y$. At an income of 200,

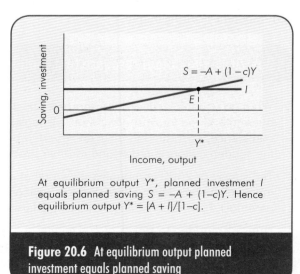

At equilibrium output Y^*, planned investment I equals planned saving $S = -A + (1-c)Y$. Hence equilibrium output $Y^* = [A + I]/[1-c]$.

Figure 20.6 At equilibrium output planned investment equals planned saving

consumption demand is 190. Add on 10 for investment demand, and aggregate demand is 200. When output and income are 200, aggregate demand is also 200. Again, this proves that equilibrium output is 200.

If income exceeds 200, households want to save more than firms want to invest. But saving is the part of income not consumed. Households are not planning enough consumption, together with firms' investment plans, to purchase all the output produced. Unplanned inventories pile up and firms cut output. Lower output and income reduces planned saving, which depends on income. When output falls back to 200, planned investment again equals planned saving.

Conversely, when output is below its equilibrium level, planned investment exceeds planned saving. Together, planned consumption and planned investment exceed actual output. Firms make unplanned inventory reductions and raise output until it reverts to its equilibrium level of 200.

Planned versus actual

Equilibrium output and income satisfy two equivalent conditions. Aggregate demand must equal income and output. Equivalently, planned investment must equal planned saving.

In the last chapter we showed that *actual* investment is *always* equal to *actual* saving, purely as a consequence of our national income accounting definitions. When the economy is not in equilibrium, planned saving and investment are not equal. However, unplanned investment in stocks and/or unplanned saving (frustrated consumers) always ensures that actual investment, planned plus unplanned, equals actual saving, planned plus unplanned.

20.5 A fall in aggregate demand

The *slope* of the *AD* schedule depends only on the marginal propensity to consume (*MPC*). For a given *MPC*, the level of autonomous spending [*A* + *I*] determines the *height* of the *AD* schedule. Autonomous spending is spending unrelated to income.

Changes in autonomous spending lead to parallel shifts in the *AD* schedule. Investment demand depends chiefly on current guesses by firms about future demand for their output. Beliefs about this future demand can fluctuate significantly, influenced by current pessimism or optimism about the future. Similarly, a fall in consumer confidence reduces autonomous consumption demand.

Suppose firms get pessimistic about future demand for their output. Planned investment falls. If autonomous consumption is unaffected, the aggregate demand schedule *AD* is now lower at each income than before. Figure 20.7 shows this downward shift from *AD* to *AD'*.

Before we go into the details, think what is likely to happen to output. It will fall, but how much? When investment demand falls, firms cut output. Households have lower incomes and cut consumption. Firms cut output again, further reducing household incomes. Consumption demand falls further. What brings the process of falling output and income to an end?

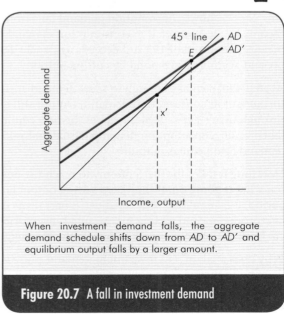

When investment demand falls, the aggregate demand schedule shifts down from *AD* to *AD'* and equilibrium output falls by a larger amount.

Figure 20.7 A fall in investment demand

PART FOUR Macroeconomics

Figure 20.7 shows that a given downward shift of the *AD* schedule reduces equilibrium output by a *finite* amount, but by an amount larger than the vertical fall in the *AD* schedule. This is because the *AD* schedule has a slope flatter than the 45° line: its slope, the marginal propensity to consume, is always smaller than unity.

Equilibrium moves from *E* to *E'*. Equilibrium output falls *more* than the original cut in investment demand, but does not fall all the way to zero.

Table 20.1 explains. Since many students find arithmetic easier than algebra, we illustrate for the particular values [$A = 10$] for autonomous consumption demand and [$c = 0.9$] for the marginal propensity to consume. Thus the particular consumption function is $C = 10 + 0.9Y$.

Table 20.1 Adjustment to a shift in investment demand

	Y	I	C = 10 + 0.9Y	AD = C + I	Y−AD	Unplanned stocks	Output
Step 1	200	10	190	200	0	Zero	Constant
Step 2	200	5	190	195	5	Rising	Falling
Step 3	195	5	185.5	190.5	4.5	Rising	Falling
Step 4	190.5	5	181.5	186.57	4	Rising	Falling
New equilibrium	150	5	145	150	0	Zero	Constant

If original investment demand is also 10, the first row of Table 20.1 shows that the original equilibrium output is 200, since consumption demand is then [$10 + 180$] and investment demand is 10. Thus aggregate demand just equals actual output.

In step 2 investment demand falls to 5. Firms did not expect demand to change, and still produced 200. Output exceeds aggregate demand by 5. Firms add this 5 to inventories, then cut output.

Step 3 shows firms making 195, the level of demand in step 2. But when firms cut output, income falls. Step 3 shows consumption demand falls from 190 to 185.5. Since the MPC is 0.9, a cut in income by 5 causes a fall in consumption demand by 4.5. The induced fall in consumption demand means that output of 195 still exceeds aggregate demand, which is now 190.5. Again inventories pile up, and again firms respond by cutting output.

At step 4 firms make enough to meet demand at step 3. Output is 190.5, but again this induces a further cut in consumption demand. Output still exceeds aggregate demand. The process keeps going, through many steps, until it reaches the new equilibrium, an output of 150. Output and income have fallen by 50, consumption demand has fallen by 45 and investment demand has fallen by 5. Aggregate demand again equals output.

How long it takes for the economy to reach the new equilibrium depends on how well firms figure out what is going on. If they keep setting output targets to meet the level of demand in the previous period, it takes a long time to adjust. Smart firms may spot that, period after period, they are overproducing and adding to unwanted inventories. They anticipate that demand is still falling and cut back output more quickly than Table 20.1 suggests.

Why does a fall of 5 in investment demand cause a fall of 50 in equilibrium output? Lower investment demand induces a cut in output and income that then induces an extra cut in consumption demand. Total demand falls by more than the original fall in investment demand, but the process does not spiral out of control. Equilibrium output is 150.

In our example, the initial change in autonomous investment demand is 5 and the final change in equilibrium output is 50. The multiplier is 10. That is why, in Figure 20.7, a small downward shift in the *AD* schedule leads to a much larger fall in equilibrium income and output.

> The **multiplier** is the ratio of the change in equilibrium output to the change in autonomous spending that caused the change.

20.6 The multiplier

The multiplier tells us how much output changes after a shift in aggregate demand. The multiplier exceeds 1 because a change in autonomous demand sets off further changes in consumption demand. The size of the multiplier depends on the marginal propensity to consume. The initial effect of a unit fall in investment demand is to cut output and income by a unit. If the *MPC* is large, this fall in income leads to a large fall in consumption and the multiplier is big. If the *MPC* is small, a given change in investment demand and output induces small changes in consumption demand and the multiplier is small.

Table 20.2 Calculating the multiplier

Change in	Step 1	Step 2	Step 3	Step 4	Step 5	*	*	*
I	1	0	0	0	0	*	*	*
Y	0	1	0.9	$(0.9)^2$	$(0.9)^3$	*	*	*
C	0	0.9	$(0.9)^2$	$(0.9)^2$	$(0.9)^3$	*	*	*

Table 20.2 examines a 1-unit increase in investment demand. In step 2, firms raise output by 1 unit. Consumption rises by 0.9, the marginal propensity to consume times the 1-unit change in income and output. At step 3, firms raise output by 0.9 to meet the increased consumption demand in step 2. In turn, consumption demand is increased by 0.81 (the *MPC* 0.9 times the 0.9 increase in income) leading in step 4 to a rise in output of 0.81. Consumption rises again and the process continues.

To find the multiplier, we add all the increases in output from each step in the table and keep going:

Multiplier = $1 + (0.9) + (0.9)^2 + (0.9)^3 + (0.9)^4 + (0.9)^5 + \ldots$

The dots at the end mean that we keep adding terms such as $(0.9)^6$ and so on. The right-hand side of this equation is called a geometric series. Each term is (0.9) times the previous term. Fortunately, mathematicians have shown that there is a general formula for the sum of all the terms in such a series:

Multiplier = $1/(1 - 0.9)$

The formula applies whatever the (constant) value of *c*, the marginal propensity to consume:

Multiplier = $1/(1 - c)$ (6)

For the particular value of $c = 0.9$, equation (6) confirms that the multiplier is $1/(0.1) = 10$. Hence a cut in investment demand by 5 causes a fall in equilibrium output by 50, as we knew from Table 20.1. Indeed, you might have guessed this from equations (4) and (5). Equilibrium output is simply autonomous demand multiplied by the multiplier!

The marginal propensity to consume tells how much of each extra unit of income is spent on consumption. Thus the *MPC* is a number between zero and unity. The higher the *MPC*, the lower is $(1 - c)$. Dividing 1 by a smaller number leads to a larger answer. The general formula for the multiplier in equation (6) confirms that a larger *MPC* implies a larger multiplier.

The multiplier and the MPS

Any part of an extra unit of income not spent must be saved. Hence $(1 - c)$ equals MPS, the marginal propensity to save.

Equation (6) says that we can also think of the multiplier as $1/MPS$. The higher the marginal propensity to save, the more of each extra unit of income leaks out of the circular flow into savings and the less goes back round the circular flow to generate further increases in aggregate demand, output and income.

> The **marginal propensity to save** is the fraction of each extra unit of income that households wish to save.

Figure 20.6 confirms that the multiplier exceeds unity. The upward-sloping line shows planned saving. Its slope, the marginal propensity to save, is less than unity since most extra income is consumed not saved. Hence the planned saving line has a flat slope. Beginning in equilibrium at E, imagine that the horizontal line, showing investment demand, shifts up by one unit. Since the planned saving line S has a flat slope, a unit increase in planned investment I must now intersect planned saving at a point more than one unit to the right of E. But that is all equation (6) says. The multiplier is $1/MPS$, which exceeds unity.

20.7 The paradox of thrift

The previous section analysed a parallel shift in the aggregate demand schedule caused by a change in autonomous investment demand. We now examine a parallel shift in the AD schedule caused by a change in the autonomous part of planned consumption and saving.

Suppose households increase autonomous consumption demand by 10. There is a parallel upward shift in the consumption function, and hence also in the aggregate demand schedule AD. Higher autonomous consumption demand implies an identical fall in autonomous planned saving. There is a parallel downward shift in the saving function.

In equilibrium planned saving always equals planned investment, and the latter is unaltered. Hence planned saving cannot change. Equilibrium income must therefore adjust to restore planned saving to the unchanged level of planned investment. Figure 20.8 illustrates. When a decline in thriftiness, or the desire to save, shifts planned saving from S to S', equilibrium income must rise from Y^* to Y^{**} to maintain the equality of planned saving and planned investment.

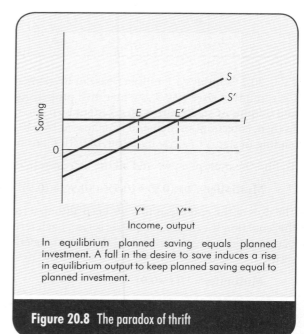

In equilibrium planned saving equals planned investment. A fall in the desire to save induces a rise in equilibrium output to keep planned saving equal to planned investment.

Figure 20.8 The paradox of thrift

The paradox of thrift helps us to understand an old debate about the virtues of saving and spending. Does society benefit from thriftiness and a high level of desired saving at each income level? The answer depends on whether or not the economy is at full employment.

When aggregate demand is low and the economy has spare resources, the paradox of thrift shows that a *reduction* in the desire to save will increase spending and increase the equilibrium income level. Society benefits from

> A change in the amount households wish to save at each income leads to a change in equilibrium income, but no change in equilibrium saving, which must still equal planned investment. This is the **paradox of thrift**.

Box 20.2 Spending like there's no tomorrow

Nowadays Nigel Lawson advertises diets. He used to be Chancellor of the Exchequer. In the Lawson boom in the late 1980s, heady optimism and easy access to credit made UK consumers spend a lot. Personal saving collapsed as people bought champagne, sports cars and houses. The boom years didn't last. As inflation rose, the government raised interest rates to slow down the economy. House prices fell. People's mortgage debt was larger than the value of their houses. To pay off this 'negative equity', households raised saving sharply in the early 1990s.

By 1997 UK households were borrowing again, as low interest rates fuelled a spending boom and a protracted rise in house prices. Reality TV shows were rivalled only by programmes showing viewers how to do up houses for subsequent letting or sale. The chart below shows that household saving, as a percentage of their disposable income, fell in 2004 to a level even below that in the Lawson boom in 1987. By 2006, the Bank of England was citing concerns about rising house prices as a reason to raise UK interest rates.

Clearly, the saving rate can fluctuate a lot. Although in this chapter we assume a constant marginal propensity to save, Chapter 24 discusses more sophisticated theories of consumption and saving.

One final remark. Does it matter whether households borrow in order to buy a foreign holiday or to buy a house for subsequent rental to others? In the former case, no asset is purchased for the future, in the latter case, the household acquires an asset that will give rise to future incomes. Simply measuring today's income and today's spending gives a misleading picture of the long-run economic position of the household. We return to this issue in Chapter 23.

Source: ONS.

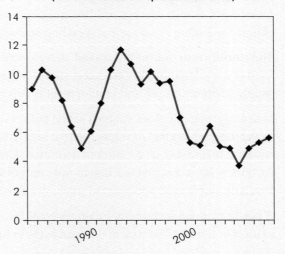

UK saving rate 1983–2007 (% of household disposable income)

higher output and employment. And since investment demand is autonomous, a change in the desire to save has no effect on the desired level of investment.

Suppose, however, that the economy is at potential output. Chapter 25 discusses how this might happen in the long run once prices and wages have time to adjust. If the economy is at potential output, an *increase* in the desire to save at each income level must increase saving, and reduce consumption, at potential output. However, investment demand *may* increase to restore aggregate demand to its full-employment level. The next few chapters explain why. Hence, in the long run society may benefit from an *increase* in the desire to save. Investment will rise and the economy's capital stock and potential output may grow more quickly.

In this chapter we have focused on the short run before prices and wages have time to adjust. Saving and investment decisions are made by different people. There is no automatic mechanism to translate higher saving into a corresponding rise in investment demand. Since planned saving depends on the level of income, income adjusts to equate planned saving and planned investment.

Summary

- **Aggregate demand** is planned spending on goods (and services). The *AD* schedule shows aggregate demand at each level of income and output.

- This chapter neglects planned spending by foreigners and by the government, studying **consumption demand** by households and **investment demand** by firms (desired additions to physical capital and to inventories). We treat investment demand as constant.

- Consumption demand is closely though not perfectly related to **personal disposable income**. Without taxes or transfers, personal disposable income and total income coincide.

- **Autonomous consumption** is desired consumption at zero income. **The marginal propensity to consume (MPC)** is the fraction by which planned consumption rises when income rises by a pound. The **marginal propensity to save (MPS)** is the fraction of an extra pound of income that is saved. Since income is consumed or saved, $MPC + MPS = 1$.

- For given prices and wages, the goods market is in equilibrium when output equals planned spending or aggregate demand. Equivalently, in equilibrium, planned saving equals planned investment. **Goods market equilibrium** does not mean output equals potential output. It means planned spending equals actual spending and actual output.

- The **equilibrium output is demand-determined** because we assume that prices and wages are fixed at a level that implies an excess supply of goods and labour. Firms and workers are happy to supply whatever output and employment is demanded.

- When aggregate demand exceeds actual output there is either unplanned disinvestment (inventory reductions) or unplanned saving (frustrated customers). Actual investment always equals actual saving, as a matter of definition. Unplanned inventory reductions or frustrated customers act as a signal to firms to raise output when aggregate demand exceeds actual output. Similarly, unplanned additions to stocks occur when aggregate demand is below output.

- A rise in planned investment increases equilibrium output by a larger amount. The initial increase in income to meet investment demand leads to further increases in consumption demand.

- The **multiplier** is the ratio of the change in output to the change in autonomous demand that caused it. In the simple model of this chapter, the multiplier is $1/[(1 - MPC)]$ or $1/MPS$. The multiplier exceeds 1 because *MPC* and *MPS* are positive fractions.

- The **paradox of thrift** shows that a reduced desire to save leads to an increase in output but no change in the equilibrium level of planned saving, which must still equal planned investment. Higher output offsets the reduced desire to save at each output level.

Review questions

To check your answers to these questions, go to page 726.

1 Suppose the consumption function is $C = 0.8Y$ and planned investment is 40. (a) Draw a diagram showing the aggregate demand schedule. (b) If actual output is 100, what unplanned actions will occur? (c) What is equilibrium output? (d) Do you get the same answer using planned saving equals planned investment?

2 Suppose the *MPC* is 0.6. Beginning from equilibrium, investment demand rises by 30. (a) How much does equilibrium output increase? (b) How much of that increase is extra consumption demand?

3 Planned investment is 100. People decide to save a higher proportion of their income: the consumption function changes from $C = 0.8Y$ to $C = 0.5Y$. (a) What happens to equilibrium income? (b) What happens to the equilibrium proportion of income saved? Explain.

4 What part of actual investment is not included in aggregate demand?

5 (a) Find equilibrium income when investment demand is 400 and $C = 0.8Y$. (b) Would output be higher or lower if the consumption function were $C = 100 + 0.7Y$?

6 **Common fallacies** Why are these statements wrong? (a) If people were prepared to save more, investment would increase and we could get the economy moving again. (b) Lower output leads to lower spending and yet lower output. The economy could spiral downwards for ever.

7 **Harder question** Could the multiplier ever be less than 1?

8 **Harder question** When could the paradox of thrift fail to be true?

9 **Essay question** 'The remarkably strong relationship between consumption and income confirms that most people want to spend most of their income as soon as they can. We are all material girls and boys at heart.' Is the inference justified?

Online **LearningCentre**

To help you grasp the key concepts of this chapter check out the extra resources posted on the Online Learning Centre. There are chapter summaries, self-test questions, an interactive graphing tool, weblinks and a searchable glossary, all for free!

To put your learning into practice and prepare for exams, an **Interactive Workbook** is also available online, containing a variety of question types and providing feedback on your answers.

If you'd like further help with economics, or have any questions, **NetTutor** is here to help! You will have a personalised tutorial service at your fingertips. Visit the online learning centre at: www.mcgraw-hill.co.uk/textbooks/begg for information on accessing all of these resources.

CHAPTER 21

Fiscal policy and foreign trade

Learning Outcomes

By the end of this chapter, you should understand:

1 how fiscal policy affects aggregate demand

2 short-run equilibrium output in this extended model

3 the balanced budget multiplier

4 automatic stabilizers

5 the structural budget and the inflation-adjusted budget

6 how budget deficits add to national debt

7 the limits to discretionary fiscal policy

8 how foreign trade affects equilibrium output

In most European countries, the government directly buys about a fifth of national output and spends about the same again on transfer payments. This spending is financed mainly by taxes. What is the macroeconomic impact of government fiscal policy?

We show how fiscal policy affects equilibrium output, then study three fiscal issues.

We analyse opportunities and limitations in using fiscal policy to stabilize output. We then examine the significance of the government's budget deficit.

When the government runs a deficit, it spends more than it earns. Deficits worry people. How can the government keep spending more than it receives? We examine the size of the deficit and ask if we should worry.

A government deficit is financed mainly by borrowing from the public by selling bonds, promises to pay specified amounts of interest payments at future dates. This borrowing adds to government debts to the public.[1]

By 2006 UK national debt was over £500 billion, or nearly £10 000 per person. The third fiscal policy issue we examine is the effect of the national debt.

> **Fiscal policy** is government policy on spending and taxes.

> **Stabilization policy** is government action to keep output close to potential output.

> The **budget deficit** is the excess of government spending over government receipts.

> The **national debt** is the stock of outstanding government debt.

---

1 Government is responsible not merely for its own deficits but also for any losses made by state-owned firms. The public sector net cash requirement (PSNCR) is the government deficit plus net losses of these firms.

Most of this chapter is about the government and aggregate demand, but we complete our model of income determination by also adding foreign trade. Exports X and imports Z are each nearly 30 per cent of UK GDP. The UK is a very open economy, and the effects of foreign trade are too important to ignore.[2]

21.1 Government and the circular flow

Government spending G on goods and services adds directly to aggregate demand. The government also withdraws money from the circular flow through indirect taxes T_e on expenditure and direct taxes T_d on factor incomes, less transfer benefits B that augment factor incomes. However, transfer payments affect aggregate demand only by affecting other components such as consumption or investment demand.

Table 21.1 shows UK government activity in 2007/08. The main components of G are health, education and defence. Social security payments – state pensions, unemployment benefit and child support – and debt interest payments are the main components of transfer payments.

The main direct taxes are income tax, corporation tax and social security contributions to state schemes for pensions and unemployment benefit. Indirect taxes include VAT, specific duties on tobacco, alcohol and fuel, and the property taxes levied by local government.

Table 21.1 UK public finances, 2007/08

Revenue	£bn	Expenditure	£bn
Direct tax		*Goods and services*	
Income tax	157	Health	104
Corporation tax	50	Education	77
Social security	95	Defence	32
		Law and order	33
Indirect tax		Housing, environment	22
VAT	80	Transport	20
Business rates	22	Industry and agriculture	21
Excise duties	41	*Transfer payments*	
Council tax	23	Social security	161
		Debt interest	30
Other receipts	84	*Other spending*	
Total revenue	553	**Total spending**	567
Deficit	14		

Source: www.hm-treasury.gov.uk.

2 In contrast, net property income is 1 per cent of GNP. We continue to treat GNP and GDP as equivalent.

21.2 The government and aggregate demand

Since it is a pain to keep distinguishing market prices and basic prices, we assume all taxes are direct taxes. With no indirect taxes, measurements at market prices and at basic prices coincide. For the moment, we still ignore foreign trade.

Aggregate demand AD is consumption demand C, investment demand I and government demand G for goods and services. Transfer payments affect aggregate demand only by affecting C or I.

$$AD = C + I + G \qquad (1)$$

In the short run, government spending G does not vary automatically with output and income. We assume G is fixed, or at least independent of income. Its size reflects how many hospitals the government wants to build and how many teachers it wants to hire. We now have three autonomous components of aggregate demand independent of current income and output: the autonomous consumption demand, investment demand I and government demand G.

The government also levies taxes and pays out transfer benefits.

With no indirect taxes, net taxes NT are simply direct taxes T_d minus transfer benefits B. Net taxes reduce personal disposable income – the amount available for spending or saving by households – relative to national income and output. If YD is disposable income, Y national income and output and NT net taxes,

> **Net taxes** are taxes minus transfers.

$$YD = Y - NT = (1 - t)Y \qquad (2)$$

where, for simplicity, we assume that net taxes are proportional to national income. Thus, if t is the *net tax rate*, the total revenue from net taxes is $NT = tY$.

Suppose taxes net of transfer benefits are about 20 per cent of national income. We can think of the (net) tax rate t as 0.2. If national income Y rises by £1, net tax revenue will rise by 20p, so household disposable income will increase only by 80p.

We still assume that households' desired consumption is proportional to their disposable income. For simplicity, suppose autonomous consumption is zero but that, as before, the marginal propensity to consume out of disposable income is 0.9. Households plan to spend 90p of each extra pound of disposable income. The consumption function is now $C = 0.9YD$.

With a net tax rate t, equation (2) says that disposable income YD is only $(1 - t)$ times national income Y. Thus, to relate consumption demand to *national* income, $C = 0.9YD = 0.9(1 - t)Y$.

If national income rises by £1, consumption demand rises by only $0.9(1 - t)$, which is less than £0.90. If the net tax rate t is 0.2, consumption demand rises by only £$(0.9 \times 0.8) = £0.72$. Each extra pound of national income increases disposable income by only 80p, out of which households plan to consume 90 per cent and save 10 per cent.

Clearly, spending £0.72 of each extra pound of national income implies a flatter consumption function, when plotted against national income, than spending £0.90 of each extra pound of national income. The effect of a positive net tax rate t therefore acts like a reduction in the marginal propensity to consume. Figure 21.1 illustrates.

Aggregate demand and equilibrium output do not depend on whether the leakage is through saving (as when the MPC is low) or through taxes (as when the MPC multiplied by $(1 - t)$ is low). Either way, the leakage prevents money being recycled as demand for output of firms.

If MPC is the marginal propensity to consume out of *disposable* income, and there is a proportional net tax rate t, then MPC', the marginal propensity to consume out of *national* income, is given by

$$MPC' = MPC \times (1 - t) \qquad (3)$$

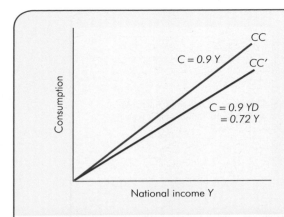

Figure 21.1 Net taxes and consumption

In the absence of taxation, national income Y and disposable income YD are the same. The consumption function CC' shows how much households wish to consume at each level of national income. With a proportional net tax rate of 0.2, households still consume 90p of each pound of disposable income. Since YD is now only 0.8 Y, households consume only $0.9 \times 0.8 = 0.72$ of each extra unit of national income. Relating consumption to national income, the effect of net taxes is to rotate the consumption function downwards from CC to CC'.

We now show how the government affects equilibrium national income and output. We start with an example in which autonomous investment demand is I and the consumption function in terms of disposable income is $C = 0.9YD$.

The effect of net taxes on output

Suppose initially that government spending is zero. Figure 21.2 illustrates. A rise in the net tax rate from zero to 0.2 makes the consumption function pivot downward from CC to CC' in Figure 21.1. We obtain aggregate demand AD by adding the constant investment demand I to the consumption function. Hence, the rise in the net rate that rotates the consumption function from CC to CC' in Figure 21.1 causes a similar rotation of aggregate demand from AD to AD' in Figure 21.2. Hence, aggregate demand equals actual output at a lower output level. The aggregate demand schedule now crosses the 45° line at E' not E. Equilibrium income and output fall.

Raising the net tax rate reduces equilibrium output. When aggregate demand and equilibrium output are below potential output, lower tax rates or higher transfer benefits will raise aggregate demand and equilibrium output.

The effect of government spending on output

Now forget taxes and think government spending. Suppose the net tax rate is zero. National income and disposable income coincide. Figure 21.3 shows that higher government spending has an effect similar to that of higher autonomous investment demand studied in Chapter 20. With a marginal propensity to consume of 0.9, the multiplier is again $1/(1 - MPC) = 10$. A rise in government spending G induces a rise in equilibrium output by 10 times that amount. In Figure 21.3 equilibrium moves from E to E' when the aggregate demand schedule shifts from AD to AD'.

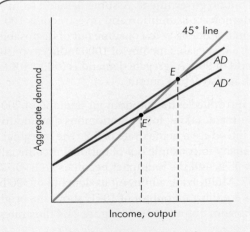

An increase in the income tax rate or a reduction in rate of unemployment benefit will increase the net tax rate t. The consumption function rotates from CC to CC' in Figure 21.1. With constant investment demand, the aggregate demand schedule rotates from AD to AD' in Figure 21.2. The equilibrium level of output falls and the equilibrium point moves from E to E'.

Figure 21.2 A higher net tax rate

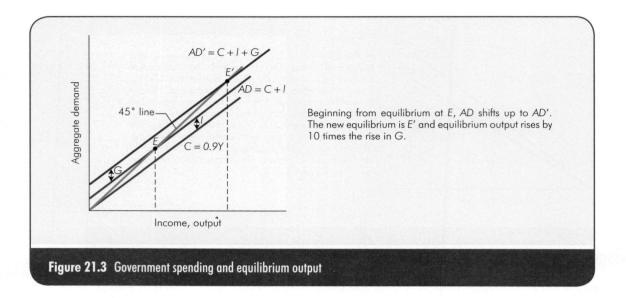

Figure 21.3 Government spending and equilibrium output

The combined effects of government spending and taxation

Suppose an economy begins with an equilibrium output of 1000 but no government. Assume demand from autonomous consumption and investment is 100. With a marginal propensity to consume out of disposable income of 0.9, a disposable income of 1000 induces consumption demand of 900. Aggregate demand is $(900 + 100) = 1000$, which is also actual output.

Now introduce extra autonomous demand of 200 from the government, taking total autonomous demand to 300. Also introduce a net tax rate of 0.2. The marginal propensity to consume out of national income falls from 0.9 to 0.72, and the multiplier becomes $1/(1 - 0.72) = 1/0.28 = 3.57$. Multiplying autonomous demand of 300 by 3.57 yields equilibrium output of 1071, above the original equilibrium output of 1000. Figure 21.4 illustrates.

The balanced budget multiplier

The economy began at an equilibrium output of 1000. With a proportional tax rate of 20 per cent, initial tax revenue was 200, precisely the amount of government spending.

This balanced increase in government spending and taxes did not leave demand and output unaltered. Figure 21.4 shows equilibrium output is larger. The new 200 of

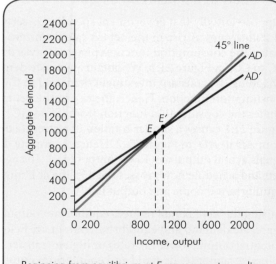

Beginning from equilibrium at *E*, government spending rises from zero to 200, shifting the *AD* schedule upwards, and the tax rises from zero to 0.2, making the new schedule *AD'* flatter. Equilibrium moves from *E* to *E'* where *AD'* intersects the 45° line. Equilibrium output increases from 1000 to 1071.

Figure 21.4 Higher spending and taxes

government spending raises aggregate demand by 200 and the tax increase cuts disposable income by 200. The *MPC* out of disposable income is 0.9, so lower disposable income reduces consumption demand by only $0.9 \times 200 = 180$.

The initial effect of the tax and spending package raises aggregate demand by 200 but reduces it by 180. Aggregate demand rises by 20. Output rises, inducing further rises in consumption demand. When the new equilibrium is reached, output has risen a total of 71, from 1000 to 1071. This is the famous balanced budget multiplier.

> The **balanced budget multiplier** says that a rise in government spending plus an equal rise in taxes leads to higher output.

Box 21.1 Land of the falling sun

Japan, after three decades of postwar success, screwed up the 1990s. A property crash made banks bankrupt. Instead of admitting this and sorting it out, policy makers ignored the problem. Consumers lost confidence and output fell. To restore confidence, Japan had big fiscal expansions to boost demand, but Japanese consumers and firms decided radical action meant things were worse than previously thought. The autonomous parts of consumption and investment demand fell more than enough to offset the fiscal expansion. Fiscal expansion failed to boost output. In macroeconomics the induced effects can outweigh the direct effect. Not until 2003 did sustainable growth return: Japan grew by 2 per cent a year between 2003 and 2007.

Japan's macroeconomic misery

	GDP growth (%)	Interest rate (%)	Budget deficit (% of GDP)	Government net debt (% of GDP)
1993	0	3	2	18
1994	1	2	2	21
1995	2	1	4	25
1996	5	1	4	29
1997	1	1	3	35
1998	–3	1	5	47
1999	0	0	7	54
2000	2	0	6	61
2001	2	0	6	66
2002	0	0	6	73
2003–07	2	0	6	82

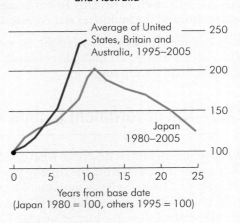

House prices in Japan, United States, Britain and Australia

Average of United States, Britain and Australia, 1995–2005

Japan 1980–2005

Years from base date
(Japan 1980 = 100, others 1995 = 100)

Sources: OECD, *Economic Outlook*, 2007; *The Economist*, 16 June 2005.

The multiplier revisited

The multiplier relates changes in autonomous demand to changes in equilibrium *national* income and output. The formula in Chapter 20 still applies, but now we use MPC', the marginal propensity to consume out of national, rather than out of disposable, income.

$$\text{Multiplier} = 1/(1 - MPC') \tag{4}$$

With proportional taxes, MPC' equals $MPC \times (1 - t)$. For a given marginal propensity to consume out of disposable income, a higher tax rate t reduces MPC', raises $(1 - MPC')$ and thus reduces the multiplier. Table 22.2 illustrates.

Table 21.2 Values of the multiplier

MPC	t	MPC'	Multiplier
0.9	0	0.90	10.00
0.9	0.2	0.72	3.57
0.7	0	0.70	3.33
0.7	0.2	0.56	2.27
0.7	0.4	0.42	1.72

In Chapter 20, without government the multiplier was simply $1/(1 - MPC)$ or $1/MPS$. With a larger marginal propensity to save, there was a larger leakage from the circular flow between firms and households, and the multiplier was correspondingly smaller.

Table 21.2 merely extends this insight. Now leakages arise both from saving and from net taxes. When both are large, the multiplier is small. The bottom row of the table has a much smaller multiplier than the top row.

21.3 The government budget

The government budget describes what goods and services the government will buy during the coming year, what transfer payments it will make and how it will pay for them. Most of its spending is financed by taxes. When spending exceeds taxes there is a budget deficit. When taxes exceed spending there is a budget surplus. Continuing to use G for government spending on goods and services, and NT for net taxes or taxes minus transfer payments,

> A **budget** is the spending and revenue plans of an individual, a company or a government.

$$\text{Government budget deficit} = G - NT \tag{5}$$

Figure 21.5 shows government purchases G and net taxes tY in relation to national income. We assume G is fixed at 200. With a proportional net tax rate of 0.2, net taxes are $0.2Y$. Taxes are zero when output is zero, 100 when output is 500 and 200 when output is 1000. At outputs below 1000, the government budget is in deficit. At an output of 1000 the budget is balanced, and at higher outputs the budget is in surplus. Given G and t, the budget deficit or surplus depends on the level of output and income.

The budget surplus or deficit is determined by three things: the tax rate t, the level of government spending G and the level of output Y. With a given tax rate, an increase in G will raise output and hence tax revenue. Could the budget deficit be *reduced* by higher spending? We now show that this is impossible.

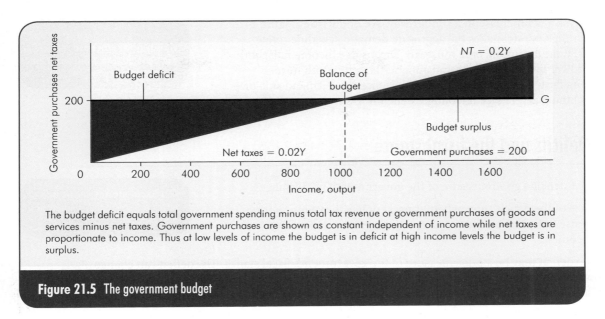

The budget deficit equals total government spending minus total tax revenue or government purchases of goods and services minus net taxes. Government purchases are shown as constant independent of income while net taxes are proportionate to income. Thus at low levels of income the budget is in deficit at high income levels the budget is in surplus.

Figure 21.5 The government budget

Investment, savings and the budget

By definition, actual leakages from the circular flow always equal actual injections to the circular flow. Payments cannot vanish into thin air. Our model now has two leakages – saving by households and net taxes paid to the government – and two injections – investment spending by firms and government spending on goods and services. Thus *actual* saving plus *actual* net taxes always equal *actual* government spending plus *actual* investment spending.

In the last chapter we saw that, when the economy is not at equilibrium income, actual saving and investment differ from *desired* or *planned* saving and investment. Firms make unplanned changes in inventories and households may be forced to make unplanned savings if demand exceeds the output actually available.

The economy is in equilibrium when all quantities demanded or *desired* are equal to *actual* quantities. In equilibrium, planned saving S plus planned net taxes NT must equal planned government purchases G plus planned investment I. Planned leakages equal planned injections:

$$S+NT=G+I \tag{6}$$

Without the government, this reduces to the equilibrium condition of Chapter 20: planned saving equals planned investment. Equation (6) implies that in equilibrium desired saving minus desired investment equals the government's desired budget deficit:

$$S-I=G-NT \tag{7}$$

Equation (7) confirms that a rise in planned government spending G must *raise* the budget deficit. For a given tax rate, a rise in G leads to a parallel upward shift in the aggregate demand schedule. This raises equilibrium income. Provided the tax rate is less than 100 per cent, disposable income must rise. Households increase both desired consumption and desired saving when disposable income rises. Some of the extra disposable income goes in extra desired saving.

Since desired investment I is independent of income, a rise in desired saving raises the left-hand side of equation (7). Hence the right-hand side must rise. Hence, net taxes NT cannot rise as G. Equation (7) promises us that the equilibrium budget deficit rises if government spending increases but the net tax rate is unaltered.

> **Higher government spending** on goods and services increases equilibrium output. With a given tax rate, tax revenue rises but the budget deficit increases (or the budget surplus falls).

We can analyse a tax increase in a similar way. We know from Figure 21.2 that a rise in the tax rate makes the aggregate demand schedule rotate downwards. Equilibrium income must fall. Disposable income falls, both because of lower national income and a higher tax rate. With lower disposable income, desired saving must fall. Hence the left-hand side of equation (7) must fall. Hence the budget deficit is lower.

> For given government spending G, a **higher tax rate** reduces both equilibrium output and the budget deficit.

21.4 Deficits and the fiscal stance

Is the budget deficit a good measure of the government's fiscal stance?

Does the size of the deficit show whether fiscal policy is *expansionary*, aiming to raise national income, or *contractionary*, trying to reduce national income?

> The **fiscal stance** shows the effect of fiscal policy on demand and output.

In itself, the deficit may be a poor measure of the government's fiscal stance. The deficit can change for reasons unconnected with fiscal policy. Even if G and t are unaltered, a fall in investment demand will reduce output and income. In turn this reduces net tax revenue and raises the budget deficit.

For given levels of government spending and tax rates, the budget has larger deficits in recessions, when income is low, than in booms, when income is high. Suppose aggregate demand suddenly falls. The budget will go into deficit. Someone looking at the deficit might conclude that fiscal policy was expansionary and that there was no need to expand fiscal policy further. That might be wrong. The deficit may exist because of the recession.

The structural budget

To use the budget deficit as an indicator of the fiscal stance we calculate the *structural* or *cyclically adjusted budget*.

> The **structural budget** shows what the budget would be if output is at potential output.

Suppose government spending is 200 and the tax rate is 0.2. As in Figure 21.4, the budget is in deficit at any income below 1000 and in surplus at any income above 1000. If, given the other components of aggregate demand, equilibrium output is 800, the actual budget will be in deficit. Net tax revenue will be $0.2 \times 800 = 160$. With government spending at 200, the budget deficit is 40.

Conversely, suppose equilibrium output is 1200. With a tax rate of 0.2, net tax revenue would be 240 but autonomous government spending would still be 200. There would be a budget *surplus* of 40.

Looking at the deficit of 40 when the actual output is 800, we might conclude that fiscal policy is too expansionary and the government should tighten fiscal policy to eliminate the deficit. Once we realize that the main cause of the deficit is low income, we are less likely to reach this conclusion. We may also recognize that tightening fiscal policy during a recession is likely to reduce output further.[3]

Inflation-adjusted deficits

> The **inflation-adjusted budget** uses real not nominal interest rates to calculate government spending on debt interest.

A second reason why the actual government deficit may be a poor measure of fiscal stance is the distinction between real and nominal interest rates. Official measures of the deficit treat all nominal interest paid by the

---

3 In this chapter we are concerned only with the impact of fiscal policy on aggregate demand. There may be other reasons to worry about a deficit. We examine these in Chapter 26.

government on the national debt as government expenditure. It makes more sense to count only the *real* interest rate times the outstanding government debt as an item of expenditure that contributes to the deficit.

Suppose inflation is 10 per cent, nominal interest rates are 12 per cent, and real interest rates are 2 per cent. From the government's viewpoint, the interest burden is only really 2 per cent on each £1 of debt outstanding. Although nominal interest rates are 12 per cent, inflation will inflate future nominal tax revenue at 10 per cent a year, providing most of the revenue needed to pay the high nominal interest rates. The real cost of borrowing is only 2 per cent.

21.5 Automatic stabilizers and discretionary fiscal policy

Table 21.2 showed that a higher net tax rate t reduces the multiplier. Suppose investment demand falls by 100. The larger the multiplier, the larger is the fall in equilibrium output. A high net tax rate reduces the multiplier and dampens the output effect of shocks to autonomous aggregate demand. A high net tax rate is a good automatic stabilizer.

Income tax, VAT and unemployment benefit are important automatic stabilizers. At given tax rates and given benefit levels, a fall in income and output raises payments of unemployment benefits and reduces tax revenue. Both effects reduce the multiplier and dampen the output response. A given shift of the aggregate demand schedule has a smaller effect on equilibrium income and output. The automatic reduction in net tax revenue acts as a fiscal stimulus. Conversely, in a boom, net tax revenue rises, which helps dampen the boom.

> **Automatic stabilizers** reduce the multiplier and thus output response to demand shocks.

Automatic stabilizers have a great advantage. They are automatic. Nobody has to decide whether there has been a shock to which policy should respond. By reducing the responsiveness of the economy to shocks, automatic stabilizers reduce output fluctuations.

All leakages are automatic stabilizers. A higher saving rate and lower marginal propensity to consume reduce the multiplier. Later in the chapter, we shall see that a high marginal propensity to import also dampens output fluctuations.

Active or discretionary fiscal policy

Although automatic fiscal stabilizers are always at work, governments also use *discretionary* fiscal policies to change spending levels or tax rates to stabilize aggregate demand. When other components of aggregate demand are abnormally low, the government can boost demand by cutting taxes, raising spending, or both. When other components of aggregate demand are abnormally high, the government raises taxes or cuts spending.

By now you should be asking two questions. First, why can fiscal policy not stabilize aggregate demand completely? Surely, by maintaining aggregate demand at its full-employment level, the government could eliminate booms and slumps altogether? Second, why are governments reluctant to expand fiscal policy and aggregate demand to a level that would completely eliminate unemployment? Box 21.2 provides some of the answers.

> **Discretionary fiscal policy** is decisions about tax rates and levels of government spending.

Box 21.2 The limits to fiscal policy

Why can demand shocks not be fully offset by fiscal policy?

1 Time lags   It takes time to spot that aggregate demand has changed. It may take six months to get reliable statistics on output. Then it takes time to change fiscal policy. Long-term spending plans on hospitals or defence cannot be changed overnight. And once the policy is changed it takes time to work through the steps of the multiplier process to have its full effect.

2 Uncertainty   The government faces two problems. First, it is unsure of key magnitudes such as the multiplier. It only has estimates from past data. Mistaken estimates induce incorrect decisions about the extent of the fiscal change needed. Second, since fiscal policy takes time to work, the government has to forecast the level that demand will reach by the time fiscal policy has its full effects. If investment is low today but about to rise sharply, a fiscal expansion may not be needed. Mistakes in forecasting non-government sources of demand, such as investment, lead to incorrect decisions about the fiscal changes currently required.

3 Induced effects on autonomous demand   Our model treats investment demand and the autonomous consumption demand as given. This is only a simplification. Changes in fiscal policy may lead to offsetting changes in other components of autonomous demand. If estimates of these induced effects are wrong, fiscal changes have unexpected effects. To study this issue, we extend our model of aggregate demand in Chapter 24.

Why not expand fiscal policy when unemployment is high?

1 The budget deficit   When output is low and unemployment high, the budget deficit may be large. Fiscal expansion makes it larger. The government may worry about the size of the deficit itself, an issue we discuss in Section 21.6, or worry that a large deficit will lead to inflation, an issue we explore in Chapter 26.

2 Maybe we are at full employment!   Our simple model assumes there are spare resources. Output is demand-determined. Fiscal expansion raises demand and output. But we could be at potential output. People are unemployed, and machines idle, only because they do not wish to supply at the going wages or rentals. If so, there are no spare resources to be mopped up raising aggregate demand. If high unemployment and low output reflect not low demand but low supply, fiscal expansion is pointless. Chapters 25, 26 and 30 discuss the supply side of the economy in more detail.

21.6 The national debt and the deficit

In recent years the UK government had a budget surplus. Historically, this is rare. Most governments have budget deficits. The flow of deficits is what adds to the stock of debt.

> The government's debts are called the **national debt**.

The UK government had large deficits in the 1970s. The nominal value of its debt soared. Yet in many of these years the nominal deficit was actually a real surplus once proper inflation accounting is used. The ratio of nominal debt to nominal income was falling because inflation was raising the value of nominal income. Moreover, when the economy is growing in *real* terms, real tax revenue is rising, and the government can service a growing real debt without having to increase *tax rates*.

Table 21.3 UK government net debt, 1973–2007 (% of GDP)

1973	1979	1989	1999	2007
60	48	15	39	44

Sources: OECD, Economic Outlook; OECD, Budget 2007.

These two arguments – inflation adjustment of the deficit, and the growth of real incomes and the real tax revenue from given tax rates – mean that in many countries debt is not out of control. Although cumulative nominal deficits dramatically raised nominal debt, the ratio of nominal debt to nominal GDP has often *fallen*, as Table 21.3 confirms. The UK debt/GDP ratio in 1989 was one-quarter its level 16 years earlier. Fears of a UK debt explosion were misplaced. However, UK government indebtedness has been steadily increasing in recent years.

There are two reasons why concerns about the national debt may be overstated. First, much of it is owed to UK citizens. It is a debt we owe ourselves as a nation. Second, some of the money borrowed by the public sector has been used to finance investment in physical or human capital, which raises *future* output and tax revenue and will help pay off the debt. Prudent businesses sometimes borrow to finance profitable investment. A prudent government may do the same. More investment in rail infrastructure would probably have been good for the UK, even if financed by greater debt.

When should a sensible economist worry about the scale of the public debt? First, *if* the debt becomes large relative to GDP, high tax rates will be needed to meet the debt interest burden. High tax rates may have disincentive effects.

Second, if the government cannot raise tax rates beyond a certain point, a large debt and hence large debt interest payments may cause large deficits that can be financed only by borrowing or printing money. Since borrowing compounds the problem, eventually it is necessary to print money on a huge scale. That is how hyperinflations start. Chapter 26 fills in the details.

By 2004 UK government debt, relative to GDP, was lower than in 1970. However, in some countries, such as Italy and Japan, it is now large, as Table 21.4 confirms. High debt levels are especially worrying when real interest rates are also high, for then the government must levy high taxes to meet the burden of paying interest on its debt.

This completes our introduction to fiscal policy, aggregate demand and the economy. We now extend our model of income determination to include the sector we have so far neglected – foreign trade with the rest of the world.

Table 21.4 Government net debt, 2007 (% of GDP)

Belgium	74
Italy	96
Netherlands	29
USA	44
UK	43
France	41
Germany	51
Japan	93

Source: OECD, Economic Outlook.

Activity box 21 'You've never had it so prudent...'

...as Prime Minister Tony Blair told the Labour Party Conference in 1999. To stop short-sighted politicians boosting the economy too much in the short run and thereby causing long-term problems, Chancellor Gordon Brown not only gave the Bank of England independent control of interest rates but also introduced a Code for Fiscal Stability.

The **Code for Fiscal Stability** commits the government to a medium-run objective of financing all current government spending out of current revenues.

Borrowing-financed deficits are allowed only to finance public-sector investment (which should eventually pay for itself by raising future output and hence future tax revenues). A medium-run perspective is needed because the actual deficit fluctuates over the business cycle even if tax rates remain constant. Chancellor Brown's 'golden rule' means that government debt accumulation in the long run (because of borrowing to finance investment) should be accompanied by higher output and tax revenue without requiring any change in tax rates.

Because tax revenues tend to fall when the economy is growing more slowly, there is always some room for dispute about whether the emergence of a tax revenue shortfall can merely be attributed to temporary cyclical factors or whether it is likely to persist and therefore require rises in tax rates to put it right again.

Some economists continue to believe that the UK's long-run budget position is sound, both because, at constant tax rates, future income growth will provide additional future tax revenue and apparently higher budget deficits reflect higher investment by the public sector.

Others have begun to disagree. For example, *The Economist* (under the theme 'Gordon and Prudence: it's so over') has in a series of articles argued that early fiscal prudence was only accomplished by stealth taxes, such as the famous raid on pension funds, but that early success then encouraged the Chancellor to become overambitious for public spending, especially on the NHS, after 2002. Overspending has therefore increasingly threatened fiscal stability.

In the 2007 Budget Statement, the Treasury tried to meet this criticism head on.

> The golden rule is being met in this cycle with a surplus of 0.1 per cent of GDP, in contrast to the last cycle's average deficit of 2.0 per cent of GDP, and the 1977–78 to 1986–87 cycle's average deficit of 1.8 per cent of GDP. Debt has remained at low and sustainable levels, while at the same time public sector net investment is now over three times higher as a share of the economy than it was in 1997–98. [...] The IMF noted in March this year, that in the UK 'shocks, such as the global downturn of 2000–03 and the increase in oil prices during 2004–06, were managed with good policy responses', and noted 'the shallowness of the UK growth slowdown during the last global downturn'. The credibility of the framework has been established not only by the performance of the key fiscal aggregates, but also by the enhanced transparency introduced by the Code for fiscal stability.

Questions

(a) Why is it important to assess the fiscal position over a complete cycle and not merely at a point in time?

Activity box 21 'You've never had it so prudent...' (Continued)

(b) Since people suspect that the government may choose the definition of the cycle's length in order to suit their own purposes, would there be any gain from a report by an independent group of experts in the same way as the Bank of England publishes an independent *Inflation Report* on monetary policy?

(c) How would you expect financial markets to react if they thought that the Treasury was cooking the books in respect of its assessment of whether the golden rule was being met?

(d) Why does the golden rule apply to current expenditure by the government but exclude spending on physical investment?

(e) Do the arguments you used in (d) in fact apply to government expenditure on human capital investment as well? Do they apply to health investment?

To check your answers to these questions, go to page 727.

21.7 Foreign trade and income determination

We now take account of exports X, goods made at home but sold abroad, and imports Z, goods made abroad but bought by domestic residents. Table 21.5 shows UK exports, imports and net exports. Two points should be noted.

Net exports are small relative to GDP. Exports and imports are about equal in size. The UK has fairly balanced trade with the rest of the world.

When a household overspends its income, it dissaves, or is in deficit, and runs down its net assets (selling assets or adding to debt) to meet this deficit. When a country runs a trade deficit with the rest of the world, the country as a whole must sell off some assets to foreigners to pay for this deficit. Chapter 28 explains how this occurs.

> The **trade balance** is the value of net exports. If this is positive, the economy has a **trade surplus**. If imports exceed exports, the economy has a **trade deficit**.

Table 21.5 shows that the UK is a very open economy. Exports and imports are each over a quarter of GDP. In the United States, exports and imports are about 12 per cent of GDP. Foreign trade is much more important for most European countries than for a huge country like the United States, which largely trades with itself.

Net exports $X - Z$ add to our income and expenditure measures of GDP. Hence, the equilibrium condition for the goods market must now be expanded to[4]

$$Y = AD = C + I + G + X - Z \tag{8}$$

What determines desired exports and imports? Export demand depends mainly on what is happening abroad. Foreign income and foreign demand are largely unrelated to domestic output. Hence we treat the demand for exports as autonomous.

---

4 This also implies $Y + Z = C + I + G + X$. Home output Y plus output Z from abroad equals final demand $C + I + G + X$.

Table 21.5 UK foreign trade, 1950–2006 (% of GDP)

	Exports	Imports	Net exports
1950	23	23	0
1960	20	21	1
1970	22	21	1
1980	27	25	2
2006	28	33	−5

Sources: ONS, *Economic Trends*; www.statistics.gov.uk/elmr.

Demand for imports rises when domestic income and output rise. Figure 21.6 shows the demand for exports, imports and net exports, as domestic income changes. The export demand schedule is horizontal. Export demand is independent of domestic income. Desired imports are zero when income is zero but rises as income rises. The slope of the import demand schedule is the marginal propensity to import.

The import demand schedule in Figure 21.6 assumes a value of 0.2 for the marginal propensity to import. Each additional pound of national income adds 20p to desired imports. One of the problems facing the UK is that the marginal propensity to import MPZ is higher than 0.2. Any increase in national income leads to a large increase in the demand for imports.

> The **marginal propensity to import (MPZ)** is the fraction of each extra pound of national income that domestic residents wish to spend on extra imports.

At each output, the gap between export demand and import demand is the demand for net exports. At low output, net exports are positive. There is a trade *surplus* with the rest of the world. At high output, there is a trade *deficit* and net exports are negative. By raising import demand while leaving export demand unchanged, higher output worsens the trade balance.

Net exports and equilibrium income

Figure 21.7 shows how equilibrium income is determined. We start from the aggregate demand schedule $C + I + G$, described earlier in the chapter, then add net exports NX. At low output, net export demand is positive. Aggregate demand $C + I + G + X - Z$ will then exceed $C + I + G$. As output rises, import demand rises and desired *net* exports fall. At the output of 250, Figure 21.6 tells us that net export demand is zero. Figure 21.7 shows the new aggregate demand schedule AD crossing $C + I + G$ at an output of 250. Beyond this output, net export demand is negative and the aggregate demand schedule is below $C + I + G$.

At a zero income, Figure 21.7 shows autonomous demand $I + G + X$. Suppose the marginal propensity to consume out of national income MPC is still 0.72. The $C + I + G$ schedule

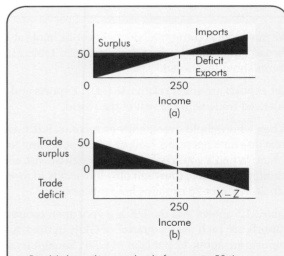

Part (a) shows the given level of exports at 50. Imports increase with the level of income. The diagram assumes a marginal propensity to import, shown by the slope of the import schedule, of 0.2. The trade balance, the difference between planned exports and planned imports, is zero at an income level of 250. Imports and exports both equal 50. At higher levels of income, imports exceed 50 and there is a trade deficit. The net export schedule $X - Z$ in part (b) shows the difference between export and import demand.

Figure 21.6 Exports, imports and the trade balance

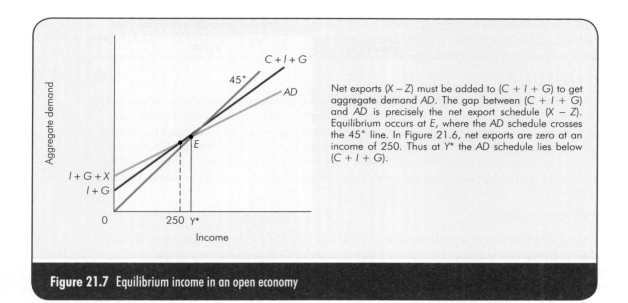

Net exports (X − Z) must be added to (C + I + G) to get aggregate demand AD. The gap between (C + I + G) and AD is precisely the net export schedule (X − Z). Equilibrium occurs at E, where the AD schedule crosses the 45° line. In Figure 21.6, net exports are zero at an income of 250. Thus at Y* the AD schedule lies below (C + I + G).

Figure 21.7 Equilibrium income in an open economy

has a slope of 0.72, but the aggregate demand schedule AD is flatter. Each extra pound of national income adds 72p to consumption demand but also adds 20p to desired imports, since $MPZ = 0.2$. Thus, each extra pound of national income adds only 52p to aggregate demand for domestic output. The AD schedule has a slope of 0.52.

In Figure 21.7 equilibrium is at E, where aggregate demand equals domestic income and output. Planned spending, actual incomes and domestic output coincide at Y*. Knowing this we can deduce the levels of tax revenue and imports, and hence compute both the budget deficit (or surplus) and the trade deficit (or surplus). Neither is automatically zero merely because the economy is at equilibrium output.

The multiplier in an open economy

Each extra pound of national income raises consumption demand *for domestically produced goods* not by MPC′, the marginal propensity to consume goods from whatever source, but only by (MPC′ − MPZ). The multiplier is lower because there are not merely leakages through saving and taxes but also through imports. In an open economy, the multiplier becomes

$$\text{Multiplier} = 1/[1 − (MPC' − MPZ)] \tag{9}$$

With a value of 0.72 for MPC′, the multiplier in the absence of foreign trade would be 3.57. If the marginal propensity to import is 0.2, the multiplier is reduced to $1/[0.48] = 2.08$. If the marginal propensity to import was as high as 0.72, equation (9) implies the multiplier would be reduced to 1, which is no multiplier at all.

For small economies, very open to international trade, this leakage through import demand is very important. Small economies that are very open thus face powerful automatic stabilizers.

Higher export demand

A rise in export demand leads to a parallel upward shift in the aggregate demand schedule AD. Equilibrium income must increase. A higher AD schedule crosses the 45° line at a higher level of income. With a higher income, desired imports rise. The analysis of what happens to net exports is very similar to our analysis of the effect of an increase in government spending on the budget deficit.

As a matter of national income accounting, total leakages from the circular flow always equal total injections to the circular flow. And in equilibrium desired spending must coincide with actual income and spending on domestic goods. Hence the amended equilibrium condition for an open economy is

$$S + NT + Z = I + G + X \qquad (10)$$

Desired saving plus net taxes plus desired imports equal desired investment plus desired government spending plus desired exports. Higher export demand X raises equilibrium domestic income and output. This raises desired saving, net tax revenue at constant tax rates and desired imports.[5] Since S, NT and Z all rise when X rises, the rise in desired imports must be smaller than the rise in desired exports. Higher export demand raises the equilibrium level of desired imports but still increases the desired level of net exports. The domestic country's trade balance with the rest of the world improves.

Imports and employment

Do imports steal jobs from the domestic economy? Final demand $C + I + G + X$ is met partly through goods produced abroad not at home. By reducing imports, we can create extra output and employment at home. This view is correct, but also dangerous. It is correct because higher consumer spending on domestic rather than foreign goods *will* increase aggregate demand for domestic goods and so raise domestic output and employment. In Figure 21.7, a lower marginal propensity to import makes the *AD* schedule steeper and raises equilibrium income and output.

There are many ways to restrict import spending at each level of output. In Chapter 28 we begin the analysis of how the exchange rate affects the demand for imports (and exports). However, imports can also be restricted directly through *import quotas* or indirectly through *tariffs*. We explore these further in Chapter 33.

The view that import restrictions help domestic output and employment is dangerous because it ignores the possibility of retaliation by other countries. By reducing our imports, we cut the exports of others. If they retaliate by doing the same thing, the demand for our exports will fall. In the end, nobody gains employment but world trade disappears. If the whole world is in recession, what is needed is a worldwide expansion of fiscal policies, not a collective, and ultimately futile, attempt to steal employment from other countries.

---

5 Since tax rates remain constant, higher domestic income raises disposable income, desired consumption and saving.

Summary

- The government buys goods and services, and levies taxes (net of transfer benefits) that reduce disposable income below national income and output.

- **Net taxes,** if related to income levels, lower the marginal propensity to consume out of national income. Households get only part of each extra pound of national income to use as disposable income.

- **Higher government spending on goods and services** raises aggregate demand and equilibrium output. A **higher tax rate** reduces aggregate demand and equilibrium output.

- An equal initial increase in government spending and taxes raises aggregate demand and output. This is the **balanced budget multiplier**.

- The **government budget** is in deficit (surplus) if spending is larger (smaller) than tax revenue. Higher government spending raises the budget deficit. A higher tax rate reduces it.

- In equilibrium in a closed economy, desired saving and taxes equal desired investment and government spending. An excess of desired saving over desired investment must be offset by an excess of government purchases over net tax revenue.

- The budget deficit is a poor indicator of **fiscal stance**. Recessions make the budget go into deficit, booms generate a budget surplus. The **structural budget** calculates whether the budget would be in surplus or deficit if output were at potential output. It is also important to **inflation-adjust** the deficit.

- **Automatic stabilizers** reduce fluctuations in GDP by reducing the multiplier. Leakages act as automatic stabilizers.

- The government may also use **active or discretionary fiscal policy** to try to stabilize output. In practice, active fiscal policy cannot stabilize output perfectly.

- Budget deficits add to the **national debt**. If the debt is mainly owed to citizens of the country, interest payments are merely a transfer within the economy. However, the national debt may be a burden if the government is unable or unwilling to raise taxes to meet high interest payments on a large national debt.

- Deficits are not necessarily bad. Particularly in a recession, a move to cut the deficit may lead output further away from potential output. But huge deficits can create a vicious circle of extra borrowing, extra interest payments and yet more borrowing.

- In an open economy, **exports** are a source of demand for domestic goods but **imports** are a leakage since they are a demand for goods made abroad.

- Exports are determined mainly by conditions abroad and can be viewed as autonomous demand unrelated to domestic income. Imports are assumed to rise with domestic income. The **marginal propensity to import** MPZ tells us the fraction of each extra pound of national income that goes on extra demand for imports.

- Leakages to imports reduce the value of the **multiplier** to $1/[1 - MPC' + MPZ]$.

- Higher export demand raises domestic output and income. A higher marginal propensity to import reduces domestic output and income.

- The **trade surplus**, exports minus imports, is larger the lower is output. Higher export demand raises the trade surplus, a higher marginal propensity to import reduces it.

- In equilibrium, desired leakages $S + NT + Z$ must equal desired injections $G + I + X$. Thus any surplus $S - I$ desired by the private sector must be offset by the sum of the government deficit $G - NT$ and the desired trade surplus $(X - Z)$.

Review questions

To check your answers to these questions, go to page 726.

1 Equilibrium output in a closed economy is 1000, consumption 800 and investment is 80. (a) Deduce G. (b) Investment rises by 50. The marginal propensity to consume out of national income is 0.8. What is the new equilibrium level of Y, C, I and G? (c) Suppose instead that G had risen by 50. What would be the new equilibrium of Y, C, I and G? (d) If potential output is 1200, to what must G rise to make output equal potential output?

2 The government spends £6 billion on rail track. The income tax rate is 0.25 and the MPC out of disposable income is 0.8. (a) What is the effect on equilibrium income and output? (b) Does the budget deficit rise or fall? Why?

3 In equilibrium, desired saving equals desired investment. True or false? Explain.

4 Why does the government raise taxes when it could borrow to cover its spending?

5 The EU's trade partners have a recession. (a) What happens to the EU's trade balance? (b) What happens to equilibrium EU output? Explain.

6 **Common fallacies** Why are these statements wrong? (a) The Chancellor raised taxes and spending by equal amounts. It will be a neutral budget for output. (b) Government policy should balance exports and imports but ensure that the government and private sector spend less than they earn.

7 **Harder question** Is the ratio of government debt to GDP a useful indicator of a government's indebtedness? When could it be misleading?

8 **Harder question** What values of the marginal propensity to save s, the marginal tax rate t and the marginal propensity to import z would be consistent with a multiplier as low as 0.67?

9 **Essay question** 'By 2007 the UK had had over 50 consecutive quarters of steady growth. This period coincides with the period in which it was decided to make the Bank of England responsible for macroeconomic stabilization. Because interest rates can be changed easily and quickly, whereas tax rates and spending programmes cannot, this example confirms the superiority of monetary policy over fiscal policy in demand management.' Is this broadly correct? Can you think of examples in which fiscal policy would still be crucial?

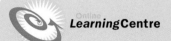

To help you grasp the key concepts of this chapter check out the extra resources posted on the Online Learning Centre. There are chapter summaries, self-test questions, an interactive graphing tool, weblinks and a searchable glossary, all for free!

To put your learning into practice and prepare for exams, an **Interactive Workbook** is also available online, containing a variety of question types and providing feedback on your answers.

If you'd like further help with economics, or have any questions, **NetTutor** is here to help! You will have a personalised tutorial service at your fingertips. Visit the online learning centre at: www.mcgraw-hill.co.uk/textbooks/begg for information on accessing all of these resources.

Money and banking

Money is a symbol of success, a source of crime, and it makes the world go around.

Dogs' teeth in the Admiralty Islands, sea shells in parts of Africa, gold in the nineteenth century: all are examples of money. What matters is not the commodity used but the social convention that it is accepted *without question* as a means of payment. We now explain how society uses money to economize on scarce resources used in the transacting process.

> **Money** is any generally accepted means of payment for delivery of goods or settlement of debt. It is the **medium of exchange**.

22.1 Money and its functions

Although the crucial feature of money is its acceptance as the means of payment or medium of exchange, money has three other functions. It serves as a unit of account, a store of value and a standard of deferred payment.

The medium of exchange

Money is used in almost half of all exchanges. Workers exchange labour services for money. People buy or sell goods for money. We accept money not to consume it directly but to use it subsequently to buy things we do wish to consume. Money is the medium through which people exchange goods and services.[1]

---

1 For an interesting account of cigarettes as money in prisoner-of-war camps, see R. A. Radford, 'The Economic Organisation of a POW Camp', *Economica*, 1945.

To see that society benefits from a medium of exchange, imagine a barter economy.

> A **barter economy** has no medium of exchange. Goods are swapped for other goods.

To see that society benefits from a medium of exchange, imagine a barter economy, in which the seller and the buyer *each* must want something the other has to offer. Each person is simultaneously a seller and a buyer. To see a film, you must swap a good or service that the cinema manager wants. There has to be a *double coincidence of wants*.

Trading is very expensive in a barter economy. People spend a lot of time and effort finding others with whom to make mutually satisfactory swaps. Since time and effort are scarce resources, a barter economy is wasteful. The use of money – any commodity *generally* accepted in payment for goods, services and debts – makes trading simpler and more efficient. By economizing on time and effort spent in trading, society can use these resources to produce extra goods or leisure, making everyone better off.

Other functions of money

In Britain prices are quoted in pounds sterling; in the United States in dollars. It is convenient to use the same units for the medium of exchange and unit of account. However, there are exceptions. During the German hyperinflation of 1922–23 when prices in marks changed very quickly, German shopkeepers found it more convenient to use dollars as the unit of account. Prices were quoted in dollars but payment was made in marks, the German medium of exchange. Similarly, during 2000–01 many EU shopkeepers quoted prices both in euros and in local currency, even though the euro did not become their medium of exchange until 2002.

> The **unit of account** is the unit in which prices are quoted and accounts kept.

To be accepted in exchange, money *has* to store value. Nobody will accept money in payment for goods supplied today if the money is worthless when they try to buy goods with it later. But money is not the only, nor necessarily the best, store of value. Houses, stamp collections and interest-bearing bank accounts all serve as stores of value. Since money pays no interest and its real purchasing power is eroded by inflation, there are better ways to store value.

> Money is a **store of value** because it can be used to make future purchases.

Finally, money is a *standard of deferred payment* or unit of account over time. When you borrow, the amount to be repaid next year is measured in pounds. This is not an essential function of money. UK citizens can get bank loans specifying in dollars the amount to be repaid next year. Thus the key feature of money is its use as a medium of exchange. For this, it must act as a store of value as well. And it is usually, though not invariably, convenient to make money the unit of account and standard of deferred payment as well.

Different kinds of money

In prisoner-of-war camps, cigarettes were money. In the nineteenth century money was mainly gold and silver coins. These are examples of *commodity money*, ordinary goods with industrial uses (gold) and consumption uses (cigarettes) which also serve as a medium of exchange. To use a commodity money, society must either cut back on other uses of that commodity or devote scarce resources to additional production of the commodity. There are cheaper ways for society to make money.

> A **token money** is a means of payment whose value or purchasing power as money greatly exceeds its cost of production or value in uses other than as money.

A £10 note is worth far more as money than as a 7.5 × 14 cm piece of high-quality paper. Similarly, the monetary value of most coins exceeds what you would get by melting them down and selling off the metal. By collectively agreeing to use token money, society economizes on the scarce resources required to produce a medium of exchange. Since the manufacturing cost is tiny, why doesn't everyone make £10 notes? The survival of token money requires a restriction on the right to supply it. Private production is illegal.[2]

Society enforces the use of token money by making it *legal tender*. By law, it must be accepted as a means of payment. However, when prices rise very quickly, domestic token money is a poor store of value and people are reluctant to accept it as a medium of exchange. Shops and firms give discounts to people paying in gold or in foreign currency.

In modern economies, token money is supplemented by IOU money.

A bank deposit is IOU money. It is a debt of the bank. When you have a bank deposit, the bank owes you money. The bank is obliged to pay when your cheque is presented. Bank deposits are a medium of exchange because they are generally accepted as payment.

> An **IOU money** is a medium of exchange based on the debt of a private firm or individual.

Box 22.1 Travellers' tales

The following contrast between a monetary and barter economy is taken from the World Bank, *World Development Report*, 1989.

Life without money

'Some years since, Mademoiselle Zelie, a singer, gave a concert in the Society Islands in exchange for a third part of the receipts. When counted, her share was found to consist of 3 pigs, 23 turkeys, 44 chickens, 5000 cocoa nuts, besides considerable quantities of bananas, lemons and oranges ... as Mademoiselle could not consume any considerable portion of the receipts herself it became necessary in the meantime to feed the pigs and poultry with the fruit.' W. S. Jevons (1898)

Marco Polo discovers paper money

'In this city of Kanbula [Beijing] is the mint of the Great Khan, who may truly be said to possess the secret of the alchemists, as he has the art of producing money. . . .

He causes the bark to be stripped from mulberry trees ... made into paper ... cut into pieces of money of different sizes. The act of counterfeiting is punished as a capital offence. This paper currency is circulated in every part of the Great Khan's domain. All his subjects receive it without hesitation because, wherever their business may call them, they can dispose of it again in the purchase of merchandise they may require.' *The Travels of Marco Polo*, Book II

22.2 Modern banking

When you deposit your coat in the theatre cloakroom, you do not expect the theatre to rent your coat out during the performance. Banks lend out some coats in their cloakroom. A theatre would have to get your particular coat back on time, which might be tricky. A bank finds it easier because one piece of money looks just like another.

> **Bank reserves** are the money available in the bank to meet possible withdrawals by depositors. The **reserve ratio** is the ratio of reserves to deposits.

Unlike other financial institutions, such as pension funds, the key aspect of banks is that some of their liabilities are used as the medium of exchange: cheques allow their deposits to be used as money.

---

2 The existence of forgers confirms society is economizing on scarce resources by producing money whose value as a medium of exchange exceeds its production cost.

At any time, some people are writing cheques on a Barclays account to pay for goods purchased from a shop that banks with Lloyds TSB; others are writing cheques on Lloyds TSB accounts to finance purchases from shops banking with Barclays. The *clearing system* is the process of interbank settlement of the net flows required between banks as a result. Thus the system of clearing cheques represents another way society reduces the costs of making transactions.[3]

> The **money supply** is the value of the stock of the medium of exchange in circulation.

Table 22.1 shows the balance sheet of UK commercial banks in 2006. The banks' assets were mainly loans to firms and households, and purchases of financial securities such as bills and bonds issued by governments and firms. Because many securities are very liquid, banks can lend short term and still get their money back in time if depositors withdraw their money.

In contrast, many loans to firms and households are quite illiquid. The bank cannot easily get its money back in a hurry. Modern banks get by with very few cash reserves in the vault. In Table 22.1 these are so small they are not even recorded separately.

> **Liquidity** is the cheapness, speed and certainty with which asset values can be converted back into money.

Liabilities of commercial banks include sight and time deposits.

Chequing accounts are sight deposits. Time deposits, which include some savings accounts, pay higher interest rates because banks have time to organize the sale of some of their high-interest assets in order to have the cash available to meet withdrawals. Certificates of deposit (CDs) are large 'wholesale' time deposits, a one-off deal with a particular client for a specified period, paying more generous interest rates. The other liabilities of banks are various 'money market instruments', short-term and highly liquid borrowing by banks.

> The money in **sight deposits** can be withdrawn 'on sight' without prior notice. **Time deposits**, paying higher interest rates, require the depositor to give notice before withdrawing money.

Table 22.1 Balance sheet of UK banking sector, August 2006

Assets	£bn	Liabilities	£bn
In foreign currency		*In foreign currency*	
Securities	546	Currency, deposits and money market instruments	2476
Loans	2096	Other liabilities	230
Other assets	39		
In sterling		*In sterling*	
Securities	186	Currency, deposits and money market instruments	1618
Loans	1693	Other liabilities	307
Other assets	71		
Total	4631	Total	4631

3 Society continues to find new ways to save scarce resources in producing and using a medium of exchange. Many people use credit cards. Some supermarket tills directly debit customers' bank accounts. And shopping by TV, telephone and the internet is growing rapidly.

The business of banking

A bank is a business making profits by lending and borrowing. To get money in, the bank offers attractive interest rates to depositors. UK banks increasingly offer interest on sight deposits and offer better interest rates on time deposits.

Banks have to find profitable ways to lend what has been borrowed. Table 22.1 shows how banks lent their money. In sterling, most is lent as advances of overdrafts to households and firms, usually at high interest rates. Some is used to buy securities such as long-term government bonds. Some is more prudently invested in liquid assets. Although these pay a lower interest rate, the bank can get its money back quickly if people withdraw a lot of money from their sight deposits. And some money is held as cash, the most liquid asset of all.

The bank uses its specialist expertise to acquire a diversified portfolio of investments. Without the existence of the bank, depositors would have neither the time nor the expertise to decide which of these loans or investments to make. UK banks hold reserves that are only 2 per cent of the sight deposits that could be withdrawn at any time. This shows the importance of the other liquid assets in which banks have invested. At very short notice, banks could cash in liquid assets easily and for a predictable amount. The skill in running a bank entails being able to judge how much must be held in liquid assets, including cash, and how much can be lent out in less liquid forms that earn higher interest rates.

> A **financial intermediary** specializes in bringing lenders and borrowers together. **Commercial banks** are financial intermediaries licensed to make loans and issue deposits, including deposits against which cheques can be written.

A commercial bank borrows money from the public, crediting them with a deposit. The deposit is a liability of the bank. It is money owed to depositors. In turn the bank lends money to firms, households or governments wishing to borrow.

Box 22.2 What is a bank?

The traditional image of a bank with long queues of account holders waiting in front of bullet proof glass to pay bills or withdraw cash has long changed. Supermarkets, including Tesco and Sainsbury's, now run banking operations. In addition, numerous insurance companies have opted to develop banking products for their customers and the age of the building society seems at an end with many having demutualized and become fully-fledged banks. At the limit, banks have also become virtual, with the likes of Intelligent Finance, Cahoot and First Direct offering telephone or online banking.

However, there are commonalities between the old traditional bank and the new financial service providers. Historically, individuals needed cash in their pocket and high street branches of national banks provided a means of collecting and distributing cash to customers. Supermarkets are equally adept at collecting and distributing cash at the checkout and have sought to develop this service with other financial products. But with the prevalence of debit cards, electronic bill payment and online banking, the collection, storage and distribution of cash becomes virtual, rather than real. Anyone with a bank of computer servers and a shed of telephone staff can operate a basic banking system.

Banks are not the only financial intermediaries. Insurance companies, pension funds and building societies also take in money in order to relend it. The crucial feature of banks is that some of their liabilities are used as a means of payment, and are thus part of the money stock.[4]

22.3 How banks create money

To simplify the arithmetic, assume banks use a reserve ratio of 10 per cent. Suppose, initially, the non-bank private sector has wealth of £1000 held in cash. This cash is a private sector asset. It is a liability of the government, who issued it, but not a liability of the private banks. The first row of Table 22.2 shows this cash as an asset of the non-bank private sector.

Table 22.2 Money creation by the banking system

| | Banks | | Non-bank private sector | |
	Assets	Liabilities	Monetary assets	Liabilities
Initial	Cash 0 Loans 0	Deposits 0	Cash 1000	Loans from banks 0
Intermediate	Cash 1000	Deposits 1000	Cash 0 Deposits 1000	Loans from banks 0
Final	Cash 1000 Loans 9000	Deposits 10 000	Cash 0 Deposits 10 000	Loans from banks 9000

Now people pay this £1000 of cash into the banks by opening bank deposits. Banks have assets of £1000 cash, and liabilities of £1000 of deposits, money owed to depositors. If banks were like cloakrooms, that would be the end of the story. Table 22.2 would end in row two.

However, banks do not need all deposits to be fully covered by cash reserves. Suppose banks create £9000 of overdrafts. This is a simultaneous loan of £9000, an asset in banks' balance sheets and the granting to customers of £9000 of deposits, against which customers can write cheques. The deposits of £9000 are a liability on banks' balance sheets. Now the banks have £10 000 total deposits – the original £1000 when cash was paid in, plus the new £9000 as counterpart to the overdraft – and £10 000 of total assets, comprising £9000 in loans and £1000 cash in the vaults. The reserve ratio is still 10 per cent in row three of Table 22.2.

It does not even matter whether the 10 per cent reserve ratio is imposed by law or is merely profit-maximizing smart behaviour by banks that balance risk and reward. The risk is the possibility of being caught short of cash, the reward is the interest rate spread.

> The **interest rate spread** is the excess of the loan interest rate over the deposit interest rate.

How did banks create money? Originally, there was £1000 of cash in circulation. That was the money supply. When paid into bank vaults, it went out of general circulation as the medium of exchange. But the public acquired £1000 of bank deposits against which cheques may be written. The money supply was still £1000. Then banks created overdrafts *not* fully backed by cash reserves. Now the public had £10 000 of deposits against which to write cheques. The money supply rose from £1000 to £10 000. Banks created money.

4 In fact, building societies now issue cheque books to their depositors. Although official UK statistics do not classify building societies as banks, this example illustrates the practical difficulty in deciding which intermediaries are banks and which of their deposits in practice are accepted as a medium of exchange. Many building societies are now changing their legal status to that of banks. The data of Table 22.1 include both banks and building societies.

Financial panics

Everybody knows what the banks are doing. Usually, people do not mind. But if people believe that a bank has lent too much and will be unable to meet depositors' claims, there will be a *run* on the bank. If the bank cannot repay all depositors, you try to get your money out first while the bank can still pay. Since everyone does the same thing, they ensure that the bank is unable to pay. Some of its loans will be too illiquid to get back in time.

> A **financial panic** is a self-fulfilling prophecy. Believing a bank will be unable to pay, people rush to get their money out. But this makes the bank go bankrupt.

Today, financial panics are rare. A key reason for this, which we discuss in the next chapter, is that the Bank of England will lend to banks in temporary difficulties. Since this is known, it helps prevent a self-fulfilling stampede to withdraw deposits before a bank cannot pay.

Activity box 22 A beginner's guide to financial markets

Financial asset   A piece of paper entitling the owner to a specified stream of interest payments for a specified period. Firms and governments raise money by selling financial assets. Buyers work out how much to bid for them by calculating the present value of the promised stream of payments. Assets are frequently retraded before the date at which the original issuer is committed to repurchase the piece of paper for a specified price.

Cash   Notes and coin, paying zero interest. The most liquid asset.

Bills   Short-term financial assets paying no interest directly but with a known date of repurchase by the original borrower at a known price. Consider a three-month Treasury bill. In April the government sells a piece of paper, promising to repurchase it for £100 in July. If people bid £98.5 in April they will make 1.5 per cent in three months by holding the bill to July, when it is worth £100. As July gets nearer, the price at which the bill is retraded climbs towards £100. Buying it from someone else in June for £99.5 and reselling to the government in July for £100 still yields 0.5 per cent in a month, or over 6 per cent a year at compound interest. Treasury bills are easily bought and sold. Their price can only fluctuate over a small range (say, between £98 and £99 in May when they expire in July), so they are highly liquid. People can get their money out easily, cheaply and predictably.

Bonds   Longer-term financial assets. Look under UK Gilts in the *Financial Times*. You will find a bond listed as 'Treasury 8pc 13'. In the year 2013 the government will buy back this bond for £100 (the usual repurchase price). Until then, the bondholder gets interest payments of £8 a year (8 per cent of the repurchase price). Bonds are less liquid than bills, not because they are hard to sell, but because the price for which they could be sold, and the cash this will generate, is less certain. To see why, we study the most extreme kind of bond.

Perpetuities   Bonds never repurchased by the original issuer, who pays interest for ever. Called Consols (consolidated stock) in the UK. Consols 2.5% pay £2.5 a year for ever. Most were issued when interest rates were low. People originally would have bid around £100 for this Consol. Suppose interest rates on other assets rise to 10 per cent. Consols are retraded between people at around £25 each so that new purchasers of these old bonds get about 10 per cent on their financial investment. The person holding a bond makes a capital loss when other interest rates rise and the price of the bond falls. Moreover, since the price of

Activity box 22 A beginner's guide to financial markets (Continued)

Consols, once £100, could fall to £25 if interest rates rise a lot, Consol prices are much more volatile than the price of Treasury bills. The longer the remaining life of a bond, the more its current price can move around as existing bondholders try to sell on to new buyers at a rate of return in line with other assets today. Bonds can easily be bought and sold, but are not very liquid. You do not know how much you would get if you had to sell out in six months' time.

Gilt-edged securities   Government bonds in the UK. Gilt-edged because the government will not go bust and refuse to pay interest.

Company shares (equities)   Entitlements to dividends, the part of firms' profits paid out to shareholders rather than retained to buy new machinery and buildings. In good years, dividends are high; in bad years dividends may be zero. Hence a risky asset that is not very liquid. Share prices are volatile. Firms could even go bust, making the shares worthless.

Questions

(a)   If cash pays no interest, why does anyone hold it?

(b)   Since firms could use bills and bonds to raise finance, what advantages do they see in raising money through issuing equities?

(c)   If it is good for firms to issue equities, can it simultaneously be good for investors?

To check your answers to these questions, go to page 727.

22.4 The monetary base and the money multiplier

Cash reserves of commercial banks are a small fraction of total bank deposits. Bank-created deposit money is much the largest part of the money supply in modern economies. You have now mastered the basics, but we now tie up some loose ends. Banks' deposits depend on the cash reserves of the banks. To complete our analysis of how the money supply is determined, we need to examine what determines the amount of cash deposited with the banking system.

Through the *central bank*, the Bank of England in the UK, the government controls the issue of token money in a modern economy. Private creation of token money must be outlawed when its value as a medium of exchange exceeds the direct cost of its production.

How much of the monetary base is held by commercial banks as cash reserves? In the previous section, we assumed that the public deposited all its cash with the banks. This was only a simplification. Everyone carries some cash around. We do not write a cheque for a bus fare. It would take too long.

The **monetary base** or stock of **high-powered money** is the quantity of notes and coins in private circulation plus the quantity held by the banking system.

There are other reasons why people hold cash. Some people do not trust banks. They keep their savings under the bed. Remarkably, only three-quarters of British households have chequing accounts. Some people hold cash in order to make illegal or tax-evading transactions in the 'black economy'.

How is the money supply related to the monetary base, the amount of notes and coin issued by the central bank? The answer to this question is the money multiplier.

> The **money multiplier** is the ratio of the money stock to the monetary base.

$$\text{Money stock} = \text{money multiplier} \times \text{monetary base} \qquad (1)$$

The value of the money multiplier depends on two key ratios: the banks' desired ratio of cash reserves to total deposits, and the non-bank public's desired ratio of cash in circulation to total bank deposits.

Banks' ratio of cash reserves to total deposits determines how much they multiply up any given cash reserves into deposit money. The *lower* the desired cash reserves ratio, the more deposits banks create against given cash reserves and the *larger* is the money supply.

Similarly, the *lower* the non-bank public's desired ratio of cash to private sector bank accounts, the *larger* is the money supply for any monetary base created by the central bank. Since more of the monetary base is deposited in banks, banks can create more bank deposits.

We give an exact formula for the money multiplier in Box 22.4. UK banks hold cash reserves equal to 1 per cent of their total deposits, and the private sector holds cash in circulation equal to 3 per cent of the value of sight deposits. The formula implies a money multiplier of 27. Each £100 rise in the monetary base increases the money supply by £2700.

Box 22.3 The money multiplier

Suppose banks wish to hold cash reserves R equal to some fraction c_b of deposits D, and that the private sector holds cash in circulation C equal to a fraction c_p of deposits D.

$$R = c_b D \quad C = c_p D$$

The monetary base, or stock of high-powered money, H, is either in circulation or in bank vaults.

$$H = C + R = (c_p + c_b)D$$

Finally, the money supply is circulating currency C plus deposits D.

$$M = C + D = (c_p + 1)D$$

These last two equations give us the money multiplier, the ratio of M to H.

$$M/H = (c_p + 1)/(c_p + c_b) > 1$$

Using the data of Table 22.3 on p. 442 below, c_p is $[45.3/1216.7] = 0.0372$, c_b is $[0.6/1216.7] = 0.0013$, and the money multiplier is

$$M/H = (1.0372)/(0.0385) = 27$$

which of course is simply 1260/45.9, the ratio of M4 to M0 in Table 22.3.

At present, it is more important to remember that a fall in either the banks' desired cash reserves ratio or the private sector's desired ratio of cash to bank deposits raises the money multiplier. For a given monetary base, the money supply rises.

What determines the cash reserve ratio desired by banks? The higher the interest rate spread, the more banks wish to lend and the more they risk a low ratio of cash reserves to deposits. Conversely, the more unpredictable are withdrawals from deposits, or the fewer lending opportunities banks have in very liquid loans, the higher cash reserves they have to maintain for any level of deposits.

The public's desired ratio of cash to deposits partly reflects institutional factors, for example whether firms pay wages by cheque or cash. It also depends on the incentive to hold cash to make untraceable payments to evade taxes. And credit cards reduce the use of cash. Credit cards are a temporary means of payment, a *money substitute* not money itself.

A signed credit card slip cannot be used for *further* purchases. Soon, you have to settle your account using money. Nevertheless, since credit cards allow people to carry less cash in their pocket, their increasing use reduces the desired ratio of cash to bank deposits.

Figure 22.1 summarizes our discussion of the monetary base and the money supply. The monetary base, or stock of high-powered money, is held either as cash reserves by the banks or as cash in circulation. Since bank deposits are a multiple of banks' cash reserves, the money multiplier exceeds unity. The money multiplier is larger (a) the lower the non-bank public's desired ratio of cash to bank deposits, giving the banks more cash with which to create a multiplied deposit expansion, and (b) the lower is the banks' desired ratio of cash to deposits, leading them to create more deposits for any given cash reserves.

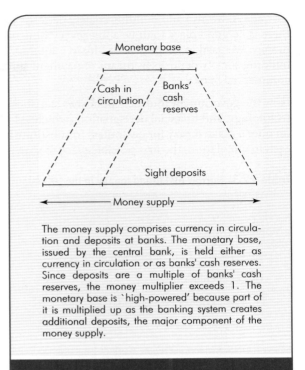

The money supply comprises currency in circulation and deposits at banks. The monetary base, issued by the central bank, is held either as currency in circulation or as banks' cash reserves. Since deposits are a multiple of banks' cash reserves, the money multiplier exceeds 1. The monetary base is `high-powered' because part of it is multiplied up as the banking system creates additional deposits, the major component of the money supply.

Figure 22.1 Money supply determination

22.5 Measures of money

Money is the medium of exchange available to make transactions. Hence, the money supply is cash in circulation outside banks, plus bank deposits. It sounds simple, but it is not. Two issues arise: which bank deposits, and why only bank deposits?

We can think of a spectrum of liquidity. Cash, by definition, is completely liquid. Sight deposits (chequing accounts) are almost as liquid. Time deposits (savings accounts) used to be less liquid, but now many banks offer automatic transfer between savings and chequing accounts when the latter run low. Savings deposits are almost as liquid as chequing accounts.

UK statistics distinguish *retail* and *wholesale* deposits. Retail deposits are made in high street branches at the advertised rate of interest. Wholesale deposits, big one-off deals between a corporate depositor and a bank at a negotiated interest rate, are also quite liquid.

Everyone used to be clear what a bank was, and hence whose deposits counted towards the money supply. Financial deregulation blurred this distinction in the UK and the USA, and is now doing so in continental Europe. Before 1980, UK banks did not lend for house purchase, and cheques on building society deposits could not be used at the supermarket checkout. Now 'banks' compete vigorously for mortgages, supermarket chains are in the banking business and building society cheques are widely accepted as a means of payment. There is no longer a reason to exclude building society deposits from measures of the money supply.

M0 is the wide monetary base: cash in circulation outside the banks, cash inside banks and the banks' own accounts at the Bank of England. M0 is the narrowest measure of money. Wider measures begin from cash in circulation. Adding all sight deposits, we get M1, which used to be considered a good measure of narrow money. Augmenting that by UK private sector time deposits and CDs gives M3, which used to be considered the best definition of broad money.

Nowadays, we also add building society deposits to get M4. Since there is a spectrum of liquidity, there is no good place to draw a line, everything narrower being money, everything wider not being money. We used to keep track of M0, M1 and M3. This approach was made obsolete by the use of building society deposits as means of payment, and by the conversion of many building societies to commercial banks.

Now the government routinely publishes statistics only for cash in circulation and M4. Advances in technology, and financial deregulation (which led to greater competition and more financial products on offer), make it easy for customers to substitute between 'broad' and 'narrow' money. Once we leave cash in circulation, the first sensible place to stop is M4. Table 22.3 gives actual data for 2005.

Table 22.3 Narrow and broad money in the UK, August 2005

	£ billion
Monetary base M0	45.9
− cash reserves of banks and building societies	0.6
= cash in circulation	45.3
+ deposits in banks and building societies	1216.7
= Money supply M4	1262.0

Sources: ONS, *Economic Trends*; Bank of England.

The reforms of 2006

London remains a pioneer of financial innovation. Financial regulation has to keep up. In April 2006 the Bank of England decided to change the system of bank reserves. Henceforth, banks and building societies will keep reserves at the Bank of England and choose a target level of reserves that they wish to hold. If they keep reserves close to the chosen target, the Bank of England will pay interest on these reserves to banks and building societies. Deviations from target will incur penalties.

Hence, in some circumstances the banking system will happily hold large amounts of interest-bearing reserves, which are now more like other assets in their portfolios. It no longer makes sense to publish statistics for M0 that combine non-interest-bearing cash held by the public and interest-bearing reserves held by the banks and building societies. Since 2006, UK monetary statistics refer only to cash in circulation outside the banking system (the part we hold on which we get zero interest), and to a wider M4 measure that also includes all deposits.

22.6 Competition between banks

Financial deregulation, allowing the entry of more and more banks, has made modern banking very competitive. Banks compete with one another both in the interest rates they offer to attract deposits and in the interest rates they charge borrowers for loans.

The interest rate spread between the lending rate and the rate paid on deposits is what covers the cost of providing banking services. When spreads exceed this amount, banks make profits. Profits are a signal for new banks to enter, which competes away spreads. With more competition, interest rates on loans fall and rates paid on deposits rise.

Equilibrium in the banking industry occurs when it is not worth attracting more deposits in order to make more loans. The marginal cost of funds, the deposit interest rate, plus the marginal cost of

CHAPTER TWENTY-TWO Money and banking

doing banking business, plus any equilibrium profit margin, just equals the marginal revenue earned on making new bank loans (inclusive of any allowance for possible non-repayment). Under perfect competition, all supernormal profits are competed away by free entry.

Although regulated less than before, banking regulation has not completely disappeared, and new banks are carefully licensed. Moreover, there are big scale economies in banking. For both reasons, competition is imperfect and equilibrium profit margins in banking are usually positive. Nevertheless, once we know the exact market structure, we have a good idea of how interest rates on deposits and loans are related. Other things equal, further deregulation of banks will reduce interest rate spreads yet more.

22.7 The demand for money

The quantity of money M4 in the UK was 76 times higher in 2006 than in 1965. Why did UK residents hold so much extra money? We focus on three variables that affect money demand: interest rates, the price level and real income.

Motives for holding money

Money is a stock. It is the quantity of circulating currency and deposits *held* at any given time. Holding money is not the same as *spending* it. We hold money now to spend it later.

Money is the medium of exchange, for which it must also be a store of value. These two functions of money provide the reasons why people wish to hold it. People can hold their wealth in various forms – money, bills, bonds, equities and property. For simplicity, assume that there are only two assets: money, the medium of exchange that pays no interest, and bonds, which we use to stand for all other interest-bearing assets that are not directly a means of payment. As people earn income, they add to their wealth. As they spend, they deplete their wealth. How should people divide their wealth at any instant between money and bonds?

> The **cost of holding money** is the interest given up by holding money rather than bonds.

People hold money only if there is a benefit to offset this cost. What is that benefit?

The transactions motive

Transacting by barter is costly in time and effort. Holding money economizes on these costs. If all transactions were perfectly synchronized, we could be paid at the same instant we did our spending. Except at that instant, we need hold no money at all.

> The **transactions motive** for holding money reflects the fact that payments and receipts are *not* synchronized.

Must we hold money between being paid and making subsequent purchases? We could put our income into interest-earning assets, to be resold later when we need money for purchases. However, every time we buy and sell assets there are brokerage and bank charges. And it takes an eagle eye to keep track of cash flow and judge the precise moment at which money is needed and assets must be sold. If small sums are involved, the extra interest does not compensate for the brokerage fees, and the time and effort. It is easier to hold some money.

How much money we need to hold depends on the value of the transactions we later wish to make and the degree of synchronization of our payments and receipts. Money is a nominal variable not a real variable. How much £100 buys depends on the price of goods. If all prices double, our receipts and our payments double in nominal terms. To transact as before we need to hold twice as much money.

> The **demand for money** is a demand for *real* money balances.

We need a given amount of real money, nominal money deflated by the price level, to make a given quantity of transactions. When the price level doubles, other things equal, the demand for nominal money balances doubles, leaving the demand for real money balances unaltered. People want money because of its purchasing power in terms of the goods it will buy.

Real GNP is a good proxy for the total real value of transactions. Thus we assume that the transactions motive for holding real money balances rises with real income.

The transactions motive for holding money also depends on the synchronization of payments and receipts. Suppose, instead of shopping throughout the week, households shop only on the day they get paid. Over the week, national income and total transactions are unaltered, but people now *hold less money over the week.*[5]

A nation's habits for making payments change only slowly. In our simplified model we assume that the degree of synchronization is constant over time. Thus we focus on real income as *the* measure of the transactions motive for holding *real* money balances.

The precautionary motive

We live in an uncertain world. Uncertainty about the timing of receipts and payments creates a precautionary motive for holding money.

Suppose you buy a lot of interest-earning bonds and get by with a small amount of money. Walking down the street you see a great bargain in a shop window, but have too little money to close the deal. By the time you cash in some bonds, the bargain is gone, snapped up by someone with ready money.

How can we measure the benefits from holding money for precautionary reasons? The payoff grows with the volume of transactions we undertake and with the degree of uncertainty. If uncertainty is roughly constant over time, the level of transactions determines the benefit of real money held for precautionary reasons. As with the transactions motive, we use real GNP to proxy the level of transactions. Thus, other things equal, the higher is real income, the stronger is the precautionary motive for holding money.

> In an uncertain world, there is a **precautionary motive** to hold money. In advance, we decide to hold money to meet contingencies that we cannot yet foresee.

The transactions and precautionary motives are the main reasons to hold the medium of exchange, and are most relevant to the benefits from holding a narrow measure of money. The wider measure, M4, includes higher-interest-earning deposits. The wider the definition of money, the less important are the transactions and precautionary motives that relate to money as a medium of exchange, and the more we must take account of money as a store of value.

The asset motive

Forget the need to transact. Think of someone deciding in which assets to hold wealth. At some distant date wealth may be spent. In the short run the aim is a good but safe rate of return.

Some assets, such as company shares, on average pay a high return but are risky. Some years their return is *very* high, in other years it is negative. When share prices fall, shareholders make a capital loss that swamps the dividends they receive. Other assets are less risky, but their average rate of return is correspondingly lower.

How should people divide their portfolios between safe and risky assets? You might like to reread Chapter 13. Since people dislike risk, they will not put all their eggs in one basket. As well as holding some risky assets, they will keep some of their wealth in safe assets.

> The **asset motive** for holding money reflects dislike of risk. People sacrifice a high average rate of return to obtain a portfolio with a lower but safer rate of return.

The asset motive for holding money is important when we consider why people hold broad measures of money such as M4.

5 By allowing us to pay all at once when the statement arrives monthly, credit cards have this effect.

The demand for money: prices, real income and interest rates

The transactions, precautionary and asset motives suggest that there are benefits to holding money. But there is also a cost, the interest forgone by not holding high-interest-earning assets instead. People hold money up to the point at which the marginal benefit of holding another pound just equals its marginal cost. Figure 22.2 illustrates how much money people want to hold.

People want money for its purchasing power over goods. The horizontal axis plots real money holdings, nominal money in current pounds divided by the average price of goods and services. The horizontal line *MC* is the marginal cost of holding money, the interest forgone by not holding bonds. *MC* shifts up if interest rates rise.

The *MB* schedule is the marginal benefit of holding money. We draw *MB* for a given real GNP measuring the transactions undertaken. For this level of transactions, it is possible but difficult to get by with low real money holdings. We have to watch purchases and receipts and be quick to invest money as it comes in and ready to sell off bonds just before we make a purchase. Nor do we have much precautionary money. We may be frustrated or inconvenienced if, unexpectedly, we want to make a purchase or settle a debt.

With low real money holdings, the marginal benefit of another pound is high. We can put less effort into timing our transfers between money and bonds, and we have more money for unforeseen contingencies. For a given real income and level of transactions, the marginal benefit of the last pound of money holdings declines as we hold more real money. With more real money, we have plenty both for precautionary purposes and for transactions purposes. Life is easier. The marginal benefit of yet more money holding is low.

Given our real income and transactions, desired money holdings are at *E* in Figure 22.2. For any level of real money below *L*, the marginal benefit of another pound exceeds its marginal cost in interest forgone. We should hold more money. Above *L*, the marginal cost exceeds the marginal benefit and we should hold less. The optimal level of money holding is *L*.

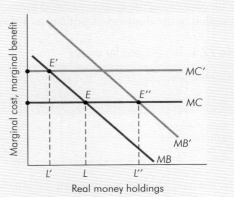

The horizontal axis shows the purchasing power of money in terms of goods. The MC schedule shows the interest sacrificed by putting the last pound into money rather than bonds. The MB schedule is drawn for a given real income and shows the marginal benefits of the last pound of money. The marginal benefit falls as money holdings increase. The desired point is E, at which marginal cost and marginal benefit are equal. An increase in interest rates, a rise in the opportunity cost schedule from MC to MC', reduces desired money holdings from L to L'. An increase in real income increases the marginal benefit of adding to real balances. The MB schedule shifts up to MB'. Facing the schedule MC, a shift from MB to MB' increases real money holdings to L''.

Figure 22.2 Desired money holdings

To emphasize the effect of prices, real income and interest rates on the quantity of money demanded, we now change each of these variables in turn. If all prices of goods and services double but interest rates and real income are unaltered, neither *MC* nor *MB* shift. The desired point remains *E* and the desired level of *real* money remains *L*. Since prices have doubled, people hold twice as much nominal money to preserve their real money balances at *L*.

If interest rates on bonds rise, the cost of holding money rises. Figure 22.2 shows this upward shift from *MC* to *MC'*. The desired point is now *E'* and the desired real money holding falls from *L* to *L'*. Higher interest rates reduce the quantity of real money demanded.[6]

6 The cost of holding money is the differential return between bonds and money. If π is the inflation rate and r the nominal interest rate, the real interest rate is $r - \pi$. In financial terms, the real return on money is $-\pi$, the rate at which the purchasing power of money is eroded by inflation. The differential real return between bonds and money is $(r - \pi) - (-\pi) = r$. The *nominal* interest rate is the opportunity cost of holding money.

Finally, consider a rise in real income. At each level of real money holdings, the marginal benefit of the last pound is higher than before. With more transactions to undertake and a greater need for precautionary balances, a given quantity of real money does not make life as easy as it did when transactions and real income were lower. The benefit of a bit more money is now greater. Hence we show the MB schedule shifting up to MB' when real income rises.

At the original interest rate and MC schedule, the desired level of money balances is L_0. Thus a rise in real income raises the quantity of real money balances demanded. Table 22.4 summarizes our discussion of the demand for money as a medium of exchange.

Table 22.4 The demand for money

Quantity demanded	Effect of rise in		
	Price level	Real income	Interest rate
Nominal money	Rises in proportion	Rises	Falls
Real money	Unaffected	Rises	Falls

So far we have studied the demand for M0, the narrowest measure of money. Wider definitions of money must also recognize the asset motive for holding money. To explain the demand for M4, we interpret MC as the average extra return by putting the last pound into risky assets rather than time deposits, which are safe but yield a lower return. For a given wealth, MB is the marginal benefit of time deposits in reducing the risk of the portfolio. If no wealth is invested in time deposits, the portfolio is very risky. A bad year is a disaster. There is a big benefit in having some time deposits. As the quantity of time deposits increases, the danger of a disaster recedes and the marginal benefit of more time deposits falls.

A rise in the average interest differential between risky assets and time deposits shifts the cost of holding broad money from MC to MC', reducing the quantity of broad money demanded. Higher wealth shifts the marginal benefit from MB to MB'. More time deposits are demanded.

Explaining the rise in money holdings from 1965 to 2006

Why were nominal money holdings 76 times higher in 2006 than in 1965? We have identified three explanations: prices, real income and nominal interest rates. Table 22.5 shows how these variables changed over the period.

Table 22.5 Holdings of M4, 1965–2006

	1965	2006
Index of		
Nominal M4	100	7600
Real M4	100	600
Real GDP	100	290
Interest rate (%)	6	5

Source: ONS, Economic Trends.

Although nominal money holdings rose 76-fold, the price level also rose a lot between 1965 and 2006. Table 22.5 shows real money rising 6-fold over the period. Real GDP was almost three times its initial level. Higher real output and income raise the quantity of real money demanded. As it happens, nominal interest rates hardly changed. But why did real money demand rise much more than real GDP?

A big rise in competition forced banks to pay higher interest rates on *deposits*, thus *reducing* the cost of holding broad money, most of which is now interest-bearing deposits. The cost of holding such a deposit is the small spread between the deposit rate and the interest rate you could earn on bonds. This cost of holding money is now much smaller than the 5 per cent shown in Table 22.5 (which implicitly assumes money earns zero interest). A lower cost of holding money made people hold more real money.

Summary

- **Money** has four functions: a **medium of exchange** or means of payment, a **store of value**, a **unit of account** and a **standard of deferred payment**. Its use as a medium of exchange distinguishes money from other assets.

- In a **barter economy**, trading is costly because there must be a double coincidence of wants. Using a medium of exchange reduces the costs of matching buyers and sellers, letting society devote scarce resources to other things. A **token money** has a higher value as a medium of exchange than in any other use. Because its monetary value greatly exceeds its production cost, token money economizes a lot on the resources needed for transacting.

- Token money is accepted either because people believe it can subsequently be used to make payments or because the government makes it legal tender. The government controls the supply of token money.

- **Banks create money** by making loans and creating deposits that are not fully backed by cash reserves. These deposits add to the medium of exchange. Deciding how many reserves to hold involves a trade-off between interest earnings and the danger of insolvency.

- Modern banks attract deposits by acting as **financial intermediaries**. A national system of clearing cheques, a convenient form of payment, attracts funds into sight deposits. Interest-bearing time deposits attract further funds. In turn, banks lend out money as short-term liquid loans, as longer-term less liquid advances, or by purchasing securities.

- Sophisticated financial markets for short-term liquid lending allow modern banks to operate with very low cash reserves relative to deposits. The **money supply** is currency in circulation plus deposits. Most is the latter.

- The **monetary base M0** is currency in circulation plus banks' cash reserves. The **money multiplier**, the ratio of the money supply to the monetary base, is big. The money multiplier is larger (a) the smaller is the desired cash ratio of the banks and (b) the smaller is the private sector's desired ratio of cash in circulation to deposits.

- **Financial deregulation** has allowed building societies into the banking business. **M4** is a broad measure of money and includes deposits at both banks and building societies.

- The **demand for money** is a demand for real money, for its subsequent purchasing power over goods. The demand for **narrow money** balances the transactions and precautionary benefits of holding another pound with the interest sacrificed by not holding interest-bearing assets instead. The quantity of real money demanded falls as the interest rate rises. Higher real income raises real money demand at each interest rate.

- For **wide money** such as M4, the asset motive for holding money also matters. When other interest-bearing assets are risky, people diversify by holding some safe money. With no immediate need to transact, this leads to an asset demand for holding interest-bearing bank deposits. This demand is larger the larger the total wealth to be invested and the lower the interest differential between deposits and risky assets.

Review questions

To check your answers to these questions, go to page 727.

1 (a) A person trades in a car when buying another. Is the used car a medium of exchange? Is this a barter transaction? (b) Could you tell by watching someone buying mints (white discs) with coins (bronze discs) which one is money?

2 Initially gold coins were used as money but people could melt them down and use the gold for industrial purposes. (a) What must have been the relative value of gold in these two uses? (b) Explain the circumstances in which gold could become a token money. (c) Explain the circumstances in which gold could disappear from monetary circulation completely.

3 How do commercial banks create money?

4 (a) Would it make sense to include (a) travellers' cheques, (b) student rail cards or (c) credit cards in measures of the money supply?

5 Sight deposits = 30, time deposits = 60, banks' cash reserves = 2, currency in circulation = 12, building society deposits = 20. Calculate M0 and M4.

6 **Common fallacies** Why are these statements wrong? (a) Since their liabilities equal their assets, banks cannot create anything. (b) The money supply has risen because of tax evasion. Since cash is untraceable, people are putting less in the banks.

7 **Harder question** Suppose banks raise interest rates on time deposits whenever interest rates on bank loans and other assets rise. Does a rise in the general level of interest rates have a big or small effect on the demand for time deposits?

8 **Harder question** Since credit cards can be used to make payments, why are they not treated as money?

9 **Essay question** Lots of institutions accept deposits and reissue them on demand – building societies, Christmas savings clubs and theatre cloakrooms. What is the key feature of banks that distinguishes them from other institutions? Why does this matter?

 *Online* *Learning Centre*

To help you grasp the key concepts of this chapter check out the extra resources posted on the Online Learning Centre. There are chapter summaries, self-test questions, an interactive graphing tool, weblinks and a searchable glossary, all for free!

To put your learning into practice and prepare for exams, an **Interactive Workbook** is also available online, containing a variety of question types and providing feedback on your answers.

If you'd like further help with economics, or have any questions, **NetTutor** is here to help! You will have a personalised tutorial service at your fingertips. Visit the online learning centre at: www.mcgraw-hill.co.uk/textbooks/begg for information on accessing all of these resources.

CHAPTER 23

Interest rates and monetary transmission

Learning Outcomes

By the end of this chapter, you should understand:

1 how a central bank can affect the money supply

2 the central bank's role as lender of last resort

3 money market equilibrium

4 an intermediate target for monetary policy

5 the transmission mechanism of monetary policy

6 how a central bank sets interest rates

7 how interest rates affect consumption and investment demand

Today every country of any size has a central bank. Originally private firms in business for profit, central banks came under public control as governments placed more emphasis on monetary policy. Founded in 1694, the Bank of England (www.bankofengland.co.uk) was not nationalized until 1947. The Federal Reserve System, the US central bank, was not set up until 1913.

This chapter examines the role of the central bank, and shows how it influences financial markets. The central bank influences the supply of money. Combining this with the demand for money, examined in the last chapter, we analyse money market equilibrium. The central bank's monopoly on the supply of cash allows it to control equilibrium interest rates. Finally, we discuss how monetary policy decides what interest rates to set.

A **central bank** is banker to the government and to the banks. It also conducts monetary policy.

23.1 The Bank of England

The Bank of England, usually known simply as the Bank, is the UK central bank. It is divided into Issue and Banking Departments. Their balance sheets are shown in Table 23.1.

Banknotes are liabilities of the Bank. To introduce notes into circulation, the Issue Department engages in open market operations (OMO) to buy financial securities issued by the government, commercial firms or local authorities. These are assets of the Issue Department.

The Banking Department is banker to the commercial banks and to the government. Advances are loans made to government or banks. Bank reserves are deposits by government and commercial banks. Other assets include buildings, equipment and securities issued by private firms.

Table 23.1 Bank of England, balance sheet, January 2007

Assets	£bn	Liabilities	£bn
Short-term OMO	36	Notes in circulation	41
Longer-term OMO	15		
Advances to government	13	Bank reserves	23
Other assets	21	Other liabilities	21
Total Assets	85	Total Liabilities	85

Source: Bank of England.

Table 23.1 resembles the balance sheet of a commercial bank, with one key difference. *A central bank cannot go bankrupt.* You take £50 to the Bank and cash it in for £50. The Bank gives you £50 in cash. It can always create new cash.

23.2 The Bank and the money supply

The money supply M4 is partly a liability of the Bank (currency in private circulation) and partly a liability of banks (bank deposits). Henceforth we talk of 'banks', without distinguishing banks and building societies.

The central bank can therefore affect broad money M4 either by affecting the cash in circulation or by affecting the number of deposits for any given amount of cash in circulation. We begin with policies that affect the latter.

> The **money supply** is currency in circulation *outside* the banking system, plus deposits of commercial banks and building societies.

Reserve requirements

Banks can hold more than the required cash reserves but not less. If their reserves fall below the required amount, they must immediately borrow cash, usually from the central bank, to restore their required reserve ratio.

> A **required reserve ratio** is a minimum ratio of cash reserves to deposits that banks are required to hold.

Suppose banks have £1 billion in cash and, for commercial purposes, want cash reserves equal to 5 per cent of deposits. Deposits are 20 times cash reserves. Banks create £20 billion of deposits against its £1 billion cash reserves. However, if there is a reserve requirement of 10 per cent, banks only create £10 billion deposits against cash reserves of £1 billion. The money supply falls from £20 billion to £10 billion.

When the central bank imposes a higher reserve requirement than the reserve ratio that prudent banks would anyway have maintained, the effect is fewer bank deposits and a lower money supply for any amount of cash in circulation. Raising the reserve requirement reduces the money supply.

The discount rate

Suppose banks think the *minimum* safe ratio of cash to deposits is 10 per cent. It does not matter whether this figure is a commercial judgement or a requirement imposed by the Bank. Banks may also hold extra cash. If their cash reserves are 12 per cent of deposits, how far dare they let their cash fall towards the 10 per cent minimum?

> The **discount rate** is the interest rate that the Bank charges when banks want to borrow cash.

Banks balance the interest rate on extra lending against the cost incurred if withdrawals push their cash reserves below the critical 10 per cent. If the central bank lend to banks at market interest rates, there is no penalty in being caught short and having to borrow from the central bank. Banks lend as much as they can and their cash reserves fall to the minimum required.

Suppose the Bank only lends to banks at an interest rate above market interest rates. Now commercial banks will not drive down their reserves to the minimum permitted. They hold extra cash as a cushion, to avoid possibly having to borrow from the central bank at penalty rates.

By setting the discount rate above general interest rates, the Bank can induce banks voluntarily to hold extra cash reserves. Bank deposits are a lower multiple of banks' cash reserves, and the money supply is lower for any given level of cash in circulation. Variations in the discount rate can change the money supply.

Open market operations

Whereas the previous two methods of monetary control alter the amount of deposits created for any given amount of cash in circulation, open market operations alter the amount of cash in circulation. Since this then affects the amount of deposits that banks wish to create, open market operations alter the money supply both directly (via the effect on cash in circulation) and indirectly (via the induced effect on the number of deposits created).

> An **open market operation** occurs when the central bank alters the monetary base by buying or selling financial securities in the open market.

The Bank prints £1 million of new banknotes and buys bonds on the open market. There are £1 million fewer bonds in private hands but £1 million more cash. Some of the extra cash is held in private circulation but most is deposited with the banks, which then expand deposit lending against their higher cash reserves. Conversely, if the Bank sells £1 million of bonds from its existing holdings, the monetary base falls by £1 million. Banks lose cash reserves, have to reduce deposit lending and the money supply falls.

Box 23.1 The repo market

In American movies, people in arrears on their loans have their cars repossessed by the repo man. In the mid-1990s, London finally established a repo market. Frankfurt and Milan had operated repo markets for years. Was the ultra-cautious German Bundesbank involved in dubious car loans?

A gilt repo is a *sale and repurchase agreement*. A bank sells you a bond, simultaneously agreeing to buy it back at a specified price on a particular future date. You have made the bank a short-term loan secured or 'backed' by the long-term bond temporarily in your ownership. Thus repos use the outstanding stock of *long-term* assets as backing for new and secured *short-term* loans.

Reverse repos work the other way. Now you get a short-term loan from the bank by initially selling bonds to the bank, plus an agreement for you to repurchase the bonds at a specified date in the near future at a price agreed now. Reverse repos are effectively secured temporary fixed-term loans by the bank.

Repos and reverse repos are very like other short-term lending and borrowing. They are now used for open market operations. The Bank of England used to conduct open market operations by buying and selling Treasury bills; the Bundesbank made much more use of repo and reverse repo transactions. But they achieved much the same purpose. Now the Bank of England also uses the repo market to conduct open market operations in order to alter cash in circulation.

Open market operations are nowadays the principal channel by which the central bank affects the money supply. Having discussed the central bank's role in monetary control, we turn next to its role in financial stability.

23.3 Lender of last resort

Modern fractional reserve banking lets society produce the medium of exchange with tiny inputs of scarce physical resources. But the efficient production of the medium of exchange yields a system of fractional reserve banking vulnerable to financial panics. Since banks have too few reserves to meet a withdrawal of all their deposits, a hint of big withdrawals may become a self-fulfilling prophecy as people scramble to get their money out before the banks go bust.

To avoid financial panics, people must believe that banks cannot get into trouble. This requires a guarantee that banks can get cash if they really need it. The central bank is the only institution that can manufacture cash in unlimited amounts. The threat of financial panics is greatly diminished if it is known that the central bank will act as lender of last resort.

> The **lender of last resort** lends to banks when financial panic threatens the financial system.

As lender of last resort, the Bank can maintain confidence in the banking system.

Prudential regulation

Last resort lending is useful in helping banks that face a temporary liquidity crisis but whose underlying balance sheet is perfectly sound. Sometimes, however, through poor decisions or bad luck, a bank has made loans that prove worthless. This raises two issues: what to do if a particular bank is in permanent trouble, and how to stop this infecting other banks.

Generally, it is the shareholders of the particular bank that bear the cost of its poor performance. To try to make sure that shareholders have sufficient funds for this purpose, financial regulations require banks to meet capital adequacy ratios.[1]

When a bank makes a small loss, this capital reserve supplied by shareholders should be sufficient to meet it. A crisis depletes this capital reserve and thereby reduces the share price of the bank. *Shareholders* suffer, but *depositors* are protected since the bank still has adequate funds to meet their liabilities.

> A **capital adequacy ratio** is a required minimum value of bank capital relative to its outstanding loans and investments.

If a bank makes larger losses it may go bankrupt. Losses incurred by rogue trader Nick Leeson brought down Barings Bank in the 1990s. Typically, governments then compensate depositors but not shareholders. Barings was actually sold to Dutch Bank ING for a notional amount and deposits were honoured in full. The knowledge that depositors are unlikely to suffer helps prevent unjustified financial panics. The knowledge that shareholders *are* likely to suffer helps keep management on its toes.

When a major bank is in trouble, the central bank may undertake last resort lending to *other* banks to prevent the particular crisis spilling over into a general panic. This may lead to a temporary rise in the money supply. When the crisis is over, a prudent central bank will then undo this effect and restore the money supply to its original level.

---

1 Financial regulation is sometimes the responsibility of the central bank, but sometimes the responsibility of a separate financial regulator. In the UK, responsibility was transferred from the Bank of England to the Financial Services Agency in 1997.

23.4 Equilibrium in financial markets

We now combine money supply and money demand to show how equilibrium is determined.

The central bank controls the *nominal* money supply. When we simplify by assuming that the price of goods is fixed, the central bank also controls the *real* money supply. In later chapters, we allow the price level to change. Changes in nominal money tend to lead to changes in prices. The central bank can still control the real money supply M/P in the short run – it can change M faster than prices P respond – but, in the long run, other forces determine real money M/P. For the moment, we treat the price level as fixed.

> The **real money supply** L is the nominal money supply M divided by the price level P.

Chapter 22 argued that the quantity of real money demanded rises when real income rises, but falls when the nominal interest rate rises.

Money market equilibrium

Figure 23.1 shows the demand curve LL for real money balances for a given real income. The higher the interest rate and the cost of holding money, the less real money is demanded. With a given price level, the central bank controls the quantity of nominal money and real money. The supply curve is vertical at this quantity of real money L_0. Equilibrium is at E. At the interest rate r_0, the real money people wish to hold just equals the outstanding stock L_0.

> In **money market equilibrium** the quantity of real balances demanded and supplied is equal.

Suppose the interest rate is r_1, below the equilibrium level r_0. There is excess demand for money AB in Figure 23.1. How does this excess demand for money bid the interest rate up from r_1 to r_0 to restore equilibrium? The answer is rather subtle. Strictly speaking, there is no market for money. Money is the medium of exchange for payments and receipts in *other* markets. A market for money would exchange pounds for pounds.

The other market relevant to Figure 23.1 is the market for bonds. Since the interest rate is the cost of holding money, people who do not hold money hold bonds. What happens explicitly in the market for bonds determines what is happening in the implicit market for money in Figure 23.1.

Real wealth W is the existing supply of real money L_0 and real bonds B_0. People divide their wealth W between desired real bond holdings B^D and desired real money holdings L^D. Hence

$$L_0 + B_0 = W = L^D + B^D \tag{1}$$

People cannot plan to divide up wealth they do not have. Equation (1) implies

$$B_0 - B^D = L^D - L_0 \tag{2}$$

An excess demand for money must be exactly matched by an excess supply of bonds. Otherwise people are planning to hold more wealth than they actually possess.

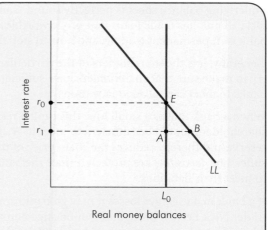

The demand schedule LL is drawn for a given level of real income. The higher the opportunity cost of holding money, the lower the real balances demanded. The real money supply schedule is vertical at L_0. The equilibrium point is E and the equilibrium interest rate, r_0. At a lower interest rate r_1 there is excess demand for money AB. There must be a corresponding excess supply of bonds. This reduces bond prices and increases the return on bonds, driving the interest rate up to its equilibrium level at which both markets clear.

Figure 23.1 Money market equilibrium

An excess demand for money at the interest rate r_1 in Figure 23.1 bids up the interest rate to its equilibrium level r_0. With excess demand for money, there is an excess supply of bonds. To make people want more bonds, suppliers of bonds offer a higher interest rate.[2] People switch from money to

Activity box 23 The big bad bubble

HOUSE prices have replaced the weather as Britain's favourite conversational standby. [...] Unlike Britain's temperate and unpredictable climate, however, the nation's housing market is reliably torrid. Another £9.3 billion ($16.7 billion) was borrowed against houses in March, taking the amount of outstanding mortgage debt past £800 billion. House prices were 18.9% higher in April than a year ago. With so much money at stake, every homeowner, house-hunter and buy-to-letter in Britain is an amateur meteorologist, watching for storms on the horizon. It falls to the Bank of England to regulate the weather and distribute the seasons, through its control of the cost of borrowing.

(The Economist, 6 May 2004)

Since the late 1990s central bankers across the world have been tasked with controlling inflation within their economies. In the UK, interest rate control and inflation management were handed to the Bank of England in 1997. Throughout most of that period UK property values have risen, often with double-digit growth per annum. Some commentators refer to this as an asset price bubble. Property prices are inflating like a bubble and the worry is that at some point the bubble will pop.

Should the Bank raise interest rates to cool down the housing market even when inflation as a whole is on target? Since the Bank has been told clearly that its job is to focus on inflation, it takes house prices into account only to the extent that they have implications for overall inflation in the economy as a whole. Sometimes, as in early 2007, inflation happens to be high when house prices are also rising rapidly. Then there is no conflict: higher interest rates help reduce inflation and cool the housing market. But on other occasions, the Bank has had to watch house prices spiral because the behaviour of overall inflation did not justify a rise in interest rates.

Questions

(a) Suppose a rise in aggregate demand makes output rise, bidding up the price of goods. Can the Bank of England use interest rates to reduce aggregate demand again? How might this work?

(b) Now suppose interest rates take up to two years to have their full effect on aggregate demand. To what indicator should today's interest rate decisions respond?

(c) Suppose higher oil prices tend to cause a rise in inflation independently of the current level of aggregate demand. Would the Bank of England have to raise interest rates even if output was simultaneously falling?

To check your answers to these questions, go to page 728.

---

2 A bond is a promise to pay a given stream of interest payments over a given time period. The bond price is the present value of this stream of payments. The higher the interest rate at which the stream is discounted, the lower the price of a bond. With an excess supply of bonds, bond prices fall and the interest rate or rate of return on bonds rises.

bonds. The higher interest rate reduces both the excess supply of bonds and the excess demand for money. At the interest rate r_0 money supply equals money demand. Bond supply equals bond demand. Both markets are in equilibrium. People wish to divide their wealth in precisely the ratio of the relative supplies of money and bonds.

From now on, we examine the implicit market for money. However, any statement about the money market is also a statement about the bond market.

Changes in equilibrium

A shift in either money supply or money demand changes equilibrium in the money market (and the bond market). These shifts are examined in Figure 23.2.

A fall in the money supply

Suppose the central bank lowers the money supply. For a fixed price level, lower nominal money reduces the real money supply. Figure 23.2 shows this leftward shift in the supply curve. Real money falls from L_0 to L'. The equilibrium interest rate rises from r_0 to r'. A higher interest rate reduces the demand for real money in line with the lower quantity supplied. Hence a lower real money supply raises the equilibrium interest rate. Conversely, a rise in the real money supply reduces the equilibrium interest rate.

A rise in real income

Figure 23.2 shows real money demand LL for a given real income. A rise in real income increases the marginal benefit of holding money at each interest rate, raising real money demand from LL to LL'. The equilibrium interest rate rises to keep real money demand equal to the unchanged real supply L_0. Conversely, a fall in real income shifts LL to the left and reduces the equilibrium interest rate.

More competition in banking

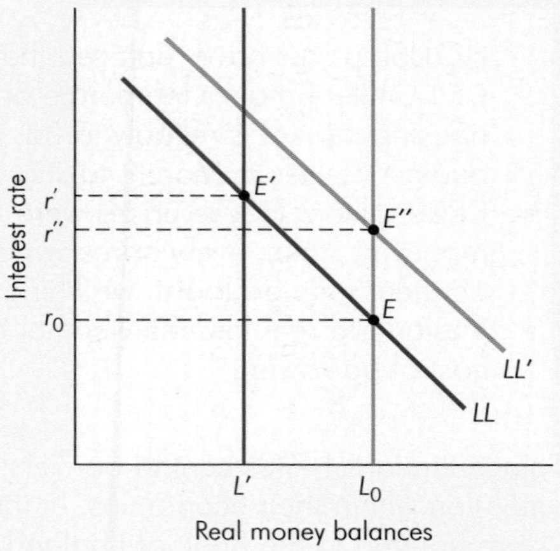

With a given real income, LL is the demand schedule for real money balances. A reduction in the real money supply from L_0 to L' moves the equilibrium interest rates from r_0 to r' to reduce the quantity of money demanded in line with the fall in the quantity supplied. With a given supply of real money L_0 an increase in real income shifts the demand schedule from LL to LL'. The equilibrium interest rates must increase from r_0 to r'. Higher real income tends to increase the quantity of real money demanded and higher interest rates are required to offer this, maintaining the quantity of real money demanded in line with the unchanged real supply.

Figure 23.2 Equilibrium interest rates

Figure 23.2 also draws money demand LL for a given interest rate paid on bank deposits. Holding this rate constant, a rise in bond interest rates r raises the cost of holding money and reduces the quantity of money demanded. This implies the economy moves up a given demand curve LL.

However, more competition between banks, reflected in permanently higher interest rates paid on bank deposits, reduces the cost of holding money at each level of r. By raising money demand at each interest rate r, this shifts the demand for money up from LL to LL'. For a given money supply, this equilibrium interest rate on bonds is higher.

To sum up, a higher real money supply reduces the equilibrium interest rate, raising real money demand in line with the higher real money supply. Conversely, higher real income, which tends to raise real money demand, must lead to a rise in the equilibrium interest rate, which tends to reduce real money demand. Only then does real money demand remain equal to the unchanged supply. An increase in banking competition has similar effects to a rise in real income.

23.5 Monetary control

The central bank can control the money supply by using open market operations to affect cash in circulation, or by using reserve requirements and the discount rate to affect the incentive of banks to create deposits. Easy in theory, but not in practice.

It is hard for the Bank to control cash because it is also lender of last resort. When the banks wish to increase lending and deposits they can *always* get extra cash from the Bank.

Nor, for any given quantity of cash, are deposits easily manipulated. To affect them, reserve requirements must force banks to hold reserves they would not otherwise have held. This is a tax on banks, stopping them conducting profitable business. Modern banks operating in global markets find ways round these controls. UK banks do business with UK borrowers using financial markets in Frankfurt or New York, and London is disadvantaged as a global financial centre.

The UK has given up required reserve ratios on banks for the purpose of monetary control. Rather, the Bank tries to forecast what ratios of cash to deposits will be chosen by banks and by households, and thus guesses the likely size of the money multiplier.

Box 23.2 The big issue

Box 22.1 showed Japan's property boom in the late 1980s and crash in the early 1990s. Japanese banks took a big hit. The value of their assets fell drastically. Fears about the health of the banks led to a collapse of both confidence and private spending.

The Bank of Japan tried to get people spending again. Interest rates fell steadily as the Bank printed money. On 3 March 1999 it issued 1800 billion yen (£9 billion), driving short-term interest rates almost to zero.

Zero interest rates failed to boost the Japanese economy because the slump was already so bad that the price level was falling. When inflation is −2 per cent and the nominal interest rate is 0, the real interest rate is +2 per cent. A bigger slump makes prices fall faster, raising the real interest rate yet more. A vicious cycle. Negative inflation is more dangerous than positive inflation.

It was therefore with some relief that during 2003 and 2004 the Japanese economy started to grow again, reducing fears of a deflationary slump.

Two lessons should be drawn from this example. First, deflation is dangerous. Second, once interest rates are already low, monetary policy has only limited power to create further boosts to the economy.

Hence precise control of the money supply is difficult. Most central banks no longer try. Instead they set interest rates. The TV news reports decisions by the Bank about interest rates, not decisions about the money supply.

Control through interest rates

Figure 23.3 shows again the market for money. We draw the money demand schedule LL for a given level of real income. If the central bank can control the money supply, then, for a given level of goods prices, it can fix the real money supply at L_0. The equilibrium interest rate is r_0.

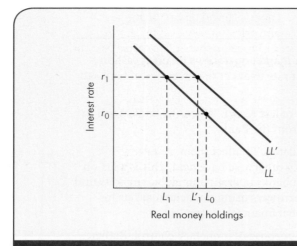

The money demand schedule *LL* is drawn for a given level of real income. If the Bank can fix the real money supply at L_0 the equilibrium interest rate will be r_0. Alternatively, if the Bank sets the interest rate r_0 and provides whatever money is demanded, the money supply will again be L_0. To control the money supply by using interest rates, the Bank must know the position of the demand schedule. Fixing an interest rate r_1, the resulting money supply will be L_1 if the demand schedule is *LL* but will be L'_1 if the demand schedule is *LL'*.

Figure 23.3 Interest rates and monetary control

Alternatively, the central bank can fix the interest rate at r_0 and supply whatever money is needed to clear the market at this interest rate. In equilibrium, the central bank supplies exactly the quantity of money demanded at the interest rate r_0. The money supply is still L_0.

The central bank can fix the money supply and accept the equilibrium interest rate implied by the money demand equation, or it can fix the interest rate and accept the equilibrium money supply implied by the money demand equation. Central banks now do the latter.

Uncertainty about the exact size of the money multiplier is now unimportant. When the interest rate starts to fall below the level r_0, either because of too little demand for money or too much supply, the Bank reduces the monetary base, through an open market operation, until the interest rate is r_0 again. Conversely, when the interest rate exceeds r_0, the Bank simply increases the monetary base until the interest rate falls to r_0.

23.6 Targets and instruments of monetary policy

Setting the interest rate not the money supply has a second advantage. When money demand is uncertain, fixing the money supply makes the interest rate uncertain, whereas fixing the interest rate makes the money supply uncertain. If the *effects* of monetary policy on the rest of the economy operate mainly via the interest rate, it is better to view monetary policy as the choice of interest rates not the money supply.

Two other concepts guide our discussion of monetary policy in later chapters. One is the *ultimate objective* of monetary policy. Possible objectives could include price stability, output stabilization, manipulation of the exchange rate and reducing swings in house prices.

To pursue its ultimate objective, what information does a central bank use at its frequent meetings to decide interest rates? It gets up-to-date forecasts of many variables. Sometimes, it concentrates on one or two key indicators.

Interest rates are the *instrument* about which policy decisions are made, but interest rates are chosen to try to keep the *intermediate target* on track.

> The **monetary instrument** is the variable over which the central bank makes day-to-day choices.

> An **intermediate target** is a key indicator used to guide interest rate decisions.

This shows how interest rates should adjust to the state of the economy. New data on the money supply (largely bank deposits) come out faster than new data on the price level or output. In the heyday of monetarism, central banks changed interest rates to try to meet medium-run targets for the path of nominal growth. In terms of Figure 23.3, it was as if they were fixing the money supply not interest rates.

Throughout the world, in the past decade there have been two key changes in the design of monetary policy. First, central banks have been told that their ultimate objectives should concentrate more on price stability and less on other things.

Second, money has become less important as an intermediate target. The financial revolution reduced its reliability as a leading indicator of future inflation. When structural changes in the financial sector are causing changes in money demand, it is hard to predict how much money will be held and how much will be spent. Increasingly, central banks use *inflation targets* as the intermediate target to which interest rate policy responds.

23.7 The transmission mechanism

The central bank sets interest rates, but how do interest rates affect the real economy?

In a closed economy, monetary policy affects consumption and investment demand by affecting real interest rates.[3] The central bank chooses the nominal interest rate. If prices are fixed, this is also the real interest rate. Once we allow prices to vary, monetary policy needs to anticipate what inflation will be. Since the real interest rate is simply the nominal interest rate minus the inflation rate, monetary policy then sets the nominal interest rate to get the desired real interest rate.

> The **transmission mechanism** of monetary policy is the channel through which it affects output and employment.

Consumption demand revisited

Chapter 20 used a very simple consumption function, an upward-sloping straight line relating aggregate consumption to the disposable income of households. The slope of this line, the marginal propensity to consume, showed the fraction of each extra pound of disposable income that households wished to spend, not save.

The height of the consumption function showed autonomous consumption demand, the part unrelated to personal disposable income. Changes in disposable income moved households *along* the consumption function. Changes in autonomous demand *shifted* the function. How can monetary policy affect autonomous consumption demand?

Household wealth

Suppose real wealth rises because of a stock market boom. Households spend some of their extra wealth on a new car. At each level of disposable income, consumption demand is higher. The entire consumption function shifts up when household wealth increases.

Money and interest rates affect household wealth, and thus consumption and aggregate demand, in two ways. First, since money is a component of household wealth, a higher real money supply adds directly to household wealth. Second, interest rates affect household wealth indirectly. The price

> The **wealth effect** is the shift in the consumption function when household wealth changes.

---

3 In Chapter 29 we show that, in an open economy, there is also a strong relationship between interest rates, the exchange rate and competitiveness. Monetary transmission then includes effects on export and import demand.

of company shares and long-term government bonds is the present value of the expected stream of divided earnings or promised coupon payments. When interest rates fall, future earnings, now discounted at a lower interest rate, are worth more today. Lower interest rates make the price of bonds and corporate shares rise and make households wealthier.[4]

Durables and consumer credit

When spending exceeds disposable income, net wealth falls. People sell off assets or borrow money to finance their dissaving. A lot of borrowing is to finance purchases of *consumer durables*, household capital goods such as televisions, furniture and cars. Splashing out on a new car can cost a whole year's income.

Two aspects of consumer credit or borrowing possibilities affect consumption spending. First, there is the quantity of credit on offer. If banks or retailers make more credit available to customers, people are more likely to buy the car or dream kitchen they have always wanted. An increase in the supply of consumer credit shifts the consumption function upwards. People spend more at any level of disposable income. Second, the cost of credit matters. The higher the interest rate, the lower the quantity that households can borrow while still being able to make repayments out of their future disposable incomes.

Money and interest rates thus affect consumer spending by affecting both the quantity of consumer credit and the interest rates charged on it. An increase in the monetary base increases the cash reserves of the banking system and allows it to extend more consumer credit in the form of overdrafts. And by reducing the cost of consumer credit, lower interest rates allow households to take out bigger loans while still being able to meet the interest and repayments.

Those two forces – wealth effects and changes in consumer credit – explain most of the shifts in the consumption function. They are part of the *transmission mechanism* through which monetary policy affects output and employment. Operating through wealth effects or the supply and cost of consumer credit, changes in the money supply and in interest rates shift the consumption function and the aggregate demand schedule, thus affecting equilibrium income and output.

Two closely related theories of the consumption function re-interpret these phenomena and make some of their subtleties more explicit.

The permanent income hypothesis

Developed by Professor Milton Friedman, this hypothesis assumes that people's incomes fluctuate but that people dislike fluctuating consumption. Because of diminishing marginal utility, a few extra bottles of champagne in the good years does not compensate for hunger in the bad years. Rather than allow fluctuations in income to induce fluctuations in consumption, people smooth out fluctuations in consumption. People go without champagne to avoid being hungry.

What determines the consumption people can afford on average? Friedman coined the term *permanent income* to describe people's average income in the long run, and argued that consumption depends not on current disposable income but on permanent income.

> The **permanent income hypothesis** says consumption reflects long-run or permanent income.

Suppose people think current income is unusually high. This temporarily high income makes little difference to their permanent income or the consumption they can afford in the long run. Since permanent income has hardly risen, they hardly increase current consumption.

---

4 When interest rates are 10 per cent, a bond paying £2.50 for ever is worth £25. New buyers get about 10 per cent a year on their investment. If interest rates fall to 5 per cent, bond prices rise to £50. New buyers still get an annual return in line with interest rates on other assets. A similar argument applies to company shares.

They save most of their temporary extra income and put money aside to see them through the years when income is unusually low. Only if people believe that a rise in today's income will be sustained as higher future incomes will their permanent income rise significantly. Only then is a large rise in current income matched by a large rise in current consumption.

The life-cycle hypothesis

Developed by Professors Franco Modigliani and Albert Ando, this theory takes a long-run approach like the permanent income hypothesis, but recognizes that changing tastes over a lifetime may undermine complete consumption smoothing.

> The **life-cycle hypothesis** assumes people make a lifetime consumption plan (including bequests to their children) that is just affordable out of lifetime income (plus any initial wealth inherited).

Each individual household need not plan constant consumption level over its lifetime. There may be years of heavy expenditure (a round-the-world cruise, sending the children to private school) and other years when spending is a bit less. However, such individual discrepancies tend to cancel out in the aggregate. Like the permanent income hypothesis, the life-cycle hypothesis suggests that it is average long-run income that determines the total demand for consumer spending.

Figure 23.4 shows a household's actual income over its lifetime. Income rises with career seniority until retirement, then drops to the lower level provided by a pension. The household's permanent income is *OD*. Technically, this is the constant annual income with the same present value as the present value of the actual stream of income. If the household consumed exactly its permanent income, it would consume *OD* each year and die penniless. The two shaded areas labelled *A* show when the household would be spending more than its current income and the area *B* shows when the household would be saving.

The household spends its income over its lifetime, but area *B* is not the sum of the two areas *A* because of compound interest. In the early years of low income, the household borrows. The area *B* shows how much the household has to save to pay back the initial borrowing *with interest* and accumulate sufficient wealth to see it through the final years when it is again dissaving.

Now let's think about wealth effects and consumer credit again. With more initial wealth, a household can spend more in every year of its lifetime without going broke. We can shift the permanent income line in Figure 23.4 upwards and consumption will rise. Although area *B* is now smaller and the areas *A* are now larger, the household can use its extra wealth to meet this shortfall between the years of saving (the area *B*) and the years of dissaving (the two areas *A*).

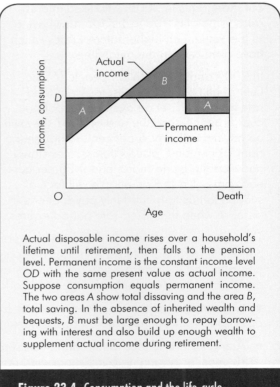

Figure 23.4 Consumption and the life-cycle

Actual disposable income rises over a household's lifetime until retirement, then falls to the pension level. Permanent income is the constant income level *OD* with the same present value as actual income. Suppose consumption equals permanent income. The two areas *A* show total dissaving and the area *B*, total saving. In the absence of inherited wealth and bequests, *B* must be large enough to repay borrowing with interest and also build up enough wealth to supplement actual income during retirement.

Again we conclude that higher wealth leads to more consumption at any current disposable income, but we pick up something we missed earlier. If households believe their *future* income will be higher than previously imagined, this also raises their permanent income. Households can spend more each year and still expect to balance their lifetime budget. They raise *current* consumption as soon as they raise their estimates of future incomes. The present value of future income plays a role very similar to wealth. It is money to be shared out in consumption over the lifetime. Friedman called it 'human wealth', to distinguish it from financial and physical assets. Rises in expected future incomes have wealth effects. They shift up the simple consumption function relating *current* consumption to *current* disposable income.

What about consumer credit? A rise in interest rates reduces the present value of future incomes and makes households worse off. In Figure 23.4, households must enlarge area *B* to meet the extra interest costs of paying back money borrowed in area *A* early in the lifetime. We must shift the permanent income line downwards. A rise in interest rates reduces current consumption not merely by reducing the market value of financial assets, but also by reducing the present value of future *labour* income. By reducing human wealth, it shifts the consumption function downwards.

Box 23.3 Transmission suspended

All good things must come to an end, concluded BBC economics correspondent Evan Davis in June 2007. People who took out mortgages in 2005, with fixed interest rates for the first two years, are now having to live with much higher interest rates which have risen a lot in the meantime.

In 2005 about 1.3 million people (65 per cent of all new mortgages) took out fixed-rate mortgages, at an average rate of just over 5 per cent. By the end of 2007 they will be paying well over 6 per cent. Although the Bank of England raised interest rates slowly and steadily, by no more than 0.25 per cent each time, 1.3 million people will face a sudden jolt as they suddenly pay 6 per cent or more when their fixed-rate period expires.

The transmission mechanism of monetary policy is delayed by mortgages offering an initial fixed-rate period. Subsequent interest rate rises bite only when the fixed-rate period is over. Other changes are also affecting the transmission mechanism, and hence the ability of the Bank of England to predict exactly how its interest rate changes will work. These include:

● Greater competition and lower margins for mortgage lenders, leading to lower mortgage interest rates for any interest rate set by the Bank of England.

● A greater use of fees rather than interest rates – banks used to charge a couple of hundred pounds for arranging a mortgage and now charge up to a couple of thousand pounds.

● A trend from repayment mortgages to interest-only mortgages that change the timing of when borrowers have to repay their loan.

For many years, we have known that interest rate changes take up to two years to have their full effect. The greater popularity of mortgages with a fixed-rate initial period, and other changes in the mortgage market, may mean that interest rates take even longer to have their full effect. With several interest rate rises behind it, the Bank of England therefore has to worry about whether it has already done enough, or whether further interest rate rises are still required.

Source: www.bbc.co.uk/blogs/thereporters/evandavis.

Finally, what about a rise in the quantity of consumer credit on offer? Figure 23.3 assumes that people spend more than their incomes early in life. Students run up overdrafts knowing that, as rich economists, they can pay them back later. What if nobody will lend? People without wealth are restricted by their actual incomes, although people with wealth can lend to themselves by running down their wealth. Hence a rise in the availability of consumer credit lets people dissave in the early years. Total consumption rises. More students run up overdrafts and buy cars.

Having discussed how monetary policy affects consumption demand, we conclude our examination of monetary transmission by analysing how interest rates affect investment demand.

Investment demand

In earlier chapters we treated investment demand as autonomous, or independent of current income and output. We now begin to analyse what determines investment demand. Here we focus on interest rates. Other determinants of investment demand are considered in Chapter 31.

Total investment spending is investment in fixed capital and investment in working capital. Fixed capital includes factories, houses, plant and machinery. The share of investment in GDP fluctuates between 10 and 20 per cent.[5] Although the total change in inventories is quite small, this component of total investment is volatile and contributes significantly to changes in the total level of investment.

In a closed economy, aggregate demand is $C + I + G$. Public investment is part of G. We still treat government demand as part of fiscal policy. Thus we assume that G is fixed at a level set by the government. In this section we focus on private investment demand I.

Investment in fixed capital

Firms add to plant and equipment because they foresee profitable opportunities to expand output or because they can reduce costs by using more capital-intensive production methods. BT needs new equipment because it is developing new products for data transmission. Nissan needs new assembly lines to substitute robots for workers in car production.

The firm weighs the benefits from new capital – the rise in profits – against the cost of investment. The benefit occurs in the future, but the costs are incurred when the plant is built or the machine bought. The firm compares the value of extra future profits with the current cost of the investment.

Will the investment yield enough extra profit to pay back *with interest* the loan used to finance the original investment. Equivalently, if the project is funded out of existing profits, will the new investment yield a return at least as great as the return that could have been earned by lending the money instead. The higher the interest rate, the larger must be the return on a new investment to match the opportunity cost of the funds tied up.

At any instant there are many investment projects a firm *could* undertake. The firm ranks these projects, from the most profitable to the least profitable. At a high interest rate, only a few projects earn enough to cover the opportunity cost of the funds employed. As the interest rate falls, more and more projects earn a return at least matching the opportunity cost of the funds used to undertake the investment. The firm invests more.

Figure 23.5 plots the investment demand schedule II relating interest rates and investment demand.

> The **investment demand schedule** shows the desired investment at each interest rate.

If the interest rate rises from r_0 to r_1, fewer investment projects cover the opportunity cost of the funds tied up, and desired investment falls from I_0 to I_1.

---

5 These numbers refer to gross investment, the production of new capital goods that contribute to aggregate demand. Since the capital stock is depreciating, or wearing out, some gross investment is needed merely to keep the existing capital stock from falling.

The height of the schedule *II* reflects the cost of new capital and the stream of profits to which it gives rise. For a given stream of expected future profits, a higher price of new capital goods reduces the return on the money tied up in investment. Fewer projects match the opportunity cost of any particular interest rate. Since desired investment is then lower at any interest rate, a rise in the cost of new capital goods shifts the investment demand schedule *II* downwards.

Similarly, pessimism about future output demand reduces estimates of the stream of profits earned on possible investment projects. The return on each project falls. At each interest rate, fewer projects match the opportunity cost of the funds. Desired investment falls at any interest rate. Lower expected future demand shifts the investment demand schedule downwards.[6]

The investment demand schedule *II* can be used to analyse both business investment in plant and machinery and residential investment in housing. What about the slope of the schedule? There is a big difference between a machine that wears out in three years and a house or a factory lasting 50 years. The longer the economic life of the capital good, the larger the fraction of its total returns earned in the distant future, and the more the original cost of the goods accumulates at compound interest before the money is repaid.

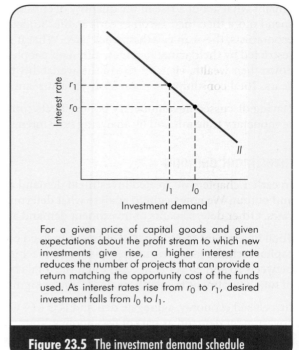

For a given price of capital goods and given expectations about the profit stream to which new investments give rise, a higher interest rate reduces the number of projects that can provide a return matching the opportunity cost of the funds used. As interest rates rise from r_0 to r_1, desired investment falls from I_0 to I_1.

Figure 23.5 The investment demand schedule

Hence a change in interest rates has a larger effect the longer the life of the capital good. The investment demand schedule is flatter, and the monetary transmission mechanism more powerful, for long-lived houses and factories than for short-term machinery.[7] A change in interest rates has more effect on long-term projects.

Inventory investment

There are three reasons why firms desire stocks of raw materials, partly finished goods and finished goods awaiting sale. First, the firm may be betting on price changes. Sometimes, firms hold large stocks of oil, believing it cheaper to buy now rather than later. Similarly, firms may hold finished goods off the market hoping to get a better price later.

Second, many production processes take time. A ship cannot be built in a month, or even a year. Some stocks are simply the throughput of inputs on their way to becoming outputs.

Third, stocks help smooth costly adjustments in output. If output demand rises suddenly, plant capacity cannot be changed overnight. A firm has to pay big overtime payments to meet the upsurge in orders. It is cheaper to carry some stocks, available to meet a sudden rise in demand. Similarly, in a

6 We can make the same points another way. Given the stream of future profits and the interest rate, a firm does all projects for which the present value of operating profits exceeds the initial price of the capital goods. A higher interest rate cuts the present value of profits. Some projects no longer cover the initial cost of capital goods. Higher interest rates reduce desired investment. Similarly, a lower expected future profit stream, or higher purchase price of capital goods, cuts the present value of operating profits relative to the initial cost, reducing investment demand.

7 Equivalently, a 1 per cent rise in the interest rate has a small effect on the present value of earnings over a three-year period but a large effect on the present value of earnings over the next 50 years. Note that this is the same argument as we used in Chapter 21, in saying that a change in interest rates would have little effect on the price (present value of promised payments) of a short-term bond but a large effect on the price of a long-term bond.

Box 23.4 The credit channel of monetary policy

Recent research emphasizes another aspect of the transmission mechanism through which monetary policy affects consumption and investment, and hence aggregate demand.

The **credit channel** affects the value of collateral for loans, and thus the supply of credit.

A lender usually asks for collateral – assets available for sale if you fail to repay the loan. Collateral is how lenders cope with moral hazard and adverse selection: borrowers who know more about their ability and willingness to repay than lenders know.

Suppose the price of goods falls, raising the real value of nominal assets. People have more collateral to offer lenders, who thus lend more than before at any particular interest rate. The supply of credit rises and aggregate demand for goods increases.

There are really two credit channels, since there are two reasons for changes in the value of collateral. First, changes in goods prices change the real value of nominal assets. Second, and quite distinct, when monetary policy changes the interest rate, this affects the present value of future income from assets and hence the market value of collateral assets themselves.

temporary downturn, it is cheaper to maintain output and pile up stocks of unsold goods than to incur expensive redundancy payments to cut the workforce and reduce production.

These are benefits of holding inventories. The cost is that, by retaining unsold goods or buying goods not yet inputs to production, a firm ties up money that could have earned interest. The cost of holding inventories is the interest forgone, plus any storage charges for holding stocks.

Thus the investment demand schedule *II* for fixed capital in Figure 23.5 also applies to increases in working capital, or inventories. Other things equal, a higher interest rate reduces desired stockbuilding, an upward move *along* the investment demand schedule. This is part of the monetary transmission mechanism. But a rise in potential speculative profits, or fall in storage costs for inventories, *shifts* the schedule *II* up and raises inventory investment at any interest rate. Not all changes in investment demand are caused by monetary policy.

Summary

- The Bank of England, the UK **central bank**, is banker to the banks. Because it can print money it can never go bust. It acts as **lender of last resort** to the banks.

- The Bank conducts the government's monetary policy. It affects the monetary base through **open market operations**, buying and selling government securities. It can also affect the money multiplier by imposing **reserve requirements** on the banks, or by setting the **discount rate** for loans to banks at a penalty level that encourages banks to hold excess reserves.

- There is no explicit market in money. Because people plan to hold the total supply of assets that they own, any excess supply of bonds is matched by an excess demand for money. Interest rates adjust to clear the market for bonds. In so doing, they clear the money market.

- A rise in the real money supply reduces the equilibrium interest rate. For a given real money supply, a rise in real income raises the equilibrium interest rate.

- In practice, the Bank cannot control the money supply exactly. Imposing artificial regulations drives banking business into unregulated channels. **Monetary base control** is difficult since the Bank acts as lender of last resort, supplying cash when banks need it.

- Thus the Bank sets the interest rate not money supply. The demand for money at this interest rate determines the quantity of money supplied. **Interest rates are the instrument of monetary policy**.

- Interest rates take time to affect the economy. **Intermediate targets** are used as leading indicators when setting the interest rate.

- A higher interest rate reduces household wealth and makes borrowing dearer. Together, these effects reduce autonomous consumption demand and shift the consumption function downwards.

- **Consumption demand** reflects long-run disposable income and a desire to smooth out short-run fluctuations in consumption. Higher interest rates reduce consumption demand by reducing the present value of expected future labour income.

- Given the cost of new capital goods and expected stream of future profits, a higher interest rate reduces **investment demand**, a movement down a given investment demand schedule *II*. Higher expected future profits, or cheaper capital goods, shift the *II* schedule upwards.

- These effects of interest rates on consumption and investment demand are the **transmission mechanism** of monetary policy.

Review questions

To check your answers to these questions, go to page 727.

1 The Bank sells £1 million of securities to Mr Jones who banks with Barclays. (a) If Mr Jones pays by cheque, show the effect on the balance sheets of the Bank of England and Barclays Bank. (b) What happens to the money supply? (c) Is the answer the same if Mr Jones pays in cash?

2 Now the Bank requires banks to hold 100 per cent cash reserves against deposits. Repeat your answers to Question 1. What is the money multiplier?

3 What are the desirable properties of a good leading indicator for interest rate decisions?

4 People previously without bank overdrafts get credit cards on which they can borrow up to £500. What happens to the consumption function? Why?

5 Why do higher interest rates reduce investment demand? Be sure to discuss all the different ways in which firms might finance their investment projects.

6 **Common fallacies** Why are these statements wrong? (a) By abolishing reserve requirements the Bank gave up any attempt to control the money supply. (b) When real interest rates are negative, people are being paid to hold cash. (c) Consumers are crazy if their spending is up when their disposable income is lower.

7 **Harder question** Why might it take up to two years for a change in interest rates fully to affect aggregate demand? What does this imply about decisions to set interest rates?

8 **Harder question** If the permanent income hypothesis is correct, we should expect to see a lower marginal propensity to consume in the short run than in the long run. Why?

9 **Essay question** Mrs Thatcher briefly tried to use the money supply as the instrument of monetary policy, and in the United States Mr Volcker tried the same experiment in the early Reagan years. Both experiments were abandoned. Why do modern central banks think of monetary policy as choosing the interest rate rather than the money supply?

 Online **Learning Centre**

To help you grasp the key concepts of this chapter check out the extra resources posted on the Online Learning Centre. There are chapter summaries, self-test questions, an interactive graphing tool, weblinks and a searchable glossary, all for free!

To put your learning into practice and prepare for exams, an **Interactive Workbook** is also available online, containing a variety of question types and providing feedback on your answers.

If you'd like further help with economics, or have any questions, **NetTutor** is here to help! You will have a personalised tutorial service at your fingertips. Visit the online learning centre at: www.mcgraw-hill.co.uk/textbooks/begg for information on accessing all of these resources.

Monetary and fiscal policy

Chapters 19 and 20 introduced a simple model of income determination, and studied how fiscal policy affects aggregate demand and equilibrium output. Since Chapter 21, we have studied the demand for money, the supply of money and the determination of interest rates. Interest rates connect the present and the future, affecting spending decisions of both households and firms. We analysed the transmission mechanism by which monetary policy affects aggregate demand.

We now examine the interaction of the markets for goods and for money. Interest rates affect the demand for goods and the level of income and output, but income and output affect the demand for money and the interest rates set by the central bank.

We need to think about both markets at once. In so doing, we explain how equilibrium income and interest rates are simultaneously determined. In this richer model, we then study changes in monetary and fiscal policy. Finally, we discuss how the mix of monetary and fiscal policy affects the composition as well as the level of equilibrium output.

This is the last chapter in which we retain the simplifying assumption that prices are fixed. The interest rate is the key variable connecting the markets for money and output. In the next chapter, we allow prices to change and introduce aggregate supply for the first time.

24.1 Monetary policy rules

> **A monetary policy rule (MPR)** specifies how the central bank adjusts interest rates in response to changes in particular economic variables.

To examine the behaviour of the economy under *given* policies, we have to say what we mean by a given policy. The central bank sets the interest rate, passively supplying whatever quantity of money is needed to equate money supply and money demand at this interest rate. At its simplest, a given monetary policy could mean a given interest rate. However, treating interest rates as fixed ignores the fact that the central bank reacts systematically to changes in economic conditions. Just as we model the behaviour of the private sector, we ought to model the behaviour of the central bank itself.

In the heyday of monetarism, central banks used to adjust interest rates to stop the money supply deviating from a given target path. For reasons explained at the end of this chapter, most central banks have abandoned this policy, preferring to target the inflation rate itself.

Inflation targeting makes no sense in a model in which we are still assuming that prices are fixed. We introduce inflation targeting in Chapter 25. In this chapter, we assume instead that the central bank pursues a monetary target. Not only is this a good way to introduce many key ideas, it is also useful in understanding how monetary policy was set in the 1980s before inflation targeting became popular.

> Following a **monetary target**, the central banks adjust interest rates to maintain the quantity of money demanded in line with the given target for money supply.

Box 24.1 Monetary intelligence

As the Iraq war showed, good intelligence is a valuable commodity. From where does the Bank of England's Monetary Policy Committee (MPC) get its briefings, and how does it check these are not being sexed up?

Teams of professional economists and statisticians scrutinize the latest data, and feed them into economic models in order to update predictions. But, as in warfare, this can usefully be supplemented by agents with their ear to the ground. The Bank of England has regional reps who tour the country talking to businesses and civic groups, gathering intelligence about local economic conditions and the latest concerns. This human intelligence is an important supplement to the volumes of statistical data that the MPC must process every month.

Mervyn King, Governor of the Bank, has earned a worldwide reputation for sound judgement and good practice, making monetary policy predictable and effective: 'For much of the postwar period, British macroeconomic policy was too exciting for comfort; we should aim to be boring.'

Choppier waters   King's life is getting more exciting. After an extended period of low interest rates and low inflation, interest rates are starting to rise around the world as high oil prices force central banks to take steps to combat incipient inflation. And with huge increases in UK house prices during the last few years, it would not take a large increase in interest rates to cause real pain in the housing market. Moreover, by 2007, higher oil prices had led inflation to exceed the permissible target range, and the Governor was forced to write a letter to Chancellor Gordon Brown explaining why the Bank had missed its target.

A political animal   Even so, there is no denying King's stature among financial policy makers. The Birmingham native, former economics professor and keen Aston Villa fan, has been a key player in modernizing Britain's once-amateurish economic policy making since he became chief economist at the Bank in 1991. 'Mervyn King developed the framework under which the bank gave advice to the chancellor,' says Alan Budd, who was chief economic adviser to the British Treasury until 1997. 'When the bank was given independence, it had a system in place.' King still keeps his lines open to the Chancellor of the Exchequer through monthly working breakfasts.

Adapted from 'Inside the Bank of England', *BusinessWeek*, 12 July 2004.

We now combine our analysis of the goods market and money market to examine interest rates and output simultaneously. Chapters 20 and 21 analysed short-run equilibrium output using a diagram with the 45° line and a straight-line aggregate demand line. The height of the aggregate demand line reflected autonomous demand from consumption, investment and government spending; the slope of the line reflected the marginal propensity to spend out of national income.

This diagram is not suitable in our extended model. As output changes, interest rates alter, affecting consumption and investment demand. And changes in monetary policy, by changing interest rates at any output level, can shift the aggregate demand schedule. To keep track of all these effects, it is easier to develop a new diagram.

24.2 The *IS–LM* model

The trick is to consider *combinations* of income and interest rates that lead to equilibrium in each of the two markets, output and money, and thus determine the unique combination of income and interest rates yielding equilibrium in both markets at the same time.

The *IS* schedule: goods market equilibrium

The goods market is in equilibrium when aggregate demand equals actual income. Hence, as shorthand, the combinations of interest rates and income compatible with short-run equilibrium in the goods market is called the *IS* schedule.[1]

> The **IS schedule** shows combinations of income and interest rates at which aggregate demand equals actual output

Figure 24.1 shows the *IS* schedule. It is drawn for a given level of present and future government spending, a given level of present and future taxes and given present beliefs about future output and income. Holding these constant, lower interest rates increase both investment and consumption demand. At an interest rate r_1, aggregate demand and short-run equilibrium output Y_1 are higher than their level Y_0 when the interest rate is r_0.

Changes in interest rates move the goods market along the *IS* curve. Anything else that affects aggregate demand is shown as a shift in the *IS* schedule.

The slope of the *IS* schedule

The *IS* schedule slopes down. Lower interest rates boost aggregate demand and output. The *slope* of the *IS* schedule reflects the sensitivity of aggregate demand to interest rates. If demand is sensitive to interest rates, the *IS* schedule is flat. Conversely, if output demand is insensitive to interest rates, the *IS* schedule is steep.

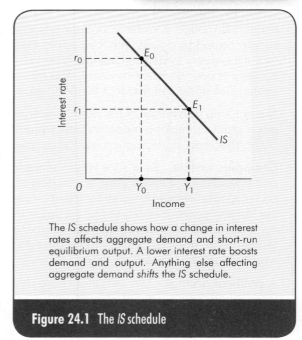

The *IS* schedule shows how a change in interest rates affects aggregate demand and short-run equilibrium output. A lower interest rate boosts demand and output. Anything else affecting aggregate demand *shifts* the *IS* schedule.

Figure 24.1 The *IS* schedule

---

1   The name *IS* schedule derives from the fact that in the simplest model without either a government or a foreign sector, equilibrium income is where planned investment *I* equals planned saving *S*. However, the *IS* schedule – combinations of income and interest rates consistent with equilibrium income – can be constructed for models including the government and foreign sector as well.

Shifts in the *IS* schedule

Movements along the *IS* schedule show how interest rates affect aggregate demand and equilibrium output. Other changes in aggregate demand shift the *IS* schedule. For a *given* interest rate, more optimism about future profits raises investment demand. Higher expected future incomes raise consumption demand. Higher government spending adds directly to aggregate demand. Any of these, by raising aggregate demand at a given interest rate, raise equilibrium output at any interest rate, an *upward shift* in the *IS* schedule.

The *LM* schedule: money market equilibrium

Pursuing a monetary target, the central bank endeavours to fix the money supply itself. In Figure 24.2, along the *LM* schedule, the demand for money (or liquidity, hence *L*) equals the given supply of money (hence *M*). Hence the shorthand *LM*.

The quantity of money demanded rises with output *Y* but falls with the interest rate *r*. In money market equilibrium, money demand equals the given money supply. Hence if output rises from Y_0 to Y_1 – tending to raise the quantity of money demanded – money market equilibrium is restored only if interest rates rise from r_0 to r_1, thereby reducing money demand back to the level of the given money supply. Figure 24.2 shows the upward-sloping schedule *LM* describing money market equilibrium. Higher output and income are accompanied by higher interest rates. When output rises, the interest rate rises to maintain money market equilibrium.

> The **LM schedule** shows combinations of interest rates and income yielding money market equilibrium when the central bank pursues a given target for the nominal money supply.

The slope of the schedule

The *LM* schedule slopes up. Following a monetary target, higher output induces a higher interest rate to keep money demand in line with money supply. The more sensitive is money demand to income and output, the more the interest rate must change to maintain money market equilibrium, and the steeper is the *LM* schedule. Similarly, if money demand is not responsive to interest rates, it takes a big change in interest rates to offset output effects on money demand, and the *LM* schedule is steep. Conversely, the more money demand responds to interest rates and the less it responds to income, the flatter is the *LM* schedule.

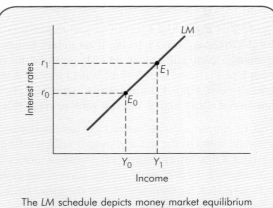

The *LM* schedule depicts money market equilibrium and is drawn for a given money supply. Higher income raises the quantity of money demanded. Only if interest rates are higher can the quantity of money demanded continue to equal the unchanged money supply.

Figure 24.2 The *LM* schedule

Shifts in the *LM* schedule

Movements along the schedule indicate interest rate changes to implement the *existing* policy as output changes. Shifts in the schedule reflect a *change* in monetary policy.

We draw an *LM* schedule for a *given* nominal money target. A rise in the target money supply means that money demand must also be increased to maintain money market equilibrium. This implies a rightward *shift* in the *LM* schedule. Output is higher, or interest rates lower, raising money demand in line with the rise in real money supply.

Conversely, a lower monetary target shifts the *LM* schedule to the left. Since money demand must also be reduced to preserve money market equilibrium, a higher interest rate is required at each income level. To sum up, moving along the *LM* schedule, higher interest rates need higher income to keep real money demand equal to the fixed supply. A higher (lower) target for money supply shifts the *LM* schedule to the right (left).

24.3 The *IS–LM* model in action

Figure 24.3 shows both the *IS* schedule, depicting combinations of income and interest rates consistent with goods market equilibrium, and the *LM* schedule, depicting combinations of interest rates and income consistent with money market equilibrium when the central bank's monetary policy rule is to pursue a fixed money supply target. Equilibrium in both the money market and the output market is at point *E*, with an interest rate r^* and income level Y^*.

Fiscal policy: shifting the *IS* schedule

Figure 24.4 shows the effect of a fiscal expansion that shifts the *IS* schedule from IS_0 to IS_1. If monetary policy is unchanged, and still shown by LM_0, equilibrium moves from *E* to E_1. Fiscal expansion leads to higher income but also higher interest rates. Higher output tends to increase the quantity of money demanded. Only higher interest rates prevent this from happening.

And, of course, a fiscal contraction has the opposite effects. The *IS* schedule shifts to the left and output falls, tending to reduce money demand. Only lower interest rates restore money demand to the unchanged level of money supply, preserving money market equilibrium. In Figure 24.4, we can view this as the move from E_1 to *E* when the *IS* schedule shifts down from IS_1 to IS_0.

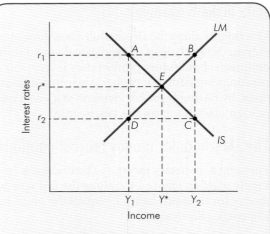

The goods market is in equilibrium at all points on the *IS* schedule. The money market is in equilibrium at all points on the *LM* schedule. Hence only at point *E* are both markets in equilibrium.

Figure 24.3 Equilibrium in the goods and money markets

A fiscal stimulus to aggregate demand **crowds out** some private spending. Higher output induces a rise in interest rates that dampens the expansionary effect on demand by reducing some components of private spending.

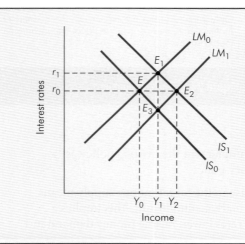

A fiscal expansion shifts the *IS* schedule from IS_0 to IS_1 but leaves the *LM* schedule unaltered at LM_0. Equilibrium moves from *E* to E_1. Output rises only from Y_0 to Y_1 because the output expansion induces a rise in interest rates from r_0 to r_1 that dampens the rise in aggregate demand. By accompanying the fiscal expansion with a monetary expansion from LM_0 to LM_1, policy could make output rise to Y_2. Fiscal expansion makes output rise more if monetary policy is loosened to keep interest rates unaltered.

Figure 24.4 Fiscal expansion shifts the *IS* schedule

Figure 24.4 makes three other points. First, crowding out is complete – extra government spending G leads to an equivalent reduction in consumption and investment $(C + I)$, leaving output unaltered – only if the LM schedule is vertical. Then, an upward shift in the IS schedule raises interest rates but not income.

In practice, the LM schedule is never completely vertical, which would occur only if it took an *infinite* rise in interest rates to offset the effect of slightly higher output on money demand. Since the LM schedule normally has a positive slope, fiscal expansion raises demand and output despite some induced rise in interest rates.

Second, fiscal policy is not the only autonomous change that is possible in aggregate demand. For example, an increase in export demand would also shift the IS schedule to the right, again inducing higher output and higher interest rates. Movements *along* the IS schedule show the effect of interest rates. All other shifts in aggregate demand imply *shifts* in the IS schedule.

Third, Figure 24.4 shows what happens if fiscal expansion is *accompanied* by a looser monetary policy. Fiscal expansion shifts IS to the right, but monetary expansion – a higher money supply target – shifts LM to the right. It is possible to loosen monetary policy just enough to keep interest rates at their original level when income expands. Fiscal expansion then leads to a new equilibrium at E_2, with interest rates unchanged at r_0.

Box 24.2 A horizontal *LM* schedule

If monetary policy is always adjusted to keep interest rates constant, we may as well view the LM schedule as horizontal at the target interest rate. The money supply is passively adjusted to whatever level of money is demanded at that interest rate. Shifts in the IS schedule no longer lead to crowding out because the money supply is adjusted to prevent interest rates from changing.

> A **horizontal *LM* schedule** implies the money supply is adjusted to keep interest rates constant.

In Chapter 29 we show that defending a fixed exchange rate may require a constant interest rate and hence a horizontal LM schedule. With other exchange rate policies it rarely makes sense to fix interest rates independently of all economic conditions.

Hence, the output effect of a fiscal expansion depends on the monetary policy in force. The more that monetary policy prevents a rise in interest rates, the more the fiscal expansion will lead to higher output.

Monetary expansion: shifting the *LM* schedule

Similarly, beginning from E in Figure 24.4, an increase in the target money supply shifts the LM schedule from LM_0 to LM_1: for any income, it requires lower interest rates to help raise money demand in line with the new higher money supply. Lower interest rates also boost income, which also helps raise money demand. Equilibrium moves from E to E_3. Conversely, a reduction in the target money supply shifts the LM schedule to the left, leading to higher interest rates but lower output.

24.4 Shocks to money demand

In the last three decades there have been major changes in the structure of the financial sector. Competition between banks has increased dramatically, raising interest rates paid on deposits. Since the opportunity cost of holding money in a bank deposit is only the differential between the deposit interest rate and the higher interest rate available on other financial assets, changes in banking competition change the opportunity cost of holding money *at any market interest rate r.*

We draw an *LM* schedule for a given nominal money target. Greater banking competition raises money demand at every combination of output and interest rates. To keep money demand in line with the unchanged supply, either output must fall or interest rates must rise. The *LM* schedule *shifts* left.

Figure 24.4 showed how changes in money *supply* shift the *LM* schedule under monetary targeting. We have now discovered that changes in money *demand*, other than those caused by changes in output and interest rates, also shift the *LM* schedule under monetary targeting.

In Figure 24.5, LM_1 corresponds to 'low' money demand and LM_2 to 'high' money demand. Suppose money demand increases but the central bank is not yet aware of the change. In choosing what monetary target to set, the central bank is expecting the schedule LM_1, which will place the economy at E_1. In fact, because of the undetected shift in money demand, the actual out-turn is at E_2, not at all what monetary policy intended when it decided what monetary target to set.

In practice, this helps explain why monetary targets were gradually abandoned by many central banks. When money demand was predictable, monetary targets worked fine. As the financial sector has become more sophisticated, more competitive and more volatile, monetary targets were gradually abandoned as the basis for the monetary policy rule.

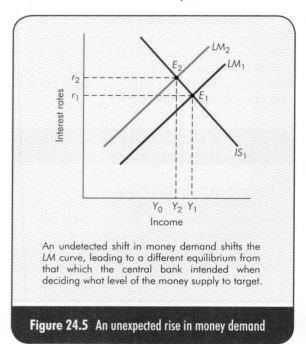

An undetected shift in money demand shifts the *LM* curve, leading to a different equilibrium from that which the central bank intended when deciding what level of the money supply to target.

Figure 24.5 An unexpected rise in money demand

24.5 The policy mix

Fiscal policy is government decisions about tax rates and spending levels. Changes in fiscal policy shift the *IS* schedule. Changes in monetary policy shift the *LM* schedule.

We now explore consequences of different *IS* and *LM* schedules. Budget deficits can be financed by printing money or by borrowing. In the latter case, there is no short-run connection between monetary and fiscal policy. The government can pursue independent monetary and fiscal policies.

Although both fiscal and monetary policy can alter aggregate demand, the two policies are not interchangeable. They affect aggregate demand through different routes and have different implications for the *composition* of aggregate demand.

> **Demand management** uses monetary and fiscal policy to stabilize output near potential output.

Figure 24.6 shows the mix of monetary and fiscal policy. There are two ways to stabilize income at Y^*. First, there is expansionary or *easy* fiscal policy (high government spending or low tax rates). This

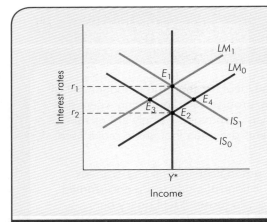

The target income Y can be attained by easy fiscal policy and tight monetary policy. Equilibrium at E_1, the intersection of LM_1 and IS_1, implies high interest rates r_1 and a low share of private sector investment and consumption in GNP. Alternatively, with easy monetary policy and tight fiscal policy, equilibrium at E_2, the intersection of LM_0 and IS_0, still attains the target income but at lower interest rates r_2. The share of private sector investment and consumption in GNP will be higher than at E_1.

Figure 24.6 The policy mix affects interest rates at any target output

leads to a high *IS* schedule, IS_1. To keep income in check with such an expansionary fiscal policy, *tight* monetary policy is needed. With a low money supply target, the schedule LM_1 is far to the left.

Equilibrium at E_1 achieves an output Y^* but also a high interest rate r_1. With high government spending, private demand must be kept in check. The mix of easy fiscal policy and tight monetary policy implies government spending G is a big share of national income Y^* but private spending $(C+I)$ a small share.

Alternatively, the government can adopt a tight fiscal policy (a low schedule IS_0) and an easy monetary policy (LM_0 far to the right). The target income Y^* is now attained with a lower interest rate r_2 at the equilibrium E_2. With easy monetary policy and tight fiscal policy, the share of private expenditure $(C+I)$ is higher, and the share of government expenditure lower, than at E_1. With lower interest rates, there is less crowding out of private expenditure.

Of course, easy monetary policy *and* easy fiscal policy together are highly expansionary. With the schedules IS_1 and LM_0 the equilibrium in Figure 24.6 is at E_4. Income is well above Y^*. Conversely, with tight monetary policy and tight fiscal policy, and schedules LM_1 and IS_0, equilibrium is at E_3, with income well below Y^*.

What should determine the mix of fiscal and monetary policy? In the long run, the government may care not just about keeping output close to potential output, but also about raising potential output. High investment increases the capital stock more quickly, giving workers more equipment with which to work and raising their productivity. Governments interested in long-run growth may choose a tight fiscal policy and an easy monetary policy. Conversely, if governments are politically weak and unable to resist demands for high government spending to pay off various factions, fiscal policy will be loose and a tight monetary policy is needed to keep aggregate demand in line with potential output.

24.6 The effect of future taxes

Chapter 23 argued that consumption demand reflects both *current* disposable income and expected *future* disposable income. Two hundred years ago, the English economist David Ricardo noticed a striking implication. Suppose the path of government purchases G is fixed over time. What path of taxes over time finances this spending?

Activity box 24 Monetary *or* fiscal policy?

Box 21.2 noted some reasons why fiscal policy may not be ideal for short-run management of aggregate demand. Some of these reasons – for example, problems in diagnosing where the economy is and forecasting where it might go if policy is left unchanged – apply just as much to monetary policy as to fiscal policy. However, two problems are often thought to make fiscal policy less suitable for short-run variation.

First, fiscal policy is difficult to change quickly. Rapid changes in hospital building or in tax rates are more costly than rapid changes in interest rates. Financial markets are accustomed to asset prices changing quickly. Second, it is politically easy to loosen fiscal policy but politically much more difficult to tighten it again later. For this reason, the most important source of short-term movements in fiscal policy is the operation of automatic stabilizers. Since tax rates are not changing, no visible decisions are being made to which voters could object. Yet tax revenue is varying with output.

It used also to be politically difficult to tighten monetary policy. For example, people (voters!) who have borrowed to buy a house get upset when interest rates rise sharply. The main reason that most countries have made their central banks independent of political control in decisions about interest rates is precisely to take the politics out of monetary policy. Nowadays, interest rates can and do change rapidly, in both directions, though usually by very small amounts, as the figure shows.

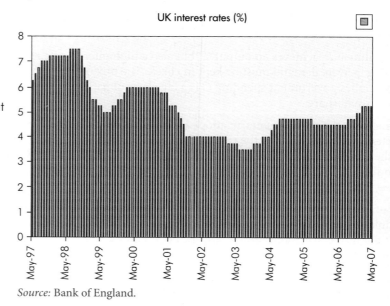

Source: Bank of England.

Questions

(a)   During which periods was the Bank of England most worried about inflation?

(b)   Was this current inflation at the time or was it the prospect of inflation in a year or two?

(c)   Should the Bank worry about changing its mind, raising interest rates only to lower them shortly afterwards if necessary, or should it act more slowly so that it rarely has to reverse its recent decisions?

To check your answers to these questions, go to page 729.

The government can lend and borrow. In some years, its spending may exceed taxes, in other years taxes must then exceed spending.

For a given planned path of spending, and a suitable planned path of tax revenue, the government cuts taxes this year, and pays for it by borrowing. It sells bonds. The tax cut is a fiscal expansion that boosts aggregate demand. Right?

> **Government solvency** requires that the present value of the current and future tax revenue equals the present value of current and future spending plus any initial net debts.

If the tax cut is £1 billion, this is also the value of bonds issued to finance it. The market value of bonds is the present value of future income to bondholders. By assumption, the path of government spending is fixed. Hence, interest payments to bondholders must be financed by higher taxes in the future.

£1 billion is the value of the tax cut, *and* the value of the new bonds, *and* the present value of the extra future taxes. The private sector gets a handout today (a tax cut) offset by a future penalty (higher taxes) of identical present value. The private sector is neither richer nor poorer. Its desired spending should not change. Today's tax cut has no effect on aggregate demand because it is matched by the *prospect* of higher future taxes.

Equivalently, the fall in government saving (larger deficit today) is exactly offset by a rise in private saving: private spending is unaltered, and larger disposable incomes (because of the tax cut) go entirely in extra saving (to pay for the future taxes).

Some people getting tax cuts today will die before future taxes arrive. But suppose these people have children and care about them. After a tax cut today, parents save more to bequeath extra money to their children, or grandchildren, to pay the higher future taxes. The extra disposable income is saved to raise the bequest for future generations.

> **Ricardian equivalence** says that it does not matter *when* a government finances a given spending programme. Tax cuts today do not affect private spending if, in present value terms, future taxes rise to match.

Ricardian equivalence does not deny that roadbuilding, financed by higher taxes, affects aggregate demand. Government spending always has real effects. Rather, for a *given* path of real government spending, it may not matter *when* people pay for it. Ricardo himself thought the equivalence hypothesis would not hold in the real world. Economists are still arguing about the extent to which Ricardian equivalence should hold.

Why Ricardian equivalence is too strong

There are three reasons why the tax cuts today *do* stimulate demand a bit even if future taxes are correspondingly higher. First, people without children get the benefit of tax cuts without paying the full burden of higher future taxes in the distant future. They spend more at once.

Second, by reducing marginal tax rates and distortions, tax cuts may increase potential output and raise income. Expecting higher incomes, people spend more immediately.

Third, solvent governments can borrow at a low interest rate. Ricardian equivalence holds only if we can borrow as easily as the government. If only! Households and firms are riskier than governments. Private people have no residual power to tax or print money when things go wrong. Hence, lenders charge private borrowers a higher rate of interest, and may refuse to lend at all.

Now do the sums again. £1 billion is the value of the tax cut, the extra government bonds and the present value of extra tax payments *discounted at the interest rate faced by the government*. We face a higher interest rate when we try to borrow. *As viewed by us, the present value of our extra future taxes is less than £1 billion because we discount at a higher interest rate.*

The tax cut is a fiscal expansion because in effect the government borrows on the good terms it enjoys, then lends to us at better terms than the capital market. It gives us a loan, tax cuts today, which we repay later in higher taxes. But we are charged the government's low interest rate for our loan. We are better off and spend more. Aggregate demand increases.

Evidence on Ricardian equivalence

Figure 24.7 shows UK evidence on Ricardian equivalence. Does private saving (by firms and households) offset government saving (taxes minus spending)? After financial markets were deregulated in the 1970s, there is *some* negative correlation between private and public saving.

Theory and evidence suggest that complete Ricardian equivalence is too extreme to fit the real world. Tax cuts do boost aggregate demand today (though higher future taxes will reduce demand at some future date). Ricardian equivalence is not completely right, but not completely wrong. Expectations of future conditions affect current behaviour. Private saving rises a bit when public saving falls. The private sector does substitute between present and future, despite obstacles to doing this easily. These obstacles make consumption demand more sensitive to current disposable income than it would be if borrowing were easy and only permanent income mattered.

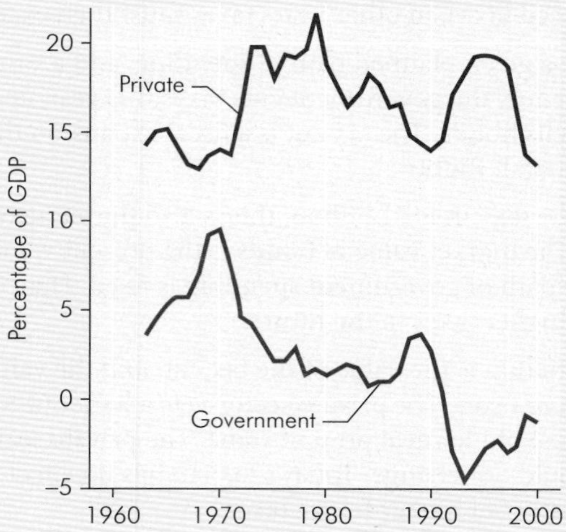

Current demand by firms and households depends both on current fiscal policy and expected future fiscal policy. Since one does not fully offset the other, for simplicity we can look at current fiscal policy in isolation. We need to remember only that some of its quantitative effects will be smaller if people expect fiscal policy to have to be reversed at some future date.

Figure 24.7 UK savings as % of GDP

Source: ONS, Economic Trends.

24.7 Demand management revisited

In the last five chapters we have studied how aggregate demand determines output and employment. Fiscal and monetary policy can manage aggregate demand, aiming to keep the economy close to its full-employment level. In periods of recession, when aggregate demand is insufficient, monetary and fiscal expansion can boost demand, output and employment.

Thus far, we have treated the price level as given. If the price level can change, boosting demand may lead not to higher output but to higher prices. In the next chapter, we begin the study of prices and inflation. In so doing, we introduce aggregate supply, and hence the balance between aggregate supply and aggregate demand.

However, you have now completed the first stage of macroeconomics, learning how to analyse the demand side of the economy. Even after mastering the analysis of supply, adjustment and price behaviour, the demand analysis of the last few chapters remains a key part of the story, especially in the short run.

Summary

- A **given fiscal policy** means a given path of government spending and tax rates. A **given monetary policy** must specify the implicit **monetary policy rule** by which interest rates are set. In this chapter, we assume that is to achieve a given **money supply target**.

- The *IS schedule* shows combinations of interest rates and output compatible with short-run equilibrium output in the goods market. Lower interest rates boost demand and output. Other causes of shifts in demand are shown as shifts in the *IS* schedule.

- The *LM schedule* shows combinations of interest rates and output compatible with money market equilibrium when the central bank pursues a money supply target. Higher output is associated with higher interest rates to maintain the equality of money supply and money demand.

- The intersection of *IS* and *LM* schedules shows simultaneous equilibrium in both goods and money markets, jointly determining output and interest rates.

- With a given monetary policy, a **fiscal expansion** increases output, money demand and interest rates, thus **crowding out** or partially displacing private consumption and investment demand.

- For a given fiscal policy, a **monetary expansion** leads to lower interest rates and higher output.

- The **mix of monetary and fiscal policy** affects the equilibrium interest rate as well as the level of output.

- **Ricardian equivalence** says that for a given present value of government spending, the private sector does not care *when* this is financed by taxes, since the total present value of taxes is the same. A tax cut today has no effect on aggregate demand since people anticipate higher future taxes to finance the extra debt interest.

- Ricardian equivalence is only true under extreme assumptions not generally true in practice. Hence tax cuts today do have some effect today. This effect is dampened by the knowledge that unless government spending is also cut, future taxes will have to rise.

- **Demand management** helps stabilize output. Fiscal policy may be difficult to adjust quickly, and may be difficult politically to reverse later: much of its impact on aggregate demand thus arises through **automatic stabilizers** with an unchanged fiscal policy.

Review questions

To check your answers to these questions, go to page 728.

1 Why do people usually save a 'once-off income tax rebate'?

2 For each of these shocks, say whether it shifts the *IS* schedule or the *LM* schedule, and in which direction: (a) an expected future fiscal expansion, (b) a higher money supply target, (c) a rise in money demand caused by higher interest rates being paid by banks on bank deposits.

3 A small country that has adopted the euro must accept the single interest rate set for the whole of Euroland. Draw the *LM* schedule relating the interest rate to that country's national output. Why would this schedule ever shift?

4 Suppose the European Central Bank has a monetary policy rule that relates Euroland's interest rate to total output in Euroland. If the small Euroland country's output is perfectly correlated with the output of all Euroland, draw the *LM* schedule (a) for Euroland and (b) for the small member country.

5 **Common fallacies** Why are the following statements wrong? (a) If tax rates never change, fiscal policy cannot stabilize output. (b) Higher government spending makes interest rates rise, which could cut aggregate demand by more than the rise in government spending. (c) Future policy cannot affect present behaviour.

6 **Harder question** Suppose mortgage lenders issued 20-year loans at fixed interest rates. (a) How would short-term changes in interest rates impact households with a mortgage? (b) Would the Bank of England have to change interest rates by more or by less to have the same effect on aggregate demand as at present?

7 **Harder question** Suppose a central bank adopts a Taylor rule in which it raises nominal interest rates by 0.8 every time inflation rises by 1. (a) How do you expect the central bank gets on in stabilizing inflation around a low level? (b) Suppose inflation is nevertheless low and stable: how might you explain this outcome?

8 **Essay question** 'If households can lend and borrow easily, their consumption and saving decisions simply offset anticipated future tax changes. The principal power of taxation policy to influence aggregate demand arises because households in practice face difficulties borrowing what would be required to implement Ricardian equivalence.' Discuss.

LearningCentre

To help you grasp the key concepts of this chapter check out the extra resources posted on the Online Learning Centre. There are chapter summaries, self-test questions, an interactive graphing tool, weblinks and a searchable glossary, all for free!

To put your learning into practice and prepare for exams, an **Interactive Workbook** is also available online, containing a variety of question types and providing feedback on your answers.

If you'd like further help with economics, or have any questions, **NetTutor** is here to help! You will have a personalised tutorial service at your fingertips. Visit the online learning centre at: www.mcgraw-hill.co.uk/textbooks/begg for information on accessing all of these resources.

CHAPTER 25

Aggregate supply, prices and adjustment to shocks

Learning Outcomes

By the end of this chapter, you should understand:

1 inflation targets for monetary policy

2 the *ii* schedule

3 the macroeconomic demand schedule *MDS*

4 aggregate supply in the classical model

5 the equilibrium inflation rate

6 complete crowding out in the classical model

7 why wage adjustment may be slow

8 short-run aggregate supply

9 temporary and permanent supply shocks

10 how monetary policy reacts to demand and supply shocks

11 flexible inflation targets

Keynesian models suggest that higher aggregate demand always raises output. However, with only finite resources, the economy cannot expand output indefinitely. We now introduce only aggregate supply – firms' willingness and ability to produce – and show how demand and supply together determine output. Aggregate demand reflects the interaction of the markets for goods and money. Aggregate supply reflects the interaction of the markets for goods and labour.

Introducing supply means that we abandon the simplifying assumption that output is determined by demand alone. With both supply and demand, we can also explain what determined prices. We no longer need to assume that prices are given. And since inflation is simply the growth of prices from period to period, a model of prices is also a model of inflation. This allows us to represent monetary policy as inflation targeting, the policy rule actually followed by most central banks today.

To get started, we swap the Keynesian extreme, with fixed wages and prices, for the opposite extreme, full wage and price flexibility.

In the classical model, the economy is *always* at full capacity. Any deviation of output from full capacity causes instant price and wage changes to restore output to potential output. In the classical model, monetary and fiscal policy affect prices but not output, which is always at potential output.

> The **classical model** of macroeconomics assumes wages and prices are completely flexible.

In the short run, until prices and wages adjust, the Keynesian model is relevant. In the long run, once all prices and wages have adjusted, the classical model is relevant. We study how the economy evolves from the Keynesian short run to the classical long run.

25.1 Inflation and aggregate demand

If a central bank behaves predictably, its behaviour should be modelled. Chapter 24 explained why the growing instability of money demand led central banks to abandon monetary targeting. Nowadays, most central banks pursue an inflation target.

> **Inflation** is the growth rate of the price of aggregate output.

Target inflation π^* varies from country to country, but is usually around 2 per cent a year. Why not a target of zero inflation? Policy makers are keen to avoid *deflation* (negative inflation), which can become a black hole. Even if the nominal interest rate r is reduced to zero, the real interest rate i, which is simply $(r - \pi)$, can be large if inflation π is large but negative.

> With an **inflation target**, the central bank adjusts interest rates to try to keep inflation close to the target inflation rate.

In turn, high real interest rates cause further contraction and make inflation more negative still, making real interest rates even higher. If nominal interest rates have already been reduced to zero, monetary policy can do nothing further to combat shrinking aggregate demand. To avoid this black hole, setting a positive inflation target leaves a margin of error. If inflation today is 2 per cent and an unforeseen shock reduces inflation by 1 per cent, there is still time for the central bank to act to boost the economy before it gets too close to a deflationary spiral.

Figure 25.1 shows how monetary policy works when interest rates are set in pursuit of an inflation target. When inflation is high, the central bank ensures that real interest rates are high, which reduces aggregate demand, putting downward pressure on inflation.

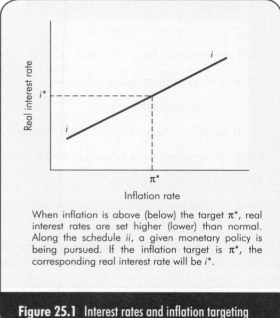

When inflation is above (below) the target π^*, real interest rates are set higher (lower) than normal. Along the schedule *ii*, a given monetary policy is being pursued. If the inflation target is π^*, the corresponding real interest rate will be i^*.

Figure 25.1 Interest rates and inflation targeting

With a vertical *ii* schedule, inflation would be completely stabilized at its target rate $\pi*$. If inflation started to rise, real interest rates would be raised by whatever was necessary to restore inflation to its target level. Conversely, if inflation started to fall, real interest rates would be reduced to whatever level it took immediately to restore inflation to target.

Such a monetary policy would be very aggressive. By the end of this chapter, you will understand why some of its side effects would be undesirable. The *ii* schedule shown in Figure 25.1 shows more moderate intervention. When inflation is too high, the central bank raises real interest rates a bit; when inflation is too low, real interest rates are reduced a bit.

> Under inflation targeting, the **ii schedule** shows that at higher inflation rates the central bank will wish to have higher real interest rates.

Although the central bank is interested in the real interest rate, which affects aggregate demand, the central bank does not directly control the price of output or the inflation rate. Hence, to achieve the *ii* schedule shown in Figure 25.1, the central bank first forecasts inflation, then sets a nominal interest rate r to achieve the real interest rate i ($= r - \pi$) that it desires.

> The central bank sets the **nominal interest rate r** not the **real interest rate i**.

One important implication of Figure 25.1 is that a rise in inflation must lead to a *larger* rise in the nominal interest rate, for only then will the real interest rate be higher when inflation is higher.[1] Merely raising nominal interest rates in line with inflation would mean a constant real interest rate.

We regard a given *ii* schedule as a given monetary policy. Moving along the schedule, the central bank is adjusting interest rates to inflation according to the policy rule already adopted. Changes in monetary policy are shown by *shifts* in the schedule. A looser monetary policy means a downward shift in the *ii* schedule, a lower interest rate at each possible inflation rate. A tighter monetary policy shifts the *ii* schedule upwards, a higher interest rate at each possible inflation rate.

If $\pi*$ is the inflation target, then the chosen height of the *ii* schedule determines the corresponding real interest rate i^* when the inflation target is being met. A tighter monetary policy (higher *ii* schedule) thus implies either accepting a higher real interest rate i^* at the given inflation target $\pi*$, or a lower inflation target at the same real interest rate i^*.

Figure 25.2 shows the level of aggregate demand for output when interest rates obey the *ii* schedule implied by inflation targeting. Movements *along* the macroeconomic demand schedule *MDS* show how inflation makes the central bank alter real interest rates and thus aggregate demand.[2] The *MDS* schedule is flat when (a) interest rate decisions react a lot to inflation and (b) interest rates have a big effect on aggregate demand. The *MDS* is steep when (a) interest rate decisions do not respond much to inflation and (b) changes in interest rates have a small effect on aggregate demand.

Shifts in the *MDS* reflect all other shifts in aggregate demand *not* caused by the effect of inflation on interest rate decisions. Thus, *MDS* shifts up if fiscal policy eases, net exports rise, or monetary policy eases (a lower *ii* schedule).

The macroeconomic demand schedule relates aggregate demand, output and inflation. Next we turn to aggregate supply.

> The **macroeconomic demand schedule MDS** shows how inflation affects aggregate demand when the interest rate is set in pursuit of an inflation target.

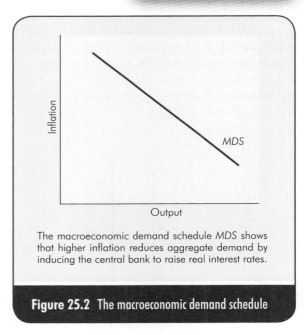

The macroeconomic demand schedule *MDS* shows that higher inflation reduces aggregate demand by inducing the central bank to raise real interest rates.

Figure 25.2 The macroeconomic demand schedule

1 Across countries, higher inflation is often matched by equally higher nominal interest rates, leaving real interest rates roughly constant. This reflects the relative constancy of i^* in the long run. For short-run data for a single country, nominal interest rates vary more than inflation, reflecting the central bank behaviour embodied in Figure 25.1. Recognizing that interest rates must rise sharply when inflation increases has been a key breakthrough of monetary policy design in the last two decades.

2 A similar *MDS* schedule exists if instead the central bank pursues a money supply target. For a given path of nominal money *M*, higher inflation, by raising prices more, reduces the real money supply *M/P* by more. With lower real money supply, interest rates rise to reduce real money demand and maintain money market equilibrium. Higher real interest rates reduce aggregate demand, just as in Figure 25.2. Under a monetary target, interest rates rise because inflation has reduced the real money supply. Under inflation targeting, interest rates rise in direct response to inflation itself, and the real money supply is then reduced to make this an equilibrium. Either way, higher inflation induces higher real interest rates and lower aggregate demand.

25.2 Aggregate supply

When prices and wages are completely flexible, output is always at potential output.

Potential output depends on the level of technology, the quantities of available inputs (labour, capital, land, energy) in long-run equilibrium, and the efficiency with which resources and technology are exploited. In the long run, investment in physical and human capital raises inputs of labour and capital, technical progress improves technology and supply-side policies reduce distortions and raise efficiency. In the short run, we treat potential output as given.

With flexible wages and prices, how does a rise in inflation (and correspondingly faster growth of nominal wages) affect the incentive of firms to supply goods and services?

Thinking in real terms, firms compare the real wage (the nominal wage W divided by the price level P) with the real benefit of labour, the extra output it makes. Similarly, workers compare real take-home pay (its purchasing power over goods and services) with the disutility of sacrificing more leisure in order to work longer. If wages and prices both double, real wages are unaffected. Neither firms nor workers should change their behaviour. Aggregate supply is unaffected by pure inflation since everything nominal rises by the same proportion, as shown in Figure 25.3.

> The **aggregate supply schedule** shows the output *that* firms wish to supply at each inflation rate.

> At **potential output** all inputs are fully employed. It is long-run equilibrium output.

> **Money illusion** exists if people confuse nominal and real variables.

> In the classical model, the **aggregate supply schedule** is vertical at potential output. Equilibrium output is independent of inflation.

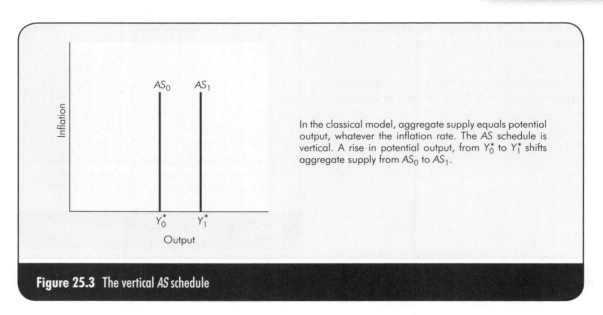

In the classical model, aggregate supply equals potential output, whatever the inflation rate. The *AS* schedule is vertical. A rise in potential output, from Y_0^* to Y_1^* shifts aggregate supply from AS_0 to AS_1.

Figure 25.3 The vertical *AS* schedule

Wage and price flexibility ensures all nominal variables rise together. Without money illusion, people see through nominal changes: real variables are unaltered. In the classical model, real things determine real things, and nominal things determine other nominal things. Better technology, more capital or greater labour supply raise potential output, shifting the vertical supply curve from AS_0 to AS_1 in Figure 25.3. However, for any given level of potential output, lower inflation does *not* reduce the real output that firms wish to supply.

25.3 Equilibrium inflation

For the classical model, Figure 25.4 shows the macroeconomic demand schedule MDS_0 and the vertical aggregate supply schedule AS_0. Output is at potential output and inflation is π_0^*. At point A there is equilibrium in all markets: for output, money and labour.

The labour market is in equilibrium anywhere on the AS_0 schedule, since the economy is at potential output and full employment. A is also on the macroeconomic demand schedule along which interest rates are adjusted in line with monetary policy and the aggregate demand for goods equals the actual output of goods.

The equilibrium inflation rate π_0^* reflects the positions of the AS and MDS schedules. Potential output Y_0^* reflects technology, efficiency and available input supplies. The macroeconomic demand schedule depends on the IS schedule showing how interest rates affect aggregate demand, and on the ii schedule of Figure 25.1, showing how interest rates respond to deviations of inflation from its target level.

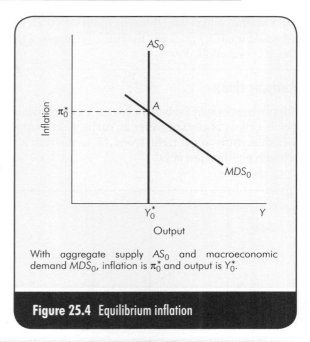

With aggregate supply AS_0 and macroeconomic demand MDS_0, inflation is π_0^* and output is Y_0^*.

Figure 25.4 Equilibrium inflation

Box 25.1 Anchors away!

When prices can change, monetary policy must anchor all nominal variables.

> A **nominal anchor** determines the *level* of other nominal variables. Market forces determine real variables.

Suppose the interest rate r is simply constant. In the classical model, output is Y^*. Y^* and r determine money demand M/P. Nominal money M is passively supplied to get the right level of real money M/P. If the market imagines prices P will be larger, the Bank supplies more nominal money M to maintain equilibrium M/P. Since prices are completely flexible, *any* price level can be the equilibrium price level! The economy has no nominal anchor, no starting point.

A target for nominal money M is one nominal anchor. Money demand determines M/P but, with M now known, the market knows where to set P. An inflation target is an alternative nominal anchor. Given *last* period's price level, now known and unalterable, an inflation target for the price increase between last period and this period is also a target for the current price level P. With money demand M/P and the price level P now known, money market equilibrium determines M. Later we show that a nominal exchange rate can also act as a nominal anchor.

Price level or inflation rate?

Since last period's price level is now known, statements about today's inflation π are equivalent to statements about today's price level P. All the diagrams in this chapter could be drawn with P rather than π on the vertical axis. We prefer to show inflation for two reasons. First, it fits more easily with inflation targeting, the actual policy of modern central banks. Second, it has a clearer link to the Phillips curve in the following chapter.

To ensure that equilibrium inflation π_0^* coincides with the inflation target $\pi*$, the central bank chooses the correct height of the *ii* schedule in Figure 25.1, thereby ensuring the *MDS* schedule has the correct height to make equilibrium inflation π_0^* coincide with the target inflation rate $\pi*$. If π_0^* is too low, the central bank loosens monetary policy, shifting the *ii* schedule down and the *MDS* schedule up. If π_0^* exceeds the inflation target, a tighter monetary policy shifts the *ii* schedule up and the *MDS* schedule down.

A supply shock

Supply shocks may be beneficial, such as technical progress, or may be adverse, such as higher real oil prices or loss of capacity after an earthquake. Suppose potential output rises. In Figure 25.5 the *AS* schedule shifts to the right, from AS_0 to AS_1. For a *given MDS* schedule, equilibrium inflation falls to π_2^* with equilibrium at *D*.

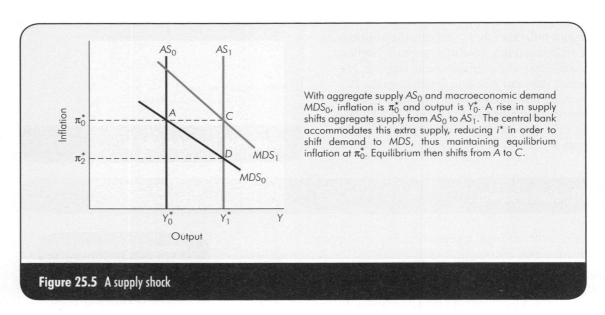

With aggregate supply AS_0 and macroeconomic demand MDS_0, inflation is π_0^* and output is Y_0^*. A rise in supply shifts aggregate supply from AS_0 to AS_1. The central bank accommodates this extra supply, reducing i^* in order to shift demand to *MDS*, thus maintaining equilibrium inflation at π_0^*. Equilibrium then shifts from *A* to *C*.

Figure 25.5 A supply shock

However, the central bank still wants a long-run equilibrium inflation rate π_0^*. Hence, in response to the supply shock, the central bank loosens monetary policy, shifting the *ii* schedule downwards and the *MDS* schedule upwards. Lower real interest rates boost aggregate demand in line with higher potential output Y_1^*. The new equilibrium is at *C* not *D*. With unchanged inflation, the lower real interest rate also implies a lower nominal interest rate.

Lower interest rates raise the demand for money. To restore money market equilibrium, the central bank must then supply more money.

Conversely, if high oil prices permanently reduce aggregate supply, this shifts AS_1 to AS_0. Beginning at point *C*, the central bank must then tighten monetary policy, so that higher real interest rates reduce aggregate demand in line with the lower aggregate supply.

> **Monetary policy accommodates a permanent supply change** by altering the real interest rate (shift in the *ii* schedule) to induce a similar change in aggregate demand.

A demand shock

Suppose aggregate demand shifts up because of easier fiscal policy or greater private sector optimism about future incomes and profits. Beginning from equilibrium at *A* in Figure 25.6, but keeping supply fixed at AS_0, a demand shift from MDS_0 to MDS_1 leads to a new equilibrium at *B*.

Box 25.2 The oil price puzzle

The figure below shows the dramatic increase in oil prices after 2003. If oil price shocks lead to inflation, why did so little inflation materialize? Was the Bank of England lulled into a false sense of security? Should we be surprised that by April 2007 the Bank had to justify why it had allowed UK inflation to exceed the target range to which it is committed.

The Bank was not entirely asleep. For example, Monetary Policy Committee member David Walton gave a speech in February 2006 entitled 'Has Oil Lost the Capacity to Shock?', concluding:

(a) *The size and nature of the shock have been different.* Relative to previous episodes, the shock had taken longer to unfold.

(b) *The UK economy had been better placed to absorb the current oil price shock.* There were few inflationary pressures in the economy when oil prices first began to rise sharply and there had been little sign subsequently of higher wage demands.

(c) *The monetary policy framework had played an important role.* Inflation targeting has helped to anchor inflation expectations, preventing it spilling over into wage claims, yet had allowed the Bank to respond flexibly to the oil shock.

To these, he might have added a fourth:

(d) *Beneficial supply shocks* (cheaper imports from China and other parts of the global economy had provided downward pressure on prices at precisely the time that adverse supply shocks (oil and commodity price rises) were providing upward pressure on prices.

By April 2007, the balance of these effects had turned clearly towards inflation. Consumer price inflation reached 3.1 per cent. On the retail price index that had previously been used to measure prices, inflation was heading up towards 5 per cent. The honeymoon for Bank of England independence was well and truly over.

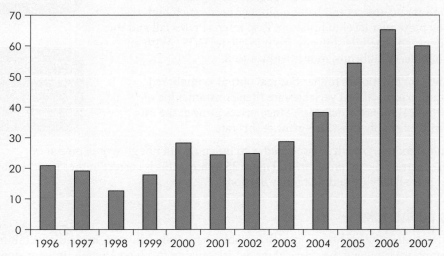

Oil price ($ barrel, Brent crude)

The central bank can continue to hit its inflation target π_0^* only by tightening monetary policy to offset the demand shock. In full equilibrium, with unchanged supply AS_0, aggregate demand must not change. By raising real interest rates, the central bank can reduce aggregate demand again. The central bank thus tightens monetary policy (upward shift in *ii* schedule) until the demand shock is fully offset and MDS_1 has shifted down to MDS_0 again. Equilibrium remains at A and the inflation target π_0^* is still achieved.

The original rise in demand could have come from the private or the public sector. If it was higher private demand, the higher real interest rate simply reduces private demand back to its original level. If it was higher government spending, the central bank raises interest rates until private spending falls by as much as government spending increased.

Note the distinction between partial crowding out in the Keynesian model and complete crowding out in the classical model. In the Keynesian model, output was demand-determined in the short run. Higher *output* induced the central bank to raise interest rates, which partly offset the expansionary effect of higher government spending.

In the classical model, aggregate supply is the binding constraint. Output does not change. When higher government expenditure raises aggregate demand, higher interest rates must reduce consumption and investment to leave aggregate demand unaltered.

We may draw a second conclusion from Figure 25.6. Suppose monetary policy changes because the inflation target is raised from π_0^* to π_1^*. With a higher target inflation rate, the central bank no longer needs such high real interest rates at any particular level of inflation. Real interest rates fall and the macroeconomic demand schedule shifts up from MDS_0 to MDS_1. With an unchanged AS schedule, equilibrium moves from A to B.

In the new equilibrium, inflation is higher but real output is unaltered. Since it is a full equilibrium, all real variables are then constant. One of these variables is the real money stock M/P. Since prices grow at the rate π_1^*, the nominal money supply must also grow at this rate.

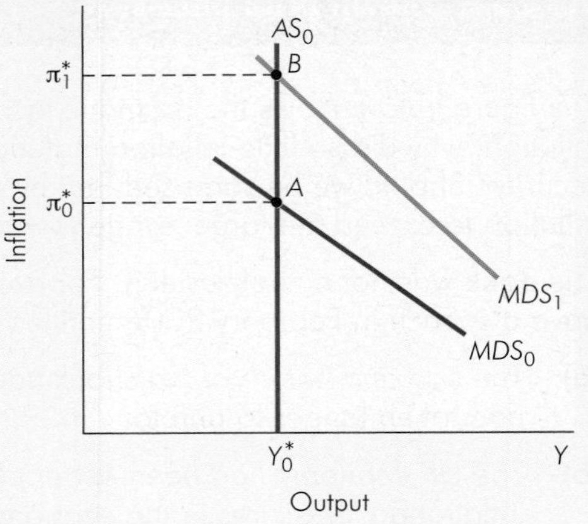

With aggregate supply AS and macroeconomic demand MDS_0, inflation is π_0^* and output is Y_0^*. For a given aggregate supply, a rise in demand from MDS_0 to MDS_1, violates the long-run inflation target at π_0^*. Thus the central bank raises i^* to shift MDS_1, back to MDS_0 and restore equilibrium at A.

Figure 25.6 A demand shock

In the classical model with a vertical AS schedule, **a rise in government spending crowds out an equal amount of private spending**. Aggregate demand remains equal to potential output.

In the classical model, **faster nominal money growth** is accompanied by higher inflation but leaves real output constant at potential output.

The idea that nominal money growth is associated with inflation, but not growth of output or employment, is the central tenet of *monetarists*. Figure 25.6 shows this is correct in the classical model with full wage and price flexibility and no money illusion.

How long does all this take?

The classical model studies the economy once all variables have fully adjusted. Instead of thinking of adjustment as instant, we can view the classical model as applying to a long enough time for slower adjustment to be completed. This means not just wage and price adjustment, but time for the central bank to work out what is going on and amend monetary policy if necessary, and time for these interest rate changes to have their full effect on private behaviour. Suppose the economy faces a fall in aggregate demand. What happens next?

The classical model

With aggregate supply unaffected, a fall in aggregate demand leads to lower inflation, to which the central bank immediately responds by easing monetary policy, reducing the real interest rate, boosting private sector demand and thus restoring aggregate demand to the unchanged level of potential output.[3]

The Keynesian model

Before wages and price adjustment is possible, there is no change in inflation to which the central bank can respond. The initial effect of lower aggregate demand is simply a fall in output. The rest of this chapter studies the adjustment process by which the economy gradually makes the transition from the Keynesian short run to the classical long run. To do so, we introduce the short-run aggregate supply curve.

25.4 The labour market and wage behaviour

Downward shocks cause recessions lasting years not weeks. Why don't changes in prices react faster, allowing changes that restore potential output? Firms relate prices to costs. Wages are the largest part of costs. Sluggish wage adjustment to departures from full employment is the main cause of slow adjustment of prices.

For both firms and workers, a job is often a long-term commitment. For the firm, it is costly to hire and fire workers. Firing entails a redundancy payment and the loss of the expertise the worker had built up on the job. Hiring entails advertising, interviewing and training a new worker in the special features of that firm. Firms are reluctant to hire and fire workers just because of short-term fluctuations in demand.

For the worker, looking for a new job costs time and effort, and throws away experience, seniority and the high wages justified by the high productivity that comes from having mastered a particular job in a particular firm. Like firms, workers care about long-term arrangements. Firms and workers reach an understanding about pay and conditions *in the medium term*, including how to handle fluctuations in the firm's output in the short run.

A firm and its workers have explicit contracts, or implicit agreements, specifying working conditions. These include normal hours, overtime requirements, regular wages and pay schedules for overtime work. The firm then sets the number of hours, within the limits of these conditions, depending on how much output it wishes to make in that week.

When demand falls, the firm initially reduces hours of work. Overtime ends and factories close early. If demand does not recover, or declines further, firms start firing workers. Conversely, in a boom a firm makes its existing workforce work overtime. Then it seeks temporary workers to supplement the existing labour force. Only when the firm is sure that higher sales will be sustained does it hire extra permanent workers.

---

3 A similar analysis applies under monetary targeting. Suppose this is 2 per cent annual growth in nominal money. Long-run inflation will also be 2 per cent. A fall in aggregate demand bids down wage and price growth *below what they would have been*. With inflation below 2 per cent but an unchanged nominal money growth of 2 per cent, the real money supply expands. This causes a fall in real interest rates and boosts aggregate demand back to potential output. Thereafter, money and prices both grow at 2 per cent. The real money supply is permanently higher and real interest rates permanently lower.

Wage adjustment

Wages are not set in a daily auction in which the equilibrium wage clears the market for labour. Firms and workers both gain from long-term understandings. This mutual commitment partly insulates a firm and its workforce from temporary conditions in the labour market.

Nor can a firm and its workforce spend every day haggling. Bargaining is costly, using up valuable time that could be used to produce output. Bargaining costs mean wages change only at discrete intervals. Immediate wage adjustment to shocks is ruled out. At best, firms must wait until the next scheduled date for a revision in the wage structure. In practice, complete wage adjustment is unlikely to take place even then. Chapter 10 discussed other reasons why involuntary unemployment is not instantly eliminated by wage adjustment.

Recap

In the short run (the first few months), changes in labour input are largely changes in hours. In the medium run (up to two years), as changes in labour demand persist, the firm begins to alter its permanent workforce. In the long run (perhaps four to six years), adjustment is complete.

In the short run, trends in wages are largely given. The firm has some flexibility over earnings, as distinct from negotiated wage rates, because fluctuations in overtime and short time affect average hourly earnings. But this flexibility is limited. In the medium run, the firm begins to adjust the path of wages. In the long run, the process is complete and the economy is back at potential output.

We now use this analysis to think about the market for output. By distinguishing supply in the short run and in the long run, our model of output reflects *both* supply and demand, even in the short run. Nevertheless, its short-run behaviour is like the simple Keynesian case in which output is demand-determined. Its long-run behaviour is fully classical.

25.5 Short-run aggregate supply

In Figure 25.7 the economy is at potential output at *A*. In the short run, the firm inherits a given rate of nominal wage growth (not shown in the figure). Previous wage negotiations anticipated remaining in long-run equilibrium at *A* with inflation π_0. By keeping up with inflation, nominal wage growth is expected to maintain the correct real wage for labour market equilibrium.

If inflation exceeds the expected inflation rate π_0, this helps firms by raising their output prices. The real wage is lower than expected. If this had been foreseen when wages were negotiated, the inherited nominal wage would have been higher; but it was not foreseen. Firms take advantage of their good luck by supplying a lot more output. They can afford to pay overtime to ensure that the workforce co-operates, and may also take on temporary extra staff.

Conversely, if inflation is below π_0, the real wage is now higher than anticipated when the nominal wage was agreed. Since labour is now costly, firms cut back output a lot. They move from *A* to *B* in Figure 25.7. Firms move along the supply schedule *SAS* in the short run.

> The **short-run supply curve SAS** shows how desired output varies with inflation, for a given inherited growth of nominal wages.

If demand and output remain low, the growth rate of negotiated nominal wages gradually falls. With lower wage growth, firms do not need to raise output prices so quickly. The short-run aggregate supply schedule shifts down from *SAS* to *SAS*$_1$ in Figure 25.7. Lower inflation moves the economy down its macroeconomic demand schedule, increasing the demand for goods. If full employment and potential output are still not restored, negotiated wage growth falls again, leading to a short-run aggregate supply schedule such as *SAS*$_2$.

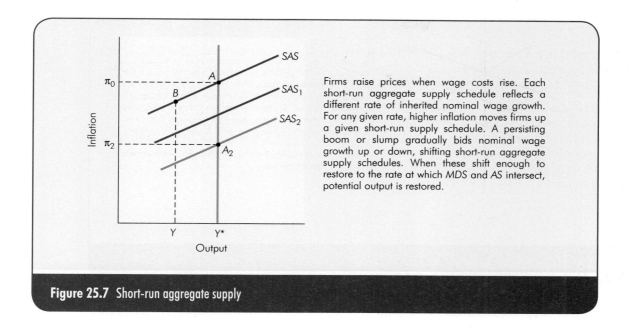

Firms raise prices when wage costs rise. Each short-run aggregate supply schedule reflects a different rate of inherited nominal wage growth. For any given rate, higher inflation moves firms up a given short-run supply schedule. A persisting boom or slump gradually bids nominal wage growth up or down, shifting short-run aggregate supply schedules. When these shift enough to restore to the rate at which *MDS* and *AS* intersect, potential output is restored.

Figure 25.7 Short-run aggregate supply

These short-run aggregate supply schedules give a realistic picture of adjustment to demand shocks. Because the short-run aggregate supply schedule is flat, a shift in aggregate demand leads mainly to changes in output not prices in the short run. This is the Keynesian feature. But deviations from full employment gradually change wage growth and short-run aggregate supply. The economy gradually works its way back to potential output. That is the classical feature. We now describe adjustment in more detail.

25.6 The adjustment process

We now combine the macroeconomic demand schedule with the short-run aggregate supply schedule to show how demand or supply shocks set up an adjustment process. In combining the *MDS* schedule and the *SAS* schedule, we assume that the goods market clears, even in the short run. Short-run aggregate supply gradually changes over time as wage growth adjusts to the rate that restores full employment and potential output, placing firms eventually on their long-run aggregate supply schedule.

Output is no longer demand-determined when aggregate demand lies below the level of potential output. In the short run, firms are also on their short-run supply schedules producing what they wish, *given the inherited nominal wages*.

However, sluggish wage adjustment prevents immediate restoration of full employment. When aggregate demand for goods falls, firms reduce output and employment. Since wages do not fall at once, there is involuntary unemployment. *Employment* is demand-determined in the short run.

Figure 25.8 shows a downward shift in the macroeconomic demand schedule from *MDS* to *MDS'* because monetary policy is tightened (a higher *ii* schedule in Figure 25.1). In the long run, aggregate demand must return to potential output, and the economy will end up at E_3. Hence, the tighter monetary policy can be viewed as a cut in the target inflation rate from $\pi*$ to π_3^*.

When monetary policy is first tightened, interest rates are initially raised since actual inflation at *E* is now above target. Macroeconomic demand shifts down to *MDS'*. In the classical model there is an

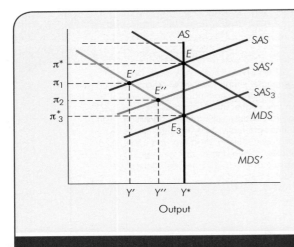

Beginning at E, a lower inflation target shifts MDS to MDS'. Given inherited wage growth, the new equilibrium is at E'. Output falls from Y^* to Y', and actual inflation is only π_1. Since wages have risen faster than prices despite the fall in output, unemployment rises. In the next wage settlement, nominal wage growth slows, and the short-run supply schedule becomes SAS'. Equilibrium is now at E'', and output recovers to Y''. Once wage growth slows enough to make SAS_3 the supply curve, long-run equilibrium is re-established at E_3.

Figure 25.8 A lower inflation target

instant adjustment of prices and wages to keep the economy at full employment and potential output. Equilibrium inflation immediately falls to π_3^* and the new equilibrium is at E_3. Output remains at potential output Y^*.

These classical results are valid only in the long run. When adjustment of wages and prices is slow, the economy faces the short-run aggregate supply schedule SAS, reflecting the nominal wages recently agreed.

In the short run, the downward shift in MDS causes a move from E to E'. Since firms cannot cut costs much, they reduce output to Y'. At E' the goods market clears at the intersection of the demand schedule MDS' and the supply schedule SAS. Inflation has fallen a little because of lower demand, but output has fallen a lot. With lower inflation than the expectation built into nominal wage agreements, *real wages have risen*, despite the fall in output. Once firms can adjust employment, some workers are fired and unemployment rises.

In the medium run, this starts to reduce wage growth. With inherited wages lower than they would have been, firms move on to a lower short-run aggregate supply schedule SAS'. The goods market now clears at E''. Output and employment recover a bit, but some unemployment persists. Since inflation has fallen, the central bank is less worried about the amount by which inflation exceeds its new target and cuts real interest rates, moving the economy down MDS' to E''.

In the long run, adjustment is complete. Wage growth and inflation fall to π_3^*. The short-run aggregate supply schedule is SAS_3 in Figure 25.8. The economy is in full equilibrium at E_3, on AS, SAS and MDS'. Output is Y^* and the labour market is back at full employment.

The real world lies between the extreme simplifications of the simple Keynesian model and classical models. In practice, prices and wages are neither fully flexible nor fully fixed. A tougher inflation target has real effects in the short run, since output and employment are reduced. But after wages and prices adjust fully, output and employment return to normal. Inflation is permanently lower thereafter.

Activity box 25   Output gaps 1989–2007

The output gap $(Y - Y^*)$ is the percentage deviation of actual output Y from potential output Y^*. Each year the Paris-based Organization for Economic Cooperation and Development (OECD) estimates potential output for all its member countries. The diagram below shows estimates for the UK and Finland. Positive output gaps are booms, negative gaps indicate slumps.

The diagram shows the UK slump in the late 1980s, at the tail end of the Lawson boom that led to renewed inflation; the Major recession in the early 1990s as policy was tightened to cut inflation again; and recovery after 1993. It confirms that the switch to inflation targeting after 1992 has generally led to a more stable macroeconomy.

We also show Finland, whose exports rose after the opening of trade with Russia, but then collapsed as the former Soviet Union imploded in the early 1990s. Since the mid-1990s, Finland has made a strong recovery, helped by high-tech firms like Nokia.

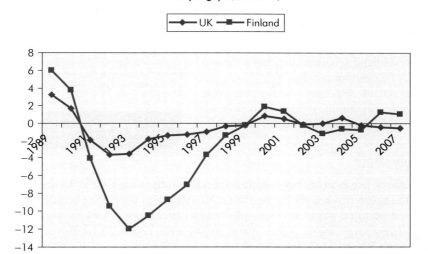

Output gaps (% of GDP)

Questions
There are two ways in which you might try to calculate potential output, and hence the output gap: (i) statistically, by fitting trend lines through previous business cycles, and (ii) economically by trying to get an idea of the balance of aggregate supply and aggregate demand.

(a)   If you wanted a quick procedure capable of being replicated across many countries, which of the two would you be inclined to choose?

(b)   How might you build up an idea of an empirical economic model of the balance between actual output and potential output?

To check your answers to these questions, go to page 730.

25.7 Sluggish adjustment to shocks

A permanent supply shock

Suppose a change in attitudes towards women working leads to an increase in labour supply. Potential output rises. In the long run, aggregate demand must rise in line with aggregate supply. Lower real interest rates allow higher aggregate demand at the unchanged inflation target $\pi*$. Provided monetary policy is loosened, the rightward shift in *MDS* can match the rightward shift in aggregate supply. By accommodating the extra supply with looser monetary policy, the inflation rate remains $\pi*$, and the economy moves directly to the new long-run equilibrium, from E_0 to E_1 in Figure 25.9.

Because of lags in diagnosing the shock, and in the response of consumption and investment demand to lower interest rates, Figure 25.9 exaggerates the ease of adjustment to a permanent supply shock. In practice, output may not jump all the way to the new level of potential output.

If the macroeconomic demand schedule does not fully and immediately shift to MDS_1, output is below $Y*_1$. This reduces inflation and the central bank responds with lower interest rates. Over time, the macroeconomic demand schedule will drift to the right until it reaches MDS_1 in Figure 25.9.

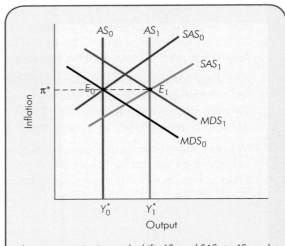

A permanent rise in supply shifts AS_0 and SAS_0 to AS_1 and SAS_1. By permanently reducing interest rates, the central bank shifts MDS_0 to MDS_1, meeting its inflation target $\pi*$ in the new equilibrium at E_1. If the central bank acts quickly, no further shifts in SAS_1 are required.

Figure 25.9 A permanent supply increase

A temporary supply shock

A temporary supply shock leaves potential output unaffected in the long run. With the vertical *AS* schedule unaltered, the short-run supply curve must shift. Although the *SAS* schedule is *mainly* influenced by inherited nominal wages, it is *also* affected by other input prices. Suppose a temporary oil price rise makes firms charge higher prices at any output level. Figure 25.10 shows a shift upwards in short-run supply, from *SAS* to *SAS'*. The new short-run equilibrium is at E'. Inflation rises but output and employment fall because the central bank raises real interest rates in response to higher inflation.

If the central bank maintains its inflation target $\pi*$, lower output and employment at E' gradually reduce inflation and nominal wage growth, shifting *SAS'* gradually back to *SAS*. The economy slowly moves down the *MDS* schedule back to the original equilibrium at E.

A different outcome is possible. When the higher oil price shifts *SAS* to *SAS'*, it is possible to *avoid* the period of low output as the economy moves along *MDS* from E' back to E. A *change* in monetary policy can *shift MDS* up enough to pass through E''. Output can quickly return to potential output, but only because the inflation target[4] has been loosened from $\pi*$ to $\pi*''$. The new long-run new equilibrium is then at E''.

A **permanent supply shock** changes potential output. A **temporary supply shock** shifts the short-run aggregate supply schedule, but leaves potential output unaltered.

Monetary policy accommodates a temporary supply shock when monetary policy is altered to help stabilize output. The consequence, however, is higher inflation.

---

4 Looser monetary policy shifts the *ii* schedule to the right in Figure 25.1. However, once long-run equilibrium is restored $i*$ must be unaltered: since aggregate supply is eventually unaltered, aggregate demand cannot eventually change. The only way for the central bank to loosen monetary policy without changing $i*$ is to accept a higher inflation target $\pi*$.

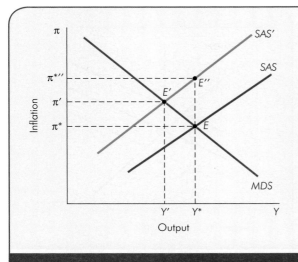

Higher oil prices force firms to raise prices. In the short-run, SAS shifts up to SAS', and equilibrium shifts from E to E'. Higher inflation reduces aggregate demand since the central bank raises real interest rates. Once the temporary supply shock disappears, SAS' gradually falls back to SAS, and equilibrium is eventually restored at E.

Figure 25.10 A temporary supply shock

A central bank caring a lot about output stability may accommodate short-run supply shocks, even if this means higher inflation. A central bank caring more about its inflation target than about output stability will not accommodate temporary supply shocks.

It matters a lot whether the supply shock is temporary or permanent. If potential output is *permanently* affected, aggregate demand *must* eventually rise to match. Once a supply side shock is diagnosed as permanent, it should be accommodated.

Demand shocks

Figure 25.11 explores demand shocks *not* caused by monetary policy. If demand is high, facing MDS' the economy moves along its short-run supply curve to point A. If demand is low, facing MDS'' the economy moves along the SAS curve to point B.

Suppose the central bank diagnoses that an expansionary demand shock has occurred. It can tighten monetary policy and shift MDS' back down to MDS again. Similarly, it can loosen monetary policy in response to low aggregate demand MDS'', restoring MDS again. The economy remains at E. Both inflation *and* output are stabilized.

It is easy for the central bank to tell where inflation is relative to its target rate. It is harder to estimate the level of potential output, which can change over time. This is part of the modern case for using inflation targeting as the intermediate target of monetary policy. When all shocks are demand shocks, it works perfectly.

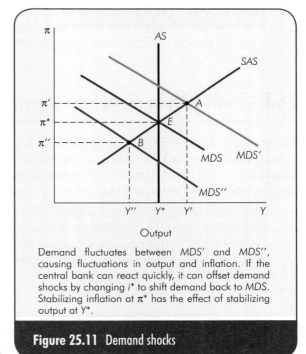

Output

Demand fluctuates between MDS' and MDS'', causing fluctuations in output and inflation. If the central bank can react quickly, it can offset demand shocks by changing i^* to shift demand back to MDS. Stabilizing inflation at π^* has the effect of stabilizing output at Y^*.

Figure 25.11 Demand shocks

When all shocks are **demand shocks**, stabilizing inflation also stabilizes output, even in a Keynesian model.

Suppose, instead, that all shocks are supply shocks. Figure 25.12 shows the long-run supply curve AS, vertical at potential output Y^*, and a set of short-run supply curves whose average level is SAS but which fluctuate between SAS′ and SAS″.

On average, output is Y^* and inflation is $\pi*$. If interest rates are varied very aggressively to stabilize inflation in the face of supply shocks, the MDS schedule is effectively horizontal at $\pi*$. Inflation is stabilized, but output fluctuates between Y' and Y'' when supply fluctuates between SAS′ and SAS″. Unlike the case of demand shocks, it is no longer possible to stabilize output *and* inflation.

Similarly, it is possible to stabilize output completely but only at the cost of allowing big fluctuations in inflation. The MDS schedule is then vertical at potential output. A rise in short-run supply to SAS′ induces a big rise in interest rates to reduce aggregate demand to Y^* again. With high supply but low demand, inflation is temporarily low (relative to inherited wage growth) and firms wish to supply only Y^*. When supply shrinks temporarily to SAS″, firms supply output Y^* only if inflation is high (relative to inherited wage growth), which needs a low interest rate to boost demand.

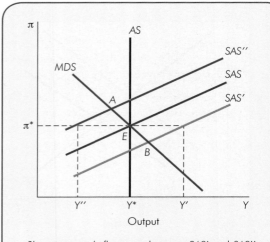

Short-run supply fluctuates between SAS′ and SAS″. If interest rates are set to stabilize inflation at $\pi*$, output fluctuates between Y' and Y''. Monetary policy cannot stabilize both output and inflation in response to supply shocks. It makes sense to set interest rates to allow some inflation fluctuations in order to reduce output a bit. For the Taylor rule implied by MDS the economy fluctuates between points A and B. A flatter MDS schedule would imply smaller inflation fluctuations but larger fluctuations in output.

Figure 25.12 Temporary supply shocks

25.8 Trade-offs in monetary objectives

Facing supply shocks, Figure 25.12 implies that it is a bad idea either to stabilize inflation completely at π^* (which induces big fluctuations in output) or to stabilize output at Y^* (which induces big fluctuations in inflation). The macroeconomic demand schedule MDS in Figure 25.12 is a particular compromise in the way interest rates are set.[5]

Any MDS schedule through point E achieves the targets $\pi*$ and Y^* on average. The particular schedule MDS in Figure 25.12 makes the economy fluctuate between A (when supply is SAS″) and B (when supply is SAS′). This achieves acceptable fluctuations in both output and inflation. A steeper MDS schedule, still through A, induces lower output fluctuations but larger inflation fluctuations. A flatter schedule has the opposite effect. The steepness of the schedule reflects the relative weight the central bank places on stabilizing inflation and output.

This trade-off does not arise for demand shocks. Figure 25.11 showed that, by fully offsetting demand shocks, the central bank stabilizes both output and prices. In reality, the central bank faces both supply and demand shocks, and cannot always diagnose which is which. It much choose a monetary rule that gives reasonable answers under both kinds of shocks.

Flexible inflation targeting commits a central bank to hit inflation targets in the medium run, but gives it some discretion about *how quickly* to hit its inflation target.

---

5 And this finally explains why in Figure 25.1 the central bank does not simply choose a vertical *ii* schedule at the target inflation rate. When adjustment is sluggish and supply shocks occur, this would imply big swings in output.

There is no conflict between output stability and inflation stability when shocks are demand shocks. It makes sense to try to hit the target as quickly as possible. Similarly, a permanent supply shock requires a permanent change in demand, which there is little reason to postpone. However, facing a *temporary supply shock*, Figure 25.12 showed that it makes sense temporarily to allow inflation to deviate from its target in order to mitigate the shock to output.

The *ii* schedule in Figure 25.1 reflects the average behaviour of the central bank under flexible inflation targeting. Deviations of inflation from target are not all immediately eliminated, but they are eventually eliminated by the policy of raising (lowering) real interest rates whenever inflation is too high (low). Temporary deviations of inflation from target are the price to be paid for ensuring that output fluctuations are not too large.

The key to successful flexible inflation targeting is that any deviation of inflation from target should be *temporary*. Credible central banks persist with high interest rates until inflation is restored to its target rate. And when credible central banks reduce interest to boost demand, nobody fears that the inflation target has been increased, and there is no reason for nominal wage bargains to fear a permanent rise in inflation.

In contrast, weak central banks that lack credibility may cause panic by easing monetary policy today. People worry that they will not be tough enough later to reverse this demand expansion. Foreseeing sustained expansion, inflation gets going. This insight places credibility centre stage, where it belongs. Chapter 26 examines the economics of credibility and its effect on inflation.

Summary

- The **classical model** of macroeconomics assumes full flexibility of wages and prices and no money illusion.

- The **ii schedule** shows, under a policy of **inflation targeting**, how the central bank achieves high interest rates when inflation is high and low interest rates when inflation is low. Central banks set nominal not real interest rates, and hence must first forecast inflation in order to calculate what nominal interest rate they wish to set.

- The *ii* schedule shifts to the left, a higher real interest rate at each inflation rate, when monetary policy is tightened, and to the right, a lower real interest rate at each inflation rate, when monetary policy is loosened.

- The **macroeconomic demand schedule** shows how higher inflation reduces aggregate demand by inducing monetary policy to raise real interest rates.

- The classical model always has full employment. The **aggregate supply schedule** is vertical at **potential output. Equilibrium inflation** is at the intersection of the aggregate supply schedule and the macroeconomic demand schedule. The markets for goods, money, and labour are all in equilibrium. Monetary policy is set to make the equilibrium inflation rate coincide with the inflation target.

- In the classical model, fiscal expansion cannot increase output. To continue to hit its inflation target, the central bank must raise real interest rates to restore aggregate demand to the level of potential output. **Higher government spending crowds out an equal amount of private spending**, leaving demand and output unaltered.

- Changing the target inflation rate leads to an equivalent change in the growth of wages and nominal money in the classical model, but not to a change in output.

- In practice, wages adjust slowly to shocks since job arrangements are long term. **Wage adjustment** is sluggish not merely because wage bargaining is infrequent, but because workers prefer their long-term employers to smooth wages.

- Prices mainly reflect labour costs. The **short-run aggregate supply schedule** shows firms' desired output, given the inherited growth of nominal wages. Output is temporarily responsive to inflation, since nominal wages are already determined. As wage adjustment occurs, the short-run supply schedule shifts.

- The **Keynesian model** is a good guide to short-term behaviour but the **classical model** describes behaviour in the long run.

- **Permanent supply shocks** alter potential output. **Temporary supply shocks** merely alter the short-run supply curve for a while.

- If its effects were instant, monetary policy could completely offset **demand shocks**, stabilizing both inflation and output. **Temporary supply shocks** force a trade-off between output stability and inflation stability. The output effect of **permanent supply shocks** cannot be escaped indefinitely.

- **Flexible inflation targeting** implies the central bank need not immediately hit its inflation target, allowing some scope for temporary action to cushion output fluctuations.

Review questions

To check your answers to these questions, go to page 729.

1 (a) Define the macroeconomic demand schedule. (b) How does a fiscal expansion affect the schedule under a flexible inflation target? (c) How would the central bank have to change monetary policy to hit its given inflation target in the long run?

2 Suppose opportunities for investing in high-tech applications boost aggregate demand in the short run, but aggregate supply in the long run. Using *AS* and *MDS* schedules, show why output might rise *without* much inflation.

3 How do the following affect the short-run supply schedule, and hence output and inflation in the short run: (a) a higher tax rate; (b) higher labour productivity?

4 An economy has the choice of having half its workers make annual wage agreements every January, and the other half make annual wage agreements every July, or instead forcing everyone to make their annual agreement on 1 July. Which system is likely to induce greater wage flexibility during a period of a few months and during a period of several years?

5 OPEC raises the price of oil for a year but then a new supply of oil from Russia bids oil prices back down again. Contrast the evolution of the economy if monetary policy follows: (a) a fixed interest rate, (b) flexible inflation targeting, or (c) a nominal money target.

6 **Common fallacies** Why are these statements wrong? (a) Fiscal expansion can increase output for ever. (b) Higher inflation always reduces output.

---

7 **Harder question** Imagine that the UK adopts the euro, and interest rates are set by the European Central Bank. (a) Are euro interest rates likely to be adjusted to help stabilize either UK inflation or UK output? (b) What automatic mechanisms, if any, can still achieve these outcomes? (c) Would UK fiscal policy be able to help more?

8 **Harder question** In 2007, the Governor of the Bank of England had to write to the Chancellor of the Exchequer to explain why UK inflation had exceeded the target range laid down by the Chancellor. (a) Why were these difficult circumstances? (b) Was the letter proof that the Bank of England had screwed up?

---

9 **Essay question** 'Climate change is essentially a permanent adverse supply shock. Production costs will rise, potential output will fall. If the private sector fails to adjust, then either monetary or fiscal policy will have to reduce aggregate demand to the required lower level.' Discuss.

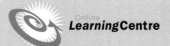

To help you grasp the key concepts of this chapter check out the extra resources posted on the Online Learning Centre. There are chapter summaries, self-test questions, an interactive graphing tool, weblinks and a searchable glossary, all for free!

To put your learning into practice and prepare for exams, an **Interactive Workbook** is also available online, containing a variety of question types and providing feedback on your answers.

If you'd like further help with economics, or have any questions, **NetTutor** is here to help! You will have a personalised tutorial service at your fingertips. Visit the online learning centre at: www.mcgraw-hill.co.uk/textbooks/begg for information on accessing all of these resources.

CHAPTER 26

Inflation, expectations and credibility

Learning Outcomes

By the end of this chapter, you should understand:

1 the quantity theory of money

2 how nominal interest rates reflect inflation

3 seigniorage, the inflation tax and why hyperinflations occur

4 when budget deficits cause money growth

5 the Phillips curve

6 the costs of inflation

7 central bank independence and inflation control

8 how the Monetary Policy Committee sets UK interest rates

On its election in 1997 the Labour government made the Bank of England independent, with a mandate to achieve low inflation.

Sustained inflation is a recent phenomenon. Before 1950, prices rose in some years but fell in other years. The UK price level was no higher in 1950 than in 1920. Figure 26.1 shows that the UK price level fell sharply in some interwar years when inflation was negative. The postwar price level has never fallen. Since 1950 the price level has risen 20-fold, more than its rise over the previous three centuries. This story applies in most advanced economies.

The effects of inflation depend on what causes inflation. We start with the causes of inflation, then examine its effects, which partly depend on whether inflation was anticipated or took people by surprise. We contrast costs that inflation imposes on individuals and costs it imposes on society as a whole. We conclude by considering what the government can do about inflation.

Inflation is a rise in the price level. **Pure inflation** means that prices of goods and inputs rise at the same rate.

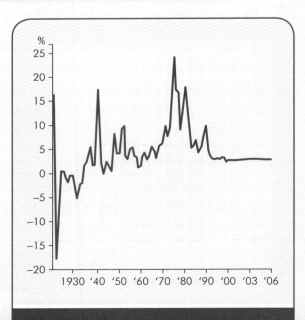

Figure 26.1 Tha annual UK inflation rate 1920–2006
Sources: R. B. Mitchell, *European Historical Statistics 1750–1970*, Macmillan, 1975; OECD, *Economic Outlook.*

26.1 Money and inflation

> The **real money supply** M/P is the nominal money supply M divided by the price level P.

There is a link between nominal money and the price level, and hence between nominal money growth and inflation.

People demand money because of its purchasing power over goods. They demand *real* money. When real income is Y and the interest rate is r, the symbol $L(Y, r)$ shows the stock of real money demanded. This rises with real income Y, since the benefit of holding money increases. It falls with the interest rate r, since the cost of holding money is higher.

$$M/P = L(Y, r) \tag{1}$$

Box 26.1 The quantity theory of money: $MV = PY$

The velocity of circulation V is nominal income PY divided by nominal money M. If prices adjust to keep real output at potential output Y^*, assumed constant, M and P must move together, *provided velocity V stays constant*. Velocity is the speed at which the stock of money is passed round the economy as people transact. If everyone holds money for less time and passes it on more quickly, the economy needs less money relative to nominal income. How do we assess whether velocity is constant, as the simple quantity theory requires?

The quantity theory equation implies $M/P = Y/V$. The left-hand side is the real money supply. The right-hand side must be real money demand. It rises with real income and falls with velocity. But real money demand rises with real income and falls with nominal interest rates. Hence velocity just measures the effect of interest rates on real money demand. Higher nominal interest rates reduce real money demand. People *hold* less money relative to income. Velocity rises.

While inflation and nominal interest rates are rising, velocity is rising. But if inflation and nominal interest rates settle down at a particular level, velocity is then constant. Thereafter, the simple quantity theory once more applies.

This assumes prices are fully flexible. In the short run, if prices are sluggish, changes in nominal money change the real money supply. Changes in nominal money are not matched by changes in prices. The quantity theory of money will fail in the short run.

In money market equilibrium, real money supply and demand are equal. Flexible interest rates maintain continuous money market equilibrium. Equation (1) always holds.

If nominal wages and prices adjust slowly in the short run, higher nominal money supply M leads initially to a higher real money stock M/P since prices P have not yet adjusted. The excess supply of real money bids down interest rates. This boosts the demand for goods. Gradually this bids up goods prices. In the labour market, nominal wages start to rise.

After complete adjustment of wages and prices, a once-off rise in nominal money leads to an equivalent once-off rise in wages and prices. Output, employment, interest rates and real money revert to their original levels. Equation (1) states this argument succinctly. After adjustment is complete, the demand for real balances is unchanged. Hence the price level changes in proportion to the original change in the nominal money supply.

> The **quantity theory of money** says that changes in nominal money lead to equivalent changes in the price level (and money wages), but have no effect on output and employment.

The theory is over 500 years old and may date from Confucius. The quantity theory is espoused by monetarists, who argue that *most* changes in prices reflect changes in the nominal money supply.

The theory must be interpreted with care. If the demand for real money is constant, the supply of real money must be constant: changes in nominal money are matched by equivalent changes in prices. This raises two issues: (a) even if the demand for real money is constant, do changes in nominal money cause changes in prices or vice versa; and (b) is the demand for real money constant?

Money, prices and causation

Suppose the demand for real money is constant over time. Money market equilibrium implies that the real money supply M/P is then constant. Monetary policy could fix the nominal money supply M, in which case money M determines prices P to get the required level of M/P implied by money demand.

Conversely, monetary policy may choose a target path for the price level P. Changes in this path then cause changes in the nominal money supply to achieve the required real money supply. Equation (1) says prices and money are correlated, but is agnostic on which causes which. That depends on the form of monetary policy pursued. With an intermediate target for nominal money, the causation flows from money to prices. With a target for prices or inflation, the causation flows the other way.

The leading monetarist, Professor Milton Friedman, always says that inflation is a monetary phenomenon. Sustained price increases, what we call inflation, are possible only if nominal money is also growing. It is always an option to change monetary policy and stop printing money. Sooner or later prices have to stop rising. Take away the oxygen and the fire goes out.

Is real money demand constant?

Table 26.1 shows nominal money, prices, real money and real income in three countries over a long period. Even in the long run, the simple quantity theory is not correct. Nominal money rose 10 times as much as prices in Japan, but less than three times as much in France. The three countries had different real income growth, affecting real money demand.

Despite recent stagnation, Japan grew by 10 per cent a year in the 1960s, and nearly 5 per cent a year during 1970–90. Huge real income growth led to an 11-fold rise in the demand for real money. To maintain equilibrium, its real money supply had to change as much. Hence its nominal money grew 11 times as much as its price level. Prices and nominal money changed by *different* amounts.

In the UK, financial deregulation and competition between banks offered depositors attractive interest rates on bank deposits (a big part of the money supply). Despite much more sluggish income growth than Japan, the demand for real money rose a lot in the UK because of banking deregulation which reduce the cost of holding money.

Table 26.1 Nominal money and prices, 1962–2007 (Each index set at 100 in 1962)

	2007		
	Japan	France	UK
Prices	447	840	1436
Nominal money stock	4966	2145	10300
Real income	1448	366	285
Real money stock	1110	260	740

Note: After France joined the eurozone in 1999, French monetary data reflect growth of eurozone money stock.
Sources: IMF, *International Financial Statistics*; OECD, *Economic Outlook*.

Another reason for cross-country differences was differences in inflation. These affect real money demand by affecting nominal interest rates. We study this effect in the next section.

To sum up, even after adjustment is complete, changes in real income and interest rates can alter real money demand. However, *if* real income and interest rates were unaltered, changes in nominal money would eventually be accompanied by equivalent changes in nominal wages and prices.

Inflation

So far we have studied levels. Now think about rates of change. Equation (1) implies that the growth in real money demand equals the growth in the real money supply, the excess of nominal money growth over the growth in prices. Hence

Inflation rate = [nominal money growth] – [real money demand growth]   (2)

Since real income and interest rates *usually* change only a few percentage points a year, real money demand usually changes slowly.[1] The essential insight of the quantity theory of money is that real variables usually change slowly.

Large changes in one nominal variable (money) are accompanied by large changes in other nominal variables (prices, nominal wages) to keep real money (and real wages) at their equilibrium values. This is a useful first look at inflation, but we have simplified too much.

26.2 Inflation and interest rates

Table 26.2 shows interest and inflation rates for selected countries. Countries with high inflation have high interest rates. An extra percentage point of inflation is accompanied by a nominal interest rate also about one percentage point higher, a proposition first suggested by Professor Irving Fisher.

Table 26.2 Inflation and interest rates 2003 (% per annum)

	Inflation	Interest rate
Turkey	10.2	25.13
Russia	10.3	14
Venezuela	23.1	14.7
Hungary	6.9	11.4
Switzerland	0.5	0.27

Source: The Economist.

Real interest rate = [nominal interest rate] – [inflation rate]   (3)

The Fisher hypothesis says that *real* interest rates do not change much. If they did, there would be large excess supply or demand for loans. Higher inflation is largely offset by higher nominal interest rates to stop the real interest rate changing much. Table 26.2 shows this is a good rule of thumb in reality.[2]

> The **Fisher hypothesis** says higher inflation leads to similarly higher nominal interest rates.

1 An exception is the hyperinflation example of the next section.
2 Chapter 25 argued that this is likely to be a long-run relationship. In the short run, higher inflation must induce a larger rise in nominal interest rates if real interest rates are to push inflation back towards its target.

Faster nominal money growth leads both to higher inflation and higher nominal interest rates. Hence a rise in the rate of money growth leads to a rise in nominal interest rates. This reduces the demand for real money, requiring money and prices to grow at *different* rates until the real money supply adjusts to the change in real money demand. To show how this works, we study a spectacular example, the German hyperinflation.

Hyperinflation

Bolivian annual inflation reached 11 000 per cent in 1985, Ukraine's inflation topped 10 000 per cent in 1993 and by 2007 inflation in Zimbabwe was heading for 5000 per cent. The most famous example is Germany in 1922–23.

> **Hyperinflation** is a period of very high inflation.

Germany lost the First World War. The German government had a big deficit, financed by printing money. Table 26.3 shows what happened. The government had to buy faster printing presses. In the later stages of the hyperinflation, they took in old notes, stamped on another zero, and reissued them as larger-denomination notes in the morning.

Table 26.3 The German hyperinflation, 1922–23

	Money	Prices	Real money	Inflation % monthly
January 1922	1	1	1.00	5
January 1923	16	75	0.21	189
July 1923	354	2021	0.18	386
September 1923	227 777	645 946	0.35	2532
October 1923	20 201 256	191 891 890	0.11	29 720

Source: Data adapted from C. L. Holtfrerish, *Die Deutsche Inflation 1914–23*, Walter de Gruyter, 1980.

Prices rose 75-fold in 1922 and much more in 1923. By October 1923 it took 192 million Reichmarks to buy a drink that had cost 1 Reichmark in January 1922. People carried money in wheelbarrows to go shopping. According to the old joke, thieves stole the barrows but left the near worthless money behind.

If inflation is π and the nominal interest rate is r, the real interest rate is $(r - \pi)$ but the real return on non-interest-bearing cash is $-\pi$, which shows how quickly the real value of cash is being eroded by inflation. The extra real return on holding interest-bearing assets rather than cash is $(r - \pi) - (-\pi) = r$. The *nominal* interest rate measures the *real* cost of holding cash. Nominal interest rates rise with inflation. In the German hyperinflation the cost of holding cash became enormous.

Table 26.3 shows that by October 1923 real money holdings were only 11 per cent of their level in January 1922. How did people get by with such small holdings of real cash?

> The **flight from cash** is the collapse in the demand for real cash when high inflation and high nominal interest rates make it very expensive to hold cash.

People, paid twice a day, shopped in their lunch hour before the real value of their cash depreciated too much. Any cash not immediately spent was quickly deposited in a bank where it could earn interest. People spent a lot of time at the bank.

What lessons can we draw? First, *rising* inflation and *rising* interest rates significantly reduce the demand for *real* cash. Hyperinflations are a rare example in which a real quantity (real cash) changes quickly and by a lot. Second, and as a result, money and prices can get quite out of line when inflation and nominal interest rates are rising. Table 26.3 shows that prices rose by six times as much as nominal money between January 1922 and July 1923, reducing the real money supply by 82 per cent, in line with the fall in real money demand.

26.3 Inflation, money and deficits

Persistent inflation must be accompanied by continuing money growth. Printing money to finance a large deficit is a source of inflation. Budget deficits may explain why governments have to print money rapidly. If so, tight *fiscal* policy is needed to fight inflation.

The level of GDP affects how much tax revenue the government gets at given tax rates. If government debt is low relative to GDP, the government can finance deficits by borrowing. It has enough tax revenue with which to pay interest and repay the debt. For governments with low debt, there may be no relation between their budget deficit and how much money they print. Sometimes they print money, sometimes they issue bonds. We do not expect a close relationship between deficits and money creation in a country like the UK.

Nevertheless, many years of deficits may make government debt large relative to GDP. The government can no longer finance deficits by more borrowing. It then has to tighten fiscal policy to shrink the deficit, or print money to finance the continuing deficit.

To ensure that the European Central Bank does not face fiscal pressure to print too much money and thus create inflation, members of the eurozone have to obey the Stability and Growth Pact, which restricts their budget deficits to less than 3 per cent of GDP, except in severe recession. Similarly, the UK's Code for Fiscal Stability commits the UK government not to keep running big deficits that steadily raise government debt relative to GDP.

Deficits, money growth and real revenue

A hyperinflation is a situation in which fiscal policy is out of control. A government with a persistently high deficit, financed by borrowing, now has so much debt that nobody will lend it any more. Instead, it prints money to finance its deficit.

How much real revenue can the government get by printing banknotes? The government has a monopoly on cash. As a token money, its production cost is tiny relative to its value as money. The government prints money for nothing, then uses it to pay nurses and build roads.

Real money demand M/P rises with real income. Long-run growth of real income allows the government some scope to raise M without adding to P. This is seigniorage. A second potential source of real revenue is the inflation tax.

> **Seigniorage** is real revenue acquired by the government through its ability to print money.

Suppose real income and output are constant but that a weak government cannot shrink its budget deficit and now has debt so large that nobody will lend to it. It prints money to cover the budget deficit. If ΔM is the amount of new cash created, this finances an amount of real spending $(\Delta M)/P$, which is the same as $(\Delta M/M) \times (M/P)$, the growth rate of cash multiplied by the real demand for cash. The rise in nominal money must feed into prices sooner or later. Suppose the rate of nominal money growth $(\Delta M/M)$ equals the inflation rate π. Thus

> The **inflation tax** is the effect of inflation in raising real revenue by reducing the real value of the government's nominal debt.

Real revenue from inflation $= [\pi] \times [M/P]$

Inflation helps the government by reducing the real value of the non-interest-bearing part of the government debt, namely cash. Think of inflation as the tax rate and real cash as the tax base for the inflation tax.

Now for the part that may be new to you. If money growth and inflation rise, does the government get more *real* revenue from the inflation tax? Higher inflation raises nominal interest rates and hence reduces the real demand for cash.

Figure 26.2 shows the answer. At low inflation, real cash demand is high, but the multiple of inflation and real cash demand is small. Similarly, at high inflation, although inflation tax rate is high, the tax base – real cash demand – is now tiny because nominal interest rates are so high. The multiple of inflation and real cash is again low. Real revenue raised through the inflation tax cannot be increased indefinitely. After a certain point, faster money growth and higher inflation shrink the tax base more than they raise the tax rate.

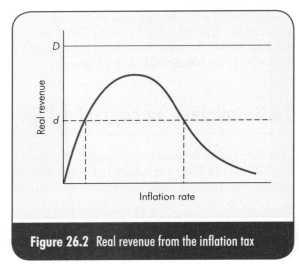

Figure 26.2 Real revenue from the inflation tax

The figure has two implications. First, if the government needs to cover a particular *real* deficit *d* by printing money, there may be two rates of money growth and inflation that do the job. Either is a long-run equilibrium in which inflation is constant.

Second, if for political reasons the government has a real deficit as large as *D*, printing money cannot do the job. The economy explodes into hyperinflation. At high inflation, real cash demand is already low. Raising inflation further causes such a large percentage fall in the tiny demand for real cash that inflation tax revenue falls, the government prints even more cash and the problem gets even worse.

That is how hyperinflation starts. The only solution is to cut the size of the deficit. Often the government does this by defaulting on its debt, which slashes the burden of interest payments.

UK money growth and inflation

The UK has never had a hyperinflation. Figure 26.3 shows UK data comparing inflation with the annual growth rate of M4 since 1970.

Even if there is a long-run relation between money growth and inflation, there need be no strong short-run relationship. Changes in interest rates and in real income lead to changes in real money demand that complicate the relationship in the short run.

Having examined the causes of inflation, we now examine its consequences. We have already seen the effect of inflation on nominal interest rates. When inflation is high, nominal interest rates are high to protect the real return earned by lenders. Otherwise there are few lenders. We look next at the effect of inflation on output and employment.

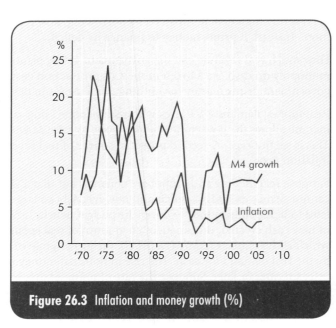

Figure 26.3 Inflation and money growth (%)

26.4 Inflation, unemployment and output

One of the most famous relationships in postwar macroeconomics is the Phillips curve.

The Phillips curve

In 1958 Professor Phillips of the London School of Economics found a strong statistical relationship between annual inflation and annual unemployment in the UK. Similar relationships were found in other countries. The Phillips curve is shown in Figure 26.4.

> The **Phillips curve** shows that a higher inflation rate is accompanied by a lower unemployment rate. It suggests we can *trade-off* more inflation for less unemployment or vice versa.

The Phillips curve seemed a useful compass for choosing macroeconomic policy. By its choice of fiscal and monetary policy, the government set aggregate demand and hence unemployment. The Phillips curve showed how much inflation then ensued. Higher aggregate demand bid up wages and prices, causing higher inflation but lower unemployment.

The Phillips curve in Figure 26.4 shows the trade-off that people believed they faced in the 1960s. In those days UK unemployment was rarely over 2 per cent of the labour force. But people believed that, if they did the unthinkable and reduced aggregate demand until unemployment rose to 2.5 per cent, inflation would fall to zero.

Since then there have been years when *both* inflation and unemployment were over 10 per cent. Something happened to the Phillips curve. The next two chapters explain why the simple Phillips curve of Figure 26.4 ceased to fit the facts.

Equilibrium unemployment is not zero, for reasons that we explore in Chapter 27. Suppose equilibrium employment and potential output are fixed in the long run, but there is sluggish wage and price adjustment. Chapter 25 discussed the vertical long-run aggregate supply curve and sloping short-run supply curve, relating output and the price level. These ideas are easily translated from inflation and output to inflation and unemployment.

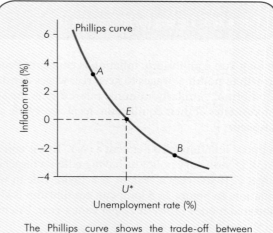

The Phillips curve shows the trade-off between higher inflation and lower unemployment. In the 1960s people believed that an unemployment rate U^* of 2.5 per cent would be accompanied by zero inflation.

Figure 26.4 The Phillips curve

The vertical long-run Phillips curve

In long-run equilibrium, the economy is at both potential output and equilibrium unemployment. Sometimes these are referred to as the natural level of output and natural rate of unemployment.

> The **natural rate of unemployment**, and **natural level of output**, are their values in long-run equilibrium.

Both are determined by real things, not nominal things. They depend on the supply of inputs, the level of technology, the level of tax rates and so on. They do not depend on inflation, provided all prices P and nominal wages W are rising together. Equilibrium unemployment depends on the real wage W/P, as we discuss in Chapter 27.

Just as long-run aggregate supply is vertical at potential output – output is unaffected by inflation – so the long-run Phillips curve is vertical at equilibrium unemployment. Equilibrium unemployment is independent of inflation. Plotting inflation and unemployment, Figure 26.5 shows the long-run Phillips curve vertical at equilibrium unemployment U^*.

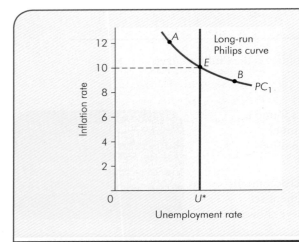

Since people care about real variables not nominal variables, when full adjustment has been completed people will arrange for all nominal variables to keep up with inflation. The vertical long-run Phillips curve shows that eventually the economy gets back to the natural rate of unemployment U^*, whatever the long-run inflation rate. There is no long-run trade-off between inflation and unemployment. The short-run Phillips curve PC_1 shows short-run adjustment as before. The height of the short-run Phillips curve depends on the rate of inflation and nominal money growth in long-run equilibrium, as shown by the position of point E on the long-run Phillips curve.

Figure 26.5 The long-run Phillips curve

In long-run equilibrium, inflation is constant. People correctly anticipate inflation, and adjust the growth of nominal wages to keep real wages constant, at the real wage required for long-run equilibrium. Similarly, nominal interest rates are sufficiently high to offset inflation and maintain real interest rates at their equilibrium level. Everyone adjusts to inflation because it can be completely foreseen.

Suppose inflation is 10 per cent a year. This is consistent with many forms of monetary policy. We can think of monetary policy as having either a target of 10 per cent annual money growth, or an inflation target of 10 per cent a year, or as a Taylor rule in which the inflation part aims for 10 per cent annual inflation. In Figure 26.5 long-run equilibrium is at E. Inflation is 10 per cent, as everybody expects. Nominal money grows at 10 per cent a year. Unemployment is at its natural rate.

The short-run Phillips curve

Beginning from E, suppose something raises aggregate demand. Unemployment falls, inflation rises and the economy is at A. Then the central bank raises interest rates to achieve its targets (in whichever form), and the economy slowly moves back down the short-run Phillips curve PC_1 from A back to E again. Since interest rates take time to affect aggregate demand, this may take one or two years.

Conversely, beginning from E a downward demand shock takes the economy to B in the short run. The central bank alters interest rates to bring the economy steadily back from B to E.

> The **short-run Phillips curve** shows that, in the short run, higher unemployment is associated with lower inflation. The height of the short-run Phillips curve reflects expected inflation. In long-run equilibrium at E, expectations are fulfilled.

The short-run Phillips curve corresponds to the short-run supply curve for output. Given inherited wages, higher prices make firms supply more output and demand more workers. For any level of last period's prices, higher prices today imply higher inflation today. In Chapter 25, the height of the short-run aggregate supply curve depended on inherited growth rate of nominal wages. Similarly, the height of the short-run Phillips curve reflects inherited nominal wage growth.

When workers and firms expect high inflation, they agree a large rise in nominal wages. If inflation turns out as expected, real wages are as forecast and the nominal wage growth was justified. If inflation is higher than expected, real wages are lower than planned. Firms supply more output and demand more labour. High inflation (relative to expectations) goes with lower unemployment. The short-run Phillips curve slopes down. Its height reflects the inflation expectations embodied in the inherited wage agreement.

This explains why most economies had high inflation at each unemployment rate in the 1970s and 1980s: the short-run Phillips curve had shifted upwards. Governments were printing money at a faster rate than before. The long-run equilibrium inflation rate was high, and expected to be so.

The point E lay further up the long-run Phillips curve in Figure 26.5. The short-run Phillips curve through this point was much higher than the short-run Phillips curve in the data originally studied by Professor Phillips. The 1970s and 1980s were a period of high inflation. The original Phillips curve data had been for a period of much lower inflation.

We draw two conclusions. First, it was wrong to interpret the original Phillips curve as a *permanent* trade-off between inflation and unemployment. It was the temporary trade-off, corresponding to a particular short-run aggregate supply schedule, while the economy adjusted to a demand shock.

Second, the speed with which the economy moves back along the Phillips curve depends on two things: the degree of flexibility of nominal wages and hence prices; and the extent to which monetary policy adjusts interest rates to restore demand more quickly. Complete wage flexibility would restore the vertical Phillips curve and the vertical aggregate supply curve. Rapid adjustment of interest rates would offset the demand shock, restoring output, unemployment and inflation to their long-run equilibrium levels.

Extreme monetarists believe that wage flexibility is very high. In the extreme version, it is only the fact that workers make annual wage settlements that prevents the economy always being in long-run equilibrium. Changes in aggregate demand unforeseen when nominal wages were set mean that wages and prices are temporarily at the wrong level. But such mistakes are rectified as soon as wages are renegotiated.

If wage and price adjustment are more sluggish than this, full employment is not immediately restored. However, we know from the previous chapter that monetary policy can completely compensate for a demand shock once it has been diagnosed. Nor is there any conflict between stabilizing inflation and stabilizing output or employment. Such conflicts arise only in response to supply shocks.

We have made considerable progress in understanding the Phillips curve, but there is more still to study. First, we need to analyse changes in long-run inflation expectations, which shift the short-run Phillips curve. Second, we need to examine supply shocks. Temporary supply shocks also shift the short-run Phillips curve. Permanent supply shocks alter equilibrium unemployment and shift the long-run Phillips curve.

Expectations and credibility

Figure 26.6 puts this apparatus to work to discuss what happens when a new government is elected with a commitment to reduce inflation. The economy begins in long-run equilibrium at E facing the short-run Phillips curve PC_1. Nominal money, prices and money wages are all rising at the rate π_1.

The government wants to reduce inflation to π_2 to reach point F. The day the government is elected it announces a cut in the inflation target from π_1 to π_2.

Overnight, firms inherit nominal wage increases that had anticipated the old inflation rate π_1. They have little scope to reduce inflation. If inflation does fall, real wages are now too high. Firms reduce output and employment. Inflation falls a little and unemployment rises. The economy moves along the short-run Phillips curve PC_1 to A.

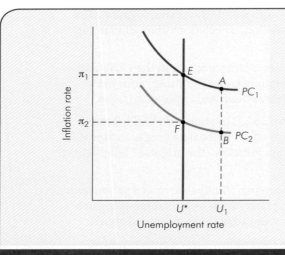

Beginning at E, the target inflation rate is cut from π_1 to π_2. Having expected inflation π_1, nominal wage growth has been too high. Firms cut back output and employment and the economy moves to A. If the new policy is credible, the next wage settlement reflects lower inflation expectations, the short-run Phillips curve shifts to PC_2 and the economy moves from A to B. Thereafter, it slowly adjusts along PC_2 to F.

However, if people doubt that the new tough policy will be sustained, nominal wages may keep growing at π_1. The short-run Phillips curve remains PC_1. Unemployment stays high, and inflation refuses to fall.

Figure 26.6 Expectations and credibility

What happens next? In the good scenario, workers believe the tighter monetary policy will last. The next wage bargain is based on inflation expectations π_2. The short-run Phillips curve shifts down to PC_2 and the economy moves from A to B. Inflation falls quickly. The economy then moves slowly along PC_2 from B to F.

Now for the bad scenario. When the economy first reaches A, workers do not believe that the tough new monetary policy will last. They think π_1 will remain the inflation rate in the long run. Thinking inflation will remain high, workers do not reduce nominal wage growth. They believe PC_1 not PC_2 will be relevant.

Suppose workers are wrong. Although nominal wages grow at π_1, the tough policy lasts and actual inflation is below π_1. Real wages rise and unemployment gets worse without much fall in inflation. The worse the slump becomes, the more likely is the government to give in, easing monetary policy to boost aggregate demand again. A belief that the government's nerve will crack can become a self-fulfilling prophecy.

> A **self-fulfilling prophecy** is an expectation that creates the incentive to make it come true.

The economy stays on PC_1 and the attempt to reduce inflation fails. Gradually the economy moves back along PC_1 to equilibrium at E.

This explains why governments go to such lengths to commit to tight monetary policy. The sooner people accept that long-run inflation will be low, the sooner nominal wage growth will slow. Making central banks independent is an institutional reform designed to increase the credibility of monetary policy by insulating it from short-term political expediency.

Supply shocks

In the long-run, the Phillips curve is vertical at equilibrium unemployment U^*. But U^* is not constant. Chapter 27 documents the rise and fall of U^* since the 1960s. In terms of Figure 26.6, a rise in equilibrium unemployment shifts the vertical long-run Phillips curve to the right. Changes in equilibrium unemployment reflect permanent supply shocks.

> A **permanent supply shock** affects equilibrium unemployment and potential output. A **temporary supply shock** leaves these long run values unaffected, but shifts the short-run Phillips curve and the short-run aggregate supply schedule for output.

The short-run Phillips curve can shift for two reasons. Inherited nominal wage growth changes if inflation expectations change, as analysed in Figure 26.6. Alternatively, a change in firms' desired supply of output and demand for workers, for a given rate of inherited nominal wage growth, shifts the short-run Phillips curve. Examples include a change in oil prices, in regulations or in tax rates.

Figure 26.7 shows an adverse temporary supply shock. The short-run Phillips curve shifts up, from PC_1 to PC_2. If monetary policy accommodates the shock, the target inflation rate rises from π_1 to π_2. The economy moves from E to F with no change in output or unemployment, but at the cost of higher inflation. Eventually the shock wear offs, since it is temporary, and the economy reverts to E, with another accommodating change in monetary policy.

Alternatively, monetary policy may *not* fully accommodate the supply shock. In Chapter 25, Figure 25.9 showed that this would mean higher inflation *and* lower output. Now, the analogue is higher inflation *and* higher unemployment. To prevent inflation shifting up by as much as the vertical shift up in the short-run Phillips curve, monetary policy makes sure that aggregate demand falls a bit. Hence inflation rises a bit and unemployment rises a bit. The economy moves from E to G in Figure 26.7. Output stagnates despite higher inflation.

Again, the credibility of policy is crucial. If workers think the government, frightened of high unemployment, will accommodate any shock, large wage rises buy temporarily higher real wages until prices adjust fully. And in the long run, monetary policy is loosened to maintain aggregate demand at full employment, so there is little danger of extra unemployment.

Once a government proves that it will not accommodate shocks, nominal wage growth slows. Workers then fear that higher wages will reduce demand and price workers out of a job.

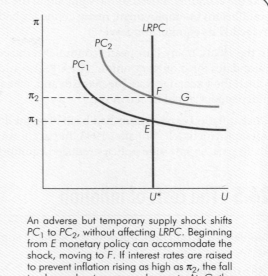

An adverse but temporary supply shock shifts PC_1 to PC_2, without affecting LRPC. Beginning from E monetary policy can accommodate the shock, moving to F. If interest rates are raised to prevent inflation rising as high as π_2, the fall in demand raises unemployment. At G the economy experiences stagflation, both high inflation and high unemployment.

Figure 26.7 Temporary supply shocks

Stagflation is high inflation and high unemployment, caused by an adverse supply shock.

Fifty years of inflation and unemployment

The original Phillips curve seemed to offer a permanent trade-off between inflation and unemployment. It also suggested both inflation *and* unemployment could be low.

At that time, governments were committed to full employment even in the short run. Any shock tending to raise inflation – including temporary supply shocks – was accommodated by a higher money supply to prevent a fall in aggregate demand. Money growth and inflation steadily rose. After the mid-1970s, government policy changed in most countries. The emphasis is now on keeping inflation low. Inflation fell after the early 1980s.

What about unemployment? We now understand that the Phillips curve is vertical in the long run at equilibrium unemployment. The rise and fall of equilibrium unemployment explained much of the rise and fall in actual unemployment. It was not the whole story.

The short-run Phillips curve is the *temporary* trade-off between inflation and unemployment while the economy adjusts to a demand shock and works its way back to long-run equilibrium. The height of the short-run Phillips curve mainly reflects anticipated inflation.

At the start of the 1980s, inflation was high because it had been high in the past. Anti-inflation policies were just beginning to bite. When tight money was first introduced, aggregate demand fell and the economy moved to the right along the short-run Phillips curve. In addition to high equilibrium unemployment, many countries had a short-run Keynesian slump. Unemployment exceeded its equilibrium level.

In the 1990s, many European economies reduced inflation to low levels to show they were fit candidates for monetary union. The UK also adopted tight policies to get inflation down. First, it joined the Exchange Rate Mechanism and, when that failed, it made the Bank of England independent of political control.

Once inflation expectations had been brought down, super-tight policies were unnecessary. British unemployment fell a lot after 1993. In part, it was a recovery from the Keynesian recession of 1990–92. In part, supply-side policies reduced equilibrium unemployment.

26.5 The costs of inflation

People dislike inflation, but why is it so bad? Some reasons commonly given are spurious.

Inflation illusion?

It is wrong to say that inflation is bad because it makes goods more expensive. If *all* nominal variables rise at the same rate, people have larger nominal incomes and can buy the same physical quantity of goods as before. If people realize that prices have risen but forget that nominal incomes have also risen, they have inflation illusion. It is real incomes that tell us how many goods people can afford to buy.

> People have **inflation illusion** if they confuse nominal and real changes. People's welfare depends on real variables, not nominal variables.

A second mistake is more subtle. Suppose there is a sharp rise in the real price of oil. Oil-importing countries are worse off. Domestic consumption per person has to fall. It can fall in one of two ways.

If workers do not ask for 'cost-of-living' wage increases to cover the higher cost of oil-related products, real wages fall. Nominal wages buy fewer goods. Suppose too that domestic firms absorb higher oil-related fuel costs and do not pass on these costs in higher prices. There is no rise in domestic prices or nominal wages. The domestic economy has adjusted to the adverse supply shock without inflation. People are worse off.

Suppose instead that people try to maintain their old standard of living. Workers claim cost-of-living rises to restore their real wages, and firms protect their profit margins by raising prices in line with higher wage and fuel costs. There is a lot of domestic inflation, which the government accommodates by printing extra money. Eventually the economy settles down in its new long-run equilibrium position.

People must still be worse off. The rise in the real oil price has not disappeared. It still takes more domestic exports, made possible by lower domestic consumption, to pay for the more expensive oil imports. In the new long-run equilibrium, workers find that their wages do not quite keep up with higher prices, and firms find that higher prices do not quite keep up with higher costs. The market has brought about the required fall in real domestic spending, letting resources go into exports to pay for the more expensive oil imports.

People notice (a) rising prices and (b) lower real incomes, but draw the wrong conclusion. It is not the inflation that has made them worse off, but the rise in oil prices. Inflation is a symptom of the initial refusal to accept the new reality.

We now turn to better arguments about the cost of inflation. Our discussion has two themes. First, was the inflation fully expected in advance? Or were people surprised? Second, do our institutions, including regulations and the tax system, let people adjust fully to inflation once they expect it? The costs of inflation depend on the answer to these two questions.

Complete adaptation and full anticipation

Imagine an economy with annual inflation of 10 per cent for ever. Everybody anticipates it. Nominal wages growth and nominal interest rates incorporate it. Real wages and real interest rates are unaffected. The economy is at full employment. Government policy is also fully adjusted. Nominal taxes are changed every year to keep real tax revenue constant. Nominal government spending rises at 10 per cent a year to keep real government spending constant. Share prices rise with inflation to maintain the real value of company shares. The tax treatment of interest earnings and capital gains is adjusted to reflect inflation. Pensions and other transfer payments are raised every year, in line with expected inflation.

This economy has no inflation illusion. Everyone has adjusted to it. This explains the long-run vertical Phillips curve in the previous section. But is complete adjustment possible?

Nominal interest rates usually rise with inflation to preserve the real rate of interest. But the nominal interest rate is the opportunity cost of holding cash. When inflation is higher, people hold less real cash.

Society uses money to economize on the time and effort involved in undertaking transactions. High nominal interest rates make people economize on real money. Using more resources to transact, we have fewer resources for production and consumption of goods and services.

> **Shoe-leather costs of inflation** are the extra time and effort in transacting when we economize on holding real money.

When prices rise, price labels have to be changed. Menus are reprinted to show the higher price of meals.

The faster the rate of price change, the more often menus must be reprinted if real prices are to remain constant. Among the menu costs of inflation is the effort of doing mental arithmetic. If inflation is zero, it is easy to see that a beer costs the same as it did three months ago. When inflation is 25 per cent a year, it takes more effort to compare the real price of beer today with that of three months ago. People without inflation illusion try to think in real terms, but the mental arithmetic involves time and effort.

> **Menu costs of inflation** are the physical resources needed for adjustments to keep real things constant when inflation occurs.

How big are menu costs? In supermarkets it is easy to change price tags. The cost of changing parking meters, pay telephones and slot machines is larger. In countries with high inflation, pay phones usually take tokens whose price is easily changed without having physically to alter the machines.

Even when inflation is perfectly anticipated and the economy has fully adjusted to inflation, we cannot avoid shoe-leather costs and menu costs. These costs are big when inflation is high, but may not be too big when inflation is moderate. However, if we cannot adjust to expected inflation, the costs are then larger.

Fully anticipated inflation when institutions do not adapt

Assume inflation is fully anticipated but institutions prevent people fully adjusting to expected inflation. Inflation now has extra costs.

Taxes

Tax rates may not be fully inflation-adjusted. One problem is fiscal drag.

Suppose income below £4000 is untaxed but you pay income tax at 25 per cent tax on all income over £4000. Initially, you earn £5000 and pay income tax of £250. After ten years of inflation, all wages and prices double but tax brackets and tax rates remain as before. You now earn

> **Fiscal drag** is the rise in real tax revenue when inflation raises nominal incomes, pushing people into higher tax brackets in a progressive income tax system.

£10 000. Paying tax at 25 per cent on the £6000 by which your nominal income exceeds £4000, you pay nominal tax of £1500. Wages and prices only doubled, but your nominal tax payment rose from £250 to £1500. Fiscal drag raised the real tax burden. The government gained from inflation. You lost.

For an inflation-neutral tax system, nominal tax brackets must rise with inflation. The real tax exemption is constant if the nominal limit rises from £4000 to £8000. Everything is then inflation-adjusted. You would pay £500 in tax, double what you paid before.

Percentage taxes on value, such as VAT, automatically raise nominal tax revenue in line with the price level. However, *specific* duties, such as £5 on a bottle of whisky, must be raised as the price level rises. In the UK there is no *automatic* formula for raising such duties. Each year the government decides.

Taxing capital

Income tax on interest income is also affected by inflation. Suppose there is no inflation. Nominal and real interest rates are both 4 per cent. With a 40 per cent tax rate, the after-tax real return on lending is 2.6 per cent. Now suppose inflation is 11 per cent and nominal interest rates are 15 per cent to keep a pre-tax real interest rate of 4 per cent. Suppose lenders must pay income tax on nominal interest income. The after-tax nominal interest rate is 9 per cent (0.6×15). Subtracting 11 per cent inflation, the after-tax *real* interest rate is −2 per cent. This compares with +2.6 per cent when inflation was zero.

When inflation was 11 per cent, nominal interest rates were 15 per cent. Eleven per cent of this was not real income, merely a payment to keep up with inflation. Only 4 per cent was the real interest rate providing real income. But income tax applied to all 15 per cent. Higher inflation reduced the real return on lending because the tax system was not properly inflation-adjusted. The government gained more real tax revenue. You lost.

Capital gains tax is another example. Suppose people pay tax of 40 per cent on any capital gain made when asset prices rise. When inflation is zero, only real gains are taxed. When inflation is 10 per cent, nominal asset prices rise merely to preserve their real value. People pay capital gains tax even though they are not making real capital gains.

Institutional imperfections help explain why inflation has real effects even when inflation is fully anticipated. These effects can be large. Usually, the government is the winner.

> **Inflation accounting** uses fully inflation-adjusted definitions of costs, income and profit.

Unexpected inflation

Previously, we assumed that inflation was fully anticipated. What if inflation is a surprise?

Redistribution

When prices rise unexpectedly, people with nominal assets lose and people with nominal liabilities gain. Nominal contracts to buy and sell, or lend and borrow, can reflect expected inflation, but cannot reflect surprise inflation.

Expecting inflation of 10 per cent, you lend £100 for a year at 12 per cent, expecting a real interest rate of 2 per cent. Unexpectedly, inflation is 20 per cent. The real interest rate on your loan is $[12 - 20] = -8$ per cent. You lose by lending. Conversely, borrowers gain 8 per cent. Their nominal income rises 20 per cent with inflation but they repay at 12 per cent interest.

For every borrower, there is a lender. One person's gain is another person's loss. In the aggregate they cancel out. But unexpected inflation redistributes real income and wealth, in this case from lenders to borrowers. This may lead to economic dislocation. Some people may have to declare bankruptcy, which then affects other people. We also have to make a value judgement about whether we like the redistribution that is taking place.

One redistribution is between the government and the private sector. *Unexpected* inflation reduces the real value of all outstanding nominal government debt. It is as if the government had taxed us in order to repay this debt.[3]

The old and the young

In practice, many savers are the old. Having paid off their mortgages and built up savings during their working life, they put their wealth into nominal bonds to provide income during retirement. These people lose out from surprise inflation.

Nominal debtors are the young and, mainly, those entering middle age with a large mortgage. They gain when surprise inflation raises house prices and nominal incomes without a matching rise in the nominal sum they owe the bank or building society.

Surprise inflation redistributes from the old to the young. We may judge this redistribution undesirable. With technical progress and productivity growth, each generation is richer than the one before. Redistribution from the old to the young raises intergenerational inequality.

Uncertain inflation

Uncertainty about future inflation has two costs. First, it makes planning more complex, raising the real resources society uses to make plans and do business.

Second, people dislike risk. Chapter 13 explained why. The extra benefits of the champagne years are poor compensation for the years of starvation. People would rather average out these extremes and live comfortably all the time. The psychological costs of worrying about how to cope with the bad years may also be important.

When people make nominal contracts, uncertainty about inflation means uncertainty about the eventual real value of the nominal bargains currently made. This is a true cost of inflation. If a lower average level of inflation also reduces uncertainty about inflation, this may be a reason to aim for low inflation. The institutions that commit the government to low inflation may also reduce the scope for uncertainty about inflation. If so, lower average inflation has a real benefit because it is also more certain.

26.6 Defeating inflation

In the long run, inflation will be low if money growth is low. This may require fiscal policy to remain fairly tight so that deficits are low. However, to get to this position from an initial position of high inflation, it may be necessary to get through an intermediate period of high unemployment.

Could this transition be made more quickly and less painfully? The more credible is the new policy, the faster the adjustment of expectations and behaviour.

Incomes policy

A freeze on wage increases certainly gets inflation down quickly. Historically, it has not been able to keep inflation down. Why were past incomes policies unsuccessful?

> **Incomes policy** is the direct control of wages and other incomes.

---

3 Why stress unexpected inflation? Because expected inflation is already built into the terms on which bonds were originally issued. Expected inflation affects nominal interest rates.

Once governments intervene in the labour market, they often cannot resist pursuing other aims at the same time. For example, they try to compress relative wages across different skills in the name of fairness. Such policies alter real wages for particular skills, causing excess supply in some skills and excess demand in others. Market forces eventually break the policy.

At best, incomes policy is a temporary adjustment device. In the long run, low nominal money growth is essential if low inflation is to be maintained. Some incomes policies failed because governments introduced a wage freeze but kept printing money, a guarantee that excess demand for workers would eventually break the policy.

Long-term incomes policies are also hard to administer because equilibrium real wages for particular skills change over time. Freezing the existing wage structure gradually sets up powerful market forces of excess supply and excess demand.

Institutional reform

This approach takes a long-run view. It is concerned not with the temporary costs of first getting inflation down, but with how to *keep* inflation down. Central bank independence is a useful pre-commitment to tight monetary policy and low inflation. Institutional pre-commitment is all the rage, as the following examples show.

The Maastricht Treaty

Signed in 1991, the treaty set out conditions both for entering the eurozone and after admission to it. The first requirement was to avoid loose fiscal policy: a ceiling of 3 per cent on budget deficits relative to GDP. High-debt countries were also supposed to initiate actions to bring their debt/GDP levels below 60 per cent. Moreover, euro entrants first had to succeed in disinflating to low levels, measured both directly by changes in price indexes and indirectly by nominal interest rates (the Irving Fisher effect again!).

Not only did EU governments have to sign up for tight policy in the 1990s and beyond, euro hopefuls had to undertake institutional reform, making their national central banks formally independent. The Maastricht Treaty also made the new European Central Bank independent of government, with a mandate to pursue price stability.

UK policy 1992–97

Despite losing the peg to the Deutschmark after leaving the Exchange Rate Mechanism (ERM) in 1992, subsequent UK inflation was remarkably low. The Chancellor announced the inflation target for the coming years. Each month Treasury and Bank officials tried to agree on a recommendation about interest rates to meet this medium-run objective while looking after the short-term needs of the real economy (an informal Taylor rule). At the monthly meeting of Chancellor and Governor, the arguments were considered, *then the Chancellor alone decided.*

Previous Chancellors always 'took the Bank's views into account'. What was new? Since the minutes of the Governor–Chancellor meeting were published a few weeks later, any objections by the Bank were highly publicized. Moreover, and separate from the monthly meetings, the Bank was given responsibility to produce a quarterly *Inflation Report*, openly published and *completely free from Treasury control.* The report quickly became very influential, because of its clear analysis, and a model for other central banks.

UK policy since 1997

In May 1997, the new Chancellor, Gordon Brown, gave the Bank of England 'operational independence' to set interest rates. The Bank aims to achieve an inflation target set by the Chancellor. In an emergency (a very adverse supply shock), the government can temporarily raise the target

Activity box 26 Central bank independence

Central bankers are cautious entities unlikely to favour rapid money growth and inflation. So why do these occur? Either because the government cares so much about unemployment that it never tackles inflation, or because it is politically weak and ends up with a budget deficit which it finances, at least to some extent, by printing money. Essentially, inflation arises when governments overrule cautious bankers. Proposals for central bank independence mean *independence from the government*. In the long run, output is at potential output, so eventually independent central banks should lead to lower inflation without a permanent fall in output. Central bank independence is a pre-commitment by government to keep money tight and inflation low.

The two figures below, shows that both predictions of the theory work out in practice – countries with more independent central banks had lower average inflation, but not lower real output growth in the long run. Since the period to which these data refer, these countries have all adopted independent central banks and enjoyed the benefits of lower inflation without adverse consequences for the real economy.

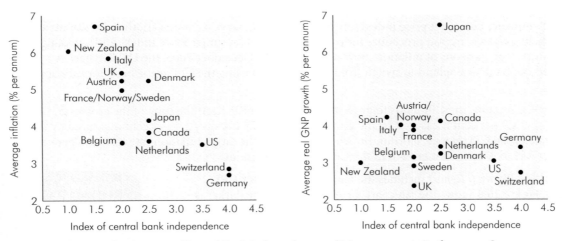

Source: A. Alesina and L. Summers, 'Central Bank Independence and Macroeconomic Performance: Some Comparative Evidence', *Journal of Money, Credit and Banking*, May 1993.

Questions

(a) What is the connection between the vertical long-run Phillips curve and the claim that independent central banks can reduce long-run inflation without reducing output or adding to long-run unemployment?

(b) The Bank of England's inflation target could in principle be changed by the Chancellor of the Exchequer. Are there any circumstances in which the government might approve (indeed, require) a temporarily higher inflation rate?

To check your answers to these questions, go to page 730.

rather than force the Bank to initiate a drastic recession merely to hit the inflation target quickly. Nevertheless, any change in the target is politically hard except in truly exceptional circumstances. Operational independence is a commitment to policies favouring low inflation.

26.7 The Monetary Policy Committee

Since 1997 UK interest rates have been set by the Bank of England's Monetary Policy Committee (MPC), which meets monthly to set interest rates to try to hit the inflation target laid down by the Chancellor. Initially, the target was 2.5 per cent annual inflation, plus or minus 1 per cent. The target applied to underlying inflation not headline inflation.

Why omit mortgage interest from the price level on which monetary policy should focus? Suppose inflation is too high. To reduce aggregate demand, interest rates are raised. But higher interest rates *raise* the retail price index RPI by raising the cost of living for homeowners. Asking monetary policy to focus on the growth of RPIX simplifies interest rate decisions. Moreover, when temporary changes in interest rates are required to get the economy back on track, it may also be more sensible to target the underlying rate of inflation.

> **Headline inflation** was actual inflation, the growth in the retail price index RPI. **Underlying inflation** was the growth of RPIX, which is the retail price index omitting the effect of mortgage interest rates on the cost of living.

Different countries construct price indexes in slightly different ways from one another. EU countries have each adopted a common procedure for calculating their Consumer Price Index (CPI), making cross-country comparisons of inflation more meaningful. In December 2003, the UK Chancellor instructed the Bank of England to switch from using RPIX to using the CPI as the basis for inflation targeting.

For statistical reasons, the CPI tends to grow less rapidly than RPIX. At the time of the crossover, UK inflation was 2.9 per cent measured by the growth rate of RPIX but only 1.3 per cent measured by the growth rate of the CPI. Hence, Gordon Brown also changed the target inflation rate from 2.5 per cent growth in RPI to 2.0 per cent growth in the Consumer Price Index.

The quarterly *Inflation Report* includes the famous fan chart for CPI inflation. Figure 26.8 shows the fan chart for August 2007. The darker is the projected line, the more likely the outcome. Figure 26.8 shows that in August 2007 the Bank was expecting UK inflation to average around 2.5 per cent in 2007, and then to revert to the 2 per cent target (with most possible outcomes within 1 per cent of this).

> A **fan chart** shows not just the most likely future outcome, but indicates the probability of different outcomes.

In this section, we discuss three questions. Why was the MPC given a target for inflation not nominal money? How does it work? And how easy has it been for the MPC to decide where to set interest rates?

Inflation targets

Without a nominal anchor, nothing ties down the price level or any other nominal variable. Market forces determine real variables such as money M divided by prices P. Setting interest rates can influence M/P but not separately determine M and P. An intermediate target – an announced path for a nominal variable – is required. For example, if we know M and can work out money demand M/P, we can deduce the price level P.

Nominal money is a logically possible nominal anchor and is attractive as an intermediate target because new data on money come out faster than data on prices or output. However, monetary targets fell out of favour because large and unpredictable changes in real money demand made it hard

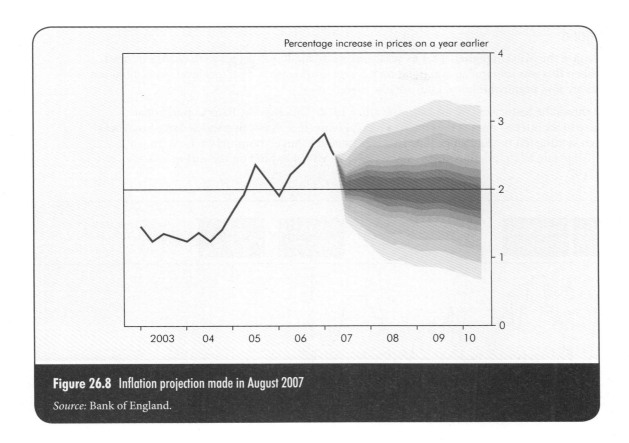

Figure 26.8 Inflation projection made in August 2007

Source: Bank of England.

to know where to set the nominal money target. When it is hard to predict M/P, it is difficult to know where to set M in order to get the desired path of P.

As explained in previous chapters, most modern central banks implicitly follow a Taylor rule but their policy is often portrayed and communicated as a flexible inflation target. This is easily understood by the public, and more easily monitored than a Taylor rule, which could lead to disputes about what the (unobservable) level of potential output really is.[4]

Back to the future

Delays in data availability mean that the MPC has to forecast where the economy is today. Moreover, the interest rate medicine takes up to two years to have its full effect on private behaviour. Hence the MPC has to *forecast* the path of prices at least two years into the future merely to know where to set interest rates *today*!

On occasion, the MPC may raise interest rates even though current inflation is under control. This means that, in the absence of any change in interest rates, the MPC is forecasting that inflation will be too high. It then has to act quickly to keep inflation on track.

---

4 Like central banks deciding where to set interest rates, academic researchers engaged in empirical evaluation of monetary policy have to make estimates of how potential output is evolving. The OECD regularly publish estimates of output gaps $(Y-Y^*)$ for the major countries.

So far so good

Most people give the MPC high marks for its performance so far. It was prepared to change interest rates even when this was unpopular, and inflation has remained close to its target level. Since inflation expectations are low, nominal interest rates are low as well.

Figure 26.9 shows the history of UK interest rates since 1974. Although the Bank's operational independence to set interest rates was granted in 1997, Figure 26.9 shows that the decisive break was in 1992 when sterling left the Exchange Rate Mechanism and changed nominal anchors from a pegged exchange rate to an inflation target. Since 1997 the MPC has built on the earlier success during 1992–97.

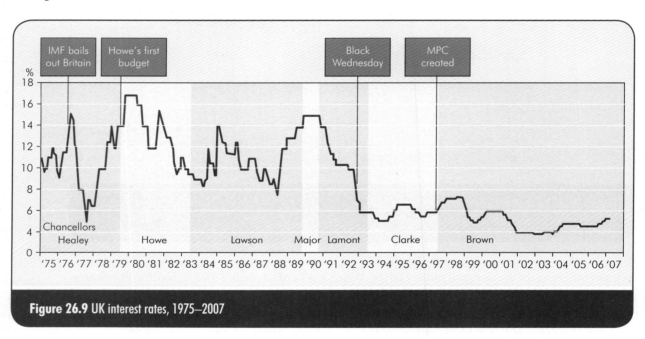

Figure 26.9 UK interest rates, 1975–2007

Summary

- The **quantity theory of money** says changes in prices are caused by equivalent changes in the nominal money supply. In practice, prices cannot adjust at once to changes in nominal money, so interest rates or income alter, changing real money demand. Nevertheless, in the long run, changes in prices are usually associated with changes in nominal money.

- The **Fisher hypothesis** is that a 1 per cent rise in inflation leads to a similar rise in nominal interest rates so real interest rates change little. Since the nominal interest rate is the cost of holding money, higher inflation reduces real money demand. The *flight from cash* during hyperinflation is a vivid example.

- For a solvent government, there need be no close relation between the budget deficit and nominal money growth. In the long run, persistent borrowing to finance large deficits may leave the government so indebted that further borrowing is impossible. It must resort to printing money or take fiscal action to cut the deficit.

- The **long-run Phillips curve** is vertical at equilibrium unemployment. If people foresee inflation and can completely adjust to it, inflation has no real effects.

- The **short-run Phillips curve** is a temporary trade-off between unemployment and inflation in response to demand shocks. Supply shocks shift the Phillips curve. The height of the short-run Phillips curve also depends on underlying money growth and expected inflation. The Phillips curve shifts down if people believe inflation will be lower in the future.

- Temporary supply shocks also shift the short-run Phillips curve. **Stagflation** is high inflation plus high unemployment.

- Some so-called **costs of inflation** reflect inflation illusion or a failure to see inflation as the consequence of a shock that would have reduced real incomes in any case. The true costs of inflation depend on whether it was anticipated and on the extent to which the economy's institutions allow complete inflation-adjustment.

- **Shoe-leather costs** and **menu costs** are unavoidable costs of inflation and are larger the larger the inflation rate. Failure fully to inflation-adjust the tax system may also impose costs, even if inflation is anticipated.

- **Unexpected inflation** redistributes income and wealth from those who have contracted to receive nominal payments (lenders and workers) to those who have contracted to pay them (firms and borrowers).

- Uncertainty about future inflation rates imposes costs on people who dislike risk. Uncertainty may be greater when inflation is already high.

- **Incomes policy** may accelerate a fall in inflation expectations, allowing disinflation without a large recession. But it is unlikely to succeed in the long run. Only low money growth can deliver low inflation in the long run.

- **Operational independence of central banks** is designed to remove the temptation faced by politicians to print too much money.

Review questions

To check your answers to these questions, go to page 730.

1 (a) Your real annual income is constant, and initially is £10 000. You borrow £200 000 for 10 years to buy a house, paying interest annually, repaying the £200 000 in a final payment at the end. (b) List your annual incomings and outgoings in the first and ninth year if inflation is 0 and the nominal interest rate is 2 per cent a year. Repeat the exercise if annual inflation is 100 per cent and the nominal interest rate 102 per cent. Are the two situations the same in real terms?

2 Does this explain why voters mind about high inflation even when nominal interest rates rise in line with inflation?

3 (a) Explain the following data taken from *The Economist* a few years ago (when some countries still had proper inflation!). (b) Is inflation always a monetary phenomenon?

	Money growth (%)	Inflation (%)
Euro area	3	2
Japan	12	–3
UK	6	2
Australia	15	3
USA	8	2

4 Looking at data on inflation and unemployment over ten years, could you tell the difference between supply shocks and demand shocks?

5 Name three groups which lose out during inflation. Does it matter whether this inflation was anticipated?

6 **Common fallacies** Why are these statements wrong? (a) Getting inflation down is the only way to cure high unemployment. (b) Inflation stops people saving. (c) Inflation stops people investing.

7 **Harder question** Professor Milton Friedman argued that money was socially useful but essentially free to create. Society should therefore reduce the opportunity cost of holding money to zero, so that people would demand it up to the point at which its marginal benefit was zero. (a) Suppose the real interest rates on other assets is around 3 per cent. Is there any way society could arrange for cash to earn a similar real return? (b) Why don't governments do this?

8 **Harder question** Inflation in Zimbabwe, high for many years, recently reached hyperinflation levels. (a) President Mugabe blames Western governments for restricting trade and driving up prices. Could a fall in supply have generated sustained high inflation? (b) Why do you think Zimbabwe has such high inflation? (c) Is inflation high enough to raise the maximum possible revenue for the government?

9 **Essay question** Does the huge success of central bank independence in so many countries suggest that other decisions should be removed from government? Your answer should include assessments of the case for (a) an independent health services board, (b) an independent budget deficit commission, and (c) a redistribution commission.

Online LearningCentre

To help you grasp the key concepts of this chapter check out the extra resources posted on the Online Learning Centre. There are chapter summaries, self-test questions, an interactive graphing tool, weblinks and a searchable glossary, all for free!

To put your learning into practice and prepare for exams, an **Interactive Workbook** is also available online, containing a variety of question types and providing feedback on your answers.

If you'd like further help with economics, or have any questions, **NetTutor** is here to help! You will have a personalised tutorial service at your fingertips. Visit the online learning centre at: www.mcgraw-hill.co.uk/textbooks/begg for information on accessing all of these resources.

Unemployment

In the early 1930s, over a quarter of the UK labour force was unemployed. Society threw away output by failing to put people to work. For the next 40 years, macroeconomic policy tried to manage aggregate demand to avoid a rerun of the 1930s. Figure 27.1 shows that until the 1970s the policy succeeded.

In the 1970s, high inflation emerged for reasons discussed in the previous chapter. Governments eventually tightened monetary and fiscal policy to get inflation under control. The mix of tighter demand policies and adverse supply shocks led to a big rise in unemployment in the 1980s.

After the economy adjusted, deficient demand was no longer the cause of high unemployment. Equilibrium unemployment remained high because of adverse changes in supply. Better supply-side policies since 1990 have reduced unemployment to levels not seen since the early 1970s.

Table 27.1 shows the fight against unemployment was even harder to win in other countries. Why did high unemployment persist so long, especially in continental Europe? What can governments do about unemployment? This chapter aims to answer these questions.

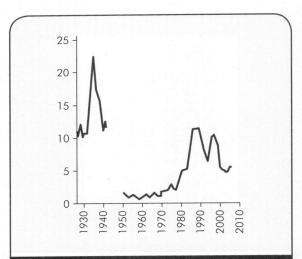

Figure 27.1 UK unemployment (%)

Sources: B. R. Mitchell, *Abstracts of Brtitish Historical Statistics* and B. R. Mitchell and H. G. Jones, *Second Abstract of British Historical Statistics*, Cambridge University Press; ONS, *Economic Trends*.

Table 27.1 Unemployment, 1972–2006 (%)

	1972	1982	1992	2006
UK	4	11	10	6
Ireland	8	14	15	4
Italy	6	8	9	6
France	3	10	10	8
Euro area	3	9	9	7
USA	5	10	8	5

Source: OECD, *Economic Outlook.*

27.1 The labour market

Not everyone wants a job. The people who do are called the labour force.

Some people looking for work do not register as unemployed. They do not appear in official statistics for the registered labour force or the registered unemployed. Yet from an economic viewpoint, such people *are* in the labour force and *are* unemployed. For the moment, our data on the labour force or the unemployed refer only to those registered.

Figure 27.1 shows that UK unemployment was high in the interwar years, especially in the 1930s. By comparison, the postwar unemployment rate was tiny until the late 1970s. In the 1980s it started to get back to prewar levels, but then fell steadily after 1990.

> The **labour force** is people with a job or registered as looking for work. The **participation rate** is the fraction of the population of working age who are in the labour force. The **unemployment rate** is the fraction of the labour force without a job but registered as looking for work.

Stocks and flows

Unemployment is a stock concept measured at a point in time. Like a pool of water, its level rises when inflows (the newly unemployed) exceed outflows (people getting new jobs or quitting the labour force altogether). Figure 27.2 illustrates this important idea.

There are three ways for workers to become unemployed. Some people are sacked or made redundant (job-losers); some are temporarily laid off but expect eventually to be rehired by the same company; and some voluntarily quit their existing jobs. But the inflow to unemployment also comes from people not previously in the labour force: school-leavers (new entrants) and people who, having left the labour force, are now returning to look for a job (re-entrants).

People leave the unemployment pool in the opposite directions. Some get jobs. Others give up looking for jobs and leave the labour force completely. Some of this latter group may simply have reached the retirement age at which they get a pension, but many are discouraged workers.

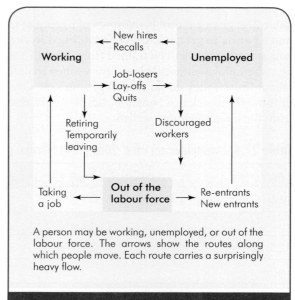

A person may be working, unemployed, or out of the labour force. The arrows show the routes along which people move. Each route carries a surprisingly heavy flow.

Figure 27.2 Labour market flows

Table 27.2 shows that the pool of unemployment is not stagnant. The stock of unemployed is 0.7 million. A much larger number, around 2.5 million people a year flow into and out of unemployment. During 2006, the inflow to unemployment was 2.6 million and the outflow 2.5 million. The net inflow of 0.1 million during 2006 meant that the 1.7 million stock of unemployed was 0.1 million higher than it had been in 2005, when the stock was 1.6 million.

Discouraged workers, pessimistic about finding a job, leave the labour force.

Table 27.2 UK unemployment, 2006 (million)

Inflow to unemployment	2.6
Outflow from unemployment	2.5
Stock of unemployed at year end	1.7

Sources: ONS, *Labour Market Trends.*

When unemployment is high, people have to spend longer in the pool before they find a way out. Table 27.3 gives data on the duration of unemployment. Unemployment is not always a temporary stopover on the way to better things. A higher unemployment rate usually also means that people are spending longer in the pool of unemployment before escaping. Table 27.3 shows how the 1.7 million UK unemployed in 2006 divide by gender and period for which they have already been unemployed.

Table 27.3 Unemployment by duration, 2006 (thousand people)

	<6 months	6–12 months	12–24 months	24+ months
Male	546	177	130	122
Female	477	126	60	45

Source: ONS, *Employment Outlook.*

The composition of unemployment

Table 27.4 gives a recent breakdown of unemployment by gender and by age. Young workers find it much harder to get a job. Unlike established workers with accumulated skills and job experience, young workers have to be trained from scratch. Youth unemployment exceeds the national average. The unemployment rate is lower for women than for men, perhaps because more women leave the labour force if they do succeed in getting jobs. Over the age of 50, both men and women tend to retire or move on to sickness benefit if they have sustained spells of unemployment, and thus disappear from the unemployment statistics.

Table 27.4 Unemployment rates, 2006 (% of relevant group)

Age	Men	Women
16–17	29	20
18–24	14	11
25–49	4	4
50+	3	3

Source: ONS, *Labour Market Trends.*

27.2 Analysing unemployment

We now develop a theoretical framework in which to analyse unemployment. We can classify unemployment by the source of the problem or by the nature of behaviour in the labour market.

Types of unemployment

Economists used to classify unemployment by source: frictional, structural, demand-deficient or classical.

Frictional unemployment includes people whose handicaps make them hard to employ. More importantly, it includes people spending short spells in unemployment as they hop between jobs in a dynamic economy.

Structural unemployment reflects the time taken to acquire human capital. A skilled welder may have worked for 25 years in shipbuilding but is made redundant at 50 when the industry contracts in the face of foreign competition. That worker may have to retrain in a new skill which is more in demand in today's economy. But firms may be reluctant to take on and train older workers. Such workers become the victims of structural unemployment.

Until wages and prices have adjusted to their new long-run equilibrium level, a fall in aggregate demand reduces output and employment. Some workers want to work at the going real wage rate but cannot find jobs. Only when demand has returned to its long-run level is demand-deficient unemployment eliminated.

Since the classical model assumes that flexible wages and prices maintain the economy at full employment, classical economists had difficulty explaining high unemployment in the 1930s. They concluded that the wage was prevented from adjusting to its equilibrium level. It can be caused either by the exercise of trade union power or by minimum wage legislation which enforces a wage in excess of the equilibrium wage rate.

The modern analysis of unemployment takes the same types of unemployment but classifies them differently to highlight the behavioural implications and consequences for government policy. Modern analysis stresses the difference between *voluntary* and *involuntary* unemployment.

> **Frictional unemployment** is the irreducible minimum unemployment in a dynamic society.

> **Structural unemployment** arises from the mismatch of skills and job opportunities as the pattern of demand and supply changes.

> **Demand-deficient unemployment** occurs when output is below full capacity.

> **Classical unemployment** describes the unemployment created when the wage is deliberately maintained above the level at which the labour supply and labour demand schedules intersect.

Equilibrium unemployment

Figure 27.3 shows the labour market. The labour demand schedule *LD* slopes down. Firms demand more workers at a lower real wage. The schedule *LF* shows how many people are in the labour force. A higher real wage increases the number of people wishing to work. However, the schedule is pretty steep. Many people are in the labour force whatever the real wage.

The schedule *AJ* shows how many people accept job offers at each real wage. The schedule is to the left of the *LF* schedule: only people in the labour force can accept a job. How far *AJ* lies to the left of *LF* depends on several things. Some people are inevitably between jobs at any instant. Also, a particular real wage may tempt some people into the labour force even though they will accept a job offer only if they find an offer with a rather higher real wage than average.

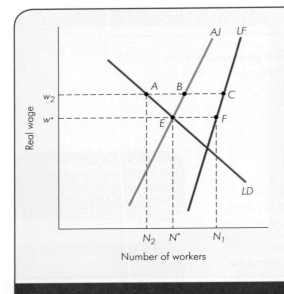

The schedules *LD*, *LF* and *AJ* show, respectively, labour demand, the size of the labour force and the number of workers willing to accept job offers at any real wage. *AJ* lies to the left of *LF* both because some labour force members are between jobs and because optimists are hanging on for an even better job offer. When the labour market clears at *E*, *EF* is the natural rate of unemployment, the people in the labour force not prepared to take job offers at the equilibrium wage *w**. If union power succeeds in maintaining the wage w_2 in the long run, the labour market will be at *A*, and the natural rate of unemployment *AC* now shows the amount of unemployment chosen by the labour force collectively by enforcing the wage w_2.

Figure 27.3 Equilibrium unemployment

We draw these schedules for a given level of jobseeker's allowance (formerly called unemployment benefit). When wages are high, jobseekers grab available jobs. The two upward-sloping schedules are close together. When wages are low (relative to unemployment benefit), potential workers are more selective in accepting job offers. People invest in searching for a good job. The two schedules are further apart.

Labour market equilibrium is at *E* in Figure 27.3. Equilibrium employment is *N**. The distance *EF* is equilibrium unemployment.

This unemployment is entirely *voluntary*.

At the equilibrium real wage *w**, N_1 people want to be in the labour force but only *N** accept job offers; the remainder do not want to work at the equilibrium real wage.

Equilibrium unemployment includes frictional and structural unemployment. Suppose a skilled welder earned £500 a week before being made redundant. The issue is not why workers became redundant (the decline of the steel industry), but why these workers will not take a lower wage as a dishwasher to get a job. Their old skills are obsolete. Until new skills are learned, dishwashing may be their only skill valued by the labour market. People not prepared to work at the going wage rate for their skills, but wanting to be in the labour force, are voluntarily unemployed.

What about classical unemployment, for example if unions keep wages above their equilibrium level? This is shown in Figure 27.3 as a wage w_2 above *w**. Total unemployment is *AC*. As individuals, *AB* workers want jobs at the wage w_2 but cannot find them. Firms wish to be at point *A*. As individuals, the workers *AB* are involuntarily unemployed.

However, through their unions, workers collectively opt for the wage w_2 above the equilibrium wage, thus reducing employment. For workers as a whole, the extra unemployment is voluntary. We include classical unemployment in equilibrium unemployment. If unions maintain the wage w_2, the economy stays at *A* and *AC* is equilibrium unemployment.

> **Equilibrium unemployment** (also called the **natural rate of unemployment**) is the unemployment rate when the labour market is in equilibrium.

> A worker is **voluntarily unemployed** if, at the given level of wages, she wishes to be in the labour force but does not yet wish to accept a job.

> A worker **involuntarily unemployed** would accept a job offer at the going wage rate.

Activity box 27 The lump-of-labour fallacy

Those without an economics training often think there is a simple solution for reducing unemployment. Shorten the working week, so that the same amount of total work is shared between more workers, leaving fewer people unemployed. What's wrong with this argument?

It presumes the demand for labour (hours × people) is fixed, whatever the cost of hiring workers or their benefit in goods produced and revenue earned. In practice, both would be affected by the proposal.

You go to work for 7 hours a day, but probably have an hour of dead time (coffee breaks, tidying your desk, being nice to colleagues, talking about sport, sneaking out to the shops). This is a fixed cost, say an hour of time. There are probably economies of scale to shift length. Shortening the shift length adds to the cost of labour, making firms less competitive and reducing their demand for labour. Moreover, if you only work 20 hours a week instead of 37, you have less money to spend. If everyone spends less, firms sell less and need fewer, not more, workers.

Few economists think compulsory reductions in the length of the working week are a promising solution to the problem of high unemployment.

Questions

(a) Suppose there was a fixed amount of work to be shared around. How would we have absorbed the population growth and productivity improvements over the last 300 years?

(b) Suppose population growth is constant over the next 100 years but new technology quadruples our productivity. What do you expect to happen to total person-hours of work?

(c) How could restrictions on hours of work add to equilibrium unemployment?

To check your answers to these questions, go to page 731.

Figure 27.4 illustrates how Keynesian or demand-deficient unemployment may arise. Initially, labour demand is LD and the labour market is in equilibrium at E with equilibrium unemployment EF. Then labour demand shifts down to LD′. Before wages or prices adjust, the real wage is still w^*. At this wage, workers want to be at E but firms want to be at A. The distance AE is demand-deficient unemployment, involuntary unemployment caused by sluggish adjustment of wages and prices. EF remains voluntary unemployment.

If labour demand remains LD′, eventually real wages fall to w^{**} to restore equilibrium at G. However, by reducing interest rates, monetary policy can shift labour demand up to LD again and restore equilibrium at E. At A, output and employment are low. Involuntary unemployment also reduces wage growth and inflation.

Thus, we can divide total unemployment into two parts. The equilibrium or natural rate is the equilibrium unemployment determined by normal labour market turnover, structural mismatch, union power and incentives in the labour market. Keynesian unemployment, also called demand-deficient or cyclical unemployment, is involuntary unemployment in disequilibrium, caused by low aggregate demand and sluggish wage adjustment.

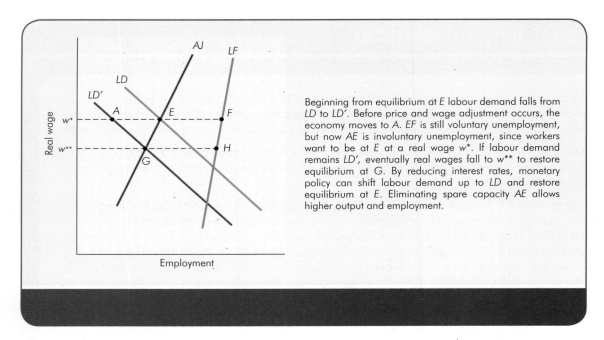

Beginning from equilibrium at E labour demand falls from LD to LD'. Before price and wage adjustment occurs, the economy moves to A. EF is still voluntary unemployment, but now AE is involuntary unemployment, since workers want to be at E at a real wage w*. If labour demand remains LD', eventually real wages fall to w** to restore equilibrium at G. By reducing interest rates, monetary policy can shift labour demand up to LD and restore equilibrium at E. Eliminating spare capacity AE allows higher output and employment.

This division helps us think clearly about the policies needed to tackle unemployment. Keynesian unemployment reflects spare capacity and wasted output. By boosting labour demand, policy can mop up this spare capacity and increase output and employment. Wage adjustment could logically accomplish the same outcome, but may take several years to do so. The more sluggish are market forces, the more it makes sense for policy to intervene. Most forms of monetary policy have the consequence that interest rates will adjust to such a situation and help offset the original demand shock. The automatic fiscal stabilizers also act in this direction.

In marked contrast, when the economy is already in long-run equilibrium, further demand expansion is pointless. Even though unemployment is not zero, there is no spare capacity. At points E or G in Figure 27.4, all remaining unemployment is voluntary.

It is true that, beginning from G, shifting labour demand up from LD' to LD achieves a small reduction in equilibrium unemployment. The distance EF is smaller than GH because the AJ and LF schedules are not parallel to one another. However the main effect of raising demand is to bid up wages not to increase output or employment.

Hence, when the economy begins with only voluntary unemployment, reductions in unemployment and increases in output are mainly accomplished not by demand policies but by supply-side policies. These policies either *shift* the supply schedules AJ and LF or they reduce distortions that prevented the economy getting to points like E or G.

The next section presents some evidence on the relative magnitude of unemployment responses to demand and supply, and then analyses these supply-side policies in more detail.

27.3 Explaining changes in unemployment

Empirical research aims to decompose causes of unemployment into those that changed equilibrium and those that caused demand-deficient unemployment. Estimates by Professors Stephen Nickell, Richard Layard and Richard Jackman of the London School of Economics are given in Table 27.5, which average UK unemployment rates during seven periods, from 1956–59 through to 1991–95.

Averaging reduces the influence of short-run fluctuations. The top row shows the sustained rise in unemployment after the late 1960s, and its steady fall after 1990.

Table 27.5 UK unemployment, 1956–95

Unemployment (year)	56–59	60–68	69–73	74–80	81–87	88–90	91–95
Actual rate (%)	2.2	2.6	3.4	5.2	11.1	7.3	9.3
Estimated natural rate (%)	2.2	2.5	3.6	7.3	8.7	8.7	8.9

Sources: R. Layard, S. Nickell and R. Jackman, *Unemployment*, Oxford University Press, 1991; S. Nickell, 'Inflation and the UK Labour Market', in T. Jenkinson, *Readings in Macroeconomics*, Oxford University Press, 1996.

The second row confirms that much of this pattern reflected the rise and fall of equilibrium unemployment, which quadrupled between the 1950s and the 1980s. Indeed, until the start of the 1980s, almost *all* the rise in unemployment reflected a deterioration of supply-side factors.

Equilibrium unemployment fell in the 1990s, and continued to fall during 1996–2004 after the end of the period studied by Nickell, Layard and Jackman. How do we know the equilibrium unemployment kept falling? Because UK unemployment fell all the way to 4 per cent by 2002 *without causing a rise in inflation*. If actual unemployment had fallen below the level of equilibrium unemployment, excess demand for workers would have started to bid up wages, causing a rise in inflation.

Moreover, since 1997 the Bank of England has been charged with achieving low and stable inflation. In order to decide at what level to set interest rates, the Monetary Policy Committee has to decide whether the economy has spare capacity or is overheating. This entails making a judgement about where actual unemployment stands in relation to equilibrium unemployment.

To the extent that the MPC has operated a sound demand management policy, we should expect actual unemployment to have been close to equilibrium unemployment for most of this period. In recent years, actual unemployment has varied between 4 and 6 per cent. It is a reasonable bet that equilibrium unemployment is close to 5 per cent.

This is not set in stone. It took good supply-side policy to reduce the equilibrium unemployment rate from the higher numbers shown in Table 27.5. A deterioration in supply-side conditions, whether from higher oil prices or poorer domestic incentives, could at some future date lead the equilibrium unemployment rate to increase again. We now discuss these issues in more detail.

Demand and unemployment

Table 27.5 shows that up to 1980 actual unemployment was close to its equilibrium rate – hardly surprising, since demand management policies aimed to keep output close to potential output. Although the rise in unemployment up to 1980 was due to supply-side factors, since 1980 the story is rather different.

Table 27.5 shows that, whenever actual unemployment rose to 10 per cent or more, much of the unemployment was Keynesian, due to deficient demand. Because inflation had been allowed to get out of control, the demand-side brakes had to be slammed on hard in the early 1980s to put downward pressure on inflation. For example, during 1981–87, of the actual unemployment rate of 11.1 per cent, only 8.7 per cent was equilibrium unemployment: the rest was due to insufficient demand. In the recession during 1990–92, when unemployment rates again reached double digits, the UK again had significant Keynesian unemployment.

However, in both episodes Keynesian unemployment did not last for ever. The late 1980s (and late 1990s) were periods in which output was at, or above, potential. Taking a 40-year view, most of the story is the rise and fall of equilibrium unemployment.

Supply-side factors

Keynesians believe that the economy can deviate from full employment for quite a long time, certainly for several years. Monetarists believe that the classical full-employment model is relevant much more quickly. Everyone agrees that long run the performance is changed only by affecting the level of full employment and the corresponding level of potential output.

We now discuss four reasons why equilibrium unemployment rose and then fell during 1970–2003.

First, increasing skill mismatch raised equilibrium unemployment after 1970.

> **Supply-side economics** is the use of microeconomic incentives to alter the level of full employment, the level of potential output and equilibrium unemployment.

Box 27.1 Globalization and labour markets

Rather than seeing globalization as a threat, OECD governments should focus on improving labour regulations and social protection systems to help people adapt to changing job markets, argues the 2007 edition of the OECD's annual *Employment Outlook*. The possibility of offshoring jobs previously within a country has probably reduced the bargaining power of low-skilled workers, and thus the vulnerability of jobs and wages in developed economies.

Wage inequality is also rising. In 18 of the 20 OECD countries where data exist, the gap between top earners and those at the bottom has risen since the early 1990s. The diagram below shows that Ireland and Spain are the only exceptions to this trend.

The OECD report makes a number of recommendations on policies that governments should put in place to create more and better jobs. Countries with high social security contributions (e.g. Belgium, France and Sweden) should adopt broader sources of financing public social protection. Social contributions act as a tax on labour, limiting job creation. Given the falling share of wages in national income, and hence the potential for revenue from social security contributions, it is critical to adopt broader tax bases, such as income taxes or VAT, to fund social protection.

Globalization requires mobility to get workers out of dead-end jobs with no future. The OECD report praises the 'flexicurity' approach in Austria and Denmark. In Austria, workers have individual savings accounts, instead of traditional severance pay schemes, that move with them as they move jobs. If they lose their job, they can choose to withdraw funds from the account or save the entitlements built up towards a future pension.

Job losers should also be compensated through social protection systems that are employment-friendly, the OECD concludes, by providing adequate benefits coupled with 'activation' policies that stimulate re-employment opportunities. Nordic countries and Australia have shown that such policies, if well designed, improve the job prospects of laid-off workers, thereby easing their fears about globalization.

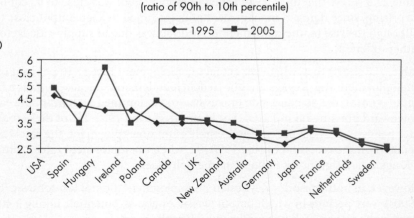

Labour market inequality
(ratio of 90th to 10th percentile)

Recent research emphasizes that the labour market is not very good at processing workers as they step out of one job and hope to step into another. The larger is mismatch, the harder the task has to perform, and the more likely it is that people get stuck in unemployment.

> **Mismatch** occurs if the skills that firms demand differ from the skills the labour force possesses.

When firms no longer want the skills possessed by the existing workforce, the labour demand curve *LD* shifts leftwards. In Figures 27.3 and 27.4 at lower equilibrium real wage, voluntary unemployment, the gap between *AJ* and *LF*, is larger. A rise in mismatch explained some of the rise in unemployment in the 1970s and 1980s.

Conversely, in the 1990s government policy has stressed reconnecting the unemployed with the labour market, rather than leaving them to languish in long-term unemployment. By offering the unemployed advice on how to get back into work quickly, government policy stopped people getting stigmatized as unemployable. This raised the demand for their labour, reducing equilibrium unemployment. At a higher real wage, *AJ* and *LF* are closer together.

A second potential explanation of a rise in equilibrium unemployment is a rise in the generosity of unemployment benefit relative to wages in work.

A higher replacement rate may entice more people into the labour force, shifting *LF* to the right. More significantly, it shifts *AJ* to the left. People spend longer in unemployment searching for the right job. For both reasons, equilibrium unemployment increases.

> The **replacement rate** is the level of benefits relative to wages in work.

Most empirical research concludes that higher benefits caused some of the increase in equilibrium unemployment, though less than sometimes supposed. In practice, UK unemployment benefit (now jobseeker's allowance) did not rise enough to explain the rise in unemployment.

However, benefits policy probably does explain some of the fall in equilibrium unemployment after 1992. First, as in other countries such as the Netherlands, the UK redefined a lot of its long-term unemployed as sick. People on sickness benefit are no longer measured as unemployed. This improves statistical unemployment, though of course in economic terms it is entirely cosmetic.

Second, Labour's employment policy viewed getting the unemployed back into work as the best form of social policy. People reacquire the work habit and rebuild their confidence. Accordingly, Labour has focused on its *Welfare to Work* and *Making Work Pay* (see Box 10.2).

> **Trade union power** is measured by the ability of unions to co-ordinate lower job acceptances, thereby increasing wages but reducing employment.

A third source of changes in equilibrium unemployment has been changes in trade union power.

Rises in union power, especially in the 1970s, had a big effect on equilibrium unemployment. Powerful unions made labour scarce and forced up its price. By shifting the *AJ* curve to the left, unions forced up real wages but increased equilibrium unemployment. Conversely, the fall in union power has shifted the *AJ* schedule right, reducing equilibrium unemployment.

Union power increased in the 1970s partly because sympathetic governments passed legislation enhancing worker protection and partly because many nationalized industries were sheltered state monopolies from which unions could extract potential profits as extra wages for their members. Their power declined after the 1980s partly because a less sympathetic government reduced the legal protection of unions, partly because privatization removed the Treasury as last-resort funder of union wage claims and partly because globalization increased competition in general.

> The **marginal tax rate** is the fraction of each extra pound that the government takes in tax. This creates a **tax wedge** between the price the purchaser pays and the price the seller receives.

The final important source of changes in equilibrium unemployment was changes in the size of the tax wedge between the cost of labour to the firm and the take-home pay of the worker. A key theme of supply-side economists is the benefits that stem from reducing the marginal tax rate.

We discussed tax rates and work incentives in detail in Chapter 10. A cut in marginal tax rates, and a consequent increase in the take-home pay derived from the last hour's work, make people substitute work for leisure. Against this *substitution effect* must be set an *income effect*. If people pay less in taxes, they have to do less work to reach any given target living standard. Thus, theoretical economics cannot prove that tax cuts raise desired labour supply. Most empirical studies confirm that, at best, tax cuts lead to only a small rise in labour supply. Further details are in Chapter 10. Figure 27.5 shows how tax rates affect equilibrium unemployment.

Suppose the marginal tax rate equals the vertical distance AB. Equilibrium employment is then N_1. The tax drives a wedge between the gross-of-tax wages paid by firms and the net-of-tax wages received by workers. Firms wish to hire N_1 workers at the gross wage w_1. Subtracting the income tax rate AB, N_1 workers want to take job offers at the after-tax wage w_3. Thus N_1 is equilibrium employment, where quantities supplied and demanded are equal. The horizontal distance BC shows equilibrium unemployment, the number of workers in the labour force not wishing to work at the going rate of take-home pay.

Suppose taxes are abolished. The gross wage and the take-home pay now coincide, and the new labour market equilibrium is at E. Two things happen. First, equilibrium employment rises. Second, although more people join the labour force because take-home pay has risen from w_3 to w_2,

Box 27.2 Did the tax carrot work?

Evidence from the past

A lower marginal tax rate makes people substitute work for leisure. But tax cuts also make workers better off. This income effect makes them want to consume more leisure and hence work less. The combined effect on hours of work is small for those already in work. Of more importance is the decision about whether to work at all. Chapter 10 showed that higher take-home pay, for example because of tax cuts, makes more people join the labour force by reducing the significance of the fixed costs of working (commuting, babysitters, giving up social security).

The UK evidence shows that tax cuts have a tiny effect on labour supply by men and single women. But for married women, higher take-home pay encourages labour force participation.

The Thatcher programme

In the 1980s the Thatcher government began a major programme of tax cuts and tax reforms. The real value of personal allowances – how much you can earn before paying income tax – rose by 25 per cent. The basic rate of income tax fell from 33 to 25 per cent and for top income-earners from 83 to 40 per cent. Many politicians anticipated a surge in labour supply. Most economists were pessimistic because of the evidence from the past.

The effect of the Thatcher programme is assessed by C. V. Brown, 'The 1988 Tax Cuts, Work Incentives and Revenue', *Fiscal Studies*, 1988. Brown finds that the big rise in tax allowances led to less than 0.5 per cent extra hours of labour supply. The cut in the basic rate of income tax had no detectable effect at all. The massive cut in the marginal tax rate of top earners had a small effect in stimulating extra hours of work by the rich. The evidence from the past stood up well to a big change of tax policy.

Implications for Labour

Gordon Brown quietly raised taxes to help the poor and provide funding for public services. Neither theory nor past evidence suggests that this will have a large and adverse incentive effect. The government's problem with tax increases is not economic but political (see Activity Box 16).

equilibrium unemployment falls from *BC* to *EF*. A rise in take-home pay relative to unemployment benefit reduces voluntary unemployment. If lower tax rates reduce equilibrium unemployment, higher tax rates increase equilibrium unemployment.

Another possible supply-side policy is to cut unemployment benefit. For a given labour force schedule *LF*, fewer people now wish to be unemployed at any real wage. The schedule *AJ*, showing acceptances of job offers, shifts to the right. This raises equilibrium employment (and hence potential output) and reduces equilibrium unemployment.

What about changes in the national insurance contributions paid both by firms and by workers? These are mandatory contributions to state schemes that provide unemployment and health insurance. They act like an income tax, driving a wedge *AB* between the total cost to a firm of hiring another worker and the net take-home pay of a worker. Figure 27.5 implies that a fall in these contributions will raise equilibrium employment and cut equilibrium unemployment.

Supply-side policies can reduce equilibrium unemployment. Where this involves being tough on those already relatively disadvantaged, there is a conflict between efficiency and fairness, and only through the political process can society express its view.

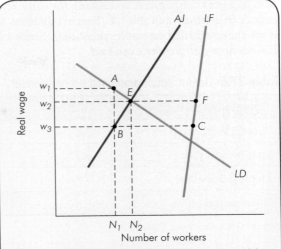

An income tax makes the net-of-tax wage received by households lower than the gross wage paid by firms. *AB* measures the amount each worker pays in income tax, and equilibrium employment is N_1, the quantity that households wish to supply at the after-tax wage w_3 and that firms demand at the gross wage w_1. At the after-tax wage w_3 the natural rate equilibrium would be at *E*. Employment would rise from N_1 to N_2 and the natural rate of unemployment would fall from *BC* to *EF*. Relative to the fixed level of unemployment benefit, the rise in take-home pay from w_3 to w_2 reduces voluntary unemployment.

Figure 27.5 A cut in marginal income tax rates

27.4 Cyclical fluctuations in unemployment

We discuss business cycles in Chapter 31. Cycles may reflect fluctuations in demand or fluctuations in supply. Since supply usually changes slowly, most of the sharp movements in the short run are caused by changes in demand.

Unless a counter-cyclical demand management policy is deliberately and successfully pursued, there may well be a business cycle. If so, there tends to be a cyclical relationship between demand, output, employment and unemployment. On average, boosting aggregate demand by 1 per cent will not raise employment by 1 per cent or reduce unemployment by 1 per cent, even if the economy begins with spare resources. Table 27.6 shows two periods of demand growth and two of demand decline. In practice, booms lead initially to a sharp increase in shift lengths and hours worked; slumps lead to the abolition of overtime, the introduction of short time and a marked decline in hours worked.

The table confirms that changes in demand and output lead to smaller changes in employment. For example, when output grew 16.8 per cent between the fourth quarter of 1992 and the second quarter of 1998, employment rose by only 6.8 per cent. Nor do changes in employment lead to corresponding changes in unemployment. The last two rows of the table show that rapid expansion or contraction of employment leads to significantly smaller changes in unemployment.

One reason is the 'discouraged worker effect'. When unemployment is high and rising, some people who would like to work get pessimistic and stop looking for work. No longer registered as looking for work, they are not recorded in the labour force or the unemployed. Conversely, in a boom, people who had previously given up looking for work rejoin the labour force since there is now a good chance of getting a suitable job. Hence in booms and slumps recorded employment data change by more than recorded unemployment data. Since 1997, the Monetary Policy Committee has kept the UK economy on a more even keel.

Table 27.6 Output, employment and unemployment

Cumulative change in	79ii–81ii	86ii–88ii	90ii–91ii	92iv–98ii
Real GDP (%)	−7.8	+9.1	−3.4	+16.8
Employment (%)	−6.3	+2.5	−2.9	+6.8
Employed (million)	−1.7	+0.5	−0.7	+1.5
Unemployed (million)	+1.4	−0.9	+0.6	−1.2

Source: ONS, *Economic Trends.*

27.5 The cost of unemployment

The private cost of unemployment

It is important to distinguish between voluntary and involuntary unemployment. When individuals are voluntarily unemployed, they reveal that they do better by being unemployed than by immediately taking a job offer that they face at the going wage rate. The private cost of unemployment (the wage forgone by not working) is less than the private benefits of being unemployed. What are these benefits?

The first is transfer payments from government. Workers who have contributed to the national insurance scheme get jobseeker's allowance for the first 12 months after becoming unemployed. Thereafter they get income support, the ultimate backstop in the British welfare state.

There are other benefits too. First, there is the value of leisure. By refusing a job, some people reveal that the extra leisure is worth more to them than the extra disposable income if they took a job. Second, some people expect to get a better job by being choosy about accepting offers. These future benefits must be set against the current cost: a lower disposable income by being out of work.

When people are involuntarily unemployed, the cost changes. Involuntary unemployment means that people would like to work at the going wage but cannot find a job because there is excess labour supply at the existing wage rate. These people are worse off by being unemployed.

The distinction between voluntary and involuntary unemployment matters because it may affect our value judgement about how much attention to pay to unemployment. When unemployment is involuntary, people are suffering more and the case for helping them is stronger.

The social cost of unemployment

Again we distinguish between voluntary and involuntary unemployment. When unemployment is voluntary, individuals prefer to be unemployed. Does this unemployment also benefit society?

An individual receives transfer payments during unemployment, but these transfers give no corresponding benefit to society as a whole. They may ease the collective conscience about poverty and income inequality, but they are not payments for the supply of any goods or services that other members of society may consume. Since the private benefit exceeds the social benefit, too many people may be voluntarily unemployed.

Box 27.3 Hysteresis and high unemployment in Europe

Supply and demand curves are supposed to be independent of one another. The labour supply curve or job acceptances schedule AJ shows the people willing to work at each real wage whatever the position of the labour demand curve LD, and vice versa. But this may be wrong.

In the diagram, the initial equilibrium is at E. Something then shifts labour demand down from LD to LD'. Suppose this causes a permanent fall in labour supply. JA shifts to JA'. When labour demand reverts to LD, the new equilibrium is at F, not E. The short-run history of the economy has affected its long-run equilibrium.

> An economy experiences **hysteresis** when its long-run equilibrium depends on the path it follows in the short run.

Hysteresis may explain high and persistent unemployment in Europe. Here are some channels through which it might work.

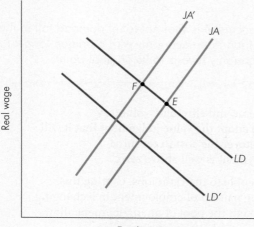

The insider–outsider distinction

Outsiders are unemployed without jobs. Only insiders with jobs participate in wage bargaining. At the original equilibrium E, the numerous insiders in work ensure that real wages are low enough to preserve their own jobs. When a recession occurs, LD shifts to LD'. Some insiders get fired and become outsiders. Eventually, as explained in Chapter 25, market forces restore labour demand to LD. But now there are fewer insiders than originally. They exploit their scarcity by securing higher wages for themselves rather than encouraging firms to rehire. The economy is trapped in the high-wage, low-employment equilibrium at F instead of the low-wage, high-employment equilibrium at E.

Thereafter, only long-run supply-side measures aimed at breaking down insider power can gradually break the economy out of this low-employment equilibrium.

Discouraged workers

Again, the economy begins at E. It has a skilled and energetic labour force. A temporary recession leads to unemployment. If the recession is protracted, we see the emergence of long-term unemployed and a culture in which people stop looking for jobs. Again, when demand picks up, labour supply has been permanently reduced and equilibrium reverts to F, not E. Only long-term supply-side measures to restore the work culture will succeed.

Search and mismatch

When employment is high at E, firms are trying to find scarce workers, and potential workers are searching hard for a job. A recession makes firms advertise fewer vacancies, and workers realize it is a waste of time searching for jobs. When demand picks up again, both firms and workers are accustomed to low levels of search. New jobs are not created.

Box 27.3 Hysteresis and high unemployment in Europe (Continued)

The capital stock

At E the economy has a lot of capital. Labour productivity is high and firms want lots of workers. During a temporary recession, firms scrap old machines. When demand picks up again, firms have permanently lower capital. The demand for labour, which depends on the marginal product of labour, never rises to its original level. Again, the economy returns to F not E.

Policy implications of hysteresis

Hysteresis means that a temporary fall in demand induces permanently lower employment and output, and higher equilibrium unemployment. There are two policy implications. First, once the problem has emerged, it is dangerous to try to break out of it simply by expanding aggregate demand. Before long-run supply can respond, you get major inflation. Supply-side policies, needed to rebuild aggregate supply, take a long time to work.

Second, because the problem is so hard to cure once it occurs, it is vital not to let demand fall in the first place. The payoff to demand management is higher than in an economy with a unique long-run equilibrium where all that is at stake is how quickly the economy reverts to its original point.

This does not mean that society should go to the opposite extreme and eliminate voluntary unemployment completely. First, society is perfectly entitled to adopt the value judgement that it will maintain a reasonable living standard for the unemployed, whatever the cost in resource misallocation. Second, the efficient level of voluntary unemployment is well above zero.

In a changing economy, it is important to match up the right people to the right jobs. Getting this match right lets society make more output. Freezing the existing pattern of employment in a changing economy leads to a mismatch of people and jobs. The flow through the pool of unemployment allows people to be reallocated to more suitable jobs, raising potential output in the long run.

Two points from our earlier discussion are also relevant here. First, even when unemployment is high, flows both into and out of the pool are large relative to the pool itself. Second, people who do not get out of the pool quickly are in danger of stagnating when unemployment is high: the fraction of the unemployed who have been unemployed for over a year was higher in the 1990s than at the end of the 1970s when unemployment was much lower.

Involuntary or Keynesian unemployment has an even higher social cost. Since the economy is producing below capacity, it is literally throwing away output that could have been made by putting these people to work. Moreover, since Keynesian unemployment is involuntary, it may entail more human and psychological suffering than voluntary unemployment. Although hard to quantify, it is also part of the social cost of unemployment.

Summary

- People are either **employed**, **unemployed** or out of the **labour force**. The level of unemployment rises when inflows to the pool of the unemployed exceed outflows. Inflows and outflows are large relative to the level of unemployment.

- As unemployment has risen, the average duration of unemployment has increased.

- Women face lower unemployment rates than men. The unemployment rates for old workers and, especially, for young workers are well above the national average.

- **Unemployment** can be classified as **frictional**, **structural**, **classical** or **demand-deficient**. In modern terminology, the first three types are **voluntary unemployment** and the last is **involuntary unemployment**. The **natural rate of unemployment** is the equilibrium level of voluntary unemployment.

- In the long run, sustained rises in unemployment must reflect increases in the natural rate of unemployment. During temporary recessions, **Keynesian unemployment** is also important.

- **Supply-side economics** aims to increase equilibrium employment and potential output, and to reduce the natural rate of unemployment, by operating on incentives at a microeconomic level. Supply-side policies include reducing mismatch, reducing union power, tax cuts, reductions in unemployment benefit, retraining and relocation grants and investment subsidies.

- A 1 per cent increase in output is likely to lead to a much smaller reduction in Keynesian unemployment. Some of the extra output will be met by longer hours. And as unemployment falls, some people, effectively in the labour force but not registered, look for work again.

- **Hysteresis** means that short-run changes can move the economy to a different long-run equilibrium. It may explain why European recessions have raised the natural rate of unemployment substantially.

- People voluntarily unemployed reveal that the private benefits from unemployment exceed the private cost in wages forgone. Society derives no output from transfer payments to support the unemployed. However, society would not benefit by driving unemployment to zero. Some social gains in higher productivity are derived from improved matching of people and jobs that temporary unemployment allows.

- Keynesian unemployment is involuntary and hurts private individuals who would prefer to be employed. Socially it represents wasted output. Society may also care about the human misery inflicted by involuntary unemployment.

- Most European countries took two decades to reverse the high unemployment of the 1980s.

Review questions

To check your answers to these questions, go to page 731.

1 What is the discouraged worker effect? Suggest two reasons why it occurs.

2 'The average duration of an individual's unemployment rises in a slump. Hence the problem is a higher inflow to the pool of unemployment, not a lower outflow.' Do you agree?

3 'The microchip caused a permanent rise in the level of unemployment.' Did it? What about all previous technical advances?

4 How is high unemployment explained by (a) a Keynesian and (b) a classical economist?

5 Explain why boosting demand sometimes fails to reduce unemployment.

6 **Common fallacies** Why are these statements wrong? (a) Unemployment is always a bad thing. (b) So long as there is unemployment, there is pressure on wages to fall. (c) Unemployment arises only because greedy workers are pricing themselves out of a job.

---

7 **Harder question** Suppose the government wants to encourage lone parents to take part-time jobs and thinks 15 hours a week is consistent with children being in a crèche for 3 hours a day, Monday to Friday. Which of the following might achieve the government's aim: (a) an additional lump-sum payment to lone parents, (b) a lower income tax rate for lone parents, or (c) a payment conditional on their taking at least 15 hours of work a week?

8 **Harder question** Why is teenage unemployment so high?

---

9 **Essay question** For two decades, unemployment in France has been significantly higher than that in the UK. If you become president of France, should you (a) blame the European Central Bank for cautious monetary policy; (b) blame the French Treasury for a fiscal policy that has been too tight; or (c) tackle labour market reform in France? Explain your answer.

Online Learning Centre

To help you grasp the key concepts of this chapter check out the extra resources posted on the Online Learning Centre. There are chapter summaries, self-test questions, an interactive graphing tool, weblinks and a searchable glossary, all for free!

To put your learning into practice and prepare for exams, an **Interactive Workbook** is also available online, containing a variety of question types and providing feedback on your answers.

If you'd like further help with economics, or have any questions, **NetTutor** is here to help! You will have a personalised tutorial service at your fingertips. Visit the online learning centre at: www.mcgraw-hill.co.uk/textbooks/begg for information on accessing all of these resources.

Exchange rates and the balance of payments

By the end of this chapter, you should understand:

1 the foreign exchange market

2 balance of payments accounts

3 determinants of current account flows

4 perfect capital mobility

5 speculative behaviour and capital flows

6 internal and external balance

7 the long-run equilibrium real exchange rate

Exports and imports are each about 10 per cent of the size of GNP in the US, 20 per cent in Japan, 30 per cent in the UK, France and Germany and well over 50 per cent in some small European economies. Even in the US, the exchange rate, international competitiveness and the trade deficit are major issues. International linkages matter even more in more open economies such as the UK, France and Germany.

> An **open economy** has important trade and financial links with other countries.

In this chapter we show how international transactions affect the domestic economy.

28.1 The foreign exchange market

Different countries use different national currencies. In the UK, goods, services, and assets are bought and sold for pounds sterling; in France they are bought and sold for euros.

> The **foreign exchange (forex) market** exchanges one national currency for another. The price at which the two currencies exchange is the **exchange rate**.

Measuring exchange rates

Suppose $2 converts to £1. We can either say the exchange rate is $2/£ or £0.50/$. Both statements contain the same information.

Thus an exchange rate of $1.5/£ is the international value of the domestic currency as viewed by a British resident, but the domestic price of foreign exchange as viewed by an American resident. Conversely, £0.50/$ is the domestic price of foreign exchange for a UK resident but the international value of the domestic currency for a US resident.

> The **international value of the domestic currency** is the quantity of foreign currency per unit of the domestic currency. The **domestic price of foreign exchange** is the quantity of domestic currency per unit of the foreign currency.

Whenever you see a table or graph with 'the' exchange rate, you need to work out which way round it has been expressed. There is no short cut. Even after years in the subject, we ourselves go slowly at that bit.

Whichever way we express the exchange rate, in practice each currency exchanges for many others, not just one.

However, for simplicity our discussion assumes only two countries, the domestic economy (say the UK) and the foreign country (say the US).

> A country's **effective exchange rate** is an average of its exchange rate against all its trade partners, weighted by the relative size of trade with each country.

Box 28.1 Effective exchange rates

Each currency has a bilateral exchange rate against each other currency. For example, we can measure the $/£ or euro/£. Sometimes it is useful to examine a single exchange rate that summarizes all the bilateral rates.

The **effective exchange rate (eer)** is a weighted average of individual bilateral exchange rates.

Usually, we use the share of trade with each country to decide the weights. Important trading partners get more weight in the effective exchange rate index. The figure on the right shows sterling's effective exchange rate since 1999, based on an index whose value is set at 1.00 in 2005. The figure also shows exchange rates for the UK's two main trading partners, the US and the eurozone. Although sterling has fluctuated against both the dollar and the euro, its effective value against all currencies has been much more stable.

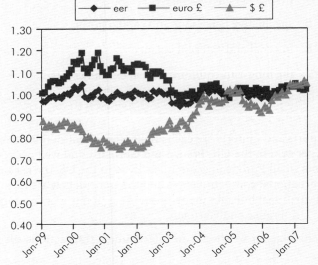

The figure shows the nominal effective exchange rate, which averages bilateral nominal exchange rates. It is also possible to compute bilateral real exchange rates. A weighted average of these yields the real effective exchange rate. Changes in the real effective exchange rate are a good indication of what is happening to competitiveness.

Source: Bank of England.

Exchanging currencies

Who supplies dollars to the forex market demanding pounds in exchange? The demand for pounds has two sources. First, US importers pay in dollars but UK exporters want to bring this money home as pounds. Second, US residents buying UK assets (shares in BT or UK bonds) must convert their dollars into pounds to buy these UK assets. Conversely, a supply of pounds reflects UK imports of US goods and UK residents buying assets in the US.

Figure 28.1 shows the supply and demand for pounds in the forex market. We begin with the demand. Suppose UK whisky costs £8 a bottle. At $2/£, it sells in the US for $16, but at $1.50/£ it sells for $12. Hence at a lower exchange rate,[1] and a lower dollar price of all UK goods, the UK exports more goods to the US. US residents buy more at a lower dollar price.

If the sterling price of UK goods is constant, a lower exchange rate, by raising the quantity of UK exports, must raise export revenue in pounds. Figure 28.1 shows that the demand schedule for pounds, DD, slopes downwards. More pounds are demanded at a lower $/£ exchange rate.

The supply of pounds SS depends on the quantity of dollars UK residents need to buy UK imports of goods or to buy dollar assets. Suppose a holiday in Florida costs $600: at $2/£ it costs £300, but at $1.50/£ it costs £400. A lower $/£ exchange rate raises the price in pounds and reduces the quantity of Florida holidays demanded by UK residents. Whether it reduces the number of pounds spent depends on the elasticity of demand for pounds.

Figure 28.1 assumes that the demand for Florida holidays and other British imports is price-elastic. For a given dollar price of Florida holidays, a lower $/£ exchange rate raises the price in pounds and reduces the sterling value of this spending. The supply of pounds SS slopes up. However, if the UK demand for US goods, services and assets is price-inelastic, a lower exchange rate and higher sterling price will raise sterling spending on these things, and the supply schedule of pounds to the forex market slopes down.[2]

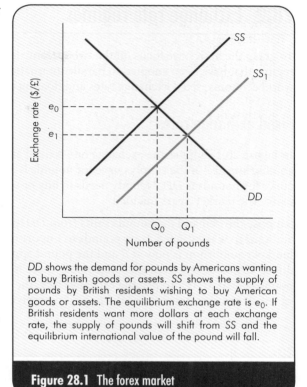

DD shows the demand for pounds by Americans wanting to buy British goods or assets. SS shows the supply of pounds by British residents wishing to buy American goods or assets. The equilibrium exchange rate is e_0. If British residents want more dollars at each exchange rate, the supply of pounds will shift from SS and the equilibrium international value of the pound will fall.

Figure 28.1 The forex market

At the equilibrium exchange rate e_0, the quantity of pounds supplied and demanded is equal. What would change this equilibrium? Suppose, at each sterling price, US demand for UK goods or assets increases. The demand pounds DD shifts to the right, raising the equilibrium $/£ exchange rate. Similarly, a fall in UK demand for US goods and assets shifts the supply of pounds SS to the left, and the equilibrium $/£ exchange rate rises.

When the $/£ exchange rate rises, the pound appreciates so the dollar depreciates. Conversely, when the exchange rate is measured the other way, a rise in the £/$ exchange rate reflects an appreciation of the dollar but a depreciation of the pound. This reinforces our earlier warning: to know whether a rise in the exchange rate reflects appreciation or depreciation, first you need to know which way round the exchange rate was measured.

The pound **appreciates** when the $/£ exchange rate rises. The international value of sterling rises. The pound **depreciates** when the $/£ exchange rate falls. The international value of sterling falls.

1 We are thus using 'the international value of sterling' as the measure of 'the' UK exchange rate.
2 The supply and demand for cars refers to physical quantities supplied or demanded at each price. However, the supply and demand schedules for pounds sterling refer to values of pounds supplied and demanded at each exchange rate. That is why the analysis can be more tricky than the analysis of the market for physical commodities. 'Number of pounds' on the horizontal axis is really a value not a quantity.

28.2 Exchange rate regimes

To grasp the basics, we focus on the two extreme forms of exchange rate regime that have been adopted to handle international transactions in the world economy: fixed exchange rates and floating exchange rates.

> An **exchange rate regime** describes how governments allow exchange rates to be determined.

Fixed exchange rates

In Figure 28.2 suppose the exchange rate is fixed at e_1. This is a free market equilibrium at A if the supply curve for pounds is SS and the demand curve for pounds is DD. Nobody needs to buy or sell pounds to the central bank. The market clears unaided.

> In a **fixed exchange rate** regime, governments maintain the convertibility of their currency at a fixed exchange rate. A currency is **convertible** if the central bank will buy or sell as much of the currency as people wish to trade at the fixed exchange rate.

Suppose the demand for pounds shifts from DD to DD_1. Americans, addicted to whisky, need more pounds to import more UK whisky. Free market equilibrium is now at B and the pound appreciates against the dollar. However, at a fixed exchange rate e_1 there is an excess demand for pounds equal to AC. To peg the exchange rate, the central bank meets this excess demand and maintains the peg e_1 by supplying an extra AC pounds to the market.

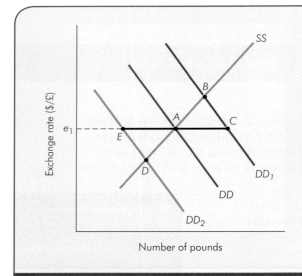

Suppose the exchange rate is fixed at e_1. When demand for pounds is DD_1, there is an excess demand AC. The Bank of England intervenes by supplying AC pounds in exchange for dollars, which are added to the UK foreign exchange reserves. When demand is DD_2, the Bank sells foreign exchange reserves in exchange for pounds. It demands EA pounds to offset the excess supply EA. When demand is DD, the market clears at the exchange rate e_1, and no intervention by the Bank is required.

Figure 28.2 Central bank intervention in the forex

The Bank prints AC extra pounds and sells them in exchange for $(e_1 \times AC)$ dollars, which are added to the UK foreign exchange reserves.

> The **foreign exchange reserves** are foreign currency held by the domestic central bank.

What if the demand for pounds now falls to DD_2? The free market equilibrium is now at D. Pegging the exchange rate at e_1 causes an excess supply of pounds EA. To defend the peg the central bank must demand EA pounds, which it pays for by selling $(EA \times e_1)$ dollars from the foreign exchange reserves.

> The **central bank intervenes** in the forex market when it is forced to buy or sell pounds to support the fixed exchange rate.

When the demand schedule is DD_1 the UK is adding to its foreign exchange reserves. When the schedule is DD_1 it is running down its reserves. If the demand for pounds fluctuates between DD_1 and DD_2, the Bank of England can sustain the exchange rate e_1 in the long run.

However, if the demand for pounds on average is DD_2, the Bank is steadily losing foreign exchange reserves to support the pound at e_1. We say that the pound is overvalued, or is at a higher international value than is warranted by its long-run equilibrium position. As reserves start to run out, the government may try to borrow foreign exchange reserves from the International Monetary Fund (IMF), an international body that exists primarily to lend to countries in short-term difficulties.

At best this is only a temporary solution. Unless the demand for pounds increases in the long run, it is necessary to *devalue* the pound. In a fixed exchange rate regime, a *devaluation* (*revaluation*) is a fall (rise) in the exchange rate governments commit themselves to maintain.

Notice that we say governments, plural. Fixing the $/£ exchange rate is possible only if both the US and UK both wish to do this. For simplicity, our discussion of Figure 28.2 supposed that only one central bank intervened. In practice, it might be both central banks.

Floating exchange rates

In a *floating exchange rate regime*, the exchange rate is allowed to find its equilibrium level *without* central bank intervention using the forex reserves. Thus, in Figure 28.2, demand shifts from DD_2 to DD to DD_1 would be allowed to move the equilibrium from D to A to B.

Of course, it is not necessary to adopt the extreme regimes of pure or clean floating on the one hand and perfectly fixed exchange rates on the other hand. *Dirty floating* implies intervention is used to offset large and rapid shifts in supply or demand schedules in the short run, but the exchange rate is gradually allowed to find its equilibrium level in the longer run.

Having examined the foreign exchange market, we look next at the balance of payments.

28.3 The balance of payments

Taking the UK as the domestic country and the US as the 'rest of the world', all international transactions that give rise to an inflow of pounds to the UK are entered as credits in the UK balance of payments accounts. Outflows of pounds are debits, entered with a minus sign. Similarly, inflows of dollars to the US are credits in the US balance of payments accounts but outflows are debits. Table 28.1 shows the actual UK balance of payments accounts in 2006.

Visible trade is exports and imports of goods (cars, food, steel). *Invisible trade* refers to exports and imports of services (banking, shipping, tourism). Together, these make up the trade balance or net exports of goods and services.

> The **balance of payments** records transactions between residents of one country and the rest of the world.

> The **current account** of the balance of payments records international flows of goods, services and current transfers.

Current transfers are transfers payments paid across borders. These include payment by the UK government of EU subsidies for agriculture, social security payments paid abroad, bilateral foreign aid payments and cross-border flows of income, profits and dividends earned on assets or debts held in other countries.

Table 28.1 shows the UK had a visible trade deficit in 2006, offset partly by surpluses on trade in services and on international transfer payments (mainly income on net foreign assets). Combining trade in goods and services with net income from transfers, the current account of the balance of payments was over £43 billion in deficit in 2006.

Table 28.1 UK balance of payments, 2006 (£bn)

Trade in goods	−83.7
Trade in services	29.6
Current transfers and other income	10.8
(1) CURRENT ACCOUNT	−43.3
(2) CAPITAL ACCOUNT	0.7
(3) FINANCIAL ACCOUNT	33.7
(4) Balancing item	8.9
(5) UK BALANCE OF PAYMENTS (1 + 2 + 3 + 4)	0
(6) Official financing	0

Source: ONS, *Economic Trends*.

A current account surplus means that a country's foreign income exceeds its foreign spending. A current account deficit means that its foreign spending exceeds its foreign income. These surpluses and deficits are saving and dissaving, and lead to purchases or sales of foreign assets.

The *capital account* of the balance of payments records the international flows of transfer payments relating to capital items. This covers payments received from the EU regional development fund for investment in infrastructure projects, the transfer of capital into or out of the UK by migrants and the forgiveness of international debt by the UK government.

Table 28.1 shows a net financial inflow of £33.7 billion in 2006. The inflow of money to the UK as foreigners bought UK physical and financial assets exceeded the inflow of money from the UK as residents bought assets abroad. The UK was a popular place in which foreigners invested money – one reason for the sharp rise in house prices.

> The **financial account** of the balance of payments records international purchases and sales of financial assets.

The balancing item, a statistical adjustment, would be zero if all previous items were correctly measured. It reflects a failure to record all transactions in the official statistics. Estimating implicit changes in the value of foreign investments, which the statistics treat as money brought home and then reinvested abroad, is particularly tricky. Adding together the current account (1), the capital account (2), the financial account (3) and the adjustment (4) we obtain the UK *balance of payments* in 2006. It so happens it just balanced in 2006.

The balance of payments shows the net inflow of money to the country when individuals, firms and the government make the transactions they wish to undertake under existing market conditions. It is in surplus (deficit) when there is a net inflow of money (outflow of money). It takes account of the transactions that individuals wish to make in importing and exporting and in buying and selling foreign assets, and the amount of transactions that governments wish to make in the form of foreign aid (transfer payments to foreigners), military spending (maintaining military bases abroad) and so on.

> The **balance of payments** is the sum of current account, capital and financial account items.

The final entry in Table 28.1 is *official financing*. This is always of equal magnitude and opposite sign to the balance of payments in the line above, so that the sum of all the entries in Table 28.1 is *always* zero. Official financing measures the international transactions that the government must take to *accommodate* all the other transactions shown in the balance of payments accounts. What is this official financing?

Floating exchange rates

If the exchange rate floats freely, there is *no* government intervention in the forex market. Forex reserves are constant. The exchange rate adjusts to equate the supply of pounds and the demand for pounds in the forex market.

The supply of pounds reflects imports to the UK and UK purchases of foreign assets. These are the outflows in the UK balance of payments accounts. Conversely, the demand for pounds reflects UK exports and sales of UK assets to foreigners. These are the inflows in the UK balance of payments accounts. With a freely floating exchange rate, the quantities of pounds supplied and demanded are equal. Hence inflows equal outflows and the balance of payments is exactly zero. There is no intervention in the forex market and no official financing.

Since the balance of payments is the sum of the current account and on the capital and financial accounts, under floating exchange rates a current account surplus must be exactly matched by a deficit on capital and financial accounts, or vice versa. This just says any unspent surplus on goods and services must be spent buying assets. A foreign deficit is financed by running down *net* foreign assets (lower assets or higher debt).

Fixed exchange rates

With a fixed exchange rate, the balance of payments need not be zero. When there is a deficit, total outflows exceed total inflows on the combined current and capital accounts. How is the deficit financed?

Since there is a deficit, the supply of pounds to the foreign exchange market, reflecting imports or purchases of foreign assets, exceeds the demand for pounds, reflecting exports or sales of assets to foreigners. The balance of payments deficit is exactly the same as the excess supply of pounds in the forex market.

To maintain the fixed exchange rate, the central bank offsets this excess supply of pounds by demanding an equivalent quantity of pounds. It runs down the foreign exchange reserves, selling dollars to buy pounds. In the balance of payments accounts this shows up as 'official financing'.

When there is a balance of payments surplus, the government intervenes in the forex market to buy foreign exchange reserves. When there is a balance of payments deficit, reserves must be sold. Table 28.2 summarizes this discussion.

Table 28.2 Balance of payments and exchange rate regimes

Fixed exchange rate	Floating exchange rate
current account	current account
+ capital account	+ capital account
+ financial account	+ financial account
= [− official financing]	= 0
= rise in forex reserves	No official financing; no change in forex reserves

28.4 The real exchange rate

In 1981, the $/£ exchange rate was $2.03/£; by 2003, it was only $1.78/£. A fall in the international value of sterling makes UK goods cheaper in foreign currencies and foreign goods more expensive in pounds. Hence, the UK became more competitive as sterling fell.

> The **real exchange rate** is the relative price of goods from different countries when measured in a common currency.

Not necessarily. The UK had more inflation than the US, so its prices rose more during 1981–2003. UK competitiveness rose because of a lower nominal or actual exchange rate, but fell because the sterling price of UK goods rose more than the dollar price of US goods. As usual, we must distinguish nominal and real variables.

Thus if $E^{\$/£}$ is the nominal exchange rate, measured by $/£ the international value of sterling, and $p_{UK}^{£}$ and $p_{US}^{\$}$ are the domestic sterling price of UK goods and dollar price of US goods,

$$\text{Real exchange rate} = \{E^{\$/£} \times p_{UK}^{£}\}/p_{US}^{\$} \tag{1}$$

Table 28.3 gives some examples. Pretend the only good is shirts. In row 1, a US shirt costs $10 and a UK shirt £6. At a nominal exchange rate of $2/£, the relative price of UK to US shirts, in a common currency, is 1.2, whether we compare the relative dollar price of shirts ($12/$10) or the relative price in pounds (£6/£5). Two things can make UK shirts more competitive with US shirts.

In row 2, a lower nominal exchange rate for sterling of $1.50/£ reduces the relative price of UK to US shirts from 1.2 to 0.9. The UK's real exchange rate depreciated in equation (1) and the UK became more competitive since its shirts became cheaper when measured in a common currency.

Table 28.3 Calculating real exchange rates

Nominal exchange rate ($/£)	UK shirt price (£)	UK shirt price ($)	US shirt price ($)	Real exchange rate
2.0	6	12	10	1.2
1.5	6	9	10	0.9
2.0	4.5	9	10	0.9
2.0	6	12	13.3	0.9

In row 3, the nominal exchange rate is $2/£, as in row 1, but now the sterling price of UK shirts has fallen from £6 to £4.50. At a nominal exchange rate of $2/£, a UK shirt costs $9. Since a US shirt costs $10, the UK real exchange rate has again fallen to 0.9. Row 4 shows that a change in US prices can have the same result.

Equation (1) makes clear that the arithmetic of real exchange rates does not care whether the nominal exchange rate E falls, the sterling price of UK shirts falls or the dollar price of US shirts rises. Any of these changes reduce sterling's real exchange rate and make the UK more competitive (and the US less competitive). Conversely, a rise in the nominal exchange rate, a rise in UK sterling prices or a fall in US dollar prices increases sterling's real exchange rate and makes the UK less competitive (and the US more competitive).

Table 28.4 shows how this works out in practice. The first row shows the nominal $/£ exchange rate in 1981 and 2003. Since the UK nominal exchange rate depreciated after 1981 we might be tempted to conclude that UK competitiveness rose during 1981–2003. The second and third rows show what happened to the price level in each country.

Although changes in the price level have been similar in the two countries since the 1990s, behaviour during the 1980s had been very different. During 1981–90, the UK price level rose from 0.54 to 1.00, whereas the US price level only rose from 0.70 to 1.00. The US had less inflation during the 1980s.

The fourth row calculates an index of the real exchange rate, using the formula of equation (1). While the nominal exchange rate depreciated from 2.03 to 1.78 between 1981 and 2003, the real exchange rate appreciated from 1.57 to 1.81. Higher inflation in the UK, especially in the 1980s, more than offset the competitiveness gain from the depreciating nominal exchange rate.

By 2007 the nominal exchange rate of $1.99/£ had returned almost to its level of 1980. The real exchange rate however had appreciated even more because now there was nothing to offset the very different behaviour of prices in the US and UK during 1981–2007.

Table 28.4 Nominal and real exchange rates

	1981	2003
$/£	2.03	1.78
Prices (1990 = 1)		
UK (in £)	0.54	1.42
US (in $)	0.70	1.39
Real $/£ rate	1.57	1.81
PPP exchange rate	1.71	1.54

Source: IMF, *International Financial Statistics.*

Purchasing power parity

What hypothetical path would the nominal exchange rate have had to follow to keep the real exchange rate at its initial level?

The PPP exchange rate offers a quick check that lets us compare the present with what we know about the past.

> The **purchasing power parity (PPP)** exchange rate path is the path of the nominal exchange rate that maintains a constant real exchange rate.

28.5 Determinants of the current account

Having defined the real exchange rate and discussed its relationship to competitiveness, we can now study what determines the current and capital accounts of the balance of payments. We begin with the current account.

Exports

Chapter 21 assumed that demand for exports was given. We now recognize that the demand for UK exports depends chiefly on two things. First, since UK exports are imports by the rest of the world, higher income abroad leads to higher UK exports. Second, the lower the UK real exchange rate, the greater is UK competitiveness and the larger are UK exports.

Exports respond quickly to changes in world income, but changes in competitiveness affect exports more slowly. Exporters may be unsure if the change in competitiveness is temporary or permanent. If they believe it to be temporary, they may change their profit margins but leave the price of their goods in foreign currency unaffected.

Even where this means losses in the short run, it may be cheaper in the long run than temporarily withdrawing from those markets and having to spend large sums on advertising and marketing to win back market share when competitiveness improves again. But if competitiveness fails to improve and the real exchange rate remains high, firms will gradually conclude that they should quit the exporting business.

Imports

Import demand is larger the higher is domestic income, as we recognized in Chapter 21 through the marginal propensity to import. But import demand is also larger the higher is the real exchange rate and the cheaper are foreign goods relative to domestic goods when both are measured in the domestic currency. Again, in practice, imports respond more quickly to changes in domestic income than to changes in the real exchange rate. However, if sustained, an appreciation of the real exchange rate eventually raises imports.

Other items on the current account

Foreign aid and spending on military bases abroad are matters of government policy. The net flow of interest, dividend and profit income between countries arises because residents of one country hold assets in another. The size of this net flow of income depends on the pattern of international asset-holding and on the level of interest rates, profits and dividends at home and abroad.

28.6 The financial account

We have distinguished between transfer payments on the capital account, for example EU subsidies for roadbuilding, and movements of financial capital to buy and sell assets on the financial account. The former are tiny and henceforth we ignore them completely, implicitly assuming that the capital account is in balance. However, financial flows on the financial account can be huge. These flows of financial capital are often called 'capital flows' even though they relate to the financial account.

Capital inflows and outflows reflect sales and purchases of foreign assets. These flows have become increasingly important. Computers and telecommunications make it as easy for a British resident to transact in the financial markets of New York or Frankfurt as in London. Moreover, controls on international capital flows have gradually been dismantled with globalization and financial integration.

The world's financial markets now have two crucial features. First, restrictions have been abolished for capital flows between the advanced countries. Funds can be freely moved from one country to another in search of the highest rate of return. Second, trillions of pounds are internationally footloose, capable of being switched between countries and currencies when assets in one currency seem to offer a higher rate of return than assets elsewhere.

Perfect capital mobility means that a vast quantity of funds flow from one currency to another if the expected return on assets differs across currencies.

Since the stock of international funds is now huge, capital flows could swamp the typical current account flows from imports and exports.

In international asset markets, capital gains arise not merely from changes in the domestic price of an asset but also from changes in exchange rates while temporarily holding a foreign asset. In Table 28.5, you can invest £100 for a year. UK interest rates are 10 per cent a year. US interest rates are zero. Keeping your funds in pounds, row 1 shows you have £110 at the end of the year.

Speculation is the purchase of an asset for subsequent resale, in the belief that the total return – interest plus capital gain – exceeds the total return on other assets.

Box 28.2 Capital flows

Flows on the financial account of the balance of payments may be short term, such as putting money in a foreign bank account, or may be long term, such as taking a permanent stake in a foreign company.

> **Foreign direct investment (FDI)** is the purchase of foreign firms or the establishment of foreign subsidiaries.

Surely globalization has made capital flows more important recently? The figure shows the scale of average annual capital flows, relative to GDP, for 12 OECD economies in peacetime years since 1870. The figure confirms that capital flows dried up in the 1930s, during the Great Depression, but today we tend to forget that the late nineteenth century was also a great period of foreign investment. By its standards, the present is unexceptional.

Such figures need to be interpreted with care, however. Since official financing is usually small, our balance of payments arithmetic guarantees that the sum of the current and financial accounts must be near zero, especially when averaged over many years. If countries cannot run large current account deficits, they cannot have large capital inflows either.

Looking at the *size* of capital flows does not itself tell us about capital mobility, which relates to the *sensitivity* of capital flows to perceived profit opportunities. If exchange rates adjust to *prevent* massive capital flows, we will never see large flows in the data whatever the degree of capital mobility.

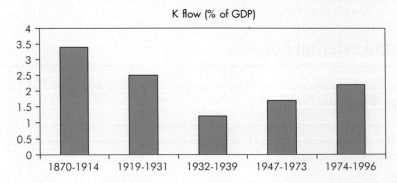

Source: M. Obstfeld, 'The Global Capital Market: Benefactor or Menace?' *Journal of Economic Perspectives*, 1999.

Row 2 shows what happens if you convert £100 into dollars at an initial exchange rate of $2/£, then lend this $200 for a year at zero interest, to get $200 by the year end. Suppose sterling depreciates 10 per cent during the year. At the year end, at the exchange rate of $1.80/£, a fall of 10 per cent on the original rate of $2/£, your $200 converts back to £110. You get 10 per cent less interest than staying in the UK, but make a capital gain of 10 per cent by temporarily holding dollars, whose value relative to pounds rises 10 per cent in the year.

Table 28.5 Lending £100 for a year

£100 lent in:	Interest rate (%)		Exchange rate ($/£)		Final wealth	
	UK	US	Initial	Final	$	£
UK	10	–	–	–	–	110
US	–	0	2.0	1.8	200	110

In this example you end up with £110 whether you lend in dollars or pounds for the year. If the pound depreciates more than 10 per cent, the capital gain on holding dollars outweighs the loss of interest, and the total return on lending in dollars is higher than in pounds. Conversely, if the pound depreciates against the dollar by less than the interest rate differential, you earn a higher total return by keeping your money in pounds.

Equation (2) summarizes this important result. The total return on temporarily lending in a foreign currency is the interest rate paid on assets in that currency plus any capital gain (or minus any capital loss) arising from depreciation (appreciation) of the domestic currency during the period.

$$\text{Return on domestic loan} = \text{Return on foreign loan} = \text{[foreign interest rate]} + \text{[domestic currency depreciation/ while funds abroad]} \quad (2)$$

Equation (2) is called the interest parity condition.

> **Interest parity** means that expected exchange rate changes offset the interest differential between domestic and foreign currency assets.

With near perfect capital mobility, there is a vast capital outflow if the total return on foreign lending exceeds the total return (the domestic interest rate) on domestic lending. There is a huge capital inflow if the return on domestic lending exceeds the return on lending abroad.

Net flows on the financial account of the balance of payments are small only when the total return on foreign lending is similar to the return on lending in the domestic currency. With no barriers to capital mobility, expected total returns are the same in assets of different currencies. Expectations about the future determine the capital gains or losses that people expect to make through changes in the exchange rate.

28.7 Internal and external balance

Next we discuss the relation between the state of the economy – boom or recession – and the current account on the balance of payments.

Figure 28.3 shows the different combinations of boom and recessions and current account surpluses and deficits. Think about demand and supply for domestic output. Equation (3) reminds us of the basic equation for goods market equilibrium:

$$Y = C + I + G + (X - Z) \quad (3)$$

Domestic output Y equals aggregate demand that arises from spending on consumption, investment, government purchases and net exports. If aggregate demand for domestic output equals potential output, firms produce the full-employment output level and in the labour market demand as much employment as workers wish to supply.

> A country is in **internal balance** when aggregate demand equals potential output.

With sluggish wage and price adjustment, lower aggregate demand causes a recession. Only when aggregate demand returns to potential output is internal balance restored.

For a floating exchange rate, the total balance of payments is always zero. Saying that the current account is in balance then also implies financial account balance.

> A country in **external balance** has a zero current account balance.

In Figure 28.3 the point of internal *and* external balance is the intersection of the two axes, with neither boom nor slump, and with the current account neither in surplus nor in deficit.

Internal balance implies aggregate demand equals potential output, and there is full employment in the labour market. External balance means current account balance. The country is neither underspending nor

> Simultaneous internal and external balance is the **long-run equilibrium** of the economy.

overspending its foreign income. Nor is it augmenting or depleting its foreign assets. Foreigners are not acquiring domestic assets without limit, nor are domestic residents acquiring ever-larger holdings of foreign assets.

Figure 28.3 shows how shocks move the economy away from internal and external balance. For example, the top left-hand quadrant shows a combination of domestic slump and current account surplus. This can be caused by a rise in desired saving (a downward shift in the consumption function) or by the adoption of tight fiscal and monetary policy. These reduce aggregate demand and thereby cause both a domestic slump and a reduction in imports.

Similarly, a higher real exchange rate (lower competitiveness) reduces export demand and raises import demand. The fall in net exports induces both a current account deficit and lower aggregate demand, leading to a domestic slump as shown in the bottom left-hand quadrant. The figure shows other shocks that move the economy into other quadrants, causing departures from both internal and external balance.

A key lesson of Figure 28.3 is that most shocks in an open economy move the economy away from *both* internal and external balance. In studying a closed economy, we examined whether the economy could return to internal balance on its own. When adjustment is sluggish, monetary and fiscal policy can speed up adjustment. In a slump, expansionary monetary and fiscal policy hasten the return to full employment.

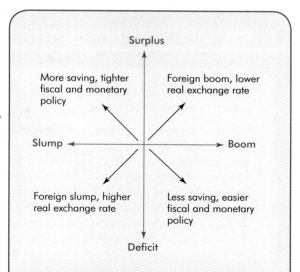

With internal and external balance there is neither a boom nor a slump, and the current account just balances. Each quadrant of the diagram identifies shocks that cause departures from internal and external balances. For example, tight fiscal and monetary policy reduce aggregate demand, creating a domestic slump but a current account surplus since import demand is reduced. However, by increasing export demand, a foreign boom leads to both a domestic boom and a current account surplus. Other possible shocks and their consequences are shown.

Figure 28.3 Internal and external balance

28.8 The long-run equilibrium real exchange rate

In long-run equilibrium, both internal and external balance must hold. Domestic output Y is at potential output Y^* and the current account is in balance. For countries with large foreign debts or foreign assets, and thus large flows of interest income, the current account can deviate a lot from trade balance. However, for most countries, the trade balance and the current account balance are similar.

Initially, we focus on this latter case. External balance then requires that net exports $X - Z$ must be zero. Long-run equilibrium then requires

$$Y^* = Y = [C + I + G] + [X - Z] \qquad (4)$$

In external balance, net exports $(X - Z) = 0$. Internal balance then requires that domestic demand $(C + I + G)$, the domestic absorption of resources, equals potential output Y^*.

Net exports depend on real income at home, real income abroad and the real exchange rate that determines competitiveness. In long-run equilibrium, both domestic and foreign income are fixed at their respective levels of potential output. Given these income levels, net exports depend only on the real exchange rate.

Activity box 28 The Balassa Samuelson effect

Paul Samuelson won the Nobel Prize for his work on many aspects of economics, including international trade.

Empirical research confirms a relation first noticed by Bala Balassa and Paul Samuelson: countries with higher per capita real incomes have a higher real exchange rate. Typically, there is more technical progress in industries making goods for trade (computers, cars, telecommunications) than in industries making services for the home economy (haircuts, laundry, crèches). Similarly, productivity-enhancing capital accumulation occurs mainly in the traded goods sector. The main difference between a rich country and a poor country is not that hairdressers or childminders are more productive in rich countries, but that industries making exports and competing with imports are more productive.

Countries with high per capita incomes therefore have high real exchange rates because their traded goods sector is more productive. Without real exchange rate appreciation such countries would be too competitive.

Questions

(a) Except for footballers, investment bankers and university professors, labour is largely a commodity that is not traded across national frontiers. Does this mean that countries with a high real exchange rate will also be ones with a high real wage rate?

(b) Rank the following countries in terms of the degree of appreciation of their real exchange rate, with the highest first: China, Greece, Italy, Switzerland.

(c) Suppose the internet allows extensive international trade in services (legal services, accounting services, software services, entertainment services). Is the Balassa Samuelson effect then likely to break down? Why, or why not?

To check your answers to these questions, go to page 732.

To check your answers to these questions, go to page 732.

Figure 28.4 shows that there is a unique real exchange rate that makes the net exports equal to zero. Given domestic and foreign levels of potential output, a lower real exchange rate raises export demand and reduces import demand. The net export schedule NX slopes down. Only at the real exchange rate R_0 are net exports zero. At a higher real exchange rate, competitiveness is too low and net exports are negative. At a lower real exchange rate, competitiveness is too high and net exports are positive.

Beginning from R_0, suppose the country gets a favourable and lasting supply shock that raises potential output Y^*. For example, the country discovers a natural resource, such as oil or gold, or develops a new high-tech industry, such as computers. Since the marginal propensity to consume is less than unity, if output and income rise by 100, aggregate demand rises by less than 100. The remaining output is exported and net exports rise.

In Figure 28.4 the favourable supply shock shifts the net export schedule to NX' and the long-run equilibrium real exchange rate appreciates from R_0 to R_1. If finding North Sea oil adds to UK net exports, only a fall in the country's manufacturing exports will prevent a permanent trade surplus. A real exchange rate appreciation – a fall in UK competitiveness – is the market mechanism that restores external balance.[3]

Large supply shocks, such as a big resource discovery, are the exception not the norm. If no shocks occur, the real exchange rate is constant in long-run equilibrium. This has two implications. First, if domestic and foreign prices grow at different rates, the nominal exchange rate has to adjust steadily to keep the real exchange rate constant. The nominal exchange rate then follows the purchasing power parity path discussed in Section 28.4.

Second, if the nominal exchange rate is fixed as an act of policy, it is possible to maintain a constant real exchange rate in the long run only if domestic and foreign prices change at the same rate. Otherwise the real exchange rate is changing in the long run, and net exports will not remain zero, as external balance requires.

Foreign debt and foreign assets

Finally, we recognize that some countries have important flows of international income or payments as a result of owning large foreign assets or having large foreign debts. The current account is net exports $(X - Z)$ plus rA the stock of net foreign assets multiplied by the interest rate r. For creditor countries A is positive, for debtor countries A is negative.

Figure 28.5 shows how inherited foreign assets or debts affect the long-run equilibrium real exchange rate. The current account CA is net exports NX, as in Figure 28.4, plus net interest on foreign assets. For current account balance, a debtor country needs a low real exchange rate R_0 to be competitive and have a sufficient trade surplus to pay interest on its foreign debts. A creditor country has a high real exchange rate R_1 to reduce competitiveness and run a trade deficit, financed by interest earned on foreign assets.

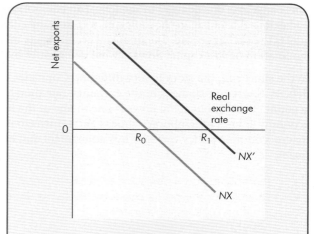

Given domestic and foreign incomes, a higher real exchange rate reduces competitiveness and net exports. Only at R_0 is there trade balance. A resource discovery, such as North Sea oil, shifts NX to NX' causing an appreciation of the real exchange rate to R_1 to maintain trade balance in the long run.

Figure 28.4 The long-run equilibrium real exchange rate

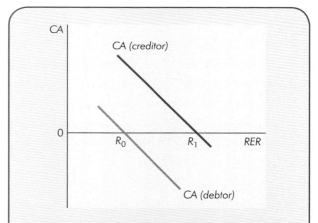

The current account CA is net exports NX plus net interest on foreign assets. For current account balance, a debtor country needs a low real exchange rate R_0 to be competitive and have a sufficient trade surplus to pay interest on its foreign debts. A creditor country has a high real exchange rate R_1 to reduce competitiveness and run a trade deficit, financed by interest earned on foreign assets.

Figure 28.5 Foreign assets and the real exchange rate

---

3 The fact that a resource discovery hurts other sectors, such as manufacturing, is sometimes called Dutch Disease. Holland's real exchange appreciated significantly after its discovery of offshore gas fields in the North Sea. Sterling also appreciated after the UK subsequently found North Sea oil.

This completes our analysis of the long-run equilibrium exchange rate, compatible with both internal and external balance. In the long run, it is thus the current account of the balance of payments that affects the exchange rate. The financial account gets into the story only to the extent that the cumulation of *past* capital flows is what determines the current stock of net foreign assets.

In the short run, the story is very different. Countries can run large current account surpluses and deficits. Short-run changes in the exchange rate then have much more to do with the financial account. The role of capital flows is one theme of the next chapter. The other themes are how the economy adjusts to temporary shocks and returns to internal and external balance, whether macroeconomic policy can ease this adjustment and how choice of exchange rate regime affects these issues.

Summary

- The **exchange rate** is the number of units of foreign currency that exchange for a unit of the domestic currency. A fall (rise) in the exchange rate is called **depreciation (appreciation)**.

- The **demand for domestic currency in the forex market** arises from exports and purchases of domestic assets by foreigners; the **supply of domestic currency** to the market arises from imports and purchases of foreign assets. **Floating exchange rates** equate supply and demand for currency in the absence of government intervention in the forex market.

- Under **fixed exchange rates**, the government meets an excess supply of pounds by running down foreign currency reserves in order to prompt demand for pounds. An excess demand for pounds, at the fixed exchange rate, raises the foreign exchange reserves as pounds are supplied to the market.

- In the **balance of payments accounts**, monetary inflows are credits and monetary outflows are debits. The **current account** shows the trade balance plus current transfer payments, which largely reflect income earned from assets owned in other currencies, payment of international subsidies and social security payments. The capital account records the transfers of capital by migrants, debt forgiveness and net grant receipts for infrastructure projects from overseas institutions. Typically, this is small and for convenience we often ignore it completely. The **financial account** shows net purchases and sales of foreign assets. The balance of payments is the sum of the current, capital and financial account balances.

- Under floating exchange rates, a current surplus must be offset by a financial account deficit or vice versa. Under fixed exchange rates, a balance of payments surplus or deficit must be matched by an offsetting quantity of official financing. **Official financing** is government intervention in the forex market.

- The **real exchange rate** adjusts the nominal exchange rate for prices at home and abroad, and is the relative price of domestic to foreign goods when measured in a common currency. A rise in the real exchange rate reduces the **competitiveness** of the domestic economy.

- The **purchasing power parity** is path of the nominal exchange rate that would keep the real exchange rate at its initial level.

- An increase in domestic (foreign) income increases the demand for imports (exports). An increase in the real exchange rate reduces the demand for exports, increases the demand for imports and reduces the demand for net exports.

- Holders of international funds compare the domestic interest rate with the total return from temporary lending abroad. This return is the foreign interest rate plus the depreciation of the international value of the domestic currency during the loan. Perfect international capital mobility means that an enormous quantity of funds shifts between currencies when the perceived rate of return differs across currencies.

- The interest parity condition says that, when capital mobility is perfect, interest rate differentials across countries should be offset by expected exchange rate changes, so that the total expected return is equated across currencies.

- **Internal balance** means output is at potential output. **External balance** means the current account equals zero. Long-run equilibrium needs both.

- Given domestic and foreign levels of potential output, there is a unique real exchange rate that achieves trade balance. An increase in domestic potential output, for example from a resource discovery, causes a real exchange rate appreciation to maintain trade balance in the long run.

- Interest flows from foreign assets and debts make the current account differ from the trade balance. The higher are net foreign assets, the higher is the inflow of interest income and the higher is the real exchange rate needed to maintain external balance.

Review questions

To check your answers to these questions, go to page 731.

1 If $1 exchanges for 1 euro and $1.40 exchanges for £1, what is the exchange rate between the euro and the £? Can the dollar appreciate against the euro but not against the £?

2 A country has a current account surplus of £6 billion but a financial account deficit of £4 billion. (a) Is its balance of payments in deficit or surplus? (b) Are its foreign exchange reserves rising or falling? (c) Is the central bank buying or selling domestic currency? Explain.

3 For decades, Japan has had a trade surplus. Must countries eventually get back to external balance? Is there more pressure on deficit countries than surplus countries to restore external balance?

4 Newsreaders say that 'the pound had a good day' if the sterling exchange rate rises. When is an appreciation (a) desirable and (b) undesirable?

5 Suppose the initial exchange rate is $4/£. After 10 years, the US price level has risen from 100 to 300 and the UK price level has risen from 100 to 200. What nominal exchange rate would preserve purchasing power parity?

6 **Common fallacies** Why are these statements wrong? (a) Countries with lower inflation gain competitiveness. (b) Current and financial accounts are equally important in determining the level of floating exchange rates. (c) UK interest rates are high. This means the pound will appreciate for the next few months.

7 **Harder question** A country discovers oil and its real exchange rate appreciates. Manufacturers go bust because their exports are no longer competitive. Could the country be worse off as a result of finding this valuable resource?

8 **Harder question** Suppose Bob Geldof and Bono succeed in getting all the debts of poor countries written off. What happens to the real exchange rate of (a) poor countries and (b) rich countries? (c) What happens to the manufacturing exports of rich countries? (d) If there were single monopoly producers of manufactures in rich countries, how would they have been lobbying their governments? (e) Why did we not see more of this in practice?

9 **Essay question** 'Capitalist firms have no problem prospering despite the volatility of stock markets. Nobody has ever suggested government policies to fix stock market prices. Exchange rates are just another asset price and it is just as silly to fix exchange rates. Let them float.' Why do governments ever want to fix exchange rates?

Online
LearningCentre

To help you grasp the key concepts of this chapter check out the extra resources posted on the Online Learning Centre. There are chapter summaries, self-test questions, an interactive graphing tool, weblinks and a searchable glossary, all for free!

To put your learning into practice and prepare for exams, an **Interactive Workbook** is also available online, containing a variety of question types and providing feedback on your answers.

If you'd like further help with economics, or have any questions, **NetTutor** is here to help! You will have a personalised tutorial service at your fingertips. Visit the online learning centre at: www.mcgraw-hill.co.uk/textbooks/begg for information on accessing all of these resources.

Open economy macroeconomics

Chapter 28 introduced fixed and floating exchange rate regimes. We now study how the exchange rate regime affects the way in which an economy operates.

Openness is often measured by the size of exports (or imports) relative to GDP. However, links through financial markets often have more impact. Large outflows of financial capital can provoke acute crises. Such crises may induce austerity measures to reassure foreign investors, devaluation of a pegged exchange rate or adoption of a completely new exchange rate regime.

> **Open economy macroeconomics** examines how the economy is affected by links with other countries through trade, the exchange rate and capital flows.

UK discussions about future exchange rate policy still recall the day in 1992 that the UK was forced off a pegged exchange rate in the Exchange Rate Mechanism. Even in the absence of crises, the choice of exchange rate regime affects the transmission mechanism of both monetary and fiscal policy. In this chapter, we study how our analysis for a closed economy must be amended for an open economy.

Initially, we examine fixed exchange rate regimes. Then we discuss the determination of floating exchange rates and the consequences for macroeconomic policy.

29.1 Fixed exchange rates

The balance of payments and the money supply

To understand the role of capital mobility, suppose initially that there are no private sector capital flows, perhaps because of controls on capital flows.

Most economies had capital controls during the period of fixed exchange rates from 1945 to 1973. Subsequent integration of global financial markets made these controls less effective and now they have been scrapped. We discuss them in more detail in Chapter 34.

> **Capital controls** are regulations preventing private sector capital flows.

With a fixed exchange rate but no private capital flows, suppose the economy has a balance of payments deficit (because it has a current account deficit). Chapter 28 showed that, to finance the deficit, the forex reserves must fall. The central bank sells foreign exchange and buys domestic currency, demanding the domestic currency that nobody else wants. In consequence, domestic money in circulation falls as pounds disappear back into the Bank of England. The balance of payments deficit reduces the domestic money supply.

Under fixed exchange rates, the money supply is not determined exclusively by the original decision about how much money to print. A balance of payments deficit reduces the domestic money supply below what it would otherwise have been. With a surplus on the balance of payments, the domestic money is higher than it would otherwise have been. This is called unsterilized intervention in the forex market.

To offset this effect, the central bank may try to sterilize the effect on the money supply.

> **Unsterilized intervention** uses the forex reserves to offset payments imbalances, consequently changing the domestic money supply.

Suppose a payments deficit is reducing domestic money supply. Allowing this to happen will mean a rise in interest rates and a recession. A recession cures the original problem, by bidding down prices and enhancing competitiveness, but a short-sighted government may want to avoid the recession. The central bank prints cash and buys domestic bonds. The domestic money supply is restored and there is no change in interest rates.

> **Sterilization** is an open market operation between domestic money and domestic bonds, to offset the change in domestic money supply that a balance of payments surplus or deficit otherwise induces.

The recession is avoided, at least for a while. The central bank now has fewer forex reserves (an asset on its balance sheet) but more government bonds (a different asset on its balance sheet). Since the recession has been avoided, the payments deficit continues. The central bank loses more forex reserves and acquires more government bonds. Eventually, it runs out of forex reserves. Adjustment cannot be postponed for ever.

The role of capital mobility

Now restore highly mobile private capital. If international investors have more funds at their disposal than central banks, central banks no longer defend exchange rates by buying and selling foreign exchange reserves. Instead, central banks set domestic interest rates to provide the correct incentive for speculators.

The interest-rate tail now wags the speculative dog. A change in interest rates manipulates capital flows and hence the financial account of balance of payments. Since these flows can be huge, in the short run this dwarfs the current account of the balance of payments.

Fixing the exchange rate is now a commitment to set the correct interest rate to eliminate one-way capital flows. This interest rate, coupled with the level of domestic income, determines money demand. This must equal real money supply. Given inherited prices, this determines the nominal money supply.

Thus, in the short run, only one level of the nominal money supply will do. Suppose the central bank tries further domestic open market operations between money and bonds. If it boosts the money supply, interest rates fall, capital flows out until the money supply falls back again and interest rates return to the only level compatible with the pegged exchange rate.

> **Sterilized intervention** does not work when there is **perfect capital mobility** because offsetting capital flows are immediately induced.

When capital mobility is high, adjustment back to long-run equilibrium no longer occurs through induced changes in the money supply and interest rates.

Adjustment to shocks

With a fixed exchange rate, how does the economy adjust to a shock when the government takes no monetary or fiscal action to accommodate the shock? Suppose there is a fall in desired consumption spending at each output level. In a closed economy, output would fall, reducing inflation. The central bank would reduce interest rates, boosting aggregate demand again. Eventually, internal balance is restored.

What happens in an open economy with a fixed nominal exchange rate and high capital mobility? After the demand shock, there is still a domestic slump. However, any fall in interest rates will generate a massive capital outflow. Interest rates cannot be reduced. Since money demand falls because of lower output, the central bank must reduce the domestic money supply, in line with lower money demand, to *prevent* a change in interest rates.

Thus the adoption of a fixed exchange rate precludes the pursuit of a Taylor rule or inflation target. Interest rate policy has to take care of the exchange rate objective. Any attempt to set interest rates at a different level immediately prompts a massive capital inflow or outflow that changes the money supply and restores the equilibrium interest rate to the required level.

> Perfect capital mobility undermines **monetary sovereignty**. If interest rates are set to maintain the pegged exchange rate, they cannot be set independently to influence the domestic economy.

With interest rates thus fixed, the adjustment mechanism of a closed economy is blocked. Lower output and falling prices no longer trigger interest rate cuts that boost aggregate demand again. So how does the economy now get back to long-run equilibrium?

Suppose initially both the domestic and the foreign country had 2 per cent inflation. With a fixed nominal exchange rate, the real exchange rate was also constant. A domestic slump then reduces domestic inflation. With a fixed nominal exchange rate, the real exchange rate depreciates, raising competitiveness and net exports. An initial fall in domestic absorption $(C + I + G)$ thus eventually induces a sufficient rise in competitiveness to raise net exports $(X - Z)$ to restore internal balance. However, higher net exports imply a current account surplus. External balance is not yet restored.

Current account surpluses raise the country's net foreign assets. By not spending all its foreign income, the country is saving and getting wealthier. Higher wealth raises consumption demand and domestic absorption. The consequent boom raises inflation, reduces competitiveness at the fixed exchange rate and net exports fall again.

Domestic absorption $(C + I + G)$ rises and $(X - Z)$ falls. Eventually, both internal and external balance are restored *without any change in interest rates during the adjustment process*. Instead, in an open economy with a fixed exchange, adjustment is achieved through temporary booms and slumps that temporarily affect inflation, with induced effects on the real exchange rate, the balance of payments and changes in external wealth.

A shock from abroad

Suppose instead of a domestic demand shock, the shock is to foreign demand, raising demand for net exports. The current account $(X - Z)$ moves into surplus. The economy has a boom and a current account surplus. It adds to forex reserves.

In a closed economy, the boom induces a rise in interest rates that eventually returns aggregate demand to potential output. In an open economy with a fixed exchange rate, interest rates remain constant. The boom gradually bids up inflation and reduces competitiveness, reversing the original rise in net exports. When prices rise enough to restore current account balance, aggregate demand reverts to its original level and internal balance is also restored.[1] Thus a

---

1 During the boom, the current account surplus adds to foreign assets, which may therefore be a little higher in the new equilibrium than in the original equilibrium. If so, restoring current account balance does not quite restore the original level of the trade balance. For internal balance, potential output equals domestic absorption plus net exports. If net exports have changed a little, so has domestic absorption. Such details belong in a more advanced course. The basic adjustment mechanism remains as described in the text.

Box 29.1 The euro's grandfather

In 1999, Bob Mundell won the Nobel Prize for helping invent open economy macroeconomics. He was the first to realize that openness in product and factor markets may create powerful pressures for monetary union. He also showed what it would be like for a small country to try to hang on to sovereignty when international capital mobility is high.

The figure shows a pegged exchange rate. The UK pegged the pound during its short membership of the ERM in 1990–92. *IS* is the usual relationship between interest rates and output consistent with goods market equilibrium. A small country can peg its exchange rate only by matching the foreign interest rate r^*. We show this as a horizontal line. The money supply adjusts to make sure this is always the domestic interest rate. Initial equilibrium is at *A*.

Any attempt to change the money supply, and hence interest rates, causes an immediate capital inflow or outflow on the financial account until the money supply and interest rates are restored to r^*. For a small open economy with a pegged exchange rate, monetary policy is powerless.

A fiscal expansion shifts *IS* to *IS'*. There is a big short-run effect on output, from *Y* to *Y'*, since interest rates cannot rise to dampen the expansion. Monetary policy is forced to create additional money supply to accommodate the extra money demand when output rises. We can think of the horizontal line for interest rates as being achieved by a shift in the implicit *LM* schedule from *LM* to *LM'*. In fact, we may as well regard the horizontal line as the *LM* schedule itself.

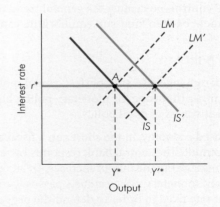

Output

Y^* is potential output. If a demand shock shifts *IS* to *IS'*, potential output is not restored by induced changes in interest rates as in a closed economy. Interest rates remain at r^*.

Rather, higher prices reduce competitiveness and hence shift *IS'* leftwards. Under a pegged exchange rate, induced changes in *IS* schedules restore output to full capacity. If this takes too long, fiscal policy must shift *IS'* back to *IS*.

temporary period of extra inflation permanently raises the price level, permanently changing the real exchange rate.

So far we have shown that an open economy *can* return to internal and external balance under a fixed exchange rate, without assistance from interest rates. Otherwise, monetary union (a permanently fixed exchange rate between member states) would be a non-starter!

However, the speed with which internal and external balance are restored depends a lot on the flexibility of wages and prices. The faster inflation adjusts, the faster the real exchange changes and the less a recession is needed to accomplish the required change in competitiveness. Can adjustment be accelerated by monetary and fiscal policy?

29.2 Macroeconomic policy under fixed exchange rates

Monetary policy

Interest rates are dedicated to defending the exchange rate when capital mobility is perfect. The higher is capital mobility, the less is the scope for an independent domestic monetary policy.

Since it would be nice to be able to use monetary policy too, countries sometimes try to reduce the degree of capital mobility. Outlawing capital flows is unlikely to work. Smart bankers find fancy ways to do the same transactions through other means that as yet are unrestricted.

The most mobile capital flows are short-term flows in and out of liquid assets. Since these assets are sometimes held for very short periods, Nobel Prize winner James Tobin suggested that a small transactions tax might be effective.

> A **Tobin tax** is a small tax on capital flow transactions.

By setting the tax at a low rate, long-term foreign investment is largely unaffected. But if you had to pay, say, 1 per cent of the value of the transaction in tax, this might prevent hopping in and out of foreign assets in an afternoon in pursuit of tiny gains.

Capital controls go against the general trend of financial integration. If monetary policy cannot speed adjustment back to long-run equilibrium, can fiscal policy do better?

Fiscal policy

A fixed exchange rate, plus perfect capital mobility, undermines the scope for monetary policy, but enhances the effectiveness of fiscal policy.

In a closed economy, in the short run a fiscal expansion raises output. The central bank responds by raising interest rates, moderating the output increase. In an open economy, monetary policy adjusts passively to keep the interest rate fixed in order to defend the pegged exchange rate. With a horizontal LM curve, fiscal expansion has a larger effect, as shown in Figure 29.1.

Hence, any fall in domestic demand can be offset by a fiscal expansion to help restore internal balance more quickly. If the change in domestic demand was the only reason that the current account departed from external balance, this fiscal expansion will also restore external balance.

Fiscal policy is potentially an important policy weapon under fixed exchange rates. It helps compensate for the fact that monetary policy can no longer be used. Automatic fiscal stabilizers play this role. Discretionary changes in government spending and tax rates are possible

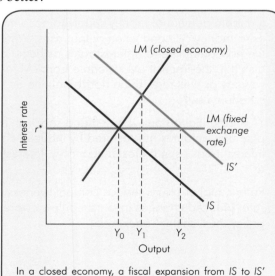

In a closed economy, a fiscal expansion from IS to IS' raises output from Y_0 to Y_1 but the induced rise in interest rates dampens the output expansion. With a pegged exchange rate, the interest rate must remain r^*. With no crowding out, fiscal expansion now raises output to Y_2 in the short run.

Figure 29.1 Fiscal policy

only if fiscal policy can respond quickly to temporary shocks. In some political systems, such as in the UK, this is feasible. In others, such as the US, in which Congress and President may be from different political parties, rapid changes in fiscal policy are harder.

Having analysed the economy with a *given* exchange rate, we now analyse changes in the pegged exchange rate.

29.3 Devaluation

Even where exchange rates are pegged at fixed values, occasional adjustments in these par values sometimes occur.

> The **par value** is the exchange rate that the government agrees to defend.

During three decades after 1945 the major countries agreed to fix their exchange rates, with occasional adjustments or realignments of these par values. Sterling was devalued in 1949 and 1967, before finally floating in 1973. The general idea was to keep exchange rates fixed for long periods if possible. We discuss exchange rate regimes more fully in Chapter 34.

Here, we assess the effects of a devaluation. A devaluation of sterling against the dollar is of course a revaluation of the dollar against sterling.

> A **devaluation (revaluation)** reduces (increases) the par value of the pegged exchange rate.

We distinguish effects in the short run, the medium run and the long run. Initially, we assume that the domestic country begins from internal and external balance. This lets us highlight the effect of the devaluation itself. Then we consider whether devaluation is an appropriate policy response to a shock that has already moved the economy from its long-run equilibrium position.

The short run

When prices and wages adjust slowly, the immediate effect of a devaluation is to reduce the real exchange rate, improving the country's competitiveness. Resources are drawn into domestic industries that compete with imports and into export industries that compete in foreign markets.

Although devaluation tends to raise the quantity of net exports $(X - Z)$, the initial response may be slow. Overnight, there are contracts outstanding that were struck at the old exchange rate. It also takes time for buyers to adjust to the new prices they face and for sellers to build up production capacity to supply more.

Hence, in the very short run, devaluation may not improve the trade balance, the value of exports minus imports. Suppose we measure the current account in pounds. If domestic prices of export goods are unchanged and the quantity of exports has yet to rise much, export revenues rise only a little in the short run. Import quantities have not yet fallen much. If their foreign prices are unchanged, their price in pounds rises by the amount of the devaluation. Hence, the value of imports in pounds may rise substantially. In *value* terms, the current account initially gets worse.[2] However, in the longer run, as quantities adjust, higher export quantities and lower import quantities improve the trade balance.[3]

---

2 The famous Marshall–Lerner condition says that devaluation improves the trade balance only if the sum of the price elasticities of demand for imports and exports is more negative than –1. Recall from Chapter 4 that, when demand is elastic, the revenue effect of changes in quantity more than offsets the effect of a change in price. In the short run, when demand is inelastic, devaluation may worsen the current account.

3 Thus a devaluation first worsens then improves the trade balance, a response known as the *J-curve*. As time elapses after the devaluation, the trade balance falls down to the bottom of the *J* but then rises above its initial position.

The medium run

Domestic output Y equals aggregate demand, which is domestic absorption $(C+I+G)$ plus net exports $(X-Z)$. Once quantities begin to adjust, devaluation increases net export demand $(X-Z)$. What happens next depends crucially on aggregate supply.

An economy with Keynesian unemployment has spare resources with which to make extra goods to meet this rise in aggregate demand. But if the economy begins at potential output, it cannot produce many more goods. Higher aggregate demand bids up prices and wages. Competitiveness falls, undoing the gain in competitiveness achieved by devaluation. When domestic prices and wages have risen as much as the exchange rate was initially devalued, the real exchange rate and competitiveness return to their original levels. If the economy began from internal and external balance, long-run equilibrium is now restored.

If devaluation is meant to raise net exports for a sustained period, for example to raise more money to service foreign debts, this is compatible internal balance $[Y^* = (C+I+G)+(X-Z)]$ only if domestic absorption $(C+I+G)$ is permanently cut, for example by tightening fiscal policy.

Thus, beginning at full employment, devaluation *accompanied* by higher taxes will raise the demand for net exports without increasing total aggregate demand. Since there is no upward pressure on domestic prices, higher competitiveness can be sustained in the medium run.

The long run

Can altering the *nominal* exchange rate permanently change the value of *real* variables? Suppose devaluation is accompanied by tighter fiscal policy to allow the economy to meet the higher demand for net exports without any direct upward pressure on prices. Although this takes care of demand-side effects on prices, we must also think about supply-side effects.

Domestic firms importing raw materials want to pass on these cost increases in higher prices. Workers buying imported TVs realize that import prices are higher and demand higher nominal wages to maintain their real wages. These price and wage rises lead other firms and other workers to react in similar fashion.

In the absence of any real change in the economy, the eventual effect of a devaluation is a rise in all other nominal wages and prices in line with the higher import prices, leaving all real variables unchanged. Eventually, devaluation has no real effect. Most empirical evidence suggests that the effect of a devaluation is completely offset by a rise in domestic prices and wages after four or five years.

In September 1992, sterling left the Exchange Rate Mechanism and quickly fell about 15 per cent against other currencies. The UK also had big devaluations in 1949 and 1967. Table 29.1 shows the effect of the sterling devaluation by 15 per cent in 1967. It took two years for the current account to move from deficit into surplus. Devaluation did not improve the current account until quantities of imports and exports had time to respond.

The public sector deficit as a percentage of GDP shows fiscal policy. In 1967, UK unemployment was low. The economy had few spare resources with which to produce extra goods for export or for import substitution. In 1969, fiscal policy was tightened substantially, reducing domestic absorption and allowing an improvement in net exports. The government (*including* the nationalized industries) actually ran a budget surplus in 1969.

The final row of Table 29.1 shows the real exchange rate, the relative price of UK goods to foreign goods when measured in a common currency. Note two things. First, instead of using the 15 per cent devaluation to cut export prices in foreign markets, UK exporters responded in part by raising prices and profit margins. Only half the competitive advantage was passed on to foreign purchasers as lower

Table 29.1 The 1967 sterling devaluation

	1967	1968	1969	1970
Current account (£bn)	−0.3	−0.2	0.5	0.8
Public sector deficit (% of GDP)	5.3	3.4	−1.2	0
Nominal exchange rate: $/£	2.8	2.4	2.4	2.4
Real exchange rate (1975 = 100)	109	102	102	103

Source: ONS, *Economic Trends*.

foreign prices for UK goods. Second, even by 1970, competitiveness was falling again. Domestic wages rose as workers asked for wage increases to meet higher import prices. By 1970, the real exchange rate had begun to rise.

Devaluation and adjustment

To sum up, once quantities begin adjusting, devaluation leads to a temporary but not a permanent rise in competitiveness relative to the path that would have occurred without the devaluation. In the long run, real variables are determined by real forces. Changes in one nominal variable eventually induce offsetting changes in other nominal variables to restore real variables to their equilibrium values.

But devaluation may be the simplest way to change competitiveness *quickly*. It is a useful policy when the alternative adjustment mechanism is a domestic slump and a protracted period of lower inflation until competitiveness is increased.

Suppose there is a permanent fall in export demand. At the original exchange rate, this generates a slump that induces a period of lower inflation that reduces wages and prices enough to boost competitiveness and restore current account balance. But this takes several years. Devaluation accomplishes an overnight improvement in competitiveness. It speeds up adjustment.

Devaluation may therefore be an appropriate response to a real shock that requires a change in the equilibrium real exchange rate. Conversely, where no real change is required, devaluation eventually generates rises in prices and nominal wages. Chapter 26 discussed inflation expectations and credibility.

Economies can get locked into self-fulfilling prophecies of high inflation. In such circumstances, maintaining a constant real exchange rate requires a steady reduction in the nominal exchange rate. One way to accomplish this is by regular devaluations.

Devaluation has a bad name because it is often associated with periods of high inflation and weak government. This is correct. However, even well-designed macroeconomic policy might choose occasionally to realign the nominal exchange rate. The appropriate circumstances would be a large and sustained shock to the trade balance.

29.4 Floating exchange rates

Having discussed fixed exchange rates, we now turn to the opposite case, freely floating exchange rates. The foreign exchange reserves remain constant, the balance of payments is zero and the government refrains from any intervention in the forex market. In this section we explain how the level of the exchange rate is determined in the short run. The next section uses this analysis to study monetary and fiscal policy in an open economy with floating exchange rates.

The long run

In long-run equilibrium the economy is at both internal and external balance. Chapter 28 analysed determinants of the real exchange rate in long-run equilibrium. Given that output is at potential output, this real exchange rate must achieve current account balance. Anything that tends to create a current account surplus (a resource discovery, a new export industry, income from foreign assets) induces a real exchange rate appreciation to reduce competitiveness. This reduces net exports until external balance is restored.[4]

When exchange rates float freely, there is no official intervention in the forex market and no net monetary transfer between countries since the balance of payments is always zero. Just as in a closed economy, the central bank controls the domestic money supply or sets it to achieve the interest rate it wishes.

> **With floating exchange rates, monetary sovereignty is restored** even under perfect capital mobility. The central bank sets the interest rate and accepts the exchange rate determined by market forces.

The monetary rule, and associated nominal anchor, then determines the domestic price level as explained in Chapter 26. For example, we can think of inflation targeting as pursuing a target path for the price level. In the long run, a Taylor rule has the same result since interest rates are adjusted until output is restored to potential output and inflation is restored to target inflation.

With perfect capital mobility, the central bank can use interest rates to peg the exchange rate, thereby giving up the independent use of interest rates to manipulate the domestic economy, or can set interest rates to manipulate the domestic economy but must then accept the level to which the exchange rate floats.

Our theory of floating exchange rates in the long run is thus easily summarized. Real forces determine the long-run equilibrium *real* exchange rate necessary for external balance. Domestic, sovereign, monetary policy determines the path of the domestic price level. Given the path of foreign prices, there is then only one path of the *nominal* exchange rate that achieves the appropriate real exchange rate in the long run.

If domestic and foreign monetary policies generate the same inflation rates, a constant real exchange rate in the long run is compatible with a constant nominal exchange rate in the long run. However, if domestic and foreign inflation rates differ permanently, the nominal exchange rate must change steadily to keep the real exchange rate at its equilibrium level.

Two examples may help reinforce this argument. Suppose first there is no inflation anywhere. A once-and-for-all change in domestic monetary policy leads to a doubling of the domestic price level. Thereafter prices are constant. To maintain the real exchange rate, there is a once-and-for-all depreciation of the nominal exchange rate by 50 per cent, say from $2/£ to $1/£.

Although domestic prices have doubled, the $ price of UK exports is unaffected in the long run. A £10 shirt used to sell for $20 at an exchange rate of $2/£. Now it costs £20 to make the shirt but it still sells for $20 since the exchange rate is now $1/£. Similarly, a US baseball bat costing $40 used to sell for £20 in the UK. After the exchange rate falls to $1/£ it still costs $40 to make but now sells for £40 in the UK. The price of UK imports doubles because the exchange rate falls by 50 per cent. Import prices rise in line with domestic prices in the UK. Whether we compare the relative price of British and American goods in dollars or in pounds, their relative price is unaltered. Competitiveness does not change.

How about continuous inflation? Suppose US inflation is zero but annual UK inflation is permanently 10 per cent. A steady depreciation of $/£ exchange rate, by 10 per cent a year, leaves the real exchange

---

4 Economists usually use devaluation (revaluation) to describe discrete falls (rises) in pegged exchange rates, but depreciation (appreciation) to describe falls (rises) in floating exchange rates.

rate and competitiveness constant. The $ price of UK goods is constant, like US prices, and the £ price of imports from the US rises annually at 10 per cent, just like UK goods.

Hence, in the long run, floating exchange rates adjust to achieve the unique real exchange rate compatible with internal and external balance. Knowing monetary policy and the price level, we know the required path for the nominal exchange rate. In the absence of real shocks, the nominal exchange rate follows the PPP path to achieve the equilibrium real exchange rate. Any real shocks that are not accommodated by changes in monetary policy and the price level will eventually induce changes in the nominal exchange to achieve the required change in the real exchange rate.

> The **purchasing power parity (PPP) path** of the nominal exchange rate is the path that offsets differential inflation rates across countries, maintaining a constant real exchange rate.

However, in the short run, the real exchange rate can fluctuate a lot. The stock of internationally mobile funds is now vast. If those funds were all to move in a short period, say an hour, between two currencies, this massive flow on the financial account could not possibly be offset by the small net flows that occur on the current account during that hour. Under freely floating exchange rates there is no government intervention and no official financing. The forex market could not clear.

But clear it does, hour by hour, and indeed minute by minute. Short-run equilibrium in the forex market is achieved because the exchange rate is capable of jumping at any instant to the level necessary to *prevent* one-way capital flows of large magnitude. To examine this process in more detail, we need to think more about capital flows.

The short run

When international capital mobility is perfect, interest parity must hold. If assets in different currencies offer different expected returns, there will be massive one-way traffic in capital flows, which is inconsistent with forex market equilibrium. Hence, expected returns are equated to *prevent* massive one-way capital flows.

Expected returns include capital gains and losses as exchange rates change while foreign assets are held temporarily. The current level of the exchange rate affects this capital gain between now and next period. Hence floating exchange rates can always be set at a level that makes expected capital gains just offset interest rate differentials across currencies, for example between UK bonds in sterling and US bonds in dollars, as interest parity requires.

Suppose UK interest rates are 2 per cent higher than US interest rates. Why do holders of funds not move all their funds into sterling? If speculators expect the pound to depreciate by 2 per cent a year against the dollar, investors in pounds get 2 per cent extra interest but lose 2 per cent a year on the exchange rate, relative to the alternative strategy of lending in dollars. The extra interest just compensates for the expected loss and most speculators will not mind where they hold their funds. Without massive flows between currencies, the forex market can be in equilibrium.

What happens if UK interest rates rise and are now 4 per cent above US interest rates? If people still think that the UK exchange rate will fall at 2 per cent a year, the extra UK interest rate more than compensates for capital losses on sterling. Everyone tries to move into pounds. Almost instantly, this bids up the $/£ exchange rate. By how much? Until it reaches such a high level that people expect the pound then to fall by 4 per cent a year thereafter. Only then are the capital losses expected on funds lent in pounds sufficient to offset the 4 per cent interest differential. This restores interest parity and ends one-way traffic.

Why does a higher value of the pound today make people expect the UK exchange rate to fall in the future? Because smart speculators figure out that eventually the exchange rate has to return to the level that achieves external balance long-run equilibrium. With the end point anchored, a higher initial value means a faster rate of subsequent fall.

Figure 29.2 sums up our theory of floating exchange rate determination. For simplicity, suppose domestic and foreign monetary policies generate similar eventual inflation rates. The constant equilibrium real exchange in the long run then implies a constant nominal exchange rate e^* to achieve external balance. In the short run the nominal exchange rate can depart a lot from e^* and can change rapidly.

A country with high (low) interest rates in the short run must have a currency expected to depreciate (appreciate) if it is not to generate one-way capital flows in or out of the currency. Figure 29.2 shows two possible paths for the nominal exchange rate. If interest rates are expected to be high by world standards, the exchange rate begins at e_0 and depreciates steadily until long-run equilibrium is reached at e^*.

At every point along $e_0 e^*$, the slope of this schedule reflects the interest differential, and the capital loss is just offsetting the interest differential.

In the long run, the nominal exchange rate can be constant only if the interest rate differential is eliminated. Recall from Chapter 26 the Fisher hypothesis which says that nominal interest rates adjust in line with inflation, since real interest rates are fairly constant. Figure 29.2 assumes the inflation differential is eventually zero, so that the nominal exchange rate can be constant. This is quite consistent with assuming that eventually monetary policies converge and the interest rate differential disappears.[5]

Conversely, if a country is expected to have abnormally low interest rates for a while, its exchange rate will begin at e_1 in Figure 29.2 The foreseen exchange rate appreciation along $e_1 e^*$ provides expected capital gains on the exchange rate to compensate for the low interest rate on sterling-denominated assets.

From time to time, financial markets change their view about the likely future path the economy will follow. This can lead to a dramatic reassessment of the current exchange rate needed to prevent massive capital flows.

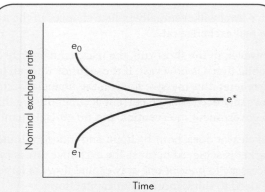

Suppose e^* is the equilibrium nominal exchange rate in the long run. To be constant, this requires there is no inflation differential across countries. The Fisher hypothesis then means that interest differentials are also eliminated eventually. For a country with temporarily high interest rates, the exchange rate begins at e_0 and moves along $e_0 e^*$. For a country with temporarily low interest rates, the exchange rate begins at e_1 and moves along $e_1 e^*$. In either case, expected exchange rate changes offset interest differentials.

Figure 29.2 Floating exchange rates

Suppose financial markets revise their expectations about the future of interest differentials. Formerly, they believed a country would have high interest rates for a while; now they believe that interest rates will be low by world standards. In terms of Figure 29.2, the appropriate path switches from $e_0 e^*$ to $e_1 e^*$ and the initial exchange rate therefore jumps from e_0 to e_1.

Any jump in an asset price is unexpected. If people had expected the exchange rate to jump from e_0 to e_1 they would already have moved out of sterling assets. People holding an asset when its price jumps up or down are either lucky or unlucky.

One reason exchange rates may jump is because of new information about the future of interest rates. Another reason is because of new information about the long-run equilibrium exchange rate. Figure 29.3 shows a country with temporarily high interest rates that was initially expected to have a long-run equilibrium exchange rate e_0^*. Its exchange rate was expected to move along $e_0 e_0^*$ as time elapsed.

> **Floating exchange rates are volatile** because they are asset prices that reflect beliefs about the entire future. Such beliefs can change a lot.

> **When new information becomes available, asset prices jump** to the level that now properly reflects the new information.

5 A different assumption about monetary policy would imply a permanently changing nominal exchange rate.

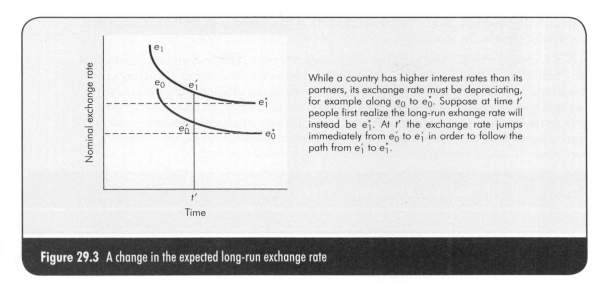

While a country has higher interest rates than its partners, its exchange rate must be depreciating, for example along e_0 to e_0^*. Suppose at time t' people first realize the long-run exhange rate will instead be e_1^*. At t' the exchange rate jumps immediately from e_0' to e_1' in order to follow the path from e_1' to e_1^*.

Figure 29.3 A change in the expected long-run exchange rate

At time t' the financial markets get information that the long-run equilibrium exchange rate will in fact be e_1^*. Had they known this all along, the exchange rate would have begun at e_1 and moved along $e_1 e_1^*$. When this is first realized at time t_1, the forex market immediately jumps the exchange rate to e_1' so that the exchange rate is appropriate from now on.

Along the path $e_1' e_1^*$ the expected capital loss on the exchange rate continues to offset the interest differential. And the path is expected to end up in the right place, namely at the long-run equilibrium exchange rate.

29.5 Monetary and fiscal policy under floating exchange rates

In a closed economy with slow wage and price adjustment, changes in monetary and fiscal policy have real effects in the short run, although the economy eventually returns to internal balance. In an open economy with fixed exchange rates, almost perfect capital mobility makes monetary policy almost powerless in the short run; however, the power of fiscal policy is enhanced since fiscal expansion no longer bids up interest rates. Under floating exchange rates the converse is true: monetary policy is powerful in the short run, but the effectiveness of fiscal policy is reduced.

Monetary policy

Figure 29.2 has already displayed the power of monetary policy to affect the real economy in the short run under floating exchange rates. Given the exchange rate expected in the long run, the anticipation of higher interest rates in the short to medium run causes an immediate appreciation of the exchange rate so it is then likely to fall thereafter. Anticipated capital losses from now on are what choke off the capital inflow that high interest rates would otherwise cause.

Conversely, the anticipation of a period of low interest rates (relative to trading partner countries) induces an initial depreciation of the exchange rate, so that it is likely to rise thereafter. The prospect of future capital gains prevents a capital outflow when interest rates are low.

Hence, beliefs about current and future monetary policy can have a dramatic effect on the initial level of the exchange rate and competitiveness. In effect, the exchange rate is pricing beliefs about the entire future of monetary policy, both at home and abroad. Changing the current interest rate for a short time will have only a small effect on this calculation. However, a credible change in monetary policy for a sustained period will cause a large re-evaluation of the correct path for the exchange rate. This can have a large effect in the short run.

Thus in an open economy with floating exchange rates, monetary policy affects aggregate demand not merely through the effect of interest rates on consumption and investment demand. Changing the anticipated path of interest rates can have a large effect on the exchange rate and competitiveness. This effect on aggregate demand may be large. Because the effect of interest rates on competitiveness operates in the same direction as the domestic effect – lower interest rates boost domestic spending, but also induce a lower exchange rate and greater competitiveness, boosting net exports – monetary policy is more powerful under floating exchange rates than in a closed economy.

Activity box 29 British shoppers cashing in on cheap dollar

'The rapid approach of the "$2 pound" is producing in Britain a curious mixture of Christmas joy and everyday despair.... The US dollar has plunged to a 14-year low against the British pound.... But the dollar's fall has already caught the attention of bargain-hunting Britons, who are deserting London's expensive Oxford Street and other pricey shopping emporiums in favor of shopping sprees in the United States.

'They are attracted by visions of men's Levis for $35 in New York, against $125 back home; a video iPod for $249, versus the $370 in London; a platinum wedding band in Tiffany's shop in the Big Apple for $700, against $945 in a shop off Oxford Street. *The Times* of London calculated that if British shoppers are planning to spend as little as $2,400 on items, they can pay for the airfare plus a weekend in a budget hotel in Manhattan and still come out ahead.

'The entrepreneurial spirit is in full flow. Travel companies report they are getting a "significant increase" in bookings for three-day weekend shopping sprees to New York. But the rush is going on all week, and both British Airways and Virgin Atlantic have added an extra flight a day. The shoe is on the other foot for American visitors in Britain, who are finding that a moderately priced London hotel room can now cost as much as $500 a night. Gasoline now runs about $6.50 a gallon, and a pub lunch for two will set them back about $80.'

(*The Washington Times*, 11 December 2006)

In this short run, sharp changes in the nominal exchange rate cause sharp changes in the real exchange rate since the prices of goods adjust much more slowly. But there is also a longer-run trend against the competitiveness of UK manufacturing, which has been declining for years under all recent prime ministers.

Questions

(a) When Gordon Brown became Chancellor in 1997, he emphasized fiscal prudence and introduced 'stealth taxes' to keep fiscal policy tighter than many people had expected. Suppose fiscal policy had been looser. How would the Bank of England have reacted? What would this have done to the exchange rate? And the effect on manufacturing?

(b) People expect Labour governments to spend more on public services such as education and health. Suppose they do, without spending less on anything else. What are the implications for monetary policy, the exchange rate and the trade deficit? Are these effects temporary or permanent?

To check your answers to these questions, go to page 733.

Fiscal policy

Under floating exchange rates, this effect of interest rate changes on competitiveness *reinforces* the power of monetary policy, but *undermines* the power of fiscal policy.

Suppose the government undertakes a fiscal expansion, raising government spending. This increases aggregate demand. Whether monetary policy follows an inflation target, a Taylor rule or a nominal money target, the boom induces the central bank to raise interest rates. The higher interest rate induces an immediate appreciation of the nominal exchange rate to choke off a capital inflow: if the exchange rate is high enough, people will believe it will fall from now on.

In a closed economy, higher interest rates partially crowd out private expenditure by reducing consumption and investment demand. But in an open economy with floating exchange rates, the induced exchange rate appreciation also reduces competitiveness and the demand for net exports, further dampening the power of fiscal expansion to stimulate aggregate demand in the short run.

29.6 The pound since 1980

Figure 29.4 shows nominal and real sterling exchange rates since 1980. We show the effective exchange rate (eer) against a basket of the currencies most important for the UK's international trade. Notice the high correlation between movements in the nominal exchange rate and real exchange rate (rer). This implies that most changes in the real exchange rate are caused by changes in the nominal exchange rate not by changes in domestic or foreign prices.

The nominal exchange rate is more volatile than the price of goods or the price of labour. This correlation got much stronger after all the major countries adopted inflation targeting with similar targets, largely eliminating differential price trends as sources of real exchange rate movements.

In 1980 a tight monetary policy had been introduced to fight inflation. The prospect of high interest rates for some time had led to a sharp appreciation in the nominal exchange rate, precisely so that it falls thereafter, as it then did. At the same time, the UK had found oil and the rise in oil prices made this oil more valuable. Figure 29.3 showed that a substantial resource discovery raises the equilibrium exchange rate in the long run. In anticipation of this, capital inflows begin immediately. Hence the exchange rate appreciates as soon as the discovery is made.

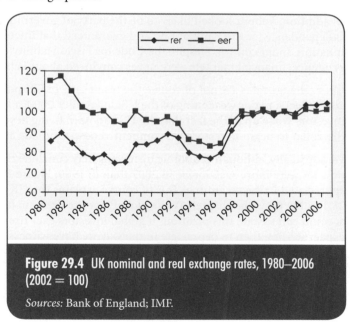

Figure 29.4 UK nominal and real exchange rates, 1980–2006 (2002 = 100)

Sources: Bank of England; IMF.

Together, tight money and North Sea oil explain why the real value of sterling was high in 1980. Competitiveness was therefore low and exports of non-oil products, particularly manufactured goods, were badly hit. After 1981, competitiveness improved for a while as the real exchange rate depreciated.

The UK boom of the mid-1980s was partly built on falls in the real exchange rate – caused by sharp falls in the nominal exchange rate with easier monetary policy – and greater competitiveness. This caused the economy to overheat. As inflation took off again, the Bank raised UK interest rates sharply in the late 1980s. As you would expect, Figure 29.4 shows that this induced a new exchange rate appreciation, of both nominal and real exchange rates, after 1987.

In 1990 the UK joined the Exchange Rate Mechanism (ERM) and pegged its nominal exchange rate to other EU countries.[6] To sustain the peg, the UK had to match interest rates in other ERM countries. The timing was lousy. Nineteen ninety was the year of German reunification. Soon Germany was giving big budget subsidies to support East Germans until their productivity caught up to West German levels. Given this fiscal expansion in Germany, it took very high interest rates in the ERM to restrain inflation in Germany.

Like many other ERM members, the UK was crippled trying to match these huge interest rates that were fine medicine for Germany but not for its partners. By 1992 the UK problem was no longer overheating but a deepening recession caused by very tight monetary policy. Since most of the UK's trading partners also had high interest rates, the pound did not appreciate much during 1990–92.

In September 1992 the UK gave up the ERM, floated the exchange rate and announced that it was cutting interest rates to end recession. Figure 29.4 shows the consequent and substantial depreciation of nominal and real UK exchange rates in late 1992. Unlike the UK, most ERM members stayed in the system and staggered on under high interest rates for several years more.

Greater competitiveness gave the UK an export boom during 1993–95 that helped pull it out of recession. However, Figure 29.4 shows that by the end of 1996 the real exchange rate had returned to its level of 1992, and continued to appreciate thereafter. Most EU countries were now tightening fiscal policy to meet the Maastricht criteria for monetary union. With tighter fiscal policy, their monetary policy no longer had to be so tight. As their exchange rates depreciated, the pound appreciated.

In addition, Labour looked likely to be the party of government for several years to come. Independence for the Bank of England guaranteed that interest rates would rise if required to keep inflation under control. Despite the Code for Fiscal Stability and the Chancellor's emphasis on prudence, financial markets were never convinced about Labour's commitment to tight fiscal policy.

UK exchange rates are not of course the result only of UK policy. In particular, the data in Figure 29.4 also reflect a major weakening of the US dollar after 2000: a low dollar means a high pound. Global investors woke up to the fact that the US had been living beyond its means. It took a depreciation of the dollar to begin to restore US competitiveness. One side effect was the rise in the pound.

Paradoxically, although economic historians may conclude that, from a domestic viewpoint, UK policies were more sustainable in 2007 than in 1980, Figure 29.4 shows just how much sterling had appreciated in the meantime. This of course explains the UK current account deficit shown in Table 28.1 in the previous chapter. While global investors remain happy to pile into London, the financial account can sustain this position. If global investors ever tire of the UK as a location for the funds, expect sterling then to depreciate in the way we have witnessed for the US dollar during 2002–06.

---

6 A different assumption about monetary policy would imply a permanently changing nominal exchange rate.

Summary

- With a **fixed exchange rate** and **perfect capital mobility**, the domestic interest rate must match foreign interest rates to prevent massive capital flows and allow equilibrium in the forex market. **Monetary sovereignty is then lost**. Monetary policy cannot be used independently to control the domestic economy.

- A **fall in domestic demand** causes a fall in output and a decline in prices. Unlike a closed economy, monetary policy cannot respond by cutting interest rates. Rather, the fall in prices boosts competitiveness and raises aggregate demand. When internal balance is restored, there is now a current account surplus. This generates greater wealth, raising domestic demand again. After a temporary boom to raise prices and reduce excess competitiveness, internal and external balance can be restored.

- A **fall in export demand** generates a slump, lower prices and higher competitiveness that restores internal and external balance. No subsequent boom is then required.

- In the short run, fiscal policy is a powerful tool under fixed exchange rates. Fiscal expansion no longer bids up domestic interest rates in the short run. Output expansion is accompanied by a rise in the money supply to maintain interest rates at the world level.

- A **devaluation** is a fall in the value of the fixed exchange rate. With sluggish price adjustment, it raises competitiveness and aggregate demand. With spare resources, output rises. But at potential output, net exports can rise only if domestic absorption is cut by tighter fiscal policy.

- In the long run, devaluation is unlikely to have much effect. Changing one nominal variable merely leads to offsetting changes in other nominal variables. In passing on higher import prices and seeking cost-of-living wage increases, firms and workers offset the competitive advantage of devaluation. But devaluation may speed up adjustment to a shock that requires a permanent change in competitiveness to restore internal and external balance.

- Under **floating exchange rates**, the long-run level of the nominal exchange rate achieves external balance, given prices at home and abroad. In the short run, the exchange rate adjusts to prevent massive flows on the capital account.

- The exchange rate must begin at a level from which the anticipated convergent path to its long-run equilibrium continuously provides capital gains or losses to offset expected interest rate differentials, thus equating the expected return on lending at home and abroad.

- Under floating exchange rates, monetary policy is a powerful short-term tool. The belief that interest rates will be higher for some time induces a sharp appreciation of the exchange rate, so that it can then credibly promise capital losses to offset high interest rates. With sluggish price adjustment, the initial appreciation of the nominal exchange rate causes a sharp fall in competitiveness. This reduction in demand for net exports reinforces other effects of high interest rates in reducing aggregate demand.

- Fiscal policy is a weaker tool under floating exchange rates. Fiscal expansion induces a boom and higher interest rates. The latter induce an exchange rate appreciation that crowds out some net exports, reinforcing domestic crowding out of consumption and investment.

● The actual path of the UK nominal exchange rate reflects changing beliefs about the future course of domestic and foreign interest rates, and about the eventual level of the exchange rate in long-run equilibrium. The latter depends on beliefs about the eventual price level at home and abroad, but also on supply shocks such as resource discoveries.

Review questions

To check your answers to these questions, go to page 732.

1 Rank the following three situations according to the ability of monetary policy to affect real output in the short run: (a) a closed economy; (b) an open economy with fixed exchange rates; (c) an open economy with floating exchange rates. Explain.

2 Beginning at internal and external balance, an economy devalues its fixed exchange rate. (a) What happens to its interest rate? (b) What happens to output? (c) What happens to inflation? (d) How are internal and external balance restored?

3 Suppose in Question 2 that the nominal exchange rate is devalued by 30 per cent. (a) What is the eventual change in the price level? In nominal wages? In the nominal money supply? (b) What is the nominal anchor in this economy?

4 A country faces a permanent fall in export demand. Would devaluation help? How else might internal and external balance be restored.

5 A country discovers a new technology that will add significantly to its export capacity in five years' time. (a) What must happen to its real exchange rate in the long run? (b) Why does the exchange rate react immediately to the news rather than waiting till the new export supply comes on stream?

6 **Common fallacies** Why are these statements wrong? (a) Collectively, global speculators have more money than central banks. Hence, central banks can no longer defend fixed exchange rates. (b) Floating exchange rates are volatile because imports and exports fluctuate a lot. (c) Exchange rate policy is really monetary policy, so it makes no difference to the impact of fiscal policy.

7 **Harder question** Because of China's sustained export success, many people in the West call for China's fixed exchange rate against the dollar to be revalued or for its currency to be floated in the expectation that it will then appreciate. (a) At its current stage of development, should China be running a deficit or surplus on the financial account of its balance of payments? (b) Given that its trade surplus in 2006 exceeded $170 billion, was China running a balance of payments surplus or deficit? (c) With such large monetary inflows, what was happening to China's foreign exchange reserves? And to the Chinese money supply? Must this be inflationary, or could the demand for money increase just as quickly?

8 **Harder question** 'Once the central bank is made independent, with a specified inflation target, the principal role of macroeconomic policy is to determine the real interest rate and hence the exchange rate.' Explain.

9 **Essay question** What do you see as the relative advantages and disadvantages of fixed and floating exchange rates?

To help you grasp the key concepts of this chapter check out the extra resources posted on the Online Learning Centre. There are chapter summaries, self-test questions, an interactive graphing tool, weblinks and a searchable glossary, all for free!

To put your learning into practice and prepare for exams, an **Interactive Workbook** is also available online, containing a variety of question types and providing feedback on your answers.

If you'd like further help with economics, or have any questions, **NetTutor** is here to help! You will have a personalised tutorial service at your fingertips. Visit the online learning centre at: www.mcgraw-hill.co.uk/textbooks/begg for information on accessing all of these resources.

Economic growth

By the end of this chapter, you should understand:

1 growth in potential output

2 Malthus' forecast of eventual starvation

3 how technical progress and capital accumulation made the forecast wrong

4 the neoclassical model of economic growth

5 the convergence hypothesis

6 the growth performance of rich and poor countries

7 whether policy can affect growth

8 whether growth must stop to save the environment

During 1870–2006 real GDP grew 11-fold and real income per person more than 5-fold. On average, we are richer than our grandparents, but less rich than our grandchildren will be. Table 30.1 shows that these long-term trends were even more dramatic elsewhere. During 1870–2002, real GDP in Japan rose 100-fold and real income per person 27-fold.

Table 30.1 prompts three questions. What is long-run economic growth? What causes it? And can economic policies affect it? We mainly focus on industrial countries. Chapter 36 examines growth, or the lack of it, in poor countries.

Economists were always fascinated by the theory of economic growth. In 1798 Thomas Malthus' *First Essay on Population* predicted that output growth would be far outstripped by population growth, causing starvation and an end to population growth, the origin of the notion of economics as 'the dismal science'. Some countries are still stuck in a Malthusian trap, others broke through to sustained growth and prosperity. We examine how they did it.

As Table 30.1 shows, an extra 0.5 per cent on the annual growth rate makes a vast difference to potential output after a few decades. By the end of the 1960s, economists had worked out a theory of economic growth. It yielded many insights but had one central failing. It predicted that government policy made no difference to the long-run growth rate.

In the mid-1980s, a simple insight spawned a new approach in which long-run growth is affected by private behaviour and government policy. We briefly explain this new approach to economic growth.

Finally, we consider whether growth is good. Might it be better to grow more slowly? Can the costs of growth outweigh its benefits?

Table 30.1 Real GDP and per capita real GDP, 1870–2006

	Real GDP		Per capital real GDP	
	Ratio of 2002 to 1870	Annual growth (%)	Ratio of 2002 to 1870	Annual growth (%)
Japan	103	3.6	28	2.6
USA	73	3.4	11	1.8
Australia	49	3.1	4.2	1.2
Sweden	36	2.8	15	2.2
France	16	2.2	10.5	1.9
UK	11	2.0	5.5	1.3

Sources: Angus Maddison, 'Phases of Capitalist Development', in R. C. O. Matthews (ed.), *Economic Growth and Resources*, vol. 2, Macmillan, 1979; updated from IMF, *International Financial Statistics.*

30.1 Economic growth

The growth rate of a variable is its percentage rise per annum. To define economic growth we must specify both the variable to measure and the period over which to measure it. Table 30.1 uses real GDP. We get similar results using real GNP or national income.

> **Economic growth** is the rate of change of real income or real output.

GDP and GNP measure the total output and total income of an economy. Even so, they are very incomplete measures of *economic* output and income. Moreover, it is hard to account for the introduction of new products. Nor does more GDP guarantee more happiness.

GDP and economic output

GDP measures the net output or value added in an economy by measuring goods and services bought with money. It omits output not bought and sold and therefore unmeasured. Two big omissions are leisure and externalities such as pollution and congestion.

In most industrial countries, average hours of work have fallen at least ten hours a week since 1900. In choosing to work fewer hours, people reveal that the extra leisure is worth at least as much as the extra goods that could have been bought by working longer. When people decide to swap washing machines for extra leisure, recorded GDP falls. GDP understates the true economic output of the economy. Conversely, the output of pollution reduces the net economic welfare that the economy is producing, and ideally should be subtracted from GDP.

Including leisure in GDP would have raised recorded GDP in both 1870 and 2006. Since the value of leisure probably rose less quickly than measured output, which rose 11-fold in the UK and 103-fold in Japan, a more comprehensive output measure might show a slower growth rate.

Conversely, pollution and congestion have increased rapidly. Allowing for them would also reduce true growth rates below the measured growth rates in Table 30.1. A measure of true economic output each year would have to allow for environmental depreciation, everything from the true cost of global warming to the reduction in genetic diversity and the loss of amenities as grasslands are replaced with urban sprawl.

New products

In 1870 people had no TVs, cars or computers. Statisticians do their best to compare the value of real GDP in different years, but new products make it hard to compare across time. We can estimate how much people's real income rises when a new product does an old task more cheaply. The calculation is harder when the new product allows a new activity not previously possible. In previous chapters, we argued that a small amount of inflation probably reflects real price increases justified by better quality or completely new products.

GDP and happiness

Even with an accurate and comprehensive measure of GDP, two problems remain. First, do we care about total GDP or GDP per capita? This depends on the question we wish to ask. Total GDP shows the size of an economy. However, if we care about the happiness of a typical individual in an economy, it is better to look at GDP per capita. Table 30.1 tells us that, although real GDP grew more quickly in Australia than in France or Sweden during 1870–2006, in part this reflected rapid population growth, largely through immigration. Sweden and France had faster growth in GDP per person over the period.

Even so, real GDP per person is an imperfect indicator of the happiness of a typical citizen. When income is shared equally between citizens, a country's per capita real GDP tells us what every person gets. But some countries have very unequal income distributions. A few people earn a lot, and a lot of people earn only a little. Such countries may have fairly high per capita real income but many citizens still live in poverty.

Finally, even when GDP is adjusted to measure leisure, pollution and so on, higher per capita GDP need not lead to greater happiness. Material goods are not everything. But they help. Movements in which people return to 'the simple life' have not had much success. Most of the poorer countries are trying to increase their GDP as quickly as possible.

A recent phenomenon?

Table 30.1 makes a final point. Even an annual growth rate of only 1.3 per cent in per capita GDP led to a 5.5-fold rise in UK per capita real GDP between 1870 and 2006. In 1870, UK per capita income was about £1900 in 2000 prices. If its annual growth rate had always been 1.3 per cent, per capita real income would have been £370 in 1750, £75 in 1630 and £16 in 1510. This is implausible. Hence, it is only in the last 250 years that per capita real income has risen steadily.

In the long run, output fluctuations around potential output are swamped by the growth of potential output itself. If potential output rises 2 per cent a year, it will increase 7-fold in less than a century. To explain growth, we must think about changes in potential output.

30.2 Growth: an overview

For simplicity, we assume that the economy is always at potential output. The production function tells us that higher potential output can be traced to more inputs of land, labour, capital and raw materials, or to technical advances that let given inputs make more output.

> The **production function** shows the maximum output obtainable from specified quantities of inputs, given the existing technical knowledge.

In the long run, population growth may be affected by per capita output, which affects the number of children people decide to have, and the health care and nutrition people then get. Nevertheless, we simplify by assuming that the rate of population growth is independent of economic factors. Thus we assume that anything that raises output also raises per capita output.

Capital

Productive capital is the stock of machinery, buildings and inventories with which other inputs combine to make output. For a given labour input, more capital raises output. However, capital depreciates over time. Some new investment is needed just to stop the existing capital stock from shrinking. And with a growing labour force, even more investment is needed if capital per worker is to be maintained. With yet faster investment, capital per worker rises over time, increasing the output each worker can produce. Higher capital per worker is a key means of raising output per worker and per capita income.

Labour

Employment can rise for two reasons. There may be population growth, or a larger fraction of a given population may have jobs. Labour input also depends on hours worked per person. For a given number of workers, more hours worked raises effective labour input, raising output.

Weekly hours worked have fallen a lot since 1870. The rise in per capita real output in Table 30.1 does not reflect longer hours. Since 1945, labour input has risen mainly because more women have joined the labour force.

Human capital

Human capital is the skill and knowledge embodied in the minds and hands of workers. Education, training and experience allow workers to make more output. For example, much of Germany's physical capital was devastated during the Second World War but the human capital of its labour force survived. Given these skills, Germany recovered rapidly after 1945. Without this human capital, there would have been no postwar German economic miracle.

Land

Land is especially important in an agricultural economy. If each worker has more land, agricultural output is higher. Land is less important in highly industrialized economies. Hong Kong and Singapore have grown rapidly despite overcrowding and a scarcity of land. Even so, more land would help.

Increases in the supply of land are pretty unimportant to growth. In theory, land is the input whose total supply to the economy is fixed. In practice, the distinction between land and capital is blurred. By applying more fertilizer per acre, the effective quantity of farming land can be increased. With investment in drainage or irrigation, marshes and deserts can be made productive. Dubai is building superstar homes, and even a new airport, on land reclaimed from the sea.

Raw materials

Given the quantity of other inputs, more input of raw materials allows more output. When raw materials are scarce and expensive, workers take time and care not to waste them. With more plentiful raw materials, workers work more quickly.

> **Depletable resources** can be used only once. **Renewable resources** can be used again if not over-exploited.

When a barrel of oil has been extracted from the ground and used to fuel a machine, the world has one less barrel of oil reserves. If the world has a finite stock of oil reserves, it will eventually run out of oil, though perhaps not for centuries.

In contrast, timber and fish, if harvested in moderation, are replaced by nature and can be used as production inputs for ever. However, if over-harvested they become extinct. With only a few whales left, whales find it hard to find partners with which to breed. The stock of whales falls.

Factor contributions and scale economies

The marginal product of a factor is extra output when that input rises by a unit but all other inputs are held constant. Microeconomics tells us that marginal products eventually decline as the input increases. With two workers already on each machine, another worker does little to raise output.

Economies of scale

Instead of increasing an input in isolation, suppose all inputs are doubled together. If output exactly doubles, there are *constant returns to scale*; if output more (less) than doubles, there are *increasing (decreasing) returns to scale*.

Scale economies reinforce growth. Any rise in inputs gets an extra bonus in higher output. There may be engineering reasons for scale economies. Simple mathematics shows that it takes less than twice the steel input to build an oil tanker of twice the capacity. On the other hand, many developing countries regret their resources tied up in huge steel mills that are now inefficient. Bigger is not always better. In practice, economists often assume constant returns to scale.

Having discussed the different production inputs, we turn now to the role of technical knowledge.

30.3 Technical knowledge

At any given time, a society has a stock of technical knowledge about ways in which goods can be produced. Some of this knowledge is written down in books and blueprints, but much is reflected in working practices learned by hard experience.

> Technical advances in productivity come through **invention**, the discovery of new knowledge, and **innovation**, the incorporation of new knowledge into actual production techniques.

Inventions

Major inventions can lead to spectacular increases in technical knowledge. The wheel, the steam engine and the modern computer are examples. Technical progress in agriculture has also been dramatic. Industrial societies began only when productivity improvements in agriculture freed some of the workforce to produce industrial goods without leaving people short of food. Before then, everyone had to work the land merely to get enough food to survive. The replacement of animal power by machines, the development of fertilizer, drainage and irrigation, and new hybrid seeds, all played a large part in improving agricultural production and enabling economic growth.

Embodiment of knowledge in capital

To introduce new ideas to actual production, innovation often requires investment in new machines. Without investment, bullocks cannot be transformed into tractors even once the know-how for building tractors is available. Major new inventions thus lead to waves of investment and innovation as the ideas are put into practice. The mid-nineteenth century was the age of the train, and mid-twentieth century the age of the car. We are now in the age of the microchip.

Learning by doing

Human capital can matter as much as physical capital. With practice, workers get better at doing a particular job. The most famous example is known as the Horndal effect, after a Swedish steelworks built during 1835–36 and kept in the same condition for the next 15 years. With no change in the plant or the size of the labour force, output per worker-hour nevertheless rose by 2 per cent a year. Eventually, however, as skills become mastered, further productivity increases are harder to attain.

Box 30.1 The road to riches

For centuries, per capita income growth was tiny. Most people were close to starvation. Now we take growth for granted. After 1750 industrialization changed everything. Capital and knowledge, accumulated by one generation, were inherited and augmented by the next generation.

Why 1750? Partly because mathematical and scientific ideas reached a critical mass, allowing an explosion of practical spin-offs. Yet many pioneers of the Industrial Revolution were common-sense artisans with little scientific training. Conversely, the ancient Greece of Pythagoras and Archimedes achieved scientific learning but not economic prosperity.

By the start of the fifteenth century, China understood hydraulic engineering, artificial fertilizers and veterinary medicine. It had blast furnaces in 200BC, 1500 years before Europe. It had paper 1000 years before Europe, and invented printing 400 years before Gutenberg. Yet by 1600 China had been overtaken by Western Europe, and by 1800 had been left far behind.

Economic historians continue to debate the root causes of progress, but three ingredients seem crucial: values, politics and economic institutions. Growth entails a willingness to embrace change. China's rulers liked social order, stability and isolation from foreign ideas: fine attitudes when progress was slow and domestic but a disaster when the world experienced a profusion of new technologies and applications.

Powerful Chinese rulers could enforce bans and block change in their huge empire. Even when individual European rulers tried to do the same, competition between small European states undermined this sovereignty and offered opportunities for growth and change. Economic competition helped separate markets from political control. Rights of merchants led to laws of contracts, patent, company law and property. Competition between forms of institution allowed more effective solutions to emerge and evolve. Arbitrary intervention by heads of state was reduced. Opportunities for business, trade, invention and innovation flourished.

The making of Western Europe

Date	Per capita income (1990 prices)	Inventions
1000	400	Watermill
1100	430	Padded horse collar
1200	480	Windmill
1300	510	Compass
1400	600	Blast furnace
1500	660	Gutenberg printing press
1600	780	Telescope
1700	880	Pendulum clock, canals
1800	1280	Steam engine, spinning and weaving machines, cast iron, electric battery
1900	3400	Telegraph, telephone, electric light, wireless
2000	17 400	Steel, cars, planes, computers, nuclear energy

Source: The Economist, 31 December 1999.

Research and development

What determines the amount of invention and innovation? Some new ideas are the product of intellectual curiosity or frustration ('There must be a better way to do this!'). But, like most activities, the output of new ideas depends to a large extent on the resources devoted to looking for them, which in turn depends on the cost of tying up resources in this way and the prospective benefits from success. Some research activities take place in university departments, usually funded at least in part by the government, but a lot of research is privately funded through the money firms devote to research and development (R&D).

The outcome of research is risky. Research workers never know whether or not they will find anything useful. Research is like a risky investment project. The funds are committed before the benefits (if any) start to accrue, but there is one important difference. Suppose you spend a lot of money developing a better mousetrap. When you succeed, everyone copies your new mousetrap: the price is bid down, and you never recoup your initial investment. In such a world, there would be little incentive to undertake R&D.

If the invention becomes widely available, society gets the benefit but the original developer does not: there is an *externality*. Private and social gains do not coincide and the price mechanism does not provide the correct incentives. Society tries to get round this *market failure* in two ways. First, it grants *patents* to private inventors and innovators, legal monopolies for a fixed period of time that allow successful research projects to repay investments in R&D by temporarily charging higher prices than the cost of production alone. Second, the government subsidizes a good deal of basic research in universities, in its own laboratories and in private industry.

30.4 Growth and accumulation

In this section we explore the links between output growth, factor accumulation and technical progress. We organize our discussion around a simple production function

$$Y = A \times f(K, L) \tag{1}$$

Variable inputs capital K and labour L combine to produce a given output $f(K, L)$. The function f tells us how much we get out of particular amounts of inputs K and L. This function f never changes. We capture technical progress separately through A, which measures the extent of technical knowledge at any date. As technical progress takes place, we get more output from given inputs: a rise in A. For simplicity we assume that land is fixed.

Malthus, land and population

Writing in 1798 and living in a largely agricultural society, Malthus worried about the fixed supply of land. As a growing population worked a fixed supply of land, the marginal product of labour would fall. Agricultural output would grow less quickly than population. The per capita food supply would fall until starvation reduced population to the level that could be fed from the given supply of agricultural land.

In terms of equation (1), starving people consume all their income. Without savings, society cannot invest in capital, so K is zero. The production function then has diminishing returns to labour: adding more workers drives down productivity.

Some poor countries today face this *Malthusian trap*. Agricultural productivity is so low that everyone must work the land to produce food. As population grows and agricultural output fails to keep pace, famine sets in and people die. If better fertilizers or irrigation improve agricultural output, population quickly expands as nutrition improves, and people are driven back to starvation levels again.

Yet Malthus' prediction was not correct for all countries. Today's rich countries broke out of the Malthusian trap. How did they do it? First, they raised agricultural productivity (without an immediate population increase) so that some workers could be switched to industrial production. The capital goods then produced included better ploughs, machinery to pump water and drain fields, and transport to distribute food more effectively. As capital was applied in agriculture, output per worker rose further, releasing more workers to industry while maintaining enough food production to feed the growing population.

Second, the rapid technical progress in agricultural production led to large and persistent productivity increases, reinforcing the effect of moving to more capital-intensive agricultural production. In terms of equation (1), rises in A and in K let output grow faster than labour, causing a *rise* in living standards.

Thus, even the existence of a factor in fixed supply need not make sustained growth impossible. If capital can be accumulated, more and more capital can be substituted for fixed land, allowing output to grow at least as rapidly as population. Similarly, continuing technical progress allows continuing output growth even if one factor is not increasing.

The price mechanism provides the correct incentives for these processes to occur. With a given supply of land, higher agricultural production raises the price of land and the rental paid for land. This gives an incentive to switch to less land-intensive production methods (heavy fertilizer usage, battery chickens) and an incentive to focus on technical progress that lets the economy get by with less land. A similar argument applies to any natural resource in finite supply.

Capital accumulation

Postwar theories of economic growth date back to work in the 1940s by Roy Harrod in England and Evsey Domar in the United States. In the late 1950s, Bob Solow of MIT assembled the nuts and bolts of the neoclassical growth theory, the basis of empirical work ever since.[1]

The theory is *neoclassical* because it does not ask how actual output gets to potential output. Over a long enough period, the only question of interest is what is happening to potential output itself. Neoclassical growth theory simply assumes that actual and potential output are equal.

In this long run, labour and capital grow. Usually, equilibrium means that things are not changing. Now we apply equilibrium not to levels but to growth rates and ratios. The steady state is the long-run equilibrium in growth theory.

> Along the **steady-state path**, output, capital and labour grow at the same rate. Hence output per worker and capital per worker are constant.

Assume that labour grows at a constant rate n. To keep things simple, we also assume a constant fraction s of income is saved; the rest is consumed. Aggregate capital formation (public and private) is the part of output not consumed (by both public and private sectors). Investment first widens and then perhaps deepens capital.

> In a growing economy, **capital-widening** extends the existing capital per worker to new extra workers. **Capital-deepening** raises capital per worker for all workers.

To keep capital per person constant, we need more investment per person the faster is population growth n (extra workers for whom capital must be provided), and the more capital per person k that has to be provided. Figure 30.1 plots the line nk along which capital per person is constant.

Adding more capital per worker k increases output per worker y, but with diminishing returns: hence the curve y in Figure 30.1. Since a constant amount of output is saved, sy shows the saving per person. Since saving and investment are equal, it also shows investment per person.

---

1 Solow won a Nobel Prize for his work on long-run growth. He is also famous for his one-liners. Since, in short-run analysis, he is an unrepentant Keynesian, many of his famous barbs are aimed at those who believe that prices clear markets quickly: 'Will the olive, unassisted, always settle half way up the martini?'

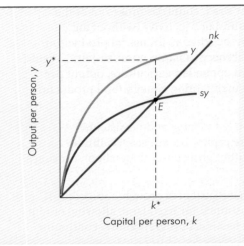

The line *nk* shows the investment per person that maintains capital per person while labour grows. *y* shows output per person, and *sy* is both saving and investment per person. At the steady state *E*, investment is just sufficient to keep capital per person constant at *k**. Per capita output is then *y**. Output and capital grow with population.

Figure 30.1 Neoclassical growth

In the steady state, capital per person is constant. Hence investment per person *sy* must equal *nk*, the investment per person needed to keep *k* constant by making capital grow as fast as labour. *k** is the steady-state capital per person and *y** the steady-state output per person. Capital, output and labour all grow at the same rate *n* along this steady-state path.

Figure 30.1 also shows what happens away from the steady state. If capital per worker is low, the economy is left of the steady state. Per capita saving and investment *sy* exceed *nk*, the per capita investment required to keep capital in line with growing labour. So capital per person rises. Conversely, to the right of the steady state, *sy* lies below *nk* and capital per person falls. Figure 30.1 says that, from whatever level of capital the economy begins, it gradually converges to the (unique) steady state.

A higher saving rate

Suppose people permanently increase the fraction of income saved, from *s* to *s'*. We get more saving, more investment and hence a faster rate of output growth. Oh no, we don't! Figure 30.2 explains why not.

There is no change in the production function relating output to inputs. At the original savings rate *s*, the steady state is at *E*. At the higher savings rate, *s'y* shows savings and investment per person. At *F* it equals *nk*, the per capita investment needed to stop *k* rising or falling. Thus *F* is the new steady state.

F has more capital per worker than *E*. Productivity and output per worker are higher. That is the permanent effect of a higher savings rate. It affects levels, not growth rates. In *any* steady state, *L*, *K* and *Y* all grow at the same rate *n*, and that rate is determined 'outside the model': it is the rate of growth of labour and population. We return to this issue shortly.

In Figure 30.2, the higher savings rate raises output and capital per worker. To make the transition from *E* to *F*,

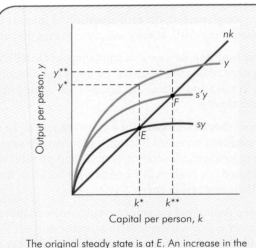

The original steady state is at *E*. An increase in the fraction of income saved, from *s* to *s'*, leads to a steady state at *F*. This raises capital and output per worker, but eventually has no effect on the growth rate. Since *y*** is constant, output and labour still grow at rate *n*.

Figure 30.2 A higher saving rate

there must be a temporary period in which capital grows faster than labour; only then can capital per worker rise as required. A higher savings rate, if successfully translated into higher investment to keep the economy at full employment, causes faster output growth for a while, but not for ever. Once capital per worker rises sufficiently, higher rates of saving and investment go entirely in capital widening, now more demanding than before. Further capital deepening, the basis of productivity growth, cannot continue without bound.

30.5 Growth through technical progress

We have made a lot of progress, but still have some problems. First, the theory does not fit *all* the facts. So far, the theory says output, labour and capital all grow at rate *n*. Although capital and output do grow at similar rates, in practice both grow more rapidly than labour. That is why we are better off than our great-grandparents.

The answer may lie in technical progress, which we ignored in trying to explain output growth entirely through growth in factor supplies (population growth and the accumulation of capital). It turns out that *labour-augmenting technical progress* would do the trick.

Population growth might eventually double the number of workers. Imagine instead that the number of workers is constant but that new knowledge allows the same workers to do the work of twice as many as before, as if the population had grown.

> **Labour-augmenting technical progress** increases the effective labour supply.

Suppose this progress occurs at rate *t*. Effective labour input grows at rate $(t + n)$ because of technical progress and population growth. Now go back to Figure 30.1 and simply put $(t + n)k$ instead of *nk*. To make this valid, we have to measure capital and output not per worker but per worker-equivalent. Worker-equivalents are created by population growth or technical progress. Otherwise the diagram is identical.

E remains the steady state. Output per worker-equivalent and capital per worker-equivalent are constant. Since worker-equivalents grow at rate $t + n$, so must capital and output. Since actual workers increase at rate *n*, output and capital per actual worker each increase at rate *t*. Now our growth theory fits all the facts. Living standards grow over time at rate *t*.

It is uncomfortable that the two key growth rates, *n* and *t*, are determined outside the model. For that reason, for the next 30 years the main use of this growth theory was in growth accounting: showing how to decompose actual output behaviour into the parts explained by changes in various inputs and the part residually explained by technical progress. We next examine the results of accounting for growth.

30.6 Growth in the OECD

The Organization for Economic Cooperation and Development is a club of the world's richest countries, from industrial giants like the United States and Japan to smaller economies like New Zealand, Ireland and Turkey. Table 30.2 shows the growth of OECD countries since 1950.

Productivity growth slowed sharply after 1973 in all OECD countries. Several explanations were put forward. Some stressed the rise in trade union power, enjoying greater legal protection in the 1970s. If this explanation is correct, the supply-side reforms of the late 1980s should have led to high productivity growth in the 1990s. There is little evidence of this.

Nineteen seventy-three was also the year of the first OPEC oil price shock, when real oil prices quadrupled. This had two effects. First, it diverted R&D to long-term efforts to find alternative

Activity box 30 Aborted take-offs on the growth runway

We assume people save a constant fraction s of their income. Even poor people earning only y save sy and consume $(1-s)y$. But if y is low enough, $(1-s)y$ is too low to stop starvation. So they consume all their income and save none. Below a critical income level y_0, saving is zero. What does the Solow diagram look like now? Suppose k_0 is the capital per person that just generates the critical income y_0. Higher capital generates savings as in previous diagrams, and nk is still the gross investment needed to maintain a given capital–labour ratio in the face of growing population. There are now three steady states!

If capital begins above k_1 the economy converges to the steady state at E. Between k_1 and k_2, saving and investment exceed the amount needed for capital widening: capital-deepening also occurs and the economy grows. Above k_2, saving and investment are insufficient to maintain the capital–labour ratio, and the economy shrinks. Either way it ends at E. This is the case analysed in Figures 30.1 and 30.2. Suppose, next, the economy begins at exactly k_1. Saving and investment just maintain the capital–labour ratio. So this is a steady state, but an unstable one. A little above k_1 the economy begins converging on E. And below k_1 there is insufficient saving and investment to provide for the growing population. Capital per person shrinks and keeps shrinking until the economy reaches $k = 0$.

In this model, countries beginning with capital below k_1 are stuck in a poverty trap. They cannot break out. All output is consumed to prevent starvation. There is never a surplus to begin accumulation and growth. This model can also explain why convergence seems to occur within the OECD (countries already above k_1), but why simultaneously many countries are stuck in poverty. Modern growth in the last two centuries began when some key events first generated the surplus to allow saving and accumulation to begin.

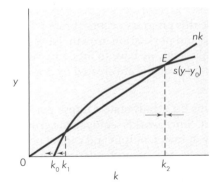

Questions

(a) Why is there no poverty trap when saving is proportional to income?

(b) When a poverty trap exists, is the payoff to overseas aid from rich countries greater if it is concentrated on helping poor countries break out of the poverty trap?

(c) The poverty trap shown above is based on there being a minimum level of per capita consumption. Could we get a poverty trap based on different population growth rates above and below some critical threshold of living standards? Is this plausible?

To check your answers to these questions, go to page 733.

Table 30.2 Average annual growth in real output per person employed (%)

	OECD	Japan	Germany	Italy	France	Sweden	UK	USA
1950–73	3.6	8.0	5.6	5.8	4.5	3.4	3.6	2.2
1973–79	1.4	2.9	3.1	2.9	3.0	1.5	1.6	0
1979–90	1.5	3.0	1.6	1.9	2.6	1.7	2.1	0.7
1990–99	1.3	0.9	3.4	1.3	1.4	1.9	1.5	1.3
2000–07	1.6	1.5	1.4	0.8	1.3	2.2	1.7	1.9

Sources: S. Dowrick and D. Nguyen, 'OECD Comparative Economic Growth 1950–85', *American Economic Review*, 1989; OECD, *Economic Outlook*.

energy-saving technologies. These efforts may take decades to pay off and raise actual productivity. Second, higher energy prices made much of the capital stock economically obsolete overnight. Energy-guzzling factories were closed. The world lost part of its capital stock, which reduced output per head. In practice, scrapping took a long time, and was given renewed impetus by another sharp rise in oil prices in 1980–81. That is why its effects were drawn out over such a long period.

Neither the internet boom nor supply-side reforms have restored the productivity growth rates that the rich countries enjoyed prior to 1973. Emerging market economies are now where the action is. We turn to their story in Part 5.

Having discussed differences in growth across periods, we now examine differences across countries. The one sheds light on the other. The fact that OECD countries move together across sub-periods shows that many aspects of growth are outside a country's own control. Technical progress diffuses across countries quite quickly, wherever it originates. Countries are increasingly dependent on the same global economy.

Even so, growth rates differ markedly across countries. Can growth theory explain why? First, it suggests that, if countries have access to the same technology, differences in output growth should reflect differences in labour force growth. Table 30.1 provides some degree of corroborating evidence: differences in per capita output growth are less marked than differences in output growth.

Second, we need to know how long it takes to get to the steady state, a question to which Figures 30.1 and 30.2 provide no direct answer. Is output growth over two or three decades an adjustment *towards* the steady state, or can we assume that an economy has reached it within that time?

The convergence hypothesis

Figure 30.1 has a unique steady state at E and, whatever the level of capital per worker with which an economy begins, the figure implies that it will eventually converge to E. Poor countries with a low inheritance of capital grow extra rapidly until they reach the steady-state growth rate of output and capital; rich countries with a very high inheritance of capital grow at below-average rates until capital per worker falls back to its steady-state level k^*.

When capital per worker is low, it doesn't take much investment to equip new workers with capital (capital-widening), so the rest of investment can go on raising capital per worker (capital-deepening). When capital per worker is already high, it takes a lot of saving and investment just to maintain capital-widening, let alone to deepen capital. This is one reason for the convergence hypothesis.

> The **convergence hypothesis** asserts that poor countries grow more quickly than average, but rich countries grow more slowly than average.

This explanation for convergence relies purely on the effect of capital accumulation. A second explanation for convergence or 'catch-up' operates through a different channel. Technical progress no longer falls out of the sky at a fixed rate. Suppose instead we have to invest real resources (universities, research labs, R&D) in trying to make technical improvements. It is rich countries that have the human and physical capital to undertake these activities, and it is in rich countries that technical progress is made. However, once discovered, new ideas are soon disseminated to other countries.

Since poorer countries do not have to use their own resources to make technical breakthroughs, they can devote their scarce investment resources to other uses, such as building machines. By slipstreaming the richer countries, they can temporarily grow faster.

Using a standard production function and data on the growth of capital and labour inputs, we can try to see how much of output growth is explained in each country by the growth of its factor inputs.

Solow naturally attributed it to technical progress. The residual is quite large and varies quite a lot across countries.

> The part of output growth not explained by the growth of measured inputs is known as the **Solow residual**.

Box 30.2 Standards of living and the convergence hypothesis

The table below shows World Bank estimates of per capita income in 1987, 2007 and the ratio of 2007 to 1987. The East Asian economies – China, Korea, Hong Kong, Thailand and Singapore – grew very quickly. India (not shown below) is also now growing steadily. Yet convergence cannot be a powerful force in the world or the very poorest countries would all be growing very rapidly. In reality, many poor countries stay poor and sometimes even decline in absolute terms.

Within the rich OECD countries, convergence is much more reliable. The richest OECD countries tend to grow less quickly than the poorer OECD countries.

Why did the East Asian 'tigers' grow so quickly in the postwar period? What was their secret? Professor Alwyn Young of MIT has shown that there is little mystery about their rapid growth, even though they did sustain dramatic rates. These economies managed rapid growth in measured inputs – labour (via increases in participation rates), capital (via high saving and investment rates) and human capital (via substantial expenditure on education). Once we allow for the rapid growth of these inputs, Young showed that the growth of output in the tigers was not very different from what standard estimates, based on OECD and Latin American countries, would have led us to expect. (See: A. Young: 'The Tyranny of Numbers: Confronting the Statistical Realities of the East Asian Growth Experience', *Quarterly Journal of Economics*, 1995.)

Generally, growth seems to be fostered by two conditions: absence of internal strife and openness to the world economy. Once China put insularity and the Cultural Revolution behind it, the potential for catching up was enormous. India had less internal strife, but took off only after it embraced the world economy and relaxed its more bureaucratic controls. Civil war held back Nigeria despite its oil wealth. Indeed, there is considerable evidence that mineral-rich countries without a long tradition of stable government suffer disproportionate incidence of civil war – fighting for the spoils – to the detriment of economic growth and higher living standards.

Note finally that Switzerland, with much the highest living standards, has one of the slowest rates of growth of per capita GNP. The Swiss are rich today because they were rich yesterday, a secret that they discovered long ago.

Box 30.2 Standards of living and the convergence hypothesis (Continued)

Per capita GNP (thousands of 1997 US $)

	Initially	1987	2007	Ratio of 2007/1987
Bangladesh	Poor	0.30	0.47	1.57
Nigeria	Poor	0.42	0.56	1.32
China	Poor	0.35	1.74	4.94
Indonesia	Poor	0.78	1.2	1.53
Philippines	Middle income	1.35	1.3	0.97
Turkey	Middle income	3.28	4.7	1.43
Korea	Middle income	6.23	15.3	2.46
Portugal	Middle income	9.92	16.2	1.63
Spain	Rich	14.84	25.4	1.71
Ireland	Rich	15.27	40.1	2.63
Italy	Rich	21.83	30.0	1.37
UK	Rich	21.23	37.6	1.77
France	Rich	27.13	34.8	1.28
USA	Rich	29.92	43.7	1.46
Switzerland	Rich	46.17	55.0	1.19

Source: World Bank, *World Development Report*, various issues.

Table 30.3 sheds some light on this issue. Professor Nick Crafts of Warwick University took the Solow residuals and tried to see how much of them could be explained by catch-up. The lower a country's per capita GDP relative to the United States' (the assumed technical leader), the larger should be the potential for catch-up. Table 30.3 shows catch-up in each sub-period, and the 'residual', i.e. that part of growth unexplained by inputs or catch-up.

The table makes several interesting points. First, on average there is a role for catch-up: countries with below-average productivity enjoy on average a faster rate of technical progress as they make use of ideas already in operation in richer countries.

Second, some countries are more able to make use of catch-up opportunities than others. Once we allow for 'average catch-up', big differences remain across countries (the residuals in the table). These may reflect the social and political framework in which the economy must operate. Change usually helps the majority but has very adverse effects on a few people whose skills are made obsolete or whose power is suddenly removed. The large number of winners should club together to buy off the few big losers, allowing change to proceed.

Table 30.3 Catch-up (CU) and residual growth (RG) (% per year)

	1950–60		1960–73		1979–88	
	CU	RG	CU	RG	CU	RG
Austria	2.8	1.0	1.3	0.0	0.5	20.9
Belgium	2.1	20.7	1.1	0.3	0.4	0.8
Denmark	1.9	21.4	1.1	0.1	0.6	20.9
France	2.1	0.2	1.0	0.6	0.3	1.1
Germany	2.9	2.0	1.0	20.3	0.3	1.1
Italy	2.4	0.2	1.2	0.8	0.4	0.1
Netherlands	1.9	20.2	0.8	20.3	0.2	0.6
Norway	1.8	21.3	0.9	20.9	0.4	0.0
Sweden	1.3	0.1	0.8	0.3	0.3	20.3
Switzerland	1.1	0.1	0.7	21.0	0.5	20.6
UK	1.6	20.8	0.8	20.6	0.5	0.8
USA	0.0	0.7	0.0	0.1	0.0	0.3
Japan	4.0	0.4	2.2	2.2	0.9	0.0

Note: CU is effect of normal catch-up, RG the residual growth unexplained by input growth or normal catch-up.
Source: N. Crafts, 'Reversing Relative Decline', *Oxford Review of Economic Policy*, 1991.

Some societies are much better than others in organizing the deals that allow catch-up to be achieved more rapidly.

An example: evaluating Thatcherism

Mrs Thatcher was elected in 1979 to breathe new efficiency and dynamism into the British economy, a long-run task properly evaluated by growth accounting. A rise in the long-run path of potential output needs the supply of more inputs or greater productivity from those inputs.

Although tax cuts aimed to raise labour supply, in fact they had little effect. Higher take-home pay provides an incentive to work longer but an equally powerful incentive for richer people to want more leisure. Nor were the 1980s a decade of high investment in the UK. Investment rates were lower than during 1950–70.

The success of Thatcherism hinged on getting higher output from given inputs. This is what the Solow residual measures. Table 30.3 shows that during 1950–70 the UK had negative residuals: allowing for input growth and 'normal catch-up', UK output grew less quickly than the norm. In contrast, the final column of Table 30.3 shows that during 1979–88 the residual increased substantially: the UK did better than the norm.

Supporters of Thatcherism take this as evidence of success. But was it a once-off improvement in output levels or the start of permanently faster growth? It will take a few more decades of data to adjudicate.

30.7 Endogenous growth

Solow's theory makes economic growth depend on population growth and technical progress. Both proceed at given rates. The subsequent literature on catch-up makes technical progress respond to economic and political factors. But it would be nice to have a stronger link between economic behaviour and the rate of economic growth. We want to make growth *endogenous*, or determined within our theory.

> **Endogenous growth** implies that the steady-state growth rate is affected by economic behaviour and economic policy.

The original insight is due to Professor Paul Romer of Chicago University. Saving, investment and capital accumulation lie at the heart of growth. In Solow's theory, applying more and more capital to a given path for population runs into the diminishing marginal product of capital. It cannot be the source of permanent growth in productivity.

We know there must be diminishing returns to capital alone at the level of individual firms; otherwise one firm would get more and more capital, become steadily more productive and gradually take over the entire world! Because diminishing returns to capital hold at the level of the firm, economists had assumed they held also at the level of the economy.

Romer's insight was the possibility (likelihood?) that there are significant externalities to capital. Higher capital in one firm increases productivity in *other* firms. When British Telecom invests in better equipment, other firms can do things previously impossible. The insight also applies to human capital. Training by one firm has beneficial externalities for others.

Thus the production function of each individual firm exhibits diminishing returns to its own capital input, but also depends on the capital of other firms. No firm, acting in isolation, would wish to raise its capital without limit. But when all firms expand together, the economy as a whole may face constant returns to aggregate capital.

Consider the following simple example of the aggregate economy. Per capita output y is proportional to capital per person k. To isolate the role of accumulation, suppose there is no technical progress. Thus $y = Ak$, where A is constant. Given a constant saving rate s and population growth at rate n, is there a steady state in which capital per person grows at rate g? If so, investment for capital-deepening is gk and investment for capital-widening, to keep up with population growth, is nk. Hence in per capita terms

Gross investment $= (g+n)k = sy = sAk =$ **gross saving**

Hence $gk = (sA - n)k$ and the steady-state growth rate g is

$$g = (sA - n) \tag{2}$$

Why does this confirm the possibility of *endogenous* growth? Because it depends on parameters that could be influenced by private behaviour or public policy. In the Solow model, without technical progress, steady-state growth is always n, whatever the savings rate s or the level of productivity A. Equation (2) says that any policy that succeeded in raising the saving rate s would *permanently* increase the *growth rate* g. Similarly, any policy achieving a once-off rise in the *level* of A, for example greater workplace efficiency, would permanently increase the growth rate of k. Since $y = Ak$, this means permanently faster output growth.

Not only can government policy affect growth in this framework, government intervention may increase efficiency. In the simple Romer model outlined above, there are externalities in capital accumulation: individual firms neglect the fact that, in raising their own capital, they also increase the productivity of *other* firms' capital. Government subsidies to investment might offset this externality.

Since Romer's original work there has been huge interest in endogenous growth. Sustaining small additions to annual growth rates eventually makes a big difference to living standards. As a result of this research we now have many potential channels of endogenous growth. For example, instead of assuming the rate of technical progress is given, we can model the industry that undertakes R&D to produce technical progress. Constant returns in this industry will generate endogenous growth. In fact, constant returns to aggregate production of any *accumulable* factor (knowledge, capital, etc.) will suffice.

Note, too, that endogenous growth models explain why growth rates in different countries might permanently be different. This might explain why convergence does not take place and why some countries remain poor indefinitely. Different countries have different growth rates *g*.

While endogenous growth theory is an exciting development, it also has its critics. Most criticisms boil down to a key point. Whatever the relevant accumulatible factor, why should there be *exactly* constant returns in the aggregate? With diminishing returns, we are back in the Solow model where long-run growth is exogenous. With increasing returns, the economy would settle not on steady growth but on ever more rapid expansion of output and capital. We know this is not occurring. So for endogenous growth only constant returns to accumulation will do. Some people think this seems just too good to be true.

30.8 The costs of growth

Can the benefits of economic growth be outweighed by its costs? Pollution, climate change, congestion and a hectic life-style are a high price to pay for more cars, washing machines and video games.

Since GNP is an imperfect measure of the true economic value of the goods and services produced by the economy, there is no presumption we should want to maximize the growth of measured GNP. We discussed issues such as pollution in Chapter 15. Without government intervention, a free market economy produces too much pollution. But complete elimination of pollution is also wasteful. Society should undertake activities accompanied by pollution up to the point at which the net marginal benefit of the goods produced equals the marginal pollution cost imposed on society. Government intervention, through pollution taxes or regulation of environmental standards, can move the economy towards an efficient allocation of resources in which marginal social costs and benefits are equalized.

The full implementation of such a policy would (optimally) reduce the growth of measured GNP below the rate when there is no restriction on activities such as pollution and congestion. And this is the most sensible way in which to approach the problem. It tackles the issue directly. In contrast, the 'zero-growth' solution is a blunt instrument.

> The **zero-growth proposal** argues that, because higher measured GNP imposes environmental costs, it is best to aim for zero growth of measured GNP.

The zero-growth approach fails to distinguish between measured outputs accompanied by social costs and measured outputs without additional social costs. It does not provide the correct incentives. The principle of targeting, a key insight of the welfare economics discussed in Part 3, suggests that it is more efficient to tackle a problem directly than to adopt an indirect approach that distorts other aspects of production or consumption. Thus, when there is too much pollution, congestion, environmental damage or stress, the best solution is to provide incentives that directly reduce these phenomena. Restricting growth in measured output is a crude alternative, distinctly second best.

Some problems might evaporate if economists and statisticians could measure true GNP more accurately, including the 'quality of life' activities (clean air, environmental beauty, sustainable climate, etc.) that yield consumption benefits but at present are omitted from measured GNP. Voters and commentators assess government performance against measurable statistics. A better measure of GNP might remove perceived conflicts between measured output and the quality of life.

This is also a good way to address 'sustainable growth'. At present, Mediterranean beauty spots become concrete jungles of hotels and bars; once the environment is spoiled, upmarket tourists move on somewhere else. An economist's advice, however, is not to abandon being a tourist destination, but to keep track of environmental depreciation and only engage in activities that show a clear return after proper costing of environmental and other damage. Embodying these costings in actual charges also provides the market incentive to look after the environment.

This also provides the answer to those who argue that tackling climate change will hamper economic growth. Growth of what? The subset of outputs that are traded anyway, and hence easily measured? Just as we want congestion charging to *reduce* some outputs (rush-hour traffic), we want environmental pricing to *reduce* some activities (greenhouse gas emissions, lax building insulation). In both cases, the objective is to get aggregate output, *properly measured*, to increase!

No matter how complete the framework, the assessment of the desirable growth rate will always be a normative question hinging on the value judgements of the assessor. Switching resources from consumption, however defined, to investment will nearly always reduce the welfare of people today but allow greater welfare for people tomorrow. Nowhere is this clearer than in the speed with which we try to deal with climate change. More sacrifice today will make life easier tomorrow; less sacrifice today will compound the problems for our children's children. The priority attached to satisfying wants of people at different points in time is always a value judgement.

Summary

- **Economic growth** is the percentage annual increase in real GNP or per capita real GNP in the long run. It is an imperfect measure of the rate of increase of economic well-being.

- Measured GNP omits the value of leisure and of untraded goods and bads that have an impact on the quality of life. Differences in income distribution make per capita real GNP a shaky basis for comparisons of the welfare of the typical individual in different countries.

- Significant rates of **growth of per capita GNP** occurred only in the last two centuries in the advanced economies. In other countries persistent growth is even more recent.

- Potential output can be increased either by increasing the inputs of land, labour, capital and raw materials, or by increasing the output obtained from given input quantities. **Technical advances** are an important source of productivity gains.

- An apparently **fixed supply of a production input,** such as a particular raw material, need not make growth impossible in the long run. As the input becomes scarce, its price rises. This makes producers substitute other inputs, increases incentives to discover new supplies and encourages inventions that economize on the use of that resource.

- The simplest theory of growth has a **steady state** in which capital, output and labour all grow at the same rate. Whatever its initial level of capital, the economy converges on this steady-state path. This theory can explain output growth but not productivity growth.

- **Labour-augmenting technical progress** allows permanent growth of labour productivity and enables the simple growth theory to fit many of the facts.

- There is a **tendency of economies to converge**, both because **capital-deepening** is easier when capital per worker is low and because of **catch-up in technology**. Implementing technical change may depend on how well society is organized to buy off (or defeat) the losers.

- Thatcherism did induce an identifiable rise in UK productivity growth, even after controlling for factor accumulation and catch-up opportunities. It is difficult to be sure whether Thatcherism changed the growth rate for ever.

- Theories of **endogenous growth** are built on constant returns to accumulation. If aggregate investment does not encounter diminishing returns to capital, choices about saving and investment can affect the long-run growth rate of productivity. An externality on a giant scale provides a powerful rationale for government intervention to encourage education, training and physical capital formation.

- Nevertheless, endogenous growth rests on the presence of constant returns to accumulation. Nobody has yet explained why this should hold.

Review questions

To check your answers to these questions, go to page 733.

1 What is the distinction between total output and per capita output? Which grows more rapidly? Why? Always?

2 'Britain produces too many scientists, too few engineers.' What kind of evidence might help you decide if this is true? Will a free market lead people to choose the career that most benefits society?

3 Name two economic bads. Suggest feasible ways in which they might be measured. Should they be included in GNP? Could they be?

4 'If the convergence hypothesis is correct, the poor African countries should have grown long ago!' Is this correct? Do newer approaches to economic growth help explain why some countries remain so poor?

5 'Because we know Malthus got it wrong we are relaxed about the fact that some minerals are in finite supply.' Is there a connection? Explain.

6 **Common fallacies** Why are these statements wrong? (a) Since the earth's resources are limited, growth cannot continue for ever. (b) If we save more, we'd definitely grow faster.

7 **Harder question** Consider a planet in which population grows at the constant rate n and people save a constant fraction s of their per capita output. Output is produced by environmental capital k, which depreciates at a constant d. Gross investment is used only to improve environmental capital, and $y = f(k)$ so that output depends on environmental capital and there are diminishing returns to environmental capital. (a) Draw a figure similar to, but different from, Figure 30.1. (b) Suppose the rate of environmental depreciation rises. What happens to the steady state level of output per person y? (c) Is it true that if recycling were to reduce environmental depreciation it would therefore raise output per person in the long run?

8 **Harder question** Can technical progress be negative?

9 **Essay question** Is growth good?

 **LearningCentre**

To help you grasp the key concepts of this chapter check out the extra resources posted on the Online Learning Centre. There are chapter summaries, self-test questions, an interactive graphing tool, weblinks and a searchable glossary, all for free!

To put your learning into practice and prepare for exams, an **Interactive Workbook** is also available online, containing a variety of question types and providing feedback on your answers.

If you'd like further help with economics, or have any questions, **NetTutor** is here to help! You will have a personalised tutorial service at your fingertips. Visit the online learning centre at: www.mcgraw-hill.co.uk/textbooks/begg for information on accessing all of these resources.

Business cycles

After a deep recession in 1990–92, the UK left the Exchange Rate Mechanism, cut interest rates and let the pound depreciate. Prime Minister Major delayed the next General Election until May 1997, in the hope that recovery would increase the 'feel-good factor' and allow a Conservative victory. It did not. Tony Blair won a landslide victory.

The incoming Labour government then made the Bank of England independent, to try to take some of the politics out of economic policy making. Gordon Brown also emphasized fiscal prudence to keep inflation expectations in check. Yet, as the 2001 election approached, Labour came under pressure to spend more money to improve the public services. Transforming the public services became the principal domestic policy of the Labour government after 2001.

In the absence of further tax increases, economists feared that the economy might overheat, or that the Bank would have to raise interest rates to high levels to prevent this. The pound remained high in anticipation of high future interest rates. When the dotcom bubble burst in 2001 and world recession was further reinforced by the terrorist attacks of 11 September, in retrospect the UK fiscal expansion looked a blessing. Coupled with rapid interest rate reductions by the Bank of England, it shielded the UK from the slowdown being felt elsewhere.

These episodes illustrate many of the issues that we examine in this chapter. First, is there a business cycle? Output fluctuates a lot in the short run, but a cycle does not mean merely temporary departures from trend: it also requires a degree of regularity. Can we see it in the data? Can monetary and fiscal policy insulate economies from business cycles? If so, should the Monetary Policy Committee or the Treasury get the credit?

We also explore the international dimension. Can a single country display cycles that are out of phase with those in its trading partners? What does this have to do with whether the UK might be able to adopt the euro? Is globalization making business cycles more correlated across countries? If they are, might a single monetary policy could become increasingly appropriate?

31.1 Trend and cycle: statistics or economics?

In practice, aggregate output and productivity do not grow smoothly. In some years they grow very rapidly but in other years they actually fall.

Actual output fluctuates around this hypothetical trend path.

Figure 31.1 shows a stylized picture of the business cycle. The black curve is the steady growth in trend output over time. Actual output follows the coloured curve. Point *A* represents a *slump*, the bottom of a business cycle. At *B* the economy has entered the *recovery* phase of the cycle. As recovery proceeds, output climbs above its trend path, reaching point *C*, which we call a *boom*. Then the economy enters a *recession* in which output is growing less quickly than trend output, and is possibly even falling. Point *E* shows a *slump*, after which recovery begins and the cycle starts again.

> The **trend path of output** is the smooth path of long-run output once its short-term fluctuations are averaged out.

> The **business cycle** is the short-term fluctuation of total output around its trend path.

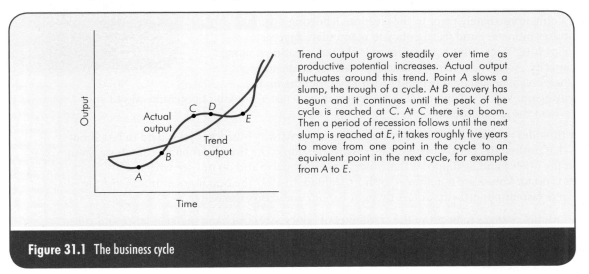

Trend output grows steadily over time as productive potential increases. Actual output fluctuates around this trend. Point *A* slows a slump, the trough of a cycle. At *B* recovery has begun and it continues until the peak of the cycle is reached at *C*. At *C* there is a boom. Then a period of recession follows until the next slump is reached at *E*, it takes roughly five years to move from one point in the cycle to an equivalent point in the next cycle, for example from *A* to *E*.

Figure 31.1 The business cycle

Figure 31.2 shows the annual percentage growth of real GDP and of real output per employed worker in the UK during the period 1975–2007. Output and productivity grew most rapidly in 1986–88 and least rapidly in 1975, 1980–81 and 1990–92. The figure makes four basic points. First, the growth of output and productivity fluctuates in the short run. Second, although cycles are not perfectly regular, there is evidence of a pattern of slump, recovery, boom and recession, with a complete cycle lasting around five or six years. Third, output and output per person are closely correlated in the short run. Fourth, cycles are less marked than they used to be. The rest of the chapter seeks to explain these facts.

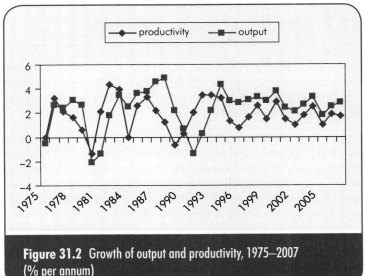

Figure 31.2 Growth of output and productivity, 1975–2007 (% per annum)

Any series of points may be decomposed statistically into an average trend and fluctuations around that trend. We initially assume that potential output grows smoothly. Later we consider whether potential output itself can fluctuate significantly in the short run.

> The **output gap** is the deviation of actual output from potential output.

Thus, we start by assuming that business cycles reflect fluctuations in the output gap. The data in Figure 31.2 show that cycles are too regular to be a coincidence. What causes business cycles?

Since we associate potential output with aggregate supply in the long run, it seems natural to think first about aggregate demand shocks as the source of cyclical deviations of actual output from potential output. We know what shifts demand. Changes in export demand, in the desire to save, in expected future profits and incomes, and in monetary and fiscal policy.

We could argue demand shocks just happen to be cyclical, generating cycles in output gaps and actual output. However, that is not an *explanation* of the business cycle: it does not tell us why demand shocks have this cyclical pattern. One version of this approach does at least claim to be a theory.

Suppose voters, having short memories, are heavily influenced by how the economy is doing immediately prior to the election. Knowing this, the government uses monetary and fiscal policy to manipulate aggregate demand. Policy is tight just after a government is elected, creating a slump and spare capacity. As the next election date approaches, expansionary policy can then create unsustainably rapid growth by mopping up the spare capacity again. Voters misinterpret this as permanently faster growth of potential output and gratefully re-elect the government.

> A **political business cycle** arises if politicians manipulate the economy for electoral advantage.

This theory provides a reason for fluctuations and also suggests why business cycles tend to last about five years – that is often the period between successive elections. The theory probably contains a grain of truth. On the other hand, it supposes that voters are pretty naive and do not see what the government is up to. Voters are not always so short-sighted. In 1997 the Major government lost the election despite fast output growth. Voters thought Labour could do even better.

Recent institutional changes to improve the credibility of policy – central bank independence and rules emphasizing fiscal prudence – act in the direction of reducing the scope for political business cycles in the future. Having discussed political causes of cycles, we now concentrate on economic causes.

31.2 Theories of the business cycle

Fluctuations in export demand might cause cycles. One country's exports are another country's imports, and these imports will fluctuate only if foreign income fluctuates. International trade helps explain how cycles get transmitted from one country to another, but we require a theory of domestic business cycles to initiate the process.

Sluggish adjustment is necessary but not sufficient to generate cycles caused by demand shocks. It is necessary because rapid adjustment would quickly eliminate output gaps and restore output to potential output. It is not sufficient because sluggishness only explains why the return to potential output takes time. An oil tanker moves sluggishly but it does not oscillate its way into port. Cycles require a mechanism by which deviations in one direction then set up forces that cause output to overshoot potential output on its return.

Having ruled out the government, a theory of domestic cycle must be based on consumption or investment spending. Investment spending is the most likely candidate, since investment spending is more likely to take time to assess and adjust. Firms do not rush into major and irreversible investment projects, nor are new factories built overnight.

Box 31.1 The real-wage puzzle

In a recession, firms employ fewer workers. A competitive firm would pay workers the real value of their marginal product. Given a diminishing marginal product of labour, cutting back on workers should raise labour's marginal product. Fewer workers have the same capital as before to work with. So real wages should rise in a slump. But they don't. They fall. This is the *real-wage puzzle* over the business cycle.

Real business cycle theorists suggest that a temporarily adverse shock may make it advisable to engage in some intertemporal labour substitution. When times are tough, you don't sacrifice much by taking time off; lifetime earnings can be rebuilt when conditions are easier. So recessions, caused by temporarily low productivity, make firms offer temporarily low wages, and households temporarily reduce their labour supply. We get low employment *and* low wages.

The Keynesian response is that recessions and unusually high unemployment reflect more than an intertemporarily optimal decision to catch up on sleep and leisure until wages improve. During a recession, utilization of capital capacity is severely cut back. There may be fewer workers, but with machines also idle, the effective input of capital falls. If the latter is sufficiently large, labour's marginal product will fall even though there are fewer workers than before; temporarily, there is even less capital.

The multiplier–accelerator model of the business cycle

The multiplier–accelerator model distinguishes the consequences and the causes of a change in investment spending. The consequence is straightforward. In the simplest Keynesian model, higher investment leads to a larger rise in income and output in the short run. Higher investment not only adds directly to aggregate demand but, by increasing incomes, it adds indirectly to consumption demand. Chapters 21 and 22 examined the multiplier effect on output.

What about the cause of a change in investment spending? Firms invest when their existing capital stock is smaller than the capital stock they would like to hold. When firms are holding the optimal capital stock, the marginal cost of another unit of capital just equals its marginal benefit, the present value of future operating profits to which it is expected to give rise over its lifetime. This present value can be increased either by a fall in the interest rate at which the stream of expected future profits is discounted or by an increase in the future profits expected.

Thus far we have focused on the role of changing interest rates in changes in investment demand. However, although nominal interest rates change a lot, real interest rates change a lot less. The simplest way to calculate the present value of a new capital good is to assess the likely stream of *real* operating profits (by valuing future profits at *constant prices*) and then discount them at the *real* interest rate.

In practice, changes in interest rates may *not* be the most important source of changes in investment spending. Almost certainly, changes in expectations about future profits are more important. The dotcom bubble collapsed not because of high real interest rates but because people realized they had been too optimistic about the future profits to be made.

More generally, if real interest rates and real wages change slowly, the main source of short-term changes in beliefs about future profits is beliefs about future levels of sales and output. Other things equal, higher expected future output raises expected future profits and raises demand for investment in new capacity. This is the insight of the accelerator model of investment.

The accelerator is only a simplification. A complete model of investment would examine changes in expected future profits and changes in (real) interest rates. Even so, many empirical studies confirm that the accelerator is a useful simplification.

How firms respond to changes in output depends on two things: first, the extent to which firms believe that current output growth will be sustained in the future; second, the cost of quickly adjusting investment plans, capital installation and the production techniques thus embodied. The more costly it is to adjust *quickly*, the more firms spread investment over a longer period.

> The **accelerator model of investment** assumes that firms guess future output and profits by extrapolating past output growth. Constant output growth leads to a constant level of investment. It takes *accelerating* output growth to *raise* desired investment.

This simple multiplier–accelerator model can lead to a business cycle. In Table 31.1 we make two specific assumptions, although the argument holds much more generally. First, we assume that the value of the multiplier is 2. An extra unit of investment raises income and output by 2 units. Second, we assume that current investment responds to the growth in output *last* period. If last period's income grew by 2 units, we assume that firms raise current investment by 1 unit.

Table 31.1 The multiplier–accelerator model of the business cycle

Period	Change in last period's output $(Y_{t-1} - Y_{t-2})$	Investment I_t	Output Y_t
$t = 1$	0	10	100
$t = 2$	0	10	120
$t = 3$	20	20	140
$t = 4$	20	20	140
$t = 5$	0	10	120
$t = 6$	−20	0	100
$t = 7$	−20	0	100
$t = 8$	0	10	120
$t = 9$	20	20	140

In period 1, the economy is in equilibrium with output $Y_1 = 100$. Since output is constant, last period's output change was zero. Investment $I_1 = 10$, which we can think of as the investment needed to offset depreciation and keep the capital stock intact.

Suppose in period 2 that some component of aggregate demand rises by 20 units. Output increases from 100 to 120. Since we have assumed that a growth of 2 units in the previous period's output leads to a unit increase in current investment, the table shows that in period 3 there is a 10-unit increase in investment in response to the 20-unit output increase during the previous period. Since the assumed value of the multiplier is 2, the 10-unit increase in investment in period 3 leads to a further increase of 20 units in output, which increases from 120 to 140.

In period 4 investment remains at 20 since the output growth in the previous period was 20. Thus output in period 4 remains at 140. But in period 5 investment reverts to its original level of 10, since there was no output growth in the previous period. This fall of 10 units in investment leads to a multiplied fall of 20 units in output in period 5. In turn, this induces a further fall of 10 units of investment in period 6 and a further fall of 20 units in output.

Since the rate of output change is not accelerating, investment in period 7 remains at its level of period 6. Output is stabilized at 100 in period 7. With no output change in the previous period, investment in period 8 returns to 10 units again and the multiplier implies that output rises to 120. In period 9 the 20 unit increase in output in the previous period increases investment from 10 to 20 units and the cycle begins all over again.

The multiplier–accelerator model explains business cycles by the dynamic interaction of consumption and investment demand. The insight of the model is that it takes accelerating output growth to increase investment. Once output growth stabilizes, so does investment. In the following period, investment must fall, since output growth has been reduced. The economy moves into a period of recession, but once the rate of output fall stops accelerating, investment starts to pick up again.

This simple model is not the definitive model of a business cycle. If output keeps cycling, surely firms stop extrapolating past output growth to form assessments of future profits? Firms, like economists, recognize that there is a business cycle. The less investment decisions respond to the most recent change in past output, the less pronounced will be the cycle.

Ceilings and floors

The multiplier–accelerator model can generate cycles even without any physical limits on the extent of fluctuations. Cycles are even more likely when we recognize the limits imposed by supply and demand. Aggregate supply provides a *ceiling* in practice. Although it is possible temporarily to meet high aggregate demand by working overtime and running down stocks of finished goods, output cannot expand indefinitely.

This tends to slow down growth as the economy reaches a boom. Having overstretched itself, the economy has to bounce back off the ceiling and begin a downturn. Conversely, there is a *floor*, below which aggregate demand cannot fall. Gross investment (including replacement investment) cannot be negative unless, for the economy as a whole, machines are unbolted and shipped abroad for sale to foreigners. Falling investment is an important component of a downswing, but investment cannot fall indefinitely, whatever our model of investment behaviour.

Fluctuations in stockbuilding

Having examined investment in fixed capital, we now look at inventory investment in working capital. Firms hold stocks of goods despite the cost, namely the interest payments on the funds tied up in producing the goods for which no revenue from sales has yet been received. What is the corresponding benefit of holding stocks? If output could be instantly and costlessly varied it would always be possible to meet sales and demand by varying current production. Holding stocks makes sense because it is expensive to adjust production *quickly*. Output expansion may involve heavy overtime payments and costs of recruiting new workers. Cutting output may involve expensive redundancy payments. Holding stocks allows firms to meet short-term fluctuations in demand without incurring the expense of short-run fluctuations in output.

How do firms respond to a fall in aggregate demand? Since rapid output adjustment is expensive, in the short run firms undertake the adjustments that can be made more cheaply. They reduce hours of overtime and possibly even move on to short-time working. If demand has fallen substantially, this still leaves firms producing a larger output than they can sell. Firms build up stocks of unsold finished output.

If aggregate demand remains low, firms gradually reduce their workforce, partly through natural wastage and partly because it becomes cheaper to sack some workers than to meet the interest payments on ever larger volumes of stocks. Once aggregate demand recovers again, firms are still holding all the extra stocks built up during recession. Only by increasing output *more slowly* than the increase in aggregate demand can firms eventually sell off these stocks and get back to their long-run equilibrium position.

Costs of employment adjustment explain both the pattern of inventories over the business cycle and the pattern of labour productivity in Figure 31.2. Output per worker rises in a boom and falls in a slump. In other words, output adjusts more quickly than employment. This is what we expect, given the costs of adjusting employment rapidly.

A fall in demand is met initially by cutting hours and increasing stocks. With a shorter work week, output per worker falls. Only as the recession intensifies do firms undertake the costlier process of sacking workers and restoring hours to their normal level. Conversely, a boom is the time when output and overtime are high and productivity per worker peaks.

Competitiveness

Chapter 29 identified another potential mechanism that could generate cycles. An economy on a fixed exchange rate experiences a downward domestic demand shock. Interest rates, fixed at world levels to peg the exchange rate, cannot be used to restore aggregate demand.

Box 31.2 Eurozone business cycles

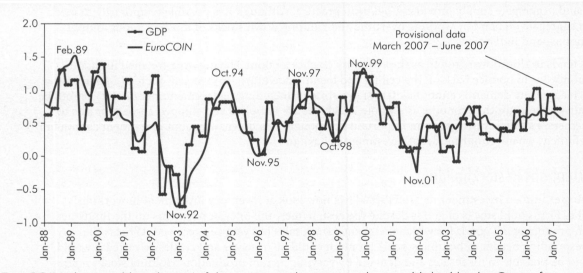

EuroCOIN, the monthly indicator of the euro area business cycle, is published by the Centre for Economic Policy Research based in London. The figure shows values of the indicator (in blue) and the growth rate of euro area GDP (in red) for January 1988–June 2007. For 1988–2003, when *EuroCOIN* was launched, the average quarterly growth rate of GDP had averaged 0.59 (the horizontal line).

Why not use changes in GDP itself to measure the business cycle? Mainly because initial estimates of GDP are unreliable and the data is often revised a lot as time elapses. The *EuroCOIN* indicator not only estimates the cyclical component of GDP more accurately but is also available monthly, whereas GDP estimates appear only quarterly. By examining past correlations of GDP growth with data that do appear monthly, the indicator provides a more frequent and more reliable picture of the euro area business cycle, helpful information for the monthly meetings of the European Central Bank at which interest rate decisions are made.

Source: http://www.cepr.org/Data/eurocoin.

Recession eventually bids down wages and prices, raising competitiveness and restoring internal balance by raising the demand for net exports. However this is not external balance, since net exports are now positive. With a current account surplus, the country gets richer, and additional wealth gradually boosts consumption demand. The economy now has a boom, which bids up prices and reduces competitiveness. Long-run equilibrium is restored when the current account falls back to zero.

This is a proper story about cycles. Output gaps induce changes in the price level that restore internal balance only by destroying external balance. This sets off a movement in the opposite direction that gradually reverses all these effects. Adjustment entails necessary overshooting of the final equilibrium.

31.3 Real business cycles

So far our analysis of business cycles focuses on demand shocks and cyclical movements in output gaps. This is compatible with our earlier analysis of sluggish wage adjustment in the short run. This view of cycles is consistent with a model that is Keynesian in the short run, but classical or monetarist in the long run.

Not all economists share our assessment of how the economy works. In particular, there is an influential school, known as the New Classical economists, whose intellectual leader is the Nobel Laureate Robert Lucas of the University of Chicago. Although we discuss competing views of macroeconomics more fully in the next chapter, one implication of the New Classical view should be discussed immediately.

A key assumption of the New Classical school is that all markets clear almost instantaneously. Effectively, output is almost always at its full-employment level.[1]

> **Real business cycle theories** explain cycles as fluctuations in potential output itself.

Proponents of the theory argue that macroeconomics should base theories of firms and households in a microeconomic analysis of choice between the present and the future. For example, this approach would view each household as making a plan to supply labour and demand goods both now and in the future in such a way that lifetime spending was financed out of lifetime income plus any initial assets. Such plans would then be aggregated to get total consumption spending and total labour supply. An equivalently complex story would apply to firms and investment.

One implication of this approach is that it is no longer helpful to distinguish between supply and demand. If labour supply and consumption demand are part of the same household decision, things that induce the household to change its consumption demand also induce it to change its labour supply.

For this reason, real business cycle theorists simply discuss what happens to actual output, which reflects both supply and demand and, by assumption, equates the two at potential output. In this view, the economy is then bombarded with shocks (e.g. breakthroughs in technology, changes in government policy) which alter these complicated plans and give rise to equilibrium behaviour that looks like a business cycle.

Why is this approach called the *real* business cycle approach? In the classical model, nominal money only affects other nominal variables. Output and employment depend only on real variables. Since real business cycle theorists believe in the classical model, they take it for granted that the source of business cycles must be in real shocks. Fancy dynamics can then explain why shocks last and have convoluted effects.

---

1 For an accessible introduction to these issues, see the lively exchange between Charles Plosser and Greg Mankiw in the *Journal of Economic Perspectives*, Summer 1989.

Intertemporal substitution: a key to persistence

Real business cycle theories need to combine rapid market adjustment to equilibrium with sluggish behaviour of aggregate output over the business cycle. Intertemporal substitution means making trade-offs over time, postponing or bringing forward actions in the sophisticated long-run plans of households and firms. This behaviour can cause effects to persist and look like part of a business cycle.

Suppose the productivity genie visits while we are all asleep. When we wake up, our productivity has doubled. But only for a year. We know that by next year our productivity will have returned to normal. We face a temporary productivity shock, a blip in our technology. What should we do?

We are definitely wealthier after the genie's visit. We are pleased it happened. We could simply behave as before, working just as hard and investing just as much. In that case, our extra productivity would make extra output this year, but it is output that we would blow entirely on consumption this year. We would get little extra utility out of the hundredth bottle of champagne, and we would be making no provision for the future. There must be a better way.

We could put in a temporary spurt of extra work while we are superproductive, but in itself that would only exacerbate the problem: even more champagne today, still nothing extra for tomorrow. In fact, because leisure is a luxury and because we are better off than before, we may feel like taking it easy and doing less work.

We need a way of transferring some of our windfall benefit into future consumption. The solution is investment. A sharp rise in the share of output going to investment will provide more capital for the future, thereby allowing higher future consumption even after our productivity bonus has evaporated. Once we get to the future, being then richer than we would have been without the genie, we may in consequence work less hard than we would have done, since leisure is a luxury.

The point of this example is to show that even a temporary shock can have effects that persist well into the future. Persistence occurs both through investment (in human as well as physical capital) and through intertemporal labour substitution – deciding when in one's life to put in the effort.

Real business cycle theories still need to be worked out fully. Apart from optimism about the speed of adjustment, they have been criticized on two grounds. First, they are usually theories of persistence not cycles. Shocks have long drawn out effects, but rarely are these cyclical. To 'explain' business cycles, so far real business cycle theorists have had to assume a cyclical pattern to the shocks themselves. The theory is therefore incomplete.

Second, and related, since the most widely researched example involves shocks to technology, a cyclical pattern of shocks implies that in some years technical knowledge actually diminishes: we forget how to do things. Not just once, but regularly every few years. This may be a bit hard to swallow.

However, this can be given a more plausible interpretation. In the dot.com bubble of the late 1990s, investors made extravagant projections about future productivity growth and associated profits from the new technologies. By 2000 evidence was accumulating that previous estimates, necessarily guesses in a new situation, were too optimistic. In 2001 investment collapsed, particularly in the United States where dotcom optimism had been greatest.

Thus, the adverse shock was not a fall in existing technology – which is indeed implausible – but in estimates about future technology, which affects current behaviour since firms, households and governments all make long-term plans.

Policy implications

Research on real business cycles has much still to accomplish, but it does have a vital message for macroeconomic policy. If the theory is right, it destroys the case for trying to stabilize output over the business cycle. Fluctuations in output are fluctuations in an *equilibrium* output that efficiently reconciles people's desires.

For example, in the parable of the genie, the induced effects on investment, labour supply, output and consumption implement people's preferred way to take advantage of the beneficial opportunity. Trying to prevent these ripples is misguided policy.

Although important, this caveat undermines the case for stabilization policy only if we buy totally the assumptions of complete and instant market-clearing and the absence of any externalities. For most economists these assumptions are too extreme to reflect the real world, which continues to exhibit Keynesian features in the short run. Valid reasons for stabilization policy then remain.

Even so, real business cycle theories force us all to acknowledge that there is no reason why potential output should grow as smoothly as trend output. The latter is a statistical artefact whose construction, averaging, forces it to be smooth.

Activity box 31 Synchronized swimming

Unlike previous recessions in recent decades, in 2001 the world's leading economies all stagnated together. The OECD's *Economic Outlook* (December 2001) identified three reasons for greater synchronization of national cycles.

First, some large shocks in the past were country specific, such as German unification. In 2001 everybody was coping with the end of the dotcom bubble and the collapse of confidence in the aftermath of the terrorist attacks.

Second, national cycles have anyway been getting smaller. This has several causes: a trend away from volatile manufacturing towards less volatile services; better inventory management made possible by information technology; less volatile consumption as financial liberalization allows consumers to borrow more easily in bad times; and better monetary policy now that central banks are independent of political control.

Third, interdependence is greater. For decades, international trade has grown faster than output, increasing interdependence. Trade liberalization has reinforced this. Financial integration has also led to smaller interest rate disparities.

The impact of a more synchronized global cycle is that regional policy makers may have to react to events that began elsewhere. US recession quickly spilled over into Europe, Latin America and Asia.

Questions

(a) If European countries had business cycles that were identical to one another, would there be much economic cost in abolishing the pound and adopting the euro?

(b) Would you expect an island such as the UK to be more or less integrated with the European economy than countries geographically at the heart of Europe?

(c) Rank the degree of market integration across countries, beginning with the most correlated: (i) unskilled labour markets, (ii) markets for financial assets, (iii) markets for goods, (iv) markets for services, (v) markets for skilled labour.

To check your answers to these questions, go to page 734.

Our discussion of supply-side economics in Chapters 27 and 30 suggested that there are forces that can change full employment and potential output, both in the short run and in the long run. The most sophisticated theory of the business cycle might involve short-term Keynesian fluctuations in aggregate demand around a path of potential output which itself was fluctuating. Nevertheless, the Keynesian component is likely to be important in the short run.

31.4 An international business cycle?

National politicians want all the credit when output is high but produce a cast-iron alibi when the economy turns sour. They say domestic difficulties were caused by a world recession. How good is their alibi?

Figure 31.3 plots data during 1980–2004 for the US and the EU. Although output fluctuations are by no means identical, they have some similarities. The 1982–83 period was one of recession, followed by rapid recovery; 1987–89 was a boom, from which there was a large crash in 1991–92. Both recovered in the late 1990s before another recession in 2001–03, followed by another recovery.

Figure 31.4 shows business cycles in the four largest countries of the EU. It confirms that countries of the EU move more closely with one another than with the USA, and suggests European integration may also be increasing over time. We discuss European integration in Chapter 35.

These patterns warn us how interdependent the leading countries have become in the modern world. Economies are becoming more open. In product markets, protectionist policies are being removed, through global institutions like the World Trade Organization and through regional integration as in the creation of a Single European Market.

Improvements in transport and telecommunications also favour greater integration of product markets. When R&D costs are large, producers need a global market if they are to recover their overheads. Product market integration provides an international transmission mechanism through exports and imports. Increasingly, we have a global financial market. Closer financial integration increases the likelihood that different countries pursue similar monetary policies.

The business cycle is transmitted from one country to another not just through private sector decisions about imports and exports (and induced effects on labour supply, investment and consumption), but also, sometimes, through induced changes in the economic policy of other governments.

Figure 31.3 Business cycles, 1980–2004 (% annual GDP change)

Source: OECD, *Economic Outlook.*

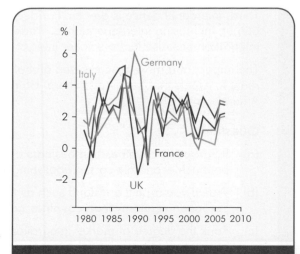

Figure 31.4 EU business cycles (% annual GDP change)

Source: OECD, *Economic Outlook.*

31.5 UK recovery after 1992

The 1980s saw financial reform in most countries. Deregulation of credit, and greater competition in its supply, was particularly marked in the US and the UK. The recession of the early 1990s was the first world recession since the financial revolution. Did it make any difference?

Imagine you had been a consumer in the boom of 1986–88. Life looked rosy, and for the first time in modern history financial institutions were competing vigorously to lend you money. So of course you borrowed. The boom surely wouldn't end just yet, would it? Table 31.2 shows the collapse of the saving rate. There was a consequent rise in UK household debt.

Perhaps if you had known more about business cycles, you would have been a bit more realistic. In any case, when the crash came, you got badly hurt. Around the world, interest rates rose as governments tried to stop economies overheating at the end of the 1980s. The interest cost of your huge debt soared.

Worse still, the collateral you had offered when you borrowed – your house or your portfolio on the stock market – was suddenly much less valuable. Higher interest rates induce lower asset prices by reducing the present value of the future income that the assets provide. In the UK, Japan and the United States, the three countries where consumer debt had risen most in the 1980s, asset prices had fallen 25 per cent by 1992.

Table 31.2 shows how consumers responded. Having acquired too much debt in the 1980s, they tried to put things right at the start of the 1990s. They saved a larger fraction of their incomes in order to try to repay some of the debt and bring it back to manageable proportions.

Table 31.2 UK household saving (% of disposable income)

1981	1988	1992	1996	2002	2005
12	6	12	9	5	5

Source: ONS, *Economic Trends*.

It can be a slow process. When debt is nearly as large as income, and only a small fraction of income is saved, debt cannot be paid off very quickly. This continuing 'debt overhang' explains why the feel-good factor was slow to return after 1992. It helps explain why consumer spending recovered only slowly and why the Major government lost the 1997 election.

Paradoxically, the success of the Major government in defeating inflation after 1992 (see Chapter 29) paved the way for reductions in nominal interest rates and a recovery in the housing market. Table 31.2 shows that by 1999, the saving rate had collapsed again as consumers went on another spending spree.

31.6 Post-2001

The twenty-first century got off to a bad start. The dotcom bubble burst, the events of 9/11 severely dented confidence, and fears that al-Qaeda might destabilize oil giant Saudi Arabia induced a dramatic rise in oil prices.

2001 was a bleak year. Growth forecasts were steadily cut back, and central banks responded with aggressive interest rate reductions to try to prevent demand falling too much. During 2001 Table 31.3 shows that interest rates were reduced by 4.5 per cent in the US where the fall in aggregate demand

Table 31.3 Interest rate cuts in 2001 (percentage points)

US	4.5
Canada	3.0
UK	2.0
Australia	1.75
Eurozone	1.5
New Zealand	1.25
Japan	0.25

Source: OECD, *Economic Outlook.*

was greatest, by 2 per cent in the UK, and by 1.5 per cent in the eurozone. Since Japanese interest rates were almost zero at the start of 2001, there was no scope to cut them further.

Japan illustrates the danger of getting into a vicious cycle of deflation. Falling prices induce consumers to postpone consumption, nominal debts rise in real value and real interest rates are uncomfortably high. Even once nominal interest rates have been cut to zero, negative inflation makes real interest rates positive.

One reason why other countries' policy makers continue to try to dampen their business cycles is to avoid falling into a black hole as Japan has done. Since Japan's difficulties were initially prompted by allowing a boom to go on too long, wise policy has to prevent the excesses of booms in order to prevent the subsequent difficulties of severe slumps.

By 2003, the powerful stimulus from monetary and fiscal expansion had restored UK output growth to normal levels, in marked contrast to the eurozone, where the European Central Bank had been slow to cut interest rates and where fiscal rules placing ceilings on budget deficits had limited the degree to which fiscal policy could come to the rescue. However, Figures 31.3 and 31.4 show that activity did recover throughout Europe by 2005.

Finally, as noted in previous chapters, the success of modern monetary policy has delivered not simply lower inflation but also greater output stability, for two reasons. First, since interest rates can be adjusted monthly – or more frequently in a crisis such as the response to 9/11 – whereas tax rates and spending plans cannot be moved up and down with such frequency, the decision to assign the principal task of demand management to central banks not treasuries has been a signal success. Monetary policy committees cannot stabilize inflation unless they accurately diagnose the relation of aggregate demand and potential output. In practice, stabilizing inflation has had the by-product of enhancing output stability.

Second, removing the politics from macroeconomic policy has also been a success. Political meddling must have been one of the main causes of shocks and one of the principal reasons why output cycles were so large in previous decades.

Summary

- The **trend path of output** is the long-run path after short-run fluctuations are ironed out. The **business cycle** describes fluctuations in output around this trend. Cycles last about five years but are not perfectly regular.

- A **political business cycle** arises from government manipulation of the economy to make things look good just before an election.

- **Persistence** requires either sluggish adjustment or intertemporal substitution. Persistence is necessary but not sufficient for cycles.

- The **multiplier–accelerator model** assumes investment depends on expected future profits, which reflect past output growth. The model delivers a cycle but assumes that firms are stupid: their expectations neglect the cycle implied by their own behaviour.

- Full capacity and the impossibility of negative gross investment provide **ceilings and floors** that limit the extent to which output can fluctuate.

- Fluctuations in **stockbuilding** are important in the business cycle. The need to restore stocks to original levels explains why output continues to differ from demand even during the recovery phase.

- **Real business cycles** are cycles in potential output itself. In such circumstances, it is not desirable for policy to dampen cycles.

- Some swings in potential output do occur, but many short-run fluctuations probably reflect Keynesian departures from potential output. Aggregate demand and aggregate supply both contribute to the business cycle.

- Increasing integration of world financial and product markets has made most countries heavily dependent on the wider world. Business cycles in the rich countries are closely correlated.

- In 2001 central banks cut interest rates to prevent recession from spiralling. Japan's difficulty escaping from the deflation trap suggests that dampening business cycles remains an important aim for other countries.

Review questions

To check your answers to these questions, go to page 733.

1 'If firms could forecast future output and profits accurately, there could not be a business cycle.' Is this true?

2 Heavily dependent on output of oil and fishing, Norway's business cycle goes the other way from that in other European countries. Why?

3 Why might voters care more about the direction in which the economy is heading than about the absolute level of its position at election time?

4 Would it help the world economy if all the largest countries elected governments on the same day? Why, or why not?

5 What is real about a business cycle?

6 **Common fallacies** Why are these statements wrong? (a) Closer integration of national economies will abolish business cycles. (b) The more we expect cycles, the more we get them. (c) Because output and labour productivity are closely correlated, fluctuations in productivity are the main cause of business cycles.

7 **Harder question** (a) Since central banks became independent, do you expect to see more or less evidence of a political business cycle? (b) Might there be an interest rate cycle instead? Why, or why not?

8 **Harder question** If the multiplier–accelerator model still fits the data quite well, does this imply that people are stupid?

9 **Essay question** 'The business cycle ought to last for different lengths depending on whether the original shocks were supply shocks or demand shocks.' Is this true?

To help you grasp the key concepts of this chapter check out the extra resources posted on the Online Learning Centre. There are chapter summaries, self-test questions, an interactive graphing tool, weblinks and a searchable glossary, all for free!

To put your learning into practice and prepare for exams, an **Interactive Workbook** is also available online, containing a variety of question types and providing feedback on your answers.

If you'd like further help with economics, or have any questions, **NetTutor** is here to help! You will have a personalised tutorial service at your fingertips. Visit the online learning centre at: www.mcgraw-hill.co.uk/textbooks/begg for information on accessing all of these resources.

Macroeconomics: taking stock

We have come a long way in our discussion of macroeconomics since Chapter 19. We have slowly built up an analysis of how the economy works, and studied the effects of government policy in both the short run and the long run. Our concluding chapter on macroeconomics sets out the main competing views of macroeconomics and their implications for government policy.

We begin by highlighting the major issues on which there is important disagreement. Different assumptions lead to different conclusions. We focus on four issues: the speed with which markets clear, whether or not equilibrium is unique, how expectations are formed, and the relative importance of the short run and the long run.

Against this background we then describe the four most prominent schools of macroeconomic thought today. We encourage you to view these competing positions not as unrelated and contradictory beliefs, but as the outcome of adopting slightly different positions within the spectrum of possible views.

This chapter defines the spectrum and indicates where different macroeconomists lie along that range of possible beliefs. In so doing, we pull together many themes of Part 4.

32.1 Areas of disagreement

Why do economists disagree at all? Surely, by looking carefully at the evidence we can say which views are correct and which are inconsistent with the facts?

In Chapter 1 we introduced the distinction between positive and normative economics. Positive economics relates to how the world actually works. Normative economics relates to different value

Box 32.1 Adjustment speeds in different markets

Our macroeconomic model now has four markets – goods, labour, money and foreign exchange – and four variables – the price of goods, the nominal wage, the interest rate and the nominal exchange rate – to respond to excess supply or excess demand in these markets. Which market adjusts most quickly?

Financial markets transact billions of pounds the minute they think an asset price is out of line. Interest rates and exchange rates are flexible. These markets clear almost instantly.

Goods markets adjust more slowly. Prices of goods are rarely set in a daily auction. Most firms quote a price and adjust it only at intervals. A decision to change the price takes time and effort. Moreover, firms with long-term relationships with regular customers are reluctant to change prices frequently.

In the labour market, long-term relations between a firm and its workforce are vital. Loyalty and trust are valuable commodities. At best, wage negotiations take time. At worst, they may involve expensive strikes and loss of output. Wages are the slowest of the four variables to adjust, and the labour market the slowest of the four markets to clear.

Few economists dispute this ordering of adjustment speeds in the four markets. The key disagreement is about the labour market, the slowest to adjust. Some economists think even the labour market adjusts quickly. Others believe it takes a very long time.

judgements about what is desirable. Some disagreements between macroeconomists reflect different value judgements. Suppose everyone agrees that more unemployment today allows more output in five years' time. Some people alive today will be dead in five years' time and some people are not yet born. The choice between the present and the future involves a choice between the welfare of different groups of people. It is a value judgement on which different people might quite reasonably disagree. Some disagreements between economists fall into this category. Since they do not arise from differing beliefs about how the world works, they cannot be settled by looking at the facts.

However, many important disagreements are disagreements in the positive economics of how the world actually works. Unlike some of the physical sciences, economists can rarely undertake controlled laboratory experiments. In practice, we have to try to unscramble historical data to make judgements about how the economy works. In Chapter 2 we indicated how econometricians attempt to undertake this task.

Even so, empirical research in economics does not always offer clear-cut answers. Suppose we want to study the economy when exchange rates are floating. Since many relevant data, such as GDP, are available only quarterly, we have only 120 separate pieces of data since floating exchange rates were adopted in 1973. For some purposes this is not enough to offer more than tentative conclusions. Economists who dispute these conclusions argue that the case against them is not yet proved.

Moreover, we live in a world that is constantly evolving. Even if we had a good estimate of the empirical magnitudes in the demand for money equation during 1950–70, would it be relevant after 2000, with credit cards and internet shopping? When behaviour is changing, although we get new data, the relevance of old data becomes suspect.

Taking a different example, much current behaviour is heavily influenced by expectations of the future. The spending decisions of firms and households depend critically on today's expectations of future incomes and profits. Purchases and sales let us measure actual spending, but we have no equivalent data on current expectations. Suppose a sharp rise in income and output is *not* preceded by a sharp increase in consumption and investment spending: do we conclude that nobody had previously expected income and output to rise, or that the rise was foreseen but had little effect on consumption and investment decisions? Different schools of economists look at the same data but view them differently.

Empirical economists do the best they can. In some cases their research is rather persuasive and their conclusions are widely accepted. Few people dispute that consumption and money demand are affected by current income. In other cases empirical research is less conclusive. Although economists agree about many aspects of positive economics, some disagreements inevitably remain. We pick out key disagreements, not mere quibbles about points of detail. The disagreements involve aspects that are fundamental to one's view of the world and the policy decisions one is likely to support.

Market clearing

A market clears when the quantity that sellers wish to supply equals the quantity that purchasers wish to demand. Whether, and if so how quickly, all markets clear remains a key issue in macroeconomics. At the one extreme, the classical analysis assumes that all markets clear. The economy is then at full employment and potential output. A monetary expansion will raise prices but not output, and a fiscal expansion will crowd out private consumption and investment until aggregate demand is restored to potential output. At the other extreme, Keynesian analysis assumes that markets, especially the labour market, do not clear. With imperfect wage flexibility, a fall in aggregate demand for goods and the demand for labour reduce output and employment. In such a situation, expansionary fiscal and monetary policy can increase real output.

Do markets clear or not? The onus of proof changes over time. Before Keynes' *General Theory*, most economists took it for granted that markets cleared and tried to explain periods of high unemployment within this framework. In the immediate postwar period, most economists took it for granted that markets did not clear continuously and interpreted macroeconomics within the Keynesian paradigm.

In the 1970s the pendulum swung back again. Many economists argued that, if wage stickiness leads to involuntary unemployment, workers will find a way to make wages more flexible, avoiding the cost of involuntary unemployment. People said the Keynesian assumption of wage stickiness could not be given plausible microeconomic foundations. Since 1980 the pendulum has been in motion again. New Keynesian economists have developed microfoundations for wage stickiness, and fewer economists presume markets automatically clear.

The attempt by some economists to explain even short-run fluctuations with market clearing models has spawned a new literature on what determines potential output and equilibrium unemployment, topics neglected when the focus of analysis was simply movements in aggregate demand. It is now generally accepted that movements in potential output may be significant, even in the short run. Whether they are the *only* source of short-run output fluctuations is essentially the same question as whether market clearing can be assumed, even in the short run.

Is long-run equilibrium unique?

Suppose an economy in long-run equilibrium then experiences a *temporary* shock which drives it to a different position in the short run. What happens once the shock disappears? Does the economy, sooner or later, go back to the original equilibrium or settle down in a new, *permanently different*, long-run equilibrium?

The latter case is *hysteresis*. We introduced it in Chapter 27 when discussing unemployment. The same argument applies to aggregate supply and potential output. Hysteresis exists when the path that an economy follows in the short run affects which long-run equilibrium it eventually reaches. This implies that there are several possible equilibria in the long run. Chapter 27 discussed mechanisms that could give rise to hysteresis.

Whether hysteresis is quantitatively an important phenomenon is a controversial issue. The more economists believe that hysteresis matters, the more they argue that the easiest way to prevent its damaging effects is to prevent the economy from entering a recession in the first place. In contrast, economists who believe that hysteresis is unimportant take a more relaxed attitude to temporary recessions, which have no long-term consequences.

Expectations formation

Most economists accept that beliefs about the future affect behaviour today. Such beliefs certainly affect consumption and investment demand. Some disagreements between economists can be traced to different beliefs about how expectations are formed. For simplicity, we divide the possible approaches into three categories.

Exogenous expectations

Some economists are agnostic on the vital question of how expectations are formed. Analysing the behaviour of the economy, they simply treat expectations as exogenous or given, one of the inputs to the analysis. The analysis can deduce *consequences* of a change in expectations – for example, a rise in expected future profits raises investment spending at each interest rate – but the analysis does not investigate the *cause* of the change in expectations. In particular, it is unrelated to other parts of the analysis. With given expectations, there is no automatic feedback from rising output to expectations of higher profits in the future.

> **Exogenous expectations** are not explained within the model.

At best, economists using exogenous expectations in their analysis give an incomplete account of how the economy works. At worst, they neglect some inevitable feedbacks from the variables they are analysing to the expectations that were an input to the analysis. On the other hand, since modelling expectations is tricky, proponents of this approach might argue that the various types of possible induced effects on expectations can be explored by ad hoc changes in expectations.

Extrapolative expectations

A simple way to make expectations endogenous, or determined by what is going on elsewhere in the analysis, is to assume people forecast future profits by extrapolating the behaviour of profits in the recent past, or extrapolate past inflation in order to form expectations of inflation in the near future.

> **Extrapolative expectations** assume that the future is an extension of the recent past.

Proponents of this approach suggest that it offers a simple rule of thumb and corresponds to what many people seem to do in the real world.

Rational expectations

Suppose you hear that half the world oil supply was destroyed by a war. You could use simple economies (supply and demand) to guess that oil prices will jump up sharply. You should raise your forecast of oil prices immediately. If you merely extrapolate past growth of oil prices, you will be knowably behind the game for a while. Many economists believe that it is implausible that people will keep using a forecasting rule that makes the same mistake (underforecasting of oil price rises, say) period after period.

They do not use forecasting rules that systematically give too low a forecast or too high a forecast. Any tendency for expectations to be systematically in error is quickly detected and put right.

> With **rational expectations,** people guess the future correctly *on average*.

This in no way says that everybody gets everything exactly right all the time. We live in a risky world where unforeseeable things are always happening. Expectations are fulfilled only rarely. Rational expectations says people make good use of information available today and do not make forecasts that are already knowably wrong. Only genuinely unforeseeable things make present forecasts go wrong. Sometimes people under-predict, sometimes they over-predict. But any systematic tendency to do one or other gets noticed and the basis of expectations formation is amended until guesses are on average correct.

Box 32.2 Policy options and constraints

The following checklist will help in working through the chapter.

Aggregate demand

The demand for domestic output. The sum of consumer spending, investment spending, government purchases and net exports.

Demand management

Using monetary and fiscal policy to try to stabilize aggregate demand near potential output.

Potential output

The output firms wish to supply at full employment after all markets clear.

Full employment

The level of employment when all markets, particularly the labour market, are in equilibrium. All unemployment is then voluntary.

Supply-side policies

Policies to raise potential output. These include investment and work incentives, union reform and retraining grants to raise effective labour supply at any real wage; and some deregulation to stimulate effort and enterprise. Lower inflation is also a kind of supply-side policy if high inflation has real economic costs.

Hysteresis

The view that temporary shocks have permanent effects on long-run equilibrium.

Short run and long run

Where policies have short-run benefits but long-run costs, or vice versa, different groups of economists may adopt differing value judgements about how these gains and losses should be traded off. In part, the differing policy prescriptions offered by different economists reflect differing judgements about the relative importance of the short run and the long run.

In practice, these judgements are closely connected with the three issues on which we have already focused. The more quickly one believes markets clear, the less scope there is for demand management in the short run and the greater the importance of supply-side policy to raise potential output in the long run. Conversely, the more one believes in the possibility of high levels of Keynesian unemployment in the short run, the more likely one is to judge that the short-run benefits of returning to full employment outweigh any tendency thus induced to reduce potential output in the long run. Similarly, the more one's horizon is short-run, the more plausible it becomes that expectations can be treated as exogenous. The more one wants to discuss the long run, the more important it is to model how expectations are changing over time. The more one believes in hysteresis, the more one must look after the short run to look after the long run.

Having identified our four areas of disagreement, we now examine the major schools of contemporary macroeconomic thought.

32.2 New Classical macroeconomics

The analysis is *classical* because it assumes that wage and price flexibility restore the economy to its position of full employment and potential output. The analysis is *new* because it assumes that expectations adjustment, as well as wage and price adjustment, is almost instant. At best, monetary and fiscal policy affect the *composition* of full-employment aggregate demand. Its *level* is necessarily potential output. This being unique, hysteresis is unimportant.

> **New Classical macroeconomics** is based on the twin principles of rapid market clearing and rational expectations.

Whereas the classical analysis was sometimes vague about the period being analysed – it was the period necessary to allow complete wage and price adjustment and hence restoration of full employment – the New Classical macroeconomics confronts this question explicitly. Wage and price adjustment is almost instant. Whatever level of unemployment is observed is thus the natural rate of unemployment. Unemployment changes over time because microeconomic incentives alter the natural rate itself.

Much of the flavour of this analysis can be understood with the following example. Nominal wages are set at the beginning of each period, then fixed for the period, since firms and workers cannot forever be arguing about the wage to be paid today. On what basis are wages set? At the level expected to clear the market for labour. Since workers and firms both care about *real* wages this requires that, after forming expectations about the likely level of prices during the period, firms and workers agree a money wage expected to give the equilibrium level of real wages.

Suppose prices turn out unexpectedly high. Firms have a good deal. With money wage fixed for the period, real wages are unexpectedly low. Firms expand output temporarily while real wages are low. But at the beginning of the following period, nominal wages are renegotiated in the light of the price expectations then prevailing for the next period, and wages are then set once again at the level expected to produce the equilibrium real wage.

Thus, in each period, any unexpectedly high prices are accompanied by unexpectedly high output. Conversely, if prices are unexpectedly low, real wages are unexpectedly high and firms temporarily cut back output. But because of the assumption that, at the start of each period, wages are set at the level expected to clear the market, there is no tendency for deviations of output and employment from their full-employment levels to persist from one period to the next.

One of the *new* things about the New Classical macroeconomics is its explicit assumption of rational expectations. The government cannot use fiscal and monetary policy systematically to fool people. Suppose the government switches to a more expansionary monetary policy. This tends to make prices rise, since the economy begins close to full employment. If the initial policy change was not foreseen, workers have not foreseen the price rise. They have settled for too low a money wage. Firms temporarily have cheap labour and expand output. Unanticipated monetary expansion causes an unanticipated rise in output and employment, above their long-run levels.

But if everyone has rational expectations, people quickly catch on to what the government is doing. When wages are renegotiated, everyone knows the money supply is expanding and prices are rising.

The next nominal wage settlement suitably reflects this and, in the absence of any further surprises, real wages are at their equilibrium level again.

The New Classical macroeconomics can be summed up thus. It is only the fact that some variables, particularly nominal wages, must be set in advance that prevents continuous full employment and potential output. Variables set in advance are set at levels expected to produce full employment. Only unexpected developments make them temporarily inappropriate, allowing output and employment to depart temporarily from their natural rates. But the government cannot use fiscal and monetary policy to make prices unexpectedly high period after period, and thus cannot hold output systematically above potential output.

If the government tries to undertake such a policy, people quickly see through it and anticipate the expansion. The expansionary policy is already incorporated in the previous wage claims. It stops being a surprise. But the combination of expected market clearing and rational expectations means that it is only surprises that move the economy away from full employment. Essentially, demand management through monetary and fiscal policy is completely impotent.

It only remains for the government to control the price level and to pursue supply-side policies to raise potential output. Supply-side policies include income tax cuts to increase the incentive to work. Tight monetary policy will keep inflation under control. It will increase potential output by reducing shoe-leather and menu costs. It will also reduce the distortions that arise when the tax system is not completely inflation-neutral. Low government spending will prevent large government borrowing from bidding up interest rates and crowding out private investment.

Nor will tight fiscal and monetary policy cause Keynesian unemployment. Wages and prices adjust to restore aggregate demand to potential output. If a switch to tighter policy takes people by surprise, at worst it has only temporary effects on output and unemployment. As soon as wages are renegotiated, they adjust to restore full employment.

Indeed, this principle can be extended. Since it is only unforeseen surprises that move the economy away from full employment in the short run, demand management should aim to minimize surprises and keep the economy as close to potential output as possible. Policies should be pre-announced so that people anticipate them, setting wages and prices at the right level.

Thus New Classical economists argue that not merely long-term trends but also short-run fluctuations have little to do with aggregate demand.

Real business cycle theorists

In the previous chapter we introduced the theory of real business cycles. This approach belongs to the same family as the New Classical macroeconomics, although its emphasis is a little different. Both believe in near-continuous market clearing and rational expectations.

The New Classicals stress the effects of temporary surprises until expectations quickly catch up, thus developing a theory of fluctuations around potential output. Real business theorists take this a stage further and seek to explain all fluctuations as fluctuations in potential output itself.

Thus, the real business cycle approach is both more extreme and more general than the New Classical macroeconomics. It is more extreme because its analysis neglects deviations from potential output even for a short time. Since changes in nominal money have no real effects in such a context, the cause of changes must be sought in shocks to real variables such as technical knowledge.

The approach is more general than the New Classical macroeconomics because it concentrates all its powers of analysis on making explicit the microeconomic foundations for the intertemporal decisions of firms, households and governments. It is in decisions to amend intertemporal plans and reallocate them over time that real business cycle theorists believe they can explain how large movements in actual output and employment could be movements in equilibrium output and employment.

32.3 Gradualist monetarists

This school is associated with Milton Friedman. We use the term 'monetarist' to mean those economists espousing the classical doctrine that an increase in the money supply leads essentially to an increase in prices rather than to an increase in output. Thus, the New Classical economists believe in almost instant monetarism.

Whereas the New Classical economists believe in only temporary departures from full employment as a result of unforeseeable shocks that cannot immediately be reflected in wages, the Gradualist monetarists accept that restoration of full employment takes a little longer. Even so, they believe that within a *few* years wage and price adjustment *will* restore full employment. Like the New Classical economists, Gradualist monetarists do not believe that hysteresis matters. When the economy gets back to full employment after a temporary shock, it returns to the *same* long-run equilibrium in real terms.

> **Gradualist monetarists** believe that full employment is restored within a few years, so the main effect of higher money supply is simply higher prices.

Thus, this school believes in some arguments for wage rigidity presented in Chapter 27, but only for a short time. Different members of this school adopt different assumptions about expectations formation. Sluggish adjustment in expectations formation may provide an extra reason for slower adjustment back to full employment.

For the New Classical macroeconomists there is no important distinction between the short run and the long run in the design of fiscal and monetary policy for demand management: the classical long run is relevant almost instantaneously. In contrast, the Gradualist monetarists believe that in the short run a fiscal or monetary stimulus would alter aggregate demand, output and employment, but that it is neither sensible nor desirable to undertake such policies. The short run must be subordinated to the interests of the long run.

Since wage and price adjustment takes a few years to complete, it follows from the analysis of Chapters 24 and 25 that expansionary monetary or fiscal policy can increase aggregate demand, output and employment in the short run. However, the Gradualists offer two reasons why policy should not be used in this way.

First, the economy will automatically return to full employment within a few years anyway. In the long run, trying to keep output above potential output leads only to inflation. Second, if instead the aim of policy is to react to shocks and reduce fluctuations around potential output, the policy may be counterproductive. By the time a shock is diagnosed and the necessary action taken, the economy may already be expanding on its own as wage and price adjustments begin to lead it back to full employment. Stabilization policy may exacerbate cycles not dampen them.

Milton Friedman frequently recommended a low but fixed rate of money growth, rejecting the 'interest rate activism' followed by the Bank of England's Monetary Policy Committee. Low money growth will keep inflation down in the long run. Constant money growth will not exacerbate the business cycle by intervening too late when corrective action is no longer required. Leading board members of the European Central Bank, such as Wim Duisenberg and Otmar Issing, have argued frequently against the overactive use of interest rate changes. Such monetarists are Gradualist because they prefer to avoid big swings in policy.

Since departures from full employment last a relatively short time, it is on the long-run classical analysis that the Gradualists place the most emphasis. The government's chief responsibility is to raise potential output by supply-side policies and the pursuit of price stability.

32.4 Moderate Keynesians

> **Moderate Keynesians**
> believe that the economy will eventually return to full employment, but that wage and price adjustment are fairly sluggish so the process could take many years.

Broadly speaking, this group are short-run Keynesians and long-run monetarists.

In the short run, a fall in aggregate demand can generate a significant recession. Although many economists in this group believe that expectations adjustment is also sluggish, some of them believe in rational expectations and hold that it is not systematic mistakes in expectations formation but sluggish wage and price adjustment that prevents rapid restoration of full employment. By sluggish we mean that they do not respond quickly to departures from potential output and equilibrium unemployment. Nominal wages may still change rapidly because of expected inflation.

Moderate Keynesians believe that recessions last a bit longer than the couple of years over which a Gradualist monetarist believes markets unaided can restore full employment. Hence, Moderate Keynesians draw a different judgement about the relative importance of the short run and the long run. Slower market adjustment reduces the danger that by the time government has diagnosed the problem the market is already fixing it. Slower adjustment also raises the need for stabilization policy. Thus Moderate Keynesians believe that the government should accept responsibility for stabilization policy in the short run.

Since Moderate Keynesians believe the economy will *eventually* return to full employment, they accept that persistent rapid monetary growth must eventually lead to inflation once the full employment position is reached. In the very long run, only supply-side policies can generate sustained economic growth by raising potential output. Thus many economists in this group argue that the government should not neglect two of the policy prescriptions of the monetarists. Supply-side policies are important in the long run – and, if high inflation reduces potential output, in the long run the average level of fiscal and monetary policy must be compatible with low inflation.

Moderate Keynesians see no conflict between this stance of policy in the long run and the recommendation that in the short run active stabilization policies should be undertaken. Credible policy makers can be active precisely because people trust that their actions will be temporary not permanent. If a current stimulus is reversed as soon as the crisis is over, it need not threaten price stability in the medium run.

New Keynesians

The Keynesian approach fell out of fashion in the 1970s for two reasons. The first was empirical and practical. Unemployment rose and the Keynesian policy response, stimulating aggregate demand, caused only inflation. Many people concluded that the Keynesian approach was wrong. And so it was: it had paid too little attention to the supply side. The rise in unemployment primarily reflected a deterioration in aggregate supply. It was an increase in the natural rate of unemployment. Moderate Keynesians now recognize the necessity of keeping track of aggregate demand as well as aggregate supply. But they continue to believe that many shocks have their origins (and solutions) in shifts in aggregate demand.

The second reason why Keynesianism fell out of favour was that its followers appeared to neglect microeconomics. Key relationships, such as the consumption function, seemed to appear out of thin air. As New Classical and real business cycle theorists developed theories with elegant microfoundations for the dynamics of choice over time, they became increasingly critical of the absence of microfoundations for Keynesian analysis. Like the boy brave enough to say that the emperor had no clothes, they had a big impact.

New Keynesians set out to provide microfoundations for Keynesian analysis. Instead of asserting that markets do not work well, they aim to deduce that markets *will* not work well. Market failures follow from problems with information, from externalities, from costs of decision making and change. Since these are all tough to analyse, it took a while to produce the rejoinder to the New Classical criticism.

Broadly, this rejoinder falls into three headings. First, economists such as Greg Mankiw of Harvard and David Romer of Berkeley analysed sluggish price and wage adjustment in greater detail. They have shown that, with one proviso, even a small amount of nominal rigidity – say, the menu costs of deciding to change prices, negotiating changes in wages and then implementing these changes – may be sufficient to produce all the standard Keynesian features described in earlier chapters. The one proviso is that we need some real rigidity in the labour market as well. Let's see why.

An adverse shock to aggregate demand, given a little price sluggishness, makes firms want to cut back output and employment. But why don't workers then take wage cuts? While prices are fixed, workers will think they are taking a real wage cut, so it is in real rigidities that we must seek the answer.

In Chapters 10 and 27 we set out some of the New Keynesian answers. The efficiency wage theory says that firms choose to set wages too high to clear the labour market, for example because this means a worker caught shirking on the job then faces a big penalty in being sacked. Another justification is provided by the insider–outsider approach, which emphasizes that the senior workers who retain their jobs place little weight on their less fortunate colleagues.

A second type of New Keynesian response is particularly associated with Nobel Laureate Joseph Stiglitz, formerly Chief Economist of the World Bank. Although agreeing that real rigidities in the labour market are an essential feature of Keynesian economics, he emphasizes that near-instant price flexibility in product markets is little help, and may actually exacerbate Keynesian problems.

Suppose there is an adverse shock to aggregate demand. For only a tiny period, prices are sluggish to adjust. During that time, real aggregate demand falls. If firms are very risk-averse, they may quickly react to this more difficult world by contracting supply: getting overextended is simply too dangerous, especially since banks get tough quickly in a recession. So, quite quickly, we reach a position in which the goods market clears. Supply and demand curves have both shifted left. From now on, price flexibility is not enough to fix things up: supply and demand clear, but at a lower level. The shift in demand has caused a shift in supply.

The New Keynesians who believe in hysteresis (see Box 27.3) go further. This shift in supply may have permanent repercussions. If so, active stabilization is desirable because it prevents short-run difficulties from becoming long-run problems which can then be broken down only by slow-working supply-side remedies.

32.5 Extreme Keynesians

> **Extreme Keynesians** not only insist that markets fail to clear in the short run, they also believe that markets do not clear in the long run.

Keynesian unemployment may persist indefinitely unless the government intervenes to boost aggregate demand.

Extreme Keynesians reject the view that slumps can eventually restore full employment via downward pressure on wages and prices. In this they agree with those New Keynesians who believe in hysteresis. But they disagree too. Whereas hysteresis suggests that, once a recession has done its damage, supply has then gone so boosting demand no longer works, Extreme Keynesians believe that boosting aggregate demand through government policy will do the trick.

Their case must therefore rest primarily on labour market rigidity. Real-wage rigidity causes excess supply in the labour market, and this pool of involuntarily unemployed workers remains available at any time to be mopped up through a demand expansion. Extreme Keynesians refer to this assumption of labour market inflexibility as the *real-wage hypothesis*.

Even if, for reasons we have discussed at length, some real-wage rigidity is plausible, why cannot all nominal variables fall to boost the real money supply, reduce interest rates and thereby eventually move the economy to full employment through market forces alone? Extreme Keynesians have several answers.

First, it is impossible to co-ordinate the changes in nominal wages and prices. If all could be cut together, no real wage need change. But in practice, some workers have to go first. Unless and until all other wages and prices come down, the first workers to cut nominal wages also cut real wages. This may be sufficient to prevent the wage cut taking place, especially if each group of workers is very sensitive about its wages relative to other groups.

Second, even if a general reduction in nominal variables could be engineered, its effect may be minimal if the economy is deep in recession. First, if interest rates are already near zero, further price falls cannot induce monetary policy to reduce interest rates any more. Second, when times are tough

Activity box 32 What can we learn from the success of demand management?

Since central banks were given operational independence from government control, they have succeeded in stabilizing inflation around low target rates, and have also dampened business cycles relative to their previous extent. We look again at Figure 31.2 showing the behaviour of output growth and productivity growth in the UK economy since 1975.

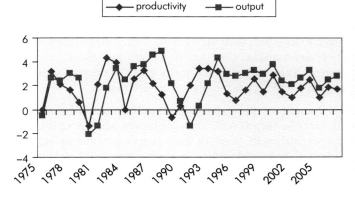

In the period 1975–95, cycles in output growth were large. There were three separate episodes in which output growth was negative, and several occasions in which output growth exceeded 4 per cent, a spurt that is unsustainable in the long run given that potential output grows by around 2.3 per cent a year.

Since 1997, fluctuations in output have been much smaller. Output has almost always grown at between 2 and 3 per cent a year, and growth has never been negative. Since output last fell in 1993, the government is fond of drawing attention to the fact that, with nearly 15 years of continuous steady growth, this is the longest period in recorded UK history without a slump.

Questions

(a) We know that the Bank of England was trying to keep the economy on an even keel, and that it essentially succeeded. Which school of economic thought does this evidence favour? Why?

(b) Why have high oil prices since 2003 not yet caused stagflation, the combination of higher inflation and output stagnation?

To check your answers to these questions, go to page 735.

and firms are losing money, they do not wish to invest, even at zero interest rates, as happened recently in Japan. Old Keynesians used to compare monetary policy to a string: you can pull tight on it in a boom, but pushing on it in a slump may have no effect. Thus, Extreme Keynesians stress the role of fiscal policy in getting the economy out of a serious recession.

Finally, a word about expectations. Just as New Classical economists are optimists about both the speed of market clearing and the ability of people intelligently to form, and rapidly to adjust, expectations about the future, Extreme Keynesians are nearly as pessimistic about expectations as they are about market clearing. Keynes himself compared expectations to a beauty contest. The modern equivalent would be a TV game show where the competitor has to guess the answer most frequently chosen by the TV audience.

In such situations, what matters is not getting the right answer (which is how economists try to evaluate rational expectations); what matters is guessing what other people guess. Multiple equilibria may be common, which undermines the ease with which we can assume that people quickly adjust expectations to *the* right answer. Through Extreme Keynesian spectacles, co-ordination failures (externalities) occur as much in expectations as in wage setting.

32.6 Summing up

We have set out the views of the competing schools of modern macroeconomics. In each case, we have sought to interpret their views against the four basic criteria set out in Section 32.1: the assumption about market clearing, the assumption about expectations formation, the assumption about hysteresis and the relative priority given to short run and long run when making policy prescriptions. Table 32.1 summarizes our discussion.

By now it should be evident that the competing views of macroeconomics rest on differing views about microeconomics as well. The economists who are optimistic about market clearing believe that markets work fairly well. Some of these economists champion free markets in general and hold that free competition is a good thing. Government should break up monopolies where they exist, and use supply-side policies to help markets function even more efficiently.

Table 32.1 A stylized picture of the competing views

	New Classical	Gradualist monetarist	Moderate Keynesian	Extreme Keynesian
Market clearing	Very fast	Quite fast	Quite slow	Very slow
Expectations adjustment	Rapid	Slower	Fast or slow	Slow
Long run/short run	Little difference since adjust fast	Long run more important	Don't forget short run	Short run vital
Full employment	Always close	Never far away	Could be far away	Could stay away
Hysteresis	No problem	No problem	Might be problem	Problem
Demand management or supply-side policy	Forget demand; supply side needed	Supply more important; avoid swings in demand	Demand matters too	Demand is what counts

In contrast, the economists pessimistic about market clearing tend to stress all the things that can inhibit markets from working efficiently. They emphasize the difficulties in acquiring the relevant information to make sensible choices and the fact that many markets for goods and labour are far from competitive. They do not believe that free unregulated markets are necessarily a good thing. Governments should intervene to help markets function in the social interest.

We discussed these issues at length in Parts 2 and 3. Fortunately, it is not necessary to divide economics arbitrarily into unconnected areas of analysis. Many of the recent developments in macroeconomics to which we have referred in Part 4 reflect the growing conviction that macroeconomists must pay close attention to what is going on at the micro level. In Chapter 19 we introduced macroeconomics by saying that sometimes we get a clearer idea of the big picture by surveying the whole scene with the naked eye. But it can be useful to have the occasional squint through binoculars to check that our interpretation of the big picture makes sense.

It is not our intention here to adjudicate between the competing views of macroeconomics, though we are probably in the Moderate Keynesian group of economists. Rather, we sought to develop a framework in which the differing positions can be interpreted. We have explained how changes in the basic assumptions, especially about the speed of adjustment, the time required for restoration of full employment and the possibility of hysteresis, allow this framework to reflect the views of the different schools of modern macroeconomics and show why they reach differing policy recommendations.

Summary

- There is much about which all economists agree. There are also differences of opinion, both in the positive economics of how the world actually works and in the normative economics of how the government should behave.

- Economic theories should be tested against the facts. In some cases, tests do not yield conclusive answers. Some variables, such as expectations, are unobservable. The world is also changing. It may be impossible to get enough data on the world as it is today to allow definitive empirical tests of competing theories.

- The major **schools of macroeconomic** thought can be viewed in relation to **four key issues**: the speed with which the labour market clears, how expectations are formed, the possibility of hysteresis, and the relative importance of short run and long run.

- **New Classical macroeconomists** assume market clearing is almost instant. Only predetermined contracts prevent continuous full employment. **Rational expectations** imply predetermined variables reflect the best guess at the time about their required equilibrium value. Any foreseeable change is already built into these variables. Only pure surprises cause temporary departures from full employment until preset variables can be altered and full employment restored. With the economy near potential output, demand management is pointless. Government policy should minimize surprises. Surprises apart, movements in output reflect movements in potential output. Policy should pursue price stability and supply-side policies to raise potential output.

- **Real business cycle theorists** neglect even temporary departures from full market clearing. They argue intertemporal decisions of households, firms and government can explain even short-term fluctuations as movements in potential output.

- **Gradualist monetarists** believe that restoration of potential output, though not instant, takes only a few years. A big rise in interest rates could induce a deep, albeit temporary, recession and should be avoided. Attempts at demand management may be counterproductive if the economy is already recovering by the time a recession is diagnosed. The government should not 'fine-tune' aggregate demand but concentrate on long-run policies to keep inflation down and promote supply-side policies to raise potential output.

- **Moderate Keynesians** believe automatic restoration of full employment can take many years but will happen eventually. Although demand management cannot raise output without limit, active stabilization policy is worth undertaking to prevent booms and slumps that could last several years and therefore are diagnosed relatively easily. In the long run, supply-side policies are still important, but eliminating big slumps is important if hysteresis has permanent effects on long-run equilibrium.

- **New Keynesians** provide microeconomic foundations for Keynesian macroeconomics. Menu costs may explain nominal rigidities. These are compounded by real rigidities in the labour market. Several channels for hysteresis have now been developed.

- **Extreme Keynesians** believe departures from full employment may be protracted. Keynesian unemployment does not make real wages fall, and may not even reduce nominal wages and prices. Even if it does, aggregate demand may not respond to lower interest rates if pessimism is high. The first responsibility of government is not supply-side policies to raise potential output that is not attained anyway, but restoration of output to potential output by expansionary fiscal and monetary policy, especially the former.

Review questions

To check your answers to these questions, go to page 734.

1 Beginning at full employment, the money supply is reduced. Explain carefully the predictions of the four schools of macroeconomics about what happens (a) in the short run and (b) in the long run. Does it matter if the lower money supply was previously foreseen?

2 How might the four schools of macroeconomics explain the fall in European unemployment after 1992?

3 Identify each statement with one of the four schools. (a) Reducing inflation is easy and will not cause higher unemployment. (b) Expansionary monetary and fiscal policy always boost output unless there is a surge of imports. (c) It is worth incurring a temporary increase in unemployment to obtain a permanent inflation reduction. (d) The government can always generate a domestic slump to reduce inflation, but the cost in output forgone could be high in the short run.

4 The first president of the European Central Bank said that interest rates should not be changed frequently, and anyway have only a limited effect on the real economy. The Governor of the Bank of England is happier to change interest rates more frequently, even though he expects the main effects of monetary policy on the real economy to wear off after a few years. Identify each with a school of thought.

5 **Common fallacies** Why are these statements wrong? (a) Rational expectations imply the economy is always at full employment. (b) There is no trade-off between inflation and unemployment. (c) Monetarists believe that the nominal money supply is the main determinant of real output.

6 **Harder question** 'The amazing thing about modern monetary policy is that it has little to do with money.' Is this true? Is monetarism discredited?

7 **Harder question** 'Despite macroeconomic stability, productivity growth in the UK remains disappointingly low. Prudence is obviously not sufficient for investment.' Explain.

8 **Essay question** 'Just as remarkable as the achievement of low inflation and steady output growth has been the sustained level of low unemployment in the UK. This shows the importance of supply-side policies and the contribution of schools of economic thought that gave prominence to supply-side economics.' Discuss.

Online **Learning**Centre

To help you grasp the key concepts of this chapter check out the extra resources posted on the Online Learning Centre. There are chapter summaries, self-test questions, an interactive graphing tool, weblinks and a searchable glossary, all for free!

To put your learning into practice and prepare for exams, an **Interactive Workbook** is also available online, containing a variety of question types and providing feedback on your answers.

If you'd like further help with economics, or have any questions, **NetTutor** is here to help! You will have a personalised tutorial service at your fingertips. Visit the online learning centre at: www.mcgraw-hill.co.uk/textbooks/begg for information on accessing all of these resources.

PART FIVE

The world economy

Part 5 focuses on the world as a whole. What determines the pattern of international trade and the tariff policies pursued by individual countries? Can free trade benefit everyone? How on earth can Europe compete with China and India? What difference does the international monetary system make? Can the IMF prevent financial crises? Part 5 also discusses how small European economies became sufficiently interdependent that they were driven to much greater policy co-operation, not just in regulatory and tax policy but in seeking exchange rate stability through monetary union. Part 5 concludes with a wider examination of transition and development, both in the former communist economies of Central and Eastern Europe, and in the poorest countries in the world.

Chapter 33 analyses why international trade takes place, studies the gains from trade and considers what this implies for trade policy of nation states. Chapter 34 examines the international monetary system through which trade is financed and discusses different types of exchange rate regime. Chapter 35 analyses European integration: the EU Single Market, monetary union and progress in Eastern Europe. Chapter 36 studies globalization, emerging markets and problems of developing countries.

Contents

International trade

International trade is part of daily life. Britons drink French wine, Americans drive Japanese cars and Russians eat American wheat. China makes European clothes but buys up raw materials that Europeans would otherwise have bought. There are two reasons why trade between the UK and Japan is different from trade between London and Birmingham.

First, because international trade crosses national frontiers, governments can monitor this trade and treat it differently. It is hard to tax or regulate goods moving from London to Birmingham but much easier to impose taxes or quota restrictions on goods imported from Taiwan or Japan. Governments have to decide whether or not such policies are desirable.

Second, international trade may involve the use of different national currencies. A British buyer of American wine pays in sterling but the American vineyard worker is paid in dollars. International trade involves international payments. We examine the system of international payments more fully in the next chapter.

This chapter concentrates on trade flows and trade policy. Who trades with whom and in what commodities? Why does international trade take place? Countries trade with one another because they can buy foreign goods at a lower price than it costs to make the same goods at home.

Is this possible for all countries? International trade reflects *exchange* and *specialization*. International differences in the availability of raw materials and other factors of production lead to international differences in production costs and goods prices. Through international exchange, countries supply the world economy with the commodities that they produce relatively cheaply and demand from the world economy the goods made relatively cheaply elsewhere.

These benefits from trade are reinforced if there are scale economies in production. Instead of each country having a lot of small producers, different countries concentrate on different things and everyone can benefit from the cost reductions that ensue.

We discuss the benefits from international trade and examine whether our analysis can explain the trade flows that actually take place. There are many circumstances in which international trade can make countries better off, but trade can also carry costs, especially in the short run. Cheap foreign cars are great for British consumers but less good for unemployed UK car workers.

Because foreign competition makes life difficult for some voters, governments are frequently under pressure to restrict imports. We conclude the chapter by discussing trade or commercial policy and whether it is a good idea to restrict imports.

33.1 Trade patterns

Every international transaction has both a buyer and a seller. One country's imports are another country's exports. To measure how much trade occurs we can measure the total value of exports by all countries or the total value of imports. Table 33.1 shows the value of world exports and, as a benchmark, the value relative to GNP in the world's largest single economy, the United States.

Table 33.1 The value of world exports

	1928	1935	1950	1973	2005
World exports (billions of 2005 £)	388	164	246	1303	6200
(% of US GNP)	57	27	20	40	80

Sources: League of Nations, *Europe's Trade,* Geneva, 1941; IMF, *International Financial Statistics; National Income Accounts of the United States,* 1928–49.

World trade has grown rapidly since 1950, at an average annual rate of 8 per cent (and by more than 11 per cent a year since 2000). International trade gets ever more important to national economies. Between 1960 and 2005, UK exports as a fraction of GNP rose from 18 per cent to 32 per cent. Details for selected countries are shown in Table 33.2. World exports are now around 20 per cent of world GNP.

Table 33.2 Exports as % of GDP

	1967	2005
Belgium	36	85
Netherlands	43	67
UK	18	28
France	14	29
Italy	17	28
USA	5	11
Japan	10	11

Source: OECD, *Economic Outlook.*

The Great Depression of the 1930s and the Second World War virtually destroyed international trade. Measured relative to US GDP, it was not until the 1960s that world trade regained its level of 1928.

As trade has grown, both in absolute terms and relative to the size of national economies, the interdependence of national economies has increased. Like many of the countries in Table 33.2,

Britain is now a very open economy. Smaller countries are usually more open. Trade between Paris and Brussels is *international* trade, but trade between New York and California is not. Events in other countries affect our daily lives much more than they did 20 years ago. We now look at the facts about who trades with whom.

World trade patterns

Table 33.3 shows the pattern of trade, which is dominated by the rich countries of Europe and North America, who are the origin of 64 per cent of world exports and receive 57 per cent of world imports. Asia, which includes mature Japan and rapidly rising China and India, accounts for around a quarter of world trade. The other countries include the former Soviet Union, Latin America, the Middle East and Africa. Many of these are classified as *less-developed countries* (LDCs), ranging from the very poor such as Bangladesh to the nearly rich such as Brazil. Having enjoyed per capita income growth of nearly 10 per cent a year for 25 years, China is breaking all records in making the transition from very poor to nearly rich.

> **Less-developed countries (LDCs)** have low per capita incomes.

Table 33.3 Trade patterns, 2005 (% of world exports)

Destination	Origin			
	E and NA	Asia	Other	Total
Europe and N. America	46	6	5	57
Asia	11	14	3	28
Other	7	4	4	15
Total	64	24	12	100

Source: GATT, *Directions of Trade.*

The commodity composition of trade

In rich countries, services are most of value added or GDP. International trade in services is growing rapidly, but from a small baseline. Trade in goods – or merchandise trade – remains important because many countries import goods, add a little value and then re-export them. The value added makes a small contribution to GDP but gross flows of imports and exports of goods are large. By importing goods, adding a little value and re-exporting, it is even possible that the value of exports exceeds the value of GDP itself.

Table 33.4 distinguishes between *primary commodities* (agricultural commodities, minerals and fuels) and manufactured or processed commodities (chemicals, steel and cars). Primary products fell from 50.5 per cent of world trade in 1955 to below 25 per cent in 2000, after which it rose a little as China searched the world for metals and fuel to sustain its industrial boom. However, over the 50-year period, the big story is the fall in primary commodity trade and the huge rise in trade in manufactures.

Although the EU mainly exports manufactures, Table 33.5 shows that primary products are a fifth of EU exports. The EU has to import many raw materials, but imports of wholly or partly finished manufactures are three-quarters of EU imports. US trade shows the same pattern.

Asian countries export fewer primary products and import more primary products than the EU or North America. Asia concentrates heavily on exports of manufactures: in Europe we buy lots of products from Sony, Canon, Mitsubishi and Daewoo.

Table 33.4 The composition of world exports

% share of	1955	2005
Primary commodities	50.5	25.6
Food, agriculture	22.3	8.4
Fuels and mining	15.0	17.2
Manufactures	49.5	72.0

Sources: GATT, *Networks of World Trade,* 1955–76; UNCTAD, *International Trade Statistics.*

Table 33.5 Trade patterns, early 2000

	EU
% of exports	
Primary	19.3
Manufactures	80.7
% of imports	
Primary	24.3
Manufactures	75.7

Source: WTO, *International Trade Statistics.*

World trade: the issues

Tables 33.1 to 33.5 set out the facts. World trade has grown faster than world income, and is increasingly important. Half of all international trade is between rich industrial countries, which are also the main export markets for emerging market economies. A quarter of world trade is in primary products, the rest in manufactures. These facts help explain some of the key issues in world trade.

Raw materials prices

LDCs claim that industrial countries exploit them by buying raw materials at a low price and returning manufactured goods at a much higher price. Producers of coffee, sugar, copper and many other products would like to be able to copy OPEC and triple the price of their primary products without suffering a significant reduction in the quantities demanded.

Agricultural protection

Farmers in rich countries not only receive agricultural subsidies, such as those through the EU Common Agricultural Policy, but also enjoy protection behind high tariffs on imported farm goods. LDCs complain that exclusion of their exports from the richest markets not merely reduces the quantity of what they can sell but also forces down the price when all their supply must be absorbed in the remaining world markets to which they have access.

Manufactured exports from emerging market economies

These countries want to make their own manufactured goods and export them to the industrial countries. Brazil, Mexico and Korea already have major manufacturing industries, China is now a powerhouse, and Indian companies such as Tata are now moving into Western markets. But exports to industrial countries have led to complaints in industrial countries that jobs are being threatened by competition from cheap foreign labour. Should Asian exports be restricted to prevent massive job losses in Western Europe and North America or should rich countries take advantage of low costs in Asia?

Globalization

Lower transport costs and better information technology are gradually breaking down the segmentation of national markets and increasing competition between countries. This trend has been reinforced by reductions in tariffs as a matter of policy. Sometimes the pace of change has been rapid.

However, poor countries feel that the process is largely dictated by rich countries according to their own self-interest. Poorer countries feel pressurized to dismantle their own tariffs and allow in foreign investors, while rich countries remain reluctant to pay attention to concerns of poor countries. By raising the demand for LDC exports, reducing agricultural protection in rich countries might do more to help LDCs than the entire programme of foreign aid.

Before examining these issues, we explain why international trade takes place at all.

33.2 Comparative advantage

Trade is beneficial when there are international differences in the opportunity cost of goods.

> The **opportunity cost** of a good is the quantity of other goods sacrificed to make another unit of that good.

Suppose a closed economy with given resources can make video recorders or shirts. The more resources used to make videos, the fewer resources can be used to make shirts. The opportunity cost of videos is the quantity of shirts sacrificed by using resources to make videos not shirts.

Opportunity costs tell us about the *relative* costs of producing different goods. We now develop a model in which international differences in relative production costs determine the pattern of international trade. The model demonstrates the law of comparative advantage.[1]

> The **law of comparative advantage** states that countries specialize in producing and exporting the goods that they produce at a lower *relative cost* than other countries.

Opportunity costs or relative costs may differ in different countries. We begin with a very simple model in which different technology explains the cost difference. Suppose two countries, the US and the UK, produce two goods, video recorders and shirts. Labour is the only input and there are constant returns to scale. Table 33.6 shows the assumed production costs. It takes 30 hours of US labour to make a video and 5 hours to make a shirt. UK labour is less productive. It takes 60 hours of UK labour to make a video and 6 hours to make a shirt.

Costs and prices

For simplicity, assume there is perfect competition. Hence the price of each good equals its marginal cost. Since there are constant returns to scale, marginal costs equal average costs. Thus, prices equal average costs of production. Because labour is the only factor of production, average cost is the value of labour input per unit of output, the unit labour cost.

---

1 This law was formulated by the great English economist David Ricardo (1772–1823), a successful stockbroker before retiring at the age of 40 to become a member of Parliament and an economist. Ricardo's arguments have a modern ring to them because he used models, clearly stating their assumptions and implications.

Table 33.6 Production techniques and costs

	USA	UK
Unit labour requirement (hours/output unit)		
Videos	30	60
Shirts	5	6
Wage per hour	$6	£2
Unit labour cost		
Videos	$180	£120
Shirts	$30	£12

Assume US workers earn $6 an hour and UK workers £2 an hour. The last two rows of Table 33.6 show unit labour costs of the two goods in each country. With no international trade, each country makes both goods. The unit labour costs are the domestic prices for which the goods are sold. Perfect competition means price equals marginal cost, and constant returns to scale means marginal cost equals average cost.

US unit labour requirements are *absolutely* lower for *both* goods than those in the UK. But US labour is *relatively* more productive in videos than in shirts. It takes twice as many labour hours to make a video in the UK as it does in the US but only 6/5 times as many hours to make a shirt. These relative productivity differences are the basis for international trade.

Allowing international trade

Now the countries trade with each other. This section makes two key points. First, if each country concentrates on producing the good that it makes *relatively* cheaply, the two countries together make more of *both* goods. Trade leads to a pure gain, extra output to be shared between the two countries. Second, the free market provides the right incentives for this beneficial trade to occur.

The countries now trade. Since they use different currencies, a foreign exchange market is set up and an equilibrium exchange rate established. A country's current account must be zero in long-run equilibrium. For simplicity, we ignore foreign debts and assets, and assume that eventually the equilibrium exchange rate adjusts to make the value of imports equal to the value of exports, thus balancing the trade account in the long run.

Table 33.7 shows the unit labour cost and price of videos and shirts in different currencies and then shows their price in pounds at three possible exchange rates: $2.50/£, $2/£ and $1.50/£. The domestic prices reflect the unit cost data in Table 33.6. The price in pounds of UK goods is unaffected by the exchange rate, but the UK price of US goods depends on the exchange rate. The more dollars to the pound, the cheaper are both US goods when valued in pounds.

At the exchange rate of $2.50, US videos are cheaper in pounds than UK videos, but the prices of UK and US shirts are the same. If the exchange rate exceeds $2.50/£, even US shirts cost less in pounds. The equilibrium exchange rate cannot lie above $2.50/£, for then nobody would buy UK goods.[2] A one-way flow in trade and foreign exchange is not an equilibrium.

2 If both US goods are cheaper than British goods when valued in pounds, they must also be cheaper when valued in dollars. We simply multiply all prices in pounds by the same exchange rate to get the corresponding dollar prices.

Table 33.7 Costs, prices and the range of equilibrium exchange rates

| | Cost in £ at an exchange rate of: | | | | | | | |
| | Domestic price | | $2.50/£ | | $2/£ | | $1.50/£ | |
	Videos	Shirts	Videos	Shirts	Videos	Shirts	Videos	Shirts
US goods	$180	$30	£72	£12	£90	£15	£120	£20
UK goods	£120	£12	£120	£12	£120	£12	£120	£12

Conversely, at $1.50/£ US shirts are dearer than UK shirts, but UK and US video prices are the same. If the exchange rate is lower than $1.50/£, both US goods are dearer than UK goods when valued in the same currency. At $1/£, US videos cost £180 and US shirts cost £30. At any exchange rate below £1.50/£ there is a one-way flow of trade and foreign exchange, though it is now UK goods everyone wants to buy.

The foreign exchange market is in equilibrium only if the value of UK imports, and hence the demand for dollars with which to purchase them, equals the value of UK exports, and hence the supply of dollars as UK exporters convert their revenues back into pounds. Hence the highest possible equilibrium exchange rate is $2.50/£, the exchange rate at which one UK good (shirts) is still just competitive with US shirts; and the lowest possible equilibrium exchange rate is $1.50/£, the exchange rate at which one US good (videos) is still just competitive with UK goods.

Comparative advantage

Table 33.7 shows an intermediate exchange rate, $2/£. The exact position of the equilibrium exchange rate depends on the demand for videos and shirts. Regardless of a country's absolute advantage in making goods more cheaply, there is always an exchange rate that lets the country make at least one good more cheaply than other countries when all goods are valued in a common currency. At the equilibrium exchange rate, the country has at least one good it can export to pay for its imports.

Although the US has a lower absolute labour requirement for both goods, the relative cost of videos is lower in the United States, and the relative cost of shirts higher, than in the UK. In the US, where videos cost $180 and shirts $30, videos cost 6 times as much as shirts. In the UK, where shirts cost £12 and videos £120, videos cost 10 times as much as shirts. Making videos costs less relative to shirts in the US than in the UK. The *opportunity cost* of videos is lower in the US, which must give up 6 shirts to make another video.

> **Absolute advantage** means a country is the lowest cost producer of that good. **Comparative advantage** means the country makes the good relatively more cheaply than it makes other goods, whether or not it has an absolute advantage. The **law of comparative advantage** says countries specialize in producing the goods they make *relatively* cheaply.

Conversely, the opportunity cost of shirts is lower in the UK than in the US. The UK must give up only 1/10 of a video to make another shirt, compared with 1/6 in the US. The law of comparative advantage says the UK will specialize in shirts, which have a low opportunity cost for UK producers, and the US will specialize in videos, which have a low opportunity cost for US producers. We discuss comparative advantage further in Box 33.1.

Production and trade patterns depend on *comparative* advantage and *relative* costs because the level of the equilibrium exchange rate takes care of differences in absolute advantage. Even if US producers have lower unit labour requirements for both goods, a sufficiently low $/£ exchange rate makes US goods dear in the UK and UK goods cheap in the US. Beginning from a high $/£ exchange rate at which no UK goods can compete with US goods, which of the UK goods first becomes competitive as the exchange rate falls? The good in which the UK has a comparative advantage or lower opportunity costs.

The principle of comparative advantage has many applications in everyday life. Suppose two students share a flat. One is faster both at making the dinner *and* at vacuuming the carpet. If tasks are allocated according to absolute advantage, the other student does nothing. The jobs get done fastest if each student does the task at which he or she is relatively good.

Box 33.1 Comparative advantage and the gains from trade

The table summarizes earlier data on unit labour requirements (ULR) in labour hours per unit of output, unit labour cost (ULC) in domestic currency and opportunity cost (OC) in domestic goods forgone. With lower ULRs, the US has an *absolute advantage* in both goods. One way to calculate *comparative advantage* is to compare ULRs across countries. Relative to the UK, the US needs less labour to produce videos than shirts. The US has a comparative advantage in videos, the UK in shirts.

Alternatively, we can compare opportunity costs, OC. By sacrificing 6 shirts, the US gets 30 labour hours that make an extra video. More simply, 6 shirts cost $180, the price of 1 video. The opportunity cost of a video is 6 shirts in the US and 10 shirts in the UK. But the opportunity cost of a shirt in the UK (1/10 of a video) is less than in the US (1/6 of a video). Again the US has a comparative advantage in videos and the UK in shirts. When there are many factor inputs, this method of calculating comparative advantage is simpler.

The gains from trade

To make 60 shirts, the UK gives up output of 6 videos. To make 6 videos, the US gives up only 36 shirts. Trade and international specialization let the world economy have an extra 24 shirts with no loss of videos. Or if the US makes another 10 videos, giving up 60 shirts, the world economy has 4 more videos with no loss of shirts. These are the *gains from trade*. Only when opportunity costs are the *same* in both countries are there no gains to exploit.

	ULR	ULC	OC
USA			
Videos	30	$180	6 shirts
Shirts	5	$30	1/6 video
UK			
Videos	60	£120	10 shirts
Shirts	6	£12	1/10 video

Many goods

The principle of comparative advantage still holds with many goods. Table 33.8 shows a range of commodities. The first two rows show unit labour requirements to make each good in the US and the UK. The third row shows unit labour requirements in the US relative to the UK.

Rank the commodities in order. Beginning at the left, the US has the largest comparative advantage in computers, where its relative unit labour requirement is only 1/6 that of the UK. Next is cars, where the US relative unit labour requirement is half that in the UK; then TVs, textiles, glass and finally shoes. The comparative advantage of the US falls as we move to the right in the table.

Table 33.8 Unit labour requirements and comparative advantage: many goods (hours of labour input per unit output)

	Computers	Cars	TVs	Textiles	Glass	Shoes
US goods	200	300	50	5	7	15
UK goods	1200	600	90	8	6	10
US/UK relative ULR	1/6	1/2	5/9	5/8	7/6	3/2

Conversely, the UK has the largest comparative advantage in making shoes, the good in which UK producers are most efficient relative to US producers. As we move to the left, the comparative advantage of the UK declines. US producers become increasingly efficient relative to UK producers.

The US has an absolute advantage in producing computers, cars, TVs and textiles. The UK has an absolute advantage in producing glass and shoes. Nevertheless, absolute advantage plays no direct part in the analysis. Comparative advantage is what counts.

The equilibrium exchange rate occurs at some intermediate level that just balances the value of trade between the two countries. Essentially, the level of the exchange rate takes care of the overall level of absolute advantage, leaving comparative advantage to determine trade patterns.

Different capital–labour ratios

Comparative advantage need not depend on technology differences. It may also reflect different factor supplies. Consider the UK and China. The UK has more capital per worker than China. Even though China's vast size may mean that it has absolutely more capital than the UK, the UK has *relatively* more capital than China.

What does this imply about the relative price of hiring labour and capital in the two countries? With more capital per worker, the marginal product of labour is higher in the UK. This makes real wages higher in the UK than in China. Conversely, the number of workers per unit of capital is lower in the UK than in China. The marginal product of capital and the rental of capital will tend to be lower in the UK, where machinery is relatively plentiful, than in China, where machinery is relatively scarce. Because the UK is endowed with more capital relative to labour than China, the cost of using labour relative to capital is higher in the UK than in China.

Relative costs of using inputs affect the relative price of the goods they produce. Goods made by labour-intensive methods cost relatively more relative to make in the UK than in China. Suppose car production is capital intensive with sophisticated assembly lines, but textile production is labour intensive with detailed tasks best done by hand. The price of cars relative to textiles is lower in the UK than in China.

Hence, a *relatively* abundant supply or endowment of one factor of production tends to make the cost of renting that factor relatively cheap. Goods that use that factor relatively intensively are thus relatively cheap. In these goods the country has a comparative advantage. Thus the UK, relatively generously supplied with capital relative to labour, exports capital-intensive cars to China. China, relatively well endowed with labour, should export labour-intensive textiles to the UK. Differences in relative factor supply are an important explanation for comparative advantage and the pattern of international trade.

Figure 33.1 supports this analysis. It emphasizes skills, or human capital, rather than physical capital, although the two are usually correlated. Countries with scarce land but abundant skills have high shares of manufactures in their exports. Countries with lots of land but few skills typically export raw materials. The figure also shows regional averages. Africa lies at one end, the industrial countries at the other end.

We now have two explanations for comparative advantage or international differences in relative production costs. The first is the Ricardian explanation, international differences in technology that cause differences in relative physical productivity and relative unit labour requirements. Second, even if countries have access to the same technology, the domestic relative price of goods may differ across countries because the relative cost of renting factor inputs differs across countries. Where a factor is in relatively abundant supply, goods that use that factor relatively intensively are likely to be relatively cheaper than in other countries.[3]

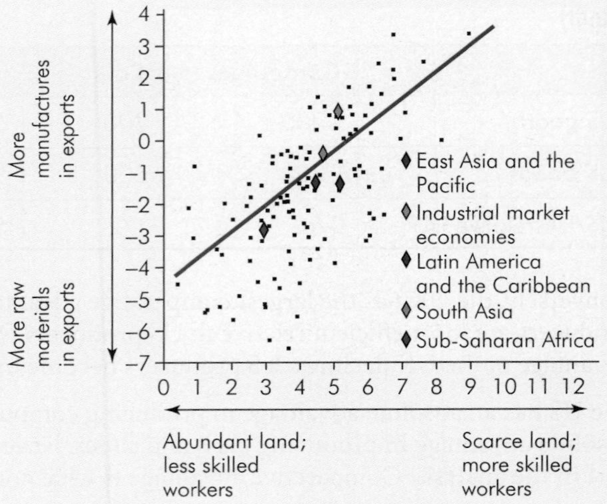

33.3 Intra-industry trade

Different countries have a comparative advantage in different goods and specialize in producing these goods for the world economy. This explains why the UK exports cars to China but imports textiles from China. It does not explain why the UK exports cars (Rover, Jaguar) to Germany while simultaneously importing cars (Mercedes, BMW, VW) from Germany.

A Jaguar is not exactly the same commodity as a Mercedes, nor is Carlsberg exactly the same as Stella. Cars and beer are industries each making a range of different, but highly substitutable, products which enjoy brand allegiance.

Figure 33.1 Comparative advantage and export composition (125 countries and regional averages)

Source: World Bank, *World Development Report*, 1995.

Intra-industry trade is two-way trade in goods made within the same industry.

Intra-industry trade reflects three factors. First, consumers like a wide choice of brands. They do not want exactly the same car as everyone else. Second, there are important economies of scale. Instead of each country making small quantities of each brand in each industry, it makes sense for the UK to make Jaguars, Germany to make Mercedes and Sweden to make Volvos and then to swap them around in international trade. Third, the tendency to specialize in a particular brand, to which the demand for diversity and the possibility of scale economies give rise, is limited by transport costs. Intra-industry trade between Germany and France is larger than intra-industry trade between Germany and Japan.

To measure the importance of intra-industry trade we define an index as zero when trade in a particular commodity is entirely one-way: a country either exports or imports the good, but not both. At the opposite extreme, the index equals 1 when there is a complete two-way trade in a commodity: a country imports as much of the commodity as it exports. Figure 33.2 shows the index for trade by the world's largest trading nation, the United States.

At one extreme, in clothing there is little two-way trade. The US imports clothing but exports very little. This trade obeys the principle of comparative advantage. At the other extreme is office

---

3 Strictly speaking, this explains differences in relative prices *before* countries start trading. Export demand may bid up the relative price of the good until relative prices are equalized across countries. This explains why trade is not infinite. Nevertheless, beginning from no trade, comparative advantage explains which goods the country then exports and which it imports.

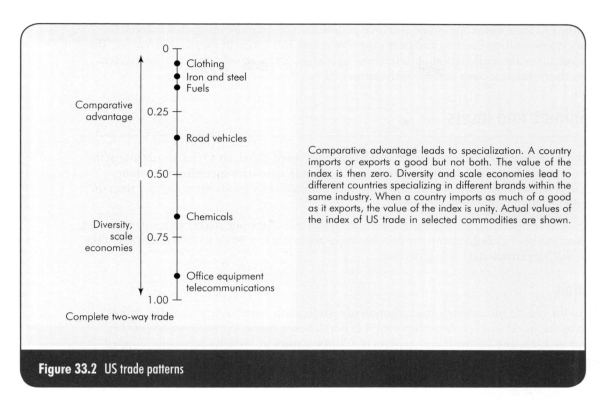

Comparative advantage leads to specialization. A country imports or exports a good but not both. The value of the index is then zero. Diversity and scale economies lead to different countries specializing in different brands within the same industry. When a country imports as much of a good as it exports, the value of the index is unity. Actual values of the index of US trade in selected commodities are shown.

Figure 33.2 US trade patterns

equipment (including telecoms). Here trade is almost completely two-way. As a general principle, the more commodities are undifferentiated goods (fuel, steel, oil), the more trade patterns reflect comparative advantage based on relative resource abundance. As we move towards finished manufactures, product differentiation becomes dominant and comparative advantage loses some of its overriding role. Intra-industry trade is more significant in cars and office equipment.

The more closely markets are integrated, and the lower the obstacles to trade – in terms both of distance and tariffs – the more intra-industry trade we expect. Table 33.9 compares intra-industry trade indices for the EU and Japan. Japan's trade is substantially one-way. Primary commodities are imported, manufactures are exported. There are few industries in which Japan simultaneously imports and exports. Hence its index of intra-industry trade is low for most goods.

Table 33.9 Index of intra-industry trade

	EU	Japan
Primary commodities	0.58	0.05
All manufactures	0.80	0.20
Road vehicles	0.70	0.02
Household appliances	0.80	0.04
Textiles	0.91	0.36
Other consumer goods	0.80	0.44
Weighted average	0.83	0.23

Source: GATT, *International Trade.*

In contrast, the EU has a more diversified resource endowment and a more integrated market, in which distance, information barriers and tariffs are now small. Intra-industry trade is extensive. The gain from trade is not the exploitation of differences in relative prices across countries but greater diversity and the lower unit costs that scale economies allow.

33.4 Gainers and losers

Countries trade because they have a comparative advantage (based either on a relative advantage in technology or on relative factor abundance) or because different countries specialize in making different brands when scale economies exist. Either way, countries buy goods more cheaply than they could have done without international trade.

Although trade is beneficial in the aggregate, this is no guarantee that trade makes *everyone* better off. Current concerns about globalization arise because there are losers too. Here are two examples of the conflicts to which international trade gives rise.

Refrigeration

At the end of the nineteenth century, the invention of refrigeration enabled Argentina to supply frozen meat to the world market. Argentina's meat exports, non-existent in 1900, rose to 400 000 tonnes a year by 1913. The US, with beef exports of 150 000 tonnes in 1900, had virtually stopped exporting beef by 1913.

Who gained and who lost in this early example of globalization? Argentina's economy was transformed. Owners of cattle and land gained; other land users lost out because higher demand bid up land rents. Argentine consumers found their steaks becoming dearer as meat was shipped abroad. Argentina's GNP rose a lot, but the gain from trade was not equally distributed. Some people in Argentina were worse off. Similarly, in Europe and the United States, cheaper beef made consumers better off. But beef producers lost out because beef prices fell.

Refrigeration opened up the world to Argentinian beef. As a whole, the world economy gained. In principle, the gainers could have compensated the losers and still had something left over. In practice, gainers rarely compensate losers. So some people lose out. In this example the big losers were beef producers elsewhere in the world and other users of land in Argentina.

The UK car industry

A second example is the UK car industry. As recently as 1971, imports of cars were only 15 per cent of the domestic UK market, while 35 per cent of UK car output was exported. The UK was a net exporter of cars. Since 1971 UK car makers have lost market share to foreign imports. Imports now exceed 60 per cent of the UK market. Exports recovered in the 1990s, in part because companies like Nissan, Honda and Toyota established UK plants to produce for the EU market.

UK car buyers and foreign car exporters benefited from the rise in UK imports of cheaper foreign cars. But UK car producers like Rover had a very tough time. The UK government faced pressure to restrict UK imports of cars to prevent further job losses in the car industry.

Restricting car imports to the UK helps the UK car industry but raises car prices to UK car buyers. Should the government please producers or consumers? More generally, how should we decide whether to restrict imports or have free trade in all goods? We now analyse the costs and benefits of tariffs or other types of trade restriction. In so doing, we move from *positive economics*, why trade exists and what form it takes, to *normative economics*, what trade policy the government should adopt.

> **Trade policy** affects international trade through taxes or subsidies, or by direct restrictions on imports and exports.

33.5 The economics of tariffs

The most common type of trade restriction is a tariff or import duty.

If t is the tariff rate as a decimal fraction (e.g. 0.2), the domestic price of an imported good is $(1 + t)$ times its world price. By raising the domestic price of imports, a tariff helps domestic producers but hurts domestic consumers.

> An **import tariff** is a tax on imports.

The free trade equilibrium

Figure 33.3 shows the domestic market for cars. The UK faces a given world price of cars, say £10 000 a car, shown by the solid horizontal line. Schedules DD and SS show the demand for cars by UK consumers and the supply of cars by UK producers. For simplicity, we assume that domestic and foreign cars are perfect substitutes. Consumers buy the cheaper one.

At a price of £10 000, UK consumers wish to buy Q_d cars, at point G on their demand curve. Domestic firms wish to make Q_s cars at this price. The gap between domestic supply Q_s and domestic demand Q_d is imported.

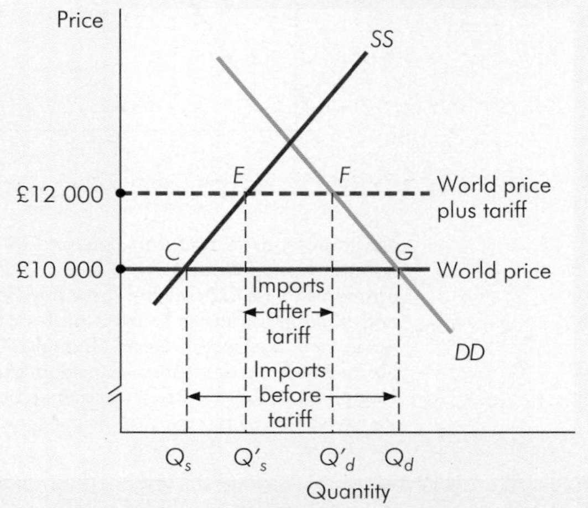

Equilibrium with a tariff

Now the government levies a 20 per cent tariff on imported cars. Car importers charge £12 000 to cover their costs, inclusive of the tariff. The broken horizontal line at this price shows that importers will sell any number of cars in the domestic market at a price of £12 000. The tariff raises the domestic tariff-inclusive price above the world price.

By raising domestic car prices, the tariff boosts domestic car production from Q_s to Q_s'. The tariff protects domestic producers by raising the domestic price at which imports become competitive. In moving up the supply curve from C to E, domestic producers with marginal costs between £10 000 and £12 000 can now survive at the higher domestic price of cars.

DD and SS show the domestic demand and supply for cars. In the absence of a tariff, consumers can import cars at a price of £10 000. In free trade equilibrium, domestic producers produce at C and domestic consumers consume at G. The quantity of imported cars is CG. Q_d is the total quantity demanded. Domestic production Q_s is supplemented by imports $(Q_d - Q_s)$. A 20 per cent tariff raises the domestic price of imports to £12 000. Domestic output is now at E and consumers consume at F. Imports fall from CG to EF.

Figure 33.3 The effects of a tariff

The higher price also moves consumers up their demand curve from G to F. The quantity of cars demanded falls from Q_d to Q_d'. For consumers, the tariff is like a tax. Cars cost more.

Figure 33.3 shows the combined effect of higher domestic production but lower domestic consumption. Imports fall because domestic production rises *and* because domestic consumption falls. The more elastic are these supply and demand schedules, the more a given tariff reduces imports. If both schedules are very steep, the quantity of imports hardly changes.

Costs and benefits of a tariff

Figure 33.4 shows the costs and benefits of imposing a tariff. We distinguish *net costs to society* from *transfers* between one part of the economy and another.

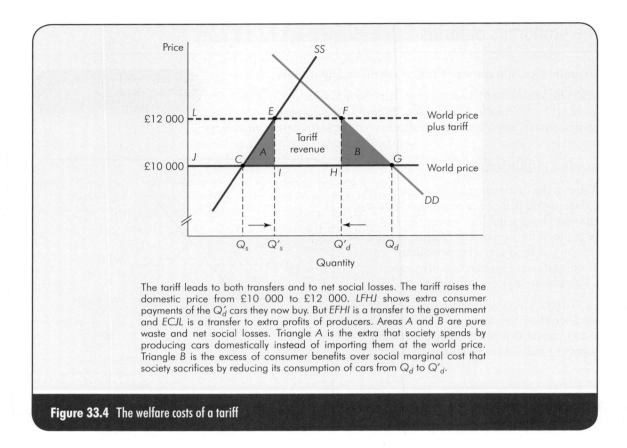

The tariff leads to both transfers and to net social losses. The tariff raises the domestic price from £10 000 to £12 000. *LFHJ* shows extra consumer payments of the Q'_d cars they now buy. But *EFHI* is a transfer to the government and *ECJL* is a transfer to extra profits of producers. Areas A and B are pure waste and net social losses. Triangle A is the extra that society spends by producing cars domestically instead of importing them at the world price. Triangle B is the excess of consumer benefits over social marginal cost that society sacrifices by reducing its consumption of cars from Q_d to Q'_d.

Figure 33.4 The welfare costs of a tariff

After the tariff is imposed, consumers buy the quantity Q'_d. Since the consumer price rises by £2000, consumers spend (£2000 × Q'_d) *more* than before to buy the quantity Q'_d. Who gets these extra payments, the area *LFHJ* in Figure 33.4.

Some of the extra consumer payments go to the government, whose revenue from the tariff is the rectangle *EFHI*, the tariff of £2000 per imported car times $(Q_d - Q'_s)$ the number of imported cars. This transfer *EFHI* from consumers to government is *not* a net cost to society. For example, the government can use the tariff revenue to reduce income tax rates.

Higher consumer payments also go in part to firms as extra profits. Firms get a higher domestic price for their output. The supply curve shows how much firms need to cover the extra cost of making Q'_s not Q_s. Hence the remaining area *ECJL* shows the extra profits, namely the extra revenue from higher prices not required to cover extra production costs. Thus *ECJL* is a transfer from consumers to the pure profit or economic rent of firms. It is *not* a net cost to society.

The shaded area A is part of the area *LFHJ* showing extra consumer payments, but is neither revenue for the government nor extra profits for firms. It is a net cost to society: the cost of supporting inefficient domestic firms.

The supply curve SS shows the marginal cost of making the last car in the home economy. But society *could* import cars from the rest of the world in unlimited quantities at the world price, which is the true marginal cost of cars to the domestic economy. The triangle A shows the resources that society wastes by making the quantity $(Q'_s - Q_s)$ at home when it could have been imported at a lower cost. The resources drawn into domestic car production could be better used elsewhere in the economy.

Triangle B is a second net loss to society. If the tariff is scrapped and free trade restored, the quantity of cars demanded rises to Q_d. The triangle B shows the excess of consumer benefits, measured by the height of the demand curve showing how much consumers will pay for the last unit demanded, over the marginal costs of expanding from Q'_d to Q_d, the world price at which imports can be purchased. Conversely, by imposing the tariff, society incurs a net loss shown by triangle B. It is the net benefit society gives up when fewer cars are bought by consumers.

To sum up, when we begin from free trade equilibrium and then impose a tariff, the rise in the domestic price leads both to transfers and to pure waste. Money is transferred from consumers to the government and to producers. The net social cost of these transfers is zero.

A tariff also involves pure waste. Society can always import cars at the world price. Efficiency requires that this marginal cost is equal both to the marginal benefit to consumers and to the marginal cost of domestic production. By raising the domestic price, to which domestic producers equate marginal cost and domestic consumers equate marginal benefit, a tariff leads to domestic overproduction and domestic under-consumption of the good. Triangles A and B measure this waste that the tariff distortion creates. Society does better to use less resources in the car industry and to transfer these resources to an export industry which could earn enough foreign exchange to import cars at the cheaper world price. This is the *case for free trade*.

Should tariffs never be imposed? We now examine common arguments in favour of tariffs.

33.6 Good and bad arguments for tariffs

Table 33.10 lists some of these arguments. We group them under several headings. The *first-best* argument is a case where a tariff is *the* best way to achieve a given objective. *Second-best* arguments are cases where a tariff is better than nothing, but where another policy is better still if it can be implemented. Non-arguments are partly or completely fallacious.

Table 33.10 Arguments for tariffs

Type	Example
First-best	Foreign trade monopoly
Second-best	Way of life, anti-luxury, infant industry, defence, revenue
Strategic	Games against foreigners
Non-argument	Cheap foreign labour

The optimal tariff: the first-best argument for tariffs

In presenting the case for free trade, we were careful to assume that the domestic economy can import as many cars as it wished without bidding up the world price of cars. For a small economy this is a reasonable assumption. However, imports by a large country may be large relative to the world market and bid up the world price of those commodities.

In this case, the world price of the last unit imported is *lower* than the true cost of the last unit to the importing economy. In demanding another unit of imports, the economy raises the price it has to pay on the quantity already being imported. But in a free trade world without tariffs, each individual thinks only about the price he or she pays. No single individual bids up the price, but collectively they bid up the price of imports.

Under free trade, each individual buys imports until the benefit to that individual equals the world price she pays. Since the collective cost of the last import exceeds its world price, the social cost of that import exceeds its benefit. There are too many imports. Society gains by restricting imports until the benefit of the last import equals its social cost.

> When imports affect the world price, the **optimal tariff** reduces imports to the level at which social marginal cost equals social marginal benefit.

A small country's imports have no effect on the world price of its imports. The marginal social cost of imports then equals the world price. Then, and only then, is the optimal tariff zero. Free trade is then first best.

The optimal tariff is a straightforward application of the principles of efficient resource allocation discussed in Part 3.

Second-best arguments for tariffs

We now introduce the principle of targeting.

The optimal tariff is a first-best application of the principle of targeting precisely because the source of the problem is a divergence between social and private marginal costs in trade itself. A tariff on trade is the most efficient solution. The arguments for tariffs that we now examine are all second-best arguments because the original source of the problem does not directly lie in trade. The principle of targeting assures us that there are ways to solve these problems at a lower net social cost.

> The **principle of targeting** says that the most efficient way to attain a given objective is to use a policy influencing that activity directly.

Way of life

Suppose society wishes to help inefficient farmers or craft industries. It believes that the old way of life, or sense of community, should be preserved. It levies tariffs to protect such groups from foreign competition.

There is a cheaper way to attain this objective. A tariff helps domestic producers but hurts domestic consumers through higher prices. A production subsidy would still keep farmers in business and, by tackling the problem directly, would avoid hurting consumers. In terms of Figure 33.4, triangle A shows the net social cost of subsidizing domestic producers so they can produce Q_s' rather than Q_s. But a tariff, the second-best solution, also involves the social cost given by the triangle B.

Suppressing luxuries

Some poor countries believe it is wrong to allow their few rich citizens to buy Rolls-Royces or luxury yachts when society needs its resources to stop people starving. A tariff on imports of luxuries reduces their consumption but, by raising the domestic price, may also provide an incentive for domestic producers to use scarce resources to produce them. A consumption tax tackles the problem directly, and is more efficient.

Defence

Some countries believe that, in case there is a war, it is important to preserve domestic industries that produce food or jet fighters. Again, a production subsidy, not an import tariff, is the most efficient way to meet this objective.

Infant industries

A common argument for a tariff is that it allows infant industries to get started. Suppose there is *learning by doing*. Only by actually being in business do firms learn how to reduce costs and become as efficient as foreign competitors. A tariff provides protection to infant industries until they master the business and can compete on equal terms with more experienced foreign suppliers.

Society should invest in new industries only if they are socially profitable in the long run. The long-run benefits must outweigh the initial losses during the period when the infant industry is producing at a higher cost than the goods could have been obtained through imports. But in the absence of any divergence between private and social costs or benefits, an industry will be socially profitable only if it is privately profitable.

If the industry is such a good idea in the long run, society should begin by asking why private firms cannot borrow the money to see them through the early period when they are losing out to more efficient foreign firms. If private lenders are not prepared to risk their money, society should ask whether the industry is such a good idea after all. And if the industry does make sense but there is a problem in the market for lending, the principle of targeting says that the government should intervene by lending money to private firms.

Failing this, a production subsidy during the initial years is still better than a tariff, which also penalizes consumers. The worst outcome of all is the imposition of a *permanent* tariff, which allows the industry to remain sheltered and less efficient than its foreign competitors long after the benefits of learning by doing are supposed to have been achieved.

Revenue

In the eighteenth century, most government revenue came from tariffs. Administratively, it was the simplest tax to collect. Today this is still true in some developing countries. But in modern economies with sophisticated systems of accounting and administration, the administrative costs of raising revenue through tariffs are not lower than the costs of raising revenue through income taxes or taxes on expenditure. The balance of tax collection should be determined chiefly by the extent to which taxes induce distortions, inefficiency and waste, and the extent to which they bring about the distribution of income and wealth desired by the government. The need to raise revenue is not a justification for tariffs themselves.

Strategic trade policy

In Chapter 9 we argued that game theory is useful in analysing strategic conflict between oligopolists. In international trade, strategic rivalry may exist either between the giant firms or 'national champions' of different countries, or between governments acting on their behalf.

Strategic international competition may justify industrial policy. For example, initial government subsidies to the European aircraft producer Airbus Industrie was a pre-commitment to deter Boeing from trying to force Airbus out of the industry.

Similar considerations arise in trade policy. Levying a tariff on imports, thereby protecting domestic producers, may deter foreigners from attempting a price war to force the domestic producers out of the industry, and may prevent foreign producers from entering the industry.

This sounds like a very general and robust argument for tariffs, but it should be viewed with considerable caution. If it is attractive for one country to impose tariffs for this purpose, it may be as attractive for foreigners to retaliate with tariffs of their own. We then reach an equilibrium in which little trade takes place, domestic giants have huge monopoly power since they no longer face effective competition from foreigners and all countries suffer.

In fact, this game has the structure of the Prisoner's Dilemma game we introduced in Chapter 9. All countries may be led to impose tariffs even though all would be better off if tariffs were abolished. This suggests there is a role for international co-operation to agree on, and subsequently enforce, low tariffs. We take up this theme shortly.

Dumping

Although the preceding discussion relates to tariffs, it can also be applied to trade subsidies.

> **Dumping** occurs when foreign producers sell at prices below their marginal production cost, either by making losses or with the assistance of government subsidies.

Domestic producers say this is unfair and demand a tariff to protect them from foreign competition. If we knew foreign suppliers would supply cheap goods indefinitely, we should say thank you, close down our more expensive industry and put our resources to work elsewhere. To this extent, dumping is a non-argument for a tariff.

However, foreign producers may be engaged in predatory pricing meant to drive our producers out of the industry. Once the foreigners achieve monopoly power in world markets, they raise prices and make big profits. If so, it may be wise for our government to resist. Even so, a production subsidy is the efficient way to insulate our producers from this threat. A tariff has the undesirable side effect of distorting consumer prices.

Non-arguments for tariffs

Cheap foreign labour

Home producers frequently argue that tariffs are needed to protect them from cheap foreign labour. Yet the whole point of trade is to exploit international differences in the relative prices of different goods. If the domestic economy is relatively well endowed with capital, it benefits from trade precisely because its exports of capital-intensive goods allow it to purchase *more* labour-intensive goods from abroad than would have been obtained by diverting domestic resources to production of labour-intensive goods.

As technology and relative factor endowments change over time, countries' comparative advantage alters. In the nineteenth century Britain exported Lancashire textiles all over the world. But textile production is relatively labour intensive. Once the countries of Southeast Asia acquired the technology, it was inevitable that their relatively abundant labour endowment would give them a comparative advantage in producing textiles.

New technology frequently gives a country a temporary comparative advantage in particular products. As time elapses, other countries acquire the technology, and relative factor endowments and relative factor costs become a more important determinant of comparative advantage. Inevitably, the domestic producers who have lost their comparative advantage start complaining about competition from imports using cheap foreign labour.

In the long run the country as a whole will benefit by facing facts, recognizing that its comparative advantage has changed and transferring production to the industries in which it now has a comparative advantage. And our analysis of comparative advantage promises us that there *must* be some industry in which each country has a comparative advantage. In the long run, trying to use tariffs to prop up industries that have lost their comparative advantage is futile and costly.

Of course, in the short run the adjustment may be painful. Workers lose their jobs and must start afresh in industries where they do not have years of experience and acquired skills. But the principle of targeting tells us that, if society wants to smooth this transition, some kind of retraining or relocation subsidy is more efficient than a tariff.

Why do we have tariffs?

Aside from the optimal tariff argument, there is little to be said in favour of tariffs. Economists have been arguing against them for well over a century. Why are tariffs still so popular?

Activity box 33 Too successful?

'China's trade surplus jumped 67 per cent in January,' reported the BBC in February 2007, 'a development that is likely to increase pressure on Beijing to allow its currency to float freely. Although the rise was inflated by seasonal factors, the West has long said the yuan is undervalued. ... China's trade surplus with the European Union reached $26.4bn in January, while that with the US totalled $23.41bn. Its overall trade surplus for 2006 hit a new record of $1777bn, up 74 per cent on 2005.'

Severe trade imbalances run the risk of provoking retaliation by countries with large trade deficits. Such retaliation may include attempts to impose tariffs or quotas.

Questions

(a) Does the supply of cheap Chinese manufactures benefit or hurt European countries?

(b) European trade unions argue that European imports from China are unfair competition because European workers enjoy greater employment rights (shorter work week, better health and safety, protection from dismissal, minimum working age) and that restricting imports of goods would provide a level playing field for European workers. How would you respond?

(c) If as a politician you decide to limit the quantity of imports from China, is it better to use a tariff or a quota? Why?

To check your answers to these questions, go to page 736.

Concentrated benefits, diffuse costs

A tariff on a particular commodity helps a particular industry. It is easy for firms and workers in an industry to organize effective political pressure, for they can all agree that this single issue is central to their livelihood, at least in the short run. But if the tariff is imposed, the cost in higher consumer prices is borne by a much larger and more diverse group of people whom it is much harder to organize politically. Hence, politicians heed the vociferous, well-organized group lobbying *for* tariffs, especially if they are geographically concentrated in an area where, by voting together, they have a significant effect on the outcome of the next election.

Tariffs versus subsidies

Why does government assistance often take the form of tariffs rather than production subsidies, frequently more appropriate? First, because if domestic industry is suffering from imports of Japanese goods, the solution seems to be to do something that hurts Japan directly. Second, because the government would have to raise taxes to finance a production subsidy. A tariff is often politically easier because it seems to augment government revenues (raising hopes of an income tax cut), whereas a subsidy seems to deplete government revenues (raising fears of higher tax rates). You now know that a tariff hits consumers directly by raising the domestic price of the good, but the government may be able to invoke impersonal 'market forces'. Tariffs cause the government less political hassle.

33.7 Tariff levels: not so bad?

In the nineteenth century world trade grew rapidly, in part because the leading country, the UK, pursued a vigorous policy of free trade. In contrast, US tariffs averaged about 50 per cent, although they had fallen to around 30 per cent by the early 1920s. As the industrial economies went into the Great Depression of the late 1920s and 1930s, there was pressure to protect domestic jobs by keeping out imports. Tariffs in the US returned to around 50 per cent, and the UK abandoned the policy of free trade that had been pursued for nearly a century.

Table 33.1 showed that the combination of world recession and increasing tariffs led to a disastrous slump in the volume of world trade, further exacerbated by the Second World War.

The World Trade Organization

After the war there was a collective determination to see world trade restored. Bodies such as the International Monetary Fund and the World Bank were set up and many countries signed the General Agreement on Tariffs and Trade (GATT), a commitment to reduce tariffs successively and dismantle trade restrictions.

Under successive rounds of GATT, tariffs fell steadily. By 1960 US tariffs were only about one-fifth their level at the outbreak of the Second World War. In the UK the system of wartime quotas on imports had been dismantled by the mid-1950s, after which tariffs were reduced by nearly half in the ensuing 25 years. Europe as a whole has moved towards an enlarged European Union in which tariffs between member countries have been abolished.

The GATT Secretariat, now called the World Trade Organization (WTO), began the latest round of negotiations – the Seattle round – in 2000. Chinese membership of the WTO has now been agreed. WTO is increasingly associated with pressure not merely to dismantle substantial protection that severely reduces efficiency but to extend trade liberalization to more and more countries. Tariff levels throughout the world are probably as low as they have ever been. Trade liberalization has been an engine of growth. World trade has seen four decades of rapid growth.

Fears about globalization often have less to do with change itself than with other distortions that it may then exacerbate. For example, when environmental protection is inadequate and corporate accountability weak, it is legitimate to draw attention to the fact that globalization may allow environmental exploitation.

The principle of targeting also tells us that the best solution may not be to hinder trade but rather to attack the problems at source. For example, strengthening environmental protection may be a more effective response than perpetuating trade restrictions.

33.8 Other trade policies

Tariffs are not the only form of trade policy. We now examine three other policy instruments: quotas, non-tariff barriers and export subsidies.

Quotas are restrictions on the maximum quantity of imports.

For example, the EU has a ceiling on imports of steel from Eastern Europe. Although quotas restrict the *quantity* of imports, this does not mean they have no effect on domestic prices of the restricted goods. With a lower supply, the equilibrium price is higher than under free trade.

Thus quotas are rather like tariffs. The domestic price to the consumer rises. It is this higher price that allows inefficient domestic producers to produce a higher output than under free trade. Quotas lead to social waste for exactly the same reasons as tariffs.

Because quotas raise the domestic price of the restricted good, the lucky foreign suppliers who succeed in getting some of their goods sold make large profits on these sales. In terms of Figure 33.4, the rectangle *EFHI*, which would have accrued to the government as revenue from a tariff, now accrues to foreign suppliers or domestic importers. It is the difference between domestic and world prices on the goods that are imported, multiplied by the quantity of imports allowed.

If these profits accrue to foreigners they are a social cost of quotas over and above the cost of an equivalent tariff. However, the government could always auction licences to import and so recoup this revenue. Private importers or foreign suppliers would bid up to this amount to get their hands on an important licence.

> **Non-tariff barriers** are administrative regulations that discriminate against foreign goods.

These barriers include delaying imports at the frontier, a home-goods bias in purchases for the government and contracts that specify standards with which domestic producers are familiar but foreign producers are not. In Chapter 35 we examine how the EU Single Market tried to end non-tariff barriers inside the EU.

So far, we have looked at restrictions on imports. Countries also use trade policy to boost exports. This can vary from outright subsidy to cheap credit or exemption from certain domestic taxes.

> **Export subsidies** are government assistance to domestic firms in competing with foreign firms.

Figure 33.5 shows the economics of an export subsidy. Suppose the world price of a computer is £5000. Under free trade, domestic consumers buy a quantity Q_d at point *G* on their demand curve, producers make a quantity Q_s at point *E* on their supply curve and a quantity *GE* is exported.

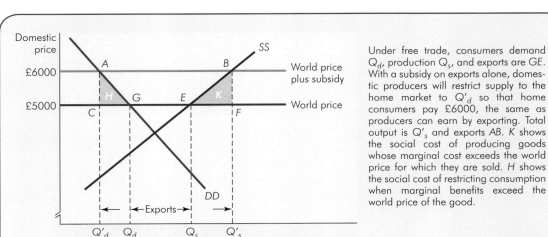

Under free trade, consumers demand Q_d, production Q_s, and exports are *GE*. With a subsidy on exports alone, domestic producers will restrict supply to the home market to Q'_d so that home consumers pay £6000, the same as producers can earn by exporting. Total output is Q'_s and exports *AB*. *K* shows the social cost of producing goods whose marginal cost exceeds the world price for which they are sold. *H* shows the social cost of restricting consumption when marginal benefits exceed the world price of the good.

Figure 33.5 An export subsidy

To help the computer industry, the government offers a 20 per cent *export subsidy* on all exported computers, on which domestic producers now earn £6000. No firm sells at home for £5000 when it can sell abroad for £6000. The supply to the domestic market is reduced to Q_d' so that domestic consumers also pay £6000. Total domestic output rises to Q_s' and exports are AB.

Although the subsidy increases exports, it entails a social cost given by the shaded triangles H and K. Triangle H is the social cost of reducing domestic consumption from Q_d to Q_d'. The consumer benefits of the extra consumption would have exceeded the world price, the social marginal cost at which the economy can obtain computers. Triangle K is the social cost of increasing output from Q_s to Q_s' when the marginal domestic cost exceeds the world price at which computers could have been imported.

Just as with a tariff, an export subsidy is usually a second-best policy. Even if a country wants to raise its output of computers, it is cheaper to use a production subsidy, incurring the cost of the triangle K, but avoiding the cost of the triangle H.

Summary

- **World trade** grew rapidly over the past 40 years, and is dominated by the **developed countries**. Primary commodities are 25 per cent of world trade; the rest is trade in manufactures.

- Countries trade because they can buy goods more cheaply abroad. Differences in costs reflect differences in technology and factor endowments. Scale economies also lead to international specialization.

- Countries make the goods in which they have a **comparative advantage** or can produce relatively cheaply. By exploiting international differences in opportunity costs, trade leads to a pure gain.

- When technology diffuses quickly to other countries, **relative factor endowments** are the main cause of different relative costs. Countries produce and export goods that use intensively the factors with which the country is relatively well endowed.

- **Intra-industry trade** occurs because of scale economies and consumer demand for diversity. The gain from this trade is cost reduction and greater diversity of products.

- If trade is to balance, and the forex market is to be in equilibrium, each country must have a comparative advantage in at least one good. The level of the equilibrium exchange rate offsets international differences in **absolute advantage**.

- Although international trade can benefit the world as a whole, trade usually hurts some groups of people, unless the gainers compensate the losers.

- By raising the domestic price, a **tariff** reduces consumption but raises domestic output. Hence imports fall.

- A tariff leads to two distortions that are social costs: overproduction by domestic firms whose marginal cost exceeds the world price, and under-consumption by consumers whose marginal benefit exceeds the world price.

- When a country affects the price of its imports, the world price is less than the social marginal cost of importing. This is the case for the **optimal tariff**. Otherwise, arguments for tariffs are usually second-best solutions. A production subsidy or consumption tax achieves the aim at lower social cost.

- **Export subsidies** raise domestic prices, reducing consumption but raising output and exports. They involve waste. Goods are exported for less than society's marginal production cost and for less than the marginal benefit to domestic consumers.

- Tariffs and other non-tariff barriers fell a lot in the last 40 years.

- Trade protection is usually costly to society. Yet governments often adopt it as an easy option politically.

Review questions

To check your answers to these questions, go to page 735.

1 (a) Why does the composition of North American and Asian trade differ in Table 33.5?
   (b) Which pattern do you expect in Brazil? Why?

2 'A country with uniformly low productivity should prevent foreign competition.' Discuss.

3 Wine, cars, steel sheeting: which have a high index of intra-industry trade? Why?

4 Making TVs has scale economies. Is this an argument for a tariff on TV imports?

5 To preserve its heritage, a country bans exports of works of art. (a) Is this better than an export tax? (b) Who gains and loses from the ban? (c) Does it encourage young domestic artists?

6 **Common fallacies** Why are these statements wrong? (a) British producers are becoming uncompetitive in everything. (b) Buy British and help Britain.

---

7 **Harder question** 'Large countries gain proportionately less from world trade than small countries.' True or false? Why?

8 **Harder question** Usually, participating in the world economy leaves a country better off, even though there may be winners and losers within the country. (a) Will workers with skills useful to the export industries be better or worse off when a country opens up to international trade? (b) What about workers in industries whose output is now displaced by imports? (c) Could technical progress in the export industry then ever leave a country worse off? Why, or why not?

---

9 **Essay question** Over the last 60 years, international trade has grown much more quickly than world output. How can this occur? Can it go on indefinitely?

To help you grasp the key concepts of this chapter check out the extra resources posted on the Online Learning Centre. There are chapter summaries, self-test questions, an interactive graphing tool, weblinks and a searchable glossary, all for free!

To put your learning into practice and prepare for exams, an **Interactive Workbook** is also available online, containing a variety of question types and providing feedback on your answers.

If you'd like further help with economics, or have any questions, **NetTutor** is here to help! You will have a personalised tutorial service at your fingertips. Visit the online learning centre at: www.mcgraw-hill.co.uk/textbooks/begg for information on accessing all of these resources.

Exchange rate regimes

Having studied trade between different countries, we now examine the corresponding system of international payments. In a closed economy, money is the medium of exchange that reduces transaction costs. An efficient monetary system promotes trade in goods, services and assets by reducing transaction costs and avoiding unnecessary uncertainty.

The exchange rate is the price at which two national currencies exchange. Chapters 28 and 29 discussed fixed and floating exchange rates, analysing how the exchange rate regime affects domestic monetary and fiscal policies in a single country. Now we are interested in how an exchange rate regime affects the world economy as a whole.

> The **international monetary system** provides a medium of exchange for international transactions.

We review different exchange rate regimes, then analyse their relative merits. Finally, we examine whether interdependence of nation states creates a motive to co-ordinate national economic policies. Table 34.1 identifies five regimes – the gold standard, a currency board, an adjustable peg, managed floating and free floating – according to the intervention obligations on the central bank. Any exchange rate involves two countries. Most regimes require that the two governments agree on which regime is in force.

> An **exchange rate regime** is a policy rule for intervening (or not) in the forex market.

Table 34.1 Exchange rate regimes

Forex intervention	Exchange rate	
	Fixed	Flexible
None	–	Free float
Automatic	Gold standard, Currency board	–
Some discretion	Adjustable peg	Managed float

34.1 The gold standard

The gold standard was in force for most of the nineteenth century, though some countries like the UK had adopted it much earlier. It had three key rules.

First, each government fixed the price of gold in its domestic currency. Second, gold was convertible domestic currency, at this fixed price, in whatever quantities people wanted to transact. Third, domestic money creation was linked to the government's stock of gold. Each pound in circulation was backed by an equivalent value of gold in the vault of the central bank. Cash could not be created unless the central bank could acquire gold.

The US gold price was $20.67 an ounce, the UK gold price was £4.25 an ounce. The $/£ exchange rate was thus fixed at $4.86/£, or $20.67 divided by £4.25. At any other exchange rate, people could sell gold in one country and buy gold in the other country, making a profit with certainty. In the forex market, the flow between currencies would be entirely one way, not an equilibrium. The equilibrium exchange rate was the relative gold price in the two currencies.

The gold standard was a monetary union based on fixed gold prices, convertible currencies, and complete gold backing for the money supply. Because monetary union is a live issue today, it is interesting to ask how the gold standard worked.

> A **monetary union** of different countries is a commitment to permanently fixed exchange rates.

Balance of payments adjustment

In long-run equilibrium, each country has internal and external balance. Each country also has a constant money supply, a given level of gold in the central bank vault, a given price level and a constant interest rate.

Suppose Americans now spend more on imports from the UK. The UK has a trade surplus. If domestic prices and wages are slow to adjust, the UK has an export-led boom in the short run. Aggregate demand for UK output rises. Conversely, the US has a recession and a trade deficit.

This provides an *automatic* adjustment mechanism. Initially, the UK has a balance of payments surplus. This causes a rise in the foreign exchange reserves. Under the gold standard, these reserves were gold. A UK trade surplus leads to more gold at the Bank of England, and a matching increase in the domestic money supply. This augments the UK boom.

As prices rise, the UK becomes less competitive: the nominal exchange rate remains fixed but the real exchange rate appreciates. This gradually eliminates the trade surplus, eventually restoring external balance.

The opposite happens in the US. With a payments deficit, the US stock of gold and money falls, raising US interest rates and reducing aggregate demand yet further. Gradually US prices and wages fall and competitiveness rises. The trade deficit is gradually eliminated and external balance restored.

The gold standard provided an automatic mechanism for adjusting imbalances in trade and payments. However, adjustment was slow. Since it depended on changes in domestic wages and prices to adjust competitiveness, the speed of adjustment reflected the speed with which domestic prices and wages adjusted to excess supply or excess demand.

Box 34.1 The gold standard and capital flows

Our discussion of the adjustment mechanism under the gold standard ignored capital flows. By treating the trade balance and the balance of payments as the same thing, our discussion made the automatic adjustment mechanism seem more effective than it really was. Capital flows frustrated adjustment in two ways.

First, countries with a trade deficit sometimes raised domestic interest rates to encourage a capital inflow. A trade deficit no longer necessarily implied a payments deficit and monetary outflow. Recession and downward pressure on domestic wages and prices could be avoided. A trade deficit could persist longer than the idealized account of automatic adjustment suggests.

Second, capital flows explain much of UK economic performance in the nineteenth century. The Industrial Revolution and access to markets in a worldwide empire caused a huge UK trade surplus, offset by a huge capital outflow, partly because of heavy investment abroad. However, investment gradually earns interest and profits. Eventually, UK foreign assets became so large that the current account inflow of interest, profits and dividends exceeded the rate at which profitable opportunities for new capital outflows could be found.

The net inflow of money started to raise domestic prices and wages and make UK producers uncompetitive. External balance now meant a big trade deficit plus large net inflows of property income. The monetary adjustment mechanism of the gold standard made inevitable a UK trade deficit in the late nineteenth century. It was not necessarily the result of laziness or decadence, as Victorians believed at the time.

The gold standard in action

The UK was on the gold standard from 1816 until 1931, apart from a gap around the First World War. The gold standard had a big benefit and a big drawback. By tying the domestic money supply to gold, it ruled out persistent large-scale money creation, and hence ruled out persistently high inflation. The UK price level in 1914 was the same as in 1816. In between, in some decades the price level rose by 20 per cent, in other decades it fell by 20 per cent.

However, since monetary policy was dictated by the flow of gold implied by the balance of payments, interest rates could not be used to counter an anticipated boom or slump. Instead, monetary policy had to wait for flows of gold to change the money supply and thus change domestic prices and wages. It could take years to adjust fully to a large fall in aggregate demand. During the gold standard, individual economies were vulnerable to long and deep recessions.

We discuss European monetary union in the next chapter. Our look at the gold standard already gives three helpful hints. First, permanently fixing nominal exchange rates does not permanently fix real exchange rates. Eventually, competitiveness can change. Second, by curtailing the role of monetary policy, a monetary union raises the significance of fiscal policy in countries that wish to manage aggregate demand. Third, monetary union is easier when wage flexibility is greater.

34.2 An adjustable peg

In operation during 1945–73, the most famous example of an adjustable peg system was called the Bretton Woods system, after the small American town where US and UK officials met in 1944 to agree its details. Because countries agreed to use dollars as well as gold as foreign reserves, the system was also called the dollar standard.

> An **adjustable peg** is a fixed exchange rate, the value of which may occasionally be changed.

Each country fixed its exchange rate against the dollar. The price of gold was fixed in dollars. Currencies were convertible against dollars or gold, which together were foreign exchange reserves. At the fixed exchange rate, central banks were committed to buy or sell domestic currency for foreign exchange reserves. They intervened in the forex market to defend the exchange rate against the dollar.

Unlike the gold standard, the dollar standard did not require 100 per cent forex reserve backing for domestic currency. Governments could print as much money as they wished. The designers of the Bretton Woods system feared that the world gold supply could not increase quickly enough to keep up with the rising demand for money that they hoped would accompany postwar prosperity.

Giving governments the discretion to print money solved that problem but created two others. First, it inhibited the adjustment mechanism built into the gold standard, in which countries with a balance of payments deficit lost gold and their domestic money supply fell. This bid down prices and boosted competitiveness. Under the dollar standard, countries with a payments deficit lost money, but the government could print more money again. This prevented higher unemployment in the short run, but also prevented long-run adjustment by stopping the fall in prices that raised competitiveness.

Such policies were not feasible for ever. If the balance of payments deficit persisted, the country ran out of foreign exchange reserves. Then it had to devalue its exchange rate to raise competitiveness and remove the underlying imbalance in international payments.

Speculators faced a one-way bet. When a country was in payment difficulties, either the exchange rate would stay the same a bit longer or it would be devalued at once. Speculators might as well bet on devaluation, since the exchange rate was unlikely to appreciate. Sometimes speculative pressure made devaluation happen earlier because countries lost reserves not only from a current account deficit but also because of a financial account outflow. Foreseeing this difficulty, the architects of the Bretton Woods system decided to solve the problem of speculative capital flows by making private capital flows illegal.

Perfect capital mobility implies interest parity. Interest differentials must be offset by expected exchange rate changes to equate expected returns in different currencies. Fixed exchange rates imply expected exchange rate changes are zero. Hence interest rates have to be equal. Countries cannot retain the sovereignty to set interest rates.

> Fixed exchange rates, perfect capital mobility and monetary sovereignty are the **impossible triad.** All three cannot co-exist at the same time.

In 1944–45, the architects of Bretton Woods decided that fixed exchange rates were important, but that countries were not ready to surrender monetary sovereignty. Hence capital mobility had to be suspended. Capital flow controls were severe until 1960, when controls on long-term capital flows were relaxed. After the adjustable peg was abandoned in 1973, the need for capital controls diminished. Capital controls were gradually dismantled and integration of global financial markets intensified.

The dollar standard had a second drawback. It led to a world of sustained inflation. Dollars had become the world's medium of exchange. A US payments deficit could be financed by printing more dollars. In the mid-1960s US payments deficits increased, partly because of heavy military spending in Vietnam. The supply of dollars rose rapidly. By raising the world's money supply, this led to inflation throughout the trading world.

Under the gold standard, national and international money supplies had risen only as quickly as new gold could be mined. This system wasted real resources. Why use scarce workers to dig up gold for use as money when money can be printed using almost no real resources? But the difficulty of augmenting the gold supply had ensured that the world money supply grew slowly. It was a commitment to low inflation.

34.3 Floating exchange rates

Pure floating implies that forex markets are in continuous equilibrium without government intervention using the forex reserves. The reserves stay constant and there is no external mechanism to change domestic money supply. The balance of payments is exactly in balance.

Chapter 28 explained how floating exchange rates are determined. In the long run, exchange rates adjust to achieve external balance. This determines the real exchange rate that has to prevail in the long run. Domestic and foreign monetary supplies determine the domestic and foreign price levels. Given these, there is only the path of the nominal exchange rate that delivers the real exchange rate required for external balance when domestic economies are also at internal balance.

In long-run equilibrium, nominal exchange rates then obey purchasing power parity.

When capital mobility is high, neither external balance nor purchasing power parity need hold in the short run. Chapters 28 and 29 discussed how exchange rates adjust to achieve interest parity and prevent massive one-way capital flows. In the short run what matters is not balancing current account flows but the need to balance the potentially much larger financial account flows that might occur when international capital is highly mobile.

> The **purchasing power parity** path of the nominal exchange rate is the path that keeps the real exchange rate constant. Nominal exchange rates offset inflation differentials between countries.

In the long run there is no conflict. Once real interest rates return to their long-run equilibrium level, nominal interest differentials reflect inflation differentials, PPP and interest parity can both be satisfied simultaneously.

Hence, a floating exchange rate does not provide continuous short-run insulation against large changes in competitiveness. Sharp changes in the expected path of interest rates, or in the eventual real exchange rate that will achieve external balance, have big effects on the real exchange rate.

However, floating exchange rates offer no one-way bet to speculators, since new information can make exchange rates jump up or jump down. Floating helps prevent massive capital flows that cause acute problems for macroeconomic management. Floating exchange rates are also the fallback exchange rate regime when countries cannot agree what other regime to adopt.

A managed float

Under a free float there is no central bank intervention in the forex market. The forex reserves are constant, the balance of payments is zero and the net monetary inflow from abroad is also zero.

In practice, exchange rates have rarely floated absolutely freely since 1973 when the Bretton Woods adjustable peg was replaced by a floating exchange rate regime.

> In a **managed float**, central banks intervene in the forex market to try to smooth out fluctuations and nudge the exchange rate in the desired direction.

Intervention may smooth day-to-day exchange rate fluctuations; in the long run it probably makes little difference to the path the exchange rate follows. Central banks have large stocks of foreign exchange reserves which they could dump on the foreign exchange market to try to alter the equilibrium exchange rate. But nowadays speculators have even larger funds at their disposal.

34.4 Speculative attacks on pegged exchange rates

National policy makers are always reluctant to admit that national sovereignty is being eroded. Capital mobility rose sharply in the last two decades of the twentieth century. Under floating exchange rates, the influence of capital flows and speculative opinion is immediately evident. Under fixed exchange rates, policy makers sometimes deluded themselves that their sovereignty was unaffected. Often, it took a crisis to convince them otherwise.

In 1990 the UK pegged its exchange rate against EU currencies in the European Monetary System (EMS), but in 1992 the UK was forced to depreciate and abandon the EMS. More recently, supposedly pegged exchange rates were successfully attacked in Mexico (1994), many Asian countries (1997), Brazil (1999) and Argentina (2002). When the speculators have more money than the central bank, the peg does not always survive.

Now that capital mobility is high, modern crises are caused not by trade deficits but by financial account outflows. These usually reflect a perception that some aspect of current policy is unsustainable. Raising interest rates to defend the currency against capital outflows may be unconvincing if the domestic economy obviously cannot stand the pain of high interest rates for long. Speculators understand that if they push hard enough, the government has to cave in.

> A **speculative attack** is a large capital outflow. If successful, it causes a devaluation. Attacks are sometimes resisted, by raising interest rates and tightening fiscal policy. This works only if it can credibly be sustained.

There are several interpretations of a speculative attack. One is that it corrects a policy mistake. If a country has such a large budget deficit that it needs to print money, it is bound to have inflation. Promising to peg the nominal exchange rate makes little sense. A speculative attack merely forces policy makers to switch to a more realistic exchange rate regime, namely floating. This is a good description of the Russian crisis in 1998 but it does not explain attacks against Asian economies, such as Korea and the Philippines, in 1997, or the attack on the UK in 1992.

A second interpretation is that there are two possible equilibrium exchange rates. Without any attack, the original peg survives. The exchange rate is a little overvalued, but the cost of devaluing (likely to raise inflation expectations) outweighs the cost of a little uncompetitiveness. However, once attacked, the cost of repelling the attack must be added to the scales. It may tip the balance, making it optimal now to accept defeat and take the (temporary) advantage of higher competitiveness that the devaluation achieves. Whether the peg survives or not depends entirely on whether speculators decide to attack.

Successful attacks may do a lot of damage. When domestic banks have borrowed in foreign currency, the domestic value of their debts rises when the exchange rate falls. This may bankrupt the banks and cause a widespread loss of confidence. If a country wants to be less vulnerable to attack, what can it do?

Repelling boarders

Three responses have been adopted. First, try to reduce capital mobility, making it easier to defend fixed but adjustable exchange rate pegs. This was the solution adopted by those designing the Bretton Woods system after the Second World War. Private capital flows were outlawed by capital controls.

> **Capital controls** prohibit, restrict or tax the flow of private capital across currencies.

Capital controls make it easier to defend pegged exchange rates. However, from the 1970s onwards, controls were progressively dismantled as a global financial system was created. It became harder and harder to enforce controls – smart bankers found offshore ways to do the same business.

One form of control that may work is a tiny tax on financial transactions, proposed many years ago by Nobel Prize winner James Tobin. Paying a tiny tax on a 10-year investment is trivial, the same tax on holding a foreign asset for two hours takes away all the profits. A Tobin tax mainly hits short-term 'hot money'.

Capital controls have been used quite successfully in Chile, and were introduced by Malaysia in 1997 after its currency was attacked. Whether the global economy is consistent with widespread controls is doubtful. Small emerging markets can probably use them. The more highly integrated a country is with the world's financial markets, the harder it is to use capital controls.

If capital controls are not to be the answer, the exchange rate regime has to become more robust. Pegged exchange rates are an uncomfortable halfway house: usually pegged, sometimes adjustable. While they are pegged, the central bank has to defend them, even when a one-way bet is emerging. But because they are not completely pegged, the speculators can win in the end.

If this is the diagnosis, the solution is to retreat to one of the safer extremes: float or peg completely. Thus, a second solution for repelling boarders and avoiding spectacular exchange rate crashes is simply to float. Let the speculators punch thin air. They can take the currency down, but, if it was for no good reason, the currency will probably come up again. Most Asian exchange rates recovered rapidly after the 1997 crisis.

The alternative is to make the peg much more credible, akin to the old gold standard. A popular device is a currency board.

A currency board removes the ability of the central bank to change the monetary base. Balance of payments surpluses (deficits) are the only source of expansion (contraction) of the monetary base. Suppose a country has a deficit because it imports too much. Importers take domestic money to the currency board to get the foreign exchange they need; the board simply keeps the domestic money which is retired from circulation. Countries using currency boards within the last 15 years included Estonia, Bulgaria and Argentina.

> A **currency board** is a constitutional commitment to peg the exchange rate by giving up monetary independence.

Like all commitments, it hurts when it has to take the strain. Since a country loses monetary independence, it cannot use interest rates for domestic reasons. To live comfortably with a fixed nominal exchange rate, it needs to avoid higher inflation than its trading partners. If it has a fiscally irresponsible government, it will require money creation and inflation that will eventually get it into trouble. Argentina's crisis in 2001–02 reflected such a trend deterioration in competitiveness. In other cases, knowledge of the monetary commitment may induce the fiscal authorities to behave responsibly, as for example in Estonia prior to its entry into the EU.

Similarly, if the country's banks get into trouble, a currency board prevents easier monetary conditions to help the banks during the crisis. If people worry that, in these circumstances, the country might find a way to give up the currency board, speculators may foresee this possibility and attack the currency anyway. Currency boards are more likely to work the better the public finances are under control and the more evident it is that the country has a sound system of bank regulation that prevents banks taking risks that may get them into trouble.

No solution is ideal. If one solution were perfect, it would have been adopted everywhere long ago. We now consider other issues in choosing between fixed and floating exchange rates.

34.5 Fixed versus floating

In this section, we consider robustness, volatility and financial discipline.

Robustness

How do different regimes cope with major strains? Nominal strains arise when different countries have very different domestic inflation rates. Real strains occur when the world economy suffers a major real shock, such as a quadrupling of real oil prices.

With fixed nominal exchange rates, countries with higher inflation than their competitors become less competitive in international markets. Unless countries pursue domestic monetary policies that lead to roughly equal inflation rates, a fixed exchange rate system simply cannot cope. If frequent devaluations are required to restore competitiveness, credibility evaporates and the country may as well float. In the long run, floating exchange rates can depreciate gently along the PPP path and 'cope' with inflation differences.

How about strains caused by real shocks? Imagine how the OPEC oil price shocks would have hit a fixed exchange rate regime. Overnight, countries that were big oil importers would have faced enormous trade deficits and speculators would have bet on these currencies to be devalued. Under a fixed exchange rate regime, the OPEC oil price shock would have led to consultations, tentative exchange rate adjustments, and further consultations to determine whether adjustments already undertaken were sufficient to achieve the adjustments required. In practice, floating exchange rates coped better.

Volatility

Floating exchange rates can be volatile. Under the adjustable peg, between 1949 and 1967 the $/£ exchange rate was rarely more than 1 cent either side of $2.80/£, and between 1967 and 1972 rarely more than 1 cent either side of $2.40/£. In contrast, Figure 34.1 shows the volatility of the $/£ exchange rates during the period of floating exchange rates since 1973. Not only did it fluctuate between $2.50/£ and $1.05/£, it sometimes moved very rapidly. Such volatility, it is argued, leads to great uncertainty, reducing both trade and foreign investment.

The volatility of floating exchange rates cannot be disputed. Is it always bad? First, it is not obvious that a system with usually fixed nominal exchange rates but occasional large crises is less uncertain than a system in which nominal exchange rates change every day.

Second, what would have happened if the exchange rate had not adjusted so much? To keep the exchange rate more stable in the face of shocks, perhaps interest rates or tax rates would have had to adjust to these shocks. Is

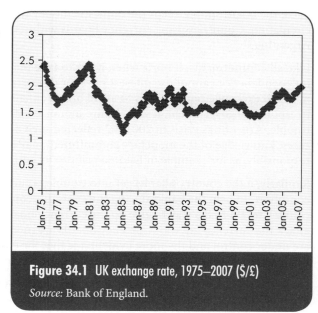

Figure 34.1 UK exchange rate, 1975–2007 ($/£)

Source: Bank of England.

uncertainty about competitiveness under floating exchange rates necessarily worse than uncertainty about interest rates or tax rates under a fixed exchange rate regime? British business was pleased when high interest rates were abandoned after the pound fell out of the Exchange Rate Mechanism in 1992.

The volatility argument may not go decisively against floating exchange rates. However, this argument also comes in a more sophisticated form. The shocks with which the world international monetary system has to deal may not be independent of the exchange rate regime in force. By their very flexibility and robustness, floating exchange rates may make shocks more likely. The most important version of this argument relates to inflation shocks and financial discipline.

Financial discipline

Floating exchange rates let different countries pursue different inflation rates indefinitely. Exchange rates of high-inflation countries depreciate to maintain purchasing power parity and constant competitiveness. Critics of floating exchange rates argue that they do not provide any financial discipline.

In contrast, with a fixed exchange rate, countries become uncompetitive if they have above-average inflation. Unless allowed to devalue, they eventually have no choice but to adopt more restrictive domestic policies to get their inflation rates back in line with the rest of the world.

Fixed exchange rates, however, are not the only route to financial discipline. Instead, the government can make domestic commitments about monetary policy. In recent years, many countries have made their central banks operationally independent of government, giving them freedom to decide interest rates in pursuit of low-inflation targets laid down by the government.

Domestic commitments are not always foolproof. But exchange rate commitments are no certainty either. The weaker EMS currencies (sterling, the lira, the peseta, the escudo) could not maintain previous fixed exchange rate commitments in September 1992. More recently, exchange rate pegs were abandoned in Mexico (1994), Korea (1997), Brazil (1999) and Argentina (2002).

Box 34.2 Thailand, a decade after the crisis

On 2 July 1997, the Bank of Thailand lost its eight-month battle against currency speculators, and abandoned the peg that tied the value of the Thai baht to the US dollar. Defence of the peg cost Thailand $37 billion in foreign reserves; less than $3 billion remained.

The country's decision set off panic. To cash in on the local property boom, local entrepreneurs had been borrowing heavily in US dollars, where interest rates were low, rather than at home, where interest rates were high. Of course, now that you have met uncovered interest parity you understand that Thai interest rates were high precisely to cover the possibility that the baht was devalued. Thais who borrowed apparently cheaply in dollars were running the risk that they might have to repay after a devaluation when their dollar loans would be much harder to repay. So financial markets recognized the danger that the peg would be abandoned, but property speculators in Thailand seemed to ignore this risk. By the end of 1997, there had been a 50 per cent devaluation of the baht against the dollar.

Sirivat Voravetvuthikun was one of those swept up in the thrill of speculation, as he caught the property bug, borrowing heavily to develop a luxury resort east of Bangkok. 'I was an honest businessman, but I was greedy … so I borrowed a lot … which brought me down on my knees.' Ten years on, he has built up a small catering business – but, unable to borrow, he has little chance of becoming the millionaire he once was. However, he thinks he is now on a firmer footing. 'This is a real business that deals with real people. It's not like a bubble business.'

Could a crisis happen again? The banking and financial systems are better regulated and, crucially, the currency now floats, making a sharp depreciation much less likely.

Adapted from: http://news.bbc.co.uk/1/hi/world/asia-pacific/6260720.stm.

Where the government is weak at home, invoking external pressures may be a useful tactic. But a tough government may be able to institute domestic forms of commitment (appointing a tough governor of the central bank or giving that bank greater independence from government control) which still leave the choice of exchange rate regime determined by other factors.

34.6 International policy co-ordination

At one extreme, this might eventually imply a supranational body to which national sovereignty is subordinated. The world economy is a long way from any such arrangement, but much of Europe has a monetary union with a single European central bank. At the other extreme, we might mean agreements to brief other governments about one's own policy and to exchange information.

> **Policy co-ordination** is a concerted attempt by some countries to formulate policy collectively.

In between lies a spectrum of arrangements which specify some 'rules of the game' subject to which national governments still have a measure of discretion. For example, under Bretton Woods, governments agreed that exchange rates would usually be fixed, but retained sovereignty over their domestic monetary and fiscal policies. On the other hand, even when floating, sterling has sometimes been driven to uncompetitive levels.

What do governments stand to gain by co-ordinating macroeconomic policy? Like oligopolists, governments are interdependent, the outcome for each depending on the policies pursued by others. Like oligopolists, they face a tension between the incentive to collude and the incentive to compete. Collusion lets them 'internalize' the externalities they otherwise impose on one another when each sets policy without regard for its impact on the welfare of others. But there is also an incentive to compete by cheating on collective agreements.

The externality argument for co-ordination

The most obvious externality occurs through the exchange rate. When countries are fighting inflation, exchange rate appreciation by one country helps reduce its import prices. But we cannot all appreciate our exchange rates. A rise in the \$/£ is a fall in the £/\$. Countries that use exchange rate appreciation to reduce their own inflation effectively export inflation abroad, by depreciating the exchange rate of trading partners. That is the externality not taken into account when a country decides to depreciate its exchange rate.

Conversely, when countries face inadequate aggregate demand, devaluation helps raise export demand. But devaluation of one exchange rate implies appreciation of another. Devaluation now means exporting unemployment to partner countries whose exchange rates have appreciated.

If national governments fail to take account of how their policies affect other countries, policy co-ordination can solve this market failure: countries can agree not to use exchange rate policy in this manner. As with other co-operative agreements, an effective punishment threat is required to prevent individual countries from subsequently cheating on the agreement. If it can be devised, the agreement will be credible and all countries may benefit.

The reputation argument for co-ordination

Earlier, we discussed financial discipline. Suppose a government would like to keep inflation under control by tight policies but cannot resist reflating the economy as the next election draws near. Because everyone knows this will happen, inflation expectations remain high and inflation is hard to control even at the start of the government's period of office.

Activity box 34 Policing competitive devaluations

The collapse of world trade in the 1930s was triggered by the Great Depression but accentuated by tariff wars and competitive devaluations as each country tried to gain an advantage over others. Collectively, this is impossible and the main result was to shrink the size of the global cake. Postwar global institutions were designed to ensure that this never happened again. For 60 years, the International Monetary Fund (IMF), based in Washington, DC, has presided over a global financial system that has fostered unprecedented trade in goods, services and assets.

In 2007, the IMF announced that it was updating its surveillance system that cracks down on foreign exchange policies causing instability in the world economy. The monitoring scheme targets currency manipulation that could destabilize trade and capital flows. The IMF's managing director, Rodrigo de Rato, said the new rules would show 'what is acceptable to the international community'.

The IMF refused to say the move was aimed at China but some US critics claim China is keeping its currency undervalued to gain an unfair competitive edge for its exports. In 2006, the US trade deficit with China rose to $232 billion.

The IMF said its framework would provide a level playing field for all its 185 members by being clearer and broader in scope. 'It reaffirms that surveillance should be focused on our core mandate, namely promoting countries' external stability,' said Mr de Rato.

Questions

(a) Why does it require an international agency to co-ordinate national exchange rate policies for the common good?

(b) Suppose international speculators believe that a currency will shortly be depreciated in order to secure a competitive advantage – how should speculators react now?

(c) If you were a government wishing to manipulate your exchange rate downwards, could you then claim that the depreciation had been caused by financial markets rather than your own policies?

(d) Suppose it becomes likely that China will allow its exchange rate to appreciate. What is likely to be the first evidence of this?

To check your answers to these questions, go to page 736.

Such a government might be glad to make a binding commitment ruling out the option to reflate as the next election draws near. Central bank independence is one such commitment; policy co-ordination may offer an alternative.

Why do people go to Weightwatchers or Alcoholics Anonymous? Because, alone, they are too weak to stick to their resolutions. Joining a club provides peer discipline. Even in everyday language, it shows commitment. You look silly if you subsequently pull out. Policy co-ordination may act in a similar way, allowing national governments to make credible the promises that would otherwise be incredible. That is the second argument for policy co-ordination.

We now examine an example of co-ordination, the European Monetary System.

34.7 The European Monetary System

In 1979, the members of the European Community set up the European Monetary System (EMS).

> The **EMS** was a system of monetary and exchange rate co-operation in Western Europe.

The system had three aspects. First, a basket of the constituent currencies, called the European Currency Unit (ECU), was used as a unit of account for transactions between EU governments (see Table 34.2). The ECU eventually became the euro in 1999.

Table 34.2 ECU composition (% share of each currency)

Deutschmark	DM	30.1	Spanish peseta	SP	5.3
French franc	FF	19.0	Danish krone	DK	2.4
Pound sterling	£	13.0	Irish punt	IP	1.1
Italian lira	IL	10.2	Greek drachma	GD	0.8
Dutch guilder	DG	9.4	Portuguese escudo	PE	0.8
Belgian franc	BF	7.6	Luxembourg franc	LF	0.3

Second, member governments agreed to lend each other foreign exchange reserves. The purpose was to make central banks more important relative to speculators. It did not really work, since the funds controlled by speculators were also growing rapidly.

The third, and crucial, aspect was the Exchange Rate Mechanism (ERM).

Each country in the ERM could let its exchange rate fluctuate within a band of ±2¼ per cent of the parities it had agreed to defend.[1] When the currency hit the edge of a band, all central banks in the ERM countries were supposed to intervene to try to defend the parity.

> In the **ERM**, each country fixed a nominal exchange rate against each other ERM participant. Collectively the group floated against the rest of the world.

Realignments of the fixed exchange rates against partner countries were possible but had to be unanimously agreed by participants of the ERM.

---

1 Italy, an especially high-inflation country in 1979, was allowed a band of 6 per cent. By the mid-1980s, it was a matter of honour for Italy not to use this wider band. Spain and the UK also joined the ERM with a wider band.

The ERM in practice

Table 34.3 shows the realignments of the major ERM currencies during 1979–91 (the UK did not join until 1990 and left in 1992.) Realignments largely restored purchasing power parity. High-inflation countries (initially Italy and France) were allowed nominal exchange rate devaluations. Notice that there was a realignment every six months between 1979 and 1983, but 1983 realignments were much less frequent. Between 1987 and 1991 there was no realignment at all.

Table 34.3 EMS realignments, 1979–91 (date and percentage realignment)

Date	DM	FF	DG	IL	BF	DK	LF	IP
Sept. 79	+2.0					–2.9		
Nov. 80						–4.8		
Mar. 81				–6.0				
Oct. 81	+5.5	–3.0	+5.5	–3.0				
Feb. 82					–8.5	–3.0	–8.5	
June 83	+4.3	–5.8	+4.3	–2.8				
Mar. 84	+5.5	–2.5	+3.5	–2.5	+1.5	+2.5	+1.5	–3.5
July 85	+2.0	+2.0	+2.0	–6.0	+2.0	+2.0	+2.0	+2.0
Apr. 86								–8.0
Jan. 87	+3.0		+3.0		+2.0			
Cumulative	+23.7	–9.3	+18.8	–20.3	–3.3	–6.2	–5.0	–9.5

Note: DM (Deutschmark), etc. refer to currencies listed in Table 34.2.

Did the ERM exert financial discipline? Were France and Italy forced to converge to low German inflation? Not initially. The old policies continued and regular exchange rate realignments fixed up competitiveness again. However, realignments did not *fully* restore competitiveness, so a little discipline was exerted. After 1983 discipline was much stricter.

Since high inflation countries needed regular devaluations, which required the consent of other ERM members, by withholding consent it was possible to put pressure on the high-inflation countries. Monetary policies steadily converged, especially after 1983.

The role of Germany was crucial. German hyperinflation in 1923 had been a disaster. Germans now hate inflation and are determined to prevent it. The Bundesbank (Buba) has a constitution mandating it to achieve price stability as its overriding objective. The Buba was never prepared to set interest rates at a level that endangered price stability in Germany.[2]

In the mid-1980s, Germany made it harder for high-inflation countries to get regular devaluations. Without them, high-inflation countries had to reduce inflation or face trend deterioration in competitiveness. They chose austerity and disinflation.

2 In 1978, during the negotiations to establish the EMS, the Buba obtained its own 'opt out' deal. The German government privately assured the Bundesbank that it had the option not to support other currencies if this threatened German price stability

By the mid-1980s the implicit deal in the ERM was simple. Germany set interest rates according to what was good for Germany alone. Other ERM members adopted German interest rates in order to keep exchange rates pegged within the ERM. In return, the other members 'borrowed' German credibility. Low inflation was expected in Spain and Italy not because their own policies were suddenly more credible but because Germany might block the devaluations that would be needed if inflationary policies ever re-emerged.

Why the ERM survived

After 1983 the success of the ERM reflected policy convergence on low inflation. Before 1983, little policy convergence had taken place. Two things explain the early survival of ERM.

First, with a band of ±2¼ per cent, there were periods when countries were effectively floating. High-inflation countries had exchange rates that started off near the top of the band and gradually depreciated, just as they would have done under floating. When they got near the bottom of the band, a devaluation soon followed. The early ERM was largely cosmetic.

Second, most countries initially had controls preventing big financial account flows. Despite differences in interest rates, fixed nominal parities survived because capital flows were prevented. Only occasionally was the prospect of a realignment so imminent that capital controls had trouble stemming the speculative tide. However, to create a single market in the EU, in 1987 countries committed themselves to the removal of capital controls within a few years.

When capital mobility is high, to peg the exchange rate between two countries, both countries need to have the same interest rate. The key issue is who chooses the common interest rate. Because of the role of Germany in ERM disinflation in the mid-1980s, Germany set the single interest rate thereafter.

After five years without any realignment during 1987–92, by mid-1992 several exchange rates appeared overvalued. Germany proposed a general ERM realignment in August, but this was declined by other countries. As speculative pressure continued, the Buba intervened heavily to support weaker currencies, as did other central banks.

Speculation persisted. Sterling and the lira were forced out of the ERM and depreciated substantially. The peseta, escudo and Irish punt were devalued but remained in the ERM. Table 34.4 shows ERM realignments during 1992–97.

Table 34.4 ERM devaluations 1992–98

Month/year	Punt	Peseta	Escudo	Lira	Pound
Sept. 92		–5		left ERM	left ERM
Nov. 92		–6	–6		
Feb. 93	–10				
May 93		–8	–6.5		
Mar. 95		–7			
Dec. 96				rejoined ERM	

A new attack on the French franc in August 1993 led to a face-saving 'redesign' of the ERM to allow the franc to survive within it. Previous narrow bands (2¼ per cent each side of the parity) were replaced by very wide bands (15 per cent each side of the parity). With such wide bands, the ERM survived thereafter. In Chapter 35 we discuss how the ERM led to the monetary union and the adoption of the euro.

Box 34.3 Capital controls and the ERM

Initially, the ERM allowed high inflation countries regular devaluations that largely shadowed the nominal exchange rate depreciation they would have had under floating. After 1983 discipline increased, and realignments got less frequent. During 1983–85 inflation rates converged substantially to the low German inflation rate.

In 1986 the Single European Act, a commitment to a Single Market, signalled the end of controls on capital flows. Yet capital controls had underpinned the early ERM. For a high inflation country, Figure (a) shows the path $ABDE$ of nominal exchange rate depreciation to maintain real competitiveness. Initially, the exchange rate is pegged within a band around central parity e_0. When the exchange rate hits the bottom of the band at B, central banks intervene to try to defend the band. As time elapses, the exchange rate moves along BC. With continuing inflation, competitiveness is now being eroded. Eventually this prompts a devaluation of the central parity from e_0 to e_1, so the whole band shifts down. The actual exchange rate jumps from C to D on the day of the realignment.

This is a one-way bet. As the exchange rate moves along BC nobody is expecting a sharp appreciation! Only capital controls prevent a massive outflow on the financial account to avoid the imminent capital loss on holding the currency. If capital controls had been removed in the early 1980s, there would have been an immediate crisis. Figure (b) explains why this did not occur after 1986.

By the mid-1980s, inflation convergence within the ERM meant even Italian inflation was nearly down to German levels. Slow depreciation of the lira could offset extra Italian inflation. The line is flatter in Figure (b) than in (a). In Figure (b) when the parity is devalued from e_0 to e_1, the actual exchange rate at B is inside both the old band and the new band. No jump is required in the exchange rate, and there is no one-way bet for speculators. A small interest differential will compensate them for the gradual depreciation.

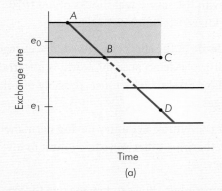

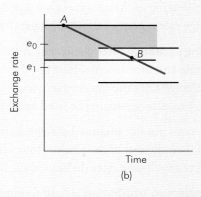

Summary

- Under the **gold standard**, each country fixed the **par value of its currency** against gold, maintained the **convertibility** of its currency into gold at this price and linked the domestic money supply to gold stocks at the central bank. It was a fixed exchange rate regime.

- Without capital flows, countries with a trade deficit faced a payments deficit, lower gold stocks and a lower money supply. Domestic recession then bid down wages and prices, raising competitiveness, an automatic adjustment mechanism. Trade surplus countries faced a monetary inflow, higher prices and lower competitiveness. In practice, this adjustment mechanism was hampered by capital flows.

- The postwar **Bretton Woods system** was an **adjustable peg** in which fixed exchange rates were sometimes adjusted. It was a dollar standard. But domestic money supplies were no longer linked to forex reserves, so the adjustment mechanism of the gold standard was weakened.

- The **purchasing power parity** path of the nominal exchange rate is the path that maintains constant competitiveness by offsetting differential inflation across countries. In the long run, floating exchange rates return to the PPP path if no real shocks occur.

- In the short run, the level of **floating exchange rates** is determined largely by speculation. Exchange rates adjust to ensure interest differentials are offset by expected exchange rate changes. This chokes off large speculative flows. In the short run, exchange rates can depart significantly from their long-run level.

- Unlike fixed exchange rates, floating exchange rates can cope with permanent differences in national inflation rates. High-inflation countries have a depreciating exchange rate in the long run. In practice, floating exchange rates also coped with the severe real shocks of the 1970s. Floating exchange rate regimes are more robust than fixed exchange rate regimes.

- Critics of **floating exchange rates** claim they are **volatile** in the short run, which discourages international trade and investment. However, they are volatile because the world is uncertain. Under fixed exchange rates the uncertainty would show up somewhere else, possibly in volatile domestic interest rates to maintain the fixed exchange rate.

- Fixed exchange rates impose **financial discipline** by preventing a country having permanently higher inflation than the rest of the world. However, there are other ways to commit to low inflation. And fixed exchange rates do not always survive!

- **International policy co-ordination** is hard to implement but allows policy makers to take account of the externalities they impose on each other. It may allow individual governments to commit themselves to policies that would otherwise not be credible.

- The UK was always a member of the **European Monetary System** but belonged to its key feature, the **Exchange Rate Mechanism**, only during 1990–92. The early survival of the ERM arose only partly from greater co-ordination of monetary policy by ERM participants. Foreign exchange controls and exchange rate bands were also important. After 1983 devaluations became harder to obtain and monetary policies had to converge on the low inflation rate in Germany.

Review questions

To check your answers to these questions, go to page 736.

1 During the First World War the gold standard was suspended. To pay for the war, Britain printed money and sold off its foreign assets. What do you think happened in 1925 when Britain tried to rejoin the gold standard at the old nominal exchange rate?

2 Contrast the dollar standard and the gold standard in terms of (a) the automatic adjustment mechanism and (b) financial discipline.

3 What are the advantages and disadvantages of a currency board?

4 If floating is so great, why did most EU countries join a monetary union in 1999?

5 When the UK left the ERM in 1992, the UK stock market and the UK bond market reacted very differently. Which market rose strongly? What was worrying the other market?

6 **Common fallacies** Why are these statements wrong? (a) Floating exchange rates make sure that exports and imports always balance. (b) Fixed exchange rate regimes prevent necessary changes in competitiveness.

7 **Harder question** You are Finance Minister of Cuba in the new government that has decided to abandon five decades of communism and move as rapidly as possible to a free market. (a) Should Cuban citizens expect rising or falling incomes in the long run? (b) If they implement lifecycle or permanent income approaches to consumption, will they wish to borrow or to lend during this transition? (c) What do you expect to happen to Cuba's international trade balance?

8 **Harder question** (a) From now on, will Cuba offer unusually good or unusually bad investment opportunities? (b) What will happen if Cuba pursues a fixed exchange rate policy during this period? (c) What will happen if Cuba follows a floating exchange rate policy? (d) Which of the two would you recommend?

9 **Essay question** 'Small open economies need fixed exchange rates, large economies need floating exchange rates.' Is this broad generalization correct? Explain why or why not.

To help you grasp the key concepts of this chapter check out the extra resources posted on the Online Learning Centre. There are chapter summaries, self-test questions, an interactive graphing tool, weblinks and a searchable glossary, all for free!

To put your learning into practice and prepare for exams, an **Interactive Workbook** is also available online, containing a variety of question types and providing feedback on your answers.

If you'd like further help with economics, or have any questions, **NetTutor** is here to help! You will have a personalised tutorial service at your fingertips. Visit the online learning centre at: www.mcgraw-hill.co.uk/textbooks/begg for information on accessing all of these resources.

CHAPTER 35

European integration

Learning Outcomes

By the end of this chapter, you should understand:

1 the EU Single Market

2 why many EU countries formed a monetary union

3 macroeconomics in the eurozone

4 UK reluctance to join

5 progress of transition in Central and Eastern Europe

The European economy of 2007 was very different from the Europe of 50 years earlier. Some developments were political, but many were economic. The economics you have learned in this book helps make sense of them. We now analyse the forces at work, and set out a checklist of what to watch for as the future unfolds.

This chapter is about three things. First, the Single European Act of 1986 committed members of the EC to a single market in goods, services, assets and people by 1992. Did it work? Second, economic and monetary union (EMU) began in January 1999. Why did EMU happen, how does it work and what difference will it make? Third, how is transition progressing in Central and Eastern Europe as these former communist economies prepare for EU entry as market economies.

35.1 The Single Market

The European Community was founded in 1957. It was a free-trade area, with some EC-wide programmes financed by (small) fiscal contributions from member states. Its largest programmes were the Common Agricultural Policy (CAP), a system of administered high prices for agricultural commodities that created excess supply and led to wine lakes and butter mountains; and the Structural Funds, providing subsidies for social infrastructure, especially in poorer areas of the EC.

Over the next 50 years, the EC was enlarged. The original six – West Germany, France, Italy, Netherlands, Belgium and Luxembourg – were joined by Denmark, Ireland and the UK in the 1970s, by Spain, Portugal and Greece in the 1980s, and by Austria, Finland and Sweden in the 1990s. The European Community (EC) became the European Union (EU). In 2004, the EU admitted the Baltic republics (Estonia, Latvia, Lithuania), the countries of Central Europe (Hungary, Poland, Czech Republic, Slovakia, Slovenia) and the Mediterranean islands of Malta and the Greek part of Cyprus. Bulgaria and Romania were admitted in 2007.

EU enlargement was not initially accompanied by any change in its fundamental structure. Member states still set national policies. Closer integration, for example the harmonization of industrial standards or national tax rates, was usually thwarted for two reasons. First, since each country did things differently, it was hard to find a single set of regulations for all member states. Second, it was political dynamite. No country wanted to adopt the policies of others.

The mid-1980s saw a breakthrough. Instead of trying to agree a single set of detailed rules, member states agreed some broad outlines for harmonizing policy. Each country then decided how to implement them. And each country recognized the validity of the regulations imposed by other member states.

For example, each country has regulations determining which institutions may register as a bank or an insurance company, and what conditions they must fulfil. Previously, a bank registered in the UK under UK law did not comply with standards laid down for banks in France, Germany or Italy. Banks in one country could not compete in other countries. National markets were segmented. Since there are economies of scale in banking, each small national market had only a few high-cost banks enjoying significant market power.

Instead, member states agreed on some general principles governing the regulation of banks – minimum standards for capital adequacy (the amount of financial backing needed to undertake particular types of risky business), for external monitoring (to check up that managers are doing their job properly), and so on. Then each government decided how to apply these general criteria and to license banks in its country. Finally, and crucially, a bank registered in Germany under German law was allowed to operate throughout the EU.

This approach had two advantages. First, it was politically acceptable. Individual governments no longer looked like they were giving up all national control. Second, it took advantage of competition. Different countries adopted different ways of implementing general principles *and then the market decided*.

Countries adopting good regulatory structures found their firms getting a bigger share of EU trade. Countries with poor systems (which might have too much regulation but might have too little: business hates anarchy, legal ambiguity and possible fraud) lost business. Thus, *competition between forms of regulation* took place.

The new approach broke the logjam. The EC ratified the Single European Act, setting 1992 as the deadline to complete the internal EU market by harmonizing regulations. Among its main objectives were: (a) abolition of remaining controls on capital flows; (b) removal of all non-tariff barriers to trade in the EU (different trademarks, patent laws and safety standards); (c) ending the bias in public sector purchasing to favour domestic producers; (d) removal of frontier controls (delays); and (e) progress in harmonizing tax rates.

35.2 Benefits of the Single Market

Table 35.1 shows that the completion of the Single Market created an economic area larger than the US or Japan, even before the accession of countries from Central and Eastern Europe. The potential gains for member states fall into three categories: more efficient resource allocation, more scale economies and more competition.

In Chapter 33 we explained how trade allows each country to specialize in the commodities that it makes *relatively* cheaply, thereby raising joint output. Although the EC was always a free-trade zone with no internal tariffs, until 1992 non-tariff barriers segmented national markets.

> A **single market** is not segmented by national regulations, taxes or informal practices.

> **Non-tariff barriers** are different national regulations or practices that prevent free movement of goods, services and factors across countries.

Table 35.1 The size of the Single Market, 2003

	EU	USA	Japan
Population (million)	376	282	127
GDP ($ billion)	8367	9817	4860

Source: World Bank, *World Development Report.*

By removing non-tariff barriers, the Single Market aimed to allow countries to exploit their comparative advantage more fully.

A second inefficiency in small and segmented national markets is that firms cannot fully exploit economies of scale. As barriers came down, firms got larger and costs fell. Two-way trade in the same industry increased, not just in goods but in services such as banking.

Third, the Single Market intensified competition in two ways. First, competition between forms of regulation led on average to lower levels of regulation. For many continental countries, the Single Market led to substantial deregulation from initial levels that had been very high. Second, a larger market enabled large firms to enjoy scale economies *without* the high market share and potential monopoly power that this would have meant in small, segmented economies.

Quantifying the gains

How large were the gains in practice? In 2002, the European Commission estimated that during 1992–2002 the first decade of the Single Market had raised members' GDP by 1.8 per cent above what it otherwise would have been (a gain of €5700 per household, which is quite substantial), and had also raised employment by 1.46 per cent.

Activity box 35 2007 Review of the Single Market

In January 2007 the DTI, together with HM Treasury, issued a report 'The Single Market: A vision for the 21st century', outlining the challenges that the Single Market faces – globalization, climate change, demographic change – and the principles needed to ensure that it continues to deliver for Europe's consumers and businesses.

The free movement of goods, persons, services and capital is a fundamental principle of the European Union. It is these four freedoms as set out in the EC Treaty which form the basis of the Single Market. The government believes that the Single European Market benefits the economy of each member state, and that the removal of trade barriers leads to a reduction in business costs as well as increasing competition and stimulating efficiency, benefiting consumers and encouraging the creation of jobs and wealth.

Benefits of the Single Market

The Single Market is a **wider market** for UK goods comprising nearly 380 million consumers and making up almost 40 per cent of world trade. Such a huge market gives consumers greater choice.

The greater **competition and liberalization** the Single Market has helped bring about have led to **lower prices**. Take air fares for example: cheap airlines such as easyJet would not have been possible without the Single Market. Airlines can now fly where they want, without national restrictions. BA has become the second largest domestic airline in France.

The Single Market provides for better **consumer protection**; for example, the Toy Directive means that all toys sold in the EU must be safe for children. Another example is the Fourth Motor Insurance Directive on which political agreement was reached by member states in December 1998. This Directive will make it easier for those involved in motor accidents in other member states to make an insurance claim when returning to their state of residence.

The Single Market principle of mutual recognition of standards means British manufacturers can sell their products all over Europe without expensive re-testing in every country. For business there has been a significant reduction in export bureaucracy. The Single Market is in effect a domestic market for European business.

UK citizens have the **right to work, study or retire** in all the other member states – there are around three-quarters of a million Britons living in other countries.

Questions

(a) How much do you think the ability of the UK to enjoy the benefits of the Single Market is affected by the fact that the UK has not adopted the euro? Name two channels through which the UK economy might be slightly quarantined by having a separate currency.

(b) What do you think are the principal benefits of belonging to a larger market?

(c) Who are the main losers in the UK from UK membership of the Single Market?

(d) Is it possible to have a single market without integration inexorably proceeding first to a single currency, then a single fiscal and regulatory policy, and finally a single government?

To check your answers to these questions, go to page 737.

In general, small countries gained more than large countries, but gains also reflected the pattern of trade. The largest gains came as the most protected activities were opened up. Not only was the Single Market good for the EU, it also boosted trade with the outside world. Fears of fortress Europe were unfounded.

35.3 From EMS to EMU

By 1988, capital controls were largely gone as part of the Single Market reforms. It was only a matter of time before speculators attacked the pegged exchange rates of the Exchange Rate Mechanism that was then in place. One solution was to go forward rapidly to completely fixed exchange rates.

A monetary union need not have a single currency. English and Scottish currencies circulate side by side in Edinburgh. What matters is that the exchange rate is certain and that a single authority (the Bank of England) sets the interest rate for both.

> A **monetary union** has permanently fixed exchange rates within the union, an integrated financial market and a single central bank setting the single interest rate for the union.

In 1988, the European heads of state established the Delors Committee to recommend how to get to European monetary union. Interestingly, the Committee was not asked to discuss whether EMU was a good idea. Small, highly integrated European economies needed to avoid large exchange rate fluctuations. With capital controls gone, there was no guarantee that the ERM could deliver. In any case, since ERM members had already given up monetary sovereignty by letting Germany set the single interest rate in the ERM, formal ratification of a monetary union did not seem such a big step.

The Delors Committee recommendations became the basis of the Treaty of Maastricht in 1991. Monetary union was to be achieved in three stages. In Stage 1, which began in 1990, any remaining capital controls were abolished, and the UK was encouraged to join the ERM (it joined in 1990). Realignments were possible but discouraged. In Stage 2, which began in January 1994, a new European Monetary Institute prepared the ground for EMU, realignments were even harder to obtain and excessive budget deficits were to be discouraged but not outlawed.

Stage 3, in which exchange rates were irreversibly fixed and the single monetary policy began, was to start in 1997 if a majority of potential entrants fulfilled the 'Maastricht criteria' (in the event they did not). Otherwise, EMU was to begin in January 1999 with whatever number of countries then met the criteria. Monetary policy in EMU was to be set by an independent central bank, mandated to achieve price stability as its principal goal.

What were the Maastricht criteria and what was their purpose? There were two sets of criteria, one for monetary policy and nominal variables, one for fiscal policy.

> The **Maastricht criteria** for joining EMU said that a country must already have achieved low inflation and sound fiscal policy.

The monetary criteria said that, to be eligible, a potential entrant had to have low inflation, low nominal interest rates (market confirmation of low inflation expectations) and two prior years in the ERM without any devaluation. This last requirement was to prevent competitive devaluations or 'last realignments' as EMU approached.

The fiscal criteria said budget deficits must not be excessive, interpreted to mean that budget deficits should be less than 3 per cent of GDP and that the debt/GDP ratio should not be over 60 per cent. Tight fiscal policy would mean there was little pressure on the central bank to print money to bail out fiscal authorities.

Many economists complained that the Maastricht criteria were caution taken to extremes. An independent central bank with a tough constitution was an adequate commitment to low inflation. It was unnecessary to constrain fiscal policy as well. Indeed, since national governments would no longer have a national interest rate or national exchange rate policy to deal with purely national circumstances, leaving them fiscal room for manoeuvre might be a good idea.

The Maastricht deal reflected the balance of power in the negotiations. At the time, Germany ran the EMS and trusted itself to do so in its own interests. Why would Germany give up such a good position? Only if EMU was going to be super safe. The Maastricht criteria were the price of getting Germany on board.

Sterling and UK membership

Why was the UK reluctant to join both the ERM and EMU? First, until the late 1980s, North Sea oil made sterling behave differently from other European currencies. As UK oil production slowed down, this objection evaporated.

Second, whereas the core countries of Europe are now very integrated with one another, offshore UK is less integrated with the rest of Europe. A common policy may be less suitable. Table 35.2 shows the composition of UK trade and how it has changed since the UK joined the EU in 1973. The trend is clear. The UK is getting more integrated with continental Europe all the time, even if from a lower baseline than some other European countries. If this trend continues, the issue is eventually not whether the UK should join but when.

Table 35.2 UK trade patterns (%)

	EU	North America	Rest of world
1970	34	17	49
2002	60	12	28

Sources: UN, *International Trade Statistics*; www.statistics.gov.uk.

Third, the UK has greater macroeconomic sovereignty: it seems to have more to lose. Whereas ERM countries had already allowed the 'single' interest rate to be set by Germany alone, sterling floated during the entire period except for the two years of its ERM membership in 1990–92.

However, the absence of capital controls and the power of the speculators limit monetary sovereignty whatever the exchange rate regime. The Bank of England has often wished to raise interest rates for domestic reasons, to cool down a housing boom, but been unprepared to do so because higher interest rates would bid up further the value of the floating pound, exacerbating the woes of UK exporters. The Bank has often found itself hoping for interest rate rises in Frankfurt and Washington that would allow it to raise sterling interest rates without causing a further appreciation of sterling.

Finally, Black Wednesday (16 September 1992) made it hard for UK politicians to enthuse about EMU. While Chancellor, John Major took the UK into the ERM in 1990 to combat rising inflation at the end of the Lawson boom. Unfortunately, this coincided with German reunification. Big subsidies to East Germany caused German overheating. When Chancellor Kohl refused to raise taxes, the Bundesbank raised interest rates to cool down the German economy. Interest rates high enough to do this job were far too high for Germany's partners in the ERM. This provoked the crisis of 1992–93. The UK and Italy left the ERM, slashed interest rates and depreciated their currencies. Other countries struggled on inside the ERM though many had devaluations (see Chapter 34).

German reunification was the biggest country-specific economic shock in postwar Europe. It may not be a good guide to how EMU will fare. Indeed, the mandate of the European Central Bank to take an EU-wide view prevents it reacting in such extreme fashion to the needs of one country. But UK voters remember the UK flirtation with a single European interest rate as an unhappy experience.

During 1996–98 EU countries scrambled frantically to get their budget deficits below the 3 per cent Maastricht limit to be eligible for EMU. There was fiscal tightening in continental Europe. Since the UK was enjoying the effects of looser policy after 1992 – the whole point of leaving the ERM had been to reduce interest rates and stimulate the economy – the UK business cycle got out of phase with the rest of Europe.

This had little to do with any structural difference. It simply reflected the fact that while the UK had its foot on the accelerator its EU partners still had the brakes on tight. By the end of the decade, the UK was worrying about overheating at a time when the rest of the EU was finally coming out of its policy-induced recession and looking forward to a period of steady growth. Eleven countries (all those wishing to go ahead) were deemed in spring of 1998 to be fit and ready for EMU at the start of 1999. Table 35.3 contrasts the healthy UK performance with the more sluggish performance of the eurozone.

Consistently superior UK performance cannot be attributed to the initial need of eurozone countries to restrain demand – the more time elapses, the less this still accounts for ongoing behaviour. Nor can it simply be attributed to the generally excellent performance of the Bank of England in stabilizing inflation and maintaining output close to potential output. The longer superior UK performance is sustained, the more one has to seek the explanation in better supply-side policies that allowed potential output to grow more quickly. Over the 12-year period, all three explanations probably played a role. Whatever the cause, it was politically impossible for a UK Chancellor to endorse entry to a club that was underperforming the UK itself.

Table 35.3 Real GDP growth rates (average % per annum)

	1996–99	2000–03	2004–07
Eurozone	2.4	1.6	2.2
UK	3.0	2.7	2.7

Source: UN, *International Trade Statistics.*

35.4 The economics of EMU

In 1999, Professor Robert Mundell won the Nobel Prize for economics, in part for his pioneering work on optimal currency areas.

> An **optimal currency area** is a group of countries better off with a common currency than keeping separate national currencies.

Mundell, and the economists who came after him, identified three attributes that might make countries suitable for a currency area. First, countries that trade a lot with each other may have little ability to affect their equilibrium real exchange rate against their partners in the long run, but they may face temptations to devalue to gain a temporary advantage. A fixed exchange rate rules out such behaviour and allows gains from trade to be enjoyed.

Second, the more similar the economic and industrial structure of potential partners, the more likely it is they face common shocks, which can be dealt with by a common monetary policy. It is country-specific shocks that pose difficulties for a single monetary policy.

Third, the more flexible are the labour markets within the currency area, the more easily any necessary changes in competitiveness and real exchange rates can be accomplished by (different) changes in the price level in different member countries.

Conversely, countries gain most by keeping their monetary sovereignty when they are not that integrated with potential partners, have a different structure, and hence are likely to face different shocks, and cannot rely on domestic wage and price flexibility as a substitute for exchange rate changes.

To these purely economic arguments, we should add an important political argument. Currency areas are more likely to work when countries within the area are prepared to make at least some fiscal transfers to partner countries. In practice, this cultural and political identity may be at least as important as any narrow economic criteria for success.

Is Europe an optimal currency area?

Those who have studied the structure of national economies, and the correlation of shocks across countries, generally reach the following conclusions. First, Europe is quite, but not very, integrated. Second, there is a clear inner core of countries – the usual suspects – more closely integrated than the rest.

However, the act of joining EMU is likely to change the degree of integration, possibly quite substantially. A common currency, by eliminating a source of segmentation into national markets, will increase integration. Moreover, there is evidence that countries that trade a lot have more correlated business cycles. And countries which belong to currency unions tend historically to trade much more with each other than can be explained simply by the fact that their exchange rates are fixed.

These bits of evidence imply that it may be possible to start a currency union before the microeconomic preconditions are fully in place. The act of starting speeds up the process.

The Stability Pact

The Stability Pact, ratified by the Treaty of Amsterdam in 1997, confirmed that the Maastricht fiscal criteria would not merely be entry conditions for EMU but would continue to apply after countries joined the monetary union. Some EMU members have debt/GDP ratios of close to 100 per cent. Reducing these towards 60 per cent may take decades. The focus has been on the 3 per cent ceiling for budget deficits.

In principle, countries exceeding the limit may have to pay fines unless their economy is in evident recession. Thus countries have to wait for output to fall before they are allowed to expand fiscal policy by having deficits above the ceiling of 3 per cent of GDP.

The pact does not preclude countries from using fiscal policies more vigorously. But to do so, they need to aim for something more like budget balance in normal times. Then they still have room to increase deficits in times of trouble without exceeding the 3 per cent ceiling.

Note that if budgets are roughly in balance over the business cycle, but output grows for ever, debt/GDP ratios should exhibit trend decline, whatever their cyclical behaviour. This may eventually lead to the tough conditions of the Stability Pact being eased.

The European Central Bank

The single monetary policy is now set in Frankfurt by the European Central Bank (ECB). National central banks have not been abolished, but the board of the ECB sets the interest rate on the euro.

The ECB mandate says its first duty is to ensure price stability, but it can take other aims into account provided price stability is not in doubt. In press conferences, officials of the ECB have emphasized that their interest rate decisions should be interpreted largely as the pursuit of price stability. Neither the financial markets nor academic economists are entirely convinced. ECB behaviour looks as if they pay some attention to output gaps as well as inflation: empirically, a Taylor rule explains their behaviour quite well.

Controversially, the ECB has adopted not one but two intermediate targets, the so-called 'twin pillars' of their monetary strategy. The first pillar is a monetary target, the growth rate of the M3 measure of nominal money. The second pillar is expected inflation. The ECB insists that it takes both pillars into account in setting interest rates in the euro area.

Figure 35.1 shows the interest rate decisions of the ECB, the evolution of inflation and the rate of nominal money growth. It is easy to see how the rise and fall of actual and expected inflation led to the rise and fall of interest rates in the euro area. It is very hard to detect any role for nominal money growth.

Far from raising interest rates when money growth is too high, the ECB has raised interest rates when money growth is low, but reduced interest rates when money growth is high. The reason is straightforward. Money demand fluctuates, and money supply growth is not a reliable guide to future inflation.

For example, after the terrorist attacks of 11 September 2001, people sold stocks and shares and put money into bank accounts. These accounts were part of the M3 measure of money. The sharp rise in the money stock reflected a rise in money demand. Money supply could safely be allowed to increase since people wanted to hold the extra money not spend it. In fact, the fall in aggregate demand for goods after 11 September meant that all central banks sensibly cut interest rates to boost aggregate demand. Figure 35.1 confirms that interest rates fell *despite* the rise in the nominal money stock.

It is precisely such swings in money demand that have made most central banks abandon monetary targeting in favour of flexible inflation targets or Taylor rules. The ECB continues to insist that monetary targets have an important role because it wants to emphasize continuity with the Bundesbank, which used monetary targets. However, as the ECB establishes it own track record, the need for links to past Bundesbank behaviour becomes less important. If the ECB is to avoid looking stupid, it may have to abandon the monetary pillar, which it has already begun to emphasize less.

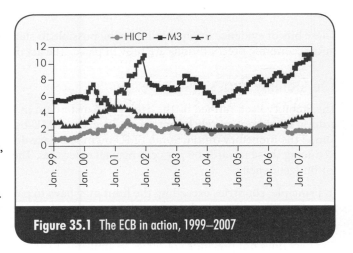

Figure 35.1 The ECB in action, 1999–2007

Fiscal federalism?

One reason for the survival of the monetary union that we call the United States is its federal fiscal structure. When a particular state has a slump, it pays less income tax revenue to Washington and gets more social security money from Washington, without any decisions having to be taken. Automatic stabilizers are at work, courtesy of federal tax rates and federal rates of social security payments. Conversely, a booming state pays more tax revenue to Washington and gets less social security money back.

When state income rises $1, the state pays an extra 30 cents in income tax and gets 10 cents less in social security. Conversely, when state income falls $1, the state pays 30 cents less in federal taxes and gets an extra 10 cents in social security. Originally, economists thought that this meant each state was effectively insured up to about 40 cents in the dollar. The euro area has no federal fiscal structure on anything like this scale. The pessimists concluded that EMU would come under pressure from country-specific shocks.

> A **federal fiscal system** has a central government setting taxes and expenditure rules that apply in its constituent states or countries.

The idea was correct but the sums were wrong. The original US calculations are relevant to a world in which state incomes are uncorrelated with each other. In practice, the correlation is quite high.

Hence, when one state slumps and gets help from Washington, many other states are slumping and also getting help. But this increases US government debt and means *every* state has to pay higher future taxes.

But an individual state could have done that on its own, without membership of the federal 'mutual insurance' club. It could have borrowed in the slump to boost its own fiscal spending, and paid it back later when times were better. Making allowance for this, US states are probably insured nearer to 10 cents in the dollar than 40 cents.

However, the Stability Pact may *prevent* individual EMU countries behaving in this way, by restricting their ability to borrow in bad times. Or else the Stability Pact may be interpreted more flexibly, having greater regard for the effect of temporary cycles in temporarily reducing tax revenue. When Germany's budget deficit rose at the start of 2002, taking it close to the 3 per cent ceiling, EU leaders agreed not to give Germany a yellow card warning it that fiscal tightening was now imperative.

Macroeconomic policy in an EMU member

Figure 35.2 shows what life is like for an EMU member. Interest rates are set by the ECB in Frankfurt. From an individual country's viewpoint, it is as if the LM curve is horizontal at r_0. Suppose the initial level of the IS curve allows equilibrium at A. Aggregate demand equals potential output.

Now the country faces a shock that shifts the IS curve down to IS_1. With full monetary sovereignty, the country might have cut its interest rate to restore full employment output at C. This might still happen in EMU if the country is highly correlated with other EMU countries. The ECB will react to what is happening throughout Euroland and cut interest rates for everybody.

However, if no other countries face the IS curve shock and the country is too small to influence Euroland data to which the ECB reacts, interest rates will remain at r_0. The country now faces two choices. Provided it does not infringe the Stability Pact, it can use fiscal policy to shift IS_1 to the right or it can wait for its labour market to do the same thing.

How does this work? At B the country is facing a slump. This gradually reduces inflation. At the fixed nominal exchange rate against its partners, this makes the country more competitive. Higher exports and lower imports shift the IS_1 curve to the right. If wage and price flexibility is high enough, there may be no need for fiscal policy. However, many European labour markets are quite sluggish. Sensible use of fiscal policy may speed up the process.

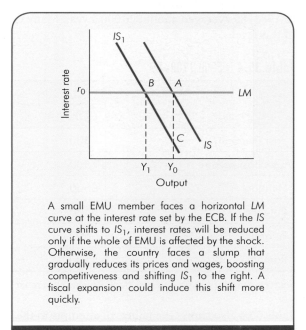

A small EMU member faces a horizontal LM curve at the interest rate set by the ECB. If the IS curve shifts to IS_1, interest rates will be reduced only if the whole of EMU is affected by the shock. Otherwise, the country faces a slump that gradually reduces its prices and wages, boosting competitiveness and shifting IS_1 to the right. A fiscal expansion could induce this shift more quickly.

Figure 35.2 A member of Euroland

One final point. If there is no discretionary change in tax rates and spending levels, fiscal relaxation in a recession is limited to the automatic stabilizers. However, these cannot see into the future. Only after income falls is revenue from income tax reduced. In 2001 Europe was hit by two demand shocks: the US recession as the dotcom bubble burst and the confidence collapse after 11 September.

Because the real economy is sluggish, it took time for these to feed through into lower output, lower employment and lower inflation. But by 12 September everyone knew these were coming. Ideally, demand policies should have been eased to offset these demand shocks. If fiscal policy is largely confined to backward-looking automatic stabilizers, the only channel for a forward-looking policy response is through interest rate cuts.

Hence, the fiscal framework in EMU raises the burden on monetary policy to react to shocks even before they have fed fully through into output and inflation.

35.5 Central and Eastern Europe

For 40 years after 1945, Central and Eastern Europe (CEE) was under rigid political and economic control from Moscow, a planned economy with only a small role for market forces. The inefficiency of planning cumulated as any market history receded. Capital was old, incentives were poor and productivity was low.

Table 35.4 confirms two points about CEE on the eve of reform. It shows the low level of living standards compared with most Western neighbours. In affluent Northern Europe, per capita incomes in 1988–89 averaged about $20 000 a year. Many CEE countries had living standards around a quarter of this level.

Table 35.4 CEE in 1988–89

	Per capita $ of	
	GDP	Foreign debt
East Germany	9300	1300
Czechoslovakia	7600	400
Hungary	6500	1900
Bulgaria	5600	1000
Poland	5600	1100
Romania	4100	0

Sources: American Express, *Amex Bank Review*, November 1989; HM Treasury, *Economic Progress Report*, 1990.

Table 35.4 also shows the failure of attempts in the 1970s to prop up planning by borrowing from the West to rebuild capital in the East. Countries such as Hungary and Poland were left with the debts but few corresponding assets: inefficiencies in planning often left investment projects unfinished and hence wasted.

Some countries, such as Poland, subsequently had part of these past debts written off by Western creditors. And the European Bank for Reconstruction and Development was set up in London to finance investment by the West in projects in the reforming economies.

Supply-side reforms

In the past, production, investment and employment decisions were made largely by planners. A larger scale of operation meant greater prestige, even if it used more inputs than it produced outputs. Supply-side reform meant allowing the price mechanism to take over the role of allocating resources. This had several aspects.

Transition economies are making the adjustment from central planning to a market economy.

> ## Box 35.2 EU accession brings burdens as well as opportunities
>
> For a decade and a half already, western companies have been exploiting the EU newcomers' proximity and cheap labour to establish low-cost manufacturing plants. Joining the Union will bring the new members a few more benefits – and some headaches.
>
> (*The Economist*, 30 April 2004)
>
> The new EU members, particularly from Eastern Europe, have benefited from $110 billion of foreign direct investment since 1989. In the main, this has come in the form of assembly plants for manufactured goods sold back into the EU. The car industry has created a significant presence in countries such as Poland, Romania and Slovakia. In the first instance, manufacturers such as Peugeot and Volkswagen were attracted by cheap labour rates, attractively set at around 10 per cent to 15 per cent of EU average wage rates. Many companies have come to recognize the high levels of education and skills within Eastern Europe: high value-added vehicles, by manufacturers such as Audi, are now being built in Eastern Europe.
>
> However, membership of the EU is bringing new problems for the transitional economies. New EU members may face pressure to raise corporate tax rates to levels of Western Europe, pressure to adopt existing EU regulations of health and safety, on a maximum working week, and other measures that effectively increase costs in the new member states.

First, prices needed to reflect true scarcity. Previously, prices were held artificially low. This made inflation look good, but such data were meaningless. Consumers could not get goods and factories could not buy inputs at these artificial prices. There was chronic excess demand.

Freeing-up prices meant that prices rose sharply.

But this was a one-off phenomenon. And it was precisely these high prices that were the market mechanism telling suppliers it was now time to increase production.

Success did not depend merely on freeing-up prices. A supply response to higher prices had to take place. Incentives had to work. Bureaucrats who ran state enterprises were not always the best people to rise to this challenge. Many enterprises have since been privatized. The aim of privatization was less the need to raise revenue for the government – consumers had little wealth with which to pay – than to put the profit motive up front for those managing the new enterprises.

Several strategies of privatization were tried. Hungary tried to find foreign buyers willing to contribute hard cash and management expertise. The Czech Republic gave citizens vouchers with which to bid for shares in firms being privatized. Although appearing to achieve rapid privatization, many of these shares were then sold back to state-owned banks. In Russia, the emphasis on privatization to existing managers led to accusations that organized crime had become too involved.

Trade and foreign investment

CEE needed markets for its output if it was to grow quickly. The pressure of external competition was a powerful force for rapid productivity improvement, even if it meant unemployment in the short run while painful adjustment took place.

The EU was the obvious market for CEE goods. Most CEE countries have now signed Europe Agreements for the associate membership of the EU. These agreements promised rapid moves to free trade in many commodities, but not in the ones that really mattered. Declining or problem industries in the West were deemed too sensitive to be subject to competition from cheap imports from CEE. This applied to textiles, steel and, of course, agriculture – three of the most obvious areas for CEE exports westwards.

EU policy was excessively protectionist. Accepting imports from CEE has three big benefits for the EU. First, EU consumers get cheap imports. Second, there is the consequent creation of economic growth in CEE as a natural export market for EU producers. Together, these two reasons are the classic case for exploiting comparative advantage. Third, if the experiment in CEE fails, the EU will face either massive immigration or a renewed political and military threat on its doorstep, probably both. Liberal trade agreements are the most effective investment the EU can make in Eastern Europe's success.

CEE has an educated workforce. Besides market access, what it needs is physical investment and the management expertise to run market-oriented businesses. Here too the West can help, and in some cases has done so with success. For example, Western investment in car plants in CEE has been extensive. Under VW ownership, Skoda has gone from ugly duckling to preening swan.

Macroeconomic conditions for success

Transition is about supply-side reform to improve potential output, but macroeconomic policy must not get in the way. Prudent monetary and fiscal policies are needed to bring inflation under control. Early in transition, inflation is high for two reasons. First, as prices are unfrozen, they surge to their equilibrium level.

Second, needing resources to invest in transition but with low potential output and hence a low tax base, it is sensible to use the inflation tax as a source of government revenue. Otherwise, needed investment has to be abandoned or else other taxes have to be so high that their distortionary effects are large.

As transition succeeds, potential output rises, and given tax rates raise more revenue. Investment also begins to encounter diminishing returns. For both reasons, the optimal inflation rate should fall. However, politicians still face many pressures to spend money and avoid taxation. Well-designed institutions help politicians to do the right thing.

Thus central bank independence has been as important in transition economies as in advanced economies. It helps ensure a responsible monetary policy. Earlier in the chapter, we noted that an independent ECB was insufficient to induce Germany to abandon the ERM for EMU. The Maastricht criteria and the Stability Pact also restrict the size of fiscal deficits, so that the central bank, even if independent, does not come under pressure to print money.

If this was true for mature Western Europe, it was even more likely to apply in transition. Monetary responsibility must be underpinned by pressure to avoid large fiscal deficits. Initially, this pressure was applied by the IMF. If countries wanted to access loans from the IMF, they had to agree and implement targets for fiscal deficits.

And of course full EU accession was the prize that kept everything on track – the clear objectives of joining the Single Market and the single currency gave CEE policy makers a clear compass reading by which to steer. Many of the CEE economies were able to join the EU in 2004, and Bulgaria and Romania followed in 2007.

If planning was so bad, why did things initially get worse?

Box 35.3 shows that the reforming economies faced falls of at least 25 per cent in measured real GDP during 1990–92 before growth resumed in 1993 or 1994. How can we explain this?

Box 35.3 CEE transition: a progress report

Countries abandoned central planning because it was not working and their economies were stagnating. The table below shows inflation and real output growth after nearly two decades of transition. What is remarkable is the similarity across countries.

During 1991–93, most countries faced huge inflation rates and suffered severe falls in output. But then the corner was turned, inflation fell rapidly and most countries have now enjoyed ten years of sustained economic growth at rates that Western Europe would envy. As monetary credibility has gradually been established, it has generally been possible to combine this with low rates of inflation.

	Annual inflation (%)				Annual real GDP growth (%)		
	91–93	94–96	97–98	99–07	91–93	94–97	98–07
Central Europe							
Czech Republic	29	10	9	3	−4.1	3.0	3.9
Hungary	27	23	16	6	−5.3	2.8	3.3
Poland	47	27	14	3	−3.4	7.8	4.4
Slovakia	27	10	7	6	−8.1	8.0	5.0
Slovenia	121	12	8	5	−3.9	4.3	3.9
S.E. Europe							
Albania	115	15	27	4	−14.8	7.7	5.3
Bulgaria	160	120	294	6	−6.8	−3.5	5.1
Croatia	777	11	5	3	−13.4	6.4	4.8
FYR Macedonia	760	22	2	3	−8.0	2.2	3.0
Romania	240	50	107	15	−4.0	2.2	5.5
Baltics							
Estonia	334	32	10	3	−12.0	4.5	7.0
Latvia	420	23	6	4	−15.0	2.9	7.7
Lithuania	561	32	7	2	−14.5	1.5	7.7

Source: EBRD Transition Report.

First, the statistics may be misleading. Before prices were freed, how should real GDP have been measured? If prices did not reflect scarcity, why value quantities at silly prices? One solution to this is to use *world prices*: simply measure quantities and then use dollar prices. Economists who have done this find that some of the old industries were producing with *negative* value added: they used more inputs than they produced output. Properly measured, output fell less than it first appears.

Second, early macroeconomic restraint was important to stop once-off price rises becoming embedded in permanent inflation expectations. For example, after price liberalization in Czechoslovakia, prices rose 25 per cent in January 1991; by July 1991, monthly inflation was down to zero.

Third, as the former Soviet Union imploded, most countries in CEE lost their major export market. Reorientation of exports to the West was not easily accomplished overnight. Even in Western Europe, Finland faced a severe recession as Russian markets collapsed.

Fourth, the key role of banks must be understood. Freeing prices does not introduce a market economy unless budget constraints bite. In the West, useless firms go bankrupt and physical resources get allocated elsewhere. In Eastern Europe, state banks had previously been passive in lending. They made loans to allow state-owned enterprises (SOEs) to meet output and investment targets laid down by the planners.

When prices were liberalized, many SOEs quickly lost money (as they should have). But nobody closed them down! State banks simply lent them new money to meet old debts and finance ongoing losses. When a giant SOE was the only employer in town, it was 'too big to fail'. Banks behaved in this way partly because they too were state-owned and still felt a responsibility to employment, but also because most of their assets – old loans to SOEs – were themselves worthless. Making a fuss might have revealed the extent of the trouble in the banks.

Governments, wisely, began tackling bad debts in the banks, and made banks early candidates for privatization. Without banks to enforce bankruptcy (in the West it is creditors who close down companies), we cannot expect prices to allocate resources more efficiently. Inefficient old firms continue and new entrepreneurs find it hard to get loans.

Finally, there was a major failure of corporate control. Even the West has trouble providing good incentives for managers (see Chapter 6). In reforming economies the problem was acute. The watchful eye of the state was removed from SOEs as governments tried to dissociate themselves from the old ways of planning. Until SOEs were privatized and monitored by informed shareholders, there was a vacuum of control. Managers could do what they liked. What they liked was an easy life or worse. Many countries faced outbreaks of 'spontaneous privatization'. In the West we call it theft.

The transition experience reminds us that adoption of markets, while perhaps necessary, is not sufficient to enjoy high living standards. Well-functioning markets, like icebergs, have a lot below the waterline: invisible but important. They have legal contracts whose impartial enforcement in courts of law has a track record that inspires confidence and trust. They have regulations mitigating market power, administered by public officials without endemic corruption. They have tax collection agencies that are fair, and an attitude of tax compliance among citizens that keeps tax evasion within tolerable bounds. They have sophisticated systems of social insurance and protection designed to prevent the emergence of an underclass that loses hope then takes revenge.

The list could be longer. Merely setting it out shows that many of its key items require expensive infrastructure and necessarily take time in which to build trust and reputation. This had two implications. First, transition takes time to succeed, especially where the social fabric is under threat. Second, establishing markets is not done on the cheap. Essential market infrastructure must be installed.

Despite these caveats, Box 35.2 shows that all these economies are now growing steadily. Our discussion of convergence and catch-up in Chapter 30 suggests that these economies may continue to grow more rapidly than Western Europe over the next decade.

EU enlargement

What transition economies in Central and Eastern Europe wanted was membership of the EU itself, which would allow full access to a huge market. This in turn became a magnet for inward investment, seeking to take advantage of low local wages but secure output markets.

Having almost all the power in the negotiations, the EU dictated the timetable of EU enlargement. From the EU viewpoint, accession countries were 'ready' when they could safely be allowed into the Single Market. Principally, this means that the EU trusted regulators in accession countries, that accession countries could cope with competition within the Single Market and that reasonable macroeconomic stability had been established.

On entry to the EU, accession countries were expected to join ERM2, an exchange rate mechanism with fixed but adjustable parities between each accession country and the euro. There are the usual bands around these parities. Accession countries will stay in ERM2 until they meet the Maastricht criteria. Then they will be allowed to adopt the euro.

Thus, different countries may remain within ERM2 for different times until ready to join the euro. The Maastricht criteria require that low inflation has been seen to be achieved, that fiscal deficits are not excessive and that no devaluation takes place in the two years before the euro is adopted. Thus two years is the minimum period of ERM2 membership.

Summary

- The **Single European Act** committed EU governments to a Single Market by 1992. The principles were common, broad outlines for regulation, national implementation, and mutual recognition of firms licensed by other member states.

- For many countries this meant substantial deregulation. Together with enlarged market size, this increased competition.

- The main winners were the small southern countries of the EU, who had relatively cheap labour and scope for scale economies. However, even the large, rich EU countries benefited.

- A **monetary union** means permanently fixed exchange rates, free capital movements and a single interest rate.

- In abolishing capital controls before 1992, the ERM had already harmonized monetary policy, under German leadership. The UK became an ERM member in 1990, but left in 1992.

- The **Maastricht criteria** say that EMU entrants, including future ones, must have shown low inflation, low interest rates and stable nominal exchange rates before entry, and must have budget deficits and government debt under control.

- EMU members must continue to obey the **Stability Pact**, which fines countries for excessive budget deficits, except if they are in recession.

- In EMU, a country's competitiveness can change through the slow process of domestic wage and price adjustment. Without a **federal fiscal system**, individual member states may want to keep control of fiscal policy to deal with crises.

- **Transition economies** in Central and Eastern Europe have begun economic reform. Supply-side reform means introducing the profit motive and deregulation, and allowing the price system to work. Because prices had been artificially low, initially there were sharp rises in prices. Tight macroeconomic policy managed to stop this turning into hyperinflation and to reduce inflation steadily thereafter.

- Output fell sharply in CEE in 1990–92. The Soviet market collapsed, banks were unable to monitor and enforce credit agreements, there was little corporate control and vital infrastructure for a market economy was lacking.

- Most CEE countries resumed growth during 1993–94 and may keep growing rapidly if sensible policies are maintained.

- Most CEE countries are at advanced stages of negotiation for EU entry. They will have to prove they can survive in the Single Market without disrupting existing EU members. They will have to join ERM2 and will be allowed to adopt the euro only after they fulfil the Maastricht criteria.

Review questions

To check your answers to these questions, go to page 736.

1 'Workers have power in the labour market only because their own firms have power in the goods market. In a perfectly competitive firm, attempts to raise wages just drive the firm out of business.' Is this correct? If 1992 increased competition in product markets, what was the effect on EU labour markets?

2 Name three EU countries you think have a comparative advantage in goods that use human capital intensively. Name three countries for which this is not the case.

3 Two countries belong to a monetary union and face a single interest rate on bank deposits. However, one government has large debts and has trouble raising taxes or cutting spending. Will government bonds in the two countries pay the same interest rate? Will there be large capital flows between the countries? Is this a monetary union? If not, why not?

4 The Stability Pact forces EMU members to maintain low budget deficits. What is the rationale for this policy? Why is it needed if the European Central Bank is independent and committed to low inflation.

5 'Transition is just a big investment project with early costs and later benefits. Transition economies should finance the whole cost of transition by foreign borrowing, and pay the subsequent interest once they are rich.' If possible, would transition economies want to do this? Why might creditors not lend this much?

6 **Common fallacies** Why are these statements wrong? (a) The EU was always a free trade zone and must always have had a single market. (b) Monetary union was a big loss of monetary sovereignty for ERM members. (c) The European Central Bank must guarantee price stability but be under democratic political control.

7 **Harder question** Suppose Spain experiences an adverse demand shock not experienced by any other eurozone country. (a) Will the European Central Bank take any action? (b) Will Spanish fiscal policy take any action? (c) What happens if there is no change in Spanish fiscal policy? If Spain began at internal and external balance, describe the full adjustment mechanism by which internal and external balance is restored.

8 **Harder question** Throughout its existence, eurozone interest rates have been lower than those in the UK. Describe what would happen if the UK joined the eurozone. What induced changes, if any, would there be in UK fiscal policy?

9 **Essay question** 'European integration has not been a pioneering vision of an optimistic future. What began as an attempt to prevent the third European war in 50 years then became the management of European decline in the face of the astonishing rise of Asia and the remarkable resilience of the United States.' Discuss.

To help you grasp the key concepts of this chapter check out the extra resources posted on the Online Learning Centre. There are chapter summaries, self-test questions, an interactive graphing tool, weblinks and a searchable glossary, all for free!

To put your learning into practice and prepare for exams, an **Interactive Workbook** is also available online, containing a variety of question types and providing feedback on your answers.

If you'd like further help with economics, or have any questions, **NetTutor** is here to help! You will have a personalised tutorial service at your fingertips. Visit the online learning centre at: www.mcgraw-hill.co.uk/textbooks/begg for information on accessing all of these resources.

CHAPTER 36

Poverty, development and globalization

Learning Outcomes

By the end of this chapter, you should understand:

1 why poor countries are poor

2 the role of exports of primary products

3 the role of industrialization and the export of manufactures

4 whether foreign borrowing promotes development

5 other avenues for poverty reduction

6 the importance of aid from rich countries

7 why globalization is taking place

8 costs and benefits of globalization

In Europe a drought is bad for the garden; in poor countries it kills people. In this chapter we examine the poorer countries in the world economy. The world's income is divided unequally between the rich industrial countries and the poor, less developed countries (LDCs).

The 2003 review by the United Nations classified countries as LDCs if they met three criteria: (i) annual average per capita below US$750; (ii) weak human resource indicators (nutrition, adult literacy, health and education); and (iii) vulnerability to natural or economic disasters. In 2006 there were around 50 LDCs, the least developed being the former French colony of Niger in West Africa.

> **Less developed countries (LDCs)** are those with low per capita income.

We review the major obstacles to economic development by poor countries, then discuss whether the world economy helps LDCs or hinders them. Many LDCs feel that the world economy is arranged to benefit the rich countries and exploit the poor countries. We examine whether or not this is true, and what can be done about it. The spectacular and sustained success of countries such as China confirms that it is possible to break out of poverty. But some countries fail persistently.

Of course, every anti-capitalist riot against McDonald's in Paris or London reveals that it is not only poor countries that have concerns about how the world economy is evolving. What exactly is globalization? Why is it taking place? Should it broadly be welcomed, or is it something generally to be feared and resisted?

36.1 World income distribution

Thirty-seven per cent of the world's people live in poor countries, with an average annual income of about £320 per person. In the rich countries, average annual income is over £19 500 per person. *Most of the world's people live in poverty beyond the imagination of people in rich Western countries.* Table 36.1 shows data on per capita income, life expectancy at birth and adult illiteracy. The low-income countries are very badly off on every measure.

Table 36.1 World welfare indicators, 2005

Country group	Poor	Middle	Rich
Per capita GNP (£)	320	1460	19 520
Life expectancy at birth (years)	59	71	79
Adult illiteracy (%)	38	10	<1

Source: World Bank, *Development Report.*

Recent progress

Nevertheless, the situation of low-income countries has improved since 1965. Table 36.2 shows a marked increase in life expectancy in low-income countries, a clear indication that the quality of life has improved since 1965. Per capita income grew in all groups of countries, yet, in absolute terms, poor countries fell even further behind the rest of the world. Thus there has been some progress in the past four decades, but the gap between low-income and other countries is wide and in most cases widening.

Table 36.2 World development, 1965–2005

Country group	Per capita real output growth (% p.a.)	Life expectancy at birth	
		1965	2005
Low	2.2	50	59
Middle	1.7	52	71
Rich	2.5	71	79

Source: World Bank, *Development Report.*

People living in rich countries may be interested in the problems of LDCs not merely out of a concern for fairness and an abhorrence of poverty wherever it occurs. In Chapter 33, we argued that a rise in world trade usually benefits all concerned. Even from a purely selfish standpoint, the rich countries have many reasons to be interested in the economic development of the LDCs.

36.2 Obstacles to development

Why do so many countries have such low per capita real GNP? To get to this position, they must have grown slowly for a long time. In this section we examine the special problems faced by countries with very low incomes.

Population growth

Per capita income grows when total income grows faster than population. In rich countries birth control is widespread; in poor countries much less so.[1] In the absence of state pensions, having children is one way people try to provide security against their old age when they are no longer able to work. In recent decades the population of low-income countries has been growing at about 2.5 per cent per annum; in rich countries annual population growth is below 1 per cent. Merely to maintain per capita living standards, poor countries have to increase total output much faster than rich countries.

A rapidly expanding labour force can allow rapid GNP growth if other factor inputs expand at an equal rate. Poor countries cannot expand supplies of land, capital and natural resources at the same rate as the labour force. Decreasing returns to labour set in.

Resource scarcity

Dubai is generously endowed with oil and has a per capita GNP in excess of the US or Germany. Most of the world's low-income countries are not so blessed with natural resources.

Capital

The rich countries have built up large stocks of physical capital which make their labour forces productive. Poor countries have few spare domestic resources to devote to physical investment. Most domestic resources are required to provide even minimal consumption. Financial loans and aid allow poor countries to buy in machinery and pay foreign construction firms. However, LDCs complain both that financial assistance is inadequate[2] and that multinational firms brought in to assist in economic development actually prevent sustained economic growth by LDCs: they use foreign workers, thus preventing domestic workers from acquiring valuable skills and experience, and they repatriate the profits to their own countries, thus preventing the accumulation of financial capital within LDCs to finance further development.

Social investment in infrastructure

Rich countries achieve scale economies and high productivity through specialization, assisted by sophisticated networks of transport and communications. Without expensive investment power generation, roads, telephone systems and urban housing, poor countries have to operate in smaller communities unable fully to exploit scale economies and specialization.

Human capital

Without resources to devote to investment in health, education and industrial training, workers in poor countries are often less productive than workers using the same technology in rich countries. Yet without higher productivity, it is hard to generate enough output (surplus to consumption requirements) to increase investment in people as well as in machinery.

---

1 There are exceptions. For example, one reason that China broke out of the group of poor countries was its one child per family policy.
2 At the 1996 Food Summit, Jacques Diouf, Director of the Food and Agriculture Organization, famously said his annual budget was 'less than what 9 developed countries spend on dog and cat food in six days, and less than 5 per cent of what inhabitants of just one developed country spend on slimming products every year.' *The Times*, 14 November 1996.

Debt

Rock stars such as Bob Geldof and Bono have drawn attention to the large amount of the income of poor countries that goes in paying interest and making debt repayments to creditors in rich countries, leaving LDCs with less to consume and invest in themselves.

Conflict

In addition to these narrow economic reasons, some people believe that the poorest regions are those where internal and international conflict has persisted. Sometimes, this reflects continuing disputes over artificial boundaries imposed during colonial rule. There is also some evidence that extreme mineral wealth can give rise to a continuing power struggle about which group should enjoy the benefits of this source of wealth.

Poor countries face many obstacles to economic development. We now examine the extent to which the world economy can help. However, we do not focus exclusively on the very poorest countries. The group of countries classified as LDCs also includes the newly industrialized countries – countries such as Mexico and China, well on their way to becoming rich countries. In some cases these middle-income countries have developed in a way the poorest countries hope to emulate. Together, the LDCs share many grievances about the way the world economy operates. In their view, it is stacked in favour of the rich industrial countries.

36.3 Development through trade in primary products

Chapter 33 analysed the gains from trade when countries specialize in the commodities in which they have a comparative advantage. We saw that relative factor abundance is an important determinant of comparative advantage. In many LDCs, the factor with which they are relatively most abundantly supplied is land. This suggests that LDCs can best take advantage of the world economy by exporting goods that use land relatively intensively.

> **Primary products** are agricultural goods and minerals, whose output relies heavily on the input of land.

Many LDCs export primary commodities, both 'soft' commodities – agricultural products such as coffee, cotton and sugar – and 'hard' commodities or minerals, such as copper or aluminium.

Traditionally, LDCs have tried to get gains from trade by exporting primary products to the rest of the world and using the revenue to import badly needed machinery and manufactures. As late as 1960, primary commodities were 84 per cent of all LDC exports. However, many LDCs have become sceptical of this route to development. Today, less than half of all LDC exports are primary products. We now explain why.

Trends in primary commodity prices

Figure 36.1 shows trends in the real prices of oil, metals and the soft commodities made into food. The real price of foodstuff commodities plummeted, reflecting both the success of LDCs in raising supply and limitations to demand for their products. LDCs raised productivity and output by better drainage and irrigation, better seeds and more fertilizers. Asian agriculture was transformed by the 'green revolution'. Similarly, producers of metallic ores developed more capital-intensive mining methods. LDCs' success in raising output and export capacity helped bid down the real price of the commodities that they were trying to sell. In agriculture, this was exacerbated by protectionist policies in Western markets that prevented poor countries accessing rich markets for their goods, thereby preventing Western demand absorbing the additional supply.

These trends in primary product prices led many poor countries to diversify out of primary product production. Paradoxically, they may have quit at the worst possible time. In recent years, the huge appetite of China for raw materials, from anywhere in the world, has provided a dramatic injection to demand. Figure 36.1 shows the spectacular hike in metal prices since 2003. Even food prices have stopped declining.

Oil is of course a special case. Nineteen eighty was the year of the second oil shock, when OPEC was at the peak of its power. As alternative oil sources were found, and the cartel was harder to hold together, real oil prices declined steadily until 2000, after which the combination of interrupted supply, because of conflict in the Gulf, and the hungry energy demand of emerging economies such as China, provided the impetus for substantially higher oil prices.

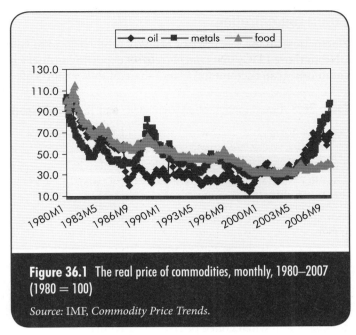

Figure 36.1 The real price of commodities, monthly, 1980–2007 (1980 = 100)

Source: IMF, *Commodity Price Trends.*

Oil-rich countries such as Russia have been major beneficiaries of higher oil prices. However, for the poorest countries in Africa that were not resource rich, this meant that they had to cope simultaneously with high energy costs and low prices for their agricultural output.

Price volatility

A second disadvantage of concentrating on the production of primary products has been that their real prices have been volatile. For both soft and hard commodities, a change of more than 40 per cent in the *real* price within a single year is not uncommon. LDCs do not know how many imports their exports will finance.

Equilibrium prices for primary products are volatile because both the supply and the demand are price-inelastic. On the demand side, people need food and industrial raw materials. On the supply side, crops have already been planted and perishable output has to be marketed whatever the price. Similarly, the supply of metals and minerals tends to be inelastic because it takes many years to develop a new copper mine or aluminium plant. Output cannot be quickly changed.

Because both supply and demand curves are very steep, a small shift in one curve leads to a large change in the equilibrium price. Demand curves shift because of business cycles in rich countries. Harvest failures and mining strikes cause shifts in supply curves.

LDCs also complain, justifiably, that agricultural protection by rich countries has been a major cause of declining real prices for agricultural products. Agriculture has been excluded from the tariff reductions negotiated in the GATT and the WTO in the last 50 years. Hence, when poor countries managed to increase supply, this extra output had to be absorbed by that part of the world economy that excludes the rich countries. In this much smaller market, extra supply bid the price down low. Had poor countries enjoyed access to the markets of rich countries, the induced change in the price would have been much less.

Export concentration

Fluctuations in the real price of primary products lead to volatile export earnings and fluctuations in GNP in those LDCs that concentrate on exporting primary products. Table 36.3 shows that a single commodity can account for a large share of total exports of some LDCs.

Table 36.3 Export concentration (commodity and % of total exports)

Guinea Bissau	Ground nuts	94
Uganda	Coffee	56
Zambia	Copper	56
Mauritania	Iron ore	52
Mali	Cotton	46

Source: Financial Times, 30 January 2002.

The real price of, say, coffee is volatile. Suppose Uganda faces a 50 per cent drop in coffee prices: its export earnings fall 28 per cent, which is catastrophic. Of course, Uganda does very well when coffee prices soar. Uganda's entire economy is buffeted by changes in the world coffee market.

The combination of a downward long-run trend in real prices and large short-term fluctuations around this trend has made LDCs reluctant to keep pursuing development through the export of primary products if this means excessive concentration on a single commodity. Diversifying production and exporting into other commodities helps to stabilize export revenue and general macroeconomic performance.

Commodity stabilization schemes

By acquiring more economic power, it is possible that primary producers could continue to pursue their natural comparative advantage but within a world economy from which they could more easily benefit. Suppose they got together to organize a stabilization scheme for a particular primary product. By stabilizing the price of the commodity, the scheme would stabilize the export earnings of countries heavily dependent on exports of that commodity.

Figure 36.2 shows how the scheme would work. *DD* shows the inelastic demand curve for the commodity. The total supply curve of competitive producers fluctuates between SS_1 and SS_2 depending on the state of the harvest. In a free market, equilibrium will oscillate between points A_1 and A_2 on the demand curve. Since demand is inelastic, these oscillations imply major changes in the equilibrium commodity price.

Now suppose a buffer stock is established.

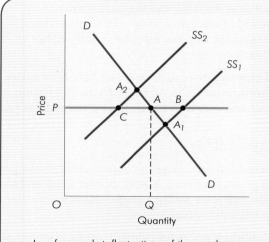

In a free market, fluctuations of the supply curve between SS_1 and SS_2 lead to movements along the demand curve between A_1 and A_2. When the supply curve is SS_1 the buffer stock scheme purchases a quantity AB. The quantity OQ is exported at a price P. When the supply curve is SS_2 the buffer stock scheme sells the quantity CA. Again a total quantity OQ is exported at a price P. Thus commodity prices and export earnings are stabilized.

Figure 36.2 Commodity price stabilization

A **buffer stock** aims to stabilize a commodity market by buying when the price is low, and selling when the price is high.

Suppose a bumper harvest means the supply curve is SS_1. In the absence of intervention, equilibrium is at A_1. The buffer stock buys a quantity AB, leaving a quantity OQ to be bought by other buyers at a price P. If the government runs the buffer stock, the country exports Q at the price P.

The buffer stock stores the commodity in warehouses. When there is a harvest failure, the producers' supply curve is SS_2. Rather than allow free market equilibrium at A_2, the buffer stock sells a quantity CA from the warehouse. Together with new production PC, this implies that again the total quantity exported is Q and the price is P. The buffer stock stabilizes the commodity price at P. By also stabilizing the quantity of exports at Q, it stabilizes export earnings.

Although Figure 36.2 illustrates fluctuations in supply, fluctuations in demand may also provide a reason for a buffer stock. The demand schedule for copper tends to fluctuate in line with the business cycle in Europe and North America where copper is a major input to production. Try drawing for yourself a figure like Figure 36.1 to illustrate how a buffer stock might work when the demand curve fluctuates.

At which price should the buffer stock aim to stabilize the market? If the only aim is to end price volatility, the price should be stabilized at the level that implies neither accumulation nor decumulation of buffer stock holdings in the long run. Suppose in Figure 36.2 that the producers' supply curve fluctuates regularly between SS_1 and SS_2. At the price P, there are as many years in which the buffer stock is buying the quantity AB as there are years in which it is selling the equal quantity CA. Stabilizing at a higher price would make AB larger than CA and imply that buffer stocks in the warehouses grow in the long run.

Ever-growing stockpiles might make economic sense. It is simply the policy of restricting supply to the market, the policy so successfully undertaken by OPEC. OPEC did not even need a warehouse. The separate producing countries formed a cartel and agreed to leave the quantity AB in the ground. Since the demand for oil and other primary products is inelastic, restricting the quantity supplied not only raises the price but also raises export earnings of commodity producers. In principle, effective cartels of producers could not only stabilize the prices of primary products, they could follow the OPEC example and combat the trend of declining real prices by restricting supply.

In recent years there have been attempts by LDCs to organize commodity price stabilization schemes in coffee, cocoa and tin. When there has been a bumper coffee crop in Brazil, the world's largest coffee producer, the Brazilian government has purchased coffee from Brazilian farmers and simply burned it. But LDCs have not generally managed to copy OPEC's example. For many primary commodities, governments have to deal not with a few large oil fields but with a large number of small producers who are much harder to organize.

We discussed cartels in detail in Chapter 9. One problem with the strategy of supply restriction to force up the price is that there is an incentive for individual producers to cheat on the collective agreement. When price is forced above marginal cost, each producer has an incentive to produce more than the agreed output. Yet if all producers cheat, either the price collapses or the buffer stock is forced to acquire enormous stocks to keep this production off the market. Even the rich countries of the EU complain about the cost of stocks such as the famous 'butter mountain'. LDCs simply cannot afford to tie up money in this way.

Since LDCs have been unsuccessful in policing their own attempts to restrict primary commodity supply, and since they cannot afford to stockpile vast quantities when individual producers refuse to cut back output, LDCs would like help from the rest of the world in establishing effective commodity stabilization schemes. By maintaining higher real prices for primary commodities, these schemes would effectively transfer purchasing power from rich industrial users and consumers to poorer producers. But, by also stabilizing real prices, LDCs argue that benefits would also accrue to industrial nations that are heavily dependent on exporting these commodities.

36.4 Industrialization

Many LDCs have now decided that industrialization is a better bet than concentration on producing primary products. Industrial development has taken two very different forms.

Import substitution

When world trade collapsed in the 1930s, many countries faced a 50 per cent cut in their export revenues and resolved never again to be so dependent on the world economy. They began a policy of import substitution.

Import substitution reduces world trade and suppresses the principle of comparative advantage. LDCs used tariffs and quotas to direct domestic resources away from the primary products in which they had a comparative advantage, into industrial manufacturing where they had a comparative disadvantage.

> **Import substitution** is the replacement of imports by domestic production under the protection of high tariffs or import quotas.

International trade theory suggests that this will be wasteful. Countries are using more domestic resources to make manufactured products than are required to make exports that would finance imports of the same quantity of manufactures.[3]

Import substitution was pursued partly because LDCs wanted to reduce dependence on particular primary commodities, and partly because they associated a developed industrial sector with the high productivity levels seen in the rich industrial countries. Embarking on import substitution has one great danger and one possible merit.

The danger is that import substitution may prove a dead end. Although domestic industry may expand quite rapidly behind tariff barriers while imports are being replaced, once import substitution has been completed economic growth may come to an abrupt halt. There are no more imports to replace and the country is now specialized in industries in which it has a comparative *disadvantage*. Any further expansion must come from expanding *domestic* demand. Moreover, since trade and foreign investment are channels through which new technologies are learned, LDCs sheltering behind a protective fortress may fall further behind in knowledge of technology.

These are real dangers of import substitution. Its possible merit is that comparative advantage is a dynamic, not a static, concept. A tariff may help an infant industry (though production subsidies would achieve the same outcome at lower social cost). By developing an industrial sector and learning to use the existing technology, LDCs may eventually come to have a comparative advantage in some industrial products.

Thus import substitution may not be an end in itself. It may be a preliminary phase in which industry gets started, as a prelude to export-led growth.

> **Export-led growth** stresses production and income growth through exports rather than the displacement of imports.

The real success stories of the last few decades are the countries that made this transition and are no longer high-tariff countries but successful exporters of manufactures. Instead of withdrawing from the world economy, they turned it to their advantage. This was particularly true in the countries of Southeast Asia, including China. Table 36.4 shows their rapid growth and the key role of exports of manufactured goods.

---

3 Closed off from the world economy, the communist bloc pursued import substitution on a grand scale. It was not an economic success.

Table 36.4 Growth and trade, Southeast Asia, 1965–2004

	Annual real growth of per capita GDP (%)		% of manufactures in total exports	
	1965–80	1980–2004	1965	2004
Indonesia	9	5	2	56
Malaysia	7	4	6	76
Singapore	10	6	34	84
S. Korea	10	7	59	93
Thailand	7	5	4	75
China	–	9	47	91

Source: World Bank, *World Development Report.*

Should producers of manufactures in the rich countries worry about competition from Asian producers of manufactures? Will the 'tigers' wipe out producers of labour-intensive manufactures in Europe, North America and even Japan?

Although we tend to think of LDCs exporting very labour-intensive low-quality manufactures such as cheap textiles, this stereotype is outdated. It remains true that textiles are the largest single manufactured commodity exported by LDCs, but exports of machinery and consumer durables are growing the most rapidly. LDCs are now major producers of everything from cars to transistors and televisions. How will the industrial countries react?

The principle of comparative advantage suggests that everyone can gain from this new trade in manufactures. The established industrial economies should reallocate factors to industries in which their comparative advantage now lies, industries such as genetics and telecommunications, which use relatively intensively the capital and technical expertise with which the rich countries are relatively well endowed.

However, the adjustment process is costly. Factories have to be closed, outdated plant written off and workers retrained. In Chapter 33 we explained why politicians may give in to pressure from declining industries to protect them through tariffs and quotas rather than insist that new industries be established.

Subsidized retraining, redundancy benefits and the closing of plants that are no longer efficient make much more sense. In the long run, protection costs more than subsidizing adjustment as comparative advantage changes.

Nevertheless, the LDCs are justifiably frightened that their strategy of economic development through industrialization and export-led growth through manufactures will be frustrated by protection in their industrial markets.

36.5 Borrowing to grow

A third route to economic development is by external borrowing, and a third complaint of LDCs about the way the world economy works is that borrowing terms are too tough. LDCs have traditionally borrowed in world markets to finance an excess of imports over exports. By importing capital goods, LDCs were able to supplement domestic investment financed by domestic savings.

Box 36.1 Fickle capital flows hurt LDCs

In the 1990s capital mobility increased. Many LDCs attracted foreign capital in large amounts. Some inflows reflected long-term investment in factories and production, but many inflows were lured by high domestic returns in 'emerging market' economies dismantling previous controls. Frequently, these economies pegged their exchange rate to the US dollar. Foreign investors thought they could grab high returns yet get their money out before any devaluation materialized.

In 1997 East Asia caught a cold. Country after country faced a speculative attack on its exchange rate peg. Even healthy countries were attacked. Since Asian banks had borrowed in foreign currency, big falls in exchange rates raised the domestic value of foreign debt, bankrupting the banking system. Real exchange rates collapsed. After the IMF organized rescue plans, the depreciated 'super-competitive' exchange rates then allowed recovery in 1998. As confidence returned, exchange rates climbed to more reasonable levels, as the table shows.

Lessons of the crisis? First, allowing massive capital inflows is dangerous: what flows in can also flow out. Floating the exchange rate would limit the capital inflow. Second, retaining some restrictions on capital flows may not be such a bad idea, at least until domestic banks are well regulated and more robust. Third, LDCs should borrow less in foreign currency, whose domestic value rises when the exchange rate plunges. Fourth, the IMF success came at a price. Bailing out foreign investors raises expectations of future bail-outs. Some critics said that if the IMF had not bailed out Mexico in 1995, the Asian crisis of 1997 would not have been so bad. And there might not have been subsequent crises in countries such as Argentina.

Real exchange rate (1990–96 = 100)	Indonesia	Korea	Malaysia	Thailand	Philippines
June 1997	105	95	111	107	115
December 1997	62	66	80	72	89
June 1998	33	76	79	87	92
December 1998	71	85	77	98	91
December 1999	62	79	77	97	98
December 2000	77	78	75	103	98

Sources: World Bank, *Global Development Finance 1999*; IMF, *International Financial Statistics.*

Foreign debt

We remind ourselves of the basic balance of payments arithmetic:

$$\textbf{Current account deficit} = \textbf{trade deficit} + \textbf{debt interest}$$
$$= \textbf{increase in net foreign debt} \tag{1}$$

The first line shows the sources of the current account deficit; the second reminds us that it has to be financed by selling domestic assets to foreigners or by new foreign borrowing. Table 36.5 shows how debt has grown in most LDCs. Table 36.6 shows debt/GDP ratios for some of the most indebted countries.

Table 36.5 LDC debt (% of GNP)

	1980	2000
All LDCs	26	41
Sub-Saharan Africa	29	69
Eastern Europe, Central Asia	24	51
Latin America, Caribbean	35	43
East Asia, Pacific	17	34
Middle East, North Africa	31	34
South Asia	17	27

Source: World Bank, *World Development Report.*

The *burden* of the debt is not measured simply by the debt/GNP ratio. Debt hurts only when the real interest rate is positive: only then does a country have to sacrifice real resources to repay the debt in the future. A crucial reason why a debt crisis emerged after 1980 was the rise in real interest rates. In several previous decades real interest rates were actually negative, and debtor countries were being subsidized in real terms by creditors.

It is also arguable that the right measure of a country's ability to pay is not its GNP but its export earnings. Instead of looking at debt/GNP ratios, we could look at the ratio of interest on foreign debt relative to exports. This ratio rises not merely because debt increases, but whenever real interest rates rise or export revenues fall.

Default and debt rescheduling

You are president of an indebted country. To keep meeting the interest on foreign debt, you need to create a deep recession that cuts imports and lets output be used to earn export revenue to pay debt interest. Politically, you are in big trouble. Voters do not like austerity for long.

Have you any other options? You can call in the IMF and the World Bank. You may get a short-term loan to pay your other creditors. But these international agencies will insist that you take tough action to get the long-run position under control.

Instead, you go to your creditors, mainly large private banks in the rich countries, to request a debt rescheduling.

Rescheduling changes when you repay, but does not change the present value of the repayments that you make. If your economy will grow in the future, this may be a good strategy.

> **Debt rescheduling** is a new agreement with old creditors to pay them less per period but for a longer payback period.

If things are more desperate, you may consider outright default, refusing to pay what you owe. This deals with the immediate burden of the debt, but what are the costs? Governments of the creditors may send in their armies, though this is rare. They may try to exert leverage through international negotiations, trade embargoes and so on.

When countries borrow in world financial markets, they do not all face the same interest rate. Like individuals, riskier countries face higher interest rates, which build in a *risk premium* to cover the possibility of default. Hence it is possible that countries that default face prohibitive risk premiums when they try to borrow in the future. The knowledge that this will happen may be sufficient to deter them from defaulting in the first place.

Activity box 36   Debt relief

Bob Geldof and Bono focused world attention on the indebtedness of poor countries and both Tony Blair and Gordon Brown have championed debt relief. Here is a way to see the magnitude of the challenge. Suppose you have just become president of a poor country, and life is tough. Your country, both public and private sectors, has borrowed a lot abroad, because foreign interest rates were lower than domestic interest rates.

Your country owes foreign banks $200 billion. This debt is unaffected by devaluation or by domestic inflation in your country. World interest rates are 5 per cent. You are supposed to pay $10 billion a year in interest. If you could pay in full, the market would value your bonds at their par value of $200 per bond, which is the present value of $10 a year for ever when the discount rate is 5 per cent a year.

Unfortunately, your country cannot pay what it owes. By imposing tough domestic policies, you have cut back consumption and imports, creating a trade surplus of $2 billion a year; but you owe $5 billion a year. You cannot squeeze the domestic economy any more: people are starving. Nor will the bankers lend you any more: they think you are going bankrupt. The secondary (second-hand) market for your outstanding bonds shows exactly what the market thinks of your chances. If it thinks you will only pay $2 billion, not $5 billion, a year for ever, each $100 bond will trade for $40 because the market expects to receive only 40 per cent of what it should.

Who lost out? The people to whom you originally issued the bond at par for $100 each. When the market figured out you were in trouble, the secondary price of your bonds fell immediately to the level then considered realistic. Your bonds are trading *at a discount*, or below par. You are less than fully creditworthy, and will find it hard to borrow any more money. Creditors will never get more than 40 per cent of what they are owed: that is the most you can pay.

Why don't creditors do what the rock stars advocate, and simply let you off 60 per cent of your debts? If creditors let you off today, they will have every other debtor government coming to them tomorrow with a similar plea. Perhaps for banks it is better simply to make a dreadful fuss and hope that governments in rich countries put up some of the money. Provided you keep paying almost $2 billion a year, any extra money from northern governments goes not to making your life easier but rather to reducing the losses of northern shareholders in northern banks.

Questions

(a)   After the write-off, what happens to bond prices in the secondary market?

(b)   Why is it necessary for *all* creditors to agree the write-off at the same instant?

To check your answers to these questions, go to page 738.

Outright defaults are quite rare. Moreover, and somewhat surprisingly, there is little evidence that, as a country's debt position becomes more risky, the financial markets substantially raise the interest rate on new borrowing. So any deterrent effect in advance is small.

In practice, much of the problem has been met by debt rescheduling. Creditors have preferred to get some money back over a longer period rather than provoke debtors to announce outright default. And, finally, under international pressure from governments, the creditor banks have actually written off much of the debt. This means they acknowledge that it is never going to be repaid even though the debtor has not explicitly announced a complete default. Many famous Western banks announced operating losses as they set off bad debts against their healthy profits from domestic operations.

The HIPC initiative

One means of co-ordinating nation efforts is to act through the IMF and the World Bank. The Heavily Indebted Poor Countries (HIPC) are poor and have high external debt. Assistance via the HIPC imitative, which has been in operation since 1996, is conditional on countries meeting targets for good governance and economic management.

The HIPC programme identifies 38 countries, 32 of which are in sub-Saharan Africa, as being potentially eligible to receive debt relief. Twenty-seven countries have so far received over $54 billion in aid, making inroads into measures of indebtedness such as the ratio of debt to GDP, or the percentage of export earnings used to pay interest to foreign creditors.

Even so, initial assistance was not sufficient for permanent sustainability. A World Bank review in 2006 concluded that 11 of the 13 HIPC countries that had completed the programme had subsequently seen indebtedness measures deteriorate again.[4] Two keys to success are providing sufficient debt relief in the first place, and ensuring that sound national policies are sustained even after debt relief has been accomplished.

Structural adjustment is the pursuit of supply-side policies aimed at increasing potential output by increasing efficiency. Examples of such policies are reductions in government subsidies to industry, privatization, lower levels of protection against imports, broader and less distortionary tax rates, and less government intervention to ration and allocate credit by quota rather than by price. This pursuit of microeconomic efficiency has usually been underpinned by a recommendation to abolish large budget deficits, financed by money creation and causing endemic inflation.

Even in OECD economies, greater stress on supply-side policies after 1980 took a long time to work and appear to have had only modest measurable success. LDCs sometimes claim that unpalatable medicine is being forced down their throats as the price for loans and aid from rich countries. Two rejoinders are possible.

First, what the doctor dispenses is rarely pleasant but often useful. Second, we have increasing evidence, for example from transition economies, that those embracing structural adjustment achieved greater subsequent economic success. In part this is a chicken-and-egg phenomenon. Countries confident of their future prospects and committed to reform may embrace structural adjustment more easily; countries fearful of the future and in which the debate still rages about which economic system is appropriate are countries more likely to find reasons to go slow on structural adjustment. Nevertheless, in economics as in medicine, we have little evidence that delaying the treatment is good for the patient.

4 http://worldbank.org/ieg.

36.6 Aid

Many of the complaints of the poor south come down to the view that the rich north should provide them with more aid.

Aid is an international transfer payment from rich countries to poor countries.

Such aid can take many forms: subsidized loans, outright gifts of food or machinery, or technical help and the free provision of expert advisers.

The basic issue is a moral or value judgement about equality. Within a country the government usually makes transfer payments to the poor, financed by taxes on the rich, thereby implementing a view of society as a whole that the income distribution thrown up by market forces is unfair and inequitable.

The same value judgement applies to transfer payments between countries. However, it is complicated by two additional factors. First, within a country with a sense of national identity and social cohesion, it may seem right that the government should be concerned with *all* its citizens. Governments of individual countries, and the citizens they represent, may feel less responsibility for the welfare of people of a different nationality in a distant country, of which they have little knowledge or experience.

Second, the issue is complicated by history. Many people in LDCs feel that the rich countries got rich by colonial exploitation of LDCs' resources. Aid seems at least partial compensation. The northern countries do not share this interpretation of history.

The recipients of aid

Does it matter in what form aid is given? Many LDCs believe the most important contribution rich countries can make is free access for LDCs to the markets of rich countries. 'Trade, not aid' is the slogan. Just as the best service a government can render to its domestic unemployed is effective retraining to allow a successful subsequent career, LDCs believe that trade rather than handouts is a better form of assistance and encouragement.

Critics of existing aid programmes also argue that donors should do more to check on who actually benefits from their transfers. It is argued that too much aid finds its way into the hands of the ruling elite in the recipient countries rather than the poorest people for whom it was intended.

Whenever aid and redistribution are discussed, it is useful to recall a leaking bucket. When transferring water in a leaky bucket, some of the water leaks out but some makes it to the other end for the purpose that was intended. Whether the process is worthwhile depends on how fast the water leaks and how urgently it is needed at the other end. And in the meantime, we should be looking for buckets with fewer holes.

Aid and migration

The quickest way to equalize world income distribution would be to permit free migration between countries. Residents of poor countries could go elsewhere in search of higher incomes. And, in emigrating, they would increase the capital and land per worker for those who stayed behind.

Nor is this idea entirely fanciful. The massive movements of population from Europe to the Americas and to the colonies in the nineteenth and early twentieth centuries represented an income-equalizing movement of this sort. Since the Second World War the major migrations have been temporary, although the steady flow of Mexicans (illegally) across the US border is one major exception. More common has been the EU's use of temporary migrant labour from Turkey, the Balkans and North Africa, which have benefited from payments sent home to their families by workers temporarily abroad. Egypt, India and Pakistan also receive significant transfer payments from workers temporarily abroad.

Yet there is no free and unrestricted immigration to the rich countries today. Indeed, even migrant workers are frequently outlawed. One difference between conditions today and conditions during the massive migrations of the nineteenth century is that there are now extensive systems of welfare and public health in rich countries. Quite apart from any racial or religious arguments, opponents of immigration say that existing residents would end up subsidizing unskilled immigrants who would spend most of their lives receiving public handouts.

The US grew extremely quickly during the period of large-scale immigration. With economies of scale, it is not clear that existing residents inevitably lose out by admitting immigrants. As populations age in the rich countries, there will come a day when immigrants get the red carpet not the cold shoulder. They will be seen as generators of income, and income tax revenue, and hence a way of financing state pensions in rich countries in which demographic changes have led to many old people but few young workers.

36.7 Globalization

The visible movement of people around the world is merely one symptom of the increasing integration of the global economy. Global brands, such as Coca-Cola and McDonald's, are another symbol. Lower transport costs, better communications, new information technology and deliberate policies to reduce trade barriers have all enhanced the size of the relevant economic market.

This erodes the sovereignty of national governments, by undermining the ability of an individual government to raise taxes, constrain firms and regulate markets. Too much intervention and business migrates to an easier location elsewhere. In turn, perceiving the erosion of the power of their national governments to influence events, voters become apathetic and lose interest in national politics. Multinational corporations (MNCs) sometimes seem to have become more powerful than governments.

Have the benefits of globalization been outweighed by its costs? Should globalization now be resisted? The next time a hamburger outlet is being trashed by anti-globalization protesters, should you be leading the charge or explaining that there is a better way to meet their concerns? To help you make up your mind, we now discuss some of the most frequent criticisms of globalization.

> **Globalization** is the increase in cross-border trade and influence on the economic and social behaviour of nation states.

Globalization is a new phenomenon, requiring a new policy response

Actually, since communications and transport have been steadily increasing for centuries, globalization is also centuries old. By many measures of trade, migration and capital flows across borders, the period 1870–1913 was comparable to the globalization of the last few decades.

Globalization is thus neither new nor irreversible. Globalization during 1870–1913 created many winners but also some powerful losers. Cheaper grain from the US drove down grain prices and land rents in Europe, prompting agricultural protection in the 1920s. Massive migration to the US drove down wages there, leading to the introduction of immigration controls in the interwar period. History warns us that sustaining the momentum for globalization requires sufficient redistribution to ensure that powerful groups of losers do not emerge to create a backlash.

Box 36.2 Internet could threaten millions of US jobs

Princeton professor Alan Blinder is one of the most eminent economists of his generation, not only a distinguished scholar but a former deputy chairman of the United States central bank, adviser to several Democratic presidential candidates, and regular columnist for *Newsweek* magazine.

The delivery of information and services via the internet could threaten as many as 40 million US jobs in the next 20 years, he told CNBC in an interview in March 2007, 'If you look back in history, [overseas job loss] has been concentrated in manufacturing, but I think as you look forward, one of the dominant forces, if not the dominant force, will be the electronic delivery of services, including upper-end services – computer programming, manuscript editing, science, accounting.'

Other jobs at risk to electronic delivery include interpreters, translators, mathematicians, economists, and financial analysts. Obviously, it is not just the United States which is at risk from this new international trade in services that allows countries such as India to exploit comparative advantage in educated workers that are inexpensive by Western standards.

Blinder, a firm believer in comparative advantage and the gains from trade, makes these points not to argue in favour of tariffs and trade barriers but rather to argue that Western governments should do more for workers whose jobs are lost to cheap foreign competition. Previously, such losses have been largely in unskilled or manufacturing jobs. Middle-class white-collar workers may be more vocal in their protests.

Western governments should revamp their education systems to prepare students for jobs that are likely to remain in the West in the long run. Blinder also suggests that the tax code be revised to encourage companies to create and maintain jobs in their home countries. In a more rapidly changing world, it is important also to make pensions and social security as portable as possible, rather than tied to a particular employer.

Source: www.cnbc.com.

Globalization increases inequality in the global economy

A few facts are helpful. Table 36.6 summarizes the last 200 years. Globalization *did* cause a big increase in inequality during 1820–1950, when the income share of the richest 10 per cent of the world population rose from 43 per cent to 51 per cent while the income share of the poorest 10 per cent of people fell from 5 per cent to 2 per cent. However, since 1950 it is *not* true that the income share of the poor has kept falling, nor has the income share of the rich risen much. Global inequality is acute, but not getting worse.

Inequality is about relative incomes. We can also ask what is happening to the absolute incomes of the poor. The number of people earning less than a dollar a day (inflation adjusted, at constant prices) has fallen since 1950, *despite* the doubling of world population in the same period. Most of us would feel happier if the conditions of the poor were improving more rapidly. But they are improving slowly, whether measured by income or by life expectancy or literacy (Table 36.1).

Why, then, do people make the connection between globalization and poverty? Nowadays, we see it on the news, on documentaries, and on charity appeals. Previously it was there, and was worse, but we were less aware of it. Similarly, people living in poor countries are much better informed about how rich the rich countries have become. Globalization of information has increased dissatisfaction about what always existed.

Table 36.6 World welfare indicators, 1820–2005

	1820	1910	1950	2005
Average income/person (1990 $000s)	1.0	2.2	3.0	7.0
World population (billion)	1.1	1.7	2.5	6.5
Income share: richest 10% of people	43	51	51	53
poorest 10% of people	5	4	2	2

Note: Latest data on income shares refer to 1992 not 2005.

Sources: World Bank, *World Development Report 2007*; Centre for Economic Policy Research, London, *Making Sense of Globalization (2002).*

Multinational corporations exploit workers and play off LDC governments against one another

Local workers employed by MNCs, whether mining minerals or producing clothes and trainers, seem to us to work for pitifully low wages and in conditions that workers in rich countries would not tolerate. However, their wages are usually higher than those earned by their compatriots in domestic industries, and working conditions in MNCs are often better than those in domestic factories.

If workers in poor countries began with much larger quantities of physical and human capital, they would be richer and more productive. In principle, rich countries could vote for a massive transfer of aid to purchase these valuable inputs for poor countries. But they never have, and the reality is that they probably never will. Without these advantages, the equilibrium wage of the disadvantaged is low but allowing them access to the world economy lets them gradually accumulate more of the valuable inputs that eventually enhance their own prosperity.

Well-meaning attempts to force 'improvements' in their wages and working conditions simply price them out of world markets and reduce their eventual prosperity. For an example closer to home, think of German reunification in 1990. West German trade unions raised wages in East Germany. But East Germans were not initially as productive as West Germans. The result was a decade of high unemployment and discontent in East Germany. So who gained? West German workers, protected from competition from cheap labour in East Germany!

What poor countries need is not less globalization but more. Here, rich countries can help a lot, principally by opening up their market in agriculture and textiles, industries in which poor countries have a natural comparative advantage. By removing tariffs, this would reduce prices in the rich countries but raise prices received by LDC exporters. Current estimates are that a 40 per cent reduction in agricultural tariffs would generate gains of $70 billion a year. Incidentally, it would also reduce the food bill of each EU citizen by £200 a year. Since the losers would be farmers in rich countries, the challenge for policy makers is to find a way to buy off these losers sufficiently.

What about the claim that MNCs play off one LDC against another. The trainers that you wear may have an American logo, but they were probably made in China or the Dominican Republic. MNCs effectively get each country to bid for hosting inward investment in a new factory. Does competition between countries ensure that the investment goes to the country with the lowest wages and lightest regulation?

Actually, it does not. MNCs like low wages, but they also like workers with education and skills, good transport infrastructure and predictable legal environments. Foreign investment has flooded into Singapore not Senegal.

Moreover, competition between countries is one disciplining force on corruption in national bureaucracies that would otherwise be sheltered monopolies. The price of abuse is the failure to attract valuable inward investment. Globalization on balance is probably a force that fosters democracy, transparency and good governance. One problem with sub-Saharan Africa is that it has been too little exposed to the global economy, not too much.

Globalization destroys the environment

Rainforests are cut down to rear beef cows for hamburgers, oil production wipes out wildlife and mining scars the landscape. All true. And all exacerbated by globalization. However, we need to remember the principle of targeting.

If the environment is wrongly priced, encouraging over-exploitation because producers do not pay the full social cost of what they do, the best solution is to encourage better pricing of the environment. Trying to suppress trade is a second-best solution.

Though logically correct, this is a counsel of perfection. Even countries rich in human capital have yet to implement sophisticated schemes that price and regulate use of the environment adequately. It is unrealistic to imagine that countries with fewer enforcement resources will do better in pricing their environments.

Global measures, such as a carbon tax that applies everywhere, may be a reasonable compromise. Not only could this protect the environment, it would be a useful source of tax revenue for poor countries. However, the failure of the US to sign up to the Kyoto Agreement indicates its current unwillingness to play a role in such agreements. History suggests that it is wrong for the winners to believe that there is no need to heed the grievances of the losers, as the collapse of globalization in the interwar period attests. If globalization is not harnessed through better political management of the process, it may eventually be undone.

Summary

- **LDCs** want a larger share of the world's income and wealth. Nearly 40 per cent of the world's population has an annual income of £320 or less.

- LDCs complain that (a) markets for their **primary products** are controlled by the north; (b) northern **protectionism** is hampering their prospects for industrial development; (c) borrowing is too expensive; (d) austere and unpopular domestic policies are being forced upon them; and (e) simple justice dictates that rich countries should take practical steps to close the gap.

- In the world's poorest countries, population growth is faster than the rate at which supplies of other factors can be increased. Hence labour productivity is low and, after provision for consumption, there are few spare resources to increase human and physical capital. It is hard to break out of this vicious circle.

- The downward trend in real prices, price volatility and danger of extreme concentration in a single commodity have made LDCs reluctant to pursue development by exploiting a **comparative advantage** in primary products. **Buffer stocks** and cartel supply restrictions have proved difficult to organize, with the conspicuous exception of OPEC.

- LDCs are increasing their export of manufactures. Although the LDCs begin from a small base, their market share could quickly become much more significant.

- Industrial countries are tempted to protect their declining manufacturing industries. They would do better by encouraging adjustment towards industries in which their comparative advantage now lies.

- **Structural adjustment** policies aim to improve incentives and the efficiency with which existing resources are used.

- LDCs ran large deficits, financed by **external borrowing**. Larger debts and high interest rates led to threats of default and an international debt crisis.

- Increasing financial market integration in the 1990s led to large **capital inflows** to LDCs. When investors got scared, many LDCs faced drastic crises.

- Trade may help the LDCs more effectively than aid. **Migration** would help equalize world incomes. Rich countries may reconsider their immigration policy once they need young, tax-paying workers.

- **Globalization**, the rise of foreign influence on domestic economic and social behaviour, is neither new nor irreversible. It is caused by cheaper transport, better communications and policies to reduce trade protection. In the absence of other distortions, this yields gains from trade and net benefits for the global economy. However, some groups may lose out.

- In the last half century, **global inequality** has not increased and the number of people in absolute poverty has fallen, despite rapid population growth. Trade is usually the route to prosperity and no country has ever got rich without international trade. However, better global information has made everyone aware of the extent of **poverty** that still exists in the world.

- Liberalizing agriculture and textile markets in rich countries would hugely benefit not only their own citizens but also potential exporters in poor countries. The gains would easily allow the losers (rich farmers) to be bought off.

- Globalization exacerbates existing distortions, for example the **over-exploitation of the environment** or **inadequate financial regulation** in poor countries. The ideal solution is to improve these by domestic policy reform, not to curtail trade. Foreign aid could usefully be channelled into these areas.

- Failing this, there is a greater role for international agencies to devise rules that offset existing market failures and allow the benefits of globalization to be enjoyed without incurring these additional costs. **Taxing pollution and environmental depreciation** would also generate useful tax revenue, in both poor and rich countries.

- Allowing powerful groups of uncompensated losers to build up is the most likely way in which globalization may eventually be arrested or even reversed. This increases the case for redistribution to allow the benefits of globalization to continue to help raise living standards in poor countries. Aid alone will never be enough.

Review questions

To check your answers to these questions, go to page 737.

1 Discuss two forces tending to reduce the real price of agricultural produce in the long run.

2 How would a world boom affect a country specializing in producing copper?

3 Why have LDCs been particularly successful in exporting textiles, clothing and leather footwear?

4 (a) Describe how a buffer stock scheme works. (b) What could go wrong?

5 Can a small LDC gain by a policy of import substitution?

6 Why might a floating exchange rate insulate an LDC from capital flows more effectively than a pegged exchange rate?

7 **Common fallacies** Why are these statements wrong? (a) Aid is all the help LDCs need. (b) Europe's problem is competition from cheap labour in LDCs. (c) LDCs do best by sticking to production of raw materials for the world economy.

---

8 **Harder question** Could the last decade of low inflation be explained by the arrival of cheap Chinese goods rather than independence of central banks?

9 **Harder question** Why does globalization undermine the sovereignty of nation states? Propose a definition of economic sovereignty, and rank the loss of sovereignty in each of the following (listing first the activity for which most sovereignty has gone): (a) taxing workers, (b) regulating banks, (c) taxing online gambling, and (d) subsidizing poor people.

10 **Essay question** Globalization was mainly caused by: (a) a fall in transport costs, (b) the internet, (c) the determination of national policy makers to remove barriers to trade. Make an assessment of the relative importance of these three forces (e.g. a = 20%, b = 50% and c = 30%) and defend your decision. Is there a (d) that should have been included in the list above?

To help you grasp the key concepts of this chapter check out the extra resources posted on the Online Learning Centre. There are chapter summaries, self-test questions, an interactive graphing tool, weblinks and a searchable glossary, all for free!

To put your learning into practice and prepare for exams, an **Interactive Workbook** is also available online, containing a variety of question types and providing feedback on your answers.

If you'd like further help with economics, or have any questions, **NetTutor** is here to help! You will have a personalised tutorial service at your fingertips. Visit the online learning centre at: www.mcgraw-hill.co.uk/textbooks/begg for information on accessing all of these resources.

Appendix: Answers to review questions and Activity boxes

Chapter 1

1 (a) A downsloping line joining 15 shirts and 20 cakes. (b) 20. (c) All points below the frontier. (d) 1.33 cakes. (e) No.
2 Informationally, too costly to plan for, deliver to and monitor individuals.
3 Wages will fall for jobs for which students wish to offer themselves.
4 (a) P. (b) N. (c) P. (d) N.
5 (a) Macro. (b) Micro. (c) Micro. (d) Macro.
6 (a) Positive economics can be tested against evidence. (b) Beginning from an inefficient point, efficiency gains yield a free lunch. (c) Can use scientific method to study human behaviour.
7 (a) High prices are also an incentive for cartel members to cheat on the collective agreement to restrict output – an individual producer that raises its output gets much higher income. Chapter 10 explains how Saudi Arabia disciplined other OPEC members to keep them in line, which was possible only because of the large oil reserves and cheap production costs of Saudi Arabia compared with other OPEC members. (b) It would fail because the UK would simply be swamped by cheap textile imports.
8 (a) Would be close to $50/barrel. (b) Yes. (c) Increase.
AB 1 (a) Health care largely rationed by price – if you could not afford it, you could not buy it. (b) NHS still rationed health care via (i) waiting lists, and (ii) not making some procedures available.

Chapter 2

1 (a) Cross-section data, e.g. by county, for crime, unemployment. (b) Collect other data to control for income, policing, inequality, urban or rural; and use econometrics to disentangle.
2 Upsloping line: rise by 1 in RPI associated with extra £1300 in house prices; time series.
3 Upsloping line: higher income associated with higher consumption of similar amount.
4 Weights reflect relative importance, so capital usually much less than rest of country.
5 Downsloping curve.
6 (a) Theory organizes facts by providing a simple framework in which to interpret them. (b) Many sciences (e.g. astronomy) cannot conduct laboratory experiments. (c) Molecules individually random but collectively predictable. People's individual whims cancel out in larger groups.
7 Higher interest rates make borrowers feel poorer, but they also make lenders feel richer. In part these two effects cancel one another out, so the effect of interest rates on overall spending (and saving) may be smaller than you had expected. Notice too that consumer spending is equivalent to around 70 per cent of national output and income, so that any induced change in consumer spending also tends to change household income within a short time, so that the relationship between the two is less affected than you might have thought.
8 Generally, our conventional wisdom at any time is a set of theories that have not yet been disproved by the evidence. If we set the bar too high, the random quirks in our particular set of

data may make us reject a theory that was in fact correct, discarding it permanently from our conventional wisdom, perhaps never to be rediscovered. Conversely, if we set the bar too low, we may fail to reject theories that should indeed have been rejected, but because they remain for now in our conventional wisdom, we will probably test them again later and get another chance to discover our mistake. Wrongly rejecting correct theories is therefore more dangerous than wrongly failing to reject theories that are in fact incorrect. Statistical testing generally sets the bar around a 5 per cent chance of falsely rejecting a theory that is in fact correct, erring on the side of making it hard to reject a theory.

AB 2 (a) 3.5. (b) 2.33. (c) Sarah. (d) Possible explanations include: Sarah is cleverer, concentrates more effectively and has a better memory; Gordon's mind is always on politics no matter how hard he studies.

Chapter 3

1 Equilibrium price £17; quantity 6.5.
2 (a) Excess demand = 5, and price rises. (b) Excess supply = 3, and price falls.
3 Demand curve for toasters shifts down. Equilibrium price and quantity of toasters fall.
4 Same as 3.
5 Drought, disease, wild dogs all shift supply curve down. Price falls move farmers down given supply curve, not a fall in supply.
6 Controlling for how much the good impresses your friends, lower prices raise your demand.
7 (a) A low enough price can fill any stadium. (b) It shows a price floor for farm goods. (c) It offers low rents to the lucky people who get housing but also reduces total supply and causes a shortage.
8 (a) You cannot be excluded from the benefit, so you get it for nothing. (b) If nobody else subscribes, your contribution will make little difference on its own. (c) Hence the private market will not exist, since everyone will decline to pay. (d) Government can co-ordinate everyone paying most easily by compulsory taxation and state provision of the police service.
9 In the long run, speculation is profitable only if it is stabilizing. However, in the short run, nobody is quite sure what the equilibrium price is – that is why armies of bright economics graduates are employed in financial services to try to use the latest information to outguess their rivals. Since nobody is quite sure what everyone else knows, herding often results, where everyone copies everyone else in case the other person has superior information. This leads to bandwagons that induce significant and sustained departures from the equilibrium price until everyone comes to their senses and there is a sharp adjustment of prices.

AB 3 (a) As European and Chinese labour markets are unified, the huge addition of Chinese labour makes the labour supply schedule shift to the right, reducing equilibrium wages. (b) With the Chinese economy growing rapidly, the demand for raw materials such as coal is enhanced worldwide. The demand curve shifts up. (c) Demand curve for Bentleys shifts down.

Chapter 4

1 (a) Vertical supply, downsloping demand. (b) To sell 10 per cent fewer peaches, raise the price 20 per cent to £1.20. Vertical supply curve now at 90 peaches.
2 (a) Inelastic. (b) More elastic. (c) More elastic still.
3 Where demand elasticity is −1. Below that point on the demand curve, demand is inelastic: higher prices add to revenue. Above that point, demand is elastic: lower prices add to revenue. If the stadium is free to operate, maximizing profits means maximizing revenue.

4 Vegetables: inelastic, necessity. Catering: elastic, luxury.

5 These data are for nominal not real spending on bread, which fell as real income rose.

6 (a) Necessity is a statement about income elasticity not price elasticity of demand. At high enough prices, demand may be price elastic. (b) If bad weather hits all farmers, it raises prices and helps incomes: 'good' weather needs insurance! (c) Not when they make inferior goods.

7 (a) Above some tax rate (and price of cigarettes) the quantity demand is likely to fall so much that further tax rises reduce tax revenue. (b) –1. (c) Cut the price to get more revenue. (d) Set a higher price than that which maximizes tax revenue because the higher price also reduces quantity of cigarettes demanded and makes people healthier.

8 (a) Income elasticity >1. (b) USA and Australia – rich countries with arid climates and hot summers. (c) Rises, rises, rises. (d) Unchecked, eventually global warming would have adverse effects on income and living standards; feeling poorer, people might then demand fewer air conditioners, other things equal. In practice, governments are likely to take action before then (higher taxes on air conditioners, dearer electricity and other measures).

AB 4

	A	B	C	D	E
(1) Initial P & Q	P = 1 Q = 10	P = 2 Q = 8	P = 2 Q = 8	P = 4 Q = 4	P = 5 Q = 2
(2) New P & Q	P = 2 Q = 8	P = 3 Q = 6	P = 1 Q = 10	P = 3 Q = 6	P = 6 Q = 1
(3) % change in P	100*(2−1)/ 1 = 100	100*(3−2)/ 2 = 50	100*(1−2)/ 2 = −50	100*(3−4)/ 3 = −33	100*(6−5)/ 5 = 20
(4) % change in Q induced	100*(8−10)/ 10 = −20	100*(6−8)/ 8 = −25	100* (10−8)/ 8 = 25	100* (6−4)/ 4 = 50	100* (1−2)/ 2 = −50
(5) PED = (4)/(3)	−0.2	−0.5	−0.5	−1.5	−2.5

Chapter 5

1 Budget line joins points of food = 10, films = 25. Fall in food price has income and substitution effects. Both raise demand for food. For films, income effect raises demand, substitution effect reduces it. When film price falls, film demand rises, food demand could go either way. Putting two price cuts together. Between e and e'' there is no substitution effect: relative prices are the same. Since both goods are normal, e'' is north-east of e since real income is higher.

2 First three statements correct. Fourth may not be. For other goods, there is a substitution effect towards them (unless, like cutlery, they are complements of food), but since real income is lower, demand for normal goods can go either way. Demand for inferior goods *must* rise.

3 Films increase as budget line moves out, transport declines.

4 (a) Both effects reduce demand. (b) Demand curve shifts down: equilibrium price and quantity fall.

5 (a) Just a device to mimic what people do instinctively. (b) Budget line unaffected.

6 (a) Quantity of coconuts and fish on the axes. Can attain the point (5 coconuts and 5 fish). Budget line slopes down through this point but kinked at the point; left of it, negative slope is flatter, right of it negative slope is steeper. (b and c) Hence indifference map likely to mean that highest indifference curve is one that touches the kink point. (d) Small change in slope means kinked point still best and behaviour unchanged.

7 Amazingly, it is not certain that you will invest more in the risky asset when its expected return rises. The reason is substitution and income effects. With a higher relative expected return than before, the substitution effect leads you towards demanding more of the risky asset. But do not forget the income effect. To the extent that you were tempted to invest in the risky asset to improve your target income, when the expected return on this asset improves you do not have to risk so much to get any particular target income. That is the income effect. In this case, it makes you demand less of the risky asset. Whether or not you end up investing more in the risky asset depends on the relative strength of the income and substitution effects, which pull in opposite directions in this case.

AB 5 (a) Not a Veblen good if the behaviour simply reflects new information about product quality; is Veblen good if people simply responding to what is fashionable. (b) Veblen good (unless people think Madonna has the best financial advisers in the world!). (c) As in previous answers, depends whether people think Rick Stein is certifying quality based on his expertise, or whether he is certifying that other people like you will also think it is trendy.

Chapter 6

1 (a) Expenses higher and pre-tax profits lower by £70 000. (b) Accounting profits change; economic profits unaffected since firm charges the opportunity cost of the money tied up in owning the office (the rental it could have got!). (c) More revenue and hence more profits.

2 Opportunity cost of owner is £40 000 and of money tied up is £24 000.

3 (a) Inventories are extra assets, extra borrowing is liability. (b) Interest on loan is a cost.

4 (a) Maybe, if we mean profits over a long period. But since managers can only be monitored imperfectly, they have some scope to pursue other aims. Profit-related bonuses and fears of takeover help keep this in check. (b) Some of these may be sound investments. Some may not. Firms tend to sponsor things popular with the board not the shareholders.

5 With an extra fixed cost of £40, 6 is still the best output level in the short run. MC and MR are unaffected. In the long run the firm is losing money and should close down.

6 (a) MR is horizontal at £13. MC is as in Table 6.4. (b) 7 units.

7 (a) They may not cover opportunity costs. (b) $MC = MR$ whenever a firm succeeds in maximizing profits. (c) Sales maximized when output expanded till $MR = 0$. Last units then fail to cover marginal cost.

8 The demand curve is kinked at an output of 50 and a price of $50 million, being flatter to the left of this point and steeper to the right of it. The corresponding marginal revenue schedules lie below these respective demand schedules but at an output of 50 the MR schedule from the left-hand demand schedule lies above the MR schedule from the right-hand demand schedule. Hence, as the firm increases output, its MR experiences a discontinuous downward jump at the output of 50. For more on the kinked demand curve, see Chapter 9.

9 (a) No change. (b) No change. (c) By reducing future total profits, a future tax reduces the payoff to investing in costly measures today in order to shift cost curves down in the future. If cost curves are different from what they would have been, profit-maximizing output is likely to be affected in the future.

AB 6 (a) A way to maximize post-tax profit is to maximize pre-tax profit – no effect on chosen output. Same answer if examine marginal profit from increasing output. At optimum output, marginal profit is zero so profit tax has no marginal effect and hence no effect on the profit-maximizing output. (b) With higher marginal cost at each output, at the previously optimal output, $MC > MR$ and hence tax makes firm reduce output.

APPENDIX: Answers to review questions and Activity Boxes

Chapter 7

1 (a) Maximum output obtainable from specified bundles of inputs. (b) Also need to know prices of inputs and of output.

2 (a) Falling *LAC*. By spreading fixed costs. (b) Columns 1, 3 and 6 are cheapest way to make 4, 8 and 12 units of output. Total costs are 33, 64, 96. Average costs are 8.25, 8 and 8. (c) There are scale economies in raising output from 4 to 8, and constant returns to scale in going from 8 to 12.

3 (a) Column 1 more capital intensive than column 2; column 3 more than 4; column 5 more than 6. (b) Away in this example.

4 (a) At output of 4, would switch from column 1 to 2. (b) Both must rise (life is harder).

5 (a)

Q	0	1	2	3	4	5	6	7	8	9
MC	0	15	13	11	9	10	10	11	13	16
AC	–	27	20	17	15	14	13.3	13	13	13.3

(b) At $Q=8$, minimum $AC=MC$. (c) Short run. In the long run, the cost of a zero output is zero.

6 (a) If covering variable costs in short run. (b) No, it exits.

7 (a) May cover short-run variable costs. (b) Not if diseconomies of scale. (c) Not if economies of scale.

8 They must be expected to make profits in the future sufficient to cover any losses today. They are borrowing or receiving injections from shareholders. Possible reasons for optimism about the future – lower oil prices (?!); opportunities in China and India; taken over by private equity who can run the companies better (?); too big to fail, and government will have to help them write off their debts at some future stage.

9 If $MC=0$ for ever, no limit on the size of the firm since no disadvantage in getting ever bigger, so one firm likely to break away from the others and become a giant monopoly. Once it has sufficient market power and customer advantage, it may be able to prevent others entering the industry and prevent excess profits being competed away. In which case, price can be set above *MC* by the eventual survivor. Alternatively, *MC* begins to rise with large scale and so do prices, and industry equilibrium allows all surviving firms to cover all their costs.

AB 7 (a) In period 2, the cost of the machine is a sunk cost and should not enter calculation of marginal cost. Since the machine ties the two periods together, the smart way for the firm to think in period 1 is not to make a single-period decision but to make a decision over the two-period horizon, foreseeing how it will itself behave once period 2 arrives and it then has a low *MC* schedule because the machine by then is a sunk cost. Forecasting its own period-2 behaviour, it can decide in period 1 what the marginal benefit of the machine is over the two periods and choose output and investment accordingly in period 1. Tough question! (b) Sunk costs are sunk. From now on, if you think you are going to lose, ignore what you have bet and quit!

Chapter 8

1 (a) Industry demand shifts down, price and quantity fall, firms lose money but may cover short-run variable costs. Eventually, enough firms leave the industry to restore original price at lower aggregate output. (b) Now industry *LRSS* curve slopes up too. In long run, higher-cost firms leave the industry, and equilibrium has lower price, fewer firms, lower total output.

2 Supply curve shifts up in short run, raising price and reducing quantity. In the long run, new entry reverses these shifts.

3 (a) Imports if domestic supply and demand intersect above world price, exports if they intersect below it. (b) Domestic price rises, so domestic output rises, domestic demand falls and imports fall.

4

Q	1	2	3	4	5	6
P	8	7	6	5	4	3
TR	8	14	18	20	20	18
MR	8	6	4	2	0	−2

Monopolist has $Q=2$, $P=7$. Competitive industry $Q=4$, $P=5$.

5 No effect. MC and MR unaltered, and profits still positive.

6 (a) Normal profit rewards all inputs properly. (b) Not if lose scale economies and raise costs.

7 Free entry and exit allow us to think about each period separately. Once exit is costly, the firm has to make a long-run decision from the outset. Even though profits are available during the period after an entrant joins the industry, the entrant has to think about how many periods it will be in the industry and whether the cumulative profit is sufficient to pay the costs of exit at the end. Clearly, entrants may not bid profits down to zero in the long run. Existing firms therefore have a degree of monopoly power. Perfect competition is no longer possible.

8 It turns out that the absolute value of the inverse of the price elasticity of demand PED equals $(P-MC)/MC$. The more inelastic is the demand curve that it faces, the larger the monopoly power of the firm. The easiest way to prove this is mathematically. MR = change in $PQ = P + Q$ (dP/dQ) where the second term is the reduction in existing revenue caused by having to cut prices to sell more output. Noting that $MC = MR$ at profit-maximizing output, we have $MC/P = 1 + (1/PED)$. Hence $(MC-P)/P = 1/PED$. Remember, price elasticities are negative, we can multiply both sides by −1 to get the result. For readers without knowledge of calculus, remember this was a harder question! We do not use calculus anywhere in the text. The intuitive idea that a more inelastic demand curve allows a firm to raise prices more above marginal cost makes perfect sense even without all the maths.

AB 8 (a) No real difference. (b) If overt price discrimination undermines the ability to charge premium prices to premium customers, a monopolist will always reconsider the wisdom of price discrimination in different markets. (c) Not interesting to look at profit margins on drugs that do succeed, since these successes need to pay for all the failures or the firm will leave the industry. Better measures are overall profits over a sustained period, or perhaps the long-run performance of the share price relative to the stock market as a whole, which should reveal what the market thinks the answer to this question is.

Chapter 9

1 (a) $Q=4$, $P=7$. (b) Same again. (c) Because each firm has $MC=3$, but will face $MR > 3$ if it alone expands: price will not fall so much since other firm not expanding too.

2 (a)

Q	1	2	3	4	5	6	7
P	8	7	6	5	4	3	2
TR	8	14	18	20	20	18	14
MR	8	6	4	2	0	−2	−4

Z makes $Q=3$, whereas in 1(b) dividing the market in half, Z made $Q=2$.

3 Certification by a reputable agency saves customers the cost of checking themselves. For mechanics, after a bad experience, you can go elsewhere. Reputation helps solve the information problem. (b) For doctors, you might be dead after a bad experience.

4 A few convey new information. Many erect entry barriers.

5 Agreeing policy with a second parent may have this effect, since you then look silly if you depart from the agreement.

6 (a) Cannot police cheating on the collective agreement. (b) Deterring entry raises profits on existing output.

7 The only smart guesses about rivals' responses are ones that are profit-maximizing for them. This rules out many guesses about how they might react. Sometimes it leaves only one guess.

8 Governments can (a) adopt and invoke international rules, such as EU or World Trade Organization prohibitions on subsidies; (b) adopt and invoke budget rules that make it harder for them to find the money; or (c) build a reputation for being tough by being seen not to bail out in other situations

AB 9   (a) No. (b) Yes. (c) Yes.

Chapter 10

1 (a) Other inputs are fixed. (b) Shifts labour demand curve up.

2 (a) Substitution effect means work more, but income effect means work less since leisure a normal good. (b) More people join labour force.

3 Industry has to pay extra to attract workers from other industries.

4 (a) Top golfers in scarce supply, but big demand. (b) Economics students have more human capital relevant to high-paying jobs.

5 (a) Since people like it, demand is high; and nobody else can supply it. (b) Income effect means want more leisure.

6 In a competitive labour market, a minimum wage below the equilibrium wage has no effect. Above the equilibrium wage, the higher the minimum wage, the higher the point on the labour demand curve and the lower the level of employment. In a monopsonistic labour market, a minimum wage above the intersection of labour demand and the marginal cost of labour to the firm simply moves the firm up its labour demand curve and again reduces jobs. A minimum wage set at a level between *MC* of labour and the wage needed to elicit that level of labour supply will actually increase equilibrium employment. A minimum wage sufficiently low simply reduces labour supply again (see Box 10.4).

7 People who pass tough degrees reveal that they are smart and work hard, general skills that are of use to many employers. University may also allow people to develop networks of friends and contacts of like-minded people that will prove valuable later on. None of this says that if you *also* study for a subject of direct use to a future employer you will not be even more valuable!

AB 10   (a) Since students will increasingly find themselves working for global companies, learning about and learning in other countries may well be valuable. (b) US universities have a long tradition of fundraising that has built up endowments that can be used to support scholarships. The culture of giving is much less developed in Europe where the state has played a larger role in funding education. (c) Institutions such as the Bank of England should attract talent from as broad a pool as possible. Sometimes, for example in the Ministry of Defence, there may be more sensitivity about nationality.

Chapter 11

1 Lose £30 000 while training. Future salary of £23 000 for 30 years repays this.

2 Restrict entry by tough exams and insisting on long working hours.

3 Yes.

4 Wages fall if less monopoly profit for unions to chase after. Larger unions would help restore workers' bargaining power but might prevent gains from competition being realized.

5 (a) Not if there are systematic reasons for women to acquire fewer attributes valued by firms. (b) Neglects the opportunity cost of wages forgone while in education. (c) Not if poor are disproportionately represented in unions in the first place.

6 For the same initial reward, you prefer general skills because they have more applications and it is less risky to be dependent on one particular firm. Firm needing specific skills could pay for training or pay a wage premium each year to the trained. Should prefer the latter since the firm too faces risks (e.g. you might have a car accident, making it impossible for the firm to recoup the cost of training).

7 (a) People in Vanuatu may consume high quantities of environmental goods that are unmeasured and excluded from conventional GDP. Proper data on environmental capital and consumption of environmental services might mean that Vanuatu was richer than you thought. Same for leisure, of which they also have lots. (b) If people care about relative incomes, then general income rises do not create extra utility and happiness. Suppose this is true. It would take higher *relative* wages to get people to work harder. Just as we get an arms race when it is relative military power that counts, a free market would lead to wage escalation as each firm tried to outbid the rest only to discover that, once all workers had high wages, nobody wanted to work after all since nobody had wages that were high relative to others. The government might then have to step in to organize multilateral wage reduction!

AB 11 (a) Adverse selection. (b) Signalling. (c) Screening. (d) Screening. (e) Signalling. (f) Signalling.

Chapter 12

1 (a) Some flows of consumption services are provided most efficiently by buying consumer durables. (b) The laundrette costs £104 a year. Buying costs £52 a year + £40 interest forgone. Better to buy.

2 You make 20 on every 90 you put in, about 22 per cent a year.

3 (£3600 × 0.91 = £3276) + (£12 600 × 0.83 = £10 458) × £13 734. Buy it!

4 It raises the present value of the existing stream of rentals, raising the incentive to build more capital assets. This slowly reduces the equilibrium rental on capital until long-run equilibrium is restored.

5 The land demand is a derived demand. If supply is fixed, only a rise in demand for land can bid up land prices. Tenant farmers face higher rentals but extra income from their crops is what started the process. Farmers lose in land prices and rentals bid up by higher demand for housing.

6 (a) It also makes future nominal income rise. (b) Higher labour productivity and wage income also raise the demand for goods. (c) True if only one possible user. Competition between users is what bids up the price.

7 Generally, by fostering trade and demand, the derived demand for land will rise, implying an increase in the price of land and other commodities (e.g. metal ores, oil) in relatively fixed supply.

However, there are also losers from globalization. Suppose Chinese textiles, based on cheap labour in China, displace European textile production from regions such as Lancashire. Other things equal, the demand for Lancashire land, and hence its price, falls.

8 (a) Running the pension scheme is easy when there are lots of young workers paying contributions and few retired people making claims. (b) Contributions must rise, pensions fall, or both. (c) Extending the retirement age would mean more workers pay in for longer and there would be fewer retired people to support. Otherwise, the government has to live with the situation or increase taxation on some population group to finance the gap between contributions and payments.

AB 12 (a) Use a zero discount rate on future utility. (b) A unit of additional future consumption yields less benefit than a unit of current consumption: using a positive discount rate for future consumption reflects this. Conversely, if the burden of global warming reduces the utility of future generations below that of current generations, the consumption of future generations should then carry more weight than current generations (a negative discount rate!). (c) At least as high a rate of return on environmental investments as investment in physical or human capital.

Chapter 13

1 A is risk-neutral, B risk-loving, C risk-averse. C insures most.
2 High. Adverse selection. Low-risk people are happy to be screened.
3 (a) Yes. (b) No. (c) Yes.
4 Negative beta: you do well in a slump, when other shares are doing less well. Your shares have high price and low expected return.
5 Fear of moral hazard – being exploited by people with better information – prevents *others* from dealing in shares.
6 (a) If all available information is already in the price, by definition only new, as yet unavailable information, can change the price. (b) Risk-pooling reduces the premium they need to charge. (c) Volatile shares are valuable if they have a negative beta!
7 You buy insurance because its payout is negatively correlated with other risks that you face, thereby reducing your total risk; you occasionally buy lottery tickets for fun despite knowing that this is an unfair gamble; and you may be tempted into risky investments either because they have low beta or because, despite their risk, their expected return is so high that it compensates for the extra risk that you take on.
8 If risk did not matter, the only equilibrium in which people would hold gold and equities is if they had the same expected return. Buying gold today at £100 you would need to expect the price next year to be £105 if this was to be as good as buying equities with an expected return of 5 per cent. (b) If gold has a negative beta, then including some gold as well as equities in your portfolio reduces the total risk of your portfolio. Since gold performs this valuable function it can pay a bit less than 5 per cent expected return and still leave you happy to hold it. So a good answer is that next year's expected gold price is, say, £103 or £104.

AB 13

Outcome	Asset price			Portfolio value		
	(a) FTSE index	(b) Low beta asset	(c) High beta asset	A ½ of (a) + ½ of (b)	B ⅓ of (a) + ⅔ of (b)	C ½% of (a) + ½ of (c)
Boom	120	90	150	105	100	135
Normal	100	100	100	100	100	100
Slump	80	110	50	95	100	65

Chapter 14

1　All three.
2　Bundling.
3　SEAT, Skoda, VW, Audi (all the same firm); regular and executive lounges in airports; standard and luxury Christmas pudding.
4　Output is higher, and those previously unwilling to pay the uniform price now do better. Those willing previously to pay it do worse, since face a higher price.
5　Cartel makes a standardized product. Strategic alliance makes a range of products that have strong complementarity.
6　(a) $MC = 0$ so price should be low. Some free pricing also to entice people into usage before prices then raised. Advertising may also support free prices, as with ITV. (b) Price discrimination requires that users cannot buy when cheap and resell when expensive. (c) High share prices could reflect expectations of high future profits.
7　You must have argued that the benefits of scale economies, incentive to invest and hence cost reduction outweigh the abuse of monopoly position (high prices, making access difficult for competitors who need to make use of Microsoft platforms); and that the threat of a future investigation would be sufficient to prevent Microsoft taking too much advantage of its market power.
8　(a) Even though everyone benefits if everyone joins, individuals may fear others will not join (because they fear others will not join) – hence two possible equilibria: everyone joins or nobody does. (b) Subsidy of 1 per person would be sufficient, since then nobody loses by switching, whether or not anyone else switches. (c) Now problem complicated by fact that men have no gain from switching. May need to subsidize them by more than 1. (d) Might offer contingent contracts that become binding *only* if everyone switches. Then in principle could extract a payment from women (for whom benefit of switch is large) in order to bribe men to switch.
AB 14　(a) Versioning. (b) Versioning but also different MC of supply (cheaper when gym not congested). (c) Versioning. (d) Different MC. (e) Bundling.

Chapter 15

1　(a) Efficient, not equitable. (b) Neither efficient nor equitable. (c) Both efficient and equitable. (d) Not efficient nor very equitable. (e) Efficient not equitable. Equitable asks 'How fair is distribution?'.
2　(a) 1 film worth 5 meals to consumer utility. (b) MC of films five times that of meals. (c) MPL in meals five times higher than in film. Equilibrium equates MSC and MSB.

3 Yes to all questions.

4 No. By insuring boilers they certified they removed any incentive to be bribed to falsify certificates, reducing moral hazard.

5 (a) Such activities waste scarce resources. (b) Yes.

6 (a) For further pollution reduction, marginal cost exceeds marginal benefit once pollution already low. (b) Monopoly, externalities, etc. are important market failures. (c) Government failures also occur.

7 Climate change does not affect a single individual, but rather a region or the entire planet. We discuss public goods in the next chapter. Essentially, if everyone gets the same quantity of the good then we need to sum the individual marginal benefits to get the total marginal benefit. And we need to add these up across current and future generations, discounting the future as we think appropriate.

8 The general principle is that things in inelastic supply or inelastic demand should be taxed more heavily for efficiency reasons. Hence (a) low, (b) high, (c) average, (d) high, not merely because of inelasticity but also because redressing an externality. Taxing some foods may be a bad idea on equity grounds, but that is a separate matter.

AB 15 (a) Separate nation states may free ride, hoping others save the planet. A world government can internalize all the benefits of costly action. However, governments need consent to rule. Outbreaks of nationalism, from Scotland to Kurdistan, remind us that large remote governments can also run into difficulties. (b) Externalities made it hard to establish markets in pollutants, though governments are now working hard to remedy this; and missing markets for future goods mean that future generations cannot express their purchasing power today. (c) Depends a lot on whether, despite global warming, future generations will be richer or poorer than us because of other technical and productivity advances – the richer they are relative to us, the harder it is to make the case for our bearing a lot of pain; conversely, if some aspects of climate change are irreversible (e.g. if Greenland melts) the case for action today is high because future welfare will be low otherwise. (d) Quotas achieve the outcome but inefficiently since there is no mechanism to equate marginal cost of cutbacks across different polluters; taxes or an induced market for carbon might be more efficient but create uncertainty about whether the overall target is achieved. Best may be tradable quotas (see Section 15.6).

Chapter 16

1 All except d.

2 Education a merit good (people do not know what is good for them); externalities (we like educated people to interact with); equity (helps promote equality of opportunity).

3 Vertical equity says take from the rich and give to the poor, but should not assess just income: ideally want to redistribute from the person getting more of all goods that they care about. Horizontal equity says treat all sunworshippers in a similar way.

4 All progressive except tax on beer, which is a larger share of poor people's income.

5 18, 24, 28.8 per cent. It is progressive, and more so the higher the exemption level. With an exemption of £1 million, the tax would only hit the rich!

6 (a) What about finance of public goods, offsetting externalities, provision of social insurance, redistribution? (b) Marginal taxes usually create distortions. (c) We can analyse the incentives for politicians to choose particular policies and for voters to elect particular parties, and hence analyse political equilibrium.

7   (a) No change in labour supplied, so no distortion triangle; burden falls on workers whose post-tax wage falls. (b) Big triangle, and firms now bear most of the tax (cost of labour rises by almost whole amount of the tax). (c) In between these cases.

8   (a) Hypothecation means that there is little welfare redistribution across groups as a result of the tax and spending policy. When politicians change things, there are winners and losers. Winners usually smile quietly, losers shout loud and make trouble. Politicians sometimes want a quiet life, or to spend their political capital on a different project. (b) Economists abstract from the political difficulties in introducing policies, and prefer to keep open the option of redistribution. Moreover, hypothecation makes no reference to efficiency since it does not assess marginal costs and benefits. The purpose of a congestion charge or tobacco tax is to reduce an activity of which too much is produced and consumed.

AB 16   (a) Party leaders prefer prospect of power to the adoption of a political position that they happen to think correct (and party members have elected leaders with these attributes). (b) Smart politicians will each locate in the centre. (c) Now locating too centrally risks losing some extremists, who will abstain from voting. How close a party should locate to the centre depends on how many votes it loses on the extreme versus how many it gains by being closer to the centre. Political equilibrium should now have some clear blue water between the two parties with neither contesting the exact centre ground. And of course all this presumes voter opinions are equally spread. If there is a big cluster of voters a third of the way from left to right, this is where the median voter will be. Parties will be trying to locate near here even though it is not halfway from left to right.

Chapter 17

1   Triangle has height of £3, and length of 200 000. Hence cost is £300 000.

2   The triangle now has height £6 and length 400 000, a cost of £1 200 000. In addition, 600 000 units are now produced at £1 more than is really necessary. Total social cost £1 800 000.

3   In essence, US presumes large size is bad, and tries to break up big firms, or regulate them if they cannot be split up. UK policy used to be on a case-by-case basis, but now increasingly emphasizes the promotion of competition.

4   Much of the promotion of small firms rests on the belief that a dynamic economy is always experiencing births and deaths, that tomorrow's successes will not all come from today's incumbents. What is the market failure? In part this might lie in the short-termism of financial markets, but the question is why governments can pick winners any better than banks and other lenders to small businesses. We would all like the consequences of successful small firms, but promoting small firms can lead to more failure as well as more success.

5   Locational externalities. But the entire cluster locates in a sensible place. High-wage Switzerland is not a good place for labour-intensive businesses.

6   (a) Profit may just reflect monopoly power. (b) Benefits of scale economies and incentive to innovate sometimes outweigh the other costs of monopoly. (c) Private benefit of mergers may include monopoly profits, which are a social cost.

7   (a) Private equity (PE) funds persuaded the market to lend to them long term (10 years at a time) so that they themselves could pursue management strategies requiring longer to pay off, thereby remedying a market failure caused by the normal failure of financial markets to be able to commit to the longer term; argued that they obtained synergies in learning how to manage portfolios of companies and projects rather than a single company; and were accused by their

detractors of breaking up viable bundles into their constituent parts for sale bit by bit. (b) Since PE funds get their finance by borrowing from the market – in effect they have much more debt and much less equity than normal companies – they are sensitive to panics in the debt market that either raise substantially the interest rate at which PE funds can borrow or impose credit rationing on PE firms.

8 (a) In principle, the UK would make a social profit if it subsidized Ferrari by anything less than the value of the beneficial externality that Ferrari's move to the UK would create. (b) Two reasons we should not expect the private sector to be as effective as the government in organizing a relocation bribe: (i) each private firm wants a free ride on the others, so none contribute, (ii) in a dynamic setting in which Ferrari's move enticed yet more inward moves, which in turn enticed yet more, not all those benefiting from the Ferrari move are incumbents, there are also future incumbents who are unrepresented today in any bribe gathering. (c) If Italy has a cluster of expertise around Ferrari's current location, Italy will suffer an adverse externality if Ferrari moves; expect retaliation from the Italian government. It is partly to prevent costly bidding wars between member states that the EU generally outlaws state aid to private firms.

AB 17 (a) If scale economies matter enough, breaking Yell up means losing the advantage of lower costs. (b) You would gather evidence on whether people use *both* the internet *and* print directories, or whether internet surfers have thrown away their print directories; you would ask firms who advertise in directories, and keep track of where they get their own new customers from, about trends in their customer responses about how people first heard of them.

Chapter 18

1 Two-part tariff yields more revenue. It cannot discriminate between existing members, can at least do so between old and new ones.

2 BA faces stiff competition. OFAIR not needed.

3 Commuters travel when MC high and ideally should pay more; but big congestion externalities on rush-hour roads could easily justify cheap rail tickets. First best is to tax the externalities appropriately (properly price car use and parking).

4 Big externalities – it helps other industries that do not use the tunnel. Could be socially desirable even if privately unprofitable.

5 (a) Encourages inward investment to build cars, only some of which exported through the tunnel. (b) Social risk premium smaller than that charged by banks (better risk-pooling and risk-spreading). (c) Reduces congestion at Heathrow and Gatwick. (d) Reduces noise pollution near these airports. (e) Provides jobs for involuntary unemployed construction workers who would otherwise make nothing.

6 (a) Might have lowest possible cost curves and be pricing at marginal cost but still losing money because $MC < AC$. (b) Might have more incentive to reduce cost curves. (c) If scale economies not too important, breaking up a large company may in fact be the easiest way in which to regulate conduct by inducing effective competition.

7 Cost-plus gives less incentive to keep costs down but prevents companies getting terrified by all the risk they bear (for which they have to charge). Fixed-price makes companies bear all risk (so raising the tender price they charge) but gives them bigger incentive to keep costs down (since they get all the benefits). Former better if little prospect of cost escalation, because easy to monitor management but large 'exogenous' uncertainties.

8   The congestion part suggests it should be expensive to use bottlenecks in the rush hour, but perhaps free to use them at 3am when nobody is around. So different streets need different prices, and these prices ideally would vary by time of day too. The issue is how users would be informed. Unless they can continuously detect the price of streets, some simplification of this system would be needed. The pollution part entails two issues. First, one might want to charge different amounts for different vehicles depending on their emissions (which themselves vary between stop-start and cruising at 60 mph. Second, you might want to think about noise pollution. Congestion arguments suggest we want inner-city shops to receive truckloads of goods at 3am, but if you live nearby you might object to being woken up. Your pricing scheme needs to trade off these different issues.

AB 18   (a) Paying upfront puts the whole cost in the current year budget. Using PFI/PPP means the payments are spread over many years. If the public finances used comprehensive accounting, these future liabilities would appear in current estimates of public sector debt, but in the current system they do not. (b) A given set of risks can always be traded in financial markets and sold for a fair price. However, nobody will trade risks that can be affected by one of the parties that has inside information about its own behaviour. As with defence procurement, these latter risks probably need to be shared by contractor and government.

Chapter 19

1   $1000 - 120 = 880$.

2   (a) £250 bn. (b) National income is net national product at basic prices. Depreciation is part of the cost of producing output. (c) They reduce the purchasing power of a given gross income.

3   (a) 210. (b) 310. (c) 1870. (d) Yes, if imports exceed exports.

4   (a) 2200. (b) 10 per cent. (c) In this example, also 10 per cent.

5   (a) Leisure is lost but investment in human capital occurs. (b) No – just a transfer payment. (c) Yes. (d) Pollution should ideally be subtracted from GNP.

6   (a) Just a transfer payment, not real output. (b) Might conceivably be undesirable if achieved by very unequal income distribution. (c) Only because people compare nominal receipts. In real terms, *Gone With The Wind* wins by a mile!

7   The place to start is that by taking leisure people reveal that this is at least as valuable to them as working more, provided they have that choice in the first place. For all such people, you would have to decide how many hours a day are the fixed cost of being alive – for sleeping, eating, washing, etc. – and hence how many hours could potentially be allocated between work and leisure. Knowing something about national wage rates and hours of work, you could have a stab at valuing total leisure hours. Some complications: (a) all the people who do not have the choice of working or not – the young, the sick, those caught in a poverty trap; (b) the distinction between those working but choosing some leisure and those on benefit schemes who simultaneously get money and leisure; and (c) how to treat parents who stay at home to look after children. Even so, it would be possible to make a guestimate.

8   Disentangle some things: (a) the nominal price has been constant therefore the real price has fallen a lot; (b) quality has improved hugely over the period. To explain both of these simultaneously, there must have been a lot of technical progress. Deciding how to revalue goods because of their superior quality is just one of the headaches of a statistician working on the national accounts.

AB 19   (a) It does not – that is why it is *gross* domestic product. (b) Net domestic product or net national income would include a deduction for capital depreciation. (c) Fairly rough and ready – assuming e.g. a lifetime of 5 years for a TV, 10 years for a car, 25 years for a factory, and writing the initial value off steadily over the period. (d) Would need to estimate the value of the stock of environmental capital – green fields, fresh air, temperate climate, etc. – and then decide each year whether reduction caused by humans (pollution, etc.) was more or less than investment made by humans (land improvement, lower emissions, etc.). (e) In practice, the best way to estimate the capital value would probably be to estimate the annual consumer benefit (e.g. of green fields) and then work out the present value using a suitable discount rate.

Chapter 20

1 (a) Intercept $= 40$, slope $= 0.8$. (b) Destocking. (c) 200. (d) Yes: $40 = 0.2 \times 200$.
2 (a) 75. (b) 45.
3 (a) Equilibrium income falls from 500 to 200. (b) $I = S = 100$. Saving is unchanged, but rises from 20 per cent to 50 per cent of income because income falls.
4 Unplanned investment (which may be positive or negative).
5 (a) 2000. (b) $200/(0.3) = 667$. Lower.
6 (a) Investment is independent of saving, and higher saving reduces aggregate demand. (b) Because $MPC < 1$, each fall in output causes a smaller fall in demand, so the process eventually comes to a halt.
7 In the simple model of this chapter, the multiplier $1/s$ is always greater than $+1$, since $0 < s < 1$. However, in later chapters, when we introduce leakages other than saving, the combined leakages may then be sufficient to reduce the multiplier below unity.
8 The paradox of thrift relies on output and income adjusting to restore desired injections and desired leakages. In the model of this chapter, that can always happen. Once we reintroduce aggregate supply, and in particular a maximum capacity for the entire economy, it is possible that there is an output ceiling above which output and income cannot go. The paradox of thrift might then be frustrated.
AB 20 (a) and (c) are shifts in AD, but (b) is a movement along a given AD schedule.

Chapter 21

1 (a) 120. (b) Output rises by 250 to 1250. Consumption rises by 200 to 1000. Investment is 130 and government spending 120. (c) $Y = 1250$, $C = 1000$, $I = 80$, $G = 170$. (d) $Y = 1200$, $C = 960$, $I = 80$, so $G = 160$.
2 Of each extra pound of national income, 0.6 goes in extra consumption, 0.15 in extra saving and 0.25 in extra taxes. Multiplier $= 1/(0.4)$. Equilibrium income rises £15 bn. Taxes rise a quarter of this, so budget deficit increases, since extra G is £6 bn.
3 In equilibrium, desired leakages equal desired injections. Desired S and I equal only when no government and no foreign sector.
4 Because eventually it would be unable to afford the interest payments on its huge debt. *You* cannot pile up huge debts either!
5 (a) EU exports fall, inducing EU slump and lower EU imports. (b) EU trade balance worsens. Although both exports and imports fall, for each unit fall in planned injections (caused by lower exports) there is a total fall of 1 unit in planned leakages. Since the latter comprises lower planned saving, lower planned taxes and lower planned imports, imports fall by less than 1 and hence less than exports fall.
6 (a) Wrong because of balanced budget multiplier. (b) As an identity, $(X - Z)$ always equals $[(T - G) + (S - I)]$.
7 Debt is a stock and a government liability; GDP a flow and a potential source of tax revenue. The

economic variable that connects real stocks and real flows is the real interest rate. If real interest rates remain constant, changes in the debt/GDP ratio do tell us what is happening to the indebtedness of the government, but if real interest rates doubled, it would take much larger GDP and tax revenue to service any given amount of debt.

8 The multiplier can be written as $1/[1 + s(1 - t) + z]$ so any values of (s, t, z) making the denominator equal to 1.5 will imply a multiplier of 2/3. For example, $z = 0.45$, $s = 0.1$, $t = 0.5$.

AB 21 (a) Because fluctuations in income alter tax revenue. (b) Could be useful, although regular IMF reports on individual countries perform some of the same function. (c) Bond markets would experience price falls and long-term interest rates would rise. (d) Government investment today adds to output and potential tax revenue tomorrow, and hence is close to self-financing from a long-run government perspective. (e) Clearly it is hard to draw a line, especially if the government believes education is the most important investment that it can make!

Chapter 22

1 (a) No. Cannot be retraded indefinitely. Nor is it pure barter unless new car has same monetary value as old. (b) Watch which is then retraded, not swallowed.
2 (a) Same value. (b) More valuable as money. (c) Less valuable as money, for example because more efficient token money now used.
3 By simultaneously creating loans and deposits to match, without requiring a cash injection.
4 (a) No. They are not subsequently retraded repeatedly. (b) No. (c) They reduce your demand for money, but do not affect supply: credit card stubs cannot be reused to purchase other goods.
5 M0 = 12 + 2 = 14, M4 = 12 + 30 + 60 + 20 = 122.
6 (a) Most of money supply is bank deposits, a liability of banks. By simultaneously expanding both sides of their balance sheet, banks increase the money supply. (b) If people put less cash in banks, banks less able to multiply up reserves into deposits.
7 Small, since opportunity cost of holding bank deposits hardly affected by rises and falls in general level of interest rates.
8 Credit cards allow you to temporarily postpone when you pay – and by affecting the synchronization of receipts and payments may therefore affect the demand for money – but do not themselves affect the supply of money.

AB 22 (a) Because cash is liquid and can be used to make transactions; also riskless and hence may be valuable as an asset. (b) The key difference between debt and equity is that equity never has to be repaid and firms can vary the level of dividends that they pay each year – in a bad year the firm can make zero dividend payments. If all its financing was debt, it might (often) be unable to meet the required interest payments and have to declare bankruptcy. (c) In exchange for absorbing this degree of risk, investors in equities demand a rate of return that on average exceeds the return on debt by several percentage points a year, though because of capital gains and losses of volatile share prices this is only true on average – particular years can be much better or much worse.

Chapter 23

1 (a) Bank of England gives cheque to Barclays in exchange for cash. Bank has now fewer securities (assets) but equivalently fewer liabilities (cash in circulation). Having lost cash reserves, Barclays has a multiplied reduction in deposits, and corresponding change in loans on the other side of its balance sheet. (b) Money supply falls by more than original open market operation. (c) No difference if pay in cash (unless changes public's desired ratio of cash to deposits).

2   The money multiplier is now 1. Money supply falls only by the value of the open market operation. No additional deposit and loan contraction at Barclays.

3   If monetary policy cares about inflation and output, but takes time to affect them, then whatever things are observable today are known to be reliably correlated with future inflation and output. This includes past values of inflation and output themselves, some financial market data (which come out fast) and survey data on business and household confidence.

4   Initially, consumption function shifts up: spend more at each income. However, once debts accumulate, more income goes on paying interest and less is available for buying goods. Consumption function eventually shifts down again.

5   Reduces present value of future profits, and hence benefit of investment. This is true whether financed by bank borrowing, new share issues or out of retained profit (when what changes is the opportunity cost of the funds employed).

6   (a) Can control money supply by relying on 'normal' reserve ratios banks want anyway. However, central banks prefer to set interest rate and supply the money the market then demands. (b) Cash pays no nominal interest. Its real return is simply $-\pi$ where π is the inflation rate. (c) Sensible if expected future incomes have risen sharply.

7   Households and firms may be locked into previous plans, may take time to re-evaluate decisions and may wait to see if the interest rate change is permanent.

8   Households should raise consumption only in response to rises in permanent income. In the long run, most changes in income are permanent, especially in the aggregate. In 2007 the UK was a lot richer than in 1907, and in 2008 it will be a lot richer than in 1908. In the short run, however, consumers are never quite sure whether an income increase is temporary or permanent, and hence increase consumption by less than their actual income has risen.

AB 23   (a) Provided interest rates affect aggregate demand – the subject of the next chapter – higher interest rates can be used to restore aggregate demand to its original position, whatever the initial shock. (b) Ideally, monetary policy should be looking two years into the future to anticipate what is going to happen to aggregate demand and respond in advance. (c) Yes, especially if its mandate is to put inflation first whenever this conflict arises.

Chapter 24

1   It adds little to permanent income, so consumption demand changes little.

2   (a) *IS* shifts up. (*b*) *LM* shifts right under a Taylor rule. (c) No effect under a Taylor rule.

3   Horizontal *LM*. Whatever the small country's output, European Central Bank (ECB) sets the single interest rate based on whole euro area, which is hardly affected by small country. Its *LM* shifts when ECB changes interest rates.

4   For Euroland, *LM* slopes up. If small country behaves like the Euroland aggregate, its output is high only when Euroland output is high, so *LM* slopes up even for the small country.

5   (a) Automatic stabilizers work at fixed tax rates. (b) If output was lower, there would have been no reason to raise interest rates, but then there would be no reason for output to fall.
(c) Consumption and investment demand based on assessment of long run.

6   (a) An expected rise in short-term interest rates may already have been built into the long-term interest rate at which households borrowed. However, an unexpected rise in short-term interest rates – for example, because new adverse information about inflation has recently become available – will leave existing borrowers unaffected, at least until their long-term loan matures and they have to renew it. Hence any given rise in short-term interest rates has less effect on aggregate

demand. (b) Hence the central bank has to raise interest rates by more in order to have the same effect. In practice, this means less effect via consumption demand and more effect via investment demand and perhaps via exchange rate effects (see Chapter 29).

7   This means real interest rates *fall* when inflation *rises*, and hence monetary policy should exacerbate departures from the inflation target rather than correcting them. (b) If inflation is nevertheless fine, the central bank must be getting some help from somewhere else, probably fiscal policy. For example, if the tax system is not inflation-neutral, higher inflation may raise real tax revenue and dampen aggregate demand – this might occur if nominal capital gains are taxed, if higher income tax thresholds are not inflation indexed. Moreover, the fiscal authorities may either have powerful automatic stabilizers (high marginal tax rates) or be successfully pursuing discretionary fiscal policy aimed at stabilizing inflation, though this is likely to be less nimble than monetary policy.

AB 24   (a) 1998, 2000, 2007. (b) Expected future inflation. (c) Lewis Hamilton does not mind turning left and then turning right shortly afterwards; however, his performance is very transparent and his skill easily assessed. Central banks need people to trust their competence, and may worry a bit more about the impact rapid reversals have on their perceived credibility. If so, they will deliberately err on the side of changing interest rates by small amounts so that the next change is likely to be in the same direction, appearing to add to their credibility. The better established their credibility, the more they might be prepared to change interest rates by a larger amount or to reverse a previous decision more quickly.

Chapter 25

1   (a) *MDS* shows how inflation affects aggregate demand via its effect on how interest rates are set. (b) Raises i^* to return *MDS* to original position. (c) Tighten monetary policy.

2   Vertical *AS* shifts right, *MDS* shifts up, equilibrium inflation unchanged. In practice, *MDS* shift likely to precede *AS* shift.

3   (a) Higher tax rate shifts it up. (b) Higher productivity shifts it down.

4   If all wages change together, in principle they could adjust quickly to a shock. When wage settlements are staggered, old wages, appropriate to old circumstances, affect where new wages are set, which in turn affects the next round of wage settlement, and so on, slowing down wage adjustment.

5   (a) With fixed nominal interest rate, higher inflation reduces real interest rate, and boosts demand: *MDS* still slopes down. *SAS* shifts up, so inflation rises and output falls. Subsequently, *SAS* shifts down when oil prices fall again, and back to full equilibrium. (b) and (c) still imply a down-sloping *MDS* schedule.

6   (a) Eventually, output restored to potential output. (b) Not in long run, unless potential output depends on inflation.

7   (a) Not unless the UK economy is so integrated with its eurozone partners that what is happening to the UK is also happening to the zone as a whole; eurozone monetary policy will react to aggregate eurozone data. (b) A UK boom, accompanied by inflation, would make the UK less competitive at its fixed exchange rate against other economies in the eurozone. Lower competitiveness would reduce net exports, reduce aggregate demand and bid down inflation. (c) If this process happens too slowly, fiscal policy could try to operate more counter-cyclically, either by designing more powerful automatic stabilizers or by discretionary changes in fiscal policy. But fiscal policy is quite difficult to adjust quickly and reversibly.

8 (a) Serious supply-side shocks such as higher oil prices and higher commodity prices caused by strong demand by China and other emerging market economies. (b) Not necessarily. If the Bank is never prepared to exceed the target, it will have to be ultra cautious, perhaps too much so. However, having exceeded the target, the Bank's credibility required taking corrective action strongly.

AB 25   (a) Statistical extrapolation of past trends and cycles requires only the macroeconomic data on output itself, is quickly implemented and easily conducted for many countries. An economist would think it a crude approximation. If there was a serious shock to the level of potential output, past extrapolation would stop working, but a statistician could always start a new extrapolation recognizing that other things were no longer equal. (b) A direct economic approach might try to use the level and rate of change of inflation to make inferences about the level of excess demand or supply, or might try to build up a more detailed model of aggregate supply based on inputs of capital, labour, technology, etc.

Chapter 26

1 (a) With zero inflation, in years 1–9 your income is £10 000, and interest payment is £4000. (b) In year 1, income £10 000, interest £204 000! By year 9, income £2 560 000, interest still £204 000.

2 Equal annual payments in nominal terms become declining annual payments in real terms. Inflation brings the real burden forward, may make early years impossibly difficult (later years very easy).

3 (a) When there is a change in real money demand, M/P, M and P grow at different rates. The imperfect correlation between money growth and inflation in the table reflects this. (b) In the long-run, if real money demand is fairly constant, sustained growth of money must be accompanied by sustained growth in prices and vice versa.

4 Initially, demand shock raises π and lowers U, supply shock raises π and raises U. Permanent demand shock has no permanent effect on U (since market forces or central bank restore aggregate demand to potential output), whereas permanent supply shock raises equilibrium U.

5 Those with fixed nominal income, those paying higher taxes because tax system not inflation-neutral, those lending at fixed nominal interest rate. For third group, if they anticipated inflation, they could set nominal interest rates appropriately higher.

6 (a) Not in long run. (b) Not if nominal interest rate adjusts to maintain real interest rate. (c) If nominal interest rate fails to keep up with inflation, real interest rates may actually be lower.

7 (a) Negative inflation of 3 per cent a year. (b) This would be first best but we live in a second-best world in which the government has few non-distortionary ways of getting the tax revenue that it needs. Rather than have heavy distortions in income tax or VAT it makes sense to keep these rates a little lower and earn a little bit on the inflation tax, thus achieving the optimal second-best compromise.

8 (a) No – could explain high prices but not continually rising prices. (b) Bankrupt government printing money to finance some activities. (c) It is far too high – in terms of Figure 26.2 the tax-revenue-maximizing inflation rate is that below the peak of the curve, but much higher inflation rates actually raise less and less revenue because people ditch cash itself.

AB 26   (a) The two are opposite sides of the same coin – only because there is no output–inflation trade-off in the long run can independent central banks succeed in permanently lowering inflation without reducing output. (b) For example, consider a huge adverse supply shock that temporarily wiped out a lot of supply capacity. Choice would be to cut aggregate demand immediately in line with supply collapse, which would prevent inflation but imply a huge output fall, or to cut demand by less knowing that the result would be inflation. If the supply decrease is permanent there is no alternative to lowering demand, but a temporary supply reduction might make it attractive to be less aggressive. If half of the UK floods tomorrow, the Chancellor might authorize the Bank to exceed its inflation target for a bit.

Chapter 27

1. Pessimistic about finding a job, people leave labour force completely. Lower morale, aware that firms, rightly or wrongly, may brand them as less good because they have been unemployed.
2. No, outflow falls a lot in slump. Rising.
3. Reduced demand for some types of labour, raised demand for others. Temporary mismatch, but eventually skills and wages adjust. Millennia of technical progress would have driven unemployment to 100 per cent if there was any permanent relationship to unemployment.
4. (a) Deficient demand in economy. (b) Real wage too high, for example because of union power or generous welfare benefits.
5. Do not begin with spare capacity. Rather high equilibrium unemployment.
6. (a) Fast flow through U pool may allow better matching of skills to jobs in changing world. (b) Not if equilibrium U. (c) Exacerbates Keynesian U. Even if equilibrium U, shifting job acceptance schedule down will only eliminate some U.
7. (a) Fails – income effect of payment makes lone parents demand leisure not more work. (b) Fails – they are unlikely to be paying much income tax. (c) Succeeds if the payment set high enough.
8. Teenagers need training from scratch – lack skills and job experience; teenage wages not low enough to compensate. Additionally, many smart teenagers choose further education, so those instead going immediately to work may get stigmatized relative to their peers.

AB 27   (a) Impossible to explain with this theory. (b) Being richer, people will demand fewer hours of work in order to have more hours of leisure for which we know demand rises strongly with income. (c) By adding to the marginal cost of labour to the firm it reduces labour demand; with lower labour demand, and lower equilibrium wages, the gap between labour force and job acceptances increases, so equilibrium unemployment is higher.

Chapter 28

1. £1 = 1.40 euro, and 1 euro = £0.71. Yes.
2. Surplus of £2bn. Rising before central bank sells this amount of sterling and buys £2bn of forex reserves to achieve forex market equilibrium at the desired exchange rate.
3. External balance refers to current account balance, not trade balance. Japan also earns income on large foreign assets, so actually has had current account surpluses. Yes, running out of forex reserves forces adjustment faster than stockpiling forex reserves.
4. Trivially, appreciation desirable if initial exchange rate too low, undesirable if initially too high. Could assess relative to likely long-run equilibrium values.
5. Inflation means US price of $4 rises to $12, UK price of £1 rises to £2. Hence need exchange rate of $6/£ to preserve original relative prices in a common currency.
6. (a) Not if nominal exchange rate depreciates enough. (b) Financial account more important in short run since flows could potentially be huge. (c) Will *already* have appreciated to high level so expected to fall from now on, offsetting from now on the benefit of high interest rates.

7 Finding the natural resource certainly leads to a big redistribution – owners of the resource are better off and others (e.g. manufacturers) worse off. However, the higher real exchange rate is not all bad: it means that consumers can import foreign goods more cheaply, and hence their domestic incomes are now worth more in international purchasing power. Countries are generally better off by finding valuable extra supplies even if particular groups within the country are made worse off.

8 Previously, debtors who were managing to service their debt must have had very depreciated real exchange rates – they needed to run large trade surpluses in order to generate the foreign exchange to meet debt repayments. Wiping out these repayments means they do not need the trade surplus any more. So their real exchange rate should appreciate (they are richer than before). Rich countries therefore experience a real depreciation against poor countries. Both this relative price change and the fact that purchasing power in poor countries has risen mean that poor countries will now demand more imports of manufactures from rich countries. A monopoly firm should have lobbied rich governments to wipe out the debt. But with many manufacturers and many governments, everyone tends to free ride on everyone else.

AB 28   (a) Yes. (b) Switzerland, Italy, Greece, China. (c) What matters for Balassa Samuelson (BS) is traded versus non-traded. Technical progress in services makes more of these tradables: if that was the only effect, it might not affect BS much. However, if it generally raises wages and productivity in non-tradeds, it erodes the distinction on which BS is based. As yet, we are not near that point in practice.

Chapter 29

1 c, a, b.

2 (a) Nothing, since interest parity must hold from now on. (b) Rises. (c) Rises. (d) Initial gain in competitiveness boosts net exports and output. Eventually, extra inflation erodes competitiveness enough to undo this. Once competitiveness back to initial level, extra inflation stops.

3 (a) All rise by 30 per cent. (b) Nominal exchange rate is the nominal anchor now.

4 Yes, as in Question 2 above. Without devaluation, slump lowers inflation and hence prices and wages, eventually adjusting competitiveness as needed.

5 (a) Since marginal propensity to import < 1, net exports rise so need real appreciation.
(b) Speculators foresee later rise and bid exchange rate up immediately – otherwise, opportunities for foreseeable large capital gains later.

6 (a) Can if set interest rate appropriately to keep speculators happy at that exchange rate.
(b) Mainly influenced by financial account in short run. (c) Affects the interest rate response (or lack of it) to a change in fiscal policy.

7 (a) With so many investment opportunities in China, would expect net inflow on its financial account as rest of world invests in China. (b) Payments surplus because of both current and financial account. (c) Rising sharply (over $250 billion in 2006). Unless this can all be sterilized, Chinese money supply must rise. Inflationary unless Chinese money demand rises as much – with economy growing at 10 per cent a year, money demand obviously rising strongly too. Chinese inflation is about the same as in the UK!

8 The stronger is aggregate demand, the more the central bank has to raise interest rates to defend the inflation target. Hence fiscal policy does not change overall level of aggregate demand but the monetary–fiscal mix, and hence the interest rate. In this chapter, we saw how interest rates then affect the exchange rate.

AB 29 (a) Looser fiscal policy would have meant monetary policy tighter and higher real exchange rate, making UK manufacturing less competitive. Fiscal expansion to finance spending on public services is one such example. (b) By adding to demand, they force the Bank of England to tighten monetary policy; in turn, higher interest rates will cause an exchange rate appreciation and increase the trade deficit. Fiscal policy crowds out other elements of aggregate demand.

Chapter 30

1 Latter is output per person. Output grows faster unless population growth negative.

2 Compare with other countries to see if factually true that Britain is different. For different countries, correlate long-run growth with usual explanations (labour input, capital input, etc.) and see if extra role for fraction of population who are scientists, engineers. Private and social benefits differ if there are externalities (some skills make it easier for people with other skills). Subsidies to education also imply discrepancy between private and social cost.

3 Pollution and congestion. Can quantify and value some (e.g. how much house prices are lower under airport flight path). As information technology lets us record data better, will get easier to include in GNP.

4 Poverty traps possible even in Solow model. Endogenous growth can also explain why growth rates permanently differ.

5 Land input has increased much less than labour, without big diminishing returns to labour. We accumulated other factors (human and physical capital) as substitutes for land, and technical progress invented ways to economize on land. Same is already happening for other scarce inputs.

6 (a) In short run, might reduce output by reducing consumption demand. (b) In long run, might just raise level of per capita output (Solow model).

7 (a) Now gross investment per person must be $(n + d)k$. This replaces the line nk in Figure 30.1, otherwise the figure the same. (b) A rise in d makes the $(n + d)k$ line steeper, and shifts the steady state to the left, reducing output per person and environmental capital per person. (c) Yes.

8 From its position of technological pre-eminence 700 years ago, China then went into a period not merely of relative decline but absolute decline. People can forget how to do things, especially if activities are prohibited for long enough. Open access to information, and the ability to use it, are usually sufficient to ensure that knowledge improves over time.

AB 30 (a) In Figure 30.1, if k and y are low, even a small amount of saving is sufficient for capital deepening, improving the future position. (b) If aid to countries in a poverty trap allows them to break out completely, the present value of the extra output and welfare is huge compared with aid that merely speeds up slightly what would have happened anyway. (c) In Figure 30.1 suppose the line nk has a larger n whenever k is below a critical amount. There are then two possible equilibria – a high n, low k equilibrium and a low n, high k equilibrium. Aid would be very valuable if it allowed the economy to increase k enough to move into the more benign regime. It might be plausible if children were seen as insurance against old age, and poor countries feared more for life in old age.

Chapter 31

1 It would kill the multiplier–accelerator model. Technology, costs and real interest rates might still induce investment fluctuations. Might also be fluctuations from C, G, X.

2 For example, higher oil prices are also a demand shock for Norway, since export revenues rise, while a supply shock for many other European countries.

3   Bygones now bygone. What matters is what can be done from now on.

4   It might accentuate a global political business cycle. With elections at different dates, pre-election booms are more diffuse.

5   Cause lies not in fluctuations in nominal money, or monetary policy, but rather in real shocks such as views about future technology and productivity growth. More generally, tries to explain cycles without nominal rigidities and constraints on adjustment speeds. Persistent is optimal because of intertemporal substitution.

6   (a) Closer integration accentuates international transmission mechanism of booms and slumps, e.g. US high-tech bust of 2001 quickly spread to Europe. (b) Multiplier–accelerator model relies on failure to forecast future output correctly. (c) Costs of adjusting labour mean output cycles induce cycles in output per worker.

7   (a) Less evidence of an output cycle since the central bank should be offsetting any cyclical aspects of fiscal policy, at least to the extent that they have inflationary implications. (b) If there are cycles in the fiscal stimulus to aggregate demand, one would expect to see the central bank raising interest rates when fiscal policy is unduly expansionary and reducing interest rates when fiscal policy is tighter.

8   The success of the multiplier–accelerator model would mean that (i) changes in income are closely related to changes in saving (that is the simple consumption function, the multiplier bit) and (ii) changes in income are closely connected with the rate of investment (the accelerator). Even if households realize that expected future income should ideally influence current consumption decisions, if they have problems borrowing because of lack of collateral, they may be driven back towards the simple consumption function not because they are stupid but because they are poor and cannot implement it. Firms may realize that changes in their ideal capital stock should depend on real interest rates, profit margins and many things besides the rate of income growth, but income growth may still be quantitatively important, especially in a period of relatively stable real interest rates.

AB 31   (a) Decisions by the European Central Bank would then suit every member of the eurozone. (b) There is a lot of evidence that geography matters for the degree of trade and integration – you would be correct to guess that Ireland, the UK and Portugal are less integrated with the EU as a whole than are France, Germany and the Benelux countries. (c) Financial markets are most integrated, then probably goods, then services or skilled labour; and unskilled labour is probably least integrated.

Chapter 32

1   New Classical: at earliest opportunity, nominal wages and prices fall by same amount, restoring all real variables to original level, so very small and temporary output fall. If anticipated, no output fall, since wages and prices already adjusted. Gradualist monetarist: bit longer for wage and price adjustment to happen, bit larger fall in output. Moderate Keynesian: bit longer still, so larger output fall and slower recovery. Extreme Keynesian: very long time indeed.

2   NC: Entirely as fall in U^* because of better supply-side policies plus maybe some intertemporal labour substitution (fewer in labour force). GM: mainly fall in U^* as above, but also recovery from very high interest rates in 1991–92 caused by German reunification (see Part 5); MK: sustained fall in U over many years must eventually be from lower U^*, but initial recession larger than GM think; EK: big Keynesian recession at start of 1990s, so mainly end of Keynesian U.

3   (a) NC. (b) MK. (c) GM. (d) EK.

4   GM, MK.

5   (a) Rational expectations possible in model with other reasons for slow wage adjustment, just happened that rational expectations was first pioneered in New Classical models. (b) Not true in short run. (c) They stress that money the main determinant of prices.

6   What is true is that central banks set the interest rate and passively supply whatever money is necessary to make this an equilibrium in the money market. If the consequence is that the nominal money supply grows faster than the demand for nominal money, this will still be inflationary – the original insight of monetarists. The part that is new is that a central bank with an inflation target will then quickly respond by raising interest rates, for which a lower money supply is then necessary, preventing the sustained monetary expansion that was possible under some previous monetary policies.

7   We know productivity fluctuates over the business cycle, but sustained productivity growth requires supply-side improvements. Except for reasons of hysteresis, demand policies should not be expected to have much supply-side effect in the longer run. We need good supply-side policies as well as good demand management. The latter is easier than the former.

AB 32   (a) A New Classical economist might try to argue that markets, not bankers, restored the economy to potential output. If all output fluctuations are to be interpreted as fluctuations in potential output, it is then difficult to explain why cycles diminished at precisely the time that central banks were given independence. If we give central banks the credit, then interest rate changes must be able to affect output reasonably quickly. Evidence consistent with Moderate Keynesian position, but not entirely at odds with Gradualist monetarist. It is not consistent with those Extreme Keynesians who believe that monetary policy is pretty powerless and that fiscal policy a more reliable demand management tool. (b) See Box 25.2.

Chapter 33

1   (a) US, with higher human and physical capital, exports more manufactures. (b) Brazil, with less than Asia, exports fewer manufactures.

2   No. Equilibrium exchange rate can be low enough to offset any absolute disadvantage. To enjoy efficiency gains from comparative advantage, should allow trade.

3   Wine and cars have high two-way trade based on choice and differentiation, steel based more on comparative advantage and one way.

4   Only if planning to become subsequent exporter in TVs, but production subsidy more efficient than tariff.

5   (a) No. Government may as well have the tax revenue too. (b) Domestic art buyers gain since prices fall. Domestic artists lose out, so too foreign art buyers. (c) Probably not.

6   (a) There always exists an equilibrium exchange rate that makes it profitable to export the goods in which they have comparative advantage. (b) International trade is generally better than no trade because countries specialize in products in which they have a comparative advantage.

7   True that gain less as percentage of their initial income: small countries cannot enjoy scale economies without international trade. Trade by large countries also bids the world price in adverse direction from their viewpoint.

8   (a) Better off, since demand for their skills rises. (b) Worse off, since demand for their skills falls. (c) If the export industry faces inelastic demand in the world economy, an increase in supply can bid down the price so much that the country gets less revenue than before (and small individual competitive producers can do nothing about it) – see the examples on primary product prices at the beginning of the chapter.

AB 33   (a) Benefits Europe provided the additional supply is permanent. (b) Rhetoric to protect European workers from competition (see the answer to Question (8b) above – as consumers, Europeans are big beneficiaries. (c) Tariff better because you get the tariff revenue; quota adds this to profits of Chinese exporters.

Chapter 34

1   Because price level had risen relative to competitors, joining at old nominal exchange rate meant a much less competitive real exchange rate. UK then had a slump.

2   Automatic adjustment better under gold standard, since money supply forced to adjust. More scope for discretion in dollar standard: could be good or bad. Financial discipline better under GS: could be good, or bad (if too tough).

3   Commitment to avoid domestic monetary expansion may help reduce inflation expectations. However, if fiscal authorities continue to have big deficits, may still bid up prices, making country increasingly uncompetitive, forcing big eventual crisis, as in Argentina 2001.

4   Because as small open economies they were interdependent and had less sovereignty anyway as separate nation states.

5   Stock market soared, anticipating low interest rates and a low exchange rate that boosted exports and profits. Bond market fell, fearing higher inflation and higher eventual nominal interest rates.

6   (a) Even in long run, only current account need balance. (b) Induced changes in domestic price level change the real exchange rate.

7   (a) In the long run, Cuba will prosper as a result of integration into international trade and the end of embargoes that inhibit its acquisition of the latest technology. However, the experience of Eastern Europe and the former Soviet Union countries is that transition is not painless and that output may fall initially before it is launched on an upward trend. (b) Richer in the future than today, they should smooth consumption across time, borrowing today in order to spend more today even if this means consuming a little less at some future date in order to repay loans. (c) The initial surge in both consumption and imported capital goods will mean a trade deficit.

8   (a) Good opportunities for investment (and hence the likelihood of inflows on the financial account of the balance of payments. (b) With a fixed exchange rate, Cuba is likely to have a balance of payments surplus because the financial inflows will probably be large, and policy makers tend to get nervous of substantial trade deficits and take other actions to limit them. (c) Exchange rate floats up because of the pressure of financial inflows. (d) Latter probably better; former leads to large increases in money supply in Cuba which may cause unnecessary inflation, as happened throughout Eastern Europe (though interestingly not in China).

AB 34   (a) Acting in isolation, each country may be tempted to depreciate its exchange rate in pursuit of short-term gain – collectively this destabilizes the system, making life worse for everyone. (b) Speculators should take their money out of the currency now before they suffer a capital loss when the exchange rate depreciates. (c) You seem to have an alibi – it was the speculators not you – but they probably only acted as they did because they knew, or thought they knew, what you were about to do. (d) Financial outflow on the balance of payments.

Chapter 35

1   Yes, wages lower.

2   Germany, France, Holland have high human capital; Greece, Spain, Portugal less so.

3 No. Equilibrium risk premium on riskier bonds to prevent capital flows by compensating properly for extra risk. Yes, a monetary union: two firms' bonds pay slightly different interest rates even within the UK.

4 If every member state has one vote on central bank board, want to prevent countries getting into fiscal trouble then voting for high inflation to help their budget position. Even with tough monetary policy, monetary–fiscal mix matters. With loose fiscal, need tight money, but then high real interest rates and real exchange rate appreciates to uncompetitive levels.

5 Yes. In practice, hard for borrowers to commit to repay and spend the money wisely. This moral hazard severely limits how much lenders will lend.

6 (a) Non-tariff barriers also important. (b) By matching German interest rates in the ERM, countries had already given up most of their monetary sovereignty. (c) Independence from political control is the best commitment to price stability if politicians are the main cause of inflationary policies.

7 (a) Hardly any – Spain has only a small effect on the aggregate eurozone data to which the ECB reacts. (b) Looser fiscal policy might offset the demand shock but fiscal policy takes longer to change than monetary policy and Spain might be close to the limits set by the Stability Pact and could find itself in a situation in which it is not allowed to loosen fiscal policy. (c) The adverse demand shock leads to a fall in output and employment, wages and prices in Spain gradually fall, competitiveness and net exports increase, demand picks up, potential output is restored, but not external balance since Spain has a trade surplus. This gradually leads to an accumulation of net foreign assets, Spaniards feel richer, consumption rises, bids up prices, erodes the competitiveness gain, and eventually external balance restored. The wealth effect and higher consumption is what ultimately has restored domestic aggregate demand.

8 UK interest rates fall to eurozone levels, causing an increase in aggregate demand. Thereafter you can use the analysis of Question 7 (but for a rise not a fall in aggregate demand). Either fiscal policy is tightened or the boom bids up prices, erodes competitiveness, reduces net exports, gradual fall in net foreign assets, until wealth effect on consumption reduces aggregate demand again.

AB 35 (a) Transactions costs of going between pound and euro, and uncertainty of future exchange rate, both act as dampener on the trade that would otherwise have occurred. Recent evidence from many countries is that these effects are potentially larger than we used to think. (b) Main benefits are being able to reconcile scale economies, diversity of choice and competition with less need for regulation. (c) Producers of goods, and workers in these industries, that UK now imports from EU. (d) It is possible but not certain. Political integration depends to a large extent on who identifies with whom, and whether or not voters acquiesce in redistribution. Greater integration tends to enhance familiarity but it is hard to say whether it will do so to a sufficient extent. Global challenges, such as global warming, may provide a different channel for greater political integration eventually. But Europe's history is about competition between small nation states.

Chapter 36

1 Man-made substitutes for raw materials (e.g. rubber) reduced demand. Productivity increases raised supply. Protection in rich countries limited markets.

2 Rise in demand, higher copper price until new copper sources found, substitutes for copper developed, or boom subsides.

3 All require intensive but low-skilled labour, which they have in relative abundance.

4 (a) Buy commodity when price low, stockpile, sell when price high. (b) Incentive for each country to 'cheat' and put all its produce on market and gain higher price at expense of others. No incentive ever to cut production: if average price wrong, as in CAP, stockpile grows without limit plus stocks accumulating.

5 Not indefinitely. Small country has to specialize to get adequate scale in some industries, and hence must export these products and import all the others.

6 Under pure float, capital account inflow = current account deficit. Latter cannot grow without bound, hence capital inflow limited. This helps prevent foreign money subsequently leaving in a rush. Bad domestic policies can still cause a crisis in which domestic citizens want to take their money out – remember the TV pictures of locked banks in the Argentina crisis of 2001.

7 (a) LDCs often argue that aid encourages dependence. They want foreign investment, less protection by rich countries, technology transfer, and debt relief to wipe out mistakes of the past. (b) Europe would make a net gain from greater exploitation of comparative advantage, even though vociferous particular losers have so far blocked the process. (c) Individually, perhaps, but collectively they bid down world prices against themselves, especially when denied access to the richest markets.

8 Increasing globalization, particularly the rise of China, with its cheap labour but thirst for raw materials, gave a series of beneficial supply shocks to the price of imported consumer goods, but a series of adverse supply shocks to the prices of commodities such as oil and metal ores. The former were initially larger and reduced Western inflation. However, poor monetary policy might have responded by cutting interest rates too much. And, as the adverse supply shocks became important, the credibility of independent central banks helped prevent higher commodity prices spilling over into inflationary wage claims.

9 Economic sovereignty is the ability of governments (and their electors) to choose tax rates, government spending and regulations. Nation states have lost most sovereignty on those things most mobile across national borders, where the attempt to behave differently in one country leads to an outflow in response to policies that penalize, or an inflow in response to policies that provide benefits. Ranking depends on assessment of degree of international mobility; internet gambling, then banking, then subsidies, then taxes (one could argue about the relative ranking about the last two of these, probably more international migration to take advantage of benefits than to avoid taxes: though, for specific mobile high-skill groups (investment bankers, rock stars, F1 drivers), location is sensitive to tax rates.

AB 36 (a) If the secondary market thinks the country can now meet in full its obligations as newly defined, bonds no longer trade at a discount in the secondary market. (b) Suppose a UK and a German bank are each owed half the money. Initially, bonds trade at 40 per cent of par value. The UK bank alone writes off all the bonds it has bought. Now all the borrower's trade surplus can go to paying off the German bank. The bonds it holds jump in second-hand value from, say, 40 to 80 per cent of par value. Since it is less than 100 per cent, the LDC is still not paying in full, and the bank still insists the LDC pay as much as it can. UK generosity (assisted by well-meaning UK taxpayers who supported the write-off) is entirely to benefit the German bank, not the LDC borrower! There is a free-rider problem. Every creditor wants every other creditor to be first to offer write-offs. Debt relief requires powerful politicians and world agencies (IMF, World Bank, UN) to shepherd creditors into the same fold at the same time to solve the free-rider problem. Making poverty history is proving as difficult as tackling climate change because it is not a problem that can be addressed by the government of a single nation state.

Glossary

Absolute advantage a country is the lowest-cost producer of that good.

Accelerator model of investment firms guess future output and profits by extrapolating past output growth. Constant output growth leads to constant investment. It takes accelerating output growth to raise desired investment.

Adjustable peg a fixed exchange rate, the value of which may occasionally be changed.

Adverse selection the use of inside information to accept or reject a contract; hence, customers are not an average sample of the population.

Aggregate demand the amount firms and households plan to spend at each level of income.

Aggregate price level the average price of goods and services.

Aggregate supply schedule the output firms wish to supply at each inflation rate.

Aggregate supply schedule in the classical model is vertical at potential output. Equilibrium output is independent of inflation.

Aid an international transfer payment from rich countries to poor countries.

Appreciation (of the exchange rate) a rise in the international value of a currency.

Asset motive reflects dislike of risk. People sacrifice a high rate of return for a lower but safer rate.

Asset price bubble a departure of the price from that justified by fundamental characteristics of the asset. Bubbles are self-fulfilling prophecies.

Automatic stabilizers reduce the multiplier, damping the output response to demand shocks.

Average tax rate the fraction of total income paid in tax.

Balance of payments records transactions between residents of one country and the rest of the world; the sum of its current account and capital account items.

Balanced budget multiplier a rise in government spending plus an equal rise in taxes leads to higher output.

Bank reserves the money available in the bank to meet possible withdrawals by depositors.

Barter economy has no medium of exchange. Goods are swapped for other goods.

Behavioural law a sensible theoretical relationship not rejected by evidence over a long period.

Benefits principle people getting most benefit from public spending should pay most tax for it.

Bertrand model each firm treats the price of other firms as given.

Beta measures how much an asset's return moves with the return on the whole stock market.

Budget spending and revenue plans of an individual, a company or a government.

Budget constraint the different bundles that the consumer can afford.

Budget deficit the excess of government spending over government receipts.

Budget share the price of a good times the quantity demanded, divided by total consumer spending.

Budget surplus (deficit) the excess (shortfall) of government spending over government revenue.

Buffer stock aims to stabilize a commodity market by buying when the price is low and selling when the price is high.

Bundling the joint supply of more than one product to reduce the need for price discrimination.

Business cycle the short-term fluctuation of total output around its trend path.

Capital account the capital account of the balance of payments records international purchases and sales of financial assets.

Capital adequacy ratio capital relative to its outstanding liabilities.

Capital controls prohibit, restrict or tax the flow of private capital across currencies.

Capital gain (loss) the rise (fall) in asset price while it is held.

Capital-deepening in a growing economy, raises capital per worker for all workers.

Capital-widening in a growing economy, extends the existing capital per worker to new extra workers.

Cash notes and coin, paying zero interest. The most liquid asset.

Cash flow the net amount of money actually received during the period.

Central bank intervention (in the forex market) buying or selling pounds to support the fixed exchange rate.

Central bank banker to the government and to the banks. It also conducts monetary policy.

Glossary

Chosen bundle the point at which an indifference curve just touches the budget line.

Circular flow how real resources and financial payments flow between firms and households.

Classical model of macroeconomics assumes wages and prices are completely flexible.

Classical unemployment arises when the wage is kept above its equilibrium level.

Closed shop an agreement that a firm's workers must be members of a trade union.

Code for Fiscal Stability commits the UK government to a medium-run objective of financing all current government spending out of current revenues; over this period, borrowing should be only to finance investment.

Collusion an explicit or implicit agreement to avoid competition.

Command economy central planning of what, how and for whom goods are produced. Detailed instructions are then issued to households, firms and workers.

Commercial banks financial intermediaries licensed to make loans and issue deposits, including deposits against which cheques can be written.

Commitment a voluntary arrangement to restrict future action.

Company an organization legally allowed to produce and trade.

Comparative advantage a country makes the good relatively more cheaply than it makes other goods, whether or not it has an absolute advantage.

Comparative static analysis examines the effect on equilibrium when conditions change.

Competition Commission investigates whether a monopoly, or potential monopoly, acts against the public interest.

Competition policy enhances efficiency by promoting or safeguarding competition.

Complements a higher price for one good reduces the demand for *complements* to this good.

Conglomerate merger union of two firms whose production activities are unrelated.

Constant returns to scale long-run average costs are constant as output rises.

Consumer surplus the excess of consumer benefits over spending.

Consumption function aggregate consumption demand at each level of personal disposable income.

Contestable market has free entry and free exit.

Convergence hypothesis poor countries grow more quickly than average but rich countries grow more slowly than average.

Convertible currency the central bank will buy or sell as much of the currency as people wish to trade at the fixed exchange rate.

Copyright see Intellectual property.

Corporate control who controls the firm in different situations.

Corporate finance how firms finance their activities.

Cost what is spent on production during a period.

Cost of holding money the interest sacrificed by not holding wealth in an asset paying more interest.

Cournot model each firm treats the output of the other firm as given.

Cream-skimming confines entry to profitable parts of the business, undermining scale economies elsewhere.

Credible promise a promise about the future that is optimal to carry out when the future arrives.

Credible threat one that, after the fact, is still optimal to carry out.

Cross-price elasticity of demand for good i with respect to changes in the price of good j, is the percentage change in the quantity of good i demanded, divided by the corresponding percentage change in the price of good j.

Cross-section data at a point in time, the way an economic variable differs across different individuals or groups.

Crowding out a stimulus to aggregate demand *crowds out* some private spending. Higher output induces a rise in interest rates that dampens the expansionary effect on demand.

Currency board a unilateral commitment to peg the exchange rate by giving up monetary independence. The money supply changes only because of balance of payments surpluses or deficits.

Current account of the balance of payments records international flows of goods, services, and transfer payments.

Data things taken as given; pieces of evidence about economic behaviour.

Deadweight burden lost social surplus by producing the wrong output level.

Debt rescheduling a new agreement with old creditors to pay them less per period but for a longer payback period.

Default refusing to pay creditors at all.

Demand the quantity that buyers wish to purchase at each conceivable price.

Demand curve the relation between price and quantity demanded, other things equal.

Demand for money is demand to hold *real* money balances. Rises with income but falls with interest rates.

Demand management use of monetary and fiscal policy to stabilize output near potential output.

Demand shock a shift in aggregate demand.

Demand-deficient unemployment occurs when output is below full capacity.

Demand-determined output since markets trade the

smaller of supply and demand, output is demand-determined when there is excess supply and wages and prices have yet to adjust to restore long-run equilibrium. Output then depends only on aggregate demand.

Depletable resources can be used only once.

Depreciation the loss in value of a capital good during the period, sometimes called capital consumption, the result of usage or obsolescence.

Depreciation of the exchange rate a fall in the international value of a currency.

Derived demand the demand for inputs reflects demand for a firm's output.

Devaluation (revaluation) a fall (rise) in the fixed exchange rate.

Diminishing marginal rate of substitution tastes exhibit this when, to hold utility constant, diminishing quantities of one good must be sacrificed to get successive equal increases in the quantity of the other good.

Diminishing marginal utility each extra unit consumed, holding constant consumption of other goods, adds successively less to total utility.

Direct taxes taxes on income and wealth.

Discount rate (in a present value calculation) the interest rate used to calculate present values of future streams of benefits or costs.

Discouraged workers pessimistic about finding a job, they leave the labour force.

Discretionary fiscal policy decisions about tax rates and levels of government spending.

Discriminating monopoly charges different prices to different people.

Discrimination the different treatment of people with the same characteristics.

Diseconomies of scale (decreasing returns to scale) long-run average cost rises as output rises.

Distortion (market failure) whenever society's marginal cost and marginal benefit diverge.

Diversification pools risk across several assets whose individual returns behave differently from one another.

Dividends regular payments of profit to shareholders.

Domestic price of foreign exchange the quantity of domestic currency per unit of a foreign currency.

Dominant strategy a player's best strategy *whatever* the strategies adopted by rivals.

Dumping foreign producers sell at prices below their marginal production cost.

Econometrics the use of mathematical statistics to quantify relationships in economic data.

Economic geography recognition that locational externalities matter in production and consumption.

Economic growth a rise in real income or real output or GNP.

Economic rent the payment a factor receives in excess of the transfer earnings needed to induce it to supply its services in that use.

Economic sovereignty the power of national governments to make decisions independently of those made by other governments.

Economics the study of how society decides what, how and for whom to produce.

Economies of scale (increasing returns to scale) long-run average cost falls as output rises.

Effective exchange rate a country's average exchange rate against all its trading partners, weighted by the relative size of trade with each country.

Efficiency wages high wages that raise productivity through their incentive effect.

Efficient asset market already incorporates existing information properly in asset prices.

Elastic demand a price elasticity more negative than −1. Quantities sensitive to prices.

Endogenous growth implies that the steady-state growth rate is affected by economic behaviour and economic policy.

Entry when new firms join an industry.

E-product can be digitally encoded then transmitted rapidly, accurately and cheaply.

Equilibrium price the price at which the quantity supplied equals the quantity demanded.

Equilibrium unemployment (also natural rate of unemployment) is the unemployment rate when the labour market is in equilibrium.

European Monetary System a system of monetary and exchange rate co-operation in Western Europe during 1979–99.

Excess demand when quantity demanded exceeds quantity supplied at the ruling price.

Excess supply when quantity supplied exceeds quantity demanded at the ruling price.

Exchange rate the price at which two national currencies exchange.

Exchange Rate Mechanism part of the EMS. Each country fixed a nominal exchange rate against each other ERM participant. Collectively the group floated against the rest of the world.

Exchange rate regime the policy rule describing how governments allow exchange rates to be determined.

Exit when existing firms leave an industry.

Exogenous expectations are not explained by the model but simply taken as given.

Experience good or service must be sampled before the user knows its value.

Export subsidies government assistance to domestic firms that compete in foreign markets.

Glossary

Export-led growth stresses production and income growth through exports rather than the displacement of imports.

Exports are made at home but sold abroad.

External balance a zero current account-balance.

Externality one person's production or consumption physically affects the production or consumption of others.

Extrapolative expectations assume that the future is an extension of the recent past.

Extreme Keynesians not only insist that markets fail to clear in the short run, they also believe that markets do not clear in the long run.

Fair gamble on average yields zero monetary profit.

Fallacy of composition what is true for one person may not be true for all, and vice versa.

Fan chart shows not only the most likely future outcome but also the probability of different outcomes.

Federal fiscal system centralized taxes and expenditure rules that apply in its constituent states or countries.

Final goods goods purchased by the end user.

Financial account the financial account of the balance of payments records international purchases and sales of financial assets.

Financial intermediary specializes in bringing lenders and borrowers together.

Financial panic a self-fulfilling prophecy. Believing a bank will be unable to pay, people rush to get their money out, which makes the bank go bankrupt.

Firm-specific skills these raise a worker's productivity only in that particular firm.

First-best allocation is fully efficient. *First-best* removes all distortions.

First mover advantage the player moving first achieves higher payoffs than when decisions are simultaneous.

Fiscal drag the rise in real tax revenue when inflation raises nominal incomes, pushing people into higher tax brackets in a progressive income tax system.

Fiscal policy government policy on spending and taxes.

Fiscal stance the effect of fiscal policy on demand and output.

Fisher hypothesis higher inflation leads to similarly higher nominal interest rates.

Fixed costs total costs do not vary with output.

Fixed exchange rate a government commitment to maintain a particular fixed exchange rate.

Fixed factor of production an input that cannot be varied.

Flexible inflation targeting commits a central bank to hit inflation targets in the medium run, but gives it some discretion about how quickly. This allows complete stabilization of demand shocks and partial stabilization of supply shocks.

Flight from cash the collapse in the demand for real cash when high inflation and high nominal interest rates make it very costly to hold cash.

Floating exchange rate regime the exchange rate is allowed to find its equilibrium level *without* central bank invervention using the forex reserves.

Flow is the stream of accounts measured over a period of time.

Foreign direct investment (FDI) the purchase of foreign firms or the establishment of foreign subsidiaries.

Foreign exchange (forex) market exchanges one national currency for another.

Foreign exchange reserves foreign currency held by the domestic central bank.

Forward market deals in contracts made today for delivery of goods at a specified future date at a price agreed today.

Free markets markets in which governments allow prices to be determined by supply and demand.

Free-rider a person unable to be excluded from consuming a good, who thus has no incentive to buy it.

Frictional unemployment the irreducible minimum unemployment in a dynamic society.

Functional income distribution the division of national income between different factors of production.

Game a situation in which intelligent decisions are necessarily interdependent.

GDP at basic prices domestic output exclusive of indirect taxes on goods and services. The former exceeds the latter by the amount of revenue raised in indirect taxes.

GDP at market prices domestic output inclusive of indirect taxes on goods and services.

General skills these enhance productivity in many jobs and can be transferred to work in another firm.

Gilt-edged securities government bonds. Gilt-edged because the government will not go bust and refuse to pay interest.

Globalization the increasing integration of national markets previously segmented from one another.

GNP deflator the ratio of nominal GNP to real GNP expressed as an index.

Government solvency the present value of the current and future tax revenue at least matches the present value of current and future spending plus any initial net debts.

Gradualist monetarists believe that full employment is restored within a few years, so the main effect of higher money is simply higher prices.

Gross domestic product (GDP) the output made in the domestic economy, regardless of who owns the production inputs. Hence, the value of total output by residents of an economy.

Gross investment the production of new capital goods and/or improvement of existing capital goods.

Gross national product (GNP or GNI) total income earned by domestic citizens regardless of the country in which their factor services were supplied. Equals GDP plus net asset income from abroad.

Growth rate the percentage change per period (usually a year).

Headline inflation actual inflation, the growth in the retail price index RPI.

Hedging the use of forward markets to shift risk on to somebody else.

Higher government spending on goods and services increases equilibrium output.

Horizontal equity the identical treatment of identical people.

Horizontal *LM* schedule the money supply is adjusted to keep interest rates constant.

Horizontal merger the union of two firms at the same production stage in the same industry.

Human capital the stock of expertise accumulated by a worker to enhance future productivity.

Hyperinflation a period of very high inflation.

Hysteresis when a particular long-run equilibrium depends on the path an economy follows in the short run.

ii schedule at higher inflation rates the central bank will wish to have higher real interest rates.

Imperfectly competitive firm faces a down-sloping demand curve. Its output price reflects the quantity of goods it makes and sells.

Import substitution the replacement of imports by domestic production under the protection of high tariffs or import quotas.

Import tariff a tax on imports.

Imports are made abroad but sold at home.

Impossible triad fixed exchange rates, perfect capital mobility and monetary sovereignty. All three cannot co-exist at the same time.

Incidence of a tax who eventually bears the burden of it.

Income distribution how total income is divided between different groups or individuals.

Income effect the *income effect* of a price change is the adjustment of demand to the change in real income alone.

Income elasticity of demand demanded divided by the corresponding percentage change in income.

Income expansion path how the chosen bundle of goods varies with consumer income levels.

Incomes policy the direct control of wages and other incomes.

Index number data relative to a given base value.

Indifference curve shows all consumption bundles with the same level of utility.

Indirect taxes taxes on spending and output.

Industrial base the existing producers available to provide locational externalities for industrial production.

Industrial policy offsets externalities affecting production decisions by firms.

Inelastic demand a price elasticity between −1 and 0. Quantities insensitive to prices.

Inferior good demand falls when incomes rise. Has a negative income elasticity of demand.

Inflation accounting fully inflation-adjusted definitions of costs, income and profit.

Inflation-adjusted budget uses real not nominal interest rates to calculate government spending on debt interest.

Inflation illusion people confuse nominal and real changes. People's welfare depends on real variables, not nominal variables.

Inflation rate the annual rate of change of the average price of goods and services.

Inflation target interest rates are adjusted by central banks to keep inflation within a narrow range.

Inflation tax the effect of inflation in raising real revenue by reducing the real value of the government's nominal debt.

Information overload arises when it is costly to process large amounts of available information. Screening devices are then very valuable.

Injection money that flows to firms without being recycled through households.

Innocent entry barrier a barrier not deliberately erected by incumbent firms.

Innovation incorporation of new knowledge into better production techniques.

Input (or factor of production) a good or service used to produce output.

Insiders those with jobs, represented in wage bargaining.

Intellectual property (patent, copyright) recognition that the creator of new knowledge may, for a period, own it as an asset from which income may be derived.

Interest parity expected exchange-rate changes offset the interest differential between domestic and foreign currency assets.

Interest rate spread the excess of the loan interest rate over the deposit interest rate.

Intermediate goods partly-finished goods that form inputs to a subsequent production process that then uses them up.

Intermediate target a key indicator used to guide interest-rate decisions.

Internal balance aggregate demand equals potential output.

International monetary system provides a medium of exchange for international transactions.

International value of the domestic currency the quantity of foreign currency per unit of the domestic currency.

Glossary

Intra-industry trade two-way trade in goods made by the same industry.

Invention the discovery of new and better knowledge.

Inventories (stocks) goods held in stock by the firm for future production or sale.

Investment the purchase of new capital goods by firms.

Investment demand firms' desired additions to physical capital, including inventories.

Investment demand schedule desired investment at each investment rate.

'Invisible hand' the assertion that the individual pursuit of self-interest within free markets may allocate resources efficiently from society's viewpoint.

Involuntary unemployment when workers want to work at the going wage but are unable to find jobs.

IOU money a medium of exchange based on the debt of a private firm or individual.

IS schedule combinations of income and interest rates at which aggregate demand equals actual output.

Isoquant shows minimum combinations of inputs to make a given output. Different points on an isoquant reflect different production techniques.

Labour force all people in work or registered as looking for work.

Labour-augmenting technical progress increases the effective labour supply.

Laffer curve how much tax revenue is raised at each possible tax rate.

Land the factor of production that nature supplies; usually treated as fixed in total quantity.

Law of comparative advantage countries specialize in producing and exporting the goods that they produce at a lower *relative cost* than other countries.

Law of diminishing returns holding constant all inputs but one, equal successive increases in the variable input steadily reduce its marginal product.

Leakage leakage from the circular flow is money no longer recycled from households to firms.

Lender of last resort central bank loans to banks during a financial panic.

Less developed countries (LDCs) these countries have low per capita incomes and output.

Life-cycle hypothesis people make a lifetime consumption plan (including bequests to their children) that is just affordable out of lifetime income (plus any initial wealth inherited).

Limited liability shareholders of a company cannot lose more than they have already invested in the business.

Liquidity the cheapness, speed and certainty with which asset values can be converted back into money.

LM schedule combinations of interest rates and income yielding money market equilibrium.

Locational externality when one firm's costs are affected by its neighbouring firms, or one consumer's costs depend on neighbouring suppliers too.

Logrolling a vote for another person's preferred outcome on one issue in exchange for their vote for your preferred outcome on another issue.

Long run the period needed for complete adjustment to changes in conditions to occur.

Long-run average cost long-run total cost (*LTC*) divided by the level of output *Q*.

Long-run equilibrium when the price equates the quantity demanded to the total quantity supplied by the number of firms in the industry when each firm is on its long-run supply curve and firms can freely enter or exit the industry.

Long-run equilibrium of an economy simultaneous internal and external balance of the economy.

Long-run marginal cost the rise in long-run total cost if output rises permanently by one unit.

Long-run Phillips curve is vertical at equilibrium unemployment. There is no trade-off in the long run.

Long-run supply curve how price affects desired output; hence, the part of a firm's *LMC* curve above its *LAC* curve.

Long-run total cost the minimum cost of producing each output level when the firm can adjust all inputs.

Luxury good has an income elasticity above unity.

Maastricht criteria (for joining EMU) a country must already have achieved low inflation and sound fiscal policy.

Macroeconomic demand schedule (*MDS*) higher inflation induces lower output because a central bank raises interest rates.

Macroeconomics the study of the economy as a system, emphasizing interactions of different parts.

Managed float central banks intervene in the forex market to smooth out fluctuations and nudge the exchange rate in the desired direction.

Marginal cost the rise in total cost when output rises by 1 unit.

Marginal firm a marginal firm in an industry just breaks even.

Marginal product of labour the extra total output when an extra worker is added, with other input quantities unaltered.

Marginal product of a variable factor is the extra output from an extra unit of that input, holding constant all other inputs.

Marginal propensity to consume the fraction of each extra pound of disposable income that households wish to consume.

Marginal propensity to import the fraction of each extra pound of national income that domestic residents wish to spend on extra imports.

Marginal propensity to save the fraction of each extra unit of income that households wish to save.